KEY SEQUENCE	COMMAND
F6	**Bold Key** Turn boldfacing on and off
Alt-F6	**Flush Right Key** Align text at the right margin
Ctrl-F6	**Tab Align Key** Align text on tab setting
Shift-F6	**Center Key** Center text between margins
F7	**Exit Key** Save and clear screen; save and exit; clear screen without saving; exit WordPerfect
Alt-F7	**Math/Columns Key** (1) turn **M**ath on, (2) create math d**E**finition, (3) turn **C**olumn mode on and off, (4) **D**efine columns
Ctrl-F7	**Footnote Key** (1) create or edit **F**ootnote, (2) create or edit **E**ndnote, (3) specify endnote **P**lacement
Shift-F7	**Print Key** Print (1) **F**ull text, (2) **P**age, or (3) **D**ocument on disk; (4) **C**ontrol printer, (5) use t**Y**pe through, (6) **V**iew document, (7) **I**nitialize printer, (**S**) **S**elect printer, (**B**) change **B**inding width, (**N**) specify **N**umber of copies, (**G**) specify **G**raphics quality, (**T**) specify **T**ext quality
F8	**Underline Key** Underline text
Alt-F8	**Style Key** (1) turn style **O**n, (2) turn style o**F**f, (3) **C**reate new style, (4) **E**dit style, (5) **D**elete style, (6) **S**ave style, (7) **R**etrieve style, (8) **U**pdate style
Ctrl-F8	**Font Key** (1) change text **S**ize, or (2) **A**ppearance; (3) change back to **N**ormal font; (4) change base **F**ont, or (5) print **C**olor
Shift-F8	**Format Key** Choose format options that affect a (1) **L**ine (hyphenation, justification, line height, line numbering, line spacing, left/right margins, tab set, widow/orphan protection); (2) **P**age (center page top to bottom, force odd/even page, headers and footers, top/bottom margins, new page number, page numbering, paper size/type, suppress); or (3) **D**ocument (display pitch, initial codes/font, redline method, summary); or use (4) **O**ther format options (advance, conditional end of page, decimal characters, language, overstrike, printer functions, underline spaces/tabs)
F9	**Merge R Key** Designate end of a field in a secondary merge file
Alt-F9	**Graphics Key** Work with (1) **F**igures, (2) **T**ables, (3) text **B**oxes, (4) **U**ser-defined boxes; (5) create a graphics **L**ine
Ctrl-F9	**Merge/Sort Key** (1) **M**erge, (2) **S**ort and select, (3) change sort **O**rder
Shift-F9	**Merge Codes Key** Display menu of 13 Merge codes
F10	**Save Key**
Alt-F10	**Macro Key** Activate a previously defined macro
Ctrl-F10	**Macro Define Key** Record keystrokes as a macro or edit a macro
Shift-F10	**Retrieve Key** Retrieve file from disk

Text Screen Setup   Alt-F1, 2, 3, 2

Graphics Screen Setup   Alt-F1, 2, 2, 2

WORDPERFECT® 5
DESKTOP COMPANION

Greg Harvey
Kay Yarborough Nelson

SAN FRANCISCO · PARIS · DÜSSELDORF · LONDON

SYBEX Ready Reference Series
Editor-in-Chief: Rudolph S. Langer
Managing Editor: Barbara Gordon
Series Editor: James A. Compton
Editor: Eric M. Stone

Cover and book design by Thomas Ingalls + Associates
Cover photography by Casey Cartwright
Screen reproductions produced by Xeı.oFont

TABLE OF CONTENTS

PART V: WordPerfect Command and Feature Reference

Appendices

Preface

The *WordPerfect 5 Desktop Companion* is designed to meet an unfulfilled need. Although a great number of excellent basic and advanced books about WordPerfect can take you through the necessary learning steps, only this book is specifically designed not only to help you while you are working on-line with the program but also to provide assistance in applying specialized tasks in the context of a practical work environment.

The idea behind this book is simple: When a function isn't working as planned, a command is producing unpredicted results, or a macro is refusing to give up its bugs, you need a single source of information that can quickly help you solve the problem at hand so that you can get on with your work.

When this book was in its planning stages, we looked carefully at alternatives for organizing and arranging its material. At first, the alternatives appeared very straightforward: either a topical reference covering the commands and functions in general discussions, or a dictionary reference listing all of the commands and functions alphabetically. To incorporate the best of both worlds, this books combines the two approaches. Parts I through IV provide a topical reference that introduces particular WordPerfect features organized according to their functions. Part V is an A–Z reference section that lists each feature and command, giving you the key sequence to follow along with a summary of its uses.

Using the Application Sections

Parts I through IV (Chapters 1 through 19) include topical material about the use of the various features in WordPerfect. For users of version 4.2 who have upgraded to 5.0, each chapter begins with an "Upgrade Notes" section that points out significant differences in the way features found in version 4.2 are handled in version 5, as well as any new features not found in version 4.2.

Each chapter introduces the use of a feature and covers its options. Many times, you will find information on how the feature can be combined with others to perform a particular task. Where appropriate, cross-references to other chapters will direct you to more detailed information about a feature that is mentioned in context.

Using the Reference Section (Part V)

You can use the reference entries listed alphabetically in Part V to refresh your memory about a certain key sequence or to review a basic technique. Each reference entry recaps the main purpose of the command, lists the key sequences used to invoke the command and the hidden codes generated (if any), summarizes the usage of the command, and refers you to related entries in Part V.

Interpreting the Key Sequence

The key sequence in each reference entry presents the keystrokes you enter at the keyboard. Function key combinations are displayed in bold and are separated by a hyphen to indicate that both keys are to be depressed. The key name assigned to the function key combination (and shown on your function key template) follows the keys in parentheses, as in

Shift-F8 (Format)

which indicates that you press one of the Shift keys and hold it down until you press F8 (then, you can release both of them).

We have presented the other keys you press, as well as option numbers and menu letters you type from the keyboard, in **boldface** type. For example, if you are to press the Enter key to confirm a choice, you will see

Enter

in boldface. If you can type either 3 or J to choose an option like Justification, the **3** and **J** will be boldfaced.

Most key sequences in WordPerfect 5.0 involve more than one menu. When you must select options from several menus, we represent the hierarchy by separating each menu level with the ▼ symbol. For example, in the reference entry for the Force Odd/Even Page feature, you will see the key sequence

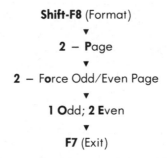

Shift-F8 (Format)
▼
2 – Page
▼
2 – Force Odd/Even Page
▼
1 Odd; **2** Even
▼
F7 (Exit)

This key sequence indicates all of the steps that you follow to use this particular feature. At each level, we show only those options that are currently of concern.

Some menus are arranged vertically, as illustrated in the key sequence for Beep Options:

Shift-F1 (Setup)

▼

5 — Initial Settings

▼

1 — **B**eep Options

▼

1 — Beep on **E**rror
2 — Beep on **H**yphenation
3 — Beep on **S**earch Failure

▼

F7 (Exit)

After you press Shift-F1 and select Initial Settings and Beep Options, you are presented with a vertical menu containing three options: Beep on Error, Beep on Hyphenation, and Beep on Search Failure. You can tell that these options constitute a single step because there is no ▼ symbol between them. Once you select the appropriate option, you then press F7 (Exit) to quit the menu.

Other menus in WordPerfect 5.0 follow the horizontal arrangement whereby individual options are presented on a line at the bottom of the screen, separated by a semicolon. This kind of arrangement can be seen in the key sequence for creating or editing a comment or converting it to text:

Ctrl-F5 (Text In/Out)

▼

5 — **C**omments

▼

1 Create; **2 E**dit; **3** Convert to **T**ext

As soon as you press Ctrl-F5 and select the Comments option, the Create, Edit, and Convert to Text options appear on a menu at the bottom of the screen.

Sometimes when executing a command sequence you need to type in some information, like a new value or a file name. When you have to enter information, the key sequence step will indicate it by describing the type of information or value required. This description is printed in italics and enclosed in angle brackets, as in

<measurement to advance> **Enter**

This sample line, which is taken from the **Advance** reference entry, instructs you to type how much the printer is to advance and then press Enter.

If you have to mark text as a block before initiating a new step, this is indicated by a description of the block. This description is printed in italics and is enclosed in square brackets, as illustrated by the following key sequence excerpt:

Alt-F4 (Block)

▼

[highlight block of text with cursor keys]

This instructs you to press Alt-F4 and then use the cursor movement keys to highlight all of the text that is to be included in the block. Certain other types of instructions are presented in the same way.

CONSISTENT TERMINOLOGY

We have endeavored wherever possible to use the same terminology as your WordPerfect 5.0 manual. However, you will find a noteworthy difference: we place the key sequence before the key name, as in *Shift-F7 (Print)* instead of *Print (Shift-F7)*. You would find this key combination referred to as *the Print key* alone only if the function key sequence and key name had been presented earlier in the same discussion.

Also, at present there is no standard terminology for the names of the menus at various levels in the program. To make it as clear as possible, we have followed the terminology used at the top of the menu screen. However, we have usually omitted punctuation in menu names.

When a new feature is introduced in the text, we list both the option number and the menu letter that can be used to select it. However, when a feature is mentioned incidentally, only the menu letter options are listed. This is in keeping with the idea that the menu letter system introduced in version 5.0 helps you remember the sequence more than the rather random numbers assigned to the options.

For example, in the discussions on desktop publishing in Chapter 19, you will find reference to using the View Document feature to preview your work. In this context, the key sequence for the feature is given simply as "press Shift-F7 V." In Chapter 7, "Printing Techniques," where the main discussion of the use of View Document takes place, we would instruct you to "press Shift-F7 (Print), then select View Document (**6** or **V**)."

SCOPE OF THE BOOK

This book is a complete reference that covers all aspects of using WordPerfect 5.0. It includes the changes incorporated in the maintenance upgrade dated 7/11/88. Because of the vast changes between versions 4.2 and 5.0, no attempt is made to indicate how a particular feature is executed or used in version 4.2.

If you have not upgraded to WordPerfect 5.0, we urge you to do so; you will have a great many more features available to you, and you will discover that many of the more unwieldy command sequences have been modified. WordPerfect Corporation is consistently upgrading this well-designed product, and it has evolved into a very sophisticated word processor that is at the same time easy to learn and use.

ORGANIZATION

Part I, "Fundamental Word Processing Features," consists of eight chapters that cover the program's basic functions. These chapters explain installing and customizing WordPerfect; basic text entry, formatting, and editing; working with fonts and styles; printing; and file management techniques. If you are only a casual user, you will probably find all the information you need within these first eight chapters.

Part II, "Specialized Word Processing Features," presents techniques used in specific tasks that not all users will need to perform. For example, Chapter 9 discusses techniques used to create indexes, tables of contents, and tables of authorities, which are widely used within the legal profession. Chapter 10 describes methods used for creating multicolumn documents such as newsletters and brochures. Chapters 11 and 12 discuss merge printing and sorting—features that offer you a variety of techniques to save a great deal of time. If your work does not require such specialized techniques, you can safely skip these chapters and return to them when you need to use them. Likewise, Chapter 13, "Performing Calculations with the Math Feature," presents techniques that will be of interest only if you need to make calculations in your documents. Chapter 14 covers drawing lines and using special characters and symbols not directly accessible from the keyboard.

Part III, "Supplemental Word Processing Features," like Part II, contains chapters that are for specialized use. Chapter 15, "Using the Speller and Thesaurus," will probably be of interest to all but the most casual of word processing users; it contains techniques you can use to produce almost error-free documents with WordPerfect. Chapter 16, "Creating and Using Macros," describes in detail how you can put the powerful Macro feature to work for you; if you've never used WordPerfect macros before, this chapter will show you how to make the most of all the macros that are presented throughout the book. Chapter 17 introduces you to the new Keyboard Layout feature, which enables you to customize the basic WordPerfect keyboard and to create specialized keyboards for easier typing of foreign-language characters or math/science symbols and equations.

Part IV, "Desktop Publishing with WordPerfect," contains two chapters that cover the program's all-new desktop publishing features. In Chapter 18, you will find detailed information on using WordPerfect's Graphics feature to combine text and graphics in your publication. In Chapter 19, you will find information and ideas for creating specific publications; this chapter outlines the design process and procedures used to produce such publications as flyers, newsletters, brochures, and longer reports in WordPerfect.

Part V, "WordPerfect Command and Feature Reference," offers a complete alphabetical reference to all of WordPerfect's features. Go to this section to look up any command for which you need just the key sequence or a quick summary of the usage.

The appendices also contain valuable information. Appendix A is a technical reference for those who import and export documents among word processing programs and spreadsheet or database management programs. In this appendix you will also find information on how to successfully import version 4.2 documents that contain font changes into version 5.0.

Appendix B lists the codes for all of WordPerfect's character sets. You can use this information to look up the codes for symbols and characters that must be inserted into the document using WordPerfect's Compose feature (which is covered in depth in Chapter 14).

Appendix C gives you a complete listing of WordPerfect's hidden formatting codes; if you ever have difficulty interpreting a code, turn to Appendix C to see what it represents. Appendix D contains a complete listing of all of WordPerfect's default settings. Appendix E illustrates and explains WordPerfect's hierarchical system for saving format settings and font changes as part of the document.

Appendix F covers the Bitstream Fontware Installation Kit, a free program available from WordPerfect Corporation. Once the Fontware program contained in this kit is installed, you can use it to make Bitstream fonts in various sizes and type styles; the fonts can then be used in WordPerfect documents. This program can be used with a wide variety of laser printers. Appendix G gives you information on using the Printer Definition program supplied with WordPerfect to customize the printer definition file used by your printer.

MACROS

WordPerfect has often been described as a feature-laden program. It contains many levels of command options, some of which are relatively undocumented. We have attempted to describe these techniques and enable you to easily use them in your work without having to go through a long learning sequence. In many cases, this requires creating a macro that carries out a sequence of instructions. You will find these macros throughout the book, near the applications to which they are related.

If you are already familiar with WordPerfect macros, you can simply incorporate them in your work without having to refer to the chapter on macros. If you are unfamiliar with WordPerfect macros, you should probably read Chapter 16, "Creating and Using Macros," before attempting to use any of the macros in this book. Using macros in WordPerfect is a simple and straightforward process, but you should be sure that you understand it before you create macros that may inadvertently damage work you have already completed. As you learn to use macros, be sure to save your document before you try to use your macro in it. That way, if the macro should produce unexpected results, you will still have a saved, correct version of your document.

In this book, all sample macros are illustrated by figures that show how they appear when edited with WordPerfect's Macro Editor. You can also use the Macro Editor to create the sample macros. To do this, first press Ctrl-F10 (Macro Define) and enter either the suggested name or one of your own. When prompted, enter the description shown in the figure or one of your own. After pressing Enter, press Ctrl-F10 to save the macro without adding any keystrokes or commands. Next, press Ctrl-F10 again and enter the name you just gave the macro. When you receive the menu options Replace and Edit, choose the Edit option by typing **2** or **E**. This takes you to the Macro Editor screen, similar to the one shown in the macro figure. Select the Action option (**2** or **A**) to place the cursor in the Macro Editor. Then, duplicate the WordPerfect commands and keystrokes just as they are in the macro figure. If you haven't used the Macro Editor before, be sure to refer to Chapter 16 for the information on using it before trying to duplicate these sequences.

HOW TO USE THIS BOOK

How you use this book depends upon your needs. If you are attempting to solve a specific problem, you will probably want to go directly to the reference entry in Part V describing the technique you are trying to use.

Most of the time, you will be able to get sufficient information from the reference entry alone to solve your problem. If, however, your problem is still unresolved, or you wish to obtain more information and see more examples of how the particular feature can be used, you should refer to the appropriate technique and application discussions in the chapters that precede Part V.

To help you locate the appropriate discussions, each chapter begins with a table of contents that lists all of the section headings.

Because of its nature, this book does not require that you use it in any specified order or that you read completely through any one chapter or section. We have endeavored whenever possible to make all discussions self-contained and to minimize cross-references that would require you to continually jump from one section to another in order to obtain the information you need.

We sincerely hope that this book provides you with a truly usable reference, and that you will turn to it time and time again as you work with this greatly enhanced and improved version of WordPerfect.

Acknowledgments

A project of this magnitude would not have been possible without the expertise and cooperation of a great many people. We were fortunate in having top-quality people to support and guide us throughout the project. This list of thanks is heartfelt and only begins to repay those involved.

First and foremost on our list are the talented people on the SYBEX staff, including editor-in-chief Dr. Rudolph S. Langer, managing editor Barbara Gordon, series editor Jim Compton, technical editor Brian Atwood, word processors Bob Myren and Jocelyn Reynolds, typesetter Cheryl Vega, proofreader Sylvia Townsend, layout artist Charlotte Carter, graphics technician Sonja Schenk, and acquisitions editor Dianne King (You were a lifesaver, Dianne!). A very special thanks is due to the copy editor on this project, Eric Stone. His patience, dedication, and skill evidenced at every turn in dealing with our manuscript are so much appreciated and are so much a part of this book (Great going, Eric!).

Next, thanks go to our indexer, Debbie Burnham-Kidwell, who heroically took on and conquered the monumental task of creating the index for this book (Thanks, Debbie!).

Also, we want to thank Susan Kelly, whose ideas and support for the project were ever so appreciated and whose outstanding work, *Mastering WordPerfect 5,* again provided an excellent base on which to build this new edition of our reference (Thanks again, Sue!).

We want to thank the software and hardware manufacturers whose loan of their excellent products gave us the tools with which to explore the heights and depths of WordPerfect 5. These include QMS, Inc. for their excellent PostScript printer, the QMS-PS 810, which was used in printing many of the figures reproduced in this book; Hewlett-Packard Company for their wonderful HP ScanJet used to produce several illustrations in the desktop publishing chapter; Bitstream, Inc. for their superior Bitstream Fontware Installation Kit; Hercules Computer Technology for their outstanding Hercules Graphics Card Plus with RamFont; Adobe Systems, Inc. for supplying many font sets from their excellent Adobe Type Library series (especially ITC Korinna, which shows up in many of our desktop publishing examples); and Aldus Corporation for Freehand, a truly superb graphics tool that was used to create the logotype exported in PostScript to our sample newsletter.

And last but never least, thanks to the dedicated people at WordPerfect Corporation for supplying us with much-needed information and with the second-to-none WordPerfect 5.0, the WordPerfect Library 2.0, WordPerfect 1.0 for the Macintosh, and the *WordPerfect Printer Definition Program, A Technical Reference* (Much appreciated, Rebecca and Jeff!).

Greg Harvey
Inverness, California
Kay Nelson
Pescadero, California
October 20, 1988

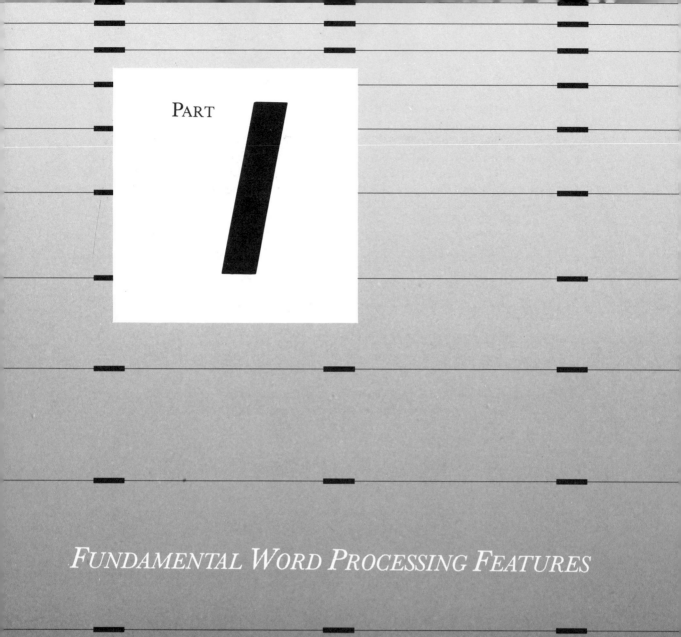

PART

1

FUNDAMENTAL WORD PROCESSING FEATURES

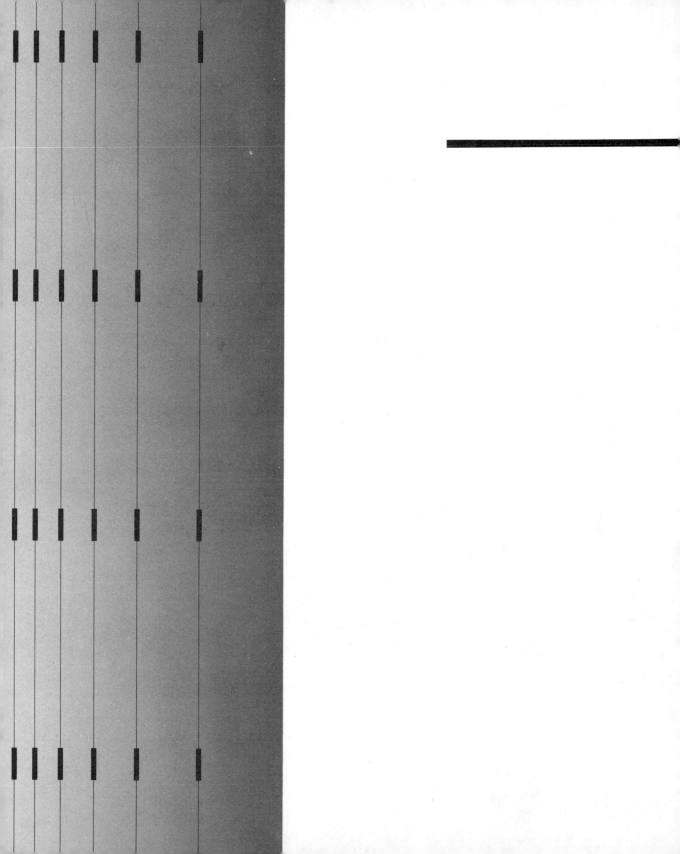

INSTALLING AND CUSTOMIZING WORDPERFECT

Installing and Customizing WordPerfect

This chapter contains the information needed to install WordPerfect on both two-disk-drive and hard disk systems. It also discusses the options that you can specify each time you issue the WordPerfect startup command. In addition, this chapter describes the default settings that you can change so that your customized settings are used each time you start WordPerfect.

Upgrade Notes

WordPerfect 5.0 comes on twelve 5¼-inch disks or seven 3½-inch disks. The program itself has become so large that it requires two program disks, labeled *WordPerfect1* and *WordPerfect2,* to start the program on a two-floppy-disk system (using the 5¼-inch format). Although it is still possible to run WordPerfect on a two-disk-drive computer, a hard disk system is now highly recommended.

Unlike earlier versions, WordPerfect 5.0 requires that the DOS file CONFIG.SYS contain a FILES = 20 statement, increasing the total number of files that can be open at one time. You can't run this version of the program with the number of files set any lower than 20. See "Installing WordPerfect" for information on how to add or change this FILES statement.

To make the installation process on a hard disk system easier, the program includes an Install program. This program automatically creates the subdirectory C:\WP50 on your hard disk and copies into it all of the files except those on the Conversion disk and the Printer disks. Because the Install program uses the C:\WP50 subdirectory that it creates, there is no need to remove version 4.2 (usually stored in the subdirectory C:\WP) from your hard disk before installing version 5.0. You may consider removing it, however, if your hard disk lacks sufficient free space to accommodate the new version. (The entire program requires about 4 megabytes of disk space.)

WordPerfect 5.0 retains most of the startup options available in version 4.2, with the notable exception of the WP/S command used to access the Setup menu. This menu has been expanded and is now accessed from within WordPerfect by pressing Shift-F1. As before, changes made to the Setup menu settings remain in effect each time you start WordPerfect. In addition, the WP/I startup command to start WordPerfect from a RAM disk is no longer available.

Version 5.0 includes some new startup options: WP/NC and WP/NK, for disabling the Cursor Speed feature and certain keyboard calls that can interfere with WordPerfect's operation when TSR (terminate-and-stay-resident) programs are loaded into RAM; WP/SS, for specifying the size of the screen (rarely needed, as WordPerfect detects the dimensions of the monitor screen); and WP/X, for restoring the program defaults changed from the Setup menu.

INSTALLING WORDPERFECT

WordPerfect runs on IBM and IBM-compatible computers, as well as on other computers. This chapter discusses installation procedures for IBM and IBM-compatible computers that operate under MS-DOS and PC-DOS. WordPerfect comes on twelve 5¼-inch floppy disks. If you have one of the IBM PS/2 computers or a laptop model that uses 3½-inch disks, you can request this format from WordPerfect Corporation. WordPerfect 5.0 comes on seven disks in the 3½-inch format. Table 1.1 lists the names of the disks supplied in each format.

	DISK	LABEL
In 5¼-inch Format:	1	WordPerfect1
	2	WordPerfect2
	3	Fonts/Graphics
	4	Speller
	5	Thesaurus
	6	PTR Program
	7	Learning
	8	Conversion
	9	Printer1
	10	Printer2
	11	Printer3
	12	Printer4
In 3½-inch Format:	1	WordPerfect1/WordPerfect2
	2	Learning/Fonts/Graphics
	3	Speller/Thesaurus
	4	Conversion
	5	Printer1/Printer2
	6	Printer3/PTR Program
	7	Printer4

TABLE 1.1: WordPerfect Program Disks

Installation on a Two-Disk-Drive System

To install WordPerfect on a two-disk-drive system, you must first make working (or backup) copies of each of the program disks (12 if you use 5¼-inch floppy disks or 7 if you use 3½-inch disks). You must also make sure that the DOS system disk that you use to start your computer contains a program file called CONFIG.SYS and that this file contains the command statement FILES = 20. If you use a DOS disk that doesn't contain this information, you will not be able to run WordPerfect. Note that there is not sufficient free space on the WordPerfect1 disk to copy COMMAND.COM on this disk. This means that you must start your computer with a separate DOS disk and then replace this disk with the WordPerfect1 disk when you want to use WordPerfect.

The complete installation procedure is outlined in the following steps:

1. Format the disks to be used as the working copies of your program disks, plus one additional disk to be used as a data disk. With your DOS disk in drive A and a blank disk in drive B, at the A> prompt enter the command

   ```
   FORMAT B:
   ```

   Follow the on-screen prompts. Type **Y** and press the Enter key when asked if you wish to format another disk. In this way, format all of the disks you need.

2. After formatting your last disk, type **N** and press the Enter key.

3. Update the FILES = statement in your existing CONFIG.SYS file or create a new one by typing

   ```
   COPY A:CONFIG.SYS + CON A:CONFIG.SYS
   FILES = 20
   ```

   and pressing F6 and the Enter key.

4. Replace the DOS disk in drive A with the WordPerfect1 disk (or the WordPerfect1/WordPerfect2 disk if you are using 3½-inch disks). Make sure that your last formatted blank disk is still in drive B, then enter

   ```
   COPY A:*.* B:
   ```

5. Repeat the process, copying each original disk to a blank formatted disk in drive B. Label each disk so that you can keep track of them. Also label the blank formatted disk that you will be using as a data disk.

6. If the DOS COPY command you entered in step 3 modified the FILES statement in your CONFIG.SYS file or created a new one, you now need to reboot the computer before running WordPerfect; the FILES statement must be read into memory. To be sure that this statement is read into memory, replace the last WordPerfect program disk with the DOS disk containing the modified or new CONFIG.SYS file and press Ctrl-Alt-Del.

7. Place your new copy of the WordPerfect1 system disk (or your WordPerfect1/WordPerfect2 system disk if you are using 3½-inch disks) in drive A, and the data disk in drive B.

You can now run WordPerfect by entering the command **WP** at the DOS prompt. If you are using 5¼-inch disks, you will be prompted to replace the WordPerfect1 disk with the WordPerfect2 disk, which will remain in drive A while you use WordPerfect.

You may want to change a few of the program's default settings. Refer to the sections later in this chapter for details about how to do so. After changing any defaults, refer to the section in Chapter 7 on installing your printer. After installing your printer, you are ready to use WordPerfect to create, edit, and print your documents.

Installation on a Hard Disk System

If your computer has a hard disk, you should install WordPerfect on it. WordPerfect Corporation has developed an automated installation program that you can use if you will be running WordPerfect from your C drive. If you need to install WordPerfect on another hard disk drive (physical or virtual), you can't use this program. (See "Installing WordPerfect on a Drive Other Than C" later in this chapter.)

When you run the Install program, it takes care of creating the necessary directory for the WordPerfect program files and tutorial files. It also automatically copies the program files onto the hard disk (in the appropriate directory) and checks your CONFIG.SYS file in the root directory to make sure that it contains a FILES = 20 statement. If this statement is missing, or if the number of files after the equal sign is less than 20, the installation program will update it for you.

Note: The Install program does not copy the files on the Conversion disk to your hard disk. If you want to have some or all of these files on your hard disk, you must copy them using the DOS COPY command. You can, however, run these utilities from a disk drive like A or B.

USING THE INSTALL PROGRAM

The automatic installation program is located on the Learning disk (or the Learning/Fonts/Graphics disk if you are using 3½-inch disks) and is named INSTALL.EXE. To run it, you must place your working copy of this disk in drive A. Before you enter the command to run this program, you must make sure that C:\ is the current or default directory. If you type **CD** and press the Enter key at the C> prompt, this directory will be current. Then follow these steps:

1. Type **A:INSTALL** at the C> prompt and press the Enter key.
2. When you see the prompt

   Do you have a hard disk (Y/N) Y

   type **Y** or press the Enter key. A new screen appears, informing you that WordPerfect will copy all program files to a directory named C:\WP50, copy all tutorial files into a directory named C:\WP50\LEARN, and insert the string FILES = 20 into your CONFIG.SYS file.
3. Type **Y** or press the Enter key to continue the installation.
4. Replace the Learning (or Learning/Fonts/Graphics) disk in drive A with the WordPerfect1 disk, press **Y**, and press any key to continue. You will see the message *Reading* filename......*please wait* and then the message *Writing* filename......*please wait.*
5. When the Install program finishes copying the program files from the WordPerfect1 disk, you will be prompted to replace it with the WordPerfect2 disk. Press **Y**, make the replacement, and press any key to have these files copied. Continue to replace each program disk with the next disk in the sequence as prompted by the Install program.

After the Install program has copied the tutorial files from the Learning disk into the directory C:\WP50\LEARN, you will see the message

   UPDATING CONFIG.SYS file

and the Install program will terminate, returning you to the C> prompt in the C:\WP50 directory.

To start WordPerfect, remove the last program disk from drive A and press Ctrl-Alt-Del to reboot the computer (to make sure that the new FILES = 20 statement in the CONFIG.SYS file is read). Then enter the date and time if prompted, and type

   CD\WP50

to make the directory containing the WordPerfect program files (WP50) current. Then type **WP** and press the Enter key to start WordPerfect.

Installing WordPerfect on a Drive Other Than C

If you need to install WordPerfect on a hard disk that uses a drive other than C (like D or E), you can't use the Install program. In such a case, you need to make a WordPerfect directory and use the COPY command in DOS to copy the WordPerfect program files into it. Also, you need to check the CONFIG.SYS file in the root directory C:\ and make sure that it contains the statement FILES = 20.

Follow these steps for installation:

1. Make the correct drive current by typing its drive letter and a colon (such as **D:** or **E:**) and pressing the Enter key.

2. Use the DOS MD (Make Directory) command to create a WordPerfect directory with a name you specify, such as **MD D:\WP50**, and press the Enter key.

3. Make this directory current with the DOS CD (Change Directory) command, such as **CD D:\WP50**, and press the Enter key.

4. Place the WordPerfect1 disk (or WordPerfect1/WordPerfect2 if you are using 3½-inch disks) in drive A, then type

   ```
   COPY A:*.*
   ```

   and press the Enter key.

5. Continue to use this command to copy all of the program disks except for the Printer disks into this directory. If you prefer, you can create a \LEARN subdirectory and copy the files on the Learning disk into it.

6. Make the directory that contains CONFIG.SYS current. This file should be located in C:\.

7. Use the DOS COPY command to update the CONFIG.SYS file so that it contains the correct FILES statement, or create this file by typing

   ```
   COPY CONFIG.SYS + CON: CONFIG.SYS
   FILES = 20
   ```

   and pressing F6 and the Enter key.

8. If the COPY command used in the last step modified your CONFIG.SYS file or created a new one, you need to reboot the computer before running WordPerfect so that the FILES statement is read into memory. To ensure that you can run WordPerfect, make sure that drive A is empty and press Ctrl-Alt-Del.

9. Enter the date and time if prompted, and then type the letter of the drive that contains WordPerfect followed by a colon, such as **D:**, and press the Enter key. Next, type

   ```
   CD\WP50
   ```

   (Substitute the name given to the directory that contains the WP.EXE file for WP50 if you used a different directory name.) This will make the directory containing the WordPerfect program files (WP50) current. Then, type **WP** and press the Enter key to start WordPerfect.

INSTALLING ONLY THE ESSENTIAL FILES TO SAVE DISK SPACE

To copy all of the program files onto your hard disk, you need at least 4 megabytes of free space. If you don't have that much room available, you can still run WordPerfect from your hard disk by copying only the essential files that are needed to make it run. Follow these guidelines:

- Copy the WP.EXE file from the WordPerfect1 disk. You can omit the .FIL files; however, you won't have access to WordPerfect's on-line help.
- Copy the WP.FIL and STANDARD.PRS files from the WordPerfect2 disk. You can omit the two .MRS files if you don't use macros. Also, you don't need the WPSMALL.DRS file when using a hard disk.
- From the Fonts/Graphics disk, copy the WP.DRS file, and then copy the .WPD file for your monitor. Likewise, copy only the .FRS file you want used by your monitor. You don't need to copy the sample graphic images or the GRAB.COM utility.

Note: There are four .FRS files, supporting different display attributes, that color monitors conforming to the EGA graphics standard are capable of producing: EGAITAL.FRS for 256 italicized characters, EGASMC.FRS for 256 small caps characters, EGAUND.FRS for 256 underlined characters, and EGA512.FRS for 512 characters. Likewise, there are two .FRS files for Hercules graphics cards that support RamFont: HRF6.FRS for 6 fonts and 512 characters, and HRF12.FRS for 12 fonts and 256 characters. If you have an EGA monitor and are only interested in seeing underlining on the screen, you need to copy only the EGAUND.FRS file. Likewise, if you have a Hercules graphics card with RamFont and only want to use 6 fonts, you copy just the HRF6.FRS file.

- Don't copy any of the files on the Learning disk.
- Copy all of the files on the Speller and Thesaurus disk(s), unless you don't plan to use spell checking or to look up synonyms.
- Don't copy any of the files on the Conversion disk. (However, you may want to copy the STANDARD.CRS file if you have problems converting version 4.2 documents to WordPerfect 5.0.)

By copying only the essential files, you can keep the amount of disk space required to about 1 megabyte.

WORDPERFECT STARTUP OPTIONS

WordPerfect provides several options that you can use with the basic WordPerfect startup command, WP. You append these options to the command, separating the command from the option with a slash. Basically, these options are designed to help you customize WordPerfect before you begin to work with the program. Depending on your computer system, they can allow you to do such things as retrieve a particular document file for editing, invoke a macro, set the Timed Backup feature, and speed up and enhance the working of the program. In Part V, under the reference entry **WordPerfect Startup Options**, you will find a complete list of all of the options supported in version 5.0. The following sections highlight the more commonly used startup options and also give you information on combining them and inserting them into your AUTOEXEC.BAT file (if you want WordPerfect to start automatically when you boot your computer).

Starting WordPerfect and Retrieving a Document to Edit

If you want to edit a particular document as soon as you load WordPerfect into the computer, you can include its file name as part of the startup command. For example, if you wish to edit a document named SEC6 located on a data disk in drive A as soon as you start WordPerfect, you can enter the startup command as

    WP A:SEC6

and then press the Enter key. As soon as WordPerfect is loaded into memory, the document SEC6 on the disk in drive A will be retrieved and displayed on your screen, and you can begin your work. If a file named SEC6 is not located on the data disk in drive A when WordPerfect is loaded, you will receive the error message

    ERROR: File not found—A:SEC6

Starting WordPerfect and Setting a Timed Backup Interval

As an alternative to permanently setting the Timed Backup feature using the Backup option on the Setup menu (Shift-F1 B—see "Timed and Original Back-ups" later in this chapter), you can specify the number of minutes between backup operations while starting WordPerfect. For example, to start Word-Perfect and set timed backups at 10-minute intervals, you type

    WP/B-10

and press the Enter key. You can substitute any number of minutes for the 10 in this example. Just be aware that you must type **WP/B-** and follow it with the number corresponding to the interval you wish to use.

How often backup copies should be made depends upon the quality of the util-ities in your area. If you experience frequent power interruptions or overloads in your building, you may want to set a very small interval between backup opera-tions. The slight inconvenience you experience when WordPerfect interrupts your editing during its save operation can be trivial in comparison to the incon-venience of reentering a long or particularly tricky section of text.

Unlike the interval set from the Backup menu (Shift-F1 B), the timed backup interval entered as part of the WordPerfect startup command is in effect only for the duration of your work session. Once you exit WordPerfect, the Timed Document Backup feature will return to its current setting (which is off unless you have changed it from the Setup menu). If you do not activate the Timed Document Backup feature using the Backup menu option, it will not be in effect at all when you use the program in a subsequent work session. This startup option is primarily intended for use when you want to temporarily override the timed backup interval defined with the Backup menu option.

Starting WordPerfect and Invoking a Macro

You can also start WordPerfect and have it invoke a macro as soon as the program is loaded into memory. For example, if you know that the first thing you need to do when WordPerfect is loaded is to change the directory, and if you have created a change-directory macro named CD, you can enter the startup command as

    WP/M-CD

and then press the Enter key. As soon as the WordPerfect program files are loaded into your computer's memory, the CD macro will be started.

You can start any macro as long as it has been saved in the directory that WordPerfect uses on startup or in the directory designated for Macro and Keyboard Layout files on the Location of Auxiliary Files menu (see ''Location of Auxiliary Files'' later in this chapter). In other words, if you use WordPerfect on a two-disk-drive system, you can make the data disk in drive B the current directory and then start WordPerfect by entering, for example,

    A>B: <Enter>
    B>A:WP/M-CD <Enter>

The macro named CD must be located on the data disk in drive B. If it is not, WordPerfect will display the message

    ERROR: File not found—CD.WPM

when it tries to invoke this macro.

If your macro is invoked using the Alt key and a letter key, you enter the macro name exactly as it is saved on your data directory. For example, if you want to invoke a macro named Alt-W upon program startup, you enter the startup command as

    WP/M-ALTW

and press the Enter key.

Starting WordPerfect
and Redirecting Overflow Files to a New Directory

As you work on a document in WordPerfect, data is moved between RAM (the temporary memory that exists only while there is power) and your data disk. How frequently data is swapped between RAM and the data disk depends upon the total amount of memory in your computer. Parts of the document currently being created or edited are saved in different temporary files when this swap occurs. This movement of text out of RAM and into such files frees necessary computer memory so that you can continue to edit or add new text to your document. (This is the reason the size of your document files is limited by the amount of storage space available rather than by the amount of memory in your computer.)

These files, called *overflow files,* are given different names, depending upon whether the text being swapped is located before or after the position of the cursor when this swapping occurs. Text located before the cursor's position is saved in a file named WP}WP{.TV1, and text located after the cursor's position is saved in a file named WP}WP{.BV1. (If you are creating or editing a document in the second window, overflow files WP}WP{.BV2 and WP}WP{.TV2 are created as well.)

When you exit WordPerfect by pressing F7 (Exit), these overflow files are closed, and the text is assembled as one document when you issue the Save command. If you do not use F7 to quit a work session in WordPerfect, these overflow files will still contain text when you next use the program. If WordPerfect detects that these files are not empty when you next use the program, it presents this prompt at the initial startup screen:

Are other copies of WordPerfect currently running? (Y/N)

When you type **N**, WordPerfect erases the contents of the overflow files and starts the program as usual by displaying the standard editing screen.

Normally, overflow files are saved in the drive or directory that WordPerfect uses at startup. (WordPerfect always lists the directory that it is using at startup on the initial screen that it displays while the program files are being loaded into memory.) You can change this so that the files are saved in a new drive or directory by appending **/D-** followed by the drive letter (and directory path name, if applicable) to the regular WordPerfect startup command. For example, if you want the overflow files saved in the directory where you will be saving the document itself and this directory is named MARY, you start WordPerfect with this command:

WP/D-C:\WP50\MARY

Not only overflow files but also buffers are redirected to this new drive or directory. This means that if you are using WordPerfect on a two-disk-drive system and start it using both the /D- and /R options (see the section that follows), you can remove the WordPerfect2 disk from drive A during program operation and replace it with a second data disk. In such a case, you would specify the startup command as

A:WP/D-B/R

The overflow files would then be saved on the data disk in drive B along with the documents you are creating and editing. The disk in drive A could then contain macros that you wish to use during the work session or a copy of the Learning disk, which contains the WordPerfect Help files that you might need to consult.

Starting WordPerfect and Loading Parts of the Program into Expanded Memory

WordPerfect 5.0 requires at least 384K of RAM to run. Of this, approximately 238K is required to load the word processor. Some of the additional memory is used by DOS, and the rest is used to maintain a minimum of editing space for your documents. If your computer is equipped with expanded memory and has at least 300K of this memory free, you can use the /R startup option to load some of the menus, error messages, and overlays into the expanded memory.

Note: The expanded memory in your system must conform to the Lotus/Intel/ Microsoft standard. Also, WordPerfect provides the /NE startup option to inhibit the use of expanded memory, should you wish that WordPerfect not use this memory.

Using the /R startup option will make parts of the program run faster. For example, you could start the program on a hard disk system using this option by typing:

WP/R

and pressing Enter. Once the additional files are loaded into expanded memory, the program can access them more quickly than it can when it simply reads the data from the system disk.

As explained in the previous discussion of the /D- startup option, if you use these options together on a two-disk-drive system, you can remove the Word-Perfect2 disk during operation. This allows you to use drive A to hold such disks as those that contain spelling dictionaries or the Thesaurus, or a disk containing macros that you use in creating and editing your documents.

Starting WordPerfect and Restoring the Default Values to the Setup Menu

You can use the startup command WP/X to restore all of the program defaults that have been changed from the Setup menu (discussed at length later in this chapter). Appendix D shows you a table listing all of the default settings for

WordPerfect. When you start the program using the /X option, all of these settings are restored regardless of the number of changes made to the program. This suppression of the changes and restoration of the default values is for that session only. The next time you start WordPerfect (without using the /X startup option), you will find all of the changes you made still in effect.

Interestingly enough, when you use the /X startup option and then look at the Setup menu options, all of their settings appear as they did when you first installed WordPerfect. It appears as though your changes are no longer saved with the program. However, when you next start WordPerfect without using the /X option and then look at the Setup menu options, all of the modifications to the default values will reappear.

Startup Options to Avoid Conflict with TSR Programs

If you use various RAM-resident utility programs referred to as *TSR* programs (terminate-and-stay-resident), in some instances you may experience trouble in starting WordPerfect or in running it. To avoid conflict between this type of software and WordPerfect, you can use the /NC or /NK startup option (or both). The /NC option disables the Cursor Speed feature (see "Setting the Cursor Speed" later in this chapter). The /NK option disables certain enhanced keyboard calls. Both the Cursor Speed feature and these keyboard calls can conflict with the use of some TSR programs. Try using these startup options if WordPerfect loads the program but freezes at the startup screen.

Combining Startup Options

Many of the startup options discussed in the preceding sections can be combined. For instance, if you want to speed up the program operation using the /R option, invoke a macro named CD at startup, and set the timed backup interval to 15 minutes, enter the command **WP/R/B-15/M-CD**. Remember not to enter spaces between the slashes and to enter a hyphen between the option letter and any particular required entry such as the macro name or the number of minutes.

Creating an AUTOEXEC.BAT File
Containing Your WordPerfect Startup Options

If you have a series of startup options that you wish to invoke each time you use WordPerfect, you can include these in the batch files that you develop to automate the startup process.

You can also add these options to the AUTOEXEC.BAT file that is automatically used each time you start the computer. You would use this method if Word-Perfect is the program that you want to work with each time you start the computer, and if you use the program on a hard disk system.

You can use WordPerfect to create the commands to be used in this file rather than using the DOS text editor. To do so, follow these steps:

1. On the first line of the document, type **DATE** and press Enter. (If your computer is equipped with a clock/calendar card, you substitute the appropriate command used to set the clock.)

2. On the second line of the document, type **TIME** and press Enter (if you don't have a clock/calendar card).

3. On the third line of the document, type **PATH C:\;C:\WP50** (or substitute the name of the directory that contains your WordPerfect program files if it is something other than WP50). Using the PATH command allows you to start WordPerfect without having to use the CD (Change Directory) command to make the WordPerfect directory current.

4. On the fourth line of the document, you can type **PROMPT $P-$G** and press Enter. This is an optional command that instructs DOS to display the current directory (including the full path name) before the greater-than symbol (>) used as the standard DOS prompt. For instance, if you include this line in your AUTOEXEC.BAT file, WordPerfect displays the prompt

   C:\WP5Ø>

   (if this is the name of the directory) instead of simply

   C>

   when you exit WordPerfect with the WP directory current. In other words, this command displays the name of the current directory, keeping you informed of where you are in the hard disk.

5. On the fifth line of the document, type the startup command, including all of the options that you wish to use each time you start WordPerfect. For instance, you can enter **WP/R/B-15/M-CD** if you wish to use the RAM option to speed up the program, set timed backup operations at 15-minute intervals, and start the CD macro mentioned previously. After entering the WP command followed by all of the startup options you wish to use, press the Enter key.

6. Save this file as a DOS text file rather than in WordPerfect's file format. To do this, you press Ctrl-F5 (Text In/Out), select the Text option (**1** or **T**), select the Save option (**1** or **S**), enter the file name as **C:\AUTO-EXEC.BAT**, and press the Enter key. This saves the file in ASCII format

in the root directory of the hard disk, as required for this file to function properly.

7. Exit WordPerfect by pressing F7 N Y. Test your AUTOEXEC.BAT file by holding down Ctrl-Alt, pressing Del, and then releasing all three keys. The computer will automatically go through the startup sequence. It will then prompt you to enter the date and the time if your computer isn't equipped with a clock/calendar that supplies this information for you. After you enter this information, WordPerfect will be loaded into the computer's memory using the startup options you specified.

Creating a Batch File to Start WordPerfect

If you don't always use WordPerfect when you first start your computer but you do want an easy way to start the program from anywhere on your hard disk, you can create a WordPerfect batch file that contains the WordPerfect startup command as well as any startup options that you use. This file works just like the AUTOEXEC.BAT file described in the previous section except that it isn't automatically executed when you start your computer.

To create the batch file, start WordPerfect as described earlier and then follow these steps:

1. On the first line, type **CD\WP50** and press Enter.

If WordPerfect is stored on a directory different from WP50, be sure to enter its name instead after the CD\ (Change Directory) command. If WordPerfect is installed on a drive other than C:, you need to add a line that changes the drive (such as D:) before you enter the CD command.

2. On the second line, type in the WordPerfect startup command, along with any startup options you wish to use, and press Enter. For example, you might type **WP** alone if you don't use any startup options, or **WP/M-CD** if you want to execute a startup macro.

3. Save the file as a DOS text file by pressing Ctrl-F5 (Text In/Out), selecting the Text option (**1** or **T**), and then selecting the Save option (**1** or **S**). Enter the file name as C:\WP5.BAT and press Enter.

4. Clear the editing screen by pressing F7 N N. You don't need to save this file in WordPerfect's file format.

From now on, you can start WordPerfect from the DOS prompt by simply typing **WP5** and pressing the Enter key. As long as you have included C:\ as part of the PATH command in the AUTOEXEC.BAT file, you can use this WordPerfect batch file to start WordPerfect from anywhere on the hard disk. (Refer back to "Creating an AUTOEXEC.BAT File Containing Your WordPerfect Startup Options" for information on setting the PATH statement.)

REDEFINING THE SHAPE OF THE CURSOR

The WordPerfect Learning disk contains a program called CURSOR.COM that you can use to change the flashing cursor indicator to a pattern other than an underline. There are a great number of other patterns to select from, but your monitor may not be able to display some of them.

When you run the CURSOR program (by typing **CURSOR** while you are in the directory in which CURSOR.COM resides), the screen shown in Figure 1.1 appears. The current cursor pattern is illustrated, and its two-letter designation is displayed at the bottom of the screen. Press the arrow keys to move the cursor to different locations on the grid and see how the cursor appears. (The differences are subtle; look carefully. As you approach the top-right corner of the grid, the cursor gets larger.) You can press the space bar to see how each pattern looks in a line of text.

To use a different cursor pattern as the default cursor, select a pattern from the grid and press Enter. (Note which pattern you have selected by copying the two-letter designation that appears at the bottom of the grid.) To use that pattern permanently, rewrite your AUTOEXEC.BAT file if you use one (see "Creating an AUTOEXEC.BAT File Containing Your WordPerfect Startup Options" earlier in this chapter) by adding the line

    <path name> CURSOR/*nn*

where *nn* is the pattern you have chosen, and *<path name>* is the full path name of the directory in which the CURSOR program is located.

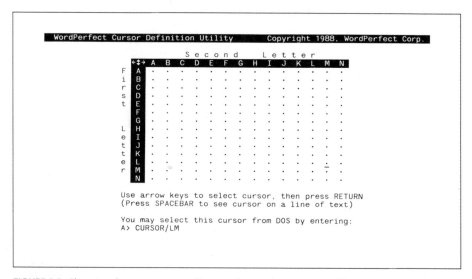

FIGURE 1.1: Changing the cursor pattern. You can change the pattern used for your cursor to a larger, much bolder block.

You cannot change the flashing cursor to a nonblinking cursor; however, if you prefer a larger, smaller, or dimmer cursor, you can select one by using this program.

CHANGING WORDPERFECT'S DEFAULT SETTINGS

One of the first things you should do after you have installed WordPerfect 5.0 on your computer and started the program is to examine the program's default settings on the Setup menu by pressing Shift-F1 (Setup). With the options available from this menu, you can customize the way WordPerfect works. Be aware that any changes you make to the default settings from this menu remain in effect each time you start WordPerfect. You can, however, return to the Setup menu at any time when using WordPerfect and make further modifications.

The Setup menu shown in Figure 1.2 contains eight options. As with any WordPerfect 5.0 menu, you can select an option by typing either its number or its menu letter. WordPerfect displays in bold the menu letter you can type to select an option (you can change this menu letter display from the Setup Display menu). All of the options on the Setup menu, with the exception of Cursor Speed and Fast Save, are attached to submenus whose options become available as soon as you select them.

The upcoming sections in this chapter cover each of the options on the Setup menu in some detail. There is no urgent need for you to modify the default settings

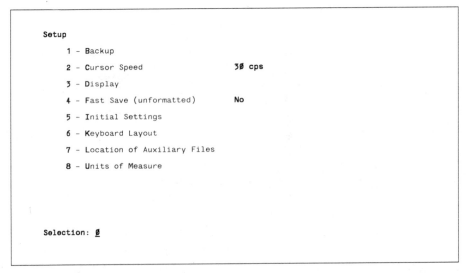

FIGURE 1.2: WordPerfect's Setup menu, accessed by pressing Shift-F1. It contains eight options for customizing the default settings of the program to suit the way you work. Any changes that you make from this menu remain in effect each time you start WordPerfect.

until you have had a chance to work with WordPerfect and determine your preferences; however, it is strongly recommended that you activate the Timed Document Backup feature on the Setup Backup menu to guard against a loss of edits due to a machine or power failure (see the following section). After that, you can exit the Setup menu and install your printer(s) for use with WordPerfect (see "Installing Your Printer" in Chapter 7), thus completing the program's installation.

Timed and Original Backups

Figure 1.3 shows you the Backup menu and its options that appear when you select Backup (**1** or **B**) from the Setup menu. When you select the Timed Document Backup option (**1** or **T**) and change No to Yes by typing **Y**, WordPerfect will automatically save your editing changes at periodic intervals under the file name WP{WP}.BK1 or WP{WP}.BK2 (for a document in the second editing window).

> *Note:* If you are working with two documents in separate editing screens, WordPerfect saves only the one in the current editing screen when the timed backup interval is reached.

When you exit WordPerfect normally (using F7—the Exit key), these timed backup files are erased. However, if you experience a power failure or machine problem that prevents you from exiting, they are retained on disk. You can then retrieve them and rename them. If you don't rename them the next time you start WordPerfect, you will receive the following message when the next timed backup interval is reached:

Old backup file exists: **1 R**ename; **2 D**elete

Select the Rename option and give the file a new name if you wish to retain it; otherwise, select the Delete option to erase it.

After turning this feature on, you press the Enter key to accept the default of 30 minutes or change to a smaller or larger interval. When setting the interval between backups, choose one that is neither too short or too long. For example, if you change the interval from 30 to 5, you will be interrupted every 5 minutes when working with WordPerfect as the program saves your new edits to disk. If, on the other hand, you change it from 30 to 50, you run the risk of losing up to 50 minutes worth of edits, for if you should experience a power failure right before the interval is up, you will lose all of the edits since the last save was made by the Timed Document Backup feature.

You can also specify whether you want to use the Original Document Backup feature. If you use this option, WordPerfect will make a backup file of the old version of your document with the extension .BK! each time you save your document. You will then have a record of the last version of your document under the name <*file name*>.BK! as well as a copy of the latest version of the document saved under <*file name*>.

```
Setup: Backup

        Timed backup files are deleted when you exit WP normally.  If you
        have a power or machine failure, you will find the backup file in the
        backup directory indicated in Setup: Location of Auxiliary Files.  .

           Backup Directory

        1 - Timed Document Backup                   No
            Minutes Between Backups                 30

        Original backup will save the original document with a .BK! extension
        whenever you replace it during a Save or Exit.

        2 - Original Document Backup                No




  Selection: 0
```

FIGURE 1.3: The Setup Backup menu with its two options, Timed Document Backup (**1** or **T**) and Original Document Backup (**2** or **O**). Setting the Timed Document Backup option to Yes instructs WordPerfect to automatically save your document at the interval specified as the Minutes Between Backups. Setting the Original Document Backup option to Yes instructs WordPerfect to save the original copy of the file under the file name with the .BK! extension before saving the edited copy in RAM under the specified file name.

Setting the Cursor Speed

The Cursor Speed option on the Setup menu is used to change the rate at which characters are repeated from the keyboard. By default, the cursor speed is set to 30 characters per second (cps), meaning that if you continue to depress a key it will move across a line of text at a rate of 30 characters per second.

To change the cursor speed, you select the Cursor Speed option (**2** or **C**). The menu options shown at the bottom of Figure 1.4 then appear. You can select 15, 20, 30, 40, or 50 characters per second, or Normal. Normal cursor speed returns the cursor speed to your keyboard's normal rate. Remember that the cursor speed set here affects not only the rate at which the cursor will move through text but also the rate at which characters will be entered if you hold down a letter or number key as well as the rate at which characters will be deleted if you press the Del or Backspace key.

Display Options

You can exert considerable control over the appearance of WordPerfect on the screen by changing the Display options that appear when you select Display

```
Setup

    1 - Backup

    2 - Cursor Speed              3Ø cps

    3 - Display

    4 - Fast Save (unformatted)   No

    5 - Initial Settings

    6 - Keyboard Layout

    7 - Location of Auxiliary Files

    8 - Units of Measure




Characters Per Second: 1 15; 2 2Ø; 3 3Ø; 4 4Ø; 5 5Ø; 6 Normal: Ø
```

FIGURE 1.4: Changing the cursor speed from the Setup menu (Shift-F1 C). Cursor speed, rated in characters per second (cps), determines the rate at which the cursor moves when you hold down a cursor movement key, the rate at which characters are entered when you press a letter or number key, and the rate at which characters are deleted when you press the Del or Backspace key. You can choose 15, 20, 30, 40, or 50 cps. Selecting the Normal option sets the cursor speed to your keyboard's normal rate.

from the Setup menu (Shift-F1 D) as shown in Figure 1.5. However, for most users, there is no need to modify any settings besides those controlled by the Colors/Fonts/Attributes option. This option leads to a hardware-specific menu whose options allow you to customize the way various screen attributes like bold-facing, underlining, italics, and highlighted blocks appear. Note that the line that holds the Graphics Screen Type option automatically displays the type of graphics card in your computer. WordPerfect automatically senses what type of video display board you are using when you start the program. There should be no need to change this selection. The following sections detail the purpose of the nine options on the Display menu.

Automatically Format and Rewrite

The default for the Automatically Format and Rewrite option is Yes. This means that WordPerfect rewrites the screen and reformats the text as you edit it. (However, word wrap still happens only when you use ↑ or ↓ to move to a new line or when you use one of the other cursor movement techniques to move somewhere else in the text.)

If you change this option to No, the program rewrites the screen and reformats the text only when you scroll through enough of the text that WordPerfect is

```
Setup: Display

        1 - Automatically Format and Rewrite     Yes

        2 - Colors/Fonts/Attributes

        3 - Display Document Comments             Yes

        4 - Filename on the Status Line           Yes

        5 - Graphics Screen Type                  Hercules 720x348 mono

        6 - Hard Return Display Character

        7 - Menu Letter Display                   BOLD

        8 - Side-by-side Columns Display          Yes

        9 - View Document in Black & White        No




    Selection: 0
```

FIGURE 1.5: The Setup Display menu options that appear when you select Display from the Setup menu (Shift-F1 D). Notice that the Graphics Screen Type option automatically displays the type of graphics card your computer is using (Hercules 720 x 348 mono, in this figure). You can use the Display options to customize the way WordPerfect appears on the screen during various phases of editing.

forced to rewrite the screen or when you press Ctrl-F3 (Screen) and select the Rewrite option (**0** or **R**). You can also force the screen to be rewritten at any time by pressing Ctrl-F3 (Screen) twice.

COLORS/FONTS/ATTRIBUTES

Colors/Fonts/Attributes allows you to choose how the font attributes available from the Size and Appearance menus (accessed with Font—Ctrl-F8), as well as the attribute used to show normal text, bold, underline, marked blocks of text, and other combinations, are displayed on your screen. The on-screen display selected for each attribute is independent of the way it will be produced by your printer.

The settings assigned to the Doc 1 screen are saved independently of those for the Doc 2 screen. After selecting your settings for the Doc 1 screen, you can press Shift-F3 (Switch) to make the selections for the Doc 2 screen. You can also use Move (Ctrl-F4) to copy the settings from Doc 1 to Doc 2 or from Doc 2 to Doc 1. After you use Switch and Move, WordPerfect will display the prompt

Copy attributes from other document? (Y/N) No

Type **Y** for Yes to have the settings from the other document window copied to the current document window.

The choices available for displaying different attributes are determined by the type of display card and monitor you are using. The differences are outlined in the following sections.

Monochrome   If you are using a monochrome monitor with a display card other than the Hercules Graphics Card Plus with RamFont capabilities (see below), you can only set the attributes using underlining, double intensity (bold), blinking, and reverse video (blocked). When you select the Colors/Fonts/Attributes option from the Display menu of the Setup key, you are presented immediately with the Set Attributes screen. There, you may alter some of the default settings by changing the Y(es) or N(o) setting for each attribute. You can use the space bar to toggle between Y and N when changing a particular attribute. As you make a change, you can see its effect by looking at the sample in the far right column of the table.

Color   If you have a color monitor, you can set different foreground/background color combinations to represent different attributes. The number of color combinations available depends upon the type of color display card you are using. If you are using an EGA (with sufficient memory) or VGA card, you can select among five different fonts (for showing italics, underline, small caps, etc.), or increase the number of displayable characters from 256 to 512. When you use these options (instead of Normal Font Only), the number of colors is limited to eight.

> *Note:* In version 5.0, for the first time, you can see underlining on the screen when using a color monitor instead of having it represented by a different color. Although this limits the number of color combinations, it may make it easier to locate this attribute in a document, especially if you have trouble remembering which color represents this attribute.

When using the Colors/Fonts/Attributes option for a color system, you can modify the Fast Text Display option. If you set this to Yes, WordPerfect will rewrite the screen faster, although you may experience "snow" on the screen.

If you have a CGA, PC3270, or MCGA (or EGA with limited memory or in a mode that displays more than 25 lines), you select colors for each attribute on the Set Screen Colors menu by assigning new foreground and/or background colors. To set a new color combination, move to the foreground color and type the letter of a listed color, then move to the background color and type its letter. As you make the change, the Sample column will immediately reflect it.

If you have an EGA (with sufficient memory) or VGA card, you select one of the fonts available by typing an asterisk (*). If the asterisk doesn't appear, there is a problem in loading the appropriate .FRS file. Make sure that all of the .FRS files that begin with EGA have been copied to your WordPerfect directory.

When you select the Screen Colors option (**1** or **S**), you set the color combinations just as described for the CGA card. If you have selected a font, you assign it to an attribute by typing **Y** for Yes or **N** for No (or use the space bar to toggle between the two) in the appropriate column.

Hercules Graphics Card with RamFont   If you have a Hercules Graphics Card Plus or InColor Card with RamFont, when you select the Colors/Fonts/Attributes option you are presented with the following menu that includes three Font/Color options. (When you select one of these options, the program marks it with an asterisk.)

1 – **S**creen Attributes
2 – 12 Fonts, 256 Characters
3 – 6 Fonts, 512 Characters
4 – **N**ormal Font only

Choose option **2** to use 12 fonts with 256 characters, or option **3** to use 6 fonts with 512 characters. If you select option 4, Normal Font Only, your display will act as though you have a standard Hercules Graphics card (even if you have a color monitor) and you must follow the procedure for a monochrome system (refer back to ''Monochrome'').

When you select the 12 Fonts, 256 Characters display option, you will be able to see most text attributes on the editing screen. Boldface, however, is not represented by double intensity but instead is displayed by a heavier version of each character (as a result, it doesn't contrast as much against normal text). Underlining and marked blocks are shown as they normally are on a monochrome monitor with a Hercules card. In addition, your monitor will display italics, double underlining, superscripts, subscripts, redlining, strikeout, outline, and small caps, as well as various size attributes such as Large, Vry Large, and Ext Large, on the screen much as they will appear when printed.

The 6 Fonts, 512 Characters display option still displays italics, double underlining, superscripts, subscripts, strikeout, and small caps. However, most of the size attributes and special appearance attributes like outline and shadow are displayed in the same way as a marked block of text. Boldface, underlining, and marked blocks are still shown as they are when you select the 12 Fonts, 256 characters display option. By selecting fewer fonts, you do, however, get to see twice the number of special characters (512 as opposed to 256) on the screen. This can be important if your work requires the use of foreign-language characters or math/science symbols.

> *Note:* Even if you select the Normal display option and can't see many of the display attributes or special characters in the document editing screen, you can still see them when you use the View Document feature (Shift-F7 V).

After selecting the number of fonts, select option **1** if you wish to change any of the predefined attributes. There are five capabilities that you can set for certain attributes, starting with Font. To change the number of the font, you can type a number between **1** and **6** if you are using 6 fonts or **1–9** and **A–C** if using 12 fonts. You can also use the space bar or the plus (+) and minus (–) keys on the numeric pad to cycle through available font choices. Of course, you can change the other capabilities as well as the font for certain attributes.

DISPLAY DOCUMENT COMMENTS

If you change the default of Yes to No for this option, all comments you have entered in the document will no longer be visible. Although they can't be seen, they still exist in the document, and you can locate them by searching for the [Comment] code in the document. See Chapter 2 for information on creating and using comments in a document.

FILENAME ON STATUS LINE

After you save your document the first time, WordPerfect displays the document file name in the lower-left corner of the editing screen (unless you switch to Typeover mode). To suppress this display, change the setting for this option from Yes to No.

Note: WordPerfect automatically suppresses the display of the file name when you switch from Insert mode to Typeover or use the ^O Merge codes or macro commands to display a message on the status line.

GRAPHICS SCREEN TYPE

WordPerfect automatically selects the correct graphics driver for the display card and monitor installed in your system. However, you may need to use this option when you have two monitors connected to your system and wish to change to a new one. When you select this option (**5** or **G**), the program displays a listing of the various screen types it supports. To change the screen type, move the highlight bar to the driver name and choose it by entering **1** or **S**. The currently selected screen type is marked with an asterisk (*) before its name.

If the graphics screen type you wish to use is not shown on the list, you may find it on the Fonts/Graphics disk. All screen type files have the extension .WPD. To make a new screen driver available, copy the appropriate .WPD file from the Fonts/Graphics disk to the directory that contains the WP.EXE (WordPerfect startup) file and then return to this menu to select it.

HARD RETURN DISPLAY CHARACTER

When you press the Enter key to end a paragraph or short line in Word-Perfect, the program inserts a Hard Return code [HRt] in the document. How-ever, because WordPerfect uses a space, which is invisible on your screen, as the default hard return display character, you can't see the location of hard returns on the editing screen.

To make hard returns visible, you select this option (**6** or **H**) and enter the character to be used. If you want to use a character that can be entered directly from the keyboard (like <), just type it in. If you want to use a character that can't be entered directly, use Compose (Ctrl-2) and the appropriate character set numbers to enter it. For example, to display the hard return as ¶, you would select the Hard Return Display Character option, press Ctrl-2, then type **4,5** and press the Enter key. The paragraph symbol will then appear on the screen.

To restore the hard return to the default of one space, return to this option and press the space bar before pressing the Enter key and Exit (F7).

MENU LETTER DISPLAY

To let you know which letter of a menu option name can be pressed to select that option, WordPerfect by default displays the letter in bold (either in double intensity, a heavier version of the character, or the color selected for boldfacing). You can change this attribute to any of the size and appearance choices on the Font menu. To change the menu letter display, select this option (**7** or **M**). Word-Perfect displays the following menu choices:

1 Size; **2 A**ppearance; **3 N**ormal: 0

To select a new size for the menu letters, choose the Size option and select the desired size from this menu. To change the appearance of the menu letter, press **2** or **A** for the Appearance option and select the desired appearance (underlining, italics, etc.). To have WordPerfect use no special enhancement for the menu let-ters (so you won't be able to tell which letter can be used), select the Normal option.

> *Note:* The attribute chosen for the menu letter display is dependent upon the selections made for it with the Colors/Fonts/Attributes option. For example, if you have a color monitor and choose to have small caps represented by red, selecting Sm Cap for the menu letter display from the Appearance menu will cause all of the menu letters to appear in red.

SIDE-BY-SIDE COLUMN DISPLAY

When you work with text columns (newspaper or parallel), WordPerfect dis-plays the columns side by side on the screen as they will be printed. However, you can scroll through columns more quickly if they are displayed as separate pages on the screen. To turn off the side-by-side column display, change this option from Yes to No. See Chapter 10 for more information on working with text columns.

VIEW DOCUMENT IN BLACK & WHITE

The last option on the Setup Display menu is View Document in Black & White. If you are using a color monitor, you can change the display in View Document mode from color to black and white by selecting this option (**9** or **V**) and setting it to Yes by typing **Y**. Note that activating this option affects the colors of the display only when you use the View Document option (**7** or **V**) on the Print menu (Shift-F7) to preview the printout. The text and graphics on the previewed page are then shown in black and the page itself is shown in white so that the colors more closely match the way they will actually appear when printed.

This black and white View Document display does not affect either of the two document editing windows; they still utilize the colors that you have chosen for the foreground and background using the Colors/Fonts/Attributes option on the Setup Display menu. If you are using a monochrome monitor and change this option from No to Yes, it will have no effect on WordPerfect's display.

Fast Save

By changing the Fast Save option from the default No to Yes on the Setup menu, you can save your documents somewhat faster than usual. There is, however, a price to be paid for the slight decrease in the time it takes to save a document: if a document has been fast-saved, it can't be printed from the disk with either the Document on Disk option on the Print menu (Shift-F7 D) or the Print option on the List Files menu (F5 Enter P) unless you save the document with the cursor at its end (Home Home ↓). Because the Fast Save option limits your printing options, it is not recommended that you turn it on. WordPerfect is no slower at saving a long document with all of its formatting codes—Fast Save saves an unformatted version—than other word processors on the market.

If you do want to spend less time waiting for a document to be saved and therefore activate the Fast Save option, be aware that you may have to take the time to retrieve the document, position the cursor at the document's end, and then resave it before you can print it from disk. Having to go through all of these steps to print just a range of pages in a document (which can only be done when printing a disk version) would waste more time than it would have taken to wait for the document to be saved with its formatting codes so that you could use the Document on Disk option on the Print menu without any interruption. To effectively make use of Fast Save, every WordPerfect user in the office must understand these steps so that everyone is still able to print from disk a document that has been fast-saved.

Initial Settings

When you choose the Initial Settings option (**5** or **I**) on the Setup menu, the Initial Settings menu options shown in Figure 1.6 become available. You can use them to change the circumstances under which the program beeps at you, change the format in which the current date is entered when you insert it with the Date/Outline key (Shift-F5), have the program automatically prompt you to enter a Document Summary the first time you save a document, enter new formatting defaults, modify the default number of times an action is repeated by the Esc key, or change the formatting for Table of Authorities citations.

BEEP OPTIONS

When you select Beep Options (**1** or **B**) from the Initial Settings menu, the menu options shown in Figure 1.7 appear. There are three conditions under which WordPerfect can beep at you: when an error results in an error message, when you turn on the Manual Hyphenation feature and the program wants you

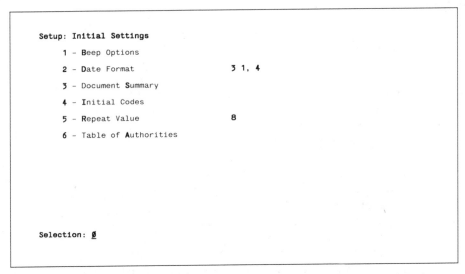

```
Setup: Initial Settings
     1 - Beep Options
     2 - Date Format                    3 1, 4
     3 - Document Summary
     4 - Initial Codes
     5 - Repeat Value                   8
     6 - Table of Authorities




     Selection: 0
```

FIGURE 1.6: The Setup Initial Settings menu that appears when you select Initial Settings from the Setup menu (Shift-F1 I). The most important option on this menu is the Initial Codes option, which allows you to permanently change the format settings like those for paper size, line spacing, and justification.

```
Setup: Beep options
       1 - Beep on Error              No
       2 - Beep on Hyphenation        Yes
       3 - Beep on Search Failure     No




       Selection: 0
```

FIGURE 1.7: The Beep Options menu, which appears when you select Beep Options from the Setup Initial Settings menu (Shift-F1 I B). Although many users dislike beeping while they work with the program, you can set any of the three options to Yes if you find that you need the sound to alert you to a particular change in the program's functioning.

to confirm the place where a word is to be hyphenated, and when you perform a search or search-and-replace operation and it fails to locate any more occurrences of the search string in the direction you are searching. Of these three, only Beep on Hyphenation is set to Yes when you first start the program. You can select any of these options and turn them off by typing **N**, or on by typing **Y**.

DATE FORMAT

The format selected by WordPerfect inserts the complete date when you use the Date Text (**1** or **T**) or Date Code (**2** or **C**) option on the Date/Outline key (Shift-F5). For example, if today's date were January 11, 1990, that is exactly how it would appear when you used either of these Date options to insert the current date in your document. This default is represented by the code numbers *3 1, 4.* Figure 1.8 shows you the Date Format options that explain how these codes result in a date format like *January 11, 1990;* code 3 inserts the name of the month, code 1 the day, and code 4 all four digits of the year. Note that the comma is inserted after code 1 with no trailing space just as it is entered in a date like *January 11, 1990.*

To change the format, select the numbers and enter the punctuation and symbols to be used as separators according to the codes listed on this screen. Note that you can set up codes that will display the current time along with the date. This menu is identical to the one that appears when you select the Date Format

```
Date Format

     Character    Meaning
         1        Day of the Month
         2        Month (number)
         3        Month (word)
         4        Year (all four digits)
         5        Year (last two digits)
         6        Day of the Week (word)
         7        Hour (24-hour clock)
         8        Hour (12-hour clock)
         9        Minute
         Ø        am / pm
         %        Used before a number, will:
                     Pad numbers less than 1Ø with a leading zero
                     Output only 3 letters for the month or day of the week


     Examples:   3 1, 4      = December 25, 1984
                 %6 %3 1, 4  = Tue Dec 25, 1984
                 %2/%1/5 (6) = Ø1/Ø1/85 (Tuesday)
                 8:9Ø        = 1Ø:55am


 Date format: 3 1, 4
```

FIGURE 1.8: The Setup Date Format menu that appears when you select the Date Format option from the Setup Initial Settings menu (Shift-F1 I D). To change the format, select the numbers and enter the punctuation and symbols to be used as separators according to the codes listed on this screen.

option from the Date/Outline key (Shift-F5 F). The only difference is that changes made to the date format from this menu remain in effect each time you start WordPerfect. Those made from the Date/Outline key remain in effect only for the duration of the current work session.

DOCUMENT SUMMARY

Document summaries allow you to maintain particular information about a document, such as its author, typist, and subject, as well as any special comments about its content or formatting. The creation date is also automatically included as part of the document summary (however, WordPerfect does not keep track of the date the document was last modified). All of these statistics are saved together at the beginning of the document, although they are not visible on the regular editing screen and, therefore, are not printed. You can, however, use the Word Search option (**9** or **W**) on the List Files menu (F5 Enter) to locate a particular document by one or more of the document summary statistics, and you can view the document summary statistics by using the Look option (**6** or **L**) on the List Files menu.

Under normal conditions, to add such a summary to your document, you must press Shift-F8 (Format), select the Document option (**3** or **D**), and then select the Summary option (**5** or **S**). However, you can have WordPerfect automatically prompt you to enter a document summary the first time you save your document by selecting the Document Summary option on the Initial Settings menu.

When you select this option, the menu shown in Figure 1.9 appears. This menu includes two options, Create on Save/Exit and Subject Search Text. When you select the first option (**1** or **C**) and change it from No to Yes by typing **Y**, WordPerfect will automatically present you with its Document Summary screen the first time you either save the document by pressing F10 (Save) or attempt to exit the document by pressing F7 (Exit). Figure 1.10 shows a sample of how this Document Summary screen appears when you set this option to Yes and save a document for the first time. The only statistic filled in is Date of Creation. As soon as you complete the save procedure, System Filename will contain the name assigned to the document rather than *(Not named yet)*. The Comments box automatically contains the first part of the text of the document. You can replace this with your own comments. (See Chapter 2 for more information on creating and using document summaries.)

The second option on the Setup Document Summary menu is Subject Search Text. By default, this search text is *RE:* (Regarding), which is used as a heading in a memorandum and, on occasion, in a business letter. This means that if the characters *RE:* exist in approximately the first 400 characters of the document, then all of the text up to the next hard return ([HRt]) will automatically be filled in as the Subject/Account in the document summary screen.

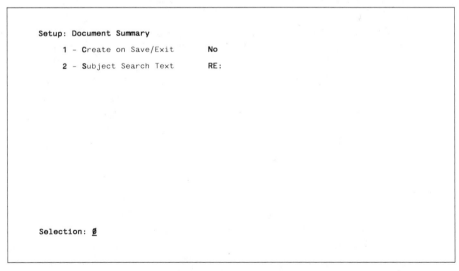

```
Setup: Document Summary

    1 - Create on Save/Exit        No

    2 - Subject Search Text        RE:

    Selection: 0
```

FIGURE 1.9: The Setup Document Summary menu that appears when you select Document Summary from the Setup Initial Settings menu (Shift-F1 I S). To have WordPerfect automatically prompt you to fill out a summary for a document, use the Create on Save/Exit option and set it to Yes. You use the Subject Search Text option to have the program use new search text. If this text is located in the first 400 characters of the document, all of the text that follows it up to the next hard return is automatically entered as the Subject/Account for the document summary.

```
Document Summary

        System Filename           (Not named yet)

        Date of Creation          April 2Ø, 1989

    1 - Descriptive Filename

    2 - Subject/Account

    3 - Author

    4 - Typist

    5 - Comments
    ┌──────────────────────────────────────────────────────────┐
    │  Document summaries allow you to maintain particular information about a │
    │  document, such as its author, typist, and subject, as well as any special │
    │  comments about its content or formatting. The creation date is also │
    │  automatically included as part of the document summary. │
    └──────────────────────────────────────────────────────────┘


Selection: Ø
```

FIGURE 1.10: The Document Summary screen as it appears when you attempt to save a document after setting the Create on Save/Exit option to Yes on the Setup Document Summary menu. Because the document was never saved before, System Filename is listed as *(Not named yet)*. This will change to the file name as soon as you fill out the document summary statistics and complete the save procedure. Also, notice that the Comments box automatically contains the first part of the text of the document. To enter your own nonprinting comments above this text, you select the Comments option on this menu, press the Enter key to push this text down, and type your comments.

You can use the Subject Search Text option to change *RE:* to some other characters or word you use more frequently. For example, if your memorandum contains the heading *Subject:* and you want the text that follows *Subject:* to be entered on the Subject/Account line in your document summaries, you would replace *RE:* with *Subject:* after selecting this option. Note that you can always replace the text chosen by the Subject Search Text string when filling out a particular document summary, if you find it to be inappropriate.

INITIAL CODES

Perhaps the most important of the Initial Settings options is the Initial Codes option (**4** or **I**). This allows you to change the formatting defaults chosen by WordPerfect. (See Appendix D for a complete list of WordPerfect's default settings.) For example, if you wish to make a left-justified and ragged-right margin the default for all new documents created in WordPerfect, you can use this option to turn off justification, which is on by default.

When you select the Initial Codes option (**4** or **I**) from the Setup Initial Settings menu (Shift-F1 I), WordPerfect splits the screen in half. The lower half is similar to the Reveal Codes screen that is accessed in a document by pressing

Alt-F3. To change various format settings, you press the Format key (Shift-F8) and select and change the defaults from the appropriate menu (Line, Page, or Document). As you make a change, the formatting codes that are inserted by WordPerfect are displayed in the lower half of the screen.

In Figure 1.11, you can see the codes for two formatting changes. The first code changes the default paper size to legal (8½" × 14"). This was done by pressing Shift-F8, selecting the Page menu, then selecting the Paper Size/Type option and changing the size to Legal, using the Standard type. The second code changes the default from right-justified to ragged-right. This was done by selecting the Line menu and then choosing the Justification option and setting it to No.

When you finish making changes from the Format menus and press F7 (Exit), you are returned to the Setup Initial Codes screen. When you press F7 (Exit) to leave this screen, you are returned to the Initial Settings menu. Any changes to the default settings made on the Setup Initial Codes screen affect all documents created from that point on. All documents created before these changes were made retain the formatting dictated by the original initial formatting codes in effect when they were created.

To bring under the new formatting defaults a document that you created before you changed the Setup initial codes, you must retrieve it and enter the changes either from the Document Initial Codes screen (Shift-F8 D C) or directly into the beginning of the document by selecting the appropriate Format menu options.

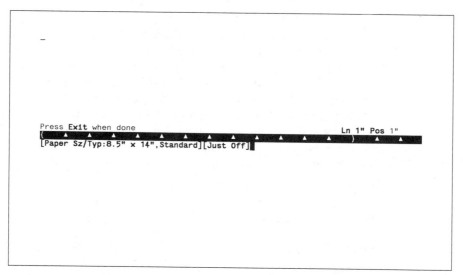

FIGURE 1.11: The Setup Initial Codes screen showing the codes for changing the default paper size to Legal and the default right margin to ragged-right. Changes made here affect all new documents created in WordPerfect.

Note: When you enter formatting changes using the Document Initial Codes options, the formatting codes are not visible in the Reveal Codes screen in the document as they are when you enter them directly into the document. You can think of such codes as "secret" codes as opposed to the "hidden" codes normally entered directly into the document at the cursor's position when you change a setting using the Format menu options. The only way to view and change "secret" codes is to select the Document Initial Codes option, where you see a Reveal Codes screen showing the codes used. This screen is identical in layout and use to the Setup Initial Codes screen. The difference is that the formatting codes in the Setup Initial Codes screen affect all new documents, while the codes shown in the Document Initial Codes screen affect only the current document. A change made to the setting of a formatting feature in the Document Initial Codes screen overrides any conflicting setting made to the same formatting feature in the Setup Initial Codes screen. See Appendix E for more information on the hierarchy of formatting codes and font changes.

To restore a formatting default to its original setting, you must return to the Setup Initial Codes screen (Shift-F1 I I) and delete it from the screen. Remember that all documents created while the change was in effect retain that formatting. The document does not automatically conform to the new WordPerfect formatting defaults when you retrieve it.

REPEAT VALUE

The Repeat Value option determines the number of times the action that immediately follows pressing the Esc key is repeated. Eight times is the default. For example, if you press the Esc key and then press the letter **R**, eight *R*'s will appear on the screen. So too, if you press Esc and then press the Del key, eight characters starting at the cursor's position will be deleted.

You can use the Repeat Value option (**5** or **R**) on the Initial Settings menu to increase or decrease this default value. You can always override this value by typing a new number after pressing the Esc key, but this new repeat value remains in effect only for the single operation you perform with it. Afterwards, it will revert to the repeat value entered on the Initial Settings menu.

TABLE OF AUTHORITIES

The Table of Authorities feature is used to mark a list of citations, such as statutes, cases, and court regulations, in a legal brief. From this list, you can generate a table of authorities. You can use the Table of Authorities option (**6** or **A**) on the Initial Settings menu to change the default style for these tables. Figure 1.12

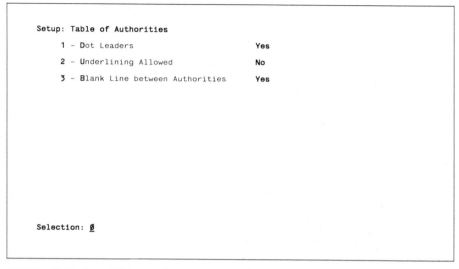

```
Setup: Table of Authorities
    1 - Dot Leaders                          Yes
    2 - Underlining Allowed                  No
    3 - Blank Line between Authorities       Yes




    Selection: 0
```

FIGURE 1.12: The Setup Table of Authorities menu, used to change the default style for tables of authorities generated by WordPerfect. As configured, WordPerfect will place periods between an authority and its page number(s) in the table, prohibit underlining in the authorities, and insert a blank line after each authority. When you change any of these settings on this menu, they affect all tables of authorities you generate in new documents.

shows you the options on the Setup Table of Authorities menu and the default values in effect when you first start WordPerfect.

The first option, Dot Leaders (**1** or **D**), is set to Yes, meaning that WordPerfect will put periods between each entry and its page number(s). The second option, Underlining Allowed (**2** or **U**), is set to No, meaning that WordPerfect won't allow you to use underlining in the table. Since it is common practice to underline case citations, you may want to change this setting to Yes. The last option, Blank Line between Authorities (**3** or **B**), is set to Yes, meaning that WordPerfect will automatically insert a blank line after each entry in the table.

You can always override the default settings entered on the Setup Table of Authorities menu by changing the style for the table you are about to generate. Press Alt-F5 (Mark Text), select the Define option (**5** or **D**), select the Define Table of Authorities option (**4** or **A**), and enter the section number. WordPerfect will then display a menu with the same three style options available on the Setup Table of Authorities menu (Figure 1.12).

Keyboard Layout

WordPerfect 5.0 allows you to create many different keyboard layouts that can customize the functioning of WordPerfect command key sequences as well as change the characters inserted into a document when you press a standard

QWERTY key. Refer to Chapter 17 for a complete account of how to create and use keyboard layouts.

To put a particular keyboard layout in effect, you select the Keyboard Layout option (**6** or **K**) from the Setup menu. Then, you highlight the name of the desired keyboard and choose the Select option. The name of the keyboard (along with the .WPK extension given by WordPerfect to all Keyboard Layout files) will appear on the Keyboard Layout option line on the Setup menu.

The keyboard selected from the Setup menu remains the keyboard that Word-Perfect uses the next time you start WordPerfect. To return to the original keyboard layout at any time when editing, press Shift-F1 K O.

Location of Auxiliary Files

The Location of Auxiliary Files option on the Setup menu is used to tell Word-Perfect where to find various files that it may have to access during program operation. Figure 1.13 shows the options that appear when you select the Location of Auxiliary Files option from the Setup menu (Shift-F1 L). If you don't specify directories for the Backup Directory, Hyphenation Module(s), Main Dictionary(s), Printer Files, Supplementary Dictionary(s), and Thesaurus options, WordPerfect will use the startup directory that contains the WordPerfect program files.

In the case of the Keyboard Layout and Macro files, these will be located in the default directory at the time they are created. (See Chapter 16 for information on using macros and Chapter 17 for information on using Keyboard Layout files.) The Style Library file is not used unless you choose the Style Library Filename option (**6** or **L**) and indicate the file (including the full path name) that is to be used. (See Chapter 6 for information on using styles and setting up a style library.)

When you install a printer (as described in Chapter 7), WordPerfect automatically copies the printer definition file into the directory used at startup. In addition, it automatically fills in the name of this directory on the Location of Auxiliary Files menu (as is the case in Figure 1.13). This is the only case in which the program indicates the location of auxiliary files automatically; for all the other options, you must select the option and type in the directory name. (In the case of Style Library Filename, you must also enter the name of the file that contains the styles to be used.)

If you wish to store supplementary files like the spelling dictionary, hyphenation module (see note below), and Thesaurus together in a directory of their own, you should first create the directory—see **Directories** in Part V for information on how to do this in WordPerfect—copy the necessary files into it, and then return to this menu and indicate the name of the directory for the appropriate options.

```
Setup: Location of Auxiliary Files
        1 - Backup Directory
        2 - Hyphenation Module(s)
        3 - Keyboard/Macro Files
        4 - Main Dictionary(s)
        5 - Printer Files                C:\WP5Ø
        6 - Style Library Filename
        7 - Supplementary Dictionary(s)
        8 - Thesaurus




    Selection: Ø
```

FIGURE 1.13: The Setup Location of Auxiliary Files menu options, which are used to tell WordPerfect where to find various files. Because a printer was installed using the Select Printer option (Shift-F7 S), WordPerfect has filled in the location of the printer files as *C:\WP50*, the directory that holds the Word-Perfect program files. If you create separate subdirectories to hold special files like macros, spelling dictionary files, and hyphenation modules, you need to indicate their location on this menu.

Note: You must purchase the hyphenation module in the language you wish to use from WordPerfect Corporation; these files are not supplied with the program. Therefore, selecting the Hyphenation Module(s) option on the Location of Auxiliary Files menu will have no effect unless you have purchased the module(s) you want to use and copied them into the directory that you enter here.

If you are using WordPerfect on a two-disk-drive system, you should indicate the letter of the drive that contains your auxiliary file(s). In most cases, this will be drive B, unless you use the /R startup option so that you can remove the WordPerfect2 disk from drive A.

Units of Measure

WordPerfect 5.0 uses inches as its default unit of measurement, both for displaying the position of the cursor on the status line and for displaying selected values for menu options that require measurements, such as left and right margins and tab settings. You use the Units of Measure option (**8** or **U**) on the Setup menu if you wish to change either display to some other unit like centimeters, points, or the column and line numbers used in version 4.2 (referred to as *4.2 units*). Moreover, you can have inches represented by either the inch symbol (the default) or the letter *i* (for *inches*).

Figure 1.14 shows you the screen that appears when you select the Units of Measure option on the Setup menu. To change the unit used for either Display and Entry of Numbers for Margins, Tabs, etc. (**1** or **D**) or Status Line Display (**2** or **S**), you select the option and then type the appropriate character according to the legend shown on this screen. For example, to set the status line display unit to points, you type **p** after selecting this option.

Regardless of the unit selected for the display and entry of number for margins, tabs, and the like, you can always enter the value in another recognized unit by terminating the value with the abbreviation shown in this legend. For instance, if inches are the selected unit for this option, you can set a new top margin of 1 inch by selecting the Margins option (Shift-F8 P M) and then entering **2.54c**, **72p**, **10u**, or **1200w** (*w* stands for *WordPerfect units*—they can be used although they aren't listed in the legend). WordPerfect will automatically convert this to *1"* (or *1i*, if you have selected *i* rather than *"* to represent the number of inches) after *Margins, Top* on the Format Page screen.

RUNNING THE TUTOR PROGRAM

WordPerfect supplies an on-line tutorial program to help you become familiar with many of its features. This program is named TUTOR.COM and is automatically copied to the C:\WP50\LEARN directory if you use the Install program to install WordPerfect on your hard disk. Before using the Tutor program on drive C, however, you must establish a path to the C:\WP50 directory so that the Tutor program can start WordPerfect and make the directory that contains the tutorial files current. You do this by adding a PATH command to your AUTOEXEC.BAT file similar to the one that follows:

```
PATH = C:\,C:\DOS,C:\WP50
```

The PATH command should include all of the directories that should be searched when a command is given in DOS. In this sample PATH statement, only the root directory C:\, the DOS directory (if you have one), and the WP50 directory are included. In your PATH statement, you may need to include other directories that should be searched.

Note that you can change the path just for the current session so that you can run the Tutor program. Simply type

```
PATH = C:\WP50
```

However, be aware that this will disable any PATH statement that was previously executed by the AUTOEXEC.BAT file (until you reboot the computer).

```
Setup: Units of Measure

      1 - Display and Entry of Numbers            "
              for Margins, Tabs, etc.

      2 - Status Line Display                     "


Legend:

      " = inches
      1 = inches
      c = centimeters
      p = points
      u = WordPerfect 4.2 Units (Lines/Columns)




   Selection: 0
```

FIGURE 1.14: The Setup Units of Measure menu. These options change the unit used when entering new values for certain menu options or displayed with the Ln and Pos indicators on the status line. To change the default unit of measure for either option, select it and then enter the symbol that represents the desired unit of measure, according to the legend shown on this screen.

After setting the path so that the C:\WP50 directory is searched when the Tutor program issues the WP startup command, you need to make the C:\WP50\ LEARN directory current before you can start the Tutor program. To do this, enter the following command from the DOS prompt:

CD \WP50\LEARN

Then press the Enter key. After that, start the lessons simply by typing **TUTOR** from the DOS prompt.

To run the Tutor program on a two-disk-drive computer, place the Word-Perfect1 disk (or the WordPerfect1/WordPerfect2 disk if you have 3½-inch drives) in drive A and the Learning disk in drive B. Type **B:** and press the Enter key to change the default drive. Then type **TUTOR** to start the lessons.

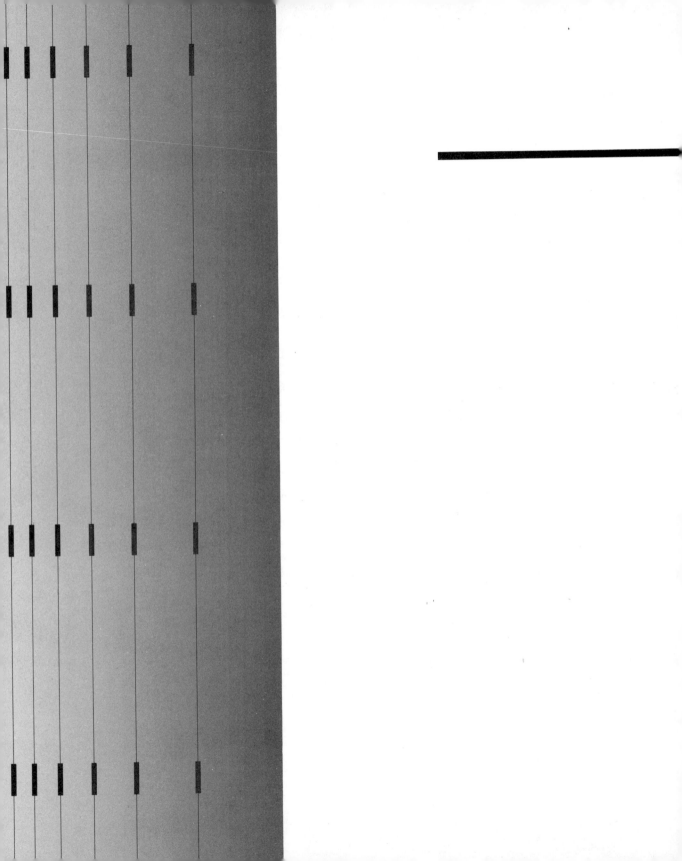

CHAPTER 2

GETTING ACQUAINTED WITH WORDPERFECT 5.0

Getting Acquainted
with WordPerfect 5.0

This chapter presents an overview of WordPerfect 5.0 and acquaints you with the basics of the program, such as entering text, moving the cursor, deleting and undeleting, working with two windows, saving documents, retrieving documents, and exiting from the program. These discussions assume that you have already installed WordPerfect. If you haven't, you may want to refer back to Chapter 1.

This chapter also orients you to WordPerfect's editing screen and the use of the IBM keyboards. These discussions introduce you to WordPerfect's appearance on the screen after you start the program and give you a sense of how you will use the keyboard to create documents.

Upgrade Notes

If you have been using an earlier version of WordPerfect, you will find that the function keys in version 5.0 have been reorganized, primarily for ease of use and graphics support. As a result, some of the functions have been reassigned to different keys. You may find the following quick summary helpful:

- **F1**—The Superscript/Subscript commands have been moved to the Font key (Ctrl-F8), which was itself previously the Print Format key. (All format functions are now on Shift-F8, which is the Format key.) Shift-F1 is Setup, which replaces the old WP/S option. Shell (Ctrl-F1), Thesaurus (Alt-F1), and Cancel (F1) remain the same.

- **F2**—Search (F2), Replace (Alt-F2), Reverse Search (Shift-F2), and Spell (Ctrl-F2) are still on this key, but some of their functions have been enhanced.

- **F3**—The Help key remains as F3, as do Reveal Codes as Alt-F3 and Switch as Shift-F3. On the Screen key (Ctrl-F3), Colors and Auto Rewrite have been moved to the Setup key (Shift-F1), and the Ctrl/Alt key's functions are now covered through the new Keyboard Layout and Compose commands.

- **F4**—Indent (F4) and Left/Right Indent (Shift-F4) remain the same. Move (Ctrl-F4) and Block (Alt-F4) are still assigned to this key, although you will find that some of their menu items have been reassigned and made easier to use.

- **F5**—This is basically a new key in version 5.0. The Text In/Out key (Ctrl-F5) now consists of three submenus. Document Summary functions are now on the Format key (Shift-F8). Date is changed to Date/Outline (Shift-F5) and the Outline and Paragraph Numbering features have been moved from Mark Text (Alt-F5) to this key. Mark Text itself has been reorganized; it now contains the Master Document, Document Compare, and Automatic Reference features. Redline and Strikeout are now on the Font key (Ctrl-F8). List Files (F5) has been enhanced, and new types of word searches are now possible.

- **F6**—The functions of this key remain essentially the same.

- **F7**—Exit (F7) is the same; however, the other functions on this key have been enhanced. Footnote (Ctrl-F7) now has footnotes and endnotes on different submenus, with new features. Print (Shift-F7) is divided into Print and Options, with renamed menu choices and new options that combine the old Print Options and Printer Control options while adding new ones. The process of installing printers has been streamlined.

- **F8**—This is also basically a new key in version 5.0. Only Underline (F8) remains the same. The program's formatting features are now on Shift-F8 (Format), which combines the old Line Format, Page Format, Print Format, and Document Format options. You will find that many formatting commands are easier to use and that new options have been made available. Shift-F8 with Block on now turns on block protection, instead of Alt-F8, which previously turned on protection. The Font key (Ctrl-F8) is a new feature that allows you to change the size and style of text directly instead of inserting a Font Change code, as you did previously. Style (Alt-F8) is a new feature that allows you to create format style sheets for the documents you write.

- **F9**—This key has changed partially. Merge Codes is now Shift-F9 instead of Alt-F9, and a new feature, Graphics (Alt-F9), which allows you to combine graphics and text, has been added. Merge E is now chosen from Merge Codes instead of being assigned to a key of its own.

- **F10**—Save (F10), Retrieve (Shift-F10), and Macro (Alt-F10) are the same; Macro Define (Ctrl-F10) now contains a macro editor.

In addition to these reassignments of the command keys, WordPerfect 5.0 contains many new features. They are listed alphabetically here. To quickly obtain more information on any of them, refer to the appropriate heading in the "WordPerfect Command and Feature Reference," Part V of this book.

Advance
Automatic Reference

Base Font
Beep Options
Cartridges and Fonts
Colors/Fonts/Attributes
Columns: Parallel Columns
Compose
Cursor Speed
Decimal/Align Character
Display Pitch
Display, Setup
Document Comments
Document Compare
Fast Save (Unformatted)
Font
Footnote: Endnote Placement
Force Odd/Even Page
Forms
Graphics
Initial Settings
Kerning
Keyboard Layout
Language
Line Height
Line Spacing
Location of Auxiliary Files
Locking a File
Margins, Top and Bottom
Master Document
Print Color
Print Quality
Printer Functions
Printer, Select
Setup
Styles
Units of Measure
View Document
Word/Letter Spacing

OVERVIEW OF WORDPERFECT

WordPerfect 5.0, like its predecessors, is a *screen-oriented* word processor, which means that as you create and edit your document, it appears on your screen pretty much as it will when it is printed: What you see is what you get. Thus, the program displays special printing attributes such as boldfacing (which appears either in reverse video or in a different color if your computer has a color card) and underlining on the screen. It also shows certain formatting effects, such as indentations, centering, newspaper columns, and double spacing, as they will appear in printed form.

WordPerfect also displays whatever attributes are supported by the video card you are using. For example, if you have a graphics card such as a Hercules Ram-Font card or its equivalent, WordPerfect will also display characteristics such as italics and large fonts. However, you do not need a graphics display to use WordPerfect 5.0. Its View Document feature allows you to see formatting features that are not presented on the editing screen, such as headers and footers, top and bottom margins, page numbers, footnotes in position, italics, graphic boxes, justification, and so forth.

WordPerfect is also *document-oriented,* which means that once you enter a setting for a format change, it will be in effect from that point on in your document, or until you change it again. This refers to changes that you make by using the Format menu (Shift-F8); changes you make by using the Setup menu (Shift-F1) are in effect each time you start WordPerfect.

However, there is a major difference between version 5.0 and earlier versions of WordPerfect in the way the program handles default settings: document format commands (made through the Format menu) are saved with the document and take precedence over any initial setup default settings (made through the Setup menu) that may have been specified. In effect, this means that you can retrieve a WordPerfect 5.0 document into any copy of WordPerfect 5.0, and it will retain the format under which it was created. (Chapters 3 and 4 will discuss formatting in greater detail.)

WordPerfect's Reveal Codes Screen

To keep the screen view of your document as similar as possible to the printed version, the WordPerfect editing screen does not display any of the special codes it uses to format the text. WordPerfect keeps all of its codes hidden until you choose to view them.

WordPerfect also differs from word processors that allow you to turn on and off the display of formatting codes normally kept invisible in the text. To view the formatting codes in WordPerfect, you must use a special key combination, Alt-F3, referred to as the *Reveal Codes* key. When you press Alt-F3, WordPerfect splits the display screen into two windows, as shown in Figure 2.1. The lower window contains a copy of the same text visible in the upper window, except that it displays all of the formatting codes that are being used.

You will often need to use the Reveal Codes key sequence (Alt-F3) to change the formatting of your document. Though WordPerfect's system of codes may

```
         You will often need to use the Reveal Codes key sequence
(Alt-F3) to change the formatting of your document. Though
WordPerfect's system of codes may appear somewhat intimidating at
first, these codes are really quite easy to read (they all use
English abbreviations rather than special graphics characters
C:\5\B\CH1                                    Doc 1 Pg 9 Ln 1.66" Pos 1"
[                  ▲   ▲   ▲   ▲   ▲   ▲   ▲   ▲   ▲   ▲   ) ▲   ▲   ]
working in the editing screen by pressing Alt-F3. In many cases[SRt]
you will need to view these codes in order to delete them.[bold][HRt]
[HRt]
        You will often need to use the Reveal Codes key sequence[SRt]
(Alt-F3) to change the formatting of your document. Though[SRt]
WordPerfect's system of codes may appear somewhat intimidating at[SRt]
first, these codes are really quite easy to read (they all use[SRt]
English abbreviations rather than special graphics characters[SRt]
such as MultiMate uses) and to manipulate. As you look up various[SRt]
word processing commands and seek out particular information[SRt]

Press Reveal Codes to restore screen
```

FIGURE 2.1: Viewing WordPerfect's hidden formatting codes. You can see WordPerfect's hidden codes at any time while working in the editing screen by pressing Alt-F3. In many cases you will need to view these codes in order to delete them.

appear somewhat intimidating at first, these codes are really quite easy to read—they all use English abbreviations rather than special graphics characters as MultiMate uses—and to manipulate. As you look up various word processing commands and seek out particular information about WordPerfect's more advanced features, you will find that this book devotes a great deal of attention to the formatting codes used by the various features. It also provides clear, concise information about what changes, if any, you should make to these formatting codes using Alt-F3 (the Reveal Codes key).

THE WORDPERFECT SCREEN

As soon as you issue the appropriate startup command and press Enter, an initial startup screen appears very briefly. This screen lists the current WordPerfect directory, although you may not always be able to read this information as it passes. Directly after the initial startup screen, you will be presented with the editing screen. This screen is shown in Figure 2.2.

The Status Line

The first indicator in the *status line* in the lower-right corner of the screen tells you the number of the document you are working with. (You can work with two documents at once, as discussed in "Working with Two Documents" later in this chapter.) The status line also indicates the page of the document you are

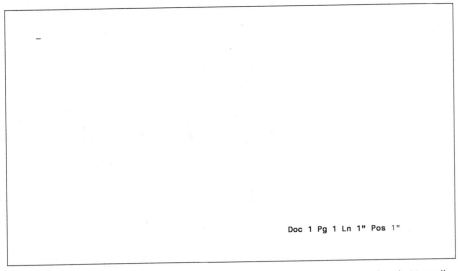

Doc 1 Pg 1 Ln 1" Pos 1"

FIGURE 2.2: WordPerfect's editing screen. The program gives you a full screen to work with. Normally the only indications you see are the document number, page number, line, and cursor position in the lower-right corner.

working on as well as the line and the cursor position. You can use the Setup menu to specify whether these measurements are in inches (the default), points, centimeters, or "WordPerfect 4.2 units" (line and column numbers). If you choose WordPerfect 4.2 units, your status line will look like the WordPerfect 4.2 status line.

Being able to work with two documents at once gives you a great deal of flexibility. For example, you can store text that you use frequently, such as standard paragraphs, product descriptions, and form letters, and switch and copy between the document you are creating and the document that holds the text. You can also use the second document as a work space to hold notes or text that you plan to use later.

The Page Indicator

The page indicator on the status line shows you the number of the page on which the cursor is located in the document you are working with. It corresponds to the number of the page that will be printed (if you specify page numbering) when you print your document. You can use the program's Go To feature (Ctrl-Home) to move directly to any page in your document (see "Cursor Movement" later in this chapter).

Page breaks in WordPerfect are shown on the screen. A page break is indicated by a line of hyphens extending across the width of the screen. You can also add your own page breaks (sometimes referred to as *hard page breaks* or *forced page breaks*) by pressing Ctrl-Enter. This type of page break appears as a line of equal signs across the width of the screen. A hard page break can be deleted by using the Reveal Codes key combination (Alt-F3) to locate the code [HPg] and then deleting the code. You can also delete a hard page break by positioning the cursor at the end of the last line of text above the page break and pressing Del. If there is a blank line above the page break display, position the cursor at the leftmost position of this blank line and press Del. You can also move to the line after the page break and press Backspace to delete the page break.

The Line Indicator

The line indicator on the status line shows the position or number of the line where the cursor is located. As you type, you will notice this indicator change whenever the cursor moves to a new line. When you use the Next Page or Previous Page function (PgDn or PgUp) or the Go To Page function (Ctrl-Home followed by the page number), the cursor will move to the first line of the page indicated.

If you accept the default Units of Measure setting on the Setup menu (see Chapter 1), the line position is displayed in inches. You can also choose centimeters, points, or WordPerfect 4.2 units (lines and columns). You may find it easier to locate a particular line if the position is displayed as a simple line number, as it was in version 4.2 of WordPerfect. In that case, you can use the Setup menu to select 4.2 Units as the unit of measure. However, all screens depicted in this book show the Ln and Pos indicators in inches, which is the default setting.

The Position Indicator

The last number on the status line indicates the position of the cursor. Your document default settings are for 1-inch right and left margins, so the right margin is at 1'' and the left is at 7.5'' if you are using the default settings.

THE KEYBOARD

The WordPerfect program is based on the use of the keyboard's function keys to carry out your commands. Because the program has no visible menu bars or ruler lines unless you call them up, you have a full screen to work with. However, you also have few reminders of the function keys and their purposes. The template that is supplied with the program explains the use of these function keys, but if you are working without a template or have forgotten some of the command keystroke sequences, you can consult the following section.

The Function Keys

Your keyboard probably resembles one of those shown in Figure 2.3. You issue commands to WordPerfect by pressing the function keys alone or in combination with the Ctrl, Shift, or Alt key.

Each of the function keys (F1 through F10) performs a special function within WordPerfect. For example, pressing F4, the Indent key, indents text according to

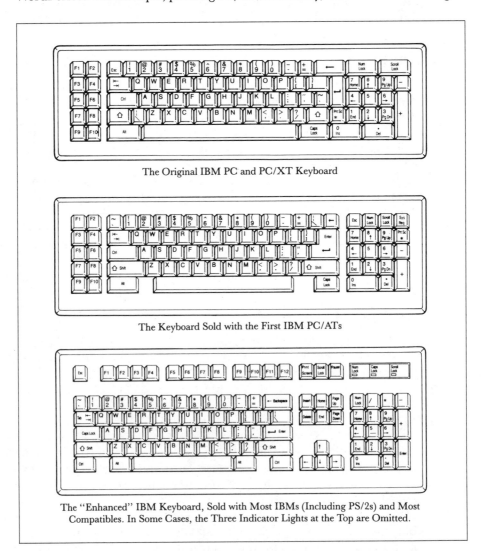

The Original IBM PC and PC/XT Keyboard

The Keyboard Sold with the First IBM PC/ATs

The "Enhanced" IBM Keyboard, Sold with Most IBMs (Including PS/2s) and Most Compatibles. In Some Cases, the Three Indicator Lights at the Top are Omitted.

FIGURE 2.3: The standard IBM keyboards. Function keys are located either at the left of the keyboard or in a row at the top of the keyboard. WordPerfect's commands are issued by pressing one of these keys alone or in combination with the Ctrl, Shift, or Alt key.

the tab settings you specify. In combination with the Ctrl, Shift, and Alt keys, these function keys take on different meanings, as summarized in Table 2.1.

The functions of each of these keys alone and in combination with the Ctrl, Shift, and Alt keys will be discussed throughout this book in the context of how you use them to perform word processing tasks.

	(ALONE)	CTRL	SHIFT	ALT
F1	Cancel	Shell	Setup	Thesaurus
F2	→Search	Spell	←Search	Replace
F3	Help	Screen	Switch	Reveal Codes
F4	→Indent	Move	→Indent←	Block
F5	List Files	Text In/Out	Date/Outline	Mark Text
F6	Bold	Tab Align	Center	Flush Right
F7	Exit	Footnote	Print	Math/Columns
F8	Underline	Font	Format	Style
F9	Merge R	Merge/Sort	Merge Codes	Graphics
F10	Save	Macro Define	Retrieve	Macro

TABLE 2.1: WordPerfect's Function Key Combinations

On the template that came with your program, a command issued through a combination of a function key and the Shift key is printed in green, a combination with the Ctrl key is red, and a combination with the Alt key is blue. The function key used alone is printed in black.

If you no longer have the function key template, you can always bring it up on your screen by pressing F3 (the Help key) twice. To obtain a hard copy for reference, turn on your printer and press Shift-PrtSc with the template displayed.

If you are using an extended keyboard—the kind in which the function keys are above the keyboard—you can order a special template from WordPerfect Corporation.

We will take a closer look at several of the special-purpose keys and the functions they serve in WordPerfect. In the following sections, refer to Figure 2.3 for the exact placement of each key on your own keyboard.

The Enter Key

The *Enter* key is marked ⏎ on many keyboards, and is sometimes called the *Return* key. It is used to indicate the end of a paragraph, to insert blank lines into a document, or, in certain cases, to confirm a menu choice.

When you reach the end of one line, WordPerfect automatically begins the next one. This is called *word wrap,* as the program "wraps" words from the end of one line to the beginning of the next. You don't have to press Enter at the end of each line. If you do, you will insert a *hard return* (a line break code), which you may not want in your document at that point.

The Escape Key

The Escape key, marked *Esc,* serves several purposes in WordPerfect. Its basic function is to repeat a command (or character) a specified number of times, although you can press it twice to cancel a command. The specified number of times that Esc repeats a command is preset to eight, but you can change this simply by typing another number. For example, pressing Esc, typing **5**, and pressing the ↑ key moves the cursor up five lines. (See "Cursor Movement" later in this chapter for a full discussion of techniques for moving the cursor.)

The repeat function of the Esc key is also quite useful for drawing boxes and lines with WordPerfect, because it lets you draw lines by repeating a single graphics character (see Chapter 14). The Esc key can also be used to repeat a macro (see Chapter 16) or to delete several lines or characters (see "Deleting Text" later in this chapter).

> *Note:* The F1 function key is used primarily as the Cancel key (although it also works as an Undelete key), a function often assigned to the Esc key in other software programs. These other programs commonly assign the Help function to F1, a function WordPerfect assigns to F3. If you choose, you can select the ALTRNAT keyboard layout so that Help is on the F1 key, as explained in Chapter 17.

The Tab Key

The Tab key, indicated by ⇆ on the left side of the keyboard, moves the cursor to the tab settings you have specified. The program's default values are tabs every ½ inch (5 spaces in 4.2 units), but you can change these settings (see Chapter 3).

You should not confuse the Tab key with the Indent key (F4) in WordPerfect. Using the Tab key moves the cursor to the next tab setting, but the Indent key inserts an Indent code into your document, telling WordPerfect to indent an entire paragraph, as discussed in greater detail in Chapter 3.

The Backspace and Delete Keys

The Backspace key, represented by ← on the upper-right side of the keyboard, and the Delete key, marked *Del,* on the lower-right side of the keyboard, are both used to delete characters. The Backspace key deletes the character to the left of the cursor, while the Del key deletes the character the cursor is on.

The "Lock" Keys

Three keys on the IBM keyboard—Caps Lock, Num Lock, and Ins—lock the keyboard into certain modes. (Scroll Lock is not used in WordPerfect.) You may sometimes press these keys inadvertently and see unexpected results on the screen.

CAPS LOCK

The Caps Lock key, as its name implies, shifts your typing mode to uppercase letters. (When the Shift key is pressed while in Caps Lock mode, letters appear in lowercase.) Pressing this key a second time returns you to normal typing mode. The position indicator on the status line changes to uppercase (for example, POS 8.04") when Caps Lock is on.

Note: When the Caps Lock key is activated (indicated by *POS* on the status line), only letters are shifted to uppercase. You still have to press one of the Shift keys to use the punctuation marks and special symbols that are on shared keys, as with the number keys in the top row. For example, even when Caps Lock is on, you must press Shift and **1** to enter the exclamation point (!).

NUM LOCK

The Num Lock key changes the keys on the numeric keypad from cursor movement keys to numeric entry keys. The position indicator on the status line flashes when Num Lock is on.

When the word *Pos* in the lower-right corner is flashing, pressing an arrow key, Home, End, PgUp, or PgDn on the numeric pad will cause numbers to be inserted into your text. Press the Num Lock key one more time to restore the cursor functions.

INSERT

The Insert key (marked *Ins*) changes the mode of operation from Insert mode, in which characters you type are inserted at the cursor's position and do not replace existing characters, to Typeover mode, in which characters you type replace existing characters. When Typeover mode is on, the word *Typeover* appears in the lower-left corner of the screen.

The Numeric Keypad

The numeric keypad, located at the right of your keyboard, contains the cursor movement keys and, when Num Lock is on, functions as a numeric entry keypad, as discussed earlier. Each of the cursor movement keys is discussed later in this chapter.

OBTAINING ON-LINE HELP AS YOU WORK

WordPerfect offers extensive on-line Help screens that you can use whenever you need additional information about a specific feature or command. The F3 function key is WordPerfect's Help key. This key may be hard to remember if you are used to other programs that use F1 as the Help key, but you can use an alternate keyboard layout that has reassigned the Help key to F1. See Chapter 17 for details.

After you press F3 (Help), you must then press another key to obtain specific help. You can use F3 alone to see what version of WordPerfect you are running. This information is always displayed in the upper-right corner of the Help screen. Right after the version number, you will see a date that further identifies the version.

If you wish to know more about how a particular function key or key combination operates in WordPerfect, you merely press the function key or combination. For example, pressing F3 followed by Ctrl-F5 displays a Help screen that tells you about document conversion, summaries, and comments—the commands associated with Ctrl-F5 (Text In/Out). On this screen you will find numbered options that you can type to obtain other, more specific Help screens. Whenever you wish to return to your document, press Enter or the space bar. Remember not to press F1 (Cancel) or Esc, or you will receive a Help screen describing the functions of these keys instead of being returned to the document.

Instead of pressing a specific function key or key combination after pressing F3, you can also type a letter. For example, if you had forgotten the function keys used to perform the search-and-replace operation in WordPerfect, you could press F3 and type **S** (for *Search*). WordPerfect would then display an alphabetical list of its features that begin with the letter *S*. This Help screen is shown in Figure 2.4.

As you can see from this figure, the Help screen is arranged in three columns listing the function keys used, the features, and the key names. In this case, you can see that to perform a search-and-replace operation in WordPerfect, you use Alt-F2. To obtain more information about how the Search and Replace feature works in the program, you can press Alt-F2 and obtain a Help screen specifically about this command.

If there are more alphabetical items available for the letter you have typed, type **1** to see the additional Help screen for that letter.

```
Key             Feature                             Key Name

F1Ø             Save Text                           Save
Ctrl-F3         Screen                              Screen
+(Num Pad)      Screen Down                         Screen Down
-(Num Pad)      Screen Up                           Screen Up
Shft-F1         Screen Setup                        Setup,3
Alt-F2          Search and Replace                  Replace
F5              Search for Text in File(s)          List Files,9
Ctrl-F9         Secondary File, Merge               Merge/Sort
Alt-F3          See Codes                           Reveal Codes
Shft-F7         Select Printer(s)                   Print
Shft-F8         Set Pitch (Letter/Word Spacing)     Format,4,6,3
Ctrl-F8         Shadow Print                        Font,2
Shft-F7         Send Printer a "GO"                 Print,4
Shft-F7         Sheet Feeder                        Print,S,3
Alt-F5          Short Form, Table of Auth.          Mark Text,4
Shft-F1         Side-by-side Columns Display        Setup,3
Ctrl-F8         Size of Print                       Font
Ctrl-F8         Small Capitalized Print             Font,2
Ctrl-F8         Small Print                         Font,1
Ctrl "-"        Soft Hyphen                         Soft Hyphen

                   Type 1 for more help: Ø
```

FIGURE 2.4: The Help screen displayed when you press F3 (Help) and type **S**. When you press F3 (Help) and type a specific letter, WordPerfect displays a Help screen organized as an alphabetical list of features. In this case, the letter *S* was used to obtain the function key combination for search-and-replace operations. As you can see, the Help screen is arranged in three columns; the first lists the function keys used, the second lists the features, and the third lists WordPerfect's names for the keys. To obtain more help about a specific feature, you need only press the function key combination. In this case, you would press Alt- F2 to access a Help screen describing search-and-replace operations.

Instead of using this method to remind you of the function key assignments, you can obtain an on-screen diagram similar to the keyboard template supplied with the WordPerfect program by pressing F3 after you have accessed the initial Help screen (in other words, by pressing F3 twice). Figure 2.5 shows this screen.

To obtain a hard copy of this screen, turn your printer on and press Shift-PrtSc with the screen displayed. To make this printout useful, you will have to mark it in some way to differentiate the various key combinations. This is because the boldface and underlining used on screen to indicate when the Ctrl and Alt keys are used with function keys are not printed when you use the Shift-PrtSc method. One way to distinguish the key combinations is to use highlighters of different colors for each combination.

CREATING A NEW DOCUMENT

As soon as you start WordPerfect and the opening screen is displayed, you are presented with an editing screen that is completely blank except for the status line in the lower-right corner. When you see this screen, you are free to begin work on a new document.

```
        WordPerfect 5.Ø Template (IBM Layout)

            ┌─────────────┬─────────────┐
            │   Shell     │   Spell     │
      F1    │   SETUP     │  <-SEARCH   │  F2
            │  Thesaurus  │   Replace   │
            │  Cancel     │  Search->   │
            │   Screen    │    Move     │            Legend:
      F3    │   SWITCH    │  ->INDENT<- │  F4
            │ Reveal Codes│   Block     │       Ctrl + Function Key
            │   Help      │  ->Indent   │       SHIFT + FUNCTION KEY
            │  Text In/Out│  Tab Align  │       Alt + Function Key
      F5    │ DATE/OUTLINE│   CENTER    │  F6   Function Key alone
            │  Mark Text  │ Flush Right │
            │  List Files │   Bold      │
            │  Footnote   │    Font     │
      F7    │   PRINT     │   FORMAT    │  F8
            │ Math/Columns│   Style     │
            │   Exit      │  Underline  │
            │  Merge/Sort │  Macro Def. │
      F9    │ MERGE CODES │  RETRIEVE   │  F10
            │  Graphics   │   Macro     │
            │  Merge R    │   Save      │
            └─────────────┴─────────────┘
```

FIGURE 2.5: The on-screen function key template accessed by pressing F3 (Help) twice. As you can see from the legend, this screen uses various print enhancements to identify the key combination (if any) used to access a particular group of features. The boldfaced labels identify function keys used with Ctrl. The capitalized labels identify function keys used with Shift. The underlined labels identify function keys used with Alt. Labels in regular text identify function keys used alone.

The Document Default Settings

If you immediately begin typing the text of a new document, it will be formatted according to WordPerfect's document default settings, which are summarized in Appendix D. If the document you are going to create requires different settings from those automatically in effect when you start WordPerfect, you can change them easily, as discussed in Chapters 3 and 4.

Tab stops are automatically set for you at 0.5-inch intervals. By pressing the Tab key, you can indent the first line of a paragraph.

Note: If you find yourself constantly reusing certain formats for many of the documents you create, you can create *macros* to save yourself time. For instance, you can create a macro that will reset the margins, set all the tab stops you need, change the line spacing, and place page numbers where you want them—all in one operation. Then, whenever you begin a new document that requires the format created by this macro, you can execute the macro before you begin entering your text. This method saves you the time required to issue all of these formatting commands separately. Macros are discussed in Chapter 16.

In addition, with version 5.0 of WordPerfect, you can set up *styles* for each element in your document and use the style instead of formatting text as you type. For instance, if you want all level-one headings to be in boldface and centered, you can define that style. Then, when you are typing a level-one heading in your text, you can simply turn on the style instead of pressing F6 for bold and Shift-F6 for center. If you work with complex design elements, such as multicolumn formats and a variety of type styles, this feature can save you many keystrokes throughout a document. See Chapter 6 for additional information about creating and using styles.

Whenever you enter text, *word wrap* is in effect. As soon as you type a word that would extend beyond the right margin, the word is placed at the beginning of the next line. You do not need to press Enter when the cursor approaches the end of the line. You should only add a carriage return to mark the end of a paragraph or to enter a short line of text whose words are to remain by themselves (as when entering a section heading or table title).

Entering the Text of the Document

After making any necessary changes to the default formatting settings, you can begin typing the text of your document. As you type, the position indicator in the extreme lower-right corner of the editing screen changes, keeping you informed of the cursor's current position as it advances across the line. When you reach the end of the line, WordPerfect will automatically advance any words that extend beyond the right margin setting to the beginning of the following line.

Because WordPerfect's Hyphenation feature is off when you first start a new document, entire words are wrapped to new lines whenever they extend beyond the right margin setting. When you enter a required hyphen between words, it will appear in the printed document. If a hyphenated expression extends beyond the right margin, it will be split at the hyphen only if the first word will fit within the line's margin setting.

When you enter or delete text that requires words to move down or up a line, WordPerfect automatically reformats the entire screen when you scroll the text up or down or press the ↑ or ↓ key. You can turn this Automatic Rewrite feature off by using the Setup menu (Shift-F1), as described in Chapter 1.

When you turn off the Automatic Rewrite feature, the program reformats the screen one line at a time (as opposed to all at once) as you move the cursor up or down. With this feature off, you can, however, reformat the entire screen by simply pressing Ctrl-F3 (Screen) twice.

The majority of the time you will want to leave the Automatic Rewrite feature active—this is the program's default setting. However, if you are working with text columns (see Chapter 10) you may want to turn off the Automatic Rewrite feature as you compose the page.

Correcting Errors

If you make a typing mistake while entering your text, you can use Backspace or Del to remove it. You use Backspace to delete any unwanted characters to the left of the cursor. Each time you press Backspace, the cursor moves to the left as it deletes the character. You use Del to delete the character the cursor is on. If you spot a character in the line that needs to be deleted, you can use the → or ← key to move the cursor to it and use Del to remove it. As you'll soon learn, you can also make cursor movements that cover more distance to place the cursor in the proper position to delete a character.

CURSOR MOVEMENT

WordPerfect has many key combinations that allow you to move the cursor through your document. These techniques are discussed in the following sections and summarized in Table 2.2. You will probably not use all of these techniques, but a few you will use over and over. You may want to write macros for some of the cursor movement sequences in combination with commands that you use frequently.

Note: Useful macros will be presented throughout this book where appropriate. For a thorough discussion of macros and how they are used, see Chapter 16, "Creating and Using Macros."

Moving Character by Character

The ← and → keys on the numeric keypad move the cursor left one character and right one character, respectively. To move the cursor a specified number of characters to the left or right, press Esc, enter the number, and press either the ← key or the → key.

Moving Word by Word

To move the cursor word by word through a line, hold down the Ctrl key and press the arrow key corresponding to the direction in which you wish to go. The cursor will jump to the first letter of the word in either direction.

To move a specified number of words to the right or left of the current cursor position, press Esc, enter the number, and press Ctrl and the right or left arrow key simultaneously. For example, to move five words to the right, press Esc, type 5, and press Ctrl-→.

Moving to the Beginning of a Line

To move to the beginning of the current line, press Home and then press the ← key.

TO MOVE	KEY SEQUENCE
Character by character	← or →
Word by word	Ctrl-← or Ctrl-→
To the beginning of a line	Home ←
To the end of a line	Home →
To the end of a sentence	Ctrl-Home .
To the next occurrence of a specified character	Ctrl-Home <*character*>
To the top of the screen	Home ↑ or − (minus)
To the bottom of the screen	Home ↓ or + (plus)
To previous screens	Home ↑ or − (minus) repeatedly
To following screens	Home ↓ or + (plus) repeatedly
To the top of the page	Ctrl-Home ↑
To the bottom of the page	Ctrl-Home ↓
To the top of the previous page	PgUp
To the top of the next page	PgDn
To a specified page	Ctrl-Home <*page number*> Enter
To the last cursor position before the cursor movement command	Ctrl-Home Ctrl-Home
To the beginning of the last defined block	Ctrl-Home Alt-F4
To the beginning of the document	Home Home ↑
To the end of the document	Home Home ↓

TABLE 2.2: WordPerfect's Cursor Movement Techniques

Moving to the End of a Line

To move to the end of the current line, press the End key (located on the numeric keypad). Alternatively, you can press Home and then the → key.

Moving to the End of a Sentence

To move to the end of a sentence (one that ends with a period), press Ctrl and Home simultaneously; then enter . (a period). You can use the same method to move to the end of a sentence that is terminated by an exclamation point by entering ! instead of a period, or to the end of a question by entering a question mark.

Moving to the Next Occurrence of a Character

To move directly to the next occurrence of any character in your document, press Ctrl-Home and then type the character. Your cursor will move to the next instance of that character in your document.

Moving Line by Line (Scrolling)

To move through your document line by line, simply hold down the ↑ or ↓ key.

Moving to the Top or Bottom of the Screen

To move to the top of the screen, press Home and then press the ↑ key. To move to the bottom of the screen, press Home and then press the ↓ key. Alternatively, you can press the − (minus) and + (plus) keys located on the right side of the numeric keypad.

> *Note:* If your keyboard has a separate cursor movement pad and 10-key number pad, you will not be able to use the − (minus) and + (plus) keys on the number pad for entering calculations into your document unless you press Num Lock, because WordPerfect uses these keys for scrolling. You will have to use the - (hyphen key) and + (Shift-=) keys on the top row of the keyboard for mathematical work.

Moving to the Previous or Next Screen

To move screen by screen, repeatedly press the + or − key on the numeric keypad.

Moving to the Previous or Next Page

To move page by page, press the PgUp or PgDn key on the numeric keypad. PgUp takes you to the beginning of the previous page; PgDn takes you to the beginning of the next page of your document.

Remember that hard page breaks (those that you add yourself) are shown by a line of equal signs, and soft page breaks (those that the program adds) are shown by a line of hyphens.

Moving to the Top or Bottom of the Page

To move directly to the beginning of the page on which you are working, press Ctrl-Home ↑. Likewise, to move directly to the end of the page on which you are working, enter Ctrl-Home ↓.

Moving to a Specific Page

To move directly to a specific page in your document, press Ctrl-Home. The prompt *Go to* will appear in the lower-left corner of your screen. Enter the number of the page to which you want to go and press Enter. The message *Repositioning* indicates that WordPerfect is repositioning the cursor during this operation.

Moving to the Previous Cursor Position

To move the cursor to the position where it was when you last used a cursor movement command, press Ctrl-Home twice. This technique is useful when you copy and paste text, as it allows you to easily return the cursor to the place where the text came from, or when you want to return to your last position during a search operation or to the first occurrence of the search string after a search-and-replace operation. Chapter 3 explains WordPerfect's search-and-replace capabilities.

Moving to the Beginning of a Block

To move the cursor to the beginning of the last block of text you defined, press Ctrl-Home (Go To) followed by Alt-F4 (Block). For information about blocking text in a document, refer to Chapter 3.

Moving to the Beginning or End of a Document

To move directly to the beginning or end of your document, press Home twice; then press either the ↑ key (to go to the beginning of your document) or the ↓ key (to go to the end). You will see the message *Repositioning,* indicating that WordPerfect is repositioning the cursor.

DELETING AND UNDELETING TEXT

One other basic operation of any word processing program, in addition to moving the cursor, is deleting text after it is typed. WordPerfect has several methods for deleting various portions of text. They are summarized in Table 2.3 for easy reference, and are discussed in the following sections.

Deleting Character by Character

To delete character by character, use Backspace or Del. Backspace deletes the character to the left of the cursor, and Del deletes the character or space the

TO DELETE	PRESS
Character by character	Backspace (deletes to left of cursor) or Del (deletes character or space cursor is on)
Word by word	Ctrl-Backspace
Several words	Esc n Ctrl-Backspace (n = number of words to left of cursor)
The word to the left of the cursor	Ctrl-← Ctrl-Backspace
The word to the right of the cursor	Ctrl-→ Ctrl-Backspace
From the cursor left to the beginning of a word	Home Backspace
From the cursor right to the end of a word	Home Del
To the end of a line	Ctrl-End
To the end of a sentence	Alt-F4 . Del 4
To the end of a page	Ctrl-PgDn
To the end of a block	Alt-F4 <highlight text> Backspace or Del Y

TABLE 2.3: Methods for Deleting Text in WordPerfect

Note: You may want to record some of the deletion methods presented in the following sections as macros to speed up your work. In particular, the deletion methods that prompt you for confirmation before making a deletion can be speeded up with macros.

cursor is on. To progressively delete to the left of the cursor, hold down Backspace. To progressively delete characters to the right of the cursor, hold down Del.

Deleting Word by Word

To delete an entire word, position the cursor anywhere in the word, hold down Ctrl, and press Backspace. If you are deleting in the middle of a line, you can continue to delete words one after another in this way, as the cursor will be positioned on the next word to the right.

Many times you will need to use Ctrl-→ or Ctrl-← to position the cursor on the first character of a word before using Ctrl-Backspace to remove the word. If you need to delete a phrase located to the left of the cursor in a line, you can press Ctrl- ← several times to place the cursor on the first word of the phrase before using Ctrl-Backspace. You can then use word-by-word deletion progressively. Each time you press Ctrl-Backspace, word wrap closes the gap caused by removing the word at the cursor. This brings into position the next word in the phrase to be removed, allowing you to delete each word without having to move the cursor.

You can also use the Esc key's Repeat function to delete a specified number of words. To do this, you press Esc, enter the number of words you wish to delete, and then press Ctrl-Backspace. For example, to delete the phrase *for a limited time only,* you would position the cursor on the *f* in *for,* press Esc, type **5** (because there are five words in this phrase), and press Ctrl-Backspace. As already discussed, you could also position the cursor on the *f* and press Ctrl-Backspace five times to remove the phrase.

Deleting the Word to the Left or Right of the Cursor

Home Backspace deletes from the cursor's position left to the beginning of the word, and Home Del deletes from the cursor's position right to the beginning of the next word.

If the cursor is positioned within the word you wish to delete, Home Backspace will remove only the characters to the left of the cursor, preserving the character the cursor is on as well as any to its right. In this way, the command differs from Ctrl-Backspace, which deletes all of the characters in a word, regardless of the character the cursor is on when the command is issued. Home Del works in the same way, except that it deletes from the cursor's position to the right. Both of these commands can be used to progressively delete several words in a single phrase.

Deleting to the End of a Line

To delete from the current cursor position to the end of the line the cursor is on, hold down Ctrl and press End. To delete several lines in this way, press Esc, specify the number of lines you want to delete, and then press Ctrl-End. When you use the Ctrl-End combination with the Esc key, include the line containing the cursor as part of the count of lines to be deleted. For example, if you want to delete to the end of the line containing the cursor as well as the next two lines of text, press Esc, type **3**, and then press Ctrl-End.

To delete the entire line that the cursor is on, move the cursor to the beginning of the line by pressing Home ← before pressing Ctrl-End.

Deleting to the End of a Sentence

You can delete to the end of a sentence by using WordPerfect's Search function (see Chapter 3). This method requires several keystrokes, so the following macro is suggested.

DES: A MACRO TO DELETE TO THE END OF A SENTENCE

To write a macro that deletes all characters from the cursor position up to and including the next period, construct the macro illustrated in Figure 2.6. It is called DES (for Delete to End of Sentence).

> *Note:* The macros in this book are presented as they appear in the Macro Editor. If you are unfamiliar with WordPerfect macros or the Macro Editor, read Chapter 16, "Creating and Using Macros," before attempting to record any of the macros presented in this book.

To record the macro, you should have a sentence ending in a period on the screen. Position the cursor within that sentence and then record the macro by pressing Ctrl-F10 (Macro), naming the macro **DES**, entering the description **delete to end of sentence**, and then performing the keystrokes Alt-F4 (Block), **.** (period), Del, and **Y** in response to the Delete prompt. Press Ctrl-F10 again to stop recording the macro.

When using this macro, remember that your sentences may not all end with a period. Some may end with a question mark or an exclamation point. If you use the DES macro to try to delete this type of sentence, it will delete all of the text from the cursor position to the first period located by the Search function; this may remove several sentences. Also, if your sentence contains a period that occurs before the period signifying the end of the sentence (as in *ABC, Inc.*), this

```
Macro: Edit

        File          DES.WPM

   1 - Description     delete to end of sentence

   2 - Action

      ┌─────────────────────────────────────────────────────────┐
      │ {Block}.{Backspace}y                                    │
      │                                                          │
      │                                                          │
      │                                                          │
      │                                                          │
      │                                                          │
      │                                                          │
      │                                                          │
      │                                                          │
      └─────────────────────────────────────────────────────────┘

   Selection: 0̲
```

FIGURE 2.6: A macro for deleting to the end of a sentence. This macro, named DES, searches for the next period and deletes the text from the cursor's position to that period.

macro will delete only to the first period, not all the way to the end of the sentence, and you will have to issue the macro a second time.

> *Note:* In general, you should not create Alt macros that delete text in WordPerfect. It is too easy to inadvertently press Alt and the letter associated with the macro when you mean to press Shift to capitalize a letter. This is why the macro that deletes to the end of a sentence is named DES instead of Alt-E or some other Alt combination. However, if you ever use a deletion macro or a delete command in error, WordPerfect's Undelete function on the F1 key (discussed later in this chapter) is available to restore your text.

Deleting a Paragraph

A quick way to delete an entire paragraph (that is, to the next hard return) is to press Alt-F4 (Block) when the cursor is on the first letter in the paragraph; then press Enter to mark the entire paragraph as a block. Delete the paragraph by pressing Backspace or Del and responding **Y** to the delete prompt.

You can also extend or contract block highlighting by pressing any of the arrow keys after you have marked a paragraph in this way.

Deleting to the End of a Page

To delete to the end of the current page, press Ctrl-PgDn. You will then see the confirmation message

Delete Remainder of Page? (Y/N) No

at the bottom of the screen. To delete the text, you must type **Y**. To cancel the command, just press Enter. Ctrl-PgDn deletes to the end of a user-defined page (marked with the formatting code [HPg] and displayed as a line of equal signs) or to the end of a system-defined page (marked with the formatting code [SPg] and displayed as a line of hyphens).

Deleting a Block of Text

To delete a block of text, first mark the block by pressing Alt-F4 and using the cursor movement keys to highlight all of the text to be included. Then press Backspace or Del. WordPerfect displays the following confirmation prompt:

Delete Block? (Y/N) No

Type **Y** to delete the block that you just marked. To cancel the command, just press Enter. (For more information about defining and using blocks in WordPerfect, refer to Chapter 3.)

DELETING FORMATTING CODES

As you saw previously in this chapter, WordPerfect inserts hidden formatting codes into your document each time you issue a formatting command—for example, when you press Enter to signal the end of a paragraph or when you press a function key such as F6 to begin or end boldfacing. You cannot see these codes as you type, but they are there. To see them, you must press Alt-F3 (Reveal Codes).

To delete hidden codes, you simply put the cursor on the code in the Reveal Codes window and then press Del. If the cursor is located to the immediate right of the code, you can press Backspace to remove the code.

After you delete any unwanted codes, you return to the normal editing screen by pressing Alt-F3 again. The window in the lower part of the screen disappears, and you can continue working on your document. However, you can continue to work on your document even with the Reveal Codes window open. In fact, working with the codes displayed is often beneficial if you are trying to position text accurately among the codes.

If two codes, such as [BOLD] and [bold], are used for a format or appearance change, the uppercase code indicates the beginning of the change—in this case, the beginning of boldfacing—and the lowercase code indicates the end of the change. To delete such formats, which include boldfacing, centering, and underlining, you need only delete one of the codes; the other will disappear as well.

Not all of the hidden codes that appear in the Reveal Codes window can be deleted. For instance, you cannot remove a soft return, marked with the code [SRt], or a soft page break, marked with the code [SPg]. If you try to delete a Soft Return code (which indicates where WordPerfect uses word wrap to reformat a line to the margin and tab settings), you will instead delete the space between the last word on the line and the first word of the following line. Likewise, if you try to delete the [SPg] code marking a soft page break, you will delete only the blank space between the last word on one page and the first word on the following page.

> *Note:* If you want to change the position of an [SPg] code (that is, where the page break occurs), you must do this by using one of the several commands for keeping text together, such as Block Protect and Conditional End of Page, as explained in Chapter 4.

You can also delete formatting codes without using Alt-F3 (Reveal Codes) if the cursor is located after the code when you press the Backspace key. However, this method is often very difficult to use, because you cannot visually locate the code in the text. For this reason, you should become familiar with the use of Alt-F3 to display the Reveal Codes window, and you should know how to identify and locate the codes to delete. All of WordPerfect's hidden codes are listed in Appendix C.

Because formatting codes can be deleted with the Backspace key, you may sometimes be prompted with a Delete message asking you to confirm the removal of a particular code when you intend to delete a character. If you do not want to delete the code, just press Enter, or press Del twice; in such cases, the No option is always the default.

For example, if you have boldfaced a word and discover that you have mistyped its final letter, you might see the following message when you press Backspace to delete it:

Delete [BOLD]? (Y/N) No

To preserve the code that turns off boldfacing, just press Backspace (since the default is No) and then press Backspace again if you want to delete the final letter of the word.

If the word that you just corrected is at the end of a line and you intend to continue typing, you must also remember to press the → key before pressing the space bar. Using → places the cursor beyond the hidden code that turns off boldfacing (though it does not change the cursor's horizontal position on the screen). If you did not use the → key before pressing the space bar and continuing to type, all of the text that you enter would be boldfaced just like the word you edited.

UNDELETING TEXT

If you delete some text in error, you can use WordPerfect's Undelete function to restore it. To implement this function, you press F1. As long as you have not just issued a WordPerfect command in which F1 acts as the Cancel key, the program will display the text last deleted in reverse video at the cursor's position. You will also be presented with two menu options: Restore and Show Previous Deletion. If you type **1** or **R** for Restore, WordPerfect will reinsert the text displayed in reverse video at the cursor's current position. If you type **2** or **S** for Show Previous Deletion, it will display any text removed in a previous deletion. You can then choose Restore to have this text reinserted. WordPerfect stores the last three text deletions.

To replace mistakes with the correct characters, you can simply type them after deleting unwanted characters. Remember, WordPerfect is in Insert mode unless you press the Ins key and see the message *Typeover* in the lower-left corner of the screen.

ADDING A DOCUMENT SUMMARY SCREEN TO YOUR DOCUMENT

You can add a Document Summary screen to any document that you create. You can use this screen to record information about the author and typist of a document as well as to enter a block of comments describing either the content or the format of the document. The Document Summary screen also automatically includes the name of the document and the date of its creation.

To add a Document Summary screen to the document you are creating or editing, press Shift-F8 (Format) and choose Document (**3** or **D**) to display the Document Format menu. Then choose Summary (**5** or **S**). A Document Summary screen similar to the one shown in Figure 2.7 will then appear on your screen. WordPerfect automatically supplies the creation date and the system file name. (If you have not yet saved the document, *Not named yet* appears on this line.) You can add a descriptive file name by typing **1** or **D** and then typing the name. Then press Enter to make another entry. For example, to enter the author's name, type **3** or **A**, type the name or initials of the author, and then press Enter. If you enter a descriptive file name and have not yet saved the document, WordPerfect will generate a suggested file name from this name and ask you whether you want to use that name when you save the document.

After you type **5** or **C** for Comments, the cursor will appear inside the Comments box. The Comments box automatically contains the first 400 characters of your document, but you can add your own comments. There is a 40-character maximum for each item except the Comments box; there, you are limited to 780 characters.

You can use the Comments box to describe the contents of the document or to annotate it in some other way that makes the document easily identifiable. When you have finished adding your comments, press F7 (Exit) to return to your document.

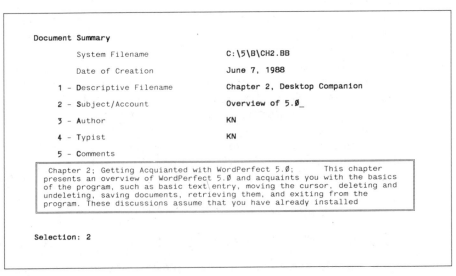

FIGURE 2.7: WordPerfect's Document Summary screen, accessed through the Format menu (Shift-F8). You can add a document summary to any document. This summary displays the file name and date of creation and can include the name of the author and the typist as well as a Comments box of up to 780 characters.

A document summary is not printed when the document is printed. The only way to obtain a printout of the Document Summary screen is by pressing the Shift and PrtSc keys simultaneously.

In version 5.0, the document summary is not displayed at the beginning of the document, as it was in previous versions. Instead, it appears only when you use the Look option on the List Files menu so that you can quickly locate the file you are looking for. You will find, as explained in Chapter 8, that the List Files menu now includes a selective Search function that allows you to search through document summaries in a directory without having to search the entire text of each file—a time-consuming process in a large directory.

You can edit the contents of the Document Summary screen from anywhere in the document by repeating the process you used to create it and replacing the old Document Summary with a new one. (You cannot change the date of creation, and it remains the same no matter when you subsequently edit the document.) After you have finished editing the document summary, press F7 (Exit). The cursor will automatically return to its original position in the document.

You can also have WordPerfect automatically prompt you to create a Document Summary screen whenever you exit and save a new document. To do this, you need to use the Setup menu (Shift-F1) and specify the Create on Save/Exit option, as explained in Chapter 1. From then on, the first time you press F10 (Save) or F7 (Exit), the Document Summary screen will appear.

You can also specify on the Setup menu a preselected character or characters called the *subject search string,* which is used to quickly locate the subject of a document when you use WordPerfect's Word Search feature on it. Chapter 8 explains Word Search in greater detail.

ADDING NONPRINTING COMMENTS TO YOUR DOCUMENT

WordPerfect also allows you to add nonprinting comments anywhere in your document. This feature is very helpful if you need to insert a comment to remind yourself to add additional text to the document when the information becomes available. You can then use the Search feature to locate the comments that you have added to the document. It is also valuable if you are circulating a document on-line for comments by others. In version 5.0, you can convert comments to text, thus speeding up the process of incorporating review comments made by others.

To add a comment to your document, press Ctrl-F5 (Text In/Out) and choose Comment (**5** or **C**) followed by Create (**1** or **C**). The Document Comment screen shown in Figure 2.8 will be displayed. The cursor will automatically appear within the Comment box bordered by double lines.

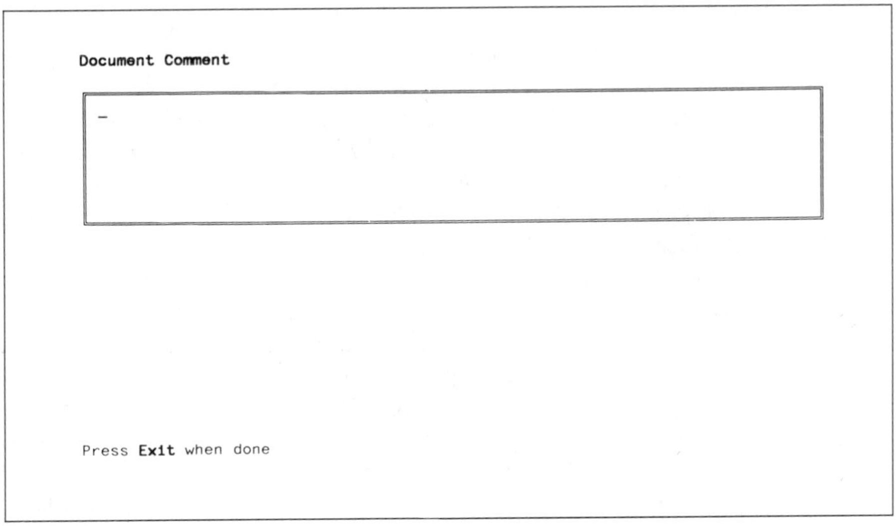

```
Document Comment


┌─────────────────────────────────────────────────────────────────┐
│  ─                                                                │
│                                                                   │
│                                                                   │
│                                                                   │
│                                                                   │
└─────────────────────────────────────────────────────────────────┘








Press Exit when done
```

FIGURE 2.8: The Document Comment screen. Once you have finished entering the comment text, press F7 (Exit). The Setup menu allows you to suppress the display of document comments.

When you have finished entering the text of the comment, press F7. A [Comment] code is inserted at that point in your text, and you can search for it (as described in Chapter 3) if you later want to revise or delete a comment. To edit a comment, locate its [Comment] code and position the cursor after it. Then press Ctrl-F5 (Text In/Out) and select Comment (**5** or **C**). Select Edit (**2** or **E**), then edit the comment.

If you want to edit a comment without using the Search feature to locate it, you must place the cursor somewhere in a line below the comment display before pressing Ctrl-F5 and choosing Edit. If the cursor is located on a line above the Comment box, WordPerfect will display the previous comment on your screen. When you exit this screen, you will find that the cursor is located right after this previous comment (which may be many pages before the comment you wanted to edit). If this happens, press Ctrl-Home twice to move the cursor to its position before you accessed the Comment Edit command. Then move the cursor to a line below the Comment box and issue the command again.

You can add comments anywhere in the text of your document. If you add a comment between the words in a single line of text, the line will be split apart by the Comment box when you have the comment displayed on your screen, but the lines will appear correctly when printed.

A comment added in the middle of a line of text is shown in Figure 2.9. Notice that the Comment box has been placed below a line of text that appears cut in half. The continuation of the sentence appears on a separate line below the Comment box. Although it appears as if the line has been broken into two by the comment, because the comment is not printed, the word processor ignores its presence; the Ln indicator on the status line does not register a change when you move the cursor from one line to the other. When you position the cursor at the end of the last word in the line before the comment and press →, the cursor jumps past the Comment box to the first character in the first word in the line below. When the document is printed, these two lines will be printed as one.

With version 5.0, you can also convert a comment to text. Simply position the cursor after the comment, press Ctrl-F5, choose Comment, and then choose Convert to Text (**3** or **T**). WordPerfect then converts the comment nearest to the cursor (above it, toward the beginning of the document) to text. It does not matter whether you are displaying comments; the first comment above the cursor will be converted to normal text.

To convert text to a comment, you first block the text that you want to use as a comment (Alt-F4); then press Ctrl-F5 and type **Y** in response to the prompt to change the highlighted text to a comment. If you change text to a comment, it will not be printed unless you change it back to text again.

WORKING WITH TWO DOCUMENTS

WordPerfect allows you to open two document windows so that you can work on two documents at one time or use the second window as a scratch area, without retrieving a document into it. These windows are identified as *Doc 1* and *Doc 2* on the status line. To work with two documents, all you have to do is

```
    Parking

    As parking is limited, please apply to the personnel office for a
    parking slot assignment.

    Hours

    Noon to 1 p.m. has been reserved as lunch hour for all employees.
    Some departments have chosen to take lunch

    ┌─────────────────────────────────────────────────────────────────┐
    │ Managers: Do you want to mention this here, or would you prefer lunch │
    │ hours to be a departmental matter?                                │
    └─────────────────────────────────────────────────────────────────┘
                                              from 12:30 to 1:30;
    check with your manager.

    Cafeteria

    The company cafeteria, located on the third floor, is open from 7
    a.m. until 2.p.m. daily. Breakfast is available for your
    convenience until 9:00. After 2 p.m., vending machines with cold
    sandwiches and salads are available.

    Recreational Facilities

                                              Doc 2 Pg 1 Ln 2.33" Pos 5.3"
```

FIGURE 2.9: A comment added in the middle of a line of text. Comments are not printed when you print your document.

retrieve your first document, switch to the second document window, and create or retrieve another document. (Retrieving and saving are discussed at the end of this chapter.)

To move to the second document window, you press Shift-F3 (the Switch key). You can keep track of which document you are working on by checking the status line. When you first press Shift-F3, the Doc indicator will change from 1 to 2. If you press this key combination again, it will change from 2 to 1. You can use Switch (Shift-F3) at any time to switch between the two documents open in the windows.

You can also retrieve the same document into the two windows, but you should be aware that WordPerfect does not update the changes you make to the document in one window whenever you change the document in the other window. When you save the document in the Doc 1 window and respond **Y** to the Replace prompt, indicating that you want to replace the previously saved version with the one you are saving, the document on the screen will overwrite the saved version on disk. However, if you have made additional changes to the same document that is being displayed in the Doc 2 window, they will not be included in the save. If you then go to the Doc 2 window and save that version of the document, it will overwrite the version you just saved from the Doc 1 window. For this reason, you should be careful to keep track of which document version—the one in the Doc 2 window or the one in the Doc 1 window—is the one that contains your current changes and revisions. Otherwise, you may wind up with a saved version that does not contain all of your editing changes. To avoid this problem, save one of the documents under a different name as soon as you retrieve it so that you can tell from the status line which is which. If you still lose track of which document contains the most current changes, you can use WordPerfect's Document Compare feature, as discussed in Chapter 3.

Splitting the Screen

You can also split the screen so that the partial contents of both windows are visible. To display parts of two documents in the same screen display, you use WordPerfect's Window feature. Press Ctrl-F3 (the Screen key) and choose the Window option (**1** or **W**). You will see the following prompt:

Number of lines in this window: 24

The cursor will be positioned under the *2* in *24*. The default value is 24 because WordPerfect allows you to use 24 of the 25 lines of text displayed on a typical monitor—it reserves the 25th line for status line information, prompts, and error messages.

To display two document windows on the same screen, you must change the number of lines to a number between 1 and 22. (If you specify 1 or 23, all you will see is the ruler line displayed at the bottom of the screen, and there will not be any lines below this for displaying the text of a second document.) If you specify 11 as the number of lines, the two document windows will be of equal size. If you specify zero or a number greater than 24, WordPerfect will ignore your entry, and the full-screen window display will not be changed.

To set the size of the windows in the display, you can either enter the number of lines or press the ↑ key. Pressing ↑ gives you visual feedback as you size the windows. This is especially helpful if you have already retrieved the two documents into the Doc 1 and Doc 2 windows before you set the sizes for the windows, because it allows you to see what sizes work best with the text you are primarily interested in comparing.

As you press the ↑ key, WordPerfect will continue to display the prompt, changing the number that follows it as you increase the size of the lower window and decrease the size of the upper window. You can always tell where the bottom of the upper window is by the position of the highlighted tab ruler displayed on the screen. As you increase the size of the lower window, you will be able to see the words *Doc 2* in the window's status line. When the document windows appear as you want them, press Enter to set the display.

Once you have set the windows, you press Shift-F3 (Switch) to move the cursor between them. Remember that the cursor must be located in the document window before you can edit the text you see displayed within it.

WordPerfect keeps you informed of which document window is current (contains the cursor) by the direction of the triangles that mark tab stops on the tab ruler. When the triangles point upward, the upper window is current, and any cursor movements or editing commands you use will affect the document this window contains. When these triangles point downward, the lower window is current. As you switch between the documents, not only will the direction of the tab triangles change, but so will their position and those of the margin settings, unless both documents use the same margin and tab settings.

When you have finished your work with the two documents, you can return the display to one full-sized window by pressing Ctrl-F3 (Screen), selecting Window (**1** or **W**), typing **24** for the number of lines, and pressing Enter. Whichever document window is current at the time you give this command will be the one whose document will be shown in the full-sized window that is created. To display the other document, press Shift-F3 (Switch).

Returning the screen display to one full-sized window does not exit or save the document that is no longer displayed. When you work with two documents in memory, you must use F7 (Exit) to close and save each one, as discussed later in this chapter.

If you exit and save a document in one of the windows when both are displayed on the screen, the window will not be automatically closed, although the cursor will return to the document left in memory. You will still have to press Ctrl-F3 (Screen) and select Window to set the window size to 24 lines and return to a single, full-screen display.

ALT-H: A MACRO TO SPLIT THE DISPLAY INTO TWO EQUAL WINDOWS

If you often use two equal-sized windows to copy, move, or compare text between documents by switching between windows, you may want to create the macro illustrated in Figure 2.10 to save keystrokes and speed up the screen-splitting process.

To use this macro after you have recorded it, press Alt-H. If you have not yet retrieved your documents, retrieve the document for the first document window, press Shift-F3, and then retrieve the second document. If you have already retrieved your two documents, parts of each will be displayed on the screen as soon as you use Alt-H.

ALT-F: A MACRO TO RETURN THE DISPLAY TO ONE FULL-SIZED WINDOW

Once you have split the screen into two equal windows, you can use the macro illustrated in Figure 2.11 to quickly return to a single full-sized window when you have finished your editing.

To use this macro after you have recorded it, press Alt-F; the document containing the cursor will be displayed on the entire screen.

SAVING A DOCUMENT AND EXITING WORDPERFECT

You should make it a practice to save your work frequently. WordPerfect provides a Timed Document Backup feature that can be extremely valuable if you

```
Macro: Edit

         File            ALTH.WPM

    1 - Description       Split screen

    2 - Action

    {DISPLAY OFF}{Screen}112{Enter}




    Selection: 0
```

FIGURE 2.10: A macro, named Alt-H (for *Half*), that splits the screen into two windows of equal size. You can retrieve a different document into each window.

```
Macro: Edit
         File            ALTF.WPM
   1 - Description        Return to full-screen window
   2 - Action

      {DISPLAY OFF}{Screen}124{Enter}




   Selection: 0
```

FIGURE 2.11: A macro, named Alt-F (for *Full*), that returns a split screen to full-screen size.

have a power loss or other computer failure, as discussed in Chapter 1, but you should get into the habit of saving regularly and often, even if you are using this automatic backup feature.

Save and Continue

To save a file while you are working on it and then return to it, press F10 (Save). WordPerfect will prompt you for a file name if you have not saved the file before. (See Chapter 8 for restrictions that apply to file names; WordPerfect basically follows the same rules as DOS.) Enter a name up to 8 characters long (plus an optional 3-character extension) and including a directory and drive designation if you want the file saved somewhere other than the current drive and directory; then press Enter.

If you press F10 (Save) after having saved the file previously, WordPerfect will provide the file name under which you previously saved the file. To save the file under the same name, press Enter and respond **Y** to the prompt

Replace <*filename*>? (Y/N) No

to indicate that you *do* want to replace the existing version of the file with the edited version you are now saving.

The default setting is No, which allows you to leave the existing file intact and save the new version under another name. If you want to rename the file—for example, if you want to keep two versions of a document—type **Y**. WordPerfect will prompt you for a new file name. Type the new name (including a drive and directory designation if you do not want to use the current ones) and press Enter.

To cancel a save sequence, use the F1 (Cancel) key. Pressing Esc simply cycles you through the screen prompts.

ALT-S: A SAVE-AND-CONTINUE MACRO

You may want to speed up the process of saving your work by writing a simple macro that saves your work and returns you to your document without your having to respond to the on-screen prompts. Such a macro is illustrated in Figure 2.12.

Save and Exit—Clearing the Screen

To save your document and exit WordPerfect or to save your document and begin work with another document, use the F7 key. This key is called the *Exit* key in WordPerfect. If you see an on-screen prompt telling you to press the Exit key, the program is referring to the F7 key.

When you press F7 during normal document editing, you will see the prompt

Save Document? (Y/N) Yes

at the bottom of your screen. Press Enter to accept the default setting, Yes, and WordPerfect will either prompt you for a file name (if you have not saved your

```
Macro: Edit

         File            ALTS.WPM

    1 - Description      Save document

    2 - Action

        {Save}{Enter}y










    Selection: 0
```

FIGURE 2.12: A macro for saving your document and continuing to work on the same document. This macro assumes that you have previously saved the document and want to save it again under the same name.

document before) or provide the file name you previously gave to your document. If you want to save your document under a different name (for example, if you want to maintain several versions of it), simply type the new name. WordPerfect will erase the name supplied in the prompt and enter the new name that you type.

If you want to save your document under the same name, simply press Enter. WordPerfect will ask you

> Replace <*filename*>? (Y/N) No

thus giving you another chance to save your file under a different name. (Remember, when you save your document under the same name, WordPerfect replaces the previously saved version.) Press Enter to give the document a different name, or type **Y** to replace the previous version of your document with this one.

If you type **Y**, WordPerfect saves the document and then displays the following prompt:

> Exit WP? (Y/N) No

(If you have two documents open, the prompt will read *Exit doc 1?* or *Exit doc 2?*. If you exit from Document 1, you will then need to repeat the process to save and exit from Document 2.) Entering **Y** returns you to DOS; pressing Enter to accept the No default clears the WordPerfect screen and puts you on line 1 of a new, blank document. You can press Shift-F10 to retrieve a previously saved document, or begin creating a new document.

To cancel a save sequence, use the F1 (Cancel) key. Pressing Esc simply cycles you through the save prompts. Table 2.4 summarizes the different methods of exiting WordPerfect.

FUNCTION	KEY SEQUENCE
Save document and clear screen	F7 Y <*file name*> N
Save document and exit	F7 Y <*file name*> Y
Clear screen	F7 N N
Exit to DOS	F7 N Y
Note: If you are saving a previously saved document, you may simply press Enter to accept the existing file name and press **Y** to replace the earlier version.	

TABLE 2.4: Methods for Exiting WordPerfect

Unlike other word processors you may have used, WordPerfect requires that you exit the program properly before you turn off your computer. With other software it does not matter if you turn off the computer without using an exit command to return to the operating system, as long as you have saved the document in memory before doing so. This is not the case with WordPerfect. Word-Perfect keeps special files, referred to as *overflow files* (see Chapter 1 for details), that are not emptied and closed until you press F7 (Exit).

If you simply use the Save command, F10, and then turn off the power, Word-Perfect will detect the presence of these files the next time you start the program and will display this prompt on the initial startup screen:

Are other copies of WordPerfect currently running? (Y/N)

You will then have to type **N** to cause WordPerfect to erase the contents of the overflow files and move on to the standard editing screen.

Alt-Q: A Save-and-Exit Macro

As you can see, several keystrokes are required to save and exit. You can reduce the number of keystrokes to two by writing a simple save-and-exit macro as illustrated in Figure 2.13 to use when you want to end your WordPerfect work session and return to DOS.

```
Macro: Edit

        File              ALTQ.WPM

    1 - Description       Save and quit

    2 - Action

        {Exit}y{Enter}
        yy




    Selection: 0
```

FIGURE 2.13: A macro for saving and exiting. This macro, named Alt-Q (for *Quit*), quickly saves your document under the name you previously gave it and then exits from WordPerfect.

Retrieving a Saved Document

The Shift-F10 key combination is used to retrieve a saved document. Press Shift-F10 and enter the name of the document; then press Enter.

If you do not enter a document name but instead press Enter at the prompt, the last text you marked as a block with Alt-F4 (Block) and deleted in the current session will be inserted at the cursor position.

You can see a list of all the files in your working directory by pressing F5 (the List Files key). WordPerfect will respond by displaying the current directory, followed by *.*, the wild-card search pattern. The *.* indicates that all files with all extensions will be displayed. (See Chapter 8 for details about directories, subdirectories, and wild cards.) Press Enter one more time to make the program display a list of all files in the directory. To retrieve a document located in another WordPerfect document directory, edit the directory name displayed and press Enter.

To retrieve a file from the alphabetical list displayed on the screen, highlight the file's name and enter **1** or **R** for the Retrieve option (listed on the menu at the bottom of the screen, as shown in Figure 2.14). To view files in the other directories listed at the top of the screen, highlight the directory name, enter **6** or **L** (for Look), and press Enter. You can also retrieve a file directly from these directories by entering **1** or **R** when the file is highlighted. See Chapter 8 for details about using the List Files screen.

```
06/07/88   14:37              Directory C:\5\*.*
Document size:     77944   Free:   2949120    Used:   3584102      Files:   267

. <CURRENT>    <DIR>                     .. <PARENT>     <DIR>
B        .     <DIR>    05/13/88  07:28   4         .LEX   289245  05/25/88  06:55
8514A  .WPD      3466   04/27/88  14:24   A)(A      .        8238  03/17/88  15:27
AIRPLANE.WPG     8484   04/27/88  14:24   ALPSALQ2.PRS      4247   04/26/88  07:23
ALTA   .WPM        79   03/17/88  09:07   ALTB      .WPM       83  03/17/88  15:57
ALTC   .WPM        83   03/17/88  09:05   ALTE      .WPM       79  03/18/88  11:50
ALTF   .WPM       101   06/07/88  14:28   ALTH      .WPM       85  06/07/88  14:28
ALTI   .WPM        77   06/02/88  06:15   ALTM      .WPM       75  05/03/88  07:46
ALTP   .WPM       100   06/03/88  08:26   ALTQ      .WPM       84  05/31/88  09:08
ALTRNAT.WPK       919   04/27/88  11:00   ALTS      .WPM       78  03/30/88  07:39
ALTT   .WPM        79   03/17/88  09:04   ALTW      .WPM      197  05/26/88  07:50
ALTX   .WPM        78   03/18/88  08:16   AND       .WPG     1978  04/27/88  14:24
ANNOUNCE.WPG     5388   04/27/88  14:24   APPAINS   .        1399  03/17/88  08:21
APPENDIX.        42148  05/29/88  15:51   APPLAUSE.WPG      1522   04/27/88  14:24
ARROW1 .WPG       366   04/27/88  14:24   ARROW2    .WPG     738   04/27/88  14:24
AUTOREF .        1784   05/30/88  08:54   AWARD     .WPG    1746   04/27/88  14:24
BACKUP1 .       29734   03/18/88  12:11   BADNEWS .WPG      3750   04/27/88  14:24
BEGIN  .WPM        59   03/30/88  07:22   BFG9-11   .CAP    4256   06/01/88  06:34
BFG9-12 .CAP     4256   06/01/88  06:33 ▼ BFG9-20   .CAP    4256   06/01/88  08:30

1 Retrieve; 2 Delete; 3 Move/Rename; 4 Print; 5 Text In;
6 Look; 7 Other Directory; 8 Copy; 9 Word Search; N Name Search: 6
```

FIGURE 2.14: Viewing the List Files screen to retrieve a file. You can also use this screen to look at the contents of other directories and retrieve files directly from them.

If you retrieve a document while you are working on another document, the retrieved document will be inserted at the current cursor position. You will see the prompt

Retrieve into current document? (Y/N) No

Type **Y** to continue with this operation and have the text of this document inserted at the cursor's position. Press the Enter key to cancel this operation.

Inserting One Document into Another

You can insert the complete text of one document into another by positioning the cursor in the place where you want the other document's text to appear and retrieving the document using one of the methods outlined previously—either the Shift-F10 (Retrieve) or F5 (List Files) command. The text located after the cursor's position in the original document will be moved down as required to accommodate all of the new text from the incoming document.

The text of the document you insert will conform to whatever format settings are in effect in the document it is brought into.

This technique for inserting the entire text of an external document file must not be confused with that for inserting only certain sections of one document file into another. The latter technique requires a copy operation between two document windows using one of WordPerfect's Block features. This kind of copy operation is discussed in Chapter 3.

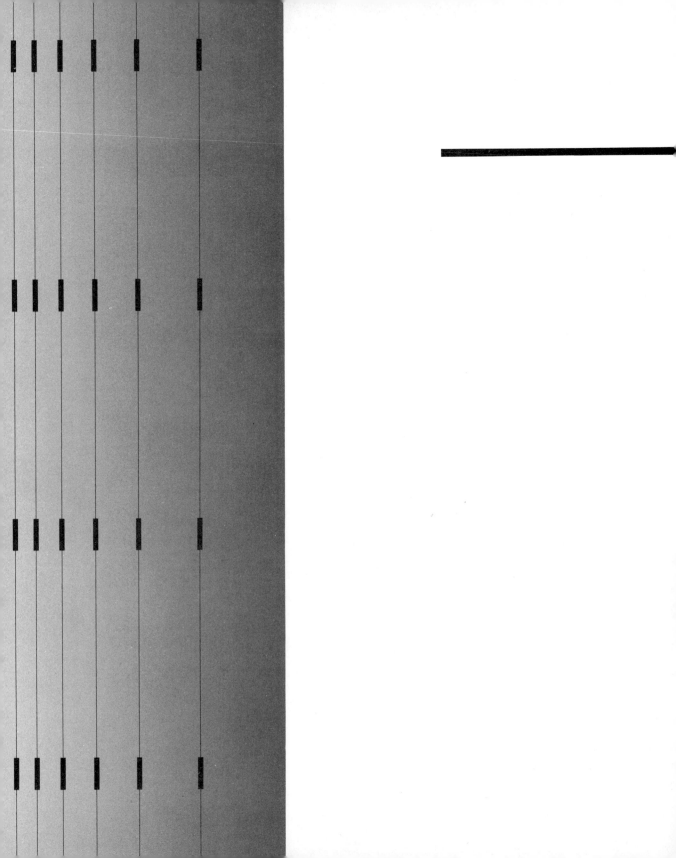

FORMATTING AND EDITING TECHNIQUES

Formatting and Editing Techniques

WordPerfect contains many functions for formatting and editing the documents you create. However, these commands are not always organized into the order you may expect, even with the improvements that have been made in version 5.0 of the program. Most of the formatting commands are now on the Format key (Shift-F8), but the submenus of the Format key do not always contain the options that you anticipate.

For example, the Widow/Orphan Protection feature, which prevents a page from ending with the first line of a paragraph or beginning with the last, is on the Line submenu instead of the Page submenu. Although it is true that this feature deals with line breaks, it also determines how pages break—probably its most important function. Conditional End of Page, which also determines how pages break, is now on the catchall submenu known as Other.

For this reason, no attempt is made in this chapter to explain each and every option of the Format key in the order in which the submenus are organized. Instead, this chapter, like all the chapters in Parts I through IV of this book, discusses the tasks that you, the user, will perform as you use WordPerfect to format and edit your documents. For step-by-step instructions organized alphabetically by feature name, see Part V, "WordPerfect Command and Feature Reference."

Most of the formatting options in the WordPerfect program have been preset for your convenience to a standard format. You can change these options for the document you are working on, as will be discussed in this chapter, or you can change them for all the documents you create by using the Setup key, as discussed in Chapter 1.

This chapter also discusses the editing techniques you can use within WordPerfect as you input and revise your documents. Knowing only a few of these basic techniques can save you a great deal of time. For example, you can use WordPerfect's Search and Replace feature when you mark passages that you want to return to and revise later. You can also, with a little imagination, use the Search and Replace feature to implement a kind of glossary containing abbreviations for words and phrases that you use often as you type, but do not want to take the time to spell out each time you type them.

This chapter discusses techniques that you can use when you create documents as well as when you revise documents you have already created. You will see techniques for block operations and for line formatting operations such as centering and indenting text. (Page formatting, such as working with headers and footers, numbering pages, and so forth, is discussed in Chapter 4, "Page Formatting Techniques.") In addition, this chapter discusses such operations as transposing words, converting text from lowercase to uppercase and vice versa, using hyphens, alphabetizing lists, and comparing different versions of documents.

UPGRADE NOTES

One major difference between version 5.0 and earlier versions of WordPerfect is that document format commands are saved with the document and take precedence over any initial setup default settings that may have been specified through the Setup menu (Shift-F1). In effect, this means that you can retrieve a WordPerfect 5.0 document into any copy of WordPerfect 5.0, and it will retain the format under which it was created.

In addition, the default unit of measurement is now inches, although you can change it to points, centimeters, or WordPerfect 4.2 units (columns and lines). The move and copy operations in WordPerfect have changed significantly. WordPerfect now expects you to move the cursor to the location in the document where you want the cut or copied text to be placed and retrieve the text immediately by pressing the Enter key; you no longer have to press the Move key and select the Retrieve option to complete the move or copy operation. You will also find that the options on the Move menu (Ctrl-F4) have been rearranged to distinguish between moving blocked and unblocked text. If text has been marked as a block, the following menu appears:

Move: **1 B**lock; **2** Tabular **C**olumn; **3** Rectangle: 0

If text has not been marked as a block, the menu appears as

Move: **1 S**entence; **2 P**aragraph; **3 P**age; **4 R**etrieve: 0

Block marking is also now automatically turned off after it has been used with a feature.

You can now search for and replace Indent, Left/Right Indent, Center, and Flush Right codes. You can also reverse the direction of the search by pressing the ↑ or ↓ key when the Search prompt is displayed.

The appearance of text (italics, small caps, and so forth), is controlled through the Font key (Ctrl-F8); however, boldfacing remains on F6 and underlining remains on F8.

Redline, Strikeout, Superscript, and Subscript have been moved to the Font key, and a new feature, Document Compare, which will often be used along with Redline and Strikeout, has been added to the Mark Text key (Alt-F5).

The program's formatting features are now on Shift-F8 (Format), which combines the old Line Format, Page Format, Print Format, and Document Format options, organized into four submenus —Line, Page, Document, and Other. The

Line Format submenu contains the version 4.2 Line Format options plus Justification, Line Numbering, Widow/Orphan Protection, and Line Height. The Page Format submenu contains the old Page Format options—some have been improved and renamed—plus two new options, Force Even/Odd Page and Paper Size/Type. The Document submenu contains options for Display Pitch (see Chapter 5), which allows you to control how your text is displayed on the screen; Initial Codes/Font, which allows you to set document defaults; Redline Method, which allows you to choose a method of redlining; and Summary (formerly on the Text In/Out key), which allows you to create document summaries. The Other submenu contains Advance (which advances the printer to a specific position, formerly on the Superscript/Subscript key); Conditional End of Page; Decimal/Align Character (formerly called the Tab Align character—this option now also includes the thousands separator); Language (for the Speller, Thesaurus, and Hyphenation files); Overstrike (formerly on the Superscript/Subscript key); Printer Functions (kerning, word spacing, etc.); and Underline Spaces/Tabs (formerly on the Print Format key), which allows you to set the underlining method.

Version 5.0 allows you to edit from the Reveal Codes screen. In version 4.2, you could only use Reveal Codes to locate the position of particular codes. As soon as you moved the cursor and then pressed a key to begin editing, Word-Perfect automatically closed the Reveal Codes window. Now when you begin editing, the Reveal Codes window remains open. This makes it possible to edit both text and hidden codes, using the Reveal Codes screen to mark your progress. As a result of being allowed to edit in Reveal Codes, you must press the Reveal Codes key (Alt-F3) to close the window; you can no longer do this by simply pressing a key or the space bar.

FORMATTING TECHNIQUES

Unlike previous versions of WordPerfect, version 5.0 saves format settings with each document so that they will be in effect each time you retrieve it. The formats that you set by using the Initial Codes/Font option (on the Document submenu of the Format menu—Shift-F8) override the codes for the settings you change on the Setup menu, so that even if you retrieve a document at another workstation that is running a copy of WordPerfect with different default values, the document will have the settings you assigned it. For example, if you have used the Initial Codes/Font option on the Format menu to specify that justification be off and double spacing be in effect, this will be the case even though the computer you are using has had its copy of WordPerfect set for right justification and single spacing. All of these initial codes are stored when you save the document and are retrieved when you retrieve it, even though they are not visible when you press Reveal Codes (Alt-F3) at the beginning of the document. Reveal

Codes shows only the codes you add to the document's initial format settings. You could check whether justification is on, however, by pressing Shift-F8 (Format) and then choosing Line (**1** or **L**).

Changing Document Initial Settings

To change the default format settings (called the *initial settings* in WordPerfect 5.0) for a single document, you use the Format key (Shift-F8), choose Document (**3** or **D**), and then choose Initial Codes (**2** or **C**). You then need to recreate the keystrokes required to produce that setting. For example, to turn justification off, you would take the following steps:

1. Press Shift-F8 (Format) and select Document (**3** or **D**).
2. Select Initial Codes (**2** or **C**). You will see a split screen, exactly as if you had pressed Alt-F3 (Reveal Codes).
3. Press Shift-F8 again to display the Format menu. You can now change any of the preset options on the Format menu.
4. To turn off justification, choose Line (**1** or **L**) and Justification (**3** or **J**). Type **N** for No, then press F7 three times to exit from the subsequent screens.

You can change as many format settings as you like while you have the Format menu displayed to generate initial codes. WordPerfect inserts the changed format codes into the bottom half of the screen.

When you change initial codes from any point in your document, they take effect throughout the document (unlike WordPerfect's other format changes).

Aligning Text

WordPerfect provides three ways of aligning a short line of text within the current left and right margins. You can center it, align it flush with the right margin, or align it flush with the current alignment character (the period, unless you designate another character).

Note that these alignments are intended for use with short lines of text, such as section headings, the date, a return address, or the closing in a letter, each of which is terminated by a carriage return (the Enter key). They are not intended for use with lines of text longer than will fit within the margins, because such lines are affected by word wrap.

You can, however, align a block of lines after they have been entered. For instance, if you want the date and the return address to appear flush with the right margin, you can enter each line (terminated by Enter), highlight all of the lines as a block, and then press Alt-F6 (Flush Right) to move all of the lines flush right at one time.

CENTERING

To center text between the margins as you type it, press Shift-F6 at the beginning of the line, just at the left margin. (Home ← moves the cursor directly to the left margin.) The text will be centered between the left and right margins until you end the line by pressing Enter.

If the cursor is not at the left margin, the text will be centered around the cursor's position when you press Shift-F6 (Center). This is useful for centering headings over columns of text that you have set up with tabs, because all you have to do is visually position the cursor over the center of the tabbed column by using the space bar or the Tab key, press Shift-F6, and type a centered heading.

If you are using WordPerfect's Columns feature for either newspaper or parallel columns, you can quickly center text by moving the cursor to the left margin of the column and pressing Shift-F6 (Center).

To center an existing line of text that has not been marked as a block, you must first end it with a Hard Return, Tab, or Flush Right code. Move the cursor to the beginning of the line, press Shift-F6 (Center), and then press ↓.

You can also indicate a block of text to be centered. First, mark the block with Alt-F4 and the cursor movement keys; then press Shift-F6 and type **Y** in response to the prompt. Each line in the block will be centered individually. WordPerfect inserts [Cntr] codes at the beginning of each line and [C/A/Flrt] and [HRt] codes at the end of each line. To edit centered text, you must make sure that the cursor is positioned between the [Cntr] and [C/A/Flrt] codes and not between the [C/A/Flrt] code and the [HRt] code. When you need to edit centered text, you should do so from the Reveal Codes window by pressing Alt-F3. After positioning the cursor within or on the correct codes, you can delete or add text without having to close the Reveal Codes window. Once you have finished editing the centered text, you can close the Reveal Codes window by pressing Alt-F3 again.

You can quickly remove the [Cntr] codes by blocking the text again, pressing Alt-F2 (Replace), pressing Enter, and then pressing Shift-F6 to generate the [Cntr] code as the string to be searched for. When you see the *Replace with:* prompt, just press F2 again, telling WordPerfect to delete all the [Cntr] codes (that is, replace them with nothing).

> *Note:* The codes that center text take precedence over the other codes in a line of text. Because of this, you may see text disappear from your screen as you center existing text. If this happens, press Reveal Codes to locate and delete the [Cntr] or [C/A/Flrt] code.

FLUSH RIGHT

WordPerfect provides a command, Alt-F6 (referred to as the Flush Right key), to automatically align your text flush with the right margin in effect. When you press Alt-F6 and you are not in Block mode, the cursor will move to the right margin setting. As you type your text, it will be entered from right to left until you press Enter to indicate the end of the line.

If you have already typed a short line of text terminated by a hard return, you can align it flush with the right margin by moving the cursor to the beginning of the line, pressing Alt-F6 (Flush Right), and then pressing ↓.

To format several lines of text flush right, mark them with Alt-F4 (Block), press Alt-F6 (Flush Right), and type **Y** in response to the prompt. WordPerfect places [Flsh Rt] codes at the beginning of each line and [C/A/Flrt] [HRt] (Hard Return) codes at the end of each line so that each line is individually formatted flush right. To revise text that has been aligned flush right, you must be careful to position the cursor between the [Flrt] and [C/A/Flrt] codes. When you need to edit right-aligned text, you should do so from the Reveal Codes window (Alt-F3). After positioning the cursor within or on the correct codes, you can delete or add text without having to close the Reveal Codes window. Once you have finished editing, you can close the Reveal Codes window (Alt-F3).

To delete the codes quickly, you can use WordPerfect's Replace feature: block the lines again, press Alt-F2 (Replace), press Enter, and then press Alt-F6 to generate the [Flsh Rt] code as the string to be searched for. When you see the *Replace with:* prompt, just press F2 again, telling WordPerfect to delete all the [Flsh Rt] codes (that is, replace them with nothing).

> *Note:* The codes that align text flush right take precedence over the other codes in a line of text. Because of this, you may sometimes see text disappear from your screen as you type text to the left of those codes. If this happens, press Alt-F3 (Reveal Codes) to locate and delete the [Flsh Rt] or [C/A/Flrt] code; then type the new text and format the line again.

THE TAB ALIGN COMMAND (DECIMAL/ALIGN CHARACTER)

The Tab Align command aligns text on the decimal/align character in effect. As when using decimal tabs, WordPerfect uses the period as the alignment character unless you specify something else. However, unlike decimal tabs, the Tab Align command works with any tab stop that is in effect.

When you press Ctrl-F6 (Tab Align), the cursor moves to the next tab stop, and the message "Align char = ." appears in the lower-left corner of the screen. Text that you type moves to the left of the cursor until you type a period (or whatever character you have set as the decimal/align character). After you type that character, text is inserted normally.

To align text on a character other than the period—for example, the colon—you first press Shift-F8 (Format), choose Other (**4** or **O**), and then choose Decimal/Align Character (**3** or **D**). Type a colon (:), then press Enter to bypass entering a thousands separator (the character used to separate each group of three numbers in numerals larger than 999). Press F7 (Exit) to return to your document.

To then align your text on the colon, you press the Tab key until you are only one tab stop away from where you want the text to be aligned. Then press Ctrl-F6 (Tab Align). The cursor will advance to the next tab stop, and you will see this message at the bottom of the screen:

Align Char = :

As you type your text, it will be entered from right to left, just as it is when you use a right-justified or decimal tab. As soon as you type the alignment character—in this case, the colon—the "Align Char = :" message disappears, and any text you then type is entered from left to right as though you were using a left-justified tab. You can thus quickly set up memo headings that are aligned on the colon, like this:

SUBJECT:
DATE:
TO:

If you do mathematical typing, you will find that Tab Align is also useful for aligning groups of equations on the equal sign.

When you use the Tab Align command to justify text on a particular alignment character, you must make sure that you have left enough space to enter all of the text that precedes the alignment character before WordPerfect reaches the left margin. If you have not, and your text is longer than can be accommodated, WordPerfect will activate the margin release when it reaches the left margin, and your text will disappear off the screen. If you continue entering characters after the line has reached the left side of the page, the text will begin to be entered from the tab alignment position to the right.

When you need to edit the text on a line that has been aligned using the Tab Align command, use the Reveal Codes window to place the cursor between the Alignment codes before inserting or deleting any text. To do this, press Alt-F3 and locate the [Align] and [C/A/Flrt] codes surrounding the text. Then move the cursor somewhere between these codes, press Alt-F3 to return to the document, and edit the text, being careful not to insert more text than can be accommodated between the tab stop for the alignment character and the left margin. When you insert new text, remember that text is entered from right to left, just the opposite of the way you are used to seeing it appear on the screen as you type.

To return text aligned with the Tab Align command to the previous tab stop, open the Reveal Codes window and delete either the [Align] code or the

[C/A/Flrt] code. If you want the text to be flush with the left margin, you should also delete the [Tab] code.

Boldfacing and Underlining Text

WordPerfect allows you to enhance parts of your documents to make them stand out from the rest of the page or to emphasize certain words or phrases in your text. In version 5.0, the Appearance menu of the Font key (Ctrl-F8) controls boldfacing, underlining, italics, outline, shadow, small caps, redline, and strikeout (as discussed in Chapter 5, "Working with Fonts"), but WordPerfect also has two keys that allow you to enter boldfacing and underlining quickly. F6 is the Bold key, and F8 is the Underline key. Both of these keys are toggles—that is, they alternate between off and on each time you press them. When bold is on, the Pos number on the status line is bold; when underlining is on, it is underlined.

When you boldface or underline text, WordPerfect surrounds it with a pair of codes. The codes for boldfacing are [BOLD] to turn the feature on and [bold] to turn it off. The codes for underlining are [UND] to turn this feature on and [und] to turn it off.

To boldface or underline text as you type it, simply press F6 for bold or F8 for underlining; then type the text. When you reach the end of the text, press the appropriate key, either F6 or F8, to turn the effect off, or simply press → to move the cursor over the final code.

To boldface or underline existing text, mark it as a block first and then press F6 or F8. To remove boldfacing or underlining, press Alt-F3 (Reveal Codes) and delete either one of the formatting codes.

CHANGING THE UNDERLINE STYLE

You can change the style of underlining from the default setting, whereby WordPerfect underlines spaces between words but not spaces between tabs, to fully continuous underlining. Continuous underlining across tab stops is sometimes useful when you are creating tables with tabs.

You can also set WordPerfect to not underline spaces entered with the space bar. For example, if you press F8, type the phrase **nolo contendere**, and then press F8 again, the phrase will be printed by default as follows:

nolo contendere

However, you may want underlined words to be underlined individually, as in

nolo contendere

To change the underlining style, press Shift-F8 (Format) and choose Other (**4** or **O**). Then choose Underline (**7** or **U**) and enter your response to the Tabs and

Spaces options. The program is preset to Yes for Spaces and No for Tabs. Press F7 (Exit) to return to your document.

USING DOUBLE UNDERLINING

The options of the Font key's Appearance submenu allow you to use double underlining if your printer supports it. To turn on double underlining, press Ctrl-F8 (Font); then select Appearance (**2** or **A**) followed by Dbl Und (**3** or **D**).

You can double-underline text as you type it, or you can mark text as a block and then double-underline it. WordPerfect inserts the codes [DBL UND] and [dbl und] around double-underlined text.

To turn off double underlining, you can press → to move over the final code, or you can select Normal from the Font menu to return to normal text attributes.

If you use double underlining for a unique item in your text, you must be careful to return to normal text. Double underlining is not displayed on the screen unless you have a color, Hercules, EGA, or RamFont card. (You can have the status line indicate the presence of double underlining if you use the Display option on the Setup menu to specify a particular attribute for it.) You may inadvertently use double underlining on a large portion of your document and not be aware of it until the document is printed.

For additional information about the Font key, refer to Chapter 5.

USING ITALICS

You may sometimes want to print text in italicized type as an alternative to underlining. To use italics, press Ctrl-F8 (Font), select the Appearance option (**2** or **A**), and then choose the Italc option (**4** or **I**). After typing all of the text that you want italicized, press Ctrl-F8 and select the Normal option (**3** or **N**) or press the → key once to move the cursor beyond the final [italc] code. You can also italicize text after it has been entered by blocking it (Alt-F4) and then selecting the Italc option from the Appearance menu of the Font key (Ctrl-F8 A I).

If your printer is not capable of printing italics or if there isn't an italic version of the current font available or installed for your printer, WordPerfect will automatically substitute underlining for the italicized text in the printed version.

Superscripting and Subscripting Text

You can have WordPerfect print a character or characters in superscript (meaning that they are printed slightly above the normal line of text in a smaller font size or in the same size) or in subscript (meaning that they are printed slightly below the normal line of text in a smaller font size or in the same size). To use superscript or subscript, press Ctrl-F8 (Font), select the Size option (**1** or **S**), and then choose either Suprscpt (**1** or **P**) to superscript the text or Subscpt (**2** or **B**) to subscript the text. After typing all of the characters that you want superscripted or subscripted, press Ctrl-F8 and select the Normal option (**3** or **N**) or press the → key once to move the cursor beyond the final [suprscpt] or [subscpt] code. You can also superscript or subscript characters after they have been entered by marking them as a block (Alt-F4) and then selecting either Suprscpt or Subscpt from the Font Size menu (Ctrl-F8 S P or Ctrl-F8 S B).

Note that WordPerfect doesn't support increasing levels of superscripting or subscripting as required when typing complex formulas and equations. To change the amount that the text is superscripted or subscripted, you must combine these attributes with the Advance feature. See Chapter 17 for more information on doing mathematical typing using superscript, and the **Advance** entry in Part V for more information on advancing the printing up or down.

Justifying Text

By default, justification is on when you begin a new document. The program aligns the right margin of each line by adjusting the spacing between its words. However, WordPerfect can't display justification on the editing screen; the right margin always appears ragged-right. To see justification and the spacing between words in each line, you need to use the View Document feature.

You can turn off justification for the entire document or only for part of it by pressing Shift-F8 (Format), choosing Line (**1** or **L**), and then choosing Justification (**3** or **J**). Type **N** to turn off justification; type **Y** to turn it back on once it has been turned off. To turn it off or back on for the entire document, position the cursor at the beginning of the document (Home Home ↑). You can also turn off justification for the whole document by using the Initial Codes option on the Document Format menu, as discussed earlier in this chapter.

When you select No for the Justification option, WordPerfect inserts a [Just Off] code in the document. Instead of using the Format menu, you can just delete this code, and your document will be justified again.

WordPerfect provides two methods for controlling the spacing between words when justification is used. You can turn on WordPerfect's Hyphenation feature and adjust the size of the hyphenation zone to reduce the amount of space between words (as discussed later in this chapter). This is especially useful when you have a short line length, as in newspaper and parallel columns.

You can also adjust the word spacing by pressing Shift-F8 (Format), selecting the Other option (**4** or **O**), selecting the Printer functions option (**6** or **P**), and finally selecting the Word Spacing Justification Limits option (**4** or **J**). The Word Spacing Justification option allows you to modify the minimum and maximum range within which WordPerfect can fit justified text. When you use a proportionally spaced font, the optimal spacing between words is built into the font (expressed by percentage as 100%). Use the Compressed To option to set the minimum word spacing percentage, and the Expanded To option to set the maximum word spacing percentage allowed. When one of these limits is reached, WordPerfect begins to adjust the spacing between letters within the words themselves.

Changing Line Height

The *line height* is the measurement from the baseline of one line of text to the baseline of the following line of text. WordPerfect automatically calculates the correct line height to accommodate the largest font that is being used in the line. The automatic line height is usually what you want, but you can override this automatic adjustment and enter a fixed line height for all of the lines in part or all of the document so that all text lines will be an equal amount of space apart no matter which font you are using or how often you change fonts. Line height is discussed in greater detail in Chapter 5.

Setting Left and Right Margins

WordPerfect is preset for 1-inch left and right margins. When you reset margins, the margins of your document are changed from the cursor position forward, so you must move to the beginning of the document (Home Home ↑) before changing margin settings if you want the new margin settings to affect the entire document. (Home Home ↑ places the cursor after any formatting codes and before the first text character, ensuring that any format changes you make will take effect in your text, even if you forget to delete the old formatting codes.)

If inches is your default unit of measurement, you can specify new margin settings as points (**p**) or centimeters (**c**), and WordPerfect will automatically translate them into inches.

To enter new left and right margin settings, press Shift-F8 (Format), choose Line (**1** or **L**) and then choose Margins, Left and Right (**7** or **M**). Enter a new value for the right margin or press Enter to enter a new value for the left margin only. Press F7 twice to return to your document.

Enter the left margin setting as the distance from the left edge of the paper and the right margin setting as the distance from the right edge of the paper. This feature is unlike previous versions of WordPerfect, in which both margins were calculated from the position of the left edge of the paper.

WordPerfect automatically adjusts the line length for the current font to maintain the left and right margin settings in effect. Therefore, you do not have to change the left and right margin settings when you change the size of the font in the document, as you did in earlier versions of WordPerfect.

When you change the left and right margin settings in a document, WordPerfect inserts an [L/R Mar:] code that includes the new settings, separated by a comma. For example, if you have specified a 1.5-inch left margin and a 2-inch right margin, the code will appear as [L/R Mar:1.5", 2"]. To revert to the default left and right margin settings of 1 inch each, locate and delete the [L/R Mar:] code in the Reveal Codes screen.

When you press Alt-F3 to see the hidden formatting codes, you can tell from the tab ruler line where your margins have been set (see Figure 3.1). The left margin is indicated by a bracket ([), or by a brace ({) if it coincides with a tab stop setting. The triangles are tab stops.

To keep the tab ruler on the screen while you are creating and editing a document, press Ctrl-F3 (Screen) and type **1** or **W** to choose the Window option. When you see the prompt

Number of lines in this Window: 24

respond by pressing ↑ once. You will then see the tab ruler displayed at the bottom of the screen, and the number of lines will change from 24 to 23. Press Enter to set the ruler in this position. To remove the tab ruler, repeat this command, this time pressing ↓ instead of ↑ before pressing Enter.

Margin Release

Margin Release (Shift-Tab) moves the cursor one tab stop to the left. It is useful for numbering paragraphs in the left margin of your document or for creating

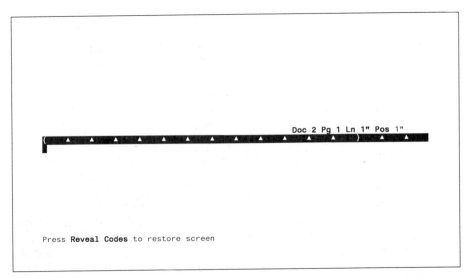

FIGURE 3.1: Viewing current margin settings by looking at the tab ruler line. The left margin ({) is set at the 1-inch position, and the right margin (}) is set at the 7.5-inch position.

hanging paragraph indents, as discussed in "Indenting Paragraphs" later in this chapter.

When you press Shift-Tab for a margin release, a [←Mar Rel] code is inserted in your document. If you are in the middle of a line of text when you press Shift-Tab, some characters may disappear from your screen as the cursor moves one tab stop to the left. If this happens, you can press Alt-F3 (Reveal Codes) to view the formatting codes and delete the [←Mar Rel] code that is causing the trouble.

Changing Line Spacing

WordPerfect allows you to set line spacing in increments of tenths of lines. The default setting is for single spacing. To change line spacing, press Shift-F8 (Format), choose Line (**1** or **L**), and then choose Line Spacing (**6** or **S**). Then enter a number indicating the line spacing you want your document to have (**1.5** for space-and-a-half, **2** for double spacing, and so forth). When you specify spacing that includes fractional increments, always enter the fraction as a decimal (**.5**).

When you set the spacing in whole-number increments such as 2 (double), 3 (triple), 4 (quadruple), and so on, WordPerfect adds the necessary blank lines on your screen to show the text of your document properly spaced.

Fractional line spacing increments cannot be properly displayed on the editing screen. Instead, WordPerfect rounds up the fraction and displays the text as it would for spacing specified as the next highest whole number. For example, if you specify one-and-a-half spacing, WordPerfect displays the text as though it were double-spaced.

The formatting code used by WordPerfect when you change line spacing is [Ln Spacing:#], where # is the line spacing. If you use this command and then enter **2.5** for two-and-a-half spacing, you will see this code in the Reveal Codes window:

[Ln Spacing:2.5]

WordPerfect obeys this code until it reaches another [Ln Spacing] code. This allows you to vary the spacing in one document as often as you need. For instance, you may want to change to single spacing whenever you enter direct quotations in an otherwise double-spaced document. To do this, you change to double spacing when you begin the document and then change to single spacing at the beginning of the first line of the quotation. After you finish typing the quotation, you change the spacing back to double.

If you have changed the line spacing many times in a document and then wish to make the spacing uniform, you must remove all of the different [Ln Spacing] codes that you have entered. To do this, you can use the Search feature to locate them. Make sure that you eliminate them all by positioning the cursor at the very beginning of the document (Home Home Home ↑ to make sure that you are at the very beginning, before any other formatting codes). Press Alt-F2 (Replace); then press Enter to replace without confirming. Press Shift-F8 (Format); then choose Line (**1** or **L**), Line (**5** or **L**), and Line Spacing (**3** or **S**). At the bottom left of the editing screen you will see

→ Srch: [Ln Spacing:]

Press F2; then simply press Enter and F2 again to replace each [Ln Spacing] code with nothing (i.e., delete it). WordPerfect will place the cursor immediately after the first Line Spacing code that it locates. To delete the code, press Backspace. Then repeat the search by pressing F2 twice, and perform the same deletion until you receive the message *Not Found.*

You can also search backward if you are at the end of the document.

S2 AND S1: DOUBLE- AND SINGLE-SPACING MACROS

If you need to vary the line spacing often in the types of documents you create, you may want to enter [Ln Spacing] codes by using macros. The macros illustrated in Figures 3.2 and 3.3 can be used to set double and single line spacing. You can use them to alternate quickly between single and double spacing in one document. You can also use these examples as models for creating your own line spacing macros. Simply choose an appropriate macro name and enter the number of line spaces you wish to associate with it.

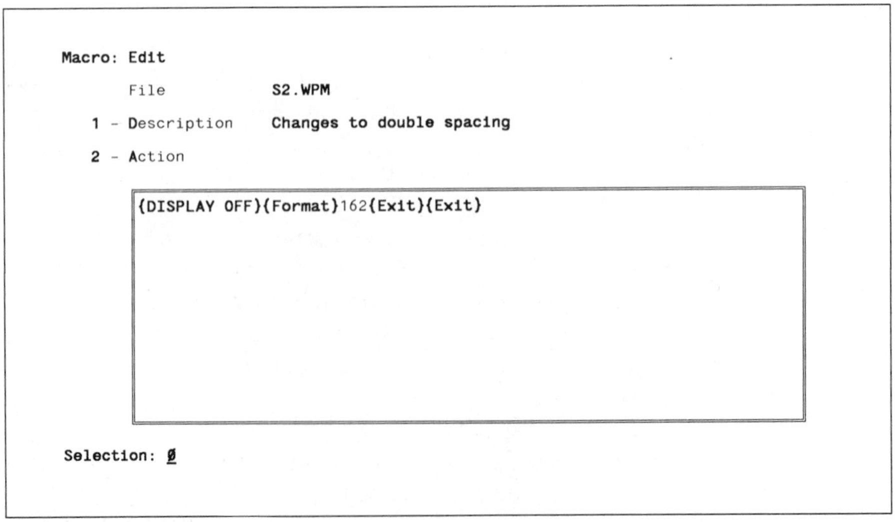

```
Macro: Edit

        File          S2.WPM

  1 - Description    Changes to double spacing

  2 - Action

  ┌─────────────────────────────────────────────────┐
  │ {DISPLAY OFF}{Format}162{Exit}{Exit}             │
  │                                                  │
  │                                                  │
  │                                                  │
  │                                                  │
  │                                                  │
  └─────────────────────────────────────────────────┘

  Selection: 0
```

FIGURE 3.2: A macro named S2 (for *double spacing*). It quickly switches from the default of single spacing to double spacing.

```
Macro: Edit

        File            S1.WPM

 1 - Description        Changes to single spacing

 2 - Action

    ┌─────────────────────────────────────────────────────────┐
    │ {DISPLAY OFF}{Format}161{Exit}{Exit}                     │
    │                                                          │
    │                                                          │
    │                                                          │
    │                                                          │
    │                                                          │
    │                                                          │
    │                                                          │
    └─────────────────────────────────────────────────────────┘

 Selection: ∅
```

FIGURE 3.3: A macro named S1 (for *single spacing*). It quickly changes your spacing back to the default of single spacing.

To use these macros, you press Alt-F10, type **S2** or **S1**, and press Enter. They will enter the appropriate [Ln Spacing] code wherever the cursor is located when you execute them.

Setting Tabs

WordPerfect is preset with left-justified tabs every ½ inch (or five spaces in 4.2 units). To change these tab settings, you press Shift-F8 (Format), choose Line, and then choose Tab Set (**8** or **T**). The screen shown in Figure 3.4 appears. To select a new tab stop, move the cursor to the position on the ruler line where you want the tab. Then type **L** (for a left-justified tab), **R** (for a right-justified tab), **C** (for a centered tab), **D** (for a decimal tab) or **.** (period, for a dot leader tab). You may use the space bar or the → key to position the cursor on the tab ruler line to see where these tabs appear in relation to your text. You can set up to 40 tabs.

To set uniformly spaced tabs, press Home Home ← to move to the beginning of the tab ruler line; then press Ctrl-End to delete all the existing tabs. If you are setting left-justified tabs at positions on or after the 1-inch mark, type the position measurement of the first tab setting, type a comma, and then type the amount of space you want to have between the evenly spaced tabs. For example, to reset tabs every inch starting 1 inch from the left margin, you would type **1,1**. If you are setting right, center, or decimal tabs, move to the position of the first tab and type **r**, **c**, or **d** before entering the position number and increment. For example,

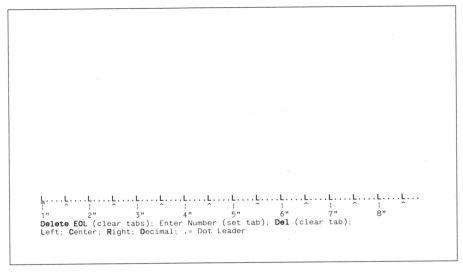

```
L....L....L....L....L....L....L....L....L....L....L....L....L....L....L....L...
  !    ^    !    ^    !    ^    !    ^    !    ^    !    ^    !    ^    !    ^
  1"       2"       3"       4"       5"       6"       7"       8"
Delete EOL (clear tabs); Enter Number (set tab); Del (clear tab);
Left; Center; Right; Decimal; .= Dot Leader
```

FIGURE 3.4: Setting tabs with the tab ruler line. You can choose four different types of tabs (left, right, center, and decimal). In addition, you can have dot leaders with these tabs.

for decimal tabs set every 2 inches starting 1 inch from the left margin, you would move to the 1-inch mark, type **d**, and then type **1,2**.

Tabs that you set go into effect from the cursor position to the end of the document or to the point where you set tabs again. A [Tab Set] code is inserted in your document. You do not have to delete old [Tab Set] codes to insert new ones. If you view the Reveal Codes screen, you can find the [Tab Set] closest to your text (just above it)—the one that is in effect.

To delete a tab when you are viewing the tab ruler line, move the cursor to it and press Del. Table 3.1 lists the various types of tab stops with examples illustrating how they work.

Left-justified tabs are the most commonly used tabs in any document. They work just like regular tabs set on a typewriter. In some other word processing programs, they are referred to as *text* tabs or *textual* tabs to differentiate them from decimal tabs.

To delete a tab indent, you can press Alt-F3 to access the Reveal Codes window and then delete the [Tab] code. You can also delete a tab by moving the cursor to the first character of the word that is indented and pressing Backspace. WordPerfect will not prompt you before removing a tab as it does when you are about to delete other formatting codes.

Right-justified tabs are used when you want all of the text to appear flush right against a particular tab stop. They are not to be confused with decimal tabs, which you use when you want to align columns of figures on the decimal point. Right-justified tabs are indicated by the letter *R* on the tab ruler.

TAB TYPE	HOW SET	EXAMPLE
Left-justified	L	First Quarter .....L...........
Right-justified	R	First Quarter ....R...........
Centered	C	First Quarter ....C...........
Decimal	D	$1,256.00 ....D...........
Dot-leader left	.L	Benefits..............Section 1.11 L....................L..........
Dot-leader right	.R	Benefits...Section 1.11 L....................R..........
Dot-leader decimal	.D	Benefits.....Section 1.11 L....................D..........
Dot-leader centered	.C	......First Quarter...... ....C...........

TABLE 3.1: Types of Tabs Supported by WordPerfect

The formatting codes for right-justified tabs are [Align] and [C/A/Flrt]. If you delete either of these codes, the tab will be removed entirely, and the text will move back to the left margin or be joined with the text that precedes it on the line.

If you set a right-justified tab too close to the left margin and then type more text than can be accommodated in the spaces between it and the left margin, your text will disappear off the screen. If you continue to type text, it will begin to move right of the tab stop as soon as the first character is pushed to the left edge of the paper. In such a case, you will have to reset the tab stop farther right to allow sufficient room for it within the current left margin setting.

Centered tabs are used to center text on a tab stop. This is especially useful when you are creating a table and want the column headings centered over the numbers in the columns. Centered tabs are indicated by the letter *C* on the tab ruler.

The formatting codes for centered tabs are [Tab][Cntr][C/A/Flrt] in the Reveal Codes window. If you delete either of the last two codes, the text will be reformatted as though you had set a left-justified tab. If you delete the [Tab] code as well, the tab will be removed entirely, and the text will move back to the left margin or be joined with the text that precedes it on the line.

Decimal tabs are most often used to align figures in columns. When you use a decimal tab, all punctuation (such as the dollar sign) and numbers are right-justified until you type a period. After that, all of the numbers you enter are left-justified. When you press the Tab key and the next tab stop is a decimal tab, the message "Align Char = ." will appear at the bottom of the screen.

You can change the alignment character to another character of your choice, as discussed earlier in this chapter in the "Aligning Text" section.

When you set decimal tabs on the tab ruler and use them in a document, their presence is indicated by the formatting codes [Align] and [C/A/Flrt]. (These are the same formatting codes used to indicate text that is formatted flush right.) The second code immediately precedes the alignment character in effect at that time. For example, if you use a decimal tab to align the number *$5,700.50* on the period, the following text and formatting codes will appear in the Reveal Codes window:

    [Align]5,700[C/A/Flrt].50

To remove the tab, you need to delete only one of these formatting codes.

In addition to these four basic types of tabs, WordPerfect has four more specialized tabs. These all add dot leaders connecting the text at the previous tab stop to the text that you enter at the current tab. These dot leaders can be added to either left-justified, right-justified, decimal, or centered tabs. You set these types of tabs by typing . (period) over the code letter (*L, R, C,* or *D*). They are indicated on the tab ruler by a highlighted rectangle.

The formatting codes for these special tabs are [Align] and [C/A/Flrt]. These are the same codes used in the Reveal Codes window to indicate the presence of right-justified or decimal tabs. (Centered tabs, of course, use the [Center] code.) To remove tab stops that use dot leaders, you can delete either of the codes.

> *Note:* When you mix different types of tabs on a single ruler line, be careful to space them so that text placed at one tab stop does not overwrite text at a neighboring tab stop. Remember that text entered at a right-justified tab moves toward the left—closer to the previous tab and to any text that you have entered there. If you find that text disappears as it encounters an entry made at the previous tab stop, reset the tabs, making sure that you space them to accommodate all of your text. To make sure that your new tab ruler takes effect, use the Reveal Codes window to place the cursor immediately after the existing [Tab Set] code.

Indenting Paragraphs

In WordPerfect, you can indent paragraphs in three ways.

- Left indent, in which all text of a paragraph is indented a certain distance from the left margin.

- Left and right indent, in which a paragraph is indented an equal distance from the right and left margins.
- Hanging indent, in which the first line of a paragraph is not indented, but the following lines are indented.

These three types of indentation are illustrated in Figure 3.5.

All three of these types of indentation are accomplished by using the F4 (Indent) key. (These examples assume you are using the default tab stops, which are set every $\frac{1}{2}$ inch.)

- For a left indent, press F4 at the beginning of your paragraph. It is then indented 0.5 inch from the left margin. If you press F4 at the beginning of an existing paragraph, it will be reformatted. If you press F4 at the beginning of a paragraph you are typing, it will be indented as you type until you press Enter again to signal the beginning of a new paragraph. Press F4 a second time to indent the paragraph 1 inch, a third time to indent it 1.5 inches, and so forth. To indent only the first line in a paragraph (as a paragraph indent in a block of quoted text, for example), use the Tab key.
- For a left and right indent, you press Shift-F4. The paragraph will be indented 0.5 inch from both the left and right margins. Continue to press Shift-F4 to indent the paragraph in half-inch increments.
- For a hanging indent, press F4 to indent the paragraph and then press Shift-Tab to remove the indentation for the first line. Shift-Tab is the

```
    —    The company cafeteria, located on the third floor, is open from 7 a.m.
         until 2 p.m. daily. Breakfast is available for your convenience until
         9:00.


         MagnaCorp participates in the city recreational plan and therefore
         its employees have access to the municipal gym located at First and
         Brannan Streets.

Full-time permanent employees are eligible for two weeks of paid vacation after
     six months of continuous employment.




C:\5\FIG3-5                                      Doc 1 Pg 1 Ln 1" Pos 1"
```

FIGURE 3.5: WordPerfect's three types of paragraph indentation: left, left and right, and hanging. In this figure, the first paragraph uses a left indent, the second paragraph uses a left and right indent, and the third paragraph uses a hanging indent.

Margin Release key. It removes the indentation for the first line only; succeeding lines will be indented (see Figure 3.5). The margin release causes the text to move back to the previous tab setting. If your tabs are uniformly spaced at 1-inch intervals, the text will move back 1 inch, and the formatting code will appear as [←Mar Rel:1"].

To remove an indentation, you backspace over it. You can also delete indentations by using Alt-F3 to identify and locate the formatting codes in the Reveal Codes window. To delete a Left Indent code, locate the [→Indent] code and delete it with either Del or Backspace.

To delete a left and right indent, locate the [→Indent←] code in the Reveal Codes window and delete it. If you used F4 to create a left indent before you pressed Shift-F4 to create a left and right indent, the text will be left-indented at the previous tab stop.

To delete a hanging indent, locate the [←Mar Rel] code and delete it. Once you delete the [←Mar Rel] code, the [→Indent] code immediately before it will cause the text to be left-indented at the tab stop. However, if you delete the [→Indent] code that precedes the [←Mar Rel] code and do not also delete the [←Mar Rel] code, the text will be reformatted to the left of the left margin setting, and it will move left the number of spaces between the tab stop used by the left indent and the previous tab on the ruler line. This will make the first part of the line of text disappear from the editing screen. To rectify this situation, delete the [←Mar Rel] code; the beginning of the line will be reformatted to the left margin setting in effect.

Beginning a New Page

You often may want to begin a new page ("force" a page break) at a certain point in your document. For example, you may want to have a table on a page by itself. To indicate the beginning of a new page, simply press Ctrl-Enter. The line of equal signs that appears on your screen indicates a hard page break. To remove the page break, move the cursor below the page break line and press Backspace.

You can also specify that a block of lines be kept together, that a page break occur when certain conditions are met, or that widows and orphans (single lines of a paragraph at the bottom or top of a page) not occur in your documents (see Chapter 4).

EDITING A DOCUMENT

After retrieving a document to be edited, you will probably use several techniques in making the necessary changes. Usually, the first order of business is to locate the appropriate place in the text where the changes are to be made. WordPerfect offers several methods for locating a particular place in the document's text:

- A Go To function (Ctrl-Home) to position the cursor at the beginning of a particular page or at the beginning of a block of text (when Block is on—see the discussion of block operations that follows).
- A Forward Search function (F2) to position the cursor at the end of particular characters, words, phrases, or formatting codes that follow the cursor's current position.
- A Reverse Search function (Shift-F2) to position the cursor at the end of particular characters, words, phrases, or formatting codes that precede the cursor's current position.
- A Replace function (Alt-F2) to replace particular groups of characters, words, or phrases with new characters, words, or phrases.

Locating Text to Be Edited by Using the Go To Page Command

If you are editing from a marked-up hard copy of a document that contains page numbers (see Chapter 4 for details about how to set page numbers), you can use the Go To function to move the cursor to the beginning of the page you want to revise. To do this, press Ctrl-Home; you will see

Go to

Enter the appropriate page number and press Enter. You will see the message *Repositioning* on your screen as WordPerfect moves the cursor to the top of the specified page.

You can use the Go To function even if you have not used page numbers in the document, because this function uses the document's Pg counter to locate pages rather than the actual page numbers WordPerfect inserts at printing time. Of course, if your printout does not have page numbers on it, you will have to manually calculate the number of the page that contains the text you want to edit.

Once the cursor is positioned on the proper page, you can use one of the cursor movement keys to move it to the specific text to be modified. If you do not see that text displayed on the first screen, you can press the plus key (+) on the numeric keypad twice to scroll up the second part of the page.

Locating Text to Be Edited by Using the Search Command

You can also use WordPerfect's Search feature to locate the specific text that you want to edit. You can search for a particular place in the text either from the cursor's present position to the end of the document (Forward Search, activated by pressing F2) or from the cursor's position to the beginning of the document

(Reverse Search, activated by pressing Shift-F2 or by pressing ↑ when the Forward Search prompt is displayed). If you have just retrieved a document, your cursor will be located at the top of the first page of the document; in this case, you will want to use the Forward Search function.

You can use either Forward Search or Reverse Search to locate particular characters, words, phrases, or formatting codes that you have entered into a document. The first time you press F2 to begin a forward search, you will see the following prompt on your screen:

→ Srch:

The cursor will appear to the right of the colon. You then enter the *search string* that you want WordPerfect to find. This string can consist of any codes, characters, words, or phrases up to 59 characters total.

> *Note:* Forward Search always remains the program default. If you want to repeat a reverse search operation using the same search string, you will find that you must still press Shift-F2 or F2 ↑ before you press F2 again to initiate the next search. There is no way to set the reverse direction once and retain it on subsequent searches.

Unlike other word processors you may have used, WordPerfect does not include special search options, such as Ignore Case, Whole Word, and so forth, that can refine your search and make it more exact. For example, if you enter the search string **ion** to find all occurrences of the word *ion* (as in "a free ion in a solution"), WordPerfect will find the three characters *i o n* wherever they appear together, even in the many words that end in *tion* (sta*tion*, rela*tion*, and so on).

You can weed out matches in larger words that contain *ion* by typing a space before and after *ion* in the search string. WordPerfect will not consider the *ion* in such words as *relation* a match because *relation* lacks one of the required spaces, the one before the *i* in *ion*.

However, entering the search string this way brings up new problems. WordPerfect will not consider the word *ion* a match if it occurs at the end of a sentence. For example, in the sentence

In this type of solution we seldom see a free ion.

WordPerfect would not consider *ion* to be a match because it is looking for <space>*ion*<space>, not <space>*ion*.; in fact, you might have quite a bit of trouble locating *ion.* in the text. Typing a space before and after letters to mark them as a word also means that you can only locate the singular form of the word. In our example, WordPerfect would not identify the plural *ions* as a match for the search string. In such a case, you should consider entering a space before but not after the search string.

Sometimes when you search for a word, you will have to perform two different searches before you find the occurrence of a word that marks the place where you want to begin editing. If you perform a search operation and WordPerfect only locates occurrences of the word that you are not interested in and then displays the *Not found* message, you can search in reverse, edit the search string, and try to find the word on a return pass through the document. Or you can search for a phrase instead of a single word (especially if the word is embedded in many other words that you have used). For example, if you specified your search string as

→ Srch: free ion

with no space after the *n* in *ion*, WordPerfect would be more likely to find the place you want on its first pass through your document. Because WordPerfect is looking for the phrase *free*<space>*ion*, it will not recognize as a match the *ion* in the ending of a word like *station*. However, it will see the occurrence of the phrase *free ions* as a match, even if it occurs at the end of a sentence and is followed by some type of punctuation. Also, it will find matches in both *free ion* and *free ions*, eliminating the problem that develops when the plural form of the word occurs.

> *Note:* WordPerfect ignores case differences in a search as long as the search string is entered in lowercase letters. To make a search case-sensitive, you must enter it using the appropriate capital letters. For example, the search string *Ion* would match only capitalized forms of the word *ion,* although it would not automatically eliminate all of the problems alluded to in the preceding discussion.

After you have entered the search string, you press F2 to make WordPerfect perform the search operation and locate the first occurrence of the string in the direction specified. (If you press Enter, you just insert [HRt] in the search string.) After WordPerfect finds the first occurrence of your search string, you must repeat the Search command to make WordPerfect locate any subsequent occurrences. (WordPerfect does not have a key whose function is to locate the next occurrence of the search string.) To reissue the command without changing the search string, just press F2 twice. If you want to edit the search string before performing the search again, press F2 once, make your changes, and then press F2 again. To stop a search operation after entering the search string, press F1 (Cancel).

Performing an Extended Search

When WordPerfect performs a standard search operation, it does not look for matches to your search string in any headers, footers, footnotes, or endnotes that you have added to the document. However, you can direct it to perform such an extended search operation. To do this, you press Home before you press F2 (Search), Shift-F2 (Reverse Search), or Alt-F2 (Replace).

If WordPerfect finds your search string in a header, footer, footnote, or endnote, it will position the cursor after the string in the appropriate function screen. To continue the extended search in the same header, footer, footnote, or endnote, you merely reenter the Search or Search and Replace command you used before. To abandon the search, you press F7 (Exit) and return to the document. To continue the extended search to include the next header, footer, footnote, or endnote, you must press Home before reissuing the Search or Search and Replace command.

> *Note:* You need to position the cursor at the very beginning of the document (Home Home Home ↑) before you begin an extended search that is to include the headers and footers you have defined for a document. If you begin a forward extended search (Home F2) from somewhere in the middle of the document—past the place where the Header and Footer Definition codes exist—WordPerfect will not include them in the search operation unless you also perform a reverse extended search (Home Shift-F2).

SEARCHING FOR FORMATTING CODES

In addition to being able to use the Search function to find text in a document, you can use it to find hidden codes that were added as you made formatting changes during the document's creation.

To have WordPerfect locate a particular hidden code, you use the appropriate Search function (Forward or Reverse) and then press the appropriate function key or key combination (including the number or letter of the menu option) instead of typing an alphanumeric search string. For instance, to perform a forward search to find the first occurrence of a hard page break (one that you entered), you press F2 and then press Ctrl-Enter (the function keys used to add a hard page break). In response, the program will display the formatting code as the search string:

→ Srch: [HPg]

You then press F2 to perform the search. WordPerfect will position the cursor right below the first hard page break it finds. To delete this page break, you then press Backspace. To find the next occurrence of a hard page break, press F2 twice.

You can also use this technique to find hidden formatting codes that require the use of menu options. For instance, to locate the place in the text where you first used WordPerfect's Columns feature (see Chapter 10), you can use the Search function to find the [Col On] code required to activate your column definitions. After you press F2 (assuming that a forward search is required), you press Alt-F7 (the Math/Columns key combination you use to define the columns and turn them on and off). You will then see the following list of options:

Math: **1** Def **2** On **3** Off **4** + **5** = **6** * **7** t **8** T **9** ! **A** N Column: **B** Def **C** On **D** Off 0

To search for the [Col On] code, type **C**; you then see the following:

→ Srch: [Col On]

Notice that because this menu line contains more than nine options, Word-Perfect uses the letters *A* through *D.* Choosing option **C** supplies the formatting code [Col On] that you need to find the beginning of text formatted as columns.

You can also use the Search function to find just the second (or lowercase) element of a code that is part of a pair—[BOLD][bold], [UND][und], and so forth. If you perform a regular search for one of these paired codes, WordPerfect positions the cursor after the uppercase code.

For instance, to find your first use of underlining in a document, you press F2 followed by F8 (Underline) to see the following prompt:

→ Srch: [UND]

If you then perform the search, and the first occurrence of underlining in the text is *Mastering WordPerfect*, WordPerfect will position the cursor under the *M* in *Mastering*. If you press Alt-F3 (Reveal Codes), you will see that the cursor is really positioned right after the [UND] code in [UND]*Mastering WordPerfect*[und]. If you press Backspace, the underlining will be removed.

To search for the [und] code, you press F2 and then F8 twice. You will see the following:

→ Srch: [UND][und]

To search for just the second code ([und]), you need to modify the codes after the Search prompt. Press ← twice and then press Del to remove the [UND] code. If you perform the search without deleting this first code, you will probably receive the message *Not Found,* because nowhere in your text will the codes [UND][und] occur together (that is, without any text between them).

Now when you press F2 to perform the search, the cursor will be positioned after the final *t* in *Mastering WordPerfect*. If you open the Reveal Codes window, you will see that the cursor is really located after the [und] code in [UND]*Mastering WordPerfect*[und].

Although this technique may not appear to be extremely useful (since you can delete underlining by locating and removing either code), it can be applied very skillfully in macros when you need to delete a paired formatting code and replace it with another set, as discussed in Chapter 16.

> *Note:* When you access command menus to generate formatting codes that will be searched for, the menu options may not appear the same as in the normal menus. All the options will be arranged horizontally, and some of them may be reworded or otherwise reorganized. In addition, some of the mnemonic shortcuts you are used to may not be in effect. You may have to enter an option number or letter different from the one that inserted the formatting code originally.

USING WILD CARDS IN SEARCHES

In WordPerfect, ^X can be used as a wild card when searching for words or phrases in your documents. (To enter ^X, press Ctrl-V first and then press Ctrl-X.) It can be substituted for any character. For example, a search for

    no^X

returns *now, not, nor, non,* and so forth. It also returns words that contain *now, nor, non,* and so forth, such as *nowadays, notable, nonapplicable, enormous, denoted,* and *anonymous.* Also note that you cannot use ^X at the beginning of a search string. Using ^X as a wild card is useful if you do not remember the exact spelling of the word you want to find. If you want to limit WordPerfect's search to complete words, you must enter spaces before and after the search string.

SEARCHING FOR SPECIAL CHARACTERS

You can search directly for special characters that you have entered with WordPerfect's Compose feature (discussed in Chapter 14, "Line Drawing and Special Symbols"). To search for one of these characters, press Search (F2) and then repeat the sequence you originally used to generate the character. For example, to search for an uppercase umlaut A (Ä), press Ctrl-2, type **1,30**, and press Enter. The Ä will appear as the search string.

Searching and Replacing

You can also search for words or phrases and replace them with substitute words or phrases that you specify. Again, the 59-character limit applies; you can search for up to 59 characters and replace them with as many as 59 characters, including spaces. When you perform a search-and-replace operation, Word-Perfect matches the capitalization of the first letter of the words it finds. For example, if you ask it to search for *file list* and replace this phrase with *list files,* it will replace *File List* with *List files, file List* with *list files,* and so forth. This feature allows you to correctly replace words and phrases that are capitalized at the beginning of a sentence as well as lowercased within the text.

You can use the Search and Replace command to significantly simplify the typing of a document by creating a kind of glossary. To do this, you enter a specific abbreviation for an often-used term throughout the document and then use the Search and Replace function to substitute each occurrence of this abbreviation with the word's unabbreviated form. For example, if you work for a firm named Nolan, Tuttle, Bronkowski and Associates, you might enter the abbreviation **NTBA** each time the firm's name is mentioned in a document. After you finish entering your text, you can then use the Replace function to search for all occurrences of *NTBA* and have the program replace them with *Nolan, Tuttle, Bronkowski and Associates.*

To perform a search-and-replace operation, press Alt-F2. WordPerfect then asks you whether you want to confirm each replacement. The following prompt appears:

w/Confirm? (Y/N) N

If you enter **Y**, WordPerfect will ask you to confirm whether you want to make the replacement each time it finds the word or phrase you specified (the search string).

To make this procedure most efficient, you can use the Replace function without requiring confirmation for each replacement. However, in such a case you must be careful that the abbreviation you have selected never occurs within other words in the document (the NTBA example meets this criterion). If it does, your replacement string will be introduced in places that are far from appropriate, and the procedure will end up wasting, instead of saving, time. For example, if you instruct WordPerfect to search for *ins* and replace it with *International Network Systems,* you will get what are euphemistically called "unexpected results" in words that contains *ins,* such as *instrumental* and *insures.* To avoid this situation, type a space before and after the search string.

To carry out a search-and-replace operation, you first respond to the confirmation prompt, as already discussed. WordPerfect then prompts you for the search string—the word or phrase to search for. When you enter the search string, be careful not to press Enter at the end unless you want WordPerfect to search for a hard return at the end of the string. Press F2 again (or press Esc) to enter the search string.

WordPerfect then prompts you to enter the replacement string. Enter it, again being careful not to enter any formatting codes unless you want those codes to be inserted in your document. Press F2 again to begin the search-and-replace operation.

To return to the place in your document where you were before you began a search or search-and-replace operation, press Ctrl-Home Ctrl-Home (that is, press Go To twice).

REPLACING FORMATTING CODES

In some cases, you can even use WordPerfect's Search and Replace function (referred to by WordPerfect Corporation simply as the Replace function) to make the program automatically replace one code with another. Table 3.2 lists the codes that you can search for and replace. Where you cannot use the Replace function, you can create a macro that uses the Search function to locate the appropriate code, performs any required deletion, and replaces the code with a new one. Chapter 16 discusses creating and using macros.

PRESS	TO GENERATE
F4	[→Indent←]
Shift-F4	[→Indent]
Ctrl-F5	[Comment]
Alt-F5	[End Def]
F6	[BOLD][bold]
Ctrl-F6	[Align]
Shift-F6	[Center]
Alt-F6	[Flsh Rt]
Ctrl-F7	[Note Num]
Alt-F7	[Math On][Math Off][+][=][*][t][T] [!][Col On][Col Off]
F8	[UND][und]
Ctrl-F8	[SUPRSCPT][suprscpt][SUBSCPT][subscpt] [FINE][fine][SMALL][small][LARGE][large] [VRY LARGE][vry large][EXT LARGE][ext large] [BOLD][bold][UND][und][DBL UND][dbl und] [ITALC][italc][OUTLN][outln][SHADW][shadw] [SMCAP][smcap][REDLN][redln][STKOUT][stkout]
Shift-F8	[Hyph On][Hyph Off][/][Just On][Just Off][Center Pg]
F9	^R
Shift-F9	^C; ^D; ^E; ^F; ^G; ^N; ^O; ^P; ^Q; ^S; ^T; ^U; ^V
Alt-F9	[Box Num]
Tab	[Tab]

TABLE 3.2: Formatting Codes That Can Be Used in a Replacement String

Making Simple Insertions and Deletions

Once you have found text to be edited, you must select the best method for changing it. If your changes consist only of simple text insertions or deletions, you can just go ahead and make them. WordPerfect is always in Insert mode unless you specifically press Ins (Insert). If you do, the message *Typeover* will appear at the bottom of the screen, replacing the name of the document you are editing. In Typeover mode, all of the characters you enter at the cursor's position replace existing ones.

Unlike some older word processors, WordPerfect does not split the text when you insert new characters. All you have to do to add new text in a particular place is position the cursor where the new text is to appear and start typing (assuming that you are not in Typeover mode). WordPerfect will use word wrap to reformat the paragraph as you type.

If you are inserting a lot of text, you may find the constant reformatting distracting. If this is the case, you can temporarily split the paragraph by positioning the cursor under the first character of the text that will remain unchanged after the insertion is made and pressing Enter (a hard return). This will move the following text down and keep it separate from the lines that you insert. After you move back up and enter all of the text you need to insert, you can rejoin the paragraph by removing the [HPg] formatting code that you entered earlier. To do this, move the cursor two spaces past the last inserted character (often a period marking the end of the last sentence inserted) and press Del. The paragraph will be rejoined, and it will be reformatted as soon as you move the cursor down one line.

When deleting text, you need to decide which of the many commands for making deletions is best suited to the task at hand. (Refer to Chapter 2 if you are uncertain of the options available to you.) Generally, the deletion commands remove discrete units of text such as individual characters and words, or they remove text from the cursor position to the end of the line or the end of the paragraph. If the text you want to delete is not such a unit, just mark the text as a block and delete it by using the appropriate command.

Because a thorough understanding of block operations is essential for getting the most from WordPerfect, the next sections discuss how to delete, copy, and move blocks of text that have already been typed, how to save blocks of text in separate files, and how to perform other specialized operations on blocks.

Working with Blocks of Text

WordPerfect's Block feature allows you to perform operations on large sections of text instead of having to work word by word or line by line. Basically, a block is an area of text that you specify. It may be as small as one character or as large as your entire document. Using the Block feature can save you much time and allow you to use the program more flexibly. For example, after you have marked text as a block, you can quickly

- Move it.
- Delete it.
- Underline it, boldface it, or change its font, size, and appearance.
- Apply a style to it.
- Center it.
- Convert it to uppercase (or lowercase).
- Print it.
- Sort the items within it.
- Search through it using Search and Replace.

- Mark it to be included in a list, table of contents, or index (see Chapter 9).
- Mark it for redlining or strikeout.
- Save it as a file by itself.
- Append it to the end of another file.
- Check its spelling (see Chapter 15).

WordPerfect allows you to mark any sized block of text— from a single character to the entire document—using its Block key combination, Alt-F4. When you press Alt-F4, the message

Block On

replaces the name of the file you are editing at the bottom of the screen. This message indicates that as you move the cursor, WordPerfect will mark the text by highlighting it. You use the cursor movement keys (see Chapter 2) to mark all of the text you want to comprise the block. If you mark too much text, use the opposite cursor movement key to reduce the limits of the block before selecting the appropriate command to perform an operation on it.

Which cursor movement key to use in marking a block depends on the extent of the block. To mark just a few words, position the cursor on the first character of the first word to be marked and press Ctrl-→ until all of the words you want to mark are highlighted.

To mark just a few lines of text, you can press ↓ several times to highlight each line to be included, or you can press Esc, type a number corresponding to the number of lines to be included, and then press ↓. Be aware that if the cursor is not positioned at the very beginning of the first line when you press Alt-F4 to turn on Block mode and you use ↓ (or ↑), the highlighting in the next line will extend only to the column position that the cursor occupied when you turned blocking on. If you want to include entire lines, you must position the cursor at the very beginning of the line.

To block a complete or partial paragraph, you can press Enter after turning Block mode on. This will extend the highlighting from the cursor's position in the paragraph to the end of the paragraph. To extend the highlighting to a particular character in the paragraph or line, type that character after turning blocking on. For example, you could mark up to the end of a sentence that ends with a question mark by typing ? after turning on Block with Alt-F4.

To cancel marking a block of text after pressing Alt-F4, you can either press F1 (Cancel) or press Alt-F4 again. (The Block key is a toggle switch.) Because you can apply so many different commands to a block of text once it has been marked, WordPerfect allows you to use Ctrl-Home (Go To) to rehighlight the same block, as long as you haven't moved the cursor. To use this technique, you must press Alt-F4 to turn blocking on and then press Ctrl-Home twice. The same block as you used in the previous command will be highlighted.

This technique has many useful applications. For instance, you can use it to mark a block of text to be centered and then use it to boldface the same block. To do this, you would press Alt-F4, use the cursor movement keys to mark the lines to be centered, press Shift-F6 and type **Y** to center the marked text, press Alt-F4 again, press Ctrl-Home twice, and then press F6 to boldface it.

ALT-M: A MACRO TO MARK BLOCKS OF TEXT

The macro named Alt-M that is illustrated in Figure 3.6 is a simple but useful macro that allows you to mark a block of text with a minimum of keystrokes. It marks the text from the cursor position to the end of the line. To extend the block forward or backward, simply press ↓ or ↑ or use any of the cursor movement keys, including PgUp/PgDn, – / + , or Home Home ↑/↓, to mark large blocks of text.

Moving and Copying Blocks of Text

Often, you will block text to move or copy it to different locations in the same document or to a document in the second window. After marking the text to be copied or moved as described in the previous section, you access the Move menu by pressing Ctrl-F4 (Move). You will then see the following menu options:

Move: **1** **B**lock; **2** Tabular **C**olumn; **3** **R**ectangle: 0

You then select Block by typing **1** or **B**.

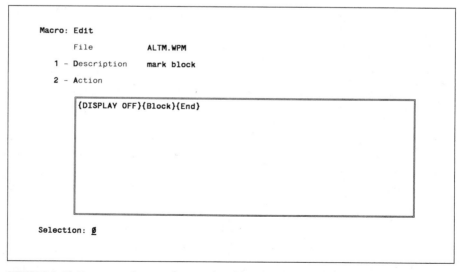

```
Macro: Edit
        File         ALTM.WPM
   1 - Description    mark block
   2 - Action

      {DISPLAY OFF}{Block}{End}




   Selection: 0
```

FIGURE 3.6: Alt-M, a macro that speeds up marking blocks of text. This macro first marks from the cursor position to the end of the line. To extend the highlighting, press any of the cursor movement keys.

Moving a Block of Text

If you want to move the block to a new location in the document (or to a document in the second window), you then type **1** or **M** to select the Move Block option. The block will then disappear from the screen—it has not been deleted, but rather is retained in a special memory location referred to as a *buffer*. You then move the cursor to the position in the document where you want the block of text to appear, and press Enter.

If you want to move a block of text to a different document currently displayed in the second window, you simply press Shift- F3 (Switch) after cutting the block. Then you position the cursor where you want the text inserted and press Enter.

The text that you cut by blocking it and choosing Move remains in the buffer until you repeat this procedure for another block of text. This means that if you move a block when you intended to copy it, you need only press Enter without moving the cursor to bring it back. (Remember, because the text has not been deleted, pressing F1, the Undelete key, will not bring it back.) You can move to another window, use the Go To function, search for a new location, and even exit to DOS temporarily (with Ctrl-F1) without altering the text in the buffer. The next time you press Enter within WordPerfect, the text will be retrieved.

You can retrieve the text that remains in the buffer at another location or in several locations by simply pressing Retrieve (Shift-F10) and Enter.

Copying a Block of Text

To copy a section of text that has been marked with Alt-F4 (Block), you simply vary the second step outlined for moving a block. After you finish marking the block, you press Ctrl-F4 and type **2** or **C** to select the Copy Block option. This copies the marked text into the same buffer that WordPerfect uses when you move text (meaning that it deletes from the buffer any text that has been cut or copied previously). The text that was highlighted is not removed from the screen as when the Move Block option is used, although the highlighting disappears.

To copy the text to a new place in the document, move the cursor to the place where you want the copied text to appear and press Enter in response to the "Move cursor: press Enter to retrieve" prompt. If you want to copy the block to a different document currently in the second document window, press Shift-F3 and move the cursor to the position where you want the text to appear before you press Enter.

You can retrieve the text that remains in the buffer at another location or in several locations by pressing Ctrl-F4 (Move), selecting the Retrieve option (**4** or **R**), and then selecting the Block option (**1** or **B**). You can also do this by pressing Shift-F10 (Retrieve) and pressing the Enter key in response to the "Document to be retrieved" prompt. This allows you to make one copy and then paste it several times.

ALT-M: A MOVE/COPY MACRO

A simple macro such as the one illustrated in Figure 3.7 can greatly speed up your moving and copying operations. This macro can be used as either a move macro or a copy macro. To use this macro to move a block, position the cursor at the beginning of the text to be moved and press Alt-M. (Choose another keystroke combination if you've already defined an Alt-M macro.) This macro then automatically marks the text from the cursor's position to the end of the line and pauses. During this pause, you can increase or decrease the limits of the marked block by using any of the cursor movement keys. After you have adjusted the size of the block so that it includes all of the text you want moved, you press Enter to end the macro pause.

The macro then executes the keystrokes Ctrl-F4 ({Move}) and selects the Block (*b*) and Move (*m*) options, thus cutting the block from the screen. The macro ends at this point, and you will see the familiar "Move cursor: press Enter to retrieve" prompt at the bottom of the screen.

To complete the move operation, you simply position the cursor in the place where you want the cut block to be inserted and press the Enter key again.

Note that you can create an almost identical macro that marks and copies a block of text by substituting *c* for *m* in the keystrokes *bm* (to select the Block and Copy options). You can also mark and copy a block of text by using the Alt-M macro exactly as shown in Figure 3.7, but you must press Enter in response to the "Move cursor: press Enter to retrieve" prompt before you move the cursor (thus reinserting the cut block in its original position). You can then copy the marked block, which remains in the buffer, to a new place in the document by moving the cursor and then pressing Shift-F10 Enter.

```
Macro: Edit

        File           ALTM.WPM

  1 - Description      A macro to move a block of text

  2 - Action

      {Block}{End}{PAUSE}{Move}bm




    Selection: 0
```

FIGURE 3.7: A macro named Alt-M that can be used for both copying and moving blocks of text.

Moving and Copying Tabular Columns

To mark a tabular column (one that has been set with tabs, not a newspaper or parallel column) for moving or copying, each column must be separated from neighboring columns by at least one tab stop. Move the cursor to the first tab stop in the first line of the column. (You may need to press Reveal Codes to see exactly where it is located.) Then press Block (Alt-F4) and move the cursor to the beginning of the last line in the column you want to move. WordPerfect will highlight more than you expect at this point, as shown in the example in Figure 3.8. However, as long as you have the cursor positioned anywhere inside the Tab codes that define a tabbed column, WordPerfect will be able to determine which column you intend to move or copy. If you are moving or copying columns that use decimal tabs, you can tell when you enter the columns that have decimal tabs because the "Align Char = ." prompt appears on your screen, as in the example in Figure 3.8.

To move, copy, or cut the column, press Move (Ctrl-F4) and select Tabular Column (**2** or **C**). WordPerfect will then highlight just the column you want to move, as Figure 3.9 illustrates. Finally, choose either Copy or Move and complete the procedure by moving the cursor to the column's new position and pressing Enter. (If you are deleting the column, choose Delete.)

In Figure 3.10, the column was moved to the far-right position by pressing End to move the cursor to the end of the line and then pressing Enter. Whenever

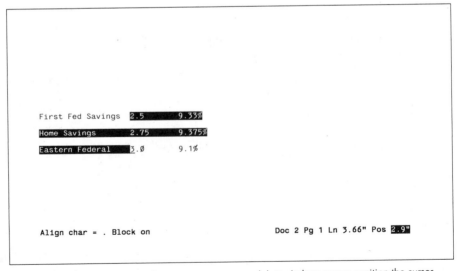

FIGURE 3.8: Marking a tabular column to move, copy, or delete. As long as you position the cursor within the same column area, when you mark it for moving, WordPerfect will be able to determine the column you want to use, although it will highlight extra material on the screen.

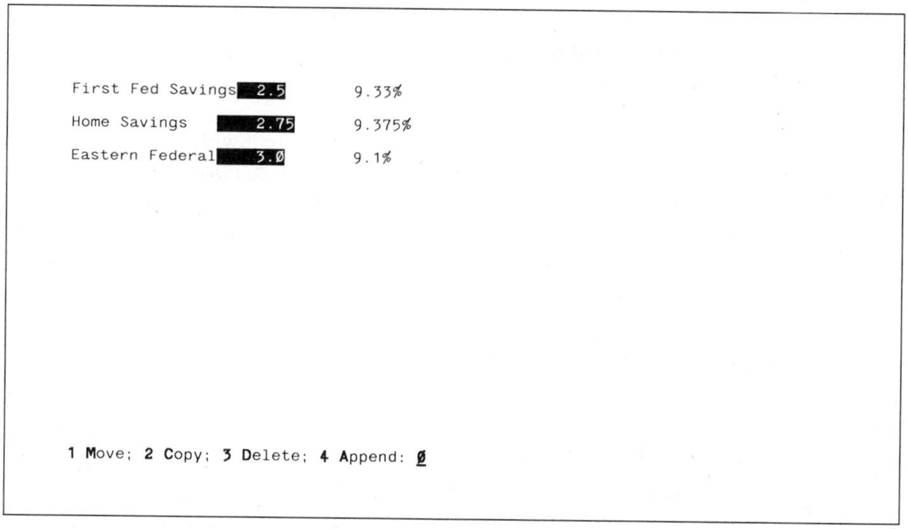

```
        First Fed Savings  2.5        9.33%

        Home Savings       2.75       9.375%

        Eastern Federal    3.0        9.1%
```

```
        1 Move; 2 Copy; 3 Delete; 4 Append: 0
```

FIGURE 3.9: Choosing Move and then Tabular Column. The correct column is now highlighted.

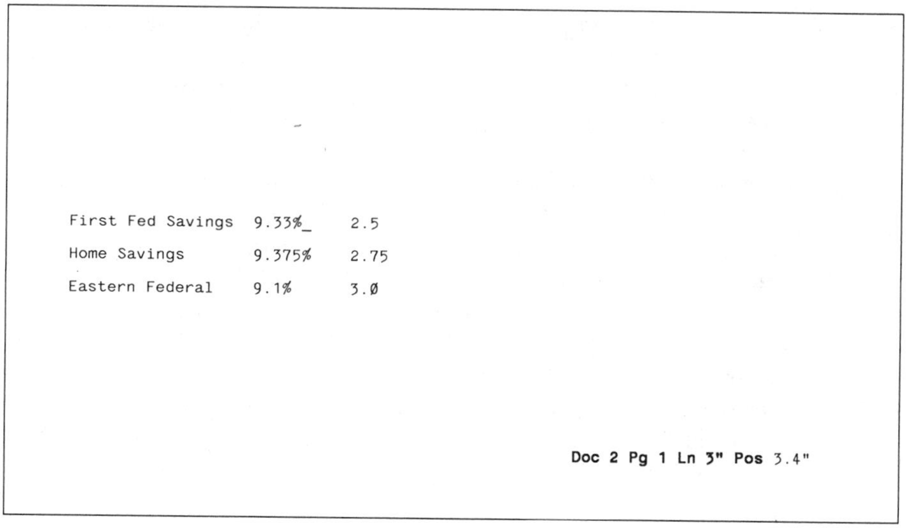

```
        First Fed Savings  9.33%_     2.5

        Home Savings       9.375%     2.75

        Eastern Federal    9.1%       3.0
```

```
                                    Doc 2 Pg 1 Ln 3" Pos 3.4"
```

FIGURE 3.10: Retrieving the moved column by pressing Enter. It is formatted correctly because its formatting codes are copied with it.

you can, use the cursor movement keys, such as End (to move to the end of a line) and Home ← (to move to the beginning of a line), when you are moving tabbed columns. That way, you can be sure that you are positioning the column at its proper location when you press Enter. If you are inserting a column between two existing columns, you will need to view the Reveal Codes screen to make sure that you position the cursor between the correct tabs before you press Enter to retrieve a moved or copied column.

> *Note:* If you delete a column and later retrieve it with WordPerfect's Undelete feature (F1), it will not appear at its original location, and your table may be reformatted incorrectly. To avoid this situation, restore the column into a blank screen and then move it as a tabular column into the position where you want it in your table.

Moving and Copying Rectangles

A rectangular block is marked for moving or copying from corner to corner. To mark a rectangle, position the cursor at any of the four corners and press Alt-F4 (Block). Then move the cursor to the opposite corner and press Ctrl-F4 (Move). Select the Rectangle option (**3** or **R**). Finally, choose either Copy or Move and complete the procedure by moving the cursor to the rectangle's new position and pressing Enter.

This feature allows you to work with blocks of text that do not extend from the left margin to the right margin. You will often use it when you are working with graphics that you have created with WordPerfect's Line Draw feature, because you can create a graphic element at the left margin and then move it as a rectangle to its final location in the graphic. You can also create duplicate graphic elements in this way, as each one is stored in the Move buffer until you retrieve it. You can continue to retrieve it by pressing Shift-F10 (Retrieve) followed by Enter.

Moving text as a rectangle is also useful if you want to cut a column but leave the space that it occupied empty, because if you delete a tabular column, the space it occupied is deleted also (see Figures 3.11 and 3.12). Be sure to press the space bar to include enough spaces in the last line to make it as wide as the longest line in the text that you are going to cut. For example, in Figure 3.11. the longest line in the column that is being cut contains the word *marketing,* so extra spaces were added in the last line of the column to accommodate that word before the [Tab] code occurs. If you highlight the [Tab] code that defines the column, WordPerfect will move the remaining columns to the left, and you will not get the empty column that you intended.

Moving and Copying Sentences, Paragraphs, and Pages

Although you can use the procedures just described to move or copy any sized block of text, WordPerfect offers you an alternative method for moving or copying entire sentences, paragraphs, or pages. If you recognize ahead of time that the text you want to move or copy is one of these discrete units of text, you can use the following method.

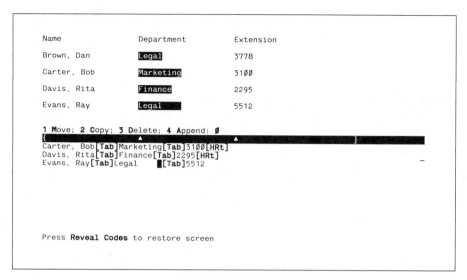

FIGURE 3.11: Creating an empty column. You use WordPerfect's Move Rectangle feature to mark the column.

FIGURE 3.12: The table from Figure 3.11 after deleting the rectangle. The space remains empty as long as you have not highlighted a [Tab] code.

First you need to position the cursor anywhere in the sentence, paragraph, or page that you want to move or copy; then press Ctrl-F4 (Move). (Notice that you do not begin this operation by using Alt-F4. You do not need to block the text when you are working with sentences, paragraphs, or pages; WordPerfect will do this for you.) When you press Ctrl-F4 (and have not marked a block previously), you will see these menu options:

Move **1** **Sentence**; **2** **Paragraph**; **3** **Page**; **4** **Retrieve**: 0

To move or copy a sentence, you choose Sentence (**1** or **S**). For a paragraph, choose Paragraph (**2** or **P**), and for a page, choose Page (**3** or **A**). If you choose Sentence, the entire sentence containing the cursor will automatically be highlighted, regardless of where the cursor is positioned within it. If you choose Paragraph, the entire paragraph will be highlighted. If you choose Page, the entire page will be highlighted. You will then see a new menu containing these options:

1 **Move**; **2** **Copy**; **3** **Delete**; **4** **Append**: 0

To move the unit of text that is highlighted, type **1** or **M** to cut it and copy it into the buffer. The highlighted text will then disappear from the document. Move the cursor to the place you want the text to appear and press Enter. If you want to move the sentence, paragraph, or page to a document in the other document window, press Shift-F3 before you press Enter.

To copy the unit of text you have chosen, you vary this procedure only slightly. After you press Ctrl-F4 and choose either Sentence, Paragraph, or Page, type **2** or **C** to choose the Copy option instead of typing **1** or **M** to choose the Move option. WordPerfect will not remove the highlighted sentence, paragraph, or page, but will copy the text to the buffer and then remove the highlighting. You then move the cursor to the place where you want the copy to appear and press Enter to insert the text.

Deleting a Block of Text

If you want to delete a block of text, you have two methods to choose from:

- If the text to be deleted is an entire sentence, paragraph, or page, you press Ctrl-F4 and type **1** or **S** for a sentence, **2** or **P** for a paragraph, or **3** or **A** for a page. Then select the Delete option (**3** or **D**) from the options that appear.

- If the text is not one of these discrete units, press Alt-F4 and mark the text to be deleted with the cursor movement keys. Then press Backspace. You will see the message

Delete Block? (Y/N) No

Type **Y** to delete the highlighted text.

It is important to remember that you can press F1 to undelete any block of text that has been deleted this way. In fact, you can use the Block Delete option as another way of moving text in a document. After deleting a block of text using one of the methods just described, you can move the cursor to the place in the document where you want the text to appear and press F1; the highlighted block just deleted will reappear on the screen. Then type **1** or **R** to undelete the block and restore it into the document at its new position. You can then copy the block elsewhere in the same document or into a document in the other document window by repeating this procedure.

> *Note:* When you delete a sentence, paragraph, or page of text by using Ctrl-F4 in this way, the text is copied into a buffer different from the one WordPerfect uses when you copy or move a sentence, paragraph, or page of text. This means that you could cut a page and then delete the next page, and the two pages would be retained in separate buffers. You could then retrieve and place the copied or moved page elsewhere in the document by pressing Enter and the deleted page by pressing F1 and typing **1** or **R**.
>
> If you want to move two separate pages (or paragraphs or sentences), you could use this technique to remove both pages, move the cursor to where you want the pages placed, and then insert both pages, using the appropriate methods, without having to move one block forward and then return to move the second one.

Saving a Block of Text in Another Document

In addition to being able to copy blocks of text to a document currently displayed in the second document window, you can mark a block of text and either save it in a new file of its own or add it to the end of an existing document file.

Saving a Block in a New File

To save a block of text in a new file, you mark it by pressing Alt-F4, highlight it with the appropriate cursor movement keys, and press F10 to save it. When you press F10, the *Block on* message changes to

Block name:

You then type the file name under which you want this block of text to be saved and press Enter. If you do not specify the drive letter and directory as part of the file name, WordPerfect will save the file in the current default directory. If you want to remove this blocked text that you just saved in a new file, block it again (Alt-F4 Ctrl-Home Ctrl-Home); then press Del or Backspace and type **Y**.

If you have made formatting changes in the document from which you copy the block, these most likely will no longer affect the text in the new file; unless you included the formatting codes used in the first document as part of the block, the text will use the new document's format settings.

APPENDING A BLOCK TO ANOTHER DOCUMENT

To copy a block of text to the end of another document, you press Alt-F4, highlight the text to be included, and press Ctrl-F4. Choose Block (**1** or **B**); then choose Append (**4** or **A**). You will see the prompt

Append to:

Type the name of the file to which you want this block of text added and press Enter.

When you next retrieve the document to which you appended the block of text, you will find the block at the very end of it. If the last sentence in the document was not terminated with a hard return, the text in the first paragraph of the added block will be joined to the last paragraph of the document. Also, the added block of text will conform to the format settings of the document to which it is appended unless the block contains its own set of formatting codes.

Adding Enhancements to Blocks of Text

You can apply boldfacing, underlining, centering, and capitalization to blocks of text after they have been marked as described earlier. (For information about using appearance and size changes such as italics and small type, as well as changing fonts, see Chapter 5.)

UNDERLINING AND BOLDFACING BLOCKS

WordPerfect lets you underline and boldface an entire block of text at one time. This feature provides a shortcut for enhancing text that you have already typed. For example, if you first mark a heading as a block (using Alt-F4), you can then indicate that the heading is to be boldfaced by pressing only one key (F6) instead of having to retype the text and insert the Boldface codes.

To delete Boldface and Underline codes from blocks of text, press Alt-F3 to see the codes, then backspace over one of them. If you backspace over one of these invisible formatting codes in the text and you don't have the Reveal Codes window open, you will see the prompt

Delete [BOLD]? (Y/N) No

at the bottom of your screen. You can enter **Y** to delete the code or press Enter to leave it in place.

You can also change the style of underlining; for details, see "Changing the Underline Style" earlier in this chapter.

CENTERING BLOCKS OF TEXT

WordPerfect allows you to center entire blocks of text, such as quotations or lists, horizontally on the page. Centering text is an effective way of calling the reader's attention to a passage and making it stand out visually on the page.

To center a block of text—a heading, a paragraph, a list, or any other text element—first mark the text as a block (using Alt-F4). Then, with the block highlighted, press Shift-F6. The prompt

[Cntr]? (Y/N) No

appears at the bottom of your screen. Enter **Y** to center the block. WordPerfect automatically calculates the center position on the text line, centers the block around that position, and inserts a hard return at the end of the line. To delete centering, press Alt-F3 to see the Center codes (they are [Cntr] at the beginning of the text and [C/A/Flrt] [HRt] at the end of the text). Position the cursor to the right of the [Cntr] or [C/A/Flrt] code and press Backspace. Press Alt-F3 to return to your document.

For information about centering text that has not been marked as a block, see "Centering" earlier in this chapter.

CONVERTING BLOCKS TO UPPERCASE FORMAT

You can also convert a marked block of text to uppercase format. This feature is useful when, for example, after entering your entire document you decide that you would like to make the text headings all capital letters. You can mark each of the headings in your document as a block and then convert it to uppercase format.

To convert a marked block of text to uppercase format, press Shift-F3 (Switch). The following message will appear in the lower-left corner of the screen:

Block: **1 U**ppercase; **2 L**owercase: 0

Enter **1** or **U** for uppercase.

To convert a block back to lowercase format, follow the same procedure, but enter **2** or **L**. When you convert blocks back to lowercase format, you lose whatever capitalization was in that block before. For example, if your heading was

New Hire Requirements

before you converted it to

NEW HIRE REQUIREMENTS

it will appear as

new hire requirements

when you convert it back to lowercase format, and you must reinsert the correct capitalization.

However, WordPerfect automatically keeps the first capital letter following a period capitalized, so if you are converting several sentences from uppercase to lowercase, each will still begin with a capital letter.

Alt-U: A Macro to Capitalize Lowercase Letters   You can write a simple macro that capitalizes the character on which the cursor rests. Such a macro is often useful when you are revising text or correcting typographical errors as well as in the situation just discussed in which you need to correct capitalization in headings that you have lowercased. Figure 3.13 illustrates such a macro.

You can write a similar macro to lowercase the character that the cursor is on. Simply substitute **2** for **1** in the preceding macro.

ALPHABETIZING LINES IN A BLOCK OF TEXT

One very useful feature of WordPerfect is its ability to alphabetize items in a block of text. This is called a *line sort* in WordPerfect. (For information about more complex sorting in WordPerfect, see Chapter 12.)

Before you use this feature, the items to be sorted must be in rows and columns, like names and phone numbers in a phone list. Separate columns from each other with at least one blank space. Then highlight the block of items you want to sort by pressing Alt-F4 (Block) and moving the cursor. When the block of

```
Macro: Edit

        File          ALTU.WPM
    1 - Description   Capitalizes current character
    2 - Action

        {DISPLAY OFF}{Block}{Right}{Switch}1




    Selection: 0
```

FIGURE 3.13: A macro to capitalize the character the cursor is on. Whenever you use this macro, named Alt-U (for *Uppercase*), the current character is automatically capitalized.

items is highlighted, press Ctrl-F9 (Merge/Sort). The screen shown in Figure 3.14 appears. To accept the default settings, which will sort your list alphabetically using the first word of each item, simply press **1** or **P**, Perform Action. Your highlighted list will be alphabetized in ascending order (A to Z).

This technique works for alphabetical entries such as employee lists. You can also specify keys on which to sort, if, for example, you want to sort first by last name and then by first name. In addition, you can sort on alphanumeric fields and even specify items to be selected from a list. (See Chapter 12 for details about how to perform such sorts in WordPerfect.)

ALF: A Macro That Alphabetizes Last and First Names Rather than having to go through the steps just described each time you want to sort a simple list, you can record the macro illustrated in Figure 3.15 to sort alphabetically by the second word in each item, which in this case is the last name. (All too often you find that the list you want to sort is not in *last name, first name* order—that's when this macro is handy. If all you want to do is sort by the first word in a list, WordPerfect's default settings will do that for you. Just mark the list as a block, press Ctrl-F9, and type **1** or **P**.)

This macro also sorts by first name within last name, making it useful for creating phone directories and similar lists. Note that this particular macro sorts only on the second and first words in a list, which is the type of alphabetizing you will usually have to do.

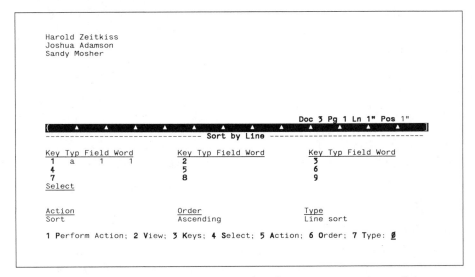

FIGURE 3.14: The Sort by Line screen. As you can see from the screen, you can also specify keys on which to sort so that you could, for example, sort by last name and then by first name within the last name category.

```
Macro: Edit

        File            ALF.WPM

    1 - Description     Alphabetic sort on second word in list

    2 - Action

    {DISPLAY OFF}{Merge/Sort}3{Right}{Right}2{Right}{Right}{Exit}1




    Selection: 0
```

FIGURE 3.15: Alphabetizing first and last names in a list. This macro, named ALF (for *Alphabetical*), sorts first on the second word (the last name) and then on the first word (the first name). It is useful for alphabetizing lists into last-name order when the list is organized with first names first and last names second.

Remember that you must mark your list as a block (Alt-F4) before you use this macro.

The macro instructs WordPerfect to sort a highlighted list (marked with Alt-F4) alphabetically (A–Z) on the second word in the line and then on the first word in the line. To use this macro, mark the list of names, press Alt-F10, type **ALF**, and press Enter.

Other Editing Techniques

WordPerfect has built-in editing aids that allow you to transpose words and characters, specify hyphenation, and keep text together on a line. It also allows you to compare different versions of the same document by using a special Document Compare feature or by marking revised text with Redline and striking out deleted text.

TRANSPOSING CHARACTERS AND WORDS

Another WordPerfect feature that you can use when editing a document transposes the positions of words or characters. This is useful, for example, when you correct typographical errors. For instance, to transpose two characters, you press

Del to delete the second character, press ← to move to the left of the deleted character, and then press F1 and type **1** to undelete the character. Figure 3.16 illustrates a macro that will do this for you quickly.

To use this macro, position the cursor under the second of the characters that need to be transposed and press Alt-T. The character will be exchanged with the one to its left.

To transpose two adjacent words, so that, for example,

> to transpose

is changed to

> transpose to

you can create the macro illustrated in Figure 3.17.

To use this macro, position the cursor on the first letter of the second word and press Alt-F10; then type **TR** and press Enter. If you ever use this macro in error, just repeat it to return the word order back to the way it was.

USING HYPHENS

WordPerfect uses several different types of hyphens:

- *Hard hyphens,* which you generate by typing - (the hyphen character). The hard hyphen is used to punctuate compound words such as *self-evaluate* and *brother-in-law.*

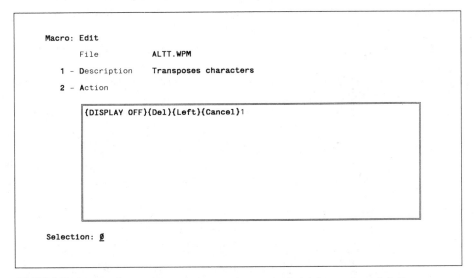

```
Macro: Edit

        File          ALTT.WPM

  1 - Description      Transposes characters

  2 - Action

     {DISPLAY OFF}{Del}{Left}{Cancel}1




  Selection: 0
```

FIGURE 3.16: A macro that transposes the current character with the character to its left. This macro, named Alt-T (for *Transpose*), can save time if you need to correct typos that WordPerfect's Speller does not automatically correct.

```
Macro: Edit

        File           TR.WPM

   1 - Description      Transposes words

   2 - Action

   ┌─────────────────────────────────────────────────────────────┐
   │ {DISPLAY OFF}{Block}{Word Left}{Del}y{Word Right}{Cancel}1    │
   │                                                               │
   │                                                               │
   │                                                               │
   │                                                               │
   │                                                               │
   └─────────────────────────────────────────────────────────────┘

   Selection: 0
```

FIGURE 3.17: A macro named TR (for *Transpose*). It exchanges the word the cursor is on with the word immediately to its left.

- *Nonbreaking hyphens* (called the *hyphen character* in the WordPerfect documentation), which you generate by typing Home before you type -. WordPerfect considers words joined by a nonbreaking hyphen to be one word; it will not break the words at the end of a line. If you are typing dates, such as **02-16-89**, proper names, such as **Lotus 1-2-3**, or mathematical expressions, such as **A1 – A2**, and you do not want WordPerfect to break them at the end of a line, press Home before you type the hyphen.

- *Soft hyphens,* which the program generates when it hyphenates a word with its Hyphenation feature. (You can also generate a soft hyphen by typing Ctrl-hyphen; for example, you may want to indicate to WordPerfect exactly where to break a word that may not be in its dictionaries, such as a new brand name or a polysyllabic pharmaceutical term.)

- *Invisible soft returns,* which are used to indicate where WordPerfect should break special symbols that occur at the ends of lines. For example, long dashes—such as these—are composed of two hyphens. To tell WordPerfect to keep both hyphens together, type the dash by pressing the hyphen key twice; then press Home-Enter to indicate an invisible soft return. You can also use invisible soft returns to indicate where phrases that use slashes, such as *either/or,* or dates, such as *2/16/45,* are to break.

In the Reveal Codes window, a nonbreaking hyphen appears as a dash (—), and a hard (breaking) hyphen appears as a hyphen enclosed in square brackets ([-]). An invisible soft return appears as [ISRt]. A soft hyphen appears as a bold hyphen. You will not see soft hyphens on the editing screen unless they are within the hyphenation zone. Soft hyphens are not fixed; they may disappear as Word-Perfect reformats lines and no longer finds it necessary to hyphenate words.

> *Note:* Do not be confused by the terminology applied to hyphenation. Because WordPerfect offers automatic hyphenation (see the next section), it differenti-ates between *soft hyphens* and *hard hyphens.* A soft hyphen (Ctrl-hyphen) is not printed if the document is edited so that the word no longer requires hyphen-ation. However, a hard hyphen (a hyphen typed by pressing the hyphen key) is always printed, whether or not the hyphenated word or phrase breaks across a line. A third type of hyphen, called a *nonbreaking hyphen,* (Home -) is also a hard hyphen in that it is always printed. However, it also binds the hyphen-ated words together as a unit, which the regular hyphen that you type by pressing the hyphen key alone does not.

USING HARD SPACES

WordPerfect allows you to apply the same kind of binding to spaces between words that it does to hyphens. WordPerfect refers to this type of space as a *hard space,* although you may know it as a *nonbreak space* if you have used other word processors. You enter this type of space by pressing Home before pressing the space bar. In the Reveal Codes window, WordPerfect differentiates a hard space from a regular space by enclosing it in square brackets ([ ]), and on the editing screen it displays a regular space just as it is in the regular document.

> *Note:* The term *hard space* used by the WordPerfect documentation is unfortu-nate because its function is not equivalent to that of a hard hyphen (see the pre-vious note). In WordPerfect, a hard space between words will not allow the words to break across lines, whereas a hard hyphen will.

You use the hard space in situations where a phrase should not be broken into two lines when it occurs at the end of a line, such as between a person's first name, middle initial, and last name, or in the spaces between elements of a date such as *July 31, 1990.*

USING WORDPERFECT'S HYPHENATION COMMANDS

Whenever your document requires hyphenation (to control the raggedness of a nonjustified right margin or the internal spacing when a document is right-justified), you can use WordPerfect's Hyphenation commands. They are located on the Line Format submenu. Press Shift-F8 (Format); select Line (**1** or **L**); then select Hyphenation (**1** or **Y**). You can then select either Manual (**2** or **M**) or Auto (**3** or **A**).

When you use manual hyphenation, WordPerfect prompts you with a *Position hyphen: Press ESC* message when it finds a word that should be hyphenated and suggests a place for the hyphen in the word. You can accept this placement for the hyphen by pressing Esc, or you can use ← or → to relocate the hyphen and then press Esc. If you do not want the word to be hyphenated, press F1 (Cancel).

When you press F1, WordPerfect enters an [SRt] formatting code at the end of the line and a [/] code (the Cancel Hyphen code) at the beginning of the following line. If you change your mind and want to hyphenate the word, delete the [/] code in the Reveal Codes window (Alt-F3). You will again see the prompt with the word to be hyphenated.

If you prefer not to be asked about where to hyphenate words, you can use automatic hyphenation. When you activate automatic hyphenation, Word-Perfect hyphenates words that require hyphenation without asking for your approval. All of the hyphens inserted using either automatic or manual hyphenation are soft hyphens (as though you had pressed Ctrl before the hyphen key).

If WordPerfect cannot decide where a word should be hyphenated according to its internal rules, it will prompt you to position the hyphen even though you have set hyphenation to automatic.

WordPerfect is preset for hyphenation to be off. To turn off hyphenation after you have turned it on, press Shift-F8 (Format), select Line, select Hyphenation, and this time select Off (**1** or **O**). To turn hyphenation off temporarily, as you would find convenient when scrolling or checking spelling, for example, move the cursor to the beginning of the document and press F7 (Exit) when the first Hyphenation prompt appears. This turns off hyphenation until the current operation (spell-checking or scrolling) is finished, at which point hyphenation will automatically come back on again.

The Hyphenation Zone   The Hyphenation Zone option (**2** or **Z**) on the Line Format menu is used to change the settings that determine the conditions under which WordPerfect will hyphenate a word. If a word begins before or right at the left zone boundary and continues past the right zone boundary, WordPerfect will either ask you where to insert the hyphen if you are using manual hyphenation or hyphenate the word immediately if you are using automatic hyphenation.

The left hyphenation zone is preset to 10% and the right hyphenation zone is preset to 4%. If you are working with the default left and right margins of 1 inch and, therefore, a line length of 6.5 inches, this means that the left zone begins .65 inch in from the right edge of the page (10% of 6.5) and the right zone begins .26 inch in from the right edge of the page (4% of 6.5). To have WordPerfect hyphenate more frequently, you need to decrease the size of the hyphenation zone by changing the left and right percentage figures. For example, you could change the left zone to 8% and the right zone to 5% by selecting the Hyphenation Zone option on the Format Line menu and entering **8** for the left and **5** for the right (the % sign is added automatically when you press Enter). Provided that you haven't changed the margins, the left zone will be set at .52 inch (8% of 6.5) and the right zone at .32 inch (5% of 6.5).

Because the left and right hyphenation zones are set as percentages of the line length, these settings automatically adjust when you change the left and right margins in the document. This means that if you decrease the left and right margins, thus increasing the line length, the hyphenation zone will also increase, although it will still maintain the same proportions as before, according to the left and right zone percentages.

WordPerfect makes all hyphenation suggestions and decisions according to the hyphenation rules in use. If you create documents that require right-justified margins, you are probably aware of how critical hyphenation can be in producing professional-looking results, as WordPerfect by default right-aligns every line by inserting spaces between words. To achieve fairly even spacing, you have to hyphenate frequently. This is all the more true when you are using several right-justified columns on a page in either newspaper or parallel style. If you use these formats in your work, you may be interested in purchasing a specialized hyphenation dictionary from WordPerfect Corporation. It contains an extensive list of proper word breaks.

You can also purchase foreign-language hyphenation modules from Word-Perfect Corporation. To have the program use one of these foreign-language hyphenation modules, you need to change the Language code on the Other Format menu, as discussed in Chapter 15, "Using the Speller and Thesaurus."

Adjusting the right hyphenation zone setting is most helpful when you are using proportional spacing with justified margins on a letter quality printer. Although your text will sometimes appear to extend beyond your right margin setting, when WordPerfect prints it, the program will try to fit all of the text within the margin by reducing the amount of space between words. Depending upon the font used and the right hyphenation zone value selected, this can help reduce uneven spacing overall. However, be aware that with some printers and fonts, changing the right hyphenation zone in this manner can cause some lines to actually extend beyond the right margin. This is especially true when you are justifying text columns. You will have to experiment with your printer and various right hyphenation zone settings to determine the balance that produces the most attractive documents.

Considerations for Hyphenating Documents   If you are typing a document in which hyphenation does not particularly matter, you can simply leave the Hyphenation feature off, turn justification off, and type your document with a ragged-right margin, in which case WordPerfect will simply wrap a word that breaks at the end of one line to the next line, not hyphenating it at all.

You can also enter your entire document and then turn on hyphenation, performing all of your hyphenation at once. To turn on hyphenation for a document that you have already entered, move to the beginning of the document (press Home Home ↑) and then turn on hyphenation.

To maintain more control over where each word is hyphenated, use manual hyphenation. Each time WordPerfect comes across a word that is to be hyphenated, it will prompt you to confirm its intended hyphenation. If you later change margin settings so that words you have indicated to be hyphenated are no longer in a position where they need a hyphen, they will not be hyphenated.

When you give the command to turn on hyphenation, WordPerfect enters the code [Hyph On] into the text. When you give the command to turn hyphenation off, WordPerfect enters the code [Hyph Off]. When you reset the hyphenation zone values, WordPerfect enters the code [HZone Set:]. Following the colon and separated by a comma, you will see the new left and right hyphenation zone values in effect.

If you ever delete a [Hyph on] code in the Reveal Codes window either deliberately or by mistake, hyphenation will immediately be turned off. However, this does not mean that the hyphens that were previously entered by the program when hyphenation was on will be eliminated; these will be affected only if you alter the [HZone Set:] settings in a way that requires rehyphenation of some of the lines.

If you intend to change the [HZone Set:] values from those you entered previously, be sure to position the cursor after the original [HZone Set:] code in the Reveal Codes window—you may even want to delete the original [HZone Set:] code—before you enter the new left and right hyphenation zone values.

If you want to rehyphenate a document that has been edited or in which you have changed the margin settings, you will probably want to first remove the Soft Hyphen and Cancel Hyphen codes that were entered during the first hyphenation operation. To do this, you must position the cursor at the very beginning of the document and turn off hyphenation. Then begin a search-and-replace operation to remove the Cancel Hyphen codes by pressing Alt-F2 and then Enter to have WordPerfect replace without confirmation. For the search string, press Shift-F8 and choose Line (**1** or **L**); then choose option **3** (/) and press F2 twice to begin the replacement.

Finally, perform a second search-and-replace operation to remove the soft hyphens by positioning the cursor at the top of the document again, pressing Alt-F2, and then pressing Enter to have WordPerfect replace without confirmation. For the search string, press Ctrl and the hyphen key. Then press F2 twice more to begin the replacement.

After all of the hyphens have been removed, reposition the cursor at the beginning of the document and turn on hyphenation once more.

> *Note:* These techniques for rehyphenating a document will not have any substantial effect if you have not made extensive editing changes or changed the right margin in a way that requires different hyphenation.

COMPARING DOCUMENT VERSIONS

Version 5.0 of WordPerfect allows you to compare the version of the document you have on the screen with a saved version on disk. When you use the Document Compare feature, redlining and strikeout are used to indicate differences in the versions. Text that is in the document version on the screen is redlined if it does not occur in the version of the document that is on disk. If text exists in the disk version but not in the on-screen version, it is copied into the on-screen version and appears in strikeout form.

Using Redlining and Strikeout

Redlining is useful for indicating revised sections to draw the reader's attention only to material that has been changed. When you redline text, a vertical bar appears in the left margin in the printed version. With strikeout, a dashed line is placed through the text you have marked for strikeout in the printed version. (On some printers, this effect may vary.) You can use the Colors/Fonts/Attributes option on the Display Setup submenu (Shift-F1 D C) to choose how redlining and strikeout appear on your screen. This feature is often used in contracts in which clauses have been deleted but must be initialed by the parties involved.

To mark text for redlining and strikeout, press Ctrl-F8 (Font) and select option **2** or **A** (Appearance). Then select option **8** or **R** for redlining or option **9** or **S** for strikeout.

You can also choose a method of redlining by using the Format key (Shift-F8). The Printer Dependent option marks the text according to how your printer is preset to handle redlining. The Left option marks redlined text with a vertical bar in the left margin, and Alternating marks it in the left margin on left-hand (even) pages and in the right margin on right-hand (odd) pages. If you have a color printer, you can choose Red to mark redlining in red.

After you have typed the text to be redlined or struck out, press Ctrl-F8 (Font) and select option **3** or **N** (Normal) to return to regular text. If you are marking text you have already typed, mark it as a block first; then mark it for redline or strikeout.

When the final version of your document is ready, you will probably want to remove redlining and delete any struck-out text. To do so, press Alt-F5 (Mark Text), select Generate (**6** or **G**), select Remove Redline Markings and Strikeout Text from Document (**1** or **R**), then type **Y** to confirm. Redline markings and text that has been struck out will be deleted from your document.

Comparing Documents

To compare the on-screen version of a document with its saved version on disk, you first choose Generate (**6** or **G**) from the Mark Text menu (Alt-F5). You then select Compare Screen and Disk Documents (**2** or **C**) and enter the name of the saved document.

If phrases that have been added to the on-screen document do not exist in the disk version, WordPerfect redlines the text in the screen version. If phrases that no longer exist in the on-screen document still exist in the disk version, the program marks the text with strikeout. In addition, if any text has been moved, you will see the messages *The Following Text was Moved* and *The Preceding Text was Moved* before and after the moved text.

WordPerfect considers a phrase to be any text between markers, including punctuation marks (comma, period, semicolon, colon, question mark, or exclamation point), hard returns, hard page breaks, Footnote and Endnote codes, and the end of the document.

Figure 3.18 illustrates a document that is being compared to its disk version. It has been printed out to show you the redlining and strikeout as they appear when printed.

After you have compared documents, you can remove the redlining marks and delete the struck-out text by following the procedure just discussed in the section "Using Redlining and Strikeout."

Version 5.0 added new capabilities to this already impressive array of reference aids. With version 5.0, you can create cross references to other areas of your document that are automatically updated as you revise the document. The program also allows you to compare two versions of a document on the screen. This sentence is in the on-screen version but not in the saved document. This sentence is in the saved document but not in the on-screen version. You can also create master documents from component WordPerfect files, which is useful if you are working with long documents, assembling documents from boilerplate, or combining the individual efforts of a work group.

FIGURE 3.18: Comparing two documents. Redlining indicates text that is not in the disk version, while strikeout indicates text that is not in the screen version.

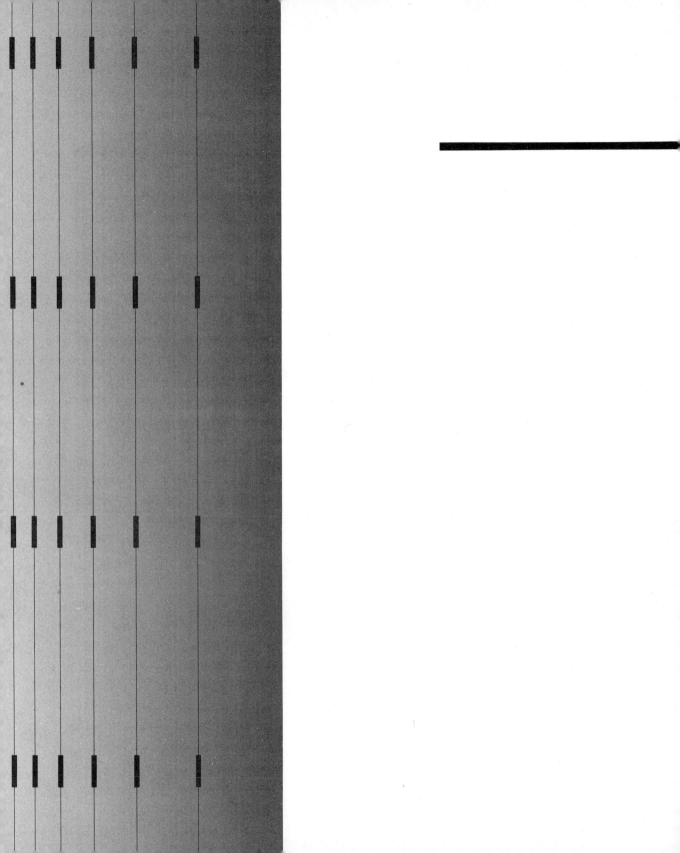

PAGE FORMATTING TECHNIQUES

Page Formatting Techniques

This chapter discusses WordPerfect's options for generating standard page layouts—using headers, footers, and page numbers, controlling how pages break, using page numbering, suppressing certain page formats, and changing the size of the paper. For information about multicolumn layouts, see Chapter 10, and for advice on combining text and graphics, see Chapter 18.

Upgrade Notes

WordPerfect 5.0 combines the previous Print Format, Line Format, and Page Format commands onto the submenus of the new Format key (Shift-F8), as illustrated in Figure 4.1. Most of the page formatting commands are on the Page submenu (**2** or **P**), but as you can see from the figure, Conditional End of Page is on the Other submenu (**4** or **O**). In addition, block protection is activated by first marking a block and then pressing Shift-F8.

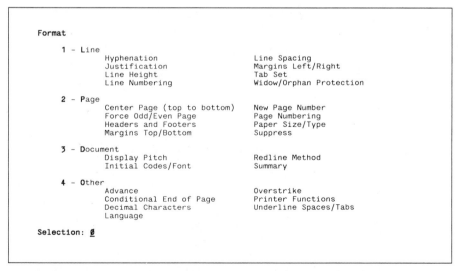

```
Format

    1 - Line
            Hyphenation                 Line Spacing
            Justification               Margins Left/Right
            Line Height                 Tab Set
            Line Numbering              Widow/Orphan Protection

    2 - Page
            Center Page (top to bottom) New Page Number
            Force Odd/Even Page         Page Numbering
            Headers and Footers         Paper Size/Type
            Margins Top/Bottom          Suppress

    3 - Document
            Display Pitch               Redline Method
            Initial Codes/Font          Summary

    4 - Other
            Advance                     Overstrike
            Conditional End of Page     Printer Functions
            Decimal Characters          Underline Spaces/Tabs
            Language

    Selection: 0
```

FIGURE 4.1: Page formatting commands, located on the Format key (Shift-F8) in WordPerfect 5.0. Most of them, including Headers/Footers and Page Numbering, are on the Page submenu (**2** or **P**).

FORCING PAGE BREAKS

WordPerfect automatically adjusts soft page breaks (those that the program inserts) as you edit your document. They are displayed as a line of dashes on the screen and indicated on the Reveal Codes screen by the [SPg] code. To change a soft page break, change the top and bottom margins as discussed in "Changing Top and Bottom Margins" later in this chapter, or delete lines of text on the page.

Hard page breaks, as discussed in Chapter 2, are those that you insert manually by pressing Ctrl-Enter at the point where you want a page break to occur. For example, you might want to end a short page at the end of one section of a report so that the next main topic begins a new page. Hard page breaks are represented by a line of equal signs across the screen and indicated on the Reveal Codes screen. Figure 4.2 illustrates both types of page breaks.

To delete a hard page break, position the cursor next to the line of equal signs that represents it and press Backspace or Delete.

Changing Top and Bottom Margins

To change the top and bottom margins for a document, first position the cursor at the beginning of the page where you want the margins to change. Then press Shift-F8 (Format), choose Page (**2** or **P**), and choose Margins (**5** or **M**). Type a new value for either the top margin, the bottom margin, or both. Press

```
    Credit Union

    MagnaCorp's credit union is located on the third floor. Hours are
    9 to 6 p.m. daily. The credit union observes all national and
    bank holidays, whereas the company may or may not follow the same
    schedule.

    ------------------------------------------------------------------------

    Holidays

    MagnaCorp designates five official holidays each year. These are
    New Year's Day, Memorial Day, Independence Day, Labor Day, and
    Thanksgiving Day. In addition, the company closes for Christmas
    week. An additional two floating holidays may be taken at your
    discretion and with the approval of your manager.

    ========================================================================

    Benefits

    Benefits programs include life insurance, health care, dental
    insurance, and travel insurance. They are available to you at no
    cost during your employment with MagnaCorp. If you leave the
    C:\5\HANDBOOK                                    Doc 1 Pg 3 Ln 1.83" Pos 1"
```

FIGURE 4.2: Hard and soft page breaks. Soft page breaks are calculated automatically and change as you add text to the document or delete text from it. Hard page breaks, represented by a line of equal signs, are inserted only when you press Ctrl-Enter.

Enter to bypass entering a new value for either setting. You can enter new settings in inches, points, centimeters, or WordPerfect 4.2 units (lines). To indicate that you are using a unit of measure different from the current default, enter the value followed by " or **i** (for inches), **p** (for points), **c** (for centimeters), or **v** (for lines).

The top margin setting is the distance from the top edge of the paper, and the bottom margin setting is the distance from the bottom edge of the paper. Any change to these settings takes effect from the cursor's position forward in the document. To set new top and bottom margins for the entire document, be sure that the cursor is at the beginning of the document before you change them.

To maintain the top and bottom margin settings in effect, WordPerfect automatically adjusts the number of lines per page according to the fonts and line heights that are being used. You do not have to change the top and bottom margin settings when you change the sizes of fonts or the line heights in the document.

When you change the top and bottom margin settings, WordPerfect inserts a [T/B Mar:] code that includes the new settings. To revert to the default top and bottom margin settings of 1 inch each, locate and delete this code in the Reveal Codes screen.

Forcing Odd and Even Pages

You can use the Force Odd/Even feature to ensure that a particular page is always given either an odd or even page number. To use this command, position the cursor at the top of the page that you want to be either odd (right-hand) or even (left-hand). Then press Shift-F8 (Format), choose Page (**2** or **P**), and choose Force Odd/Even Page (**2** or **O**). Type **1** or **O** to force an odd page, or **2** or **E** to force an even page. When you select the Odd option and the page number is already an odd number (as indicated on the status line), selecting this option has no effect on the page number. If, however, the page number is currently an even number, WordPerfect will insertt a soft page break at the cursor's position, thus increasing the page number by one and making it an odd page. The soft page break is indicated on the editing screen by a line of hyphens. The program also inserts an [SPg] code, which can be found in the Reveal Codes screen (Alt-F3). The same thing happens when you choose the Even option: if the page number is already even, no page number change occurs in the document. If, on the other hand, the page number is currently odd, the program will insert a soft page break, making the page number even.

If you later add text in front of a forced page break, you can wind up with short pages in your document, as WordPerfect will break the page at the [Force:Odd] or [Force:Even] code. For this reason, it's best to decide on forced page breaks as one of the final steps in preparing a document.

If you decide later that you want to return to regular page numbering, locate and delete the [Force] code in the Reveal Codes screen. You can search for it by pressing

F2 (Search), pressing Shift-F8, typing **2** or **P**, and typing **2** or **O**. You will also have to delete the [Spg] code inserted by the Force Odd/Even command.

NUMBERING PAGES

There are two ways of adding page numbers to a document; you can either use the Page Numbering command or add the page number to the header or footer you are using throughout the document. However, you should not use these techniques together; if you do, you will have two sets of page numbers on every page.

Automatic Page Numbering

To add automatic page numbers, press Shift-F8 (Format), choose Page (**2** or **P**), and then choose Page Numbering (**7** or **P**). You will see the Page Numbering Position menu, from which you can select where you want page numbers to appear on the page. Choose options **1–3** and **5–7** for page numbers to appear on every page. Options **4** and **8** will insert page numbers on alternating left and right pages. Option **9** turns off page numbers. After you select the numbering position, WordPerfect inserts a [Pg Num Pos] code into the document. Following the code, you will see the position that determines where the page numbers are placed on the page.

When you return to your document by pressing F7 (Exit), you will not see page numbers on the screen, but they will appear when the document is printed. You can use the View Document feature, discussed later in this chapter, to view page numbers in position on the screen.

The one drawback to using the Page Numbering command as opposed to including page numbering as part of a header or footer is that you cannot add a word such as *Page* or *Chapter* to the number—for example, *Page 1* or *Chapter 4-1*. The Page Numbering command adds only the numeral that WordPerfect supplies for the page number in its appropriate position on the page. If you want to add a word to the page number, you need to put the page number in a header or footer, as you will learn how to do later in this chapter.

If you want your entire document to be numbered, position the cursor at the very beginning of the document before using the Page Numbering command. If you don't want the page numbering to begin on the first page (if the first page of your document is a title page, table of contents, or list of figures, for instance), position the cursor at the beginning of the page on which numbering is to begin—right after the [HPg] or [SPg] formatting code in the Reveal Codes window—and then issue the command.

If you don't want a page number to appear on the first page and don't want to include the first page in the page number count, you must also adjust the beginning page number. For example, if your report contains a title page that should not have a page number printed on it or be included in the page count, you must use the New Page Number option, as discussed later.

Using Page Numbers in Headers and Footers

You can also turn on page numbering by inserting the code ^B (Ctrl-B) or ^N (Ctrl-N) in your document. Wherever the ^B or ^N code appears, the current page number will be printed. For example, if you want your headers or footers to contain page numbers, enter **^B** (Ctrl-B) at the position where you want the page number to occur. To specify the position of page numbers in headers and footers, press Alt-F6 (Flush Right) or Shift-F6 (Center) before you enter **^B**. (Headers and footers are discussed later in this chapter.)

Starting Page Numbers with a Specific Number

To start page numbering with a number that you specify, choose the New Page Number option (**6** or **N**) on the Page Format menu. If you have saved a document in several separate files, this option allows you to number the pages sequentially. When you type the number that you want numbering to start with, you can use either Arabic numerals (1, 2, 3, etc.) or Roman numerals (i, ii, iii, etc.). Most of the time you will use Arabic numerals, but if you are numbering front matter such as a preface, introduction, table of contents, or list of figures, you may want to switch to lowercase Roman numerals and then change back to Arabic numbers on the first text page.

When you begin numbering with a new page number, you will see the change reflected on the status line after you return to your document.

Note: The Pg indicator on the status line functions even if you do not add page numbers to the document. However, if you add page numbers and set a new beginning page somewhere after the first page, the Pg indicator will change, and in the same document you may have two different pages that have the same page number. For instance, if you turn on page numbering at the beginning of the document and later use the New Page Number command to start numbering again from page 1, as you scroll from the beginning of the document you will see the Pg indicator increase from *1* until it reaches the [Pg Num:1] formatting code, where you will see it change back to *1* again. If you use the Go To function (Ctrl-Home) to move to the beginning of a page by entering its page number in a document that has duplicate page numbers, you could find yourself at the wrong page.

To indicate that page numbering is to begin by using the Page Numbering command, press Shift-F8 (Format), choose Page (**2** or **P**), and choose Page Numbering (**7** or **P**). You will see the screen shown in Figure 4.3.

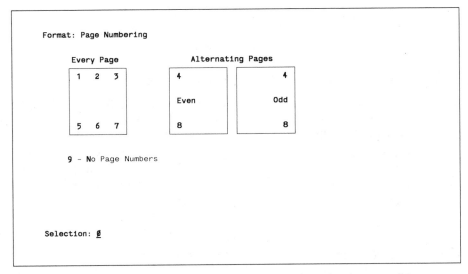

FIGURE 4.3: The Page Numbering screen. The various numbers indicate the placement of the page number in your document; choosing **6** centers the page number at the bottom of the page, choosing **8** places the page number in the lower-left corner of even pages and in the lower-right corner of odd pages, and so forth.

WordPerfect inserts a [Pg Num] code into your document when you indicate a new page number. You can use the Search feature to find this code. Press F2, press Shift-F8, type **2** or **P,** and then type **6** or **N**. Press F2 again to initiate the search.

Be sure to move the cursor to the beginning of the page where you want numbering to start when you use the Page Numbering or New Page Number option.

If you are using Roman-style numbering for just part of the document, remember to change the New Page Number style when you come to the first page that is to be numbered using Arabic numerals. When you make the transition to Arabic numerals, remember to set the page number to *1*.

Numbering Blank Pages

If you want your report to contain blank pages where illustrations, figures, or charts from another source will appear, you may want to add a blank page that will still contain a page number (use the Suppress feature to suppress the page number), or you may want to skip printed page numbers and then number the one containing the artwork with a typewriter or by hand.

If you want to include a blank page that contains only the page number, position the cursor beneath the soft page break (shown by a line of hyphens) and press Ctrl-Enter to insert a hard page break (shown by a line of equal signs). Make sure that no text is included between these two lines. The best way to accomplish this is to open the Reveal Codes window (Alt-F3), position the cursor right after the [SPg] code, and press Ctrl-Enter to add the [HPg] code. In the editing screen, the blank page will be represented by a blank line between a line of hyphens and a line of equal signs. When you position the cursor on this blank line, you will see the Pg indicator on the status line change to a new page number. To remove such a blank page, all you have to do is delete the [HPg] code.

> *Note:* If you are not only adding a blank page for art but also assigning the page a special page number out of sequence with the previous pages, make sure that the [Pg Num] formatting code that is added when you use the New Page Number command is between the [SPg] and [HPg] codes in the Reveal Codes window.

Suppressing Page Numbering

To suppress page numbering on any particular page of your document, first select the Suppress option (**9** or **U**) on the Page Format menu. If you want to turn off only the page numbering, you then select Suppress Page Numbering (**4** or **P**) from the list of menu options that appears. If you also want to suppress the headers and footers that occur on the page, select Suppress All Page Numbering, Headers and Footers (**1** or **A**). No page number will appear on the page where you use the Suppress command, but it will be counted in the numbering sequence. Before you use this command, you should make sure that the cursor is positioned at the top of the page (right after the [SPg] or [HPg] code in the Reveal Codes window).

If you want to suppress headers and footers but still have a page number on the page, choose Print Page Number at Bottom Center (**3** or **B**).

WORKING WITH HEADERS AND FOOTERS

Headers are headings that appear at the tops of pages, and *footers* are headings that appear at the bottoms of pages. WordPerfect separates the header from the main body of the document text by adding a single blank line. Likewise, it separates a footer from the main body of text by adding one blank line after the document text and before the text of the footer.

Before adding a header or footer to your document, position the cursor at the top of the first page that the header or footer is to appear on. Then press Shift-F8 (Format), choose Page (**2** or **P**), and choose either Headers (**3** or **H**) or Footers (**4** or **F**). Then choose **A** or **B**. You will see the following menu line:

1 **D**iscontinue; **2** **E**very **P**age; **3** **O**dd Pages; **4** **E**ven Pages; **5** **E**dit:0

Type **2** or **P** for the footer or header to appear on every page, or type *3* or **O** or **4** or **V** for it to be only on odd or even pages.

You will then have a full editing screen on which to enter the text of the header or footer. Your header or footer can use as many lines as you need.

You enter the text of multiple-line headers and footers exactly as you want it to appear on the page. The left and right margin settings that are currently in effect for the text of the document also rule the alignment and word wrap of the header and footer text.

You can also add any text enhancements (such as boldface or a smaller font size) or formatting (such as centering or flush right) that you wish. To insert automatic page numbering into your headers and footers, press Ctrl-B (or Ctrl-N) at the position in the header or footer where you want the page number to appear. For details about using page numbering in headers and footers, see "Adding Automatic Page Numbering to Headers and Footers" later in this chapter.

You can create two headers (A and B) or footers (A and B) if you want their text to alternate on even- and odd-numbered pages of a document. You can also create two headers or footers on the same page. When you use two headers (or footers) on the same page, place one flush left and the other flush right or place them on separate lines. For details about using multiple headers and footers, see "Alternating Headers and Footers" and "Using Two Nonalternating Headers and Footers" later in this chapter.

Headers begin printing on the first line below the top margin, and WordPerfect places 0.16 inch between the last line of the header and the last line of the text. Footers begin printing on the first line above the bottom margin, and the program places 0.16 inch between the first line of the footer and the body of the text.

If you want to increase the amount of blank space between a header and the main body of text, you need only add extra blank lines by pressing Enter after you type the header text and before you exit the definition screen. To increase the amount of blank space between the main body of text and a footer, add these blank lines at the beginning of the Definition screen before you enter the footer text.

Alternating Headers and Footers

WordPerfect allows you to use two headers and two footers for each document. It refers to these as Header A, Header B, Footer A, and Footer B, respectively. Normally, a report requires only one header, especially because the program allows you to create multiple-line headers containing various types of identifying information.

However, one common situation usually requires two headers or footers: when your report is going to be reproduced on both sides of a sheet of paper and later bound. In such a situation, you need to define one header for odd-numbered pages and another for even-numbered pages (as defined by the Page Numbering options where those override the default settings). Sometimes these two headers may contain slightly different information. The first header (which appears on odd-numbered pages) might identify the name of the report, and the second header (on the even-numbered pages) might identify the current chapter or section.

Even if your headers contain exactly the same identifying text, they require different formatting if you want them to appear at different locations. For instance, sometimes you may want Header A (for the even-numbered pages) to be justified with the left margin, and Header B (for the odd-numbered pages) to be justified with the right margin.

If you want your headers or footers to contain page numbers, place a ^B or ^N Page Number code (see "Adding Automatic Page Numbering to Headers and Footers" later in this chapter) before the text of the header or footer for even-numbered pages and after the text of the header or footer for odd-numbered pages. For example, to add alternating headers that include page numbers to a business plan, you move the cursor to the beginning of the second page (assuming that the document has a title page) and enter the text for Header A on the Definition screen as follows:

^B   BUSINESS PLAN

(You enter **^B** by pressing Ctrl-B.) Then you move the cursor to the beginning of the third page, press Alt-F6, and enter the text for Header B as follows:

BUSINESS PLAN   ^B

(If you do not press Alt-F6 (Flush Right) before you enter the text for the odd-page header, WordPerfect left-aligns it.)

When you define alternating Headers A and B, not only do you format their text, but you also specify that one header (A or B) occurs only on even-numbered pages and that the other occurs only on odd-numbered pages. Remember that when you print a report containing alternating headers or footers, you can set the binding width to allow sufficient room on even- and odd-numbered pages for three-ring or spiral binding. To do this, you press Shift-F7 and type **B** to select the Binding Width option (see Chapter 7, "Printing Techniques," for details).

Using Two Nonalternating Headers or Footers

You can also define and use two headers on pages of a report that is not going to be reproduced on both sides of the paper. Defining both Header A and Header B (or Footer A and Footer B) in a single document allows you to discontinue one of the headers while still printing the other. If you define a two-line header with the first line as Header A and the second line as Header B, you can discontinue Header B somewhere in the text while retaining Header A, whereas if you define both lines in Header A, you cannot display one part without the other (so if you discontinue Header A, no heading of any sort will be printed from that point forward in the text).

When you define two headers (or footers), you must separate them in some way. If both headers are to occur on the same line, their text must remain separate and not overlap in any way. For example, you can enter the text for Header A flush left and the text for Header B flush right, as long as they do not overlap when printed. If you want to place the two headers on separate lines, you can enter Header A on the first line and a blank on the second line and then, when defining Header B, enter a blank line with a hard return followed on the second line by the text of Header B.

You can also separate elements within the same header or footer, as has been done in Figure 4.4. Here, the phrase *First Draft* is flush left and *Company Confidential* is flush right.

Adding Automatic Page Numbering to Headers and Footers

Instead of using the Page Number command, you can have WordPerfect automatically number the pages of your report in the header or footer you define. To do this, enter the code **^B** (Ctrl-B) or **^N** (Ctrl-N) into the header or footer text. The Page Number code consists of a caret (or circumflex) preceding the capital letter *B* or *N*, depending upon which you use. (Ctrl-N is a little easier to remember if you think of *N* as representing *Number.*)

When you have WordPerfect number the pages in a header or footer, you can also add text before the numerals. For instance, to print the page number preceded by the word *Page* in Footer A, centered on every page, choose Header A (**1** or **A**) and then choose Every Page (**2** or **V**). Press Shift-F6 (Center) and enter

Page ^N

When the report is printed, the ^N code will be replaced by the appropriate page number, and the headers will appear as *Page 1, Page 2,* and so on.

To enter a starting number different from the one that the program would use automatically, select New Page Number on the Page Format menu before you create the header or footer. Then enter the page number you want to begin with. (See "Numbering Pages" earlier in this chapter for details about the New Page Number option.)

Suppose, for example, that you keep various chapters of a report in separate files but want to number all pages of the report consecutively. After determining the last page number in the first chapter, you would edit the file containing the second chapter and then use the New Page Number command to indicate the appropriate number for the first page of this chapter before creating the header or footer. Remember that you can always verify the page number assignment by checking the Pg indicator

MagnaCorp Employee Handbook

WELCOME

Welcome to MagnaCorp. We hope this employee handbook will help to guide you through your first few days here. In addition, it contains valuable information about employee services and benefits available to you. Ask your manager or call the personnel office if you have any questions for which you cannot find the answers in this handbook.

Work Day

The official work day at MagnaCorp is 8:30 a.m. to 5:00 p.m. Flexible hours can be arranged with your manager.

Parking

As parking is limited, please apply to the personnel office for a parking slot assignment.

Hours

Noon to 1 p.m. has been reserved as lunch hour for all employees. Some departments have chosen to take lunch from 11:30 to 12:30 or from 12:30 to 1:30; check with your manager.

Cafeteria

The company cafeteria, located on the third floor, is open from 7 a.m. until 2 p.m. daily. Breakfast is available for your convenience until 9:00. After 2 p.m., vending machines with cold sandwiches and salads are available.

Recreational Facilities

MagnaCorp participates in the city recreational plan and therefore its employees have access to the municipal gym located at First and Brannan Streets. The jogging track and par course in Grant Park are also nearby. Showers and lockers for company employees are located near the south entrance of the main lobby.

Vacation

Full-time permanent employees are eligible for two weeks of paid vacation after six months of continuous employment. During the first five years of service, you earn three weeks of vacation per year. After five years of service, you receive four weeks of vacation.

Credit Union

First Draft   Company Confidential

FIGURE 4.4: Using formatting codes for flush right text within the same header or footer to position separate elements. Here, *Company Confidential* is flush right in the same footer as *First Draft*.

on the status line. If you use the New Page Number command to change the starting number of the second chapter from 1 to 43, the Pg indicator will then display *43* instead of *1*.

Inserting the Date and Time in Headers and Footers

In addition to adding automatic page numbering to the header or footer of a report, you can also insert the date or time. WordPerfect provides two options for inserting the current date and time: the Insert Text and Insert Function options. Selecting Date Text (**1** or **T**) after pressing Shift-F5 (the Date key) enters today's date, which remains the same each time you retrieve or print the document. The Date Code option (**2** or **C**) inserts a date that is updated whenever you retrieve or print the document.

If you want to date-stamp your document so that the date is current whenever you print a copy of it, use the Date Code command instead of the Date Text command. You can also time-stamp your document by using the Date Code option; the Date Format option (**3** or **F**) that is in effect determines whether the date or time is inserted, and in what format.

CHANGING THE DATE FORMAT

You can format the date in a variety of ways by using the Date Format option. The default format is *Month Day, Year* as in *August 15, 1990*. However, you can specify whether

- The month appears as a number or as a word.
- Four digits or two digits of the year are used.
- The day of the week is spelled out or abbreviated.
- A 12-hour clock or a 24-hour clock is used.
- Minutes and A.M. or P.M. are used.

Refer to the **Date, Inserting the** entry in the "WordPerfect Command and Feature Reference," Part V of this book, for a table of possible formats and examples of their use. Unless you specify a time format, WordPerfect will insert only the date.

To change the default date format permanently, select the Initial Settings option (**5** or **I**) from the Setup menu (Shift-F1).

HDR: A MACRO TO ENTER A HEADER (OR FOOTER)

You can write a macro to automate the process of inserting headers or footers into standard documents you create. The macro illustrated in Figure 4.5 takes advantage of WordPerfect's ability to pause during a macro so that you can insert text—in this case, the chapter number. This macro inserts a header that will appear in the upper-right corner of each page of your document. It will also contain the Date function so that the document is date-stamped each time you retrieve or print it.

To use this header, position the cursor at the very beginning of the document (by pressing Home Home ↑), press Alt-F10, type **HDR**, and press Enter. When the macro pauses, type the number of the chapter and press Enter. The macro will then insert the automatic page numbering symbol (^B) and enter the word *Version:* along with the date.

You can easily customize this macro to your own needs by substituting *Section* for *Chapter* (or some other more appropriate heading) and deleting *Version:* or omitting the current date. These keystrokes for entering the header can also be combined with those that set the margins and tab stops when you start a new document. For more information about creating and using macros, especially macros that pause for user input, see Chapter 16.

Editing Headers and Footers

To edit the text of a header or footer, press Shift-F8 (Format), choose Page, and then choose either Headers (**3** or **H**) or Footers (**4** or **F**). Then select either **A** or **B**, depending on which one you want to edit. When the menu appears, select

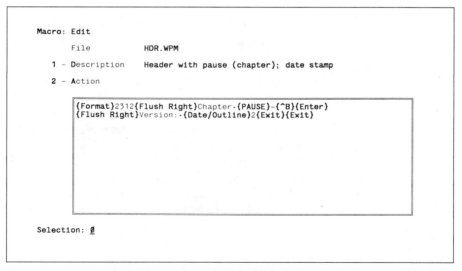

FIGURE 4.5: A macro, named HDR, that pauses for you to indicate the chapter number and then inserts the page number, the word *Version:*, and the date the document is printed, in the upper-right corner of each page.

the Edit option (**5** or **E**). You will see the text of the header or footer, and you can edit it in any way you like, including adding font size and appearance changes. Press F7 (Exit) when you have finished editing the text of the header or footer.

> *Note:* Because you can select only two headers or footers (regardless of whether you have them printed on every page or on alternating pages), you cannot keep changing the text of the header or footer to reflect each new section in a document unless you discontinue one header or footer and then restart it with new text. By doing this, you can have a report in which Header A identifies the chapter and Header B identifies each subsection. In such a case, although Header A would remain unchanged throughout the chapter, Header B might have to change every several pages. If you use the Edit option (**5**) to change the subsection name, the text of Header B changes throughout the document, not just on the page where you entered it.

Searching for Headers and Footers

To search for a header or footer in a document, press F2 (or Shift-F2 if you are searching backward), then press Shift-F8 and type **2** or **P**. Choose either Header or Footer and then choose **A** or **B**. Finally, press F2 to initiate the search.

WordPerfect then locates the [Header] or [Footer] code. To delete the header or footer located by the program, press Backspace. If you turn on the Reveal Codes window by pressing Alt-F3 when you perform the search, you can view the text of the header or footer. This will help you determine if you want to delete or edit the header or footer.

UPDATING MARGIN CHANGES IN HEADERS AND FOOTERS

When you change the left and right margin settings in a document, you must take care that the margins of the headers and footers on the page are included. Otherwise, the margins for the text of the header and footer will not match the new margins set for the document. In order to ensure that the margins match, you must insert the [L/R mar] code that changes the margins for the text of the document before the [Header] and [Footer] codes. To do this, press Alt-F3 (Reveal Codes) and position the cursor on or before the first [Header] or [Footer] code in the Reveal Codes window. Then, press Shift-F8 L M and enter your new left and right margin settings. Note that you can always check the alignment of a header or footer in relation to the current left and right settings by using the View Document feature (Shift-F7 V).

Discontinuing and Suppressing Headers and Footers

To discontinue a header or footer from a specific page to the end of the document, press Shift-F8 (Format), choose Page (**2** or **P**), and select either Header or

Footer, depending on which you want to discontinue. Type **1** or **A** or **2** or **B** for Header A or B or Footer A or B, then choose Discontinue (**1** or **D**).

To suppress a header or footer on a specific page, use the Suppress option (**9** or **U**) on the Page submenu of the Format key. Choose option **1** or **A** to suppress headers, footers, and page numbers, or option **2** or **S** to suppress only headers and footers. To suppress individual headers and footers, choose Header A (**5** or **H**), Header B (**6** or **E**), Footer A (**7** or **F**), or Footer B (**8** or **O**).

The Discontinue command has a different effect from the various options accessed by selecting the Suppress option. The Discontinue option suppresses the type of header selected from the specified page through the rest of the document, whereas Suppress discontinues the header only on the specified page.

Deleting Headers and Footers

To delete a header or footer, locate and delete the [Header/Footer] code associated with it. WordPerfect displays the first 50 characters of the header or footer in the Reveal Codes screen, so you can tell which header or footer you are deleting.

TECHNIQUES FOR KEEPING TEXT TOGETHER ON A PAGE

When you are checking the pagination of a document before printing, you may find instances where soft page breaks (those entered by the program) split text that you want to remain on a single page. Common bad page breaks that you usually want to correct involve widow and orphan lines, section headings at the bottom of a page separated from any of their accompanying text, and tables that are split apart.

WordPerfect offers several methods for controlling these types of page break problems. To avoid widows and orphans (stray single lines at the tops or bottoms of pages), you can use WordPerfect's Widow/Orphan Protection feature. To avoid headings at the bottom of a page separated from their text, you can use the program's Conditional End of Page command. And to avoid splitting a table across two pages, you can use the program's Block Protect command.

Avoiding Widow and Orphan Lines

To prevent the occurrence of widow and orphan lines throughout a document, turn on widow/orphan protection at the beginning of the document. To do this, position the cursor at the very beginning of the document (by pressing Home Home ↑), press Shift-F8 (Format), choose Line (**1** or **L**), and then choose Widow/Orphan Protection (**9** or **W**). Type **Y** to turn the feature on. After you have turned on widow/orphan protection, WordPerfect will automatically paginate the document so that the first line of any paragraph does not appear alone at the end of a page and the last line of any paragraph does not appear alone at the top of a new page. This means that you may get occasional short pages in the document.

If you later edit the document in such a way that widows or orphans no longer occur in pagination, WordPerfect will ignore the Widow/Orphan formatting code, and the pages previously affected will again have the standard number of lines.

Using the Conditional End of Page Command

To get rid of other kinds of unwanted page breaks, such as those that occur when a section heading is placed on the last line of a page separated from any of its accompanying text, you can use the Conditional End of Page option (**2** or **C**) on the Other Format submenu. When you select this option, you are prompted to enter the number of lines to be kept together.

To use this command, position the cursor on the heading that is not to appear alone on the page and then enter the number of lines to keep together.

If you are using line spacing other than single spacing, you may need to calculate the number of lines to be kept together. First, place the cursor on the heading; then press ↓ to move to the last line you want to keep with it. For instance, if you are using one-and-a-half spacing and you pressed ↓ six times to reach the last line, enter the number of lines to keep together as **9** (1.5 × 6). If you are using double spacing, enter **12** (2 × 6), and so on.

If you want to keep a specific block of text together—for instance, a section heading and the entire first paragraph that occurs below it—you use this same technique for determining the number of lines to be kept together. In this case, however, you must position the cursor at the beginning of the last line of the first paragraph before you press ↑ to reach the line where you enter the Conditional End of Page command.

Using the Conditional End of Page command is preferable to adding hard page breaks (by pressing Ctrl-Enter) because its use will never cause an additional short page to be introduced into the text. If you insert a hard page break and then add a few lines of text to sections that precede it, you can end up with a very short page, containing only a few lines, that is inserted between the last soft page break the program added and the hard page break you added.

Using Block Protection

Although you can use the Conditional End of Page command to keep lines together, WordPerfect offers an alternative means for keeping a block of text from ever being split across two pages: the Block Protect command. This command is easier to use than the Conditional End of Page command because it requires no line number calculations.

To use Block Protect, you must first mark the block using Alt-F4 and the appropriate cursor movement keys. Then press Shift-F8. You will see the prompt

Protect Block? (Y/N) No

To protect the highlighted text, type **Y**. The highlighting disappears, and Word-Perfect places two Block Protect codes around the text: a [Block Pro:On] code before the beginning of the block and a [Block Pro:Off] code at its end. You can remove the block protection by deleting either of these two codes in the Reveal Codes window.

The major difference between the Conditional End of Page command and the Block Protect command is that when you use block protection, you can edit the block freely and still be assured that it will always be printed together on a page. For example, if you use the Conditional End of Page command to protect the present number of lines in a table and then add several new lines to the end of it, you could end up with the new lines orphaned on a new page. However, if you use the Block Protect command and then enter these lines (as long as they are entered before and not after the [Block Pro:Off] code), this situation will never occur.

Normally, you will find it most efficient to use Conditional End of Page to eliminate widowed headings at the bottoms of pages and Block Protect to prevent tables and similar units of text from being split by page breaks.

When you use the Block Protect command with a table or some other unit of text, be careful if you ever move the table to a new place in the document. It is very easy to forget to include one or the other of the [Block Pro] codes when marking the text to be relocated. You should use the Reveal Codes window to locate these codes and position the cursor immediately in front of the [Block Pro:On] code before you use Alt-F4 to highlight the block. Likewise, make sure that the cursor is positioned right after the [Block Pro:Off] code when you mark the text for moving or copying.

If you ever move a protected block and find that it is missing either the [Block Pro:On] or [Block Pro:Off] code, delete the code that remains and then mark the block and reissue the Block Protect command.

CENTERING TEXT VERTICALLY ON A PAGE

In WordPerfect, you can easily center title pages and short, one-page letters vertically between the top and bottom margins of the page (see Figure 4.6). To do this, you must first position the cursor at the very top of the page. You will almost always use vertical centering on the first page of the document, so this will usually correspond to the beginning of the document. To move the cursor to the top of the document, you press Home Home ↑.

After you have positioned the cursor, press Shift-F8 (Format), type **2** or **P** to select the Page submenu, and then type **1** or **C** for the Center Page (top to bottom) option. Then press Enter twice to return to the document. When you do this, WordPerfect adds the formatting code [Center Pg] to your document. However, you will not see the effect of this code on the text. To see how the page will appear when printed, you can use the View Document feature, as discussed later in this chapter.

When you are working with a title page that is followed by full pages of text, be sure to add a hard page break (by pressing Ctrl-Enter) after the text that is to appear on the title page. If you don't, WordPerfect will include the text from subsequent pages in its vertical centering.

To eliminate vertical centering, display the Reveal Codes window, position the cursor right after the [Center Pg] code, and delete the code by pressing the Backspace key.

Changing Paper Size and Type

It's most likely that you'll be using a standard 8.5-by-11-inch page for most of your documents, but WordPerfect has several other paper sizes built into the program. To select any of these, you use the Paper Size/Type command, which is on the Page Format menu (Shift-F8 P S). The Paper Size options are:

1 - Standard	8.5" x 11"
2 - Standard Landscape	11" x 8.5"
3 - Legal	8.5" x 14"
4 - Legal Landscape	14" x 8.5"
5 - Envelope	9.5" x 4"
6 - Half Sheet	5.5" x 8.5"
7 - US Government	8" x 11"
8 - A4	210 mm x 297 mm
9 - A4 Landscape	297 mm x 210 mm

The Landscape choices on the menu refer to the printing orientation of the page. For example, if you're printing extra wide tables or figures sideways on the page, you would select one of the Landscape options.

The other sizes are fairly self-explanatory, except for A4, which is a paper size popular in Europe. In inches, it's approximately 8.25" by 11.67".

```
Memo to:  All departments
From:  Business office

Effective immediately, the following procedures are necessary to
obtain work requisitions for hiring contract employees:


1.  Notify the business office 30 days before any new-hire
contract employee begins employment.

2.  Prepare a Cost Estimate worksheet showing projected
length of employment, renumeration, and estimated
termination date.

3.  Obtain signoffs from the relevant department managers in
whose departments the contract employee will be working (see
Form 23-799).

4.  Submit a completed Form 34-110 indicating that the
proposed employee is a bona fide contractor; attach local
business license if required.
```

FIGURE 4.6: Centering text vertically on a page. This is useful for title pages and business letters as well as short memos like this one.

Once you've selected a paper size, WordPerfect automatically presents another menu called Paper Type. You can select Standard (**1** or **S**), Bond (**2** or **B**), Letterhead (**3** or **H**), Labels (**4** or **L**), Envelope (**5** or **E**), Transparency (**6** or **T**), Cardstock (**7** or **C**), or Other (**8** or **O**) from this menu.

When selecting the paper type from this menu, you must keep in mind how the paper will be fed to the printer. For example, for most printers, when you choose the Standard type from this menu, this indicates to WordPerfect that the paper (in the size you just selected from the Format Paper Size menu) will be continuously fed to the printer, either from a paper bin or by tractor feed. On the other hand, when you select some of the other Paper Type options like Letterhead, Labels, and the like, WordPerfect assumes that the paper must be fed to the printer manually. As a result, when one of these paper types is selected, the program will automatically pause before printing each page of the document so that you can insert a sheet of paper (of the size chosen on the Format Paper Size menu) in the printer. After inserting the page, you must then select the Go (start printer) option from the Control Printer menu (Shift-F7 C G).

To check how WordPerfect expects a particular paper type to be fed to your printer, you need to select the Forms option on the Select Printer Edit screen (Shift-F7 S E F). Then, look under the Location column on the Select Printer Forms screen. This screen shows you all of the predefined forms for your printer (they vary according to the printer you have installed). If you see *Contin* in the Location column for a form like Standard, you know that WordPerfect will expect the paper to be continuously fed whenever you select the Standard or Standard Landscape option on the Format Paper Type screen. If you see *Manual* in the Location column for a predefined form like Envelope, you know that the program will expect the paper to be manually fed to the printer whenever you select the Envelope paper type. The Location listed for the [ALL OTHERS] form on this menu determines the type of feed expected when you choose a paper type not covered by one of the predefined forms.

If you want to use legal size paper for a document and this size of paper will be continuously fed to your printer, you select the Legal option (**3** or **L**) from the Format Paper Size menu and then select the Standard option (**1** or **S**) from the Format Paper Type menu. (If your printer is capable of printing in the Landscape orientation and you want the printing to run with the long side of the paper, you would select the Legal Landscape option for Paper Size and the Standard option for Paper Type.) If you use the Standard paper type for legal size, you must then make sure that the legal size paper tray is in place or that you have loaded you tractor feed with 8.5-by-14-inch paper prior to printing. If your printer is equipped with multiple paper bins, and legal size paper is supplied from a bin other than bin 1, you must create a special form definition that tells WordPerfect to get the paper from this bin. (See Chapter 7 for complete information on how to create such form definitions for your printer.)

When you select a paper type (or simply press Enter to keep the default choice of Standard), WordPerfect inserts a code into your document. For example, if you change to legal size, you see the code

[Paper Sz/Typ:8.5″ × 14″,Standard]

You also see the margins change in your document on the screen if the paper size you select is wider or narrower than 8.5″. You don't see any margin changes if you select Legal size, because it is 8.5″ wide, the same as a standard 8.5-by-11-inch page.

To print the document, WordPerfect tries to match the Paper Size/Type code with a form definition in your printer definition file. (Different printers come with different predefined forms.) If there is no form definition for the paper type, the program either uses an [ALL OTHERS] form definition that comes with some types of printers, or substitutes the form definition that is nearest in size to what you have specified in the Paper Size/Type code.

You may want to define special forms for use with WordPerfect. For example, your company letterhead may use 8.5-by-11-inch paper but require you to leave 3 inches of space at the top of the page. You can set up the Letterhead form so that WordPerfect will use this format when you select the Letterhead paper type. Defining forms is explained in Chapter 7, "Printing Techniques."

Once you've inserted a Paper Size/Type code, it remains in effect from the cursor's position forward. In some situations, you'll need to remember to switch back to another paper size. If you're printing one page as Letterhead, for example, you'll need to switch back to Standard at the top of the second page of any letter.

REVIEWING PAGE FORMATTING

When you have finished entering and editing the text of your document, you may find it beneficial to review its page layout before you print your work. You can do this by using WordPerfect's View Document feature, which you access through the Print menu by pressing Shift-F7 (Print) and choosing the View Document option (**6** or **V**). You will see almost exactly how the document will appear when it is printed, complete with text elements that are not normally visible on the screen, such as page numbers, headers, and footers. If you have a graphics card, you can select 100% (option **1**) to view the document at its actual size or 200% (option **2**) to see it at twice its actual size. Full Page (option **3**) is the default. If you select Facing Pages (option **4**), you will see odd-numbered pages on the right and even-numbered pages on the left. You will also be able to see font sizes and graphics, and you will be able to manipulate the document's display size.

Once you have displayed a page or pages, you can use the cursor movement keys to scroll through the document, or use the PgUp, PgDn, Screen Up, and Screen Down (+ / −) keys.

When you check the pagination, you should make sure that no widow or orphan lines have occurred and that no tables or sections of text that must be kept together on a page have been broken across two pages.

If your document contains headers and footers, you should make sure that their contents are correct and that they appear in the proper position on the page. This is especially true if you are using two headers or footers that alternate left and right on even- and odd-numbered pages of the document and in situations where you suppress them either temporarily or permanently.

If you notice page layout changes that must be made before you print, make them and then preview the page or document once more. Regular use of the View Document feature will save you a great deal of printing time, to say nothing of wasted paper. You can use the information in this chapter to help you diagnose and correct particular page format problems.

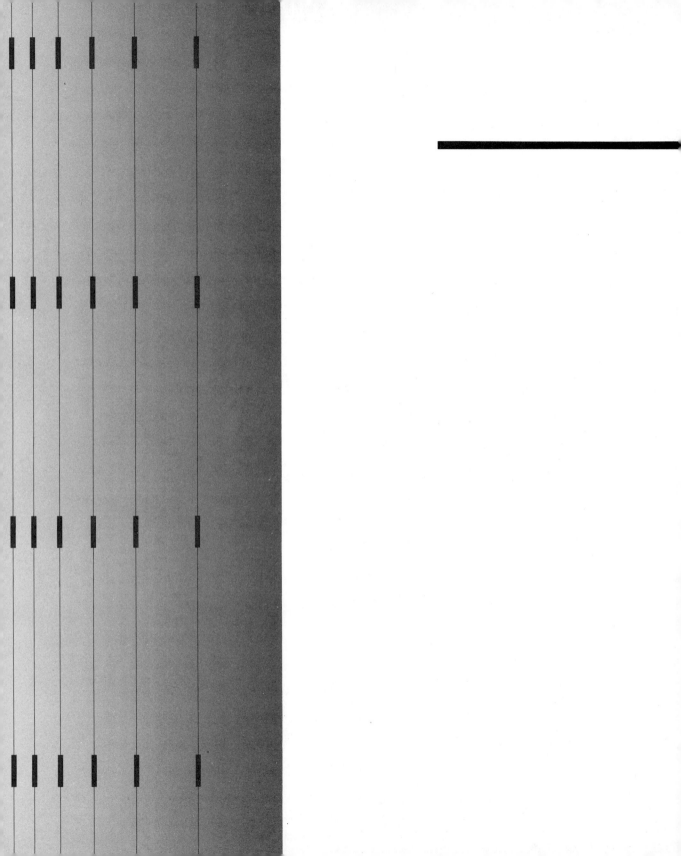

CHAPTER 5

WORKING WITH FONTS

WORKING WITH FONTS

WordPerfect allows you a great deal of freedom in selecting and combining different fonts (typefaces, type sizes, and type styles) in a document. In fact, the real limitation on the number and type of fonts that you can use is imposed by the printer you are using. This chapter presents information on how to install, select, and combine different fonts in a single document. It also explores aspects of controlling the line, word, and letter spacing when you use different fonts in one document.

The subject of fonts is necessarily tied to that of installing and selecting a printer. If you need information on installing your printer, please refer to Chapter 7 before trying to follow the instructions on selecting and using different fonts. In Chapter 6, you will learn how to create and use styles, a new WordPerfect feature that can greatly simplify changing from one font to another in a document by automating this process.

After reading the discussion of fonts, you may also want to refer to Part IV on desktop publishing (Chapters 18 and 19) for ideas on when and how to combine different fonts in a publication. In Chapter 19, you will also find valuable material on how to combine different fonts with graphics to achieve the effect you want in a particular desktop publishing application.

UPGRADE NOTES

The way you select and assign fonts in WordPerfect 5.0 has changed radically from the methods you used in version 4.2. No longer are you restricted to eight predefined fonts for your printer. As you may have already noticed, the key combination Ctrl-F8 is now called Font instead of Print Format, which is now located on a submenu of the Format key—Shift-F8. The options on the Font menu are entirely new. They enable you to change the basic font used to print the text and to assign different type sizes and type styles to particular portions of text.

Perhaps the most important improvement to using different fonts in Word-Perfect is the program's ability to automatically adjust the line length as required by the font (or fonts) used in that line to maintain the left and right margin settings. This means that when you change fonts, you no longer have to calculate the number of characters that fit on the line and manually change the left and right margin settings to accommodate this new number. Likewise, WordPerfect automatically calculates and adjusts the amount of space between lines (referred to as the *line height*) to maintain the appropriate amount of space between lines.

This line height is based on the largest type size used, if multiple sizes are combined in the line, and remains tied to the line spacing in use (single, double, and so on).

You will also find it much easier to assign new fonts to the text of your document. You no longer have to puzzle through assigning the correct pitch number to match the font number selected; you simply highlight the name of the font to use as it appears on the Base Font menu and choose the Select option to put it in effect. Moreover, you will find changing the size of the type and assigning new attributes (like italics, outline, and shadow) an effortless procedure. So many attributes are now directly supported that you will probably never have to resort to looking up complex Escape-sequence Printer Control codes and entering them as Printer commands in the document to get a desired printing effect.

How WordPerfect Defines a Font

Before you learn how to change and combine fonts in a document, you must be clear about how WordPerfect defines a font. A font in WordPerfect represents a certain set of characters (including letters, numbers, punctuation, and other special symbols—called *dingbats* by the publishing industry) of a particular type style and size.

Figures 5.1 and 5.2 show you two different fonts in the Helvetica family. As you can see, they differ only in the type style; the one in Figure 5.1 is Helvetica Upright (also referred to as *roman*) while the one in Figure 5.2 is Helvetica Italic (referred to as *oblique* when the letter forms are simply slanted 45 degrees to the right rather than redesigned to form a new typeface based on the upright letter forms as is the case in this figure). Otherwise, these fonts are identical in terms of the size and the characters (symbols) they contain.

In addition to their character set, style of type, and size, fonts are also described by their character spacing, either *monospaced* or *proportionally spaced*. One of the most commonly used monospaced fonts is the Courier type that almost all typewriters produce (in fact, it is so popular that it is built into the LaserJet printers). Courier type is classified as monospaced because each of its characters takes up the same amount of horizontal space on the page. This is not to say that you can't get Courier type in different sizes; you can. But within a particular size of Courier type, each of the characters takes up the same amount of space on the line (see Figure 5.3).

Proportionally spaced fonts are quite different, in that various characters within a font require different amounts of horizontal space when printed. In this way, proportionally spaced fonts are much more like handwriting or calligraphy because in our alphabet, characters like *i* and *t* take up roughly the same amount of space, which is almost one-third less than the space required by characters like *m* and *w*. The type that you are reading right this minute is a proportionally

Helvetica Upright, Medium 24pt

ABCDEFGHIJKLMNOPQRSTUVWXYZ
abcdefghijklmnopqrstuvwxyz
0123456789:; < = > ?·@^
!"#$%'()*+,-./]'~{|}_ ▓

FIGURE 5.1: Helvetica Upright, Medium 24pt, a single font in WordPerfect 5.0. The *pt* after the *24* stands for *point*, which describes the size of the type. A font in WordPerfect represents a typeface (Helvetica), a type style (Upright), and a type size (24pt). All of the characters (symbols) included in this font are shown in this figure. As you can see, this includes all of the letters of the alphabet (in uppercase and lowercase), the numbers, the standard punctuation, and a few special symbols. In addition, this font includes a graphics character (the checkerboard at the end of the last line) that is used to designate redlined text.

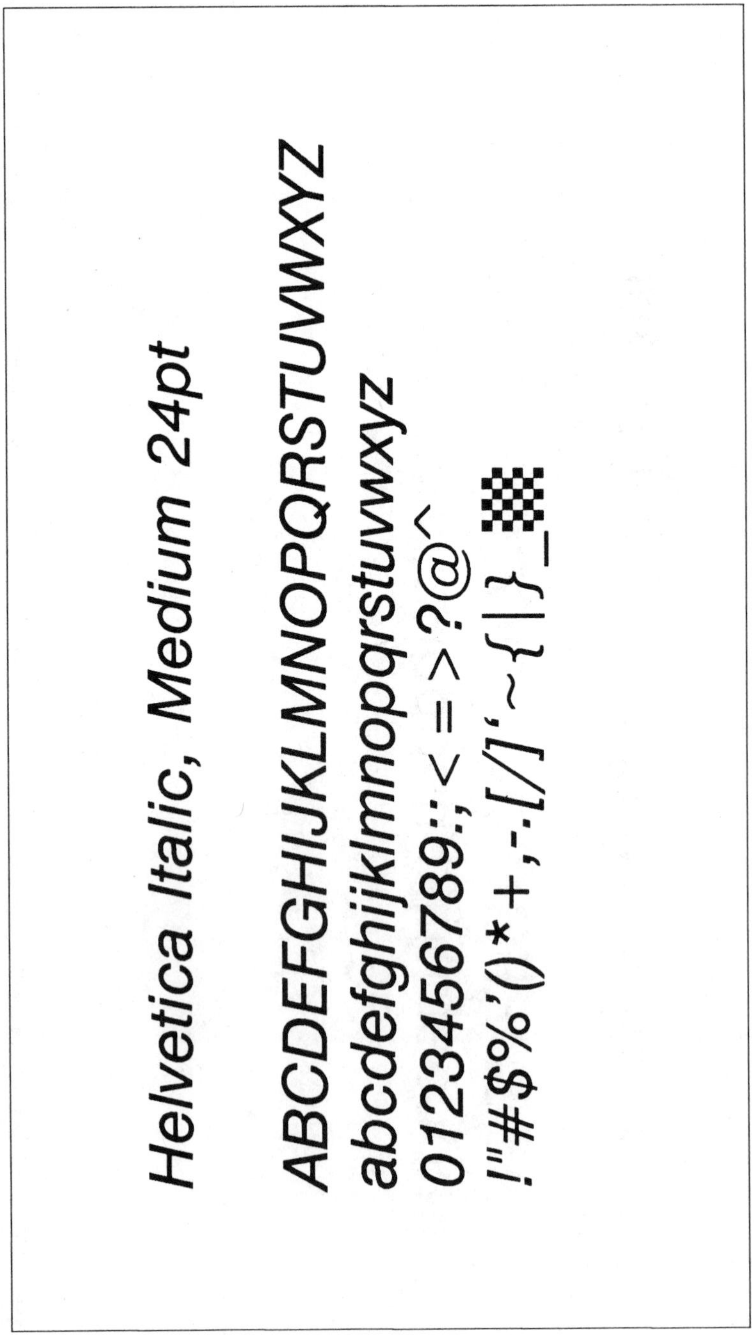

Helvetica Italic, Medium 24pt

ABCDEFGHIJKLMNOPQRSTUVWXYZ
abcdefghijklmnopqrstuvwxyz
0123456789:;<=>?@^
!"#$%'()*+,-[/]'~{|}_

FIGURE 5.2: Helvetica Italic, Medium 24pt, which WordPerfect considers a different font from the one shown in Figure 5.1, although they vary only in type style; this font is italic, while the font shown in the previous figure is upright (or roman).

spaced font called *Baskerville*. Look at the word *minute* in the previous sentence. Notice how much wider the *m* is than the *i* next to it, and that the *i* takes up about the same space as the *t*.

You can also see the dramatic variation between using a monospaced font and a proportionally spaced font in Figure 5.3, where the same paragraph is printed in Courier 10 pitch and 11 point Century Schoolbook. Although the vertical size of the type is roughly the same and the line length is identical, you will immediately notice that there are fewer words per line in the first paragraph, which uses the Courier monospaced font, than there are in the second, which uses the Century Schoolbook proportionally spaced font. This is due in large part to the variable character spacing that is utilized by a proportionally spaced font. The end result of fitting more words per line is that it takes fewer lines to print the same amount of text. In addition, some people find proportionally spaced text easier to read, especially when the text is justified, as it is in these two paragraphs.

> *Note:* All of the text that you type in a WordPerfect document is displayed on your computer monitor in a monospaced type even if you specified that a proportionally spaced font be used to print it. When you are using a 10 pitch monospaced font, all of the characters that you enter advance the cursor exactly $1/10$ inch as indicated by the Pos indicator on the status line. When you are using a proportionally spaced font, the amount of advancement displayed by the Pos indicator varies according to the character you are entering. Nevertheless, the appearance of the characters on the editing screen does not vary, only the length of the line. To get a more accurate view of how the document will look when printed, you must use the View Document feature (Shift-F7 V).

Almost all professionally published material uses proportionally spaced fonts instead of monospaced fonts. Currently, many types of printers—not just laser printers but also dot matrix and impact printers that use print wheels or thimbles—can use proportionally spaced fonts. This means that you can use these types of fonts in documents that call for the ''published'' look.

The last thing you need to know about fonts is how their size is measured. Here, things get a bit trickier simply because two very different systems are in use; one was developed to describe the monospaced fonts produced by typewriters and rates the type size by a horizontal measurement, while the other was developed to describe proportionally spaced fonts used in typesetting and rates the type size by a vertical measurement! Because monospaced fonts do not contain variable-width characters, it is convenient to describe their size by the number of characters used to produce a horizontal inch of type. This is the *pitch* of the type, so that in a font described as 10 pitch, you know there are 10 characters in every inch of type. You may also see pitch described by the abbreviation *cpi* (characters per inch), so that 12 cpi means 12 characters per inch or 12 pitch. Often, 10 pitch type is called *Pica* type and 12 pitch type is called *Elite* type.

Unfortunately, this system won't work when applied to a proportionally spaced font because of its varied character spacing—it may take 10, it may take

The paragraph to the right is printed in the monospaced font called Courier in 10 pitch (that is, 10 characters per inch).

WELCOME

Welcome to MagnaCorp. We hope this employee handbook will help to guide you through your first few days here. In addition, it contains valuable information about employee services and benefits available to you. Ask your manager or call the personnel office if you have any questions for which you cannot find the answers in this handbook.

The paragraph to the right is printed in the proportionally-spaced font called Century Schoolbook in 11 point.

WELCOME

Welcome to MagnaCorp. We hope this employee handbook will help to guide you through your first few days here. In addition, it contains valuable information about employee services and benefits available to you. Ask your manager or call the personnel office if you have any questions for which you cannot find the answers in this handbook.

FIGURE 5.3: A paragraph printed in Courier 10 pitch (a monospaced font) and again in Century Schoolbook 11 point. Although the vertical size of the type is roughly the same, Courier accommodates fewer words per line than Century Schoolbook. More words can fit into the same line length with a proportionally spaced font primarily because of the variable character spacing it uses. As a result of fitting more words into the same line length, it requires two fewer lines to print the same paragraph in Century Schoolbook than it takes to print it in Courier.

15, it may even take 22 characters to produce an inch of type, all depending upon which characters in the set you are using. These kinds of fonts are rated according to a vertical measurement called the *point* size (a single point being about $^1/_{72}$ inch). A common point size for the body of text in a book is anywhere from 10 to 12 point—this book uses 11 point—depending upon the type style used.

Monospaced fonts can be described by both their point size (which measures the height of the characters) and their pitch, or cpi (characters per inch). You will find that WordPerfect uses all of these measurements to list different fonts available to your printer. For example, it lists the condensed print built into the HP LaserJet printers as

Line Printer 08.5pt 16.66 pitch (PC-8)

This tells you that the Line Printer font is 8$^1/_2$ points high (approximately $^9/_{72}$ or $^1/_8$ inch) and that it takes 16.66 characters to fill each line inch. (The *PC-8* indicates the character set.) In contrast, the program uses only the point size when referring to the Courier 10 pitch (or Pica type), the most popular font that is built into all of the LaserJet printers:

Courier 10 pitch (PC-8)

(*PC-8* refers to the character set supported by this font). However, if you are using an Epson FX-80 or FX-100 and wish to select 10 pitch or Pica type, Word-Perfect will list it as

10 CPI

using, instead, the characters per inch rating.

Proportionally spaced fonts are usually listed by name and point size or, for built-in fonts in PostScript printers like the LaserWriter, just by name (in which case you indicate the point size after you select the name of the font to use). However, with some printers, like the Epson FX-80 or FX-100, the program will differentiate proportionally spaced fonts from monospaced fonts by placing *(PS)* at the end of the name.

SELECTING FONTS

When you install your printer (see Chapter 7 for specific information on this procedure), WordPerfect selects the most commonly used font that it supports and designates it as the *initial font* (Figure 5.4). Whenever you begin a new document, the initial font is used. The program controls the horizontal and vertical spacing according to this font.

All printers support multiple fonts, although they differ greatly in the number and type of fonts supported and how these fonts are installed. If you are using a letter quality printer like a Diablo 635, you must change print wheels to change

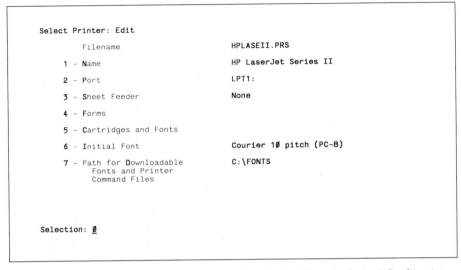

```
Select Printer: Edit

        Filename                    HPLASEII.PRS

    1 - Name                        HP LaserJet Series II

    2 - Port                        LPT1:

    3 - Sheet Feeder                None

    4 - Forms

    5 - Cartridges and Fonts

    6 - Initial Font               Courier 1Ø pitch (PC-8)

    7 - Path for Downloadable      C:\FONTS
        Fonts and Printer
        Command Files




    Selection: Ø
```

FIGURE 5.4: The Printer Edit screen showing the initial font for the HP LaserJet Series II. For this printer, the initial font is Courier 10 pitch, a monospaced font that is resident in the LaserJet.

to a new font. This type of printer has no resident or built-in fonts, although WordPerfect will expect the font that it selects as the initial font to be used when you print your document unless you indicate a font change.

If you are using a dot matrix printer, like an Epson FX-80 or FX-100, you can choose from a number of resident fonts that are built into the printer (see Figure 5.5). A few dot matrix printers not only support several resident fonts but also give you the option of purchasing additional fonts that are stored on cartridges. To be able to use a font on a cartridge, you must insert the cartridge into the slot provided prior to print time.

If you are using a laser printer that doesn't support PostScript (a page description language built into the printer), like one of the HP LaserJet models, you can choose among a small number of resident fonts, fonts that come on cartridges, and fonts that come on disk (referred to as *soft* fonts or, sometimes, *downloadable* fonts). When you purchase soft fonts for your laser printer, you receive a number of different fonts on a set of disks, usually in a couple of typefaces (like Times Roman and Helvetica or Letter Gothic and Presentation).

WordPerfect 5.0 does not directly support all of the soft font sets available for the LaserJet printers, although it does support a fair number of them. Word-Perfect Corporation will send you the Bitstream Fontware package free of charge. This package includes three typefaces—Charter, Dutch (Times Roman), and Swiss (Helvetica)—and a utility that enables you to create these soft fonts in different sizes. To get this package, call the toll-free number listed at the beginning of the "Getting Started" section of your WordPerfect manual. Refer to Appendix F for information on using this utility.

```
Select Printer: Initial Font
    Ø5 CPI
    Ø6 CPI
    Ø8.5 CPI
*   1Ø CPI
    12 CPI
    12pt (PS)
    17 CPI
    Italic 12pt (PS)
    Subscript (Ø5 CPI)
    Subscript (Ø6 CPI)
    Subscript (1Ø CPI)
    Subscript (12 CPI)




    1 Select; N Name search: 1
```

FIGURE 5.5: Sample listing of resident fonts. With an Epson FX-80/100 printer, you may select from several built-in fonts and styles.

If you have a laser printer that uses PostScript, like one of the LaserWriter models, you can choose between a wide variety of resident fonts (the LaserWriter Plus has 35 of them). Laser printers that don't support PostScript limit a particular font to a single point size, while PostScript printers allow you to set the type size (in points) when you select a particular font. This is due to PostScript's ability to scale a font at print time. Because you are free to select from an almost unlimited assortment of type sizes for any resident font, you have many more choices available than when using a non-PostScript laser printer like the HP LaserJet.

In addition to using the resident fonts, PostScript laser printers also support the use of soft fonts, thus further increasing your choice of typefaces and type styles. Note, however, that WordPerfect does not yet support all of the soft fonts that can be purchased and used with a PostScript laser printer. When you install the printer, the help notes that are displayed tell you which soft fonts are supported.

Installing Fonts for Use in WordPerfect

If you are using a printer that accepts fonts either on cartridge or on disk (soft fonts), you must install the fonts on them individually before using them in a document. Otherwise, your selection of fonts will be limited to those that are resident in the printer.

Note: Although WordPerfect lists all of the cartridge fonts and soft fonts that it supports for a particular printer on the Printer Edit menu (Shift-F7 S E C), this does not mean that the fonts themselves are supplied with the WordPerfect program. You must still purchase the appropriate cartridge or soft font disk set containing the fonts you want to use from a third-party vendor and make them available to the printer at print time.

To install nonresident fonts, press Shift-F7 and choose the Select Printer option (**S**). This brings you to a screen that lists all of the printers you have installed. Use the ↑ or ↓ key to move the highlight bar to the name of the printer that uses the fonts you are about to install. Next, select the Edit option (**3** or **E**) on the menu at the bottom of the screen. From the Printer Edit screen, choose the Cartridges and Fonts option (**5** or **C**).

Note: If you receive the "Printer file not found" screen (which prompts you to indicate the name of the directory that contains the printer definition file) after selecting the Cartridges and Fonts option, place the Printer disk that contains this file for your printer in one of your disk drives and then enter the appropriate drive/directory path before pressing the Enter key.

This brings you to the Cartridges and Fonts screen, which contains the menu options

1 Select Fonts; **2** Change **Q**uantity; **N N**ame Search: 1

at the bottom. At the top of the screen, you will see the categories of the fonts that you can install for the printer you are using. These categories vary according to the type of printer selected. (If the printer you have selected does not support any additional cartridges or fonts, you will see the message "This printer has no other cartridges or fonts" when you use the Cartridges and Fonts option.) For example, Figure 5.6 shows you the Cartridges and Fonts screen for the HP LaserJet Series II. This printer allows you to install either cartridge fonts or soft fonts. Figure 5.7 shows you the Cartridges and Fonts screen for the LaserWriter Plus. Notice that this printer supports only the use of soft fonts (here called downloadable fonts).

The Cartridges and Fonts screen lists not only the types of fonts supported, but also, in the case of soft fonts, how much printer memory is available for their installation. This figure, stated in kilobytes, is not the same as the total amount of memory that your printer has. For instance, LaserJet printers come with a standard 512K (kilobytes or thousand bytes) of printer memory, although, as you can see in Figure 5.6, only 350K of this memory is available for installing soft fonts. In the case of the LaserWriter Plus, which comes with 1.5 Mb (megabytes or million bytes), only 120K is available for downloadable fonts; the rest of the printer memory is used by the PostScript language built into it to scale and produce the resident fonts.

If you have equipped your LaserJet with extra memory beyond the standard 512K or you have one of the LaserWriter II models (the NT or NTX), you need to select the Change Quantity option (**2** or **Q**) and indicate the additional amount

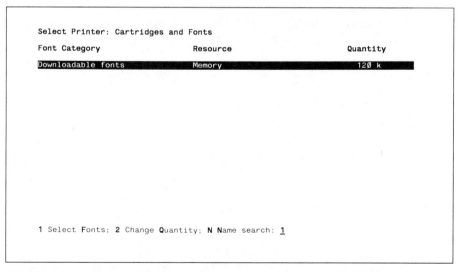

```
Select Printer: Cartridges and Fonts

Font Category                   Resource                    Quantity

Cartridge Fonts                 Font Cartridge Slot             2
Soft Fonts                      Memory available for fonts    350 K
```

```
1 Select Fonts; 2 Change Quantity; N Name search: 1
```

FIGURE 5.6: The Cartridges and Fonts screen for the HP LaserJet Series II. The top of this screen shows you that this printer will accept up to two cartridges and that there is 350K of printer memory available for their installation. If you have installed additional memory in your LaserJet (beyond the 512K that is standard), you need to select the Change Quantity option (**2** or **Q**) and indicate the additional amount of memory available (like **1350** if the printer has 1.5 Mb of memory).

```
Select Printer: Cartridges and Fonts

Font Category                   Resource                    Quantity

Downloadable fonts              Memory                        120 k
```

```
1 Select Fonts; 2 Change Quantity; N Name search: 1
```

FIGURE 5.7: The Cartridges and Fonts screen for the LaserWriter Plus. This printer uses only soft fonts (called downloadable fonts), and there is only 120K of printer memory available for their installation. Although the LaserWriter Plus comes with a standard 1.5 Mb of memory, only 120K can be used for installing soft fonts; the rest of the memory is used by the PostScript language to produce the resident fonts. If you have a LaserWriter II NT or NTX, both of which have 2 Mb of memory, you need to select the Change Quantity option (**2** or **Q**) and enter **632** as the amount (the 120K available plus the 512K additional).

of memory in response to the Quantity prompt. Type in the number of kilobytes and press the Enter key. For example, if your LaserJet has 1.5 Mb of total memory, you have approximately 1000K (or 1 Mb) of additional memory available. You would then enter **1350** for the quantity—the 350K available plus the 1000K additional.

> *Note:* If you will be printing graphics with this type of printer, WordPerfect recommends that a minimum of 1 Mb of total printer memory be installed. Printing a page that contains both graphics and text (especially if the text is set in different fonts) requires a lot of memory. If your LaserJet has only 512K of printer memory, you will almost always still be able to print text and graphics, but this may require that you print the graphics separately from the text. See Chapter 7 for details on how this is done.

If your printer uses print wheels and Quantity is set at 1 on the Cartridges and Fonts menu, you use the Quantity option to indicate the number of print wheels you own.

SELECTING CARTRIDGE FONTS

You use the first option on the Printer Edit menu, Select Fonts (**1** or **F**), to see which of the fonts that your printer supports can be used in WordPerfect and to indicate which of these you will be using. To select the cartridges you will be using, make sure that the highlight bar is on the Cartridge Fonts line before choosing the Select Fonts option. Figure 5.8 shows you the screen, containing the first part of the cartridge font choices for the HP LaserJet Series II, that comes up when you do this.

If the printer file (using the .ALL file extension) that holds the information on the cartridge fonts to be installed is not found, you will receive a full-screen message indicating this with the prompt

Directory for printer files:

at the bottom of the screen. Place the Printer disk that you used originally to install the printer in one of your disk drives (the LaserJet printer file is on Printer disk 1). Then type the name of the drive (such as **A:** or **B:**) that holds this disk and press the Enter key. If you have copied this file into a directory of your hard disk, you enter its path name. When you have indicated the correct disk or directory, a full-screen list of cartridges supported by the program will appear.

> *Note:* You can use the Location of Auxiliary Files option (**7** or **L**) on the Setup menu (Shift-F1) to indicate the directory in which you keep all of the printer files. Select the Printer Files option (**5** or **P**) on the Location of Auxiliary Files menu and enter the full path name. WordPerfect will then automatically look in this directory for the printer file(s) containing the font information it requires.

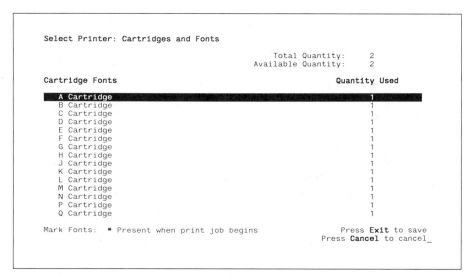

FIGURE 5.8: Selecting cartridge fonts for the HP LaserJet Series II. To select a cartridge that you have, position the highlight bar on its name and type an asterisk (*). Because Total Quantity is 2, Word-Perfect will only allow you to mark two of the cartriges on this list. If you own more than two and want to use one that has not been installed here, you must remember to return to this screen, deselect the one you aren't using, and select the one that has replaced it.

WordPerfect supports all of the cartridge font sets currently available for the HP LaserJet printers. (The cartridges from R through Z1A are not visible on the initial screen—you must scroll the list to select one of them.) Because the HP LaserJet Series II has two slots, you can select up to two cartridges from this list. To select a cartridge you want to use, move the highlight cursor to its name using the cursor movement keys and type an asterisk (*). The asterisk will then precede the cartridge, indicating that it is selected.

Note that WordPerfect will expect this cartridge to be present when the print job that uses it begins. This means that you can't insert the correct cartridge during the print job, so be sure that everything is properly set up before sending the document to be printed.

If you mark a cartridge in error, you can deselect it by typing a second asterisk when the highlight bar is on it. After marking the cartridge fonts, be sure to press F7 (Exit). If you press F1 (Cancel), WordPerfect will not update the printer definition file with the font selections you have just made.

Note: Remember that you must take the LaserJet off line by pressing the On Line button on the front panel before you insert a cartridge in one of the slots. After you have seated the cartridge in its slot, be sure to put the printer back on line by pressing the On Line button again.

SELECTING SOFT FONTS

The process of selecting soft fonts for your printer is very similar to that of selecting cartridge fonts. With the highlight bar positioned on the Soft Fonts or Downloadable Fonts line in the Cartridges and Fonts screen, you choose the Select Fonts option (**1** or **F**). Figure 5.9 shows you the first screen that appears when you select soft fonts for the HP LaserJet Series II.

Notice that the screen for selecting soft fonts lists not only the name of the font but also the amount of printer memory that it takes to load it (the larger the point size, the more memory required). At the top, above these two columns, Word-Perfect tells you the total amount of printer memory available and keeps you informed about how much your selections use up (Figure 5.10). WordPerfect will not allow you to install more fonts that are to be present when the print job begins than can be accommodated in the total amount of memory available on this screen. If you try to install a font with an asterisk that requires more memory than you have left, the font will not accept the mark you give it.

Notice also that you mark soft fonts in a slightly different manner than you do for cartridge fonts. You type an asterisk to indicate that the font will be present (downloaded) when the print job begins and a plus sign to indicate that it can be downloaded during the print job. Marking fonts as present when the print job begins speeds up the printing process, because WordPerfect doesn't have to

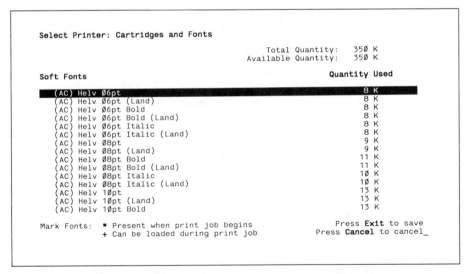

FIGURE 5.9: Selecting soft fonts for the HP LaserJet Series II. Along with the font set, name, type style, and orientation of the font, this screen lists the amount of printer memory used to load it. Type an asterisk (*) to mark all of the fonts that will already be downloaded to the printer before you print the document that uses them. Mark all of the fonts that WordPerfect should download as part of the print job with a plus sign (+).

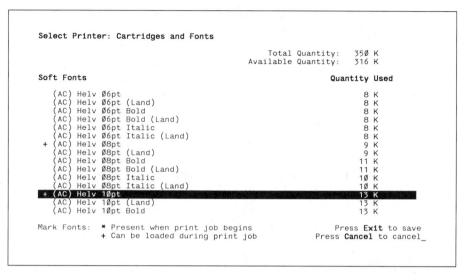

```
Select Printer: Cartridges and Fonts

                                          Total Quantity:   350 K
                                      Available Quantity:   316 K

Soft Fonts                                           Quantity Used

      (AC) Helv Ø6pt                                      8 K
      (AC) Helv Ø6pt (Land)                               8 K
      (AC) Helv Ø6pt Bold                                 8 K
      (AC) Helv Ø6pt Bold (Land)                          8 K
      (AC) Helv Ø6pt Italic                               8 K
      (AC) Helv Ø6pt Italic (Land)                        8 K
   +  (AC) Helv Ø8pt                                      9 K
      (AC) Helv Ø8pt (Land)                               9 K
      (AC) Helv Ø8pt Bold                                11 K
      (AC) Helv Ø8pt Bold (Land)                         11 K
      (AC) Helv Ø8pt Italic                              10 K
      (AC) Helv Ø8pt Italic (Land)                       10 K
   +  (AC) Helv 1Øpt                                     13 K
      (AC) Helv 1Øpt (Land)                              13 K
      (AC) Helv 1Øpt Bold                                13 K

Mark Fonts:  * Present when print job begins          Press Exit to save
             + Can be loaded during print job       Press Cancel to cancel_
```

FIGURE 5.10: Marking the soft fonts to be installed. Marking a font as present when the print job begins reduces the amount of memory available. In this figure, with just two fonts selected, the available quantity of memory has been reduced from 350K to 316K. As you continue to select soft fonts with an asterisk, the available memory will continue to be reduced. WordPerfect will not allow you to mark a new font if you don't have sufficient memory left for it as Available Quantity.

download these fonts to the printer to be able to print the page that uses them. On the other hand, marking fonts to be downloaded during printing saves on the amount of printer memory used by soft fonts, since these fonts can be flushed from the printer's memory after the document is printed, freeing up some memory. As a rule, it is a good idea to mark all of the fonts that you routinely use in printing with an asterisk (provided that your printer has sufficient memory). Then, mark those fonts that you just use occasionally with the plus sign. After you have marked all of the soft fonts you want to use, be sure to press F7 (Exit) and not F1 (Cancel) to have your printer definition updated.

> *Note:* The HP LaserJet Series II will only accept a total of 32 different soft fonts regardless of how much memory your printer has. Also, it will only allow you to mix a total of 16 different fonts on a page in a WordPerfect document.

Fonts Already Present at Print Time   You must have downloaded all fonts marked with an asterisk prior to sending the print job to the printer. To do this, you use the Initialize Printer option on the Print menu (Shift-F7 I). After you download the fonts that you have marked with an asterisk (*), you must be sure that you don't turn off the printer before you print the document that uses these fonts.

Fonts Downloaded at Print Time   All fonts that are marked with a plus sign are downloaded during the print job. WordPerfect automatically downloads the fonts as long as you have correctly indicated the directory that contains the font files that must be used to print the document. You will receive a printer error message if a required font file is not located when you send a document to be printed.

You indicate the location of the font files by selecting the Path for Downloadable Fonts and Printer Command Files option (**7** or **D**) on the Printer Edit menu (Shift-F7 S E). If you have a hard disk, you should create a separate directory and copy all of the soft font files into it. After choosing this option on the Printer Edit screen, enter the full path name for this directory. If the soft fonts will be downloaded from a separate disk, enter the name of the drive that will contain it—make sure that this disk contains all of the necessary font files. Be sure that you press F7 (Exit) rather than F1 (Cancel) when you are ready to leave this screen; otherwise WordPerfect won't update this information.

Locating and Identifying Soft Fonts   The list of soft fonts for the LaserJet that can be used in WordPerfect is quite long. In Figure 5.9, you saw only the first selections for the Helvetica font (sizes 6 to 10 point) in the AC set. Soft fonts are sold in sets that usually contain many sizes and type styles for a couple of typefaces. The AC set from Hewlett-Packard contains Helvetica and Times Roman typefaces in even-point sizes including 6, 8, 10, 12, 14, 18, 24, and 30 point. Some of these font sizes are available in medium and bold, while others (the 18, 24, and 30 point) are available only in bold. Some sizes (6, 8, 10, 12, and 14 point) are also available in italic type. Each type size and style variation has its own font file that must be selected to be installed.

In addition, some of the fonts are available in *landscape* mode as well as the normal *portrait* mode. In portrait mode the orientation of the printing is in line with the short side of the paper. In landscape mode, it is turned 90 degrees so that it is in line with the long side of the paper. Landscape mode is useful when you are creating a table or figure and you need to take advantage of the long line length (11 inches if you are using 8½-by-11-inch paper) that is possible in this orientation.

You can use the cursor keys to scroll this list of font files, and you can also use Name Search. For instance, if you want to go directly to the Times Roman soft fonts in the AC set to select some of them, you press F2 (Search), and the prompts at the bottom of the screen are replaced with

(Name Search; Enter or arrows to Exit)

at the right side of the screen. Then type (**ac**) **t** as the first characters to search for and WordPerfect will take you directly to the first font in the AC set whose name begins with *T.* This happens to be

(AC) Tms Rmn 06pt

as shown in Figure 5.11.

```
Select Printer: Cartridges and Fonts

                                              Total Quantity:   350 K
                                          Available Quantity:    31 K

Soft Fonts                                       Quantity Used

     (AC) Helv 18pt Bold (Land)                        29 K
     (AC) Helv 24pt Bold                               46 K
     (AC) Helv 24pt Bold (Land)                        46 K
     (AC) Helv 30pt Bold                               68 K
     (AC) Helv 30pt Bold (Land)                        68 K
     (AC) Tms Rmn 06pt                                  8 K
     (AC) Tms Rmn 06pt (Land)                           8 K
     (AC) Tms Rmn 06pt Bold                             8 K
     (AC) Tms Rmn 06pt Bold (Land)                      8 K
     (AC) Tms Rmn 06pt Italic                           8 K
     (AC) Tms Rmn 06pt Italic (Land)                    8 K
     (AC) Tms Rmn 08pt                                  9 K
     (AC) Tms Rmn 08pt (Land)                           9 K
     (AC) Tms Rmn 08pt Bold                            10 K
     (AC) Tms Rmn 08pt Bold (Land)                     10 K


 (ac) t                          (Name Search; Enter or arrows to Exit)
```

FIGURE 5.11: Using Name Search to locate the Times Roman soft fonts in the AC set. To initiate a name search on this screen, press F2 and type the first few characters. Because this list of soft fonts begins with the name of the set in parentheses, you must enter this designation before you enter the first letter or letters of the name of the typeface. To exit Name Search, press one of the arrow keys or the Enter key.

A word is in order here about the character set information that is included in the soft font listing. You already know that the first part of the listing in parentheses tells you the name of the font set. The font set determines not only what type families, sizes, and styles are available, but also the symbol (or character) set that they use.

The three most common character sets are Roman-8, USASCII, and Roman-Ext (Roman extended). The USASCII symbol set includes the uppercase and lowercase letters, numbers, and punctuation marks that are available from your keyboard (which represents the ASCII character set used in the United States—thus the name USASCII). The Roman-Ext symbol set includes only accented letters and special symbols (dingbats) used to represent European languages that use the Roman alphabet (accented characters like é and dingbats like the Pound symbol). The Roman-8 character set includes all of the characters available in both the USASCII and Roman-Ext character sets.

All of the fonts in the AC set use the USASCII symbol set, while fonts from the AD soft font set use the Roman-8 symbol set. This is the only difference between the AC and AD sets; they are the same in all other respects. If you have only selected the USASCII version of a font, be sure you don't attempt to use special symbols or accented characters included in the Roman-Ext symbol set, as they won't be printed.

The character set information is followed by the name of the type (*Tms Rmn* stands for *Times Roman*), the point size, and, sometimes, the pitch of a font. In

Figure 5.11, you can see that 6 point Times Roman is also listed with *(Land)* at the end of the description. You select this font if you want to print the type in landscape (Land) mode. Any font that doesn't have *(Land)* listed at the end is printed in portrait mode.

After you select all of the soft fonts that you plan to use and press F7 (Exit), you are returned to the previous screen, which allows you to choose between installing cartridge fonts or soft fonts. To have your soft font selections updated, you must also press F7 to exit this screen rather than F1 (Cancel). You will see a brief message informing you that WordPerfect is updating the fonts (listed by font number) before you are returned to the Printer Edit screen.

Selecting a New Initial Font for the Printer Once you are back at the Printer Edit menu, you should verify that the font listed as the initial font (option **6**) is the one you want to use. The initial font represents the default font that WordPerfect uses for all text in every document you create using this printer. It remains in effect unless you change it to one of the other fonts you have installed for the printer. Select a new initial font for the document, or select a new base font. (See the next two sections for details.)

To change the initial font, you select the Initial Font option (**6** or **I**) from the Printer Edit menu. This takes you to a listing of all of the fonts you have selected

```
Select Printer: Initial Font

* Courier 10 pitch (PC-8)
  Courier 10 pitch (Roman-8)
  Cou er Bold 10 pitch (PC-8)
  Hel  14.4pt Bold (B)
  Line Printer 16.66 pitch (Roman-8)
  Solid Line Draw 10 pitch
  Solid Line Draw 12 pitch
  Tms Rmn 08pt (B)
  Tms Rmn 10pt (B)
  Tms Rmn 10pt Bold (B)
  Tms Rmn 10pt Italic (B)




  1 Select; N Name search: 1
```

FIGURE 5.12: Selecting a new initial font for the LaserJet Series II. The list of fonts that appears when you choose the Initial Font option (**6** or **I**) on the Printer Edit menu shows you all of the fonts that are available with your printer. This includes both those fonts that are resident and all of the fonts that you have installed using the Cartridges and Fonts option (**5** or **C**) on this menu. To choose a new font, move the highlight bar to its name and type **S** or press the Enter key. The font chosen will be the default font for all new documents you create in WordPerfect.

for use with your printer, similar to the one shown in Figure 5.12 for the LaserJet Series II. Notice that the font descriptions in this list are not presented in the same manner as they are when you install the fonts. In this listing, the font set is displayed at the end of the description, making it easier to do a name search for the font you want to select.

Move the highlight bar to the font you want to make the new default and then press the Enter key or choose the Select option by typing **1** or **S**. You will be returned to the Edit menu screen and you will see the name of the initial font you just chose, now listed after the Initial Font option on this menu.

To return to the editing screen from the Edit menu, press F7 (Exit) three times. Do not press the Cancel key from the Edit menu after changing the initial font, or WordPerfect will not update your change and the originally selected initial font will stay in effect. If you change the initial font while you have a document in the editing screen, the change won't affect that document. To change the initial font for existing documents, you must change the initial font for the document, as described below.

Selecting a New Initial Font for the Document   You can change the initial font in just the document you are creating. To do this, you press Shift-F8 (Format) and select the Document option (**3** or **D**) followed by the Initial Font option (**3** or **F**). This takes you to the same full-screen listing of all of the available fonts. The highlight bar will be on the current initial font and its name will be preceded by an asterisk. Move the highlight bar to the name of the font you want to make the initial font in the document you are creating; then choose the Select option (**1** or **S**). You can use Name Search (**N** or F2) to quickly locate a particular font in a long list.

After you select a new initial font, you are returned to the Document Format menu. Press F7 (Exit) to return to the document editing screen. The font selected here becomes the initial font only in the document you are creating. Changing the font in this document does not change it for any other documents you create in the future.

When you change the initial font, either for the document as described here or for the printer as described in the previous section, WordPerfect doesn't insert any hidden codes in the document. This means that there is no way to tell that a different initial font is in use even if you look at the Reveal Codes screen. The only way you might suspect that the initial font has been changed is if you notice a change in the line length (caused if the new font happens to accommodate more or fewer characters per line).

Therefore, if you change the initial font for the printer rather than just for the document, your fellow workers might be surprised when they use your computer and printer to produce and print a new document. For example, assume that you change the initial font from Courier 10 pitch to Times Roman 10 point for the printer rather than for the document to produce a special report that requires proportional spacing. If, after printing the final draft of the report, you forget to change the initial font back to Courier 10 pitch, your printer will still be set to produce all new documents in Times Roman 10 point. Then, if someone else in the office, who knows nothing of this change, uses your computer to produce a business letter, they will be surprised by the printout they receive. To get the letter printed in Courier 10 pitch as they want, they will have to take the extra step of changing the initial font for the document back to that font or issuing a base font change at the beginning of the document (discussed in the following section) before reprinting the letter.

To avoid such problems, you should use the Initial Font option on the Document Format menu to change the default font for the current document only. Use the Initial Font option on the Printer Edit menu only when you really aren't satisfied with the font selected by WordPerfect for your printer. If your office seldom, if ever, uses the font selected by the program, then you should change it permanently for the printer.

Using Different Fonts in the Document

When you use a new font that changes the type size or the type style (except for a boldface type), WordPerfect isn't able to display the effect of the change on the editing screen on most monitors. The only graphics cards capable of displaying changes to a font's size and style on the display screen are the Hercules graphics cards that support RamFont. (Hercules makes a monochrome and color graphics card with RamFont.) If your computer uses such a graphics card, you can see the effect of most changes on the editing screen. (See Chapter 1 for information on how to set WordPerfect to display different fonts with a Hercules RamFont graphics card.)

If you aren't fortunate enough to have one of these graphics cards, you won't be able to tell just by looking at the editing screen where a change to the font size or style has taken place. However, provided that your computer has a regular Hercules graphics card (or clone) or a color/graphics card, you can see the effect of a font change when you use the View Document feature (Shift-F7 V). Figure 5.13 shows you how various changes to the size and appearance of a type appear when previewed in this manner.

If your computer uses a standard monochrome card that doesn't have graphics capabilities, you will have to rely on the Reveal Codes screen to locate and verify where you have made font changes in the document and what kind. You can always use WordPerfect's Search feature to locate the Font Change codes that the program inserts when you make a font change. To do this, press F2 (→Search) or Shift-F2 (←Search) and then press Ctrl-F8 (Font). Select the appropriate option: Size (**1** or **S**), Appearance (**2** or **A**), or Base Font (**4** or **F**). If you select either Size or Appearance, you must select a suboption that further describes the change to be located.

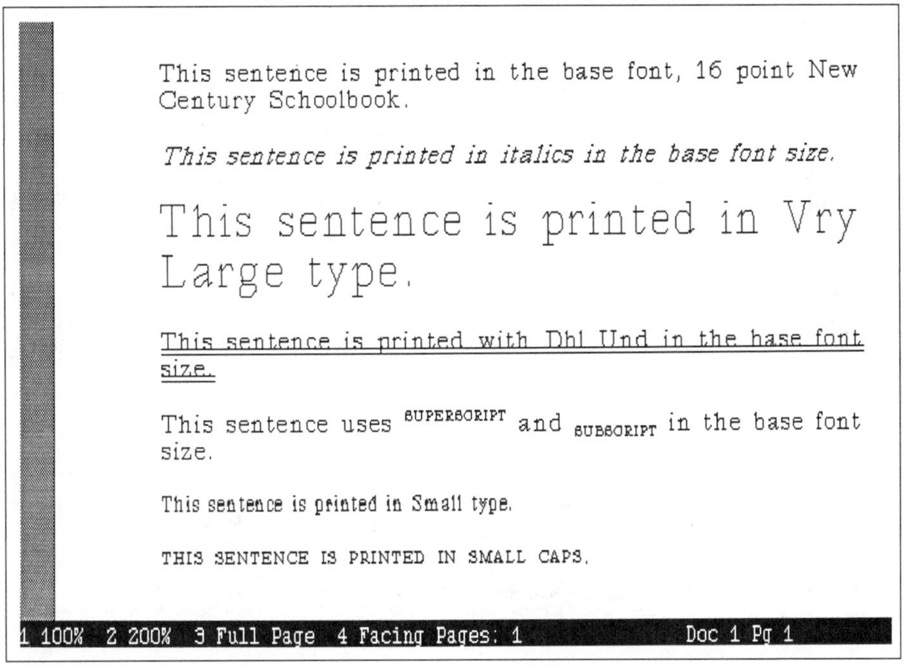

This sentence is printed in the base font, 16 point New Century Schoolbook.

This sentence is printed in italics in the base font size.

This sentence is printed in Vry Large type.

This sentence is printed with Dbl Und in the base font size.

This sentence uses SUPERSCRIPT and SUBSCRIPT in the base font size.

This sentence is printed in Small type.

THIS SENTENCE IS PRINTED IN SMALL CAPS.

1 100%   2 200%   3 Full Page   4 Facing Pages: 1   Doc 1 Pg 1

FIGURE 5.13: How various changes to the size and style of the type appear when previewed with the View Document feature (Shift-F7 V) at 100% (full size). In the regular document editing screen, none of these font changes are displayed—all of the type appears in the standard 10 pitch monospaced type. It is only in the View Document screen or in the printout that you can see the effect that each change to the size or appearance has on the type to be used.

After selecting the correct option, press F2 to have WordPerfect search for the first occurrence of its hidden code in the document.

WordPerfect gives you many methods for changing to different fonts within a document. When you want to change just the type size or type style (such as from medium to bold or from upright to italic) but retain the typeface designated as the initial font, you usually need to use only the Size and Appearance options on the Font menu (Ctrl-F8). When you want to intermix different typefaces (using the same or different type sizes and type styles), you use the Base Font option on the Font menu.

Changing the Base Font

The *base* font is so called because WordPerfect bases different type size and type style changes on it. Figures 5.14 and 5.15 illustrate this point.

In Figure 5.14, the first part of the sample employee manual was printed with the HP LaserJet Series II. The initial font selected by WordPerfect for this

WELCOME

Welcome to MagnaCorp. We hope this employee handbook will help to guide you through your first few days here. In addition, it contains valuable information about employee services and benefits available to you. Ask your manager or call the personnel office if you have any questions for which you cannot find the answers in this handbook.

ITEMS OF INTEREST

Work Day

The official work day at MagnaCorp is 8:30 A.M. to 5:00 P.M. Flexible hours can be arranged with your manager.

Parking

As parking is limited, please apply to the personnel office for a parking slot assignment.

Hours

Noon to 1:00 P.M. has been reserved as the lunch hour for all employees. Some departments have chosen to take lunch from 11:30 to 12:30 or from 12:30 to 1:30; check with your manager.

Cafeteria

The company cafeteria, located on the second floor, is open from 7:00 A.M. until 2:00 P.M. daily. Breakfast is available for your convenience until 9:00 A.M. After 2:00 P.M., vending machines with cold sandwiches and salads are available.

Recreational Facilities

MagnaCorp participates in the city recreational plan and therefore its employees have access to the municipal gym located at First and Stone Streets. The jogging track and par course in Grant Park are also nearby. Showers and lockers for company employees are located near the south entrance of the main lobby.

Vacation

Full-time permanent employees are eligible for two weeks of paid vacation after six months of continuous employment. During the first five years of service, you earn three weeks of vacation per year. After five years of service, you receive four weeks of vacation.

Credit Union

MagnaCorp's credit union is located on the third floor. Hours are from 9:00 A.M. to 6:00 P.M. daily. The credit union observes all national and bank holidays, whereas the company may or may not follow the same schedule.

FIGURE 5.14: The first part of the employee manual printed with the HP LaserJet Series II with 10 point Helvetica used as the base font. All of the text is printed in the Helvetica typeface instead of Courier because the base font overrides the initial font assigned to the printer. WordPerfect also assigned the sizes of the headings on this page (12 and 14 point) according to the type size of the base font.

WELCOME

Welcome to MagnaCorp. We hope this employee handbook will help to guide you through your first few days here. In addition, it contains valuable information about employee services and benefits available to you. Ask your manager or call the personnel office if you have any questions for which you cannot find the answers in this handbook.

ITEMS OF INTEREST

Work Day

The official work day at MagnaCorp is 8:30 A.M. to 5:00 P.M. Flexible hours can be arranged with your manager.

Parking

As parking is limited, please apply to the personnel office for a parking slot assignment.

Hours

Noon to 1:00 P.M. has been reserved as the lunch hour for all employees. Some departments have chosen to take lunch from 11:30 to 12:30 or from 12:30 to 1:30; check with your manager.

Cafeteria

The company cafeteria, located on the second floor, is open from 7:00 A.M. until 2:00 P.M. daily. Breakfast is available for your convenience until 9:00 A.M. After 2:00 P.M., vending machines with cold sandwiches and salads are available.

Recreational Facilities

MagnaCorp participates in the city recreational plan and therefore its employees have access to the municipal gym located at First and Stone Streets. The jogging track and par course in Grant Park are also nearby. Showers and lockers for company employees are located near the south entrance of the main lobby.

Vacation

Full-time permanent employees are eligible for two weeks of paid vacation after six months of continuous employment. During the first five years of service, you earn three weeks of vacation per year. After five years of service, you receive four weeks of vacation.

Credit Union

MagnaCorp's credit union is located on the third floor. Hours are from 9:00 A.M. to 6:00 P.M. daily. The credit union observes all national and bank holidays, whereas the company may or may not follow the same schedule.

FIGURE 5.15: The first part of the employee manual, this time printed with 10 point Times Roman as the base font. The typeface and type sizes used for the headings and the body on this page are now all based on the new font used.

printer is Courier 10 pitch. However, in this figure, 10 point Helvetica was selected as the base font. Furthermore, the size of the headings was changed with two of the Size options available from the Font menu. The main section headings, *WELCOME* and *ITEMS OF INTEREST,* are formatted with the Vry Large Size option in boldface. The secondary headings (*Work Day, Parking,* and so on), are formatted with the Large Size option.

As a result, the body is printed in 10 point Helvetica (the base font), the main headings are printed in 14 point Helvetica Bold, and the secondary headings are printed in 12 point Helvetica. The type size and style of both types of headings were automatically chosen by WordPerfect according to the base font selected. Both types of headings are printed in the Helvetica typeface because the base font is Helvetica. The 12 point size is assigned for Large and 14 point for Vry Large based on the 10 point size of the base font. In addition, the bold type style for the main headings in 14 point Helvetica was selected because the boldface soft font was installed instead of the regular typeface—WordPerfect selects sizes from among those that are installed for the printer.

Figure 5.15 shows you what happens if you change the base font. In this figure, the base font was changed from 10 point Helvetica to 10 point Times Roman. No other change was made; the codes for using the Vry Large and Large type sizes for the headings were not modified. In this printout, all of the type is now based on the Times Roman typeface in the 10 point type size. As a result, the main headings are printed in 14 point Times Roman Bold and the secondary headings are printed in 12 point Times Roman.

> *Note:* The type size and type style selected when you use the Size and Appearance options on the Font menu are based on the initial font for the printer or for the document (if you have changed the document initial font), if you don't insert a base font change in the document.

Changing the base font in a document is very easy. You simply position the cursor at the place in the document where you want the new font to begin printing and press Ctrl-F8 (Font). The following menu then appears:

1 Size; **2 A**ppearance; **3 N**ormal; **4 B**ase **F**ont; **5 P**rint **C**olor: 0

When you select the Base Font option (**4** or **F**), you see a full-screen list showing as many as possible of the resident fonts and fonts that you have installed. (This listing is identical to the one you see when changing the initial font, either for the printer or for the document.) Move the highlight cursor to the font you wish to use, and type **S** or press Enter to select it.

To locate a particular font on the list quickly, type **N** or press F2 for Name Search and type the first few characters of the font's name. To exit Name Search and leave the highlight bar on the font, press the Enter key or press one of the four cursor keys. Then, select the font as described above.

Changing the Font Size

WordPerfect gives you a wide range of choices in type size. To change the type size for the base font or initial font in effect, you press Ctrl-F8 (Font) and select the Size option (**1** or **S**) from the Font menu. When you do, the following menu options appear:

1 Suprscpt; **2 Su**bscpt; **3 F**ine; **4 S**mall; **5 L**arge; **6 V**ry Large; **7 E**xt Large: 0

The first two options, Suprscpt and Subscpt, are used to superscript and subscript text in a document. They print selected characters in a smaller size either above or below the line of type, if your printer has this capability. For information on how to add superscripts and subscripts to your text, refer to the section "Changing the Size of the Font" in the reference entry **Font** in Part V.

The Fine, Small, Large, Vry Large, and Ext Large options are used to change the type size without shifting the characters up or down on the line. All of the options on the Size menu work very much like the Bold key (F6) or the Underline key (F8). They put in a pair of codes (the first marking where the size change begins and the second marking where it ends) and position the cursor between them. For example, if you select the Small option (**4** or **S**) and you look at the Reveal Codes screen (Alt-F3), you see that WordPerfect has inserted the codes

[SMALL][small]

and located the highlight cursor on the [small] code. When you are finished entering the text that is to be affected, you must be sure to move the cursor beyond the last code by selecting the Normal option on the Font menu (Ctrl-F8 N). You can accomplish the same thing by pressing the → key one time.

You can also add these size changes to existing text in the document. To do this, you press Alt-F4 (Block) and mark the text, press Ctrl-F8 (Font), select the Size option (**1** or **S**), and choose the number or letter of the appropriate option from the Size menu.

The actual size of the type used when you select one of the Size options depends upon the base font (or initial font, if no base font is selected) as well as the capabilities of your printer and the number and types of fonts you have installed for it. Figures 5.16 and 5.17 illustrate this point.

In Figure 5.16, sample sentences have been printed using the QMS-PS 810 laser printer (a PostScript laser printer that is comparable to the Apple LaserWriter Plus or II NT) using 12 point ITC Avant Garde Gothic Book as the base font. The first sentence has been sized by selecting the Fine Size option. The second sentence has been sized by selecting the Small Size option. The third sentence is printed using the base font, which was designated as 12 point. The last three sample sentences were printed by selecting the Large, Vry Large, and Ext Large Size options respectively. Because the QMS-PS 810 is equipped with PostScript, it is able to scale the size of the font at print time. It is WordPerfect, however, that selects the actual sizes to be used, based on the size selected for the base font.

Note: PostScript printers like the LaserWriter and the QMS laser printers allow you to specify the font size in points when you select a particular typeface as the base font or initial font. Non-PostScript printers like the HP LaserJet printers don't have this capability; to change the type size for a typeface, you must select a separate font on the Base Font menu.

In this figure, the type size of the base font was specified as 12 point, using the ITC Avant Garde Gothic Book typeface (one of those that is resident in the QMS-PS 810). Based on the 12 point size, WordPerfect selected 10 point in this typeface as the type size when the Small Size option was used in the second sentence and 8 point when the Fine option was selected in the first sentence. For the larger sizes, still based on the 12 point size of the base font, the program selected 14 point when the Large Size option was used in the fourth sentence, 24 point when the Vry Large option was used in the fifth sentence, and 30 point when the Ext Large option was used in the last sentence.

Note: The point size of a typeface is not based on the size in points of its upper-case letters. Instead, it is the measurement in points from the tip of an *ascender* (a letter, like lowercase *d* or *t*, that extends above the standard height or *x-height* of the other lowercase letters) to the tip of a *descender* (a letter, like lowercase *p* or *g*, that extends below the baseline of the other letters). Therefore, to accurately determine the type size in these sample sentences (shown full size in Figure 5.16), you would need to use a point scale and measure the distance from the bottom of the lowercase *p* to the top of the *t* in the word *printed* in each sentence.

Figure 5.17 demonstrates what happens if you just change the size of the base font. In this figure the same size options are assigned to the sample sentences as were assigned in Figure 5.16. However, because the size of the base font was increased from 12 point to 14 point, the type sizes assigned by the Fine, Small, Large, Vry Large, and Ext Large Size options increased as well. As a result, the type printed with the Fine option in this figure is now 10 point, that produced with the Small option is 12 point, that with the Large option is 18 point, that with the Vry Large option is 30 point, and, finally, that with Ext Large option is 36 point.

Changing the Appearance of the Font

The Appearance option (**2** or **A**) on the Font menu (Ctrl-F8) controls the style of the printing. When you select Appearance, the following options become available:

1 Bold; **2 U**ndrln; **3 D**bl Und; **4 I**talc; **5 O**utln; **6 S**hadw; **7 S**m **C**ap; **8 R**edln; **9 S**tkout: 0

The first two options, Bold and Undrln, can also be accessed by pressing their own keys: F6 to boldface text and F8 to underline text. All nine of these options work like F6 or F8; when you select an enhancement (like italics, by pressing **4** or **I**) WordPerfect puts in a pair of codes—the first turns on the enhancement and

This sentence is printed in *FINE* size.

This sentence is printed in *SMALL* size.

This sentence is printed in the size of the *BASE FONT*.

This sentence is printed in *Large* size.

This sentence is printed in *Very Large* type.

This sentence is printed in *Extra Large* type.

FIGURE 5.16: Samples of the type sizes produced when using the Size options from Fine to Ext Large with 12 point ITC Avant Garde Gothic Book as the base font. Using the Fine option produces 8 point type, Small produces 10 point type, Large produces 14 point type, Vry Large produces 24 point type, and Ext Large produces 30 point type.

This sentence is printed in *FINE* size.

This sentence is printed in *SMALL* size.

This sentence is printed in the size of the *BASE FONT.*

This sentence is printed in *Large* size.

This sentence is printed in *Very Large* type.

This sentence is printed in *Extra Large* type.

FIGURE 5.17: Samples of the type sizes produced with the Size options from Fine to Ext Large when the ITC Avant Garde Gothic Book base font is increased from 12 point to 14 point. Because of the increase of 2 points in the size of the base font, using the Fine option here produces 10 point type, Small produces 12 point type, Large produces 18 point type, Vry Large produces 30 point type, and Ext Large produces 36 point type.

the second turns it off—and positions the cursor between them. When you are finished entering the text that is to be affected by the enhancement, be sure to position the cursor beyond the second code by pressing Ctrl-F8 (Font) and selecting the Normal option (**3** or **N**). You can also do this by pressing the → key one time.

If you want to use one of these enhancements on existing text, press Alt-F4 (Block), mark the text, and then press Ctrl-F8 (Font). Select the Appearance option (**2** or **A**) and then choose the number or letter of the enhancement you want to apply to the marked text.

Figure 5.18 shows you a sample printout that uses each of the nine print enhancements (or attributes) that you can choose from the Appearance menu. This figure was printed with the QMS-PS 810 laser printer with 16 point Palatino selected as the base font. (This is one of the resident fonts built into PostScript printers like this one and the Apple LaserWriter Plus and II NT and NTX.)

Many printers aren't capable of producing all of the enhancements available from the Appearance menu, especially small caps, italic, outline, and shadow type. If you select an attribute that your printer isn't capable of producing, WordPerfect will try to substitute another that is supported. For example, if you specify italics for a portion of your text and your printer or the font you've selected isn't capable of printing italics, WordPerfect will underline the text that has been assigned this enhancement. If this type of substitution isn't possible, the text enhancement will be ignored and the designated text will be printed in the base font (or initial font, if you haven't used a base font).

Determining What Effects Your Printer Can Produce

You can use the PRINTER.TST file, located on the WordPerfect Conversion disk, to help you determine which features your printer can produce with the program. The PRINTER.TST file will print special features such as superscripts and subscripts, underlining, redline and strikeout, tab aligning and columns, advance up and down, and a figure containing a graphic (if your printer is capable). To use it, just retrieve the PRINTER.TST file to the editing screen (using Shift-F10) and print it by pressing Shift-F7 (Print) and selecting the Full Document option (**1** or **F**). You should try printing the PRINTER.TST document with each of the printers you have installed for WordPerfect. You can also try printing it after selecting a new base font to find out what difference, if any, the font change has on WordPerfect's printing capabilities as well as to judge how your printout will appear using that particular font.

Mixing Fonts in a Document

WordPerfect makes it very easy to mix different fonts in the same document by changing the base font. Each time you change the base font, WordPerfect

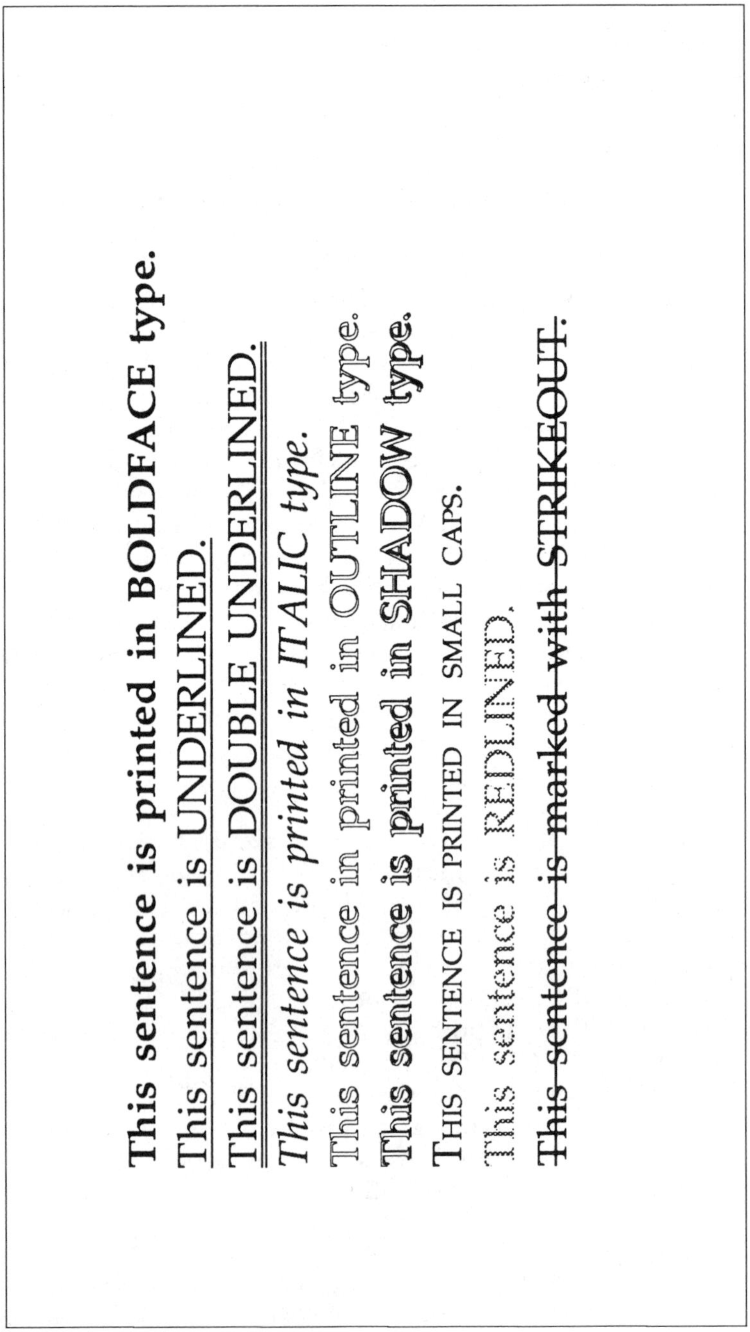

This sentence is printed in **BOLDFACE type.**

This sentence is UNDERLINED.

This sentence is DOUBLE UNDERLINED.

This sentence is printed in ITALIC type.

This sentence in printed in OUTLINE type.

This sentence is printed in SHADOW type.

This sentence is printed in small caps.

This sentence is REDLINED.

This sentence is marked with STRIKEOUT.

FIGURE 5.18: Samples of the text enhancements possible when using the options available on the Appearance menu. The text in this figure was printed by the QMS-PS 810 PostScript laser printer using 16 point Palatino (one of its resident fonts) as the base font.

inserts a Font Change code that describes the new typeface, type size, and type style (if applicable). The font that you choose with the Base Font option affects all of the text from the cursor's position to the end of the document (or to the next Font Change code, if one occurs).

To verify that a font change has been made (and where it has been made), you can use the Reveal Codes key (Alt-F3) to locate this code. For instance, if you select 12 point Times Roman as the new base font, you will see the code

[Font:Tms Rmn 12pt (AC)]

in the Reveal Codes screen at the place in the document where the cursor was positioned when you selected the Base Font option (Ctrl-F8 F). Remember that changing the base font in a document also affects the fonts that WordPerfect uses when you select different text sizes with the Size options and text enhancements with the Appearance options.

You can use the Base Font option on the Font menu to continue to add new fonts as needed. However, you must be mindful of the total number of different fonts that your printer will support in WordPerfect. (For example, the maximum is 16 for the HP LaserJet Series II.) Normally, you will not want to mix more than two different typefaces on the same page, although you may find the need to use these typefaces in different sizes and styles. (See Chapter 19 for more information on selecting the appropriate typeface for the publication you are designing in WordPerfect.)

Figure 5.19 illustrates how you can combine two different fonts in a document to add interest. This figure shows the first part of a page of the sample employee manual, printed with the QMS-PS 810 using its resident fonts. The headings are printed in ITC Bookman Demi, upright and italic. The first main heading, *WELCOME,* is printed in 24 point, and the second main heading, *ITEMS OF INTEREST,* is printed in 16 point. The secondary headings, printed in the italic type style for this typeface, are printed in 14 point. The body copy is printed in 10 point ITC Avant Garde Book.

If you ever select a font incorrectly when using the Base Font option, you can just locate the Font Change code in the Reveal Codes screen and delete it. To return to the use of a base font selected earlier in the text, just select the Base Font option and choose the name of the font selected previously.

Font Substitution

When you switch to a new printer, WordPerfect will substitute the fonts selected according to the capabilities of that printer. For example, if you create a document with the Epson FX-80 dot matrix printer as the selected printer and change the base font or the initial font for the document to 12 cpi (that is, 12 pitch) and later select a laser printer for final printing, WordPerfect will substitute the Line Printer font in 16.66 pitch. Because the HP LaserJet Series II

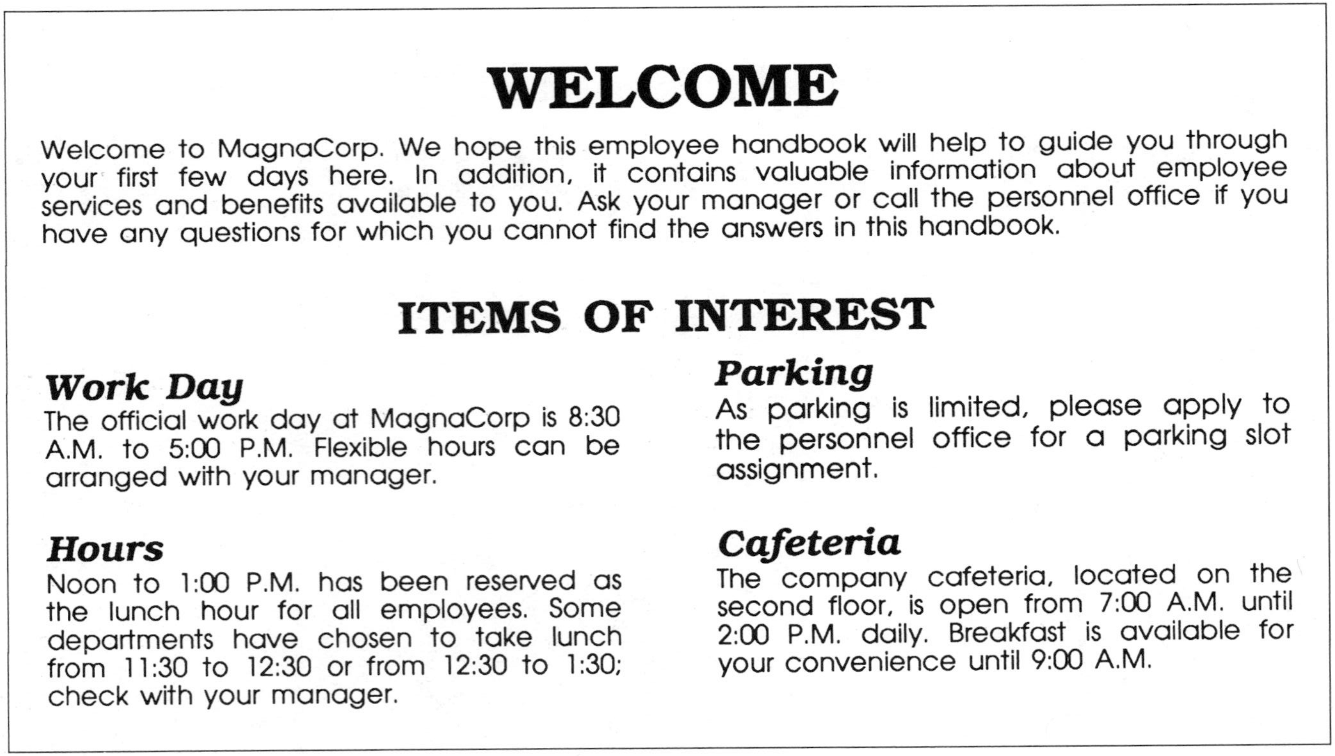

WELCOME

Welcome to MagnaCorp. We hope this employee handbook will help to guide you through your first few days here. In addition, it contains valuable information about employee services and benefits available to you. Ask your manager or call the personnel office if you have any questions for which you cannot find the answers in this handbook.

ITEMS OF INTEREST

Work Day

The official work day at MagnaCorp is 8:30 A.M. to 5:00 P.M. Flexible hours can be arranged with your manager.

Hours

Noon to 1:00 P.M. has been reserved as the lunch hour for all employees. Some departments have chosen to take lunch from 11:30 to 12:30 or from 12:30 to 1:30; check with your manager.

Parking

As parking is limited, please apply to the personnel office for a parking slot assignment.

Cafeteria

The company cafeteria, located on the second floor, is open from 7:00 A.M. until 2:00 P.M. daily. Breakfast is available for your convenience until 9:00 A.M.

FIGURE 5.19: Combining different typefaces to add interest to the first page of the sample employee manual. This page was printed on a QMS-PS 810 PostScript printer using some of its resident fonts. The headings are printed in ITC Bookman Demi, upright and italic. The body text is printed in 10 point ITC Avant Garde Book.

doesn't have a built-in 12 pitch font, its resident compressed font in 16.66 pitch is the closest possible match.

Figure 5.20 illustrates an example of font substitution, this time involving soft fonts. It shows the editing screen for the first part of the sample document (whose printout is shown in Figure 5.19) after the printer was changed from the LaserWriter Plus to the HP LaserJet Series II. The document was originally created with the LaserWriter Plus as the selected printer, using various resident downloadable fonts as described in the previous section. Because the HP LaserJet Series II does not support these fonts, new fonts were substituted as soon as the HP LaserJet Series II was selected.

Notice in the Reveal Codes screen in Figure 5.20 that each of the names of the fonts shown in the [Font] codes is now preceded by an asterisk. This indicates that these fonts were substituted and are not the original fonts selected with the Base Font option (Ctrl-F8 F). Any time WordPerfect performs font substitution, it will place an asterisk in front of the font name when viewed in the Reveal Codes screen.

Figure 5.21 shows you the printout of the document using the new printer. Contrast the fonts used in the printout shown in this figure with those in Figure 5.19. The first heading, *WELCOME,* is now printed in Times Roman in the same size as the heading in Figure 5.19, which used ITC Bookman Demi. Times Roman is the closest to the ITC Bookman Demi that is available for this printer. Notice, however, that the heading *ITEMS OF INTEREST* in Figure 5.20 does

```
                           WELCOME
_
Welcome to MagnaCorp. We hope this employee handbook will help to guide you thr
days here. In addition, it contains valuable information about employee service
you. Ask your manager or call the personnel office if you have any questions fo
answers in this handbook.
                      ITEMS OF INTEREST
Work Day                          Parking
The official work day at MagnaCorp As parking is limited, please apply to the
to 5:00 P.M. Flexible hours can be personnel office for a parking slot assignme
your manager.

D:\WP\WDC\FIG5-17.DOC                          Doc 2 Pg 1 Ln 1" Pos 1"
(       ▲    ▲    ▲    ▲     ▲    ▲      ▲    ▲    ▲    ▲    )    ▲        ▲
[Font:*Tms Rmn 24pt Bold (AC)][Cntr]WELCOME[C/A/Flrt][Ln Height:0.62"][HRt]
[Font:*Helv 10pt (AC)][Ln Height:Auto]Welcome to MagnaCorp. We hope this employe
e handbook will help to guide you through your first few[SRt]
days here. In addition, it contains valuable information about employee services
 and benefits available to[SRt]
you. Ask your manager or call the personnel office if you have any questions for
 which you cannot find the[SRt]
answers in this handbook.[HRt]
[Ln Height:0.62"][Font:*Helv 18pt Bold (AC)][Cntr]ITEMS OF INTEREST[Ln Height:0.
62"][C/A/Flrt][HRt]

Press Reveal Codes to restore screen
```

FIGURE 5.20: Reveal Codes screen demonstrating font substitution. Fonts that were substituted by WordPerfect rather than selected by the user are marked with an asterisk.

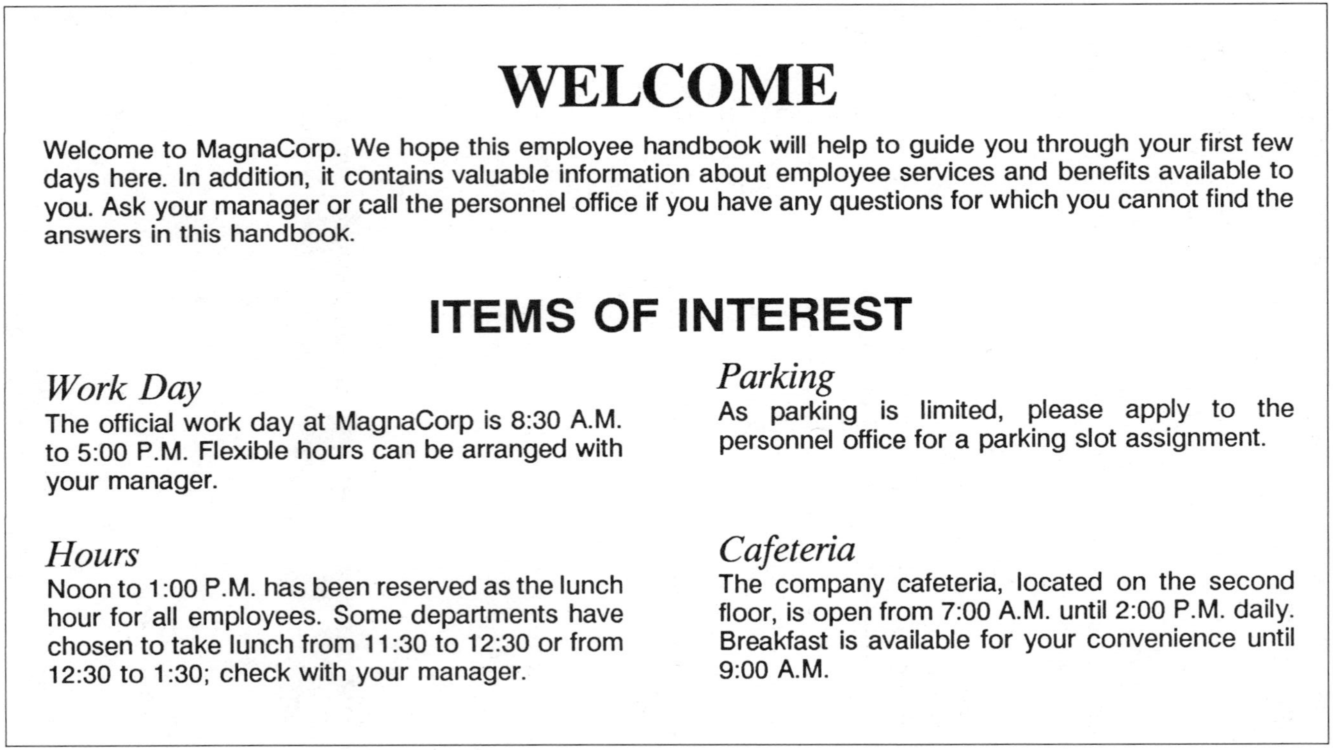

WELCOME

Welcome to MagnaCorp. We hope this employee handbook will help to guide you through your first few days here. In addition, it contains valuable information about employee services and benefits available to you. Ask your manager or call the personnel office if you have any questions for which you cannot find the answers in this handbook.

ITEMS OF INTEREST

Work Day

The official work day at MagnaCorp is 8:30 A.M. to 5:00 P.M. Flexible hours can be arranged with your manager.

Hours

Noon to 1:00 P.M. has been reserved as the lunch hour for all employees. Some departments have chosen to take lunch from 11:30 to 12:30 or from 12:30 to 1:30; check with your manager.

Parking

As parking is limited, please apply to the personnel office for a parking slot assignment.

Cafeteria

The company cafeteria, located on the second floor, is open from 7:00 A.M. until 2:00 P.M. daily. Breakfast is available for your convenience until 9:00 A.M.

FIGURE 5.21: Printout of the document in Figure 5.19, showing the effects of font substitution. For this printout, the printer was changed from the LaserWriter Plus to the HP LaserJet Series II.

not use Times Roman, although it too was printed in ITC Bookman in the original printout. Instead, it uses Helvetica in the same size. This occurred because Times Roman was not installed for the HP LaserJet Series II in the same size as specified in the original document. Whenever WordPerfect can't find an analogous type style in the specified size, it substitutes another type style that is available in the required size.

Notice also that the italicized headings were not printed in boldface when the HP LaserJet Series II was used. This is because there are no italic bold type styles available for this printer. Rather than resort to an upright bold type, Word-Perfect has retained the italics in normal weight during font substitution.

> *Note:* When you switch back to the printer under which the fonts were originally selected, the asterisks shown in the Reveal Codes screen disappear—sometimes you have to move the cursor on or over the font before this happens—and the fonts originally selected are used when you next print the document on the original printer.

If you change to a new printer, you should use the Reveal Codes screen to check what font substitution has taken place. If you see a [Font] code that contains only an asterisk, it will expand to show you the name of the substituted font when you position the cursor on it. If necessary, you can override the automatic substitutions by inserting a base font change immediately after the substituted font. That way, you can ensure that the fonts used in the printout with the new printer match as closely as possible those originally selected.

To minimize font substitution problems when you use a dot matrix printer for rough drafts and a laser printer for final printouts, you should select the laser printer before you create the document and choose your fonts according to the printer's capabilities. Although font size and attribute substitutions will often occur in the rough draft printout made with the dot matrix printer, you will then experience no problems with formatting and font changes in the final printed version. This technique of creating the document and selecting the fonts for the printer that is ultimately to be used to produce the final output should even be followed when you are planning to use a laser printer you don't own (such as one at the local copy service) to print the final version of a document.

REGULATING THE LINE, WORD, AND LETTER SPACING

WordPerfect automatically adjusts the spacing between the lines, words, and letters within words when you select a new font. You may sometimes want to modify the spacing between lines of type, between the words in a line, and even between letters within a word. WordPerfect includes commands that give you control over all of these, allowing you to further refine the final look of your document.

Line Height

The line height is the distance from the baseline of one line to the baseline of the next line. Figure 5.22 illustrates what is meant by the baseline; the lines drawn beneath each line of type in this figure represent the baselines. WordPerfect automatically determines the line height for the size of the font you are using. If you increase the line spacing from single spacing to double spacing, WordPerfect increases the line height to suit.

When you use different sizes of fonts in the same line, the program will base the line spacing on the largest size used. Figure 5.23 illustrates this point. In this figure, the type size has been increased from 12 to 24 point (bold italic) type for part of the text. WordPerfect automatically increases the line height between the first four lines to accommodate the mix of 24 point and 12 point type. In the third line, which contains both sizes of type, the line height is based on the largest type (24 point) in the line.

In publishing, the difference in points between the line height (the distance between the baselines of two lines of type) and the type size is referred to as the *leading* (or *ledding*). For example, if you use 10 point type in a paragraph, Word-Perfect assigns a line height of 11 points between the lines, giving you a leading of 1 point. If you change the type size to 12 points, WordPerfect assigns a new line height of 13 points, again maintaining a leading of 1 point (although the leading will eventually increase as you continue to increase the type size).

When you want to maintain a constant line height between one line of type and the next, or within a group of lines, you use the Line Height option on the Line Format menu. To get to this option, you press Shift-F8 (Format) and select the Line option (**1** or **L**) followed by the Line Height option (**4** or **H**). The default setting for this option is Auto, which means that WordPerfect automatically determines the line height according to the sizes of type used. When you select this option, you see that you can also select Fixed line spacing by typing **2** or **F**.

1 Auto; **2** Fixed: 0

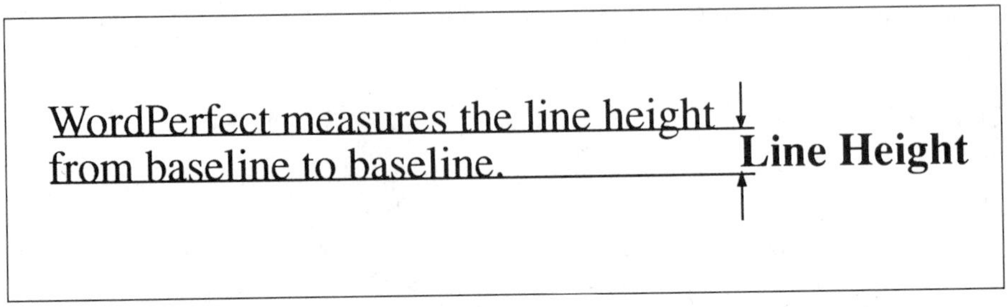

WordPerfect measures the line height from baseline to baseline. **Line Height**

FIGURE 5.22: How line height is measured by WordPerfect. In this figure, the baselines of the two lines of type are drawn. The vertical distance between these two lines represents the line height that is designated either by you or by WordPerfect.

Welcome to MagnaCorp. We hope this employee handbook will help to

guide you through your first few days here. In addition, it contains valuable information about employee services and benefits available to you. Ask your manager or call the personnel office if you have any questions for which you cannot find the answers in this handbook.

FIGURE 5.23: The effect of mixed font sizes on the line height selected by WordPerfect. The line heights between the first and second, second and third, and third and fourth lines of type have been increased to accommodate the mix of 24 point and 12 point type. In the third line, which contains both sizes of type, the line height is based on the largest type (24 point) in the line.

When you select the Fixed option, the program displays the current line height, using the unit of measure in effect for the display of numbers, and positions the cursor on it. You are then free to type in a new line height measurement. You can enter this distance in inches or points. If the default unit of measure for the display of numbers is inches and you want to enter the line height in points, you must terminate the number with a *p* as in **24p**. If the default unit of measure for the display of numbers is points and you want to enter the line height in inches, you must terminate the number with the quotation mark as in **.25"** or an *i* as in **25i**. Press F7 (Exit) to return to the document when you have entered the correct line height.

WordPerfect inserts a Line Height code in the document at the cursor's position. For example, if you change the line height to a fixed distance of .25 inch, you will see

[Ln Height:0.25"]

when you press Alt-F3 (Reveal Codes) to display the Reveal Codes screen.

When you change the line height in this manner, it remains in effect from that point forward in the document until you change it again. To have WordPerfect once again determine the line height, you repeat the key sequence (Shift-F8 L H) and select the Auto option (**1** or **A**).

When you return to the document editing screen after changing the line height, you will not be able to distinguish the new line height on the screen. To see the effect of changing the line height, you must use View Document (Shift-F7 V) and change the view to full size (100%), or print the document. You will, however, notice a difference on the Ln indicator on the status line when you move the cursor up and down the lines.

Figure 5.24 shows the effect of increasing the line height between lines of body copy for four identical paragraphs. The first paragraph uses the automatic line height assigned by WordPerfect. Because the body type is 12 point and the automatic line height is 13, the leading is only 1 point, which is somewhat tight when a person is reading a great deal of copy. The second paragraph increases the leading to 2 points by assigning a fixed line height of 14 points to the text. The last two sample paragraphs increase the leading to 3 and 4 points by increasing the fixed line height to 15 and 16 points, respectively.

Many times, you can use the Line Height feature instead of increasing the line spacing to enlarge the amount of space between two lines. This is particularly effective in cases where you use a large type size for a heading to contrast with a smaller type size for the body copy. If you add an extra blank line between the heading and the body text, you can end up with too much space between them. However, if you change the line height between the heading and the body text, you can precisely control the distance between the two.

The paragraph to the right uses the automatic line height assigned by WordPerfect. The type size used is 12 point and the line height is 13 point, giving you a leading of 1 point.

The paragraph to the right increases the line height by using a fixed line height of 14 points. With 12 point type, this gives you a leading of 2 points.

Welcome to MagnaCorp. We hope this employee handbook will help to guide you through your first few days here. In addition, it contains valuable information about employee services and benefits available to you. Ask your manager or call the personnel office if you have any questions for which you cannot find the answers in this handbook.

Welcome to MagnaCorp. We hope this employee handbook will help to guide you through your first few days here. In addition, it contains valuable information about employee services and benefits available to you. Ask your manager or call the personnel office if you have any questions for which you cannot find the answers in this handbook.

FIGURE 5.24: The effect of progressively increasing the line height on four identical paragraphs printed in 12 point type. The first paragraph uses the automatic line height assigned by WordPerfect, 12/13 ("12 on 13"), for a leading of 1 point. The second increases the leading to 2 points by using a fixed line height of 14 points (12/14). The third paragraph increases the leading to 3 points by using a fixed line height of 15 points (12/15). Finally, the fourth paragraph increases the leading even further to 4 points by using a fixed line height of 16 points (12/16).

The paragraph to the right increases the line height by using a fixed line height of 15 points. With 12 point type, this gives you a leading of 3 points.

Welcome to MagnaCorp. We hope this employee handbook will help to guide you through your first few days here. In addition, it contains valuable information about employee services and benefits available to you. Ask your manager or call the personnel office if you have any questions for which you cannot find the answers in this handbook.

The paragraph to the right increases the line height by using a fixed line height of 16 points. With 12 point type, this gives you a leading of 4 points.

Welcome to MagnaCorp. We hope this employee handbook will help to guide you through your first few days here. In addition, it contains valuable information about employee services and benefits available to you. Ask your manager or call the personnel office if you have any questions for which you cannot find the answers in this handbook.

FIGURE 5.24: The effect of progressively increasing the line height on four identical paragraphs printed in 12 point type (continued).

Figure 5.25 illustrates this situation. It shows three identical paragraphs with a heading. The heading is printed in Palatino Bold and the paragraph text is printed in ITC Bookman Light. In the first example, WordPerfect's automatic line height is used, and the heading is quite close to the body of the text in the paragraph. In the second example, WordPerfect's automatic line height is still used, but this time a blank line is entered between the heading and the text of the paragraph. This places too much space between the heading and its text. In the third example, the line height between the heading and the text of the paragraph is controlled with a fixed line height that separates the heading sufficiently from the body of the text without separating it too much.

Welcome

Welcome to MagnaCorp. We hope this employee handbook will help to guide you through your first few days here. In addition, it contains valuable information about employee services and benefits available to you. Ask your manager or call the personnel office if you have any questions for which you cannot find the answers in this handbook.

Welcome

Welcome to MagnaCorp. We hope this employee handbook will help to guide you through your first few days here. In addition, it contains valuable information about employee services and benefits available to you. Ask your manager or call the personnel office if you have any questions for which you cannot find the answers in this handbook.

Welcome

Welcome to MagnaCorp. We hope this employee handbook will help to guide you through your first few days here. In addition, it contains valuable information about employee services and benefits available to you. Ask your manager or call the personnel office if you have any questions for which you cannot find the answers in this handbook.

FIGURE 5.25: Controlling the vertical spacing between specific lines that use two different type sizes. In all three examples in this figure, the heading is printed in Palatino Bold and the body text is printed in ITC Bookman Light. In the first example, WordPerfect's automatic line height is used, and the result is that the heading is quite close to the body text. In the example below it, automatic line height is still used and an extra blank line is inserted to increase the spacing between the heading and the body text. The result here is that the heading is too far from the body text. In the third example, fixed line height is used to place the heading exactly where it is wanted in relation to the text of the paragraph.

Controlling the Word and Letter Spacing

The vertical spacing between lines is not the only spacing you can control in WordPerfect. You can also modify the horizontal spacing between words in a line and the spacing between letters in a particular word. However, you must realize that WordPerfect doesn't give you anything like the degree of control over word and letter spacing that is possible with stand-alone desktop publishing programs like PageMaker or Ventura Publisher, let alone with typesetting equipment.

CHANGING TO A RAGGED-RIGHT MARGIN

Most word spacing problems in WordPerfect are encountered when you format your text with justification activated (the program default). In order to right-justify the text, WordPerfect must fill out the line with white space between words. Many times, this causes unsightly rivers of white space that angle down the paragraph. This problem is exacerbated when you format the text in columns or are forced to use wide left and right margins, resulting in a relatively narrow line length.

The easiest way to cure this kind of problem is to turn off justification so that the document has a ragged-right margin. When you turn off justification, the spacing between words in all lines of the text is uniform, regardless of whether you are using a monospaced font or a proportionally spaced font for the text.

Figures 5.26 and 5.27 illustrate the difference between right-justified and ragged-right margins for text that is formatted in a narrow column. In the first figure, where justification is turned on, some of the words are spaced too far apart because of the short line length. In the second figure, where justification is turned off, the spacing between the words is uniform, making it a little easier to read. However, the right margin is very ragged due to the short line length.

You can use WordPerfect's Hyphenation feature to help control the spacing between words. By breaking words at the end of the line, you can often reduce extra white space between words when justification is turned on, and reduce the raggedness of the right margin when justification is turned off. See Chapter 3 for complete information on how to use the Hyphenation feature.

ADJUSTING THE WORD/LETTER SPACING

WordPerfect automatically sets the spacing between words and between letters within a word. You can modify the spacing by pressing Shift-F8 (Format), selecting the Other option (4 or **O**), and then choosing the Printer Functions option (6 or **P**). From the Printer Functions menu, you then select the Word Spacing option (3 or **W**). When you do, you are presented with these menu options for

Recreational Facilities

MagnaCorp participates in the municipal recreational plan and therefore its employees have access to the city gymnasium located at First and Stone Streets. The jogging track and par course in Grant Park are also nearby. Showers and lockers for company employees are located near the south entrance of the main lobby.

Vacation

Full-time permanent employees are eligible for two weeks of paid vacation after six months of continuous employment. During the first five years of service, you earn three weeks of vacation per year. After five years of service, you receive four weeks of vacation.

Credit Union

MagnaCorp's credit union is located on the third floor. Hours are from 9:00 A.M. to 6:00 P.M. daily. The credit union observes all national and bank holidays, whereas the company may or may not follow the same schedule.

FIGURE 5.26: Justified text, formatted in a narrow column. In this figure, the shortness of the line length combined with the use of justification causes irregularities in word spacing. Refer to Figure 5.27 to see the effect that changing to ragged-right margins has on legibility.

Recreational Facilities

MagnaCorp participates in the municipal recreational plan and therefore its employees have access to the city gymnasium located at First and Stone Streets. The jogging track and par course in Grant Park are also nearby. Showers and lockers for company employees are located near the south entrance of the main lobby.

Vacation

Full-time permanent employees are eligible for two weeks of paid vacation after six months of continuous employment. During the first five years of service, you earn three weeks of vacation per year. After five years of service, you receive four weeks of vacation.

Credit Union

MagnaCorp's credit union is located on the third floor. Hours are from 9:00 A.M. to 6:00 P.M. daily. The credit union observes all national and bank holidays, whereas the company may or may not follow the same schedule.

FIGURE 5.27: Ragged-right margins used on text in a narrow column to correct the word spacing problems. Changing from justification to this formatting ensures that all word spacing will be equal. Unfortunately, it also results in an extremely ragged right margin. The best way to combat this problem is to use WordPerfect's Hyphenation feature to help even out the lines.

controlling the word spacing:

Word Spacing: **1 N**ormal; **2 O**ptimal; **3 P**ercent of Optimal; **4 S**et Pitch: 2

After you select one of the options on this menu, you see a Letter Spacing menu containing the same four options.

The Optimal option is the default for both word and letter spacing. This represents what the software engineers at WordPerfect Corporation feel is the best word/letter spacing for the printer you are using. However, in a few cases, this may differ slightly from the printer manufacturer's suggested word and letter spacing. Therefore, WordPerfect provides the Normal option (**1** or **N**), which allows you to pick the manufacturer's spacing rather than WordPerfect's. (For most printers, changing either the word or letter spacing to normal will have no effect.)

To override either the manufacturer's or WordPerfect's word or letter spacing, you can use either the Percent of Optimal option (**3** or **P**) or the Set Pitch option (**4** or **S**). To enter a new word or letter spacing using the Percent of Optimal option, you enter a number that represents the percentage of the optimal setting. If you enter a percentage below 100 (100 percent is the same as optimal), WordPerfect will reduce the amount of space between words if you are setting the word spacing or between letters within words if you are setting the letter spacing. Entering percentages above 100 has the opposite effect of increasing the space.

To enter a new word or letter spacing using the Set Pitch option, you enter a number that represents the new pitch in characters per inch. The pitch that you specify is automatically translated to the correct percent of optimal spacing required to maintain it for the font you are currently using.

You will probably find the Percent of Optimal option better suited for adjusting the word or letter spacing for a font on a laser printer. On the other hand, you will probably find the Set Pitch option better suited for adjusting the word or letter spacing for a font on a dot matrix printer. Note, however, that not all printers are able to adjust the spacing as precisely as the new word or letter spacing setting indicates. This is just one of those features that you must experiment with to see what works best with the type of printer you are using.

Figures 5.28 through 5.30 illustrate a typical situation under which you would use this feature to override the default optimal spacing assigned by WordPerfect. The sample sentence in Figure 5.28 is printed in 24 point Palatino type on a QMS-PS 810 laser printer with justification activated. Notice that the word spacing in the first line is a little too loose.

To tighten it up, the Word/Letter spacing option is selected and the Percent of Optimal option is used to set the word spacing at 60 percent of the optimal. (The letter spacing is kept at optimal, since the problem is between words and not between the letters within words.) Figure 5.29 shows you the result of this change. When you use the Word/Letter spacing option on the Printer Functions

WordPerfect 5.0 allows you to modify both the spacing between words in the line and the spacing between letters in the words.

FIGURE 5.28: A single sentence printed in 24 point type using WordPerfect's optimal word and letter spacing. Notice that the first line is set a little too loose. See Figure 5.29 to observe the effect that changing the word spacing for this sentence has on this problem.

WordPerfect 5.0 allows you to modify both the spacing between words in the line and the spacing between letters in the words.

FIGURE 5.29: The same sentence as used in Figure 5.28, this time with the word spacing set to 60 percent of optimal and the letter spacing kept at optimal. Although changing the word spacing for the sentence takes care of the looseness in the first line, it creates a new problem of a stack at the beginning of the second and third lines—the phrase *the spacing between* is repeated in the sentence, and the two occurrences are now set directly on top of each other.

WordPerfect 5.0 allows you to modify both the spacing between words in the line and the spacing between letters in the words.

FIGURE 5.30: A third example, in which the word spacing in the first line is still set to 60 percent of optimal to tighten up the spacing there. However, the word spacing has been set back to 100 percent in the second and third lines to take care of the stack that appeared in Figure 5.29.

menu, WordPerfect inserts a hidden code at the cursor's position. In this case, the code

[Wrd/Ltr Spacing:60% of Optimal,Optimal]

is inserted immediately ahead of the *W* in *WordPerfect* following the Font Change code. The first figure in the Word/Letter spacing code, *60% of Optimal,* describes the new word spacing, while the second, *Optimal,* describes the letter spacing.

Notice in Figure 5.29 that changing to 60% of Optimal has tightened the word spacing enough that the word *both* has been pulled up to the first line. Although this takes care of the looseness of the first line, it creates another problem. Observe that the phrase *the spacing between,* repeated twice in the sentence, is now exactly aligned in the second and third lines, creating a "stack." This kind of alignment is to be avoided at all costs because it is far too easy for the reader to lose his or her place in the sentence. Often, when readers are confronted with a stack at the beginning of lines in a paragraph, they skip to the second of the lines, missing the text in the line above.

To eliminate this problem, the cursor is positioned at the beginning of the second line, and the Word/Letter Spacing option is used again. This time, both the word and letter spacing are set to optimal. Figure 5.30 shows the result of this change: although the last two lines are now set looser than the first line, the stack has been taken care of.

When you use the Word/Letter Spacing option to loosen or tighten words or letters in lines of text, you will not be able to see the results of the change on the editing screen (which remains monospaced no matter what typographic change is made to a font). Moreover, you are often not able to discern the difference even when you use the View Document option (Shift-F7 V) to preview it at 100 or 200 percent before printing, unless the change to the word or letter spacing is fairly radical. (It will show you if you have squashed the letters or words together or spaced them extremely far apart.)

Change only the word spacing when the internal spacing between letters in words is fine but you need to adjust the spacing between words in a line. Change only the letter spacing when you want to create a special visual effect for a particular word, phrase, or title without changing the space between the words. Change both the word and letter spacing when you must fit copy within a fixed space and it is not sufficient to adjust the word spacing alone (but be very careful when decreasing the letter spacing). Be sure to return to optimal (or normal) word and/or letter spacing at the place in the text where the tightening or loosening is no longer required. Very seldom will you want to print an entire document with other than optimal word and letter spacing.

Figure 5.31 illustrates a situation in which you need to increase the word and letter spacing to expand a headline so that it fills out the line. The headline as first printed uses the optimal spacing. To get it to fill out the entire line as shown in

Figure 5.32, the following Word/Letter Spacing code was entered at the beginning of the headline:

[Wrd/Ltr Spacing:175% of Optimal,175% of Optimal]

By increasing both the word and letter spacing, the program maintains the necessary extra space between the two words so that they are legible, while inserting sufficient space between each letter to fill out the line. The 175% figure was arrived at by trial and error.

KERNING

Kerning refers to the process of decreasing the spacing between specific pairs of letters. It can provide you with an alternative to adjusting the letter spacing using the Word/Letter Spacing option on the Printer Functions menu.

When particular letters of the alphabet are paired, the normal letter spacing used for the font is too great. The extra white space between the letter pairs is especially noticeable when you use larger type sizes in your document. Figure 5.33 shows you a sample page that contains the most problematic letter pairs, often referred to as *kern pairs*.

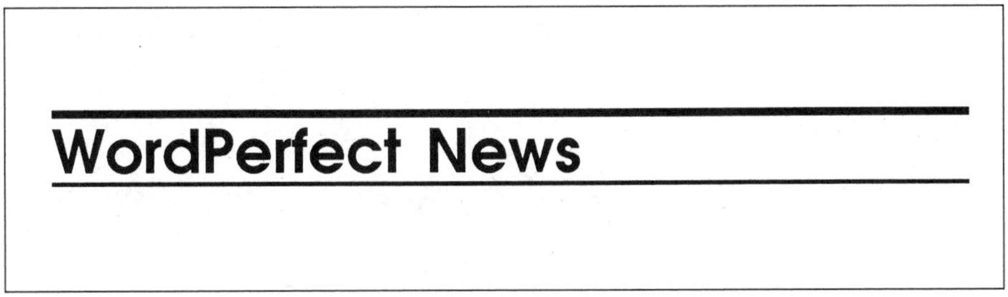

WordPerfect News

FIGURE 5.31: Headline that must be expanded to fill out the entire line. In order to do so, you must increase both the word and letter spacing. If you increase only the letter spacing, it will be very difficult to discern the two words. Figure 5.32 shows you the result.

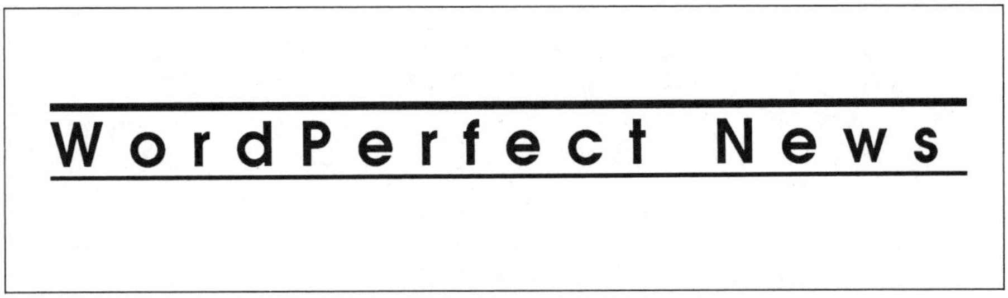

W o r d P e r f e c t   N e w s

FIGURE 5.32: Word and letter spacing used to form a headline to fill out the entire line. Both the word and letter spacing were increased to 175% of optimal to achieve this effect.

This figure also shows the result of using WordPerfect's Kern feature. The first line of each of the four paired sample lines (the first three containing sample kern pairs and the last containing a sample sentence that uses many of these kern pairs) is printed without using the Kern feature. The duplicated lines below are printed with the Kern feature turned on. You can see that, although the kerning of some pairs is more conspicuous than others, WordPerfect has reduced the amount of space between all of the letter pairs.

When you use WordPerfect's Kern feature, you can only turn it on and off. There is no way in version 5.0 to control the amount of kerning that takes place. This is controlled by kerning tables in the .PRS (printer definition) file that is used by your printer and supplied by WordPerfect. These tables don't exist for all fonts that may be used by your printer. When you use the Kern feature on a font that doesn't have a kerning table, it will have no effect on the letter spacing in the printout. In such a case, you can try to use the Word/Letter Spacing option to change the letter spacing as described in the previous section.

AT AY AV AW LT LY
AT AY AV AW LT LY

LV PA TA VA WA YA
LV PA TA VA WA YA

Ay To Tr T. P.
Ay To Tr T. P.

The Way To Go is HOT.
The Way To Go is HOT.

FIGURE 5.33: The effect of using the Kern feature in WordPerfect 5.0. The first line of each pair of examples is printed without using kerning. The second line is printed with the use of the Kern feature. Notice how WordPerfect reduces the space between these traditional kern pairs. In the very last line, which contains a sample sentence, notice the overall effect of using kerning on the line of text.

ADJUSTING THE DISPLAY PITCH TO CONTROL THE SCREEN DISPLAY

When you work with smaller font sizes in a document, as when creating forms or setting up publications, WordPerfect automatically adjusts the display pitch; this is an attempt to avoid the overlapping on the document editing screen that can occur between text separated by tabs, indents, or column settings. The program automatically extends the line horizontally so the characters that you enter after one tab stop or in one column don't disappear underneath the characters at the next tab stop or in the next column. It does this by automatically decreasing the display pitch setting—that is, the amount of space that one character takes up on the editing screen. The effect on the editing screen is to increase the amount of space between tab settings or columns. As a result, some of the characters at the ends of lines will extend beyond the right edge of the editing screen, seeming to have disappeared until you scroll across the line horizontally.

Despite WordPerfect's automatic adjustment of the display pitch, you may come upon situations in which you need to manually adjust the display pitch setting to avoid overlapping in the editing screen display. Figure 5.34 illustrates such a case. In the table shown in this figure, there are two tabs set, a left-aligned tab at 2 inches and a right-aligned tab at 5.44 inches. You can see that overlapping has occurred between the part description and its part number on the last line that has been entered. Such a situation makes it very difficult to edit any of the part descriptions, and impossible to tell when real overlapping of the text will occur. You can see from the Reveal Codes screen shown in this figure that although the word *software* appears to have been cut off after the *w* in the editing display, the word and the right parenthesis are entered correctly.

Figure 5.35 shows you a part of the same document using the View Document feature at 200% (twice the normal size). Here, you can see that at the 10-point type size there is, in fact, no actual overlapping occurring between the description and the part number on the last line entered. It only appears that there is insufficient room to accommodate the modem description and part number in the document editing screen because the display pitch is too large.

Figure 5.36 shows you the document editing screen after the display pitch has been decreased manually. Notice that WordPerfect has now put enough space between the part descriptions and the part numbers so that you can read the modem description on the last line. This adjustment was made by pressing Shift-F8 (Format), selecting the Document option (**3** or **D**), then choosing the Display Pitch option (**1** or **D**). Next, the default response of Yes for Automatic was changed to No by typing **N**. After Enter was pressed, the Width setting was changed from 0.07'' (set by WordPerfect) to 0.06''. Upon pressing F7 to return to the document editing screen, you would see that this small adjustment to the display pitch was sufficient to prevent the overlapping of the part description and the part number in the last line of the table.

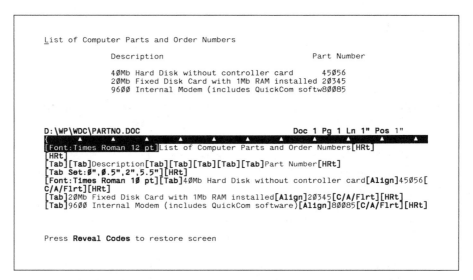

FIGURE 5.34: A table with two columns, one set with a left-aligned tab and the other with a right-aligned tab. The text in these columns is entered in a 10-point type size. Although there is sufficient room at this point size to accommodate both the part description and the part number in the last line, WordPerfect has not automatically adjusted the display pitch width sufficiently to prevent apparent overlapping of the last few characters of the part description and part number.

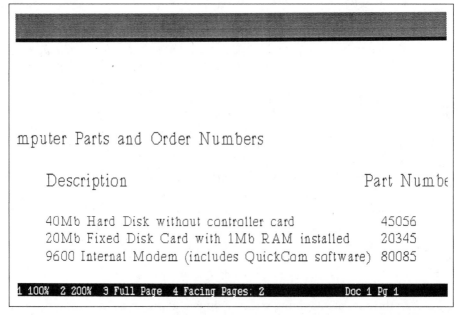

FIGURE 5.35: Part of the table shown in Figure 5.34 in the View Document display at 200%. Here, you can see that although the part description and part number on the last line appear to overlap in the document editing display, there will be, in fact, no overlapping in the printout at this point size.

```
 List of Computer Parts and Order Numbers

              Description                                   Part Number

              40Mb Hard Disk without controller card            45056
              20Mb Fixed Disk Card with 1Mb RAM installed       20345
              9600 Internal Modem (includes QuickCom software)  80085




 D:\WP\WDC\PARTNO.DOC                         Doc 1 Pg 1 Ln 1" Pos 1"
```

FIGURE 5.36: The table shown in Figure 5.34 after setting the Display Pitch option to Manual and decreasing the display pitch width by 0.01 inch. When you decrease the display pitch width for this table, WordPerfect increases the space between the columns in the document editing screen. This makes it much easier to edit the text and determine when real overlapping will occur.

When you need to manually adjust the display pitch, you can do it from anywhere in the document, and it affects the display of the entire document. WordPerfect doesn't insert any type of hidden code to signify a change in the display pitch width; however, if you save the document after changing the display pitch settings, these settings are saved as part of the document.

You can also use the Display Pitch option to bring the display of text in columns or separated by tabs closer together on the document editing screen. You would do this when you change the font and then find that WordPerfect's automatic display pitch width has increased the amount of space between tabbed items or items in columns so that some of the text on a line now extends beyond the right edge of the display screen. To counter this, you set the display pitch to Manual and increase the display pitch width. Provided that increasing the display pitch width doesn't result in overlapping when you press F7 to return to the document editing screen, you will find that this makes editing easier by reducing the amount of horizontal scrolling that you have to do.

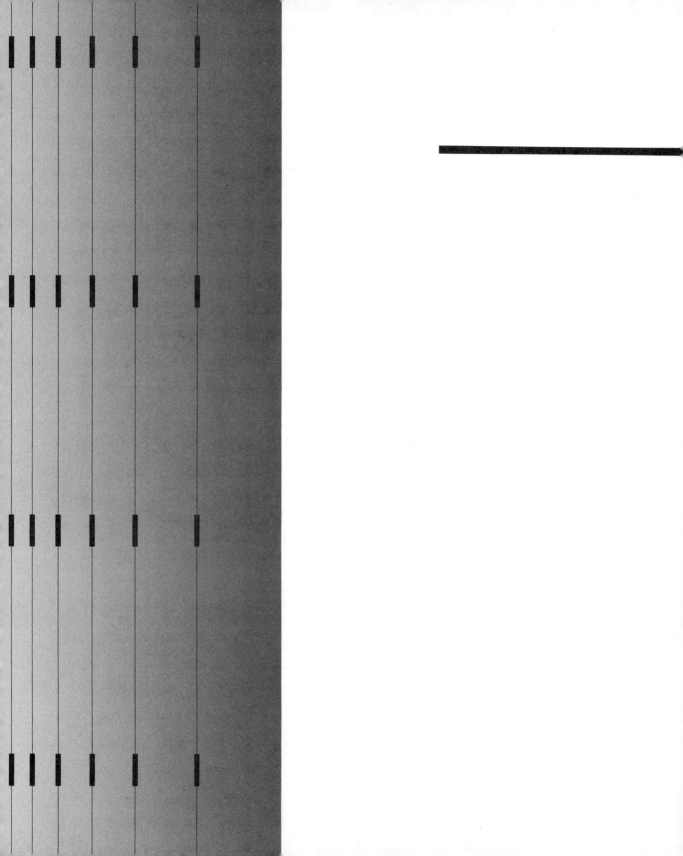

CHAPTER 6

FORMATTING WITH STYLES

Formatting with Styles

WordPerfect 5.0 allows you to set up *styles* to automate many of the formatting changes that you routinely use in a document. When you use styles to introduce formatting changes, you realize two important benefits: you can be sure that each element in the document requiring special formatting is treated exactly the same way throughout, and you can update all the formatting changes applied to each element merely by editing the style used.

In this chapter, you will find detailed information on creating, modifying, and using styles to perform all types of document formatting. As you will discover, styles provide an easy and extremely efficient method of doing repetitive document formatting. You can take advantage of them when you are creating all types of documents, from single-page forms to multipage desktop-published reports.

Upgrade Notes

WordPerfect 5.0 introduces styles to the program for the first time; anything like this feature is totally absent from version 4.2. Although you could use macros in earlier versions to insert particular formatting changes in a document, this did not give you the benefit of being able to universally update the formatting codes throughout the document. If you insert formatting changes via a particular style, they can be changed simply by modifying the contents of that style on the Styles menu. If you insert such formatting changes with a macro, you must edit the contents of the macro, use the Search feature to locate the placement of each group of formatting codes, delete them, and then reinsert them with the macro.

To make room for the Styles and Font menus, WordPerfect 5.0 placed all of the Format menus (Line, Page, Document, and Other) on the Format key, Shift-F8.

Creating and Using Styles

To select, create, or edit a style, you use the Styles menu, accessed by pressing Alt-F8. The Styles menu contains the following options:

1 On; **2 O**ff; **3 C**reate; **4 E**dit; **5 D**elete; **6 S**ave; **7 R**etrieve; **8 U**pdate: 1

Notice that the default selection for this menu is the On option (**1**). If you press the Enter key from this menu, you turn on the style that is currently highlighted on this screen.

WordPerfect supports two types of styles, *open* and *paired*. Once an open style is turned on, it remains on. Whatever formatting codes it contains (like changing to double spacing or using a new base font) affect the entire document from the place at which the style is selected. Because of their nature, open styles are usually selected at the beginning of the document.

A paired style, as the name implies, is turned on and off. Whatever formatting codes it contains (like changing the size or appearance of the base or initial font) affect only the text that lies between the codes that turn the style on and off. Paired styles are particularly useful when a document contains different levels of headings, each of which requires a little different treatment.

Open and paired styles can be, and often are, combined in a single document. In such a case, the open style at the beginning of the document sets the basic formatting changes to which you return when the paired styles are turned off.

Different types of documents will require different sets of styles. To help you organize related styles, WordPerfect allows you to save them in a single file. When you retrieve the style file, all of the styles (both open and paired) that it contains will be available for selection within the document you are creating. Further, the program allows you to create a *style library* containing the styles you use most often in various types of documents. The styles in the style library are available for selection any time you create a new document. To be available for use, they don't have to be retrieved as do styles in a saved file.

Creating an Open Style

To illustrate the steps involved in creating styles in WordPerfect, we will begin with examples of open styles. You can create a new style from anywhere in a document or from a blank document editing screen. Press Alt-F8 (Style) and select the Create option (**3** or **C**).

When you select the Create option, you are presented with the Styles Edit menu shown in Figure 6.1. This menu has five options. Select the Name option (**1** or **N**) to name your style. You can enter up to 11 characters for the style name. This name plus the description entered for the Description option (**3** or **D**) will be displayed on the Styles menu. You use this information to identify the style you want to select.

The default type of style is the paired style. To create an open style, you select the Type option (**2** or **T**). You are then presented with the options

Type: **1 P**aired; **2 O**pen: 0

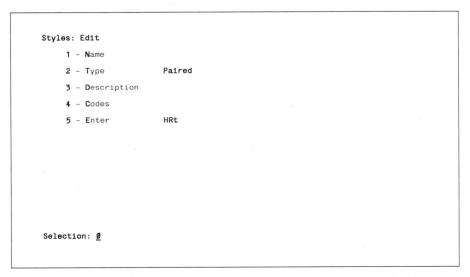

```
Styles: Edit

    1 - Name

    2 - Type          Paired

    3 - Description

    4 - Codes

    5 - Enter          HRt




    Selection: 0
```

FIGURE 6.1: The Styles Edit menu, which appears when you create a new style (Alt-F8 C). This menu contains five options. The name and description you give the style here will be displayed on the Styles menu. You use this information to identify the style you wish to select. The Type option (**2** or **T**) is used to choose between the Open and Paired types of styles. You select the Codes option (**4** or **C**) to enter the formatting codes that are to be inserted in the document when you select this style.

Select the Open option by typing either **2** or **0**. When you change the type from paired to open, the fifth option on the Styles Edit menu, Enter, showing the HRt (Hard Return) code, disappears.

Figure 6.2 shows you the Styles Edit menu for a sample open style called Manuscript. When you enter a style name with the Name option, you can enter a name up to 11 characters long. The description lists the formatting functions of the open style. In this case, it tells you that the style automatically turns off justification and selects double spacing for the document. You can enter a functional description up to 53 characters long when you use the Description option.

After you enter a name and description and select the type of style to be created, you are ready to choose the Codes options (**4** or **C**) and enter the formatting codes that it is to contain. Figure 6.3 shows you the screen where you enter the codes. This screen is split in two, with the Reveal Codes screen at the bottom of the editing screen. This is because a style in WordPerfect can contain text as well as formatting codes. When you press a formatting key sequence, you see its hidden codes in the Reveal Codes screen. When you enter text, you see it in the editing window above.

As you can see from Figure 6.3, the Manuscript style consists of only two formatting commands, whose codes are displayed in the Reveal Codes window below. When you select this style, it inserts codes to turn justification off and to double-space text in the document at the cursor's position.

```
Styles: Edit
        1 - Name              Manuscript
        2 - Type              Open
        3 - Description       Just. off, double-spacing
        4 - Codes




        Selection: 0
```

FIGURE 6.2: The Styles Edit screen for a sample open style called Manuscript. When you create a style, you can enter a style name up to 11 characters long and a description up to 53 characters long. Both the name and the description are used to identify the style for selection from the Styles menu.

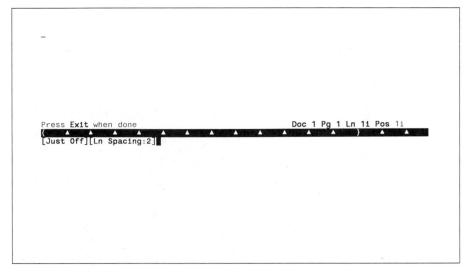

```
        —

Press Exit when done                    Doc 1 Pg 1 Ln 11 Pos 1i
[Just Off][Ln Spacing:2]
```

FIGURE 6.3: The Codes screen for the Manuscript open style. This style inserts two formatting codes; the first turns justification off, and the second changes to double spacing. These codes were entered here by pressing Shift-F8 (Format), selecting the Line option, and then selecting the appropriate formatting options from the Line Format menu.

The formatting codes are entered into the Manuscript style just as they would be in the document itself: by pressing Shift-F8, selecting the Line option, and then selecting the Justification and Line Spacing options. If you enter the wrong formatting code when defining a style, delete it in the Reveal Codes screen and replace it with the appropriate code.

When you are finished entering all of the commands as well as any standard text, press F7 (Exit) to exit the Codes screen. This returns you to the Styles Edit menu screen; when you exit this menu, you are returned to the Styles menu screen, where you will see the style name, type, and description (Figure 6.4). As you create more styles, their names, types, and descriptions are added to this screen. WordPerfect maintains the list of styles in alphabetical order by style name.

TURNING ON AN OPEN STYLE IN THE DOCUMENT

To use an open style, you need to return to the document editing screen by pressing F7 (Exit), and then locate the cursor at the place in the document where you want the style's formatting to take effect. If you have created an open style that is to be used to format the entire document, you position the cursor at the beginning of the document (Home Home ↑). Then press Alt-F8 (Style), move the highlight bar to the name of the style to be used, and select the On option (**1**, **O**, or Enter). Doing this returns you to the document editing screen.

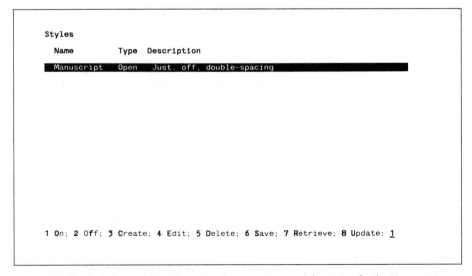

FIGURE 6.4: The Styles menu, displaying the style name, type, and description for the Manuscript style. When you define a new style, these statistics are added to the list on this screen (maintained in alphabetical order by style name). You move the highlight bar to the name of the style when you want to select, edit, or delete it.

WordPerfect inserts a [Style] code in the document at the cursor's position whenever you choose On from the Styles menu. For example, if you locate the cursor at the beginning of the document after creating the Manuscript open style and press Alt-F8 and select the On option, the program inserts the code

[Open Style:Manuscript]

in the document. If you open the Reveal Codes screen and locate the cursor on the [Open Style] code as shown in Figure 6.5, the code automatically expands to show the formatting codes it contains. When you move the cursor beyond this code, it collapses again to display only the code and the style name.

The ragged-right margin and double spacing initiated by the [Just Off] and [Ln Spacing:2] codes will remain in effect for the rest of the document until you do one of three things:

- Select a new style containing formatting codes that either turn justification back on or change the line spacing to some other value.
- Manually select the Justification option and turn it back on or select the Line Spacing option and enter a new line spacing from the Line Format menu (Shift-F8 L).

```
The Speller menu also offers a word count option, which is useful

in two very different situations. First, and most obviously, it

allows you to get a count of the words in your document, which can

be useful if you are writing a document of a specific number of

words for a journal or term paper. However, getting a word count

of your document is also a quick way to make sure that any changes
D:\WP\WDC\FIG6-5.DOC                              Doc 2 Pg 1 Ln 11 Pos 1i
{         ▲    ▲     ▲     ▲      ▲      ▲      )      ▲          }
[Open Style:Manuscript;[Just Off][Ln Spacing:2]]The Speller menu also offers a w
ord count option, which is useful[SRt]
in two very different situations. First, and most obviously, it[SRt]
allows you to get a count of the words in your document, which can[SRt]
be useful if you are writing a document of a specific number of[SRt]
words for a journal or term paper. However, getting a word count[SRt]
of your document is also a quick way to make sure that any changes[SRt]
you have made in margin settings are reflected in the document's[SRt]
headers and footers.[HRt]
Because you will probably often use words WordPerfect's Speller[SRt]

Press Reveal Codes to restore screen
```

FIGURE 6.5: Using the open style at the beginning of a document immediately after creating it. In this figure, you can see the Reveal Codes screen showing the [Style] code. Because the cursor is on this code, it is expanded to display the formatting codes it contains. The ragged-right margin and double spacing initiated by this style will remain in effect for the rest of the document, unless you either turn on a new style, override one of the formatting changes from the appropriate menu, or change the contents of the Manuscript open style.

• Edit the contents of the Manuscript open style and remove or override the formatting codes it contains. This can be done from anywhere in the document.

Note: If you ever turn on a style in the wrong place in the document, you can delete it by opening the Reveal Codes window, locating the [Open Style] code, and pressing the Del key. The document will immediately return to its default formats. You can then turn the style on at the correct location by moving the cursor to the place in the Reveal Codes screen where the style should begin, pressing F1 (Cancel/Undelete), and typing **R**. You can use this method to restore, move, or copy any type of hidden codes that you have deleted.

Creating a Paired Style

The paired style is invaluable when you are formatting a document that contains many structured elements, like a report with several levels of headings, each of which must be visibly distinguished from other levels and must also stand out from the body of the text. When you work with desktop publishing applications in which the different headings can use different type sizes and type styles, as well as fixed line heights, you will really come to appreciate the power and flexibility of formatting with paired styles.

The initial steps involved in creating a paired style are identical to those used to create an open style. You press Alt-F8 (Style), select the Create option, and then enter the name and description for your style using the Name and Description options. As paired is the default type of style, you don't have to use the Type option.

When you select the Codes option (**4** or **C**) to enter the formatting codes or standard text to be included in the style, you are confronted with a slightly different Codes screen from the one presented when you create an open style. As shown in Figure 6.6, the top window of this Codes screen contains the comment

Place Style On Codes above, and Style Off Codes below.

In the Reveal Codes screen below, you can see the [Comment] code. All of the text and codes you enter before the [Comment] code in the Reveal Codes screen are inserted by the paired style when you turn it on. Any codes or text entered after the [Comment] code are inserted in the document as soon as you turn the paired style off.

Figure 6.6 also shows you the codes in the paired style that will be used in the document to format all level-one headings. There, you can see that the [BOLD] code that turns on boldfacing is inserted when this style is turned on (because it precedes the [Comment] code in the Reveal Codes screen). When the style is turned off, the complementary code [bold], which turns off this attribute and returns to normal text, is inserted in the document.

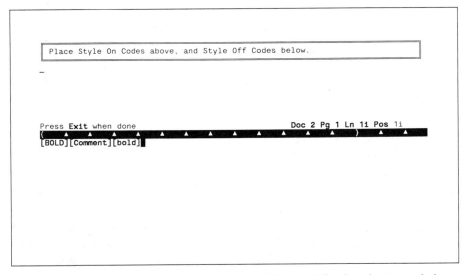

FIGURE 6.6: The Codes screen for defining a paired style. This screen differs from the one used when you create an open style in that it contains a comment telling you that all text and formatting codes inserted above the on-screen comment (that is, before the [Comment] code in the Reveal Codes window) will be inserted in the document when you turn the paired style on; any codes or text below the on-screen comment (that is, after the [Comment] code in the Reveal Codes screen) will be inserted when you turn the paired style off. In this paired style, the code for turning on boldfacing is inserted as soon as the style is turned on. The complementary code for turning it off is inserted when the style is turned off.

DEFINING THE FUNCTION OF THE ENTER KEY IN A PAIRED STYLE

The last option on the Styles Edit menu, Enter (**5** or **E**), is used to determine the function of the Enter key in a paired style. When you select this option, you are presented with the following three options:

Enter: **1** HRt; **2** Off; **3** Off/**O**n: 0

The default, HRt (also **1** or **H**), means that pressing the Enter key will insert a Hard Return code into the document as usual. If you select the Off option (**2** or **F**), pressing the Enter key will turn off the paired style by inserting any codes that follow the [Comment] code in the style. If you select the Off/On option (**3** or **O**), pressing the Enter key will first turn the style off (inserting any codes after the [Comment] code) and then immediately turn it back on (inserting the codes that precede the [Comment] code).

TURNING ON AND OFF A PAIRED STYLE IN THE DOCUMENT

To use a paired style in a document before you've entered the text that it will format, you first position the cursor at the place where the Style On codes are to be inserted. Press Alt-F8 (Style), move the highlight bar to the name of the style to be used, and select the On option (**1**, **O**, or Enter). This inserts all of the [Style On] codes in the document. For instance, if you are adding a level-one heading to the document and have turned on the sample paired style, called 1st Level, you will see

[Style On:1st Level]

in the Reveal Codes screen. If the cursor is still on the [Style On] code, it will expand, and you will see the formatting codes that the style contains (before the [Comment] code), as in

[Style On:1st Level;[BOLD]]

When the cursor is moved off of the [Style On] code, it will be compressed again.

After turning the style on, you type the text of the heading. You then have to remember to turn off the 1st Level paired style; otherwise the text will continue to be boldfaced. If the definition of the paired style does not modify the function of the Enter key, you must press Alt-F8 and select the Off option (**2** or **F**).

> *Note:* When you turn on a paired style that doesn't change the function of the Enter key, WordPerfect inserts both the [Style On] and [Style Off] codes and positions the cursor on the [Style Off] code, allowing you to enter text that is to be affected by this style. When you are finished entering your text, you can press the → key once to move the cursor beyond the [Style Off] code instead of having to press Alt-F8 and select the Off option. This is exactly what Word-Perfect does behind the scenes when you turn off the style by selecting the Off option from the Styles menu.

If the definition modifies the function of the Enter key so that it turns off the style, you don't have to take the time to press Alt-F8 F to turn it off. You simply press the Enter key as soon as you have finished typing the text. To avoid having to press the Enter key a second time to terminate the line containing the heading and move the cursor to the beginning of the next line, you could insert a Hard Return code ([HRt]) or two if you want to skip a line in the document, after the [Comment] code in the style definition. If you don't, you will find yourself having to press the Enter key twice in a row each time you've finished entering the text of a level-one heading, once to turn off the style, and another time to move the cursor to the next line.

Figure 6.7 shows you a level-one heading that has been added to a sample document on spell-checking. It also displays the Reveal Codes screen so that you can see the [Style On] and [Style Off] codes surrounding the heading *The Speller Menu*. Notice in this figure that the [Open Style] code precedes the paired Style On and Off codes. It still controls the nonjustified and double-spaced formatting of the body of the text in this document. This particular paired style does not modify the function of the Enter key, so you have to use the Off option on the Styles menu after you finish typing it in and pressing Enter.

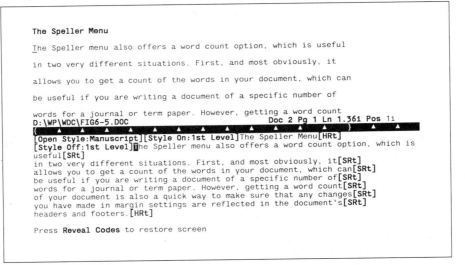

FIGURE 6.7: Using the 1st Level paired style to format a section heading. The Reveal Codes screen at the bottom of this figure shows the [Style On] and [Style Off] codes that control where the style is turned on and off. Because the definition of this paired style doesn't modify the function of the Enter key, to turn off the style you have to press Alt-F8 and type **F** to insert the [Style Off] code shown here. Refer to Figure 6.6 to see the formatting codes inserted by the 1st Level paired style.

Applying Paired Styles to Existing Text   You use a slightly different method to apply a paired style to existing text in a document. To indicate where the style is to be turned on and off, you mark the text as a block (Alt-F4) and then select the style from the Styles menu (press Alt-F8, highlight style name, press **O** or Enter). There is no need to use the Off option on the Styles menu when you apply the style to existing text. The style is always turned off immediately after the end of the block marking.

If you ever find that you have marked the block incorrectly when applying a paired style, you need to locate its [Style On] or [Style Off] code and delete it. You only need to delete one of these codes, for as soon as you delete one of these codes, the other disappears. (Sometimes this doesn't happen in the Reveal Codes screen until the cursor passes over the remaining code.)

Using the Off/On Enter Option   The third Enter option on the Styles Edit menu for paired styles, Off/On, is particularly useful when you are using styles to format an outline or some similar document that continues to use the same style. Because the Off/On option turns the paired style off and then right back on when you press the Enter key, the style is immediately available when you type your next point or subject heading; you don't have to use the Styles menu.

For example, you could create an Outline style that uses this Off/On option for the Enter key. The Style On codes (those that precede the [Comment] code) might be [Tab][Par Num:Auto], which insert a tab and then turn on automatic paragraph numbering. The Style Off codes (those that follow the [Comment] code) will be [HRt][HRt], which simply terminate the current line and add a blank line between each item in the outline.

To use this Outline style in creating a document, you simply turn it on. Word-Perfect inserts a tab and *A.* (unless you modify the paragraph numbering style). You then press F4 (→Indent) and type your first entry. When you press the Enter key, the program automatically inserts two hard returns (in turning the Outline style off) and then a tab and *B.* (in turning the Outline style back on). If you want to change the level of the outline, you press ← once, press the Tab key, press the End key (this will change the *B.* to *1.*), and type your next point. When you again press the Enter key, WordPerfect repeats the process of inserting two hard returns and automatically adding the next paragraph number (*C.*) to your outline. When you are finished entering all of the items in the outline and no longer need the Outline style, you press Alt-F8 F to turn it off in the rest of the document.

Figure 6.8 shows another example that makes good use of the On/Off function in a paired style. The title page shown in this figure was created with a paired style named Title. When turned on, the Title style automatically centers the text on each line and changes the size of the font to Large. (The base font used in this example is 14 point ITC Zapf Chancery Medium Italic.) When the Title style is turned off, it enters two hard returns.

Because the Enter key turns off the Title style and then turns it back on, all six lines for this page were centered in the chosen font size simply by turning on the Title font at the top of the page and then entering each line terminated by a hard return. After the user typed the first line and pressed the Enter key, centering was turned off by the first hard return, and a blank line was entered by the second hard return (accomplished with the [Style Off] code). The cursor was automatically centered on the third line (accomplished by the [Style On] code), waiting for the next line of the title to be entered. After the last line of text was entered and the Enter key was pressed, the Title style was turned off by pressing Alt-F8 and selecting the Off option (**2** or **F**).

Figure 6.9 shows you the codes for this title page that uses the Title style. At the beginning of the Reveal Codes screen, you can see the [Font] code that makes 14-point ITC Zapf Chancery Medium Italic the base font and the [Center Pg] code that centers the title page information vertically. Notice that the only other codes are the [Style On] and [Style Off] codes for the Title style. The horizontal centering, the change in font size, and the blank line between each line are handled by these codes.

The Art of Desktop Publishing

with WordPerfect 5.0

by

Gregory Alan Harvey

and

Kay Yarborough Nelson

FIGURE 6.8: A title page entered with the use of a paired style that is turned off and then on again when the Enter key is pressed. When the style is turned on, centering is turned on and the font size is changed to Large. When the style is turned off, one hard return that terminates centering is entered, followed by another that enters a blank line. Because pressing the Enter key turns the style off and then on again, all of the lines for this title page could be entered without having to continually access the Styles menu to reselect the style and the On or Off option.

LOCATING STYLES IN A DOCUMENT

WordPerfect allows you to search for hidden style codes in the document. To locate a code, you press F2 (→Search) followed by Alt-F8. You then select the code you wish to locate from this menu of options:

1 Style **O**n; **2** Style O**ff**; **3** Open **S**tyle: 0

After you select one of these three options, WordPerfect will insert the appropriate style code as the search string; you then press F2 again to begin the search. Remember that you can press ↑ to reverse the direction of the search and locate the code you have selected before the cursor's position. Notice, however, that you can't search for a particular open style or paired style by name. The program will only locate the first occurrence of the style code. To locate this code for a particular style you have used, you may have to repeat the search several times.

Creating Styles from Existing Formatting Codes

WordPerfect allows you to create a style from existing formatting codes in a document. To do this, turn on the Reveal Codes window (Alt-F3), move the cursor onto the first code you want to include, press Alt-F4 (Block), and mark the block so that the cursor is located immediately after the last code you wish to include. Press Alt-F8 (Style) and select the Create option (**3** or **C**). This takes you

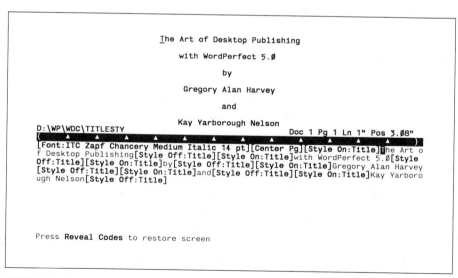

FIGURE 6.9: The codes used to produce the title page shown in Figure 6.8. At the top of the Reveal Codes screen, you see the codes that insert the base font and vertically center the text. Notice that the only other codes used are those that turn on and off the Title style.

to the Styles Edit screen, where you can name a style, change the type, enter a description, or change the function of the Enter key.

However, you don't have to use the Codes option, because all of the codes included in the marked block will already be included. Note that any text within the marked block will not be added to the style. If you want to add standard text to the style, you must select the Codes option and enter it manually in the Codes editing screen.

Modifying a Style

In the introduction to this chapter, it was emphasized that the real power of formatting with styles comes from the fact that you can modify the formatting controlled by the style anywhere it has been used in the entire document simply by modifying the style itself. This saves you the time and trouble of searching for each and every occurrence of the format you wish to change and then issuing the required formatting commands to make these changes. Not only does this save a great deal of editing time, it also guarantees that you will not overlook a part of the document that needs changing, thus ensuring stylistic uniformity in the document.

To modify a style, you press Alt-F8, move the highlight bar to its name and description, and select the Edit option. This returns you to the Styles Edit menu, where you can modify the name, type, description, and codes, and reset how the Enter key functions (if you are editing a paired style and don't change a paired style to an open style).

To change the way the style formats the text, you choose the Codes option (**4** or **C**). This returns you to the Codes screen for that style, where you can add new codes as well as delete existing ones. After you have finished modifying the codes, press F7 (Exit) to return to the Styles Edit screen. After you have completed all necessary changes to the name, description, and, perhaps, the Enter key function, press F7 again to save the changes. This returns you to the Styles menu. To return to the document screen, you press F7 a third time. As soon as you do, WordPerfect will reformat the text of your document according to the changes made to the style.

To illustrate how changes to the applied style can affect the formatting of a document, let's look at the sample document on using WordPerfect's Speller (referred to in Figure 6.7) and make some changes to its styles. Currently, the level-one headings are formatted in boldfaced type using the 1st Level paired style. The body of the text is formatted with a ragged-right margin and double-spaced through the use of the Manuscript open style. Now, after printing a copy of this document, you decide that you wish to see how the document would look with a justified margin setting and each paragraph of text that follows a section heading formatted with a hanging indentation.

To restore right justification (the program default) requires that you edit the Manuscript style codes; press Alt-F8, highlight *Manuscript* on the screen, type **E**, select the Codes option by typing **C**, and simply delete the [Just Off] code in the Reveal Codes window by pressing the Del key. Press F7 three times to return to the document and have it reformatted according to the change to the Manuscript style. Because you can't see justification on the screen, you need to use the View Document feature (Shift-F7 V) to see the effect of this change before printing your document (Figure 6.10).

To change the format of each paragraph of text that follows a level-one section head, you need to modify the formatting codes that are inserted when the paired style is turned off. To do this, you edit the 1st Level style (Alt-F8 E) and select the Codes option (**C**). To add the Indent and Margin Release commands, you press the End key to move the cursor directly to the end of the codes in the Reveal Codes screen (after the closing bracket in the [bold] code) and press F4 (→Indent) and Shift-Tab (Margin Release), as shown in Figure 6.11.

To apply the new formatting to the document, you press F7 three times to return to it. Figure 6.12 shows the new formatting in the View Document screen

```
The Speller Menu

The Speller menu also offers a word count option, which is useful
in two very different situations. First, and most obviously, it
allows you to get a count of the words in your document, which can
be useful if you are writing a document of a specific number of
words for a journal or term paper. However, getting a word count
of your document is also a quick way to make sure that any changes
you have made in margin settings are reflected in the document's
headers and footers.

Because you will probably often use words WordPerfect's Speller
does not know- -especially proper names and specialized terms you
use in your work- -the program makes it easy for you to add words
```

1 100% 2 200% 3 Full Page 4 Facing Pages: 1   Doc 2 Pg 1

FIGURE 6.10: The sample Speller document after the Manuscript style has been edited so that the text is now right-justified. Because you can't see justification in the document editing screen, you have to use the View Document feature (Shift-F7 V) to see the change to the style—deleting the [Just Off] code. Here, you see the document at full size (100%).

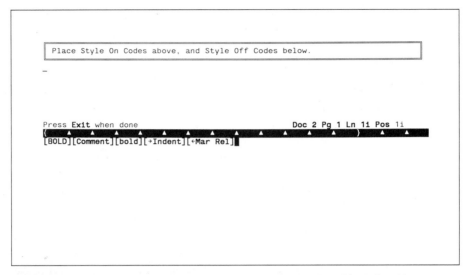

FIGURE 6.11: Modifying the formatting accomplished with the 1st Level paired style by adding new formatting codes. To add the [→Indent] and [←Mar Rel] codes, you move the cursor just beyond the [bold] code and press F4 and Shift-Tab. When you press F7 three times to update the style and return to the document, the style reformats the paragraphs after the level-one headings so that they have hanging indentations (see Figure 6.10).

(Shift-F7 V) at 100%. You can see that the first paragraph now sets off the first sentence with a hanging indentation.

Suppose that you want to make a further change to the formatting. Instead of having the level-one headings set off with boldfacing, you now want them underlined, and instead of using a hanging indentation for the first line of the accompanying paragraphs, you want them to be simply indented with a tab. To make this change, you again edit the codes for the 1st Level style. Once you are in the Codes screen, you move the cursor to the [BOLD] code before the [Comment] code in the Reveal Codes section and replace it with an [UND] code by pressing Del and F6. Then you move the cursor to the [bold] code after the [Comment] code, delete it, and replace it with an [und] code by pressing F6 again. Then you delete the [→Indent] and [←Mar Rel] codes and replace them with a [Tab] code by pressing the Tab key.

When you save the change to the 1st Level style and return to the document (by pressing F7 three times), not only will the appearance of level-one headings be changed—they will no longer appear boldfaced—but the first line of each paragraph below will also be tabbed instead of using a hanging indentation. Figure 6.13 shows how this appears in the View Document screen at full size.

As you can see from these simple examples, you can continue to modify the styles that are used in a document and preview the formatting changes they effect in the document until you are completely happy with the overall results.

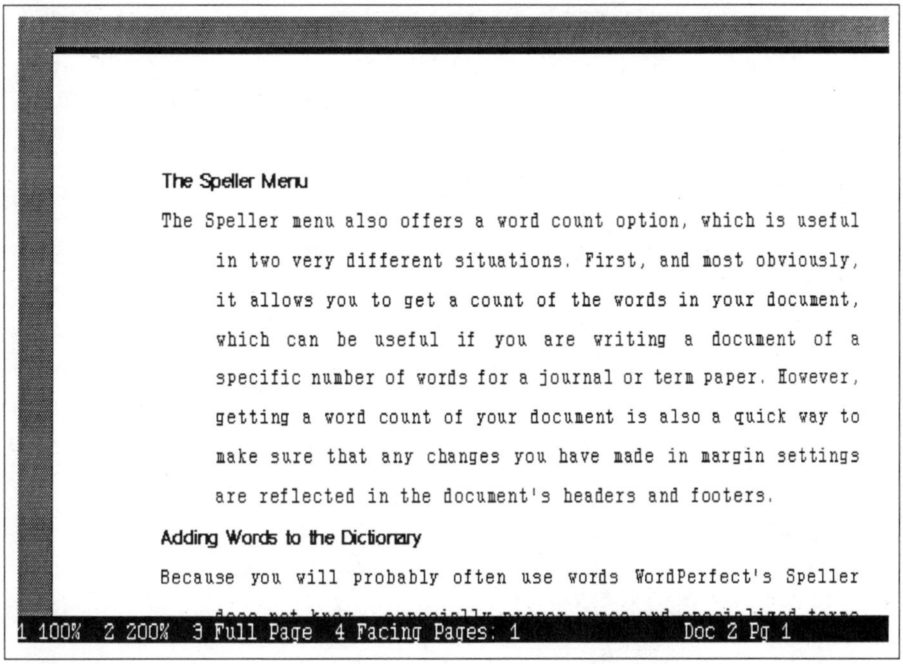

> **The Speller Menu**
>
> The Speller menu also offers a word count option, which is useful
> in two very different situations. First, and most obviously,
> it allows you to get a count of the words in your document,
> which can be useful if you are writing a document of a
> specific number of words for a journal or term paper. However,
> getting a word count of your document is also a quick way to
> make sure that any changes you have made in margin settings
> are reflected in the document's headers and footers.
>
> **Adding Words to the Dictionary**
>
> Because you will probably often use words WordPerfect's Speller

`1 100%  2 200%  3 Full Page  4 Facing Pages: 1                    Doc 2 Pg 1`

FIGURE 6.12: The first part of the sample document in the View Document screen at full size (100%) after changing the 1st Level style. The paragraph now uses a hanging indentation because the formatting codes that are inserted when the 1st Level paired style is turned off now include the [→Indent] and [←Mar Rel] codes.

CHANGING STANDARD TEXT IN A STYLE

When you create a style that contains any kind of standard text and use it in a document, you can't edit it as you can the text that you enter from the keyboard. If you find that you need to modify standard text included in a style, you must press Alt-F8 (Style), highlight the name of the style that includes the text, and select the Edit option (**4** or **E**) followed by the Codes option (**4** or **C**). Only when you are in the Codes screen can you edit the text using the same editing keys used in normal document editing.

If you use a style to insert a header or footer in the document, you can edit the contents of the header or footer without having to edit the style that contains it. Select the Header (**3** or **H**) or Footer (**4** or **F**) option on the Page Format menu (Shift-F8 P), indicate the letter (**A** or **B**) of the header or footer, and then select the Edit option (**5** or **E**). Once you are in the Header or Footer Edit screen, you can make any changes you want to its contents. Any changes made to it here will be reflected in the contents of the style that uses the particular header or footer.

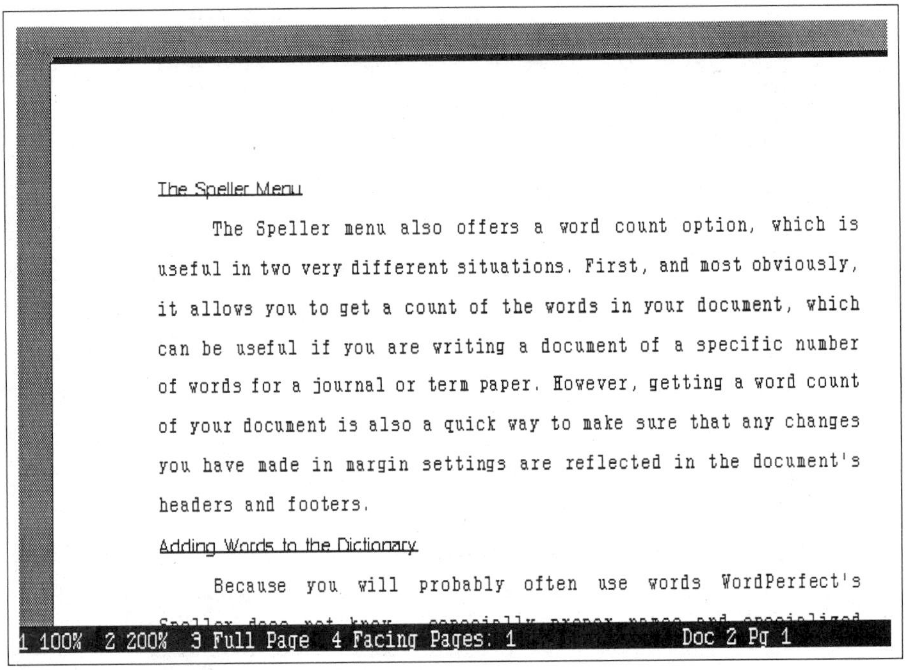

The Speller Menu

     The Speller menu also offers a word count option, which is useful in two very different situations. First, and most obviously, it allows you to get a count of the words in your document, which can be useful if you are writing a document of a specific number of words for a journal or term paper. However, getting a word count of your document is also a quick way to make sure that any changes you have made in margin settings are reflected in the document's headers and footers.

Adding Words to the Dictionary

     Because you will probably often use words WordPerfect's

1 100% 2 200% 3 Full Page 4 Facing Pages: 1   Doc 2 Pg 1

FIGURE 6.13: The first part of the sample document in the View Document screen at full size (100%) after changing the 1st Level style still further. The section headings are underlined instead of bold-faced because the [BOLD] code before the [Comment] code is replaced with an [UND] code and the [bold] code after the [Comment] code is replaced with an [und] code. The paragraphs now use simple tabs instead of hanging indentations to set off the first line because the formatting codes that are inserted when the 1st Level paired style is turned off now include the [Tab] code.

Saving Styles in a File

When you create styles for a document and save that document, the styles are saved with it. When you retrieve that document (Shift-F10 or F5 Enter R), the styles saved with it are also retrieved and are available when you press Alt-F8 (Style). However, if you want to be able to reuse the styles that you create for one document in a different document, you need to save those styles in a separate file.

To do this, you select the Save option (**6** or **S**) on the Styles menu. You will be prompted to enter a name for the new file. To differentiate style files from regular document files, it is suggested that you add the extension .STY to the file name. (WordPerfect, however, will save your styles under any valid file name).

As soon as you press the Enter key after typing the file name, all of the styles listed on the Styles menu screen are saved together in the same file; there is no way to select just certain styles from this screen to be saved. This file will be saved in the default directory unless you enter the full path name when giving the file name.

If you create a particular WordPerfect directory to keep all of your style files and it is not the current directory when you use the Save option, be sure to enter this directory path name. For example, if you are about to save the styles you have created to format your outline in a file and want to add this file to the special STYLES directory set up to hold all of your styles, you would enter

C:\WP50\STYLES\OUTLINE.STY

when prompted for the file name.

If you try to save a group of styles under a file name that already exists, you will receive the message

Replace <*file name*>? (Y/N) No

warning you that you are about to replace the contents of an existing file. To continue the save operation and replace the file with the styles, you must type **Y**. Be forewarned that if the file you are about to replace contains text and you type **Y** to continue the save operation here, it will contain only styles when you next open it. You can't add styles in this way to an existing document that contains text. (See the following section on retrieving style files for information on how to do this.)

Retrieving Styles Saved in a File

To use the styles saved in a file and apply some or all of them to sections of a document, you select the Retrieve option (**7** or **R**) from the Styles menu (Alt-F8). In response to the Filename prompt, enter the name of the file that contains the styles you want to use and press the Enter key. You will see all of the styles in that file listed on the Styles menu screen. You are then free to edit them and select them as you want for the document you are creating or editing.

If you want to apply styles to an existing document, first retrieve the document (Shift-F10 or F5 Enter R) and then retrieve the style file to use (Alt-F8 R). Exit to the document in the editing screen and then apply the styles to sections of the text by marking as a block (Alt-F4) the text that is to be formatted with one of the styles and then selecting the style to be used by turning it on (Alt-F8, highlight style name, **O**). If you want to apply the styles saved in a file to a new document, you simply switch to a blank editing screen (if necessary), retrieve the style file (Alt-F8 R), and then apply the style by turning it on before entering the text. (If you are applying a paired style, you must also remember to turn it off.)

> *Note:* If you retrieve a file of styles (Shift-F10 or F5 Enter R), you will see only a blank editing screen. When you press Alt-F8 (Style), you will then see all of the styles saved in the file. From the Styles menu, you can edit them (**E**) or add to them (**C**) before saving the file again (F10). Use the List Files menu options (F5 Enter) if you need to move or rename the styles file (**M**) or if you want to delete it entirely (**D**). Because you can't see the styles in the file unless you press Alt-F8, you can't use the Look option (**L**) on the List Files menu to determine which styles the file contains.

RETRIEVING MULTIPLE STYLE FILES

You can have access in a single document to styles saved in multiple style files. To do this, you simply continue to retrieve all of the style files that contain the styles you wish to have available. Each time you use the Retrieve option (**7** or **R**) on the Styles menu (Alt-F8) and name a new style file, WordPerfect adds the styles in this file to the current list.

However, if the style file you are about to retrieve contains a style whose name is identical to one currently on the Styles menu list, you will receive the following prompt:

Style(s) already exist. Replace? (Y/N) No

If you type **N** or press the Enter key, the style in the file you are retrieving will not replace the style that has the duplicate name on the list, although all nonduplicate styles from this file will be retrieved and added. If you type **Y**, the style in the file you are retrieving will replace its duplicate on the list (and if it has not already been saved in a style file, its definition will be lost).

When you save the document (F10 or F7 Y), all of the styles brought in from separate style files will be saved with it. You can also combine all of these styles into their own style file by using the Save option (**6** or **S**) on the Styles menu (Alt-F8) and giving this file a new name.

Using a Style Library

WordPerfect allows you to turn a particular style file into the default, which is then available whenever you create a new document. It refers to this file as the *Style Library*. To create a Style Library, you select the Location of Auxiliary Files option (**7** or **L**) on the Setup menu (Shift-F1). Then you select the Style Library Filename option (**6** or **L**) and enter the name of the style file along with its complete path name.

This Location option differs from all of the others on the Location of Auxiliary Files menu in that it indicates not only the path name of a particular directory but also the name of a particular file. For example, if you want the default styles to be the ones saved in a file named BUSINESS.STY that is located in your C:\WP50\STYLES directory, you enter

C:\WP50\STYLES\BUSINESS.STY

after selecting the Style Library Filename option on the Location of Auxiliary Files menu. After indicating the file name and its location in this manner, press the Enter key and then F7 to return to the document editing screen.

After you indicate the style file to be used as the Style Library, you have to retrieve its styles by selecting the Update option (**8** or **U**) on the Styles menu (Alt-F8) if you wish to use them in the document you are currently editing. As soon as you type **8** or

U, all of the styles in the Style Library file are added to the list currently on the Styles menu. If, during the same editing session, you change the Style Library file, you will also have to use the Update option to retrieve the styles from the new file and make them available.

If you retrieve a document that has been saved with styles, you will also have to use the Update option to add the styles contained in the Style Library. However, when you begin a new document (in the same editing session or subsequently), the styles in the Style Library will be automatically listed on the Styles menu as soon as you press Alt-F8; there will be no need to use the Update option.

USING STYLES TO MAKE FONT CHANGES IN A DOCUMENT

One of the most important applications for styles is to control font changes in a document that uses different type sizes and/or attributes to differentiate various levels of headings from each other and from the body type. When you perform this kind of format change through a style, you can easily experiment with different typefaces and styles until you have the "right" look for the document.

Figures 6.14 and 6.15 illustrate how using styles to format design elements makes it easy to experiment with the use of different fonts in a document. This particular document (of which you see only one page) uses four styles:

- An open style called Body that determines the base font to be used for the body of the document.

- A paired style called A Head that determines the font and size of all level-one headings. *Master Menu* represents a level-one heading in this particular document.

- A paired style called B Head that determines the font and size of all level-two headings. *Using the {CASE} Command* represents a level-two heading in this document.

- A paired style called Program that determines the font and size of all programming examples in the text. The commands following {CHAR}, {CASE}, and IF represent program listings in this document.

In Figure 6.14, ITC Bookman Light was assigned to the Body style, Palatino to the A Head style, a smaller sized Palatino to the B Head style, and Helvetica Bold to the Program style. In Figure 6.15, ITC Bookman Light was assigned to the Body style, Times Roman Bold Italic to the A Head style, a smaller sized Times Roman Bold Italic to the B Head style, and ITC Bookman Demi to the Program style. Various point sizes were assigned.

All of these font changes were accomplished by editing the codes of the four styles used in the document. As this document is many pages long, making the font changes by changing the fonts used by each of the four styles was much

Master Menu

The Master Menu displayed when you execute the MASTER macro allows the user to choose between document assembly tasks using particular primary and secondary merge files and secondary file maintenance tasks like adding, editing or deleting records as well as printing a data report.

The Master Menu is created with the {CHAR} command that allows the user to enter a single character in response to the prompt entered in the *message* argument. When you use this macro command, you enter the number of the variable in which the user's response is to be stored followed by the prompt message. As usual, each argument is terminated with the tilde (~).

In this case, the menu options as well as the prompt are placed within the *message* argument as follows:

```
{CHAR}1~{Del to EOP}
·················M·A·S·T·E·R··M·E·N·U
{Enter}
{Enter}
·················1·~·Document·Assembly
{Enter}
{Enter}
·················2·~·Maintain·Secondary·Files
{Enter}
{Enter}
·················3·~·Quit·Menu
{Enter}
{Enter}
Enter·number·or·letter·of·your·choice:·~
```

Using the {CASE} Command

The {CASE} command is used to determine what the macro is to do in response to the key pressed by the user. The {CASE} command can be read like an IF statement. For example, the first case condition in the MASTER macro is:

```
{CASE}{VAR 1}~1~Assembly~
```

which can be interpreted as,

```
IF {VAR 1} = 1 THEN do the subroutine named Assembly
```

Because there are three menu choices, we need to have at least two other conditions, one that instructs the program what to do if the response entered into {VAR 1} is 2 and another that tells it what to do if the response is 3.

FIGURE 6.14: A sample page of a document formatted with WordPerfect's Styles feature.

quicker and easier than having to locate each [Font] code in the document and change it by deleting the existing code and replacing it with a new [Font] code.

Using styles also allows you to modify the fonts to suit the capabilities of the printer you are using at the time. For example, if you use a dot matrix printer to

Master Menu

The Master Menu displayed when you execute the MASTER macro allows the user to choose between document assembly tasks using particular primary and secondary merge files and secondary file maintenance tasks like adding, editing or deleting records as well as printing a data report.

The Master Menu is created with the {CHAR} command that allows the user to enter a single character in response to the prompt entered in the *message* argument. When you use this macro command, you enter the number of the variable in which the user's response is to be stored followed by the prompt message. As usual, each argument is terminated with the tilde (~).

In this case, the menu options as well as the prompt are placed within the *message* argument as follows:

```
{CHAR}1~{Del to EOP}
····················M·A·S·T·E·R··M·E·N·U
{Enter}
{Enter}
··················1···Document·Assembly
{Enter}
{Enter}
··················2···Maintain·Secondary·Files
{Enter}
{Enter}
··················3···Quit·Menu
{Enter}
{Enter}
Enter·number·or·letter·of·your·choice:·~
```

Using the {CASE} Command

The {CASE} command is used to determine what the macro is to do in response to the key pressed by the user. The {CASE} command can be read like an IF statement. For example, the first case condition in the MASTER macro is:

```
{CASE}{VAR 1}~1~Assembly~
```

which can be interpreted as,

IF {VAR 1} = 1 THEN do the subroutine named Assembly

Because there are three menu choices, we need to have at least two other conditions, one that instructs the program what to do if the response entered into {VAR 1} is 2 and another that tells it what to do if the response is 3.

FIGURE 6.15: The pages from Figure 6.14, with the styles changed.

produce a draft of the document and a laser printer to produce the final draft, you can first set up styles to take advantage of the dot matrix printer's more limited font capabilities, and then modify the styles used in the document to take full advantage of the laser printer's more developed font capabilities when you are ready to produce the final output.

Remember that if you switch printers and don't edit the Font codes in the styles used, WordPerfect will perform font substitution, trying to match the font selections to the printer's capabilities. If the changes made automatically by the program are not to your satisfaction, you will need to modify the style codes by making explicit choices in the typefaces, type styles, and fixed line heights, as you see fit. For more information on using styles to make font changes in a document, refer to Chapter 19, "WordPerfect's Desktop Publishing Capabilities."

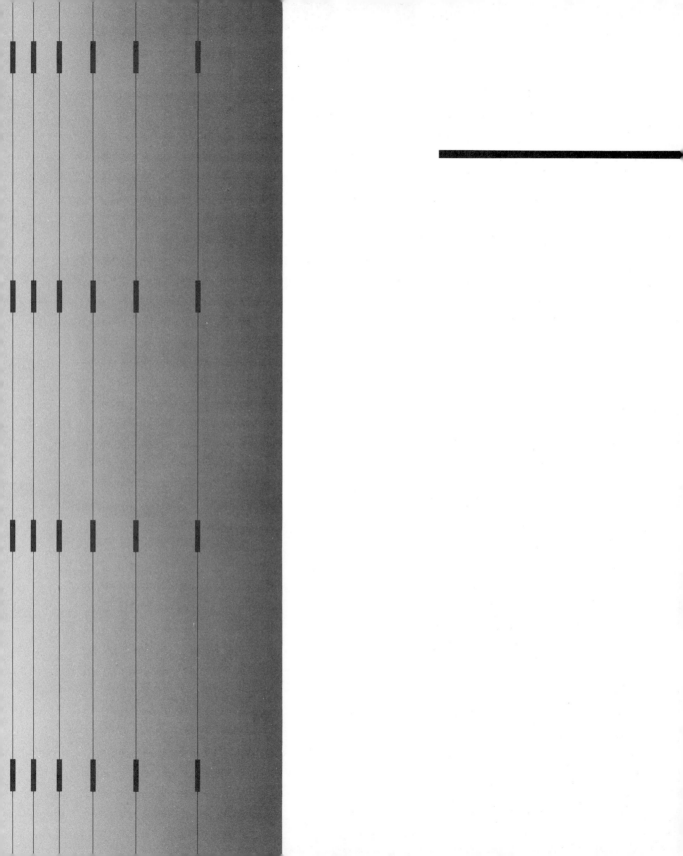

PRINTING TECHNIQUES

Printing Techniques

WordPerfect gives you a variety of methods with which to print your documents—so many, in fact, that they may be confusing at first. However, each of these printing methods is designed to handle a particular task and thus give you more flexibility with the program. You can, for example, print

- An entire document that you have retrieved into the computer's memory (Shift-F7 F).
- All pages, selected pages, or a range of pages of a document that's on disk (Shift-F7 D or F5, highlight file, P).
- The current page on your screen (Shift-F7 P).
- A marked block of text (Alt-F4, highlight block, Shift-F7 Y).
- The contents of the current screen (Shift-PrtSc).

This chapter details all of these methods by which you can print in Word-Perfect and explains how to install your printer and use the print options that are available to you. These options include changing printers that are already installed, setting the number of copies, adding a binding width, and selecting different print qualities. You will also find information on previewing a document before sending it to the printer as well as using the new Master Document feature to print several different documents as one ("chain printing").

For information on installing and using different fonts supported by your printer, see Chapter 5, "Working with Fonts." For information on printing to disk to create an ASCII file, see Appendix A, "Importing and Exporting Documents."

Upgrade Notes

Version 5.0 retains all of the printing methods that you used in version 4.2; you can print all of the document or the current page in the editing window, or all or part of a document on disk. However, the Print menu, accessed by pressing Shift-F7 (Print), has been completely reorganized. In place of a horizontal line of options, WordPerfect now uses a full-screen menu containing all of the options on the version 4.2 Print menu, some that were located on the Printer Control screen, and some new ones not previously available.

In addition, the Print menu contains the printing options that were formerly on a separate menu accessed by selecting *3* for Options. You will notice that in version 5.0 the options stay in effect for the entire work session with Word-Perfect; you no longer have the option of using them for one print job only.

Besides the changes to the Print menu, you will also notice modifications to the Printer Control screen (now referred to as the Control Printer screen). The menu options on this screen control only the print queue; they include the familiar Cancel Job(s), Display Jobs, Rush Job, Stop, and Go (start printer) options. Although the print queue options have not changed, you will find that the Control Printer screen gives more information than before about the status of the printer and the print jobs in the queue.

Printer installation in version 5.0 is much easier than it was in version 4.2. To install a printer, you simply select it from a listing of the printers available on the Printer disks that accompany the program. As part of the installation, you can edit the printer definition from a full-screen menu immediately after selecting the printer or at any time after that. Instead of having to assign a number to a printer definition as you did in 4.2, you simply select it by name from a menu showing all of the installed printers when you want to use it for a particular printing job.

The method of selecting the fonts you want to use with an installed printer has changed greatly in version 5.0. No longer are you restricted to the use of eight predefined fonts. Instead, you can install as many fonts as you have and your printer is capable of using. Only one font is preselected as the initial font, which becomes the default font for each document you created with that particular printer. (See Chapter 5 for information on installing and selecting fonts for use with your printer.)

As part of the printer definition, you can create form definitions that tell WordPerfect what paper size, method of paper feed, and offsets will be required for specialized forms like those required to print the first page of a business letter on letterhead, the second page of the letter on plain bond, memoranda on half-sheets, and so on. If your printer has a sheet feeder, you use this new Forms feature in version 5.0 to indicate the bin to be used rather than using a Sheet Feeder Bin Number option as you did in the past.

The version 4.2 Preview option on the Print menu is called View Document in WordPerfect 5.0. If your computer is equipped with a graphics card, this feature will display different font sizes and graphic images that are brought into the document (see Chapter 18 for more details on how to do this) as well as page numbers, headers and footers, footnotes, and right justification as it did in version 4.2. Moreover, View Document allows you to resize the page image to full size (100%) or twice full size (200%), and to view the layout of two facing pages in the document.

Version 5.0 also introduces a new printing feature called Master Document that allows you to chain-print several separate documents as one. This feature permits you to edit smaller individual documents while still being able to apply automatic references (such as indexes and tables of contents) and to use continuous page numbering for the entire composite document. This feature is covered in some detail later in this chapter.

INSTALLING YOUR PRINTER

Before printing the documents you create in WordPerfect, you must install and select your printer. If you have several different printers to choose from, you should install all of them. Then you can switch printers at print time, as when using a dot matrix printer for a rough draft and a laser printer for the final printout.

The procedure for installing a printer is very easy. You need to have the Printer disks—there are four if you use 5¹/₄-inch disks or three if you use 3¹/₂-inch disks—handy unless you have copied all of their files onto your hard disk. WordPerfect stores individual printer definitions in files named WPRINT followed by the number of the Printer disk and the .ALL extension, such as WPRINT1.ALL on the Printer1 disk. Each of these files takes up nearly as much space as there is on a Printer disk.

It's not necessary to copy all of these .ALL files from the Printer disks onto your hard disk. You only really need to have the files that contain the specific definitions for the printers you have available; copying all of these files is a waste of a great deal of disk space that can better be used for document storage.

> *Note:* If you have sufficient disk space, you can create a directory such as C:\WP50\PRINTER and copy all of the .ALL files into it. That way, all of the printers supported by WordPerfect will be listed during the installation procedure. After installing all of the printers you have and all of the fonts you use with these printers, you can then erase the .ALL files from this directory to restore the disk space. You will not need the .ALL files again unless you need to install a new printer or add new fonts to one you've already installed, in which case you would simply place the disk containing the appropriate .ALL file in drive A.

Setting Up the Location for the Printer Files

During printer installation, WordPerfect copies the printer definition files into the directory or disk that contains the WordPerfect program files. If you are using WordPerfect on a hard disk system, you can create a separate directory just for the printer files. After creating this directory—see Chapter 8 or **Directories** in Part V for information on creating a new directory in WordPerfect—and before beginning the printer installation, press Shift-F1 and select the Location of Auxiliary Files option (**7** or **L**). Then, select Printer Files (**5** or **P**) and enter the full path name of this directory. For example, if you create a WordPerfect subdirectory named \PRINTER and you keep your WordPerfect program files in C:\WP50, you would enter

    C:\WP50\PRINTER

as the path name. After entering the path name, press the Enter key and F7 (Exit) to return to the document editing screen. Then begin the printer installation procedure.

Note: If you use the Bitstream Fontware Installation Kit, you can't use a separate PRINTER directory for your printer files. Instead, you must copy the WPRINT1.ALL file into the same directory that contains the WP.EXE file. See Appendix F for details on installing and using this utility.

Locating and Copying the Printer Definition Files

To start the installation procedure, press Shift-F7 and choose the Select Printer option by typing **S**. This takes you to a Print Select Printer screen similar to the one shown in Figure 7.1. If you are using a two-disk-drive system, place the working copy of the Printer1 disk in drive B. If you are using a hard disk system, place this Printer1 disk in drive A. Then select the Additional Printers option by typing **2** or **A**.

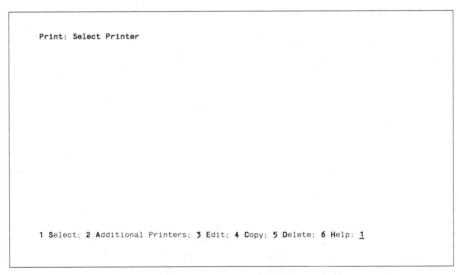

```
   Print: Select Printer




















       1 Select; 2 Additional Printers; 3 Edit; 4 Copy; 5 Delete; 6 Help: 1
```

FIGURE 7.1: The Print Select Printer screen, accessed by pressing Shift-F7 S. The screen shown in this figure is as it appears prior to installing any printers for use with WordPerfect. The program does not come with a default printer installed. Therefore, to do any printing in version 5.0, you must first install your printer.

If the default directory is the one that contains the Printer1 disk, you will see the screen that appears in Figure 7.2. If the default directory is not the same, you will see the screen shown in Figure 7.3, indicating that the files were not found and that you must select the Other Disk option (**2** or **O**). When you do, you receive the prompt

Directory for printer files:

followed by the name of the current directory. If you have the Printer1 disk in drive A or drive B, just type in the drive letter followed by a colon before pressing the Enter key.

If your printer isn't among those listed on the Printer1 disk, you need to replace this disk with the next one in the sequence and select the Other Disk option again. WordPerfect will retain the drive and directory path that you first entered. As long as this information hasn't changed, you just press the Enter key to view the printers listed on the next printer disk. Continue this procedure of exchanging printer disks and examining the list of printers until you locate your printer.

There are too many printers listed on Printer disks 2 through 4 to be displayed in a single screen. To locate your printer on one of these lists, you can use Name Search by typing **N** followed by the first few characters of the printer's name. This will locate the highlight cursor on the appropriate printer. You can also use ↑ and ↓, − (Screen Up) and + (Screen Down), PgUp and PgDn, and Home Home ↑ and Home Home ↓ to move the highlight cursor through the list of printers.

```
Select Printer: Additional Printers

  ▌Dataproducts LZR-1230                    ▐
   HP LaserJet
   HP LaserJet 2000
   HP LaserJet Series II
   HP LaserJet+, 500+
   LaserImage 1000
   NEC Silentwriter LC-860+
   Okidata LaserLine 6
   Olympia Laserstar 6




   1 Select; 2 Other Disk; 3 Help; 4 List Printer Files; N Name Search: 1
```

FIGURE 7.2: The listing of the printers located on the Printer1 disk. If your printer doesn't appear on this list, you need to select Other Disk (**2** or **O**), indicate the drive/directory for the printer files, replace the Printer1 disk with Printer2, and press the Enter key. (If you have 3½-inch disks, you have Printer1/Printer2 on same disk.)

```
Select Printer: Additional Printers

Printer files not found

        Use the Other Disk option to specify a directory for the printer
        files. Continue to use this option until you find the disk with the
        printer you want.
```

```
    1 Select; 2 Other Disk; 3 Help; 4 List Printer Files; N Name Search: 1
```

FIGURE 7.3: The *Printer files not found* screen, which will appear if the default directory doesn't contain any printer files (that is, files named WPRINT, followed by the disk number and .ALL). Use the Other Disk option (**2** or **O**), indicate the drive/directory for the printer files, insert the Printer1 disk in the indicated drive (if necessary), and press the Enter key.

When you have located your printer on the list and highlighted it with the cursor, choose the Select option (**1** or **S**) from the menu. You will be prompted to confirm the file name for the printer that you have selected. For instance, if you have highlighted the HP LaserJet Series II on the list for the Printer1 disk, you will see the following prompt:

Printer filename: HPLASEII.PRS

All printer definition files carry the extension .PRS. When you press the Enter key, the program will copy the .PRS file to your disk. (Refer back to "Setting Up the Location for the Printer Files" for information on how to set a default directory for this file.) Press the Enter key to accept this file name.

> *Note:* You can edit the printer file name; however, the file name cannot exceed eight characters and must have the .PRS extension. If you have already installed the printer definition file, you will see a prompt similar to this

Replace HPLASEII.PRS? (Y/N) No

If you press the Enter key or type **N**, you will be given another opportunity to change the file name before copying it. If you type **Y**, the printer definition file on the Printer disk will replace the one currently in your WordPerfect directory or printer directory (if you have created one). For more information on renaming a printer definition file, see "Setting Up Multiple Definitions for the Same Printer" later in this chapter.

After copying the printer definition file, WordPerfect updates the resident fonts for the printer and displays a Printer Helps and Hints screen for the newly installed printer. Figure 7.4 shows you this screen for the HP LaserJet Series II printer. You can print this screen by pressing Shift-PrtSc. To see a Helps and Hints screen for the sheet feeder available with your printer, press Shift-F3 (Switch). Press F7 (Exit) when you are finished reading the information on this screen or have made a printout of it with Shift-PrtSc.

Note: You can return to the Printer Helps and Hints screen for your printer at a later time by selecting the Help option (**6** or **H**) on the Print Select Printer screen (Shift-F7 S). You can get the Help screen on the sheet feeder (if one is available) by selecting the Sheet Feeder option (**3** or **S**) on the Printer Edit menu and then selecting the Help option (**3** or **H**) from the Sheet Feeder menu.

The Printer Edit Screen

When you quit the Printer Helps and Hints screen, WordPerfect displays the Printer Edit screen, similar to the one shown in Figure 7.5 for the HP LaserJet Series II. At the top, it displays the file name of the Printer Definition file as you accepted it during installation. Below that, it shows you the name of the printer as it appeared on the Printer disk, and it shows the port as LPT1, the default. This screen also shows the name of the initial font selected by WordPerfect for your printer.

```
 Printer Helps and Hints:   HP LaserJet Series II

  _·  If you choose the option to initialize the printer, all soft fonts in its
      memory will be erased and those fonts marked with an asterisk (*) will be
      downloaded.

   ·  The graphics feature is not supported in landscape mode.

   ·  Do not set any margins less than 1/4 of an inch.

   ·  Line draw does not work correctly with proportionally spaced fonts.






      Press Exit to quit, Cursor Keys for More Text, Switch for Sheet Feeder Help
```

FIGURE 7.4: The Printer Helps and Hints screen for the HP LaserJet Series II. To obtain a hard copy of this screen for your records, press Shift-PrtSc. To obtain on-line help regarding the sheet feeder used by your printer, press Shift-F3 (Switch).

You can change any of these default settings, select the sheet feeder that your printer uses, define special forms to use with your printer (and the bins that they use), select additional cartridges and fonts for your printer, and designate the location of any downloadable (soft) fonts your printer uses. (For more information on using each of these options, see. "Editing the Printer Definition" later on in this chapter.)

To complete the installation of your printer, you don't have to specify this information when the Printer Edit screen first appears. You can return to the Printer Edit menu at any time when using WordPerfect by pressing Shift-F7, highlighting the printer's name on the Print Select Printer menu, and then selecting the Edit option (**5** or **E**). However, before leaving this screen, you need to modify the Port setting if your printer is connected to any port besides LPT1. (See "Specifying the Printer Port" later in this chapter for details on how to do this.)

Selecting Your Printer

After verifying the information on this screen and modifying it as required, press F7 (Exit) to return to the Print Select Printer screen. Before you can use the printer that you just installed, you must select it with the Select option (**1** or **S**). If

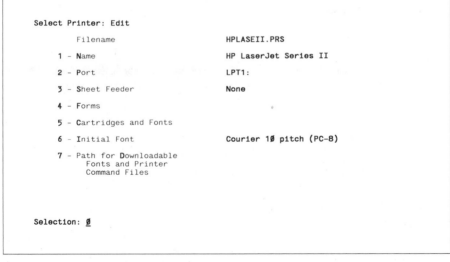

FIGURE 7.5: The Printer Edit screen for the HP LaserJet Series II. Initially, this screen shows you the file name, printer name, *LPT1* as the printer port, and the name of the initial font selected for the printer, such as *Courier 10 pitch (PC-8)* for the HP LaserJet Series II. You can modify these and the other settings on this menu when this screen first appears or return to it later by selecting the Edit option (**3** or **E**) on the Print Select Printer menu (Shift-F7 S).

you don't take this step, and you try to print the document, you will receive the error message

ERROR: Printer not selected

even though you have successfully installed the printer.

To select a printer, make sure that the highlight cursor is on it, and then type **1** or **S**. You will be returned to the Print menu, where you will see the name of the printer you selected after the Select Printer option. From here, you can either use one of the print options to print all or part of a document, or press F7 (Exit) to quit this screen and return to the document editing screen.

EDITING THE PRINTER DEFINITION

You can edit the printer definition during the initial printer installation after selecting it from the printer disk, or at any time thereafter. To edit a printer definition during a work session, you press Shift-F7 (Print), move the highlight bar to the name of the printer on the Print screen, choose the Select option (**1** or **S**), and then choose the Edit option (**3** or **E**) from the Print Select Printer menu. This takes you to the Printer Edit menu, similar to the one shown in Figure 7.5.

Changing the Printer's Name

Select the Name option (**1** or **N**) to modify the name of the printer. When you change the name of the printer definition, the new name will appear on the Print Select Printer screen that comes up when you press Shift-F7 and choose the Select option (**1** or **S**). You only need to change the name of the printer when you are setting up different printer definitions for the same printer. (See "Setting Up Multiple Definitions for the Same Printer" later in this chapter.)

Specifying the Printer Port

The IBM PC and PS/2 computers allow you to connect your printers using different printer ports. To have your printer work properly, the printer definition must indicate the port to which your printer is actually connected. When you select the Port option (**2** or **P**), you are presented with the following choices:

Port **1** LPT 1; **2** LPT 2; **3** LPT 3; **4** COM 1; **5** COM 2; **6** COM 3; **7** COM 4; **8 O**ther: 0

The default is LPT1:, which stands for *Line Printer 1* and indicates that the computer and printer communicate with each other via a parallel cable, using a parallel port. IBM personal computers support up to three different parallel ports, LPT1 through LPT3. If your printer uses a parallel interface, you select the appropriate LPT option from options **1** through **3** on the Port menu.

IBM personal computers also support four different serial ports, COM1 (*COM* stands for *Communications*) through COM4, and your printer can be connected to the computer through one of these. If your printer uses a serial interface, you choose the appropriate COM option from options **4** through **7** on the Port menu.

When you select one of the COM options, you are presented with a new menu of options as shown in Figure 7.6. As you can see from this figure, the defaults for a serial interface are a baud rate of 9600, parity none, stop bits 1, character length 8, and XON/XOFF off. You will have to refer to your printer manual to obtain the correct settings for the printer you are installing. If your printer requires different settings, select the appropriate option(s) and enter the new values. If you don't know what values your printer requires when connected by a serial interface to a COM port, leave the COM port default settings as they appear on this menu and try printing a document using them. To exit this menu and return to the Printer Edit screen, press F7 (Exit). The Port option on the Printer Edit screen will then display the COM port number followed by a listing of these settings separated by commas, as in

COM1:9600,N,8,1

if you select option **4**, COM1:, from the Port menu and don't make any changes to the COM port default settings.

> *Note:* The Other option on the Port menu is used only if you are printing to another device rather than through the printer. It is most often used to print a document to disk. This technique is discussed at length in the section "Printing to Disk" later in this chapter.

Selecting Your Sheet Feeder

If your printer is equipped with a sheet feeder, you need to indicate the model it uses as part of the printer definition. When you select the Sheet Feeder option on the Printer Edit screen, you are presented with the screen shown in Figure 7.7. If your sheet feeder is listed on this screen, move the highlight bar to it and choose the Select option to install it.

If your model isn't listed, select the Build Your Own option. This definition should work as long as the sheet feeder you are installing doesn't have more than six bins. To use this definition, you must use the Forms option on the Printer Edit menu to indicate which bin will be used for each of the forms that you use in printing (see "Creating Forms for Your Printer" just ahead).

```
Select Printer: COM Port

        1 - Baud                          9600

        2 - Parity                        None

        3 - Stop Bits (1 or 2)            1

        4 - Character Length (7 or 8)     8

        5 - XON/XOFF                      No




    Selection: 0
```

FIGURE 7.6: The Printer COM Port menu that appears when you select one of the serial port options, COM1: through COM4:, after selecting the Port option (**2** or **P**) on the Printer Edit menu. Change the baud rate, parity, stop bits, character length, and XON/OFF settings to match the specifications set in your printer documentation for your printer when using a serial interface. If you don't have access to your printer manual, leave these defaults in effect.

```
Select Printer: Sheet Feeder

    BDT MF 830 (6 Bin)
    BDT MF 850 (3 Bin)
    Build Your Own
    Dataproducts LZR-1230 Multi-Bin
    HP LaserJet
    HP LaserJet 2000
    HP LaserJet 500+
    Mechanical
    NEC LC-860+
    Ziyad PaperJet 400










    1 Select; 2 None; 3 Help; N Name search: 1
```

FIGURE 7.7: Selecting a sheet feeder for your printer. When you select the Sheet Feeder option on the Printer Edit screen (Shift-F7 S E), you are presented with the options shown in this figure. If your sheet feeder is not listed on this screen, select the Build Your Own option by moving the highlight bar to it and choosing the Select option.

Use the Help option (**3** or **H**) if you need more information on how Word-Perfect uses the bins for the selected sheet feeder. Note that before you can use any forms that specify a particular bin to be used in printing, you must first install your sheet feeder by using the Sheet Feeder option and selecting the correct model.

Creating Forms for Your Printer

The Forms option (**4** or **F**) on the Printer Edit screen is used to create definitions for specialized forms that you use with your printer. At the most basic level, a WordPerfect form definition specifies the size of the paper to be used and the type of feed required to print the chosen paper size. The form definition can also specify the orientation of the printing on the page or offsets required to adjust the position of the printhead when printing begins.

Note: Orientation is specified as either portrait or landscape mode, which describes the direction of the printing in relation to the width and length of the page. In portrait mode, the printing parallels the width of the page. In landscape mode, it parallels the length of the page.

Figure 7.8 shows you the Printer Forms screen that appears when you first select the Forms option for the HP LaserJet Series II. WordPerfect supplies three predefined forms: one called Envelope for printing business envelopes, another called Standard for printing 8½-by-11-inch pages, and a third called [ALL OTHERS] for all other types of printing. Notice that this screen tells you the paper size, the orientation, whether the form will be initially present during printing, the location of the paper (meaning the type of paper feed), and any special offsets used.

For the HP LaserJet Series II, only the Standard form uses continuous feed (meaning that it is fed from the paper tray). Both the Envelope and [ALL OTHERS] forms are manually fed. The notes at the bottom of the screen inform you that if you try to use any other form (that is, one that has not been added to this list), WordPerfect will halt the printing and expect the paper to be fed at the location defined for the [ALL OTHERS] form; in this case the paper would be manually fed. Also, it will use the maximum width for the [ALL OTHERS] form, which is 8½ inches.

CREATING A FORM DEFINITION

To create a new form definition, you select the Add option (**1** or **A**) on the Printer Forms menu. When you do, the screen shown in Figure 7.9 appears. When creating a new form, you may select the name of the form from the first eight options (Standard through [ALL OTHERS]) or select the Other option

```
Select Printer: Forms

Form type                Size          Orient  Init
                                       P L     Pres  Location   Top     Side
                                                                 Offset
Envelope                 4" x 9.5"     N Y     Y     Manual     Ø"      Ø"
Standard                 8.5" x 11"    Y Y     Y     Contin     Ø"      Ø"
[ALL OTHERS]             Width ≤ 8.5"          N     Manual     Ø"      Ø"




        If the requested form is not available, then printing stops and WordPerfect
        waits for a form to be inserted in the ALL OTHERS location.  If the requested
        form is larger than the ALL OTHERS form, the width is set to the maximum width.

        1 Add; 2 Delete; 3 Edit: 3
```

FIGURE 7.8: The predefined forms for the HP LaserJet Series II and the Printer Forms screen. Word-Perfect comes configured with three predefined forms whose definitions can be edited. You can also create new definitions from this screen. A form definition describes the paper size, the orientation, whether the form will be initially present, the location of the paper (that is, the type of paper feed), and any offsets required to adjust the position of the printhead.

```
Select Printer: Form Type

        1 - Standard

        2 - Bond

        3 - Letterhead

        4 - Labels

        5 - Envelope

        6 - Transparency

        7 - Cardstock

        8 - [ALL OTHERS]

        9 - Other




Selection: 1
```

FIGURE 7.9: The Form Type menu that appears when you create a new form for your printer by selecting the Add option—**1** or **A**. You select the form name from the first eight options or assign a name of your choice by selecting the Other option and typing it in. Note that WordPerfect has assigned specific paper sizes to the first eight form types only. Therefore, if you choose the Other option, you will be asked to select the paper size.

and give it a name of your choice. After you choose one of the form types, Word-Perfect takes you directly to the Printer Forms screen shown in Figure 7.10.

Figure 7.10 shows you the Printer Forms screen for a new form definition called Letterhead. This form will be used when the document is to be printed on the company letterhead stationery. To create this form, the Add option on the Printer Forms screen was selected (Figure 7.8), followed by the Letterhead option (**3** or **H**) on the Form Type menu (Figure 7.9). Notice in Figure 7.10 that the form size assigned to the Letterhead form is 8½ by 11 inches.

Form Size   If you need to change the size of the form, select the Form Size option. When you do, the Form Size menu shown in Figure 7.11 appears. If the size you wish to use is listed as one of the menu options, all you have to do is select its number or menu letter. However, if the dimensions of your form are not listed on this menu, select the Other option (**O**) and type in the width followed by the length when prompted to do so. Note that the paper width always refers to the dimension of the inserted edge.

Orientation   The default orientation for a new form is portrait. If you need to change this, select the Orientation option (**2** or **O**) on the Printer Forms screen. When you do, you are presented with the following options:

Orientation: **1 P**ortrait; **2 L**andscape; **3 B**oth: 0

```
Select Printer: Forms

        Filename            HPLASEII.PRS

        Form Type           Letterhead

    1 - Form Size           8.5" x 11"

    2 - Orientation         Portrait

    3 - Initially Present   Yes

    4 - Location            Continuous

    5 - Page Offsets - Top  Ø"
                     Side   Ø"




    Selection: Ø
```

FIGURE 7.10: The Printer Forms screen and menu options used to define a new form. You can use the options on this menu to change the default size, orientation, location, and offsets for the form, and to indicate whether the form will be initially present when the printing begins.

```
Select Printer: Form Size
                              Inserted
                                Edge

        1 - Standard          8.5"    ×    11"

        2 - Standard Wide     11"     ×    8.5"

        3 - Legal             8.5"    ×    14"

        4 - Legal Wide        14"     ×    8.5"

        5 - Envelope          9.5"    ×    4"

        6 - Half Sheet        5.5"    ×    8.5"

        7 - US Government      8"      ×    11"

        8 - A4                210mm   ×    297mm

        9 - A4 Wide           297mm   ×    210mm

        0 - Other

    Selection: 1
```

FIGURE 7.11: The Form Size menu, which allows you to modify the size of the form you are creating or editing. If the size you wish to assign to your form is not one of the listed options, select the Other option and input the width and length.

Choose the Landscape option (**2** or **L**) to have the printing run perpendicular to the inserted edge of the paper. For example, if you are creating a form that uses the standard paper size of 8¹/₂ by 11 inches and you want the printing to run with the 11-inch side, you select the Landscape option with 8¹/₂ inches representing the width (that is, the dimension of the inserted edge). If the printer you use to print the form is incapable of rotating the printing on the page, any Landscape setting in the form definition will be ignored.

Use the Both option (**3** or **B**) if you want to be able to switch between portrait mode and landscape mode when printing the form and to determine which orientation is used by the way you manually feed the paper to the printer. For example, if you are creating a Half Sheet form with a width of 8¹/₂ inches and a length of 5¹/₂ inches and you select Both, you can print in portrait mode by inserting the 8¹/₂-inch side in the printer. To switch to landscape mode, you rotate the paper and insert the 5¹/₂-inch side in the printer.

When you select the Both option, WordPerfect always uses the width of the form size in determining the line length, according to the left and right margin settings in effect. Therefore, it is possible for the line of type to extend beyond the edge of the paper when you manually switch from portrait to landscape mode. For example, if you create and use the Half Sheet form as described above, the document's line length will be 6¹/₂ inches if you use 1-inch left and right margins. If you switch to landscape mode, the width of the paper will only be 5¹/₂ inches and part of each line will be printed beyond the edge of the paper. Be very aware of this potential problem when you apply a form definition that uses the Both orientation option. It is up to you to make sure that the line length can be accommodated by the orientation you choose at print time.

> *Note:* You can avoid this problem by creating two forms, Half Sheet Wide and Half Sheet Narrow, both of which use the portrait orientation. Choose 8½ by 5½ inches as the form size for the Half Sheet Wide form and 5½ by 8½ inches as the form size for the Half Sheet Narrow form; choose Manual as the location for both. When you apply the Half Sheet Narrow form to a document, WordPerfect will use a line length of 3½ inches, as opposed to the 6½-inch line length it uses when you apply the Half Sheet Wide form (assuming that you still maintain 1-inch left and right margins). The only thing that you have to remember is to insert the correct edge for the form you have used when you manually feed the paper to the printer at print time.

Initially Present   The Initially Present option (**3** or **I**) on the Printer Forms menu is set to either Yes or No. If you leave this option set to Yes, the default, WordPerfect will expect to find the paper at the designated location (see "Location" just ahead). If you change it to No, WordPerfect will halt the printing when it encounters the Paper Size/Type code that uses this form; it will then wait for you to insert the paper you want to use for the form and choose the Go option on the Control Printer screen (see "Managing the Printer" later in this chapter) before attempting to print the document.

This option is especially useful if you know that the form you are creating will use some special paper (like a different color or letterhead) that is not normally loaded into the bin you designate as the location for the form. By setting Initially Present to No, you are given an opportunity to load the required paper into the bin before the printing of your form begins. That way, you won't end up with multiple copies of a form printed on the wrong type of paper.

Location   There are three Location options that appear when you select Location (**4** or **L**) on the Printer Forms menu:

Location: **1 C**ontinuous; **2 B**in Number; **3 M**anual: 0

If your printer uses a feed mechanism like a tractor feed or has only one bin (like the HP LaserJet Series II) and your form is to be printed on the paper this mechanism supplies, leave the Location option set to Continuous. If your printer has multiple bins and your form will use paper from a particular bin (such as letterhead in bin 1 and plain bond in bin 2 or standard 8½-by-11-inch paper in bin 1 and legal paper in bin 2), select the Bin Number option. When you do, you will receive the prompt

Bin Number:

At this point, you enter its number. (Remember that you must also select a sheet feeder for your printer as part of the definition before WordPerfect can respond properly to a Bin Number setting. See "Selecting Your Sheet Feeder" earlier in this chapter.) If you will have to manually insert the form, as when printing envelopes, select the Manual option.

> *Note:* If you are using the HP LaserJet Plus or Series II, you may select the HP LaserJet sheet feeder for the Printer Forms Sheet Feeder option, in which case you can then designate bin 1 as the location for all forms that are fed from the internal paper cassette, bin 2 for all forms that are fed manually, and bin 3 for envelopes that are fed with the envelope feed, if you have one (otherwise, use bin 2 if you manually feed your envelopes).

Page Offsets   The Page Offsets option allows you to adjust where the printing begins on the form by entering a measurement that tells WordPerfect how much to shift the position up or down and/or left or right on the page. This can be useful if you need to control exactly where the printing begins when using a form type like Letterhead, where you want the printing to start below the company name and logo. To shift the printing position up or down, you select the Page Offsets option (**5** or **P**) and enter a new measurement for the top. Entering a positive number for the top offset shifts the printing position up on the page, while entering a negative number shifts it down on the page. To shift the printing position to the left or right on the page, you enter a new side offset measurement. Here, entering a positive number shifts the position to the right on the page, while entering a negative number shifts it to the left.

Note that adding a top or side offset for your form in no way affects the top and bottom or left and right margins used in the document. WordPerfect will continue to apply the margins used in the document to the printed form in addition to any top or side offset. This means that you must make sure your offset measurements are small enough so that all of the text on the page still fits on the sheet of paper. For example, if you enter a top offset measurement of −**1**" and the document maintains a 1-inch top margin, WordPerfect will begin applying that top margin of 1 inch *after* shifting the printing position 1 inch down from the top of the first sheet of paper. This would cause the text to begin printing 2 inches down from the top of that sheet of paper. Therefore, if you had a footer on this page, it would no longer fit at the bottom of the page and would be shifted to the next page (or printed on the platen, if there were no next page), causing continuous pagination problems for the printing of the rest of the document!

Editing a Form Definition

After you have all of the options on the Printer Forms menu set the way you want them for the particular form you are creating, press F7 (Exit) to save the definition. This returns you to the Printer Forms screen, which displays all of the forms available for your printer, similar to the one shown in Figure 7.12.

Then press F7 (Exit) again to save the form as part of the printer definition. Don't use the F1 (Cancel) option to leave this menu; if you do, the new form definitions that you added will not be saved with the printer definition.

You can edit a form definition from the Printer Forms screen (Shift-F7 S E F) at any time after defining it. To edit the settings for a particular form from this screen, move the highlight bar to it and select the Edit option (**3** or **E**). This returns you to the Printer Forms screen for that particular form, where you can modify any of its settings.

Note, however, that you can't edit the name of the form. After you assign the name by selecting one of the available form types or entering one of your own (Figure 7.9), there is no way to modify it later on. If you want to change the name of the form (that is, the form type), you must create a new one using the same settings with the Add option (**1** or **A**) and then delete the old form definition using the Delete option (**2** or **D**) on this menu. Before you use the Delete option, make sure that the highlight cursor is on the correct form type. If you do delete a definition in error, press F1 (Cancel) instead of F7 (Exit) to leave this screen and then return to it by selecting the Forms option (**4** or **F**) from the Printer Edit screen.

USING A FORM DEFINITION IN THE DOCUMENT

To have WordPerfect print your document using one of the form definitions that you have created, you use the Paper Size/Type option on the Format Page

```
Select Printer: Forms                         Orient Init           Offset
                                              P  L   Pres Location  Top    Side
   Form type                    Size

   Bond                         8.5" x 11"    Y  N   Y    Bin 2     Ø"     Ø"
   Envelope                     4" x 9.5"     N  Y   Y    Manual    Ø"     Ø"
   Half Sheet Narrow            5.5" x 8.5"   Y  N   N    Manual    Ø"     Ø"
   Half Sheet Wide              8.5" x 5.5"   Y  N   N    Manual    Ø"     Ø"
   Letterhead                   8.5" x 11"    Y  N   Y    Bin 1     Ø"     Ø"
   Standard                     8.5" x 11"    Y  Y   Y    Contin    Ø"     Ø"
   [ALL OTHERS]                 Width ≤ 8.5"          N    Manual    Ø"     Ø"




   If the requested form is not available, then printing stops and WordPerfect
   waits for a form to be inserted in the ALL OTHERS location.  If the requested
   form is larger than the ALL OTHERS form, the width is set to the maximum width.

   1 Add; 2 Delete; 3 Edit: 3
```

FIGURE 7.12: The Printer Forms menu showing all of the forms added for the HP LaserJet Series II.

menu (Shift-F8 P). The basic procedure for selecting a new paper size and type is discussed in "Changing Paper Size and Type" in Chapter 4, and you can refer to that section for more information on using this option when you only need to choose a new paper size; the procedure for applying this feature to use a form definition is outlined below.

When you select the Paper Size/Type option, you are presented with a menu of various paper sizes, as shown in Figure 7.13. In fact, this menu has the same options and works the same way as the Form Size menu; the only difference between this menu and the Paper Size menu is the heading at the top of the screen and the fact that one menu is accessed through the Page Format menu (Shift-F8 P) and the other is accessed through the Print Select Printer menu (Shift-F7 S). You can verify this by comparing the menu shown in Figure 7.13 with the one shown in Figure 7.11.

Be sure to select the correct size for the form you want to use. If the size of your form conforms to one of the sizes listed to the right of the first eight options, select that option. Otherwise, select the Other option (**O**) on this menu and manually enter the width and length. If you choose a paper size from this menu that doesn't match the paper size used in the form definition, WordPerfect will format the text of the document using the paper size selected from this menu instead of the size called for by the form definition.

For example, if you have created a Half Sheet Narrow form definition that designates the width as 5½ inches and the length as 8½ inches, you need to select the Half Sheet option (**6** or **H**) from the Paper Size menu when using this form to

```
Format: Paper Size

     1 - Standard              (8.5" x 11")

     2 - Standard Landscape    (11" x 8.5")

     3 - Legal                 (8.5" x 14")

     4 - Legal Landscape       (14" x 8.5")

     5 - Envelope              (9.5" x 4")

     6 - Half Sheet            (5.5" x 8.5")

     7 - US Government         (8" x 11")

     8 - A4                    (210mm x 297mm)

     9 - A4 Landscape          (297mm x 210mm)

     0 - Other

 Selection: 1
```

FIGURE 7.13: The Format Paper Size menu, used to designate the size of the form used to print the document. If your form doesn't use one of the predefined sizes (options **1** through **8**), select the Other option and type in the width followed by the length.

maintain the proper line length according to the margins set for the document that is to be printed using this form. If you selected the Standard option (**1** or **S**), which uses the size 8½ by 11 inches, the line length in your document would conform to the 8½-inch width even though the form definition uses a 5½-inch width. Your line length would then be too long for the width of the paper that you will actually insert in the printer.

> *Note:* Having to designate the paper size on the Paper Size menu (Shift-F8 P S) is redundant since the form definition already specifies the paper size. Nevertheless, you can't indicate which form is to be used without first specifying the paper size on this menu.

After you select the paper size, the Format Paper Type menu will appear, as shown in Figure 7.14. Select the option that corresponds to the name of the form type you want to use. If this is not one of the first seven options listed on this menu, select the Other option (**8** or **O**). The names of the other form types that you created will appear beneath the heading *Defined Form Types* as shown in Figure 7.15. To use one of the nonstandard form types that you created, move the highlight bar to it and choose the Select option (either by typing **1** or **S** or by pressing the Enter key). In Figure 7.15, there are two nonstandard form types defined for the printer: Half Sheet Narrow and Half Sheet Wide. (Refer to Figure 7.12 to see the descriptions for these forms.)

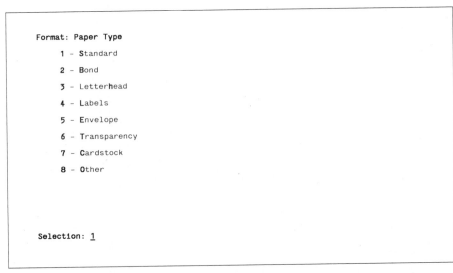

```
Format: Paper Type

        1 - Standard

        2 - Bond

        3 - Letterhead

        4 - Labels

        5 - Envelope

        6 - Transparency

        7 - Cardstock

        8 - Other




    Selection: 1
```

FIGURE 7.14: The Format Paper Type menu that appears after you designate the paper size of your form. If the name of the form type you wish to use is listed among the first seven options, select the appropriate option. If not, select the Other option, and a screen similar to the one shown in Figure 7.15 will appear.

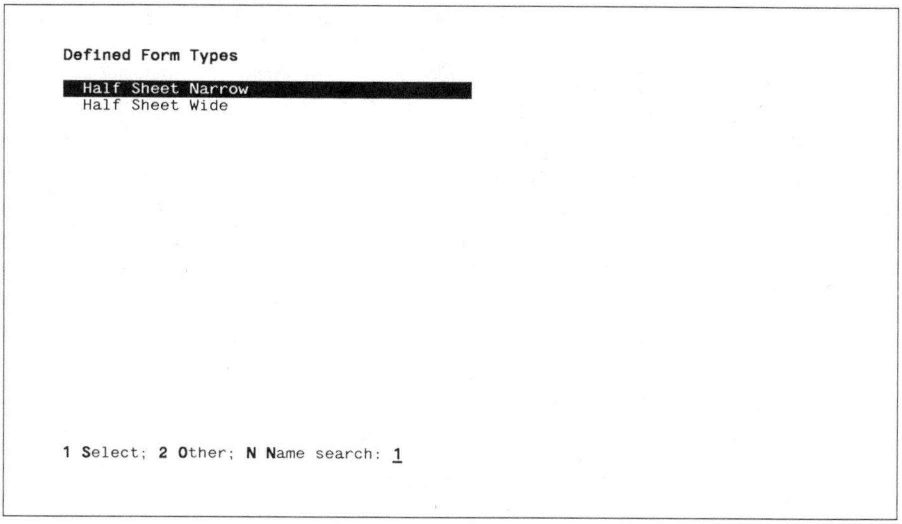

```
Defined Form Types

   Half Sheet Narrow
   Half Sheet Wide
```

```
1 Select; 2 Other; N Name search: 1
```

FIGURE 7.15: Selecting a nonstandard form type by using the Other option on the Format Paper Type menu. When you select this option, you see a list of all of the forms that you have defined whose names don't correspond to the first seven paper type options. In this case, there are two nonstandard form types defined for the printer: Half Sheet Narrow and Half Sheet Wide. To select one of these, you move the highlight bar to its name and choose the Select option.

Note: You can use the Other option (**2** or **O**) on the Defined Form Types menu to type in the name of the form type. This allows you to enter the name of a standard form type, if you select the Other option from the Format Paper Type menu before realizing that you should have selected one of the Form Type options on this menu. That way, you don't have to redo the entire command sequence in order to use the desired form, for if you press F1 (Cancel) from the Defined Form Types menu, you will be returned to the Format Page menu, and no form type will be selected.

After selecting the form type, you are returned to the Format Page menu. When you press F7 (Exit), you are returned to the document editing screen. WordPerfect inserts a code at the cursor's position, indicating the paper size and form type selected. This code affects the printing of the rest of the document until you select a new paper size and form type. For instance, if you had selected the Half Sheet Narrow form type shown in Figure 7.15, you would see the following code in the Reveal Codes screen upon returning to the document editing screen:

[Paper Sz/Typ:5.5″ × 8.5″,Half Sheet Narrow]

The positioning of the Paper Size/Type code depends on the function of the form type you are using. If you are selecting a form type that should be applied to the entire document, place the cursor at the very beginning of the document before selecting the paper size and form type. If you are selecting a form type that should be applied to just a single page or a group of pages, place the cursor at the top of the page that the code is to control.

For example, suppose that you are creating a two-page business letter; for the first page, you want to use the Letterhead form type that takes letterhead paper from the first bin, and for the second page, you want to use the Bond form type that takes plain bond from the second bin. At the top of the first page, you insert the code to use the Letterhead form type by selecting the Standard Paper Size option (**1** or **S**) and the Letterhead Form Type option (**3** or **H**). Then, at the top of the second page (beneath the [SPg] code), you insert the code to use the Bond form type by selecting the Standard Paper Size option (**1** or **S**) and the Bond Form Type option (**2** or **B**).

Installing the Fonts for Your Printer

The last three options on the Printer Edit menu deal with the fonts your printer can use. The Cartridges and Fonts option (**5** or **C**) is used to install any nonresident fonts that your printer can use. If you have a laser printer, these fonts can come on either a cartridge or a disk. (Disk fonts are referred to alternatively as downloadable or soft fonts.) The fonts from either source must be purchased separately and must be installed using this option before they can be used in your documents.

The Initial Font option (**6** or **I**) allows you to select a new font that your printer will continue to use as the default. You only change this option if you are dissatisfied with the selection made by WordPerfect, shown to the right of this option on the Printer Edit screen.

The Path for Downloadable Fonts and Printer Command Files option (**7** or **D**) is used to designate the directory in which WordPerfect will find any soft fonts that you wish to use with your printer. Remember that you must use the Cartridges and Fonts option to install all of the fonts that you have copied to this directory. This directory can also contain special printer command files whose instructions can be used in the printing of a document (see "Entering Printer Codes in a Document" later in this chapter).

Because of the importance of this subject, an entire chapter of this book is devoted to the use of fonts in a document. For detailed information on installing and using fonts in a document, please see Chapter 5, "Working with Fonts."

Installing Several Printers

To install more than one printer for use with WordPerfect, you simply repeat the installation procedure by choosing the Additional Printers option (**2** or **A**) from the Print Select Printer menu (Shift-F7 S). It is advisable to install all of the printers that you will be using in one session while you still have the Printer disks handy.

If you have a hard disk, you can copy the .ALL files that contain the printers' .PRS files on your hard disk, either in the WordPerfect directory or in a special printer directory that you create. For example, if you use an Epson FX-80 for rough drafts and an HP LaserJet Series II for final output, you would copy both the WPRINT1.ALL and WPRINT3.ALL files in your directory since the HPLASEII.PRS file is located in the WPRINT1.ALL file and the EPFX-80.PRS file is located in the WPRINT3.ALL file. After installing the HPLaserJet and Epson FX-80 printers, you then delete the two .ALL files from the hard disk. If you don't have the disk space to copy these two large files, you can still install these printers by placing the Printer1 and Printer3 disks in drive A and using the Other Disk option (**2** or **O**) after selecting the Additional Printers option (**2** or **A**) from the Print Select Printer menu.

The .PRS files, which define how WordPerfect will utilize the printer's capabilities and which are copied from the appropriate .ALL file, are displayed when you obtain a directory listing of your printer directory using List Files (F5). You can also see which printer definition files have been copied to this directory from within WordPerfect by using the List Printer Files option (**4** or **L**) available on the Additional Printers menu (Shift-F7 S A). Use the List Files Delete option to remove any of these files from within WordPerfect. (The List Printer Files menu doesn't include a Delete option.)

Setting Up Multiple Definitions for the Same Printer

In addition to installing all of the different printers you have attached to your system, you can set up several definitions for the same printer. For example, for the HP LaserJet Series II you could set up one definition that uses 10 pitch Courier as the initial font and another definition that uses 10 point Times Roman as the initial font. Then, when you are about to begin a document that you want proportionally spaced, you can select the HP LaserJet Series II definition that uses 10 point Times Roman as the initial font. There are two methods that you can follow to set up an additional definition for a printer; they are both outlined below.

In the first method, you select the Additional Printers option (**2** or **A**) from the Print Select Printer menu (Shift-F7 S) and then copy the .PRS file a second time from the appropriate .ALL file by choosing the same printer name with the Select option (**1** or **S**). For example, to set the alternate definitions for the HP LaserJet Series II as described above, you highlight *HP LaserJet Series II* on the printer list and type **S**. Then, upon receiving the prompt

Printer filename: HPLASEII.PRS

you edit the file name (being careful not to exceed eight characters or to modify the .PRS extension). After you edit the file name and press the Enter key, the

Printer Edit screen (similar to the one shown in Figure 7.5) appears. Here, you should edit the name of the printer by selecting the Name option (**1** or **N**) and entering a name up to 36 characters long. Then, make your changes to the default font by selecting the Initial Font option (**6** or **I**). After you have made all of the modifications to this printer definition, be sure to press F7 (Exit) to save it and return to the Print Select Printer menu.

In the second method, you create an alternate printer definition for the same printer by using the Copy option (**4** or **C**) on the Print Select Printer menu. To do this, you press Shift-F7 S, highlight the name of the printer whose definition you want to use, and type **C**. For instance, to copy the HPLASEII.PRS file used by the LaserJet Series II, you would highlight *HP LaserJet Series II* on the Print Select Printer menu and type **C**. Then, edit the file name and press the Enter key. This takes you to the Printer Edit screen, where you rename the printer definition; you can also install new cartridge fonts or soft fonts and change the initial font to the one you wish this printer definition to use. When you are finished editing the new printer definition and return to the Print Select Printer screen, you will see this new definition listed under the name you assigned to it. To switch to this alternate printer before you begin a new document that is to use it, you move the highlight cursor to it and choose the Select option (**1** or **S**).

Figure 7.16 shows you the Printer Edit screen for an alternate HP LaserJet Series II printer definition. This definition was created by copying the original printer definition from the Print Select Printer menu. That way, all of the

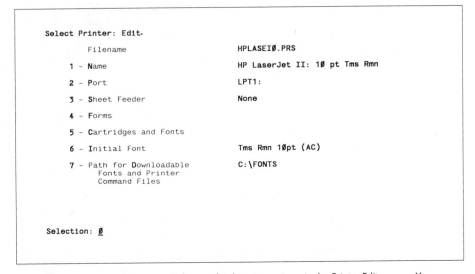

FIGURE 7.16: Creating an alternate definition for the same printer in the Printer Edit screen. You can create such a definition by copying the existing definition and then making whatever changes are required by using the various options on the Printer Edit screen for that printer definition.

installed cartridge fonts and soft fonts saved in the HPLASEII.PRS file were copied over to the new .PRS file used by this definition (in this example, named HPLASEI0.PRS); thus it was unnecessary to use the Cartridges and Fonts option on the Printer Edit screen to reinstall all of these fonts. This new definition has been renamed HP LaserJet II: 10 pt Tms Rmn to differentiate it from the original HP LaserJet Series II printer definition (which has been renamed HP LaserJet II: 10 pitch Courier—see Figure 7.17) on the Print Select Printer menu. In addition, the initial font has been changed from 10 pitch Courier (PC-8) to Tms Rmn 10pt (AC). Figure 7.17 shows you the Print Select Printer screen after this alternate HP LaserJet Series II printer definition has been saved and after the original definition has been renamed HP LaserJet II: 10 pitch Courier.

PRINTING METHODS—AN OVERVIEW

Because there are numerous ways with which to print in WordPerfect, we will examine each of them before going on to discuss the printer control and print options available to you. Regardless of the printing method chosen, WordPerfect performs all of its printing in the background, allowing you to return to editing as soon as you have issued the appropriate printing command. Because all printing methods support background printing, there is seldom any need for you to wait until a print job has finished before returning to WordPerfect either to create a

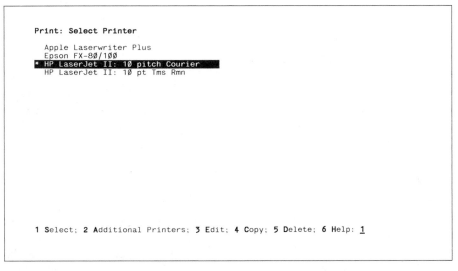

FIGURE 7.17: The Print Select Printer screen after adding the alternate printer definition for the HP LaserJet Series II and after renaming the original definition HP LaserJet II: 10 pitch Courier.

new document or to edit an existing one. However, if a page of the document you are printing contains complex graphic images, you may want to refrain from editing until that page is printed. In early releases of WordPerfect 5.0, attempts at doing even simple background editing while printing graphics were known to cause WordPerfect to crash.

Printing the Document on the Editing Screen

WordPerfect allows you to print the document that is currently in RAM—the document you are working on—even if you have not saved it. You can print the entire document or print only the current page. If you want to print less than the entire document but more than the current page, you must block the text and then press Shift-F7 when using this method (See "Printing a Block of Text" later in this chapter.)

To print the document currently in memory, press Shift-F7. The Print menu shown in Figure 7.18 appears on the screen. Select the Full Document option (**1** or **F**) to print the entire document, or the Page option (**2** or **P**) to print the current page only. You can suspend printing by selecting the Control Printer option (**4** or **C**) and then selecting the Stop option (**5** or **S**) on the Printer Control screen. This technique for stopping the printer is discussed in more detail later in this chapter.

By using the options on the Print menu before you make your printout, you can change the printer, the number of copies, the binding width for the printed

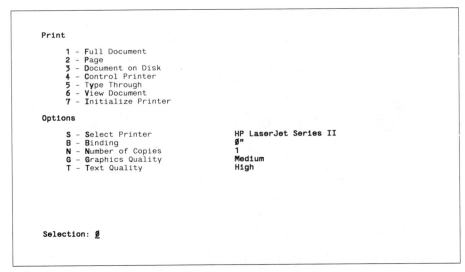

```
Print

        1 - Full Document
        2 - Page
        3 - Document on Disk
        4 - Control Printer
        5 - Type Through
        6 - View Document
        7 - Initialize Printer

   Options

        S - Select Printer          HP LaserJet Series II
        B - Binding                 Ø"
        N - Number of Copies        1
        G - Graphics Quality        Medium
        T - Text Quality            High




   Selection: Ø
```

FIGURE 7.18: The Print menu in WordPerfect 5.0. To print the entire document on the document editing screen, select the Full Document option (**1** or **F**). To print just the current page, select the Page option (**2** or **P**).

document, or the print quality of the text or graphics in the document. (See "Using the Print Options" later in this chapter for details on how to use each of these options.) You can also obtain an on-screen preview of the printed document by selecting the View Document option (**6** or **V**) from this menu. (See "Previewing the Printout with View Document" later in this chapter for more information on using this feature.)

When you print either the full text or the current page of the document in memory, WordPerfect creates a temporary copy of the file in RAM or, if there is insufficient free memory, on the current disk. If you are printing the full text of a particularly long document, you may run into a situation in which you receive the error message telling you that the disk is full when you press Shift-F7 and type **F**. This occurs whenever the current disk does not have enough free space to accommodate the temporary copy of the file that's in RAM. In such a case, you will have to use one of the two methods for printing a document that has been saved on disk (see "Printing a Document on Disk" just ahead).

Printing a Document on Disk

WordPerfect gives you two methods for printing a document that has already been saved on disk: you can use the Print option on the List Files menu (F5 Enter P), or you can use the Document on Disk option on the Print menu (Shift-F7 D). When you use either of these methods, remember that WordPerfect will print the document as it was last saved on disk. If you have the document you want to print in RAM and have made editing changes that have not been saved, these changes will not be reflected in the printout unless you save the document again before using either of these printing commands.

PRINTING FROM THE LIST FILES SCREEN

You can print all or part of a single document from either the List Files screen or the Print menu. However, you will usually find it much easier to use the List Files screen when you want to print several documents at one time because you do not need to type the file name; it is also a faster method for adding files to the queue when you want to print a group of files in the same directory.

To print a single document located in the current directory or on the active data disk, you press F5 (List Files) and the Enter key. Then move the highlight cursor to the name of the file that you want printed and select the Print option (**4** or **P**). You receive the prompt

Page(s): (All)

To print the entire document, press the Enter key. If you want to print a single page, enter its page number (as it appears on the status line of the document), and press the Enter key. To print a range of pages, enter the starting and ending page numbers separated by a hyphen, as in **3–7** to print pages 3 through 7 inclusive, and press the Enter key. As soon as you press Enter, you may return to work and create or edit another document by pressing F1 (Cancel). For more information on specifying selected pages to print, see "Specifying the Pages to Print" later in this chapter.

To have more than one file printed, you can mark each file name listed by moving the highlight cursor to it and typing * (the asterisk). To mark the file, WordPerfect will place an asterisk right after the byte count in the file listing. To select all of the documents in the directory, press Alt-F5. After you have marked all of the files you want printed in this manner, select the Print option. You will receive the message

Print Marked Files? (Y/N) No

You type **Y** to have WordPerfect place the marked files in its print queue (in alphabetical order) and begin printing the first one.

If you need to suspend the printing, cancel a print job, delete one of the files in the queue, or advance one of the files to the head of the queue, you must do this from the Control Printer screen. To access this screen, you press Shift-F7 and select the Control Printer option (**4** or **C**). See the following section for a discussion of how you would accomplish these tasks using the options listed on this menu.

You can also print documents in other subdirectories. With the List Files screen displayed (F5 Enter), highlight the subdirectory name and press the Enter key twice. Then highlight the document file you want to print and type **4** or **P**. Again, if you want to print a group of files listed in this subdirectory, mark all of the files with an asterisk before typing **4** or **P**. If you want to return to the current directory, highlight .. *<PARENT> <DIR>* and press the Enter key. (See Chapter 8 for more information on changing directories in WordPerfect.)

When you have finished selecting documents to be printed, press F1, the Cancel key, to return to your document or to begin work on a new document.

PRINTING A DOCUMENT ON DISK FROM THE PRINT MENU

You can also print all or part of a document on disk by selecting the Document on Disk option (**3** or **D**) from the Print menu (Shift-F7). When you select this option, you receive the prompt

Document name:

where you type in the name of the document you wish to print. If the document is not located in the current directory, include the full path name. If the document is in the current directory, you need not include the drive and directory specifications as part of the name.

If you misspell the name of the file, or if the file name you enter is not located in the directory that you specified, you will receive the message

ERROR: File not found

when you press the Enter key. If you cannot figure out your error and need to refer to a directory listing, you must exit the Print screen by pressing F1 twice. You can then use the List Files screen (F5 Enter) to find the file name. Once you locate it, you can print it directly from the List Files screen by selecting the Print option (**4** or **P**).

Specifying the Pages to Print   After you enter a valid file name and press the Enter key, you receive the prompt

Page(s): (All)

To have the entire document printed, all you have to do is press the Enter key. However, if you want to print only a range of pages, you indicate this by entering the first and last pages to be printed, separated by a hyphen. For example, if all you wanted to print were pages 48 through 50, you would indicate this by typing **48–50** over the *(All)* displayed after *Page(s):* on the screen. You can specify a starting page with no ending page, or an ending page with no starting page. For instance, to print from page 10 to the end of the document you enter **10–**, while to print from the beginning of the document up to and including page 15 you enter **–15**.

You can also specify individual, discontinuous pages and ranges of pages to be printed. For example, to print just pages 6, 9, and 21–24 from a document, you enter **6,9,21–24** in response to the Page(s) prompt. Table 7.1 shows you examples of the kinds of page selections you can enter in response to the Page(s) prompt.

ENTRY	RESULT
Page(s): 4	Prints only page 4 of the document.
Page(s): 6,12	Prints pages 6 and 12 of the document.
Page(s): 2-6,17	Prints pages 2 through 6 and page 17 of the document.
Page(s): 10-	Prints from page 10 to the end of the document.
Page(s): -5	Prints from the beginning of the document through page 5.
Page(s): x-xii	Prints Roman numeral pages 10 through 12.
Page(s): iv,2-5,iv-x	Prints the first Roman numeral page iv, Arabic numeral pages 2 through 5, and finally the second Roman numeral pages iv through x.

TABLE 7.1: Entering Selected Pages to Be Printed

Printing a Block of Text

You can also quickly print a specified block of text without going through the Printer Control screen. To do so, mark the block (Alt-F4) and then press Shift-F7. Enter **Y** to the prompt

Print block? (Y/N) No

You do not have to wait until the block is printed before returning to your document.

Printing the Screen Contents

You can also print out the contents of the current screen. To do so, press Shift-PrtSc. Your printer may translate some graphics characters that appear on your screen into symbols it can print. Also, the printout will contain the information on the status line at the bottom of the screen.

This procedure does not go through WordPerfect's printer control; to cancel printing before the current screen is printed, you must press Ctrl-Break.

Note: If you want to obtain a printout of all of the files in the List Files screen, you don't have to use the Shift-PrtSc method. WordPerfect will print out the entire contents of the List Files screen (including those that are visible and any that are not) if you press Shift-F7 after bringing up the List Files screen (F5 Enter).

Using WordPerfect as a Typewriter

You can use WordPerfect as a typewriter by selecting the Type Through option (**5** or **Y**) from the Print menu. If the printer you are using doesn't support the Type Through feature, you will receive the following message at the bottom of the Print screen:

Feature not available on this printer

Note: The Type Through feature works with fewer dot matrix printers in version 5.0 than it did in version 4.2. For example, you could perform type-through printing with the Epson FX-85 in version 4.2, whereas you get the "Feature not available on this printer" message when you select Type Through in WordPerfect 5.0.

If your printer does support type-through printing, you will find it is most useful when you only need to print an incidental envelope or mailing label that you have no intention of saving. When using type-through printing, you can choose between having each character echoed to the printer as you type it, or each line.

These two options are selected from the following menu, which appears when you press Shift-F7 and type **5** or **Y**:

Type Through by: **1** Line; **2 C**haracter: 0

Once you have selected either line-by-line or character-by-character typing, you will see a screen similar to the Line Type Through printing screen shown in Figure 7.19.

If you receive the message

ERROR: Printer not ready

instead, check to make sure that the printer cable is properly connected to both the computer and the printer, and that the printer is on.

Most of the time you will find it more convenient to print line by line rather than character by character. This is because you cannot correct any typing mistakes when you use character-by-character printing; each character you type is immediately printed. Also, you may find that your printer will not support WordPerfect's character-by-character type-through printing. To clear the screen of the characters that have already been sent to the printer, press Ctrl-PgDn (Delete to End of Page).

When you use line-by-line type-through printing, the line of text that you enter is not printed until you press the Enter key. This gives you time to catch any typing errors and correct them on the line before you use the Enter key to send the line to the printer and advance the printhead to the next line.

To align the printhead on the proper line, you can press the ↓ or Enter key to move down a line. On some printers, pressing the ↑ key will move the printhead up a line. To begin printing in some distance from the left edge of the paper, move the cursor to the proper horizontal position on your monitor by pressing

```
—


Line Type Through printing

Function Key          Action

Move                  Retrieve the previous line for editing
Format                Do a printer command
Enter                 Print the line
Exit/Cancel           Exit without printing




                                                              Pos 1
```

FIGURE 7.19: The Line Type Through printing screen. When you use Line Type Through, you can edit each line before sending it to the printer. When you use Character Type Through, each character is sent directly to the printer, so you have no opportunity to correct any typing errors.

the space bar. If you make a typing error on a line before you press the Enter key, you can use the ← or → key to move the cursor to the place where you need to make the correction. You can also use Home ← or Home → to move to the beginning or end of the line. However, you can't use Ctrl-← or Ctrl-→ to move one word at a time on the line.

Note that when you use the Type Through feature, the program is always in Typeover mode, and there is no way to put it into Insert mode. Also, while you can still delete characters on the line with either Del or Backspace, you can't use Ctrl-Backspace to delete a word.

You can use Move (Ctrl-F4) to insert a copy of the previous line into the current line that contains the cursor. You can also use Format (Shift-F8) to enter a printer code that will change the print style. For example, you could change to expanded or condensed print when typing a mailing label or envelope. When you press Shift-F8 in Type Through, WordPerfect responds with

Command:

Type in the printer code for turning on the kind of printing you want to use and press the Enter key. (See "Entering Special Printer Commands in Your Document" later in this chapter for more information about entering printer control codes.)

You can type up to 250 characters on a line when using the Type Through feature. However, you must be using wide paper (14" × 11") and have the printer in compressed mode before it will be able to print a single line with so many characters. If you press the Enter key to print and your printer can't accommodate the number of characters you have entered on a line, you will see the message

Printer not accepting characters. Press EXIT or Cancel to quit or fix printer and then press any other key to continue.

In such a case, press either F7 or F1 and then reenter fewer characters on the line before pressing the Enter key. Word wrap is not in effect when you use Type Through; if you type more than 80 characters, the screen will scroll to the right.

To quit type-through printing and return to the regular document editing window, press either F7 (Exit) or F1 (Cancel).

Chain Printing with the Master Document Feature

You can print any number of separate documents in succession as though they were all part of the same document by using the Master Document feature. With this feature, you indicate the documents and the order in which they are to be chain-printed by adding Subdoc (Subdocument) codes to a master document that contains the documents' file names. A master document can consist of Subdoc codes only, or it can contain new text interspersed with these Subdoc codes.

Assembling a master document is quick and easy. After starting a new document, you simply position the cursor where the text of the first subdocument is to be printed, press Alt-F5 (Mark Text), and select the Subdoc option (**2** or **S**). You are then prompted to enter the name of the document:

Subdoc Filename:

Enter the file name (including the drive and directory path if the file is not located in the current directory) and press Enter.

WordPerfect then places the name of the subdocument in a box. Figure 7.20 shows five subdocuments added to a master document in this way. In addition to the box that you can see on the editing screen identifying the name of the subdocument, WordPerfect inserts a [Subdoc] code into the document. For example, the code for the INTRO subdocument at the beginning of the master document appears as

[Subdoc:INTRO]

in the Reveal Codes screen.

Before you can print a master document, you must expand it by pressing Alt-F5 (Mark Text) and then selecting the Generate option (**6** or **G**) followed by the Expand Master Document option (**3** or **E**). When you select this option, Word-Perfect locates each [Subdoc] code and inserts the actual text of the named file in that location. In addition, the program replaces the [Subdoc] code with a [Subdoc Start] code and places a [Subdoc End] code at the end of the document; both

```
┌─────────────────────────────────────────────────────────────────────────┐
│                                                                           │
│    ┌──────────────────────────────────────────────────────────────────┐  │
│    │ Subdoc:  INTRO                                                     │  │
│    └──────────────────────────────────────────────────────────────────┘  │
│    ┌──────────────────────────────────────────────────────────────────┐  │
│    │ Subdoc:  LESSON1                                                   │  │
│    └──────────────────────────────────────────────────────────────────┘  │
│    ┌──────────────────────────────────────────────────────────────────┐  │
│    │ Subdoc:  LESSON2                                                   │  │
│    └──────────────────────────────────────────────────────────────────┘  │
│    ┌──────────────────────────────────────────────────────────────────┐  │
│    │ Subdoc:  LESSON3                                                   │  │
│    └──────────────────────────────────────────────────────────────────┘  │
│    ┌──────────────────────────────────────────────────────────────────┐  │
│    │ Subdoc:  LESSON4                                                   │  │
│    └──────────────────────────────────────────────────────────────────┘  │
│    _                                                                      │
│                                                                           │
│    D:\WP\WDC\MASTER.DOC                          Doc 2 Pg 1 Ln 1" Pos 1"   │
│                                                                           │
└─────────────────────────────────────────────────────────────────────────┘
```

FIGURE 7.20: A master document with five subdocuments. The text of each subdocument shown in this figure will be printed in the order shown here.

of these codes include the name of the subdocument. It is important that you not delete either of these codes. If you do, WordPerfect won't be able to condense the text of the subdocument when you use the Condense Master Document option on the Mark Text Generate menu after printing the master document.

If WordPerfect can't find a file that matches the document name you indicated for a subdocument, you will receive the message

Subdoc not found (Press Enter to skip):

The message will include the name of the subdocument. In such a case, you may press the Enter key so that WordPerfect will continue to expand the master document with the remaining subdocuments or press F1 (Cancel) to stop the expansion. If you find that you have entered the file or directory path name in error, delete the existing [Subdoc] code and then create a new subdocument using the correct file name.

> *Note:* If you press the Enter key to skip the subdocument that is not found, you can later replace the incorrect [Subdoc] code with one containing the correct subdocument name and again choose the Expand Master Document option on the Mark Text Generate menu (Alt-F5 G E) to have the correct file expanded.

While the master document is expanded, you can make any necessary editing changes or enter any footnote, endnote, index, list, table of contents, or automatic reference markings that you want generated for the master document prior to printing. (See Chapter 9 for more information about using these reference utilities.) When you are ready to print the master document, you press Shift-F7 (Print) and select the Full Document option (**1** or **F**).

You can only print the master document successfully when it is expanded. This means you can't print a master document from disk either from the List Files screen (F5 Enter P) or from the Print menu (Shift-F7 D) unless you save the expanded version on disk. If you do try printing the condensed version using either of these options, your printout will consist only of any text that you have added to the master document. If your master document consists of just Subdocument codes, you will get a blank sheet of paper. Because you have to print the document in memory, you can't print just a selected range of pages in the master document; you must print either the entire document (Shift-F7 F) or just the current page (Shift-F7 P) or a block of text (Alt-F4, shift-F7 Y).

To save the expanded version on disk, press F10 (Save). WordPerfect will present the prompt

Document is expanded, condense it? (Y/N) Yes

Type **N**, enter the file name you wish to give to the expanded version, and press Enter. The program will save all of the text in the subdocuments (along with the [Subdoc Start] and [Subdoc End] codes) and any text that exists only in

If it is the first time you have issued the PRINT command during a work session, you will receive the prompt

Name of list device [PRN]

Press Enter if the printer is attached to the first parallel port. Indicate a different device by entering the port type and number, as in LPT2, LPT3, COM1, COM2, and the like.

> *Note:* Do not use the PRINT command to print your DOS text file if you have temporarily exited WordPerfect to get to the operating system by using the Shell (Go to DOS) command (Ctrl-F1 G). If you do use the PRINT command from the shell, WordPerfect will lock up on you when you return to the program after typing EXIT and pressing Enter. You will then have to reboot the computer and restart WordPerfect. You can, however, safely use the COPY command to print your DOS text file and afterward return directly to Word-Perfect without causing the program to crash.

WordPerfect offers another way to create a DOS text file that can be printed directly from the operating system instead of from within WordPerfect. To use this method, you first install and select the DOS Text Printer as the printer to use. This printer definition is located on the Printer3 disk under the name DOS Text Printer. Install it as you would any other printer to use with WordPerfect (refer back to "Installing Your Printer" for details on this procedure).

After copying the DOS Text Printer definition file (DOTEXPRI.PRS) during installation of the DOS Text Printer, you select the Port option (**2** or **P**) on the Printer Edit screen. Then, select the Other option (**8** or **O**) and enter the name you want to give to the resulting DOS text file in response to the Device or Filename prompt (such as LETTER.TXT).

Press F7 (Exit) to leave the Printer Edit screen and return to the Print menu. From this menu, choose the Select Printer option (**1** or **S**), then use the ↑ or ↓ key to highlight *DOS Text Printer* on the Print Select Printer menu and choose the Select option (**1** or **S**). This returns you to the Print menu, where you select the Full Document option (**1** or **F**). WordPerfect will then print the document currently in the document editing screen to disk under the name you specified in response to the Device or Filename prompt.

After creating a DOS text file in this manner, you can use the COPY or PRINT command in DOS to print its contents directly from the operating system prompt. When you print the file, you will find that it is formatted as it appeared on screen. However, the printout will lack any special print enhancements that you used, like boldface and underlining. If the document you wish to print from DOS contains such print enhancements, you must use the first method, whereby you define the appropriate printer definition to use and assign the DOS text file a new name.

After printing the file to disk using the DOS Text Printer definition, remember to return to the Print Select Printer screen and select the printer you normally use. If you forget to do this and try printing another document that you create during the same work session, it too will be saved as a DOS text file using the same name that you gave the previous file in response to the Device or Filename prompt. If this happens, the contents of the document you are currently working on will replace the DOS text file you created earlier.

It is important to note that you can't successfully print a DOS text file created with either of these methods using one of WordPerfect's Print commands. If you try to, you will receive the following error message:

ERROR: Incompatible file format

Documents printed to disk are to be printed only from DOS. You don't need to go through this procedure if you can print the document directly from within WordPerfect.

Also, if you need to make editing changes, do so from the original document saved as a WordPerfect file. After you complete your changes and have saved the document, repeat the procedure for printing a copy to disk as a DOS text file and then print it as outlined above.

GETTING READY TO PRINT

Before you actually send a document to your printer using any of WordPerfect's printing methods, you may need to further refine the printout by adjusting the settings of some of the Print options on the Print menu. For example, if you are producing the final draft of a document, you may need to select a new printer and change the print quality to near-letter-quality mode. If you are going to make two-sided copies of the document, you may want to set a binding width to adjust the printing position of even-numbered and odd-numbered pages. If you want WordPerfect to print more than one copy of the document, you need to reset the number of copies. If you are printing a rough draft of a document and using a dot matrix printer, you should change the text print quality so that WordPerfect doesn't use near-letter-quality mode. If your document contains graphic images, you may need to print them separately from the text.

If your document uses fonts that are not built into the printer and you have marked them as being present when the print job begins, you also need to select the Initialize Printer option to have WordPerfect download these fonts to your printer if this has not been done before. You will also often find it useful to select the View Document feature to preview the printout and make sure that everything is the way you want it.

Previewing the Printout with View Document

WordPerfect's View Document option (**6** or **V**) on the Print menu allows you to preview all of the document, or specific pages, to see how they appear when printed. This option is very useful because it approximates the printed page much more closely than is possible in the normal editing screen. The View Document display shows you the text of any headers, footers, and footnotes used on the page as well as the actual page number, if one of the automatic page numbering methods is used. It also displays justification if you've used it in the document, which is not the case in the normal document editing screen.

If your computer is equipped with graphics capabilities, the preview will show you the position of these types of elements. It will also display the paragraphs on the page in relation to the edges of the page. If you have selected a new paper size and type, the preview will show you this paper size and the text in relation to its edges. For example, if you have selected Envelope as the paper size and type, the page displayed when you select View Document will approximate that of the standard business envelope, $9\frac{1}{2}$ inches wide by 4 inches long.

In addition, if the document contains graphic images such as a Lotus 1-2-3 graph in a Figure box, you will be able to see all of the elements of the graph as well as any caption you have assigned to it. (In the document editing screen, you see only the outline of the Figure box and its number.) WordPerfect also displays different font sizes and styles used in the document. Here, the preview is not exact; it differentiates Helvetica from Times Roman by showing Helvetica as a sans serif type and Times Roman as a serif type. It cannot, however, accurately display the difference between Times Roman and Century Schoolbook type (both of which are serif types). In addition to displaying the size of the font used, the View Document feature shows the line height used.

THE VIEW DOCUMENT SIZE OPTIONS

You are also able to adjust the size of the displayed page when using View Document on a computer with graphics capabilities. There are four size options available from the View Document display screen:

1 100%   2 200%   3 Full Page   4 Facing Pages

Option **3**, Full Page, is the default. Figure 7.21 shows you the first page of a document using the Full Page display. This display is useful when you are interested in checking the layout of the page, not when you want to examine its text. To see the text at full size, you need to select option **1**, 100%, as illustrated in Figure 7.22. At 100%, you can't see all of the text on a page. You can scroll through the text using the same cursor movement keys that you use to scroll through a document in the normal editing screen. If you need to inspect a part of the page up

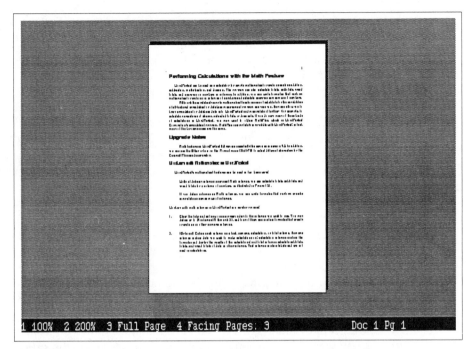

FIGURE 7.21: Preview of the first page of a sample document, using the View Document option (Shift-F7 V) with the Full Page option (the default) selected.

close, you select option **2**, 200%, which displays a portion of the page at twice normal size (as illustrated in Figure 7.23).

To check the layout of a two-page "spread," you select option **4**, Facing Pages. If you select this option when the cursor is on the first page of the document, WordPerfect will show only the full-page display of page 1 shifted to the right of the screen. This is because WordPerfect always assumes that the first page of the document is a right-hand page. However, if you press PgDn, you will then see pages 2 and 3 (on the left and right, respectively) in the display screen, as shown in Figure 7.24. Obviously, you only use the Facing Pages option when your document contains more than two pages of text.

You can switch to a new display size at any time while still in View Document mode by selecting another of the four options.

USING THE VIEW DOCUMENT OPTION

Using the View Document option can save you from wasting paper when you must reprint part or all of a document that contains errors. You can use it to check alignments, positioning, text attributes, and the like. If you spot an error, you can then return to the document editing screen and fix it before sending the document to the printer.

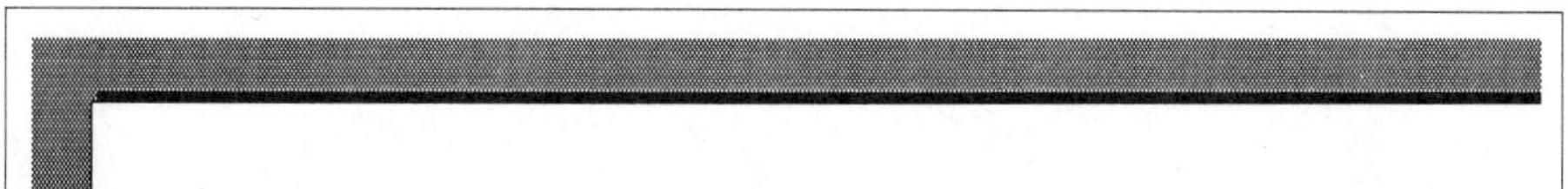
1

Performing Calculations with the Math Feature

WordPerfect can be used as a calculator for simple mathematical operations such as addition, subtraction, multiplication, and division. The program can also calculate totals, subtotals, grand totals, and averages on numbers in columns. In addition, you can write formulas that perform mathematical operations on columns of numbers and calculate averages across rows of numbers.

Although these relatively simple mathematical functions cannot substitute for the capabilities a full-featured spreadsheet or database management program can give you, they can allow you to bring spreadsheet or database data into WordPerfect and manipulate it further- -for example, to calculate percentages of change, extended totals, or discounts. If you do very many of these kinds of calculations in WordPerfect, you may want to obtain MathPlan, which is WordPerfect Corporation's spreadsheet program. MathPlan is completely compatible with WordPerfect; in fact, many of the key sequences are the same.

Upgrade Notes

Math features in WordPerfect 5.0 remain essentially the same as in version 4.2. In addition, you can use the Other option on the Format menu (Shift-F8) to select different characters for the

1 100% 2 200% 3 Full Page 4 Facing Pages: 1 Doc 1 Pg 1

FIGURE 7.22: Preview of the first page of a sample document, using the View Document option (Shift-F7 V) with the 100% option selected. This shows part of the text of the document at full size.

To use this feature, move the cursor to the page you want to preview, press Shift-F7, and select the View Document option (**6** or **V**). To see the next page of the document, press the PgDn key. You can also use the Go to Page feature (Ctrl-Home followed by the page number) to preview a specific page. To see more of the page, press ↓ or the Screen Down key (+ on the numeric pad). You can also scroll the text up by pressing ↑ or the Screen Up key (– on the numeric pad), or go to the previous page by pressing PgUp. As discussed earlier, you can also change the size of the display by selecting another of the four size options.

Remember, however, that you can't edit the text shown in the View Document display. When you are finished previewing the document, press F7 (Exit) to return to the normal document editing screen. The cursor's position in the editing screen will be the same as in the View Document screen.

Note: You may experience a bug in the program whereby you receive the prompt to save the document (as though you had pressed F7 to clear the document editing screen) when you press the Enter key after returning to the document from the View Document display. If this happens, press F1 (Cancel) right away, unless you want to save the document and clear the editing screen.

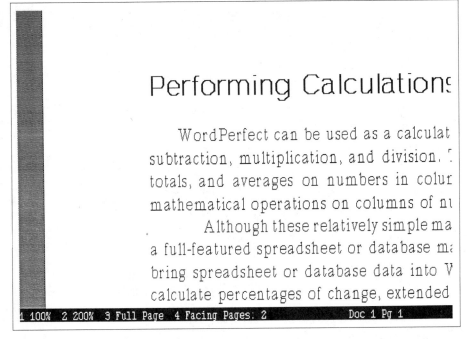

FIGURE 7.23: Preview of the first page of a sample document, using the View Document option (Shift-F7 V) with the 200% option selected. This shows part of the text of the document at twice full size.

A VIEW DOCUMENT MACRO

You can create a macro that takes you into the View Document screen. With the macro constructed in Figure 7.25, you need only press Alt-V to preview the current page. When you are finished examining the document in View Document mode, you can press Enter (instead of F7) to return to the normal document editing screen because of the {PAUSE} added before the {Exit} command. See Chapter 16 for a complete description of WordPerfect macros.

Initializing the Printer

The Initialize Printer option (**7** or **I**) on the Print menu (Shift-F7) is used to have WordPerfect download soft fonts that are not built into your printer and that you have indicated will already be present when the print job begins (by marking them with an asterisk when installing the fonts). You only have to use this option once during a work session unless you cancel the print job and Word-Perfect instructs you to select the Cancel option a second time (see "Managing

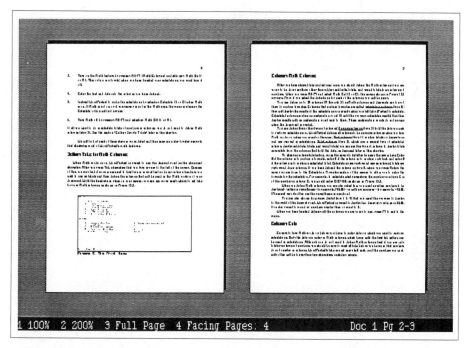

FIGURE 7.24: Preview of the second and third pages of a sample document, using the View Document option (Shift-F7 V) with the Facing Pages option selected. When you use the Facing Pages option, the even-numbered page is always shown on the left side and the odd-numbered page is always shown on the right side of the display screen.

```
Macro: Edit

        File            ALTV.WPM

  1 - Description     View Document

  2 - Action


    ┌──────────────────────────────────────────────────┐
    │ {Print}v{PAUSE}{Exit}                            │
    │                                                  │
    │                                                  │
    │                                                  │
    │                                                  │
    │                                                  │
    │                                                  │
    └──────────────────────────────────────────────────┘




  Selection: 0
```

FIGURE 7.25: A View Document macro to take you to the preview display screen when you press Alt-V. To exit this display and return to the normal editing screen, you simply press the Enter key.

the Printing'' later in this chapter). If this happens, you will see a message at the bottom of the Control Printer screen warning you that you will have to reinitialize the printer before printing again.

Obviously, you don't have to use the Initialize Printer option unless you have a laser printer and are printing a document that uses soft fonts that are not built into the printer. You don't need to use this if your printer doesn't use soft fonts or if your document uses fonts that are supplied on a cartridge.

When you select the Initialize Printer option, WordPerfect creates a print job called *(Initialize)* and downloads each soft font that you indicated must be present in the printer's memory at print time (see Chapter 5, ''Working with Fonts''). These fonts stay in the printer's memory until you use the Initialize Printer option again or turn off the laser printer.

Remember that in order for the downloading to take place, you must have indicated the correct location of the Font files (not supplied with WordPerfect) using the Path for Downloadable Fonts and Printer Command Files option (**7** or **D**) on the Printer Edit screen (Shift-F7 S E). This directory must also contain the correct Font file for each of the fonts installed with an asterisk; otherwise, WordPerfect will halt the *(Initialize)* print job when it tries to download a missing font. You will then have to access the Control Printer screen (Shift-F7 C) and select the Go (start printer) option (**4** or **G**).

Using the Print Options

The Options section on the Print menu screen allows you to select a printer to use, specify the number of copies to be printed, specify any extra binding width you may need if your document is to be bound, or vary the print quality of the text or graphics in the document. These print options you select are only temporary; they stay in effect until you quit WordPerfect. To change print options so that they will be in effect each time you use WordPerfect, you can create a macro that selects the appropriate settings and then execute that macro when you start WordPerfect. (See ''DRAFT: A Macro to Select Draft Printing'' later in this chapter for more details on this technique.)

SELECTING A NEW PRINTER

Only one printer at a time can be selected. To use a new printer to print a particular document, you use the Select Printer option (**S**), the first of the Print options listed on the Print menu screen. This takes you to the Print Select Printer screen. Remember that upon completion of the installation of a new printer, its name is added to the list that appears on this screen.

The printer that is currently selected is marked with an asterisk immediately before its name on this menu. To select a new printer, use the ↑ or ↓ key to move the highlight cursor to its name and type **1** or **S** for the Select option. This returns you to the Print menu, where you will see the printer's name alongside the Select Printer option on this screen. From here, you can choose one of the other Print options or press F7 to return to document editing.

When you select a new printer, it remains the selected printer for the current and future work sessions with WordPerfect until you return to this menu and change to some other printer on the list. All new documents that you create will be formatted for this printer. This means that whatever font is defined as the initial font for the selected printer will be the default font assigned to the document (refer back to "Installing the Fonts for Your Printer").

If you try to print from disk a document that was created and saved with a printer that's not currently selected, you will receive the message

Document not formatted for current printer. Continue? (Y/N) No

If you press Enter, WordPerfect will cancel the printing command. If you type **Y**, WordPerfect will print the document in a font as close as possible to the initial font assigned by the original printer from among those fonts available on the current printer. For example, assume that you have installed both the Epson FX-80 with 10 CPI as the initial font and the HP LaserJet Series II with 10 pitch Courier as the initial font. Then, you select the Epson FX-80 as the default printer, create a letter, and print a rough draft of it. After making any final corrections to it and saving it, you choose the HP LaserJet Series II as the default printer for the final printout. Next, you select Print from the List Files screen (F5 Enter P) and type **Y** in response to the "document not formatted for current printer" message to have the document printed by the HP LaserJet. This time WordPerfect will print it in 10 pitch Courier.

The program does not print the document in 10 pitch Courier on the HP LaserJet Series II because this is the initial font for that printer, as you might think. Rather, it chooses 10 pitch Courier for the document because this font most closely matches the 10 CPI—the initial font for the Epson FX-80—under which the document was originally created.

You would have received the same results if you had installed an Epson FX-80 with 10 CPI as its initial font and an HP LaserJet Series II, this time with 12 point Times Roman as its initial font. When the document is created with the Epson as the default printer, the 10 CPI initial font is assigned to it. When you make the HP LaserJet Series II the default printer, even though 12 point Times Roman is its initial font, the document will still print the document in 10 pitch Courier because 10 pitch Courier most closely matches the 10 CPI font on the Epson. (See "Font Substitution" in Chapter 5 for more information.)

Note: If you wanted the final version of the letter printed in 12 point Times Roman on the HP LaserJet Series II after it was originally created with the Epson FX-80, you would have to change the document's initial font (Shift-F8 D F) to 12 point Times Roman after selecting the HP LaserJet Series II as the default printer (Shift-F7 S). You could also accomplish this by moving the cursor to the beginning of the file and changing the base font to 12 point Times Roman (Ctrl-F8 F).

CHANGING THE BINDING WIDTH

When a two-sided document is bound, especially if it is very large, it may be difficult to open it sufficiently to read all the text that is near the inside margins (the "gutter"). WordPerfect allows you to shift text that is on even-numbered (left-hand) pages to the left and to shift odd-numbered (right-hand) pages to the right to provide wider inside margins.

To do so, select the Binding option (**B**) on the Print menu and then enter the size of the inside margin you wish to use. For example, to increase the default 1-inch margin by ¼ inch on the inside, you would type **.25** and press Enter after selecting the Binding option. Remember to set this option back to 0'' if you want to print a page or entire document during the same work session without a binding width.

SPECIFYING THE NUMBER OF COPIES TO PRINT

You may often want to specify that more than one copy of your document be printed. WordPerfect will print as many copies as you indicate, while freeing you to return to other documents or begin work on a new document.

To change the number of copies, select the Number of Copies option (**N**) and type in the number you want printed. Then select the Full Document (**1** or **F**) or Page (**2** or **P**) option from the Print menu. Don't forget to change the number of copies back to 1 if you don't want multiple copies of a page or entire document that you print later in the same work session.

GRAPHICS QUALITY

If your document contains graphic images, you can control the quality of their printing. When you select the Graphics Quality option (**G**) on the Print menu, you are presented with the following options:

Graphics Quality: **1 Do Not Print; 2 Draft; 3 Medium; 4 High**: 3

The default setting for your printer depends upon the printer selected. For example, High is the default if you are using a LaserWriter, while Medium is the default if you are using the HP LaserJet Series II printer. Setting the Graphics Quality option to High will slow down the print job appreciably, as it takes longer for your printer to print the graphic images at high resolution.

Use the Do Not Print option (**1** or **N**) when your printer doesn't have sufficient memory to print both the text and the graphics on a page or in the entire document. After selecting this option and printing the document, you can reinsert the page or pages and reprint the document after selecting the Do Not Print option that appears when you select Text Quality (see the section that follows) and selecting the Graphics Quality option and resetting it to High. This technique of printing graphics separate from text in a document works well if you are using a laser printer where the paper is supplied from a paper cassette. However, it works less well if you are printing the document with a dot matrix printer that uses friction feed; it is very difficult to properly align a single page, to say nothing of several pages of the document.

> *Note:* Some dot matrix printers are incapable of printing complex graphic images even when you select the Do Not Print option for Text Quality. If you are using an HP LaserJet, you should consider getting more memory for the printer if your documents often combine text and graphics so that you don't have to use this technique of printing the same page or document twice.

TEXT QUALITY

The Text Quality option (**T**) on the Print menu uses the same options as the Graphics Quality option discussed above:

Text Quality: **1** Do **N**ot Print; **2 D**raft; **3 M**edium; **4** High: 4

If you are using a dot matrix printer, you can choose Medium (**3** or **M**) or Draft (**2** or **D**) to produce quicker rough drafts, or High to produce slower final printouts in near-letter-quality mode. If you are using a letter quality printer (with printwheels) or a laser printer, setting Text Quality to Medium or Draft has no effect: your printer is only capable of high-resolution text printing.

Select the Do Not Print option (**1** or **N**) to print only the graphic images in the document or on the page without the text when you need to print documents that combine text and graphics in two passes, as described in the previous section.

DRAFT: A MACRO TO SELECT DRAFT PRINTING

If you are using a dot matrix printer whose printer definition defaults to High (near-letter-quality mode) for text printing, you can easily forget to select the Text Quality option from the Print menu and set it to Medium or Draft before you begin printing. If you do most of your printing in draft mode and can't afford the time and ribbons to print your work in near-letter-quality mode, you can create and use a macro similar to the one shown in Figure 7.26. Further, you can run this DRAFT macro on startup by entering

WP/M-DRAFT

when you start WordPerfect. That way, you can be sure that any printing you do during that work session will be in draft mode unless you deliberately access the Print menu and change the Text Quality option to High for a final printout.

You can enter the startup command shown above manually, or you can insert it into a batch file or your AUTOEXEC.BAT file if you use either of these types of files to start WordPerfect. (See Chapter 1 for specific information on using WordPerfect startup options and creating and using an AUTOEXEC.BAT file.)

> *Note:* You can also overcome this problem by using the Printer Definition program (named PTR.EXE) that comes with WordPerfect. Refer to Appendix G, "Using the Printer Definition Program," for information on how to change the Text Quality default setting for the fonts that you use.

MANAGING THE PRINTING

Whenever you send an entire document or just a page of it to your printer using any of the printing methods described in this chapter, WordPerfect puts it in a "queue" (meaning a line of things waiting to be brought into service), thereby generating a print job for it. You can therefore continue to select files to be printed; as you select each file, it will be the next one placed in the print queue.

```
Macro: Edit

         File            DRAFT.WPM

    1 - Description      Select Draft Printing

    2 - Action

    ┌──────────────────────────────────────────────────────────┐
    │ {DISPLAY OFF}{Print}tm{Exit}                             │
    │                                                          │
    │                                                          │
    │                                                          │
    │                                                          │
    │                                                          │
    └──────────────────────────────────────────────────────────┘

    Selection: 0
```

FIGURE 7.26: The DRAFT macro, which selects Medium as the Text Quality option. You can use this macro if you have a dot matrix printer and do most of your printing in draft mode. See the accompanying text for ideas on how to use DRAFT as your startup macro.

When you select a group of files from the List Files screen and then choose the Print option, the files are placed in the print queue in alphabetical order.)

From the Control Printer screen, you can manage the print jobs in the queue or stop and restart the printing of the current print job. To reach this screen and its menu options, you press Shift-F7 (Print) and select the Control Printer option (**4** or **C**). This screen allows you not only to control the printing of the current job but also to see the current status of your print jobs and verify or change the print queue. The Control Printer screen and menu options are illustrated in Figure 7.27.

The first document listed in the job list is always the one that is currently being printed. The top section of the Control Printer screen gives you information about the status of the current print job. This includes the job number, the number of the page being printed, the size of the paper used, the number of the copy being printed, and the location (or source) of the paper. In addition, WordPerfect will display error messages, as well as messages informing you of any action you should take regarding the printer. This information is very useful, for it can help you gauge how long it will be before the document finishes printing and the next copy of it or the next document in the queue will begin.

Below the information on the current job, this screen shows the first three print jobs in the print queue. This section of the screen informs you of the job number assigned to each print job in the queue, the source of the document—either by file name or by *(Screen)* if you are printing the document in the editing screen—

```
Print: Control Printer

Current Job

Job Number: None                           Page Number:  None
Status:     No print jobs                  Current Copy: None
Message:    None
Paper:      None
Location:   None
Action:     None


Job List

Job   Document                Destination        Print Options




Additional Jobs Not Shown: Ø


 1 Cancel Job(s); 2 Rush Job; 3 Display Jobs; 4 Go (start printer); 5 Stop: Ø
```

FIGURE 7.27: The Control Printer screen (Shift-F7 C) without any print jobs. The options on this screen enable you to control the printing of all of the documents or pages that you have sent to the printer. No matter what method of printing you use (except Shift-PrtSc to print the screen contents), you use this screen to halt printing, view the status of your print jobs, or change the print queue.

the destination in terms of the printer port used, and any print options that have been selected (like *Graphics = High*)

At the bottom of the Control Printer screen, you will see the options

1 Cancel Job(s); **2 R**ush Job; **3 D**isplay Jobs; **4 G**o (start printer); **5 S**top: 0

Each of these options is described in the following sections.

Canceling Print Jobs

To take a job out of the queue, you use the Cancel Print Job(s) option. When you type **C**, you receive the prompt

Cancel which job? (* = All Jobs) 1

(where *1* is the number of the current print job) at the bottom of the screen. If you just want to cancel the current print job, you press Enter. If you want to cancel a single print job other than the current one, type its number and press Enter. If you want to cancel all of the jobs in the queue (including the current one), you type *. When you do so, you must then type **Y** to confirm this cancellation in response to the prompt

Cancel all print jobs? (Y/N) No

Be careful that you do not press the Enter key out of habit after you type * for this would answer No to canceling all print jobs.

After you type **Y**, you may see the warning message shown in Figure 7.28 at the bottom of your screen. To cancel the printing at this point, you must type **Y** to confirm the cancellation and then type **C** to select the Cancel option as indicated by the Action message. However, after doing this, you must remember to select the Initialize Printer option (**7** or **I**) on the Print menu before trying to reprint the document or any other document that uses the same soft fonts with this printer.

Rushing a Print Job

If you ever want to speed up the printing of a document in the queue by sending it to the top, you use the Rush Print Job command. When you select this option, you are prompted

Rush which job?

WordPerfect displays the next job number as the suggested one to send to the top of the queue. If you wish to rush a different print job, you type in its number over the number that is currently displayed. As soon as you press Enter, you receive a second prompt

Interrupt Current Job? (Y/N) No

```
Print: Control Printer

Current Job

Job Number: 1Ø                                    Page Number:  1
Status:      Trying to cancel job                 Current Copy: 1 of 1
Message:     Completing line
Paper:       Standard 8.5" x 11"
Location:    Continuous feed
Action:      Press "C" to cancel job immediately


Job List

Job  Document              Destination          Print Options
1Ø   D:\...\LESSON1        LPT 2
11   D:\...\LESSON2        LPT 2                 Graphics=High
12   D:\...\LESSON3        LPT 2                 Graphics=High

Additional Jobs Not Shown: 1


WARNING:  If you use this option, you will need to initialize your printer
before you can continue printing.  You will also need to make sure all forms
are in their original positions.  Are you sure? (Y/N) No
```

FIGURE 7.28: Control Printer screen with warning message. Sometimes when you select the Cancel option to cancel a particular print job, you must confirm this action by typing **Y** and then select the Cancel option a second time. Notice that WordPerfect informs you that you must reinitialize the printer if you go ahead with canceling the print job.

If you wish to print your rush job right away, you type **Y**. WordPerfect will respond by suspending the printing of the current document and will begin printing your rush job. As soon as the rush job is finished, it will return to the document whose printing was suspended and finish it before printing the other jobs left in the queue. If you just press Enter, the program will not begin printing your rush job until after it has finished printing the job that was current when you selected the Rush Print Job command.

The Display Jobs Option

The job list near the bottom of the screen contains information for only three print jobs—the current job and the next two in the queue. If you specify that a document be printed from memory (from document window 1 or 2), Word-Perfect will indicate this by displaying *(Screen)* in the Document column of the job list in place of the document's file name. If you specify that a document be printed from disk, the program will display its file name (abbreviating the path name) under the Document column.

Because there is room to display only the top three print jobs in the queue, this screen includes the indicator

Additional Jobs Not Shown: 0

at the bottom of the job list. If the number shown after the colon displays some number other than zero, this indicates that there are other print jobs that are not currently visible on screen. If you have additional print jobs, you can select the Display Print Jobs option (**3** or **D**), which displays a full-screen list of all print jobs (similar to the one shown in Figure 7.29).

Pausing and Restarting the Printing

If you ever have to pause the printing to make some adjustment with the paper or ribbon, you type **S** to select the Stop option. As soon as you select this option, WordPerfect quits sending data to the printer. The printer, however, will continue to print until all of the data in its buffer has been emptied.

Whenever you use this command, the Job Status message will show *Stopped* and the Action message will read

Adjust paper (press FORM FEED or advance paper to top of page)
Press "G" to continue

as shown in Figure 7.30. You would then fix the problem, advance the paper to the top of the form, and type **G** to select the Go (start printer) option. Word-Perfect will restart the printing, the Job Status message will return to *Printing,* and the Action message will say *None.*

```
Job List

Job  Document            Destination    Print Options
 3   D:\...\LESSON4      LPT 2          RUSH,Graphics=High
 1   D:\...\LESSON2      LPT 2          Graphics=High
 2   D:\...\LESSON3      LPT 2          Graphics=High
 4   D:\...\LESSON5      LPT 2          Graphics=High
 5   (Screen)            LPT 2          Graphics=High




      Press any key to continue_
```

FIGURE 7.29: Additional print jobs in the print queue. When you select the Display Jobs option (**3** or **D**) on the Control Printer screen, WordPerfect displays a full screen showing the remaining jobs in the queue. Here, you see five jobs in the queue. Notice that job 3 has just been rushed to the head of the queue (indicated by *RUSH* in the Print Options column).

```
Print: Control Printer

Current Job

Job Number: None                          Page Number:  None
Status:     Stopped                       Current Copy: None
Message:    None
Paper:      None
Location:   None
Action:         Adjust paper (press FORM FEED or advance paper to top of page)
                Press "G" to continue

Job List

Job   Document              Destination      Print Options
 3    D:\...\LESSON4        LPT 2            RUSH,Graphics=High
 1    D:\...\LESSON2        LPT 2            Graphics=High
 2    D:\...\LESSON3        LPT 2            Graphics=High

Additional Jobs Not Shown: 2




 1 Cancel Job(s); 2 Rush Job; 3 Display Jobs; 4 Go (start printer); 5 Stop: 0
```

FIGURE 7.30: Control Printer screen after pausing the current print job. When you select the Stop option, WordPerfect quits sending data to the printer, and the printing halts as soon as the printer buffer is empty. You fix the printer problem and select the Go (start printing) option after making sure that the paper is at the top of the form.

ALT-I: A MACRO TO IMMEDIATELY INTERRUPT THE PRINTING

Unlike other programs that require only two keystrokes like Ctrl-Break to interrupt or suspend printing, WordPerfect requires four keystrokes to invoke this command (Shift-F7 C S). To speed up this process and, perhaps, make it a little easier to remember (especially if you are panicking over a paper jam), you can create a macro under a name like Alt-I, containing the keystrokes shown in Figure 7.31.

To use this macro, you must first be in one of the document windows. If you are at the List Files screen, you must press F1 before you use this macro. To stop the printing, press Alt-I. This takes you immediately to the Control Printer screen and enters *S* to stop the printing. Don't press the Enter key until you have fixed the problem, because this macro contains the keystroke *G* to restart the printing as soon as you press Enter to end the macro pause.

TESTING YOUR PRINTERS

Before you print with WordPerfect, you may want to test your printer's capabilities with the PRINTER.TST file on the Conversion disk. This allows you to see whether your printer is capable of printing such effects as boldface, italics, underlining, overstrike, superscripts and subscripts, double underlining, tab aligning, column centering, redlining, graphics, and line drawing.

```
Macro: Edit

          File            ALTI.WPM

   1 - Description    Interrupt Printer

   2 - Action

       {Print}cs{PAUSE}g




   Selection: 0
```

FIGURE 7.31: A macro to interrupt the printing of the current print job when you press Alt-I. To restart the printing and return to the normal editing screen, you simply press the Enter key.

To test your printer, place a copy of your WordPerfect Conversion diskette in one of your floppy disk drives (drive A or B) and press Shift-F10 (Retrieve). Then type **PRINTER.TST** prefaced by the appropriate drive letter in response to the *Document to be retrieved* prompt. For example, if you have placed the Conversion disk in drive B, you would enter

    B:PRINTER.TST

as the file to retrieve. If you have copied the PRINTER.TST file onto your hard disk, you can retrieve it and print it from the directory that contains it. You may briefly see the message *document being formatted for default printer* at the bottom of the screen. Then press Enter followed by Shift-F7 (Print) and select the Full Document option.

If you have installed more than one printer, you should reprint this file using the other printers attached to your system. To do this, press Shift-F7 and choose the Select Printer option (**S**). Then, move the highlight cursor to the name of the printer you want to use and choose the Select option (**1** or **S**). Then, reprint the PRINTER.TST file by pressing Shift-F7 and selecting the Full Document option again.

ENTERING SPECIAL PRINTER COMMANDS IN YOUR DOCUMENT

If the printer definition supplied by WordPerfect does not support a printing enhancement you wish to use, you can enter the appropriate Escape or Control code directly in the text. To enter a printer code in your document, you press Shift-F8 (Format), select the Other option (**4** or **O**), select the Printer Functions option (**6** or **P**), and then select the Printer Command option (**2** or **P**). When you select the Printer Command option, you are presented with the following options:

1 Command; **2 F**ilename: 0

When you select the Command option, you see

Command:

At this prompt, you enter the appropriate printer command in ASCII code. To find the appropriate code, you must look it up in your printer manual. Most printer codes are initiated by the ASCII code for the Escape key; thus they are referred to as "Escape sequences."

Many times your printer manual will list the appropriate Escape sequence in three different ways: ASCII, decimal, and hexadecimal code. For example, you might see the following alternative codes for turning near-letter-quality mode on and off listed in a manual for a dot matrix printer:

ASCII — ESC x n
DEC. — 27 120 n
HEX. — 1B 78 n

In this example, you substitute either **1** or **0** for n in the code. Entering **1** turns on near-letter-quality mode, while entering **0** turns it off. If you were to use Word-Perfect's Printer Command option to turn on near-letter-quality mode, you would have to mix the ASCII and decimal code forms. This is because of the following simple rule for when to use the ASCII form and when to use the decimal code form: any character whose ASCII code number is less than 32 or greater than 126 must be entered in decimal form. Any character whose ASCII code number is between 32 and 126 (inclusive) can be entered in either ASCII or decimal form.

When you enter an ASCII code in decimal form, you must enter its decimal number enclosed in a pair of angle brackets. For instance, in the previous example, the Escape printer sequence to turn on near-letter-quality mode is ESCx1. The ASCII decimal code for ESC is 27, x is 120, and 1 is 49. Because 27 is less than 32, you must enter it in angle brackets as **<27>**. Because both x and 1 are between 32 and 126, you can enter them as ASCII characters (i.e., exactly as they would be entered into the text of any document). Thus, you would enter the following Escape sequence after the Command prompt:

<27>x1

It is important to note that the case (upper or lower) of letter characters (like *x* in this example) entered into a printer Escape sequence is crucial. This printer command would not work if you entered **X** in place of **x**. This is because *X* has the ASCII code number 088 while *x* has the number 120.

After you enter a printer code in this manner, it will not be visible in the text of your document. In order to verify that it has been entered correctly, you must access the Reveal Codes window by pressing Alt-F3. The formatting code for sending a printer command is [Ptr Cmnd:]. The code you entered will appear after the colon and before the last square bracket. For example, if you look at the Escape sequence to turn on near-letter-quality mode in the Reveal Codes window, it will appear as

[Ptr Cmnd:<27>x1]

It is also possible to use the Printer Command feature to have WordPerfect read in a program file such as one that downloads certain soft fonts into the printer's memory (a technique that can also be accomplished with the Initialize Printer option). If you have created a BASIC program that sends the necessary Escape sequences required to load soft fonts, you can have WordPerfect send it to the printer when it encounters the appropriate [Ptr Cmnd:] code.

To do this, you select the Filename option (**2** or **F**) from the Printer Command menu. When you select this option, WordPerfect displays

Document name:

as the prompt. Here, you type in the complete name of the program file. Make sure that you include the drive letter and path as part of the file name if the file is not located on the same disk or directory as the document in which you enter this special printer code. After entering the name of the program file, press Enter. When you look at the code in the Reveal Codes window (Alt-F3), you will see the file name listed in the [Ptr Cmnd:] code after the colon.

To locate special printer codes that you have entered into the text of your document, you may use the Search function (either forward or backward, as required). To do so, press F2, press Shift-F8, select the Other option (**3** or **O**), select the Ptr Fnc option (**7** or **P**), and, finally, select the Ptr Cmnd option (**2** or **P**). You will see [Ptr Cmnd] entered as the search string. Printer Command codes can be deleted by positioning the cursor in the Reveal Codes window either immediately before or immediately after it and then pressing Del or Backspace.

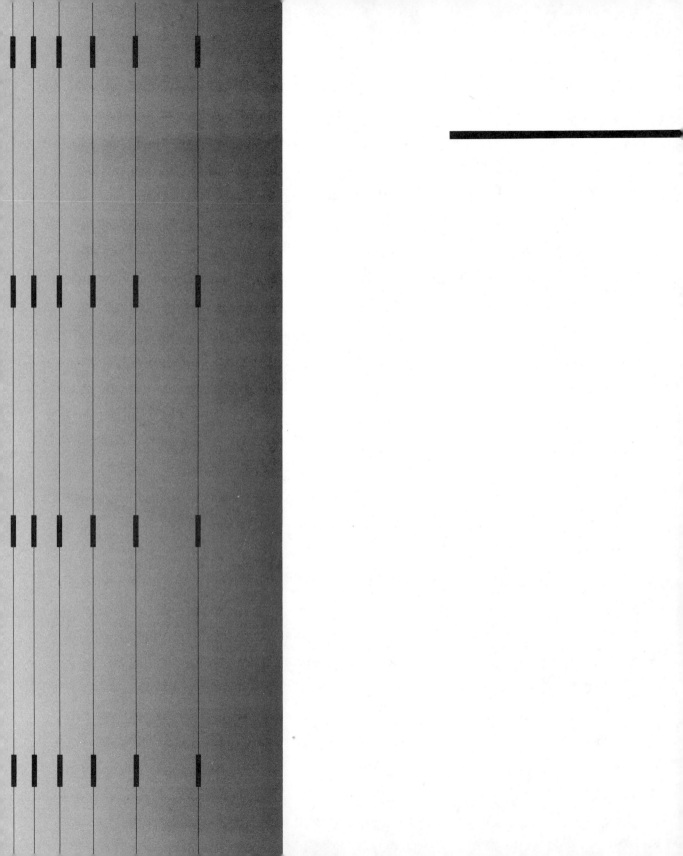

CHAPTER 8

FILE MANAGEMENT TECHNIQUES

FILE MANAGEMENT TECHNIQUES

T his chapter presents techniques for managing the document files that you create with WordPerfect. The file management topics covered in this chapter include

- Locating specific documents for editing.
- Creating and organizing document files in directories.
- Performing housekeeping chores such as deleting files, renaming documents, and making backup copies of your data disks.
- Protecting documents with passwords.
- Temporarily exiting to DOS.

In Chapter 2 you will find information about saving and retrieving the document files that you create in WordPerfect. Chapter 7 contains information about printing files, and Appendix A contains information about importing files created in other programs, including WordPerfect's Macintosh version, and exporting WordPerfect files to other programs. You will find all of the other pertinent information about managing WordPerfect documents in this chapter.

UPGRADE NOTES

File management techniques are essentially the same in WordPerfect 5.0 as in version 4.2, although version 5.0 uses a different underlying file structure. If you attempt to retrieve a WordPerfect 4.2 document into 5.0, it will automatically be converted to the new format.

On version 5.0's List Files screen, an arrow appears at the top or bottom if there are more files that you can scroll to see. Retrieve and Text In/Out now ask you for confirmation after you select them if you have already retrieved or begun a new document in the current document window. The Rename option has become the Move/Rename option and it now allows you to move a file to a new directory, rename it, or both rename and move it at the same time. You now access Name Search by typing **N** and then typing a letter. Extended word search pattern options are possible in version 5.0 so that you can perform selective searches through groups of files.

Password protection, now located on the Text In/Out key (Ctrl-F5), has been enhanced so that once you protect a document, any files associated with that document, such as backup files, the original disk file, and so forth, are also locked when you retrieve the document. In addition, the procedure for removing a password is slightly different.

Using the List Files Screen

To get an alphabetical list of all files on the disk in the default drive (if you save your documents on a floppy disk) or on the default directory (if you save your documents on a hard disk), press F5 (List Files); then press Enter.

The List Files screen (Figure 8.1) that you then see is divided into three parts:

- A header section that gives you the date, time, name of the default directory, size in bytes of the current file in memory, and amount of unused space in bytes remaining on the default drive.

- A directory listing section that gives you a complete two-column list of the files on the default directory. This listing begins with the names of any directories attached to the default directory; this includes the parent directory as well as any subdirectories. Directories are indicated by <*DIR*>. The list of files that follows includes the file name, file name extension, size in bytes, and date and time of the last update. This list is arranged alphabetically by file name. If additional file names are available but you must scroll to see them, an arrowhead appears at the top or bottom of the screen.

- A menu line containing the command options available on the List Files screen. There are ten options on this menu:

    1 Retrieve; **2** Delete; **3** Move/Rename; **4** Print; **5** Text In; **6** Look; **7** Other Directory; **8** Copy; **9** Word Search; **N** Name Search: 6

To move the highlighting through the list of file names on the screen, you can use the ↑ and ↓ keys to move up and down one file at a time, or Screen Up and Screen Down (− or + on the numeric keypad), PgUp and PgDn, or Home ↑ and Home ↓ to move the highlight up and down one screen at a time. To move directly to the last file name in the list, press Home Home ↓. To move up to the first file, press Home Home ↑. To move the highlight back and forth between the two columns, use the ← and → keys.

You can also quickly locate a particular file in the list just by typing **N** and the first few characters of its name. WordPerfect's Name Search feature is activated as soon as you type **N**. It tries to match the letters you enter with files in the listing. For example, to locate a file named TABLE2-1 that is not visible in the first List Files screen display, you need only type **T**. This takes the highlight bar to the first file that begins with the letter *T*. If TABLE2-1 is not the first file in the directory that begins with *T*, you can continue typing more letters (such as **ABL**), or you can use the ↓ key to exit Name Search and move the highlight directly down to the name of the file you want.

```
09/22/89  10:07                Directory C:\WPROC\WP5\*.*
Document size:        Ø   Free:  415744  Used:  4489418          Files:  134

  . <CURRENT>    <DIR>                    .. <PARENT>    <DIR>
LEARN    .       <DIR>    06/28/88 09:24   8514A    .WPD    3466  04/27/88 14:24
AIRPLANE .WPG     8484    04/27/88 14:24   ALTRNAT  .WPK     919  07/28/88 11:39
ALTS     .WPM       89    09/15/88 15:02   AND      .WPG    1978  04/27/88 14:24
ANNOUNCE .WPG     5388    04/27/88 14:24   APLASPLU .PRS   34991  05/11/88 08:21
APPLAUSE .WPG     1522    04/27/88 14:24   ARROW1   .WPG     366  04/27/88 14:24
ARROW2   .WPG      738    04/27/88 14:24   AWARD    .WPG    1746  04/27/88 14:24
BADNEWS  .WPG     3750    04/27/88 14:24   BEAR     .PIC    3630  04/11/88 16:11
BOOK     .WPG     1800    04/27/88 14:24   BORDER   .WPG   13518  04/27/88 14:24
CHARACTR .DOC    67149    07/28/88 11:39   CHARMAP  .TST   15239  07/28/88 11:39
CHECK    .WPG     1074    04/27/88 14:24   CLIP_ART .PIC    2474  12/10/85 02:01
CLOCK    .WPG     6234    04/27/88 14:24   CONFIDEN .WPG    3226  04/27/88 14:24
CONVERT  .EXE    80937    07/28/88 11:39   CURSOR   .COM    1452  07/28/88 11:39
DATA     .         446    07/24/88 23:43   DIAB620  .PRS    1345  09/21/88 11:41
DIR      .         318    07/22/88 00:43   EGA512   .FRS    3584  04/27/88 14:24
EGAITAL  .FRS     3584    04/27/88 14:24   EGASMC   .FRS    3584  04/27/88 14:24
EGAUND   .FRS     3584    04/27/88 14:24   ENHANCED .WPK    3375  07/28/88 11:39
EPLQ800  .PRS     9406    08/23/88 13:13   FC       .DOC    1953  07/28/88 11:39
FC       .EXE    23552    07/28/88 11:39 ▼ FIXBIOS  .COM      50  07/28/88 11:39

 1 Retrieve; 2 Delete; 3 Move/Rename; 4 Print; 5 Text In;
 6 Look; 7 Other Directory; 8 Copy; 9 Word Search; N Name Search: 6
```

FIGURE 8.1: A sample List Files screen (F5). This screen lists the names of all files stored in the default directory as well as their sizes and the amount of space available on disk.

To confirm that a file is the one you are looking for, you can press Enter (or **6** or **L**) when its name is highlighted. WordPerfect 5.0 is preset to use the Look option, which displays the contents of files and directories, when you press Enter while in the List Files screen. WordPerfect will then present the contents of the file on the screen, as shown in Figure 8.2. Although you cannot edit the file, you can view it to make sure that it is the one you are looking for. If you have added a Document Summary screen to your document, you will see it displayed before the first text in the document, even if you have turned off its display. To see more of the file, scroll through it by using any of the cursor keys. To return to the List Files screen, press F7 (Exit).

Restricting the List Files Display

You can restrict the List Files display to a particular group of files among those in the current directory by using the asterisk and/or the question mark (the DOS wild-card characters) when entering the directory name. Use the asterisk (*) to denote any type and number of characters before and/or after the period in the file name. Use the question mark (?) to denote a single character of any type. For example, to restrict a List Files display to documents that carry the .RPT file extension, you would press F5, then type

*.RPT

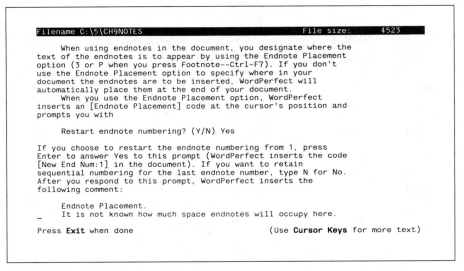

```
Filename C:\5\CH9NOTES                                    File size:      4523

        When using endnotes in the document, you designate where the
    text of the endnotes is to appear by using the Endnote Placement
    option (3 or P when you press Footnote--Ctrl-F7). If you don't
    use the Endnote Placement option to specify where in your
    document the endnotes are to be inserted, WordPerfect will
    automatically place them at the end of your document.
        When you use the Endnote Placement option, WordPerfect
    inserts an [Endnote Placement] code at the cursor's position and
    prompts you with

        Restart endnote numbering? (Y/N) Yes

    If you choose to restart the endnote numbering from 1, press
    Enter to answer Yes to this prompt (WordPerfect inserts the code
    [New End Num:1] in the document). If you want to retain
    sequential numbering for the last endnote number, type N for No.
    After you respond to this prompt, WordPerfect inserts the
    following comment:

        Endnote Placement.
    _   It is not known how much space endnotes will occupy here.

    Press Exit when done                    (Use Cursor Keys for more text)
```

FIGURE 8.2: Viewing the contents of a document before retrieving it. You can use the Look option of the List Files menu to view a document's contents before you retrieve it, to make sure it is the document you want.

and press Enter. WordPerfect would then list only those documents in the current directory whose extensions are .RPT. To restrict the listing to those documents whose names begin with *LTTR* regardless of what characters follow, you would press F5, type

LTTR*.*

and press Enter. To restrict the listing to those files named LTTR followed by a single character (such as *LTTR1, LTTR2,* etc.), you would press F5, type

LTTR?

and press Enter.

Creating and Using Document Directories

As you can see from looking at the List Files screen, WordPerfect documents are stored in directories. When you start WordPerfect, all of the documents you create are automatically saved in the current directory. If you are using Word-Perfect on a hard disk system, you can keep your documents in subdirectories below the one that contains the WordPerfect program files. In fact, you can set up many such subdirectories in which you keep related documents. For example, if you do word processing for many people in the office, you can have a directory for each person. When you type a letter or memo for one person, you make his or her directory current before creating the document. You can also set up subdirectories based on the type of document. For instance, you can have a directory for proposals, another for letters, and so on.

CREATING A NEW DIRECTORY

You may often want to create a new directory to store groups of related files. WordPerfect allows you to create new directories from within the program instead of having to exit to DOS.

To create a new directory, press F5 (List Files); then press Enter to see the List Files screen. Select the Other Directory option (**7** or **O**). When the prompt

New Directory =

appears, enter the name of the new directory you wish to create. If you have highlighted a directory name, you will see its full path name. You will be asked to confirm whether you want to create a new directory. Type **Y** to confirm your selection and tell WordPerfect to create the new directory.

The new directory name will then appear on the List Files screen. Remember, it will be a subdirectory of the directory you are currently in. For example, if you are in a subdirectory named \WP50\FILES and you type **Book** as the name of your new directory, this new directory will be a subdirectory of the FILES subdirectory, and its path name will be \WP50\FILES\BOOK.

You can also press F5 (List Files) and type = followed by a new directory name. When you press Enter, WordPerfect prompts you to create a new directory if it finds that the directory does not currently exist. For example, if you press F5, type = , and then type

C:\WP50\DOUG

and you have not yet created a directory for Doug, WordPerfect will respond with

Create C:\WP50\DOUG? (Y/N) No

To create this new directory, type **Y**. WordPerfect will then create a new subdirectory named DOUG. However, it will not simultaneously make this directory current. If you want to change to this directory, you must use one of the methods for changing directories, as described in the following section.

CHANGING THE CURRENT DIRECTORY

One way to change the current or default directory is to press F5 (List Files) and type = (the equal sign). When you first press F5, WordPerfect displays the name of the current directory at the bottom of the editing screen, and the message *(Type = to change default Dir)*, as shown in Figure 8.3.

```
        You can rename a file that you have already named either by

using the DOS RENAME command (see "Renaming a File from DOS"

later in this chapter) or by selecting Move/Rename (3 or M), from

the List Files screen. You may, for example, want to rename files

when you move them to a different directory or subdirectory (see

"Working with Directories" later in this chapter), or you may

want to assign more meaningful names for long-term storage.

        To rename a file,


        1. Press F5 (List Files). A prompt appears at the bottom

of the screen asking if you want to search the default directory,

which is the directory you specified to hold the program files

Dir C:\5\*.*                              (Type = to change default Dir)
```

FIGURE 8.3: Using the List Files key (F5). The prompt that appears when you press F5 (List Files) in effect asks whether you want to list the contents of the default directory.

For example, if you press F5 after starting WordPerfect in the directory named WP50, you will see

    Dir C:\WP50*.*

in the lower-left corner of the screen. (The *.* is a DOS convention that means "Show all of the files regardless of file name or extension.") If you press Enter at this point, WordPerfect will display an alphabetical list of all program files in this directory.

To change the current directory, type = (the equal sign from the top row of the keyboard). This changes the screen display to

    New directory = C:\WP50

and places the cursor beneath the *C*. To change directories, you can completely retype the directory name or simply edit it. For example, if you want to create a new letter for Bob and you have set up a directory to contain all of his documents, you can type

    C:\WP50\BOB

and press Enter, or you can use the ← or End key to move the cursor to the end of *C:\WP50* and just type **\BOB** before pressing Enter.

As soon as you press Enter, WordPerfect displays the new directory, including the DOS wild-card characters; as in

    C:\WP50\BOB*.*

Press Enter again to display all of the files in this directory that can be accommodated in one screen view. The files in the directory are listed in alphabetical order, from left to right and down each line. If there are more files to view, an arrowhead will appear at the top or bottom of the screen, and you can scroll to see them. You can press F1 (Cancel), F7 (Exit), Esc, the space bar, or **0** to return to the document editing screen, where you can begin your new document.

Once you are viewing the List Files screen, you can change directories by selecting Other Directory (**7** or **O**). When you are prompted, enter the new directory name and press Enter.

When WordPerfect presents the List Files screen, it displays all of the subdirectories attached to the current directory. To view the contents of that directory, highlight its name and press Enter twice.

Regardless of the method you use, once you have made a particular directory current, all of the documents you create and save will automatically be located in it.

LOCATING FILES IN OTHER DIRECTORIES

You can locate files that are stored in other directories without having to change the current directory. Remember that when you press F5 = from the editing screen or select the Other Directory option (**7** or **O**) on List Files and then enter a new directory name, you are actually changing the current, or default, directory. If all you want to do is locate a file in a different directory, either to look at its contents or to retrieve it, you don't have to change the current directory. Instead, you can look at the contents of the directories in one of the levels above or below the current directory, searching each one until you find the document you want to use.

To do this, you press F5 Enter. If there are directories on a level below the current directory, you will see their names at the top of the List Files screen. Directories are indicated by <DIR> after the name. To move to one of these directories, you move the highlight cursor to its name and press Enter. At the bottom of the List Files screen, you will then see the full path name of the directory. Press Enter a second time; WordPerfect will display the List Files screen for this directory (without changing the current directory).

To move the directory to a level above the current directory, move the highlight cursor to the directory displayed as

    .. <PARENT> <DIR>

This directory is always located in the first row on the right (across from <CURRENT> <DIR>, which is the directory now shown in the List Files screen). After moving the highlight cursor to the parent directory, press the Enter key twice; WordPerfect will display the List Files screen for the directory on the next highest level.

When you are finished examining the contents of any of these directories, you can press F1 (Cancel), F7 (Exit), **0**, or the space bar to return to the current document editing screen. Note too that you can also retrieve a document into the current editing screen (assuming that it's empty) by selecting the Retrieve option (**1** or **R**) on the List Files menu.

DIRECTING DOCUMENTS TO OTHER DIRECTORIES

Normally, once you name a document when saving it, the name of the document, including the full path name, is displayed on the last line of the editing screen. (You can choose to suppress this display by using the Setup key.) If you want to save the edited document in a directory different from the one in which it was created, you must edit its file name by modifying the directory path when saving the file.

For instance, if you retrieve a document named C:\WP50\BOB\IBMPROP and you want to save the edited version in Mary's directory, you must modify its name to C:\WP50\MARY\IBMPROP when you save it. The file name at the bottom of the screen will appear as *C:\WP50\MARY\IBMPROP.* However, the current directory will continue to be *C:\WP50\BOB.* If you were to start a new document in the second window and then save it, it would be located in Bob's directory.

DELETING A DIRECTORY

You can delete an empty directory from within WordPerfect or from DOS (see "Temporarily Exiting to DOS" later in this chapter). You must delete all files within a directory (except the **.** and **..** directories, which simply represent the current and parent directories) before you can delete the directory itself. (See "Deleting Files" later in this chapter for information about deleting files.)

To delete a directory, highlight its name on the List Files screen by pressing F5, pressing Enter, and then moving the cursor to the appropriate directory. Choose Delete (**2** or **D**) and type **Y** to confirm. If the directory still contains files, you will receive the prompt

ERROR: directory not empty

Go to the directory by using the Look option (or simply by pressing Enter twice when the directory name is highlighted); then delete any files the directory contains. You can then return to the parent directory (marked .. *<PARENT> <DIR>*) and delete the directory you have just emptied.

Deleting Files

To delete files from within WordPerfect, you use the List Files key (F5) and specify the directory containing the file(s) you want to delete. When the List Files screen appears, highlight the file you want to delete, choose Delete (**2** or **D**), and type **Y** to confirm the deletion. To delete several files, move the highlight to each one and type * (asterisk), as shown in Figure 8.4. Then choose Delete. You will be prompted to confirm whether you want to delete the files you have indicated.

Note: You may want to use the Look option to verify that a certain file is the one you want to delete before actually selecting the Delete option.

Copying Files

WordPerfect's List Files screen also allows you to copy files. This feature is very useful when you need to copy a document into a different directory or copy a file onto a floppy disk. You can also use this feature to rename a document by making a copy of it under a different name.

If you only want to copy a file to a different drive or directory under the same name, you do not have to retype the name. Simply indicate the drive or directory onto which you want the file copied.

```
06/05/88  12:56              Directory C:\5\*.*
Document size:     45200   Free:   3829760   Used:     55752        Marked: 7

  BOOK     .WPG     1800   04/27/88 14:24     BORDER   .WPG    13518   04/27/88 14:24
  BORDER   .WPM      103   05/26/88 15:20     BYE      .WPM       82   03/12/88 14:48
  CD       .WPM       93   05/31/88 09:12     CH10INS  .         1225   05/25/88 13:01
  CH11INS  .        3499*  05/28/88 12:37     CH12INS  .          771   04/28/88 07:20
  CH1INS   .       36749   05/25/88 06:27     CH2INS   .        15804*  06/02/88 08:07
  CH5INS   .        6460   05/31/88 13:15     CH6INS   .         1102   03/19/88 15:28
  CH7INS   .       25680*  05/31/88 09:08     CH8INS   .         2546*  06/01/88 09:04
  CH9INS   .        8033*  05/28/88 12:45     CH9NOTES.          3701   05/30/88 07:15
  CHAP1    .          95   03/18/88 08:05     CHAP2    .           95*  03/18/88 08:05
  CHAP3    .          95*  03/18/88 08:05     CHARACTR .DOC     52655   04/27/88 11:00
  CHARMAP  .TST    15239   04/27/88 11:00     CHECK    .WPG      1074   04/27/88 14:24
  CLOCK    .WPG     6234   04/27/88 14:24     COMPARE  .         1348   03/17/88 16:26
  COMPDOC  .         927   05/25/88 13:59     CONFIDEN .WPG      3226   04/27/88 14:24
  CONTENTS .WPM      124   05/31/88 12:08     CURSOR   .COM      1452   04/27/88 11:00
  DATE     .WPM       96   03/30/88 07:42     DES      .WPM       96   03/30/88 07:39
  EGA512   .FRS     3584   04/27/88 14:24     EGAITAL  .FRS      3584   04/27/88 14:24
  EGASMC   .FRS     3584   04/27/88 14:24     EGAUND   .FRS      3584   04/27/88 14:24
  ENHANCED .WPK     3375   04/27/88 11:00     EPFX85   .PRS      5256   05/04/88 08:00
  EPFX86   .PRS     5256   05/03/88 07:52     EPFX87   .PRS      5256   05/13/88 10:55


  Delete marked files? (Y/N) No
```

FIGURE 8.4: Marking several files to be deleted. You can delete several files at a time by marking each with an asterisk before typing **2** or **D**. You can also use this method to copy or print several files at the same time.

You can copy several files at once by marking each with an asterisk (*) before choosing Copy (**8** or **C**).

To copy a file (or several files):

1. Press F5 (List Files), press Enter, and either highlight one file to copy or mark several files with asterisks.

2. Type **8** or **C** for Copy. The following prompt will appear:

   Copy this file to:

   You can simply type a drive name followed by a colon to copy the file(s) under the same name to a disk on another drive. For example, if you want to copy a file named LTTR27 to a floppy disk in drive A, you type **A:** at the prompt, and the file will be copied under the name LTTR27 onto the disk in drive A.

   If you want to copy a file to another directory, you must use the path name that indicates where you want the file to be copied. For example, to copy LTTR27 to a subdirectory named BOB on drive C (your current location), you type **BOB**.

You can rename the file by giving it a new name at the prompt. For example, to rename LTTR27 as BOB27 and copy the file to the BOB subdirectory, you enter **BOB\BOB27**.

When you have finished copying files to their appropriate directories, use the Delete option if you want to delete the files from the directory you have just copied them from.

Renaming Files

You can move or rename a file that you have already named by selecting Move/Rename (**3** or **M**) from the List Files screen. You may, for example, want to move files to a different directory or subdirectory, or you may want to assign them more meaningful names for long-term storage.

To rename a file

1. Press F5 (List Files). A prompt appears at the bottom of the screen asking if you want to see the contents of the default directory. To see a list of the files in this directory, press Enter. Alternatively, you can type the path name of the directory you want to search.

2. When the List Files screen appears, move the highlight to the file you want to rename. Type **3** or **M** to select Move/Rename.

3. Enter the new file name, as shown in Figure 8.5; then press Enter. The file listing changes to reflect the new name. Press F1 (Cancel), F7 (Exit), Esc, or **0** to return to your document.

Moving Files

The Move/Rename option, as its name implies, not only lets you give a file a new name (as described above), but also allows you to move it to a new disk or to another directory on the same disk. When you use this option to move a file, it combines two operations: the program first copies the file to the new location, and then it deletes it from its present location. To move a file to a new disk or directory, move the highlight cursor to its name on the List Files screen and then select the Move/Rename option (**3** or **M**). Next, use the cursor movement keys to position the cursor on the drive letter or the beginning of the directory name and edit this part of the complete file name as required.

For example, assume that you want to move a letter file (SMITH-1.LTR) currently located in your WordPerfect LETTER directory to another Word-Perfect directory called CLIENT on your hard disk. After highlighting the letter's file name on the List Files screen for the C:\WP50\LETTER directory, you select the Move/Rename option. The following prompt then appears at the bottom of the screen:

New Name: C:\WP50\LETTER\SMITH-1.LTR

```
06/04/88  08:45                Directory C:\5\*.*
Document size:     20122   Free:  4118528   Used:  3323779     Files:   246

.  <CURRENT>   <DIR>                    ..  <PARENT>   <DIR>
B        .     <DIR>    05/13/88 07:28   4       .LEX   289245  05/25/88 06:55
8514A    .WPD    3466   04/27/88 14:24   A)(A    .          8238  03/17/88 15:27
AIRPLANE .WPG    8484   04/27/88 14:24   ALPSALQ2.PRS    4247  04/26/88 07:23
ALTA     .WPM      79   03/17/88 09:07   ALTB    .WPM       83  03/17/88 15:57
ALTC     .WPM      83   03/17/88 09:05   ALTE    .WPM       79  03/18/88 11:50
ALTH     .WPM     119   05/19/88 07:08   ALTI    .WPM       77  06/02/88 06:15
ALTM     .WPM      75   05/03/88 07:46   ALTP    .WPM      100  06/03/88 08:26
ALTQ     .WPM      84   05/31/88 09:08   ALTRNAT .WPK      919  04/27/88 11:00
ALTS     .WPM      78   03/30/88 07:39   ALTT    .WPM       79  03/17/88 09:04
ALTW     .WPM     197   05/26/88 07:50   ALTX    .WPM       78  03/18/88 08:16
AND      .WPG    1978   04/27/88 14:24   ANNOUNCE.WPG     5388  04/27/88 14:24
APPA     .       42148  05/29/88 15:51   APPAINS .         1399  03/17/88 08:21
APPLAUSE .WPG    1522   04/27/88 14:24   ARROW1  .WPG      366  04/27/88 14:24
ARROW2   .WPG     738   04/27/88 14:24   AUTOREF .         1784  05/30/88 08:54
AWARD    .WPG    1746   04/27/88 14:24   BACKUP1 .        29734  03/18/88 12:11
BADNEWS  .WPG    3750   04/27/88 14:24   BEGIN   .WPM       59  03/30/88 07:22
BFG9-11  .CAP    4256   06/01/88 06:34   BFG9-12 .CAP     4256  06/01/88 06:33
BFG9-20  .CAP    4256   06/01/88 08:30 ▼ BIGBOX  .WPM      111  05/26/88 15:21

New name: C:\5\appendix_
```

FIGURE 8.5: Renaming a file. The name you type for the file at the prompt in the lower-left corner will be the one it will have until you change it again. Be sure to include any extension you want the file to have. For example, if the file is a DOS text file, you may want to give it the extension .ASC (for *ASCII*). WordPerfect will automatically give the extension .WPM to any macro files you create.

and the cursor is located under the *C*. You press the → key until the cursor is positioned under the *L* in *LETTER*, press the Del key until this directory name is erased, and then type **CLIENT.** The new file name will appear as

New Name: C:\WP50\CLIENT\SMITH-1.LTR

When you press the Enter key, the SMITH-1.LTR file will disappear from the List Files screen. (To verify that this file is now in the CLIENT directory, you need to move to that directory—see "Locating Files in Other Directories" earlier in this chapter.)

The Move/Rename option can also be used to simultaneously rename and move a file. To change the name of the file and move it, you need to edit both the drive/directory and the file name before pressing Enter to carry out the move operation. Remember, however, that the file will be listed under the new file name assigned to it when you view the List Files screen for its new directory; you won't find it listed any longer under its old file name.

To move a group of files to a new disk or directory, you mark each one with an asterisk and then select the Move/Rename option. The following prompt will appear at the bottom of the screen:

Move marked files? (Y/N) No

To continue with the move operation, you must type **Y**. If you press the Enter key, the move operation will be canceled. After you type **Y** for Yes, the prompt immediately changes to

Move marked files to:

Here, you type in the drive letter and/or directory name representing the new location for all of the files that are marked with an asterisk. You don't have to type in the full path name if you are moving the files to a directory level below the current directory. You should enter the full path name, however, if you are moving the files to a directory on the same level or to a directory on a different drive. If you want to move the files to a new disk (in the root directory), you only have to type in the drive letter followed by a colon (such as **A:** or **B:**).

For instance, assume that when you installed WordPerfect, you copied all of the sample graphics files into the C:\WP50 directory along with all of the other WordPerfect program files. Now, after creating a new GRAPHICS directory (C:\WP50\GRAPHICS), you want to move all of these graphics files into it. After marking each of the files to be moved on the List Files screen, you select the Move/Rename option and answer yes to the "Move marked files?" prompt. In response to the "Move marked files to" prompt, you just need to type

GRAPHICS

and press Enter. All of the files will then be moved to the C:\WP50\ GRAPHICS directory that you set up. Remember that to mark all of the files in the List Files screen, you press Alt-F5. You can use this command if you ever want to move all of the files in the current directory to a new disk or directory that you have created.

The Move/Rename option is very effective when you want to archive particular files on the hard disk that are no longer being actively used. By moving such files to floppy disks, you can free up valuable storage space on the hard disk. (Note that you should still have backup copies of each of these files on floppy disks before removing them from the hard disk.) When you are moving files from the hard disk to a floppy disk, you only need to enter the drive letter followed by a colon in response to the "Move marked files to" prompt.

Naming Files

To name a file in WordPerfect, you follow the DOS file-naming conventions. WordPerfect follows the same rules that DOS does for naming files; they are summarized here for your reference.

- A file name can consist of one to eight characters.
- These characters may be the letters A–Z or the numerals 0–9.
- In addition, you can use the following symbols: $ ~ # @ ! ' ' ( ) { } - _ ^
- You cannot use these symbols: ? . " / \ [ ] : | < > + = , *
- You cannot use spaces within a file name.
- You may add an optional extension consisting of a period (.) followed by one to three additional permitted characters, as defined above.

In general, a file name cannot exceed eight characters (before the extension) and may consist of any combination of letters, numbers, and symbols, with the exceptions listed above. You can enter a file name in lowercase letters; Word-Perfect will automatically convert them to uppercase letters.

WordPerfect does not automatically assign extensions to the files it creates (other than macro files, to which it automatically gives the extension .WPM). If you are creating a file for a special purpose—for example, a DOS text file to be used in another program—you may want to assign it a three-letter file extension such as .ASC (for *ASCII*) so that you can quickly identify such files later.

Meaningful File Names

Eight characters are not a lot in which to communicate what a file contains. The name 10-27LTR may help you remember that you wrote a letter on the 27th of October, but it does not tell you to whom you wrote the letter or why. As a general rule, use abbreviations that are meaningful to you. If you write few letters, and if October 27 was a special day, 10-27LTR may be a perfectly meaningful name for you.

Searching Files for Specific Contents

You can have WordPerfect search files for a particular word or phrase. This helps you quickly locate files whose names you no longer remember but for which you know some identifying phrase or keywords. You can mark specific files that you want WordPerfect to search by typing an asterisk (*) when they are highlighted. If you do not mark any files, WordPerfect will search all the files in the directory.

To have the program list only those files that contain the keywords or phrase you remember, you use the Word Search option (**9** or **W**) on the List Files screen. When you select this command, you will see the following menu:

Search: **1 D**oc Summary; **2 F**irst Page; **3 E**ntire Doc; **4 C**onditions

If you choose Doc Summary (**1** or **D**), you can enter a word, phrase, or word pattern to search for throughout the document summaries in the current directory or in the files you have marked in that directory. If you make it a habit to create a document summary for each of your documents, you can use this feature to quickly locate files you use regularly. By choosing First Page (**2** or **F**), you search only the first page of each document. Choosing either of these options— Doc Summary or First Page—greatly speeds up the process of searching through a directory.

If you choose Entire Doc (**3** or **E**), WordPerfect will search through the documents you have marked or through all the documents in the directory.

If you choose Conditions (**4** or **C**), you can selectively restrict searches, as discussed in the section "Restricting Searches" later in this chapter.

ENTERING SEARCH STRINGS

The search string you enter can contain up to 20 characters. When entering this search string, be aware that uppercase and lowercase letters are considered to be the same by the program.

For example, you can use Word Search to locate all documents that have anything to do with the Apple LaserWriter by selecting the Word Search option from the List Files screen and entering **"Apple LaserWriter"** in response to the prompt

Word Pattern:

(You must enclose the word pattern in quotation marks if it contains a space, comma, semicolon, or single or double quotation marks.) After you press Enter, WordPerfect searches all of the files in the current directory for the phrase *Apple LaserWriter*. After it has finished, it will mark with an asterisk only those files that contain these words.

When using Word Search to locate specific files, you can use the * and *?* wild-card characters. For example, if you have forgotten exactly how to spell *Hewlett* in the company name Hewlett-Packard, you can enter the word pattern as

H?wl*

WordPerfect will match the search string if you began the name with *He* or *Hu,* or if you ended it with *let, lat,* or *lett.*

Also, this feature allows you to use the logical operators AND and OR, repre-sented by the semicolon (or single blank space) and comma, respectively. For instance, if you want to narrow the search to only those documents in which you mention both the Apple LaserWriter and the HP LaserJet printer, you enter the word pattern as

"Apple LaserWriter";"HP LaserJet"

On the other hand, to locate documents in which you mention either the Apple LaserWriter or the HP LaserJet, you can modify the word pattern to

"Apple LaserWriter","HP LaserJet"

Once WordPerfect searches all of the files, it marks those files that contain your search string. The number of files that have been marked appears in the upper-right corner of the List Files screen. If you press Tab or Shift-Tab, you can move among the marked files. To locate a specific document within this restricted list, you can use the Look option to review the contents of each one.

Note that you can use more than a single AND or OR logical operator in the search string you enter, as long as it does not exceed 20 characters. However, you must understand the logic you employ. Consider these examples:

- If you enter **Ash,Berry,Singer** your document must contain the name Ash, Berry, *or* Singer.
- If you enter **Ash;Berry;Singer** your document must contain all three names, Ash, Berry, *and* Singer.
- If you enter **Ash;Berry,Singer** your document must contain *either* both the names Ash and Berry *or* just Singer alone.
- If you enter **Ash,Berry;Singer** your document must contain *either* the names Ash and Singer, *or* Berry and Singer.

RESTRICTING SEARCHES

Version 5.0 of WordPerfect allows you to set restrictions on searches so that in effect you can selectively sort subsets of files until you have located the ones you want to use. You can search for all the files containing a pattern, then search only those files for another pattern, and then enter a third pattern to restrict the search even further. For example, you might search for all files containing the word *customer* on the first page, then search the resulting files for *new account,* and then search for a particular state. You can also search files by date to locate the oldest or the most recent files that have been created, or the files that were created during any given period.

When you select Conditions (**4** or **C**) from the Search menu, you will see a screen like the one in Figure 8.6. WordPerfect lists the number of files in the current directory and is preset to search them all. After subsets of files have been selected, this number will change. For example, if the program locates five files in the first search, the number *5* will appear, and the next search will take place through these files unless you select Undo Last Search (**2** or **U**), which resets the search to the files that were located in the previous search.

The Reset Search Conditions option (**3** or **R**) clears the search criteria you have set so that you can enter new conditions.

You can search files by date with the File Date option (**4** or **D**). When you select the File Date option, the *No* listed on the File Date line changes to *Yes* and the cursor is located under the *Y.* When you press Enter, the cursor moves to the *FROM* line, and the *(All)* disappears. Here, you type in the starting date. Then press Enter again and type in the ending date. You can enter a date with leading zeroes, as in *01/01/89,* or you can omit the zeroes and use the form *1/1/89.* You can also enter a date using hyphens instead of slashes to separate the elements.

If you want to find all of the files created within a particular period, enter both the starting date (on the *FROM* line) and the ending date (on the *TO* line). For

```
Word Search

   1 - Perform Search on          All 250 File(s)

   2 - Undo Last Search

   3 - Reset Search Conditions

   4 - File Date                   No
       From (MM/DD/YY):            (All)
       To   (MM/DD/YY):            (All)

                   Word Pattern(s)

   5 - First Page
   6 - Entire Doc
   7 - Document Summary
       Creation Date (e.g. Nov)
       Descriptive Name
       Subject/Account
       Author
       Typist
       Comments

   Selection: 1
```

FIGURE 8.6: The Word Search screen. You can restrict searches to progressively smaller subsets of files as well as select files by creation date.

example, to locate files created between May 1, 1989 and May 15, 1989 (inclusive), you enter **5/1/89** as the starting date and **5/15/89** as the ending date.

To find all of the files created before a particular date, you enter only a starting date. For example, to locate all of the files created before June 1, 1989, you leave the starting date on the *FROM* line blank by pressing Enter—the default setting of *(All)* then reappears on this line. Then, type **6/1/89** as the ending date on the *TO* line and press Enter. When you perform the Word Search, WordPerfect will mark only those files that were created before June 1, 1989.

To locate all of the files that were created after a particular date, you enter only the ending date. For example, to locate all of the files created after June 15 1989, you enter **6/15/89** as the starting date on the *FROM* line and leave the ending date on the *TO* line blank (by pressing the Enter key).

You may have to use the Reset option (**3** or **R**) on the Search Conditions menu to erase a previously used date on the *FROM* and *TO* settings and return them to *(All)* defaults before using either of these two methods. If you aren't concerned about a particular date within a given month, you can leave it blank, as in **6//89** (signifying any date in June, 1989). If you aren't concerned about a particular month or date in a year, you can omit these parts of the date, as in **//89** (signifying any date in 1989). Note that you can't use this method to omit *any* part of the date if you choose to use hyphens instead of slashes when entering the starting or ending date. For example, WordPerfect will not understand a file date entered as **6- -89**.

The remaining options allow you to specify whether to search the first page, the whole document, or the document summary screen of each document in the directory. You can combine the search conditions to restrict searches very tightly. For example, you could search for all the files created by Jeff during the month of August that contain the words *"new account"* or *"Net 30 days."*

PROTECTING YOUR FILES WITH PASSWORDS

WordPerfect allows you to protect your document files by creating passwords. In the parlance of the program, this is referred to as "locking a file." The options for locking a file are accessed by pressing Ctrl-F5 (Text In/Out). From this screen, you select Password (**2** or **P**). To indicate a new password, you then choose Add/Change (**1** or **A**). WordPerfect prompts you for a password:

Enter Password:

You can enter a password up to 24 characters long. (WordPerfect masks the display of the characters you enter for the password on the editing screen, so you will be typing "blind.") After you press Enter, you are prompted to reenter the password you just typed:

Re-Enter Password:

You must type the password exactly as you just entered it. (Note that Word-Perfect matches only the sequence or spelling of the letters and disregards any difference in case.) Again, WordPerfect does not display the characters that you enter on your screen.

If you fail to correctly reenter the password in this manner, you will receive the message

ERROR: Incorrect Password

You will receive the original Password prompt, where you can enter another password that you will then have to verify.

If you verify the password, WordPerfect will prompt you to enter a document name if the document has not been saved before. If the document has already been saved, WordPerfect will suggest the original file name. If you want to save the document under the same name, you type **Y** in response to the Replace prompt. However, you may save the password-protected file under a new file name if you want. To do this, you simply edit the file name that is displayed on the screen.

When you retrieve a locked file, you will be asked for the password after you enter the file name. You can also retrieve a password-protected file by highlighting its name on the List Files screen (F5), selecting Retrieve (**1** or **R**), and then entering the password.

Regardless of the retrieval method you use, if you do not enter the password correctly, you will receive an error message and be prompted to enter the file name again. If you cannot reproduce the password that you assigned to the document, you will not be able to retrieve the document for editing or printing.

WordPerfect does not allow you to print a password-protected document from disk by using either the Print menu (Shift-F7) or the List Files screen. The only way to print a locked file is by retrieving it with the correct password, then pressing Shift-F7 (Print) followed by either Full Text (**1** or **F**) or Page (**2** or **P**). If you forget the password, you cannot obtain another printout of the document. Also, you can't use the Look option (**6**, **L**, or Enter) on the List Files menu (F5 Enter) to view the contents of a locked document. When you select this option, Word-Perfect will prompt you to reenter the password for this file. If you don't enter it correctly, you won't be able to view its contents.

> *Note:* You can still rename, copy, and delete password-protected files without giving the password. However, files that you rename or copy to new disks or directories are still password-protected; you must enter the correct password before you can retrieve them for editing or printing.

To remove password protection, or "unlock" a file, you must retrieve the file. Then press Ctrl-F5 (Text In/Out), select Password (**2** or **P**), and select Remove (**2** or **R**). From then on, you will be able to retrieve the file without having to enter a password, and you can print the file from disk.

TEMPORARILY EXITING TO DOS

If your computer has sufficient RAM, you can temporarily exit to DOS while in WordPerfect. You may, for example, need to format some disks or use another DOS command like CHKDSK or COPY. You can also run other programs from the new DOS shell, provided that your computer has sufficient memory. Unfortunately, you won't be able to run programs like Lotus 1-2-3 or dBASE III Plus as you could with version 4.2, because WordPerfect now requires too much memory to fit both programs in RAM. Also, don't start any RAM-resident utilities (which will probably still fit in the remaining memory) when you use the Go to DOS command. If you start one of these so-called TSR (terminate-and-stay-resident) programs, you will crash WordPerfect. Never use this command until after you have saved the document or documents (if you are using both editing windows) that you are working on. If anything prevents you from successfully returning to WordPerfect, your edits will be lost.

To exit to DOS through the Shell command, press Ctrl-F1 (Shell) and select Go to DOS (**1** or **G**). While you are in DOS you can use most of its commands to carry out tasks. For example, you can copy, rename, or delete files, or format new data disks. However, don't use the DOS PRINT command, as this will crash WordPerfect. When you have finished working in DOS, type **EXIT** to return to WordPerfect.

If you type **WP** to return to WordPerfect from DOS instead of typing **EXIT**, you will start a new copy of WordPerfect. You will receive a *Program too big to fit in memory* message if you do not have sufficient RAM to run both copies of Word-Perfect simultaneously.

MAKING BACKUP COPIES

WordPerfect gives you several ways to safeguard your work by backing up files to another disk and by creating duplicate copies of files on the same disk. The following sections examine these methods.

Disk Backup Copies

You should always back up your work by making a copy of it and keeping the copy in a place separate from where you normally store your files. If you are using a two-disk-drive system, this means copying important files onto other floppy disks and storing them in a covered place away from heat, light, and magnetic sources. If you are using a hard disk system, this means establishing a backup system whereby you copy important files to floppy disks and store those disks in a location separate from your hard disk. (See ''Backing Up a Hard Disk'' later in this chapter.) Backing up your disks is a precaution you should take in addition to backing up your files. If a disk gets damaged, the files it contains may be unusable. Keeping a separate disk backup can save you from having to recreate a great deal of work.

Automatic Backup

The WordPerfect program can create automatic backup files for you on the disk you have specified to contain your program files. The program provides an automatic Timed Document Backup feature that allows you to set the number of minutes between each automatic save operation.

If you save the document when you exit the program at the end of your work session, the special backup file named WP{WP}BK.# (where # is either 1 or 2 depending upon which document editing window you are currently working in), in which your edits are automatically saved, is erased. However, if you experience some kind of problem that prevents you from exiting WordPerfect normally, this special file is retained. You can then rename it and use it as your working copy of the document. Using this feature means that the only edits you can possibly lose are those you made between the time the last automatic save operation occurred and the time you experienced the power interruption or computer failure.

Original Backup

WordPerfect also provides an Original Backup feature to automatically save two copies of a document that has been edited: one in its original form and the other containing all of your editing changes. If you use this feature, you must have sufficient storage space on your data disk to accommodate both an edited version and an unedited version of the document.

Note: Both the Timed Backup and Original Backup features are inactive when you first use WordPerfect. To activate them, you must use the Setup key (Shift-F1), as explained in Chapter 1.

BACKING UP A HARD DISK AND RESTORING FILES

If you are using WordPerfect on a hard disk, you will sometimes need to back up files from the hard disk. In addition, you will often need to transfer files to floppy disks so that you can move them to a different workstation—to a computer in a colleague's office or at home, for example.

In an office environment, you should make it a practice to back up files to floppy disks daily, just in case of a hard disk failure. For your own personal use, follow this rule of thumb: Back up what you do not want to lose. If you have spent a long time creating a file and do not want to lose that work and effort, be sure to back it up.

These backup copies are in addition to the backup files WordPerfect creates and saves for you. The WordPerfect backup files are also stored on the hard disk, so this will not do you any good if you have a hard disk failure. (See "Making Backup Copies" earlier in this chapter, as well as Chapter 1, for details about using the Setup menu to specify automatic backups.)

You can back up the contents of an entire hard disk (as you might want to do before physically moving the computer, for example). You can also back up the contents of a directory or document file. The following sections briefly explain the procedures used to back up and restore files in each of these situations. For additional information, refer to the *Power User's Guide to Hard Disk Management* by Jonathan Kamin (SYBEX, 1987).

Backing Up a Hard Disk

Note: Always have sufficient blank formatted disks on hand before you begin any backup operation. You cannot interrupt the backup to format more disks.

To back up the entire contents of a hard disk (drive C), including all subdirectories, use the following command in DOS:

```
BACKUP C:\ A: /S
```

If your hard disk is drive D or some other drive, you would use that drive letter instead of the *C* in the preceding command. The /S argument ensures that all subdirectories are backed up. You will be prompted to insert additional floppy disks as necessary.

To back up only those files that have been modified since the last backup, use the command

```
BACKUP C:\ A: /S/M
```

To use this command effectively, you must always answer the date and time prompts accurately. Otherwise the system has no way of keeping track of when each file was last modified.

Restoring files to the hard disk follows a similar procedure. Use the command

```
RESTORE A: C:\ /S
```

to restore files (including the contents of subdirectories) contained on a floppy disk in drive A to a hard disk named drive C.

Backing Up a Directory

To back up only the contents of a certain directory to a floppy disk in drive A, you use the command

BACKUP C:<*directory name*> A:

This backs up all the files in the directory whose name you specify. You will be prompted to insert additional floppy disks as necessary.

To restore a backed-up directory to a hard disk (if, for example, you are transferring files from one hard disk to another), you use the command

RESTORE A: .C:<*directory name*> /P

The /P argument tells DOS to prompt you for each file to restore. You may, for example, want to restore some files but not others.

Backing Up a File

You can also choose to back up only one file from the hard disk to a floppy disk. The command to do this is

BACKUP C:<*file name*> A:

This backs up a file on the hard disk (drive C) to a floppy disk in drive A. If the floppy disk in drive A already has files on it, use the command

BACKUP C:<*file name*> A: /A

The /A argument tells DOS to append files to the contents of the floppy disk, not overwrite them.

Likewise, to restore a file to the hard disk, you can use either the COPY command or the RESTORE command. You can simply enter

COPY A:<*file name*> C:

to copy the specified file to the current directory in drive C (the hard disk), or you can use

RESTORE A: C:<*file name*>

to accomplish the same thing.

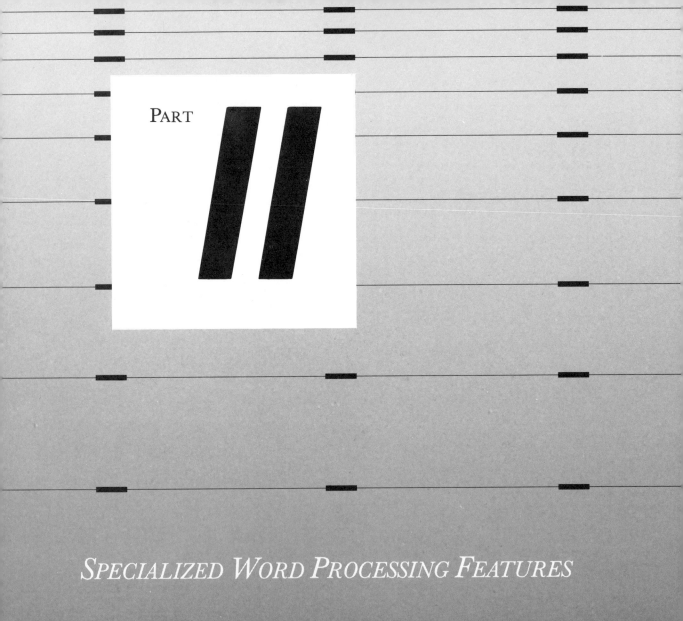

PART

II

SPECIALIZED WORD PROCESSING FEATURES

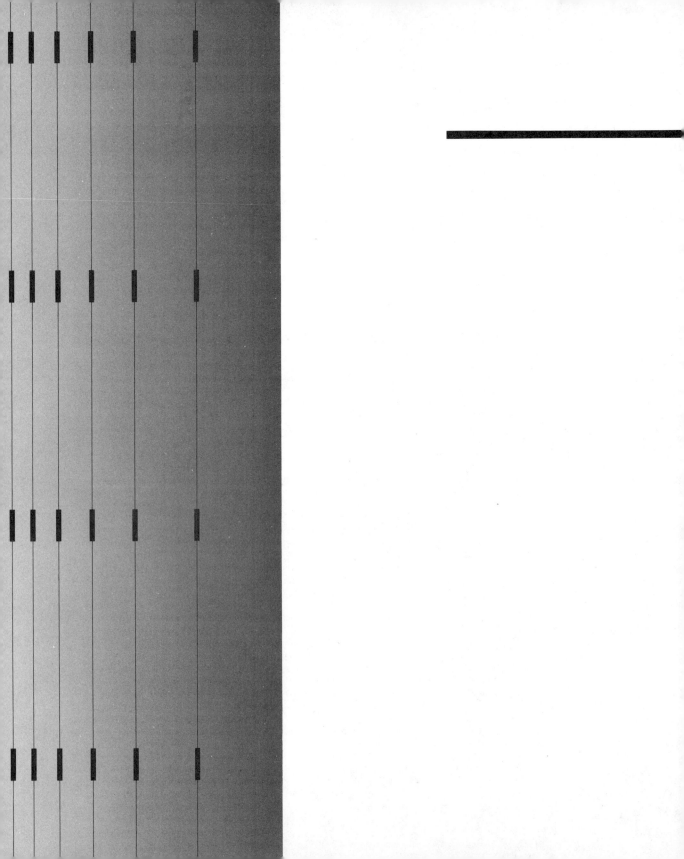

CREATING AUTOMATED REFERENCES

CREATING AUTOMATED REFERENCES

WordPerfect contains several built-in functions that streamline specialized word processing tasks required in certain occupations. For example, it can:

- Create footnotes and endnotes.
- Maintain automatic cross-references.
- Create tables of contents.
- Create and reorganize lists.
- Generate outlines.
- Generate indexes.
- Number lines.
- Create tables of authorities.

If your work calls for any of these specialized functions, you will appreciate the tools WordPerfect gives you. For example, if you create documents such as long business reports or professional papers that require a table of contents as well as footnotes, indexes, and lists of tables and figures, you will find WordPerfect's specialized features indispensable. If you are in the legal profession, you will often use WordPerfect's automatic Line Numbering feature as well as its ability to mark citations and generate tables of authorities.

This chapter discusses the techniques used to generate these special formats in your documents. If you do not use any of these formats in your work, you may wish to turn to another chapter that discusses a specialized technique applicable to the tasks you do. Chapter 10 discusses multicolumn layouts, which you will find useful if you prepare newsletters, manuals, or brochures. Chapters 11 and 12 explain techniques used for merge-printing and sorting, which have a variety of applications in many fields; Chapter 13 contains information about using mathematics within WordPerfect, and Chapter 14 discusses line drawing and special symbols.

UPGRADE NOTES

If you have been using WordPerfect 4.2, you will find several changes to the keystrokes required to use reference aids in version 5.0. Outline and paragraph numbering have been moved from Mark Text (Alt-F5) to Date/Outline

(Shift-F5). The Mark Text key itself has been reorganized; it now contains the new Master Document, Document Compare, and Automatic Reference features. Redline and Strikeout are now on the Font key (Ctrl-F8).

On the Footnote key (Ctrl-F7), footnotes and endnotes are now on different submenus. An Endnote Placement code, which allows you to generate endnotes at any point in your document, has been added.

Because moving these features to other keys and adding new features has also affected the related options, you will probably want to review the material in this chapter even if you are already familiar with the corresponding feature in WordPerfect 4.2.

FOOTNOTES AND ENDNOTES

If your work requires you to create footnotes (notes that appear at the bottom of the page) and endnotes (notes that appear at the end of a document or at the end of each chapter or section in a document) you will appreciate the many features that WordPerfect provides.

When you add or delete a note, WordPerfect automatically renumbers all of your notes for you. That way you never have to worry about searching through your documents and changing the note numbering each time you change your notes.

When you create footnotes, WordPerfect automatically inserts them at the bottom of the page. Figure 9.1 illustrates an example of a page with several footnotes.

The default settings for footnotes create notes like the ones shown in Figure 9.1. Numbering begins with an Arabic *1,* footnotes appear at the bottom of the page, a 2-inch rule separates footnotes from the text of the document, the footnote number is superscripted, and footnotes are single-spaced with one line between notes. You have several options for changing these default settings, as will be explained later in this chapter.

Endnotes are simply notes that are printed at the end of a document rather than as footnotes on the page where their reference occurs. When endnotes are printed, their reference numbers normally appear as Arabic numerals with periods, on the same line as the note (Figure 9.2), whereas footnote numbers are superscripted if your printer can print superscripts. If you want endnotes to appear on a page by themselves, you need to move the cursor to the end of your document (Home Home ↓) and press Ctrl-Enter to insert a new page before you print the document.

You can use both footnotes and endnotes within the same document; footnotes can explain or further clarify material on the page, and endnotes can provide a list of references or suggestions for further reading. If you choose to use this system, you will want to change the system of footnote numbering to use different symbols from those you use for endnotes; you may also want to specify that footnote marking start over again on each new page; see ''Numbering Footnotes by Page'' later in this chapter.

A business, once it gets beyond the entrepreneurial stage,[1] next faces the challenge of organizing and managing itself as a stable company.[2] Managers who heretofore were rewarded for initiative and ingenuity are now penalized for outstepping the boundaries of corporate rules; employees who in the past were rewarded for their willingness to challenge established theory must now follow corporate canons. In this stage of business growth a radical change in the employee-manager mix may be noted.[3]

At the same time the business is facing this challenge, it meets yet another challenge: managing for future growth. A dynamic business cannot be allowed to stagnate; it must always be planning for the future. The future, in such a case, may mean diversification rather than the former concentration on a narrow set of goals. Yet another type of managerial thinking is required: that of long-range planners.[4]

These different types of idealists must manage a new set of assumptions to manage for current stability while planning for future expansion. Such planners must be able to juggle one set of conservative assumptions while at the same time exercising a plan of highly imaginative proportions that concerns five- and ten-year growth plans and beyond. Such thinkers are scarce; when found, they command excellent salaries.

---

[1]See Paul L. Salomon, <u>The Entrepreneurial Mind</u> (Chicago: Row-Martin, 1987).

[2] Saul C. Guttman, <u>Stages in Business Growth</u> (Hoffman: Baltimore, 1987), p.198

[3]This is also the time of most rapid employee expansion, so the mix in personality types may pass unnoticed.

[4]Eldon R. WainWright, <u>Long-Range Planning for Corporate Policy</u> (Harrison & Ball: New York, 1987).

FIGURE 9.1: Footnotes on a printed page. WordPerfect will break pages to keep footnotes on the page to which they refer unless you instruct it otherwise. You can also change the default 2-inch rule that separates footnotes from text.

1.Carruthers, R. M., et al., Establishing a Value-Added
Performance Appraisal System (New York: Abbott Press, 1987).

2.Stein, J. M., "A Dual System of Performance Appraisal," in The
Immediate Manager 18:22-35 (April 1987).

3.McKnight, S. L., and Harrington, T.L., Corporate Strategies
for the Twentieth Century (Indianapolis: Hubris Publishers, 1987).

4.Stephens, R. W., Motivation: The Inner-Directed Search (New
York: Abbott Press, 1986).

FIGURE 9.2: Endnotes printed at the end of a document. WordPerfect automatically numbers endnotes for you. If you delete a note or add a new one, WordPerfect adjusts the numbering system.

When you create a note, WordPerfect gives you a full screen in which to type it. There is, practically speaking, no limit to the length of the footnote you create—WordPerfect allows you to create a 16,000-character footnote if you choose. When you press F7 to return to the editing screen, you see only the footnote number, not the text of the footnote itself. You can press Alt-F3 (Reveal Codes) to see the first 50 characters of the note. To see the note in its entirety, you can choose to edit it, as discussed later in this chapter. To see how it will appear on the printed page, you can preview the page by pressing Shift-F7 (Print) and choosing View Document (**6** or **V**).

> *Note:* If you change the margins of a document that contains notes, the program does not automatically reset the margins of footnotes and endnotes for you. To make sure your footnote and endnote margins are correct, move to the beginning of your document (Home Home ↑) and search for your margin change (F2 Shift-F8 L M F2). Open the Reveal Codes window (Alt-F3) and make a note of the setting; then move to the beginning of the document and change its initial codes to match your margin change. For example, if you have reset the left margin to 2'', press Shift-F8, type **D C**, press Shift-F8 again, type **L M 2''**, and press F7 four times to return to your document.

The upcoming sections explain the techniques used in working with footnotes and endnotes. As the procedures are the same in both cases—with the exception of certain option numbers—both footnotes and endnotes will be referred to as *notes* unless one or the other is specifically meant.

Creating a Note

You can create a note at any position in your text. To create a note, press Ctrl-F7 (Footnote). The following menu appears:

1 **F**ootnote; **2** **E**ndnote; **3** **E**ndnote **P**lacement: 0

When you choose Footnote (**1** or **F**), a second menu appears:

Footnote: **1 C**reate; **2 E**dit; **3 N**ew Number; **4 O**ptions: 0

If you select Create (**1** or **C**), the screen shown in Figure 9.3 appears. (The screen is identical for endnotes, except that the *1* in the upper-left corner has a period following it because endnotes are not numbered with superscripts.)

You can enter a footnote of any length that you wish. When WordPerfect formats the page, it subtracts the number of lines the footnote requires from the number of text lines, including the headers and footers that must appear on the page. If WordPerfect cannot fit all of the footnote on the page that contains the line to which it refers, it will keep a minimum of $1/2$ inch of the footnote on the page, plus a blank line to separate the footnote from the rule, before beginning a new page. (How many lines of text this is depends on the font and printer your are using.) You can change the minimum amount of footnote text to be kept on the first page; you can also specify that WordPerfect insert the message *(Continued...)* when it breaks footnotes. See "Specifying How Footnotes Break" later in this chapter.

When you press F7 (Exit) to return to the editing screen after creating a note, the note number appears, as shown in Figure 9.4. When your document is printed, footnote numbers (or letters or symbols) will be printed as superscripts—assuming your printer has that capability—in both of the places where they appear; endnotes will be referenced in text as superscripts, but in the reference list their numbers will be on the same line as the text (see Figure 9.2).

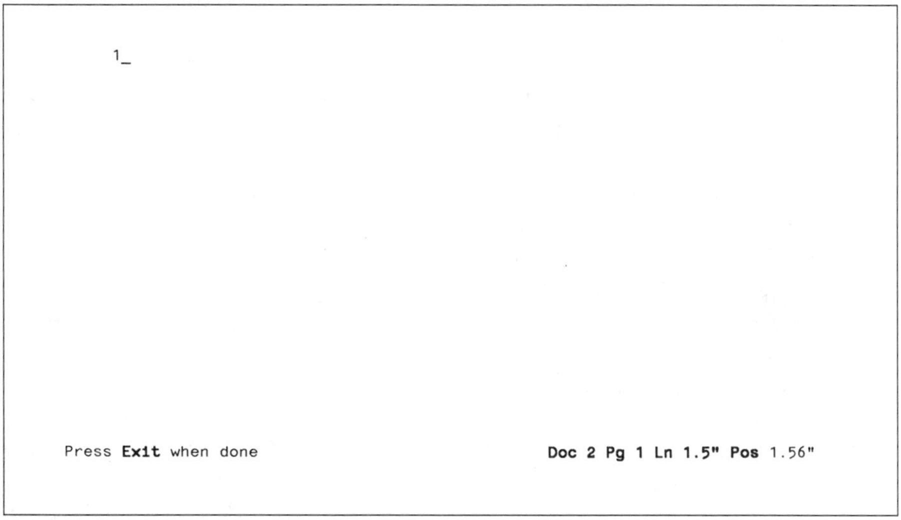

```
   1_




















   Press Exit when done                    Doc 2 Pg 1 Ln 1.5" Pos 1.56"
```

FIGURE 9.3: The Footnote screen. There is almost no limit to the size of the notes you can create in WordPerfect. The screen for creating and editing endnotes is the same except that the *1* in the upper-left corner is followed by a period (*1.*).

```
A performance appraisal system has, among others, the following
goals1:
        To assess actual performance
        To motivate employees
        To provide a system of rewards (and punishments)2
        To open a channel of feedback between employee and manager

A well-designed performance appraisal system has as its foremost
characteristic that there be no surprises--that is, that ongoing
communication between employee and manager be so thorough as to
let both know where they stand at all times.

Scheduling Performance Appraisals

Such results can only be achieved by a system of frequent
meetings, both formal and informal, between employees and their
managers. Securing commitment to the goals of this process
facilitates communication and establishes a climate that is
conducive to change and growth within a corporation3.

In technical white-collar industries, many companies have found
that a bi-weekly system of informal meetings combined with a
formal review every six months produces satisfactory results.
Usually, however, a system in which formal meetings occur more
                                        Doc 1 Pg 1 Ln 2.16" Pos 1"
```

FIGURE 9.4: Note numbers as they appear in your document on the editing screen. These numbers (or symbols, if you are not using the default numbering system) normally appear as superscripts in the printed document.

Endnote Placement

If you are using endnotes, WordPerfect will automatically place them at the end of your document, but you can specify another placement by inserting an Endnote Placement code where you want them to occur. For example, if you are writing a document that is organized into sections, you may want endnotes at the end of each section instead of at the end of the document. To insert an Endnote Placement code, move the cursor to the page where you want the endnotes to appear. (If you want them on a separate page, create a blank page for them.) Then press Ctrl-F7 (Footnote) and select Endnote Placement (**3** or **E**). You can choose whether to start a new numbering system or to continue with the next endnote number in your document.

In a subdocument, the Endnote Placement code takes effect where it occurs, so when you expand the master document, the endnotes (up to the Endnote Placement code) will be generated at that point. Any endnotes after that point will appear at the end of the master document. (See "Chain Printing with the Master Document Feature" in Chapter 7 for information on expanding a master document.)

When you press Enter, you will see a message that acts as a placeholder until you actually generate the endnotes. You may want to insert a Page Break code before the Endnote Placement code so that the next text will start on a new page. If you want the new page to be a right-hand page, press Shift-F8 (Format), select Page (**2** or **P**), select Force Odd/Even Page (**2** or **O**), and then select Odd (**1** or **O**) to make the next page a right-hand page.

Editing a Note

To edit a note, you do not have to position the cursor on the note number. When you press Ctrl-F7 (Footnote) and select first Footnote (**1** or **F**) and then Edit (**2** or **E**), you will see the prompt

Footnote number?

Type the number of the note you wish to edit.

Likewise, when you edit an endnote, you receive the prompt

Endnote number?

By entering a progressively higher number at each prompt, you can step through all the notes in your document if you choose, and review or edit the contents of all of the notes.

When you edit a note, all of WordPerfect's features, including any macros you have created, are available to you. When you spell-check a page or an entire document using the Spell feature, WordPerfect checks each note in the order it occurs in your text.

Deleting a Note

To delete a note from a document, position the cursor on the note number and then press Del. You can also press Alt-F3 (Reveal Codes) to see the code Word-Perfect has inserted for the note and simply backspace over it. Each time you insert a note into your document, WordPerfect inserts a [Footnote] or [Endnote] code, as shown in Figure 9.5. You can use the program's Search feature (F2) to search for each occurrence of the [Footnote] or [Endnote] code and delete the notes. WordPerfect automatically renumbers notes each time you delete one.

To search for a Footnote code, you must generate its formatting symbol at the Search prompt.

1. Position the cursor at the beginning of the document (Home Home ↑) and press F2 (Search).

2. When the Search prompt appears, press Ctrl-F7 and select Footnote or Endnote. The Search prompt will then display

1 Note; **2** Number **C**ode; **3** New **N**umber; **4 O**ptions: 0

Choose Note (**1** or **N**) to search for the next footnote or endnote. Choose New Number (**3** or **U**) to search for the point where you began a new note numbering system. Options (**4** or **O**) searches for the location where you defined the style of the footnotes or endnotes.

```
A performance appraisal system has, among others, the following

goals:1_

        To assess actual performance

        To motivate employees

        To provide a system of rewards and punishments

        To open a channel of feedback between employee and manager
                                        Doc 2 Pg 1 Ln 1.33" Pos 1.65"
```
```
A performance appraisal system has, among others, the following[SRt]
goals:[Footnote:1;[Note Num] See Carruthers, et al., Establishing a Value[-]Add
...][HRt]
[Tab]To assess actual performance[HRt]
[Tab]To motivate employees[HRt]
[Tab]To provide a system of rewards and punishments[HRt]
[Tab]To open a channel of feedback between employee and manager


Press Reveal Codes to restore screen
```

FIGURE 9.5: Using Reveal Codes (Alt-F3) to display the codes associated with a footnote. WordPerfect automatically supplies the number of the footnote in the code. To delete a footnote from your document, you can display the Footnote codes, position the cursor to the right of the codes, and press Backspace. You can also search your document for [Footnote] or [Endnote] codes and delete them without displaying them.

3. When WordPerfect finds a note, you can delete it by pressing Backspace. The program displays the prompt

   Delete Note? (Y/N) N

   Enter **Y** to delete the note. Press F2 again to have WordPerfect search through your document for the next occurrence of the [Footnote] or [Endnote] code.

Changing Note Options

When you select Footnote (**1** or **F**) from the Footnote/Endnote menu (Ctrl-F7) and then choose Options (**4** or **O**), the screen shown in Figure 9.6 appears. If you have chosen Endnote (**2** or **E**) first, the screen in Figure 9.7 appears. As you can see, there are many options you can use with footnotes and endnotes. The following sections explain each of these and illustrate how you can use them in documents you create.

Be sure to return to the beginning of your document (by pressing Home Home ↑) before you change note options so that the options you select will apply to all the notes in your document.

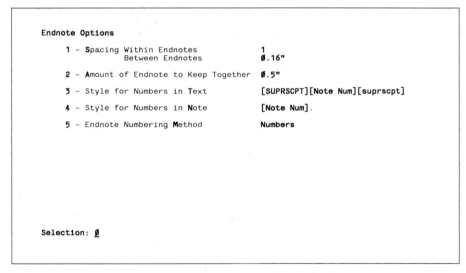

```
Footnote Options

    1 - Spacing Within Footnotes       1
                 Between Footnotes      Ø.16"

    2 - Amount of Note to Keep Together  Ø.5"

    3 - Style for Number in Text        [SUPRSCPT][Note Num][suprscpt]

    4 - Style for Number in Note              [SUPRSCPT][Note Num][suprscp

    5 - Footnote Numbering Method       Numbers

    6 - Start Footnote Numbers each Page   No

    7 - Line Separating Text and Footnotes  2-inch Line

    8 - Print Continued Message         No

    9 - Footnotes at Bottom of Page     Yes



    Selection: Ø
```

FIGURE 9.6: The Footnote Options screen. WordPerfect allows you to style many different aspects of notes, including how they are printed and what numbering system they use.

```
Endnote Options

    1 - Spacing Within Endnotes         1
                 Between Endnotes        Ø.16"

    2 - Amount of Endnote to Keep Together  Ø.5"

    3 - Style for Numbers in Text       [SUPRSCPT][Note Num][suprscpt]

    4 - Style for Numbers in Note       [Note Num].

    5 - Endnote Numbering Method        Numbers





    Selection: Ø
```

FIGURE 9.7: The Endnote Options screen. You can also specify several different style options for endnotes in WordPerfect.

CHANGING LINE SPACING IN NOTES

The default spacing for both types of notes is single spacing; you can select other line spacing for your notes, using half-line increments. For example, to use one-and-a-half spacing in notes, enter **1.5**, for double spacing, enter **2**, and so forth.

CHANGING LINE SPACING BETWEEN NOTES

The default setting for spacing between notes is .16 inch. If you would like additional space between notes, enter the amount of space you would like. The number you enter here will automatically be converted to the default units of measurement.

SPECIFYING HOW FOOTNOTES BREAK

WordPerfect will keep at least ½ inch of note text on the same page as its reference before beginning a new page unless you specify otherwise. You can enter a new number for the minimum amount of text you want to appear together on the same page.

CHANGING THE STYLE OF NOTES

If you redefine the style of footnotes and endnotes by using either Style for Number in Text (**3** or **T**) or Style for Number in Note (**4** or **N**) on the Footnote Options and Endnote Options menus, you will get a *replace with* prompt at the bottom of the screen. You can enter a word such as *Note:* and use font style changes like italics and boldface or insert format changes such as indents by pressing the space bar. To indicate where the note number itself should occur, press Ctrl-F7 (Footnote), select Footnotes or Endnotes, and then select Number Code (**2** or **C**) to insert the [Note#] code into your new style.

CHANGING THE NOTE NUMBERING STYLE

WordPerfect is preset to number both footnotes and endnotes in Arabic numerals. You can change this to letters or characters. If you choose characters, you can enter up to five different characters. After each character is used once, it will be doubled, then tripled, and so forth. For example, if you use two characters, the asterisk (*) and the pound sign (#), they'll alternate like this:

Note 1   *

Note 2   #

Note 3   **

Note 4   ##

Note 5   ***

Note 6   ###

Note: Your readers will get hopelessly confused if you use the same numbering style for footnotes and endnotes within the same document. Change one of them to either letters or characters.

NUMBERING FOOTNOTES BY PAGE

WordPerfect allows you to specify whether it is to number footnotes consecutively throughout a document (the default setting) or to begin numbering with *1, a,* or your beginning symbol each time it begins a new page. Choose Start Footnote Numbers Each Page (**6** or **P**) on the Footnote Options menu and enter **Y** to restart numbering each time the program begins a new page.

CHANGING THE LINE THAT SEPARATES FOOTNOTES FROM TEXT

WordPerfect allows you to change the default 2-inch rule that separates footnotes from text either to no rule or to a rule that extends across the page. You can also specify whether to have the program insert *(Continued...)* when a footnote must be split to another page. If you select this option, the text of a footnote that is split ends with *(Continued...)* and begins with *(...Continued)* on the next page.

PLACING FOOTNOTES IN TEXT

WordPerfect is preset to print footnotes at the bottom of the page, even when there is not enough text to fill the page completely. If you want to have footnotes moved up near the last line of text on short pages, you can change the footnote placement setting by selecting Footnotes at Bottom of Page (**9** or **B**) on the Footnote Options menu. If you enter **N**, WordPerfect places footnotes two lines below the last text on the page, even if it is not a full page.

CREATING A TABLE OF CONTENTS

WordPerfect can create tables of contents for you and print them when your documents are printed. For the program to create a table of contents, you must mark each heading that you want to appear in the table of contents by using the Mark Text key sequence (Alt-F5).

> *Note:* Alt-F5 presents options for marking items for tables of contents only if you have first marked a block of text. If you have not marked a block of text, the program assumes that when you press Alt-F5 you want to use one of WordPerfect's other Mark Text options.

You can mark up to five levels of headings to be included in the table of contents. Because you probably will not want to take the time to do this as you are writing, it's a good idea to make a habit of marking the headings you wish to appear in the table of contents with a special attribute—such as boldface or underlining—that you do not use anywhere else in your document. (You will probably want to use some special attribute to set off headings from text, anyway.) That way you can quickly search for the [BOLD] or [UND] code and mark the headings for the table of contents when you are ready to create it. You can also write a macro to search for the headings—assuming you have used a unique text attribute or symbol in them—and generate the table of contents for you.

After you have marked the headings you wish to include in the table of contents, you define how you want the table of contents page to be formatted. Each level of heading can use one of five different numbering and formatting styles. Figure 9.8 illustrates some of the various formats you can use in a table of contents.

Marking Text for a Table of Contents

For each heading you want included in the table of contents, follow these steps:

1. Press Alt-F4 and mark the heading as a block.

2. Press Alt-F5 (Mark Text). The following prompt appears:

   Mark for: **1** To**C**; **2** **L**ist; **3** **I**ndex; **4** To**A**: 0

3. Select ToC (**1** or **C**). The following prompt appears:

   ToC Level:

Enter the level of the heading (from **1** to **5**). WordPerfect inserts formatting codes as shown in Figure 9.9.

```
            _                   CONTENTS


   WELCOME  . . . . . . . . . . . . . . . . . . . . . . . . . .   1
            Work Day  1
            Parking  1
            Hours  1
            Cafeteria  1
            Recreational Facilities  1

   PAID LEAVE . . . . . . . . . . . . . . . . . . . . . . . . .   1
            Vacation  1
            Holidays  1
            Personal Leave  2
                Bereavement Leave (2); Military Leave (2); Jury
                Duty (2)
            Leave for Illness  2

   CREDIT UNION . . . . . . . . . . . . . . . . . . . . . . . .   2

   BENEFITS . . . . . . . . . . . . . . . . . . . . . . . . . .   2

   PERFORMANCE APPRAISALS . . . . . . . . . . . . . . . . . . .   2
            Opportunities for Advancement  3
                                            Doc 1 Pg 1 Ln 1" Pos 1"
```

FIGURE 9.8: Various table of contents formats. You can use no page numbers, or place page numbers in parentheses. Page numbers can follow the entries or appear flush right preceded by dot leaders as shown. You can have the lowest defined level of heading displayed in wrapped format, as is shown here. Each level of heading can use a different style.

```
         let both know where they stand at all times.


         Scheduling Performance Appraisals_


         Such results can be achieved only by a system of frequent
         meetings, both formal and informal, between employees and their
                                                Doc 2 Pg 1 Ln 1.66" Pos 4.3"
         let both know where they stand at all times.[HRt]
         [HRt]
         [Mark:ToC,2]Scheduling Performance Appraisals[End Mark:ToC,2][HRt]
         [HRt]
         Such results can be achieved only by a system of frequent[SRt]
         meetings, both formal and informal, between employees and their



         Press Reveal Codes to restore screen
```

FIGURE 9.9: Formatting codes inserted when you mark text for a table of contents. WordPerfect keeps track of each level of heading by the level number you assign to it.

Defining the Style for a Table of Contents

You need to create a page for the table of contents, which normally appears near the beginning of a document. If you want a title page as the first page of your document, create the title page first; then insert a hard page break (Ctrl-Enter) and position the cursor just below the break so that the table of contents will follow the title page. (When you generate a table of contents, it appears at the position where you define its style.) If you are not using a title page, move the cursor to the beginning of the document (Home Home ↑) and then insert the hard page break for the table of contents. You will also probably want to center a heading—such as **CONTENTS**—for the table of contents.

To define the format of the contents page,

1. Press Alt-F5 (Mark Text) and select Define (**5** or **D**). The Mark Text Define screen appears (Figure 9.10).

2. Select Define Table of Contents (**1** or **C**). The Table of Contents Definition screen appears (Figure 9.11).

3. Select Number of Levels (**1** or **N**) and enter the number of heading levels you are using in the table of contents (**1–5**).

4. If you want the last level of your headings presented as one wrapped line, with the headings and page numbers separated by semicolons, select Display Last Level in Wrapped Format (**2** or **D**) and type **Y**. Otherwise WordPerfect will display each heading on a separate line.

5. Select Page Numbering (**3** or **P**); then select the page number position style you wish to use for each level by entering the appropriate code.

The None option (**1** or **N**) prints headings only, with no page numbers. If you choose Pg# Follows (**2** or **P**) or (Pg #) Follows (**3** or **(**), page numbers will occur next to headings, and with (Pg #) Follows they will be in parentheses. Flush Rt (**4** or **F**) and Flush Rt with Leader (**5** or **L**) place page numbers flush right, with or without dot leaders.

Generating a Table of Contents

When you have defined a style for your table of contents, press Alt-F5 (Mark Text), select Generate (**6** or **G**), and then select Generate Tables, Indexes, Automatic References, etc. (**5** or **G**). If you have marked text for other lists or tables, such as a table of authorities, or if you have marked index entries, WordPerfect will generate those at the same time. It is not necessary, however, to wait until you have marked these other tables and index entries so that everything is generated at once; you can generate a table of contents before you have marked any of the other items. WordPerfect generates a table of contents, list, or index for each [Def Mark] code it finds.

You will be prompted that existing tables and lists will be replaced. Type **Y** or press Enter to generate the table, or type **N** to return to your document.

The prompt

Generation in progress: Counter: *<number>*

```
Mark Text: Define

      1 - Define Table of Contents

      2 - Define List

      3 - Define Index

      4 - Define Table of Authorities

      5 - Edit Table of Authorities Full Form




      Selection: 0
```

FIGURE 9.10: The Mark Text Define screen. You also use this screen to define formats for indexes, lists, and tables of authorities.

```
Table of Contents Definition

     1 - Number of Levels                    1

     2 - Display Last Level in              No
           Wrapped Format

     3 - Page Numbering - Level 1    Flush right with leader
                          Level 2
                          Level 3
                          Level 4
                          Level 5




Selection: 0
```

FIGURE 9.11: The Table of Contents Definition screen. You can specify a different numbering style for each of five levels of headings. The None option (**1** or **N**) prints headings only, with no page numbers. If you choose Pg # Follows (**2** or **P**) or (Pg #) Follows (**3** or **( )**), page numbers will occur next to headings, and with option **3** they will be in parentheses. Flust Rt (**4** or **F**) and Flush Rt with Leader (**5** or **L**) place page numbers flush right, with or without dot leaders.

appears while the program is generating the table of contents. If your computer does not have sufficient RAM to hold the entire table in memory, you may be asked to close the Doc 2 window so that WordPerfect can use more memory for generating the table.

If you attempt to print a document for which you have defined a table of contents without generating it, you will get a warning that you have not generated the document.

Deleting Existing Tables of Contents, Lists, and Indexes

Each time WordPerfect generates a table of contents—or any other kind of list, such as a table of authorities or an index—it searches for a [Def Mark] code and uses that code to generate the list.

To delete a table of contents, be sure to delete both the [Def Mark] code and the [End Def] code marking the end of the table. If WordPerfect finds a [Def Mark] code but no [End Def] code, it will continue to generate a table of contents each time you generate your tables and lists. If it finds two [Def Mark] codes, it will generate two tables of contents.

To remove the old [Def Mark] code from previously defined lists, tables of contents, or indexes,

1. Press F2 (Search); then press Alt-F5 (Mark Text).
2. Select Defs and Refs (**5** or **D** or **R**) from the menu that appears.
3. Choose Def Mark (**1** or **D**).
4. Press F2 to begin the search.
5. When the program locates the [Def Mark] code, delete the code (by backspacing over it). You will see the prompt

   Delete [Def Mark]? (Y/N) N

   Enter **Y** to delete the code.
6. Press Alt-F5 (Mark Text) and choose Define (**5** or **D**) to define the new style where you want the table of contents to appear.
7. Select Generate (**6** or **G**) to generate the new tables and index.

If you have any difficulty generating subsequent tables of contents, lists, or indexes, there may be extra [Def Mark] codes in your text. Use the procedure just described to find and delete them. Remember, after you generate the first table of contents, list, or index at the position of the cursor, subsequent tables, lists, and indexes will be generated at that same location, because it will contain a [Def Mark] code.

Revising a Table of Contents, List, or Index

If you have changed the text in your document since you last generated a table of contents, list, or index, you may need to mark the entries again. WordPerfect allows you to search for the particular [Mark] code for each entry you have marked.

1. Press F2 (Search); then press Alt-F5 (Mark Text).
2. From the following menu, select the appropriate option to find the [Mark] code that begins the item you want to search for, such as items marked for a table of contents or index entry:

   1 ToC/List; **2** End Mark; **3** Index; **4** ToA; **5** Defs and Refs; **6** Subdocs:0

3. Press F2 to begin the search.
4. When the program finds the [Mark] code, delete it (by backspacing over it) and confirm the deletion by typing **Y** when you are prompted.

If you want to change the style of a table of contents, list, or index, you need to search for its [Def Mark] code, delete it, and define the new style as described in the previous section. The new table, list, or index will be generated at the point in your document where the style is defined.

CREATING AND REORGANIZING LISTS

WordPerfect can create lists for you. It will keep track of up to five lists that you specify—each as long as you like—for each document you write. In addition to the five lists you may mark yourself, WordPerfect automatically maintains separate lists of the captions assigned to figures, tables, Text boxes, and User-Defined boxes created with the Graphics feature (see Chapter 19, ''WordPerfect's Desktop Publishing Capabilities'') in the lists numbered 6 through 9, respectively. For example, to generate a list composed of all of the captions for the text boxes in a document, you simply define the style for list 8 and generate it. There is no need to mark any of the captions assigned to each of these text boxes as you do with the first five lists.

The items in a list do not have to be next to each other but can be scattered throughout your document. However, an item can be included in only one list, such as a list of key terms, for example.

The procedure for marking a list and having WordPerfect generate it is similar to that used for creating a table of contents. You mark the items to be included in the list, define the style of the list, and then instruct WordPerfect to generate the list for you. The sections that follow explain the procedure for creating and reorganizing lists.

Creating a List

You can mark up to five separate lists in a document, in addition to those you create with the Graphics feature. You can use WordPerfect's Search feature (F2) to locate list items if you have previously marked them with a special character, such as @, or have used a unique text attribute that does not appear anywhere else in your document, such as boldfacing or underlining. For each list item that you want to include, follow these steps:

1. Press Alt-F4 and use the cursor movement keys to mark the list item as a block.

2. Press Alt-F5 (Mark Text). The following prompt appears:

   Mark for **1** To**C**; **2** List; **3** Index; **4** To**A**: 0

3. Select List (**2** or **L**). When the following prompt appears, enter the number of the list (from **1** to **5**):

   List Number:

You can enter numbers **6** through **9**, but WordPerfect automatically takes care of marking these items for you, so there is no need to mark special boxes to be included in lists, as discussed in Chapter 18.

Defining the Style for a List

You will probably want to create a page for your list, usually at the end of the document, but at the beginning if you are manually creating a list of figures or tables. You may want to insert a hard page break (Ctrl-Enter) so that the list begins on a new page. Move the cursor to the end of the document (Home Home ↓) and then insert the hard page break.

To define the format of the list,

1. Press Alt-F5 (Mark Text) and select Define (**5** or **D**). The Mark Text: Define screen appears.

2. Select Define List (**2** or **L**). The following prompt appears:

   List Number:

3. Enter the number of the list you want to define. The List Definition screen appears (Figure 9.12).

4. Select the style you wish to use by entering the appropriate option number, as shown in Figure 9.12.

The No Page Numbers option (**1** or **N**) prints list items only, with no page numbers. If you choose Page Numbers Follow Entries (**2** or **P**) or (Page Numbers) Follow Entries (**3** or **(**), page numbers will occur next to list items; with option **3** or **(**, they will be in parentheses. The final two options place page numbers flush right, with or without dot leaders.

```
List 1 Definition

    1 - No Page Numbers

    2 - Page Numbers Follow Entries

    3 - (Page Numbers) Follow Entries

    4 - Flush Right Page Numbers

    5 - Flush Right Page Numbers with Leaders









    Selection: 0
```

FIGURE 9.12: The List Definition screen. You will most often use the No Page Numbers option (**1** or **N**), which generates list items without page numbers. The other options create lists similar to tables of contents, with page numbers that indicate which page of your document each item is on.

Generating a List

When you have marked all the items to be included in a list and have defined the style for each list, you can generate the lists by pressing Alt-F5 (Mark Text), selecting Generate (**6** or **G**), and then selecting Generate Tables, Indexes, Automatic References, etc. (**5** or **G**). If you have marked text for other lists or tables, such as a table of authorities, or if you have marked index entries, WordPerfect will generate those at the same time. It is not necessary, however, to wait until you have marked those items so that all of the lists and tables are generated at once; you can generate a list before you have marked any of the other items. WordPerfect will generate a list, table of contents, or index for each [Def Mark] code it finds.

The prompt

Generation in progress: Counter: <*number*>

appears while the program is generating the list. The counter number indicates the number of list items in your document.

Revising or Deleting a List

To delete a list, you need to delete the [Def Mark] code that generates it. If you want to change the style of a list, you need to locate its [Def Mark] code, delete it, and define a new style. See the sections ''Deleting Existing Tables of Contents, Lists, and Indexes'' and ''Revising a Table of Contents, List, or Index'' earlier in this chapter; the procedure is the same for all.

USING AUTOMATIC REFERENCING

The Automatic Reference feature maintains and automatically updates references to other pages, outline or paragraph numbers, note numbers, graphics or text boxes, and figures. As you add or delete pages, WordPerfect keeps track of each element you've marked with a Reference code. You can refer to more than one item in a reference, as in *See page 314, figure 7-9.* You can also have references in separate documents that you later plan to combine into one document by using WordPerfect's Master Document feature, as discussed in Chapter 7. When you generate lists in the expanded master document, all references will be automatically updated.

When you mark a reference, you use a Reference code instead of a reference number and indicate a *target*—the actual item you are referencing, which in this case would be the discussion on the page you are making the reference to. You don't have to know in advance where that page is; in fact, if you know you are going to be adding the material you are referring to later, you can go ahead and mark the reference now and fill in the target later. For example, assume you want to create an automatic reference in the paragraph illustrated in Figure 9.13. After you type the word *page* and press the space bar, press Alt-F5 (Mark Text), select Auto Ref (**1** or **R**), and select Mark Both Reference and Target (**3** or **B**) if you have already typed the material you are referring to. Then select the type of reference you want to use—page number, paragraph or outline number, footnote or endnote, or graphics box.

You will then be allowed to move the cursor to the item that's being referred to, but there are a few variations in how you target an item, depending on what that item is. If the target is in a footnote or an endnote, you will need to display the note in the note editing screen as described in "Editing a Note" earlier in this chapter. You can then mark both the target and the reference for footnotes and endnotes by pressing Enter and entering a short ID name. If you are targeting an endnote page number, you will have to generate the endnotes so that WordPerfect knows which page they are going to appear on. If you want to refer to the page on which the endnote number occurs, not the page on which the actual endnote text appears, position the target immediately after the endnote number.

If you are referencing a graphics box, you will also need to indicate which type of graphics box it is (Text, Figure, Table, or User-Defined) and you will have to mark the reference and target separately, as discussed later.

When you have located the target, press Enter to mark it. WordPerfect then lets you enter an ID name so that you can keep track of what's being referred to.

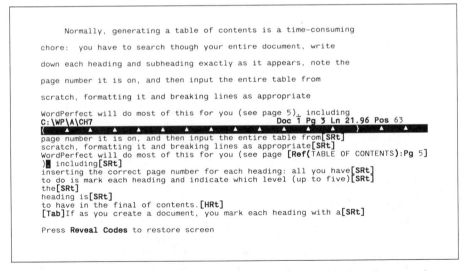

FIGURE 9.13: Creating an automatic reference. WordPerfect lets you mark both a reference and a target, or simply mark a reference and indicate the target later.

If you press Reveal Codes, you can see both the name and the Target code, as illustrated in Figure 9.14.

If you have not typed the material you want to refer to, you can choose to mark the reference only. You will need to select the type of reference you are going to use and enter an ID name for it, but you will not have to move to the target and mark it. A question mark will appear in place of the reference number. After you mark a target with the same ID name that you used for the reference, the question mark will change to a reference number.

You can mark all your references separately and then mark their targets, if you like. To mark a target separately, choose Mark Target (**2** or **T**) after pressing Alt-F5 (Mark Text) and selecting Auto Ref (**1** or **R**) when the cursor is positioned at the target. You can then enter an ID name corresponding to the one you used earlier when you marked the reference. When you generate your references, targets and references with the same ID name will be matched.

To refer to more than one target when the targets are of different types, create a reference and target for each one. For example, if you want to insert an automatic reference such as *see also page 34, Table 10,* you would need to mark a reference and target both for page 34 (a page number) and Table 10 (a graphics box). However, if you are referring to one topic that appears on several different pages (such as *see pages 145, 200, 203*), you can just mark the reference once and use the same ID name to mark each target on pages 145, 200, and 203.

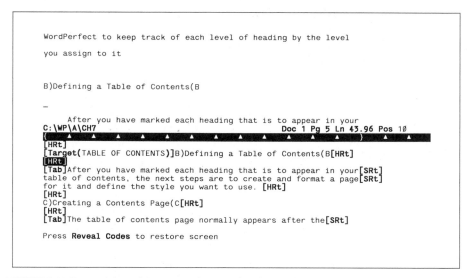

FIGURE 9.14: Target code and ID name in the Reveal Codes window. The target is the item you are making the reference to.

Automatic references will be generated and updated when you generate tables, lists, and indexes, as described earlier in the chapter.

WORKING WITH OUTLINES

Many people who write find that outlining is a useful aid in organizing their work. However, they often avoid the task because of the difficulty in manually keeping an outline accurate. WordPerfect can automatically maintain outlines you create with the program and change the level and numbering of items as necessary. Of course, you can also create short outlines by simply typing the material as you want it to appear, but when you work with long outlines, you will probably want to use WordPerfect's built-in Outlining feature.

In fact, you can use WordPerfect's Outlining feature as an idea processor, similar to programs such as ThinkTank. After you have created a basic outline, you can add major points to it, indenting sublevels as ideas occur to you. You can then write the document by following the outline, and you can be assured that all the points you listed are covered. If you are maintaining "boilerplate" or standard text in separate files, you can even insert Merge codes to have the program insert the appropriate paragraphs or sections at print time. (See Chapter 11 for additional ideas regarding how you can use WordPerfect's Merge feature.)

As you soon discover when you use Outline mode, the Tab and Enter keys work differently from the way they usually do. Pressing Enter adds an outline level number to a paragraph, and pressing Tab lowers a paragraph to the next outline level (for example, from *1* to *a*). This allows you to quickly reorganize your work, with WordPerfect keeping track of the outline level numbers for you.

WordPerfect's default outlining style is the one you probably learned in school:

     I.
         A.
             1.
                  a.
                       (1)
                            (a)
                                 i)
                                     a)

There are other numbering styles built into the program; for example, *paragraph* style uses the system 1., a., i., (1), (a), (i), 1), a), and *legal* style (sometimes called *mil spec*) numbers each paragraph and level sequentially as 1, 1.1, 1.1.1, and so forth. You can change the system of numbering and punctuation; see "Customizing a Numbering Style" later in this chapter.

Creating an Outline

After you have turned on Outline mode by pressing Shift-F5 and selecting Outline (**4** or **O**), each time you enter characters or a space and then press Enter, a new outline number is generated in your text. To generate a number at a lower level, you press the Tab key. For example, to create an entry numbered *1* (assuming you are using the default style for outlining), you press Tab three times after pressing Enter for the first-level number.

As long as you are in Outline mode, the message

Outline

appears in the lower-left corner of your screen. To turn off Outline mode, press Shift-F5 (Date/Outline) and select Outline again.

To indent text without entering an outline number or letter when you are in Outline mode, press the space bar before you press the Tab key. You can also use the Indent key (F4) to indent text without inserting outline numbers.

To create the short outline shown in Figure 9.15, you follow these steps:

1. Press Shift-F5 (Date/Outine) and select Outline (**4** or **O**). Press Enter to insert the first level number, *I*.

2. Press the space bar; then enter the first heading, *Year-End Results*. Press Enter and then press Tab to change the *II* that appears to *A*.

3. Press the space bar; then enter the heading *Comparison with Fiscal 1988*. Press Enter and then Tab to see the *B*.

4. Enter the heading *Estimate for Fiscal 1989*. Then press Enter. This time, press Tab twice to indent to the next level.

5. Press the space bar; then enter *Best Case:* and press the space bar followed by the Tab key to insert a tab.

6. Enter *Early/Late Analysis* and press Enter. Then press Tab twice, press the space bar, and enter *Worst Case*.

7. Press Enter to insert the *II;* then press the space bar and enter the heading *General Market Trends*.

8. Press Enter to insert the *III;* then press the space bar and enter the heading *Outlook for the Future*.

You can continue to outline eight different levels in this way until you turn Outline mode off.

When you delete or insert items in an outline, WordPerfect automatically renumbers your outline for you.

To delete an outline number, position the cursor on it and press Del. You can also backspace over an outline number to delete it.

```
    I. Year-End Results

        A. Comparison with Fiscal 1988

        B. Estimate for Fiscal 1989

            1. Best Case:  Early/Late Analysis

            2. Worst Case

   II. General Market Trends

  III. Outlook for the Future_




Outline                                Doc 2 Pg 1 Ln 3.33" Pos 3.7"
```

FIGURE 9.15: A short outline created with the Outlining feature. In Outline mode, pressing the Enter and Tab keys enters outline numbers for you. Pressing Enter enters a number at the first level; the program then indents the cursor and inserts a lower-level number each time you press Tab.

NUMBERING PARAGRAPHS

WordPerfect can automatically number paragraphs for you. You can use this feature to number paragraphs or items in a list, and it will keep track of the numbers for you. When you add or delete items or paragraphs, WordPerfect renumbers the rest of them. The paragraphs or items you number do not have to be next to each other; they can be scattered throughout your document.

If you are writing numbered instructions or test questions, this feature is especially useful because you can insert or delete steps or questions and the program will automatically correct the numbering system.

If you use automatic paragraph numbering, each time you press the Tab key WordPerfect inserts a paragraph number at a progressively lower level. The numbering style the program uses depends on the tab stop the cursor is at. For example, if the cursor is at the left margin, WordPerfect inserts *I.* (for level 1). If you have pressed Tab once, it labels the paragraph *A.* (level 2); if you have pressed Tab twice, it labels the paragraph *1.* You can also use *fixed* paragraph numbering, in which case WordPerfect also automatically inserts a new number, but the style of the paragraph level does not change. See "Using Fixed Numbering" later in this chapter.

Automatic Paragraph Numbering

To number paragraphs automatically, press Shift-F5 and select Para Num (**5** or **P**). The prompt

Paragraph Level (Press Enter for Automatic):

appears. When you press Enter, WordPerfect will insert a paragraph number. To enter progressively lower levels of paragraph numbers, press the Tab key until you reach the level you want. Then press Shift-F5, select Para Num, and press Enter. An important difference from Outline mode is that here, pressing the Tab key *after* you enter a paragraph number does not change the paragraph number level but does insert a tab indent.

Using Fixed Numbering

The Reveal Codes screen for the outline shown in Figure 9.15 is presented in Figure 9.16. The code

[Par Num:Auto]

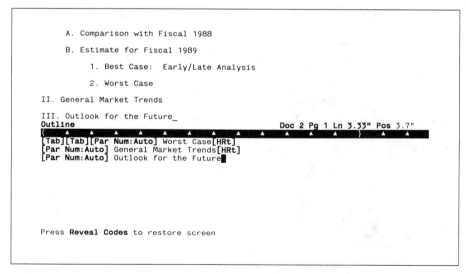

FIGURE 9.16: The Reveal Codes screen for part of the outline shown in Figure 9.15. The word *Auto* in the code indicates that WordPerfect is using automatic outline numbering. To use fixed numbering, press Shift-F5 (Date/Outline) and select Para Num (**5** or **P**). Then enter the number of the level or style you want to use.

indicates that WordPerfect is automatically numbering for you. You can avoid automatic numbering so that each time you enter a paragraph number, it will be generated at the same level. Fixed numbering is the method you normally use when you are writing numbered test questions or preparing a questionnaire, for example, and you want to be able to renumber quickly when adding to or deleting from the list.

When you use fixed numbering, WordPerfect does not change the level of paragraph numbers automatically if you press Tab in front of them. However, it still adjusts all paragraph numbers if you delete or add a new numbered paragraph. (It does not change paragraph numbers until you press Enter for the new addition or deletion.)

The level you indicate at the prompt determines the style of numbering the program uses. It uses whatever style you have chosen for that level. For example, to enter Arabic numerals you enter **3**, because level 3 of the default numbering style is Arabic numerals. See "Changing the Style of Outline and Paragraph Numbering" later in this chapter for details about how to change the numbering style or specify a custom style to suit your needs.

Figure 9.17 illustrates the results you can get by using fixed numbering. In this figure, the fifth level of outline style—in which numerals are enclosed in parentheses—was indicated by entering **5** at the prompt

Paragraph Level (Press Enter for Automatic):

```
(1) Define the term recession and explain its probable

consequences.

(2) What historical evidence is presented by the monetarists to

support the argument that the money supply is the key to the

monetary system?

(3) In what year was the Federal Reserve Board created?




Paragraph Level (Press Enter for Automatic): _
```

FIGURE 9.17: The prompt for using fixed numbering. If you turn off automatic numbering by entering a level number (from **1** to **7**), the number the program enters stays in the same style when you press the Tab key. (With automatic numbering, the numbering level changes when you move the cursor to the left of the number and press Tab.)

Figure 9.18 illustrates the results of inserting a new paragraph in the list. WordPerfect automatically renumbers the rest of the numbered items for you.

ALT-P: AN AUTOMATIC PARAGRAPH NUMBERING MACRO

If you use fixed paragraph numbering often, you may want to write a macro to speed up entry of the key sequences each time you create a new numbered paragraph. The macro Alt-P, illustrated in Figure 9.19, automates the process for you. It assumes that you are using the default style for paragraph/outline numbering and that you want to number paragraphs with Arabic numerals and periods (1., 2., 3., and so forth).

CHANGING THE STYLE OF OUTLINE AND PARAGRAPH NUMBERING

The program contains many options for paragraph numbering, as shown in Figure 9.20. You can use six different styles, including a user-defined style, using five punctuation options and six numbering styles. The default style is style 3,

```
(1) Define the term recession and explain its probable
consequences.
(2) What historical evidence is presented by the monetarists to
support the argument that the money supply is the key to the
monetary system?
(3) Define the term inflation and discuss its effects.
(4) In what year was the Federal Reserve Board created?_




                                      Doc 2 Pg 1 Ln 3" Pos 6.5"
```

FIGURE 9.18: Inserting a new numbered paragraph. If you insert a new paragraph by pressing Shift-F5 (Date/Outline), selecting Para Num (**5** or **P**), and pressing Enter (or entering a fixed level), Word-Perfect will automatically renumber paragraphs you have entered in this way when you delete one or add a new one to the list.

```
Macro: Edit

        File          ALTP.WPM

   1 - Description     Automatic paragraph numbering

   2 - Action

   {DISPLAY OFF}{Date/Outline}53{Enter}




   Selection: 0
```

FIGURE 9.19: The macro Alt-P, which automatically inserts paragraph numbers as 1., 2., 3., and so forth. You can edit it to use a different style, such as (1), (2), (3), by changing the final *3* in the macro to *5*.

Outline; in this style, the eight different levels are represented as

> I.
>> A.
>>> 1.
>>>> a.
>>>>> (1)
>>>>>> (a)
>>>>>>> i)
>>>>>>>> a)

If you select the Paragraph style (**2** or **P**), your outlines and paragraphs will be numbered in the style 1., a., i., (1), (a), (i), 1). Legal numbering (**4** or **L**) provides the sequence 1., 1.1., 1.1.1., and so forth. You can also choose to use a sequence of bullets, which is useful if you are creating outlines for presentation graphics.

To use the Paragraph style instead of the default Outline style, follow these steps:

1. Press Shift-F5 (Date/Outline) and select Define (**6** or **D**).

2. Select Paragraph (**2** or **P**).

To use legal style, choose Legal (**4** or **L**), then enter the paragraph number at which you want numbering to start. If you are numbering book chapters that are kept in separate files, you can enter **5** to begin numbers in Chapter 5 with *5* (5.1, 5.1.1, and so on).

Restarting the Numbering System

You can also start the numbering at any number that you specify. You will find this feature useful if you are continuing a numbering system in two documents and you want the second to start where the first left off.

To reset the numbering system, select Starting Paragraph Number (**1** or **S**) from the Paragraph Number Definition screen. Then enter the number you want WordPerfect to begin with. For example, entering **5** starts outline numbering at *V.* and legal numbering at *5.* Entering **5.2.4** starts outline numbering at *V.B.4* and paragraph numbering at *5.b.iv.*

If you have reset the numbering system in a document, remember to press Tab the correct number of times to get to the correct level before you begin making entries with the new numbering system.

If you are combining subdocuments into a master document, remember that Numbering codes will continue to operate as they do within a single WordPerfect document. A code that changes the numbering system will take effect from the cursor position forward until it reaches a new Definition code. Therefore, if you have reset numbers at the beginning of each chapter, they will remain accurate.

```
Paragraph Number Definition

     1 - Starting Paragraph Number          1
         (in legal style)

                                        Levels
                           1    2    3    4    5    6    7    8
     2 - Paragraph         1.   a.   i.  (1)  (a)  (i)  1)   a)
     3 - Outline           I.   A.   1.   a.  (1)  (a)  i)   a)
     4 - Legal (1.1.1)     1    .1   .1   .1   .1   .1   .1   .1
     5 - Bullets           •    o    -    ▮    *    +    ·    ×
     6 - User-defined

     Current Definition    I.   A.   1.   a.  (1)  (a)  1)   a)

         Number Style               Punctuation
         1 - Digits                 #   - No punctuation
         A - Upper case letters     #.  - Trailing period
         a - Lower case letters     #)  - Trailing parenthesis
         I - Upper case roman      (#)  - Enclosing parentheses
         1 - Lower case roman       .#  - All levels separated by period
         Other character - Bullet        (e.g.  2.1.3.4)

     Selection: 0
```

FIGURE 9.20: The Paragraph Number Definition screen. These definitions may be used in outlines as well. You can customize the numbering system if you prefer.

Customizing a Numbering Style

You can instruct WordPerfect to use a numbering system of your own for paragraph and outline numbering. To do so, press Shift-F5 (Date/Outline) and select Define (**6** or **D**). Then select User-defined (**6** or **U**). Enter any combination of styles and symbols from the choices available to you for the seven levels. When you select User-defined, the cursor moves to the current definition that is displayed in the middle of the screen. Press Enter or Tab to move from level to level on that line. When the cursor is on the level you want to change, type the number or letter of the style you want to change to. For example, to change the outline style to begin with *(A)*, type **3** (for Outline), then **6** (User-defined). Type a left parenthesis, type **A**, and then type a right parenthesis.

CREATING INDEXES

You create an index of a document you have written in WordPerfect by marking each occurrence of the items you want to include in the index. The program prompts you for the heading you wish the item to appear under in the index and also allows you to specify a subheading for the entry. It inserts an [Index] code for each entry you make and keeps track of the page numbers on which the entries appear. When you ask WordPerfect to generate the index, it searches for the [Index] codes and creates the index in the style you have selected. Figure 9.21 shows a sample index.

```
Communication
     Employee-manager   2
     Facilitating   3
Corporate goals
     As superset of employee goals   4
     Setting of   4
Performance Appraisal System   2
     Formal review   3
     Goals of   2
     Informal meetings   3
Performance Appraisals
     Bi-weekly system   3
     Scheduling of   2
Perspective, manager-employee   4
Productivity   3
```

FIGURE 9.21: A sample index created with WordPerfect. You can select the numbering style that is to be used for headings and subheadings (note that headings and subheadings must use the same style). Selecting no page numbering is useful if you want to create a list of key words rather than an index.

You can select several different index styles, just as you can select different styles for tables of contents and lists.

The word or phrase as it is listed in the index does not have to be the same as it appears in the text. For example, you might want to index *John Smith* as *Smith, John.* WordPerfect allows you to change the phrasing of the index item when it prompts you for the index heading and subheading (see Figure 9.22). It also allows you to indicate more than one heading under which to index the item.

The Concordance feature allows you to list separately all the words or phrases that you want to include in the index. If you create a concordance file, Word-Perfect will search your document for each occurrence of the words in the concordance file and mark it for inclusion in the index. If you have specified that the item be indexed under another word or phrase, WordPerfect will use the word or phrase you have specified instead of the exact wording of the item that it finds in the text. However, a concordance file has its limitations; it will automatically mark all occurrences of the word or phrase, no matter the context in which they occur. When you create an index yourself by marking the individual entries, you can decide which occurrences of the entry are significant.

It is generally wise to plan an index before beginning to mark entries for it. Keeping a list of headings under which you want to organize your entries helps you avoid entries that are worded differently but actually cover the same material. For example, you might decide to create an entry for *Twentieth-century economists* but halfway through the process change the wording to *Economists,*

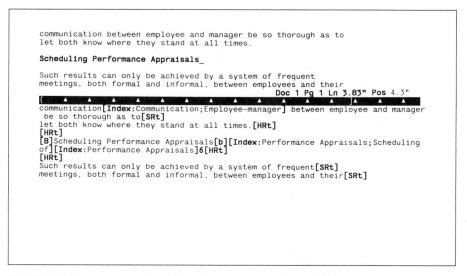

FIGURE 9.22: Changing the wording of an index entry from the way it appears in the text. In this figure, *Scheduling Performance Appraisals* has been marked to appear in two different ways in the index.

twentieth-century. Keeping such a list—perhaps in a second window for easy reference—can help you remember how you have organized your entries.

Marking Items for an Index

You can mark items for an index in one of two ways: by following the procedure outlined here, or by creating a concordance file, as discussed later in this chapter.

To mark items for an index,

1. Locate the word or phrase you wish to include in the index. Position the cursor on it or on the space following it. If you are indexing a phrase, you must first mark it by pressing Alt-F4 (Block) and highlighting the phrase.

2. Press Alt-F5 (Mark Text). The following menu appears:

    Mark for: **1** To**C**; **2 List**; **3 Index**; **4** To**A**: 0

3. Select Index (**3** or **I**). The following prompt appears:

    Index Heading:

    This prompt is followed by the phrase you marked or the word the cursor is on. If you want the entry to appear in the index just as it does where it is highlighted, press Enter. WordPerfect automatically capitalizes the first letter of an index heading and lowercases subheading entries unless the word was capitalized in the text. If you want the word or phrase to appear differently in the index, type it or edit it as you wish it to appear. For example, if WordPerfect presents

    Index Heading: John Kenneth Galbraith

    and you wish the entry to be

    Galbraith, John Kenneth

    enter **Galbraith, John Kenneth** as the index heading. (You can also enter any *See* and *See also* references at this point by typing them at the appropriate heading or subheading level.)

4. The program then prompts you for a subheading. If you accepted the default word or phrase as the heading, you can type a subheading or simply press Enter for no subheading. If you entered a different word or phrase for the heading, WordPerfect will present the default word or phrase as the subheading. You can press Enter to accept it, type over the word WordPerfect presents and substitute the one you wish to use, or delete the subheading if you do not want one.

5. Repeat this process for each word or phrase you want to include in your index.

In Figure 9.22 you saw how WordPerfect inserts formatting codes with your index entries.

Deleting Items from an Index

To delete a term from an index, you must delete the [Index] code associated with it. To search for these codes, press F2 (Search); then press Alt-F5 (Mark Text) and select Index (**3** or **I**). You can also search directly for the word or phrase you wish to delete or change and then delete its [Index] code.

Creating Concordance Files

A concordance file is simply a file containing all the words and phrases you wish WordPerfect to search for and mark as index entries. To use such a file, you specify the name of the concordance file associated with a document when you define the style of your index. When WordPerfect generates the index, it uses the named concordance file as the basis on which to search your document, mark index entries, and generate the index. Both the concordance file and the document you are indexing should be in your default directory.

Although you can automate the indexing process by creating a concordance file, creating one can be very time-consuming if you have a large number of cross-references or references that should appear in a form different from the way they appear in the text (as *Smith, John* instead of *John Smith* for example). Such complex concordance files can also be tedious to revise. The most efficient use of a concordance file is to index specific words and phrases exactly as they appear in the text.

It is easy to create very large concordance files, especially if you are indexing many entries under several different headings. The size of the concordance file WordPerfect can handle is limited only by the amount of memory available when you generate the index. If the program does not have sufficient memory, it will ask whether you want to continue. If you enter **Y**, the amount of material that you have marked for the index up to that point will be created as an index. Typing **N** cancels the process of index generation. If memory limitation is a problem, you may need to close the Document 2 window; WordPerfect will give you a message to do so.

If you use large concordance files, you can speed up the process of generating indexes by sorting the concordance file alphabetically before generating the index. (Refer to Chapter 12 for more information on sorting.)

To use a concordance file, enter the words or phrases you wish to index exactly as they appear in your document, including any hyphenation. If you want an entry to appear in the index with a different wording or under a different heading, you must also use Alt-F5 (Mark Text) to define these forms as index entries. For example, in Figure 9.23, *John Kenneth Galbraith* is the phrase as it appears in the document. By looking at the formatting codes, you can see that the phrase has been marked in the index as a heading as well as a subheading under *Economists, twentieth-century*. The name *Galbraith* has also been specified as a search string in the concordance file. When the index is generated, all occurrences of *John Kenneth Galbraith* or *Galbraith* will be indexed under *Galbraith, John Kenneth* or *Economists, twentieth-century*. The form of the entry in the final index (Figure 9.24) follows the capitalization of the coded index entry, although WordPerfect will search for instances of both uppercase and lowercase words in the document.

To create a concordance file,

1. Open a new document.

2. Enter the words or phrases you want to use in the index as headings or as subheadings. Press Enter after you type each one.

3. Go back and mark each entry with the appropriate index marks by pressing Alt-F5 (Mark Text) and selecting Index (**3** or **I**). You will need to block phrases first; see "Marking Items for an Index" earlier in this chapter. If you want an entry to appear as a subheading under another heading, mark it as a subheading for that heading. If you want the item also to appear as an entry by itself, you must mark it as a heading as well.

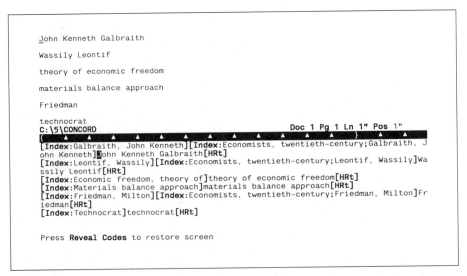

FIGURE 9.23: Marking items in a concordance file. You mark items in a concordance file in the same way that you mark items in a document you are indexing. The program uses this file as the basis on which to search the actual document and mark the occurrences of the words and phrases that are listed in the concordance file. In this figure, the item *Galbraith, John Kenneth* has been marked both as a heading and as a subheading under *Economists, twentieth-century*. Figure 9.24 illustrates the index entries that were generated from this concordance file.

```
     During the twentieth century, several economists became known for
     their work on the materials balance approach. In particular,
     Wassily Leontif expounded the theory that...
     =================================================================
     Milton Friedman and John Kenneth Galbraith became known for their
     innovative theories in...
     =================================================================
     The concept of the technocrat encompasses several aspects of...
     =================================================================
     Friedman's solution to the problem was to...
     =================================================================
     Economists, twentieth-century  2, 4
          Galbraith, John Kenneth  2
          Leontif, Wassily  1
     Friedman, Milton  2, 4
     Galbraith, John Kenneth  2
     Leontif, Wassily  1
     Materials balance approach  1
     Technocrat  3


                                            Doc 2 Pg 5 Ln 1" Pos 1"
```

FIGURE 9.24: The index generated from the concordance file shown in Figure 9.24. This partial document illustrates that the program recognizes possessives (*Friedman's* on page 3) as well as complete words and phrases listed in the concordance file. Note also that because of the way the index entries were listed in the concordance file, the format *last name, first name* has been generated in the index, although in the document the first name appears before the last name.

Defining the Style of an Index

Before defining an index style, move the cursor to the end of the document you are indexing (Home Home ↓) and press Ctrl-Enter to insert a hard page break. The index will be generated at the point where you define the index style, so if you do not move to the end of your document, some terms that you have marked may not be included in the index.

To define the style of an index:

1. Press Alt-F5 (Mark Text) and select Define (**5** or **D**).

2. Select Define Index (**3** or **I**). The following prompt appears:

   Concordance Filename (Enter = none):

   If you are using a concordance file, enter its name; otherwise, press Enter. The screen shown in Figure 9.25 appears.

3. Select the option number corresponding to the style you wish to use.

The index style options are similar to the list style options. Select No Page Numbers (**1** or **N**) if you do not want WordPerfect to print the page number on which the index entry appears. (This is the style you would use if you were preparing a list of key words rather than an index.) If you select Page Numbers Follow Entries (**2** or **P**), page numbers follow the index entries. Selecting (Page Numbers) Follow Entries (**3** or **(**) produces page numbers after entries also, but

```
Index Definition

      1 - No Page Numbers

      2 - Page Numbers Follow Entries

      3 - (Page Numbers) Follow Entries

      4 - Flush Right Page Numbers

      5 - Flush Right Page Numbers with Leaders




      Selection: 0
```

FIGURE 9.25: The Index Definition screen. The options available here are similar to the Page Number Definition options you can select for tables of contents, except that you cannot use different numbering styles in heading and subheading entries, and you cannot wrap subheadings as you can the lowest level of headings in tables of contents.

the page numbers will be in parentheses. Selecting Flush Right Page Numbers (**4** or **F**) or Flush Right Page Numbers with Leaders (**5** or **L**) produces page numbers flush right on the index page, with or without dot leaders.

If you want a columnar index, you must define newspaper columns and turn the Columns feature on in the text just before the [Def Mark:Index] code. See Chapter 10 for details about working with columns.

Generating an Index

Any indexes you have defined and marked text for will automatically be generated when you press Alt-F5 (Mark Text), select Generate (**6** or **G**), and then select Generate Tables, Indexes, Automatic References, etc. (**5** or **G**).

WordPerfect will generate one index for each [Def Mark:Index] code that it finds. If you are getting too many indexes, it means that there is an extra [Def Mark:Index] code in your document.

Deleting an Index

To delete an index from your document, delete both its [Def Mark] and [End Def] codes. If you do not delete the [End Def] code, WordPerfect will continue to generate an index when you select Generate.

AUTOMATIC LINE NUMBERING

WordPerfect allows you to specify that lines be automatically numbered in the documents you create. Although the line numbers do not appear on the editing screen, they will be present when your document is printed (see Figure 9.26), and you can view them with the View Document feature (Shift-F7 V).

You can select whether to exclude blank lines from the line count (the default is to count them). You can also specify the starting line number and whether numbering begins with *1* when a new page begins (the default) or continues consecutively throughout the document. Another option lets you specify how often you want line numbers to appear—for example, every fifth line. You can also specify how far from the left edge of the paper you want the line numbers to appear.

To number the lines in a document, move the cursor to the position in your document where you want line numbering to begin. Press Shift-F8 (Format); then choose Line (**1** or **L**) followed by Line Numbering (**5** or **N**). The screen shown in Figure 9.27 appears.

If you want blank lines to be skipped, type **1** or **C** and enter **N** at the Count Blank Lines option. WordPerfect automatically includes blank lines as it numbers lines unless you tell it not to.

You can also choose to have line numbers appear in increments you specify. For example, suppose you want only every other line or every fifth line to appear with a number. To do so, type **2** and enter the number of lines you want WordPerfect to skip before it numbers the next line. To have the program number every five lines, enter **5**; WordPerfect will number lines 5, 10, 15, 20, and so forth.

The third option on the Line Numbering menu allows you to indicate where you want WordPerfect to print the line numbers. WordPerfect automatically inserts line numbers $6/10$ inch from the left margin unless you specify otherwise.

To specify a starting number other than 1, choose Starting Number (**4** or **S**) and enter the new starting number.

If you want line numbering to continue sequentially throughout your document, enter **5** or **R** and type **N**. WordPerfect begins line numbering with *1* on each new page unless you change this option.

To stop line numbering, position the cursor at the point where you want line numbering to stop, press Shift-F8 (Format), choose Line, and then choose Line Numbering. Type **N** to turn numbering off. You can also search for the [Ln Num] codes within your document and delete them.

USING CITATIONS AND TABLES OF AUTHORITIES

If you work in the legal profession, you will appreciate WordPerfect's built-in Table of Authorities feature. It allows you to search a legal document for citations that you specify and mark them wherever they occur in the document, including in

```
1   Carney & Kellahan

2   125 West Main St.

3   Redwood City, CA 94035

4

5   (415) 555-1244

6

7   Attorneys for Petitioner

8

9

10              SUPERIOR COURT OF THE STATE OF CALIFORNIA

11

12                      COUNTY OF SAN MATEO

13
14  Estate of       )
15  Wilma M. Cohen,)                          No. 774921
16       deceased.)
17  _____)
18

19              PETITION FOR PROBATE OF WILL

20

21          To the Honorable Superior Court of the State Of

22  California in the County of San Mateo:

23              The petition of RALPH W. PATTON respectfully shows:

24              That WILMA M. COHEN died on the 30th day of October,

25  1986, in the City of Half Moon Bay, County of San Mateo, State of

26  California; that said decedent was at the time of her death a

27  resident of the County of San Mateo, State of California, and

28  left an estate therein consisting of real and personal property;
```

FIGURE 9.26: Line numbering in a legal document. You can also number lines in selected portions of a document if you do not want each line in the entire document to be numbered.

```
Format: Line Numbering
        1 - Count Blank Lines                        Yes
        2 - Number Every n Lines, where n is         1
        3 - Position of Number from Left Edge        Ø.6"
        4 - Starting Number                          1
        5 - Restart Numbering on Each Page           Yes




        Selection: Ø
```

FIGURE 9.27: The Line Numbering screen. The default condition is that blank lines are to be numbered.

footnotes and endnotes. WordPerfect can then generate a table of authorities that lists each citation in the document and the page numbers on which it appears.

In a table of authorities, citations are usually grouped into sections by type: statutes, cases, articles, text, and so on. You can specify up to 16 different sections for the table, and you can define a different format for each section. Within each section, WordPerfect sorts the authorities alphanumerically.

After you have marked all the citations that you want included in the table of authorities, you create a page for the table. You then define the style for the table, just as you do for tables of contents, lists, and indexes, and instruct WordPerfect to generate the table for you. A sample table of authorities is shown in Figure 9.28; the exact format for legal citations varies from state to state, but you can define Word-Perfect's format to meet your needs.

Marking Citations for a Table of Authorities

To generate an accurate table of authorities, WordPerfect has to know where each citation occurs. You can mark citations in the body of the document as well as in any footnotes or endnotes you have created.

If the document you are working with contains footnotes and endnotes, you should use WordPerfect's Extended Search feature to search for citations; it searches through notes as well as headers and footers. To specify an extended search, press Home and then press F2 (Search).

```
                        TABLE OF AUTHORITIES

STATUTES                                          Page:

Business and Professional Code, Section 6009 . . . . . . . . .  2

Business and Professional Code, Sections 2-101 and 2-102 . . .  1

CASES

Adams v. State Bar of California, 811 Cal. 933 (1986) . . . .  1

Belli v. State Bar of California, 609 Cal. 788 (1985) . . . .  1

ARTICLES

Martin, Legal Advertising, 13 A.B.A.J. 110 (1986) . . . . . .  2


=============================================================================
                SUPREME COURT FOR THE STATE OF CALIFORNIA
MARTIN ERICKSON,                  )
             Petitioner,          )        NO. 956201
                                        Doc 2 Pg 1 Ln 3.66" Pos 1"
```

FIGURE 9.28: A sample table of authorities. A table of authorities lists all the citations referred to in a legal document. Citations are grouped into sections by type—for example, federal and state statutes, cases, and secondary sources such as legal encyclopedias and periodicals.

When you have located a citation you wish to mark for inclusion in the table of authorities, be sure to mark it as a block (Alt-F4) before you press Alt-F5 (Mark Text). If you have not marked a block in your document, the correct Mark Text menu will not appear.

The first occurrence of a citation should be marked in its entirety—that is, using its full form. This is the way the citation will be listed in the table of authorities. After you have specified the full form, you can specify a short form, which is an abbreviated version of the full form. Thereafter you can use the short form in place of the full form by pressing Alt-F5 (Mark Text) and selecting ToA Short Form (**4** or **A**). WordPerfect presents the last short form you defined, and you can simply press Enter to accept it.

WordPerfect also expects you to indicate in which section of the table of authorities you want each citation to be included—whether it is a federal or state statute, a case, or another type of citation. You are prompted for the appropriate section number when you mark the citation. You can keep a list of the section types by number in a second window for easy reference.

To mark citations for inclusion in a table of authorities,

1. Move to the beginning of the document (Home Home ↑). You can press F2 (Search) or Home F2 (Extended Search) and specify the citation you wish to find in the document, or simply move to the first occurrence of the citation.

2. Mark the first occurrence of the citation in its full form by pressing Alt-F4 (Block) and highlighting the entire citation.

3. Press Alt-F5 (Mark Text). The following menu appears:

    Mark for: **1** To**C**; **2** **L**ist; **3** **I**ndex; **4** To**A**: 0

    Select ToA (**4** or **A**).

4. The following prompt appears:

    ToA Section Number (Press Enter for Short Form Only):

    For the first occurrence of the citation, enter the number of the section in which you want the citation to be listed in the table of authorities. If this is not the first occurrence and you have already defined a short form, then you simply press Enter to have WordPerfect mark the citation and its section number for you.

5. For the first occurrence of the citation, WordPerfect presents you with an editing screen in which you can edit the full form of the citation. At this point you can insert text attributes such as boldfacing or underlining and style the citation as you want it to appear in the table of authorities. A full form can contain up to 30 lines. A sample full-form citation on the editing screen is shown in Figure 9.29.

6. When you have edited the full form of the citation, press F7 (Exit). Word-Perfect then presents you with a suggested short form on the prompt line (see Figure 9.30). You can shorten the short form even further or accept the program's suggestion by simply pressing Enter.

7. Press F2 (or Home F2) to resume the search or change the search string; press F2 again to actually begin the search.

8. When the program stops at the next occurrence of the citation, press Alt-F5 (Mark Text) and select ToA Short Form (**4** or **A**). The program displays the short form you have defined. Press Enter to accept it and mark the citation in the document.

Continue in this way until all occurrences of the citation in your document have been marked. Then move to the beginning of your document and search for the next citation that you wish to include in the table of authorities.

Defining the Style of a Table of Authorities

Formatting a table of authorities is slightly different from formatting other special pages in your document, such as tables of contents, lists, and indexes. You need to define the sections the table is to contain (up to 16) as well as specify the table style—whether it is to use dot leaders between citations and page numbers, and how much space to allow between citations, for example.

In addition, a table of authorities is normally placed after a cover sheet and table of contents (which may be called an *index* or *subject index*), so you may wish to define

```
Business and Professional Code, Sections 2-1Ø1 and 2-1Ø2




















Press Exit when done                                    Ln 1" Pos 1"
```

FIGURE 9.29: A citation editing screen. WordPerfect presents an editing screen like this so you can edit the first occurrence of a citation. The full form of any citation may be up to 30 lines long.

```
                        STATEMENT OF THE CASE
              The California State Legal Advisory Board has
     recommended that Martin Erickson be suspended from the practice
     of law for an alleged violation of the Business and Professional
     Code, Sections 2-1Ø1 and 2-1Ø2. Erickson petitions the California
     Supreme Court to review the Board's recommendation.
              The California State Legal Advisory Board heard the
     case pursuant to American Bar Association regulations.  The
     California Supreme Court is authorized to hear this petition for
     review under Business and Professions Code Section 6ØØ9.
                        STATEMENT OF FACTS
              Petitioner, MARTIN ERICKSON, placed advertisements in
     the Palo Alto Times Tribune and the Peninsula Register offering
     his services to the public in the event of a DWI (Driving While
     Intoxicated) arrest. These advertisements appeared on Wednesday,
     March 18, 1986, in the Business sections of both publications.
              On July 5, 1986, after an evidentiary hearing, the Legal
     Advisory Board issued a recommendation suspending petitioner from
     the active practice of law for a period of three months on the
     basis that he had violated the Business and Professional Code.
     Motion was then made to the Superior Court of the County of Santa
     Clara to issue such a ruling.  The Court so ruled on August 1,
     1986.
     Enter Short Form:  Business and Professional Code, Sections
```

FIGURE 9.30: The prompt to enter the short form of a citation. Using the short form speeds up the process of marking text for a table of authorities. Each citation may have only one unique short form associated with it. You may want to use a second window to keep track of the short forms you have assigned.

these pages first. You will then need to change the page numbering of your document so that numbering begins with *1* on the first page of the actual document. If you do not start with a new page number between the definition of the table of authorities and the first text that has been marked for inclusion in the table, your page number references may not be accurate, and WordPerfect will warn you if it does not find a New Page Number code. To insert this code, press Shift-F8 (Format), select Page (**2** or **P**), and then select New Page Number (**6** or **N**).

To define the style of a table of authorities,

1. Move to the beginning of your document (Home Home ↑) or to the location where you want the table of authorities to be generated.

2. Press Ctrl-Enter to insert a hard page break. Position the cursor on the new page and type the heading you want for the table, such as **Table of Authorities**; press Enter twice to move to a new line.

3. Define each section you want included in the table. First enter the section name (such as **CASES** or **STATUTES**). Press Alt-F6 (Flush Right) to align the heading *Page:* at the right margin and enter **Page:**. Press Enter to move to a new line. Then press Alt-F5 (Mark Text) and select Define (**5** or **D**). Select Define Table of Authorities (**4** or **A**), enter the section number at the prompt, and press Enter.

4. Select the style you wish to use in that section from the options that appear (see Figure 9.31). You can choose whether to use dot leaders, allow underlining, and allow space between citations. WordPerfect then prepares a table of authorities similar to the one in Figure 9.30. Press Enter to return to the document.

Repeat this process for each section you want to include in the table of authorities.

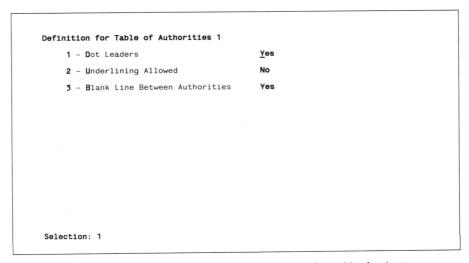

```
Definition for Table of Authorities 1

    1 - Dot Leaders                         Yes

    2 - Underlining Allowed                 No

    3 - Blank Line Between Authorities      Yes
```

```
Selection: 1
```

FIGURE 9.31: Defining the style of a table of authorities. The options for a table of authorities are more limited than those for other types of tables and lists. You can choose whether to use dot leaders, allow underlining, and allow space between citations.

Generating a Table of Authorities

When you have marked each citation and specified the style for the table of authorities, press Alt-F5 (Mark Text) and select Generate (**6** or **G**). Then select Generate Tables, Indexes, Automatic References, etc. (**5** or **G**), to generate the table of authorities as well as any other tables, lists, or indexes you have defined. See "Deleting Existing Tables of Contents, Lists, and Indexes" earlier in this chapter for a discussion of other factors you should take into account when generating tables in a document that already contains tables and lists.

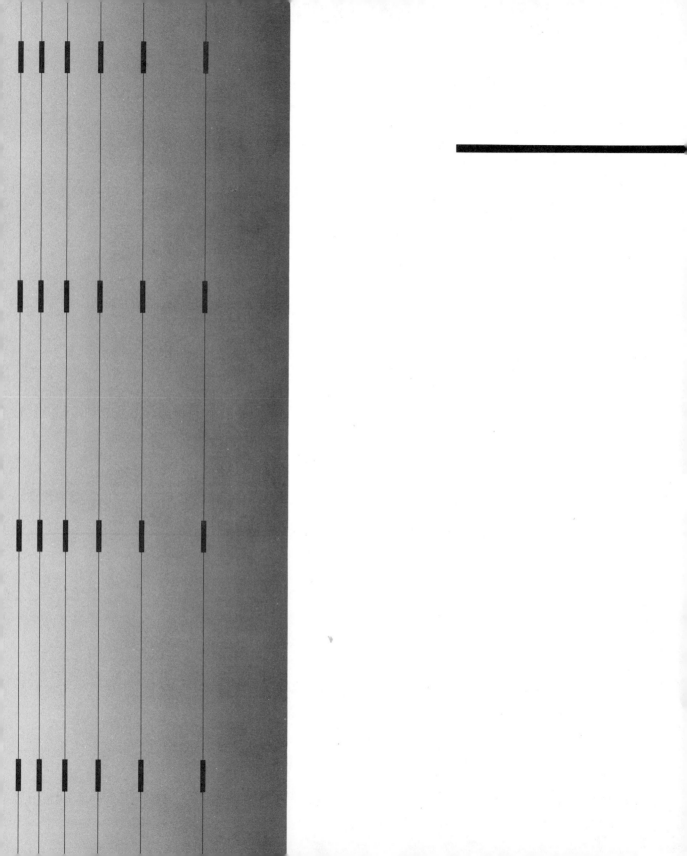

CHAPTER 10

WORKING WITH TEXT COLUMNS (NEWSPAPER AND PARALLEL)

WORKING WITH TEXT COLUMNS (NEWSPAPER AND PARALLEL)

WordPerfect can automatically format two different types of text columns for you: *newspaper* columns (sometimes called *winding* or *snaking* columns) and *parallel* columns. The term *text columns* is used to differentiate these types of columns from those that you create with tab stops.

Newspaper columns are used whenever it does not matter where the material in the column ends, because the program wraps the text to the top of the next column. Parallel columns are used whenever the material in the columns consists of items that should remain next to each other on the same page.

For example, you will probably want to use WordPerfect's newspaper columns to create columns of text for a newsletter or handbook, or to generate a multicolumn index. Parallel columns can be very useful for such items as brochures, in which product descriptions and prices must stay next to each other, or agendas, in which dates and times must stay parallel to notes on what is taking place. Parallel columns are also often used in script-writing, in which stage directions occupy one parallel column while dialogue is presented in a second column. Indeed, you will want to use parallel columns to construct tables whenever the data in one or more columns requires more than a single line. If you set up such tables using tabs or temporary indents (F4), you don't get the benefit of having word wrap operate only within a particular column. As a result, you often end up having to format the text by inserting extra hard returns and tabs that make further editing very difficult.

This chapter discusses how you use both types of text columns and shows you how changes you make to text in one column can affect text in other columns as well. As you can imagine, both types of columns are used heavily in desktop publishing applications. For more information on desktop publishing, refer to Chapter 19, "WordPerfect's Desktop Publishing Capabilities."

It is important to note that in WordPerfect, text columns are not the same as columns you set with tabs or columns you define as Math columns, and the techniques you use with each of these types of columns are slightly different. For information on working with tabs, see Chapter 3, "Formatting and Editing Techniques"; for techniques involving Math columns, refer to Chapter 13, "Performing Calculations with the Math Feature."

UPGRADE NOTES

Newspaper and parallel columns in version 5.0 operate much the same as they did in version 4.2. However, you will notice that the Text Column Definition screen has been rearranged so that it now contains four menu options: Type, Number of Columns, Distance between Columns, and Margins. Here, you specify essentially the same information that you did when setting up newspaper or parallel columns on the old Text Column Definition screen, although you are no longer asked if you want to have evenly spaced columns (instead, you specify the kind of column you want to define by using the Type option—see below).

You will discover the biggest change in text columns when you use the Type option. In version 4.2, you could choose only between Newspaper and Parallel with Block Protect. WordPerfect 5.0 now gives you a choice between three types of text columns: Newspaper (**1** or **N**), Parallel (**2** or **P**), and Parallel with Block Protect (**3** or **B**). If you select the Parallel option, block protection will not be in effect, meaning that a block of text in a column can be split across two pages when WordPerfect inserts a soft page break.

Also, instead of specifying the number of the column or the amount of spaces, you enter column margin settings and distances between columns in inches, points, or centimeters.

Finally, a couple of editing capabilities have been added to text columns. You can now intermix different line spacing and use decimal tabs (as well as all the other types of tabs) within text columns. Both of these abilities were absent in version 4.2.

PAGE COMPOSITION

Because you can mix text columns with regular one-column formats, Word-Perfect gives you a great deal of flexibility in page composition. For example, you could begin a page with a one-column format, switch to two or three newspaper-style columns, switch back to a one-column format, and then change to two parallel columns, all on the same page. Figure 10.1 illustrates a sample page that uses a mix of column layouts in the editing screen. Figure 10.2 shows you the full-page display of the same document, using the View Document feature (Shift-F7 V).

Unlike many other programs, WordPerfect displays columns on the screen as they will be formatted on the printed page, so you can see the effects of changes you make in page layouts. You can, however, change this so that you only view one column at a time on your screen.

WordPerfect also automatically calculates and displays column margin settings for you, so the only kind of copy-fitting you have to do is to look at the screen and make any adjustments you think are necessary. The program will

```
        _                    WELCOME

        Welcome to MagnaCorp. We hope this employee handbook will help to
        guide you through your first few days here. In addition, it
        contains valuable information about employee services and benefits
        available to you. Ask your manager or call the personnel office if
        you have any questions for which you cannot find the answers in
        this handbook.


                          ITEMS OF INTEREST

        Work Day                         Recreational Facilities

        The official work day at         MagnaCorp participates in the
        MagnaCorp is 8:30 A.M. to 5:00   city recreational plan and
        P.M. Flexible hours can be       therefore its employees have
        arranged with your manager.      access to the municipal gym
                                         located at First and Stone
        Parking                          Streets. The jogging track and
                                         par course in Compton Park are
        As parking is limited, please    also nearby. Showers and
        apply to the personnel office    lockers for company employees
        for a parking slot assignment.   are located near the south
        D:\WP\WDC\HANDBOOK                        Doc 2 Pg 1 Ln 1.51 Pos 1i
```

FIGURE 10.1: Intermixing columns with regular text. The columns were specified as newspaper-style columns, which means that WordPerfect will continue to wrap text from one column to the next until you turn Column mode off. When Column mode is on and you wish to return to regular text format, press Alt-F7 and select the Column On/Off option (**3** or **C**).

automatically calculate evenly spaced columns for you and adjust the distance between columns to whatever measurement you specify.

Along with text columns, WordPerfect contains several other features you can use for page composition to create various effects. These include:

- Setting different headers and footers for right (even) and left (odd) pages (see Chapter 4).
- Changing fonts for larger headings (see Chapter 5).
- Changing the binding width for documents that are going to be printed and bound (see Chapter 7).
- Creating borders and using graphics characters (see Chapter 14).
- Inserting graphics in or between text columns that you have set up (see Chapter 18).

After you review the material in this chapter, you may want to explore some of these additional techniques to use with text columns.

WORKING WITH COLUMNS

The basic process of creating text columns in WordPerfect is straightforward; you define the type of columns you want to use—including the number of

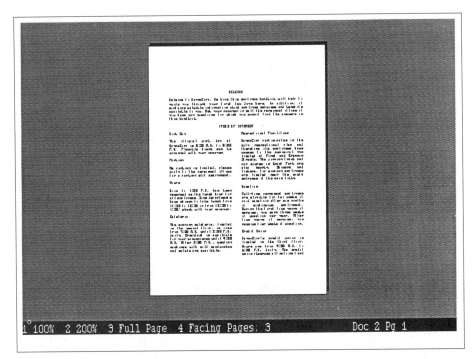

FIGURE 10.2: A full-page preview of a document that mixes regular text with newspaper columns. Although you can't read the text in this view, you can see the contrast between the standard format of the first paragraph and the two-column layout of the newspaper columns used for the rest of the paragraphs on this page.

columns per page, the distance between them, and so forth—turn Column mode on, type the text for the columns, and turn Column mode off again. Once you have created a column definition, you can use it anywhere in your text by simply turning Column mode on.

Because the program treats each type of text column—newspaper and parallel—in a slightly different way, you may have unexpected results when you edit your document unless you understand just how the program handles each type. The upcoming sections discuss how WordPerfect treats newspaper and parallel text columns.

Newspaper Columns

With newspaper-style columns, when you reach the bottom of the first column, the cursor moves to the top of the next column on the same page. When you fill one page with columns, the cursor moves to the beginning of the first column on the next page. When you add text to the columns, text below the new text is pushed down through the columns and to the next page if necessary. If you look at the Reveal Codes screen for newspaper-style columns, you will see that WordPerfect is inserting a Soft Page code, [SPg], at the end of each column (Figure 10.3).

When you fill one page with newspaper-style columns, WordPerfect moves the cursor to the leftmost column at the beginning of the next page. In this way, you can continue to write columnar material or add to existing material, and it will automatically flow through the columns. Newspaper-style columns are therefore very easy to edit and manipulate.

Because the program treats each newspaper-style column as a separate page, you will notice that some commands operate a little differently from the way they do in normal editing mode. If you press the delete-to-end-of-page key sequence (Ctrl-PgDn) while in newspaper-style columns, the program will delete the lines from the cursor position to the end of the column. It will not remove text in the other columns on the same page.

With newspaper columns, you can instruct the program to keep a block of text together and not divide it between columns by turning on block protection (Alt-F4 Shift-F8 Y). If you do so, WordPerfect will keep the text you marked as a

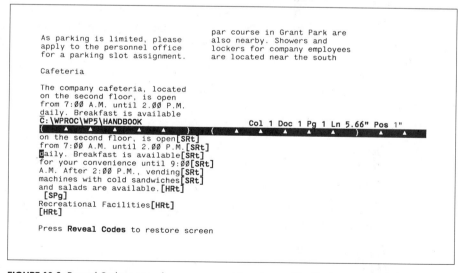

FIGURE 10.3: Reveal Codes screen for newspaper-style columns. WordPerfect inserts a Soft Page code ([SPg]) at the end of each column.

block within the same column, but it may have to break a column early to do so, resulting in a short column.

To end a newspaper-style column at a specific point, simply position the cursor where you want the column to end and press Ctrl-Enter. If you are not in the rightmost column, this does not force a page break, as you might expect, but inserts a Hard Page code, [HPg], in the text at the bottom of that column. The cursor then moves to the top of the next column, where you can enter more text or revise the text that is already there. If you press Ctrl-Enter while you are in the rightmost column of newspaper-style columns, the program breaks the page and moves the cursor to the beginning of the next page.

Parallel Columns

When using parallel columns, WordPerfect behaves in a slightly different way. Instead of inserting a soft page break at the end of each column, it defines each parallel column with a [Col On] and [Col Off] code. WordPerfect now supports two types of parallel columns: parallel columns without block protection (referred to by WordPerfect simply as *Parallel*) and parallel columns with block protection.

When you enter text in parallel columns of either type, you indicate the end of one item (sentence, paragraph, group of paragraphs, etc.) and the beginning of the next by pressing Ctrl-Enter (Hard Page). You must always insert a Hard Page Break code by pressing Ctrl-Enter at the end of each item that is to be formatted into a parallel column. Newspaper columns, by contrast, will continue to flow to the correct column.

When you press Ctrl-Enter at the end of the last item in a parallel column, the cursor wraps to the beginning of the first column. If you are entering parallel columns that don't use block protection, you will see the codes

[Col Off]
[HRt]
[Col On]

in the Reveal Codes screen. If, however, you are entering parallel columns with block protection, you instead will see

[BlockPro:Off][Col off]
[HRt]
[BlockPro:On][Col on]

in the Reveal Codes screen.

PARALLEL COLUMNS WITHOUT BLOCK PROTECTION

Figure 10.4 shows you the benefits section of an employee manual formatted into two parallel columns. In the Reveal Codes screen shown at the bottom of this figure, you can see the Column Definition code, [Col Def], displaying the number of columns and their margin settings. Immediately after this, you can see the [Col On] code that turns on the parallel columns. To format each heading and its associated paragraph of text into parallel columns, a hard page break (Ctrl-Enter) is entered at the end of the paragraph.

Figure 10.5 shows you the Reveal Codes screen at the end of the first parallel columns and the beginning of the next ones. Here, you can see the [Col Off] code that WordPerfect automatically places at the end of the first two columns when you press Ctrl-Enter. The cursor returns to the far left column and the program turns on Column mode again ([Col On]) after inserting a hard return ([HRt]). Figure 10.6 shows you the full-page layout of the first page of the employee manual when it's formatted using two parallel columns.

With parallel columns that don't use block protection, text that extends beyond the end of a page will be split between two pages by a soft page break, as illustrated in Figure 10.7. While this may be fine in an application like script-writing where you don't care if the dialog in the second column continues to the top of the next page without the character's name, there are many applications

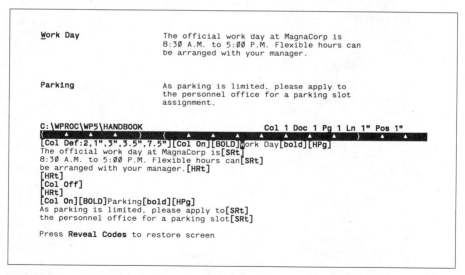

FIGURE 10.4: Part of the first two items in the employee manual and the beginning of the Reveal Codes screen for parallel columns (without block protection). Here you can also see the [Col Def] code that WordPerfect inserts when you define this type of parallel columns. The first number indicates the number of columns; the rest are the left and right margin settings of each pair of columns.

```
Work Day                 The official work day at MagnaCorp is
                         8:3Ø A.M. to 5:ØØ P.M. Flexible hours can
                         be arranged with your manager.


Parking                  As parking is limited, please apply to
                         the personnel office for a parking slot
                         assignment.
D:\WP\WDC\HANDBOOK                            Col 2 Doc 1 Pg 1 Ln 3.511 Pos 3.5i
(    ▲    ▲   ▲   }   (     ▲    ▲    ▲    ▲    ▲    ▲   }   ▲    ▲
The official work day at MagnaCorp is[SRt]
8:3Ø A.M. to 5:ØØ P.M. Flexible hours can[SRt]
be arranged with your manager.[HRt]
[HRt]
[Col Off]
[HRt]
[Col On][BOLD]Parking[HRt]
[bold][HRt]
[HPg]
As parking is limited, please apply to[SRt]

Press Reveal Codes to restore screen
```

FIGURE 10.5: The Reveal Codes screen at the end of the first two parallel columns and the beginning of the next ones. WordPerfect turns the column definition off ([Col Off]) and then on again ([Col On]) whenever a new set of parallel columns begins.

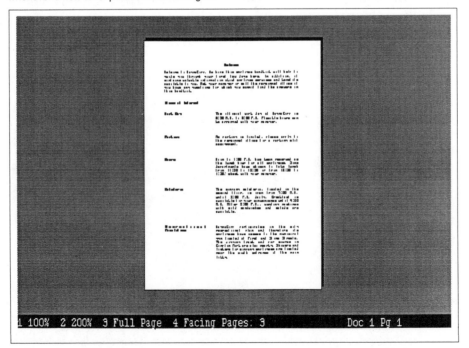

FIGURE 10.6: A full-page preview of the first page of the employee manual showing the benefits section, formatted with parallel columns. Although you can't read the text in this view, you can observe the effect of this layout, which places each heading and associated item side by side across and down the page. Contrast this layout with the one shown in Figure 10.2, which mixes a standard paragraph layout with newspaper columns.

(like complex tables and schedules) where this kind of split is not desirable. To avoid having an item split by a soft page break, use parallel columns with block protection. (See the following section for more information on this type of parallel columns.)

PARALLEL COLUMNS WITH BLOCK PROTECTION

The best way to avoid having any text in parallel columns split by a soft page break is to use parallel columns with block protection as illustrated in Figure 10.8. This relieves you of having to manually insert hard page breaks to keep items of text together on a page.

Because each parallel column on the page is surrounded by Block Protection On and Off codes, you never have to worry about the effect that editing changes might have on the way text is paginated. Whenever any text in one of the items in a particular parallel column extends beyond the end of the page, all of the items in that column are pushed to the next page. You can always be sure that they will appear on the same page in the appropriate column across from one another.

Working in Column Mode

When you are in Column mode, WordPerfect provides a slightly different status line that indicates the current column, as well as the document, page, current

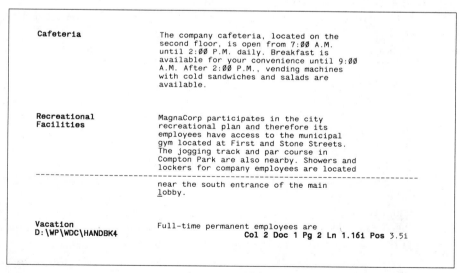

FIGURE 10.7: The text of the last item extending beyond the end of the page and therefore split across two pages when using parallel columns without block protection. To avoid this situation, use parallel columns with block protection.

```
Items of Interest


Work Day                        The official work day at MagnaCorp is
                                8:30 A.M. to 5:00 P.M. Flexible hours can
                                be arranged with your manager.




D:\WP\WDC\HANDBK4                         Col 2 Doc 1 Pg 1 Ln 3.341 Pos 3.5i

[BOLD][Col Def:2,1",3",3.5",7.5"][Block Pro:On][Col On]Work Day[HPg]
[bold]The official work day at MagnaCorp is[SRt]
8:30 A.M. to 5:00 P.M. Flexible hours can[SRt]
be arranged with your manager.[HRt]
[HRt]
[HRt]
[BOLD][HRt]
[Block Pro:Off][Col Off]
[HRt]
[Block Pro:On][Col On]Parking[HRt]

Press Reveal Codes to restore screen
```

FIGURE 10.8: Reveal Codes screen for parallel columns with block protection. WordPerfect turns on block protection at the beginning of each set of parallel columns, uses a soft page break between columns within the parallel column area, and turns off block protection at the end of the parallel column area when you press Ctrl-Enter.

line, and position, to help you keep track of where the cursor is (line and position are indicated in inches). If you have several columns on the screen, you may need to check the status line from time to time to determine the location of the cursor. This is especially true if you are using Reveal Codes, because Word-Perfect displays only the codes for the column the cursor is on (Figure 10.9). Although the codes are presented under the leftmost column, they may apply to material in other columns.

When you are in Column mode in WordPerfect, a few of the program's other features do not operate. The Footnote feature is not available; neither is the program's Sort feature. If you need to sort columnar material—as, for example, in a glossary or index—be sure to sort it before you convert it to columns, or change the columns back to regular text format by deleting the [Col On] code. (See Chapter 12 for more information about sorting.)

If you are working with newspaper-style columns, you may often run across a situation in which columns are not of equal length on the same page. If you want equal columns, you can press Shift-F8 (Format), select the Page option (**2** or **P**) followed by the Margins option (**5** or **M**), and reset the top and/or bottom margin to reduce or increase the number of text lines on the page.

You can have up to 24 columns on a page, but if you are printing on standard 8½-by-11-inch paper, you will find that four columns is about the maximum you will want to use, unless you are working with very short entries, such as an index.

```
    Employee              brief summary of your work experience to the rest
    Relations             of the group.
    Council
                          Coffee break will be scheduled after the film
                          presentation.

                          Call-forward phones to extension 355Ø.

    11:3Ø-12:3Ø           Half an hour extra will be allowed for returning
    Lunch                 calls, etc. Try not to leave the premises;
                          meeting will resume promptly at 1 P.M.
  D:\WP\WDC\ORIENT.SCH                         Col 2 Doc 1 Pg 1 Ln 3.Ø11 Pos 2.75i
Lunch[HPg]
Half an hour extra will be allowed for returning[SRt]
calls, etc. Try not to leave the premises;[SRt]
meeting will resume promptly at 1 P.M.[Col Off]
[HRt]
[Col On][HPg]
[Col Off]
[HRt]
[UND]Friday, September 18[und][HRt]
[HRt]

Press Reveal Codes to restore screen
```

FIGURE 10.9: Using Reveal Codes with two columns. The program displays the codes for the column the cursor is in, but they appear under the leftmost column. Check the status line to make sure which column you are viewing. You can also press Shift-F1 (Setup), select the Display option (**3** or **D**) and then select the Side-by-side Columns Display option (**8** or **S**) and type **N** to display only one column at a time on the screen.

With three or four columns ½ inch apart, lines are long enough to be easily readable without too much hyphenation. To improve hyphenation, you may want to turn right justification off in narrow columns by pressing Shift-F8 (Format) and selecting the Line option (**1** or **L**) followed by the Justification option (**3** or **J**), which you set to No. With over three columns per page, you will probably also want to adjust the hyphenation zone so that word spacing will be more equal when columns are right-justified (see ''WordPerfect's Hyphenation Commands'' in Chapter 3).

When you work with columns, you may also want to set a tab for paragraph indents. Figure 10.10 illustrates a situation in which paragraph indents were used within columns. If you are working with very narrow columns, however, you may want to simply press the Enter key one extra time at the end of each paragraph to insert an additional line of space between paragraphs. Otherwise the first line in each paragraph will be even shorter than the rest of the lines in the column, possibly causing difficulties in formatting right-justified material.

WordPerfect will calculate and display margin settings for equal columns. If you wish, you can override them. For example, you may want the columns to have different column widths, as shown in Figure 10.11. To create unequal columns, you must reset the left and right margins for each column. In this example, the left margin for the first column remains at 1'' (flush with the left margin) while its right margin is reset to 2'', thus giving you a column length of 1½ inches. The left margin of the second column is reset at 2.5'' and the right margin remains at 7.5'' (flush with the right margin setting). This gives you ½ inch between the columns and a second column width of 5 inches.

Moving Between Columns

Cursor movement in Column mode is a little different from normal editing mode. Instead of using the Tab key to move between columns, you use the Go To key sequence (Ctrl-Home) plus the → or ← key. In addition, Ctrl-Home Home plus the ← key moves the cursor to the first column on the page, while Ctrl-Home Home plus the → key moves the cursor to the last column on the page. You will find that these key sequences are much faster than moving the cursor through the text to reach the beginning or end of the columns. Table 10.1 summarizes all of these cursor movement key sequences.

You may also find it less confusing to work in Column mode with the side-by-side column display disabled (Figure 10.12). This makes it faster to scroll through the text, and you don't have to press Ctrl-Home (Go To) followed by → or ← to move the cursor back and forth between columns. This can make editing the text item in a particular column much easier.

KEY SEQUENCE	RESULT
Ctrl-Home → or ←	Moves cursor between columns
Ctrl-Home Home ←	Moves to the first column
Ctrl-Home Home →	Moves to the last column
→	Moves to the first character of the next column when the cursor is on the last character in one column
←	Moves to the last character of the previous column when the cursor is on the first character in one column
Ctrl-Enter	Ends a column and moves to the next column; in a rightmost newspaper-style column, also creates a page break

Note: Other cursor control key sequences work as they do in editing mode and scroll all columns simultaneously.

TABLE 10.1: Cursor Movement in Column Mode

```
Items of Interest

    Work Day                The official work day at MagnaCorp is
                            8:30 A.M. to 5:00 P.M. Flexible hours can
                            be arranged with your manager.




    Parking                 As parking is limited, please apply to
                            the personnel office for a parking slot
                            assignment.




    Hours                   Noon to 1:00 P.M. has been reserved as
                            the lunch hour for all employees. Some
                            departments have chosen to take lunch
                            from 11:30 to 12:30 or from 12:30 to
D:\WP\WDC\HANDBK4                        Col 1 Doc 1 Pg 1 Ln 3.171 Pos 1.31
```

FIGURE 10.10: Using tabs for paragraph indents within columns. Although WordPerfect treats each column as a separate page, you can set new tabs to indent text in each column by modifying the tab stops on the ruler (Shift-F8 L T) after the place in the document where you turned on Column mode. Here tab stops are set at 1.3″ and 3.7″ to indent the heading and first line of the paragraph in each column. You can see these two tab stops on the tab ruler shown at the bottom of this figure.

```
Items of Interest

    Work Day        The official work day at MagnaCorp is 8:30 A.M. to
                    5:00 P.M. Flexible hours can be arranged with your
                    manager.




    Parking         As parking is limited, please apply to the
                    personnel office for a parking slot assignment.




    Hours           Noon to 1:00 P.M. has been reserved as the lunch
                    hour for all employees. Some departments have
                    chosen to take lunch from 11:30 to 12:30 or from
                    12:30 to 1:30; check with your manager.




    D:\WP\WDC\HANDBK4                    Col 1 Doc 1 Pg 1 Ln 3.171 Pos 11
```

FIGURE 10.11: Mixing different column margin settings. Although this technique is more often used with parallel columns as shown here, you can also create newspaper columns of varying width to add interest and variety to your page layouts. In this example, the first column is 1½ inches long, and the second column is 5 inches long; there is a distance of ½ inch between them.

To disable the side-by-side display, you press Shift-F1 (Setup), select the Display option (**3** or **D**), select the Side-by-side Columns Display option (**8** or **S**), and type **N**. After you are finished adding and editing the text of the columns, you can then use the View Document feature (Shift-F7 V) to preview how the columns will appear when printed. If you wish to change back to the side-by-side display in the document editing screen, you repeat the key sequence initiated with Setup (Shift-F1). After selecting the Display option again, you type **Y** instead of **N** after choosing the Side-by-side Columns Display option.

Defining Text Columns

When you make a column definition, you do not have to use it right away. Instead, you can set up your page layout at the beginning of a document and then switch to the column format you have defined at any point in the document by turning Column mode on. This allows you to alternate between standard paragraphs and text columns in the document without having to redefine columns each time you use them.

You use the same general procedure to define newspaper-style columns and parallel columns. To define any type of text column, you follow these steps:

1. Position the cursor at the beginning of the area you want to define. (To create a column definition, you can actually position the cursor at any earlier point in the document, including the beginning of the document.) When you turn Column mode on (by pressing Alt-F7 and selecting the Column On/Off option—**3** or **C**), the last column definition you specified will be used.

2. Press Alt-F7 and select the Column Def option (**4** or **D**). The screen shown in Figure 10.13 appears.

3. If you need to change the type of column (newspaper is the default), choose the Type option by typing **1** or **T**. The program will display the following options:

   Column Type: **1** **N**ewsaper; **2** **P**arallel; **3** Parallel with **B**lock Protect: 0

   Type the appropriate number or letter, depending on the kind of columns you wish to create.

4. If you need to increase the number of columns (the default is 2), select the Number option by typing **2** or **N** and enter a number up to 24. WordPerfect will automatically calculate the length and left and right margin settings for each column, leaving ½ inch between them.

```
Thursday, September 17

9 A.M.
Employee
Relations
Council
=================================================================
                        New employee orientation. Be prepared to give a
                        brief summary of your work experience to the rest
                        of the group.

                        Coffee break will be scheduled after the film
                        presentation.

                        Call-forward phones to extension 3550.

11:30-12:30
Lunch
=================================================================
                        Half an hour extra will be allowed for returning
                        calls, etc. Try not to leave the premises;
                        meeting will resume promptly at 1 P.M.


D:\WP\WDC\ORIENT.SCH              Col 2 Doc 1 Pg 1 Ln 3.17i Pos 2.75i
```

FIGURE 10.12: Parallel columns as they appear when the side-by-side display is turned off. The lines of equal signs represent the hard page breaks that separate each of the text items in a parallel column. When you move the cursor through this display, you can go from one column to the next just by pressing → and ←; there is no need to press Ctrl-Home (Go To) as is the case when the side-by-side display is active.

```
Text Column Definition

    1 - Type                              Newspaper

    2 - Number of Columns                 2

    3 - Distance Between Columns

    4 - Margins

    Column    Left     Right     Column    Left      Right
      1:      1"       4"          13:
      2:      4.5"     7.5"        14:
      3:                           15:
      4:                           16:
      5:                           17:
      6:                           18:
      7:                           19:
      8:                           20:
      9:                           21:
     10:                           22:
     11:                           23:
     12:                           24:

Selection: 0
```

FIGURE 10.13: The Text Column Definition screen. WordPerfect allows you to define up to 24 columns per page. The default is two newspaper columns. If you are using 8½-by-11-inch paper with left and right margins of 1 inch, both columns will be 3 inches long and there will be ½ inch between them. As you can see from this figure, WordPerfect automatically calculates and sets the left and right margins for each of these columns.

5. If you wish to change the spacing between the columns from the default of
   $1/2$ inch, select the Distance between Columns option and enter the new
   measurement. WordPerfect will recalculate the left and right margin settings to maintain equal columns as soon as you press the Enter key.

6. If you wish to create unequal columns, select the Margins option (**4** or
   M). Use the cursor movement keys to move the cursor to the left and right
   margin settings you wish to modify; then enter the new measurement.
   Press F7 (Exit) when you are finished defining the margins.

7. Press F7 to exit and insert your column definition into the document at
   the cursor's position (or press F1—Cancel—if you wish to abandon the
   definition). This takes you back to the Math/Columns menu.

8. Select the Column On/Off option (**3** or **C**) to turn on the column definition you just created. Simply press the Enter key to return to the document if you don't want to create the columns at the cursor's current
   position. (You may return to this menu and turn Column mode on at any
   time as long as the cursor is positioned after the Column Definition code.)

After changing the left and right margins for columns using the Margins
option, you may receive the following error message:

ERROR: Text columns can't overlap

This message appears when you have set column margins so that the right and
left margin settings intersect. When this happens, you will be returned to the
margin settings for the columns, where you can reset the offending margins.
When you have finished, press F7 (Exit) to leave this screen. If you are through
defining the columns, press F7 again to return to the Math/Columns menu.

If you try to turn Column mode on before you have defined the type and number of columns to be used (i.e., before WordPerfect meets a [Col Def] code), you
will receive the error message

ERROR: No text columns defined

To delete the column format in effect (either newspaper or parallel) and return the
text to regular line formatting, press Alt-F3 (Reveal Codes) and then locate and
delete the [Col On] code positioned before the text that is formatted in columns.

Entering Text in Columns

To enter text in either style of columns, you simply begin typing in the leftmost
column on the page. If you want to end a column and begin a new one, press Ctrl-
Enter. In Column mode, this does not cause a page break, as you might expect,

unless you are in a rightmost column. It simply moves the cursor to the top of the next column and begins a new column. If you press Ctrl-Enter when the cursor is in the rightmost column on a page, the cursor moves to the beginning of the first column on the next page, and the program inserts a hard page break.

If you are working with parallel columns, you always end them by pressing Ctrl-Enter at the end of each text item to insert a Hard Page Break code. (See "Parallel Columns" earlier in this chapter for an illustration explaining why.)

You may also notice that WordPerfect does not allow you to move the cursor through an empty column. You may want to press Enter to insert a blank line in an otherwise empty column if you wish to move through it to enter text in another column to its right.

In Column mode, most of the cursor movement key sequences operate normally (exceptions are listed in Table 10.1). Pressing End moves the cursor to the end of the line, Home Home ↑ moves the cursor to the beginning of the document, and so forth.

Mixing Columns and Standard Text

In WordPerfect, it is easy to intermix standard text that flows from the left to the right margin with text that is presented in columns. After you have set column definitions (which can be done at any point earlier in the document), you can simply turn Column mode on (Alt-F7, option **3** or **C**) and begin typing text in columns. When you finish entering text for columns, turn Column mode off by pressing Alt-F7 and selecting option **3** or **C** again. If you want columns of even lengths, you may wish to change the top and bottom margin settings, or simply press Ctrl-Enter at the end of each column where you want it to break.

Converting One-Column Text to Two Columns

You may often want to convert text that has already been entered in one column into a two-column format, or, for ease in entering text, you may want to enter text in one column and then convert it to two or three columns. When setting the width for your columns, use the length of the longest line as a guide.

After you have inserted a new column definition for text that has already been entered in one-column format, remember that you must turn Column mode on (the Column On/Off option on the Math/Columns menu). To reformat the text to the new column definition without having to move the cursor through the text, you can press Ctrl-F3 (Screen) twice or press Ctrl-F3 and the Enter key. Otherwise, press ↓ to move the cursor into the text area in order for the reformatting to take place.

If you have defined newspaper columns, you may also want to press Ctrl-Enter at appropriate places in the reformatted material to produce better column breaks and more even column alignment. If you have defined parallel columns (with or without block protection), your text will all be reformatted into one long column flush with the left margin. To position individual items across from one another in the parallel layout, you need to position the cursor at the beginning of each text item and then press Ctrl-Enter. If the text items don't line up properly, delete or add blank lines as required.

Mixing Line Spacing in Text Columns

You can easily intermix different spacing, like single and double spacing, when using any of the text column formats. Changing line spacing when using newspaper or parallel columns was a particular problem in version 4.2, but WordPerfect 5.0 enables you to modify the line spacing just as you do with a standard layout. Figure 10.14 shows you newspaper columns that use both single and double spacing. To change the line spacing, you simply position the cursor at the place where the new line spacing is to take effect, press Shift-F8 (Format), select the Line option (**1** or **L**) followed by the Line Spacing option (**6** or **S**), enter the spacing you wish to use, press the Enter key, and press F7 (Exit). When you return to the document, WordPerfect will reformat the text that occurs after this line spacing change according to the number you entered.

```
Work Day                      Cafeteria

The official work day at      The company cafeteria, located
                              on the second floor, is open
MagnaCorp is 8:30 A.M. to 5:00    from 7:00 A.M. until 2:00 P.M.
                              daily. Breakfast is available
P.M. Flexible hours can be    for your convenience until 9:00
                              A.M. After 2:00 P.M., vending
arranged with your manager.   machines with cold sandwiches
                              and salads are available.


Parking                       Recreational Facilities

As parking is limited, please    MagnaCorp participates in the
                              city recreational plan and
apply to the personnel office    therefore its employees have
                              access to the municipal gym
for a parking slot assignment.   located at First and Stone
                              Streets. The jogging track and
                              par course in Compton Park are
                              also nearby. Showers and
Hours                         lockers for company employees
D:\WP\WDC\HANDBK4                    Col 1 Doc 1 Pg 1 Ln 4.341 Pos 1i
```

FIGURE 10.14: Mixing single and double spacing in text columns. To change the line spacing, you simply position the cursor at the place in the column where the new line spacing is to take effect, select the Line Spacing option (**6** or **S**) from the Line Format menu (Shift-F8 L), and enter the number of the spacing you wish to use. When you press Enter and F7 (Exit), WordPerfect will reformat the rest of the text in that column, as well as the text in succeeding columns, according to the new line spacing.

Retrieving Material into Text Columns

When the cursor is positioned in the column where you want retrieved text to appear, you can simply retrieve a file into that position. You can also open a new document window (Shift-F3), retrieve a file, and move or copy selected portions of it into your column. When Column mode is on, WordPerfect will reformat the new text according to the [Col Def] code that appears before the columns in the text.

Editing Columns

To cut or copy a text column in WordPerfect, you mark the text as a block (Alt-F4), press Ctrl-F4 (Move), and select the Block option (**1** or **B**) followed by either Move (**1** or **M**) or Copy (**2** or **C**). You don't use the Tabular Column or Rectangle option to perform these operations. (The Tabular Column option works only on columns you have set with the Tab key or have defined as Math columns.) You define a block in Column mode by using the same cursor movement keys that you do when marking a standard block of text.

Note: If you want to move or copy a discrete section of text like a particular sentence or paragraph in a column, you can press Ctrl-F4 (Move) and select either Sentence (**1** or **S**) or Paragraph (**2** or **P**) to mark it. You can also use the Page option (**3** or **A**). However, when you choose this option, WordPerfect marks all of the text on the page (regardless of the number or type of columns used), just as it does when marking a standard page of text. It does not, as you might expect, mark only up to the next hard page break used to separate columns.

If you are editing text columns, simply make whatever additions or deletions you think are necessary. WordPerfect reformats columns automatically, wrapping each one down throughout the columns and between pages of columns. You may not see all the reformatting until you move the cursor through the columns. (You can press Ctrl-F3 twice to have all of the text reformatted at one time.)

Because WordPerfect considers a text column to be a page, all the page commands (such as delete-to-end-of-page) work within columns. For example, pressing Ctrl-PgDn deletes all the lines from the cursor position to the end of the column instead of all the lines from the cursor position to the end of the page.

You can set widow/orphan protection within a column (Shift-F8 L W) so that single lines will not be left at beginnings or ends of columns. See Chapter 4 for more information about using WordPerfect's Widow/Orphan feature.

You can shorten the length of columns by changing the top and bottom margins of the page (Shift-F8 P M).

To return columnar material to the normal one-column format, delete the [Col On] code. Press Alt-F3 to reveal the codes, position the cursor to the right of the [Col On] code, and press Backspace.

Changing Column Definitions

To change a column definition, locate the existing definition, then insert the new definition to its right and delete the old Column Definition code. You can use WordPerfect's Search feature to locate any [Col Def] codes you may have inserted into your text. To do so:

1. Press F2 (Search); then press Alt-F7. The following menu appears:

   Math: **1** Def **2** On **3** Off **4** + **5** = **6** * **7** ↑ **8** T **9** ! **A** N
   Column: **B** Def **C** On **D** Off: 0

   Select option **B**. WordPerfect will locate the next occurrence of a Col Def code in your text.

2. Press Alt-F3 to see the codes. Position the cursor to the right of the existing [Col Def] code and set up your new column definition (refer back to "Defining Text Columns").

3. Press the Backspace key to delete the existing code that you are replacing.

When you delete a column definition, the page is reformatted to whatever one-column text format you are using. After you set a new column definition and move the cursor through the text, it will be reformatted back into columns.

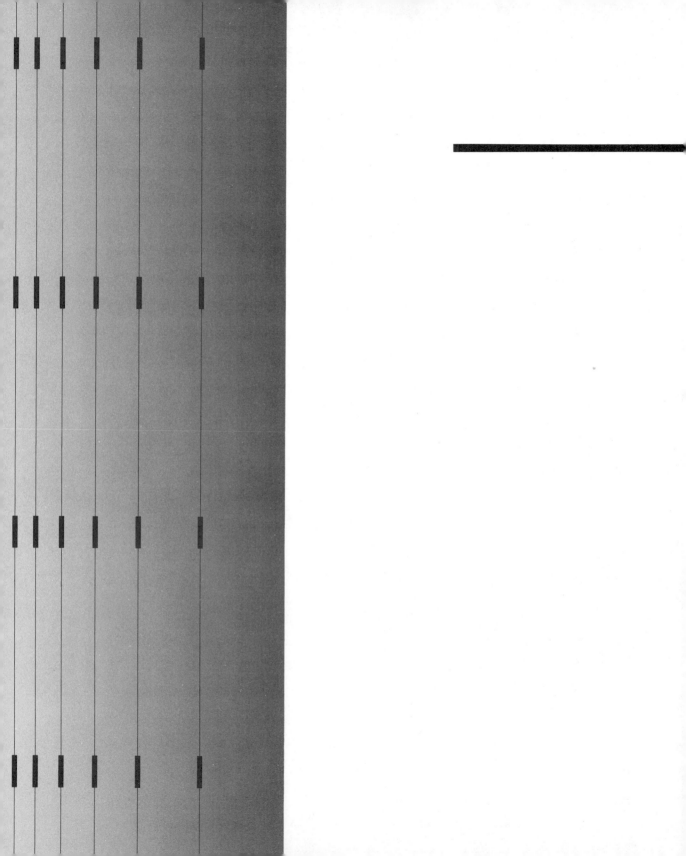

CHAPTER 11

PERFORMING MERGE OPERATIONS

PERFORMING MERGE OPERATIONS

This chapter covers WordPerfect's merge capabilities, starting with the traditional mail merge applications such as the production of form letters and mailing labels, form printing, and the creation of reports. In addition, you will find information about using the Merge feature to perform document assembly using standard text from several different files.

WordPerfect's Merge feature includes many options that can enhance the basic merge procedure. In this chapter, you will find information on performing the merge directly from the keyboard, sending merged information directly to the printer, executing macros from a merge operation, and even creating menu-driven merge operations.

Many times you will want to have the data in a secondary merge file sorted before you execute the merge. To do this, you use WordPerfect's Sort feature. For specific information about this kind of sorting, refer to Chapter 12, "Sorting Text."

If you use other software programs like Lotus 1-2-3 or dBASE III Plus and you maintain data that you wish to use in WordPerfect merge operations, you must first convert this data into the format used by the secondary merge file. To find out how you do this, refer to Appendix A, "Importing and Exporting Documents."

UPGRADE NOTES

WordPerfect's merge operations have changed little in version 5.0. The biggest change has occurred in the reassignment of the functions of Alt-F9 and Shift-F9 as outlined below:

KEY	VERSION 4.2	VERSION 5.0
F9	Merge R	Merge R
Shift-F9	Merge E	Merge Codes
Alt-F9	Merge Codes	Graphics
Ctrl-F9	Merge/Sort	Merge/Sort

With the inclusion of the Graphics key and its assignment to Alt-F9 in WordPerfect 5.0, Shift-F9 is now used to insert all Merge codes—except for Merge R (still F9)—into the primary or secondary document. This means that to insert a Merge E code (^E) to end a record in the secondary file, you must now press Shift-F9 and type **E**. You will also notice that WordPerfect automatically inserts a hard page break (indicated by a line of equal signs) whenever you insert a Merge E code in this manner.

Because of the reassignment of Merge Codes from Alt-F9 to Shift-F9, you will need to change any 4.2 macros that contain the old Merge Codes keystroke of Alt-F9. Also, any Merge E codes must now contain the keystrokes Shift-F9 E instead of just Shift-F9.

COMPONENTS OF THE BASIC MERGE OPERATION

At their most basic level, WordPerfect merge operations involve two files: a secondary merge file that contains a list of data items arranged in an unvarying order, and a primary merge file that contains both standard text and data variables that will be replaced with specific data items from the secondary merge file when the merge is performed. During the merge operation, WordPerfect creates a new file that contains information from both the secondary and primary merge files. For instance, if you are creating form letters, the new file created during the merge operation will contain one letter for each set of data (or *record*) in the secondary merge file. In each letter generated, all data variables that you designated in the primary merge file will be replaced with the appropriate data items from the secondary file. Once the merge file has been created, you can print it or edit it just as you would any other document in WordPerfect.

Preparing the Secondary Merge File

To prepare the secondary merge file, you must select the data items you wish to include and decide upon the order in which they are to be maintained. Both aspects of the secondary merge file are important. Because this file represents a special kind of data file, the elements it contains and the way they are structured must not vary throughout the file.

For instance, suppose that you are creating a client address file that you will ultimately use to generate form letters as well as to print mailing labels or to address envelopes. Undoubtedly, you will want to include the company name, street address, city, state, and zip code for each of your clients. In addition, you may want to include the name of your primary contact at the company and the appropriate personal title like *Mr., Ms.,* or *Mrs.*

Each of these items of information has to be represented in the same way in the new secondary merge file. However, not all of these items will require their own data variable, or *field*. A single field can contain several items of information as long as they will always be used as a single unit in the ensuing merges.

For example, the city, state, and zip code for each client will always be substituted as a unit either in the inside address in the form letters, or on the envelopes or mailing labels generated through merging. However, the contact person's first and last name and personal title will not always remain a unit. In the salutation of the letter, you would use either just the personal title and the person's last name or just the first name. For instance, you might address the letter to Mr. Smith (as in *Dear Mr. Smith*) or directly to John (*Dear John*), but not to Mr. John Smith (as in *Dear Mr. John Smith*) as it would appear on the mailing label. When you set up a secondary merge file, you must look very carefully at which items must be kept separate and which can be combined into single fields in the secondary merge file.

> *Note:* If you will be taking data into the secondary merge file from other sources like databases maintained in Lotus 1-2-3 or stand-alone database management systems like dBASE III Plus or R:base, the structuring of fields in the secondary merge file must be modeled after that of the source database. For example, if the client database is maintained in dBASE III Plus and the city, state, and zip code data are maintained in their own separate fields there, they will have to have the same individual fields in the secondary merge file.

However you finally decide is best to set up the fields, you will need to reserve a place for each of them in the secondary merge file even when you do not yet have information for them. Taken together, all of the fields that you maintain for each of your clients in the secondary merge file are referred to as a record. Each record in the secondary merge file must always have the same number of fields even if some of them are empty.

WordPerfect has its own way of identifying the fields and records in the secondary merge file. All data entered in each field must be terminated by a Merge R (Return) code. However, the data that you enter for a single field can be entered on multiple lines terminated by Hard Returns [HRt]. WordPerfect considers all data between Merge R codes to belong to that field regardless of how many lines it uses. To designate the end of one record and the beginning of another, you must terminate the field information with a Merge E (End) code. When you insert a Merge E code, WordPerfect automatically inserts a hard page break (displayed on the screen by a line of equal signs and in the Reveal Codes screen by an [HPg] code).

You can enter the Merge R code by pressing either F9 (marked *Merge R* on the keyboard template) or Ctrl-R. Using the F9 key is more convenient because WordPerfect will enter not only the Merge R code but also a hard return when you press it. If you use the Ctrl-R method, you must press the Enter key yourself to get to the next line for entering a new field or a Merge E code.

On screen, Merge R is displayed as ^R. However, you cannot produce this code by entering the caret (Shift-6) and the letter **R**. Although the result of using this key combination appears identical on the screen, WordPerfect does not recognize ^R as a Merge R code unless it is produced by pressing F9 or Ctrl-R.

To enter the Merge E code to mark the end of a record, you press either Shift-F9 E or Ctrl-E Ctrl-Enter (to insert an [HPg] code in the document). Again, using Shift-F9 E to select Merge E is more convenient than Ctrl-E because WordPerfect automatically enters the Merge E code and a hard page break at the same time. If you use the Ctrl-E method, you must manually press Ctrl-Enter to achieve the same result.

Figure 11.1 shows you the structure of the Merge codes in the client secondary merge file. Notice that when there is no information for field 1 (company name), as is the case for the second record, there is still a Merge R code marking its place. If this Merge R were omitted from the secondary merge file, its absence would adversely affect any use of the subsequent fields in this record. Word-Perfect keeps track of individual fields by numbering their placement in the record (see "Preparing the Primary Merge File"). Without a Merge R code for the empty field 1, the street address field (2) would become the first field, the city, state, and zip would become the second, and so on. This would also mean that there would be no sixth field for this record. As a result, the wrong information in this record would be merged into the primary file whenever fields 2 through 6 were used.

The number of records that a secondary merge file can hold is limited only by available disk space. Nevertheless, when you maintain truly large data files with thousands of records, you will probably find that the size of the file makes it unwieldy to edit and maintain. In that event, you will find it advantageous to divide the secondary merge file into several smaller files. For instance, if you maintain the records in a client file by company name in alphabetical order (see Chapter 12 for information on sorting secondary merge files), you can split the file in two so that one contains those companies whose names begin with the letters A–M and the other contains those which begin with N–Z.

```
Speedo Printing^R
1345 Seventh Street^R
Berkeley, CA 94704^R
Mr.^R
Jim^R
Waggoner^R
^E
=================================================================
^R
221 Avenue of the Americas
Suite 210^R
New York, NY 10010^R
Mr.^R
Allan^R
Grill^R
^E
=================================================================
Toys N' Things^R
302 West Elm Street^R
Alameda, CA 94501^R
Ms.^R
Grace^R
Fraesir^R
^E
D:\WP\WDC\CLIENTS.SF                          Doc 1 Pg 1 Ln 11 Pos 1i
```

FIGURE 11.1: The secondary merge file for the client addresses. This file keeps track of six fields (or items) of information for each record (or client) in it. Notice that information for each of the fields is terminated with a Merge R (Return) code shown as ^R. Even when there is no information for a particular field, as is the case for the company name field (1) in the second record, a Merge R code must still be entered to mark the place for that field. Also, notice that the end of each record is marked with a Merge E code (shown as ^E) and a hard page break.

When you save the data you have entered in a secondary merge file (just as you save any WordPerfect document, by using either F10 or F7), you may want to give an .SF extension to mark it as a secondary merge file. Although it is not required, adding this extension to all secondary merge files makes it easy to distinguish them from regular documents in a directory listing.

Preparing the Primary Merge File

You can create several different primary merge files to be used with a single secondary merge file. In the example of the client data file, you might use it to generate form letters to your customers as well as to prepare the mailing labels for these letters. In such a case, you would set up two primary merge files, the first of which generates a letter for each client in the secondary merge file and the second of which addresses the mailing label for the letter.

The primary merge file that contains the "form" letter will include both standard text, which does not vary from letter to letter, and data variables (fields), which are taken from each record in the secondary merge file and, therefore, change as each letter is generated. It is the appropriate use of these data variables throughout the letter that "personalizes" its content.

To indicate where the contents of a particular field will be merged into the text of the letter, you use WordPerfect's Merge Codes key, Shift-F9. When you press Shift-F9, you are presented with the following merge options:

^C; ^D; ^E; ^F; ^G; ^N; ^O; ^P; ^Q; ^S; ^T; ^U; ^V:

As with Merge R (^R), these are preceded by the symbol for the Ctrl character (^) to mark them as Merge codes. From this menu, you select ^F by typing **F** (for *Field*). As soon as you do, you see the following prompt:

Field:

In response, you enter the number of the field whose data variable you want inserted into the text. Fields in the secondary merge file are numbered sequentially from 1. The numbering of the fields ends when WordPerfect reaches the Merge E (^E) and hard page break marking the end of one record and the beginning of the next in the file.

Figure 11.2 shows you a sample primary merge file that will generate a form letter for each record in the client secondary merge file. Below the Date code, you can see the Merge codes to insert fields 1 through 6. Together, these fields make up the inside address and salutation.

To add the Merge code to insert field 4 on the first line of the inside address, you place the cursor at the beginning of the line, press Shift-F9, type **F** followed by **4**, and press the Enter key. WordPerfect automatically adds the carets before the *F* and after the *4* so that the code is entered in the letter as *^F4^*. The fourth

```
^D

^F4^ ^F5^ ^F6^
^F1?^
^F2^
^F3^

Dear ^F4^ ^F6^:

        Please take a moment out of your busy schedule to look over
the enclosed price list, which contains many exciting specials that
I can offer your firm for a limited time only. As you will see,
most of our paper products are offered at prices well below retail
(and some are just pennies above wholesale cost!).

        Thank you for your time. I look forward to serving your firm
and hope to take care of all of your paper product needs.

Sincerely,


Jason Stanford
Corporate Account Executive
D:\WP\WDC\FORMLTR.PF                            Doc 2 Pg 1 Ln 11 Pos 1i
```

FIGURE 11.2: Sample form letter to be used with the client secondary merge file to generate personalized letters to each customer. Each of the ^Fn^ Merge codes (where *n* is the number of the field) will be replaced during the merge with the data entered into that field in the secondary merge file. Notice that the ^F4^ and ^F6^ Merge codes are used twice (in the inside address and the salutation). In each of these positions, the personal title and last name to which the letter is addressed will appear. Also, notice that it uses the ^D Merge code at the top to insert the current date at the time of the merge.

field in the client secondary merge file contains the client's personal title (*Mr.,
Ms.,* or *Mrs.*). When WordPerfect generates the letters for each customer during
the merge operation, it will replace the *^F4^* with either *Mr., Ms.,* or *Mrs.,*
according to the title that has been entered in the fourth field.

The codes for the fifth and sixth fields follow that for the fourth field on the
same line. They are separated by spaces and are entered in the same manner as
field 4. When you enter field codes into the primary file, use the same spacing
and punctuation as you would when typing an actual letter. If you normally add
a comma between two words (such as the city and state in an address), you type
this comma between the two field codes that will insert these items for you when
the merge is performed.

Notice, however, that the Merge code for field 1 on the second line of the inside
address contains a question mark immediately before the final caret (^F1?^).
This was done by pressing Shift-F9, typing **F**, and then entering **1?** before pressing the Enter key. The question mark prevents WordPerfect from adding a blank
line in a letter when the first field in the record is blank. It is added to field 1
because not all of the records have a company name. Similarly, in your merge
applications, you will want to add a question mark to the ^F Merge codes of all
field numbers that you use in a primary merge file whenever any of its entries in
the secondary merge file are empty (marked only by a Merge R code).

If you add the question mark to a field number and then use that field code with others on the same line in a primary document (rather than on a line by itself), WordPerfect will suppress every field substitution on that line; it won't just suppress the field code that contains the question mark. However, if you use such a field in the primary document on a line that contains only standard text (and no other field codes), it will suppress only the field entry and will not affect the standard text that you typed.

In the salutation of this letter, fields 4 and 6 are reused. The colon, the standard punctuation used in a business letter salutation, immediately follows the ^F6^ field entry, just as it would if you were typing an actual salutation such as *Dear Ms. Johnson:* in a typical business letter. As a result of using the personal title and last name fields here, the salutation will give a more polite greeting that addresses the person by title and last name.

When you insert Merge codes, you must be careful that you enter the correct field number in each case. As you create the primary merge file, you should probably refer to a printout of your secondary merge file that has all of the fields of a sample record numbered. Then, you should also double-check your work by printing a copy of the primary merge file (Shift-F7 F) and substituting live data from each of the fields used on the copy.

You save a primary merge file just as you would any other WordPerfect document. When naming the file, you may want to give the file name the extension .PF to mark it as a primary merge file. Just as adding the extension .SF to a secondary merge file makes its function clear, so too adding the .PF extension will alert you to the fact that it contains data variables and should only be used with WordPerfect's Merge feature.

Performing the Merge

After you have prepared both the primary and secondary merge files, you can perform the merge at any time. However, before you actually give the Merge command, you will want to be in a blank editing window. If you still have the text of your primary or secondary merge file (or any other document) displayed on your screen, you will want to either use Exit (F7) to clear it or switch to the other document window (Shift-F3).

This is because WordPerfect, unlike most other word processors, does not output the results of the merge operation directly to the printer. Instead, in the current document window it creates a new file containing a copy of the primary merge file for each record in the secondary file. After this file has been created, you can save and/or print it just as you would any other WordPerfect document.

To perform the merge, you press Ctrl-F9 (Merge/Sort). When you do, you are presented with these three options:

1 Merge; **2 S**ort; **3 S**ort Order: **0**

After you type **1** or **M** to initiate the merge, you are prompted to enter the name of the primary merge file to use:

Primary file:

After you enter the name of your primary merge file—be sure to add the .PF extension if you used it and the path name if the file is on a different disk or in a different directory—and press the Enter key, you are prompted to enter the name of the secondary merge file:

Secondary file:

As soon as you type the file name of the secondary merge file you wish to use, WordPerfect begins the merge.

While data from the two files is being processed and the new file is being generated, you will see the message *Merging* in the lower-left corner of the screen. As soon as the merge is completed, the cursor will be placed at the very end of the file. During the merge, WordPerfect will automatically place a hard page break after each copy of the contents of the primary merge file (each letter, form, report, envelope, mailing label, and so on).

Figure 11.3 shows the first letter generated when the form letter in Figure 11.2 is merged with the records in the client data file shown in Figure 11.1. Notice in Figure 11.3 where the replacements were made in the primary merge file to create the final letter.

```
April 30, 1989

Mr. Jim Waggoner
Speedo Printing
1345 Seventh Street
Berkeley, CA 94704

Dear Mr. Waggoner:

    Please take a moment out of your busy schedule to look over
the enclosed price list, which contains many exciting specials that
I can offer your firm for a limited time only. As you will see,
most of our paper products are offered at prices well below retail
(and some are just pennies above wholesale cost!).

    Thank you for your time. I look forward to serving your firm
and hope to take care of all of your paper product needs.

Sincerely,



Jason Stanford
Corporate Account Executive
                                    Doc 1 Pg 1 Ln 11 Pos 1i
```

FIGURE 11.3: The first form letter created with WordPerfect's Merge feature. In this letter to Speedo Printing, all six fields in the first record of the secondary file are used. Notice that the data from fields 4 and 6 is used twice, once at the top of the inside address (along with the fifth field) and again in the salutation. The ^D Merge code in the primary file supplied the date (and will supply your computer's current system date when you run your own applications).

In Figure 11.4, notice that the use of the question mark in field 1 (*^F1?^* in Figure 11.2) has prevented a blank line from being inserted between the line containing the person's name and the street address. Also, notice that the street address in this letter occupies two lines, although only one field was used in the merge.

To stop a merge operation before it is finished, you can press Shift-F9 and type **E** at any time. This causes WordPerfect to stop merging and write whatever letters or forms have been completed to the screen. To redo the merge, you can then press F7 (Exit) and answer no to saving the new document. Then you can make whatever changes are required to either the primary or secondary merge file and reissue the Merge command (Ctrl-F9 M).

After you have checked over the results of the merge, you can print the file right away (Shift-F7 F) or save it under a new file name and print it later.

Merging Directly to the Printer

When you perform a merge, the entire file generated by the merge in the current document window is held in the computer's memory, not on disk (so if you lose power before you have a chance to save the new document, it will be lost). If the number of records in your secondary merge file is quite large, your computer

```
April 3Ø, 1989

Mr. Allan Grill
221 Avenue of the Americas
Suite 21Ø
New York, NY 1ØØ1Ø

Dear Mr. Grill:

        Please take a moment out of your busy schedule to look over
the enclosed price list, which contains many exciting specials that
I can offer your firm for a limited time only. As you will see,
most of our paper products are offered at prices well below retail
(and some are just pennies above wholesale cost!).

        Thank you for your time. I look forward to serving your firm
and hope to take care of all of your paper product needs.

Sincerely,




Jason Stanford
Corporate Account Executive
                                    Doc 1 Pg 2 Ln 11 Pos 1i
```

FIGURE 11.4: The second form letter created with WordPerfect's Merge feature. Notice that the only difference between this letter to Mr. Grill and the one to Mr. Waggoner (shown in Figure 11.3) is that its inside address doesn't contain a company name. However, it still occupies four lines like the first letter because the street address requires two lines. Whenever you perform a merge in which some of the copies require data from a particular field and others do not, you need to enter the **?** after the field number in the primary merge file in order to accommodate both situations.

could run out of memory before WordPerfect has generated all of the merged copies. If this happens, WordPerfect terminates the merge operation as soon as the computer's available memory is used up, much like when you press Shift-F9 E to abort a merge.

To avoid having only a part of your secondary merge file processed, you can add special Merge option codes at the end of the primary merge file to have each merged form sent directly to the printer as soon as it is generated. You can add these codes on the last line containing text if you put a space between them and the last part of the text on the line, or you can add them on their own line at the very end of the file.

The first Merge code that you must add, ^T (for *Type*), instructs WordPerfect to send all of the merged text up to its occurrence to the printer and then to clear this text out of the computer's memory. In addition, you must add the Merge codes ^N and ^P^P to instruct WordPerfect to move to the next record and print the letter for it until all of the records in the secondary merge file have been processed. The ^N Merge code (for *Next*) tells WordPerfect to proceed to the next record in the file. The pair of ^P Merge codes (for *Primary*) tells WordPerfect which primary merge file to use next. When you do not enter any file name between the pair of ^P codes, WordPerfect uses the same primary merge file again.

The ^N^P^P Merge code combination is required with the ^T code to prevent WordPerfect from entering an extra page break. When the ^T Merge code is used alone, the printer automatically advances to the beginning of the next page when it finishes printing each merged document. This page break sends an unwanted form feed to the printer, resulting in a blank page after each merged document. When you enter the entire sequence

    ^T^N^P^P

at the end of your primary merge file, extra blank pages are suppressed as Word-Perfect prints each of your merged documents. The printing automatically stops when the program processes the last record or reaches a ^Q code (for *Quit*) in the secondary merge file.

When you use this method to send your merged documents directly to the printer, you can stop the printing at any time by pressing Shift-F7 (Print), selecting the Control Printer option (**4** or **C**), and then selecting the Stop option (**5** or **S**). When you are ready to begin merge-printing once again, reset the printhead at the top of the form, press Shift-F7, type **C** (Control Printer) and then type **G** to select the Go (start printer) option from the Control Printer menu. If you wish to cancel the merge-printing, you do so from this screen by selecting the Cancel Job(s) option (**1** or **C**). Press the Enter key if the print job document is listed as (Merge). You may have to press the Enter key a second time to stop the printer.

However, if you did not terminate the merge itself before you stopped the printing, WordPerfect will restart the merge operation as soon as you return to the editing screen. In this event, press Shift-F9 and type **E** to cancel the merge and then return to the Control Printer screen again. Once there, select the Cancel Job(s) option a second time. When you then return to the editing screen, the merge will not commence again.

Merging from the Keyboard

When you have only a few letters, forms, or reports to generate and you do not need to save the variable data, you can enter data directly from the keyboard during the merge operation. You do this by entering a special Merge code, ^C (for *Console*), wherever you want WordPerfect to pause the merge operation to allow you to manually enter text. After you have entered the text, you press F9 (Merge R) to have WordPerfect continue the merge operation.

The ^C code can be used in either the primary or secondary merge file. You use it in the primary file when you need to fill in the text for a particular field for all of the documents generated by the merge. To use the ^C Merge code, you simply enter it in the text of the primary merge file where you would normally enter a field code. For example, assume that you replace the ^F1?^ field code with a ^C Merge code in the primary merge file as shown in Figure 11.5.

When you run the merge (using the client secondary merge file), WordPerfect will generate the current date (because of the ^D Merge code) and the personal title, first name, and last name of the client on your screen. With the cursor positioned at the beginning of the line below (and the ^C Merge code gone), the merge will be paused. At that point, you type in the name of the company, if it is known to you. Press F9 (Merge R) to continue the merge; the rest of the substitutions in the inside address and salutation will be made, and the next letter will be generated on your screen. Again the merge will pause when it encounters another ^C code, positioning the cursor after first line of the inside address and waiting until you press F9. The merge operation will continue in this manner until all of the records in the secondary merge file have been processed. Note, however, that if you don't enter a company name during the pause and just press F9, the letter will contain a blank line in the inside address unless you press the Del key before you press F9 to continue the merge operation.

You use the ^C Merge code in the secondary merge file when you want Word-Perfect to pause the merge operation to allow you to enter text for a field or fields of just specific records. Rather than pausing as it generates the merged document for each record, as is the case when you use ^C in the primary file, WordPerfect will stop only when it processes a record in which one or more of the fields that are used in the merge contain the ^C code.

For instance, assume that you edit the secondary merge file containing the client records and replace the entries for fields 4 (personal title), 5 (first name), and 6 (last name) with ^C Merge codes just in the third record (see Figure 11.6). When you perform the merge with the form letter primary file that uses fields

```
^D

^F4^ ^F5^ ^F6^
^C
^F2^
^F3^

Dear ^F4^ ^F6^:

     Please take a moment out of your busy schedule to look over
the enclosed price list, which contains many exciting specials that
I can offer your firm for a limited time only. As you will see,
most of our paper products are offered at prices well below retail
(and some are just pennies above wholesale cost!).

     Thank you for your time. I look forward to serving your firm
and hope to take care of all of your paper product needs.

Sincerely,



Jason Stanford
Corporate Account Executive
D:\WP\WDC\FORMLTR.PF                          Doc 2 Pg 1 Ln 11 Pos 1i
```

FIGURE 11.5: Using the ^C Merge code in the primary merge file. Here, a ^C code has been substituted for the ^F1?^ field code in the primary merge file. Instead of letting WordPerfect take the company name for each merged letter from the records of the secondary file, the operator will have to enter this information when the merge pauses. During this pause, the cursor will be located in the position where you currently see the ^ (control character) of the ^C code. Once the operator types the company name and presses F9, the merge will generate a new letter, pausing again at the same position.

```
Speedo Printing^R
1345 Seventh Street^R
Berkeley, CA 94704^R
Mr.^R
Jim^R
Waggoner^R
^E
==================================================================
^R
221 Avenue of the Americas
Suite 210^R
New York, NY 10010^R
Mr.^R
Allan^R
Grill^R
^E
==================================================================
Toys N' Things^R
302 West Elm Street^R
Alameda, CA 94501^R
^C^R
^C^R
^C^R
^E
D:\WP\WDC\CLIENTS.SF                           Doc 1 Pg 1 Ln 11 Pos 1i
```

FIGURE 11.6: Using the ^C Merge code in the secondary merge file. Here, the code replaces the entries for the personal title, first name, and last name only in the record for Toys N' Things (at the bottom of the figure). During the merge, WordPerfect will pause to allow the operator to input these items only when it generates this particular merged letter. The first two records don't contain any ^C codes, so their letters will be generated without any input from the keyboard.

4 (^F4^), 5 (^F5^), and 6 (^F6^), WordPerfect will still generate the first two letters using the data from these records automatically.

However, when WordPerfect processes the record for Toys N' Things, it will generate the text on your screen, position the cursor at the beginning of the first line of the inside address, and pause the merge operation. At that point, it will wait for you to enter the person's title from the keyboard. (The ^F4^ field code will no longer be seen on screen, although the ^F5^ and ^F6^ codes will still be visible.) As soon as you enter it and press F9 (Merge R), the ^F5^ code will disappear, the cursor will move to the right one space, and the merge will pause again. Here, you enter the last name of the person you are addressing in the salutation. When you press F9 to continue the merge, WordPerfect will pause again to allow you to enter the last name. After you press F9, the program will take over making the rest of the substitutions for the inside address. When it reaches the salutation, the program will pause to allow you to enter the personal title and last name. After you press F9 the last time, WordPerfect will go on to generate the rest of this letter as well as the letters from any remaining records in the secondary file.

Displaying Messages on Screen

You can use another Merge code, ^O (for *On-screen*), with the ^C Merge code to have WordPerfect display a particular message or prompt whenever it pauses the merge. For example, if you were using the ^C code to allow you to enter the company name in form letters from the keyboard (as shown in Figure 11.5), you could also have WordPerfect display a message indicating that the merge has been paused and prompting you (or a fellow worker) to enter the name of the firm, if applicable.

To do this, you enter your message or prompt enclosed in a pair of ^O Merge codes followed by the ^C code in the primary merge file. For example, you could enter the following message and pause in the sample form letter. This would be entered on the second line of the inside address:

^OMerge Pause! Enter company & press F9^O^C

When you perform the merge, the message

Merge Pause! Enter company & press F9

will be displayed on the last line of the screen in bold. The cursor will also be positioned immediately after the beginning of the second line of the inside address to allow you to enter this information.

When you create your on-screen messages and prompts using the ^O codes followed by the ^C Merge code, you can use up to 37 characters. Any characters beyond the 37th will automatically be truncated. For this reason, you must keep these on-screen messages brief.

The ^O Merge codes can be combined with other WordPerfect merge options. You can use them to display a message that prompts you to enter the name of the primary and secondary files to be used in an upcoming merge operation, or you can even use them to display a message prompting you to enter the name of a macro that is to be executed at the end of the merge. For more information on possible applications, see "Filling In Forms," "Macros in Merges," and "Creating Menus" later in this chapter.

Envelopes and Mailing Labels

Once you have created the secondary merge file containing all of the records you need to use in a merge operation, you can use this file not only to generate the form letters but also to create the mailing labels or to address the envelopes needed to send these letters. To do so requires only that you create an additional primary merge file with all of the field codes you need in the correct order and then select the appropriate format settings.

For example, if you were going to generate mailing labels or envelopes for the advertising letters generated from the client secondary merge file, you would begin by entering the following field codes in a new document:

```
^F1?^
^F2^
^F3^

Attn: ^F4^ ^F5^ ^F6^
```

The field codes on the first three lines must each be entered on their own line, terminated with a hard return (Enter). To enter the field number, you press Shift-F9, type **F** and the number of the field you wish to use, and press the Enter key.

Once you had created this new primary file containing only the fields to be inserted, you would save it and run the merge (Ctrl-F9 M) using this new file as the primary file and the file containing the client records as the secondary file. Figure 11.7 shows the result of this merge operation.

Once the merge had ended, all you would have to do is establish the correct format settings for the size of mailing labels or envelopes you were using prior to sending this new document to the printer. This could be done by adjusting the margins and changing the paper size and type.

Determining the Format Settings for Envelopes

To position the address correctly on an envelope, you must adjust the left and top margin settings. You should set the top margin setting from the Page Format menu before changing the paper size and type. To do this, press Shift-F8 (Format) and select the Page menu (**2** or **P**). Then select the Margins option (**5** or **M**)

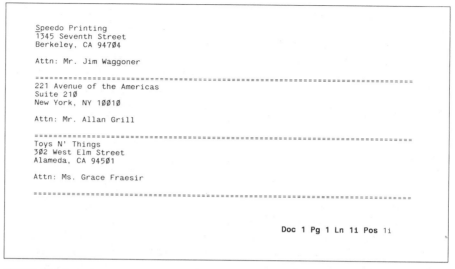

```
    Speedo Printing
    1345 Seventh Street
    Berkeley, CA 94704

    Attn: Mr. Jim Waggoner

    ======================================================================
    221 Avenue of the Americas
    Suite 210
    New York, NY 10010

    Attn: Mr. Allan Grill

    ======================================================================
    Toys N' Things
    302 West Elm Street
    Alameda, CA 94501

    Attn: Ms. Grace Fraesir

    ======================================================================



                                         Doc 1 Pg 1 Ln 11 Pos 1i
```

FIGURE 11.7: Executing a merge to print mailing labels or envelopes for the form letters. This figure shows three addresses that can be printed on mailing labels or directly on envelopes. These addresses were generated by using a new primary merge file. This file contains essentially just the proper field codes (except for the text *Attn:* in the last line) arranged to fit the mailing address format.

and enter a new top margin setting according to the capabilities of your printer. If you must hand-feed the envelope to the printer and you can manually adjust where the first line of the address is printed, set a top margin of 0″.

If you are using a printer like a laser printer, where you can't manually determine where the first line is printed (regardless of whether you hand-feed the envelope or have a special envelope feeder do it for you), you need to set an appropriate top margin (a top margin setting of 1.5 inches is usually fine, unless your address has many more lines than the ones shown in Figure 11.7). With such printers, you may also want to reduce the bottom margin setting, if your addresses are long and you don't care how little space there is between the last line and the bottom edge of the envelope. The last thing you want is to have WordPerfect insert a soft page break and start a new page containing only a line or two of the address information. Remember that the page length for the Envelope paper size is only 4 inches—you are no longer working with the 8½-by-11-inch paper size.

To address legal-size envelopes, you will then have to change the paper size and type from Standard (8½ × 11 inches) to Envelope (9½ × 4 inches). From the Page menu, select the Paper Size/Type option (**8** or **S**). From the Paper Size and Paper Type menus, select the Envelope option (**5** or **E**).

After setting the page size and type, press the Enter key to return to the main Format menu. From there, you can adjust the left margin setting by selecting Line (**1** or **L**), choosing the Margins options (**7** or **M**), and increasing the left margin setting. (A left margin of 3.75 inches is used with the sample addresses shown in Figure 11.8.)

After you set a new left margin and press F7 (Exit) to return to the editing screen, the addresses will appear shifted to the right, reflecting the new left margin. Figure 11.8 shows you the sample addresses with new format settings as indicated above. To see the effect of changing the top margin setting, you must use the View Document feature (Shift-F7 V). Figure 11.9 shows you the first envelope, using View Document.

To print your envelopes with a printer where you manually determine where the first line of the address is printed, place the first envelope in the printer and move it up so that the printhead is at the exact place where you want the first line of the address to appear. Make sure that the cursor is located on the first address in the editing screen (press Home Home ↑ if necessary). Then, press Shift-F7 and select Page (**2** or **P**). Finally, press Shift-F7, select the Control Printer option (**4** or **C**), and from this screen select the Go (start printer) option (**4** or **G**) to print the first envelope. After the first address has been printed, press PgDn to move the cursor to the second address, position your next envelope as before, and repeat the key sequence indicated above. Repeat this procedure until all of your envelopes have been addressed.

If your printer requires hand feeding but doesn't allow you to adjust the position of the printhead, you follow essentially the same procedure as outlined above after placing the first envelope in the manual feed. Note, however, that the envelope will

```
            Speedo Printing
            1345 Seventh Street
            Berkeley, CA 94704

            Attn: Mr. Jim Waggoner

=====================================================================
            221 Avenue of the Americas
            Suite 210
            New York, NY 10010

                                Doc 1 Pg 1 Ln 1.51 Pos 3.75i
▲    ▲     ▲    ▲     ▲    ▲│     ▲      ▲         ▲      ▲  )
[T/B Mar:1.5",1"][Paper Sz/Typ:9.5" x 4",Envelope][L/R Mar:3.75",1"]Speedo Print
ing[HRt]
1345 Seventh Street[HRt]
Berkeley, CA 94704[HRt]
[HRt]
Attn: Mr. Jim Waggoner[HRt]
[HPg]
221 Avenue of the Americas[HRt]
Suite 210[HRt]
New York, NY 10010[HRt]

Press Reveal Codes to restore screen
```

FIGURE 11.8: The addresses generated by the second merge operation with new format settings for printing on envelopes. As you can see in the Reveal Codes screen (in the lower half of this figure), the left, right, top, and bottom margins have been adjusted to reflect the dimensions of the envelope (9½ × 4 inches), which has been selected as the paper size and type.

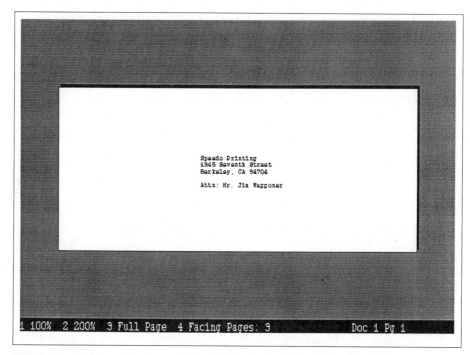

FIGURE 11.9: The first envelope as it appears in the View Document screen (Shift-F7 V). Previewing the envelope with the View Document feature gives you a good idea of whether an address is properly formatted.

not begin to go through the feeder until you select the Go (start printer) option after giving the command to print the first page (that is, the first address).

DETERMINING THE FORMAT SETTINGS FOR MAILING LABELS

Changing the format settings for mailing labels is a little bit more involved than for envelopes. WordPerfect doesn't have a predefined paper size for mailing labels, as their dimensions vary according to the type of labels you are using. Because the "page size" of a typical label is quite small (a size of 4 × 1½ inches is large), you *must* change the top and bottom margin settings before the program will permit you to change the paper size to reflect the overall dimensions of the label. In addition, you must remember to change the left and right margin settings to accommodate the new size or you may find that extra lines have been added to your addresses because of word wrap and, in the worst case, that your address is split up on two pages (that is, two mailing labels).

To get a feel for how this is done, follow along the procedure for formatting the sample addresses shown in Figure 11.7. Assume that these addresses will be printed on tractor-fed mailing labels that measure 4 inches wide by 1½ inches long. To accommodate the length and width of the longest address, the top margin will be set at ⅜ inch (.37") and the bottom margin at ¼ inch (.25"). Likewise, the left margin will be set at ¾ inch (.75") and the right margin at ¼ inch (.25").

The first step is to set the new top and bottom margins. To do this, you press Shift-F8 (Format), select the Page menu (**2** or **P**), and then the Margin option (**5** or **M**). Enter **.37** for the top margin and **.25** for the bottom margin (be sure to type " after these dimensions if you have changed WordPerfect's units of measure for the display of numbers to points, or centimeters, or 4.2 units). After resetting the margins, select the Size/Type option (**8** or **S**) from this menu. Because there is no predefined size for 4-by-1½-inch paper, you need to select the Other option (**0**). WordPerfect displays the prompt

    Width: 8"

at the bottom of the screen. After you type **4** (which replaces the 8" default) and press the Enter key, the prompt

    Length: 11"

appears. Here, you type **1.5** over the 11" default. When you press the Enter key, the Type menu appears. From this menu, you select the Labels option (**4** or **L**). This returns you to the Page menu, where you press the Enter key to return to the main Format menu.

The next step is to change the left and right margins for the addresses. To do this, select the Line menu (**1** or **L**). From this menu, select the Margin option (**7** or **M**) and enter **.75** for the left margin and **.25** for the right margin. After changing these margins, press F7 (Exit) to return to the document editing screen.

As you scroll through the document (or press Ctrl-F3 twice to rewrite the screen), you will see that soft page breaks precede each of the hard page breaks inserted between the addresses during the merge operation (see Figure 11.10). The soft page breaks are a result of the greatly reduced page length (from 11 inches to 1½ inches). Even with the smaller top and bottom margin settings, this new page length is just sufficient to have each address printed on a single page (that is, label). However, before printing the labels, you must delete the hard page breaks.

The simplest and fastest way to delete the hard page breaks is by using Word-Perfect's Search and Replace feature. You position the cursor at the beginning of the document and press Alt-F2 (Replace) and the Enter key to replace without confirmation. Press Ctrl-Enter to insert the [HPg] code as the search string, then press F2 (Search). When prompted for a replacement, you simply press F2 to initiate the search and replacement throughout the document. All of the hard page breaks will then disappear from the editing screen.

```
Speedo Printing
1345 Seventh Street
Berkeley, CA 94704

Attn: Mr. Jim Waggoner
-------------------------------------------------------------------

===================================================================
221 Avenue of the Americas
Suite 210
New York, NY 10010
                                        Doc 1 Pg 1 Ln 0.371 Pos 0.75i
 ▲    ▲    ▲    ▲    ▲    ▲    ▲    ▲    ▲    ▲    ▲
[T/B Mar:0.37",0.25"][Paper Sz/Typ:4" x 1.5",Labels][L/R Mar:0.75",0.25"]Speedo
Printing[HRt]
1345 Seventh Street[HRt]
Berkeley, CA 94704[HRt]
[HRt]
Attn: Mr. Jim Waggoner[SPg]
[HPg]
221 Avenue of the Americas[HRt]
Suite 210[HRt]
New York, NY 10010[HRt]

Press Reveal Codes to restore screen
```

FIGURE 11.10: The first complete address and part of the second, generated by the second merge operation with new format settings for printing on mailing labels. Notice that the change in the paper size (to 4" × 1½", the dimensions of a single mailing label) has caused WordPerfect to insert a soft page break (the line of hyphens) above the hard page break (the line of equal signs) inserted by the merge. You can see the changes to the format settings in the Reveal Codes screen.

Before you send the newly formatted document containing the addresses to the printer, you should use the View Document feature to check the layout of the addresses on the mailing label. Figure 11.11 shows you the first address in the View Document screen.

If everything appears as you want it, you are ready to print the mailing labels. Remember to load your printer with the mailing labels of the size specified when changing the paper size and type. If your printer allows you to position the paper in relation to the printhead, line it up so that the printhead is at the very top of the first label before you give the Print command. Otherwise, just press Shift-F7 (Print) and select the Full Document option (**1** or **F**). If you think that you may need to rerun these labels before you update the secondary file and perform the merge again, you should save the document before exiting WordPerfect.

> *Note:* If your secondary file contains so many records that WordPerfect cannot complete the merge with the primary file that contains Merge codes for your labels due to insufficient computer memory, you will have to send each label to the printer by adding the ^T^N^P^P Merge codes to the end of the file. Refer back to "Merging Directly to the Printer" for details on how to use these codes.

To print addresses on sheets of labels that have multiple columns (usually two or three columns across a sheet), you use WordPerfect's Parallel Columns feature. The number of labels across the page determines the number of columns to

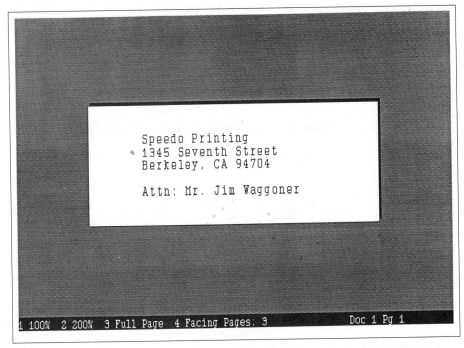

```
            Speedo Printing
          • 1345 Seventh Street
            Berkeley, CA 94704

            Attn: Mr. Jim Waggoner
```

```
1 100%  2 200%  3 Full Page  4 Facing Pages: 3          Doc 1 Pg 1
```

FIGURE 11.11: The first mailing label as it appears in the View Document screen (Shift-F7 V). Word-Perfect automatically adjusts the view to 100% (full size) for such a small paper size (4 by 1½ inches).

specify when defining the parallel columns. Figure 11.12 shows you a sample layout of six addresses designed for printing on a laser printer with 8½-by-11-inch sheets of adhesive labels, arranged in three columns and ten rows.

Each label on the sheet measures 2⅝ inches wide by 1 inch long. Because each label is so small, the addresses must be printed in a smaller font (10 point Times Roman, in this case) to fit within the dimensions of the label. After the merge operation is completed, you insert this font change at the beginning of the merged document. You do this by pressing Ctrl-F8 (Font), selecting the Base Font option (**4** or **F**), highlighting any small font you have available on the list—*Tms Rmn 10pt (AC)* in this case—and then choosing the Select option (**1** or **S**). (See Chapter 5 for more information on working with different fonts.)

The top edge of the first row of labels starts ½ inch down from the top of the sheet, and the bottom edge of the last row ends ½ inch up from the bottom of the sheet. To accommodate this arrangement, you set both the top and bottom margins to .62" (⅝ inch). The left edge of the first column of labels and the right edge of the last column of labels are both ³⁄₁₆ inch in from the left and right edges of the page, respectively. Therefore, you set both the left and right margins at .25".

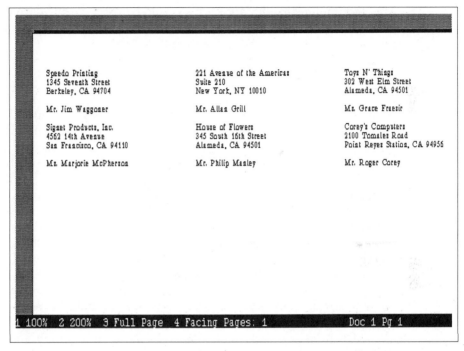

FIGURE 11.12: Mail merge addresses laid out in three columns and two rows as they appear in the View Document screen (Shift-F7 V) at 100% (full size). This layout was created with parallel columns after the merge operation. The addresses will be printed on a laser printer using an 8½-by-11-inch sheet of 30 adhesive labels, arranged in three columns and ten rows. Each label measures 2⅝ inches wide by 1 inch long.

After inserting the font change and modifying the margin settings, you define the parallel columns. Press Alt-F7 (Math/Columns) and select the Column Def option (**4** or **D**). Then, select the Type option (**1** or **T**) and change the Newspaper default to Parallel. Use the Number of Columns option (**2** or **N**) to change the default of 2 to 3. Finally, select the Distance between Columns option (**3** or **D**) and specify **.25"** as the distance between each column. WordPerfect automatically calculates the correct margin settings for the three columns. After pressing F7 (Exit), turn on the parallel columns by selecting the Column On/Off option (**2** or **C**). (See Chapter 10 for more details on setting and using parallel columns.) After you turn the columns on, WordPerfect reformats the addresses in the three-column, two-row arrangement shown in Figure 11.12.

Note: You may experience formatting problems when WordPerfect reaches the second row of addresses. (It has been known to take out the [HPg] codes that separate each address and format the remaining addresses in a single column.) In such a case, you must locate the cursor on the first character of each address that needs to be reformatted and press Ctrl-Enter to insert a hard page break. When you do this, the address will be reformatted immediately in the proper column.

After ascertaining that the labels are formatted correctly (using the View Document feature), you load the laser printer with the sheets of labels and give the command to print the entire document (Shift-F7 F).

Filling In Forms

In addition to creating form letters, generating mailing labels, and addressing envelopes, you can use WordPerfect's merge capabilities to fill in forms. These forms may be either preprinted, such as tax forms, or created by you or a colleague in WordPerfect. The information that is entered into particular blanks of the form can come from a secondary merge file, the keyboard, or even a combination of these sources.

When using the Merge feature to complete forms that you have designed in WordPerfect, you will want to set up the form, including all headings and tab stops, before you insert the required Merge codes. If you will be using a secondary merge file to complete part or all of the blanks in the form, you will want to use the field code (Shift-F9 F) and enter the appropriate field number right where you want the text to begin. The same is true if you will be entering ^C Merge codes to allow you to fill in some or all of the blanks from the keyboard.

Figure 11.13 shows a simple form, designed and executed in WordPerfect, that uses data from various fields of a secondary merge file to fill in all but the last blank. When WordPerfect comes to this blank during the merge, the on-screen prompt

Enter "Yes" or "No" - Press F9

is displayed and the program pauses to allow you to enter a yes or no response.

Using Preprinted Forms

If you are using WordPerfect's Merge feature to fill in preprinted forms or forms that you create with WordPerfect (see Chapter 19 for information on using the desktop publishing features to create your own forms), your primary file will contain only the appropriate Merge codes, much like the primary files for printing mailing labels or addressing envelopes. When you enter the Merge codes, either to insert a specific field from a secondary file or to pause the merge to allow you to enter information from the keyboard, their placement in the primary file is critical. If you enter the codes on the wrong line or beginning at the wrong horizontal position, the merged data will not properly "fill in the blanks" when you print the merged document.

To identify the correct position for each Merge code, measure the form's margins, the location of the lines containing blanks, and the position on each line where the code is to be placed. Be sure that you take into account WordPerfect's

```
                   ‾
                        B U S I N E S S   D A T A


            LEGAL NAME: ^F1^

               ADDRESS: ^F2^

                  CITY: ^F3^

                 STATE: ^F4^

              ZIP CODE: ^F5^

        TAX ID NUMBER: ^F6^

                   SSN: ^F7^

          INCORPORATED?: ^OEnter Yes or No - Press F9^O^C



    D:\WP\WDC\FORM1Ø99.PF                          Doc 1 Pg 1 Ln 11 Pos 1i
```

FIGURE 11.13: A simple form that is filled out by a combination of data from a secondary file and information typed from the keyboard. Notice that the last entry (where the operator designates whether or not the business is incorporated) contains not only a ^C code to temporarily pause the merge operation but also a prompt enclosed between a pair of ^O codes. This instruction on how to fill in the blank and proceed with the merge appears on the last line of the screen when the merge operation is paused.

default left, right, top, and bottom margin settings of 1 inch and change them if necessary in the primary document. You may also have to insert font changes to use a smaller size of a particular type style so that the responses fit within the pre-printed lines. Although it may take some experimentation to get all of these set-tings just right, once you have worked out the proper placement for each code, you will never have to change your settings unless the preprinted form is revised.

If you will be merging data from a field in a secondary merge file, be sure that none of the entries for that field contain more characters than will fit in the length of the blank where it will be merged. You will also need to be aware of the maxi-mum number of characters that you can enter for the size of font you are using when you are filling in the blank from the keyboard (remember, you will not see the blank form on your computer screen).

If you wish, you can enter a short message between a pair of ^O Merge codes for each blank, indicating the type of entry that is required from the keyboard. The ^O Merge codes enclosing your messages are placed immediately before the ^C codes that pause the merge operation.

If you are going to add message prompts, do not add them until after you have made sure that all of the ^C codes for each blank in your preprinted form are cor-rectly positioned. Then, make sure that WordPerfect is still in Insert mode, position the cursor beneath the caret of each ^C, and then enter the first **^O** (Shift-F9 O or Ctrl-O) followed by the text of your message and the final **^O** code. Do the same thing for each blank to which you wish to add a message. Adding message prompts will displace the ^C codes on your screen. However, when you run the merge, the messages between the ^O codes will appear only at the bottom of the screen, and the ^C codes will return to their correct placement.

Creating Reports

You may find it beneficial, from time to time, to obtain a complete report listing all of the records that you are maintaining in a secondary merge file. To do this, you first need to create a primary merge file that lists the fields in the order in which you want them to appear in printed form. Often, you will want to have all of the information in each record arranged on a single line of the report. In addition, you will probably want to include column headings that identify each item. After you have created this file, you simply run the merge, designating it as the primary file and selecting the requisite secondary file to be used.

For example, to obtain a report that lists all of the clients in the secondary file, you might set up the following primary file:

```
Company          Address          Contact
^F1^             ^F2 ^F3^         ^F4^ ^F5^ ^F6^
^N^P^P
```

When you do, you must make sure that your left and right margin settings are small enough to accommodate the entire record on a single line in the font you are using. In addition, you need to make sure that there is enough space between the groups of fields so that they can be accommodated. The ^N^P^P codes at the end of the file suppress a page break between each record. If you did not do this, the resulting merged document would have each record on its own page.

PERFORMING MORE COMPLEX MERGE OPERATIONS

WordPerfect includes other Merge codes that make it possible to accomplish much more complex operations than we have looked at thus far. In the upcoming sections, you will find information on performing merges that assemble the merged document from several different primary files, creating a secondary file through a merge operation, specifying macros to be executed when the merge operation terminates, and creating menu-driven merge operations.

Assembling Documents

You can use WordPerfect's Merge feature to automatically assemble documents whose parts are stored in their own separate files. This application is often useful when you construct form letters or legal documents made up of standard paragraphs that require only slight modification during the merge.

To have WordPerfect assemble a final document from several different primary files during a merge, you use a pair of ^P Merge codes enclosing the name of the primary file to be used. The ^P code is always paired, like the ^O code. Between the ^P codes, you enter the complete file name of the primary file to be used.

Figure 11.14 shows a primary merge file, named ASSEMBLE.PF, that constructs a merged document from three different primary files. The first file, called HEADING.PF, contains a Merge code (^D) that inserts the system date into the letter as well as several field codes that create the inside address and salutation from data in the client secondary merge file (used in the previous merge examples). Its contents are shown in Figure 11.15.

The second file, LTRBODY.PF, contains the bulk of the standard text for the letter. It also holds a ^C code that allows you to specify how long the special prices are in effect, as well as two field codes (^F4^ and ^F6^) that supply the personal title and last name of the person to whom the letter is addressed. The contents of this file are shown in Figure 11.16. The third file, CONCLUS.PF, contains two on-screen messages that prompt you to enter the name and business title of the salesperson sending the letter. Its contents are shown in Figure 11.17.

Notice in Figure 11.14 that ASSEMBLE.PF is itself listed between a matched pair of ^P codes at the bottom of the file after a hard page break (designated by the line of equal signs). Adding this page break and these ^P codes causes the

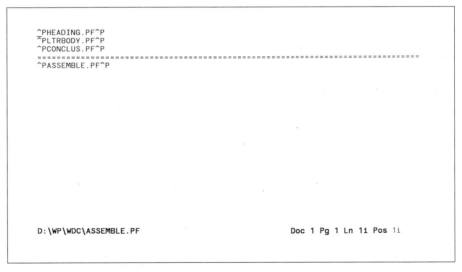

FIGURE 11.14: The ASSEMBLE.PF primary merge file creates merged letters by using the contents of three external primary merge files: HEADING.PF, LTRBODY.PF, and CONCLUS.PF. The ^P Merge codes that surround each of these file names instruct WordPerfect to bring their contents into the merge. In addition, as WordPerfect processes their contents, it will follow whatever Merge codes they contain. The hard page break (shown by the line of equal signs) and the ^PASSEMBLE.PF^P Merge codes chain the merge operation, causing it to repeat the document assembly until the operator terminates the merge (Shift-F9 E).

```
^D

^F4^ ^F5^ ^F6^
^F1?^
^F2^
^F3^

Dear ^F4^ ^F6^:
```

D:\WP\WDC\HEADING.PF   Doc 1 Pg 1 Ln 11 Pos 1i

FIGURE 11.15: The contents of the HEADING.PF primary merge file used in the document assembly. It creates a standard inside address and salutation using data from each record in the secondary file.

```
       Please take a moment out of your busy schedule to look over
the enclosed price list, which contains many exciting specials that
I can offer your firm only until ^C. As you will see, most of our
paper products are offered at prices well below retail (and some
are just pennies above wholesale cost!).

       In addition, if you order now, I will send you, ^F4^ ^F6^, a
free thank you gift. I look forward to serving your firm and hope
to take care of all of your paper product needs.
```

D:\WP\WDC\LTRBODY.PF   Doc 1 Pg 1 Ln 11 Pos 1i

FIGURE 11.16: The contents of the LTRBODY.PF primary merge file used in the document assembly. It contains a ^C Merge code to allow the operator to slightly alter the text of each letter generated, tailoring it to the company it is sent to. The ^F4^ and ^F6^ codes take the addressee's personal title and last name from the same record that is used to generate the inside address. The contents of the heading will be visible on the screen when the operator enters the date upon which the "exciting specials" will expire.

```
        Sincerely yours,


        ^OEnter name & press F9^O^C
        ^OEnter business title & press F9^O^C

        .encls




        D:\WP\WDC\CONCLUS.PF                    Doc 1 Pg 1 Ln 11 Pos 1i
```

FIGURE 11.17: The contents of the CONCLUS.PF primary merge file used in the document assembly. This primary file contains the Merge codes that not only pause the merge but also prompt the operator, instructing him or her to enter the salesperson's name and business title. These prompts will appear on the last line of the screen.

merge operation to loop continuously, allowing you to construct merged letters from these component files until WordPerfect reaches the end of the secondary merge file or until you press Shift-F9 and type **E** to terminate the merge. To perform this merge, you press Ctrl-F9, select the Merge option (**1** or **M**), then give **ASSEMBLE.PF** as the name of the primary file and **CLIENTS.SF** as the name of the secondary file.

SELECTING THE PRIMARY FILES TO BE USED

The document assembly performed in the preceding example does not vary. During the merge, WordPerfect always uses the same primary files. The only differences between the letters produced by this operation result from the various data variables taken from the records in the client secondary merge file and the individual responses that are entered from the keyboard.

However, you can easily make this type of merge more flexible by combining the ^O, ^P, and ^C Merge codes in a slightly new way. The purpose of combining them is to have WordPerfect prompt you during the merge for the names of the different primary files to be used. This makes the document assembly a dynamic process, allowing you to select from among a variety of prepared primary files that suit the particular document you are constructing.

You could use this technique to allow you to choose the appropriate text for each letter in the preceding example as it is being assembled during the merge. Instead of always using the text in the file LTRBODY.PF, as it does now, WordPerfect would allow you to designate the primary file (and therefore, the text) to be merged for the body of the letter.

Figure 11.18 shows how this is done. Notice that in place of the Merge codes ^PLTRBODY.PF^P in the third line, this line in the ASSEMBL1.PF primary file now contains

^U^OEnter name of letter file to use: ^P^C^P^O

The ^U code (for *Update*) writes the contents of the merged letter on the screen. This is done to show you to whom the letter is addressed, thus enabling you to make the appropriate decision as to which primary file should be used (that is, which type of letter the addressee should be sent).

After the ^U code, notice that an on-screen message prompt is introduced with the use of the ^O code. When the merge is run, the prompt without the ^O codes will appear as

Enter name of letter file to use:

at the bottom of the screen.

```
^N
^PHEADING.PF^P
^U^OEnter name of letter file to use: ^P^C^P^O
^PCONCLUS.PF^P
================================================================================
^PASSEMBL1.PF^P




D:\WP\WDC\ASSEMBL1.PF                          Doc 1 Pg 1 Ln 11 Pos 1i
```

FIGURE 11.18: Creating a more flexible document assembly. This figure shows essentially the same Merge codes as Figure 11.14, with one significant difference. During this document assembly, the operator will be prompted to enter the name of the primary file to be used for the body of the letter. This allows him or her to choose from various "boilerplates" that contain slightly different versions. The ^U Merge code writes the contents of the heading on the screen while the ^C code pauses the merge to allow the operator to enter the name of the primary file to be used. WordPerfect takes the entry as the name of the primary file because the ^C is between a pair of ^P codes.

However, notice that the pair of ^O codes encloses not only this prompt but also a pair of ^P codes which themselves enclose a ^C code. The ^C code pauses the merge operation to allow you to respond to the prompt that is still displayed on the screen. (This is why the ^P^C^P codes come before the final ^O code.) The response that you enter is interpreted by WordPerfect as being the name of a primary merge file because it is enclosed in a pair of ^P codes.

When you initiate the merge using this version of the ASSEMBL1.PF file, WordPerfect generates the heading of the letter from the HEADING.PF file and then displays the inside address and salutation on the screen. It then pauses and prompts you for the name of the primary file to use in generating the body of the letter (shown in Figure 11.19). After you enter the name of the appropriate primary merge file (assuming that you have prepared several alternative primary files) and press F9, WordPerfect uses the CONCLUS.PF file to generate the conclusion of the letter. After you enter the correct signature name from the keyboard and press F9 again, WordPerfect repeats the entire process for a new letter. This continues until either all of the records in the secondary merge file are used or you press Shift-F9 E.

> *Note:* You can adapt this technique easily to other applications, from assembling contracts to preparing examinations, making them as complex as you need to. Although this example was purposely kept simple and therefore employs only one prompt for the correct primary file to be used, you can add as many of these prompts as required to assemble the final document.

SELECTING THE SECONDARY FILES TO BE USED

The preceding examples have all assumed that you only need to use a single secondary merge file during the entire merge operation. This may not always be the case. To change the secondary file, you use a pair of ^S Merge codes. These work just like the ^P codes, only here you enter the name of the secondary merge file to be used.

When you use the ^S Merge codes to switch to a new secondary file (different from the one you name when you initiate the merge operation with Ctrl-F9 M), you should place them before any field codes (^F*n*^ where *n* is the field number) in the primary file that will take data from this new secondary file.

In addition to entering the name of the secondary file to be used, you can have WordPerfect prompt the operator for the name of the secondary file by adapting the technique introduced in the preceding section. You just use ^S codes instead of ^P codes. For example, you could enter

```
^U^OEnter name of secondary file to use: ^S^C^S^O
```

```
May 30, 1988

Mr. Allan Grill
221 Avenue of the Americas
Suite 210
New York, NY 10010

Dear Mr. Grill:

^OEnter name of letter file to use: ^P^C^P^O
^PCONCLUS.PF^P
=========================================================================
^PASSEMBL1.PF^P




    Enter name of letter file to use: ADLTR2.PF_
```

FIGURE 11.19: The flexible document assembly merge in progress. Here, the contents of the heading primary file have been written to the screen and the prompt to enter the name of the primary file to be used in generating the body of the letter can be seen. In this case, the primary file ADLTR2.PF has been entered by the operator. As soon as he or she presses F9, WordPerfect will insert the text of this primary file into the body of the letter, and the merge operation will continue. Just as before, the merge will repeat for each record in the secondary file. However, each time a new letter is being created, the operator will have to name the primary file that is to generate the body of the letter.

to have the merge paused and the on-screen message

Enter name of secondary file to use:

displayed. During this pause you can designate the new secondary merge file to be used as soon as you press F9 to continue the merge operation.

Creating a Secondary File Through a Merge

You can use WordPerfect's Merge feature to help you build your secondary files. By combining the ^O and ^C Merge codes with a new code, ^V, you can essentially automate the procedure of adding records to any of your secondary merge files. The ^V Merge code (for *Insert* because Ctrl-V toggles Insert mode on and off in many programs) is used to insert Merge codes into the file you are creating.

Figure 11.20 illustrates this technique, here applied to adding records for the original client secondary merge file (see Figure 11.1). Notice the general pattern used to prompt you as to the kind of data you should enter for each field in the record:

^O<*message*>^O^C^V^R^V

You are already familiar with the ^O and ^C Merge codes. These merely display the message between the ^O codes at the bottom of the screen and pause the merge to allow you to enter the required text.

A pair of ^V codes surrounding an ^R code has been added to the ^O and ^C codes. As soon as you enter the text and press F9 to continue the merge, the ^V codes insert the ^R at the end of your entry. In effect, this automates the process of terminating each field entry with the ^R Merge code (entered by pressing F9 when you add records to a secondary merge file manually).

To use this primary merge file to create the client secondary file, you simply press Ctrl-F9 and type **M** to start the merge. When prompted for the name of the primary file to use, you would enter **CLIENT.INP** (the file name given to this sample file—the .INP extension marks this as an input file). When you are prompted for the name of the secondary file to use, you just press the Enter key to bypass the prompt.

As soon as this file is loaded, you will see the prompt

Enter the company name

without the ^O codes on the last line of the screen. Only the ^V^R^V codes remain on the first line of the file. As soon as you enter the name of the company

```
    ^OEnter the company name^O^C^V^R^V
    ^OEnter the street address^O^C^V^R^V
    ^OEnter the city, state (as CA) & Zip^O^C^V^R^V
    ^OEnter Mr., Ms., or Mrs.^O^C^V^R^V
    ^OEnter first name^O^C^V^R^V
    ^OEnter last name^O^C^V^R^V
    ^V^E^V
    =========================================================================
    ^OShift-F9 E if done - F9 for next rec^O^C^PCLIENT.INP^P



    D:\WP\WDC\CLIENT.INP                          Doc 1 Pg 1 Ln 11 Pos 1i
```

FIGURE 11.20: Using a merge with on-screen prompts to build a secondary merge file. This file is named CLIENT.INP. The .INP extension marks it as a special primary file that facilitates the inputting of data into the client secondary merge file. The ^V Merge code seen here inserts the Merge codes (either ^R or ^E) into the document as soon as F9 is pressed to continue the merge. Notice that the operator is prompted when entering data for each field in the record. The ^PCLIENT.INP^P in the last line causes the entire merge operation to repeat until the operator presses Shift-F9 and types **E**, thus allowing the entry of multiple records without having to run a macro or reexecute the merge.

and press F9, WordPerfect inserts the ^R code immediately after your entry and displays the prompt for the street address, pausing to allow you to make this entry on the second line of the file.

This process of prompting you, pausing, and inserting the ^R code continues until WordPerfect reaches the line containing

^V^E^V^
==

The ^V codes insert the ^E (Merge End) code that marks the end of the record in the secondary file. The on-screen prompt is then displayed on the bottom of the status line as

Shift-F9 E if done - F9 for next rec

(shown in Figure 11.21) when WordPerfect executes the

^OShift-F9 E if done - F9 for next rec^O^C

codes. If you press F9, the ^PCLIENT.INP^P codes on the line below start the merge process all over again. If you press Shift-F9 and type **E**, the merge is terminated.

```
        Signet Products, Inc.^R
        4562 14th Avenue^R
        San Francisco, CA 94110^R
        Ms.^R
        Marjorie^R
        McPherson^R
        ^E
        ============================================================================
        ^PCLIENT.INP^P




















        Shift-F9 E if done - F9 for next rec              Doc 1 Pg 2 Ln 11 Pos 1i
```

FIGURE 11.21: Finishing the first record in the merge that adds records to a secondary file. In this figure, the operator has responded to all of the prompts for entering specific field data. In addition, the ^V^E^V Merge codes have entered the ^E code in the file. Currently, the prompt indicating how to exit or add another record is displayed at the bottom of the screen. If the operator presses F9, the ^PCLIENT.INP^P codes repeat the merge. If he or she presses Shift-F9 and types **E**, the merge terminates and these codes are ignored. However, the operator would have to erase them before appending the record to the secondary file.

After you terminate the merge, all that is required is for you to erase the ^PCLIENT.INP^P in the last line and append the records you have created to the secondary file (CLIENT.SF in this case). To do this, you first mark the new records as a block by positioning the cursor at the beginning of the file (Home Home ↑) and then pressing Alt-F4 and Home Home ↓. Then press Ctrl-F4 (Move), select the Block option (**1** or **B**) followed by the Append option (**4** or **A**), and enter **CLIENT.SF**, the name of the secondary merge file. These steps can be accomplished by using a macro. See the following section for details.

Macros in Merges

You can have a macro executed upon the termination of any merge operation. To do this, you enclose the name of the macro within a pair of ^G Merge codes (for *Go To Macro*). When entering the macro name between the pair of ^G codes, you enter its file name exactly as it appears in the macro directory listing, but omitting the file extension .WPM. For example, if your macro were named ALTL.WPM (executed manually by pressing Alt-L), you would enter it as **^GALTL^G** in the merge file. If your macro were named SORT.WPM (executed manually by pressing Alt-F10, typing **SORT**, and pressing the Enter key), you would enter it as **^GSORT^G**.

It is important to understand that, regardless of where these ^G codes are placed in the primary merge file, the macro they contain will not be executed until the merge operation is terminated. In other words, there is no way to have WordPerfect execute the macro at the onset of the merge or during the merge operation. Also, you can only call for the execution of a single macro at the completion of a merge (although the macro can itself call other macros—see Chapter 16 for more information on chaining macros).

In some primary merge files, the placement of the macro enclosed in ^G Merge codes within the file is crucial. For example, if your primary file assembles documents or loops continuously by using a pair of ^P codes (surrounding the file name of a new primary file or without a file name if it uses the same primary file), you will want to place the Go To Macro statement before the pair of ^P codes. That way, WordPerfect will read the Go To Macro statement before it uses the new primary file (or files). Although the macro will not be executed until the merge called for in the new primary file is completed, because WordPerfect reads (and remembers) the Go To Macro statement before it reads and executes the ^P Merge codes, the macro will not be overlooked.

Figure 11.22 shows the primary merge file, introduced in the previous discussion, that facilitates the addition of records to the client secondary merge file, this time with a Go To Macro statement. The ^GAPPEND^G, added immediately after the hard page break entered by the ^E code, executes the macro named APPEND whenever the user terminates the merge by pressing Shift-F9 and typing **E**. Notice that the pair of ^G codes surrounding this macro name is placed before the ^PCLIENT.INP^P codes on the last line. This ensures that the macro will be read before the merge repeats. If the ^G codes were placed after the pair of ^P codes, the APPEND macro would never be executed.

When you terminate the merge, signaling that you do not want to add any more records to the secondary file, the macro APPEND is executed. Figure 11.23 shows the keystrokes of the macro in the Macro Editor. As you can see, the macro first turns off the display and then deletes the ^PCLIENT.INP^P Merge codes on the last line ({Del to EOL}). Then it moves the cursor to the beginning of the file ({Home}{Home}{Up}), turns on the Block feature ({Block} or Alt-F4), and highlights all of the text to the end of the document ({Home}{Home}{Down}{Left}). Finally, it accesses the Move menu ({Move} or Ctrl-F4), selects the Block option (b) followed by the Append option (a), inserts the name of the file to be appended to as CLIENT.SF, and presses the Enter key ({Enter}) to perform the append operation. In effect, this macro performs all of the cleanup tasks that you would normally do by either executing such a macro or manually performing these keystrokes once you had run this merge.

```
^OEnter the company name^O^C^V^R^V
^OEnter the street address^O^C^V^R^V
^OEnter the city, state (as CA) & Zip^O^C^V^R^V
^OEnter Mr., Ms., or Mrs.^O^C^V^R^V
^OEnter first name^O^C^V^R^V
^OEnter last name^O^C^V^R^V
^V^E^V
================================================================================
^GAPPEND^G^OShift-F9 E if done - F9 for next rec^O^C^PCLIENT.INP^P



             D:\WP\WDC\CLIENT.INP                        Doc 1 Pg 1 Ln 11 Pos 1i
```

FIGURE 11.22: Adding a macro to be executed upon the termination of a merge that adds records to the client secondary merge file. This macro, APPEND, is only executed when the operator presses Shift-F9 and types **E** to terminate the merge. The macro then deletes the ^PCLIENT.INP^P Merge codes, blocks the records that have been created, and appends them to the client secondary merge file. Notice the placement of the ^GAPPEND^G codes. They are placed before the on-screen message codes or those that repeat the merge to ensure that the macro is not ignored.

```
Macro: Edit

        File            APPEND.WPM

  1 - Description     Append records to CLIENT.SF

  2 - Action

    ┌─────────────────────────────────────────────────────────────┐
    │ {DISPLAY OFF}{Del to EOL}{Home}{Home}{Up}{Block}{Home}{Home}{Down}│
    │ {Left}{Move}baclients.sf{Enter}                               │
    │                                                               │
    │                                                               │
    │                                                               │
    │                                                               │
    │                                                               │
    └─────────────────────────────────────────────────────────────┘

     Selection: 0
```

FIGURE 11.23: The contents of the APPEND macro as displayed in the Macro Editor. This macro does the necessary cleanup after the operator inputs all of the new records and then appends these records to the CLIENT.SF file.

Creating Menus

You can also run your merge operations from menus that you create by a skillful combining of the ^O, ^C, and ^G Merge codes. When you create a menu for a merge application, you display the entire menu, including all of its options, on the screen by placing it between a pair of ^O codes. Within the ^O codes, you place the ^G codes. Within the pair of ^G codes, you enter the first part of the macro name followed by a ^C code.

The simplest menu to create uses number options from which you select. The number chosen then determines which macro is executed. To have this work, you name all of the macros associated with the menu the same except for the last character, which is a number. The macro name will be fed in automatically as part of the merge, and the number added to the macro name corresponds to that of the menu option it runs.

Figure 11.24 shows you an example of this type of menu. Here you see a simple menu with five options that execute the most common tasks associated with performing various merge operations using the client secondary file. Notice that the entire menu, including the title, numbered options, and prompt, is enclosed within the ^O Merge codes. If you center your menu options on the screen as was done in this example, you must use spaces instead of tab stops. You can always use the repeat function of the Esc key, as in pressing Esc, typing **25**, and pressing the space bar, to help you make these indentations. Also, you can't use any of the text attributes like boldface or underlining to enhance the menu text.

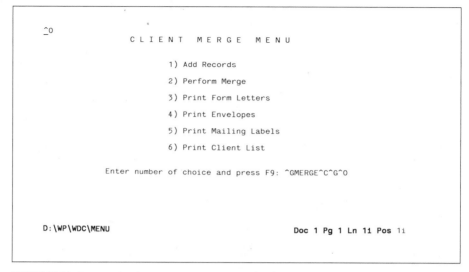

```
^O
                    C L I E N T   M E R G E   M E N U

                        1)  Add Records

                        2)  Perform Merge

                        3)  Print Form Letters

                        4)  Print Envelopes

                        5)  Print Mailing Labels

                        6)  Print Client List

          Enter number of choice and press F9:  ^GMERGE^C^G^O




   D:\WP\WDC\MENU                                    Doc 1 Pg 1 Ln 11 Pos 1i
```

FIGURE 11.24: Creating the client merge menu. Notice that the entire menu, including the title, the options, and the prompt, is enclosed in ^O Merge codes. In addition, the ^GMERGE^C^G codes are placed before the final ^O code. When the menu merge is executed, this puts the first part of the macro name (MERGE) with the cursor immediately after it on the last line of the screen with the rest of the prompt (see Figure 11.25).

Immediately before the second ^O code, you can see the ^G Merge codes surrounding the macro name, MERGE, followed by a ^C code. This pauses the merge to allow you to enter the number of the option you wish to use. Figure 11.25 shows you how the menu appears when the merge operation containing the menu Merge codes is run. When you select a number and press F9, the number is appended to MERGE. For example, if you type **1** to choose the option *Add records,* the macro named MERGE1 is executed. If you type **2** to select the *Perform merge* option, the macro named MERGE2 is executed, and so on.

Each macro created for this menu begins a different merge operation. For example, MERGE1, executed by selecting option **1**, *Add records,* contains the keystrokes

{DISPLAY OFF} {Merge/Sort} mCLIENT. INP{Enter} {Enter}

which initiate the merge, enter CLIENT.INP as the primary file to be used, and bypass the prompt for the name of the secondary file. At that point, the MERGE1 macro terminates and the merge operation controlled by the Merge codes in CLIENT.INP takes over. Remember, this is the merge that prompts you as you add new records to the client secondary file. (To review the functioning of the CLIENT.INP primary file, refer back to the discussion and figures in "Creating a Secondary File Through a Merge.")

```
C L I E N T   M E R G E   M E N U


            1) Add Records

            2) Perform Merge

            3) Print Form Letters

            4) Print Envelopes

            5) Print Mailing Labels

            6) Print Client List


    Enter number of choice and press F9: MERGE_
```

FIGURE 11.25: The client merge menu as it appears on the screen during execution. Notice that the cursor is located immediately following the macro name, MERGE. When the operator enters the number of the option he or she wishes to use, it is appended to the macro name. When the operator then presses F9 to continue, WordPerfect executes that macro, which in turn initiates the appropriate merge operation. (See the accompanying text for details on how these macros work.)

If you choose the second option, *Perform merge,* the MERGE2 macro is executed. This macro contains the keystrokes

{DISPLAY OFF} {Merge/Sort} mASSEMBL1.PF{Enter} {Enter}

which start the merge operation, and then enter ASSEMBL1.PF as the primary file and bypass the secondary file to be used. At that point, the MERGE2 macro terminates and the merge operation controlled by the Merge codes in ASSEMBL1.PF takes over. Remember that the merge operation in the ASSEMBL1.PF file allows you to choose from among various primary merge files that are used to tailor the letter to the particular addressee retrieved from the client secondary file. (To review the functioning of the ASSEMBL1.PF merge, refer back to the discussion and figures in "Assembling Documents.")

In a similar manner, the macros for options **3, 4, 5,** and **6** (named MERGE3, MERGE4, MERGE5, and MERGE6 respectively) initiate specific merge-print operations. The macro MERGE3, executed when you choose option **3,** initiates a merge using a primary file that sends each of the merged letters to the printer (using the ^T^N^P^P Merge codes—refer back to "Merging Directly to the Printer" to review their use).

The macro MERGE4, executed when you choose option **4,** begins a merge operation using another merge file. This merge file contains the codes to create addresses from the client data using ENVELOPE.PF and CLIENT.SF and then send them to the printer. The ENVELOPE.PF file contains the correct left, right, top, and bottom margin settings and selects the Envelope paper size and type. The macros MERGE5 and MERGE6 are very similar to each other except that each uses a primary file with the appropriate field codes and format settings to print either addresses on mailing labels or a standard report listing all of the clients in the secondary file.

If you wish to have your menu redisplayed after you use one of its options, you merely create a macro that starts the merge and then insert the ^G Merge codes to have that macro executed when the particular merge operation terminates. For example, the menu shown in Figure 11.25 can be activated by executing an Alt-M macro containing the following commands:

{DISPLAY OFF}{Merge/Sort}mMENU{Enter}{Enter}

This macro, similar to those that execute its various menu options, simply initiates the merge operation, supplies the name of the primary file containing the menu (MENU in this case), bypasses the prompt for a secondary file, and then terminates.

To have the merge menu activated, you simply add the following statement to the merge file that runs a particular menu option:

^GALTM^G

You must make sure that this pair of ^G Merge codes is placed in the primary merge file so that WordPerfect reads this statement before it executes any codes that initiate the use of new primary or secondary files (refer back to "Macros in Merges" for details).

Not all of the menus that you create will have options that are executed by macros enclosed in ^G Merge codes. In fact, you may create some menus in which it makes more sense to have each menu option execute a merge operation, using a specific primary or secondary file. In such cases, you nest a pair of ^P or ^S codes that contain the ^C pause within the ^O codes that display the menu structure and list its options. For example, you could place the statement

^PMERGE^C^P

before the final ^O code. In this case, the menu option number you select completes the name of the primary file that is executed. This merge file could itself contain the appropriate Go To Macro codes that reactivate the menu or activate a new menu containing various suboptions.

By transferring control in this way, from macro to merge file and back to macro, you can create sophisticated menu systems that include as many levels and suboptions as you find necessary.

WordPerfect's new macro command language greatly expands your possibilities in creating menu-driven merge applications. For information on how to use the macro command language to control your merge operations, see Chapter 16, "Creating and Using Macros." For further ideas on how to create menu-driven merge applications using macro commands, see *WordPerfect Tips and Tricks,* Third Edition, by Alan R. Neibauer, SYBEX, 1988.

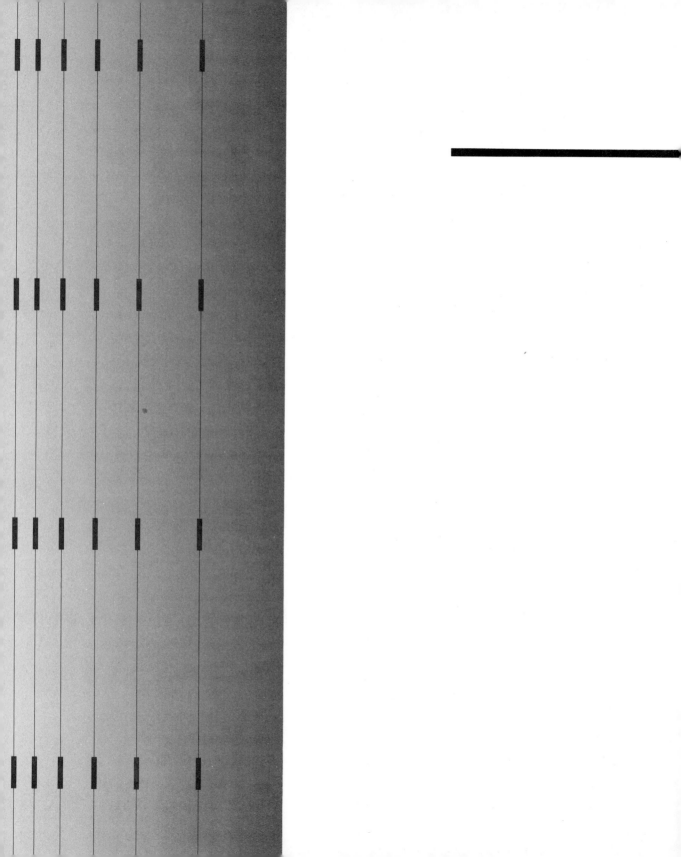

SORTING TEXT

SORTING TEXT

ou can use WordPerfect's Sort feature to order text or numbers in tables, to reorder paragraphs throughout the document, or to sort records in your secondary files, by selecting among these three kinds of sorts:

- The *line sort,* which is performed on data organized into tables.
- The *paragraph sort,* which is performed on text separated by at least two hard returns or a hard page break.
- The *merge sort,* which is performed on records in a secondary merge file.

If your work involves regular use of mail merge, you will find the merge sort invaluable. In addition to making it possible to order the records in the secondary file in the way you want the letters and mailing labels produced (such as in order by zip code), it also allows you to select just those records that you want to use (such as only those addresses where the state is Ohio). For more information on mail merges with WordPerfect, see Chapter 11, "Performing Merge Operations."

UPGRADE NOTES

The Sort feature in WordPerfect 5.0 has not changed, except that you can select a particular option from the Sort menu by typing either the option number or the menu letter—a universal change in this version. Regardless of how you select them, these options function as they did in version 4.2.

PRINCIPLES OF SORTING

Before you begin using WordPerfect's Sort feature, you will want to be familiar with the terms that it uses. Without a background in data processing, you may find the Sort menu a little daunting at first. However, once you grasp the underlying principles and gain a little experience performing various kinds of sorts, you will find sorting a quite straightforward process.

Sort Keys

The fundamental element in sorting is the *key.* In a line sort, the key is the data item in the column (or field) that determines the new order for all of the data that is sorted. Suppose that you have just entered the following list of names:

Elizabeth Mundel
Allan Grill
Jay Schnyder
Susan Kelly
Shane Gearing
Judy Ziajka
Susan Nurse
David Kolodney

and you now want to arrange them alphabetically by last name. Your list contains a single field for each person, consisting of two words: the first and last name. Either name in the list can be used as a sorting key. To have WordPerfect sort this list for you by last name, you would designate the second word of the field, the last name, as the sorting key. Using the last name as the key would sort the list as follows:

Shane Gearing
Allan Grill
Susan Kelly
David Kolodney
Elizabeth Mundel
Susan Nurse
Jay Schnyder
Judy Ziajka

However, if you change the key to the first word, consisting of the first name, the sort produces this list:

Allan Grill
David Kolodney
Elizabeth Mundel
Jay Schnyder
Judy Ziajka
Shane Gearing
Susan Nurse
Susan Kelly

When you sort, you may need to use more than one key. In the preceding example, all of the last names in the list are unique. However, not all of the first names in the list are unique, as there are two *Susan*s in the list. Notice that the final order in which the two *Susan*s appear is not completely alphabetical (with *Nurse* listed before *Kelly*) when WordPerfect sorts the list using just the first name as the key.

If you want to make sure that the list is arranged in a completely alphabetical order regarding both the first and last names, you have to sort the list again. You will still use the first word of the first field as the first (or primary) key and, in addition, you will designate the second word of the first field (the last name) as the second (or secondary) key. When the list is sorted using two keys, the placement of the duplicates in the primary field (the *Susans*) will be determined by the ordering of the secondary key (the last name) so that *Susan Kelly* precedes *Susan Nurse*.

WordPerfect allows you to use up to nine different keys in sorting. Very seldom, if ever, do you need to use all nine keys in order to have all of the duplicates in a list arranged the way you want. However, there are many situations that require the use of multiple keys.

For instance, suppose that you have a table listing the employees and their supervisors for all of the departments in a company, and that currently it is arranged in no particular order. If you want to arrange the table alphabetically, first by department, then by supervisor, and finally by the employee's last name, you have to use at least three, and possibly four, sort keys.

First, you can designate the word in the column containing the department as the primary key. To order the employees within each department, you would designate the key column containing the supervisor's last name as the secondary key. Again, there are bound to be many employees who have the same supervisor. To order the employees who have the same supervisor, you would define the word in the column holding the last name as the third key. Finally, if some of the employees have the same last name (as with common last names like Smith and Jones), you would have to define the word in the column containing first names as the fourth key.

When you sort data in WordPerfect, you will have to make these types of determinations in all but a few cases. Only when you know the data that you want the list sorted on contains no duplicates (as when you sort by social security number or account number) can you be sure that using just one key will result in the desired arrangement.

Ascending Versus Descending Order

Another important principle in sorting is the *order*. There are two basic orders: ascending (from lowest to highest) and descending (from highest to lowest). When you sort data in ascending order, WordPerfect follows a sequence in which punctuation and special symbols (like @, #, and $) precede numbers (arranged from lowest to highest), which in turn precede letters (arranged in alphabetical or A–Z order). When you sort data in descending order, this sequence is reversed. Letters (arranged in Z–A order) precede numbers (arranged from highest to lowest), which in turn precede punctuation and symbols.

Ascending order is the default for any sort in WordPerfect; you can change it to descending. WordPerfect uses whatever order you select in all subsequent sort operations performed during your work session until you change it.

Alphanumeric Versus Numeric Sorting Keys

WordPerfect supports two different types of sorting keys: *alphanumeric* and *numeric*. The default is alphanumeric. An alphanumeric key can consist of any type of character (letters, numbers, and symbols). However, when you use the alphanumeric key and the data consists of numbers, all of the numbers must be of the same length to be sorted correctly. Because numbers like zip codes and social security numbers are always of equal length, you can sort them using the alphanumeric key.

If the data you want sorted consists of numbers of unequal length, you need to designate the key to be a numeric key. The data in a numeric key can contain dollar signs, commas, and periods, as is often the case in a column of financial figures. Be aware, however, that WordPerfect will ignore any letters in a numeric key when performing a sort or selection operation. Therefore, you want to make sure that any key containing both text and numbers is designated as an alphanumeric key and not as a numeric key.

When you sort a numeric key in ascending order, WordPerfect arranges its data in a strict lowest-to-highest progression. This means that any negative values (prefaced by a minus sign) would come before positive values, however small. When you sort a numeric key in descending order, just the opposite is true, as WordPerfect arranges its data in a strict highest-to-lowest sequence.

THE LINE SORT

The line sort is used when your data is arranged in a tabular format consisting of columns and rows. Each field is placed in its own column of the table, separated by at least one tab setting (either a Tab or an Indent). Each row thus contains a complete record, divided by tabs into fields. Any word in any field in the table can be used as a sorting key. However, in order for this to work, each field must always contain the same type of information. For example, recall the sort-by-department example mentioned earlier. It can be sorted correctly if all employee records list the department first and the supervisor second, but not if any single record lists the fields in a different order from the rest. You can also use the line sort when you have only a single column of items that are all aligned with the left margin.

When laying out a table that consists of multiple columns of data, you must make sure that the number of tab settings between the columns in the table and the number of spaces between words in each column remain constant. To make it easy to create the table, you should clear the tabs and set only those tabs required to reach each column. When doing this, make sure that these tab stops are spaced far enough apart to accommodate all of the entries in any one column.

Figure 12.1 shows a vacation accrual table containing seven different fields, from the employee's identification number in the first column to the number of vacation days in the seventh column. Each field is separated by a single tab setting. All of the columns except for that of the vacation days field are created with left-aligned tabs separated by the [TAB] format code. The last field uses a decimal tab, which separates it from the previous field with the [Align] and [C/A/Flrt] codes.

To sort the information in this table, you use WordPerfect's line sort. If you want to arrange it alphabetically by the employee's name, you designate the second field, that of the last name, as the primary key. Notice, however, that there are three people whose last name is Smith. To order these duplicates, you also define a secondary key, the third field (or column), containing the first name.

To do this, you press Ctrl-F9 (Merge/Sort) and select the Sort option (**2** or **S**) from the following menu:

1 Merge; **2 S**ort; **3 S**ort **O**rder: 0

When you do, you see the prompt

Input file to sort: (Screen)

```
     1004    Nelson       Steven   F.   11   06-02-84   14.3
     1324    Carrington   Neil     T.   10   03-02-86    7.1
     1073    Smith        Thomas   A.   12   10-03-83   14.3
     1289    Tudor        Carol    M.   10   12-03-84   17.8
     1233    McGill       David    P.   10   01-04-84   16.8
     1323    Wadsworth    Sharon   G.   12   01-04-86    7.1
     1415    Watson       Sean     A.   10   07-05-85   14.3
     1325    Smith        Mary     A.   11   03-05-86    7.1
      233    Smith        Sandra   B.   12   02-16-80   31.4
      788    Kaye         Peter    A.   11   05-16-82   29.4
     1066    Olsen        Phyllis  G.   12   04-17-83   26.4
     1059    Allen        Holly    M.   11   03-18-83   23.4
     1407    Farner       Kenneth  E.   12   04-20-85   14.3
      534    Drew         Mary     J.   10   03-24-81   26.4




     D:\WP\WDC\VACATION                          Doc 1 Pg 1 Ln 1" Pos 1"
```

FIGURE 12.1: The vacation accrual table before line sorting. When performing a line sort, you must arrange each of the fields in columns separated by the same number of tabs or indents. In this table, each column except the last is separated by a single left-aligned tab. Notice that each column contains the same type of information. During sorting, the rows (records) will be reordered according to the key that is defined.

If you just press the Enter key without typing a file name, WordPerfect will apply the sort you are about to define to all of the data in the document in the current document window (editing screen). If you want to sort a file that is on disk and not currently in the document window, you type its complete file name over the default of *(Screen)*. Most of the time, you will want to retrieve the document that contains the data you want to sort before you begin the sort operation, and, therefore, will accept the Screen default by simply pressing the Enter key.

> *Note:* You will always want to make sure that you have saved the document in memory before you sort its information using the Screen default for the input file. That way, if you make a mistake when defining the sorting parameters, you will still have a copy of the information in its original order.

When you press the Enter key, you receive a similar prompt for the name of a new file to which the sorted data should be output:

Output file for sort: (Screen)

Again, WordPerfect defaults to the screen. If you do not wish to save the sorted data in a new disk file, you simply press the Enter key. If you want the sorted file to be saved, type in a new file name over the Screen default.

Often, you will want to accept the Screen default here, too. That way, you can view the results of the sort and make sure that the information is arranged exactly as you want it before you decide to save the file. If you find that you mistakenly used a key or did not define enough keys to obtain the desired sort, you could then abandon the file in memory (F7 N N), retrieve the original file, and redefine the sort operation.

After you press the Enter key, WordPerfect will automatically split the editing window display. In the lower window, it will display the Sort by Line screen, which is the default (shown in Figure 12.2). At the bottom of this screen, you will see the Sort menu options displayed as follows:

1 Perform Action; **2** View; **3** Keys; **4** Select; **5** Action; **6** Order; **7** Type: 0

WordPerfect supports three types of sorts: line, paragraph, and merge. It always tells you the type of sort it will perform in two places in the lower window. You will see the type of sort listed immediately below the ruler line that divides the windows, centered between a line of hyphens, and you will also see it listed under the heading *Type* on the right side of the screen above the Sort menu options.

Although the line sort is the default type of sort, WordPerfect retains any change made to this setting during the current work session. Therefore, you should make it a practice to always check these areas to make sure that the program is set to perform the kind of sort you want. If it is not, you select the Type option (**7** or **T**) and select the correct option from among these choices:

Type: **1** Merge; **2** Line; **3** Paragraph: 0

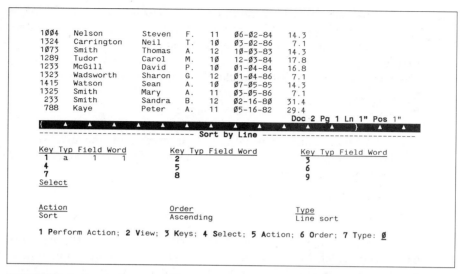

```
1004    Nelson      Steven  F.  11  06-02-84  14.3
1324    Carrington  Neil    T.  10  03-02-86   7.1
1073    Smith       Thomas  A.  12  10-03-83  14.3
1289    Tudor       Carol   M.  10  12-03-84  17.8
1233    McGill      David   P.  10  01-04-84  16.8
1323    Wadsworth   Sharon  G.  12  01-04-86   7.1
1415    Watson      Sean    A.  10  07-05-85  14.3
1325    Smith       Mary    A.  11  03-05-86   7.1
 233    Smith       Sandra  B.  12  02-16-80  31.4
 788    Kaye        Peter   A.  11  05-16-82  29.4
                                    Doc 2 Pg 1 Ln 1" Pos 1"
```

```
( ▲    ▲    ▲    ▲    ▲    ▲    ▲    ▲   ▲  ▲    } ▲    ▲
--------------------------------- Sort by Line ---------------------------------

Key Typ Field Word          Key Typ Field Word          Key Typ Field Word
 1   a    1     1             2                           3
 4                            5                           6
 7                            8                           9
Select


Action                      Order                       Type
Sort                        Ascending                   Line sort

 1 Perform Action; 2 View; 3 Keys; 4 Select; 5 Action; 6 Order; 7 Type: 0
```

FIGURE 12.2: Starting the line sort of the vacation accrual table. When you define a sorting operation, WordPerfect splits the editing screen into two windows as shown. The default is Sort by Line. The program also provides default settings for the first key. To change these, or to define other keys to be used, you select the Keys option (**3** or **K**) from the Sort menu. Notice that, below the keys, the Sort by Line screen displays the action, order, and type of sort. You can change any of these defaults by choosing the appropriate Sort menu options.

Notice in Figure 12.2 that WordPerfect has already entered default values for the first key while leaving all of the other eight keys blank. The information for the first key appears as follows:

Key	Typ	Field	Word
1	a	1	1

The heading *Typ* stands for *Type*. It currently contains an *a,* indicating an alphanumeric sort. When you redefine these values for this key, or add new keys, you can also indicate numeric sorts by entering an **n** instead of an **a** in this column.

The next two columns for the first key both contain the number *1.* When you define a line sort, you can indicate not only the number of the field (column) to be used as the key, but also the number of the word in that field.

Fields and words are numbered sequentially from left to right across the line. For example, in Figure 12.1, the column containing the employees' identification numbers is field 1, while the one containing their last names is field 2, and so on.

None of the fields in the vacation accrual table have more than one word as WordPerfect counts them. In order for WordPerfect to consider an item a single word in a field, it must be separated from others in the same field by spaces. If the field entries contain individual elements separated by punctuation, like commas or hyphens, WordPerfect does not consider them to contain separate words.

For instance, although the date-hired field is made up of three elements (month, day, and year), because they are separated by hyphens and not spaces, the elements cannot be counted as individual words. You cannot use the Word setting to put the table in order by the year hired (in field 6) unless you replace the hyphens with spaces. For example, if the dates hired were entered as

06 02 84
03 02 86

and so on, you could sort the table by year hired, using the third word (the digits of the year) of the sixth field as the sorting key. This key would be designated in the Sort by Line screen as

Key	Typ	Field	Word
1	a	6	3

In fact, if the date were entered with spaces, you could easily arrange this table by the entire date hired (month, day, and year). To do this would require the use of three keys, each using field 6 with a different word. The keys for this sort would appear as follows in the Sort by Line screen:

Key	Typ	Field	Word	Key	Typ	Field	Word	Key	Typ	Field	Word
1	a	6	3	2	a	6	1	3	a	6	2

Key 1 sorts the table by the digits for the year hired (word 3). Key 2 sorts those records that share the same year by the month (word 1). Finally, key 3 sorts by day those records which share both the same year and month.

> *Note:* Even though the dates in field 6 are entered entirely with numbers, the type of sort does not have to be changed from *a* (alphanumeric) to *n* (numeric) to have WordPerfect sort correctly, because the numbers are of equal length. Do not forget that *a* stands for *alphanumeric* and not for *ascending order.*

When the fields in your table have only one word, as they do in the vacation accrual table, you need not change the default of 1 for Word. However, to have WordPerfect sort the vacation accrual table in alphabetical order by employee name, you do have to change the number of the field for key 1 and add the information for key 2.

To do this, you select the Keys option (**3** or **K**) from the Sort menu. When you do, WordPerfect places the cursor under the Typ column for key 1. You can press either the Enter key or → to move to the next key column. If you need to move to a previous key column, you press the ← key. If you have defined keys in the rows below, you can use the ↑ and ↓ keys to move the cursor back and forth between keys on different lines.

Figure 12.3 shows how the keys for this sort must be filled out. For this sort, you are using two alphanumeric fields, the last name and the first name, so you do not change the default of *a* (for *alphanumeric*). To move to the column for the field number, you press →. To change the field number for key 1 from 1 to 2, you press → and type **2**. Even though the cursor is placed immediately after the *1,* when you type **2**, the *2* replaces the *1* as the field number.

Then, you press → twice, once to move to the Word column and a second time to bypass it and move to the key 2 definition. As soon as you press → a second time, WordPerfect fills in its default settings of *a* for Typ, *1* for Field, and *1* for Word for this key. Here, you need to change the field number from 1 to 3. After moving the cursor to the Field column for this key and entering the new value, you press F7 (Exit) to return to the Sort by Line menu options.

Before you perform any sorting operation by selecting the Perform Action option (**1** or **P**) from the Sort by Line menu, you should always check the key definitions and the Action, Order, and Type of Sort settings that are listed immediately above them, at the bottom of the Sort screen.

The Action column tells you if you are about to perform just a Sort, a Sort and Select, or just a Select operation. (See ''Selecting Records'' later in this chapter for information about using the Select feature.) The Order column tells you whether the sort will be arranged in ascending or descending order. To change Order from the default setting of Ascending to Descending, you select the Order option (**6** or **O**). WordPerfect displays the following options:

Order: **1 A**scending; **2 D**escending: 0

To select the Descending option, you type **2** or **D**.

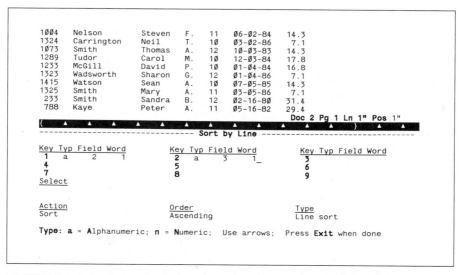

FIGURE 12.3: Defining the keys for the line sort. As this table is to be sorted alphabetically by last name and first name, two keys are defined. The first key uses field 2, which contains the last names. The second key uses field 3, which contains the first names. Both of these fields in the table contain only one word, so the Word setting is left at 1 for both keys. Because both of these keys contain only alphabetical information, the Typ setting is left at the default of *a* (for *alphanumeric*).

The Type of Sort column tells you the type of sort, which must be Line Sort in order to correctly sort this table. To change this from the default of Line Sort, you select the Type option (**7** or **T**). To set it to Paragraph sort, you then type **3** or **P**. (See ''The Paragraph Sort'' later in this chapter for information on when and how to use this type.) To set it to Merge Sort, you type **1** or **M**. (See ''The Merge Sort'' later in this chapter for information on when and how to use this type.)

Figure 12.4 shows the table after the sort has been performed by selecting the Perform Action option (**1** or **P**) from the menu. As soon as you choose this option, WordPerfect displays a counter, indicating the number of records sorted. (This may appear too briefly for you to read if there are few records to sort.) Once the sorting operation is finished, WordPerfect automatically clears the Sort window and returns to the normal full-screen document window, displaying the sorted data.

Because WordPerfect uses a split-screen window arrangement whenever you sort data, the Sort menu contains a View option (**2** or **V**). You can use this option to move the cursor to the data in the window above. This allows you to scroll through the data using all of the normal scrolling keys. However, you cannot edit the data in this window. If you see something that requires editing, you must exit the sorting operation completely by pressing F1 (Cancel). To return to the Sort menu after scrolling through the document to be sorted, you press F7 (Exit).

```
1059    Allen        Holly    M.   11   03-18-83   23.4
1324    Carrington   Neil     T.   10   03-02-86    7.1
 534    Drew         Mary     J.   10   03-24-81   26.4
1407    Farner       Kenneth  E.   12   04-20-85   14.3
 788    Kaye         Peter    A.   11   05-16-82   29.4
1233    McGill       David    P.   10   01-04-84   16.8
1004    Nelson       Steven   F.   11   06-02-84   14.3
1066    Olsen        Phyllis  G.   12   04-17-83   26.4
1325    Smith        Mary     A.   11   03-05-86    7.1
 233    Smith        Sandra   B.   12   02-16-80   31.4
1073    Smith        Thomas   A.   12   10-03-83   14.3
1289    Tudor        Carol    M.   10   12-03-84   17.8
1323    Wadsworth    Sharon   G.   12   01-04-86    7.1
1415    Watson       Sean     A.   10   07-05-85   14.3



D:\WP\WDC\VACATION                        Doc 1 Pg 1 Ln 1" Pos 1"
```

FIGURE 12.4: The vacation accrual table after sorting. Notice that all of the records have been re-arranged. The primary key, which used the last name, controlled the new order of the records except in the case of the three duplicate last names of Smith. Their order was controlled by the secondary key, which used the first name.

Sorting a Block

In the sort outlined in the previous discussion, the entire document (which contained only the tabular data to be sorted) was used. Sometimes when you use the line, paragraph, or merge sort, it will not be appropriate to sort all of the records or to include all of the text in the document.

In such cases, you will alter the sorting procedure slightly by first marking the data to be included with WordPerfect's Block feature before selecting the Sort feature. For example, Figure 12.5 shows the vacation accrual table sorted by employee name; this time you also see the column headings, line separators, and table numbering required for the final report. To use the Line Sort feature to sort the employee data again, this time by department number and number of vacation days accrued, you have to sort a block that contains just the data, rather than sorting the entire document.

To do this, you position the cursor at the beginning of the first identification number in the first line of data and press Alt-F4 (Block). Then, you use the ↓ key to highlight all of the records down to that of Sean Watson. Once the block is correctly marked, you press Ctrl-F9 (Merge/Sort). This time, WordPerfect opens

```
┌─────────────────────────────────────────────────────────────┐
│   ←─────────────────────────────────────→                     │
│                      Vacation Accrual                         │
│                    Departments 1Ø - 12                        │
│   ←═════════════════════════════════════→                     │
│   ID.     Last          First  M    Dept  Date     Vacation   │
│   No.     Name          Name   I    Code  Hired    Days       │
│   ←─────────────────────────────────────→                     │
│   1Ø59    Allen         Holly   M.   11   Ø3-18-83   23.4      │
│   1324    Carrington    Neil    T.   1Ø   Ø3-Ø2-86    7.1      │
│    788    Kaye          Peter   A.   11   Ø5-16-82   29.4      │
│   1233    McGill        David   P.   1Ø   Ø1-Ø4-84   16.8      │
│   1ØØ4    Nelson        Steven  F.   11   Ø6-Ø2-84   14.3      │
│   1Ø66    Olsen         Phyllis G.   12   Ø4-17-83   26.4      │
│   1325    Smith         Mary    A.   11   Ø3-Ø5-86    7.1      │
│    233    Smith         Sandra  B.   12   Ø2-16-8Ø   31.4      │
│   1Ø73    Smith         Thomas  A.   12   1Ø-Ø3-83   14.3      │
│   1289    Tudor         Carol   M.   1Ø   12-Ø3-84   17.8      │
│   1323    Wadsworth     Sharon  G.   12   Ø1-Ø4-86    7.1      │
│   1415    Watson        Sean    A.   1Ø   Ø7-Ø5-85   14.3      │
│   ←─────────────────────────────────────→                     │
│          TABLE 6.2: Accrued Vacation                          │
│                                                               │
│   D:\WP\WDC\TABLE6.VAC              Doc 1 Pg 1 Ln 1" Pos 1"    │
└─────────────────────────────────────────────────────────────┘
```

FIGURE 12.5: Finalized vacation accrual table as it appears in the text of the report. Titles, columns headings, a table number, and even line separators (created with the Line Draw feature) have now been added to the table data. If the records in the table require a different ordering, you must limit the sort to just those records by defining them as a block (Alt-F4) before using the Sort command (Ctrl-F9).

the Line Sort window without requiring you to select the Sort option from the Merge/Sort menu.

To sort records in the table by department number and vacation days, you enter **5** (the fifth column contains department numbers) as the Field for key 1, and you enter **7** (the seventh column contains vacation days) as the Field for key 2. Leave the Word set to 1 for both. However, because the vacation days field contains fractions and, therefore, numbers of unequal length, you must change the Typ setting from *a* (alphanumeric) to *n* (numeric).

You can only apply the alphanumeric type of sort to fields containing numbers when the values are of equal length. Whenever the numbers contain decimal points, as in this case, or when the field contains dollars and cents figures (even with the *$* symbol), you change to the numeric type of sort. Figure 12.6 shows you the key definitions used to perform this new record sort.

Figure 12.7 shows the records in this table after the sort has been performed. Notice that only the records included in the block (those between the line separators) were reordered. If the line sort had been performed on the entire document, WordPerfect would have rearranged not only these records but also the title, the column headings, and even the line separators, with disastrous consequences for the table.

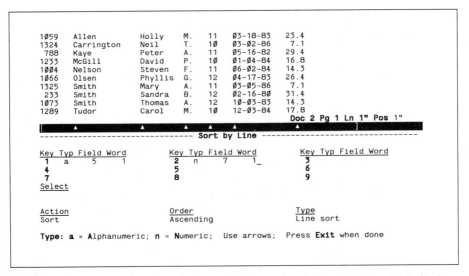

```
1059    Allen        Holly    M.   11   03-18-83   23.4
1324    Carrington   Neil     T.   10   03-02-86    7.1
 788    Kaye         Peter    A.   11   05-16-82   29.4
1233    McGill       David    P.   10   01-04-84   16.8
1004    Nelson       Steven   F.   11   06-02-84   14.3
1066    Olsen        Phyllis  G.   12   04-17-83   26.4
1325    Smith        Mary     A.   11   03-05-86    7.1
 233    Smith        Sandra   B.   12   02-16-80   31.4
1073    Smith        Thomas   A.   12   10-03-83   14.3
1289    Tudor        Carol    M.   10   12-03-84   17.8
                                        Doc 2 Pg 1 Ln 1" Pos 1"
```

```
------------------------------- Sort by Line -------------------------------

Key Typ Field Word        Key Typ Field Word        Key Typ Field Word
 1   a    5     1           2   n    7     1_          3
 4                          5                          6
 7                          8                          9
Select


Action                    Order                     Type
Sort                      Ascending                 Line sort

Type: a = Alphanumeric;  n = Numeric;   Use arrows;  Press Exit when done
```

FIGURE 12.6: The key definitions required for sorting the records in the vacation accrual table first by department number and then by the number of vacation days accrued. Before the sorting operation was begun and these two keys were defined, just the records in the table were marked as a block. Notice that the type of the secondary key using the vacation days field (the last one in the table) has been changed from alphanumeric to numeric (*n*). This was necessary because this field contains fractional numbers of various lengths.

```
┌─────────────────────────────────────────────────────────────────┐
│                                                                   │
│  ←─────────────────────────────────────────────→                 │
│                    Vacation Accrual                               │
│                  Departments 1Ø - 12                              │
│  ←─────────────────────────────────────────────→                 │
│  ID.     Last         First    M   Dept  Date      Vacation       │
│  No.     Name         Name     I   Code  Hired      Days          │
│  ←─────────────────────────────────────────────→                 │
│  1324    Carrington   Neil     T.   1Ø   Ø3-Ø2-86    7.1          │
│  1415    Watson       Sean     A.   1Ø   Ø7-Ø5-85   14.3          │
│  1233    McGill       David    P.   1Ø   Ø1-Ø4-84   16.8          │
│  1289    Tudor        Carol    M.   1Ø   12-Ø3-84   17.8          │
│  1325    Smith        Mary     A.   11   Ø3-Ø5-86    7.1          │
│  1ØØ4    Nelson       Steven   F.   11   Ø6-Ø2-84   14.3          │
│  1Ø59    Allen        Holly    M.   11   Ø3-18-83   23.4          │
│   788    Kaye         Peter    A.   11   Ø5-16-82   29.4          │
│  1323    Wadsworth    Sharon   G.   12   Ø1-Ø4-86    7.1          │
│  1Ø73    Smith        Thomas   A.   12   1Ø-Ø3-83   14.3          │
│  1Ø66    Olsen        Phyllis  G.   12   Ø4-17-83   26.4          │
│   233    Smith        Sandra   B.   12   Ø2-16-8Ø   31.4          │
│  ←─────────────────────────────────────────────→                 │
│           TABLE 6.2: Accrued Vacation                             │
│                                                                   │
│                                                                   │
│  D:\WP\WDC\TABLE6.VAC                    Doc 1 Pg 1 Ln 2.17" Pos 1"│
│                                                                   │
└─────────────────────────────────────────────────────────────────┘
```

FIGURE 12.7: The vacation accrual table after the records were sorted by department number and vacation days accrued. Now the records in this table are in order by department number and vacation days in ascending order. Because this sort was applied only to the records in the table, and not to the entire file, none of the headings are disturbed by this operation.

THE PARAGRAPH SORT

The paragraph sort is used when the data items consist of paragraphs separated from each other by at least two hard returns, one to end the paragraph and the other to enter a blank line. The data can also be separated by hard page breaks, entered by pressing Ctrl-Enter (and shown in the Reveal Codes screen as [HPg]). This kind of sort can also be applied to the entire document (in other words, all of the paragraphs) or just to specific paragraphs that have been previously marked as a block.

The paragraph sort differs only slightly from the line sort discussed in the previous section. Figure 12.8 shows a document containing several descriptions for a movie guide. As you can see, these were not entered in alphabetical order. However, because each description is entered as a paragraph (below a single-line heading), you can use WordPerfect's paragraph sort to order them.

In sorting the paragraphs, you will want to use the movie title, entered as a short line, as the key. Even though the titles are followed by a hard return, the descriptions below them will move with the titles when the document is sorted. This is because WordPerfect's paragraph sort marks the information to be rearranged by at least two hard returns, one to end the paragraph and another to enter a blank line. Because the movie titles are terminated by a single hard return, they and their descriptions will be considered a single unit for purposes of sorting.

To begin the paragraph sort, you mark the paragraphs (assuming that just this group of movies beginning with the letter *C* is to be sorted) and press Ctrl-F9.

```
The Clairvoyant
TV reporter sets out to find the truth when a psychic art student
draws sketches of three murder victims before their gruesome
murders. R-Language, violence. (1983). June 20.

Cocoon
Ron Howard's heartwarming look at age and extraterrestrials. Don
Ameche won the Academy Award for Best Supporting Actor for his
portrayal of the leader of an older set in search of the fountain
of youth. PG13-Language. (1985). June 1, 9.

The Candidate
Robert Redford stars as an ambitious young lawyer who runs for
senator and, in the process, alienates his wife and finds himself
alienated from his own views on the world. PG. (1972). June 15.

Camelot
Lerner and Loewe's acclaimed musical with Richard Harris as the
ill-fated King Arthur of the Round Table. G. (1967). June 18.

Cimmarron
Heroic family adventure set during the last days of the American
frontier. Based on Edna Ferber's great novel of the same name.
With Irene Dunne. PG. (1931). June 3, 6.
D:\WP\WDC\GUIDE                              Doc 1 Pg 1 Ln 1" Pos 1"
```

FIGURE 12.8: Movie descriptions before sorting with the paragraph sort. Each description, including the title and its accompanying paragraph, is separated from the next by two hard returns. The first one marks the end of the paragraph, and the second enters a blank line.

When WordPerfect opens the Sort window, it will still be set for line sort, the program default. In addition, if you have done any previous sorting during the work session, the key settings for the last sort that you defined will still be displayed. WordPerfect remembers all sort settings until you exit the program.

To change the type of sort from line to paragraph, you select the Type option (**7** or **T**) followed by the Paragraph option (**3** or **P**). Once you do this, you will see *Paragraph Sort* listed under the heading *Type of Sort,* and *Sort by Paragraph* displayed under the ruler line demarcating the windows.

The columns for the key definitions are slightly different for a paragraph sort. To the three columns of information, *Typ, Field,* and *Word,* the paragraph sort adds a fourth, *Line.* The definition for the first key therefore appears as

Key	Typ	Line	Field	Word
1	a	1	1	1

When you define a key for paragraph sorting, you designate not only the number of the field and the word within it, but also the number of the line that is to be used. In a paragraph, lines are counted sequentially from the first line of the paragraph (below the blank line containing the second hard return) to the last line of the paragraph (containing the first hard return and immediately above the blank line containing the second hard return). Also note that since fields are defined by tab settings, and there are no tabs within paragraphs, the field number is always 1.

Reverse Field Sorting

To sort the movie descriptions by title, you only need to define a single key. For this key, you will use line 1 and field 1 (the default settings). To have these titles ordered correctly, you will want WordPerfect to ignore the definite article, *The,* whenever it occurs first in the movie title (so that *The Candidate* precedes *Cimmarron* and *The Clairvoyant* precedes *Cocoon*). WordPerfect will not do this if you use *1* as the setting for Word. It will observe a strict alphabetical order for the first word in each title, resulting in *The Candidate* and *The Clairvoyant* at the end of the document.

To get around this problem, you can use WordPerfect's *reverse field sorting.* In this type of sorting, you designate which word is to be used in a particular field by entering the Word setting as a negative value. This tells WordPerfect to reverse the word count, thus counting from right to left from the end of the field. The number you enter after the minus sign tells WordPerfect how many words to advance to the left. When you apply reverse field sorting to a specific field in a line, merge, or paragraph sort, WordPerfect counts backward from the end of the field, advancing left one word (marked by spaces) for each number after the minus sign.

For example, entering a value of −**1** for Word while retaining 1 for Line and Field when defining the key for this paragraph sort tells WordPerfect to use the first word to the right of the end of the first line of field 1. When the movie title in the first line consists of just a single word, this amounts to the same thing as designating *1* for Word. However, when the title contains two words, *The* followed by the movie's name, the program uses the second word (the movie's name, beginning with *C*) instead of the first word (*The*) in the first field in the first line of each paragraph.

> *Note:* This technique of using a reverse word order only works when all of the fields have the word you want used as the key in the same relative position when counted from right to left. In other words, it works in the preceding example because the name of the movie starting with *C* is always picked up by the −1 setting, whether or not its title is preceded by the definite article. However, if the paragraphs included a description for the movie *Citizen Kane,* this technique would not work for it. The −1 setting would tell WordPerfect to sort the paragraph by the word *Kane* instead of *Citizen,* thus placing the movie's description at the very end of the sorted titles beginning with the letter *C.*

Figure 12.9 shows the final definition for key 1 required to sort the movie descriptions in the correct alphabetical order. Figure 12.10 shows the descriptions after they have been sorted using this key. Notice that because reverse field sorting was used in defining the word to be used in line 1 and field 1, the movie titles and summaries are in the proper order even when their titles begin with *The.*

THE MERGE SORT

If your work involves mail merge operations, you will undoubtedly come to rely very heavily upon WordPerfect's third kind of sort, the merge sort. This

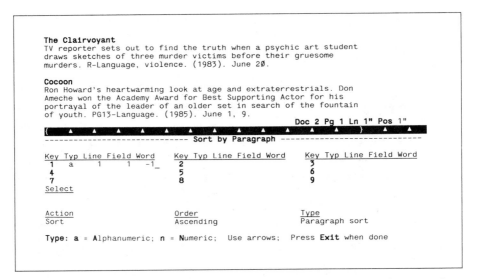

The Clairvoyant
TV reporter sets out to find the truth when a psychic art student
draws sketches of three murder victims before their gruesome
murders. R-Language, violence. (1983). June 2Ø.

Cocoon
Ron Howard's heartwarming look at age and extraterrestrials. Don
Ameche won the Academy Award for Best Supporting Actor for his
portrayal of the leader of an older set in search of the fountain
of youth. PG13-Language. (1985). June 1, 9.

                                              Doc 2 Pg 1 Ln 1" Pos 1"

-------------------------- Sort by Paragraph --------------------------

Key Typ Line Field Word   Key Typ Line Field Word   Key Typ Line Field Word
1   a   1   1   -1   2   3
4   5   6
7   8   9
Select

Action   Order   Type
Sort   Ascending   Paragraph sort

Type: a = Alphanumeric; **n** = Numeric; Use arrows; Press **Exit** when done

FIGURE 12.9: The sorting key definition required to sort the paragraphs alphabetically by movie title. In order to sort the movie descriptions by the part of the name that begins with the letter *C* and ignore any titles that use the definite article *The,* the number of the Word is given as − 1. This tells the program to count each word from right to left from the end of the first line of the field.

Camelot
Lerner and Loewe's acclaimed musical with Richard Harris as the
ill-fated King Arthur of the Round Table. G. (1967). June 18.

The Candidate
Robert Redford stars as an ambitious young lawyer who runs for
senator and, in the process, alienates his wife and finds himself
alienated from his own views on the world. PG. (1972). June 15.

Cimmarron
Heroic family adventure set during the last days of the American
frontier. Based on Edna Ferber's great novel of the same name. With
Irene Dunne. PG. (1931). June 3, 6.

The Clairvoyant
TV reporter sets out to find the truth when a psychic art student
draws sketches of three murder victims before their gruesome
murders. R-Language, violence. (1983). June 2Ø.

Cocoon
Ron Howard's heartwarming look at age and extraterrestrials. Don
Ameche won the Academy Award for Best Supporting Actor for his
protrayal of the leader of an older set in search of the fountain
of youth. PG13-Language. (1985). June 1, 9.
C:\WPROC\WP5\GUIDE   **Doc 1 Pg 1 Ln 1" Pos 1"**

FIGURE 12.10: Movie descriptions after sorting with the paragraph sort. Notice that because reverse field sorting was used with respect to the word (− 1), the movie descriptions are now arranged in proper order because any occurrence of *The* as the first word in the title was ignored in the sort.

type of sorting is specially designed to be used only with secondary merge files. It recognizes individual fields within each record by the Merge R code and individual records within the file by the Merge E code (and the hard page break it inserts). See Chapter 11 for specific information on setting up secondary merge files and performing merge operations.

When defining the sort keys for the merge sort, just as when defining them for the paragraph sort, you can designate the type (either *a* or *n*), as well as the number of the field, the number of the line in the field, and the number of the word within the field to use. The only difference between defining a key for a merge sort and for a paragraph sort is that, in the merge sort, the column for the number of the field precedes that for the line.

When WordPerfect counts fields in the merge sort, the field number is the equivalent of the number you would use to designate that field in a primary document. You only change the line number from the default of 1 when the field consists of multiple lines terminated by hard returns but not Merge R codes.

To select a merge sort, you select the Type option (**7** or **T**) from the Sort menu followed by the Merge option (**1** or **M**). The default settings for key 1 will appear as follows (unless you have changed the key settings previously in the same work session):

Key	Typ	Field	Line	Word
1	a	1	1	1

You can perform a merge sort on just a particular set of records by marking them as a block, or on the entire secondary merge file. Most of the time, you will perform the merge sort on the contents of the entire secondary file. This is an occasion when you might want to output the results of the sort not to the screen, but rather to a new file.

Figure 12.11 shows you the first few records of the client secondary file (used in the examples on merge operations in Chapter 11) before any of its records have been sorted.

To sort these records in alphabetical order by company name, the merge sort is used, with the first key left to the default settings. These call for an alphanumeric sort using the first word in the first line of the first field. The first field in the secondary file contains the name of the company. Because the first field of this file contains only one line, the Line setting is left at 1, and because the first word of the company name is the most significant, the Word setting is left at 1. Figure 12.12 shows you some of the results of this sort.

If you were about to use this secondary file in a mail merge, you would probably want to sort it again, this time ordering its records by zip code. To do this, you would use another merge sort, this time defining the zip code as the key. In

```
Speedo Printing^R
1345 Seventh Street^R
Berkeley, CA 94704^R
Mr.^R
Jim^R
Waggoner^R
^E
================================================================
^R
221 Avenue of the Americas
Suite 210^R
New York, NY 10010^R
Mr.^R
Allan^R
Grill^R
^E
================================================================
Toys N' Things^R
302 West Elm Street^R
Alameda, CA 94501^R
Ms.^R
Grace^R
Fraesir^R
^E
D:\WP\WDC\CLIENTS.SF                          Doc 1 Pg 1 Ln 11 Pos 1i
```

FIGURE 12.11: The first few records of the client secondary merge file before sorting. When you sort these records, fields are counted by Merge R codes (^R), just as they are when you insert fields into a primary merge file.

```
^R
221 Avenue of the Americas
Suite 210^R
New York, NY 10010^R
Mr.^R
Allan^R
Grill^R
^E
================================================================
ABC Contracting^R
2021 Parker Street
Berkeley, CA 94704^R
Mr.^R
David^R
Thompson^R
^E
================================================================
Corey's Computers^R
2100 Tomales Road^R
Point Reyes Station, CA 94956^R
Mr.^R
Roger^R
Corey^R
^E
D:\WP\WDC\CLIENTS.SF                          Doc 1 Pg 1 Ln 11 Pos 1i
```

FIGURE 12.12: The first part of the client secondary file after its records have been sorted alphabetically by company name. To accomplish this sort, it was only necessary to define a primary key (key 1). The first word in field 1 was defined as the primary key. This sorted the records by the first name of each company. Notice that the first record in the sorted list is the one where the first field is blank. Blanks and punctuation always precede the letter *A* in an ascending sort.

these records, the zip code is always the last word in the third field. You would then define the first sorting key, using reverse field sorting, as follows:

Key	Typ	Field	Line	Word
1	a	3	1	−1

After the sort is performed and the secondary file is used in a mail merge operation, each form letter and mailing label will be generated in ascending order by zip code, making it easier to bundle and send out the mass mailing.

SELECTING RECORDS

WordPerfect's Select feature can be used to restrict the sort to just those records that meet specific conditions. Most of the time, you will need to use the Select feature when performing a merge sort, although it is also possible to use Select when performing a line or paragraph sort. You can also use Select to create a special file that contains just part of the records without sorting them at all.

When you use the Select feature (either with sorting or without), WordPerfect eliminates from RAM all those records that don't meet your condition(s). This means that if you save the document under the same name after performing a Select or Select and Sort operation, you will lose the data that wasn't selected. To avoid this, always save the selected file under a new file name.

Sorting and Selecting Records with Simple Conditions

When you set up the conditions by which records are selected, you use the number of one of the keys followed by the condition that must be met. When you construct this condition, you use one of the logical operators recognized by WordPerfect. Table 12.1 shows you the special symbols and logical operators used by WordPerfect when setting up conditions for the Select feature.

In order for the selection to work, you must have already defined the key (using the Keys option on the Sort menu) before trying to enter a selection condition. If you have not previously defined the key, you will receive the error message

ERROR: Key not defined

when you go to construct the condition.

To set up a selection condition after you have defined all of the sorting keys, you choose the Select option (**4** or **S**) from the Sort menu. The cursor is then moved to the first position below the heading *Select,* where you type in the condition. When you enter your condition, spaces are not required before and after

SYMBOL	FUNCTION	EXAMPLE
=	Equal to	key1 = IL
< >	Not equal to	key1 < >CA
>	Greater than	key1 >M
<	Less than	key2<50.00
> =	Greater than or equal to	key1 > =74500
< =	Less than or equal to	key2< =H
*	Logical AND	key1 = IL * key2<60600
+	Logical OR	key1 = IL + key3>1000.00
g	Global select	keyg = Mary

TABLE 12.1: The Symbols and Logical Operators Used in Selecting Records

the operators that you use, although they can be entered if it makes it easier for you to read.

The first part of the condition always consists of the word *key* followed by the number of the sorting key that the selection is to be applied to. Then you enter the symbol for the logical operator you wish to use, followed by the value that the key is to be compared to. This value can be a number or letter if you are using an alphanumeric sort, or any type of number if you are using a numeric sort.

For example, if you want to sort and include only those records in the client secondary file where the zip code is greater than or equal to 94500, you first set the type of sort to Merge (Ctrl-F9 T M). Then you define the first key to sort by zip code by selecting the Keys option (**3** or **K**) and entering the following values:

Key	Typ	Field	Line	Word
1	a	3	1	−1

Finally, you choose the Select option (**4** or **S**) and enter the following condition for key 1:

key1> =94500

After entering this condition, you press F7 (Exit) to return to the Sort menu.

As soon as you press F7, the Action setting changes from *Sort* to *Sort and Select* on the Merge Sort screen. When you choose the Perform Action option (**1** or **P**), WordPerfect not only sorts all of the records where the zip code is 94500 or greater, but also eliminates from the file any records where the zip code is less than 94500.

Figure 12.13 shows the first part of the client secondary file after performing this sort-and-select operation. Notice that none of the records where the zip code is below 94500 appear here, and that all of the records visible are properly sorted according to zip code.

```
        House of Flowers^R
        345 South 16th Street^R
        Alameda, CA 94501^R
        Mr.^R
        Philip^R
        Manley^R
        ^E
        =====================================================================
        Toys N' Things^R
        302 West Elm Street^R
        Alameda, CA 94501^R
        Ms.^R
        Grace^R
        Fraesir^R
        ^E
        =====================================================================
        Speedo Printing^R
        1345 Seventh Street^R
        Berkeley, CA 94704^R
        Mr.^R
        Jim^R
        Waggoner^R
        ^E
        =====================================================================
        D:\WP\WDC\CLIENTS.SF                      Doc 1 Pg 1 Ln 11 Pos 1i
```

FIGURE 12.13: The first part of the client secondary file after the records have been selected by zip code greater than or equal to 94500 and then sorted. Notice that no records with zip codes below 94500 now appear at the beginning of this file. Also, notice that the remaining records visible in this figure (those with zip codes above 94500) are now sorted in strict zip code order.

Sorting and Selecting Records with Compound Conditions

When you prepare selection conditions, you can create compound conditions by using the logical AND and OR operators between simple conditions. Word-Perfect uses the asterisk (*) for the AND logical operator and the plus sign (+) for the OR logical operator. Be careful that you do not confuse + for AND when setting up compound conditions.

When you set up a compound AND condition, both parts of the condition must be met. For example, you might want to restrict the sorted records to those where the zip code is between 94500 and 94800. To do this, you would enter the following compound condition using the AND logical operator (*):

    key1> = 94500 * key1<=94800

This statement means "Select only those records where the zip code (defined in key 1) is greater than or equal to 94500 *and* less than or equal to 94800." When the sort-and-select operation is performed, WordPerfect will sort only those records where the zip code entry is between (or includes) these values. All of the other records will be discarded.

You can also create compound conditions using the OR logical operator to join simple conditions. For example, you might want to use only those records where the state field is UT, CA, or WA in a mail merge operation. To select these records and still sort them by zip code, you would again use the zip code field as the primary key, but, in addition, you would define a second key for the state field. (This key will not affect the outcome of the sort; it does allow you to set up the selection condition.)

After defining these two keys, you would enter the following compound select condition, using simple conditions referring to key 2, which defines the state field, separated by the OR logical operator (+):

key2 = UT + key2 = CA + key2 = WA

This statement means "Select only those records where the state (defined in key 2) is *either* UT *or* CA *or* WA." When these records are selected, they are still sorted by the primary key, which represents the zip code.

The foregoing examples have all used the same key number in the compound conditions. This does not have to be the case. You may have conditions where a value must be met or exceeded in one key field and must also equal another value in a second field. For example, if you have a secondary file that tracks the credit limit of each customer as well as address information, you can set up a condition where only records in which the credit limit is $2,500.00 or more and the state is New York are selected. Assuming that you have defined the state field as key 1 and the credit limit field as key 2, the selection statement would be entered as

key1 = NY * key2 > = 2500.00

This means "Select only those records where the state (defined in key 1) is NY *and* the credit limit (defined in key 2) is greater than or equal to $2,500.00." Remember, because the credit limit field contains dollars and cents figures that may be of unequal length, you need to set the type of sort for key 2 to *n* (for *numeric*) to have the operation work properly.

Sometimes when constructing compound conditions, you will have to alter the phrasing of the simple conditions by the use of parentheses. When WordPerfect evaluates a selection condition, it does so from left to right. To have the program evaluate a pair of simple conditions as a unit before it evaluates other conditions in the statement, you enclose that pair of conditions in parentheses. For instance, if you want to expand the selection cited in the last example so that you select the records in which the state is either New York or Massachusetts and the credit limit is between $2,500.00 and $5,000.00, you enter the following compound statement:

(key1 = NY + key1 = MA) * key2 > = 2500.00 * key2 < = 5000.00

This statement means "Select only those records where the state (defined in key 1) is *either* NY *or* MA *and in either case* where the credit limit (defined in key 2) is greater than or equal to $2,500.00 *and* less than or equal to $5,000.00." Without the parentheses around the first OR condition of the statement, WordPerfect would interpret the condition to mean "Select only those records where the state is NY (and the credit limit is anything) *or* the state is MA *and* the credit limit for these records is also between $2,500.00 and $5,000.00." The AND condition defining the range for the credit limit would be applied only to those customers who live in Massachusetts. When creating complex compound conditions, consider the phrasing if the records selected are not the ones that you thought you'd get.

Performing a Global Selection

In addition to the operators illustrated in the previous examples, there is one more special character that you should be familiar with. This is the global select character, *g*. The *g* is entered in place of a key number as **keyg**. When you use *keyg,* you do not have to have already defined any sorting keys for it to work. This is the only time that you need not have previously defined the keys when using the Select command.

The global select character instructs WordPerfect to select all records where the condition following *keyg* is met, regardless of the field in which this occurs. For example, the statement

keyg = Smith

will select all records where *Smith* occurs, in any field. It will select the record if *Smith* is the second word in the company name (as in *The Smith Company*), if *Smith* is the surname in the contact name field, and so on.

Once you have performed a sort-and-select operation, you will probably want to save the results in a new file. If you did not change the default for the output of the sort from Screen to a new file name when you began the sort operation, you could still save the results in a new file by pressing F7 (Exit), typing **Y**, and then editing the suggested file name before pressing the Enter key. Then, you could use the records in this new file when needed in your merge operations.

Selecting Records Only

Most of the time, you will want to sort the records at the same time that you select them. However, if this is not the case, you can have WordPerfect just select the records that meet your conditions without sorting them. To do this, you define your keys and selection conditions just as you do when you both sort and select records. However, after you have finished both these steps and have returned to the Sort menu, you select the Action option (**5** or **A**). When you choose this option, you are presented with these two menu options:

Action: **1 S**elect and Sort; **2** Select **O**nly: 0

To just select the records according to the condition you have set up, you choose the Select Only option (**2** or **O**) from this menu. As soon as you choose this option, you are returned to the Merge Sort screen. Beneath the *Action* heading, you will see that the word *Select* has replaced the words *Sort and Select.* When you select the Perform Action option (**1** or **P**) from the Sort menu, WordPerfect will eliminate from the file all records that do not meet the selection condition. However, those records that remain will still be in the same order as they were before you ran the selection.

CHANGING THE SORTING SEQUENCE

The Merge/Sort menu includes an option that allows you to change the normal US/European sorting sequence to Scandinavian. You need to change to the Scandinavian sorting sequence when the data you are about to sort contains digraphs like æ and Æ, diacritics like Ö and ê, and the like.

To do this, you press Ctrl-F9 and select the Sort Order option (**3** or **O**). When you do, you are presented with these options:

Sort Order: **1** **U**S/European; **2 S**candinavian: 0

To select the alternate sort order, select the Scandinavian option (**2** or **S**) from this menu. To return to the normal sort order (the normal dictionary sort order for languages using the Roman alphabet without any foreign language characters), select the US/European option (**1** or **U**).

Note: To produce certain digraphs and diacritics, you use Compose (Ctrl-2) and simply enter the two characters (in either order) that make up the symbol. To produce special characters like the Thorn (equivalent of *Th* at the beginning of a word), which some Scandinavian languages use, you press Ctrl-2 and enter the number of the character set, a comma, and the number of the symbol. See Chapter 14 for more information on using Compose, and Appendix B for a complete list of the WordPerfect character sets.

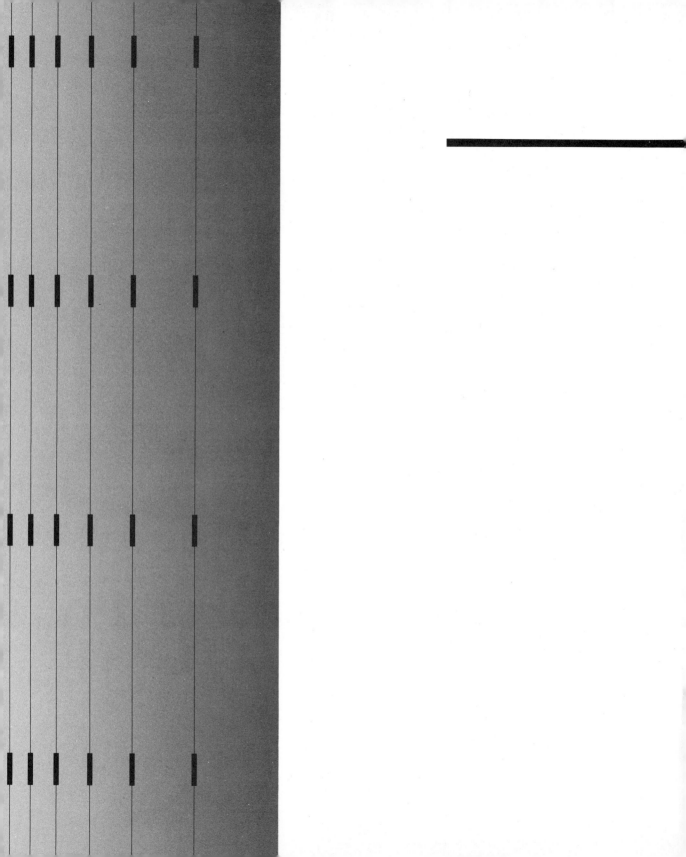

CHAPTER 13

PERFORMING CALCULATIONS WITH THE MATH FEATURE

PERFORMING CALCULATIONS
WITH THE MATH FEATURE

WordPerfect can be used as a calculator for simple mathematical operations such as addition, subtraction, multiplication, and division. The program can also calculate totals, subtotals, grand totals, and averages on numbers in columns. In addition, you can write formulas that perform mathematical operations on columns of numbers and calculate averages across rows of numbers.

Although these relatively simple mathematical functions cannot match the capabilities of a full-featured spreadsheet or database management program, they allow you to bring spreadsheet or database data into WordPerfect and manipulate it further—for example, to calculate percentages of change, extended totals, or discounts. If you do very many of these kinds of calculations in WordPerfect, you may want to obtain PlanPerfect, which is WordPerfect Corporation's spreadsheet program.

UPGRADE NOTES

Math features in WordPerfect 5.0 remain the same as in version 4.2. In addition, you can use the Other option on the Format menu (Shift-F8) to select different characters for the decimal and thousands separators.

WORKING WITH MATHEMATICS IN WORDPERFECT

WordPerfect's Math features can be used in two basic ways:

- Without defining columns as special Math columns, you can calculate totals, subtotals, and grand totals for a column of numbers, as illustrated in Figure 13.1.
- If you define columns as Math columns, you can write formulas that perform specific computations across rows of columns.

Working with Math columns in WordPerfect is a six-step process:

1. Clear the tabs and set new ones corresponding to the columns you wish to use. You may define up to 24 columns (A through X), and four of them can contain formulas that specify operations on other numeric columns.

```
        _       Order A      Order B

                $7.98        $15.60

                88.90        101.28

                33.56         11.01
    Subtotal    130.44+      127.89+

                $55.98       $75.98

                -7.45         -6.98
    Subtotal    48.53+        69.00+
    Total       178.97=      196.89=




    Math                                          Doc 2 Pg 1 Ln 1" Pos 1"
```

FIGURE 13.1: Performing calculations on simple columns of numbers. You can calculate totals, sub-totals, and grand totals for columns of numbers without first defining the columns as special Math columns. The **+** and **=** symbols will not appear when the document is printed.

2. (Optional) Define each column as a Text, Numeric, Calculation, or Total column. Numeric columns contain data you wish to make calculations on, Calculation columns contain the formulas and display the results of the calculations, and Total columns calculate subtotals, totals, and grand totals of data in other columns. Text columns contain labels and are not used in calculations.

3. Turn on the Math feature by pressing Alt-F7 (Math/Columns) and choosing Math On (**1** or **M**). This option is a toggle; when you have finished your calculations, you should turn it off.

4. Enter the text and data into the columns you have defined.

5. Instruct WordPerfect to make the calculations by selecting Calculate (**2** or **A**) when Math is on. If Math is not on, or if the cursor is not in the Math area, the menu containing the Calculate option will not appear.

6. Turn Math off by pressing Alt-F7 and selecting Math Off (**1** or **M**).

If all you want to do is calculate totals of numbers in columns, you do not need to define Math columns (step 2). Instead, follow the procedures in the next section.

Getting Simple Totals

To get totals, subtotals, and grand totals from simple columns of numbers (not predefined as Math columns):

1. Clear and then reset the tabs for your Math columns.

2. Turn the Math feature on by pressing Alt-F7 (Math/Columns) and selecting Math On (**1** or **M**). The following message appears in the lower-left corner of the screen:

   Math

3. Press the Tab key to move to the first column. Then enter the numbers you are going to work with. When you type a period (.) to indicate a decimal point, the numbers will align on that decimal point.

4. Wherever you want a subtotal to be calculated in that column, insert a plus sign (+), either from the numeric keypad or from the top row of your keyboard. When you choose Calculate, WordPerfect will subtotal each number in the column after the last plus sign. Where you want a total of the subtotals, enter an equal sign (=). If you want any numbers to be considered as totals or subtotals even if no calculation has been performed on them—which may be useful if you are working with imported data on which totals and subtotals have already been calculated—enter **t** (lowercase) before any additional subtotals, and **T** (uppercase) before any additional totals. If you want to calculate a grand total—the total of all the totals—enter an asterisk (*). Entering **N**, a minus sign, or parentheses surrounding a number indicates a number that is to be considered negative.

5. To tell WordPerfect to make the calculations you have specified, press Alt-F7 (Math/Columns) and select Calculate. (You can select this option at any time to have the program perform calculations—for example, as you enter the numbers.)

6. Turn Math off by selecting Math Off from the Math/Columns menu.

Turning Math on and off inserts the codes [Math On] and [Math Off] into your document. If you later need to change your figures, you can search for these codes by pressing F2 (Search), then pressing Alt-F7 and selecting option **2** or **3**.

However, if you define Math columns first, the program offers you several more sophisticated options. We will look at each of the steps involved in defining Math columns and then examine a step-by-step example that illustrates most of WordPerfect's Math features.

Setting Tabs for Math Columns

When Math mode is on, WordPerfect is preset to use the decimal point as the alignment character. After you press Tab, characters that you type appear to the left of the cursor. Because of this, you may find it more convenient to first type any column headings in normal text mode and then define the columns that will be used in the Math portion of your document. With the headings in place on your screen, you can see more easily where to set tabs for your Math columns, as shown in Figure 13.2.

Defining Math Columns

After you have cleared tabs and set new ones, you should define the Math columns if you are going to be doing anything other than adding subtotals, totals, and grand totals down columns of numbers. When you press Alt-F7 and select Math Def (**2** or **E**), the screen shown in Figure 13.3 appears. From it, you select the definitions for each of the columns you will be using.

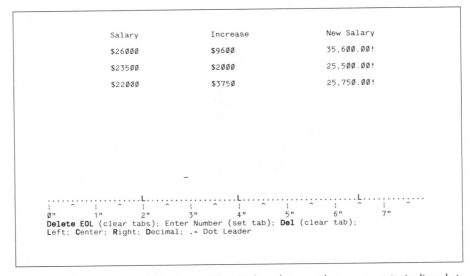

FIGURE 13.2: Setting tabs for Math columns. When Math mode is on, whatever you enter is aligned at the tab setting. When you set up Math columns, be sure to clear all tabs on the line and then set new ones at the positions where you want each column to end; otherwise, your columns will not align as you want them to. (The exclamation points in the figure indicate calculations that WordPerfect has made; they will not be printed.)

```
Math Definition                  Use arrow keys to position cursor

Columns                          A B C D E F G H I J K L M N O P Q R S T U V W X

Type                             2 2 0 2 2 2 2 2 2 2 2 2 2 2 2 2 2 2 2 2 2 2 2 2

Negative Numbers                 ( ( ( ( ( ( ( ( ( ( ( ( ( ( ( ( ( ( ( ( ( ( ( (

Number of Digits to              2 2 2 2 2 2 2 2 2 2 2 2 2 2 2 2 2 2 2 2 2 2 2 2
  the Right (0-4)

Calculation    1      C      B/C*100_
   Formulas    2
               3
               4

Type of Column:
     0 = Calculation      1 = Text      2 = Numeric    3 = Total

Negative Numbers
     ( = Parentheses (50.00)           - = Minus Sign  -50.00


Press Exit when done
```

FIGURE 13.3: The Math Definition screen. Here column C has been defined as a Calculation column (type 0). You can use from one to four Calculation columns to perform calculations on Numeric columns (type 2). You enter the formulas you want to use in the Calculation Formulas area, using the column letters as the variables in the formula. In the figure, column B will be divided by column C and multiplied by 100.

You can define up to 24 columns (A through X) as Math columns and designate any four of them to contain formulas. Columns that contain formulas are called *Calculation columns* (type 0); they will display the results of the calculations you specify when you tell WordPerfect to calculate. Calculation columns contain an exclamation point (!) until the program calculates results; they then display results with an exclamation point next to them. These exclamation points do not appear when the document is printed.

You can define three other types of columns. *Numeric columns* (type 2) hold the data you wish to perform calculations on. WordPerfect defines all columns to be Numeric columns when you turn Math mode on unless you specify otherwise. *Text columns* (type 1) contain labels or descriptions and are ignored in calculations. *Total columns* (type 3), which are a special type of calculated column, display subtotals, totals, and grand totals; you can use this type of column to display totals separately from the columns that hold the data, as discussed later in this chapter.

To change a column's definition, move the cursor to its letter by using the arrow keys. Enter **0** if the column is to contain a formula, enter **1** if the column is to contain only text, and enter **3** if the column is to contain a calculated total. Calculations are performed across columns; totals are performed down columns. If you have defined the column as type 0, when you press Enter the cursor moves down to the Calculation Formulas section of the screen to allow you to enter the formula for the calculation. For example, to calculate what percentage of the number in column C is represented by the number in column B, you would enter **B/C*100** as shown in Figure 13.3.

When you define Math columns, you can also select how you want negative numbers to be displayed—either in parentheses, as in *(48.00)*, or with a minus sign, as in *– 48.00*. (Financial reports often use parentheses.)

You can also choose how many digits (from one to four) you want the program to display to the right of the decimal point. WordPerfect is preset to display two decimal places, as in *55.55*. It is also preset to round up numbers greater than or equal to 5.

When you have finished defining all the columns you are going to use, press F7 to exit to the menu.

Entering Data

Be sure to turn Math mode on before you begin to enter data on which you want to perform calculations. Only the data you enter in Math columns, which begin with the first tab setting, can be used in calculations. Although you do not need to define Math columns first if you are only totaling columns of numbers, you should be sure to reset all tabs before you begin so that numbers do not overlap in columns. WordPerfect's tabs are set every $1/2$ inch by default, and the numbers you work with will often occupy more space than that.

When you move the cursor to a column you have defined as a Calculation column, an exclamation point (!) appears. This indicates that WordPerfect is going to perform a calculation in that column, so do not enter anything there.

You will need to enter any currency symbols (such as *$*) manually; unlike many spreadsheet programs, WordPerfect's Math feature does not have an option that defines entries as currency and formats them for you.

You can designate any number in a column to be considered a negative number when it is used in calculations by entering **N** before the number, placing a minus sign before it, or enclosing it in parentheses. The *N* will not be printed, but the minus sign and parentheses will be printed.

MAKING CALCULATIONS

WordPerfect contains built-in formulas that allow you to calculate subtotals, totals, grand totals, and averages. If you are totaling numbers down a column, you do not need to define Math columns first. You simply enter the symbol for the operation at the point in the column where you wish the operation to be performed. A plus sign calculates subtotals, an equal sign calculates totals, and an asterisk calculates grand totals. You can also enter **T** (uppercase) before a number to indicate that it is to be considered a total when the results are calculated, or you can enter **t** (lowercase) to indicate that a number is to be considered a subtotal.

Displaying Totals in Separate Columns

If you have defined Math columns, you can perform more complex operations. For example, you can display subtotals, totals, and grand totals in separate columns. To do so, you simply define the column or columns that you wish to hold the total calculations as Total columns (type 3) and type the +, =, or * symbol in your document in the column where you want the calculation to appear. You will see how to do this shortly in a step-by-step example.

Getting Averages and Total Across Rows

Once you have defined Math columns, you can also use certain special operators to compute the totals and averages of rows, as illustrated in Figure 13.4, where averages have been calculated across rows. To do so, define the column that is to hold these special operators as a Calculation column (type 0). Then, when the cursor moves to the Calculation Formulas area of the Math Definition screen, enter any one of the following special operators:

- The + symbol calculates the total of all the numbers in the row that are in Numeric columns (type 2).
- The + / symbol calculates the average of all the numbers in the row that are in Numeric columns (type 2).
- The = symbol calculates the total of all the numbers in the row that are in Total columns (type 3).
- The = / symbol calculates the average of all the numbers in the row that are in Total columns (type 3).

These special operators work on numbers to their right and left, across the entire row—not just on numbers to the left. If you are not aware of this, you can obtain confusing results.

If you do not want a calculation to be performed on a certain row, you can delete the exclamation point that appears in the Calculation column for that row. These special formulas should be used by themselves; no other formulas should appear in the columns that contain them.

Making Other Calculations

You can specify other types of calculations, such as formulas that involve multiplication, division, addition, and subtraction, on Numeric columns (type 2). To do so, you define the column in which you want these calculations to occur as type 0 (Calculation) and enter the formula you want to use in the Calculation

```
          Sales Summary--Third Quarter
            August      September    October        Average

            99.89        77.56        45.09          74.18!

            45.78        78.54        76.09          66.80!

            98.23       129.98       120.65         116.29!_




   Math                                     Doc 1 Pg 1 Ln 2.33" Pos 6.9"
```

FIGURE 13.4: Making calculations across rows. WordPerfect provides four special operators that make calculations across rows. These calculations are made either on every number in each Numeric column or on every number in each Total column, depending on the operator you select. The **+** symbol operates on Numeric columns, and the **=** symbol operates on Total columns. Here, averages have been computed by using the **+ /** symbol.

Formulas part of the Math Definition screen. When you write formulas, do not use any spaces in them—for example, write **C/B + D**.

WordPerfect calculates from left to right. To tell WordPerfect to calculate a sequence of operations first, enclose them in parentheses. For example, the expression **3*(5 − 2)** returns 9, not 13. You cannot nest parentheses, however, so the complexity of formulas you can enter is limited.

To indicate a fraction, enclose it in parentheses, as in **(1/2)**, or use its decimal equivalent, as in **.5**.

The program displays double question marks (*??*) if it cannot make a calculation. If this occurs, recheck your Math Definition screen to make sure that the column references in any formulas you have written are correct.

Example: **Working with Math Columns**

To illustrate how WordPerfect's Math features work, here is a simple example that incorporates most of the program's basic math techniques. You can apply these same techniques to more complex Math columns that involve additional computations.

This example demonstrates

- Clearing and setting tabs for Math columns.
- Defining a Math column.

- Turning Math on and off.
- Entering data in Math columns.
- Getting a subtotal and total.
- Displaying a total in a separate column.
- Indicating an additional subtotal.
- Using a formula for computation.

To create the example shown in Figure 13.7, take the following steps:

1. Set tabs at positions 1", 3", 4.4", and 5.5". These tabs will be used for the headings in the table, not for the numbers that WordPerfect will act upon.

2. Enter the headings **Order Number**, **Amount**, **Total**, and **Plus 6% Tax**, as shown in Figure 13.5.

3. To set Math tabs, press Shift-F8 (Format), then select Line (**1** or **L**) and Tab Set (**8** or **T**). Press Home Home ↑ to make sure you are at the beginning of the tab ruler line, then press Ctrl-End to delete all tabs to the end of the line. Set new tabs at positions 3.5", 5", and 6.5". Then press F7 (Exit). Any tabs you set while in Math mode will be considered decimal tabs unless you change the alignment character. (See Chapter 3 for a more detailed discussion of setting tabs.)

4. Press Alt-F7 (Math/Columns) and choose Math Def (**2** or **E**) to define the Math columns. When the Math Definition screen appears, fill it out as shown in Figure 13.6. Column B is a Total column, so it is type 3; column C holds a formula, so it is type 0. (Because the leftmost column does not occur after a tab, WordPerfect ignores it in any calculations it makes. If you have columns that contain headings or labels that occur after a tab setting, you can define them as text columns—type 1—and WordPerfect will ignore them in calculations too.)

5. When the cursor moves to the Formula Calculation area, enter the formula for column C as **1.06*B**. Press F7 to exit the Math Definition screen and enter the [Math Def] code into your document.

6. Turn Math mode on by pressing **1** or **M**.

7. Enter the data as shown in Figure 13.5. After you enter the last number in each row, press Enter. The *t* before the *From P04485* figure indicates that WordPerfect is to consider this number a subtotal, even though it has not calculated it.

8. After you type **Total**, enter an equal sign (=) in the Total column to indicate that WordPerfect should calculate the total of all the subtotals here. Then press Tab again. WordPerfect inserts an exclamation point in the *Plus 6% Tax* column to indicate that a calculation will be made here.

```
        Order Number        Amount      Total      Plus 6% Tax


          Ø21389             54.54

          912670            190.75

          667120             25.51

          Subtotal          270.80+

          From PO#4485      t217.89

          Total                _          =               !




   Math                                     Doc 1 Pg 1 Ln 3.33" Pos 3.7"
```

FIGURE 13.5: Sample Math columns example. Although relatively simple, this example illustrates the basic techniques required to create more complex Math columns and formulas. Follow the step-by-step instructions in the text to practice these techniques.

```
   Math Definition           Use arrow keys to position cursor

   Columns                   A B C D E F G H I J K L M N O P Q R S T U V W X

   Type                      2 3 Ø 2 2 2 2 2 2 2 2 2 2 2 2 2 2 2 2 2 2 2 2 2

   Negative Numbers          ( ( ( ( ( ( ( ( ( ( ( ( ( ( ( ( ( ( ( ( ( ( ( (

   Number of Digits to       2 2 2 2 2 2 2 2 2 2 2 2 2 2 2 2 2 2 2 2 2 2 2 2
     the Right (Ø-4)

   Calculation    1     C    1.Ø6*B_
      Formulas    2
                  3
                  4

   Type of Column:
        Ø = Calculation    1 = Text      2 = Numeric    3 = Total

   Negative Numbers
        ( = Parentheses (5Ø.ØØ)        - = Minus Sign  -5Ø.ØØ


   Press Exit when done
```

FIGURE 13.6: The Math Definition screen for the example. Column A has been left as a numeric column (type 2). Column B has been defined as a total column (type 3), and column C, which contains the formula 1.06*B, is a calculation column (type 0). In any math definition, only four columns can hold formulas.

9. When your table resembles the one in Figure 13.5, press Alt-F7 (Math/ Columns) and select Calculate (**2** or **A**) to make the calculations. Your screen should then look like the one in Figure 13.7. After the calculations have been made, press Alt-F7 and select Math Off to turn Math off.

TIPS ON USING WORDPERFECT'S MATH FEATURE

Although most of these suggestions have been mentioned earlier in this chapter, they are presented here in concise form so that you can review them quickly if you are having difficulty with Math operations:

- When you use WordPerfect's Math feature, be sure to delete all tab settings and set new ones before you begin. Even if you are using the Math feature only in its simplest form, the preset tab stops are too close together for most columns of numbers. WordPerfect considers whatever is between two tab stops to be a column, starting with the first tab stop. In other words, column A begins at the first tab stop, and what is typed at the left margin before a tab stop is set is not considered to be a column. If you write formulas involving columns without understanding this distinction, you may wind up with inaccurate results, because your column designations will not be correct.

- It's a good idea to sketch your columns on a sheet of paper before you begin so that you can keep track of which is column A, which is column B, and so forth, or label each column outside the [Math On] area as you

```
Order Number        Amount        Total        Plus 6% Tax

Ø21389               54.54
912670              190.75
667120               25.51
Subtotal            270.80+
From PO#4485        t217.89
Total                             488.69=        518.Ø1!




                                              Doc 1 Pg 1 Ln 1" Pos 1"
```

FIGURE 13.7: The completed example with the subtotal, total, and calculation.

work and delete the letter designator later. The columns themselves will not be visible when you use the Math Definition screen.

- If you reset any tabs while you are working—for example, if you realize you need to add a new column—be sure to press Alt-F3 (Reveal Codes) to check the placement of the new [Tab Set] code. WordPerfect uses the code that is closest to the data in your document.

- Do not enter any numbers that are to be calculated unless you see the *Align Char* = message in the lower-left corner of the screen. It indicates that you are in a column on which the Math feature can operate instead of in a column next to the left margin.

- When you write a formula that contains column letters as variables, do not use any spaces in the formula.

- WordPerfect performs calculations from left to right. To tell WordPerfect to calculate a sequence of operations first, enclose the sequence in parentheses.

- In columns where calculated values are to appear (those columns that you define as Calculation columns), WordPerfect will insert an exclamation point when you press Tab to enter the column. Anything you enter into these columns will be disregarded, as they are to hold calculated values only. If you do not want a row in that column to be used in the calculation, delete the ! before you select Calculate from the Math/Columns menu.

- If you have difficulty getting calculations to appear, it may be because you did not press Tab to enter each Calculation column you defined before you selected Calculate. Before you calculate, make sure that an exclamation point is visible in each column that is to hold calculations, including columns you have defined as Total columns. Also remember that you must be within the area defined as a Math area—between the [Math On] and [Math Off] codes—in order to make calculations.

- Any time you change numbers in Numeric columns or formulas in Calculation columns, or when you move, cut, or copy Math columns, be sure to recalculate your results by pressing Alt-F7 and selecting Calculate. Option 2 will not appear as Calculate unless you are within the Math area and can see the Math prompt in the lower-left corner of the screen.

- Once you have defined Math columns (inserted a [Math Def] code into your document), that definition will be used each time you turn Math on, even if you are in a different part of your document, unless you specify another Math definition.

CHANGING MATH DEFINITIONS

WordPerfect enters special codes when you define Math columns. If you need to revise the Math definition later, you can use the program's Search feature to

search for the [Math Def], [Math On], [Math Off], + (subtotal), = (total), *
(grand total), *t* (subtotal designator), *T* (total designator), ! (calculation), or *N*
(negative number designator) codes. To use this feature, press F2 (Search); then
press Alt-F7. The following menu appears:

Math: **1** Def **2** On **3** Off **4** + **5** = **6** * **7** t **8** T **9** ! **A** N
Column: **B** Def **C** On **D** Off: 0

You can press the number or letter of the option to search for the next occurrence
of it in your document. (Only options 1 through A pertain to Math features.) For
example, to search for the next Math definition, you enter **1**; to search for the
next Calculation column, you enter **9**.

You often will want to change the definitions of Math columns so that you can
add new columns of data, delete columns, or move columns to new locations.
With your cursor positioned before the [Math On] code—press Alt-F3 to see the
codes—you can delete the old [Math Def] code. Then press Alt-F7 and select
Math Def to change any column definitions that you wish. Remember to recalculate before you move to another part of your document.

To revise a Math Definition screen that you have already defined, delete the
old [Math Def] code, select Math Def from the Math Columns menu, and create
a new Math definition in the same location.

Remember that if you add, delete, or move columns, you will also need to
revise the formulas that involve them.

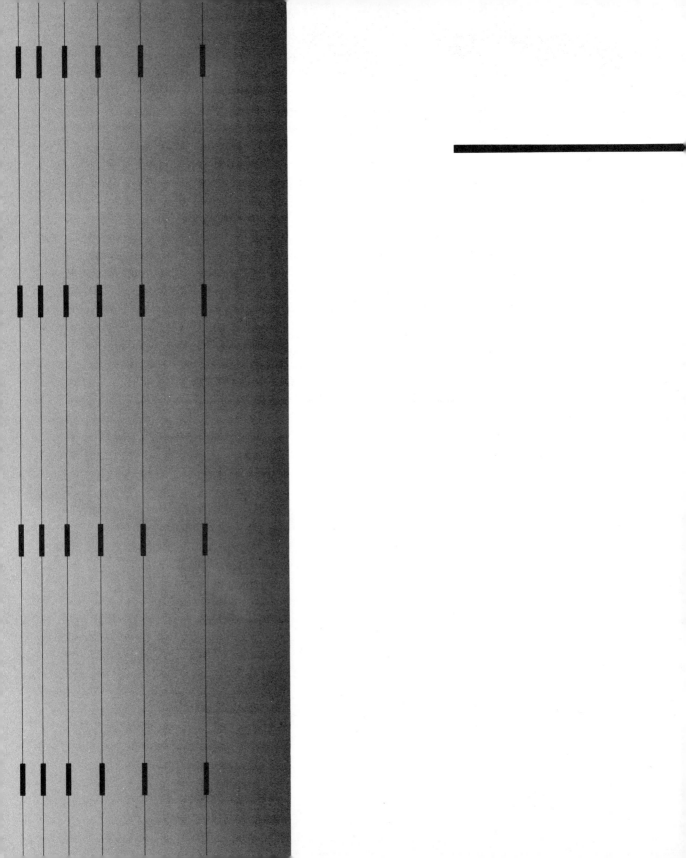

CHAPTER 14

LINE DRAWING AND SPECIAL SYMBOLS

LINE DRAWING
AND SPECIAL SYMBOLS

Not only does WordPerfect process words for you, but it also allows you to create simple line drawings—such as charts, forms, and graphs—in your documents. If you are creating newsletters or brochures, you can use the program's Line Draw feature to add interest to your page layouts, create borders around areas where artwork will be inserted, and highlight portions of the page to attract the reader's attention. You can even use WordPerfect to create fairly complex forms, complete with boxes and rules.

Because you can save the drawings you create, you can use simple shapes over and over again without having to create them each time from scratch. If you use standard shapes often—such as in organizational charts that change monthly—you may want to use WordPerfect's macro capabilities to generate these shapes wherever you need them in your documents.

In addition to creating simple shapes with line drawing, you can use the new Compose feature to insert special symbols, such as brackets for large matrices, in your documents. You can also use it to type in foreign language characters or mathematical and scientific symbols. Moreover, if your work requires that you use these characters often, you can map them onto a keyboard layout of your own design (see Chapter 17).

Do not confuse the drawings you create by using the Line Draw feature with graphics boxes. You create a graphics box when you want to retrieve a graphic image from another source, such as a graphics program, as discussed in Chapter 18. Also, do not confuse the Line option (**5** or **L**) on the Graphics key (Alt-F9) with the Line Draw feature. The Line option refers to the program's capabilities of creating horizontal and vertical lines, such as those that separate columns of text. It is also discussed in Chapter 18.

UPGRADE NOTES

Line drawing in version 5.0 works exactly the same way it did in version 4.2. However, the method for inserting special graphics characters and symbols has changed radically. WordPerfect 5.0 no longer uses Ctrl/Alt key mapping. Instead, it uses the Compose feature (Ctrl-2), which allows you to combine certain pairs of standard characters into special characters, or to choose from a vast array of special characters and symbols in 12 predefined character sets. These can be used as the line draw character to create borders, or they can be entered directly into the text of your document.

USING LINE DRAWING IN WORDPERFECT

WordPerfect's Line Draw feature allows you to use the graphics characters that your printer is capable of printing to create a variety of relatively simple graphs, charts, and forms, such as the one illustrated in Figure 14.1. You can draw using single lines, double lines, or asterisks, or you can select other drawing characters.

Printer Considerations

Most dot matrix printers can print many of the IBM graphics characters, but letter quality printers, such as daisy wheel printers, are limited to the characters that are on their print wheels.

If you have a laser printer, you can only print line drawings with a monospaced font, like the internal Courier 10 pitch font in the LaserJet printers. (See Chapter 5 for detailed information on using different fonts in a document.) If you use a proportionally spaced font (either on a cartridge or as a soft font), you need to use the Graphics feature to draw vertical and horizontal lines or boxes

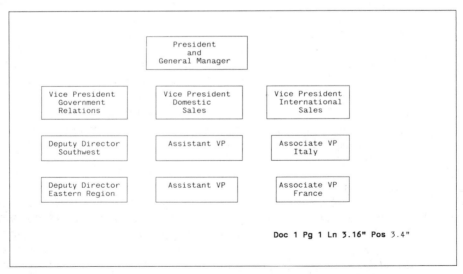

FIGURE 14.1: Sample chart created with WordPerfect's Line Draw feature. You can draw "freehand" on the screen, or you can create a variety of shapes and store them in a file from which you cut and paste the shapes you need. If you use graphics often, you can write macros that generate basic shapes for you.

instead of the Line Draw feature. (See Chapter 18 for information on using the Graphics feature.)

You will want to test your printer to determine the correct vertical-to-horizontal ratio to use for drawing squares. Boxes that appear square on the screen may not be square when they are printed because the representation on the screen does not show the same ratio used for a printed document. Moving the cursor a certain number of spaces vertically is not the same as moving it the same number of spaces horizontally; the cursor moves a greater distance vertically. You can try out your printer by drawing what appears to be a square on the screen and then pressing Shift-F7 (Print) and choosing the Page option (**2** or **P**) to see immediately whether the box you have drawn is printed as a square. Many dot matrix printers use a 5:3 vertical to horizontal ratio; that is, a box that is 5 spaces deep by 3 spaces wide (or 10 spaces by 6 spaces, or 15 spaces by 9 spaces, and so forth) will be printed as a square. Figure 14.2 illustrates the differences in screen representation and printed results using an Epson FX-85 dot matrix printer. Use a similar test with your own printer to determine the correct ratio for squares.

Getting Ready to Draw

Any complex drawing or form you want to create requires a little forethought. You may find it convenient to sketch a diagram on graph paper before you begin

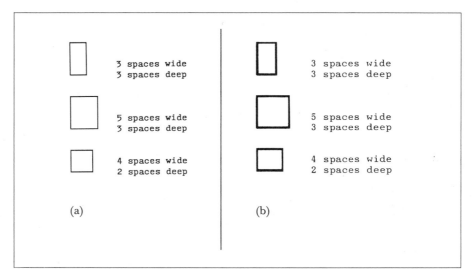

FIGURE 14.2: Determining the correct way to draw rectangles so that they will be printed as squares. Rectangles as represented on the monitor screen do not have the same proportions when they are printed. Part (a) of this figure illustrates a variety of shapes as they appear on the screen; part (b) shows how they appear when printed. Exact proportions may vary, depending on the type of printer you are using.

so that you can determine the exact inch mark or line number on which to place graphic elements. The default document page size (for 8½-by-11-inch paper) is 6.5 inches wide by 9 inches high. You may find it helpful to keep the units of measure for the status line in inches when working with line drawing, rather than changing it to 4.2 units. (See "The Status Line" in Chapter 2 for information on the Units of Measure feature and how it applies to the status line.)

Even if you decide not to sketch out your form or chart completely, you should estimate the longest line of text that each box or area needs to contain. You can simply type a sample entry on the screen and use Line Draw to draw a box around it; in most cases, this is the fastest way to estimate length.

When you draw within WordPerfect, you are in Typeover mode. Characters that you draw replace any other characters that may be on the screen. Because of this, you may want to enter text for your charts and forms first and then draw the rules around them.

If you return later to add text to drawings, you must be sure to press the Ins key to go into Typeover mode. (When Typeover mode is on, the word *Typeover* appears in the lower-left corner of the screen.) If you remain in Insert mode, you will get unexpected results, as illustrated in Figure 14.3.

Any format codes you have inserted on the screen can also produce unexpected results in Line Draw mode. For example, if you use Shift-F6 to center text and then later attempt to enclose this text in a box, the rule you draw will not extend over the Center code on the line where it is present. You will need to exit

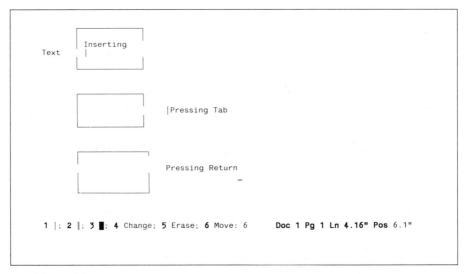

FIGURE 14.3: Entering text into box drawings while in Insert mode. As you can see, inserting text or pressing Tab or Enter destroys the graphic arrangement. For this reason, be sure to enter text such as labels into graphics you create in WordPerfect by first pressing Ins to go into Typeover mode. In Typeover mode, you can add many enhancements, such as legends, to graphs.

Line Draw mode by pressing F7, then press Alt-F3 to view the codes, position the cursor to the right of any codes that are causing trouble, and press Backspace to delete these codes. You can then reposition any text that has gotten out of alignment or redraw misaligned lines. For this reason, it is better to first create the shape that you want to center and then mark it as a block (with Alt-F4) before you press Shift-F6 to center it.

Because format codes can get in the way of line drawings, it is usually wise to create your graphics in a separate document—perhaps in a second window—and cut and paste them into the location where you want them in a document. See "Revising Graphics" later in this chapter for more information about cutting and pasting line draw graphics in a document.

DRAWING SIMPLE GRAPHICS

To draw simple graphics in WordPerfect, press Ctrl-F3 (Screen) and select the Line Draw option (**2** or **L**). When you are in WordPerfect's Line Draw mode, the following menu line appears:

1 │ ; **2** │ │ ; **3** ∗; **4** Change; **5** Erase; **6** Move: **1**

Selecting option **1**, **2**, or **3** allows you to choose among drawing single lines, double lines, or asterisks, as shown in Figure 14.4. Option **4** allows you to select up to eight different types of alternate drawing characters, as shown in Figure 14.5. You can select one of these to replace option **3** on the previous menu, or you can select option **9** (Other) to enter another character from the font you are using. If you want to use a simple keyboard character, like > (greater than), you simply type it from the keyboard after selecting the Other option. If you want to use a special graphics character or symbol, you use the Compose feature as described later in this chapter. (See "Creating Symbols with Compose" and "Using WordPerfect's Character Sets.")

If you select option **5**, the cursor will erase each character it passes through. Selecting option **6** allows you to move the cursor through your drawing without changing anything. When you are in Line Draw mode, the option you have selected appears at the end of the menu line, as shown in Figure 14.4. To exit Line Draw mode and enter text in editing mode, press F7 (Exit) or F1 (Cancel).

To enter text in drawings you have created, you should be in Typeover mode. (Press Ins to go into Typeover mode; you will see the word *Typeover* in the lower-left corner of the screen.) If you remain in Insert mode, which is WordPerfect's default setting, lines will be pushed to the right as you type, and pressing Enter, Tab, or the space bar will insert spaces into your graphics.

You can also type text for your graphics first, enter Line Draw mode, and then draw lines around the text you have already entered.

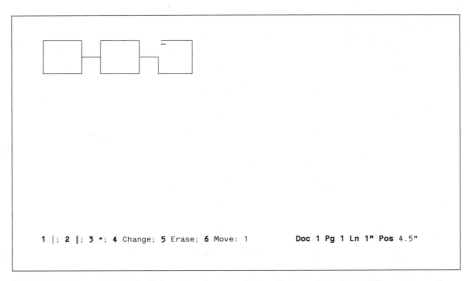

FIGURE 14.4: Using WordPerfect's Line Draw feature. Options **1**, **2**, and **3** indicate different types of lines you can draw. You can change option **3** to another character or symbol. While you are in Line Draw mode, the number at the end of this menu indicates the option you have chosen. Press F7 (Exit) to leave Line Draw mode.

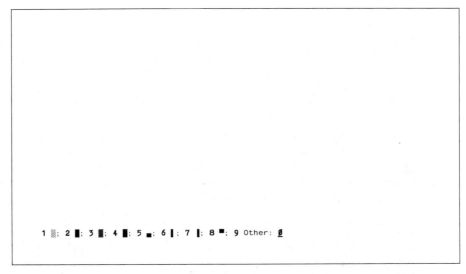

FIGURE 14.5: Selecting alternate graphics characters. You can select any of these characters to be used as option **3** on the Line Draw menu, or you can specify another character or symbol by pressing its key on the keyboard or by entering its code with Compose (Ctrl-2), as described later in this chapter.

Creating Forms

WordPerfect's Line Draw feature can be very useful for creating forms. You can use graphics characters to draw attention to important areas of the form that must be filled in, or to block out sections that are to be kept blank, as shown in Figure 14.6. You can even create forms that will perform calculations on the screen. For example, in Figure 14.6 it would be quite simple to insert codes that will subtotal down the columns and across the rows and produce a total at the bottom. Other applications include calculating the prices of orders (price × quantity), adding sales tax to subtotals, adding standard shipping and handling charges to totals, and so forth. Chapter 13 discusses how you set up columns of numbers so that WordPerfect can make simple calculations on them.

WordPerfect's Advance feature allows you to command the printer to advance to a certain position or line on the page without having to repeatedly press the Enter key to insert hard returns. If your printer supports this feature (not all printers do), you can use it to insert text within boxes drawn with the Line Draw feature. Figure 14.7 shows you an example in which the Advance feature is used to advance the double-line box so that the heading, WEEKLY LABOR REPORT, is printed within it. In this figure you can see the Reveal Codes screen showing the Advance to Line code that is used to situate the box so that it encloses the heading. Figure 14.8 uses the View Document feature to show how the box and heading will actually appear in the printout.

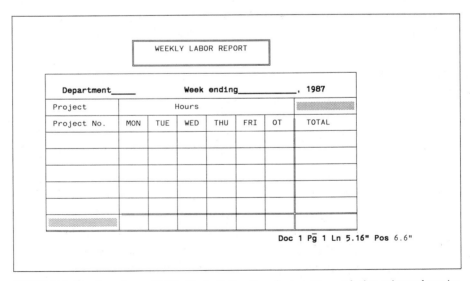

FIGURE 14.6: Creating a form with WordPerfect's Line Draw feature. You can further enhance forms by using Merge codes to insert additional information or by using WordPerfect's Math feature to perform calculations on columns of numbers.

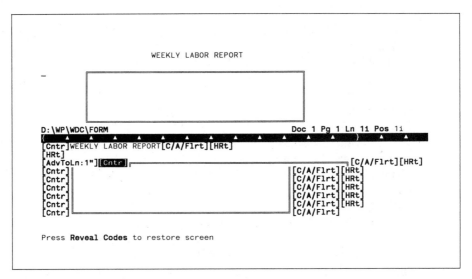

FIGURE 14.7: Using the Advance feature with Line Draw to correctly align a heading inside a double-line box. The Advance feature (here, the Advance to Line option was used) allows you to position text in boxes created by Line Draw without having to worry about disturbing the graphics characters when you enter the text. Refer to Figure 14.8 to see how the heading and box will appear in the printout.

When you use the Advance feature, changes to the placement of text or graphics are indicated on the status line but are not visible on the editing screen. You must use View Document to preview the final result. (See Chapter 18, "Combining Graphics and Text in a Publication," or the **Advance** reference entry in Part V, if you need specific information on how to use the Advance feature.)

Creating Graphics Macros

If you often use a standard set of graphics symbols—such as rectangles for charts—you may want to either create macros that produce them or store the shapes in separate files and cut and paste them from these files as needed. Several graphics macros that you can use or modify for your own needs are presented here.

BIGBOX: A MACRO FOR A LARGE RECTANGLE

The macro shown in Figure 14.9 creates a large rectangle 25 characters wide by 9 characters deep (approximately 2½ by 1½ inches on most printers, assuming that you are using a "normal" font). It is suitable for use in charts and diagrams in which you need several lines of text within a box. The {Esc} and number sequence tells WordPerfect to repeat an operation the number of times you define for the Esc key. The keys {Down}, {Right}, {Up}, and {Left} indicate the direction in which the line is drawn. Figure 14.10 illustrates the results of

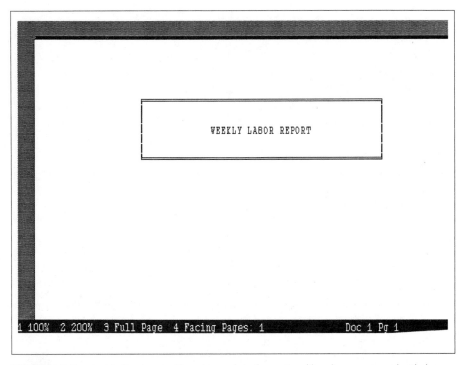

FIGURE 14.8: The double-line box positioned to enclose the centered heading, previewed with the View Document feature at 100% (full size). The [AdvToLine:1″] code inserted before the double-line box positions this graphics box correctly so that the heading appears to have been entered inside. Actually, as you can see in Figure 14.7, the heading was entered and centered on the line 1½ inches down from the top of the page, two lines before the box was drawn with WordPerfect's Line Draw feature.

this macro, which you activate by pressing Alt-F10 (Macro), typing **BIGBOX**, and pressing the Enter key.

SMBOX: A MACRO FOR A SMALL RECTANGLE

Similar to the BIGBOX macro presented above, this macro, shown in Figure 14.11, creates a small rectangle at the point in your document where the cursor is when you invoke it. This smaller rectangle is suitable for use in charts that contain two lines of text—for instance, organizational charts that contain a person's name and title. This macro will draw a box that is 15 characters wide by three lines deep (approximately 1½ by ½ inch on most printers). To increase the width of the box for longer names and titles, use a number larger than 15 in the macro. Remember, these rectangles will have slightly different proportions when printed; test them on your printer and adjust the proportions accordingly.

Figure 14.10 illustrates the results of this macro.

```
Macro: Edit

        File            BIGBOX.WPM

    1 - Description     Draw rect. box: 2 1/2" x 1 1/2"

    2 - Action

    ┌─────────────────────────────────────────────────────────┐
    │ {DISPLAY OFF}{Screen}11{Esc}9{Down}{Esc}25{Right}{Esc}9{Up}{Esc}25 │
    │ {Left}{Exit}                                              │
    │                                                           │
    │                                                           │
    │                                                           │
    │                                                           │
    │                                                           │
    └─────────────────────────────────────────────────────────┘

Selection: 0
```

FIGURE 14.9: The keystrokes of the BIGBOX macro shown in the Macro Editor. This macro initiates Line Draw with {Screen}l and then selects option **1**, the single line. The {Esc}-number sequences followed by the cursor movement direction tell WordPerfect the number of repetitions for the graphics character as well as the direction.

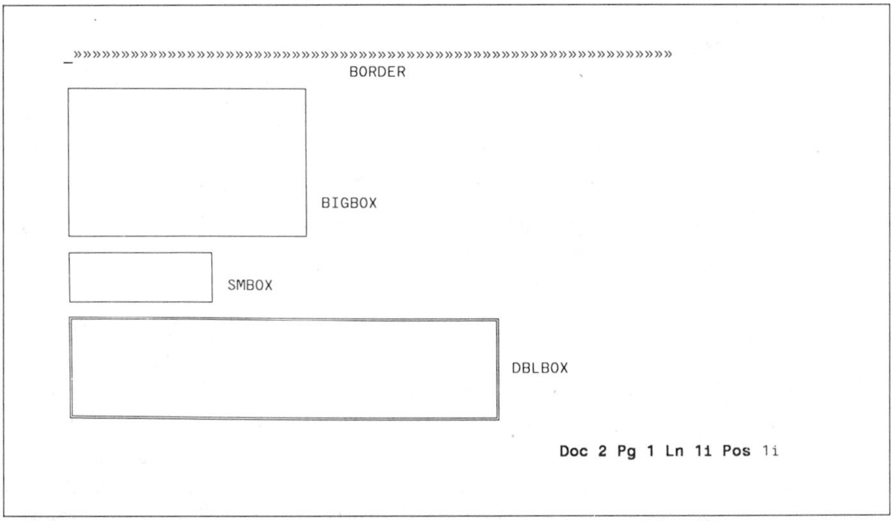

FIGURE 14.10: Using the macros described in the text. BIGBOX was used to create the large box, and SMBOX was used to create the smaller box. The double-rule box was created with DBLBOX, and the border was generated with BORDER. You can save these shapes in a file, perhaps naming it GRAPHICS, and copy them into your documents wherever you choose, or you can simply invoke the macro to create each shape in your documents.

```
Macro: Edit

        File            SMBOX.WPM

   1 - Description      Draw rect. box: 1 1/2" x 1/2"

   2 - Action

        ┌──────────────────────────────────────────────────────────────┐
        │{DISPLAY OFF}{Screen}11{Esc}3{Down}{Esc}15{Right}{Esc}3{Up}{Esc}15│
        │{Left}{Exit}                                                    │
        │                                                                │
        │                                                                │
        │                                                                │
        │                                                                │
        │                                                                │
        │                                                                │
        └──────────────────────────────────────────────────────────────┘

   Selection: 0
```

FIGURE 14.11: The keystrokes of the SMBOX macro shown in the Macro Editor. This macro initiates Line Draw with {Screen}1 and then selects option **1**, the single line. The {Esc}-number sequences followed by the cursor movement direction tell WordPerfect the number of repetitions for the graphics character as well as the direction.

DBLBOX: A MACRO FOR A RECTANGLE WITH A DOUBLE BORDER

You may often want to highlight graphics boxes—to draw attention to the portion of a chart containing sales totals, for example, or to point out the major topics on an overhead transparency. This macro, shown in Figure 14.12, uses the double-rule character to create a banner-type box with a double border. To change the proportions of the box, simply use other numbers in place of the 6 (depth) and 12 (width) in the macro.

To center this box in a chart or document, mark it as a block (Alt-F4); then press Shift-F6 (Center) and respond **Y** to the [Cntr]? prompt.

BORDER: A MACRO FOR A CHARACTER BORDER RULE

This macro, shown in Figure 14.13, demonstrates how you can change the graphics character presented in option **3** of the Line Draw menu to create other graphics effects in your text. It uses the right angle bracket (>) to create a horizontal 65-character border in your documents. If you work with newsletters or brochures, you may want to enhance them with such borders and rules. You can select any character in the fonts available to you.

```
Macro: Edit

       File          DBLBOX.WPM
  1 - Description     Draw dbl. line box: 4 1/2" x 1"
  2 - Action

  ┌─────────────────────────────────────────────────────────────┐
  │ {DISPLAY OFF}{Screen}12{Esc}6{Down}{Esc}45{Right}{Esc}6{Up}{Esc}45 │
  │ {Left}{Exit}                                                  │
  │                                                               │
  │                                                               │
  │                                                               │
  │                                                               │
  │                                                               │
  └─────────────────────────────────────────────────────────────┘

Selection: 0
```

FIGURE 14.12: The keystrokes of the DBLBOX macro shown in the Macro Editor. This macro initiates Line Draw with {Screen}l and then selects option **2**, the double line. The {Esc}-number sequences followed by the cursor movement direction tell WordPerfect the number of repetitions for the graphics character as well as the direction.

```
Macro: Edit

       File          BORDER.WPM
  1 - Description     Draw 6 1/2" fancy border
  2 - Action

  ┌─────────────────────────────────────────────────────────────┐
  │ {DISPLAY OFF}{Home}{Home}{Left}·{Screen}149»3{Esc}65{Right}{Exit} │
  │ {Right}{Enter}                                                │
  │                                                               │
  │                                                               │
  │                                                               │
  │                                                               │
  │                                                               │
  └─────────────────────────────────────────────────────────────┘

Selection: 0
```

FIGURE 14.13: The keystrokes of the BORDER macro shown in the Macro Editor. This macro positions the cursor at the beginning of the line ({Home}{Home}{Left}) and adds a space (shown by the dot). It then initiates Line Draw with {Screen}l, selects option **4**, Change, and then option **9**, Other. The new character is selected from character set 6 with Compose (Ctrl-2 6,18). The new graphics character then replaces the asterisk, and option **3** selects it. The {Esc}65{Right} sequence tells WordPerfect to repeat the graphics character 65 times to the right.

Creating a Graph

WordPerfect's Line Draw feature allows you to create bar and stacked-bar graphs. You will have to calculate the relative proportions for the graphic depiction of your data outside WordPerfect, however; the program cannot automatically create graphs from sets of data, as some graphics and spreadsheet programs can. The program also cannot connect lines at any angle other than 90 degrees, however, so you cannot create pie charts or line graphs.

Figure 14.14 illustrates a sample graph you can create with WordPerfect. Options **1**, **2**, and **4** from the menu presented when Change (option **4**) is selected from the Line Draw menu were used to create the bars in the graph and the legend indicators in the upper-right corner. After the lines and bars were drawn, F7 was pressed to exit Line Draw mode; Ins was then pressed to enter Typeover mode, as indicated in the lower-left corner of the screen. The text for the figure title and labels was then entered.

Revising Graphics

To erase lines when the Line Draw feature is on, select the Erase option (**5** or **E**) on the menu line. Then simply move the cursor over the lines and text you wish to erase. If Line Draw is off, you can erase by using the space bar to type over graphics or by using the Del or Backspace key.

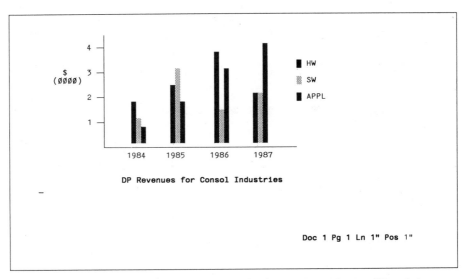

FIGURE 14.14: Sample graph you can create with WordPerfect's Line Draw feature. Although the program does not support pie charts and line graphs, which require slanted or curved lines, you can create bar and stacked-bar graphs such as this one to enhance your WordPerfect documents.

To cut and paste a graphics drawing, you simply mark its beginning and end (opposite corners) with Block (Alt-F4), press Ctrl-F4 (Move), select the Rectangle option (**3** or **R**), and then select the Move option (**1** or **M**). Position the cursor at the location in your document where you want the graphic image and press the Enter key. You can also copy graphics by following this key procedure, only selecting the Copy option (**2** or **C**) instead of the Move option.

If you look at the Reveal Codes screen for a graphic image, as shown in Figure 14.15, you will see that WordPerfect inserts [HRt] at the end of each line you draw. You can therefore cut or copy portions of your drawings also by simply marking the portion you want as a block.

CREATING SYMBOLS WITH COMPOSE

Version 5.0 gives you a way to create special characters by using the Compose key, which is Ctrl-2 (be careful you don't press Ctrl-F2, the Spell key). Note that you must press the Ctrl key and the number **2** on the top row of the QWERTY keyboard; you can't press Ctrl and the number **2** key on the numeric keypad. (You can also press Ctrl-V instead of Ctrl-2, if you prefer.)

After you press Ctrl-2, the next two characters you type will create a special character. You can create digraphs (characters that are joined together) as well as diacritics (accents) for letters. For example, you can create a digraph like Æ by pressing Ctrl-2 and then typing **AE**. (You can also produce this digraph by typing **EA**; the order does not matter.) As soon as you type **AE** after pressing Ctrl-2,

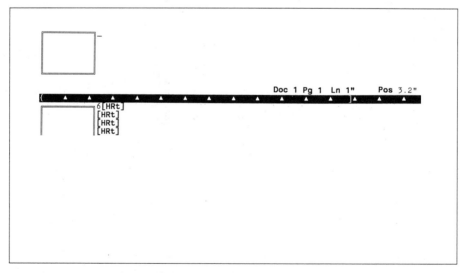

FIGURE 14.15: Reveal Codes screen for a graphic image. WordPerfect inserts a hard return ([HRt]) at the end of each line you draw, thus creating a rectangle. These shapes can then be cut and copied using the program's Move Rectangle key sequence.

the character Æ will appear at the cursor's present position in the document. However, if your printer is not capable of printing this digraph, you will see a solid rectangle on the screen instead. (This happens whenever you use Compose to enter a character that your printer can't reproduce—see below.)

Using WordPerfect's Character Sets

In addition, WordPerfect 5.0 comes with 12 different predefined character sets, most of which won't be printable with your printer. Character sets 0 through 10 contain special symbols, digraphs, and diacritical characters; character set 11 is Japanese Hiragana or Katakana. Set 12 is a user-defined set that you can create by using the printer definition program supplied with WordPerfect. If you are doing mathematical typing, you'll find most of the scientific and mathematical symbols in character sets 6 and 7, and character set 8 contains the Greek alphabet.

These character sets, which are reproduced in Appendix B, contain almost any character or symbol you may need. However, few printers are currently capable of reproducing many of them (especially those in sets 6 through 11). To determine which characters can be printed, you can retrieve the CHARACTR.DOC file on the Conversion disk (when you retrieve it, it will automatically be formatted for your printer). As you scroll through the file, you can tell which characters your printer definitely can't produce because each of these will be represented by a solid rectangle instead of the character described (see Figure 14.16).

You will also notice that some of the characters in a set are not displayed on the screen as they are described, so you will need to proof any documents that contain these symbols as hard copy. For example, the uppercase *U* with a circumflex in the first character set (1,68) may be displayed as a plain uppercase *U* lacking this mark. The composite character can't be shown correctly on your screen because it's not part of the IBM Extended Character Set. However, you can't be sure that your printer will not produce the character correctly until you try it. (Rather than waste paper by printing the entire text of the CHARACTR.DOC file, you should just print certain sections or even just certain pages of it.)

To insert a character from one of the sets that your printer can produce, you press Ctrl-2 and then type the number of the set followed by a comma and the number of the character in that set. It will not be displayed on the screen, however, until you press the Enter key or the space bar. For example, to produce the infinity symbol (∞), which is the 19th character in character set 6, you simply press Ctrl-2; type **6**, a comma, and **19** (no spaces); and press the Enter key or the space bar.

You can get the set and character number of a character either by referring to Appendix B of this book or by retrieving the CHARACTR.DOC file from the

```
**************************************************************
Charset:  1
Contains: Common capitalizable multinational characters,
          diacriticals, and non-capitalizable multinational
          characters.
**************************************************************
1,0     ▮    Grave

1,1     ▮    Centered Dot

1,2     ~    Tilde

1,3     ^    Circumflex

1,4     -    Horizontal Bar

1,5     /    Forward Slash

1,6     ▮    Acute

1,7     ▮    Diaeresis (Umlaut)

1,8     ▮    Macron
D:\WP\CHARACTR.DOC                      Doc 1 Pg 5 Ln 2.51 Pos 1i
```

FIGURE 14.16: The first part of Character Set 1 as displayed in the CHARACTR.DOC file when formatted for the LaserJet Series II with Courier 10-pitch as the initial font. Notice that this printer is only capable of printing the tilde, circumflex, horizontal bar, and forward slash in this font. It can't produce any of the other characters shown in this screen (indicated by the solid rectangle immediately preceding the character's description).

Conversion disk. If there are special characters you use regularly, you can record a macro to create them or map them onto a particular key or key sequence using WordPerfect's Keyboard Layout feature (see Chapter 17).

PART

III

SUPPLEMENTAL WORD PROCESSING FEATURES

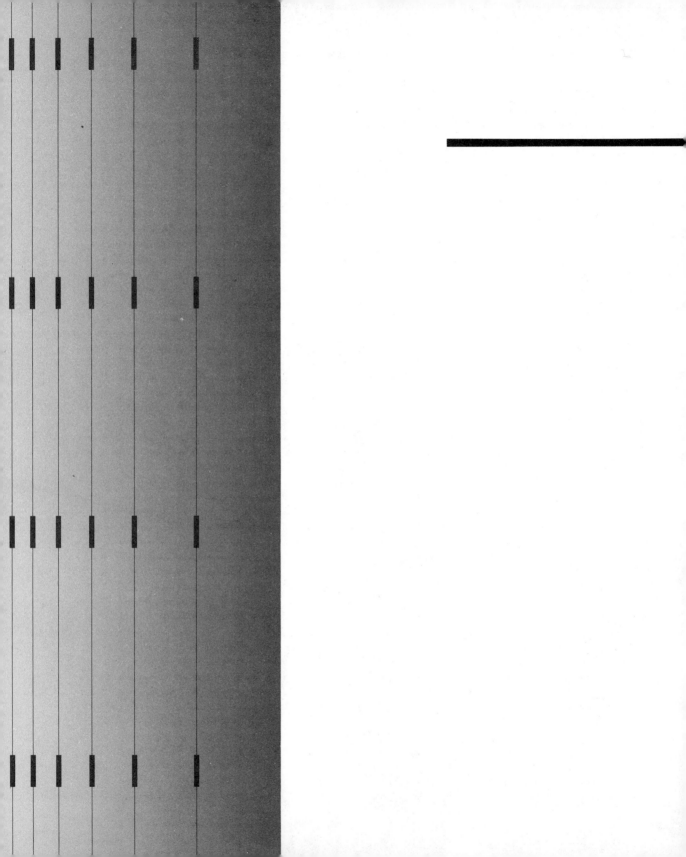

USING THE SPELLER AND THESAURUS

USING THE
SPELLER AND THESAURUS

WordPerfect contains both a built-in dictionary and a thesaurus to help you as you write and to check your work when it is done. You can use the Speller to check your documents for typographical errors after you have finished writing; because you can specify a word to look up, you can also use it to check the spelling of words you are unsure about as you write. You can use the Thesaurus to see alternative adjectives, nouns, and verbs for a word (synonyms) as well as words that have an opposite meaning (antonyms). This feature can be especially helpful if you are struggling for just the right word in a particular context.

UPGRADE NOTES

WordPerfect 5.0's Speller works much the same way as the previous version's; the differences are subtle. Phonetic alternatives are now automatically presented; there is no longer a menu option for them. You press F7 (Exit) to return to the Speller after correcting a word manually. The main dictionary has been named WP{WP}US.LEX, and the supplemental dictionary is WP{WP}US-.SUP. The Speller Utility contains an option for converting WordPerfect 4.2 dictionaries to 5.0 format.

OVERVIEW OF WORDPERFECT'S SPELLER AND THESAURUS

WordPerfect's Speller actually uses three dictionaries: a common list of 1,550 of the most often used words, a main list of approximately 100,000 more words, and a supplemental dictionary consisting of all the words you add as you write. You can create additional custom dictionaries to suit your needs, as you may want to do if you write in a specialized field. In addition, you can tailor Word-Perfect's dictionary to suit your own needs by adding the words you habitually mistype to its common word list, thereby speeding up the spell-checking process.

The Thesaurus consists of approximately 10,000 *headwords,* which are the basic words you can look up. WordPerfect will display many more words as suggested alternatives, but the headwords are linked to other references, meaning that you can continue to explore alternative words until you find the one that best suits your needs. Figure 15.1 illustrates a Thesaurus screen presenting suggested alternatives for the word *stage.*

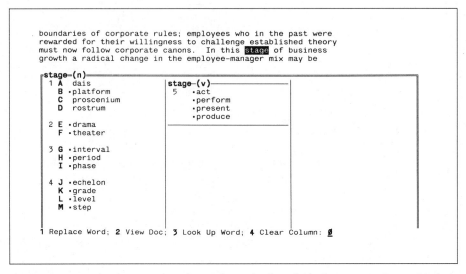

```
      boundaries of corporate rules; employees who in the past were
      rewarded for their willingness to challenge established theory
      must now follow corporate canons.  In this  stage  of business
      growth a radical change in the employee-manager mix may be

  ┌stage-(n)────────────────┬──────────────────────────┬────────────────
    1 A   dais              │ stage-(v)────             │
      B •platform           │ 5     •act                │
      C  proscenium         │       •perform            │
      D  rostrum            │       •present            │
                            │       •produce            │
    2 E •drama              │                           │
      F •theater            │                           │
                            │                           │
    3 G •interval           │                           │
      H •period             │                           │
      I •phase              │                           │
                            │                           │
    4 J •echelon            │                           │
      K •grade              │                           │
      L •level              │                           │
      M •step               │                           │

  1 Replace Word; 2 View Doc; 3 Look Up Word; 4 Clear Column: 0
```

FIGURE 15.1: Using the Thesaurus. Here the word *stage* has been looked up. As you can see, Word-Perfect presents alternative nouns and verbs that could be used in place of the word in your document. Words with dots next to them, such as *period* and *level* in the figure, are cross-referenced to other word lists.

Use the Speller if

- You are unsure about the spelling of a word.
- You want to correct typographical errors and misspelled words in your document.

Use the Thesaurus if

- You are unsure which word to use in a particular context.
- You are unsure about the meaning of a word, and seeing other related words, including any antonyms (opposites), would help you define it.
- You would like to see a group of related words (nouns, verbs, and adjectives) that could be used in place of or along with a word already in your document.

Changing the Language Code

In version 5.0, if you are checking documents written in foreign languages, you may change the Language code so that WordPerfect uses a different version of the Speller and Thesaurus. To change the Language code, press Shift-F8 (Format); then select Other (**4** or **O**). Select Language (**5** or **L**) to change the Language code to the one you want to use. WordPerfect comes with only one version of the Speller and Thesaurus, but you can order versions in the following languages:

Language	Code
British English	UK
Canadian French	CA
Danish	DA
Dutch	NE
Finnish	SU
French	FR
German	DE
Icelandic	IC
Italian	IT
Norwegian	NO
Portuguese	PO
Spanish	ES
Swedish	SV
U.S.A. English	US

HOW WORDPERFECT'S SPELLER WORKS

When checking the spelling of a word, WordPerfect's Speller first checks a common list of approximately 1,550 words. If it does not find the word there, it next checks its main list of over 100,000 more words.

When you use the Speller, WordPerfect checks your document for words it does not recognize. When it encounters one of these, it presents the message *Not Found!* and displays a list of possible spellings (if it finds any near matches), as shown in Figure 15.2. You can simply press the letter corresponding to the correct word; WordPerfect then inserts it into the document for you so that you do not have to manually correct the spelling. WordPerfect 5.0 automatically searches for words that sound like the word it has highlighted and queries you on words that contain numbers. You can disable alphanumeric checking by selecting Ignore Numbers (option 6). In Figure 15.2, for example, WordPerfect has presented phonetic alternatives for the highlighted word.

The Speller menu also offers a Word Count option that allows you to get a count of the words in your document, which can be useful if you are writing a document of a specific number of words for a journal or term paper.

Because you will probably often use words that WordPerfect's Speller does not know—especially proper names and specialized terms you use in your work—the program makes it easy for you to add words to the dictionary. Each time you

```
Don't use more than a 10% screen if you want text and graphics to be

legible. Use the heavier screens for special effects in your documents,

such as decorative borders, but don't try to ▊puit▊ text in them.



Before You Begin

=====================================================================================
     A. pit                    B. puis                   C. punt
     D. put                    E. putt                   F. pad
     G. paid                   H. pat                    I. pate
     J. path                   K. pawed                  L. payout
     M. pd                     N. peat                   O. pede
     P. pet                    Q. pete                   R. peyote
     S. pied                   T. pith                   U. pod
     V. poet                   W. pot                    X. pott
Press Enter for more words

Not Found: 1 Skip Once; 2 Skip; 3 Add; 4 Edit; 5 Look Up; 6 Ignore Numbers: 0
```

FIGURE 15.2: Presenting a list of suggested alternatives for a mistyped word. If WordPerfect presents a full screen of alternatives (A through X), press Enter to scroll up any additional alternatives.

select Add (*3*) from the Speller menu, WordPerfect adds that word to its supplemental dictionary, WP{WP}US.SUP. You can view this supplemental dictionary and edit it as you would any other document you create in WordPerfect. The dictionary WP{WP}US.SUP is automatically created in the directory containing WordPerfect utilities the first time you use the Add Word option. You can also create other custom supplemental dictionaries of your own and specify that they be used instead of the regular supplemental dictionary. If you are working with two floppy drives instead of a hard disk and use a large supplemental dictionary, you may want to create several smaller supplemental dictionaries and copy the main dictionary plus your specialized dictionary onto one floppy disk.

Note that WordPerfect's Speller cannot check words that you have spelled correctly but may have used incorrectly, such as *weather* and *whether*. If you are in doubt about the use of such words, you may want to use the Speller's Look Up option (*5*) to look them up; WordPerfect will then present you with a list of possible alternatives, even if the words are spelled correctly.

When you look up a word, you can use the question mark (?) and asterisk (*) wild-card characters in place of letters you are unsure of. The question mark stands for any one letter, and the asterisk represents any sequence of letters.

USING THE SPELLER

Although the Speller checks the version of your document that is on the screen (in RAM), it is wise to save your document first when you use WordPerfect's

Speller. Also remember to save your document after you have spell-checked it so that the changes you indicated as you used the Speller will become part of the saved version of your document.

To use WordPerfect's Speller, press Ctrl-F2 (Spell). You are then presented with the following menu options:

Check: **1 W**ord; **2 P**age; **3 D**; **4 N**ew Sup. Dictionary; **5 L**ookup; **6 C**ount: 0

You can select whether to check the word the cursor is on (**1** or **W**), the page the cursor is on (**2** or **P**), or the entire document as it appears on the screen (**3** or **D**). (When you instruct WordPerfect's Speller to check an entire document, it checks all portions of your document, including headers and footers, but it does not check index entries.) In addition, you can have the program use another supplemental dictionary that you have created (**4** or **N**). You can also instruct Word-Perfect to look up a word that you type in response to a prompt or to count the words in your document (**5** or **L**). Finally, you can get a count of the number of words in the document (**6** or **C**).

If you want to check the spelling for a portion of the document, press Alt-F4 (Block), mark all of the text to be included (Alt-F4), and press Ctrl-F2 (Spell).

When you use WordPerfect's Speller to check the word at the cursor, Word-Perfect skips the cursor to the next word in the text if the word is spelled correctly. When a word is not found in the dictionary, you are presented with a screen whose lower half contains the suggested alternatives for any incorrect word WordPerfect finds, as was shown in Figure 15.2. The top half shows where in your document WordPerfect found the suspect word. You can easily toggle between the two screens to edit your document, however. To enter the document portion of the screen, just press the → or ← key. (You can also select Edit, but pressing → or ← is faster.) While you are working with the Speller, only the → and ← keys, along with Backspace and Del, are available as cursor movement keys. You cannot use most of the other cursor movement techniques, such as Go To (Ctrl-Home) and End. You can, however, change from Insert to Typeover mode. When you have finished editing, press F7 (Exit) to return to the Speller.

The Not Found menu at the very bottom of the screen includes the following options:

Not Found: **1** Skip Once; **2** Skip; **3** Add; **4** Edit; **5** Look Up; **6** Ignore Numbers: 0

Select the Skip Once option (**1**) to have WordPerfect skip just the current occurrence of the word in the document. If there are any further occurrences and you use this option, WordPerfect will stop and flag them. If you want this word to be skipped throughout the rest of the document, select the Skip option (**2**) instead. If you want to add this word to the supplementary dictionary, select the Add option (**3**). If you want to edit the word, select the Edit option (**4**), make your changes, and then press F7 (Exit) to continue the spell-checking. If you want to look up the spelling of a related term, select the Look Up option and type in the word to be looked up. If WordPerfect has flagged a word with a number in it, like *B12*, and you want it and other words that contain numbers to be ignored during the spell-checking, select the Ignore Numbers option (**6**).

> *Note:* The Ignore Numbers option (**6**) was not included in the first shipments of WordPerfect 5.0 in May, 1988. It was first added to the maintenance upgrade dated 7/11/88. (To check the date of your copy of 5.0, press F3 and look at the date in the upper-right corner of the screen.) Call WordPerfect Corporation to receive a copy of the latest version of WordPerfect 5.0.

To exit from the Speller, press F1 (Cancel). The program automatically presents a word count of the text it has checked up to that point. Save your document if you want the changes introduced with the Speller to be incorporated into the saved version.

Because the Speller basically matches patterns, it quickly finds words in which only one or two letters are incorrect or out of place—such as *atble* for *table* or *procided* for *provided*. It also catches more complex typographical errors and misspellings—it will suggest *document* as a replacement for *dicumenty,* for example.

The Speller ignores numbers when used alone, but it will stop at alphanumeric words, such as *F3* unless you select the Ignore Numbers option (**6** or **I**). It will not suggest appropriate replacements for mistyped words containing symbols, such as *l;etter;* it considers only the portion of the word occurring before or after the symbol. It will query these words, but you must correct them manually. Likewise, it does not suggest appropriate replacements for words that have been run together, such as *specifythat.* It will query them, but you must correct them manually by pressing →, moving the cursor to the letter where the next word is to begin, pressing the space bar, and pressing F7 (Exit) to accept the new words.

The Speller will locate words that occur twice in a row. When it does, it presents the following menu:

Double Word: **1 2** Skip; **3** Delete 2nd; **4** Edit; **5** Disable Double Word Checking

You can select the Delete 2nd option (**3**) to delete the second occurrence, or you can leave the words in place (the Skip option, **1** or **2**). Disable Double Word Checking (**5**) allows you to turn this feature off so that the program will not query you at double words.

You may notice as you use the Speller that sometimes the choices are presented in alphabetical order and sometimes they are not. This is because WordPerfect looks first in the common word list and then in the main word list. Both lists are stored in alphabetical order. You may also sometimes see duplicate words presented as choices if a word you have added to a supplemental dictionary is in one of the other word lists as well, or if a word is in both the main and common word lists. After you have used the Speller for a while, you will be able to tell which list your commonly mistyped words are in by the amount of time it takes the program to display the choices on the screen. You can speed up the checking process by using the Speller utility (as described later in this chapter) to move words you habitually mistype to the common word list.

If one of the words the Speller presents is the word you want, press the letter next to the word. WordPerfect then inserts the word into your text; you do not have to manually retype it or correct the incorrect letters. The program automatically capitalizes the word as the misspelled version had been typed in your document. If you have mistyped *The* as *Hte,* WordPerfect will correct it as *The,* although its suggested replacement will be *the.*

If none of the words match the one you intended, press Enter to see any additional words WordPerfect may find. For example, if WordPerfect presented you with a full screen of words, pressing Enter may bring up additional alternatives that could not be displayed. WordPerfect sometimes will also present words beginning with other letters if you press Enter. If words beginning with *c* are displayed, for example, pressing Enter may bring up a list of words beginning with *k.*

If the Speller cannot locate a near match for a word, the blinking cursor moves from just under the double-dashed line to the *0* at the end of the first menu line. If the cursor moves to this position, you know that WordPerfect has checked all of its lists and cannot match the word. If the word needs to be edited, press the → key to move to the document screen and begin correcting the word manually, then press F7 (Exit) to return to the Speller.

"Dictionary Full" Messages

As you use the Speller, WordPerfect adds the words you specify to a supplemental dictionary called WP{WP}US.SUP. It also adds the words you skip to a list that it keeps in memory. When the RAM space you are working with becomes full—as it may when you are working with a large document—you will receive the message *Dictionary Full.* In such a case, you should add the words in the supplemental dictionary to the main dictionary by using the Speller Utility, as described later in this chapter.

USING THE THESAURUS

WordPerfect's Thesaurus provides a quick way to see a list of nouns, adjectives, and verbs that have meanings similar to that of a word in your document. To use the Thesaurus, you can first position the cursor on or after the word you wish to look up. When you press Alt-F1 (Thesaurus), you will see three columns containing various words as well as several lines of your text surrounding the word you are looking up. (If you are using a floppy disk system, the Thesaurus disk must be in drive B before you press Alt-F1.)

The word you are looking up is presented in boldface at the beginning of each group of nouns, adjectives, or verbs. WordPerfect then presents several alternatives that have the same or similar meaning. A word with a dot to its left (like *history* in Figure 15.3) is a headword, and you can look up additional references to it through the Thesaurus. If you press the letter next to any of the headwords, a further list of suggested alternatives will appear. For example, to see the screen shown in Figure 15.4, the letter *G* for *over* was pressed from the screen in Figure 15.3.

You can move between the columns by using the ← and → keys. The ↑ and ↓ keys as well as the PgUp and PgDn keys scroll the columns vertically. The Home Home ↑ and Home Home ↓ key combinations take you to the beginning and end of the Thesaurus entry.

You can replace the word in your document with any of the words in the list by selecting Replace Word (**1**) from the Thesaurus menu and typing the letter corresponding to the word you wish to use. You can also return to view your document—for example, to get a better idea of the context in which the word was used—by selecting the View Doc option (**2**). Although you cannot edit your document while using View Doc, you can return to the Thesaurus by pressing F7 (Exit), or you can continue to use the Thesaurus by pressing Alt-F1 again to look up another word. If you decide to make extensive editing changes, press F7 twice to exit from the Thesaurus.

If the word you are looking for is not on the list, try selecting other headwords (those with a dot next to them) and looking up their synonyms. You can also have the Thesaurus look up a word that is not presented as a headword by using Look Up Word (**3**). If you use this method, you will find that the Thesaurus is a very

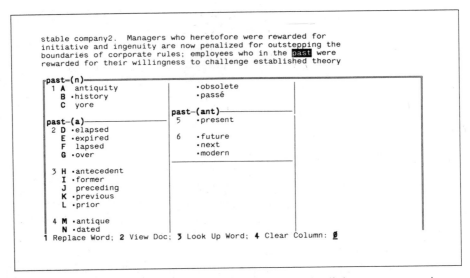

FIGURE 15.3: Using the Thesaurus. Here WordPerfect is presenting a list of alternative nouns and adjectives for the word *past*, as well as antonyms—words such as *future* and *present* that mean the opposite of *past*.

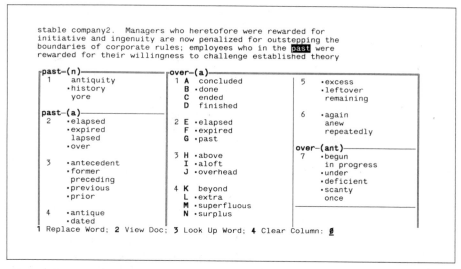

stable company2. Managers who heretofore were rewarded for
initiative and ingenuity are now penalized for outstepping the
boundaries of corporate rules; employees who in the `past` were
rewarded for their willingness to challenge established theory

```
┌past=(n)────────   ┌over=(a)─────────
 1    antiquity       1 A  concluded      5   •excess
      •history          B  •done              •leftover
      yore               C  ended              remaining
                         D  finished
past─(a)───────                           6   •again
 2    •elapsed       2 E  •elapsed              anew
      •expired         F  •expired             repeatedly
       lapsed         G  •past
      •over                               over─(ant)────────
                     3 H  •above          7   •begun
 3    •antecedent      I  •aloft               in progress
      •former          J  •overhead            •under
       preceding                               •deficient
      •previous      4 K   beyond              •scanty
      •prior           L  •extra                once
                       M  •superfluous
 4    •antique         N  •surplus
      •dated
1 Replace Word; 2 View Doc; 3 Look Up Word; 4 Clear Column: 0
```

FIGURE 15.4: Looking up a headword. Headwords, which are identified by a dot next to them, are connected to lists of related words. To see synonyms for a headword, press the letter corresponding to the word. WordPerfect's Thesaurus contains approximately 10,000 headwords. In this figure, the letter *G* was typed to see related words for the headword *over* (listed in Figure 15.3). Notice that the related words for *over* in the second and third columns include a group of antonyms, listed under 7.

useful tool and will take you through many different levels of meanings. If your screen becomes cluttered with too many alternative words, you can use the Clear Column option (**4**) to clear the column the cursor is in and make room for more synonyms of another headword.

To use the Thesaurus with a two-floppy-disk system, replace the data disk in drive B with the Thesaurus disk when you are ready to use the Thesaurus. When you have finished looking up words and making any replacements within your document, replace your data disk in drive B and save your document.

If you are using the Thesaurus on a hard disk, WordPerfect will first look for WP{WP}US.THS, the Thesaurus program, in the same directory as the Word-Perfect program, WP.EXE, or in the directory designated on the Setup Location of Auxiliary Files menu (see the next section). If it does not find it there, it will prompt you for the full path name of the location where the Thesaurus is stored.

INSTALLING THE SPELLER AND THESAURUS

When you use WordPerfect with a floppy disk system, the WordPerfect Program disk is in drive A and the data disk is in drive B. You must use the Setup key (Shift-F1) to tell WordPerfect that the main dictionary and the Thesaurus will also be in drive B (see **Setup** in Part V, "WordPerfect Command and Feature Reference"). When you want to use the Speller or Thesaurus, you must remove your data disk from drive B and insert the Speller disk. You can then press Ctrl-F2 to use the Speller or Alt-F1 to use the Thesaurus. When you have corrected your document, remove the Speller disk and reinsert the data disk in drive B before you save your document. If you forget to remove the Speller disk and you save the corrected document on the Speller disk instead of on the data disk, simply insert the data disk, save the document again, insert the Speller disk, and delete the saved document from it. (See Chapter 8 for details about saving and deleting files.)

If you have a hard disk and you intend to keep the Speller and Thesaurus in a directory other than the default directory, you need to tell WordPerfect which directory contains the Speller and Thesaurus. You do this by using the Setup key (Shift-F1) to specify the location of the main dictionary and the Thesaurus (see **Setup** in Part V, "WordPerfect Command and Feature Reference").

THE SPELLER UTILITY

A separate program, the Speller Utility (SPELL.EXE), is provided on the Speller disk. This program allows you to create new dictionaries and to edit both the common word list and the main word list in WordPerfect's built-in dictionary. It also allows you to display the common word list on the screen and to look up word patterns and phonetic alternatives.

Because you may sometimes inadvertently add misspelled words to the dictionary by selecting the Add option (3) from the Speller menu and then adding the supplemental dictionary to the main dictionary, the ability to delete words from the dictionary can be very useful to you. Likewise, it can be very useful for deleting words that you never use but which WordPerfect maintains as correct in the main dictionary. For example, *id* is a common typing error for *is,* but because the main dictionary lists *id* as a correct word (which it is, if you are writing in the field of psychology or related sciences), WordPerfect will not query you for the typographical error *id.* If you never use *id* or other main-dictionary words likely to appear in your documents as typing errors, you can delete them from the dictionary, and WordPerfect will query them as mistakes.

It is also handy to add words directly to either the main dictionary or the common word list. WordPerfect's Speller Utility allows you to add or delete words directly from the keyboard or from a file containing a word list. When you create such a file, each word must be followed by a hard return, but the words do not have to be alphabetized.

You can also increase the speed of the spell-checking process by adding words you habitually mistype or misspell to the common word list instead of the main dictionary. The Speller Utility allows you to determine which list a word is in, as well as to look up a word directly.

You can use the Speller Utility to

- Change dictionaries that you use, or create new dictionaries.
- Add words to the main dictionary's word lists.

- Delete words from the main dictionary's word lists.
- Optimize new dictionaries (by locating and formatting their words).
- Display the common word list.
- Check the location of a word—whether it is in the common word list or the main word list.
- Look up words using wild-card characters, if you are unsure of the exact spelling.
- Look up words phonetically.
- Convert WordPerfect 4.2 dictionaries to WordPerfect 5.0 format.

The Speller Utility's main menu (Figure 15.5) allows you to perform many housekeeping functions for the dictionaries you use.

USING THE SPELLER UTILITY

To use the Speller Utility, you must first exit to DOS either by exiting Word-Perfect (F7) or using the Shell command (Ctrl-F1 1). If you are using a floppy disk system, you then insert the Speller disk in drive A and a data disk in drive B. When WordPerfect executes the Speller Utility to create a new dictionary, it creates it in drive B. It then deletes the old version of the main dictionary from the Speller disk in drive A and recopies the dictionary in drive B back into drive A.

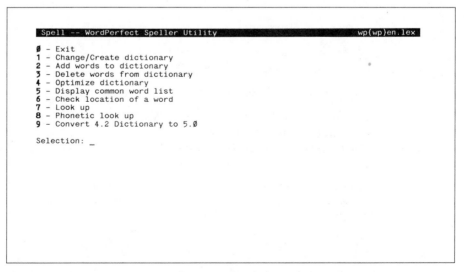

FIGURE 15.5: WordPerfect's Speller Utility. This menu allows you to perform housekeeping duties for the dictionaries you create and maintain in WordPerfect.

Note: If the disk in drive A does not have sufficient space, WordPerfect will cancel the transfer of the new dictionary from drive B to drive A. In such a case, you need to delete extra files that may be on the Speller disk and then use the DOS COPY command to transfer the updated dictionary from the disk in drive B to the disk in drive A. You can also simply use the dictionary disk that is in drive B as your dictionary disk. Remember to label the disk properly if you choose to use this method.

If you are using WordPerfect on a hard disk system, make sure that the directory containing the WP{WP}US.LEX file is current before issuing the Speller Utility startup command.

To use the Speller Utility at the DOS prompt,

1. Type **SPELL** and press Enter.
2. When the Speller Utility's main menu (shown in Figure 15.5) appears, select the option(s) you wish to use, one at a time, and supply any other necessary information the program prompts you for. (The options are presented in the upcoming sections.)
3. When you have selected all the options you wish to use, enter **0** (Exit).

Changing and Creating Dictionaries

To create a new dictionary or switch to another existing one, press **1** to select the Change/Create Dictionary option on the Speller Utility menu. The prompt

You may now safely exchange diskettes in any drive

Name of dictionary to use: wp{wp}us.lex

appears. Enter the file name of the dictionary you wish to create or switch to. If you are creating a new dictionary, WordPerfect displays the following prompt:

Create a new dictionary named *<file name>* (Y/N)

Press **Y** to create the new dictionary, which will be empty at this point.

The name of the current main dictionary is displayed in the upper-right corner of the screen. When you change to or create another dictionary, its name is displayed there.

Note: When you create a new dictionary, it will not contain the 100,000 or so words in WordPerfect's main dictionary. You can accidentally delete the main dictionary by naming another, smaller dictionary WP{WP}US.LEX. To be safe, always work with a copy of the main dictionary on a separate floppy disk or in a separate directory on the hard disk. If space is not a consideration, it is best to simply add words to your main dictionary. If you work with a floppy disk system, you may wish to create different versions of the main dictionary and keep them on separate floppy disks.

You must then add words to your new dictionary (see the sections that discuss editing dictionaries later in this chapter). After you have added words, select the Optimize Dictionary option (**4**) to optimize the new dictionary. During this process, WordPerfect alphabetizes the dictionary entries and formats them so that they may be used.

If you wish to switch the current dictionary to another existing one, enter its name—for example, **LEGAL.LEX**—at the "Name of Dictionary" prompt. WordPerfect will recognize the file name and carry out all the options you subsequently select from the Speller Utility menu on the dictionary you specify here.

Creating a New Supplemental Dictionary

To create a new supplemental dictionary, you simply create a new document containing the words you want to include, each followed by a hard return. *Make sure that the words are spelled correctly.* When you save the document, give it a name, such as LEGAL.SUP, that helps you remember that it is a supplemental dictionary.

To use a different supplemental dictionary, select New Sup. Dictionary (**4**) when you run the Speller. When you are prompted to do so, enter the full path name of the supplemental dictionary you wish to use.

Editing a Main Dictionary

You can add words to a dictionary—either the main dictionary, which is called WP{WP}US.LEX, or other main dictionaries you have created—and delete words from it either directly from the keyboard or from a file containing the words you wish to add or delete. You may, for example, inadvertently add a misspelled word to the supplemental dictionary while spell-checking your document and then later add the supplemental dictionary to the main dictionary, thus inserting a misspelled word into the main dictionary. You can use the Speller Utility to delete those words.

You may also want to add words you often mistype to the common word list to speed up the spell-checking process.

When you select the Add Words to Dictionary option (**2**) from the Speller Utility main menu, the Add Words menu appears on the screen, as shown in Figure 15.6. The Delete Words from Dictionary option (**3**) presents the Delete Words menu; it works the same way and has the same options as the Add Words menu.

From the Add Words menu, you can select Add to Common Word List (**1**) to add words to the common word list from the keyboard. The common word list is the one that WordPerfect checks first, so if you are adding words that you will use often, select one of these options. (If you are adding words to the common word list from the default supplemental dictionary, select option **2** and enter **WP{WP}US.SUP** as the name of the file when prompted to do so.)

```
Spell -- Add Words                                          wp{wp}en.lex

0 - Cancel - do not add words
1 - Add to common word list (from keyboard)
2 - Add to common word list (from a file)
3 - Add to main word list (from keyboard)
4 - Add to main word list (from a file)
5 - Exit

Selection: _
```

FIGURE 15.6: The Add Words menu. This menu allows you to add words to the main dictionary. If you receive the message *Dictionary Full* as you work, you need to add the words contained in the supplemental dictionary (WP{WP}EN.SUP) to the main dictionary. This menu allows you to do so.

The Add to Main Word List options (**3** and **4**) allow you to add words directly from the keyboard or from a file to the main word list. If you are updating the main dictionary from the default supplemental dictionary, use option **4** and enter **WP{WP}US.SUP** when prompted for a file name. Otherwise, enter the name of the file containing the words you wish to add. The words in the file should be separated by hard returns, but they do not need to be in alphabetical order. If you want to add words to a dictionary other than the main dictionary, you must first use the Change/Create Dictionary option (**1**) on the main Speller Utility menu to change to that dictionary.

Select Cancel (**0**) on the Add Words menu to return to the Speller Utility menu without making any changes; select Exit (**5**) to run the Add Words program and to exit from the Add Words menu.

When you use the Speller Utility to add words to or delete words from a dictionary, no matter how few or how many words, the process will take up to 20 minutes (a shorter time for the smaller common word list) because WordPerfect must re-sort the entire dictionary. The program does not execute the add or delete operation until you exit from the Add or Delete menu.

Editing a Supplemental Dictionary

You can edit the default supplemental dictionary, WP{WP}US.SUP, or any other supplemental dictionary you create, just as you would any other

WordPerfect document. Simply retrieve it by using List Files (F5 Enter) or by pressing Shift-F10 (Retrieve).

Optimizing Dictionaries

The Optimize Dictionary option (**4**) is used when you create a new dictionary. It instructs WordPerfect to alphabetize the words the new dictionary contains and format them properly. You should use this option only when you are creating a new dictionary.

Displaying the Common Word List

Because WordPerfect's Speller checks the common word list first, you may want to view the contents of this list and add to it words that you habitually mistype in order to speed up the checking process. For example, *document* is a word often mistyped by authors of word processing books, but because of the time WordPerfect takes to match its pattern and suggest alternatives for it, this word is in the main word list instead of the common word list.

When you select Display Common Word List (**5**) from the Speller Utility menu, WordPerfect displays the common word list in alphabetical order, one screen at a time (Figure 15.7). You can press any key to move through the list (in a forward direction only). To exit from the list, press F1 (Cancel). You cannot edit this list directly; to add words to it or delete words from it, use the Add Words to Dictionary or Delete Words from Dictionary option (**2** or **3**) on the Speller Utility menu.

Checking the Location of a Word

The Check Location of a Word option (**6**) on the Speller Utility menu allows you to determine whether a word is in WordPerfect's dictionary, and if it is, whether it is in the common word list or the main word list. When you select this option, you receive the prompt

Word to check:

Enter the word you want to check. WordPerfect responds with either

Found in main dictionary

or

Found in common word list

You can check any number of words. Press F1 (Cancel) to return to the Speller Utility menu.

```
╔══════════════════════════════════════════════════════════════════════╗
║ Spell -- List Common Words                                wp{wp}en.lex ║
║                                                                        ║
║ ====================================================================== ║
║                                                                        ║
║     1. a                    2. ability             3. able             ║
║     4. about                5. above               6. accept           ║
║     7. accepted             8. according           9. account          ║
║    10. across              11. act                12. action           ║
║    13. actions             14. active             15. activities        ║
║    16. activity            17. actual             18. actually         ║
║    19. add                 20. added              21. addition         ║
║    22. additional          23. address            24. administration   ║
║    25. advantage           26. affairs            27. after            ║
║    28. afternoon           29. again              30. against          ║
║    31. age                 32. ago                33. agreed           ║
║    34. agreement           35. ahead              36. aid              ║
║    37. air                 38. all                39. allow            ║
║    40. allowed             41. almost             42. alone            ║
║    43. along               44. already            45. also             ║
║    46. although            47. always             48. am               ║
║    49. america             50. american           51. among            ║
║ Press Enter for more words                                             ║
║ Press any key to continue_                                             ║
║                                                                        ║
╚══════════════════════════════════════════════════════════════════════╝
```

FIGURE 15.7: Viewing the common word list. If you habitually mistype certain words, you may want to check this list to be sure that these words are included in it. WordPerfect checks this list first, so adding the words you typically misspell may speed up the spell-checking process.

Looking Up Words with the Speller Utility

You can also use the Speller Utility to look up a word directly, using the Look Up and Phonetic Look Up options (**7** and **8**). You can use the question mark (**?**) and asterisk (*****) wild-card characters in place of letters you are unsure of. The question mark stands for any one letter, and the asterisk represents a sequence of letters. For example, if you want to check the spelling of *reprieve* but are unsure whether the word is spelled *repreieve, repreive,* or *reprieve,* you can enter **repr*ve** to see a list of correctly spelled words beginning with *repr-* and ending with *-ve* (Figure 15.8).

Use Phonetic Look Up (**8**) to look up a word phonetically. WordPerfect will present a list of suggested words that sound like the word you have typed.

Converting WordPerfect 4.2 Dictionaries

If you have created dictionaries with WordPerfect 4.2, you can convert them to version 5.0 by using Convert 4.2 Dictionary to 5.0, option **9** on the Speller Utility menu. WordPerfect will prompt you for the name of the 4.2 dictionary you want to convert and the name you wish it to have in version 5.0. In version 4.2, the main dictionary was named WP.LEX, so enter this name, including the full path name where the dictionary is located, if you want to convert it for use with version 5.0.

```
┌──────────────────────────────────────────────────────────────────────────┐
│ ▐ Spell -- Match Pattern ▌                              wp{wp}en.lex       │
│ Word Pattern: _                                                            │
│                                                                            │
│ ==========================================================================│
│    1. reprehensive      2. representative      3. repressive               │
│    4. reprieve          5. reprobative         6. reproductive             │
│    7. reprove                                                              │
│                                                                            │
│                                                                            │
│                                                                            │
│                                                                            │
│                                                                            │
│                                                                            │
│                                                                            │
│                                                                            │
└──────────────────────────────────────────────────────────────────────────┘
```

FIGURE 15.8: Looking up a word through the Speller Utility. This process works the same way as looking up a word in the Speller program.

You can also use this method to convert any dictionaries you have created with the Macintosh version of WordPerfect and saved in WordPerfect 4.2 format. Refer to Appendix A for information about transferring documents between Macintosh and IBM WordPerfect.

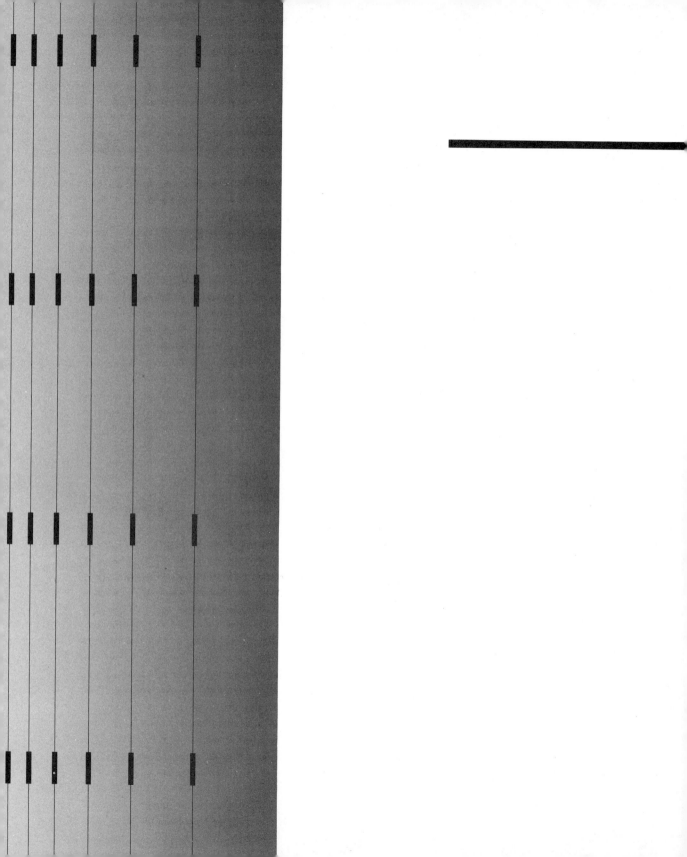

CHAPTER 16

CREATING AND USING MACROS

CREATING AND
USING MACROS

WordPerfect macros can be used to customize word processing command sequences, enter repetitively typed text, or both. Because WordPerfect macros are so versatile, there are almost no applications or areas of the program in which they cannot be used.

Throughout this book, you will find sample macros that you may want to use in your work. If you are new to WordPerfect macros, you should first read the material in this chapter. Afterward, you can consult the index to locate specific macros that occur throughout the text. By following the steps outlined for each macro, and with proper testing, you will soon be able to incorporate the macros that interest you into your everyday work.

UPGRADE NOTES

The biggest change in WordPerfect's macro capabilities from version 4.2 to 5.0 is the addition of a Macro Editor, complete with a macro command language that allows you to create very sophisticated programmed macros.

There are also a few changes in how you create and use temporary macros—those that are removed from memory when you exit the program. First, only one-character temporary macros are allowed now; you assign them to the Alt key plus a number key from *0* to *9*. In addition, you assign these temporary macros by using the Ctrl-PgUp key (Macro Commands). Second, macros you assign to the Enter key are no longer temporary but are stored as WP{WP}.WPM (note also that the file name extension for macros has been changed from .MAC to .WPM). If you reassign another macro to the Enter key, however, it will overwrite the one that is there without prompting you.

You can also now create a macro directory for storing your macros and specify its location with the Setup key (Shift-F1). Once you have done so, you can edit and execute your macros from any directory.

Version 4.2 macros are not compatible with Version 5, but you can use the MACROCNV.EXE utility discussed at the end of this chapter to convert them so that they can be used in WordPerfect 5.0.

DEFINING AND EXECUTING MACROS

A macro is simply a sequence of keystrokes, recorded and saved under a particular name. When you invoke the Macro command and enter a macro's name,

WordPerfect replays all of the macro's keystrokes exactly as they were originally entered. The keystrokes can contain text, WordPerfect command sequences, or a combination of text and commands. You can also create programmed macros that use the commands in a special macro command language, which is available when you use WordPerfect's Macro Editor.

To create a macro, you press Ctrl-F10 (Macro Define). WordPerfect displays the prompt

Define macro:

You then enter the name you want to assign to the macro and press Enter. (You can also assign a one-letter macro to an Alt key combination, as you'll see shortly.) You may enter a name containing up to eight characters, which is the maximum allowed for any file name, as long as there are no spaces between the characters. Normally, you should keep your macro names short—perhaps two or three characters. What you want is a name that readily reminds you of the macro's function but is quick and easy to enter.

After you enter the macro name, WordPerfect prompts you to enter a description for the macro:

Description:

This description can contain up to 39 characters. You can bypass the description by pressing the Enter key. After you type in the description, the program displays the Macro Definition prompt

Macro Def

which on most monitors flashes on and off continuously. This tells you that WordPerfect is now recording each keystroke you make in your document. This prompt continues to be displayed until you press Ctrl-F10 again to stop recording the macro.

As soon as you press Ctrl-F10 the second time, the Macro Def prompt disappears, and WordPerfect automatically saves the macro keystrokes you just entered under the name you assigned to the macro. WordPerfect gives all macro files the extension .WPM to distinguish them from regular document files.

The macro file is saved in the current directory, unless you select another directory by using the Keyboard/Macro Files option (**3** or **K**) on the Location of Auxiliary Files menu (Shift-F1 L) and enter its path name. Once you specify this directory, WordPerfect will automatically save all of your macro files in it. This means that they will always be available for execution any time you are using the program (see "Indicating the Location of Macro Files" later in this chapter).

To execute a named macro, you press Alt-F10 (Macro), enter the name of the macro, and press Enter. WordPerfect then enters all of the keystrokes precisely as you entered them. If you make a mistake and enter the name of a macro that does not exist, WordPerfect displays the error message

ERROR: File not found — <*file*>.WPM

where <*file*> represents the macro name you mistyped. If you receive this message, you will have to reexecute the macro. If you ever want to terminate the execution of a macro while it is underway, simply press F1 (Cancel). This stops the macro at whatever keystroke it was entering when you pressed Cancel.

If, when you execute a macro, you find that it does not work as you intended, you will have to modify it. Macro files can either be reentered (replaced) or edited in WordPerfect (see "Using the Macro Editor" later in this chapter). You cannot edit a macro by retrieving the macro file as you would any normal document file (Shift-F10 or F5 Enter); the only way that the contents of a macro can be edited is by using the Macro Editor, which can be accessed when you redefine a macro.

To replace or edit a macro, repeat the definition procedure as though you were defining the macro for the first time. When you enter the macro name and WordPerfect finds that the macro file already exists, it will prompt you with

<*file*>.WPM is Already Defined. **1 R**eplace; **2 E**dit: 0

where <*file*> is the file name of the macro that you entered and want to redefine. To record the macro again, select the Replace option (**1** or **R**). To edit the contents of the macro with the Macro Editor, select the Edit option (**2** or **E**). To cancel this procedure, press the Enter key.

Alt Macros

In addition to standard macros, which you execute by pressing Alt-F10 (Macro), entering the macro name, and pressing the Enter key, you can create special macros that you can execute simply by pressing the Alt key and entering a single letter of the alphabet. These special Alt macros can be created only with the letters *A* through *Z*, not with numbers or punctuation marks. However, the 26 Alt macros that you can create are very useful because they can be invoked much more easily than regular macros; you just press the Alt-key combination.

To create an Alt macro, you press Ctrl-F10 to start the macro definition just as you do when creating standard macros. However, instead of typing a full macro name in response to the Define Macro prompt, you press the Alt key and then type the letter you want to use. You will not see the macro name on your screen after the Define Macro prompt as you do when you are creating a regular macro. Instead, WordPerfect immediately prompts you to enter a description for the macro. (If you have already used the letter you entered in an Alt macro, Word-Perfect will instead ask you whether you want to replace or edit the macro that it represents.) After you type in the description (optional) and press Enter, the program displays the Macro Def prompt to let you know that it is now recording your keystrokes.

After you enter the keystrokes you want to save in the Alt macro, you press Ctrl-F10 again to terminate keystroke entry, just as you do to terminate a regular macro definition. To execute the macro, simply press Alt and the letter key. An Alt macro file appears in a directory listing as ALT$<L>$.WPM, where $<L>$ is the letter of the alphabet assigned by pressing the Alt key and one of the letter keys. For instance, if you create an Alt-M macro by pressing the Alt key and **m**, its file name will appear as

ALTM.WPM

Alt macros are very convenient to use. However, it is easy to invoke an Alt macro in error. Because the Alt key is located near the Shift key on many IBM and IBM-compatible keyboards, you could easily execute an Alt macro when you intended to capitalize a letter. For that reason, you should not assign Alt macros to particularly complex, powerful, or destructive tasks. For example, if you create a macro to mark citations in tables of authorities, you would not want to name it Alt-T; someday you may execute it when trying to capitalize the letter *t.* It would be safer to use a multiple-character macro name, such as TOA, so that you would have to execute the macro by pressing Alt-F10 and entering its three-character name.

The Enter Key Macro

The macro assigned to the Enter key represents a special kind of macro in WordPerfect 5.0. Although the Enter key macro is permanent in the sense that it is available each time you use WordPerfect, you can never edit its contents; you can only replace them. To create a macro for the Enter key, you press Ctrl-F10 (Macro Define) and press the Enter key. You are not prompted to enter a description for the Enter key macro as you are with all other macros that you create. Instead, the Macro Def message is immediately displayed in the lower-left corner of the screen. After you enter all of the WordPerfect commands and/or text to be stored in this macro and press Ctrl-F10 to turn off the macro recording, the Enter key macro is stored in the file WP{WP}.WPM. To execute an Enter key macro, you press Alt-F10 followed by the Enter key.

If you want to replace the contents of the Enter key macro, repeat the procedure of pressing Ctrl-F10 and the Enter key. This time, instead of informing you that this macro is already defined and giving you a chance to replace or edit it, the program simply displays the Macro Def prompt and begins to record all the keystrokes and/or WordPerfect commands that you enter until you press Ctrl-F10 again to turn off the macro recording.

Indicating the Location of Macro Files

For WordPerfect to execute a particular macro, its file normally must be in the default drive or directory. If you are using WordPerfect on a computer with two floppy disk drives, your default drive will be drive B, where you save your documents. As a result, the macros you save on your data disk reduce the amount of free space you have for saving the documents you create. Also, you will have to copy macros that you regularly use onto new data disks to make them available to the program (unless you want to go to the trouble of redefining them each time you change to a new data disk).

If you are using a hard disk system, the default directory normally must contain the macros you wish to use. However, you can get around this limitation by pressing Shift-F1 (Setup), selecting the Location of Auxiliary Files option (**7** or **L**), selecting the Keyboard/Macro Files option (**3** or **K**), and entering the path name of the directory that is to hold both your Keyboard Layout files (with the file extension .WPK) and your macro files (with the extension .WPM). After typing in the full name of the directory (including the drive letter, if your hard disk is partitioned and you wish to use a directory on a virtual drive different from the one that WordPerfect uses), press Enter and then press F7 (Exit).

From that point on, all the macros you create will be saved in this directory. You can use the Move/Rename option (**3** or **M**) on the List Files menu (F5 Enter) to move any macro files to this new macro default directory, if you created any macros before designating the directory to contain your Keyboard Layout and macro files.

To obtain a directory listing of all of the macros in this default directory, press F5 and then type in its path name. If the keyboard layout and macro directory is a subdirectory of the current directory, you need only complete the path name. Use the asterisk and the extension .WPM to filter out any Keyboard Layout files that you may have created. For example, if you designated C:\WP50\MACROS as the default directory for your Keyboard Layout and macro files on the Location of Auxiliary Files menu and the current directory is C:\WP50, you would press F5, type

MACROS*.WPM

and press Enter to obtain a listing of only the macro files.

If you use the Look option (**6** or **L**) on the List Files menu to attempt to see the contents of a macro, you will instead see the description you assigned to the macro followed by a hard page break (indicated by a line of equal signs). You will not be able to make out the WordPerfect commands or text that you have assigned to the macro below this line of equal signs. If you have only entered text for a particular macro, you will see nothing below the hard page break; if you have entered WordPerfect commands as part of the macro, you will see various symbols, none of which will be comprehensible. To review the contents of a macro, you must use the Macro Editor; you can't do it by using the Look option on the List Files menu.

To delete a macro, however, you must use the Delete option (**2** or **D**) on the List Files menu or the DELETE or ERASE command from the operating system.

Repeating a Macro

You can use WordPerfect's built-in Repeat function (the Esc key) to repeat a macro any number of times. Just follow these steps:

1. Press Esc. You'll see the prompt

   Repeat Value = 8

2. Enter the number of times you want the macro to repeat. Don't press Enter.

3. Press Alt-F10 (Macro), enter the macro's name, and press Enter. If you're repeating an Alt macro, just press Alt and the letter of the macro.

For example, if you've recorded a macro named Alt-U that capitalizes the character the cursor is on, capitalize three characters in a row by pressing Esc, entering **3**, and pressing Alt-U.

Temporary Macros

In WordPerfect 4.2, you could create temporary macros whose definitions were not likely to be reused and, therefore, did not warrant saving on disk. You did this by assigning a one- or two-character macro name to the macro during definition. In WordPerfect 5.0, all of the macros (including the Enter key macro) are permanent. This means that their keystrokes are saved in macro files and that they are available to you each time you use WordPerfect, regardless of the number of characters used in their names.

You can, however, have WordPerfect temporarily store 120 characters of text. If you mark the text as a block first, you can store a few formatting codes ([-], [Tab], [←Indent], [HRt], and [HPg]) with it. You then assign the text and codes to one of the ten macro variables, 0–9, which can then be accessed by pressing the Alt key in combination with the particular number used (on the top row only—you can't use the numbers on the ten-key numeric pad). Any keystrokes assigned to one of the ten variables are temporary, meaning that they are not saved on disk and remain in the computer's memory only until you exit Word-Perfect or reassign new text to the variable. You can perform automatic typing in a document by creating a temporary macro to insert text that you want typed only during the current work session. Remember, however, that these variables can't contain WordPerfect commands as can normal macros; they must be used in the more limited role of inserting text into the document.

To assign text to a variable, press Ctrl-PgUp (Macro Commands). You then receive the prompt

> Variable:

Press the number key (**1–0**) that you want to use. Be sure to use the top row of the keyboard, not the keypad. The prompt immediately changes to

> Value:

When you see this prompt, type all of the text that you want to assign to the variable number that you just entered. After you finish typing the text, press the Enter key. Note that the text that you typed will not be inserted in the current document during this definition process. You must press Alt plus the number assigned to insert this text in the document you are creating.

You can also assign text to a variable by typing it in the editing screen, marking it as a block (Alt-F4), pressing Ctrl-PgUp, and entering the variable number in response to the Variable prompt that appears. As soon as you type the number, the block highlighting disappears. You don't see the Value prompt because you have already designated the text to be assigned to the variable by marking it as a block.

If you want to insert text that consists of more than 120 characters and/or contains formatting codes that are not stored, you will have to create permanent macros to do the job.

Pausing a Macro for Input

WordPerfect allows you to insert a pause for input in the macros you create. During this pause, you can manually enter text and commands that you don't want the macro to enter automatically. The macro pause ends as soon as you press the Enter key (even if it's in response to a program prompt) and the program continues to replay any keystrokes that you recorded after the pause.

To enter this type of pause in a macro, begin defining the macro as you would any other. When you reach the place in the macro where the pause should occur, press Ctrl-PgUp. If you are in the document editing screen when you press Ctrl-PgUp, the following menu options appear at the bottom of the screen:

> **1 P**ause; **2 D**isplay; **3 A**ssign; **4 C**omment: 0

If you are in one of the menu screens when you press Ctrl-PgUp, you see only the two options

> **1 P**ause; **2 D**isplay

To insert the command to pause the macro, you select the Pause option by typing either **1** or **P**. The menu will disappear and the macro will remain paused until you press the Enter key, just as the macro will perform when you later play it back.

If you are pausing the macro at a point during its creation where you must select a response to a WordPerfect command before you can continue to record subsequent commands, go ahead and enter any appropriate response before pressing the Enter key to end the pause. The response that you enter when inserting the pause in macro creation is not saved as part of the macro, but it will affect the document in which you're recording the macro. When you execute the macro, you will find that WordPerfect has stored only the pause that gives you the opportunity to choose the appropriate response when executing the macro. If you don't want or need to enter a response during the pause, you can just press the Enter key to end the pause.

After you end the pause, you continue to enter the keystrokes for your macro as usual, terminating its definition by pressing Ctrl-F10. When you execute a macro that contains a pause for user input, WordPerfect will execute all of the keystrokes up to the point where you pressed Ctrl-PgUp and entered the pause. The macro's execution will then be suspended. During this time, you can enter whatever text or WordPerfect commands you want. To resume macro execution, press Enter.

Making Macros Visible

When WordPerfect executes a macro, it normally operates too quickly to see. When you execute a macro that contains only a few keystrokes and commands, it may seem almost instantaneous. To slow a macro so that you can follow its progress on the screen—this can aid in debugging a macro so that you can see what is going wrong—you can make a macro's execution visible so that you can see it as it operates. To do this, just press Ctrl-PgUp as you're recording the macro. You'll see the prompt

1 Pause; **2 D**isplay; **3 A**ssign; **4 C**omment: 0

Type **2** or **D** to insert a {DISPLAY OFF} command in the macro. You'll then see the prompt

Display Execution? (Y/N) N

Type **Y** to display the macro's execution.

You can combine the commands that make the macro visible, pause it, and make it invisible. For example, you might want to record a macro that types the standard text of a business letter at a pace at which you can read it by turning the display on. At the places where you need to insert text, the macro can pause for your input. As soon as you type the last input and press Enter, you can have the macro execute the F10 command to save the file as LTR and pause again for you to type an ending to the file name, such as **822** for August 22. You can then return the macro to invisible speed by turning off the display and have it execute the keystrokes needed to print the letter (Shift-F7 1).

You can also insert pauses and display instructions by using the Macro Editor, which is discussed in the next section.

USING THE MACRO EDITOR

Version 5.0 of WordPerfect has added a Macro Editor so that you can edit macros after they have been recorded. In addition, it allows you to nest macros inside each other. This enables you to record short macros that perform simple tasks and link these sets of instructions together to carry out more complex tasks. The short macros can be used in many larger macros, so you can create a library of short routines and assemble them to create complex macros as needed.

To edit a macro, you simply enter its name at the Define Macro prompt. When you enter the name of a macro that has already been defined, WordPerfect displays the prompt

<*File*>.WPM Is Already Defined. 1 **R**eplace; 2 **E**dit: 0

where <*File*> is the name of the macro. If you want to redefine the macro, select Replace (**1** or **R**). If you select the Edit option (**2** or **E**), you will see a screen similar to the one in Figure 16.1, which you can use to edit the macro. It is displaying an Alt-S macro that resaves a previously saved document.

```
Macro: Edit

        File          ALTS.WPM
    1 - Description    saves document
    2 - Action

      ┌──────────────────────────────────────────────────────┐
      │ {DISPLAY OFF}{Save}{Enter}                            │
      │                                                      │
      │                                                      │
      │                                                      │
      │                                                      │
      │                                                      │
      │                                                      │
      │                                                      │
      └──────────────────────────────────────────────────────┘

    Selection: 0
```

FIGURE 16.1: The macro editing screen. The Macro Editor allows you to change steps in a macro without having to record the macro from scratch.

When the macro editing screen appears, type **2** or **A** for Action. (Typing **1** or **D** allows you to change the macro's description, or to enter a description if one is not already there.) Once you choose Action, you're in normal editing mode, so pressing Backspace or Del deletes characters, pressing End takes you to the end of the line, and so forth.

To insert certain types of macro instructions, such as {Enter} or {Tab}, or any of the special macro commands, such as {DISPLAY ON} or {PAUSE}, you have to be in Macro Command mode, which you can enter in either of two ways:

1. You can press Ctrl-F10 (Macro Define) so that all the keys you press until you press Ctrl-F10 again will be entered as instructions in the macro. Once you press Ctrl-F10 in the Macro Editor, you will see a "Press **Macro Define** to enable editing" prompt. It indicates that all of the keys you press will be interpreted as commands. Pressing End, for example, inserts an {End} command into the macro instead of moving the cursor to the End of the line. To return to normal editing mode, press Ctrl-F10 again. This method works best if you're entering several steps in the macro.

2. You can press Ctrl-V so that only the next key you press is entered as an instruction in the macro. This method is best if you're entering only one or two steps.

The Macro Editor doesn't represent codes as the Reveal Codes screen does. Formatting codes and other codes are shown in a macro within curly braces; both menu selections and text that you type are represented by their characters. Spaces are represented by centered dots.

To exit from the Macro Editor and return to your document, press F7. If you have chosen Action and have been editing a macro, press F7 twice: once to exit from the macro edit screen and a second time to exit from the Macro Editor itself.

Inserting Special Commands

If you press Ctrl-PgUp, which is called the Macro Commands key, while in the Macro Editor, the Macro Commands menu appears in the upper-right corner of the screen. You can scroll through it with the Home, ↑, ↓, Screen Up, Screen Down, PgUp, and PgDn keys. To insert any of the special commands listed there into your macro, highlight the command and press Enter. (To exit the Macro Commands menu without selecting a command, press F1 or Esc.) The menu has a built-in Name Search feature, so typing the first letter of the command you want to use will take you to the command quickly.

These commands are in WordPerfect's macro command language, which is summarized later in this chapter. Unless you're going to write programmed macros, you will probably never need to use more than a few of these commands. However, several of the commands are easy to use and understand even if you have no programming background, and they can be executed from the keyboard without using the macro command language. They include those that chain and nest macros as well as those that pause macros and display their execution, as already discussed. (To see how to perform any of these functions by using the command language, refer to "Using the Macro Command Language" later in this chapter.)

NESTING AND CHAINING MACROS

WordPerfect 5.0 allows for both nested and chained macros. There is a difference between the two: with nested macros, one macro starts another macro whenever it occurs; with chained macros, the program waits until it completes the first macro before it starts the second. Nested macros thus allow you to start one process and branch to another process.

You will find as you use the program that this nesting and chaining capability allows you to create and maintain a library of short macro routines, unlike the relatively complex macros you may have created with earlier versions of Word-Perfect. You can simply nest short macros—such as a macro that prints the document or moves to the beginning of the document—in other macros as you need them. Because you can use one macro in many other macros, you can pick and choose from your macro library and assemble complex macros out of relatively simple building blocks.

If you do much nesting and chaining with macros, you will probably want to use the Macro Editor with its built-in command language. However, you can nest and chain macros as you're recording them from the keyboard.

- To chain one macro to another, press Alt-F10 as you're recording the first macro; then enter the name of the macro you want to chain. If you haven't recorded the second macro yet, you can record it after you finish recording the first one; press Ctrl-F10 (Define Macro), enter the macro's name, and then choose to edit it.

- To nest one macro inside another, just press Alt and the letter of the macro as you're recording the first macro. The second macro will be executed at that point, *as you're recording the macro,* so you have to have recorded a nested macro before you nest it. You can nest named macros by using the Macro Editor's {NEST} command.

Nesting a Macro

For example, if you've recorded the Alt-S macro that saves your document, as shown in Figure 16.1, you can nest it inside another macro that prints the document so that the document will be saved before it is printed. You'll need to have a short, previously saved document on the screen to create this macro.

1. To create the print macro, press Ctrl-F10, name it **print**, and enter **Saves and prints document** as the description.
2. Press Home Home ↓ to record the keystrokes that move to the end of the document. This will format your document even if you've saved it with Fast Save on, so that you can print it later from disk.
3. Next, you will nest the macro that saves the document into this macro. You created the Alt-S macro earlier, so just press Alt-S. You will see a *Please Wait* message, and WordPerfect will save the document without your having to do anything.
4. Next, you need the keystrokes that print the document, so press Shift-F7 and type **1** or **F** to print the entire document. WordPerfect will print the document at that point unless you use Printer Control to cancel the print job.
5. Press Ctrl-F10 to end macro definition.

When you press Alt-F10, type **print**, and press Enter to execute the macro, WordPerfect first saves the document on the screen and then prints it (if your printer is turned on).

If you were to retrieve the macro into the Macro Editor, the keystrokes would be the same as those in Figure 16.2 (unless you used letters instead of numbers as your menu choices).

Chaining a Macro

To see how chaining macros works, you can record a short macro that searches for a pattern and then instruct it to repeat itself until it no longer locates what it's searching for. Since you've still got a document on the screen from the last example, just move to the top of it (Home Home ↑) and then take the following steps:

1. Press Ctrl-F10, type **breakup** as the macro's name, and press Enter.
2. Type **Breaks document into sentences** as the description and press Enter.
3. Press F2 (Search) and type a period (**.**) as the pattern to search for.
4. Press F2 again to start the search.

```
Macro: Edit

        File            PRINT.WPM
    1 - Description      saves and prints document
    2 - Action

    ┌──────────────────────────────────────────────────────────────┐
    │ {DISPLAY OFF}{Home}{Home}{Down}{ALT S}{Print}1                │
    │                                                                │
    │                                                                │
    │                                                                │
    │                                                                │
    │                                                                │
    │                                                                │
    │                                                                │
    └──────────────────────────────────────────────────────────────┘

    Selection: 0
```

FIGURE 16.2: Retrieving the print macro. The nested macro is indicated by the command {ALT S}.

5. Press Enter twice so that WordPerfect inserts a blank line when it locates a period. Then press Del to delete the extra space (or press Del twice if you use two spaces between sentences).

6. To chain the macro to itself, press Alt-F10 and enter the name of the macro you're defining, **breakup**; then press Enter.

7. Press Ctrl-F10 to stop recording the macro.

Now press Alt-F10, enter **breakup**, and press Enter. Your short document will be broken into its component sentences (that end with a period), as the example in Figure 16.3 shows. Figure 16.4 illustrates the keystrokes of the completed macro. The {Macro} instruction indicates that the breakup macro is to repeat.

> *Note:* You can also chain and nest macros by using the macro command language. To chain the breakup macro this way, you would press Ctrl-Pgup (Macro Commands) in the Macro Editor, type **ch** for *chain* (activating the Name Search feature, which takes the highlighting directly to the {CHAIN} command), then press Enter to insert the {CHAIN} command in the macro and type breakup ~ as the macro's name. Note the tilde (~) at the end; it indicates the end of the macro's name. To nest a macro by using the macro command language, instead choose the {NEST} command from the menu that is activated when you press Ctrl-PgUp in the Macro Editor.

Replacing Paired Format Codes by Using Macros

When you delete one of a pair of codes, WordPerfect also deletes the other member of the pair, so you can't simply replace all instances of [BOLD] with

```
Combined with WordPerfect's Search feature, macros become a
powerful tool. Because you can have a macro locate something,
such as a word or even a format code, by searching for it, search
macros give you a way of moving around in a document. When the
macro locates what it's searching for, you can have the program
change that item to something else.




                                        Doc 2 Pg 1 Ln 1" Pos 1"
```

FIGURE 16.3a: Sample paragraph to be separated into individual paragraphs by the breakup macro. The macro searches for each period, inserts a blank line, and repeats until no more periods are found.

```
Combined with WordPerfect's Search feature, macros become a
powerful tool.

Because you can have a macro locate something, such as a word or
even a format code, by searching for it, search macros give you a
way of moving around in a document.

When the macro locates what it's searching for, you can have the
program change that item to something else.

—




                                        Doc 2 Pg 1 Ln 2.66" Pos 1"
```

FIGURE 16.3b: The sample paragraph after the breakup macro was applied.

[ITALC], for example. If you did, you would turn on italics type but never turn it off, and the rest of your document would be in italics. You could use the Search feature to search for each [BOLD] code individually so that you could delete it,

```
Macro: Edit

        File            BREAKUP.WPM

   1 - Description       breaks document into sentences

   2 - Action


   {DISPLAY OFF}{Search}.{Search}{Enter}
   {Enter}
   {Del}{Macro}breakup{Enter}




   Selection: 0
```

FIGURE 16.4: The keystrokes for the breakup macro. The chained macro is indicated by the {Macro} command, and {Enter} indicates pressing Enter.

mark the text to be italicized, and generate the [ITALC][italc] codes by pressing Ctrl-F8 (Font), choosing Appearance (**2** or **A**), then choosing Italc (**4** or **I**), but in a long document, this could take some time. Instead, you can record a macro that searches for the first one of these codes, turns on Block mode, searches for the second code in the pair, inserts the new Size or Appearance codes, and deletes the old ones.

The following pattern can be used in any macro in which you want to change one of WordPerfect's paired sets of codes to another:

1. Search for the first part of the code that you want to replace. For example, to search for boldface, search for the [BOLD] part of the [BOLD][bold] pattern by pressing F2 (Search), pressing F6, and then pressing F2 to start the search.

2. When the program locates the first code in the pair, turn on Block mode (Alt-F4) and search for the second code in the pair—in this case, [bold]. Press F2 (Search), then press F6 a second time to generate the [bold] code.

Note: If you're generating codes from the Ctrl-F8 key, you'll need to go through the sequence twice to generate the second code in the pair. For example, pressing Ctrl-F8 AI generates an [ITALC] code the first time; repeat the sequence Ctrl-F8 AI again to generate an [italc] code.

Press ← to move back over the [bold] code, press Backspace to delete the [BOLD] code; then press F2 to search for the [bold] code.

3. When the program locates the second code in the pair, the entire phrase is highlighted, because you have marked from the first code in the pair to the second. Now you can press the keys that insert the pair of codes for the new effect you want. In this example, since we are changing boldface to italics, you would press Ctrl-F8 (Font), choose Appearance (**2** or **A**), and choose Italc (**4** or **I**).

4. After you have applied the new size or appearance change, delete the old codes (unless you are instead adding them to the existing effect—in this case, specifying bold italics) by pressing ← to move the cursor onto or next to the last old code (in this case, [bold]). Then press Delete or Backspace to delete it. WordPerfect will automatically delete the first code in the pair also.

To have a macro such as this one repeat until all of the codes are replaced, chain it to itself, as previously discussed.

Terminating Chained Macros

WordPerfect's Search feature automatically terminates a search macro when no more occurrences of the pattern it is searching for can be located. This allows you to chain search macros that will stop when the last instance of what's being searched for is found. However, if you try to chain a macro that doesn't contain a search instruction, you set up an endless loop from which you have to exit by pressing F1 (Cancel). For this reason, don't ever create a self-chaining macro (one that calls for its own execution) without adding an instruction that makes it visible on the screen (either {DISPLAY ON} or {SPEED}). Without visibility, you'll only see the * *Please Wait* * prompt on the screen as the macro continues to execute. Unless you can see what the macro is doing, you won't know when to press F1 to terminate the macro at the proper time in its execution.

For example, suppose you create a self-chaining macro that first retrieves a file containing a blank form for you to later fill in manually, then enters a hard page break, and finally calls for its own reexecution. If you don't turn on the display or enter a speed value, WordPerfect will continuously read in page after page of the blank forms without your knowing how many times this procedure has been repeated. However, if you turn on the display as the first step in the macro, you will see each form being retrieved and each hard page break being entered. Also, the delay will give you time to press F1 to stop the process when you see that you have a sufficient number of blank forms in the file.

Planning Macros

You can create WordPerfect macros by simply having the program record your keystrokes as you work with the program itself, or you can create macros entirely within the Macro Editor. When you record a macro, each keystroke you type is both recorded in the macro and entered into the document window where you are working. Before you enter a new macro, you may want to switch to an unused document window (Shift-F3). You can then use this window as a "scratch pad" where you can enter your standard text and format changes without affecting any of your existing documents.

However, it isn't always possible to record the keystrokes of a macro in a blank editing screen. Many macros require text to process during definition; for example, to create a macro that cuts a block of text, you must have on the screen some text that has previously been marked as a block and can be cut when you define the macro's keystrokes. Before you test any macro that you have created, you should always save the document that you will test it on. That way, you will not introduce changes that you have to edit manually.

Macros that require text to process during definition always assume that the conditions under which they were created will exist in the document when they are executed. For instance, if you execute the macro that cuts a marked block without first marking the block, or if you execute it in a new document window where no text yet exists, it won't operate properly.

When planning your macro, before you actually begin to define it, you must also decide how much of a procedure should be automated. If you plan to manually move the cursor into the proper position each time you execute a particular macro, you will not include the keystrokes to reach the sample text you use in the macro's definition as part of the macro. However, if you always begin a procedure by moving the cursor to the very beginning or end of the document, you will want to include these cursor movement keystrokes in the first step of the macro.

Sometimes you must resist the temptation to automate too much of a procedure. If you make the macro too specific to the particular document you are working with, you may find it of limited or no value when you work on a new document. If you find yourself redefining a favorite macro each time you begin work on a new document, you may want to find ways to make it more versatile. Often you can accomplish this by retaining in the macro only those keystrokes that never vary.

Another way to make a macro more versatile is to enter pauses for input whenever possible. For instance, if you often change the spacing in a document from single to double and back, you can use a macro that enters the Line Spacing commands (Shift-F8 L S), pauses for input (Ctrl-PgUp P) so you can enter the line spacing number, then includes a final Enter to enter the new value, and then presses F7 four times to return to your document. You can then use this one macro whenever you change line spacing, regardless of whether you want single spacing, double spacing, one-and-a-half spacing, or any other spacing.

USING THE MACRO COMMAND LANGUAGE

If you're familiar with a programming language such as BASIC or Pascal, you may want to create programmed macros in WordPerfect by using its built-in macro command language. These types of macros allow you to perform much more sophisticated tasks than simply recording keystrokes. For example, you can test whether certain conditions exist (such as whether Block mode has been turned on) and take an appropriate action, you can write subroutines that will be used to handle exceptions, and you can create IF-THEN-ELSE statements that determine which instructions are to be executed depending on the outcome of an action.

Using Variables

WordPerfect has ten built-in variables ({VAR 0} through {VAR 9}) that can contain either text or numbers, called *values*. After you've assigned a value to a variable, you can use the variable anywhere that you want the text or numbers to appear in a document.

Variables can be used not only as "temporary" macros, as you saw earlier, but also within the Macro Editor to perform conditional testing, control the flow of the macro, and handle certain conditions as they arise. For example, you can use the {CHAR} command to produce a menu and assign the character that the user enters to a variable. Depending on what that character was, the macro could use the {CASE} command to execute one set of instructions or another. Likewise, you can use the {IF} and {CASE} command to test whether certain conditions exist and perform different sets of instructions.

To enter the value of a variable in a document, you press Alt plus the number of the variable. For example, if you've assigned the phrase *Thorton Stock Industries Ltd.* to variable 1, pressing Alt-1 inserts that phrase in your document.

As you saw earlier, to assign a variable to a value while you're in the editing screen, you press Ctrl-PgUp, type a variable number (from **0** to **9**) at the Variable prompt, and then type the text or numbers that you want the variable to contain at the Value prompt. You can enter up to 120 characters and use the format codes [Tab], [→Indent], [HRt], [HPg], and [-]

You can also block text and then assign a variable to it by simply pressing Ctrl-PgUp and entering a variable number from **0** to **9**.

While you're defining a macro, you can assign a value to a variable by pressing Ctrl-PgUp and typing **3** or **A** for Assign. You'll then be prompted for the variable number and the value.

In the Macro Editor, you assign values to variables either by entering the instructions to mark text as a block and then using the {ASSIGN} command to assign that block to a variable number, or by using several of the other macro commands. The {ASSIGN} command also lets you set the value of a variable to text or numbers that you specify without using block marking. The {CHAR} and {LOOK} commands assign a single character, typed by the user, to a variable. The {TEXT} command prompts the user for text that is then assigned to a variable.

To insert the value of a variable in a macro by using the Macro Editor, you press Alt plus the number of the variable. For example, inserting Alt-1 in a macro would produce the phrase *Thorton Stock Industries Ltd.* at that point when the macro is executed. To insert the number of a variable, press Ctrl-V before pressing Alt and the number of the variable. For example, if you press Ctrl-V Alt-2, the program will insert {VAR 2} in the macro.

The following sections summarize each of the commands in the macro command language. Follow the syntax of each command to use the appropriate variable notation.

{;}(Comment)

The {;}(Comment) command lets you add descriptive comments to your macros. The text of the comments will appear on the Macro Editor screen, but it isn't part of the macro and WordPerfect won't interpret its text as commands to be executed. An example of a comment line explaining the {Right} command is shown below:

{Right}   {;}Moves cursor right ~

To add a comment to a macro as you're recording it, press Ctrl-PgUp and choose Comment (**4** or **C**). The program gives the prompt *Comment:*. When you press Enter, WordPerfect inserts a semicolon (;) in the macro; anything after it is treated as a comment until you press Enter.

If you type a comment while you're recording a macro, you won't be able to see the comment text after the cursor reaches the right edge of the screen, but you can insert longer comments by using the Macro Editor. To insert a comment with the Macro Editor, press Ctrl-PgUp (Macro Commands), type **;** (a semicolon), and press Enter. Anything you type after that until you type a tilde (~) will be considered a comment.

{ASSIGN}

The {ASSIGN} command allows you to assign a value to a variable (from 0 to 9) from within a macro. Its syntax is

{ASSIGN} variable ˜ value ˜

For example, if you assign variable 2 (Alt-2) the value of 50, pressing Alt-2 displays *50* on your screen.

Once you have assigned a value to a variable, you can use it in another command, such as {IF}, {CALL}, or {IF EXISTS}, or you can insert it into a document or prompt. The value can be text or numbers.

This value can be entered literally or as the result of an arithmetic or logical expression. The following expressions can be used:

OPERATOR	RESULT
value1 + value2	Adds two values together and assigns the sum to the variable.
value1 − value2	Subtracts one value from another and assigns the difference to the variable.
value1 * value2	Multiplies two values together and assigns the product to the variable.
value1 / value2	Divides two values together and assigns the integer result to the variable.
value1 % value2	Divides two values together and assigns the remainder to the variable.
− value	Assigns the negative value to the variable.
!value	Returns the logical NOT (bitwise).
value1 $ value2	Returns the logical AND (bitwise).
value1 | value2	Returns the logical OR (bitwise).
value1 = value2	If the values are equal, assigns − 1 to the variable; otherwise, assigns 0 to it.
value1 ! = value2	If the values not are equal, assigns − 1 to the variable; otherwise, assigns 0 to it.
value1 > value2	If value1 is greater than value2, assigns − 1 to the variable; otherwise, assigns 0 to it.
value1 < value2	If value1 is less than value2, assigns − 1 to the variable; otherwise, assigns 0 to it.

While recording a macro, you can mark text as a block and assign it to a variable by pressing Ctrl-PgUp and choosing Assign (**3** or **A**). You will then be prompted to assign a variable number (0 to 9). If you haven't marked text as a block, you can enter a variable number at the Variable prompt, press Enter, and enter a value of up to 120 characters at the Value prompt.

If you've assigned a value to a variable and then want to cancel that assignment, type the variable number with no value. For example, to cancel the assignment of variable 2, enter the command as

{ASSIGN}2~ ~

{BELL}

The {BELL} command instructs WordPerfect to beep at a certain step in a macro. Its syntax is simply

{BELL}

This command sounds a beep when the macro executes the step where the command is inserted. For example, you might want to sound a beep when a pause is encountered for keyboard input.

To have the bell sound several times in succession, insert the {BELL} command the number of times you want the bell sounded.

{BREAK}

You use the BREAK command to break out of an {IF} command sequence. Its syntax is simply

{BREAK}

{CALL}

The {CALL} command is similar to the {GO} command. It branches to a subroutine identified by a label and executes the instructions that it finds there. When it finishes carrying out those instructions and finds a {RETURN}, {RETURN CANCEL}, {RETURN ERROR}, or {RETURN NOT FOUND} instruction, it will return to its original position and carry out the next instruction that it finds there. Its syntax is

{CALL}label ~

You can use the {CALL} command to carry out subroutines that you use frequently, without having to repeat the instructions in the macro. For example, you may have a fairly complex subroutine that you use several times in a macro, identified by the label *doit*. You can simply call that subroutine by using the {CALL} command each time you need it, as long as somewhere in the macro you have the subroutine identified by the label *doit*.

{CANCEL ON}, {CANCEL OFF}

The {CANCEL ON} and {CANCEL OFF} commands are used to indicate whether you want WordPerfect to allow the user to use the Cancel key (F1) to cancel a macro. Their syntax is

```
{CANCEL ON}
{CANCEL OFF}
```

With {CANCEL ON} (the default), pressing F1 cancels the macro in progress. With {CANCEL OFF}, pressing F1 has no effect. Use it whenever the macro you're writing executes a routine that you don't want to allow the user to interrupt.

{CASE}

The {CASE} command compares a value to a list of other values, each identified by a label, and instructs the macro to branch to the subroutine identified by the label that matches the initial value. Its syntax is

```
{CASE}value ~
case1 ~ label1 ~
case2 ~ label2 ~

. . .

casen ~ labeln ~ ~
```

Note that the entire command must end with an additional tilde as well as each case and label within it.

The {CASE} command is generally used to evaluate user input from a menu. Depending on which key the user pressed, the macro branches to the subroutine identified by the label.

For example, a macro can display a menu with three options, such as

1 - Sort by name and address
2 - Print report
3 - Quit

In this case, you would set up a {CASE} command to interpret the user's response, as follows:

```
{LABEL}options ~
{CASE}{VAR 1} ~ 1 ~ sort ~ s ~ sort ~ S ~ sort ~
```

```
2 ˜ print ˜ p ˜ print ˜ P ˜ print ˜
3 ˜ end ˜ q ˜ end ˜ Q ˜ end ˜ ˜
{GO} options
```

If variable 1 contains *1, s,* or *S,* the macro executes the subroutine identified by the label *sort.* If it contains *2, p,* or *P,* it goes to the *print* subroutine. If it contains *3, q,* or *Q,* it goes to the *end* subroutine. If no matches are found, the macro executes the {GO} command followed by the *options* subroutine. This creates a closed loop whereby the user must select one of the nine valid choices or press the Cancel key to have the program progress to the rest of the commands in the macro. This technique is most useful for keeping a menu displayed until the user makes a valid selection.

{CASE CALL}

The {CASE CALL} command compares a value to a list of other values and then calls a subroutine, depending on the matches that it finds. Its syntax is

```
{CASE CALL} value ˜
case1 ˜ label1 ˜
case2 ˜ label2 ˜
. . .
casen ˜ labeln ˜ ˜
```

This command is generally used to evaluate user input from a menu. Depending on which key the user presses, the macro branches to the subroutine identified by the label. If no matches are found, the macro simply executes the next step that follows the {CASE CALL} command.

The {CASE CALL} command is similar to the {CASE} command. If the case value is the equivalent of the value of the variable, the macro executes the subroutine identified by the label. When it reaches a {RETURN} command in the called subroutine, it executes the next step that follows the {CASE CALL} command.

{CHAIN}

The {CHAIN} command allows you to indicate the name of a macro to execute as soon as all the steps of the current macro are carried out. Its syntax is

```
{CHAIN} file ˜
```

where *file* is the name of another WordPerfect macro. You don't have to enter the .WPM extension.

For example, to execute a macro named **print** as soon as the current macro finishes, you would enter

{CHAIN}print˜

The **print** macro will not be executed until the current macro finishes, no matter where you put the {CHAIN} command in the macro. If you want the macro to be executed at a certain point in the current macro, use the {NEST} command instead.

{CHAR}

The {CHAR} command displays a prompt at the bottom of the screen and pauses until the user presses a key, such as **Y** or **N**. The text that the user types in response to the prompt is stored in a variable (0 through 9). The syntax of the command is

{CHAR}variable˜message˜

It can be used either with prompts that require a Yes/No response or with menus that require a letter or number choice. For example, the following command will produce a menu at the bottom of the screen and will store the user's response in variable 2:

{CHAR}2˜**1 D**elete Record;**2 S**ort:˜

Use the {DISPLAY OFF} command before the {CHAR} command so that WordPerfect won't display the menu lines after the menu has been used.

You can control where and how the {CHAR}, {TEXT}, and {PROMPT} commands place text on the screen by using the control characters shown in Table 16.1. To enter the commands that position the cursor in the Macro Editor, press the appropriate keys with Macro Command mode on. The ^H, ^J, ^K, ^L, ^W, ^Z, ^X, and ^Y keystrokes are alternatives for generating some of the cursor positioning commands, as shown in the table. For example, to position the cursor in the upper-left corner of the screen, you must generate the {Home} command. With Macro Command mode on, you can either press Ctrl-H to generate the {Home} code, or press the Home key. To position the cursor at the beginning of the current line, you will need to enter {^M} by pressing Ctrl-M. To position the cursor at a specific row and column position, insert a {^P} code; then insert the ASCII character or code equivalent of the column (0–79) and row (0–24) positions as shown in Table 16.2. For example, to display the prompt

"One moment, please!" starting in column 24 on line 10, you would enter

　　{PROMPT}{^P}{^X}{^I}One moment, please! ~

To enter display attribute codes such as **{^R}** and **{^T}**, press Ctrl-R and Ctrl-T in the Macro Editor.

TO POSITION THE CURSOR	PRESS
In the upper-left corner of the screen	^H or Home
At the beginning of the current line	^M
At the beginning of the next line	^J or Enter
Up one line	^W or ↑
Down one line	^Z or ↓
Right one character	^X or →
Left one character	^Y or ↓
At a column and row position	^P plus ASCII character and code equivalent of column and row positions (see Table 16.2)
At the bottom of the screen with the message in the upper-left corner	^L or Ctrl-PgDn (DELETE TO EOP)
At the bottom of the screen without moving the cursor	^K or Ctrl-End (DELETE TO EOL)
TO USE DISPLAY ATTRIBUTES	**PRESS**
Bold on	^]
Bold off	^\
Reverse video on	^R
Reverse video off	^S
Underline on	^T
Underline off	^U
To turn on display for text that follows	^N plus ^L for bold, ^N for underlining, ^P for blinking, and ^Q for reverse video
To turn off display for text that follows	^O
To turn off all display attributes	^Q
To turn on the attribute specified for menu letter options on the Setup menu	^V

TABLE 16.1: Control Characters for Displaying Messages

1	^A	17	^Q	33	!	49	1	65	A
2	^B	18	^R	34	"	50	2	66	B
3	^C	19	^S	35	#	51	3	67	C
4	^D	20	^T	36	$	52	4	68	D
5	^E	21	^U	37	%	53	5	69	E
6	^F	22	^V	38	&	54	6	70	F
7	^G	23	^W	39	'	55	7	71	G
8	^H	24	^X	40	(	56	8	72	H
*9	^I	25	^Y	41	)	57	9	73	I
*10	^J	26	^Z	42	*	58	:	74	J
*11	^K	27	^[	43	+	59	;	75	K
*12	^L	28	^\	44	,	60	<	76	L
13	^M	29	^]	45	–	61	=	77	M
14	^N	30	▲	46	.	62	>	78	N
15	^O	31	▼	47	/	63	?	79	O
16	^P	32	Space	48	0	64	@	80	P

TABLE 16.2: ASCII Character and Code Equivalents. (To enter asterisked codes, press Ctrl-V first. To enter codes 30 through 80, hold down Alt while entering the number from the numeric keys pad.)

{DISPLAY OFF}, {DISPLAY ON}

The {DISPLAY OFF} and {DISPLAY ON} commands determine whether macro execution is visible on the screen (DISPLAY ON) or whether you simply see the *Please Wait* message as the macro is executed ({DISPLAY OFF}). The default is for the display to be on for macros that you create within the Macro Editor but for the display to be off for macros that you record in the editing screens, outside the Macro Editor. Their syntax is simply

{DISPLAY ON}
{DISPLAY OFF}

You can insert these commands as you record a macro as well as from within the Macro Editor. To do this, just press Ctrl-PgUp as you're recording the macro. You'll see the prompt

1 Pause; **2 D**isplay; **3 A**ssign; **4 C**omment: 0

Type **D**. You'll then see the prompt

Display Execution? (Y/N) N

Type **Y** to display the macro's execution. Typing **N** inserts a {DISPLAY OFF} command in the macro.

Macros that repeat certain processes such as searching, marking, and copying text will run much faster with the display off. However, if you're having trouble debugging a macro that isn't working correctly, you may want to turn the display on, slow down the macro's execution with the Speed command, or use the Step command to see one step of the macro at a time.

{GO}

The {GO} command passes control to the commands identified by a {LABEL} command. Its syntax is

{GO}label ˜

When a macro reaches a {GO} command, it branches to the {LABEL} command in the macro and executes the first instruction that it finds there, so you must have a {LABEL} command for each {GO} command. Any instructions between the {GO} command and the {LABEL} command are not executed.

For example, the command

{GO}generate ˜

branches to the subroutine identified by the *generate* label, which might be a set of instructions for generating tables, indexes, and automatic references at a certain location in the document.

The {GO} command is also used to repeat a subroutine until a search fails. To do this, you have the {GO} command branch to a subroutine named *tab* that includes a Search command. For example,

{LABEL}tab ˜
 {SEARCH}{Tab}·{SEARCH}
 {Backspace}{Left}
{GO}tab ˜

searches for all the Tab codes followed by a space in a document and deletes the space.

If you want the {GO} command to execute the {LABEL} subroutine and then return to where it was in the macro, use the {CALL} command instead.

If you want to branch to another macro, use the {NEST} or {CHAIN} command instead.

{IF}

See {IF}{ELSE}{ENDIF}.

{IF}/{ELSE}/{ENDIF}

The {IF} command tests to see if a condition exists. Used with the {ELSE} and {END IF} commands, the {IF} command can be used to check whether a condition exists; if it does, the macro can perform one operation, and if the condition does not exist, it can perform another. The syntax of the {IF} command is

```
{IF}value ~
     <commands to carry out if the condition exists>
{END IF}
```

or, if you are specifying that actions take place if the condition does not exist, the syntax is

```
{IF}value ~
     <commands to carry out if the condition exists>
{ELSE}
     <commands to carry out if the condition does not exist>
{END IF}
```

The value is either zero or not zero. A value of zero indicates that the condition is false (does not exist); a nonzero value indicates that it is true (does exist). If the value is false (0), the commands after the {IF} command are not carried out. If the value is true (– 1 or some other nonzero value), the steps after the {IF} command are carried out, but if there is an {ELSE} command, the actions following it are performed.

In WordPerfect macros, the {IF} command is frequently used to check the state of the program (see {STATE}) and execute (or not execute) steps that depend on this condition. The following lines tell the macro to check if a prompt is being displayed. If it is, the macro goes to the subroutine labeled *stop*:

```
{IF}{STATE}&1024 ~
     {GO}stop ~
{END IF}
```

Note: If your variable contains text (as opposed to numbers) or WordPerfect codes and is used with one of the program's logical operators, you must enclose both the name of the variable and its equivalent in a pair of quotation marks (single or double), as in the following example using nested {IF} constructions:

```
{IF}"{VAR 3}" = "done" ~
     {GO}quit ~
{ELSE}
     {IF}"{VAR 3}" = "{Cancel}" ~
          {GO}cancelmsg ~
     {ENDIF}
{ENDIF}
```

{IF EXISTS}

The {IF EXISTS} command tests to see if a value is stored in a variable. Its syntax is

```
{IF EXISTS}variable ~
     <commands to perform if variable exists>
{END IF}
```

Its usage is very similar to that of the {IF} command (see {IF}{ELSE}{END IF}). For example, you could write a macro that checks to see if a value has been entered at a prompt and, if one has not been entered, go to a subroutine labeled *end*:

```
{IF EXISTS}0 ~
{ELSE}
     {GO}end ~
{END IF}
```

{LABEL}

The {LABEL} command identifies a subroutine by name. It is used with the {GO}, {CALL}, {CASE}, and {CASE CALL} commands.
Its syntax is

```
{LABEL}label ~
```

Where *label* is the name given to the subroutine that follows it.

When a macro reaches a {LABEL} command, it executes the instructions it finds there.

For example, you could assign the label *menu* to a set of commands that produces a menu on the screen:

```
{LABEL}menu ~
{CHAR}1 ~ 1 Delete Record;2 Sort: ~
```

The label you assign can consist of any characters and be as long as you want.

{LOOK}

The {LOOK} command checks to see if the user has pressed a key. If so, the command assigns that character to a variable number. Its syntax is

```
{LOOK}variable ~
```

The {LOOK} command is similar to the {CHAR} command. The difference is that the {CHAR} command waits for the user to type a character, while the {LOOK} command tests to see whether a character has been typed. If a character has been typed, the {LOOK} command places its value in the variable (0 through 9).

For example, the command

```
{LOOK}1 ~
```

places the character that the user has typed into variable 1. You can then use the {IF EXISTS} and {GO} commands to branch to different processes. For example, the following lines tell the macro to assign the keystroke that the user has pressed to variable 1. If there is a value in variable 1, the macro branches to the subroutine called *doit*. If there is no value in variable 1, the macro ends with

```
{LABEL}doit ~
{LOOK}1 ~
{IF EXISTS}1 ~
     {GO}doit ~
{END IF}
```

In the next example, the macro is waiting for the user to press a key. The {LOOK} command checks to see whether a key was pressed and, if it was, stores that value in variable 0. The {IF EXISTS} command then checks to see if variable 0 exists. If there is no variable 0, the macro returns to the label *wait* and executes the {LOOK} command again, continuing until the user finally presses a key.

```
{LABEL}Wait ~
     {WAIT}1 ~
     {LOOK}0 ~
     {IF EXISTS}0 ~
     {ELSE}
          {GO}wait ~
{END IF}
```

{NEST}

The {NEST} command indicates to a macro that it should execute another macro at the point where the {NEST} command occurs. Its syntax is

```
{NEST}file ~
```

where *file* is the name of another WordPerfect macro. You don't have to enter the .WPM extension.

You can also nest Alt macros as you're recording other macros, but this technique is a little different from using the {NEST} command. When you press Alt and the letter of a previously recorded macro while recording a new macro, the keystrokes of that macro are executed immediately as you're recording the macro, and the command to execute the macro is placed in the macro. For example, if you've recorded an Alt-S macro that saves and prints the document, your document will be saved and printed at that point. An {ALT S} command will also be inserted in the macro.

{ON CANCEL}

The {ON CANCEL} command, along with the {ON ERROR} and {ON NOT FOUND} commands, is used as an exception handler, which means that it tells WordPerfect what to do if a certain condition arises. In the case of the {ON CANCEL} command, it indicates the action that the macro should take when the user presses the Cancel key (F1). The syntax of the {ON CANCEL} command is

{ON CANCEL} action ˜

The *action* portion of the command can be either a {BREAK}, {CALL}, {GO}, {RESTART}, {RETURN}, {RETURN NOT FOUND}, or {QUIT} command.

For example, you might want to have a macro branch to a set of commands with the {GO} or {CALL} command if the user presses the F1 key. The subroutine could ask for confirmation of the cancel action. Depending on the response, the macro could return to where it left off (with the {RETURN} command), or quit ({QUIT}).

If you want the {ON CANCEL} command to be active throughout a macro, be sure to place it near the beginning of a macro so that the program is instructed about what action to take if the Cancel key is pressed.

{ON ERROR}

The {ON ERROR} command is used to instruct a macro what to do if an error message is generated as the macro executes. Its syntax is

{ON ERROR} action ˜

where *action* can be a {BREAK}, {CALL}, {GO}, {RESTART}, {RETURN}, {RETURN NOT FOUND}, or {QUIT} command.

For example, if during a macro the user performs some action that results in an error message such as "Not enough memory," which can occur if the user is attempting to sort on the screen a file that is too large to fit in RAM, you can use an {ON ERROR} command to tell WordPerfect what to do. In this case, you would probably use a {GO} command to display a prompt telling the user to sort the input file to a disk file. Unfortunately, the macro has no way of knowing which of the many errors could have occurred.

If you want the {ON ERROR} command to be active throughout a macro, be sure to place it near the beginning of the macro so that the program is instructed what to do if an error condition occurs at any point.

{ON NOT FOUND}

The {ON NOT FOUND} command is used to instruct a macro what to do if a Not Found condition occurs, as in a search. Its syntax is

{ON NOT FOUND}action ~

where *action* can be a {BREAK}, {CALL}, {GO}, {RESTART}, {RETURN}, {RETURN NOT FOUND}, or {QUIT} command.

For example, after a search fails—indicating that all the instances of the search pattern have been located—you might want to go to a set of instructions to save and print a document.

If you want the {ON NOT FOUND} command to be active throughout a macro, be sure to place it near the beginning of the macro so that the program is instructed what to do if a Not Found condition occurs at any point.

{ORIGINAL KEY}

The {ORIGINAL KEY} command tells WordPerfect to use the original definition of a key, not any definition that you may have subsequently assigned to that key with the Keyboard Layout feature. Its syntax is simply

{ORIGINAL KEY}

For example, if you have reassigned Ctrl-B to a macro that inserts boldfacing in your text but you want to use Ctrl-B to insert the current page number (which is its original definition), you would insert the command in the macro as

Ctrl-B{ORIGINAL KEY}

The {ORIGINAL KEY} command comes after the key sequence; it tells Word-Perfect to use the original definition of the last key you pressed only for this one time.

{PAUSE}

The {PAUSE} command allows you to pause a macro and wait for the user's input from the keyboard. When the user presses Enter, the macro resumes. Its syntax is

{PAUSE}

You can also insert a pause as you're recording a macro. To do this, just press Ctrl-PgUp. You'll see the prompt

1 Pause; **2 D**isplay; **3 A**ssign; **4 C**omment: 0

Type **P** to insert {PAUSE} in the macro. While a macro is paused, any keys you press are not recorded. As soon as you press Enter, the macro resumes.

While recording certain macros from the keyboard, you'll need to enter something at this point for the macro to work on. For example, if you're pausing the macro so that you can highlight text and the macro will move the text when it resumes, you'll need to highlight some text at this point as you record the macro. No keystrokes you make will be recorded while the macro is paused.

You may want to use the {BELL} command with pauses in your macros to alert the user that the macro is waiting for input.

{PROMPT}

The {PROMPT} command allows you to write macros that display a message on the screen. Its syntax is

{PROMPT}message ˜

The message itself normally appears in boldface at the bottom of the screen. If the prompt is longer than one line and includes hard returns, WordPerfect will scroll the prompt up until its last line is at the bottom of the screen.

You can use special position and display commands that control where and how the text appears on the screen (Table 16.1). For example, to position the cursor in the upper-left corner and display the prompt *Please wait* in reverse video, you would supply a {PROMPT} command as follows:

{PROMPT}{HOME}{^N}{^Q}Please wait ˜

{QUIT}

The {QUIT} command terminates a macro at the point that the command is encountered. Its syntax is simply

{QUIT}

The {QUIT} command can be used at any point within a macro. It's often used if a TRUE condition has been returned by an IF statement, in which case it can immediately terminate the macro.

{RESTART}

The {RESTART} command terminates a macro when the subroutine that is currently running is finished. Its syntax is simply

{RESTART}

It terminates the execution of the macro as soon as the keystrokes and commands in the current subroutine or macro have finished executing.

{RETURN}

The {Return} command is used to return from a subroutine to the next higher level. It can also be used to return to a main macro from a nested macro.

{RETURN CANCEL}

The {RETURN CANCEL} command resumes a macro's execution after a {CALL} or {CASE CALL} and indicates a cancel condition, as though the Cancel key (F1) had been pressed by the user. Its syntax is simply

{RETURN CANCEL}

If an {ON CANCEL} command has been used elsewhere in the macro, the subroutine that it specifies will be carried out. Otherwise, the macro terminates.

{RETURN ERROR}

The {RETURN ERROR} command resumes a macro's execution after a {CALL} or {CASE CALL} and indicates an error condition. Its syntax is simply

{RETURN ERROR}

If an {ON ERROR} command has been used elsewhere in the macro, the subroutine that it specifies will be carried out. Otherwise, the macro terminates.

{RETURN NOT FOUND}

The {RETURN NOT FOUND} command resumes a macro's execution after a {CALL} or {CASE CALL} and indicates a Not Found condition. Its syntax is simply

{RETURN NOT FND}

If an {ON NOT FOUND} command has been used elsewhere in the macro, the subroutine that it specifies will be carried out. Otherwise, the macro terminates.

{SPEED}

The {SPEED} command indicates how fast macros are to be executed. Its syntax is

{SPEED}100ths ~

where the speed you enter is in hundredths of a second. For example, to have a macro execute its steps one second at a time, enter **100**; for a speed of ½ second, enter **50**, and so forth.

The {SPEED} command can be used to slow macro execution so that text can be read as it is written on the screen. For example, if the speed provided by the {DISPLAY ON} command is still too fast, you can use the {SPEED} command to display a document at a readable rate as it is written but resume top speed for the part of the macro that saves and prints it.

{STATE}

The {STATE} command tests which state WordPerfect is in. For example, if Block mode is active, the current state is identified as 128. If the main document editing screen is active, the state is 4. The syntax for the {STATE} command requires you to enter an ampersand (&) after the {STATE} command and before the number representing the state to test for, so you would represent the Block On state, for example, as

{STATE}&128

Other states are represented according to the following list:

1,2,3   Current document number
4   Main editing screen

8	Editing screen (other than main document, such as footnote or header editing screen)
16	Macro definition
32	Macro execution (always set)
64	Merge execution
128	Block on
256	Typeover on
512	Reveal Codes operative
1024	Yes/No question operative

Note: More than one state can be active at a time. In such cases, the individual state numbers are summed. For example, if the macro is performing a merge operation in document window 2, the state is 102. This figure represents the sum of 2 (Current document number) plus 4 (Main editing screen) plus 32 (Macro execution) plus 64 (Merge active).

{STEP OFF}, {STEP ON}

The {STEP ON} and {STEP OFF} commands allow you to debug macros by telling WordPerfect to execute the macro one step at a time. Their syntax is

```
{STEP ON}
{STEP OFF}
```

When WordPerfect reaches a {STEP ON} command, it executes the macro one keystroke at a time. It displays the step that it is executing at the bottom of the screen. When you press any key, it executes the next step.

{TEXT}

The {TEXT} command displays a prompt at the bottom of the screen and pauses until the user presses Enter. The text that the user types in response to the prompt is stored in a variable (0 through 9). The syntax of the command is

```
{TEXT}variable ˜ message ˜
```

You can use the {TEXT} command to request user input, such as document names and other text that is to be entered from the keyboard. It can also be used for menus whose responses require more than one character. (Use the {CHAR} command for one-character menu responses.)

For example, you can use the following {TEXT} command to prompt the user to enter a name that is to be stored in variable 1:

{TEXT}1 ˜ Type the client's full name: ˜

After the name is typed, it is stored in variable 1, so you can use the command {VAR 1} anywhere else in the macro to produce the client's full name.

Table 16.1 (see the "{CHAR}" entry earlier in this chapter) summarizes the commands that you can use with the {TEXT} command to display text on the screen.

{WAIT}

The {WAIT} command tells WordPerfect to pause for a certain time that you indicate in tenths of a second. Its syntax is

{WAIT}10ths ˜

For example, you might want to have a macro retrieve a document consisting of one screen of text, wait until the user has time to read it, clear the screen, and retrieve another document, thus creating a "slide show" effect. To have a macro wait for 1 second, you would enter **10** as the value for the {WAIT} command; to have it wait for 5 seconds, enter **50**, and so forth.

PROGRAMMING WITH THE MACRO COMMAND LANGUAGE

In Chapter 11, you were introduced to techniques for building a menu system to perform merges; the system was created solely with WordPerfect's Merge commands. However, you can use the macro command language to build an even more powerful and versatile menu system that both merges primary and secondary files and performs routine maintenance tasks on the secondary files such as adding, editing, and deleting records. The system outlined here is intended to further illustrate how the macro command language is used, as well as to give you ideas for creating a menu-driven merge system of your own.

The Merge Menu System

The merge system relies upon a hierarchy of menus. Each of these menus allows the user to select any of its options either by number or by a menu letter, just as the standard WordPerfect command menus do. Moreover, each option number and menu letter choice is displayed on the screen in bold, just like menu options on WordPerfect's standard command menus (unless the user has changed the menu letter display default on the Setup menu).

The menu system is invoked with the MASTER.WPM macro. This displays a menu (shown in Figure 16.5) that allows the user to select one of three options: Perform Merge, which displays the Merge Menu (shown in Figure 16.6), Maintain Secondary Files, which displays the Maintenance Menu (shown in Figure 16.7), or Quit Master Menu, which terminates the menu system, displays a termination message, and returns the user to the document editing screen.

As you can see from Figures 16.6 and 16.7, the user can return to the Master Menu from either submenu by selecting the Return to Master Menu option (option **4** on the Merge Menu and option **5** on the Maintenance Menu). The user cannot, however, exit the menu system from the submenu level. The Quit Master Menu option on the Master Menu is the only exit point from this system. The user can, however, press the Cancel key (F1), as the macros don't disable this function by using the {CANCEL OFF} command.

THE MASTER MENU MACRO

The complete program listing for the Master Menu macro named MASTER.WPM is shown in Listing 16.1. The Master Menu is displayed on the screen using the {CHAR} command. Remember that this command records a

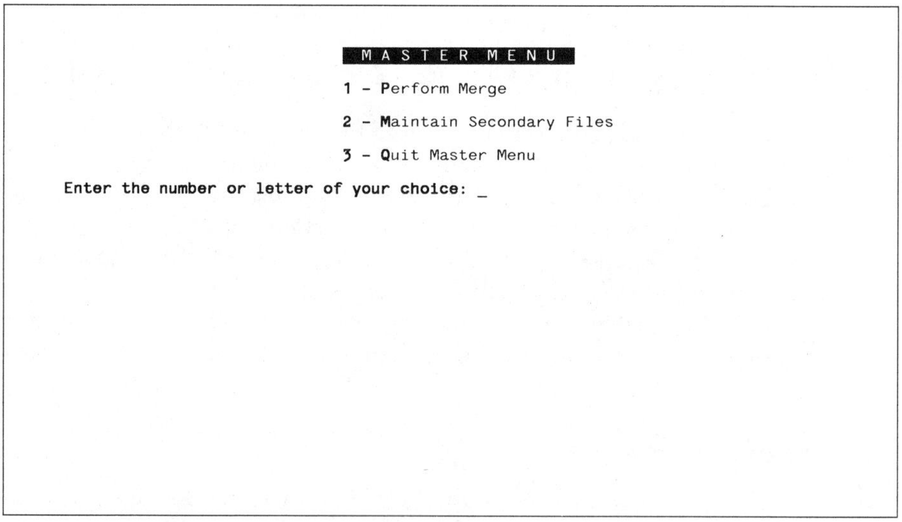

```
                          M A S T E R   M E N U

                    1 - Perform Merge

                    2 - Maintain Secondary Files

                    3 - Quit Master Menu

            Enter the number or letter of your choice: _
```

FIGURE 16.5: The Master Menu displayed when the user executes the macro called MASTER.WPM. From this menu, the user can choose to perform various merge operations (**1** or **P**) or a number of routine maintenance tasks (**2** or **M**).

```
                    M E R G E   M E N U

            1 - Select Primary File

            2 - Select Secondary File

            3 - Merge Files

            4 - Return to Master Menu

     Enter the number of letter of your choice: _
```

FIGURE 16.6: The Merge Menu displayed when the Perform Merge option (**1** or **P**) on the Master Menu is selected. The user, once finished with this menu, can return to the Master Menu by selecting the Return to Master Menu option (**4** or **R**).

```
                M A I N T E N A N C E   M E N U

            1 - Select Secondary File

            2 - Add New Record

            3 - Edit Record

            4 - Delete Record

            5 - Return to Master Menu

     Enter number or letter of your choice: _
```

FIGURE 16.7: The Maintenance Menu displayed when the Maintain Secondary Files option (**2** or **M**) on the Master Menu is selected. Once finished with this menu, the user can return to the Master Menu by selecting the Return to Master Menu option (**5** or **R**).

```
{;}MASTER.WPM displays a menu of options for maintaining primary
{;}and secondary files and for performing merges

{DISPLAY OFF}
{LABEL}mainmenu~
{CHAR}1~{Del to EOP}
                {^R}M A S T E R   M E N U{^S}
{Enter}
{Enter}
                {]}1  P{^\}erform Merge
{Enter}
{Enter}
                {]}2  M{^\}aintain Secondary Files
{Enter}
{Enter}
                {]}3  Q{^\}uit Master Menu
{Enter}
{Enter}
{]}Enter the number or letter of your choice:\~\} ~
{CASE}{VAR 1}~1~assembly~p~assembly~P~assembly~
2~maintenance~m~maintenance~M~maintenance~
3~end~q~end~Q~end~~
{GO}mainmenu~

{LABEL}assembly~{NEST}assembly~

{LABEL}maintenance~{NEST}maintain~

{LABEL}end~{CHAIN}thatsit~
```

LISTING 16.1: Program listing for the Master Menu macro.

single keystroke response given by the user in the variable entered as its first argument (variable 1, in this case). The menu title, the menu options, and the prompt for the user to enter a choice by number or letter are all included as part of the {CHAR} command message argument. Appropriate spacing is maintained between the menu title, the menu options, and the prompt by the use of {Enter} commands (inserted by pressing Ctrl-V followed by the Enter key in the Macro Editor).

The document editing screen is cleared and the Master Menu is positioned by the use of the {Del to EOP} command, inserted by pressing Ctrl-L in the Macro Editor. This command clears the screen and positions the cursor at the upper-left corner. Note that this can also be accomplished by placing a {Home} (Ctrl-H) command in the {CHAR} message argument, since the {DISPLAY OFF} command is left in the macro. Either way, it is important that the editing screen be cleared each time the Master Menu is displayed, to ensure that none of its messages overlap characters displayed previously.

There are two visual effects used in this menu (and subsequent menus) for the merge system. The menu title is highlighted by the use of the {^R} and {^S} display attribute control characters, which turn on and off reverse video. The option number or menu letter choice and the message prompt are displayed in bold by enclosing them in the {^]} and {^\} display attribute control characters, which turn on and off the bold display.

The {CASE} command is used to indicate which choices are valid and which subroutine is to be executed when one of these valid choices is made. To allow the user to type the number of the option or its lowercase or uppercase menu letter, three choices are covered for each menu item, making a total of nine valid cases.

The menu continues to be displayed until the user presses one of the nine allowable choices because of the {LABEL}mainmenu˜ and {GO}mainmenu˜ commands that enclose the entire {CHAR} and {CASE} commands. Any keystroke other than one of those explicitly covered by the {CASE} command causes the {GO}mainmenu˜ command to be executed. The {LABEL}mainmenu˜ statement indicates where the subroutine *mainmenu* is located in the program.

When the user selects the Perform Merge option by typing **1** or **p** or **P**, the {CASE} command tells WordPerfect to go to the subroutine labeled *assembly* and to execute the commands that it finds there. In this case, the {NEST} command is used to immediately execute the macro named ASSEMBLY.WPM. This macro displays the Merge Menu shown in Figure 16.6.

When the user selects the Perform Merge option by typing **2** or **m** or **M**, the {CASE} command tells WordPerfect to go to the subroutine labeled *maintenance* and execute the commands that it finds there. In this case, the {NEST} command is used to immediately execute the macro named MAINTAIN.WPM. This macro displays the Maintenance Menu shown in Figure 16.7.

When the user selects the Quit Master Menu option by typing **3** or **q** or **Q**, the {CASE} command tells WordPerfect to go to the subroutine labeled *end* and execute the commands that it finds there. In this case, the {CHAIN} command is used to immediately execute the macro named THATSIT.WPM. This macro contains the following commands:

```
{DISPLAY OFF}{PROMPT}{Del to EOP}
    This concludes the merge program{Enter}{Enter}
    Come back soon!  ˜
{WAIT}10˜
{QUIT}
```

This macro uses the {PROMPT} command to clear the screen of the Master Menu and display a brief termination message. The {WAIT} command instructs the program to wait 1 second (ten tenths) before terminating the macro with the {QUIT} command.

THE MERGE MENU MACRO

The Merge Menu program is very similar to the Master Menu program. Its program listing is shown in Listing 16.2. The Merge Menu program employs

```
{;}ASSEMBLY.WPM displays a menu that allows the user to
{;}select the primary and secondary files to be merged
{;}and then performs the merge and saves the merged data
{;}upon confirmation by the user

{DISPLAY OFF}
{LABEL}mergemenu~
{CHAR}1~{Del to EOP}
               {^R}M E R G E  M E N U{^S}
{Enter}
{Enter}
               {]}1 -{^\} Select {]}P{^\}rimary File
{Enter}
{Enter}
               {]}2 -{^\} Select {]}S{^\}econdary File
{Enter}
{Enter}
               {]}3 - M{^\}erge Files
{Enter}
{Enter}
               {]}4 - R{^\}eturn to Master Menu
{Enter}
{Enter}
{]}Enter the number or letter of your choice:{^\} ~
{CASE}{VAR 1}~1~primary~p~primary~P~primary~
2~secondary~s~secondary~S~secondary~
3~merge~m~merge~M~merge~
3~return~r~return~R~return~~
{GO}mergemenu~

{LABEL}primary~{NEST}primary~

{LABEL}secondary~{NEST}secondar~

{LABEL}merge~{NEST}merging~

{LABEL}return~{CHAIN}master~
```

LISTING 16.2: Program listing for the Merge Menu macro.

the same techniques for displaying the menu, highlighting the title, and bold-facing the menu options and prompt message.

In fact, this menu is so similar in structure and commands that it was created by first copying the MASTER.WPM macro and renaming it ASSEMBLY-.WPM on the List Files screen. Then, the ASSEMBLY.WPM macro was edited, and the commands and prompts were changed as required for the new menu program.

Selecting the Primary and Secondary Files to be Merged To simplify the selection of the primary and secondary files to be used in a merge operation, the user selects the files by menu option rather than typing in the file name. Figure 16.8 shows you the menu that is displayed when the user chooses the Select Primary File option (**1** or **P**) from the Merge Menu. It allows him or her to select among five different primary files or to return to the Merge Menu. When the user selects one of the first five options, the program selects the correct primary document by file name and assigns this file name to variable 2.

```
╔══════════════════════════════════════════════════════════════╗
║                     ▐ P r i m a r y  F i l e s ▌              ║
║                                                              ║
║                 1 - Customer Form Letter                     ║
║                                                              ║
║                 2 - Invoice Form                             ║
║                                                              ║
║                 3 - Overdue Form Letter                      ║
║                                                              ║
║                 4 - Mailing Labels                           ║
║                                                              ║
║                 5 - Envelopes                                ║
║                                                              ║
║                 6 - Return to Merge Menu                     ║
║                                                              ║
║   Enter the number or letter of the primary file to use in   ║
║   the merge: _                                               ║
║                                                              ║
╚══════════════════════════════════════════════════════════════╝
```

FIGURE 16.8: The Primary Files Menu accessed by choosing the Select Primary File option on the Merge Menu. To select the primary document to be used in the merge, the user simply types the number or menu letter of the appropriate option. The program chooses the correct primary file based on this entry.

The PRIMARY.WPM macro uses the {CHAR} command to get the user's menu selection just as the Master Menu and Merge Menu programs do. The program also uses the {CASE} command to evaluate the choice made by the user and branch to the appropriate subroutine. The six subroutines use the {ASSIGN} command to insert the correct primary file name into variable 2. These subroutines are entered in the program as follows:

```
{LABEL}customer ~ {ASSIGN}2 ~ formltr.pf ~ {GO}end ~
{LABEL}invoice ~ {ASSIGN}2 ~ invoice.pf ~ {GO}end ~
{LABEL}overdue ~ {ASSIGN}2 ~ overdue.pf ~ {GO}end ~
{LABEL}mailing ~ {ASSIGN}2 ~ mailing.pf ~ {GO}end ~
{LABEL}envelope ~ {ASSIGN}2 ~ envelope.pf ~ {GO}end ~
{LABEL}end ~ {CHAIN}assembly ~
```

To print standard form letters in a merge, the user would select the Customer Form Letter option (**1** or **C**). The program branches to the *customer* subroutine and assigns the file name FORMLTR.PF to variable 2. Then, it executes the *end* subroutine, which returns the user to the Merge Menu. From there, the user can next select the secondary file to be used in the merge (assuming that one is necessary).

The Select Secondary File option (**2** or **S**) on the Merge Menu leads to a very similar menu that displays choices for the secondary file (Figure 16.9). When the user selects any of the first four menu options, the program assigns the associated secondary file name to variable 3.

```
                    ╔══════════════════════════╗
                    ║  S e c o n d a r y  F i l e s ║
                    ╚══════════════════════════╝
                         1 - Client List

                         2 - Vendor List

                         3 - Sales List

                         4 - Employee List

                         5 - Return to Merge Menu

      Enter the number or letter of the secondary file to use in the merge: _
```

FIGURE 16.9: The Secondary Files Menu accessed by choosing the Select Secondary File option on the Merge Menu. To select the secondary document to be used in the merge, the user simply types the number or menu letter of the appropriate option. The program chooses the correct secondary file based on this entry.

To merge the standard form letter with the client file, the user would select the Client List option (**1** or **C**) from this menu. The SECONDAR.WPM macro contains subroutines similar to those used in the PRIMARY.WPM macro. In this case, the program would execute the subroutine

{LABEL}client ˜ {ASSIGN}3 ˜ client.sf ˜ {GO}end ˜

which assigns the secondary file name CLIENT.SF to variable 3. The program returns the user to the Merge Menu, where he or she can select the Merge Files option to have WordPerfect perform this merge operation.

Merging the Files   After selecting the primary and secondary files to use in the merge, the user can select the Merge Files option (**3** or **M**) to perform the merge. Listing 16.3 shows the program listing for the MERGING.WPM file, which is executed when this option is selected.

Figure 16.10 shows you the prompt that appears when the user has selected the Customer Form Letter option from the Primary Files menu and the Client List option from the Secondary Files menu before choosing the Merge Files option. As you can see from the program listing, it uses {VAR 2} and {VAR 3} highlighted with reverse video to show the user the files that are currently selected.

```
(;)MERGING.WPM performs the merge using the primary and secondary
(;)files previously selected by the user, then prompts the user to
(;)save the merged file. If Yes, the program prompts the user for
(;)file name and saves the file.

(DISPLAY OFF)
(LABEL)message~
(CHAR)5~(Del to EOP)
        Merge primary file (^])(VAR 2)(^\)
(Enter)
(Enter)
        with secondary file (])(VAR 3)(^\)? (Y/N) ~
(CASE)(VAR 5)~y~mergeit~Y~mergeit~
n~return~N~return~~
(GO)message~

(LABEL)mergeit~
(Switch)(Exit)nn
(Merge/Sort)m(VAR 2)(Enter)(VAR 3)(Enter)

(DISPLAY ON)
(LABEL)mergesave~
(CHAR)6~Save this file? (Y/N) ~
(CASE)(VAR 6)~y~saveit~Y~saveit~
n~nosave~N~nosave~~
(GO)mergesave~

(LABEL)saveit~
(TEXT)7~Enter a new name for this file: ~

(IF EXISTS)7~
    (Exit)y(VAR 7)(Enter)n
    (Switch)
    (DISPLAY OFF)
(ELSE)
    (GO)saveit~
(END IF)

(LABEL)nosave~(Switch)

(LABEL)return~(CHAIN)assembly~
```

LISTING 16.3: Program listing for the Merging macro.

If the user doesn't designate a secondary file (some merge operations don't require them), its absence will be indicated on the second line by a highlight bar two spaces wide without a file name. If the user has specified the wrong files or has forgotten to select a primary file (WordPerfect won't perform a merge without a primary file), the user can type **n** or **N** and cancel the merge. This brings back the Merge Menu, where the user can select the appropriate option(s) to rectify the mistake.

If the selected files shown in this display are correct, the user types **y** or **Y** to have the program merge the files. The program performs the merge according to the *mergit* subroutine that contains the following commands:

```
{LABEL}mergeit ~
{Switch}{Exit}nn
{Merge/Sort}m{VAR 2}{Enter}{VAR 3}{Enter}
```

```
                  Merge primary file  formltr.pf
                  with secondary file  client.sf ? (Y/N)  _
```

FIGURE 16.10: The prompt that appears when the Merge Files option is selected from the Merge Menu. In this figure, the user first selected the Customer Form Letter option from the Primary Files menu and the Client List option from the Secondary Files menu before choosing the Merge Files option. The MERGING.WPM macro begins by forcing the user to confirm the previous selections.

The routine begins by switching to the other document screen with the {Switch} command and clearing it of any document that it might contain with {Exit} command. It then performs the merge with the file name in {VAR 2} as the primary file and the file name in {VAR 3} as the secondary file.

After the merge operation has been completed, the routine turns on the display so that the user can see the part of the last form letter created and prompts the user to save this merged document, as seen in Figure 16.11. The commands for this part of the program are presented by a *mergesave* and *saveit* routine as follows:

```
{DISPLAY ON}
{LABEL}mergesave ~
{CHAR}6 ~ Save this file? (Y/N) ~
{CASE}{VAR 6} ~ y ~ saveit ~ Y ~ saveit ~
n ~ nosave ~ N ~ nosave ~ ~
{GO}mergesave ~
```

First, the program asks the user whether this file should be saved. If the user responds by typing **n** or **N**, the program executes the *nosave* subroutine, which uses the {CHAIN} command to execute the ASSEMBLY.WPM macro, displaying the Merge Menu. If the user enters **y** or **Y**, the program executes the *saveit* subroutine as follows:

```
{LABEL}saveit ~
{TEXT}7 ~ Enter a new name for this file: ~
```

```
    Susan Kelly
    PC Teach
    P.O. Box 1175
    Point Reyes Station, CA 94956

    Dear Ms. Kelly:

        Please take a moment out of your busy schedule to look over
    the enclosed price list, which contains many exciting specials that
    I can offer your firm for a limited time only. As you will see,
    most of our paper products are offered at prices well below retail
    (and some are just pennies above wholesale cost!).

        Thank you for your time. I look forward to serving your firm
    and hope to take care of all of your paper product needs.

    Sincerely,



    Jason Stanford
    Corporate Account Executive

    Save this file? (Y/N) _
```

FIGURE 16.11: The prompt that appears after the merge has been completed. Because of the {DISPLAY ON} command, the user can now see the last letter that has been created with the merge. If **y** or **Y** is entered, the program will prompt the user to enter a file name under which to save the merged data. If **n** or **N** is typed, the program will redisplay the Merge Menu.

```
{IF EXISTS}7 ~
        {Exit}y{VAR 7}{Enter}n
        {Switch}
        {DISPLAY OFF}
{ELSE}
        {GO}saveit ~
{END IF}
```

To avoid an error caused when the user doesn't enter a new file name but just presses the Enter key, the {IF EXISTS} command is employed. This command evaluates the contents of variable 7. If it contains something, the save-and-exit command sequence is executed, using variable 7 for the file name. However, if variable 7 is empty, the {ELSE} statement is used, and the program reexecutes the *saveit* subroutine. This means that the only way the user can get back to the Merge Menu after confirming that the merged file should be saved (short of pressing Cancel and terminating the macro) is to enter some kind of file name.

> *Note:* The *saveit* subroutine does not guard against the possibility that the user will enter a file name that already exists. If this happens, the keystrokes for the save-and-exit command in this routine will not be correct because of the extra Replace File prompt that WordPerfect displays in this situation. The user of this menu system must be aware of this potential problem, or the program code must be changed to avoid this possibility entirely.

THE MAINTENANCE MENU MACRO

The Maintenance Menu (shown in Figure 16.7) gives the user a choice of three routine tasks: adding a new record, editing a record, or deleting a record from a secondary file. The user can also return to the Master Menu. The MAINTAIN.WPM macro that displays this menu uses the same programming techniques as the Master Menu and Merge Menu to display its options. It, too, uses the {CASE} command to determine which subroutine is executed when a particular option is selected by number or menu letter.

Selecting the Secondary File to Edit   To select the secondary file to be edited, the user first chooses the Select Secondary File option (**1** or **S**). This brings up the menu of choices shown in Figure 16.12.

Just as with the Secondary Files menu attached to the Merge Menu, this menu program selects the correct secondary file according to the option chosen by inserting the file name in variable 3. This file is then retrieved when the user selects the Add New Record, Edit Record, or Delete Record option from the Maintenance Menu. To edit a new secondary file, the user must choose the Select Secondary File option (**1** or **S**) on the Maintenance Menu.

```
                        Secondary Files

                    1 - Client List

                    2 - Vendor List

                    3 - Sales List

                    4 - Employee List

                    5 - Return to Maintenance Menu
    Enter the number or letter of the secondary file to edit: _
```

FIGURE 16.12: The Secondary Files menu for the Maintenance Menu. This menu appears when the user chooses the Select Secondary File option (1 or S) from the Maintenance Menu. The file selected from this menu is then used when the user selects the Add New Record, Edit Record, or Delete Record option from the Maintenance Menu, until he or she returns to this menu and selects a new file for editing.

The Add Record Macro When the user chooses the Add New Record option (**2** or **A**) on the Maintenance Menu, the program first checks to see if a secondary file has been selected. If it has not, it prompts the user to choose a secondary file and then returns to the Maintenance Menu. If the program finds that a secondary file has been selected, it chooses the appropriate macro to execute, depending upon which secondary file has been chosen. This is done by placing a {CASE} statement within an {IF EXISTS} condition as shown below:

```
{LABEL}add ~
{IF EXISTS}3 ~
    {CASE}{VAR 3} ~ client.sf ~ client ~ vendor.sf ~ vendor ~
    sales.sf ~ sales ~ employ.sf ~ employee ~ ~
{ELSE}
    {PROMPT}Please select a secondary file to edit ~
    {WAIT}10 ~
    {GO}maintainmenu ~
{END IF}
```

If the {IF EXISTS} command finds a value in variable 3 (meaning that the user has selected a secondary file with the Select Secondary File option), the {CASE} command branches to the appropriate subroutine based on variable 3's current value. If the {IF EXISTS} command finds no value in variable 3 (meaning that the user has not yet selected a secondary file), it displays the prompt to select a secondary file and redisplays the Maintenance Menu.

The subroutines attached to the {CASE} command indicate, as follows, which of the four add-record macros to use:

```
{LABEL}client ~ {NEST}addclrec ~
{LABEL}vendor ~ {NEST}vendrec ~
{LABEL}sales ~ {NEST}salesrec ~
{LABEL}employee ~ {NEST}emplyrec ~
```

Because the structure of the four secondary files is slightly different, a separate macro is used to add records to each one of them. Listing 16.4 shows the ADD-CLREC.WPM macro that is used to add a new record to CLIENT.SF file. The other three macros for adding records are similar to this program; the major differences between them are the type and number of prompts displayed, reflecting the type and number of fields contained in the secondary files they use.

This macro begins by informing the user that records will be added to the Customer List. The second line of the prompt shows the user the secondary file that is currently selected. The user must signal the confirmation to continue by typing **y** or **Y** in response to the prompt (shown in Figure 16.13). If the wrong secondary file has been chosen, the user can terminate the add- record operation by typing **n** or **N**.

```
You have chosen to add a record to the Customer List.

The currently selected secondary file is client.sf.

Do you want to continue? (Y/N): _
```

FIGURE 16.13: The prompt displayed when the user selects the Customer List option from the Secondary Files menu and then selects the Add New Record option on the Maintenance Menu. To continue, the user must type **y** or **Y**. To abort the operation, the user can type **n** or **N**.

When the user signals to continue, the macro displays seven prompts in succession, using the {TEXT} command. Each prompt is keyed to a particular field in the order it occurs in the CLIENT.SF file. Notice that the variables chosen to store the text for each of the seven fields in this secondary file purposely omit variable 3. At this point in the program, this variable stores the name of the currently selected secondary file. If it were used with one of the {TEXT} commands, this file name would be replaced by the user's response. If this happened, the program could no longer use this variable to retrieve the secondary file as it does in the line

{Retrieve} {VAR 3} {Enter}

When creating your own menu systems, be very careful that your programs never reuse a variable whose initially assigned value is required later on in a subroutine.

Note: You can't use the technique illustrated in this program to enter data in a secondary file that uses more than nine fields. This is due to the fact that Word-Perfect limits you to ten total variables (0–9). Because you must use one of these variables (variable 3 in this example) to store the name of the secondary file used in the retrieve and save commands, you can only prompt for field entries for nine fields before you have used all ten. Also, this system restricts the data entry for each field to one line only; when the user presses Enter, the program always inserts an ^R code and displays the prompt to enter data for the next field.

```
{;}ADDCLREC.WPM is used to add records to the CLIENT.SF file
{;}The program prompts the user to enter the information for
{;}each of its seven fields. It then saves the data in the
{;}CLIENT.SF file and returns the user to the Maintenance Menu.

{DISPLAY OFF}
{LABEL}message~
{CHAR}9~{Del to EOP}
You have chosen to add a record to the Customer List
{Enter}
{Enter}
The currently selected secondary file is {^R}{VAR 3}{^S}.
{Enter}
{Enter}
Do you want to continue? (Y/N): ~
{CASE}{VAR 9}~y~addrec~Y~addrec~
n~end~N~end~~
{GO}message~

{LABEL}addrec~
{TEXT}0~Enter the customer (record) number: ~
{TEXT}1~Enter the name of the company: ~
{TEXT}2~Enter the street address: ~
{TEXT}4~Enter the city, state, and zip code: ~
{TEXT}5~Enter the title (Mr., Ms., or Mrs.): ~
{TEXT}6~Enter the customer's first name: ~
{TEXT}7~Enter the customer's last name: ~
{Exit}nn
{Retrieve}{VAR 3}{Enter}
{Home}{Home}{Down}
{VAR 0}{Merge R}
{VAR 1}{Merge R}
{VAR 2}{Merge R}
{VAR 4}{Merge R}
{VAR 5}{Merge R}
{VAR 6}{Merge R}
{VAR 7}{Merge R}
{Merge Codes}e
{Exit}y{Enter}yn

{LABEL}end~{CHAIN}maintain~
```

LISTING 16.4: Program listing for the Add Client Record macro.

After retrieving the CLIENT.SF file and positioning the cursor at the end of the file with {Home}{Home}{Down}, the program inserts the text entered for each field as well as an ^R code to mark its end and begin a new line in the secondary file. This is done by entering the variable and the Merge R code, as in

{VAR 0}{Merge R}

which inserts the text contained in variable 0, ^R, and a hard return.

After all of the text for the seven fields has been inserted into the file in this manner, the program adds a Merge E code to mark the end of the record:

{Merge Codes}e

This inserts an ^E code and a hard page break. The macro then saves the file under the same name, clears the screen, and redisplays the Maintenance Menu.

The Edit Record Macro   The EDIT.WPM macro is executed when the user selects the Edit Record option (**3** or **E**) on the Maintenance Menu. Its listing is shown in Listing 16.5. This macro uses WordPerfect's Search feature to locate the particular record that the user wants to edit. Because the record number is the first field in all of the secondary files that can be selected from the Secondary Files menu, the same macro can be used to edit any of them.

The first commands after the {DISPLAY OFF} command in the edit-record macro tell the program what to do if a search fails—that is, if the user enters a nonvalid record number:

```
{ON NOT FOUND}{RETURN NOT FND} ~
{ON NOT FOUND}{GO}Notfound ~ ~
```

The {ON NOT FOUND}{RETURN NOT FND} ~ statement is entered to counter a bug in some earlier versions of WordPerfect 5.0 that causes the {ON NOT FOUND} command to be ignored. The first statement tells WordPerfect to return the value "Not Found" when a search fails. The second statement uses the {GO} command to have the program execute the *Notfound* subroutine upon a search failure.

> *Note:* Theoretically, the {ON NOT FOUND}{RETURN NOT FND} ~ commands are not required in order to make the subsequent {ON NOT FOUND}{GO}Notfound ~ ~ statement work. You can try programming your {ON NOT FOUND} routines without it. However, if you find that they are ignored by WordPerfect, try adding the first line that uses the {RETURN NOT FND} command.

The *Notfound* subroutine informs the user that the record number was entered in error and urges the user to try again as follows:

```
{LABEL}Notfound ~
{PROMPT}Record number as entered does not exist...Try again! ~
{WAIT}20 ~
{Exit}nn
```

After displaying the prompt for 2 seconds (twenty tenths), it clears the editing screen of the secondary file and redisplays the Maintenance Menu, where the user can select the Edit Record option again and enter a new record number.

The main processing routine in the macro (called *Editrecord*) prompts the user with the {TEXT} command to enter the number of the record to edit. It then clears the editing screen and retrieves the selected secondary file (again using the file name stored in variable 3).

The record number entered by the user is stored in variable 4. Therefore, the program searches for this record number terminated by a Merge R code as follows:

{Search} {VAR 4} {Merge R} {Search}

Adding the Merge R code at the end of the search string ensures that the program doesn't locate the number stored in variable 4 somewhere else in the secondary file, like in a street address or social security number field. For example, when the user enters **132** as the record number, the program inserts *132^R* as the search string, guaranteeing that WordPerfect won't consider *132* in the street address field containing *132 Elm Street* to be a match.

As soon as the program locates the record number, the macro pauses to allow the user to make editing changes to the record that is now on the document editing screen. As soon as the user presses Enter to end the pause, the program saves the record, clears the editing screen, and returns the user to the Maintenance Menu.

The Delete Record Macro   The DELETE.WPM macro that is executed when the Delete Record option (**4** or **D**) is selected from the Maintenance Menu works very much like the EDIT.WPM macro described above. It is shown in Listing 16.6.

As you can see, this macro uses the same {ON NOT FOUND} commands and *Notfound* subroutine to indicate what is to happen if the user enters a nonvalid record number. Likewise, the *Getrecord* subroutine prompts the user to enter

```
{;}EDIT.WPM allows the user to locate a specific record
{;}in the selected secondary file by record number and edit it.

{DISPLAY OFF}
{ON NOT FOUND}{RETURN NOT FND}˜
{ON NOT FOUND}{GO}Notfound˜˜

{LABEL}Editrecord˜
{TEXT}4˜Enter the number of the record to edit: ˜
{Exit}nn
{Retrieve}{VAR 3}{Enter}
{Search}{VAR 4}{Merge R}{Search}
{Pause}
{Exit}y{Enter}yn
{GO}end˜

{LABEL}Notfound˜
{PROMPT}Record number as entered does not exist...Try again! ˜
{WAIT}20˜
{Exit}nn

{LABEL}end˜{CHAIN}maintain˜
```

LISTING 16.5: Program listing for the Edit Record macro.

```
{;}DELETE.WPM allows the user to locate a specific record,
{;}view it, and delete it upon confirmation.


{DISPLAY OFF}
{ON NOT FOUND}{RETURN NOT FND}~
{ON NOT FOUND}{GO}Notfound~~

{LABEL}Getrecord~
{TEXT}7~Enter the number of the record to delete: ~
{Exit}nn
{Retrieve}{VAR 3}{Enter}
{DISPLAY ON}
{Search}{VAR 7}{Merge R}{Search}
{Home}{Left}{Block}{Search}{Merge Codes}e{Search}

{LABEL}Deletemsg~
{CHAR}8~You are about to delete record {VAR 7} - Continue? (Y/N)
{CASE}{VAR 8}~y~Yes~Y~Yes~
n~No~N~No~~
{GO}Deletemsg~

{LABEL}No~
{Cancel}{Exit}nn{GO}return~

{LABEL}Yes~
{Backspace}y{Down}{Backspace}
{Exit}y{Enter}yn
{GO}return~


{LABEL}Notfound~
{PROMPT}Record number as entered does not exist...Try again! ~
{WAIT}20~
{Exit}nn

{LABEL}return~{CHAIN}maintain~
```

LISTING 16.6: Program listing for the Delete Record macro.

the record number of the record to be deleted and then uses the same type of search command sequence to locate that record. Notice, however, that the {DISPLAY ON} command is used after the program retrieves the secondary file into the current editing screen. This is done so that the user can view the record before giving the confirmation to have it deleted.

Once the record is located, the program uses the following commands to block the record in preparation to delete it:

{Home}{Left}{Block}{Search}{Merge Codes}e{Search}

Because the cursor is located immediately following the ^R merge code, the {Home}{Left} commands position it at the very beginning of the line. Next, the program turns on Block mode and searches for the ^E (Merge E) code, thus extending the highlighting to the end of the record.

Now, with the blocked record in view on the screen, the user is prompted to confirm its deletion from the file. Figure 16.14 shows you this situation. In the

```
Grace^R
Fraesir^R
^E
===============================================================
134^R
Signet Products, Inc.^R
4562 14th Avenue^R
San Francisco, CA 94110^R
Ms.^R
Marjorie^R
McPherson^R
^E
===============================================================
200^R
House of Flowers^R
345 South 16th Street^R
Alameda, CA 94501^R
Mr.^R
Philip^R
Manley^R
^E
===============================================================
400^R
Corey's Computers^R
You are about to delete record 134 - Continue? (Y/N) _
```

FIGURE 16.14: The prompt to delete the record that is highlighted. To confirm the deletion, the user must type **y** or **Y**. To cancel the deletion, the user must type **n** or **N**.

figure, the user has selected record number 134. This record is now highlighted, and the prompt

> You are about to delete record 134 - Continue? (Y/N)

is displayed at the bottom of the screen. This is done with the *Deletemsg* subroutine, which contains the following commands:

> {LABEL}Deletemsg ˜
> {CHAR}8 ˜ You are about to delete record {VAR 7} - Continue? (Y/N)
> {CASE}{VAR 8} ˜ y ˜ Yes ˜ Y ˜ Yes ˜
> n ˜ No ˜ N ˜ No ˜
> {GO}Deletemsg ˜

To go ahead and remove the record from this file, the user must type either **y** or **Y**. If this is not the record that the user intended to delete, he or she can type **n** or **N** to cancel the delete sequence.

When the user types **y** or **Y**, the *Yes* subroutine, which contains the following commands, is executed:

> {LABEL}Yes ˜
> {Backspace}y{Down}{Backspace}
> {Exit}y{Enter}yn
> {GO}return ˜

This subroutine backspaces to delete the highlighted block and types **y** to confirm its removal. It then moves the cursor down one line below the hard page break and backspaces, thus deleting the [HPg] code. It terminates by saving the file and returning the user to the Maintenance Menu in the *return* subroutine.

When the user types **n** or **N** to avoid deleting the marked record, the program executes the *No* subroutine, which contains these commands:

```
{LABEL}No ~
{Cancel}{Exit}nn{GO}return ~
```

This subroutine presses the Cancel (F1) key to unmark the highlighted block, then clears the screen and redisplays the Maintenance Menu after executing the *return* subroutine.

REFINEMENTS FOR THE MERGE MENU SYSTEM

There are several enhancements and refinements that could be planned for the merge menu system presented here. For one thing, a Sort Records option could be added to the Merge Menu, as the sorting operation is difficult for most Word-Perfect users, new and experienced alike. A Sort Record option added to the Merge Menu would eventually lead to a menu of sorting options something like this:

> SORTING MENU
> **1** - Sort in **L**ast name, First name order
> **2** - Sort in **F**irst name, Last name order
> **3** - Sort in **Z**ip Code order
> **4** - Sort in **C**ity, State order
> **5** - Sort in Record **N**umber order
> **6** - **R**eturn to Merge Menu

A {CASE} command would cause the program to branch to the appropriate sorting subroutine depending upon the option selected by the user. Each of these subroutines would contain the appropriate command sequence required to sort the selected secondary file by the designated key field or fields (see Chapter 12 for information on sorting in WordPerfect).

A Print Report option could also be planned for the Maintenance Menu. This option would allow the user to obtain a complete, up-to-date printed listing of all of the records in the selected secondary file. Such an option might be attached to a menu that presented a number of choices for the style and type of report to be printed. It would then select the primary file that formats this report, based on the user's selection.

Note: Any printing option that you add to your own menu systems should include a prompt to have the user check that the printer is on and that paper is available. This reminder can avoid many problems that come up when the user tries to print and the printer isn't ready.

Besides additional options, the macros in this menu system could also eventually include {ON ERROR} and {ON CANCEL} subroutines so that the system can't be terminated due to pressing the Cancel key (F1) or due to some type of error generated by WordPerfect. When creating your own menu systems, it is wise to start from the assumption that users of your system will make mistakes and that it is your duty to take all necessary steps to have the system deal with any conditions that result from them.

CONVERTING WORDPERFECT 4.2 MACROS TO WORDPERFECT 5.0

WordPerfect provides a macro conversion program called MACRO-CNV.EXE on the Conversion disk; it converts version 4.2 macros (which have the extension .MAC) to 5.0 format (.WPM). To run this utility from the DOS prompt, type

macroconv *macroname*

where *macroname* is the name of the WordPerfect 4.2 macro you want to convert. (You don't have to enter the .MAC extension unless you're converting several macros by using wild-card characters.) The utility will convert the 4.2 macro to 5.0 format, automatically giving it the .WPM extension. After the macro is converted, you'll see a status report showing the number of characters and functions processed, as Figure 16.15 illustrates.

Some 4.2 features, notably Font Change codes, can't be converted directly to 5.0 format. If there are features in the 4.2 macro that have no equivalents in WordPerfect 5.0, you will receive a message at the DOS prompt after you convert the macro. If this occurs, return to WordPerfect 5.0 (by typing **exit** if you've exited to DOS temporarily) and retrieve the macro for editing. You can then delete the commands that are marked with a *Bad!* comment and insert the correct 5.0 commands.

For example, Figure 16.16 illustrates a HEAD macro that originally changed pitch and font in version 4.2 (indicated by the <Chng Font> commands in the macro). The comment line (beginning at {;}{:}) indicates the unusable portion of the macro, and the comment *Bad!* indicates the keystrokes that must be replaced.

To get additional help on the use of the macro conversion utility, enter its startup command as

macrocnv /h

at the DOS prompt.

```
The IBM Personal Computer DOS
Version 3.3Ø (C)Copyright International Business Machines Corp 1981, 1987
            (C)Copyright Microsoft Corp 1981, 1986

Enter 'EXIT' to return to WordPerfect
C:\5>macrocnv head

WP 4.2 to WP 5.Ø Macro Conversion Utility.
Copyright (C) 1988 WordPerfect Corp., All Rights Reserved.
Version 1.4


Done.  Conversion statistics for: head.MAC
          Number of characters processed: 7.
          Number of ctrl characters processed: 2.
          Number of functions processed: 5.

          This macro will not work properly without major modifications
          to 2 function(s) which require extensive hand fix-up.
          In the output macro these functions have been appended with the
          comment:{;}      BAD!    ~.

Enter 'EXIT' to return to WordPerfect
C:\5>_
```

FIGURE 16.15: Converting a 4.2 macro to 5.0 format. If any features cannot be converted directly, you will receive a message stating that you must edit the macro manually.

```
Macro: Edit

        File          B:HEAD.WPM

    1 - Description    WP 4.2 Converted Macro:head.MAC

    2 - Action

        ┌──────────────────────────────────────────────────────────┐
        │ {DISPLAY OFF}{;}{;}<Chng-Font>~{;}   Bad!   ~1Ø8{Enter}    │
        │ {Exit}{End}{;}{;}<Chng-Font>~{;}  Bad!   ~14*1{Enter}      │
        │ {Exit}                                                     │
        │                                                            │
        │                                                            │
        │                                                            │
        │                                                            │
        │                                                            │
        └──────────────────────────────────────────────────────────┘

    Selection: Ø
```

FIGURE 16.16: Retrieving a converted macro for editing. The comment lines indicate the portions of the macro that must be manually edited for the macro to operate correctly in version 5.0.

Note: You will need DOS 2.0 or higher to run MACROCNV.EXE. In addition, if the macro you're converting is larger than 4K, the conversion utility will break it into two or more macros, named MACRO1.WPM, MACRO2.WPM, and so forth, and chain them. You can use wild-card characters to convert a group of macros. For example, entering **macrocnv *.mac** will convert all the 4.2 macros in the current directory to their equivalents in WordPerfect 5.0.

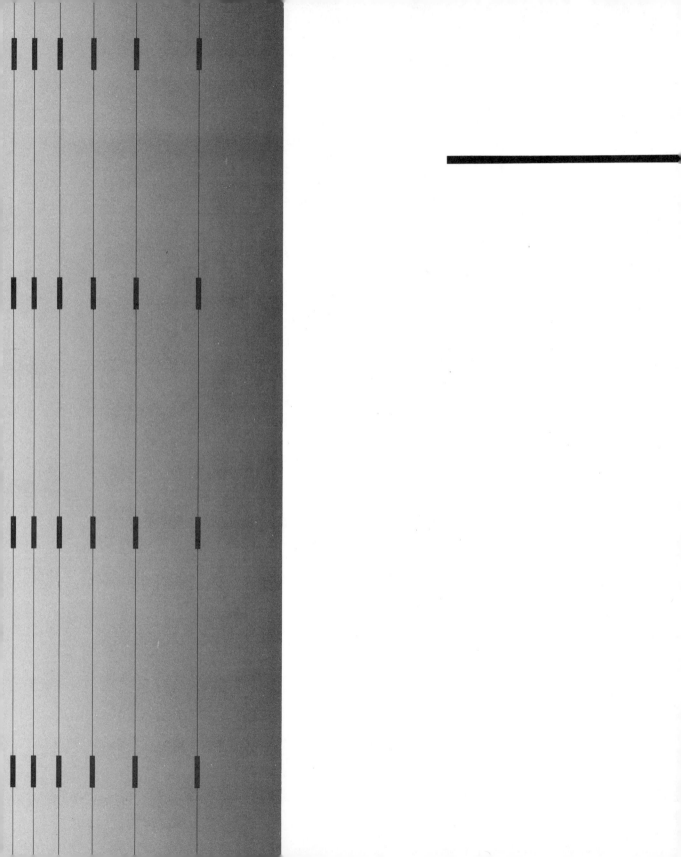

CHAPTER 17

CREATING YOUR OWN KEYBOARD LAYOUTS

CREATING YOUR OWN KEYBOARD LAYOUTS

WordPerfect's new Keyboard Layout feature performs two powerful functions: it allows you, through keyboards that you create, to customize WordPerfect's commands, and to simplify specialized typing that requires the use of special foreign-language characters or math/science symbols. In this chapter, you will find information on how to create, edit, and select keyboards. In addition, you will find application sections designed to give ideas on how to make effective use of this very versatile feature.

UPGRADE NOTES

The Keyboard Layout feature is completely new to WordPerfect 5.0. When used with the Compose feature (see the reference entry **Compose** in Part V) to map new characters onto particular Ctrl- and Alt-letter key combinations, it takes the place of Ctrl/Alt key mapping, which was done in version 4.2 with the Screen key and the Ctrl/Alt Keys option. However, the Keyboard Layout feature can be used for more than mapping special characters onto Ctrl and Alt key combinations. Through a keyboard layout, you can completely reassign all of the WordPerfect commands and assign macros to new key combinations.

USING THE KEYBOARD LAYOUT FEATURE

When you start WordPerfect, the program automatically assigns specific word processing commands to each of the function keys F1 through F10, used alone and in combination with the Ctrl, Shift, and Alt keys. Along with these standard function key assignments, the program assigns its own cursor movement and deletion functions to the keys on the numeric pad (or cursor pad, if they are separate on your keyboard), used alone and in combination with the Ctrl key. In addition, Word-Perfect uses the ASCII code system to assign the correct values to the number, letter, and symbol keys on the keyboard (the so-called QWERTY keys).

In WordPerfect 5.0, you can change the function of any of these keys or key combinations by creating a new keyboard layout. When you select a keyboard layout that you have created, the symbol or command function assignments that you have defined for each key or key combination replace the default definitions assigned by WordPerfect Corporation.

603

You can use the Keyboard Layout feature to create many different types of keyboards used for different purposes. For example, if you aren't comfortable with particular WordPerfect command assignments (or the lack of them), you can set up a keyboard that reassigns them (such as pressing Ctrl-B to mark a block, normally Alt-F4) or adds new commands (like Ctrl-Y to delete a line of text, as it does in WordStar—you must press Home ← Ctrl-End in WordPerfect).

If you do foreign-language typing, you can create special keyboards for typing German, Spanish, or French. For instance, you could select the German keyboard to provide key combinations for producing letters with accents, like Ctrl-O to produce ô, and special characters, like Ctrl-S to produce ß (the German double S). This kind of special key mapping can also be applied to creating a keyboard that produces mathematical symbols for equations and other types of statistical and scientific typing.

Selecting a Keyboard

WordPerfect includes three sample keyboard layouts (all located on the Conversion disk), called ALTRNAT, ENHANCED, and MACROS. You can use them as is or modify them to your own needs. To select one of these keyboards, or one of your own creation, for use, you press Shift-F1 (Setup) and select the Keyboard Layout option (**6** or **K**). This brings up a screen (shown in Figure 17.1) that shows a list of all of the existing keyboards as well as the following menu options:

1 Select; **2 D**elete; **3 R**ename; **4 C**reate; **5 E**dit; **6 O**riginal; **N N**ame Search: 1

Move the highlight bar to the name of the keyboard you want to use and then choose the Select option (**1** or **S**). This returns you immediately to the Setup menu (shown in Figure 17.2), where you will see the name of the new keyboard in effect listed next to *Keyboard Layout*. (This area is blank when you are using the default keyboard supplied with WordPerfect.) From there, you can press F7 (Exit), F1 (Cancel), or the Enter key to return to the document editing screen. Besides placing the keyboard's name next to *Keyboard Layout* on the Setup menu, WordPerfect marks the selected keyboard with an asterisk (*) before its name on the Keyboard Layout menu.

When you select a new keyboard layout in this manner, it remains in effect each time you start WordPerfect. To return to the default keyboard arrangement supplied with WordPerfect, you must press Shift-F1 (Setup), select the Keyboard Layout option (**6** or **K**), and select the Original option (**6** or **O**). In the course of a work session, you may need to change keyboards many times. If you want the standard keyboard layout operative when you next use WordPerfect, you must remember to select the Original option before exiting the program. To change to a new keyboard, you press Shift-F1, type **6** or **K**, highlight the name of the new keyboard, and type **1** or **S** or press the Enter key.

Figure 17.1 shows you the Keyboard Layout screen that appears when you follow this key sequence. If you press the Enter key with the highlight bar on *ALTRNAT* as it is in this figure, ALTRNAT will become the selected keyboard. (The default response to these menu options is **1**, which chooses the Select option.) This would return you immediately to the Setup menu shown in Figure 17.2. When you press F7 (Exit) to return to the document editing screen, the key reassignments contained in the ALTRNAT keyboard will be operative.

The ALTRNAT keyboard layout makes just three changes to the default keyboard layout: it reassigns the on-line Help feature to F1, the Cancel feature to the Esc key, and the Esc (Repeat) feature to F3. If you regularly use other software programs that assign the Cancel function to the Esc key and Help to F1, you may want to select this keyboard layout so that WordPerfect works just as those other programs, at least in this respect.

The ENHANCED keyboard is designed for use with the IBM enhanced keyboard (see Figure 2.3 in Chapter 2). This keyboard has 12 function keys instead of the standard 10, and this keyboard layout assigns commands to them. In addition, there are several special cursor movement commands (like moving up or down a sentence or paragraph at a time) that aren't available when using the original keyboard layout.

The MACROS keyboard contains sample macros that are assigned to various Alt- and Ctrl-letter key combinations. For example, when this keyboard is

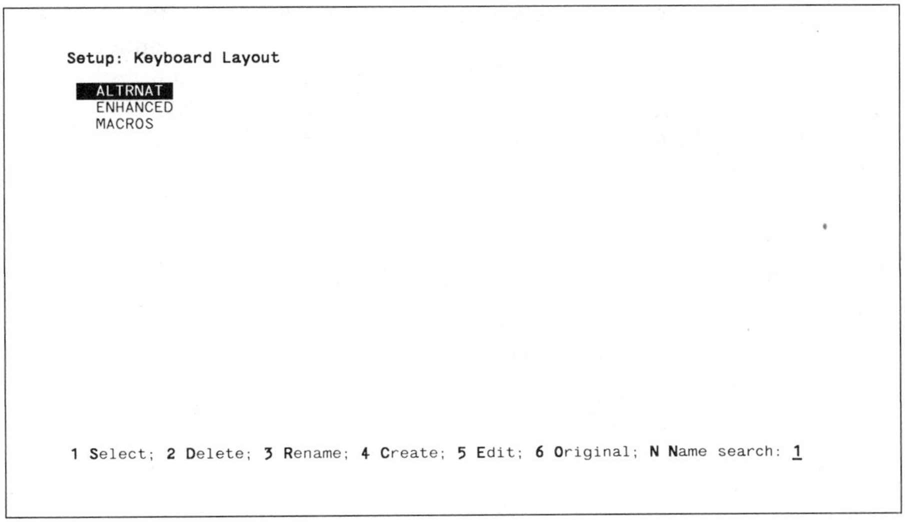

```
  Setup: Keyboard Layout
        ALTRNAT
        ENHANCED
        MACROS



















  1 Select; 2 Delete; 3 Rename; 4 Create; 5 Edit; 6 Original; N Name search: 1
```

FIGURE 17.1: The Keyboard Layout screen as it appears when you first use the Keyboard Layout option. WordPerfect Corporation supplies three sample keyboard layouts that you may use as is or edit. You can also create your own keyboard layouts from this screen.

```
Setup

     1 - Backup

     2 - Cursor Speed                    5Ø cps

     3 - Display

     4 - Fast Save (unformatted)         No

     5 - Initial Settings

     6 - Keyboard Layout                 ALTRNAT.WPK

     7 - Location of Auxiliary Files

     8 - Units of Measure




  Selection: Ø
```

FIGURE 17.2: The Setup menu with the ALTRNAT keyboard layout selected. After you select a new keyboard layout, you are returned to the Setup screen. To return to your document, you can press F7 (Exit), F1 (Cancel), or the Enter key. The selected keyboard remains in effect each time you start WordPerfect. To change back to the standard keyboard arrangement, you need to select the Original option on the Keyboard Edit menu (Shift-F1 K O).

selected, pressing Ctrl-C brings up an on-line calculator that you can use to perform simple calculations while editing in WordPerfect. Other macros include an Alt-C macro to capitalize the first letter of the word that contains the cursor and an Alt-G macro to select the Go option on the Print menu from the editing screen when you need to restart the printer. (See "Assigning Macros to Keys" later in this chapter for more information on this topic.)

Creating a Keyboard

To create a new keyboard layout, you press Shift-F1 (Setup), select the Keyboard Layout option (**6** or **K**), and select the Create option (**4** or **C**). When you select the Create option, you are prompted to enter a name for the keyboard file as follows:

Keyboard Filename:

WordPerfect saves your keyboard layout in its own file. The file name that you enter here must obey the DOS naming conventions (no more than eight characters, with no spaces). The program automatically appends the extension .WPK to the file name that you type, so don't enter a file name extension for the keyboard files that you create.

You can specify that Keyboard Layout files be saved on the same disk or in the same directory as your macros. To designate this drive or directory, you need to select the Location of Auxiliary Files option (**7** or **L**) on the Setup menu (Shift-F1). Then, select the Keyboard/Macro Files option (**3** or **K**) and enter the drive letter or path name where you want your keyboard layouts and macro files stored. If you haven't used this option to designate a location for these files, they will be saved on the drive or directory that contains your WordPerfect program files (drive A on a two-disk system, or the directory C:\WP50 on a hard disk if you ran the Install program).

After you assign a name to your Keyboard Layout file, you are presented with the Keyboard Edit screen and menu (similar to the one shown in Figure 17.3). The menu at the bottom of the screen contains the following options for defining the functions of the keys:

Key: **1** Edit; **2** Delete; **3** Move; **4** Create; Macro: **5** Save; **6** Retrieve: 1

To begin defining the keys for your new keyboard, you then select the Create option (**4** or **C**). The menu options at the bottom of the screen are replaced by the prompt

Key:

In response to this prompt, press the key or key combination that you wish to define. For example, if you wish Ctrl-Y to delete the entire line that the cursor is on (as it does in WordStar), you press Ctrl-Y.

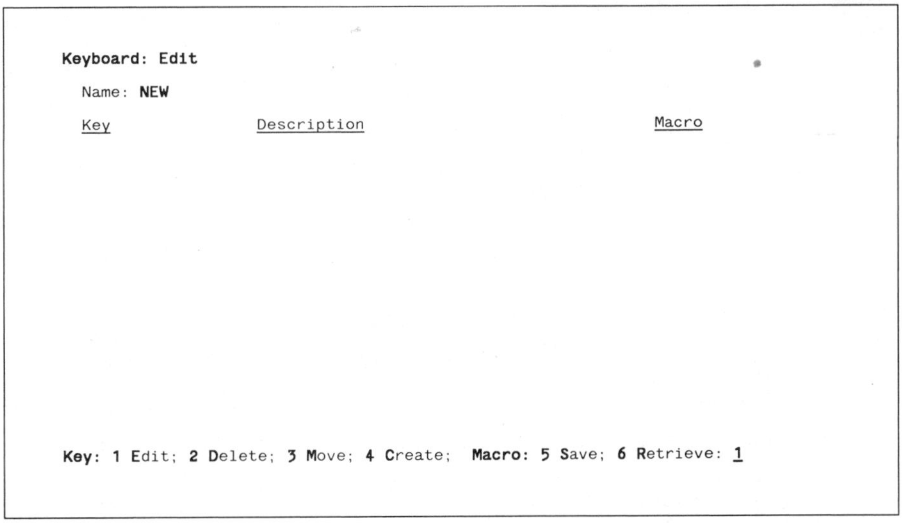

```
Keyboard: Edit

 Name: NEW

 Key              Description                    Macro












 Key: 1 Edit; 2 Delete; 3 Move; 4 Create;  Macro: 5 Save; 6 Retrieve: 1
```

FIGURE 17.3: The Keyboard Edit screen that appears when creating a keyboard layout called NEW. To create new definitions for particular keys, you select the Create option (**4** or **C**) on this menu and press the key or key combination you want to define.

This takes you to the Key Edit menu, which is identical in appearance and function to the Macro Editor (see "Editing Macros" in Chapter 16). This screen is illustrated in Figure 17.4. Here, you enter the description for the key combination (Ctrl-Y in this example) and redefine its function in the editing area.

It is very important that you enter a description for your new key assignment(s) because only this description is displayed in the Keyboard Edit screen. If you don't enter one, you can easily forget what function you gave to the key or key combination listed on this screen. Select the Description option on the Key Edit screen by typing **1** or **D**. Then type in a verbal description up to 37 characters long. Make this description as complete as you can in the space provided.

WordPerfect shows you the current definition for the key or key combination you are creating (or editing), using the same key notation as the Macro Editor. For instance, in Figure 17.4 you can see that Ctrl-Y moves the cursor one space to the left in the original keyboard. If WordPerfect has not assigned a function to the particular key combination you are defining, you will see just those keys represented in the editing area. For example, if you were creating a new definition for the key combination Alt-F, which has no function in WordPerfect, you would simply see {Alt F} in the double-lined editing box.

Just as when editing macros, you must select the Action option (**2** or **A**) in order to define the function of the key you are creating. When you select this option, WordPerfect places the cursor inside the double-lined editing box.

```
Key: Edit
          Key            Ctrl-Y

    1 - Description

    2 - Action

         ┌─────────────────────────────────────────────┐
         │ {Left}                                       │
         │                                              │
         │                                              │
         │                                              │
         │                                              │
         │                                              │
         │                                              │
         │                        .                     │
         │                                              │
         └─────────────────────────────────────────────┘

    Selection: 0
```

FIGURE 17.4: Creating a new definition for the key combination Ctrl-Y in the NEW keyboard. After selecting the Description option (**1** or **D**) and entering a description up to 37 characters long, you need to use the Action option (**2** or **A**) to revise its definition. As you can see, the default definition for Ctrl-Y in WordPerfect is to move the cursor one space to the left.

Assuming that you don't want to retain the current key assignment, the first thing you do is delete the contents of this box—press the Del key until it is empty.

If you have already worked with the Macro Editor, you will have no trouble defining key assignments here. If you have never used the Macro Editor or are still uncertain about aspects of its operation, you should read the information in the section "Editing Macros" in Chapter 16 before attempting to create a new keyboard layout. To provide a brief review of how you switch between function mode and editing mode, the general steps followed in assigning the delete-current-line function to Ctrl-Y are outlined below.

When you first enter the key definition area, the program is in editing mode. To delete the existing {Left} key definition, you simply press the Del key. The new assignment for Ctrl-Y is to delete the entire line that the cursor is on. The easiest way to have WordPerfect do this is to position the cursor at the very beginning of the line (Home ←) and then delete to the end of the line (Ctrl-End). To add these keystrokes, you press Ctrl-F10 (Macro Define) to enter the function mode. Then, when you press the Home and ← keys, WordPerfect inserts {Home}{Left} into the key definition. When you press Ctrl-End, the program inserts the functional notation {Del to EOL} in the definition, as shown in Figure 17.5.

These are all of the keystrokes required to make Ctrl-Y delete the current line. However, to exit the editing area and save the keystrokes, you must first press Ctrl-F10 to return to editing mode; otherwise, pressing F7 to exit will insert

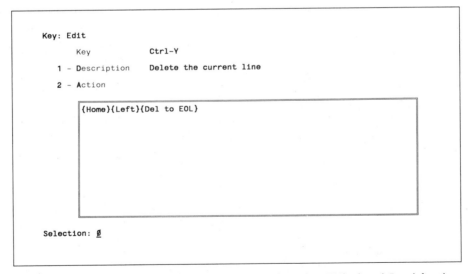

FIGURE 17.5: The complete definition and description for Ctrl-Y in the NEW keyboard. To redefine the function for Ctrl-Y, you first delete the existing definition {Left} (see Figure 17.4). Then, press Ctrl-F10 (Macro Define) to put the Editor into function mode, and press Home ← Ctrl-End. To exit and save this definition, you need to press Ctrl-F10 again (to return to editing mode) followed by F7 (Exit) twice.

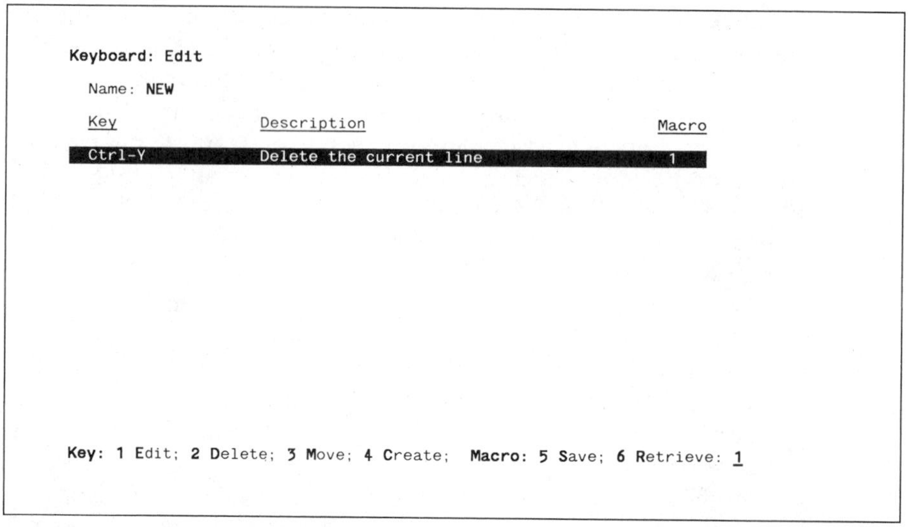

```
Keyboard: Edit

  Name: NEW

  Key                    Description                              Macro

  Ctrl-Y                 Delete the current line                    1
```

```
Key: 1 Edit; 2 Delete; 3 Move; 4 Create;  Macro: 5 Save; 6 Retrieve: 1
```

FIGURE 17.6: The Keyboard Edit screen showing the newly defined key, its description, and the macro number assigned to it. Whenever you save a key definition that you created, its description is added to the list. Only a key definition consisting of more than one keystroke is assigned a macro number; WordPerfect assigns these numbers sequentially according to when the key was defined. To move, delete, or edit a key definition, move the highlight bar to its description before selecting the appropriate option.

{Exit} in the definition instead of returning you to the Selection prompt. Then you press F7 to return the cursor to the Selection prompt at the bottom of the Key Edit screen and press F7 once again to save the new description and definition for Ctrl-Y.

This returns you to the Keyboard Edit screen, where you will see the new key definition and description listed at the top, as shown in Figure 17.6. Note in this figure that WordPerfect has also assigned the number *1* to this key combination in the Macro column. As you continue to define new functions to specific keys and key combinations, the key descriptions are maintained in alphabetical order by key. This means that their positions in the listing may change as you define new keys or key combinations for your keyboard.

> *Note:* WordPerfect only assigns macro numbers to key definitions that use multiple WordPerfect commands. If your key definition simply maps a single character onto a key with the Compose feature or uses a single command like F6, WordPerfect will not assign it a macro number, and this third column will remain blank in the Keyboard Edit screen.

KEYS THAT CAN'T BE DEFINED

Almost all of the keys and key combinations on the keyboard can be redefined when creating a keyboard layout. However, there are a few exceptions, and the great majority of these have to do with combining the Ctrl key with other keys. WordPerfect won't allow you to assign new definitions to the Ctrl key when used with the numbers 0 to 9, the equal sign (=), semicolon (;), apostrophe ('), grave accent (`), comma (,), period (.), or slash (/). You can, however, reassign the functions of these characters when combined with the Alt or Shift key.

USING MACRO COMMANDS IN KEY DEFINITIONS

When you are creating (or editing) a key definition, you are in essence creating a macro containing the keystrokes that redefine its function in WordPerfect. As when creating any macro in version 5.0, you can use any of the macro commands as part of the definition. To insert a particular macro command in the definition, you select the Action option (**2** or **A**) on the Key Edit screen and press Ctrl-PgUp. This brings up a box containing a scroll menu of macro commands. Highlight the one you want to use and press the Enter key to select it and insert it into the definition (at the cursor's position). See Chapter 16 for information on how to use the macro commands, and Appendix E for a complete list of them.

Make sure that you are in editing mode when you press Ctrl-PgUp or this will insert {Macro Commands} into your definition instead of accessing the menu containing the macro commands.

Modifying a Keyboard Layout

You can continue to modify a particular keyboard layout as you work with it. You can add new key definitions to the keyboard, change the function of a key definition, delete a key definition, or even move an existing definition to a new key or key combination. To edit a keyboard, you press Shift-F1 (Setup), select the Keyboard Layout option (**6** or **K**), highlight the name of the keyboard to be modified, and then choose the Edit option (**5** or **E**). This takes you directly to the Keyboard Edit screen, which shows you all of the keys that you have already defined.

To locate the key description for the key or key combination you wish to modify, you can use the Name Search function by pressing F2 (→Search). However, Name Search here is somewhat different from Name Search in List Files or in the Base Font screen; instead of typing the first few matching characters as you do with those menus, you press the key or key combination. For example, if you want to use Name Search to locate the key description for Ctrl-Z, you hold down the Ctrl key and type **Z** instead of typing **ctrl-z**, as you normally would.

To edit the function of a particular key definition, you first position the highlight bar on its description and select the Edit option (**1** or **E**) from the Keyboard Edit menu. This takes you to the Key Edit screen for that key definition. There, you can change its description by selecting the Description option (**1** or **D**) or its keystrokes or commands by selecting the Action option (**2** or **A**). When you are finished modifying the key definition, press F7 (Exit) to save the changes and return to the Keyboard Edit menu.

To delete a key definition entirely, move the highlight bar to its description and select the Delete option (**2** or **D**). You will be asked to confirm the deletion. For example, if you highlight the Ctrl-Y key description and type **D**, you will see

Delete Ctrl-Y? (Y/N) No

at the bottom of the screen. Type **Y** to remove the key definition or press the Enter key or type **N** to abandon the deletion.

To move an existing key definition to a new key or key combination, you position the highlight bar on the key description to be changed and select the Move option (**3** or **M**). WordPerfect responds with the *key:* prompt. Here, you press the key or key combination that you now wish to use. WordPerfect immediately assigns the description and keystrokes to this key combination. On the Keyboard Edit screen, you will see the key description and macro number assigned to the key or key combination you just pressed. The former key(s) will no longer be listed on this menu. This key or key combination can then be reassigned to some new function.

To save the modifications you make to the existing key definitions as well as any new definitions you've added, you must press F7 (Exit) to return to the Setup menu. If you press F1 (Cancel), you receive the message

Cancel changes? (Y/N) No

If you type **Y** in response to this prompt, the changes you have made will not be saved, and you will be returned to the Setup menu. Answering **Y** to this prompt will restore any key definitions that you removed with the Delete option.

WordPerfect also allows you to rename a keyboard layout or delete it entirely. To rename the Keyboard Layout file, you select the Rename option (**3** or **R**) from the Keyboard Layout menu (Shift-F1 K). WordPerfect displays the prompt

Keyboard Filename:

with the current name of the file (but without the .WPK extension). Remember, if you are renaming the Keyboard Layout file you must obey the DOS file-naming conventions. After you type in the new keyboard name and press the Enter key, the new name will replace the old name on this screen; the list may also be realphabetized in the process.

To delete a Keyboard Layout file, you select the Delete option (**2** or **D**) on the Keyboard Layout menu. Before you select this option, position the highlight bar on the name of the keyboard to be removed. For example, to delete the NEW keyboard layout used as a sample in this chapter, you would move the highlight bar to it and type **D**. WordPerfect then displays a confirmation prompt:

Delete NEW.WPK? (Y/N) No

When you type **Y**, WordPerfect deletes the file. If you have not made a backup copy of this file, it is gone forever.

Macros and Key Definitions

As stated earlier, key definitions that utilize WordPerfect commands are essentially macros that describe the function of a particular key or key combination. However, although they are defined and edited with a screen just like the Macro Editor and their files are stored in the same location as your macro files, they nevertheless represent a special set of macros whose definitions will take precedence over any existing macros that have been assigned the same key combination.

> *Note:* The only key combinations that macros and key definitions for a keyboard can share are Alt-letter key combinations; WordPerfect won't allow you to assign any other key (like Ctrl or Shift) and single-letter combination as a macro name. In fact, it is by using the Keyboard Layout feature that you overcome this limitation (see "Assigning Macros to Keys" later in this chapter).

To illustrate this point, assume that previously you have created an Alt-C macro to copy a block of text, that you are now creating a French-language keyboard, and that you assign the Compose sequence 1,39 to the key combination Alt-C to produce the lowercase letter *c* with the cedilla (ç) so that you can type words like garçon by typing **gar**, pressing Alt-C, and then typing **on**. After you finish assigning other special characters to your French keyboard, you select it.

As you might expect, when you return to the editing screen and press Alt-C, it will produce the lowercase *c* with the cedilla instead of copying a block of text. However, the original Alt-C macro that copies text has not been replaced by the new Alt-C definition in the French keyboard. If you deselect the French keyboard by selecting the original keyboard (Shift-F1 K O) or any other keyboard that doesn't redefine Alt-C, pressing Alt-C will once again copy a block of text.

This, of course, means that you can give different assignments to the same key or key combination as long as they are in different Keyboard Layout files. However, it also means that you might disable the functioning of a favorite Alt-letter macro and get unexpected results when you go to use it.

Saving a Key Definition as a Macro

WordPerfect includes two Macro options on the Keyboard Edit menu, Save (**5** or **S**) and Retrieve (**6** or **R**). You use the Save option when you have created a key definition that you would like to be able to use even when the keyboard is not selected. For example, if you add to the MACROS keyboard layout (supplied by WordPerfect Corporation) an Alt-Z key definition that automatically restores the last block of text that you deleted, you might very well want to have access to this macro at all times, even when the MACROS keyboard is not selected.

If you don't save Alt-Z as a macro as well as a key definition in the MACROS keyboard, and you press Alt-Z when MACROS isn't selected, you will receive the error message

ERROR: File not found — <u>ALTZ.WPM</u>

To create an ALTZ.WPM file that contains the same keystrokes as the Alt-Z key definition, you edit the MACROS keyboard layout that contains this definition (Shift-F1 E). Move the highlight bar to the Alt-Z key description in the Keyboard Edit screen and select the Save option (**5** or **S**). WordPerfect will respond with

Define macro:

You then press Alt-Z to give the same name to the macro. This copies the Alt-Z key definition

{Cancel}r

to the Alt-Z macro (saved in the file ALTZ.WPM).

You can, of course, name the macro differently from the key definition. In fact, if you are saving a key definition whose key combination represents an unacceptable macro name, like Ctrl-Z or Shift-Z, you *must* save it under a new name at the Define Macro prompt. (See "Defining and Executing Macros" in Chapter 16 for more details on legal macro names.)

Once you have saved a key definition as a macro using the Save option, you can edit it as you can any macro that you create from the keyboard with Ctrl-F10 (Macro Define).

ASSIGNING MACROS TO KEYS

You use the Retrieve option (**6** or **R**) to assign an existing macro to a particular key combination (or key, but you will almost never want a macro executed when you press a single key like *H*). This option allows you to execute macros with Ctrl-letter key combinations, which is not possible when you create a macro using Ctrl-F10 (Macro Define) with the keyboard selected.

To illustrate how you can use this option, assume that you have created a macro called MSFORM that automatically sets up the document formatting defaults required for typing a manuscript (such as double spacing, justification off, page numbering center bottom, widow/orphan protection on, etc.). Assume that you would like to use this macro without having to press Alt-F10, type **msform**, and press the Enter key, but you can't call it Alt-M because you already have an Alt-M macro that moves a block of text and you use it all of the time.

To map the MSFORM keystrokes onto Ctrl-M (so that you can still use Alt-M) in the keyboard you use when typing manuscripts—here we'll call that keyboard MANUSCPT—you can use the Retrieve option on the Keyboard Edit menu. To do this, you edit the MANUSCPT Keyboard Layout file (Shift-F1 K E) and select Retrieve (**6** or **R**). When you choose this option, WordPerfect first displays the prompt

Key:

Here, you press Ctrl-M. As soon as you do, a second prompt appears:

Macro:

Here, you enter **msform** and press the Enter key. On the Keyboard Edit screen, you will now see Ctrl-M listed. The description for this key will be copied from the macro definition. (If you didn't enter a description when creating the MSFORM macro, this area will be blank on the Keyboard Edit screen.)

Remember that, although you can now activate this macro simply by pressing Ctrl-M, this works only as long as the MANUSCPT keyboard is selected. If you return to the original keyboard layout or select another keyboard that you have created (and that doesn't use Ctrl-M), nothing will happen when you press Ctrl-M. You can, however, always execute the macro that you assign to a particular key combination in a keyboard layout in the usual way (Alt-F10, **msform**, and the Enter key, in this case), whether or not that keyboard layout is currently selected.

Typical Uses for the Keyboard Layout Feature

There are many applications for the new Keyboard Layout feature. The following sections outline some of the more prominent uses to which you can put this very versatile feature. Broadly speaking, there are two uses for the Keyboard Layout feature. You can create Keyboard Layouts that customize WordPerfect commands by incorporating a special set of macros, and you can design keyboards that simplify specialized typing by mapping special characters and symbols to keys and key combinations. In each of the following sections, you will find outlines of sample keyboard layouts that you can use as models to adapt to your own needs.

Customizing WordPerfect Commands

WordPerfect lacks very few of the editing commands that you will ever need when creating documents. Nevertheless, you may find some editing features offered by another word processor that aren't supported by WordPerfect. Moreover, there may be some commands that you routinely use whose key combinations you find ill-placed on the keyboard; this is especially true if you are using the IBM enhanced keyboard, which has the function keys on the top in a single row, making them harder to reach without having your fingers leave the

QWERTY keyboard. In either case, you remedy the situation by creating a keyboard layout that adds special commands or simply rearranges them to your liking on the keyboard.

Figure 17.7 shows the first part of the Keyboard Edit screen for the completed NEW keyboard, which was used as an example earlier in this chapter. This keyboard layout reassigns a number of WordPerfect editing commands to various Alt- and Ctrl-letter key combinations. Some of the reassignments add new editing commands, like Ctrl-N, which inserts a blank line and repositions the cursor on the line above (whereas pressing the Enter key inserts a blank line but leaves the cursor on it), and Ctrl-Y, which deletes the entire line that the cursor is on (rather than just to the end of the line). Others, like Alt-R, which rewrites and reformats the screen by invoking Ctrl-F3 (Screen) twice, and Alt-U, which begins underlining with F8 (Underline), merely reassign often used editing commands to key combinations that are easier to invoke when typing.

In creating your own keyboard layouts that customize and enhance WordPerfect's commands, you have a great deal of freedom in designing the system that best fits the way you work. Remember, however, that when creating a keyboard layout it is possible to inadvertently disable commands that you may need when editing. For example, Ctrl-B is used to place page numbers in headers or footers in a document. If you assign a new key definition, like inserting a bullet into the document, to Ctrl-B without reassigning the Page Number function to

```
Keyboard: Edit

   Name: NEW

   Key                 Description                         Macro

   Alt-R               Rewrite screen                      5
   Alt-T               Transpose characters                7
   Alt-U               Underline                           1Ø
   Alt-I               Italics                             9
   Alt-P               Print document in editing screen    12
   Alt-D               Insert today's date as text         4
   Alt-F               Flush right
   Alt-Z               Undo most recent deletion           3
   Alt-X               Subscript                           13
   Alt-C               Center
   Alt-B               Boldface                            11
   Alt-.               Move cursor to end of next sentence  14
   Ctrl-D              Insert today's date as code         6
   Ctrl-I              ->Indent
   Ctrl-N              Insert line, cursor up              2
   Ctrl-P              Print current page of document      15
   Ctrl-T              Transpose words                     8

   Key: 1 Edit; 2 Delete; 3 Move; 4 Create;  Macro: 5 Save; 6 Retrieve: 1
```

FIGURE 17.7: The first part of the Keyboard Edit screen for the complete NEW keyboard layout. The key definitions shown here add some new editing features (like Alt-T, which transposes two characters) and reassign standard editing features (like Alt-C, which begins centering) to key combinations that are easier to use when touch-typing.

another key combination, you will not be able to use Ctrl-B to put page numbers into any headers or footers you create while using this keyboard layout. To avoid this situation, you would first have to reassign ^B to a new key combination (like Alt-B) before you assign the bullet function to Ctrl-B. (You could also use Ctrl-N unless you have also reassigned it to a new key definition.)

Specialized Typing

You can put WordPerfect's Keyboard Layout feature to good use when your work requires special characters that are created with the Compose feature. (See Chapter 14 for more information on using Compose.) By using the Keyboard Layout feature to map particular characters from one of 12 predefined character sets onto a key or key combination, you can have easy access to them when creating and editing a document. The next two sections look at two types of specialized typing; the first covers foreign-language typing, and the second covers typing equations.

Foreign-Language Typing

The entire ASCII character set and the IBM Extended character set are included within the character sets created by WordPerfect (see Appendix B for the ASCII Table and Appendix C for the WordPerfect character sets). Between these two, you will find most of the special characters and symbols needed to type in European languages that use the Roman alphabet, like French, German, Italian, and Spanish. This means that most of the accented letters and punctuation symbols used by these languages can be displayed on the editing screen as they will be printed (though this doesn't ensure that your printer will be able to print them correctly).

Even when characters or symbols you need are not found within the ASCII or IBM Extended character sets, and therefore can't be displayed on the screen, chances are that they can be found in one of the WordPerfect character sets, and your printer may still be able to accurately produce them. You must experiment with the characters and symbols in question to verify whether your printer can produce them.

By using the Compose feature when creating a foreign-language keyboard layout, you can make a very straightforward procedure out of what otherwise would be a very laborious typing task. Figure 17.8 shows you a sample French keyboard that maps almost all of the accented characters onto Alt- and Ctrl-letter key combinations. As you can see from this screen, most of these characters can be displayed on the monitor; the exceptions are the four capital letters that are followed by verbal descriptions of the kind of accents they use. Although these characters can't be properly displayed on the screen, they can be printed with a laser printer like the LaserWriter Plus. (See the last line in Figure 17.10 to verify this.)

Both for the majority of the descriptions shown in the Keyboard Edit screen and for the key definitions themselves, the Compose feature was used to produce the accented character. For example, to use Alt-W to produce the uppercase *E* with an acute accent, which is the 42nd character in the first character set, you select the Create option (**4** or **C**) on the Keyboard Edit menu and press Alt-W. Then, first after selecting Description (**1** or **D**), and again after selecting Action (**2** or **A**), you press Ctrl-2, type **1,42** and press the Enter key. The same procedure was used to create all of the other key definitions for this keyboard.

> *Note:* This French keyboard layout only maps the most used accented French characters onto key combinations that are comfortable for an English-speaking typist who is used to the QWERTY keyboard arrangement. It does not attempt to rearrange the basic keyboard to the AZERTY keyboard used in French-language typing, although this arrangement can be set up with the Keyboard Layout feature, if desired.

Figure 17.9 shows you a document containing sample French sentences that use many of the key definitions assigned in the French keyboard layout. Before creating

```
Keyboard: Edit

  Name: FRENCH

  Key                 Description                          Macro

  Alt-W               É
  Alt-E               é
  Alt-U               ù
  Alt-I               î
  Alt-O               ô
  Alt-A               à
  Alt-Z               A  (uppercase A, accent grave)
  Alt-C               ç
  Ctrl-A              â
  Ctrl-C              Ç
  Ctrl-E              è
  Ctrl-I              I  (uppercase I, circumflex)
  Ctrl-O              O  (uppercase O, circumflex)
  Ctrl-U              û
  Ctrl-W              ê
  Ctrl-Z              A  (uppercase A, circumflex)

  Key: 1 Edit; 2 Delete; 3 Move; 4 Create;   Macro: 5 Save; 6 Retrieve: 1
```

FIGURE 17.8: The Keyboard Edit screen for the French keyboard layout created with the Compose feature. To create these key definitions, the Compose sequence (Ctrl-2) along with the appropriate character set and character codes are used both for the descriptions and for the actual key definitions. When creating a foreign-language keyboard for a European language that uses the Roman alphabet, you use characters from the Multinational character set (1).

this document, you must remember to select the keyboard (Shift-F1 K S). To help remember the key assignments (not all of them can be mnemonic due to the number of accents given to some vowels like *E* and *A* in this language), prepare and print a symbol key document that shows the Ctrl- and Alt-letter key combination in one column followed by the accented letter it produces in the other column.

After you are finished typing in French, remember to return to the Keyboard Edit menu and select the original keyboard (Shift-F1 K O) or select another keyboard layout that you normally use. Otherwise, you may end up with accented characters when you go to use some of your favorite macros that use the same Alt-letter key combinations.

Figure 17.10 shows you the printed version of the document shown in Figure 17.9. Notice in the last sentence that one of the accented characters (the uppercase *A* with the acute accent) that couldn't be displayed on the screen was nevertheless successfully printed on a laser printer. Also, notice that the guillemets (used as we use quotation marks to set off direct address) are not directly supported by the WordPerfect character sets and had to be simulated by using double < < (greater than) and > > (less than) symbols.

You can, of course, easily create keyboard layouts for other European languages like Spanish and German, each of which uses its own accented characters and special punctuation contained in the Multinational character set (1). In theory, it is even

```
Si vous plaît, où est la Côte d'Azur?

Il dit rien â moi.

Ça c'est ma tâche prochaîne.

Que vous êtes belle!

Malgré tout, j'ai été surpris.

Qu'est que veut dire <<éphémère>>?

Voilà! D'après cet homme, nous avons perdu l'élection!

C'est le coup de pied de l'âne!

Bien sûr, je suis très honnête.

<<A la mode>>. Tous les Américains utilisent l'expression <<à la mode>>.



D:\WP\WDC\FRKEY                              Doc 2 Pg 1 Ln 11 Pos 1i
```

FIGURE 17.9: The document editing screen showing sample French sentences created with the French keyboard layout selected. All of the accented characters were produced by pressing the new Ctrl- and Alt-letter key combinations assigned to them under this keyboard. Note that all characters but the uppercase *A* with an acute accent in the last sentence are displayed on the screen as they will be printed, thanks to their inclusion in the IBM Extended character set.

S'il vous plaît, où est la Côte d'Azur?

Il ne dit rien á moi.

Ça c'est ma tâche prochaîne.

Que vous êtes belle!

Malgré tout, j'ai été surpris.

Qu'est que veut dire <<éphémère>>?

Voilà! D'après cet homme, nous avons perdu l'élection!

C'est le coup de pied de l'âne!

Bien sûr, je suis très honnête.

<<À la mode>>. Tous les Américains utilisent l'expression <<à la mode>>.

FIGURE 17.10: The printed version of the document containing the sample French sentences printed in 12 point Palatino type. Notice that, although the uppercase *A* with an acute accent wasn't displayed properly on the screen (Figure 17.9), it has been correctly reproduced in the printout. When using any of the special characters or symbols in WordPerfect's character sets, you must always experiment with your printer to make sure that it is capable of reproducing those characters that you wish to use.

possible to use the method outlined here to create special foreign language keyboard layouts for languages that don't use the Roman alphabet, like Greek, Hebrew, and Russian, as their letters are included in their own character sets. Moreover, the last two predefined character sets, 10 and 11, support the Japanese Hiragana and Katakana symbols.

There are, however, major problems involved with setting up and using keyboard layouts for non-Roman alphabets, because the IBM family of personal computers is not equipped to display more than a handful of such characters (most of which are Greek letters supported because they are used to enter equations for math and science work). Even if your printer were capable of producing them, you would not be able to see them on the screen, meaning that all foreign typing in Greek, Russian, or

Japanese would have to be done blindly. (All you would see on the screen would a line of solid rectangles, indicating that the character can't be properly displayed.) The situation worsens when trying to use Hebrew; not only is its alphabet not displayed, but its characters are entered from right to left, just the opposite of the way WordPerfect is set up to enter characters!

Typing Equations

WordPerfect's character sets 6 and 7 contain a wide variety of mathematical symbols that can be used when creating a math keyboard layout for work that requires complex equations. In addition, character set 8 contains the complete Greek alphabet. If you will be creating formulas that use particular Greek letters, you can map them onto key combinations when setting up such a keyboard layout. (See Appendix C for a list of these characters and their code numbers.) Before you take the time to map such characters onto key definitions in a keyboard layout, you should make sure that your printer is capable of producing them.

Many equations and formulas can be entered without the use of special symbols from these character sets. Instead of special symbols, they require only the use of multiple levels of superscripted and subscripted characters and, perhaps, italics to denote the variables in the equation. You can also use WordPerfect's Advance feature to precisely control the vertical placement of the elements in the formula. Horizontal separators in the formula can be drawn either with the Line Draw feature (Ctrl-F3 L) if you are using a monospaced font, or with the Horizontal Line feature on the Graphics key (Alt-F9 L H) if you are using a proportionally spaced font.

Figure 17.11 shows a sample math keyboard layout. It contains not only the symbols and characters like $\cong$ (approximately equal), $\geqslant$ (greater than or equal to), π (pi), θ (theta), and so on, but also macros for the Superscript, Subscript, Advance Up, and Advance Down functions. Because these WordPerfect commands are often required to correctly position parts of formulas and equations, they are as necessary as the special mathematical symbols.

The superscript macro, Ctrl-X, contains the following keystrokes:

{Font}sp{Pause}{Right}

It invokes the Font menu (Ctrl-F8), selects the Size option (S) and then the Superscript option (P), pauses to allow you to enter the character or characters to be superscripted, and then positions the cursor after the last Superscript code by moving the cursor one space to the right when you press the Enter key to continue the execution of the key definition's keystrokes (after the {Pause}). The subscript macro, Alt-X, is the same, except that it chooses the Subscript option (B).

```
Keyboard: Edit

 Name: MATH

 Key             Description                              Macro

 Alt-T           Lowercase Theta
 Alt-U           Advance Up                                 2
 Alt-P           π (lowercase PI)
 Alt-A           ≈ (approximately equals)
 Alt-D           Advance down                               1
 Alt-X           Subscript                                  3
 Alt-N           Not equal to
 Alt-.           ≥ (greater than or equal to)
 Alt--           - (minus sign)
 Alt-=           ∞ (infinity)
 Ctrl-A          → (approaches)
 Ctrl-D          Delta
 Ctrl-P          Uppercase PI
 Ctrl-S          Σ (Sum)
 Ctrl-X          Superscript                                4



 Key: 1 Edit; 2 Delete; 3 Move; 4 Create;   Macro: 5 Save; 6 Retrieve: 1
```

FIGURE 17.11: The Keyboard Edit screen for a sample keyboard layout called MATH. This keyboard maps various math symbols onto key definitions for easy use. In addition, it maps the en dash Compose character 4,33 onto Alt-– (Alt-minus), and it designates macros for using superscripts and subscripts and the Advance Up and Advance Down commands.

The Advance Up macro, Alt-U, contains the following keystrokes:

{Format}oau{Pause}{Enter}{Exit}

It invokes the Format menu (Shift-F8), selects the Other option (O) and then the Advance (A) and Up (U) options, pauses to allow you to enter the distance that the characters are to be advanced, and then presses the Enter key to enter this number and the Exit key (F7) to return to the document editing screen when you press the Enter key to continue the execution of the key definition's keystrokes (after the {Pause}). The Advance Down macro, Alt-D, is the same, except that it chooses the Down option (D).

Figure 17.12 shows the first two of four sample formulas created with the MATH keyboard. Below these formulas, you can see the Reveal Codes screen for the first one. This screen includes [AdvUp] and [AdvDn] codes for the I as well as the horizontal rule (drawn with the Graphics key). It also includes an [AdvLft] code to reposition the I slightly to the left so that it will be aligned over the I (and subscripted 0) below it.

Note: Remember that you can use the Line Draw feature (Ctrl-F3 L) to insert line separators in formulas and equations if you are using a monospaced font, but you must use the Horizontal Line feature on the Graphics Key (Alt-F9 L H) to create them if you are using a proportionally spaced font.

```
              I
 L = 10 log10
               IØ




                    π
 tan ▌ → + ∞ as
                    2
 D:\WP\WDC\MATH.TST                          Doc 2 Pg 1 Ln 1.291 Pos 2.29i
 ▲      ▲    ▲    ▲     ▲    ▲     ▲    ▲    ▲    ▲    ▲     )    ▲    ▲
 [Font:Times Roman 14 pt][HRt]
 [Tab]          [AdvDn:Ø.Ø8"] [AdvLft:Ø.Ø1"]▌[AdvUp:Ø.Ø8"][HRt]
 L = 1Ø log[SUBSCPT]1Ø[subscpt] [AdvUp:Ø.Ø2"][HLine:2.19",Ø.25",Ø.Ø1",1ØØ%][AdvDn
 :Ø.Ø2"][HRt]
                  I[SUBSCPT]Ø[HRt]
 [HRt]
 [HRt]
 [HRt]
  [subscpt][HRt]
                   [AdvDn:Ø.Ø8"] π[AdvUp:Ø.Ø8"][HRt]

 Press Reveal Codes to restore screen
```

FIGURE 17.12: Creating formulas with the MATH keyboard layout. The lower part of this screen shows the codes for the first formula. There, you will notice that the Advance Up and Advance Down commands have been used to refine the position of both the *I* and the horizontal separator. In addition, the Advance Left command was used to align the *I* over the *I* with subscripted *0*.

When entering an equation or formula, you will need to rely on the Ln and Pos indicators to help you properly align its elements. If you are drawing rules with the Horizontal Line option on the Graphics key (Alt-F9 L H), you need to select the Horizontal Position option (**1** or **H**), choose the Set Position option (**S**) on its menu, and then press the Enter key to accept the measurement supplied by WordPerfect. Make sure that the cursor is at the appropriate place on the line where you want the horizontal separator to begin when you do this. Before you leave the Horizontal Line menu, select the Length of Line option (**2** or **L**) and enter its measurement. Also, you will often want to use the View Document feature (Shift-F7 V) at 100% or 200% to preview the positioning of the elements in a formula or equation before printing.

Figure 17.13 shows you the final printed result. This particular page was printed in 14 point Times Roman with the QMS-PS 810 PostScript laser printer. If you use the HP LaserJet, you should probably stick to the 10 pitch Courier monospaced font (though HP also offers all of the math symbols as part of its Prestige Elite soft font set in 10 point). If you change to one of the proportionally spaced fonts on cartridge or disk in a larger point size (like 12 or 14 point), you will find that the special math characters remain in 10 point. Sizing is not a problem on PostScript printers because of their ability to scale the font, although you must make sure that the typeface used contains all of the math symbols you use, as not all of them do.

$$L = 10 \ \log_{10} \frac{I}{I_0}$$

$$\tan \theta \rightarrow + \infty \ \text{as} \ \frac{\pi}{2}$$

$$\tan \theta \rightarrow - \infty \ \text{as} \ - \frac{\pi}{2}$$

$$t = \frac{ln \ P}{- \ 0.00012}$$

FIGURE 17.13: The sample formulas created with the MATH keyboard when printed. This page was printed in 14 point Times Roman on the QMS-PS 810 (a PostScript laser printer). Times Roman was chosen because it includes all of the mathematical and Greek symbols needed to produce these formulas. Not all of the resident fonts in the QMS laser printer—the same fonts as are included in the LaserWriter Plus—include all of the necessary symbols.

PART **IV**

DESKTOP PUBLISHING WITH WORDPERFECT

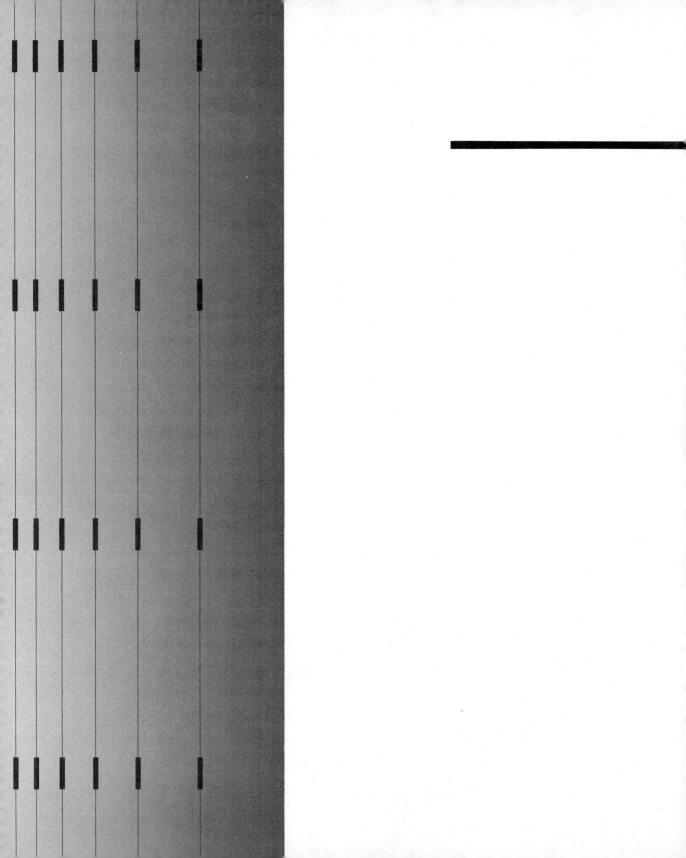

COMBINING GRAPHICS
AND TEXT IN A PUBLICATION

COMBINING GRAPHICS
AND TEXT IN A PUBLICATION

WordPerfect 5.0 has added graphics capabilities that make the program much more than a full-featured word processor. Using these graphics options, combined with features you've seen in other chapters, such as kerning, letter spacing, fonts, and text columns, you can create newsletters, advertisements, pages for catalogs, handbooks, and other publications.

To get the most from WordPerfect as a desktop publishing program, you'll need some fairly sophisticated hardware. First, you'll need a monitor that's capable of showing graphics so that you can use the View Document feature to preview pages before you print them. You can choose either a color monitor or a monochrome monitor, but you'll need a graphics card such as the Hercules card or the EGA card.

Second, you'll need a printer of good quality. For serious desktop publishing, that means a laser printer. Laser printers produce 300 dots per inch on the printed page, whereas most dot matrix printers print 72 dots per inch. You may also need to purchase additional fonts, but that depends on which printer you choose and what you plan to publish with it.

Third, you may also want to invest in a scanner to convert printed images into files that WordPerfect can read. WordPerfect can use computer files created by many different graphics programs, but if the images you're planning to use are photographs or printed pages, a scanner may be a wise investment. If you have access to an optical scanner, you can scan your company logo or digitize photographs for use in your documents.

UPGRADE NOTES

All of WordPerfect 5.0's graphics features are new. They are located on the Graphics key (Alt-F9).

SOURCES FOR GRAPHICS

In WordPerfect 5.0, you can easily merge text with graphics from a variety of sources. The program comes with 30 images from Publisher's PicturePaks (Figure 18.1 illustrates a few of them), and you can also use images created by most of the popular graphics and spreadsheet programs as well as by optical scanners.

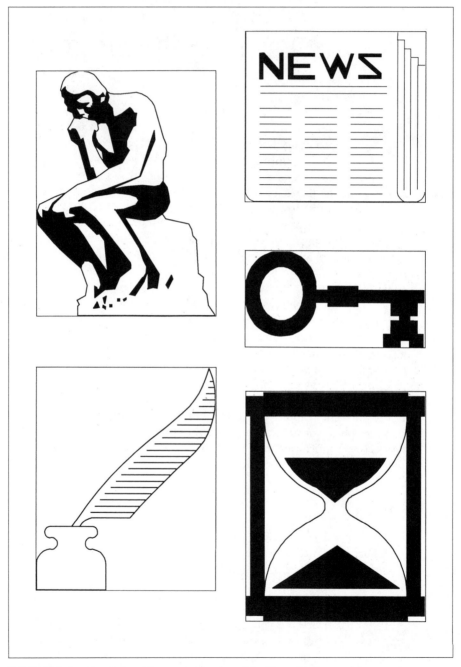

FIGURE 18.1: Sample graphics. These are only a few of the 30 graphic images that are on the Fonts/Graphics disk supplied with your program.

Files from certain sources can be converted to a format that WordPerfect supports, and files from other programs can be used by WordPerfect directly. Consult your graphics program's manual to see if the graphics it produces can be converted to a type of file that WordPerfect can use. Compatible formats include:

CGM	Computer Graphics Metafile
DHP	Dr Halo PIC format
DXF	AutoCAD format
EPS	Encapsulated PostScript
HPGL	Hewlett-Packard Graphics Language Plotter File
IMG	GEM Paint format
MSP	Microsoft Windows Paint format
PCX	PC Paintbrush format
PIC	Lotus 1-2-3 PIC format
PTNG	MacPaint format
PPIC	PC Paint Plus format
TIFF	Tagged Image File format
WPG	WordPerfect Graphics format

Once you have a graphic image in WordPerfect, you can resize it, scale it, rotate it, move it, and even invert it. You can surround graphics with borders, create shaded boxes, and insert rules in text.

This chapter will look at some specific considerations you should keep in mind as you mix text and graphics in almost any type of document. These examples will not attempt to teach you how to design a newsletter or a manual; Chapter 19 will illustrate a few of these projects. However, the examples do explain how to create specific types of graphics effects, and they should be enough to get you started producing fairly complex documents that mix text and graphics.

WORDPERFECT'S NEW GRAPHICS KEY

The Graphics key, Alt-F9, contains the following choices:

1 Figure; **2** Table; **3** Text **B**ox; **4 U**ser-defined Box; **5 L**ine:0

These choices refer to the type of graphics box you select. The fifth option, Line, allows you to create horizontal and vertical rules in your text.

You can fill a graphics box with graphics from other sources, or you can simply type them in. The major difference between these graphics boxes and the boxes you create with Line Draw is that graphics boxes are usually going to contain graphics from another source, whereas graphics you create with Line Draw are ones that you create yourself. You can easily resize and reposition graphics boxes, whereas Line Draw graphics can be difficult to position accurately and are impossible to resize without redrawing. Graphics boxes also allow text to flow around them, whereas Line Draw graphics don't.

Selecting a Box Type

Figure boxes are often used for graphic artwork and charts; Table boxes can be used for tables and statistical data; Text boxes often contain quotations and sidebars; and User-Defined boxes can hold anything else, or all of the above. The only differences between them are in their default styles. The type of box you use doesn't really matter as far as the type of graphic is concerned, but WordPerfect automatically maintains lists of its graphics box captions, so if you want an automatic list of figures and tables, you should be careful to place your figures in figure boxes and your tables in table boxes so that those lists will be accurate. WordPerfect won't print the lists unless you define and generate them just as you do other special lists, as you'll see in "Creating Lists of Graphic Elements" later in this chapter. If you don't need those lists, you can choose the type of box according to which default style you want; this will save you the additional step of specifying new options for the graphics box.

You can create graphics boxes almost anywhere in your document, including in headers, footers, footnotes, and endnotes, but you can't create them in tables of authorities, in document comments, or inside other graphics boxes.

Graphics Box Styles

The default settings for the different types of boxes are slightly different (all are illustrated in Figure 18.16).

- Figure boxes are bordered on all four sides with a thin rule; their default numbering style is numbers (*Figure 1, Figure 2,* and so forth). Their default size is 3.25" × 3.25", a square.

- Text boxes are bordered at the top and bottom with a thick rule and are shaded 10% gray; their default numbering style is also numbers (*1, 2,* and so forth). Their default size is 3.25" × 0.6", a wide, narrow rectangle.

- Table boxes are bordered at the top and bottom with a thick rule but are not shaded; their default numbering style is Roman numerals (*Table I, Table II,* and so forth). Their default size is 3.25" × 3.37", a tall rectangle.

- User-Defined boxes have no borders and are not shaded; their default numbering style is numbers. Their default size is the same as Figure boxes, 3.25" × 3.25", a square.

For example, if you want your graphic to use a thick top and bottom border and to carry 10% gray shading, select the Text box style and retrieve your graphic into it. If you want to insert text in a box that will be bordered on all sides, choose a Figure box instead. The box type doesn't refer to what the box contains, but rather to which of the four lists—Figure, Table, Text, or User-Defined—it belongs.

You will see examples of the different boxes and their styles later in the chapter. Once you select a box type from the Graphics menu, you'll see this menu:

<box type>: **1 C**reate; **2 E**dit; **3 N**ew Number; **4 O**ptions:0

If you're changing the border style, the space surrounding the border, the caption style, or the shading of the graphics box, you should choose Options (**4** or **O**) before you create the graphics box. If you've already created a graphic and want to specify options for it, be sure to move the cursor to the left of or before the code for the graphics box—[Figure], [Table], [Text Box], or [User Box]—before you choose Options (**4** or **O**). Like many other WordPerfect features, graphics options take effect at the cursor's position, so if they occur after the code for the graphics box, you won't get the effects you wanted. We'll look at graphics options in more detail later in this chapter, but first we'll look at the basics of graphics.

CREATING A GRAPHICS BOX

If you're creating a new graphics box, choose Create (**1** or **C**). You will then see a screen like the one in Figure 18.2. As you see, you can indicate the graphic image you want to retrieve, specify a caption for it, and position it on the page, among other things. If you want the graphics box to contain text, you can choose Edit (**8** or **E**) and type the text that you want it to contain.

Choosing a Graphic Image

You can enter the file name of a graphics file and use it by choosing Filename (**1** or **F**). For example, to retrieve the WordPerfect Graphic file shown in Figure 18.3, you would select Filename and enter **COMPASS.WPG**. It's necessary to enter the three-character extension here so that WordPerfect can locate the right type of graphics file. Be sure to include the full path name for graphics stored in other directories. For example, to retrieve a Lotus 1-2-3 graph called OCT-SALES in a main directory named LOTUS on your C drive, you would enter

LOTUS\OCTSALES.PIC

(Graphs created with Lotus 1-2-3 use a .PIC extension.)

```
Definition: Figure
        1 - Filename
        2 - Caption
        3 - Type                    Paragraph
        4 - Vertical Position       Ø"
        5 - Horizontal Position     Right
        6 - Size                    3.25" wide x 3.25" (high)
        7 - Wrap Text Around Box    Yes
        8 - Edit




   Selection: Ø
```

FIGURE 18.2: The Figure Definition screen. When you create a graphics box, you see a screen similar to this one. The choices that you see depend on the type of graphics box you have chosen.

FIGURE 18.3: The COMPASS.WPG graphic. Thirty different graphic images are supplied on the Fonts/Graphics disk.

To see the graphics files available to you, choose Filename, press F5 (List Files), and then either press F5 again to see the contents of the current directory or enter the path name of the directory you want to view. If you have trouble with this feature, you may be working with an early copy of WordPerfect 5.0; contact WordPerfect Corporation or your dealer for a corrected version.

When you have defined a graphics box and pressed F7 to exit, WordPerfect inserts either a [Figure], [Table], [Text Box], or [User Box] code in your text.

You will see a box outline indicating the position of the box in your text, as Figure 18.4 shows. To delete the box, you will have to delete the code. You can search for these codes by pressing F2 (Search) and then pressing Alt-F9, or you can open the Reveal Codes window to view them. If the Reveal Codes window is closed when you try to delete a graphics box (or if you backspace over one accidentally), you'll get a typical *Delete?* prompt.

> *Note:* Once you've chosen to create any type of graphics box, you can't cancel the creation of the graphic by pressing F1 (Cancel) from its Definition screen. If you decide that you don't want the graphics box, you must exit by pressing F7 (Exit) and then delete the code that WordPerfect inserts when you open and close a graphics definition screen.

Using Caption Text

If you want the graphics box to have a caption, select Caption (**2** or **C**). You will see an editing screen with the default style of box number, as shown in Figure 18.5. Here a Figure box was chosen, so the caption reads *Figure 1*. If you were creating a Table box, it would read *Table I,* and a Text box or User-Defined box would read simply *1*.

To change the style of these captions, you must use the Options command on the Graphics menu. For example, if you want to use a two-level numbering system so that your figures will be numbered as *Figure 1-1, Figure 1-2,* and so forth,

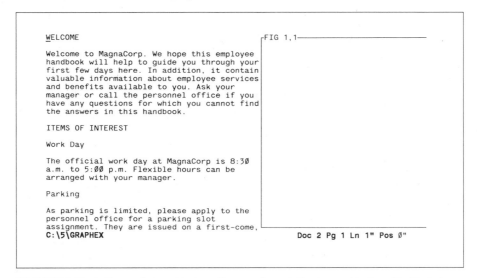

FIGURE 18.4: The indicator of a graphics box. Once you have defined a graphics box, WordPerfect indicates its position by an outline on the screen. To see the contents of the box, use the View Document feature (Shift F7 V).

you need to set Figure options before creating the figure, as you will see in "Working with Graphics Options" later in this chapter.

You can change fonts, sizes, or attributes in graphics box captions, just as you can in regular WordPerfect text. If you change fonts, you don't need to change back to Normal for the body of your text. WordPerfect recognizes that a font change in a graphics caption applies only to that caption.

You can also center captions by pressing Shift-F6 (Center) or make them flush right by pressing Alt-F6. You can begin a new line to separate the text from the figure, box, or table number by pressing Enter. Later, when we look at changing figure options, you will see a few more of the things you can do with graphics captions.

After you have typed the text of the caption and formatted it as you want it to appear, press F7 (Exit).

Choosing a Type for the Box

You can use the Type option (**3** or **T**) to select a type for the box itself, no matter whether it's a Figure, Table, Text, or User-Defined box. You can select either a Page, Paragraph, or Character box. The type you select is important for the way WordPerfect treats it in terms of the rest of your document's text:

- If you select a Page box, you must select it at the beginning of a new page, before you have entered or retrieved any text into the page, or WordPerfect

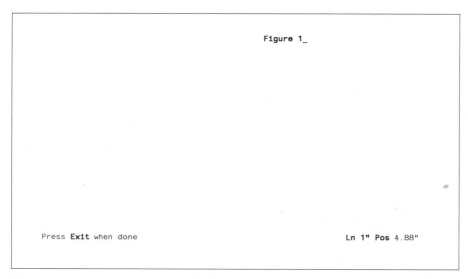

FIGURE 18.5: Creating a figure caption. To change the style of the numbering system, you must set Figure options first.

will move the box to the next page on which you enter text. Choose this style if you want the graphics box to remain in place on the page.

- If you select a Paragraph box, WordPerfect inserts a code at the beginning of the paragraph the cursor is in, and the graphics box stays with that paragraph, even if the paragraph moves on the page. Choose this style if you want the graphics box to move with the text that is wrapped around it.

- If you select a Character box, WordPerfect treats it as if it were a single character, so that if the text that contains it is wrapped to the next line, the line after that will start below the graphics box. Character boxes are the only kinds that you can use in footnotes and endnotes. Choose this style if you want the graphics box to be treated as part of the text on a line.

Specifying the Box's Position on the Page

The Vertical and Horizontal options both depend on the type you choose with the Type option. To specify a vertical position for a Paragraph box, you enter an offset measurement from the beginning of the paragraph that accompanies the graphic. For example, if you want the graphics box to be even with the first line of the paragraph, use 0″ (the default) as the offset. To position it 0.25″ below the first line of the paragraph, enter **.25″** as the offset. If the paragraph is too close to the bottom of the page so that the box won't fit next to it, WordPerfect will try to keep both the box and the paragraph together by moving the graphics box up. You can control how far the box can move without breaking the page and moving the paragraph and its box to the next page by using the Minimum Offset option on the Options menu. For example, you can specify a minimum offset of 1″ if you are willing to allow the program to move graphics boxes 1 inch upward in order to keep them with their related paragraphs before the page is broken.

If you are using a Page graphic, you have a different set of Vertical Position options. If you choose Vertical Position (**4** or **V**), the following menu appears:

1 Full Page; **2 T**op; **3 C**enter; **4 B**ottom; **5 S**et Position: 0

You can choose to align the graphic with the top (the first line) or the bottom (the last text line, above any footnotes or footers) of the page, or have it centered on the page or offset from the top edge of the paper by an amount that you specify. If you choose Full Page (**1** or **F**), the graphics box fills the page within the margins. You can't have additional text on a full-page graphics box, just the graphic itself, plus any border and/or caption that you may be using.

The Horizontal Position options also differ, depending on the type of graphics box you're using. If you are using a Paragraph graphics box, you will see the following menu if you choose Horizontal Position (**5** or **H**):

1 Left; **2 R**ight; **3 C**enter; **4 B**oth Left & Right: 0

You can align the box with the left or right edge of the text area, or you can have it centered in this area. You can also specify whether the text fills the area by choosing Both Left and Right (**4** or **B**).

If you are using a Page graphics box, you can choose either Margins, Columns, or Set Position:

- Choosing Margins (**1** or **M**) allows you to align the box with the left or right margin, center it, or expand it to fill the area between margins.

- Choosing Columns (**2** or **C**) allows you to align the box with the left or right edge of a column or to center it between columns. You will be asked to enter the number of the column and then specify how you want it to align (left, right, or centered). To align the graphics box on more than one column, specify a range by separating the column numbers with a dash. For example, to align a graphic between columns 1 and 2, as in Figure 18.6, choose Horizontal Position (**5** or **H**); then choose Column (**2** or **C**), enter **1-2**, and choose Center (**3** or **C**). If you choose Both Left and Right (**4** or **B**), the box will be expanded to fill the space defined by the columns.

- Choosing Set Position (**3** or **S**) allows you to enter a measurement from the left edge of the paper. As with WordPerfect's other measurements, you can specify a unit of measure other than the default unit by entering the measurement followed by **p** (for points), **c** (for centimeters), **u** (for WordPerfect 4.2 units), or **"** or **i** (for inches). For example, to specify that a Page box be 15 points from the left edge of the paper, enter **15p**.

If you are using a Character box, you don't have to worry about its horizontal position; it will always be positioned just after the character that is to its immediate left.

> *Note:* To move a graphic image, highlight its code in the Reveal Codes screen; then delete it. Move the cursor to the new position where you want it and press F1 (Cancel). Choose Restore (**1** or **R**) to paste the graphic image in the new location.

Selecting a Size

After you choose Size (**6** or **S**) from the Definition menu, you can set a graphics box's height, width, or both. If you choose to set a width (option **1** or **W**), you can enter a specific width, such as **2"**, and WordPerfect will calculate the height automatically to preserve the box's default proportions (square for Figure boxes and User-Defined boxes; rectangular for the others). Likewise, you can specify a height (option **2** or **H**) and WordPerfect will calculate the proportional width. If you choose Both Height and Width (**3** or **B**), you can enter sizes for both dimensions.

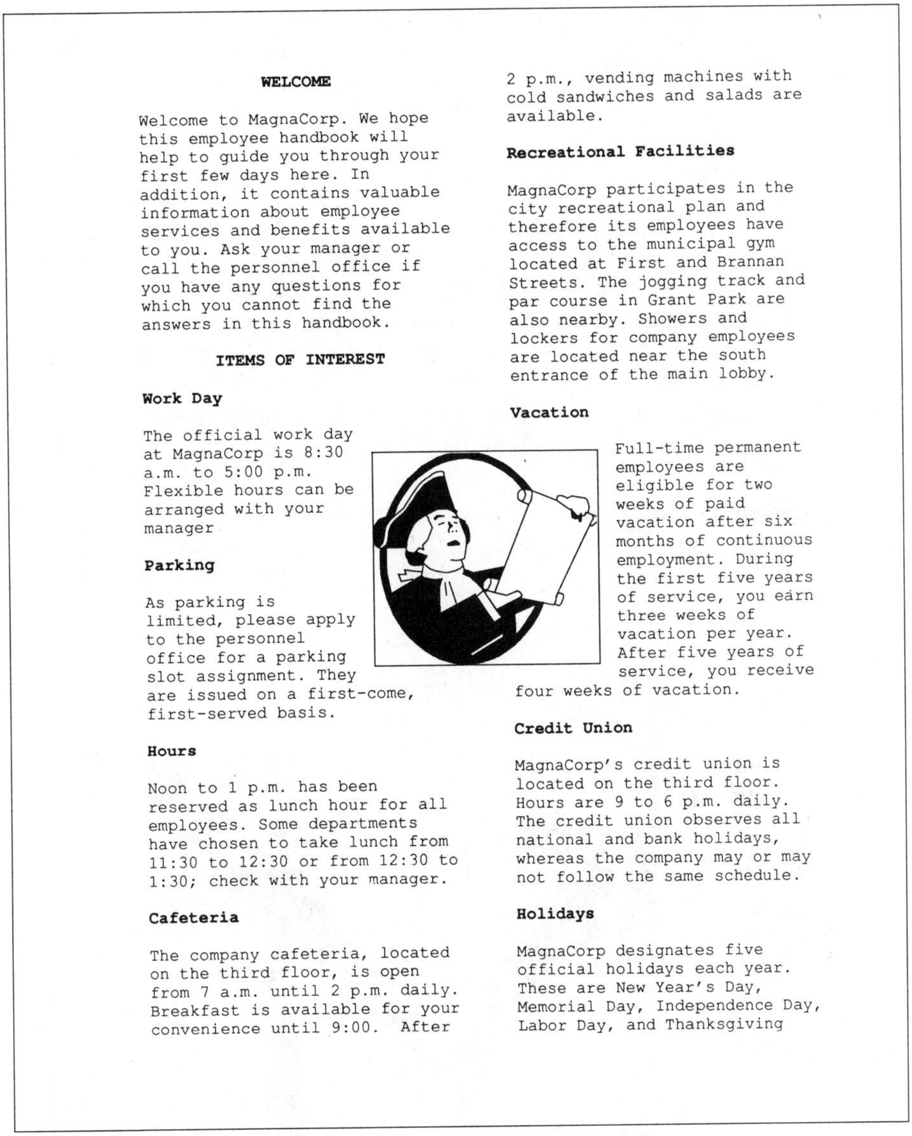

WELCOME

Welcome to MagnaCorp. We hope this employee handbook will help to guide you through your first few days here. In addition, it contains valuable information about employee services and benefits available to you. Ask your manager or call the personnel office if you have any questions for which you cannot find the answers in this handbook.

ITEMS OF INTEREST

Work Day

The official work day at MagnaCorp is 8:30 a.m. to 5:00 p.m. Flexible hours can be arranged with your manager

Parking

As parking is limited, please apply to the personnel office for a parking slot assignment. They are issued on a first-come, first-served basis.

Hours

Noon to 1 p.m. has been reserved as lunch hour for all employees. Some departments have chosen to take lunch from 11:30 to 12:30 or from 12:30 to 1:30; check with your manager.

Cafeteria

The company cafeteria, located on the third floor, is open from 7 a.m. until 2 p.m. daily. Breakfast is available for your convenience until 9:00. After

2 p.m., vending machines with cold sandwiches and salads are available.

Recreational Facilities

MagnaCorp participates in the city recreational plan and therefore its employees have access to the municipal gym located at First and Brannan Streets. The jogging track and par course in Grant Park are also nearby. Showers and lockers for company employees are located near the south entrance of the main lobby.

Vacation

Full-time permanent employees are eligible for two weeks of paid vacation after six months of continuous employment. During the first five years of service, you earn three weeks of vacation per year. After five years of service, you receive four weeks of vacation.

Credit Union

MagnaCorp's credit union is located on the third floor. Hours are 9 to 6 p.m. daily. The credit union observes all national and bank holidays, whereas the company may or may not follow the same schedule.

Holidays

MagnaCorp designates five official holidays each year. These are New Year's Day, Memorial Day, Independence Day, Labor Day, and Thanksgiving

FIGURE 18.6: Centering a graphic between columns. Choose the Page type for your graphic if you want to be able to center it between columns.

Wrapping Text Around Graphics

WordPerfect automatically wraps text around graphic images as shown in Figure 18.6 unless you set the Wrap Text Around Box option to No. After you have set this option to No, you won't see any indication of your graphics boxes on the screen unless you use View Document to see how they are being positioned on the page and how your text is continuing from margin to margin. Text may overprint graphic images unless you leave this option set to Yes.

Editing Graphics

The Edit option (**8** or **E**) on the Definition menu allows you either to edit graphic images or to enter text in graphics boxes that are not going to use graphic images, as you will often do if you are creating tables of text or sidebars of displayed quotes. You'll see how to use it for text later in this chapter; for now, we'll look at how you can use it to view the image (with a graphics monitor), scale it, rotate it, and invert it.

After you have entered a file name for your graphic image by using the Filename option on the Definition screen, you can select Edit. In these examples we will use the CHECK.WPG graphic that is located on your Fonts/Graphics disk and treat it as a figure using the Paragraph type. If you like, you can retrieve this graphic and follow along in the examples. Figure 18.7 shows it at its default size and printed with its default options of thin borders and no caption.

FIGURE 18.7: The CHECK.WPG graphic. The examples that follow will illustrate how to edit this graphic image.

Note: To view any of the graphics that you will be experimenting with in the next sections, you will need to exit from the graphics editing screen by pressing F7 (Exit) twice. Then view the document (Shift-F7 V) and return to the editing screen by pressing Alt-F9 (Graphics), typing **F E 1** (assuming your graphic image is Figure 1), and pressing Enter. If you find yourself switching from screen to screen often as you edit graphics, you can record an Alt macro to take you back and forth quickly (see Chapter 16).

Once you select Edit, you will see a special graphics editing screen. The legend at the top of the screen indicates which keys to use for the various effects:

- The arrow keys move the image within the box.
- The PgUp and PgDn keys scale the image (change its size within the graphics box).
- The + and – keys on the numeric keypad rotate the image.
- The Ins key changes the percentage of change that is used if you move, scale, or rotate the image. It changes from the default of 10% to 5%, 1%, or 25%.
- The Go To key (Ctrl-Home) resets the image to its original version.

MOVING AN IMAGE WITHIN A BOX

For example, suppose that you want to move the image within its box. You can do this either by using the arrow keys or by using the Move option. Using the Move option lets you move the image a fixed amount horizontally, vertically, or both. Using the arrow keys moves the figure a certain percentage each time you press the arrow key.

1. To get the effect shown in Figure 18.8, first change the percentage of movement to 25% by pressing Ins three times. You will see the percentage in the lower-right corner change.

2. To move the figure to the right, press → four times. Notice that the image has been cropped on the right.

3. To reset the figure to its original version, press Ctrl-Home (Go To). Resetting the figure does not change the percentage in the lower-right corner. However, if you exit from this screen and return to it later, the percentage will revert to the default of 10%.

4. To move the figure upward, select Move (option **1**), press Enter to bypass setting a horizontal distance, enter the amount of vertical space by which you want the figure to move up, and press Enter again. You will see an effect similar to the one in Figure 18.9. (To move the figure down, you would enter a negative vertical distance.)

FIGURE 18.8: Moving a figure within its box. In effect, this lets you crop out unwanted parts.

FIGURE 18.9: Using the Move option. You can enter a fixed amount by which to move the image, either horizontally, vertically, or both.

Note: You can't move an image by one amount and then add an increment to it in a subsequent move. You have to enter the total amount by which to move the image from its original position each time. For example, to move the image 2.5 inches to the left, you can't move it 2 inches and then move it another 0.5 inch. If you have moved it 2 inches and decide that it needs to move another 0.5 inch, enter the amount as **2.5"** the second time.

SCALING AN IMAGE

You can also use the Edit options to scale an image (reduce or enlarge it to a certain percentage of its original size). Each time you press PgDn or PgUp, the image is reduced (or enlarged) by the percentage shown in the lower-right corner. Figure 18.10 illustrates the CHECK.WPG graphic figure scaled to 50% by pressing PgDn five times with the percentage set to 10%.

Note: When you scale an image, you are only adjusting how large the graphic will be in its box, not the size of the graphics box on the page.

The Scale option works much the same way, except that it lets you specify a factor for both the x-axis and the y-axis, so that you can create special effects with distortion. Choose the Scale option (**2**); then enter **100** for the x-axis and **50** for the y-axis to get the effects shown in Figure 18.11. (If you didn't want distortion, you would scale both axes by the same amount.)

ROTATING IMAGES

As long as you aren't using a bitmapped image (one that is created by a paint program such as PC Paintbrush or GEM Paint), you can rotate the graphic any

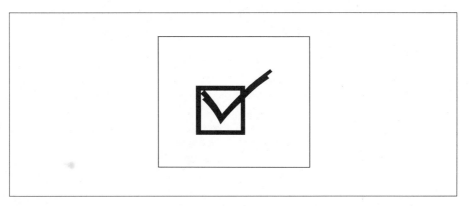

FIGURE 18.10: Scaling the image. An image is scaled like this by using the PgUp and PgDn keys.

FIGURE 18.11: Creating special effects with the Scale option. You can distort graphic images by entering different scaling percentages for the right and left axes.

number of degrees or create a mirror image (change it to "opposite hand," as architects say). Bitmapped images are composed of dots, and resizing them often produces unacceptable results. However, you can invert bitmapped images, creating a special effect called "reversing out."

CREATING MIRROR IMAGES

To create a mirror image of a graphic, choose the Rotate option (3), press Enter, and type **Y.** By leaving the number of degrees set to 0, you create a mirror image, as Figure 18.12 shows.

You can choose to rotate the image instead by pressing the + and − keys on the numeric keypad. With the percentage left at 25%, pressing either key four times brings the image full circle. If the percentage is at 10%, pressing either key ten times turns it completely around.

To change the rotation of the image by a fixed number of degrees (from 1 to 360), use the Rotate option on the menu instead of the + and − keys.

REVERSING OUT IMAGES

You can invert (or "reverse out") bitmapped images, such as those created by a paint program or digitized through an optical scanner, so that black becomes white and vice versa. However, the graphic images that come with the Word-Perfect program are not bitmapped images. If you try using this option with the CHECK.WPG image, you will see no change. However, if you have access to a paint-type program, you can try inverting an image on your own. In fact, if you

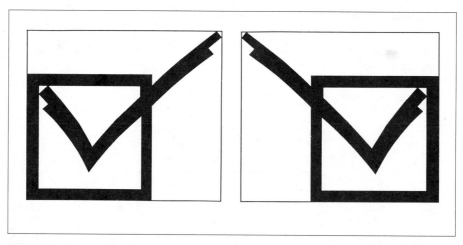

FIGURE 18.12: Creating mirror images. The Rotate option lets you rotate the orientation of graphic images.

want to create reversed-out type in your publications, this is the way to do it: create the image in the paint program, even if it consists only of type; then bring it into WordPerfect and invert it.

WORKING WITH GRAPHICS OPTIONS

Now that you've seen a few of the basic things you can do with graphics and their boxes, we can look in more detail at some of the other special techniques that you may often want to use with your graphics. For example, you may want to use captions with them, change the default borders, and specify a percent of shading ("screen") to use within them.

To change graphics options once you have set them, you will first need to delete the [Opt] code that represents them; then press Alt-F9, select the graphics type, and select Options to specify new ones. You can't simply edit graphics options as you can graphics definitions.

To specify graphics options, press Alt-F9 (Graphics) and select Options (**4** or **O**). You will then see one of the screens illustrated in Figures 8.13 through 8.15, which show the default options for the various types of graphics boxes. Options for the User-Defined box are not illustrated, as they are similar to those for the Figure box. Figure 18.16 shows a sample of each default box style.

The differences are subtle on these screens, but they can affect the appearance of your graphics considerably. For example, as noted earlier in the chapter, Figure boxes are square in proportion and are surrounded by a single rule, while

```
Options:    Figure

      1 - Border Style
            Left                          Single
            Right                         Single
            Top                           Single
            Bottom                        Single
      2 - Outside Border Space
            Left                          Ø.16"
            Right                         Ø.16"
            Top                           Ø.16"
            Bottom                        Ø.16"
      3 - Inside Border Space
            Left                          Ø"
            Right                         Ø"
            Top                           Ø"
            Bottom                        Ø"
      4 - First Level Numbering Method    Numbers
      5 - Second Level Numbering Method   Off
      6 - Caption Number Style            [BOLD]Figure 1[bold]
      7 - Position of Caption             Below box, Outside borders
      8 - Minimum Offset from Paragraph   Ø"
      9 - Gray Shading (% of black)       Ø%

      Selection: Ø
```

FIGURE 18.13: The Figure Options screen. You can use this screen to change the borders, the caption style, and the percent of shading.

```
Options:    Text Box

    1 - Border Style
            Left                            None
            Right                           None
            Top                             Thick
            Bottom                          Thick
    2 - Outside Border Space
            Left                            0.16"
            Right                           0.16"
            Top                             0.16"
            Bottom                          0.16"
    3 - Inside Border Space
            Left                            0.16"
            Right                           0.16"
            Top                             0.16"
            Bottom                          0.16"
    4 - First Level Numbering Method        Numbers
    5 - Second Level Numbering Method       Off
    6 - Caption Number Style                [BOLD]1[bold]
    7 - Position of Caption                 Below box, Outside borders
    8 - Minimum Offset from Paragraph       0"
    9 - Gray Shading (% of black)           10%

Selection: 0
```

FIGURE 18.14: The Text Box Options screen. Similar to the Figure Options screen, this screen lets you change the style of Text boxes.

```
Options:    Table

    1 - Border Style
            Left                            None
            Right                           None
            Top                             Thick
            Bottom                          Thick
    2 - Outside Border Space
            Left                            0.16"
            Right                           0.16"
            Top                             0.16"
            Bottom                          0.16"
    3 - Inside Border Space
            Left                            0.16"
            Right                           0.16"
            Top                             0.16"
            Bottom                          0.16"
    4 - First Level Numbering Method        Roman
    5 - Second Level Numbering Method       Off
    6 - Caption Number Style                [BOLD]Table 1[bold]
    7 - Position of Caption                 Above box, Outside borders
    8 - Minimum Offset from Paragraph       0"
    9 - Gray Shading (% of black)           0%

Selection: 0
```

FIGURE 18.15: The Table Options screen. This screen allows you to set the style for Table boxes.

text boxes are shaded 10% gray and have thick borders at the top and bottom. Table boxes resemble Text boxes but carry no default shading, as Figure 18.15 shows. In the following sections, we will see the effects of changing these options.

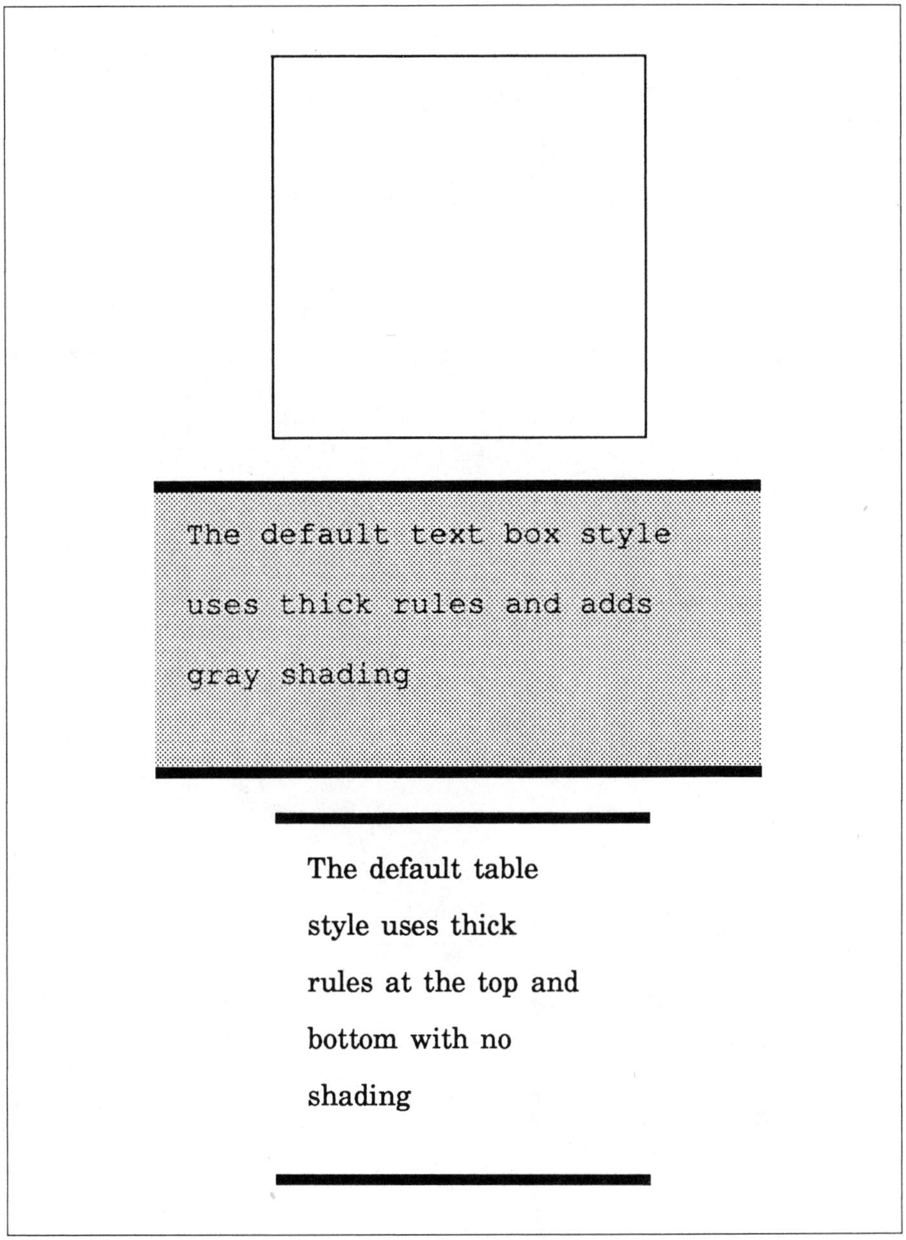

FIGURE 18.16: Default styles for graphics boxes. Using the default settings for Figure, Text, and Table boxes produces effects like these.

Using Borders

WordPerfect has several built-in options for changing the border style from the default style to a double rule or a dashed, dotted, thick, or extra thick rule. In addition, you can change the amount of space that separates the border from the text and the image from the border within the box.

Figure 18.17 illustrates many of the possibilities that are available. These depict the Figure box proportions, but you can create these effects in any size or type of graphics box.

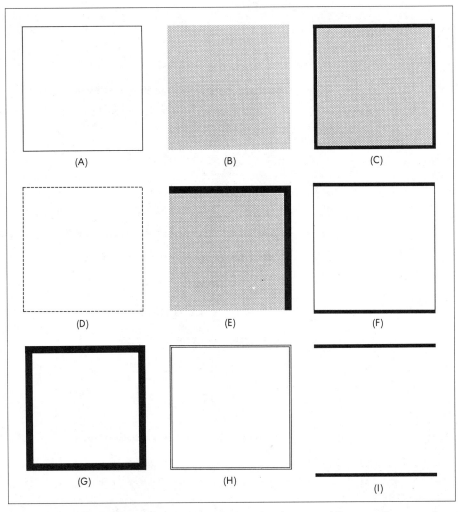

FIGURE 18.17: Using different graphics box options. You can select many different combinations of borders and screens to create different effects in your text.

Part (a) of Figure 18.17 shows the default Figure box style of four thin-ruled borders. In (b), the borders have been deleted and a 10% gray screen is being used. In (c), thick rules are used on all four sides, with a 10% gray screen. In (d), a dashed rule is used on all four sides. Part (e) illustrates how you can create a three-dimensional effect by using an extra thick border at the top and right and filling in the box with a 10% screen. A more restrained approach is shown in part (f), where a thick rule is used at the top and bottom and normal rules are used on the right and left sides. In part (g), thick borders are used on all sides, creating a picture-frame effect. Part (h) shows the effects of using double borders on all sides, and part (i) illustrates how you can use a figure definition to create the same style as the default table style—two thick rules at the top and bottom of the figure.

To change the border style, press Alt-F9 (Graphics), choose Figure (or the type of box you are using), and then choose Options (**4** or **O**). You can then select Border Style (**1** or **B**) and pick a combination of styles for the top, bottom, left, and right rules.

Options **2** and **3** (Outside and Inside Border Space) let you select the amount of white space that is used to surround the box and to surround the graphic image inside the box.

Changing any of these Figure options changes them for all the figures in your text from the cursor's position forward, not just the one that is nearest the cursor. For example, if you change the border style to a double rule on the top and bottom, all the figures in your document after the [Fig Opt] code that WordPerfect inserts will change also. If you want your figures to use a consistent style, be sure to put the [Fig Opt] code at the beginning of your document.

If you experiment with changing Figure options and decide that you want to return to the default, just delete the [Fig Opt] code that WordPerfect inserts. All your figures will return to the default style. The options include:

- The border style.
- Inside and outside border space.
- The figure numbering method.
- The caption numbering style.
- The percent of gray shading.
- The minimum amount of space to be offset from the paragraph.

Creating Shaded Boxes

As you saw in Figure 18.17, you can specify a percentage of gray shading ("screen") to use in your figures. Entering **100%** makes the box black; **10%** fills it with a very light gray. However, a few words of warning apply. If you are using a dot matrix printer, you may get unwelcome effects, as these printers have a lower resolution than laser printers, so you will get a coarser, grainier screen. Also, be careful about how heavy a screen you use. Figure 18.18 illustrates the use of a 10% screen as well as a 20% screen. Anything over about 20% can cause the text that it covers to be illegible when printed. Be sure to test-print a sample figure to see the screen effect your printer can produce before you set up a document to use screened graphics.

WORKING WITH TEXT BOXES

Most of the illustrations in this chapter have used Figure boxes, but you may want to create Text boxes in your documents for sidebars, displayed quotations, and so forth. To create a Text box, you follow the same procedure as for creating a Figure box, except you choose Text Box (**3** or **B**) from the Graphics menu (Alt-F9) instead. To type text that is to go into a Text box, you choose the Edit option (**8** or **E**) on the Text Box Definition menu. To retrieve an existing Word-Perfect document into a text box, you enter its name at the Filename option. WordPerfect will perform word wrap on whatever you type within the dimensions of the box you are using. You can press Ctrl-F8 (Font) and change fonts or font styles as often as you like for the text that is to go within the box. After you have typed text for the graphic and pressed F7 to exit, the Filename option on the definition screen reads *(Text)*.

Figures 18.19 and 18.20 illustrate some of the effects you can get by using Text boxes for displayed text. To get the effects shown in Figure 18.19, you simply set Text Box options (Alt-F9 B O) for the borders and the shading. Then create the box itself (Alt-F9 B C) and choose the Edit option.

For example, here are the steps required to create the box in part (a) of Figure 18.20:

1. Position your cursor in the document where you want the sidebar to go.
2. Press Alt-F9 (Graphics). Then select Text Box (**3** or **B**) and select Create (**1** or **C**).
3. Choose Edit (**8** or **E**).

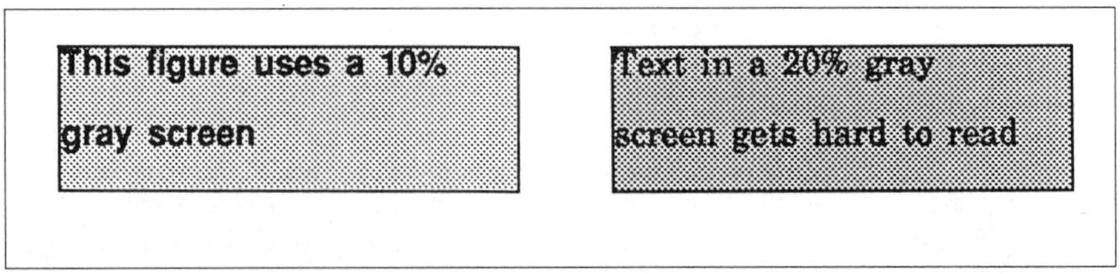

This figure uses a 10% gray screen

Text in a 20% gray screen gets hard to read

FIGURE 18.18: Using screens. The box on the left uses a 10% screen; the one on the right uses a 20% screen.

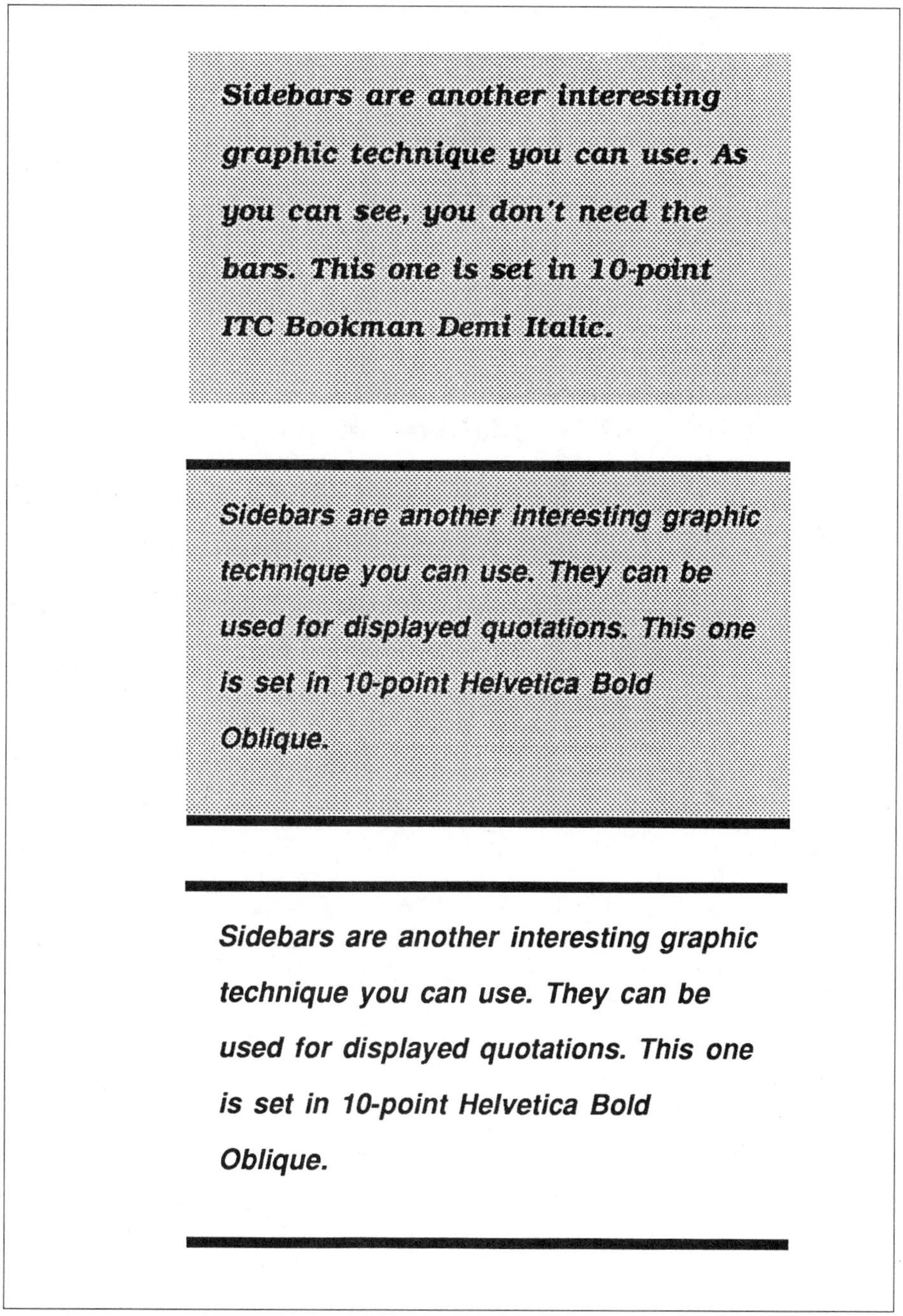

Sidebars are another interesting graphic technique you can use. As you can see, you don't need the bars. This one is set in 10-point ITC Bookman Demi Italic.

Sidebars are another interesting graphic technique you can use. They can be used for displayed quotations. This one is set in 10-point Helvetica Bold Oblique.

Sidebars are another interesting graphic technique you can use. They can be used for displayed quotations. This one is set in 10-point Helvetica Bold Oblique.

FIGURE 18.19: Various styles of Text boxes. You can use Text boxes for displayed quotations and sidebars.

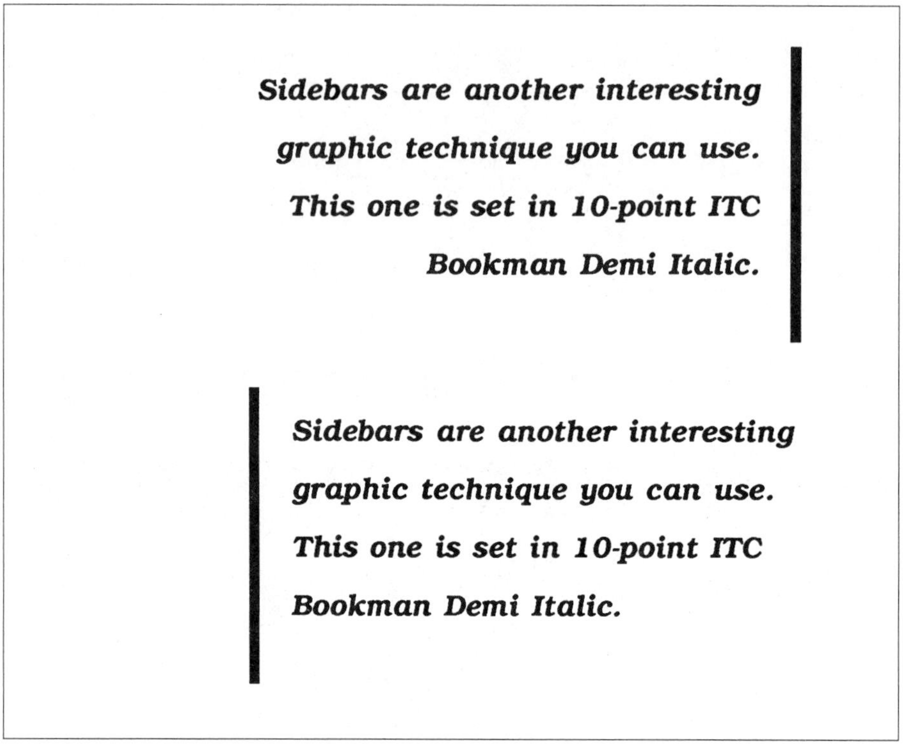

Sidebars are another interesting graphic technique you can use. This one is set in 10-point ITC Bookman Demi Italic.

Sidebars are another interesting graphic technique you can use. This one is set in 10-point ITC Bookman Demi Italic.

FIGURE 18.20: Using sidebars. These graphic elements can be used effectively in columns of text.

4. Press Alt-F6 (Flush Right).

5. To set the sidebar in a different font, press Ctrl-F8 (Font) and select a new base font (**4** or **B**). Here, 10 point ITC Bookman Demi Italics was used. Then type the text of the sidebar and press Enter. You don't have to return to Normal after switching fonts in a graphics box and before returning to your document; WordPerfect will automatically return you to the font you were using in the document when you return to it.

6. Press F7 until you get back to your document.

7. Since you don't want to use the default options of thick rules and 10% shading for this Text box, press Alt-F3 (Reveal Codes) and move the cursor to the left of the Text Box code. You can then change the Text Box options so that they will affect the box you just created.

8. Press Alt-F9, choose Text Box, and choose Options.

9. Select Border Style (**1** or **B**) and set the top, bottom, and left borders to None and the right border to Thick.

10. Select Gray Shading (**9** or **G**) and type **0** to remove the 10% gray shading.

11. Press F7 to return to your document.

You can now view the document or print it to see the sidebar you have created, as Figure 18.20 illustrates. Depending on the type of page layout you are using, you may want to change the size of the text box to make it deeper or wider.

These examples illustrate only a few of the formatting commands you can used on text within graphics boxes. You can change fonts, sizes, and appearances as well as use the program's built-in formatting commands, such as Center, Left-Right Indent, and so forth.

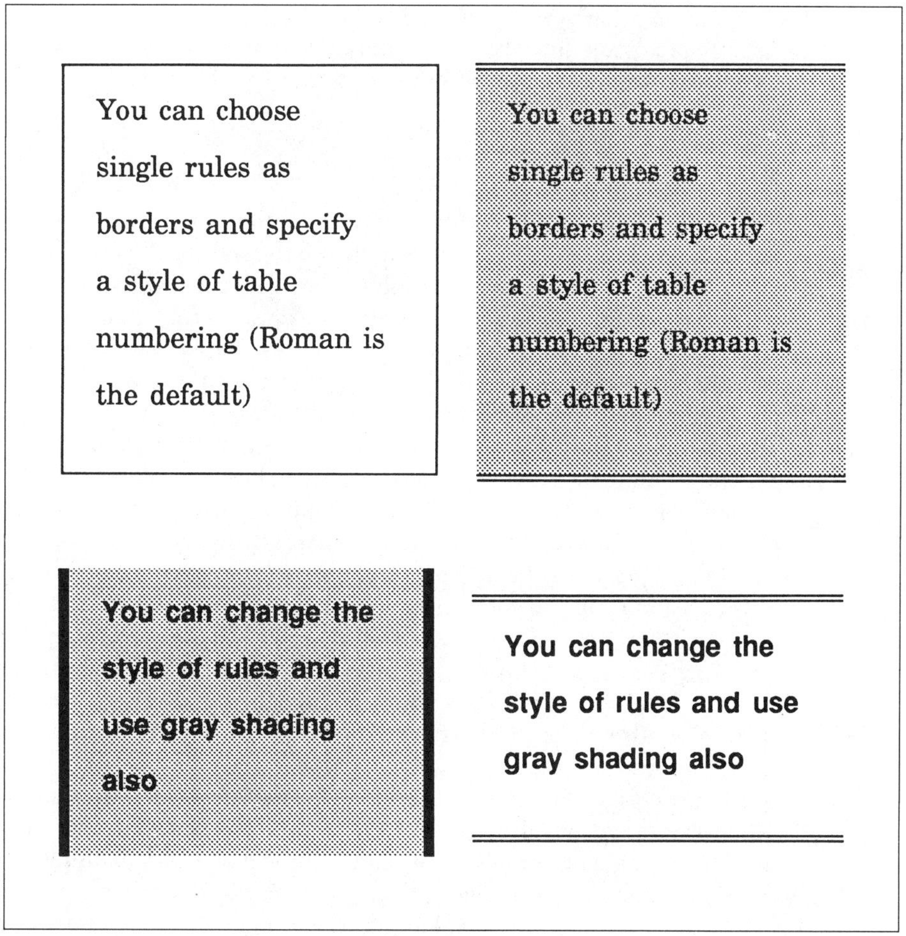

You can choose
single rules as
borders and specify
a style of table
numbering (Roman is
the default)

You can choose
single rules as
borders and specify
a style of table
numbering (Roman is
the default)

You can change the
style of rules and
use gray shading
also

You can change the
style of rules and use
gray shading also

FIGURE 18.21: Using Table boxes to hold text. You can retrieve graphics into this type of box also.

You don't have to put text into a Text box; instead, you can use Text boxes to create small shaded areas in forms that you are designing to indicate which areas should be filled out and which should be left blank. In fact, you can even retrieve graphics into text boxes.

WORKING WITH TABLE BOXES

Table boxes are often used to hold tables of text or data. You have already seen the default Table box style, but you can choose other combinations of styles from the Table Options screen. Figure 18.21 illustrates only a few of the combinations. Like the other types of graphics boxes, Table boxes can contain either text or graphics that you retrieve, as Figure 18.21 illustrates.

As both tables and figures often require you to use captions, the following sections will explore some of the Caption options available to you.

WORKING WITH CAPTIONS

You'll probably want to use a caption for many of the graphics boxes you create. The trick to using captions is to define the style of the numbering system with the Options option on the Graphics menu first and then use the Captions option on the Definition screen to write the caption and format it. Even if you don't want text with your graphics captions but simply want them to be numbered as *Figure 1, Table I,* and so forth, you must use the Caption option on the Definition screen to generate the [Box Num] code.

For example, WordPerfect uses a default caption style of boldface for the word *Figure* and its number. However, you can use the Figure Options menu to change the caption numbering style, change the caption style in print, and change the position of the caption itself. To use this menu, press Alt-F9 (Graphics), select Figure (**1** or **F**), select Edit (**2** or **E**), and type **1** (or the number of the figure you want to create a caption for); then press Enter to once again edit the graphic image. This time, choose Options (**4** or **O**). You will see the Options screen, as Figure 18.13 illustrated. Options **4** through **7** on this menu control captions. In particular, options **4** and **5** allow you to change the numbering style used for the first and second levels of captions, which you may want to do if you are creating a long or complex document.

For figures, the default style is numbers for the first level of captions (option **4** or **F**). However, you can indicate that you want the program to use a second level of numbering for captions as well by using option **5** or **S**. For example, you might want to have the first figure labeled as *Figure 1a,* the second as *Figure 1b,* and so forth. You can choose numbers, letters, or Roman numerals. However, the system that you set up with these two options helps you keep track of the figures only on the screen, not in the printed document.

If you want to change the style of the captions that are printed in your document, you must *also* use option **6**, Caption Number Style. You can change the caption style from the default of boldface in the base or initial font that you are using to a different font and size if you prefer, or you can use two levels of numbering, as illustrated in Figure 18.22. WordPerfect will use the second level of numbering that you indicated in option **5**.

For example, to number your figures so that they appear as *Figure 1-1, Figure 1-2,* and so forth, in the italic style of your base or initial font, you would take the following steps:

1. Choose Second Level Numbering Method (**5** or **S**); then choose Numbers (**2** or **S**).

2. Choose Caption Number Style (**6** or **C**); then press Ctrl-F8 (Font).

3. Choose Appearance (**2** or **A**); then choose Italics (**4** or **I**).

4. Type **Figure 1-2**. The *1* stands for level 1, and the *2* stands for level 2. Since you chose numbers for level 2, your figures will be numbered as *Figure 1-1, Figure 1-2,* and so forth. If you had chosen letters for level 2, they would be numbered as *Figure 1-a, Figure 2-a,* and so forth. Roman numerals would produce the system *Figure 1-i, Figure 1-ii,* and so forth.

5. Press Ctrl-F8 and choose Normal (**3** or **N**). Then press Enter. You will see that the line for option **6** now reads [ITALC]Figure 1-2[italc].

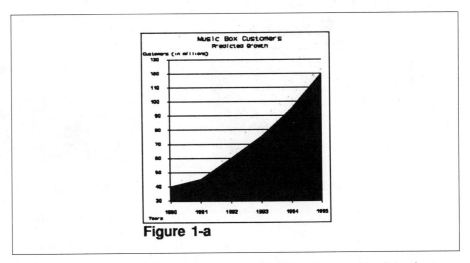

Figure 1-a

FIGURE 18.22: Using two levels of numbering in captions. To indicate the second level's numbering style, carefully follow the steps given in the text.

There are a couple of limitations on what you can do about styling captions in this screen. First, you can't change fonts for this part of the caption (it will use the base or initial font you have selected for the document), and you can only choose a Size or Appearance option, not both. If you want to change the font for the caption or select another Size or Appearance option, you can do that in the Definition screen when you choose the Caption option.

Option **7**, Position of Caption, lets you position the caption either above or below the Figure box, and either inside it or outside it. The default for figures is for captions to be below and outside the box. However, you can position captions above figures or below them, as Figure 18.23 shows. In that figure, note also that the caption style has been changed to *A-1* (in the first part) and that you can specify various sizes and type styles for captions.

The default settings for table captions use Roman numerals set in boldface type above the table. Figure 18.24 illustrates a few of the other effects you can get with different styles of table captions.

There are a few interesting things demonstrated by the captions in the sample tables in Figure 18.24. First, although different fonts were used for the captions themselves, the body of the table material reverted to the base font, New Century Schoolbook, chosen for the document. Second, any type of formatting code

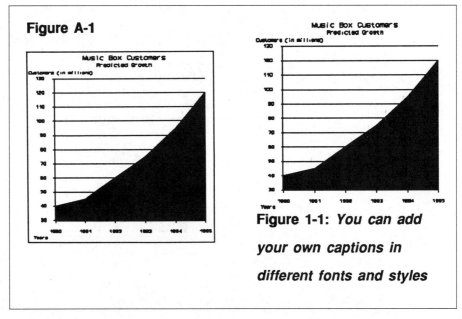

FIGURE 18.23: Positioning a caption. You can change the style of numbering as well as the position of the caption.

Table 1-1

Annual Exports

Animal products	Cotton goods
Soybeans	Sugar cane
Handicrafts	Tobacco products

Table 1

Primary Exports

Annual Exports

Animal products	Cotton goods
Soybeans	Sugar cane
Handicrafts	Tobacco products

Table I-a: Primary Products Used for Export

Annual Exports

Animal products	Cotton goods
Soybeans	Sugar cane
Handicrafts	Tobacco products

FIGURE 18.24: Different styles of table captions. As with the other types of graphics boxes, you can use a dual numbering system to number table captions.

you use for centering or flush right alignment must be done in the Definitions screen, not in the Options screen. Third, WordPerfect wraps any caption that is longer than one line correctly onto the next line. Fourth, if you are changing a font's appearance in the Options screen, you can't block the text and apply the appearance change to it; instead, press Ctrl-F8 (Font), choose Appearance, and type the number of letter of the appearance change you want. Then move to the end of the caption, press Ctrl-F8, and repeat the process. WordPerfect will insert an [ITALC] code (for example) first, and then it will insert an [italc] code the second time.

Creating Lists of Graphic Elements

WordPerfect automatically maintains lists of the captions you use for graphics boxes. To have the program generate these lists, you must insert a List Definition code at the place in the document where you want the list to appear. For example, to create a list of figures on a separate page at the end of a document, you would use Ctrl-Enter to create a blank page at the end of the document and then press Alt-F5 (Mark Text) and choose Define (**5** or **D**) to define the list with or without page numbers. (Figure boxes are maintained as list 6, Table boxes as list 7, Text boxes as list 8, and User-Defined boxes as list 9.) When you have created all of your graphics boxes, you can generate the lists by selecting Generate from the Mark Text menu.

If you add or delete graphics, you will need to keep your lists up to date manually by selecting Generate, as WordPerfect does not automatically update lists as new elements are added to or deleted from them.

Additional information on defining, styling, and generating automated reference lists is in Chapter 9, ''Creating Automated References.''

CREATING HORIZONTAL AND VERTICAL RULES

You can also create different types of horizontal and vertical rules to enhance the appearance of your printed documents. Figure 18.25 illustrates a vertical rule in a layout that uses two columns.

If you're using rules with columns, you should define your columns first and get the page the way you want it to appear before you begin to insert the rules. In Figure 18.25, the vertical rule was inserted by positioning the cursor after the [HPg] code, then pressing Alt-F9 (Graphics), choosing Line (option **5** or **L**), choosing Vertical Line (option **1** or **H**), and pressing Enter to accept the default settings.

To create vertical rules along the left margin, you have to position the cursor to the right of the [Col On] code. If you don't want the rule to run the full vertical

*No other company surpasses **MagnaCorp** when it comes to*

employee benefits: credit union, extended leave

Vacation

Full-time permanent employees are
eligible for two weeks of paid vacation
after six months of continuous
employment. During the first five years
of service, you earn three weeks of
vacation per year. After five years of
service, you receive four weeks.

FIGURE 18.25: A vertical rule. WordPerfect's Graphics feature will insert rules as well as graphics boxes.

length of the page, you can't accept the default settings. Instead, you have to take
these steps:

1. With the cursor immediately after the [Col On] code, press Alt-F9,
   choose Line (**5** or **L**) and choose Vertical Line (**2** or **V**).

2. Since you want the horizontal position of the rule to start at the left margin, you do not need to change that setting. However, you may not want
   the rule to run vertically down the entire page, but rather to start below a
   horizontal rule that you have inserted. Choose Vertical Position (**2** or **V**);
   then choose Set Position (**5** or **S**). WordPerfect will suggest the current
   cursor position. Press Enter to accept it.

3. Press Enter again to create the vertical rule at the left margin.

4. Then, to create a second vertical rule between the columns, press Alt-F9
   and choose Vertical Line again.

5. This time, you want the horizontal portion of the rule to begin between
   the two columns instead of at the left margin, so choose Horizontal Position (**1** or **H**) and then choose Between Columns (**3** or **B**). Press Enter to
   insert the line after column 1.

6. You want the line to start below the horizontal rule, so choose Vertical
   Position, choose Set Position, and press Enter to accept the current cursor
   position.

7. Press Enter again to return to your document. You can then view the document or print it to see the rules you have inserted.

Note: Once you have determined the layout of a publication designed with Word-
Perfect, you can save each design element—such as the level-one headings, the
level-two headings, and so forth—as a style, as discussed in Chapter 6. You can
include vertical and horizontal lines in styles, but you can't include a graphics
box. You will need to position the cursor at the appropriate place between the Style
On and Off codes and then retrieve the graphic image.

USING ADVANCE TO POSITION TEXT

WordPerfect's Advance feature can be used to fine-tune the placement of text in a box. To see how this works, you can create a borderless shaded box and position some text within it. This type of box can be used as a masthead for a newsletter, as you see in Figure 18.26 and in Chapter 19.

To create this effect, you would take the following steps:

1. Press Alt-F9 (Graphics) and choose Line (**5** or **L**).
2. Choose Horizontal (**1** or **H**).
3. The default setting for lines is Left and Right, which is what you want for a line running across the page, so you can leave that setting alone. However, the width (.01'') is much too small for a masthead, so choose Width (**3** or **W**) and change it to 1''.
4. Choose Gray Shading (**4** or **G**) and change it to 10%.
5. This time, you want the line to go between the columns, so choose Horizontal Position (**1** or **H**) and then choose Between Columns. Since you want it to go to the right of column 1, press Enter at the prompt.
6. You want the vertical line to begin at the cursor's position, so choose Vertical Position and choose Set Position. Press Enter to insert the current cursor position.
7. Press Enter again to return to your document. You can then view the document or print it to see the rules you have inserted.
8. Press Enter twice more to return to your document.
9. Now you can type the text that you want to have in the masthead. To center it, press Shift-F6 (Center). In Figure 18.26, the font was changed to ITC Zapf Chancery Medium Italic by pressing Ctrl-F8 (Font), selecting that typeface in the 12-point size, and then selecting Large. You can choose any typeface available on your printer.

Harshaw's Harness Horses

October 28, 2001　　　*All That's Fit to Rent*　　　*Vol. 22, No. 900*

FIGURE 18.26: Using Advance to position text. This shaded box is actually a horizontal line in which text is centered with WordPerfect's Advance feature.

10. When you have selected a typeface and a size, type the text that is to be centered and press Enter. In this masthead, it's **Harshaw's Harness Horses**.

11. Press Enter and type the date.

12. Press Shift-F6 (Center), type the text that you want to have centered on the second line, **All That's Fit to Rent**, and press Enter.

13. Press Alt-F6 (Flush Right) and type the text that you want to be flush right, **Vol. 22, No. 900**.

You can now use the View Document feature to preview the masthead, or you can test-print it. Once you've created a masthead that you like, you can save it and use it many times.

The Advance feature will let you move text right, left, and down as well as up. The amount that you enter is relative to the place where your cursor is. For example, to move text right 1.5 inches from the cursor, you would enter the Advance Right command as **1.5"**.

You can also choose Set Position (**3** or **S**) on the Advance menu to advance lines of text to an absolute horizontal position on the page. For example, if you want to position text at a certain horizontal location, move the cursor to that location, check the status line, move the cursor to the beginning of the text, and then advance the text to that position by choosing Set Position and entering the position measurement that you noted on the status line. The main difference between this command and the Advance Up, Down, Left and Right commands is that you enter the exact position where you want the text to appear, not the relative position from the cursor.

You can't block several lines of text and then move them with the Advance feature; you have to move each line individually. If you try blocking text first, you will see that the *Block Protect?* prompt comes on when you press Shift-F8 (Format).

Once you've used any of the Advance features, remember to advance back to your original position by using the feature again, specifying the opposite direction in this case.

USING THE SCREEN CAPTURE UTILITY

The WordPerfect 5.0 Graphics disk comes with a screen capture utility called GRAB.COM that you can use to capture whatever is on your screen (if it's in graphics mode) as a graphic image that can be used in other documents. You can use this utility not only with WordPerfect but also with many graphics and spreadsheet programs. GRAB.COM will work with most graphics adapter cards, such as the EGA, Hercules, and CGA graphics cards, but it does not work with the Compaq Portable in 640 × 400 mode. It does not operate in text mode (that is, if you are in WordPerfect's normal editing screen), but it will, for example, capture images from the View Document screen, which is a graphics display.

You can use this utility to capture up to 9999 images (the files will be named GRAB.WPG, GRAB1.WPG, GRAB2.WPG, and so forth) before you need to delete or rename any of them. However, you will probably find it easier to work with the images you capture if you rename them after each session to reflect what they contain. For example, it will be more meaningful later to retrieve a graphic named SALESUM.WPG or even FIG1-2.WPG than to keep track of the graphics by number. Just remember to keep the .WPG extension so that WordPerfect can tell which type of graphic it is. You can use either the DOS REN (rename) command or the Move/Rename option on the List Files screen to rename the graphics files.

Once you've captured a screen image, you can retrieve it into a graphics box and use it just as you would any other graphic.

To use GRAB.COM, you must be at the DOS prompt, without WordPerfect running. You should be in the directory that contains GRAB.COM, or you should copy GRAB.COM into the directory that you are using. Enter

    GRAB

and press Enter.

Once you have installed GRAB.COM, you can start WordPerfect in the usual way. Then, when you have a screen that you want to capture, press Alt-Shift-F9. A two-tone chime indicates that GRAB.COM is ready, and you will see a box on the screen. (If you hear a buzz, either your monitor doesn't support GRAB.COM, or you aren't in graphics mode.)

You can use the ↑ and ↓ keys to move the box. Press Shift with the arrow keys to resize the box. Press Ins to toggle between coarse and fine increments as you move or resize the image. When you have the image as you would like it, press Enter. Press Esc if you decide that you don't want to capture the image.

When you press Enter, GRAB.COM takes a few seconds to capture the image and then sounds another two-tone chime, indicating that it has finished. You can then capture another image.

You will need to load GRAB.COM each time you start a session in which you want to use the utility. However, if you exit from WordPerfect to run other programs and then return to WordPerfect, GRAB.COM will still be in memory. It is not automatically cleared from memory until you turn off your computer.

GRAB.COM may conflict with other TSR (terminate-and-stay-resident) programs that are running. If it does, you can clear it from memory without turning off your machine. To clear it from memory, enter

    GRAB/R

at the DOS prompt.

When you install GRAB.COM each time, you can direct the images it captures to another directory by entering the startup command as

GRAB/D = *PATH*

where *path* is the path name of the directory where you want to store the captured images. If you capture a lot of images, you may find it easier to work with them if they're kept in a separate directory. For example, you could keep figures for Chapter 1 in one directory, for Chapter 2 in another, and so on.

If you want to change the name under which the images are stored, start GRAB.COM with

GRAB/F = *NAME*

where *name* is a name up to four characters that replaces *GRAB*. For example, you could enter **GRAB/F = FIG**, and they would be labeled FIG1.WPG, FIG2.WPG, and so forth.

For additional information on GRAB.COM, type

GRAB/H

at the DOS prompt after you have loaded GRAB.COM into memory.

Printing Bitmapped Graphics

GRAB.COM captures the screen as a bitmapped image at the same resolution that your monitor provides. For example, with an EGA graphics monitor, this resolution is 640 dots per line (high) by 350 dots per line (wide). Practically speaking, this means that the images GRAB.COM produces are about the same quality as what you see when you view a document at 100% with the View Document feature. However, the resolution you get in your printed documents depends, of course, on the quality your printer can provide. A laser printer capable of 300 dots per inch will definitely give you better graphics than a 72-dpi dot matrix printer.

To get even better quality in printed bitmapped graphics, consider scaling them down. Enlarging a bitmapped graphic is usually not a good idea, because they are composed of dots, and increasing the size of the dots only magnifies the imperfections. Reducing a bitmapped image smoothes out the dot patterns, so you get the impression of higher quality.

One other thing you need to keep in mind if you're printing bitmapped graphics, either captured with GRAB.COM or brought in from another source such as a painting program or a scanner, is that what you see on your screen is not always what you get when you print. The aspect ratios for monitors and printers are different; for example, boxes that appear square on the screen will probably not be square when they are printed. You can demonstrate this for yourself by using WordPerfect's Line Draw feature (Ctrl-F3 L) and drawing a small box. You'll find that moving the cursor a certain number of spaces vertically is not the same as moving it the same number of spaces horizontally. If you try to print a "square" that's on the screen, it will come out as a rectangle.

Practically speaking, this means that you may have to do some test-printing with bitmapped images to get the results you want. Use the Size option on the Definition screen to set either the width or the height that you want, and let WordPerfect calculate the other dimension so that the proportions remain the same. With bitmapped images, you will probably find that a slightly smaller size than the original will produce graphics of better quality in your printed documents.

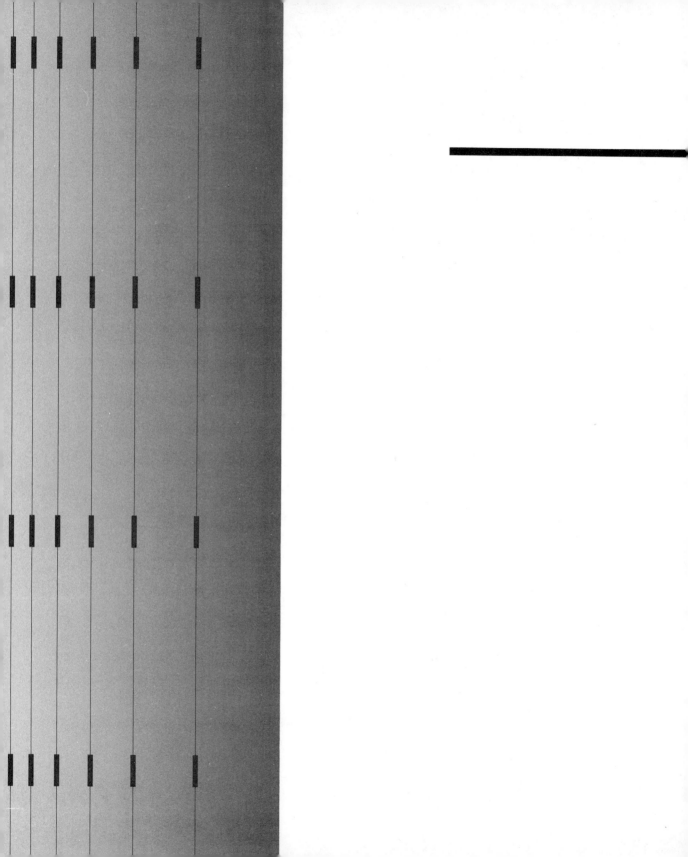

CHAPTER 19

WORDPERFECT'S DESKTOP PUBLISHING CAPABILITIES

WordPerfect's
Desktop Publishing Capabilities

This chapter outlines the steps you need to take when planning and producing publications with WordPerfect. The first part discusses layout and design concepts as they relate to using WordPerfect for desktop publishing. There, you will find many pointers on achieving good designs suited to the publication you want to create.

The second part of this chapter concentrates on specific examples of just some of the types of publications you can create with WordPerfect. You will find detailed information on how WordPerfect was used to create the final sample publication. This information is intended not only to stimulate ideas for your own publications but also to make clear the process involved in their creation.

Upgrade Notes

Although desktop publications using Line Draw and different fonts were possible in version 4.2, the desktop publishing capabilities of WordPerfect's former version were a far cry from those of version 5.0. As a result of the dramatic enhancements in the area of graphics and text manipulation (outlined in detail in Chapter 18), this chapter's material on utilizing the desktop publishing capabilities will be as fresh to experienced 4.2 users as it is for the new users of WordPerfect 5.0.

Planning a Publication

The first step you must take in producing any desktop publication is to plan it. Before planning the actual layout, you need to consider the audience that you are addressing as well as the message that you want to communicate. Look over as many samples as possible of the type of publication you are producing.

During the planning stage, you should keep the following questions in mind:

- Which printer will you use to produce the final printout of the publication? Do you have this printer in house or will you be renting one at a service such as your local copy center?

- Will this publication require you to create a custom form for your printer in order to have WordPerfect print it? (See Chapter 7 for details on how to go about this.)

- Which fonts will you be using in the publication? Do you already possess these fonts for your printer, or are they fonts that will be available only when the final printout is made?

- What graphic images are to be included in the publication? Are these images in graphics files directly supported by WordPerfect, or will some or all of them require translating? (See Chapter 18 for a list of supported graphics formats.) Do you own the programs in which these graphics will be produced? If you don't, how can you have the graphics revised, if this becomes necessary?

- What layout is best suited to this publication? Should it use newspaper or parallel columns? Will it benefit from the use of WordPerfect's Styles feature (see Chapter 6)?

- Will the design of this publication be reused, as is the case with a monthly or quarterly newsletter, or will it be used one time only? If you do plan to reuse it, will it save you time in the long run to create a template and then add the text and graphics to a copy of the template document rather than creating the actual publication and then revising it each time you print the publication?

Some of these planning considerations—what basic design or layout to use, what particular fonts and graphics to include, and whether to work from a template—need to be determined before producing any desktop publications, even those produced with desktop publishing programs like Ventura Publisher or PageMaker. Other considerations—which final printer to use, whether a form (or forms) must be created to print the publication, how to translate the graphics files into a new format, and whether to format the publication with styles—are related more closely to WordPerfect's capabilities in producing desktop publications.

WordPerfect Versus Desktop Publishing Programs

Before taking up the more general planning and design guidelines, we need to summarize the way WordPerfect is used as a desktop publisher and look more closely at these program-specific considerations. Keep in mind that Word-Perfect 5.0 is a word processor with desktop publishing capabilities, not a desktop publisher with word processing capabilities.

As a word processor, WordPerfect doesn't give you direct access to what is often referred to as WYSIWYG (what-you-see-is-what-you-get) desktop publishing. The most accurate on-screen representation of the final publication comes when you use View Document, a feature on which you will rely often. Because the publication as viewed in WordPerfect's document editing screen often bears little resemblance to the finished product, it is somewhat more difficult to design a publication with WordPerfect than with a desktop publishing program that uses the WYSIWYG system throughout the design process.

Also, when using WordPerfect to create a publication, you don't have access to any kind of grid system onto which you place blocks or columns of text and graphic images as you do with desktop publishing software. Not having this ability makes it more difficult to change the page layout and design. For example, you won't always be able to reposition a layout element, such as a Figure box containing a graphic image, on the page without disturbing the layout of the remaining elements on the page, as you usually can with dedicated desktop publishers.

These differences underscore the need to know how to best combine Word-Perfect's many formatting features with its new desktop publishing features to create an effective layout and design. They should not, however, imply that you can't create great-looking desktop publications with WordPerfect.

Elements of Design

Although the final product must please your artistic sense, deciding on the design for your publication is not simply a matter of aesthetics. Remember that the layout chosen, the figures used, and the type selected all serve only one goal, to clearly and effectively communicate the subject matter of your publication. While it is well beyond the scope of this book to teach layout and design, there are some tried-and-true design principles that you need to keep in mind.

The first principle is to establish unity or consistency in the design. The publication needs to have coherence; that is, to demonstrate its underlying plan at a glance. To achieve unity, you need to create a certain amount of sameness throughout the publication, especially among like elements. You can do this by establishing a basic design for each element—like the headlines, headers and footers, sidebars, figures, and body copy—and then using these designs each time the element occurs. Resist the temptation to change the type style for each new heading. Minimize changes to the Figure Box options each time you use a figure. Make the style of the body type for each story or part of the publication consistent.

The second principle is to counterbalance the unity by establishing tension or contrast in the design. If the design is too consistent, it tends to be uninteresting. This is the last thing you want, because such a design can bore the reader, thus interfering with the communication of your message. To achieve contrast within the unity that you establish, you need to introduce a certain amount of difference, even between like elements in the publication. You do this by relying on the principle of proportion: vary the size of a particular element like a headline or figure in proportion to its importance in the publication. With type, you can also use a different style, like boldface or italics in the same typeface, to establish a hierarchy of importance. This has two beneficial effects: it creates more interest in the message, and it helps the reader to find his or her way around the publication.

Tension is heightened when the overall value of the page does not appear gray, as it does when the page consists entirely of plain text on a white background. (You can judge the gray value of the page by squinting at it when you hold it at about arm's length.) The easiest way to change the value is to introduce bold headlines and/or figures that use high black and white contrast.

If you are creating a publication like an advertising flyer or a newsletter, some contrast is usually very desirable, but it can be overdone. If your page is too brilliant (that is, uses too much black on white), it can become hard for the reader to follow its flow. On the other hand, if you are creating longer publications like training manuals or annual reports, you will probably have some pages that don't contain high contrast but instead are completely gray in value. In such cases, it is not advisable to add unnecessary figures or to manufacture bold headings in an attempt to increase the contrast on the page. Remember, the purpose of a publication is the clear communication of your message, not the creation of fine art.

DECIDING ON THE LAYOUT TO USE

The term *layout* describes how you use and choose to fill or not fill the white space on the page. The layout of the various elements on the page is another important factor that contributes to the unity and diversity of the design. The amount of information that you must accommodate on the page often becomes a determining factor in the final layout that you use. If you must fit a lot of information on a single page (as when creating a one-page flyer), you cannot leave a great deal of white space. However, you must at all costs avoid overcrowding the information or resorting to a type size that is too small to be read comfortably.

The layout must also make it easy to follow the flow of information. Make use of the English-language reader's natural tendency to read from left to right and from top to bottom. Don't place figures in such a way that they interrupt this rhythm. If anything, you want to engineer their placement so that they help guide the readers in finding and maintaining their place as they read. This is especially important with newsletters, where you may have figures combined with several stories in columns that begin on the page and whose text may or may not continue on subsequent pages. While you would never place a figure in the middle of the text, you might find that placing a figure at the bottom of the column underscores that the story does not continue on a later page.

The placement of the elements on the page is influenced by several interrelated factors:

- The size of the type and the line length used for the body copy.
- The size of type used for headlines.
- The size and number of figures.

- The addition of graphics like vertical and horizontal rules.
- The use of newspaper or parallel columns.
- The size of the page and the margins required.
- Whether the layout spans two facing pages or uses just a single page.

Ideally, you select the size for the type and figures independently of the page size and margins. Their sizing should reflect more their relative importance to the overall message than whether or not they will fit on the page. Once the type and figures have been sized, you can determine how they can best be arranged on the page.

Your arrangement should attempt to use the positive space (the figures and text) and the negative space (the white space that remains on the page) in such a way that it heightens the reader's interest in your message. Some designs, like those for newsletters, benefit most by a careful balancing of the white space with the text and figures, giving almost equal weight to the positive and negative space.

Other designs, like those for flyers and advertisements, can sometimes have greater impact if you leave more white space on the page, adding text and figures very judiciously. This can call more attention to the text and figures that you do include. Just remember that in order for this to work as planned, you may have to increase the value of the text and figures by using a bolder type or a figure with fewer gray tones. Otherwise, the positive elements can end up being overpowered by the negative space, thus diminishing their impact.

If you can't leave much white space and still accommodate all of the required information (as is often the case when designing a form), you need to work carefully with the size and placement of the text and figures to minimize crowding that will increase the gray value of the page and detract from its legibility. This is especially true if the publication uses a lot of graphic elements like rules and boxes, which tend to be naturally darker in contrast.

Selecting the Right Fonts

The fonts that you choose for your publication do, of course, depend greatly on which ones you have available for your printer (see Chapter 5 for information on installing fonts). Beyond that, at the design stage you are concerned primarily with the legibility of the text. Several factors determine the legibility of type:

Serif Versus Sans Serif Type   When choosing fonts, you must first decide between serif and sans serif type. *Serif type* refers to a typeface using short cross-strokes that project from the main stroke. Times Roman (referred to as *Dutch* in Bitstream fonts) is an example of a serif type. Sans serif typefaces (*sans* means *without* in French) don't use these terminating cross-strokes on the letter forms. Helvetica (called *Swiss* in Bitstream fonts) is an example of a sans serif type.

Most often, a serif type is chosen for smaller body type because the serifs tend to aid the reader in differentiating between letters, thus increasing legibility. Sans serif types, therefore, are usually reserved for *display type*—that is, larger type used for headlines and other types of headings.

Type Size   Another important factor in legibility is type size. Body type should be between 9 and 12 points. Traditionally, display type is any size of 14 points or larger. When choosing the type size for the publication, you need to indicate the relative importance of headings by increasing the type sizes.

Sometimes, you can do this by using WordPerfect's Font Size attributes (Ctrl-F8 S), which allow you to specify large, very large, and extra large type based on the size of the base font. By using the Base Font command (Ctrl-F8 F) to assign the type size for the body text, you can let WordPerfect assign the type size for the Large, Vry Large, and Ext Large options simply by selecting the appropriate Size option. In other situations, you have to continue to use the Base Font command to assign the specific type size you want for each heading. This is especially true when your publication calls for a larger display type than Word-Perfect would automatically assign with the Large, Vry Large, or Ext Large option.

Type sizes smaller than 9 points should be used judiciously in the design. Such small sizes usually form the "fine print" that readers often ignore. However, you will find that you need smaller sizes when creating forms or business cards in order to accommodate all of the required information.

Line Height   As a necessary part of choosing the fonts for your publication, you need to think about the line height required by the types sizes chosen. *Line height* (referred to as *leading* in traditional typesetting) refers to the vertical distance between the baselines of each line of type (refer to Chapter 5 for an illustration of how the program measures line height). WordPerfect automatically assigns a line height for each type size you use in a document. When you use sizes of type smaller than 30 points, however, WordPerfect uses the minimum line height measurement that you would want to assign (unless you were creating a special effect). If you print a paragraph of 10-point type and measure the line height in points, you will find a distance of 10 points between each baseline. Traditionally, the minimum line height should be at least 12 points (120 percent of the type size). This means that you will usually want to increase the line height by choosing a fixed line height (Shift-F8 L H F) for the text you are setting.

Remember that line height is an important factor in balancing positive and negative space in the publication. It also influences the legibility of the text. Large, solid-looking sections of type are less inviting to the reader.

The Value and the Shape of the Type   As mentioned earlier, regular type, balanced with the white space between letters, words, and lines, results in a fairly neutral gray tone for the page. To increase the contrast, heighten interest, and call attention to the important parts of your message, you can use a bold version of the type you have chosen. In most cases, you can do this by using WordPerfect's Bold command (F6).

Italic type normally appears lighter than regular type. Italics are generally used to emphasize a word or phrase, or to call out the title of a publication. You can also use them to emphasize small sections of the publication. However, be aware of the effect italics have on the gray value of the page. Italic type was designed to fit more letters in the same space. With smaller type sizes, you can fit more type in the same space when you change to italics. Italics also emphasize movement from left to right across the line or page.

With some printers, you can choose between regular and bold italic type. Bold italics can often be effectively used for headlines and other types of headings. They tend to be somewhat easier to read with a sans serif type than with a serif type.

WordPerfect supports several other effects, like outline and shadow lettering. Both of these effects should be reserved for larger sizes of type. Outline type is very light in value because it traces the outer edges of each letter form, leaving the core blank. Shadow type adds depth to the letter form by creating a "shadow" for each outlined letter. While both can be used as special effects to heighten interest, you must balance the benefits of their use against a potential reduction in legibility.

Uppercase Versus Lowercase   Body type is set using uppercase and lowercase letters as dictated by the rules of English grammar. However, when it comes to display type used for headlines and other headings in the publication, emphasis traditionally is added by capitalizing each important word in the sentence or phrase, or by setting the entire heading in uppercase letters.

While these techniques can be quite effective, they also tend to reduce legibility. This is especially true when the heading is set in all uppercase letters. Although this has the effect of heightening the contrast, it also takes most people a longer time to comprehend the message. Therefore, restrict the use of all-uppercase headings to those that are composed of very few words; also, whenever possible, set such headings on one line.

In longer headings that only capitalize important words, legibility is hampered by the "bounce" effect as the eye goes up and down the line to follow the interplay of uppercase and lowercase letters. More modern typographic design avoids this effect entirely by merely capitalizing the first word in the headline and setting the rest of the line (except letters that must be uppercase) in lowercase letters.

The Shape of the Text   Another important factor in legibility is the length of the line. If the line of type is too long, the eye becomes tired and the reader's interest wanes, especially with a longer publication like a report or manual in which there is a great deal of plain text.

The optimal line length is determined by the size of the type. Ideally, the line length (measured in picas) should be between 1.5 and 3 times the type size. For instance, if you are using 10-point type, the line should be between 15 and 30 picas long. The pica is a standard typesetting unit of measurement; there are almost 6 picas per horizontal inch of type. Therefore, if you are using inches as your default unit of measurement, the line length should be between 2.5 and 5 inches. WordPerfect also allows you to use points as the default unit of measurement. There are exactly 12 points to each pica, so a line set in 10-point type should be between 180 and 360 points long.

All sections of type in a publication form different shapes that can be manipulated in the layout. After deciding on the type size and line length, you need to consider whether the type within a section should be right-justified (WordPerfect's default) or ragged-right.

Traditionally, right justification is used almost exclusively in typeset publications. When used, it gives the text a solid, boxy shape that reinforces the vertical and horizontal lines of the page. This is especially true for newsletters in which the articles are formatted into newspaper columns.

You should be aware, however, that using a ragged-right margin instead of right justification has little effect on legibility; if anything, it increases it slightly. Also, using right justification in a publication created with WordPerfect can create some word spacing problems that can be avoided by using a ragged-right margin. In order to fill out a right-justified line so that the left and right margins are even, WordPerfect often varies the amount of space between words. This variance becomes greater when a shorter line length is used. This is an almost inescapable problem when setting text using newspaper columns, and therefore it occurs quite commonly in newsletters.

Unequal word spacing tends to decrease the legibility of the line and can result in unsightly "rivers" of white space cascading through the paragraph. It is very time-consuming to use WordPerfect's Word/Letter Spacing option (Shift-F8 O P W) to correct this problem.

Regardless of the type of right margin you select for the text, you should probably use WordPerfect's Hyphenation feature, especially when you are setting text that uses a short line length. This can help minimize the word spacing problem that happens with right-justified lines and decrease the amount of unevenness in lines that use a ragged-right margin.

You also need to decide what kind of indentation, if any, you want to assign to each paragraph in any given section of the publication. The most common way to set off the beginning of each paragraph is by using a simple tab. You can also choose to outdent the first line of the paragraph (see the **Margin Release** entry in Part V). Another technique is to leave the first line of each paragraph flush left but increase the line height between the end of one paragraph and the beginning of the next. Regardless of the method you settle on, you should somehow indicate the start of a new paragraph.

Word and Letter Spacing   As noted in the preceding section, word spacing plays an important role in the legibility of the type. You can use the Word/Letter Spacing option to either condense or expand the line of type. This can be used to fill out a line, to fit text within a narrow space on the page, or just to reduce the amount of white space between words. Often, you will find that the word and letter spacing percentage must be applied on a line-by-line basis, especially when you're trying to reduce the amount of white space. This is because reducing the word spacing in one line may result in poor word spacing in the following line or lines. These lines, in turn, must then be adjusted with a different percentage figure. (See Chapter 5 for more information on adjusting the word and letter spacing.)

The Impact of Type   You must select a typeface whose design is appropriate to your message. Typefaces vary greatly in their visual impact. Some, like Times Roman and Helvetica, are very formal and can be used in almost any kind of publication. Others, like Palatino and ITC Avant Garde, are more informal and may not be appropriate for all types of publications. For example, they may not look "serious" enough for a financial report that is to be submitted to the board of directors, but they could really enhance the monthly newsletter.

Still others, like ITC Zapf Chancery (a cursive font), have a very specialized design, appropriate to fewer publications. While ITC Zapf Chancery would be completely inappropriate for the annual report, it is a natural choice for office party invitations or a luncheon menu. When selecting a typeface, always consider the potential impact of its design on your audience.

CHOOSING YOUR GRAPHICS

Graphics form a tremendously important component of most publications. They not only heighten interest in the subject matter being discussed, but also inform the reader in their own right. The graphics you use in your publication can come from many sources; you can scan photographs, purchase sets of ready-made images, or even draw an illustration using one of the paint programs supported by WordPerfect. If your publication requires graphs, these can be created with spreadsheet programs like Lotus 1-2-3 or Quattro and then imported directly into your document.

As indicated in Chapter 18, WordPerfect accepts a large number of graphics formats. These include both bitmapped graphics (composed of dots) like those produced by GEM Paint, PC Paintbrush, MacPaint, Lotus 1-2-3, and so on, and object-oriented graphics (composed of shapes) like those produced by Auto-CAD and the sample Publisher's PicturePak images included with WordPerfect.

In addition, WordPerfect accepts scanned images saved in Tagged Image File Format (TIFF) and Encapsulated PostScript (EPS) files created by programs like Freehand and Adobe Illustrator 88. The TIFF file format gives you a bitmapped image, while Encapsulated PostScript represents a special object-oriented image. Both of these types of files are very large and tend to slow down printing considerably.

Note: Remember that in WordPerfect you can invert (or reverse out) only bitmapped images. Though they can't be inverted, object-oriented images can be cropped, rotated, scaled, or mirrored just like bitmapped images. Encapsulated PostScript images, however, can't always be edited, as they aren't always visible.

As a rule, object-oriented images are reproduced better than bitmapped images, especially when the illustration contains curves. Therefore, if you have a choice for the source of your illustrations, choose object-oriented over bitmapped images.

Sizing and Placing Graphics on the Page   After you collect the graphics files that you want to use, you need to decide which type of graphics box to use for each. Chapter 18 outlines the uses and default settings for each of the four types of graphics boxes supported by WordPerfect. As you import a graphics file into a WordPerfect graphics box, you need to decide how to size the box and where to place it in relation to the surrounding text.

If your publication is going to use text columns, you can use the column width to help you determine the sizing and placement of your figures. For example, if you are designing a newsletter on an 8½-by-11-inch page with left and right margins of ⅝ inch, divided into three columns 2¼ inches wide with ¼ inch between each column, the smallest graphics box in the publication will be

2¹/₄ inches wide, placed in line with any one of the columns. The next size will be 4³/₄ inches wide (2 columns wide plus the ¹/₄ inch space between them), placed in line with any two of the three columns. The largest figure will be 7¹/₄ inches wide (3 columns wide including the spaces between them).

You can let WordPerfect automatically decide the vertical dimension for the graphic image based on the width that you enter. This is not always appropriate for the particular illustration or graph, however. You may encounter situations in which you prefer to determine the vertical dimension yourself.

WordPerfect is always preset to wrap text around the graphic image that you place on the page. If you want to try to shape the text around the graphic image, you must remember to edit the graphics box, select the Wrap Text Around Box option, and indicate No. To prevent the text from overlapping with part of the graphic image, you must terminate each line with a hard return (Enter) at the appropriate place. You will have to use the View Document feature (Shift-F7 V) to find the exact place at which to terminate each line. Don't attempt to create such a special effect until you have spell-checked and proofread the document so you are certain that there will be no further changes to the text.

Using Rules in the Publication   WordPerfect allows you to draw horizontal and vertical rules that can help call out new sections on a page and otherwise enhance the look of a publication. The default thickness for each type of rule is 1 point, and you can increase or decrease the thickness as you see fit. Note that if inches are the default unit of measure and you want to draw a thinner horizontal or vertical line, you'll have to enter the measurement in points, such as **.5p**; note that WordPerfect would then show a width of *0"* at the Width of Line option.

You can also use the Graphics Line feature to draw thick rules that appear as rectangles or square boxes (depending upon their length). You can achieve a nice effect by decreasing the shading percentage for thick rules so that they don't overpower the other elements on the page.

Typical Steps in Executing a Design

Each publication that you create with WordPerfect will require a slightly different treatment. There are, however, some typical steps that you will have to take in executing any design. These steps are outlined below:

- Decide on the basic page layout for your publication. Be sure to take into consideration the capabilities of the printer you will be using. For example, if your printer isn't capable of printing in landscape mode, you will have to design the publication so that it works in portrait mode.

- Decide which paper size and type your design requires. If these aren't covered by a predefined form for your printer, you will have to create it. (See Chapter 7 for a discussion on the creation and use of forms.)

- Decide on all four margins (top, bottom, left, and right). Take into consideration any special margins required by your printer to reproduce the final artwork.

- Open a new document in WordPerfect and select the printer that will be used to produce the final printout. Then, type in all of the copy (that is, the text to be included). At this stage, don't worry about assigning different fonts to the text, using the final margin settings, or formatting the text beyond the basic paragraph format. Just use WordPerfect's default settings and the printer's initial font. After spell-checking and proofreading the text, save this document in its own file.

- Select the files containing the graphic images to be used (if any). Convert any files that WordPerfect can't read directly. (See Chapter 18 for details on which graphics files are directly supported.) To make it as easy as possible to import these graphics files into your publication, copy all of them onto the same diskette or into the same directory that contains the text for the publication.

- Open another new document and select the final printer, if it is not the default. Make any required changes to the margin settings and the paper size and type, and create any column definitions or headers and footers that will be used. If the publication's design is to be reused, as with a newsletter, save this file under a new name. This will then become the template file that contains only the elements that are common to each issue of the publication.

- Retrieve the file containing the text for the publication into your template file. If the text is to be formatted into columns, turn them on before retrieving the text.

- Add all of your font changes to the text. Create an open style (see Chapter 6) containing the base font and standard line height for the body of the text and apply the style. If different fonts and/or line heights are to be used for different level of headings that reoccur in the publication, create paired styles for each level and apply them.

- Add graphic images at the appropriate places in the text. Choose the type of graphics box whose default settings most closely match those that you want to use. When creating the box, designate the file that contains the graphics image you want to use, create the caption, make any changes to the size and position of the box, and then edit the image itself as required.

- Preview the page design with the View Document feature (Shift-F7 V). If necessary, change the options for the type of box you selected (be sure that the Options code precedes the Graphics Box code in the Reveal Codes window).

- If you are happy with the layout at this stage, consider whether you need to work with the word and letter spacing of the text. If you want to cut down on white space in the body copy, try using WordPerfect's manual hyphenation. If you still need to work with white space, use the Word/ Letter Spacing feature to adjust it. You can also use this command to adjust the spacing for all of the headlines that you feel have either too little or too much white space.

- Save the document under a new name and then print a copy of it. If you don't have the printer that will be used to produce the final printout, you can try printing a rough draft using a printer that you do own. However, unless this printer uses similar fonts and can print graphics, you will have to rely mostly on View Document to make sure that the publication is the way you want it.

Producing Publications with WordPerfect

To give you a more concrete understanding of the desktop publishing capabilities of WordPerfect, the remaining sections of this chapter cover specific applications created with WordPerfect. By reading through these sections, you will not only get some idea of the program's great potential but also gain some insight into the steps involved in using WordPerfect as a desktop publisher.

Flyers

One of the simplest desktop publishing applications to produce is the one-page flyer. Figure 19.1 shows you such a flyer for a wine merchant, listing special wines by category along with their prices. This flyer relies largely on type for its impact. The typeface used throughout the flyer is ITC Zapf Chancery, a cursive typeface meant to mimic calligraphy. It lends a refined look to the flyer, in keeping with the audience for fine and expensive wines.

The flyer uses an illustration to form the right border. This graphic image was scanned on an HP ScanJet from the book *Art Nouveau Display Alphabets 100 Complete Fonts,* by Dover Press. The image was saved on a Macintosh in the TIFF file format. This file was then transferred to the IBM and brought directly into WordPerfect.

FIGURE 19.1: Wine merchant's flyer. This one-page flyer uses ITC Zapf Chancery Medium Italic as the typeface throughout. It uses one graphic image that was scanned on an HP ScanJet; the TIFF file was brought into this WordPerfect document in a Figure box.

Figure 19.2 shows the definition for this figure. As you can see, the image was saved in the file NOUVEAU1.TIF, shown here without the file extension. The Figure box uses the Page type aligned with the top and right margins (which were changed from the default before the figure was created). The width of the figure (3.25'') was originally selected by WordPerfect when the graphic image was assigned to the Figure box. It was retained when the length was increased using the Both Width and Height option. Notice, too, that the Wrap Text Around Box option for this figure is set to No. This allows the column of wine prices to be entered within the border of the figure.

Figure 19.3 shows you the first part of this flyer as it appears in the document editing screen with the Reveal Codes screen visible. The [Fig Opt] code sets Border Style for the four borders to None and sets Inside Border Space to 0'' in all four directions. This allowed the text of the flyer to be moved as close to the illustration as was considered desirable.

The formatting of the text is accomplished with tab settings except for the name of the wine merchant. The Advance Right command controls its horizontal placement in relation to the top of the illustration. As you would expect, the wine titles and descriptions in the first and second columns are aligned with left tabs and the wine prices in the third column are aligned with decimal tabs.

The flyer uses three styles to change the size and style of the ITC Zapf Chancery font. The Open Style called Base Type, shown after the Margin Change codes in Figure 19.3, sets the base font to a 14-point size. The main heading, *Shane's Wine Cellar,* is formatted with a paired style called Title Type. This style changes the font to 36 point ITC Zapf Chancery and turns boldfacing on and off. The wine types, such as Chardonnay, Sparkling Wine, and so on, are formatted with a paired style called Wine Type that changes the point size to 18.

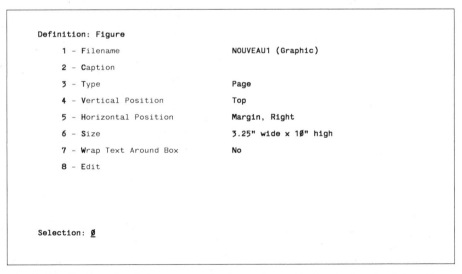

FIGURE 19.2: The Figure Box Definition screen for the graphic used in the wine merchant's flyer. The Figure box uses the Page type and is aligned with the top and right margin settings. Note that the Wrap Text Around Box option is set to No so that the column of wine prices can be set inside its borders (which were set to None) by changing the Figure options.

```
    —

Shane's Wine Cellar

        Chardonnay
             1985  Chalone                                  $50.00
             1981  Kenwood/Beltane Ranch                    $40.00
             1985  Flora Springs/Napa                       $30.00
             1985  Acacia/Carneros                          $30.00
             1986  Goosecross/Napa                          $30.00
D:\WP\WDC\WINE.FLY                            Doc 2 Pg 1 Ln 1" Pos 1"
▲      {      ▲      ▲       ▲      ▲      ▲      ▲      ▲      ▲      ▲      ▲
[T/B Mar:Ø.37",Ø.37"][L/R Mar:Ø.5",Ø.5"][Open Style:BASE TYPE][Fig Opt][Figure:1
;NOUVEAU1;][HRt]
[HRt]
[HRt]
[AdvRgt:Ø.5"][Style On:TITLE TYPE]Shane's Wine Cellar[Style Off:TITLE TYPE][HRt]

[Tab Set:Ø",Ø.5",1.33",1.91",6.25"][HRt]
[Tab][Style On:WINE TYPE]Chardonnay[Style Off:WINE TYPE][HRt]
[Tab][Tab]1985   Chalone[Align]$50[C/A/Flrt].ØØ[HRt]
[Tab][Tab]1981   Kenwood/Beltane Ranch[Align]$40[C/A/Flrt].ØØ[HRt]

Press Reveal Codes to restore screen
```

FIGURE 19.3: First part of the flyer in the document editing screen with the Reveal Codes screen visible. Here, you can see that an open style is used after the Margin Change codes. This open style sets the point size for the body of text to 14 point. The point size and bold style of the wine cellar title is set with a paired style called Title Type. The wine titles are set to 18 points with a paired style called Wine Type.

Styles, even when used to make simple font changes like those in this one-page flyer, make designing an easier task. With the styles in place, the point size, the alignment, and even the typeface to be used can be changed repeatedly from the Styles menu.

Newsletters

The newsletter is perhaps the most common desktop publishing application for businesses of all sizes and types. The layout of the standard newsletter is based loosely on that of the daily newspaper. Because of this influence, newsletters almost always use a columnar layout, which is accomplished in WordPerfect with the program's Newspaper Columns feature.

Figure 19.4 shows you the printout of the first page of a newsletter called *PC Teach Perspectives*. As you can see, this particular newsletter uses three newspaper columns, mainly because of the size of the page used (8½ by 11 inches). The use of any more than three columns on an 8½-inch width would force the columns to be very narrow. If the columns are too narrow, you must hyphenate much more often, diminishing the legibility of the text. If you plan to print your newsletters on a larger size of paper, you can probably use up to four columns in the newsletter layout.

PC *Teach* Perspectives

| Vol. 1 No. 1 | OCTOBER |

Upgrading to WordPerfect 5.0

New Course for 4.2 Users

PC Teach has developed a complete training course for all experienced 4.2 users who have upgraded to WordPerfect 5.0. "Upgrading to WordPerfect 5.0," by Susan Kelly (author of *Mastering WordPerfect 5*) and Greg Harvey (author of *WordPerfect 5 Instant Reference* and *WordPerfect 5 Desktop Companion*).

This course includes a 65 page workbook and lesson disk with many exercises designed to get you familiar with all the important new features. The workbook is divided into the following eight lessons:

1. Changes to keys, menus, and hidden codes
2. Modifications to basic editing
3. Modifications to formatting Lesson
4. Modifications to printing and fonts
5. Formatting with Styles Lesson
6. Macros in WordPerfect 5.0 Lesson
7. Using Different Keyboard Layouts
8. Desktop Publishing with WordPerfect 5.0

Individual workbook and lesson disk are offered at a cost of $25.00. Call (415) 663-9430 to order or for information on our discounts for dealers and nonprofit educational institutions. ◆

Courtesy of Symbols, Signs & Signets, Dover Press

Desktop Publishing Comes to WordPerfect 5.0

WordPerfect 5.0's graphics and desktop publishing features have opened up a whole new world for WordPerfect users. You can now create horizontal and vertical rules, and boxes containing text, figures, or tables, and you can use illustrations created in other programs such as Lotus 1-2-3, as well as scanned images or photographs. Combined with WordPerfect's font capabilities, you can create newsletters, forms, and presentation graphics of all kinds.

WordPerfect supports a wide variety of graphics formats, from Lotus 1-2-3 .PIC graph files to Encapsulated PostScript files. Moreover, if you create a graphics image that can't be directly imported into a WordPerfect graphics box, you can use the GRAB utility that comes with the program to save the screen image so that it can be imported.

Once you bring a graphic image into a WordPerfect graphics box, you can crop the image, scale it, rotate it, or produce its mirror image.

WordPerfect provides for four different types of graphics boxes, each with its own box options. You can choose between a Figure, Table, Text, or User-Defined box. Each box type has its own default settings, which you can modify as required for the particular illustration or table that you are placing in the document.

You can also use the program's auto reference feature to indicate the page numbers where figures continued on page 4

| PC Teach Perspectives | Page 1 |

FIGURE 19.4: First page of the *PC Teach Perspectives* newsletter. This newsletter uses a three-column layout. The PC Teach logotype was created in Freehand on the Macintosh and was then brought into the document as a PostScript file. The figure of the men at the printing press was scanned from the Dover Press book *Symbols, Signs & Signets,* with an HP ScanJet on the Macintosh. This scanned image was then saved as a TIFF file, transferred to the IBM, and brought into this WordPerfect document exactly as it was captured.

The first page of *PC Teach Perspectives* incorporates both a PostScript file and a TIFF file in the two figures it uses. The newsletter also contains two Text boxes; the first one occurs in the masthead and gives the volume, issue number, and date, and the second one is inserted into Footer A and gives the name of the publication and the page number. There are two stories on page 1 of this newsletter. The story on the "Upgrading to WordPerfect 5.0" course takes up the first column, and the story on desktop publishing with WordPerfect 5.0 takes up the other two columns and is continued on page 4 of the newsletter.

Figure 19.5 shows you the first part of the newsletter as it appears in the WordPerfect document editing screen. Notice that Figure 1 occurs at the very top of the page, followed by the word *Perspectives*. This first figure contains the *PC Teach* logotype that was designed in Freehand on the Macintosh. A copy of the final image was then saved as a PostScript file, which was transferred to the IBM, brought into WordPerfect, and placed in a Figure box in the newsletter.

This particular PostScript image is not visible in Graphics Edit mode or in View Document mode. Figure 19.6 shows the first half of the newsletter in the View Document screen. Notice that the *PC Teach* logotype is not visible even though it was printed correctly in Figure 19.4.

Not all PostScript images can be previewed, so it is necessary to rely on printouts to check the effect that any cropping, scaling, or rotating has on the figure.

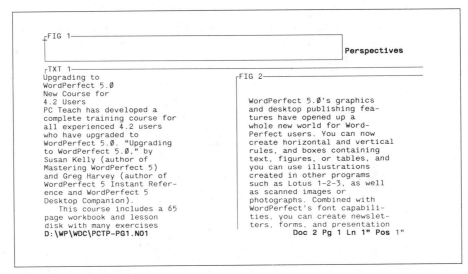

FIGURE 19.5: The top part of the first page of the newsletter as it appears in the document editing screen. This shows you the placement of the first and second figures in the newsletter. Notice that you can only see the first two columns in the editing screen and that the first part of the second column appears to overlap with the second figure.

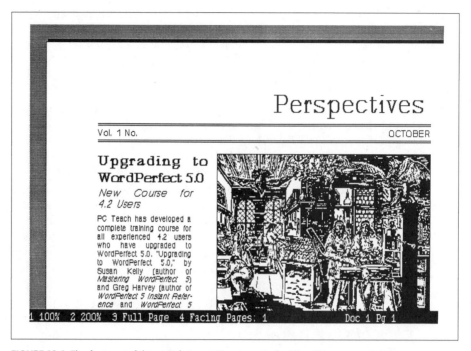

FIGURE 19.6: The first part of the newsletter as it appears in the View Document preview screen at 100% (full size). Notice that the PostScript image (preceding the word *Perspectives*) that contains the *PC Teach* logotype doesn't appear in this screen. Because the borders have been removed from its Figure box, you can't tell where it is located until the page is printed.

Because of this possibility, you should use the features of the graphics program with which the PostScript image is created to achieve any of these special effects before exporting the PostScript file to WordPerfect.

Because the image itself does not show up in the preview, the borders around it were removed from this figure (by setting Border Style to None with the Figure options) only after it was placed in its final position on the page. After the Figure box was correctly placed in relation to the word *Perspectives,* the borders were removed.

The Text box that displays the volume number, issue number, and date is contained in a paired style called Volume. The codes for this paired style are shown in Figure 19.7. There, you can see the [AdvUp], [Txt Opt], and [Text Box] codes that are entered when the style is turned on. The [Txt Opt] code changes the default border style to None for the left and right sides and uses Double for the top and bottom sides. It also reduces the inside border space for the top to 0.06'' and for the bottom to 0'' and sets Gray Shading to 0%.

Note: The change in the base font back to Helvetica 10 point when the Volume paired style is turned off is added as a precaution. Although WordPerfect is supposed to automatically return to this font because it is set by the open style called Text Type (which is turned on at the very beginning of the document), this does not always happen. In earlier versions of WordPerfect 5.0, the program was known to return to the initial printer font instead.

The newsletter footer is formatted by the [FooterA] code in the newsletter. This footer consists of a Text box that contains the font change to Helvetica 12 point, the text *PC Teach Perspectives* left-aligned, and **Page** ^**B** (the Page Number code) flush right. The default settings for this Text box have been changed to match those for the Text box used in the masthead.

The first headline for the story in column 1 of the newsletter is formatted with a paired style called Headline, which changes the base font to 20 point New Century Schoolbook Bold. Notice in Figure 19.8 that the Word/Letter Spacing feature was used to spread out the first line and compress the second line of the headline. You will often have to use this feature to obtain the proper spacing for headlines and titles in your publications. The default word spacing used by WordPerfect often appears to be too great, especially for newsletters.

The second headline for the first story is formatted by a paired style called Subhead that changes the font to 14 point ITC Avant Garde Gothic Book. The body copy for both stories uses Helvetica 10. This base font change is made by an

```
 ⌐TXT 1─────────────────────────────────────────────────

   ┌──────────────────────────────────────────────────┐
   │ Place Style On Codes above, and Style Off Codes below. │
   └──────────────────────────────────────────────────┘




   Press Exit when done                    Doc 2 Pg 1 Ln 1" Pos 1"
        ▲      ▲       ▲      ▲      ▲       ▲              ▲
   [AdvUp:Ø.5"][Txt Opt][Text Box:1;;][Comment][Font:Helvetica 1Ø pt]
```

FIGURE 19.7: The codes for the Volume style. This paired style is used to enter the Text box that contains the volume and issue number and the date. The [Txt Opt] code changes the default settings for the border style, using Double for Top and Bottom and None for Left and Right. It also sets the inside border space to 0″ for all settings except for Top, which is set to 0.06″ to increase slightly the space between the double line at the top of the Text box and the text it contains.

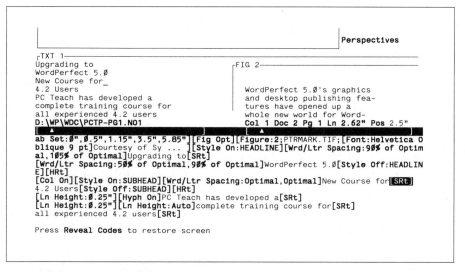

```
                                                            Perspectives

 ┌TXT 1─────────────────────────
 Upgrading to                          ┌FIG 2─────────────────────
 WordPerfect 5.Ø
 New Course for_
 4.2 Users                                WordPerfect 5.Ø's graphics
 PC Teach has developed a                 and desktop publishing fea-
 complete training course for             tures have opened up a
 all experienced 4.2 users                whole new world for Word-
 D:\WP\WDC\PCTP-PG1.NO1                    Col 1 Doc 2 Pg 1 Ln 2.62" Pos 2.5"

 ab Set:Ø",Ø.5",1.15",3.5",5.85"][Fig Opt][Figure:2;PTRMARK.TIF;[Font:Helvetica O
 blique 9 pt]Courtesy of Sy ... ][Style On:HEADLINE][Wrd/Ltr Spacing:9Ø% of Optim
 al,1Ø5% of Optimal]Upgrading to[SRt]
 [Wrd/Ltr Spacing:5Ø% of Optimal,9Ø% of Optimal]WordPerfect 5.Ø[Style Off:HEADLIN
 E][HRt]
 [Col On][Style On:SUBHEAD][Wrd/Ltr Spacing:Optimal,Optimal]New Course for[SRt]
 4.2 Users[Style Off:SUBHEAD][HRt]
 [Ln Height:Ø.25"][Hyph On]PC Teach has developed a[SRt]
 [Ln Height:Ø.25"][Ln Height:Auto]complete training course for[SRt]
 all experienced 4.2 users[SRt]

 Press Reveal Codes to restore screen
```

FIGURE 19.8: The Reveal Codes screen for the newsletter showing the Word/Letter Spacing codes used to position the two-line headline for the first story. The first line of the headline is extended by decreasing the word spacing to 90% and the letter spacing to 105% of Optimal. The second line is compressed by decreasing the word spacing to 50% and the letter spacing to 90% of Optimal. The word and letter spacing is then returned to Optimal in the next line before entering the subheading with the Subhead paired style.

open style called Text Style that is turned on at the beginning of the document right after the margin changes. Each story was typed and saved in a separate file. Columns were turned on immediately after the headline and subheading were entered, and then the file containing the story on the WordPerfect course was retrieved into this file. It happened to fit entirely within the first column. After that, the file containing the story on desktop publishing with WordPerfect was retrieved, whereupon it was automatically formatted into the next two adjoining columns. After it was determined where the story should break on page 1, the continuation message was added. The remaining text of the story was blocked and saved in its own file, which was then retrieved when laying out page 4 of the newsletter.

The figure of the men at work at an old-style printing press was created by scanning an illustration from the Dover Press book *Symbols, Signs & Signets* with the HP ScanJet on the Macintosh. The resulting TIFF file was then transferred to the IBM and taken into WordPerfect in a second Figure box.

This Figure box is designated as a Paragraph-type box with the vertical position set at 0'' and the horizontal position set to Right (to align it with the right margin setting). The width of the figure was manually sized so that it would take up two columns of the newsletter. Its length was determined automatically by the program.

This figure uses two captions: the first uses small italic type to give credit for the source of the illustration, and the second forms the headline for the story on desktop publishing with WordPerfect. With newspaper columns turned on, placing the headline in the figure caption allows you to have it extend across the width of two columns (as the figure itself does) without disturbing the flow of the text in the last two columns.

The headline is placed farther from the first caption line and from the figure itself and closer to the text of the story by using the Advance Down feature before entering the text of the headline. The base font is also changed to 20 point New Century Schoolbook, and the Word/Letter Spacing feature is used on the first line of the headline to make it extend fully across the two columns, and on the second line to decrease the word spacing between *WordPerfect* and *5.0*.

> *Note:* Be very careful about how many lines of text you attempt to add to figure captions—especially if you're using different fonts and varied spacing. You can very easily encounter a situation in which WordPerfect gives you the error message "Too much text" when you try to delete part of the caption. When the program has to deal with a complex graphic plus a caption, it can make it difficult not only to make editing changes to the caption, but even to save the document.

Volume 1 of the *PC Teach Perspectives* newsletter, with all of its text and graphics, is stored in a file called PCTP-PG1.NO1. The basic layout or template, however, is stored in a file called PCTP.TMP. This file contains only the following elements:

- The top and bottom margin settings.
- The open style that sets the base font of the body copy to the Helvetica 10 point font.
- The footer that contains the newsletter title and page number contained in a Text box, along with the Box Options code for this Text box.
- The masthead for the newsletter consisting of the *PC Teach* logotype figure, the word *Perspectives,* and the Volume style that places the volume, issue number, and date in a Text box and changes the Text Box options.
- The column definition that sets up the three newspaper columns.
- The tab settings used in the three newspaper columns.

This template file contains none of the headlines, story text, or illustrations used in an actual issue of the newsletter. The purpose of the template file is to provide the layout for all subsequent issues. To create the first page of the second issue of this newsletter, this file will be retrieved, and the headlines, text, and figures to be used will then be added to this file. After these are formatted, the file will be saved under a new file name like PCTP-PG1.NO2.

Brochures

Many styles of brochures can be produced using a single sheet of paper. One of the easiest brochures to design is one that uses an 8½-by-11-inch page in landscape mode, folded into thirds. Figures 19.9 and 19.10 show the final printouts for the inside and outside of such a brochure. If you are printing the brochure in landscape mode on 8½-by-14-inch paper, you can use four panels and fold the page into fourths.

The brochure is stored in three different files: PCTBROCH.INS contains the text and graphics for the inside of the brochure, formatted in three columns; PCTBR1&3.OUT contains the first and third columns of text for the outside of the brochure; and PCTBRO2.OUT contains the Text box with the return address.

All three files use a change in paper size and type, inserted at the beginning of the file. The paper type uses a custom form definition called Standard Landscape that was added to the LaserWriter Plus printer definition. This form sets Paper Size to 11" × 8.5", Portrait to No, Landscape to Yes, Present to Yes, and Location to Manual; the offsets remain at 0". To use this form, the Paper Size/Type option on the Page menu is first selected (Shift-F8 P S). Then, the Standard Landscape option (**2** or **T**) on the Format Paper Size menu is chosen, followed by the Other option on the Format Paper Type menu. To select the Standard Landscape form shown on the screen, you highlight it and then choose the Select option (**1** or **S**). Doing this inserts the code

[Paper Sz/Typ:11" × 8.5",Standard Landscape]

into the document at the cursor's position when the Format Page menu is exited.

The information for the inside of the brochure is stored in a single file. This document uses three newspaper columns. The headline that extends across the entire width of the page and the horizontal rule beneath it are entered before these columns are turned on. The information on the teachers and classes and the course descriptions are entered using three styles: Headline, Leadin, and Text. After the text was entered and formatted, a Text box was entered at the end of the third column. This Text box changes the default Box options so that Border Style is Single for the left and top, and Thick for the right and bottom sides. This adds depth to the box containing the information on the cost of the classes and the monthly calendar.

The information for the outside of the brochure is stored in two files, making it necessary to put the same page through the printer twice. One of the files contains the information on the training policies and the name of the training company. This information is formatted by using a newspaper column definition with three columns. The training policies are entered in the first column and the name of the training company in the third.

PCTeach — WordPerfect Training for Users at All Levels

About Our Teachers:

Susan Baake Kelly has been providing WordPerfect training for business clients and college students in the Bay Area for the last three years. She is the author of the best-selling *Mastering WordPerfect* (for versions 4.2 and 5.0) by SYBEX Computer books.

Greg Harvey has been training business clients in the Bay Area in all levels of WordPerfect for the last three years. He is the author of the *WordPerfect Desktop Companion* (for version 4.2) and *WordPerfect Instant Reference* by SYBEX Computer books (for versions 4.2 and 5.0).

About Our Classes:

PCTeach specializes in Word-Perfect training for all levels of users. Currently, we offer classes at the introductory and intermediate levels for both WordPerfect 4.2 and 5.0. In addition, we offer an Upgrading to WordPerfect 5.0 for 4.2 users who need to become familiar with the changes to the program.

Course Descriptions:

Introduction to WordPerfect 5.0.
Learn basic editing and formatting with WordPerfect 5.0. Features learned include inserting, deleting, & undeleting text; copying, moving, deleting, and undeleting blocks; enhancing text; setting tabs; using indents, search & replace, page numbering, headers & footers, merge, and introduction to file management.

Intermediate WordPerfect 5.0
Learn advanced editing and formatting with WordPerfect 5.0. Features learned include keeping text together on a page; creating macros; newspaper & parallel columns; sort & select; using styles; creating keyboard layouts; installing & using fonts; and combining graphics & text.

Introduction to WordPerfect 4.2.
Learn basic editing and formatting with WordPerfect 4.2. Features learned include inserting, deleting, & undeleting text; copying, moving, deleting, and undeleting blocks; enhancing text; setting tabs & using indents; search & replace; page numbering; headers & footers; merge; and introduction to file management.

Intermediate WordPerfect 4.2
Learn advanced editing and formatting with WordPerfect 4.2. Features learned include keeping text together on a page; creating macros; newspaper & parallel columns; sort & select; Ctrl/Alt key mapping; line drawing; and changing pitch & selecting new fonts.

Upgrading to WordPerfect 5.0
Use your WordPerfect 4.2 skills and knowledge to quickly learn the new features added WordPerfect 5.0. Features learned include selecting options by menu letter; setting new program defaults; editing in Reveal Codes; page formatting in version 5.0; installing printers and fonts; formatting with styles; macro conversion and editing; creating and using keyboard layouts; and introduction to desktop publishing.

> **All classes cost $195.00**
>
> **Consult our monthly calendar for the date and time of the class you want to take.**

FIGURE 19.9: Interior copy of a brochure printed on 8½-by-11-inch paper in landscape mode. This layout uses newspaper columns to format the text into three panels. After the headline that extends across the entire width of the page was entered, the columns were turned on. The third panel uses a Text box with 10% gray shading and a thick border for the right and bottom sides.

PCTeach
*Your WordPerfect
Training Experts*

PCTeach Training Policies

All classes include a workbook
and training disk that is the
student's to keep. All classes
are conducted at the training
room at MicroAge Computer
in San Rafael. Each class is
limited to 10 students total,
with one student at each computer. Pre-registration is en-
couraged as classes tend to fill
up quickly.

In addition to the materials
provided as part of the class
fee, students may purchase
any of our WordPerfect books
at our cost.

To help our students put the
skills they acquire in our
classes into immediate use, we
provide continued telephone
support for any problems encountered with using the
WordPerfect features covered
in the course you completed.

Corporate classes can be arranged
in advance. Such classes can
be conducted on-site or at the
MicroAge Computer training
room. Call for information on
our corporate discounts or to
discuss any specialized Word-
Perfect training and consulting
needs that you might have.

With **PCTeach,**
Your satisfaction is guaranteed.

PCTeach
P.O. Box 1175
Point Reyes Station, CA 94956

FIGURE 19.10: Exterior copy of a brochure printed on 8½-by-11-inch paper in landscape mode. When the inside is printed back-to-back to this page, the brochure is folded into thirds so that the last panel, with *PC Teach Your WordPerfect Experts,* is on top. After the brochure is folded and stapled, an address label is attached to the second panel, which is made to look like an envelope with the return address in the upper-left corner.

The second file contains just the Text box with the return address in the upper-left corner. Figure 19.11 shows how this Text box appears in the View Document screen with the Full Page option selected. This Text box uses the Page type with Vertical Position set to Top and Horizontal Position set to 4''. The size of the box is set to 3'' wide × 7.83'' high. This Text box is preceded by a [Txt Opt] code that changes Border Style to Single for the left and bottom sides and Thick for the right and top sides. It also sets Gray Shading to 0%.

The return address is rotated up 90 degrees so that it runs parallel with the long side of the Text box. To accomplish this, you use the Edit option (**8** or **E**) on the Text Box Definition screen and enter the three lines for the return address. At the bottom of the screen, you will see the message

Press **Exit** when done, **Graphics** to rotate text

When you press the Graphics key, Alt-F9, the following menu options appear:

Rotate Text: **1** 0°; **2** 90°; **3** 180°; **4** 270°: 1

Then, you select option **2** to rotate the text 90 degrees.

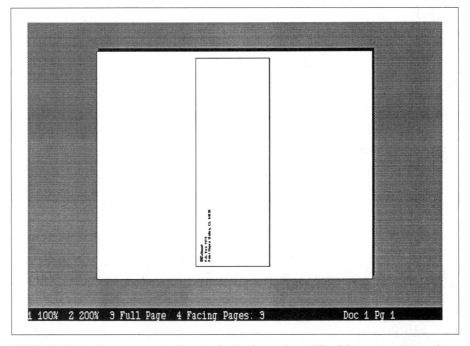

FIGURE 19.11: View Document screen showing the Text box in the middle of the page containing the return address. This Text box uses the Thick border style for the top and right sides and the Single border style for the bottom and left sides (not discernable in this figure using the Full Page option). The text for the return address is rotated 90 degrees so that it runs parallel with the long (left) side of the box.

To print the master for the outside of the brochure, you need to print the page twice: once using the file that contains the information on the training policies and the name of the business, and a second time using the file that contains this Text box. After printing the master for the inside page, you produce the final brochure by photocopying the two pages on a single sheet, back to back.

Manuals and Reports

Longer documents, like training manuals and annual reports, sometimes rely more on the skillful use of type to set off each element than on the use of illustrations. However, even when your report is basically text-based and makes little or no use of figures, you can make good use of WordPerfect's Graphics features by using rules, shaded Text boxes, and simple graphics to emphasize certain elements.

Figures 19.12 and 19.13 show you the first two pages of a PC Teach training manual that illustrates such a situation. The left-hand page contains the lesson opener and the right-hand page contains the first page of the lesson.

The lesson opener (shown in Figure 19.12) uses large, sans serif type with the Shadow appearance attribute to announce the lesson number. The name of the lesson is set off in a Text box that uses 10-percent gray shading. The objectives for the lesson are set off by shaded arrows. These were created by using the ARROW1.WPG file—one of the sample graphics files shipped with Word-Perfect. This arrow was placed in a Figure box that is .5" wide and .25" high. A [Fig Opt] code was inserted, setting the border style for all sides to None. After the first Figure box was created, the others were created by copying it down the page four times.

The exercises in the lessons use a two-column format created with parallel columns. In Figure 19.13, you can see part of the first exercise beneath the introductory paragraphs. These columns are separated by a vertical rule to emphasize that the steps to be performed by the student occur in the left-hand column, with any accompanying explanations appearing in the right-hand column.

Notice that both of the pages are bordered by a box. To achieve this effect, a file containing only this Text box was created, and multiple copies of this document were printed. Then, these sheets with the printed border were loaded into the printer and used in printing the pages for Lesson 8. You can't place the Text box that creates the border on the same page as the lesson opener because Word-Perfect won't accept Figure boxes and rules to be inserted in a Text box. For this reason, the effect must be created by printing on the same sheet of paper twice.

All of the text in the lesson is formatted with styles. An open style called Body Text changes the base font to 12 point Times Roman. Two paired styles called A Head and B Head are used to change the font and line height for all major headings and subheadings in the lesson (only the major heading *Using the Graphics Key* is visible in Figure 19.13). A paired style called Step is used to make another

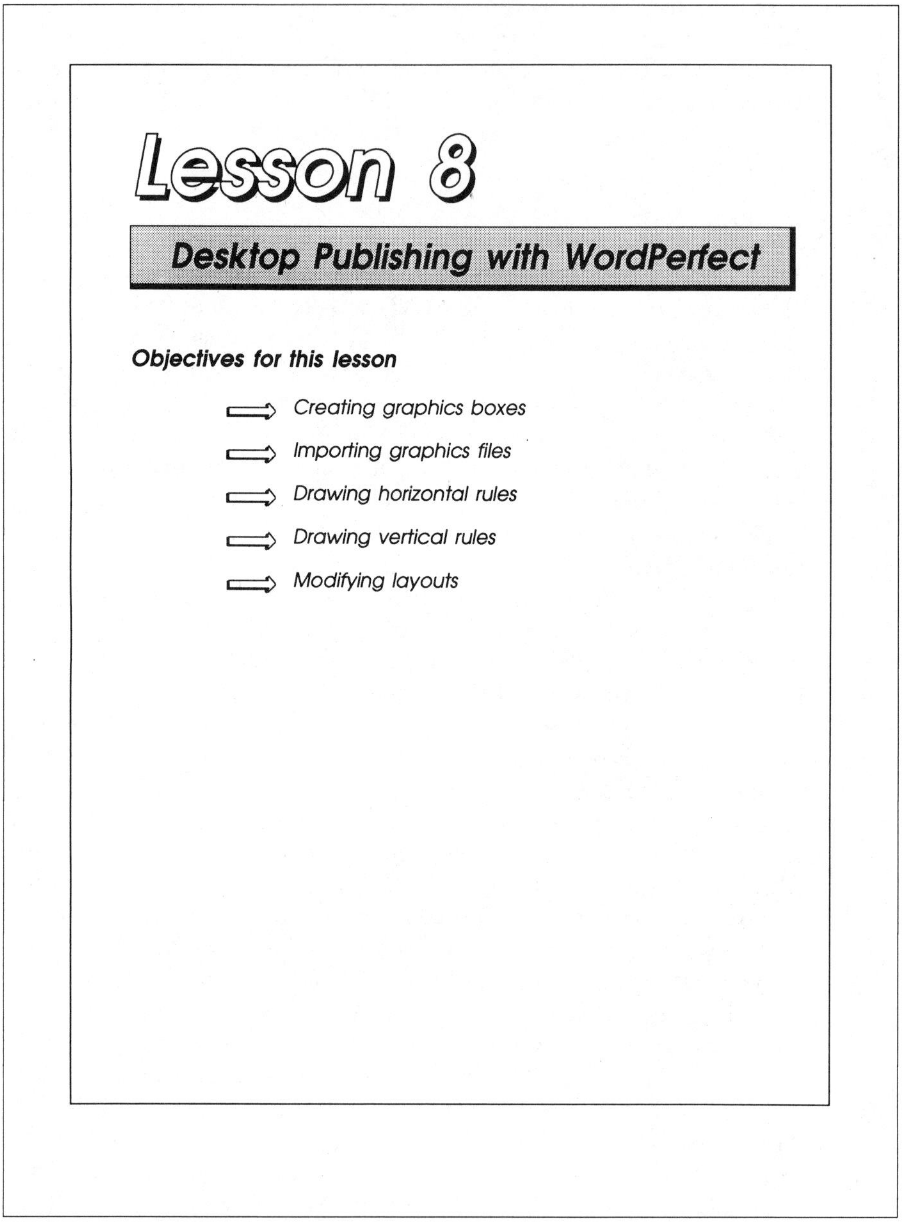

Lesson 8

Desktop Publishing with WordPerfect

Objectives for this lesson

⇨ Creating graphics boxes

⇨ Importing graphics files

⇨ Drawing horizontal rules

⇨ Drawing vertical rules

⇨ Modifying layouts

FIGURE 19.12: Opening page for Lesson 8 in a PC Teach training manual. This design uses the Shadow appearance attribute with a large type to emphasize the lesson number. The name of the lesson is entered in a Text box that sets Border Style to Thick for the right and bottom sides to carry through the three-dimensional effect set up by the Shadow attribute. The arrows that point out the lesson's objectives are contained in small Figure boxes that use the ARROW1.WPG file supplied with the program.

WordPerfect 5.0's graphics and desktop publishing features have opened up a whole new world for WordPerfect users. You can now create horizontal and vertical rules, and boxes containing text, figures, or tables, and you can use illustrations created in other programs such as Lotus 1-2-3, as well as scanned images or photographs.

Using the Graphics key

In this exercise, you will learn how easy it is to retrieve graphic images created in a different program. You will retrieve a WordPerfect file from the data disk, and import an Lotus graph into it on the second page.

1. **Press Retrieve (Shift-F10) and type *LOTUSGRA.LES***	Begin by retrieving the file named LOTUSGRA.LES from your data disk. Notice that it is a two-page document that explains how to create a simple bar graph using the Lotus 1-2-3 spreadsheet.
2. **Place the cursor in the blank line under the heading EXERCISE 15: LOTUS GRAPHICS**	In the next step, you will create a horizontal rule under the heading.
3. **Press Graphics (Alt F9) and select Line**	The Line option is used to create horizontal or vertical rules; here you will use it to create the horizontal line at the top of the page.
4. **Select the Horizontal Line option**	The Graphics: Horizontal Line menu appears, and you can use it to change the position, length or width of the line, or the amount of gray shading it will have.
5. **Select Horizontal Position, then select Left**	The default setting of Left and Right means the line starts at the left margin and stretches across the entire page. Changing it to Left starts it at the left margin, and allows you to end it before the right margin using the Length of Line option.

Page 58   *Upgrading to WordPerfect 5.0 - PC Teach Workbook 4.99*

FIGURE 19.13: First page of Lesson 8 in a PC Teach training manual. The design of the lesson itself uses only one graphic element: a vertical rule to separate the exercise steps from the accompanying explanations. All of the text elements in the lesson are formatted with styles.

font and line height change for the steps required to complete the exercise. This style also contains an Automatic Paragraph Numbering code to number each step. A paired style called Small is used to set the font and line height for the explanatory text that is entered in the second parallel column. Finally, there are also paired styles called FooterA and FooterB that contain the text, font changes, and formatting for the lesson footers. The FooterA style inserts a footer that is printed only on odd pages, while the FooterB style inserts a footer that is printed only on even pages.

Business Forms

WordPerfect's desktop publishing capabilities can be used to create all kinds of business forms required by your office. Once you create the form template, you can then photocopy the form and use it in printing WordPerfect documents prepared with the Merge feature. Figure 19.14 shows you an invoice form template created with Text boxes and vertical rules.

Figure 19.15 shows you a sample invoice that was prepared by using a merge document named INVOICE.PF. This document uses the ^C Merge code to allow the user to enter all of the required information. It also uses WordPerfect's Math feature to create the subtotal and total amount due. The Advance to Line feature is used to correctly position each ^C code vertically on the page. The tab settings have been modified to correctly position this code horizontally on each line.

Four separate Text boxes were created to make up the body of the invoice (see Figure 19.16). The first Text box is 6.33 inches wide and .25 inch high. It contains the labels *BILLING DATE, CUSTOMER NUMBER,* and *INVOICE NUMBER.* The second Text box is the same size as the first, and it contains no text. The Advance Up feature is used to move the second Text box up so that it touches the first. The vertical lines that separate the three labels were created with the Vertical Line feature. Their horizontal and vertical positions were calculated using a printed copy of the form up to this point. The Text Box options were changed so that Single is used as the border style for all four sides of both boxes.

The third Text box is 6.33 inches wide and 4.5 inches high. Gray Shading was set to 0%. The fourth Text box is 6.33 inches wide and 1.12 inches high. It contains the headings *SUBTOTAL, SALES TAX,* and *AMOUNT DUE,* along with the notice about the late charge. Both of these Text boxes were moved up with the Advance Up feature so that they touch each other. The Text box options for the fourth Text box were changed so that Gray Shading is once again set to 10%.

Before the merge is performed, the printer is loaded with copies of the invoice form printed from the master shown in Figure 19.14. After the merge is completed, the invoice is saved and printed, with the result seen in Figure 19.15.

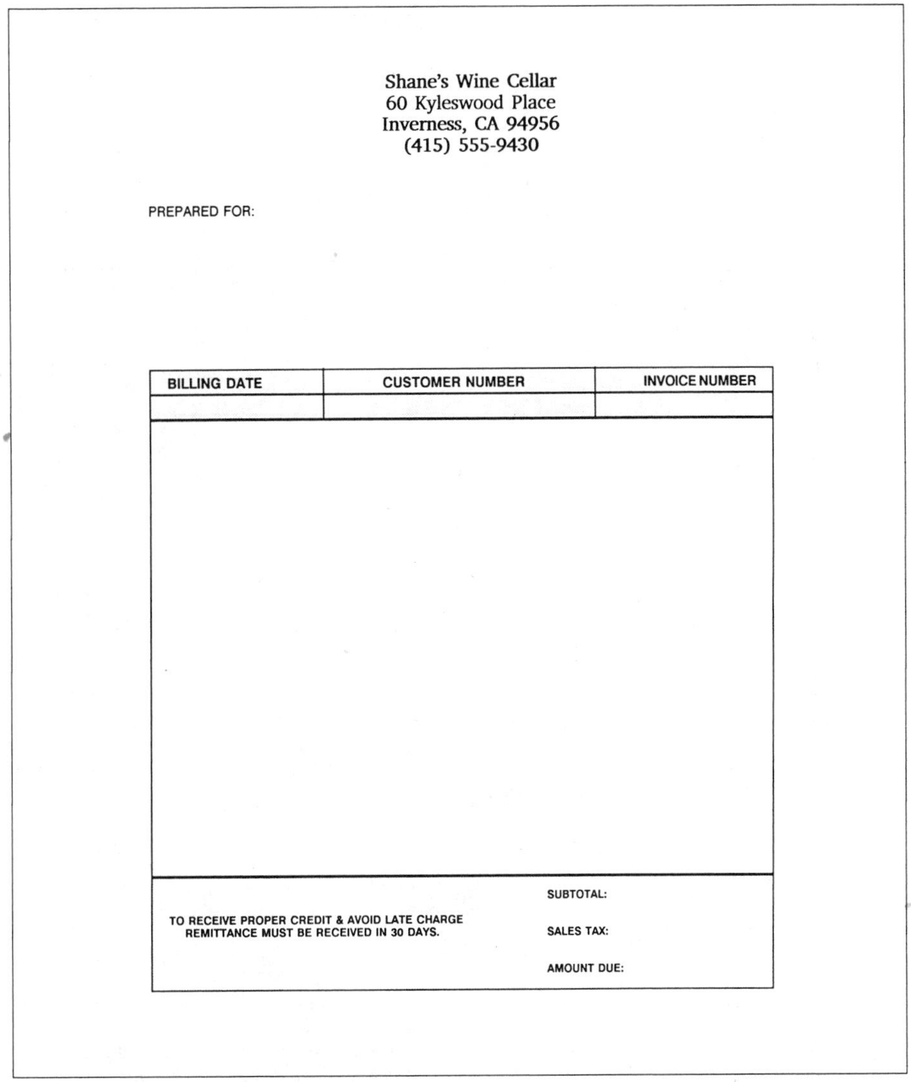

Shane's Wine Cellar
60 Kyleswood Place
Inverness, CA 94956
(415) 555-9430

PREPARED FOR:

BILLING DATE	CUSTOMER NUMBER	INVOICE NUMBER

TO RECEIVE PROPER CREDIT & AVOID LATE CHARGE
REMITTANCE MUST BE RECEIVED IN 30 DAYS.

SUBTOTAL:

SALES TAX:

AMOUNT DUE:

FIGURE 19.14: Printed invoice form template for the wine merchant. This form was created by making four Text boxes and moving them up with the Advance Up feature so that they all touch. The vertical lines separating the *Billing Date, Customer Number,* and *Invoice Number* headings were created with vertical rules.

Shane's Wine Cellar
60 Kyleswood Place
Inverness, CA 94956
(415) 555-9430

PREPARED FOR:

Samuel P. Taylor
1011 Ridge Valley Road
Santa Cruz, CA 94435

BILLING DATE	CUSTOMER NUMBER	INVOICE NUMBER
08-04-89	OMT78056-3	10201

2 bottles	1985 Chalone	$100.00
3 bottles	1984 Meeker-Sonoma	$45.00
1 bottle	1985 Vose-Napa	$20.00

TO RECEIVE PROPER CREDIT & AVOID LATE CHARGE
REMITTANCE MUST BE RECEIVED IN 30 DAYS.

SUBTOTAL:	$165.00
SALES TAX:	$9.09
AMOUNT DUE:	$174.09

FIGURE 19.15: Sample invoice printed using the invoice form. This invoice was created with a merge operation using a primary file that correctly positions the cursor and then pauses for the user to enter each item of information. This primary file also uses the Math feature to calculate the subtotal and total. After the merge is completed, the invoice is printed on a copy of the invoice form shown in Figure 19.14.

```
 ┌TXT 1────────────────────────────────────────────────
 ┌TXT 2────────────────────────────────────────────────
 ┌TXT 3────────────────────────────────────────────────
 ┌TXT 4────────────────────────────────────────────────
 D:\WP\WDC\WINEBILL.TMP                    Doc 2 Pg 1 Ln 1" Pos 1"
 ▌    ▲     ▲     ▲    ▲    ▲    ▲    ▲    ▲    ▲    ▲
 [HRt]
 [HRt]
 [Txt Opt][Text Box:1;;][VLine:2.75",3.7",0.25",0.01",100%][VLine:5.5",3.7",0.25"
 ,0.01",100%][AdvUp:0.21"][Text Box:2;;][VLine:2.75",3.95",0.25",0.01",100%][VLin
 e:5.5",3.95",0.25",0.01",100%][Txt Opt][AdvUp:0.21"][Text Box:3;;][Txt Opt][AdvU
 p:0.25"][Text Box:4;;]█



 Press Reveal Codes to restore screen
```

FIGURE 19.16: Reveal Codes screen for the form template showing the codes for the Text boxes used. Notice the [Adv Up] codes that precede the [Text Box] codes in this screen; they move the boxes up so that they touch each other. The [VLine] codes create the vertical rules that appear in the first and second Text boxes.

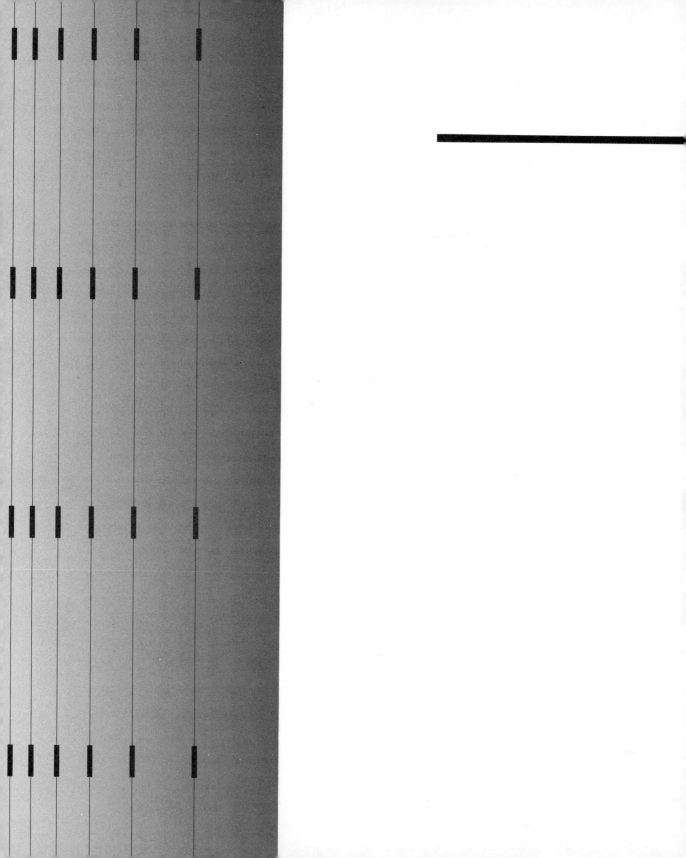

PART V

WORDPERFECT COMMAND AND FEATURE REFERENCE

ADVANCE

Advances the printer to a specific line or position on the page.

KEY SEQUENCE

Shift-F8 (Format)

▼

4 – Other

▼

1 – Advance

▼

1 Up; **2 D**own; **3 L**ine; **4 L**eft; **5 R**ight; **6 P**osition

▼

<measurement to advance> **Enter**

▼

F7 (Exit)

REVEAL CODES

[AdvDn]	Advance Down
[AdvLft]	Advance Left
[AdvRgt]	Advance Right
[AdvToLn]	Advance to Line
[AdvToPos]	Advance to (horizontal) Position
[AdvUp]	Advance Up

USAGE

The Advance feature advances the printer to a specific position on the page. To advance the printer up, down, left, or right of the current printing position (that is, the place where the [Adv] code is entered), you enter a distance that is relative to the cursor's position when you use the command. To advance the printer to a specific line or column, you enter a measurement that is an absolute

705

position on the page. When using the Advance to Line option, you enter the distance from the top of the page. When using the Advance to Position option, you enter the distance from the left edge of the page.

To use the Advance feature, move the cursor to the place where you want the advance to begin and follow the key sequence shown at the beginning of this section. After you press F7 (Exit), type the text to be advanced.

Although the status line will reflect the advance position, the cursor does not move when you use this command. To return to the original position when using Advance Up, Down, Left, or Right, select the opposite Advance option (down if you used up, right if you used left, etc.) and enter the same distance you specified earlier. To return to the original line or column when using Advance to Line or Advance to Position, repeat the advance procedure, selecting the same Advance option but entering the original line or offset position as the distance. To prevent the text from being advanced as indicated, locate and delete the appropriate [Adv] code in the Reveal Codes screen.

The Advance feature is especially useful in layout work involving text and graphics on a page. You can use it to fine-tune the placement of headings in Text boxes and to position text that overlays other types of graphics on the page (see **Graphics**).

Alignment Character

See **Decimal/Align Character**.

Append Block

Adds a marked block of text to the end of another document.

KEY SEQUENCE

To append a sentence, paragraph, or page:

Ctrl-F4 (Move)

▼

1 Sentence; **2 P**aragraph; **3 P**age

▼

4 Append

▼

Append to: <*file name*>

To append a marked block, column, or rectangle:

Alt-F4 (Block)

▼

[highlight block of text with cursor keys]

▼

Ctrl-F4 (Move)

▼

1 Block; **2** Tabular **C**olumn; **3 R**ectangle

▼

4 Append

▼

Append to: *<file name>*

USAGE

When you append a block of text, WordPerfect adds it to the end of a document saved on disk. You can append a discrete block of text like a sentence, paragraph, or page without using Block (Alt-F4) to mark it first. When appending any other type of block (like several words but not an entire sentence, several lines but not an entire paragraph or a tabular column or rectangle), you must use Block to mark the text to be appended before you use Move (Ctrl-F4).

When using either method, you indicate the type of block and select the Append option. You are then asked for the name of the file to which this text will be appended. Type in the file name. If this file is not in the current (default) directory, include the path name. After entering the name, press Enter to have the text added to the end of the disk file.

NOTE

You can also append the text of a disk file to the end of the document currently in the editing screen. To do this, you move to the end of the document (Home Home ↓), select Retrieve Text (Shift-F10), and enter the name of the document whose text you want appended. The same thing happens when you use the Retrieve option on the List Files menu and have a document on the editing screen.

SEE ALSO

Block Operations
Cut and Copy Text
Retrieve

AUTOMATIC REFERENCE

Allows you to mark cross-references that are automatically updated.

KEY SEQUENCE

To mark both the reference and target:

[move to the place where the reference is to appear]

▼

Alt-F5 (Mark Text)

▼

1 Auto **R**ef

▼

3 — Mark **B**oth Reference and Target

▼

1 — **P**age Number
2 — Paragraph/**O**utline Number
3 — **F**ootnote Number
4 — **E**ndnote Number
5 — **G**raphics Box Number

▼

[position the cursor immediately after the target] **Enter**

▼

Target Name: *<target name>* **Enter**

To mark only the reference:

[move to the place where the reference is to appear]

▼

Alt-F5 (Mark Text)

▼

1 Auto **R**ef

▼

1 — Mark **R**eference

▼

1 — **P**age Number
2 — Paragraph/**O**utline Number
3 — **F**ootnote Number
4 — **E**ndnote Number
5 — **G**raphics Box Number

▼

Target Name: *<target name>* **Enter**

To mark only the target:

[position the cursor immediately after the target]

▼

Alt-F5 (Mark Text)

▼

1 Auto **R**ef

▼

2 – Mark **T**arget

▼

Target Name: <*target name*> **Enter**

To generate the automatic references for those where the reference and target were marked separately:

Alt-F5 (Mark Text)

▼

6 Generate

▼

5 – Generate Tables, Indexes, Automatic References, etc.

▼

Existing tables, lists, and indexes will be replaced.
Continue? (Y/N) **Enter** *or any key except N*

REVEAL CODES

[Ref]	Reference (Automatic Reference)
[Target]	Target (Automatic Reference)

USAGE

The Automatic Reference feature maintains and automatically updates references to areas of text, footnotes, endnotes, headers, footers, graphics boxes, or the captions attached to graphics boxes. The place in the document where the reference number will appear when the document is printed is the *reference*. The place in the document that contains the text referred to is the *target*.

You can mark the reference and target at the same time except when referencing a graphics box caption. In this case, you must mark the reference and the target separately. When you mark a reference only, a question mark appears in place of the reference number. This question mark is replaced with the actual figure, note, or page number when you generate the references.

SEE ALSO

Graphics
Mark Text
Master Document

BACKUP, TIMED AND ORIGINAL DOCUMENT

Automatically saves your document at intervals of your choosing or saves a copy of the original document each time you save the document on the editing screen.

KEY SEQUENCE

Shift-F1 (Setup)

▼

1 – Backup

▼

1 – Timed Document Backup
Minutes Between Backups
2 – Original Document Backup

▼

F7 (Exit)

USAGE

WordPerfect periodically saves your document to a temporary backup file if you turn on the Timed Document Backup feature. This guards against a loss of edits should you experience either a machine failure or a loss of power when working. When you exit WordPerfect normally, these backup files are deleted.

The document that is being edited in document window 1 (Doc 1) is saved as WP{WP}.BK1, and the one being edited in document window 2 (Doc 2) is saved as WP{WP}.BK2. If you should be prevented from exiting normally, you can retrieve either of these documents from the directory where they are stored. Then, you can save them under a new name using Save (F10) or Exit (F7).

With the Original Document Backup option, you can have WordPerfect save a copy of the document before your most recent editing changes to it. When you activate this feature, any time you save a document under the same name by answering Yes to the Replace? (Y/N) question, it first saves a copy of the document as it was last saved, using the same file name with the extension .BK!. Then it saves the document on your editing screen, with all of the changes you have made, to disk.

To specify where the backup files made by the Timed Document Backup and Original Document Backup are to be stored, you need to set the Backup Directory from the Setup menu (see **Location of Files**). Note that even when using both of these backup methods, you should still keep backup copies of your work on a different disk. See **Copying Files** for information on how to make these backup copies from within WordPerfect.

SEE ALSO

Copying Files
Location of Auxiliary Files

BASE FONT

Changes the basic font used in printing the document from the cursor's position forward.

KEY SEQUENCE

Ctrl-F8 (Font)
▼
4 Base **Font**
▼
[highlight font with cursor keys]
▼
1 Select; **N N**ame Search

REVEAL CODES

[Font]   Base Font

USAGE

The *current font* represents the font in which the text is normally printed. This font depends upon the printer that you have selected and the initial font that you have assigned to it (see **Printer Selection**) or the initial font selected for the document. To switch to a new basic font in the document, you use the Base Font option on the Font menu (Ctrl- F8). When you select a new font in this way, it becomes the new current font from the cursor's position forward in the document.

The current font also determines what sizes will be used when you select different font size options such as Fine, Small, or Large, or different attribute options like Bold or Italics (see **Font**). For example, if you select a new base font of Times Roman 10 point, WordPerfect will use Times Roman 10 point bold to print boldfaced text in the document, Times Roman 10 Italic to print italicized text, and so on. Likewise, when you make a change to the size, it will use different sized fonts in the Times Roman family, such as Times Roman 6 point for Fine, Times Roman 8 point for Small, Times Roman 12 point for Large, and so forth. The actual sizes chosen for each change in size depend upon the fonts your printer supports and the fonts you have selected for that printer. Moreover, the font choices available when you change the current font with the Base Font option are determined by the fonts you have selected for the printer you are using (see **Cartridges and Fonts**). To prevent a font change from taking place, locate and delete the [Font] code in the Reveal Codes screen.

SEE ALSO

Cartridges and Fonts
Font
Printer Selection: Initial Font

BEEP OPTIONS

Determines whether WordPerfect beeps when an error occurs, a word is to be hyphenated, or a search fails.

KEY SEQUENCE

Shift-F1 (Setup)
▼
5 — Initial Settings
▼
1 — **B**eep Options
▼
1 — Beep on **E**rror
2 — Beep on **H**yphenation
3 — Beep on **S**earch Failure
▼
F7 (Exit)

USAGE

By default, WordPerfect beeps only when prompting you to hyphenate a word if you are using the Hyphenation feature (see **Hyphenation**). You can, however, also have it beep when an error occurs or when a search operation fails. If you don't want to be disturbed by any beeps, you can turn off the beep on the Hyphenation option and leave the others off.

BINDING

Shifts text to the right on odd-numbered pages and to the left on even-numbered pages.

KEY SEQUENCE

Shift-F7 (Print)

▼

B — **B**inding *<measurement for binding width>* **Enter**

▼

F7 (Exit)

USAGE

You use the Binding option on the Print menu (Shift-F7) when your document is going to be reproduced on two-sided copies to ensure that there is sufficient room to bind the document. You set a binding width to determine how far the text is shifted to the right on odd-numbered pages and to the left on even-numbered pages.

The binding width is entered as an absolute measurement from the left or right edge of the paper and overrides the left and right margin settings that are in effect. You can enter the binding width any time prior to printing the document.

If you intend to reproduce the document on just one side of the paper, you can ignore the Binding option; just increase the left margin setting to allow sufficient room for binding.

To remove the binding width before printing a document during the same work session, you need to select the Binding option from the Print menu and enter **0** as the binding width measurement.

BLOCK OPERATIONS

Defines a block of text on which you can perform a number of operations.

KEY SEQUENCE

Alt-F4 (Block)

▼

[highlight block with cursor keys]

▼

[select the operation to be performed on the block]

REVEAL CODES

[Block]   Block on

USAGE

The Block command (Alt-F4) is used to highlight (mark) a section of text for use with other WordPerfect commands. Once you have marked a block of text, you can use any of the following WordPerfect features:

Bold
Center
Delete
Flush Right
Font: Appearance and Size
Format
Macro
Mark Text: Index, List, Table of Authorities, Table of Contents
Move: Block, Tabular Column, Rectangle
Print
Replace
Save
Search
Shell (if using the WordPerfect Library)
Sort
Spell
Style
Switch
Text In/Out
Underline

Marking a Block

To mark a block of text, you position the cursor at the beginning of the block and press Block (Alt-F4). The message

Block on

appears in the lower-left corner of your screen. Position the cursor at the end of the block; as you move the cursor, the text included will be highlighted. Then select the operation you want applied to the block.

When marking the block, you have several options for positioning the cursor. You can use the Search feature to move the cursor forward or backward to a particular place in the document. Press Enter to extend the block to the next [HRt] code (hard return). Type a particular character to extend the block to that character—like a period to include text up to the end of the sentence. Press ↑ or ↓ to extend the block up or down to include a number of lines. Press Ctrl-→ to extend the block to include several words.

Rehighlighting a Block

After you mark the block and select a WordPerfect feature, the highlighting and the *Block on* message will disappear. To rehighlight the block you just used, you press Block (Alt-F4) and then Go To (Ctrl-Home) twice. To move the cursor directly to the beginning of the block, press Go To (Ctrl-Home) followed by Block (Alt-F4).

Press Cancel (F1) or Block (Alt-F4) to turn off the *Block on* prompt and cancel the intended block operation.

SEE ALSO

Bold
Center
Cut and Copy Text
Mark Text
Save Text
Sort
Speller
Underline

BLOCK PROTECT

Prevents a marked block of text from being split by a page break.

KEY SEQUENCE

Alt-F4 (Block)
▼
[highlight text of block with cursor keys]
▼
Shift-F8 (Format)
▼
Protect block? (Y/N) **Y**

REVEAL CODES

[Block Pro:On]	Block Protection On
[Block Pro:Off]	Block Protection Off

USAGE

You can use block protection to ensure that any block of text is not split between pages. If you make editing changes that would split the protected text between pages, WordPerfect will shift the entire block to the following page. This feature can be used effectively to keep tables on a single page.

To block-protect text, move the cursor to the beginning of the block, press Alt-F4 (Block), and move the cursor to the end of the block. Then, press Shift-F8 (Format). WordPerfect will display the prompt

Protect block? (Y/N) No

Type **Y** to have the block protected.

To remove block protection, locate and delete the [Block Pro:On] or [Block Pro:Off] code in the Reveal Codes screen.

SEE ALSO

Conditional End of Page
Page Breaks
Widow/Orphan Protection

BOLD

Enhances the selected text by printing it in a boldface font or with doublestrike.

KEY SEQUENCE

To boldface text as you type it:

F6 (Bold)
▼
[type text to be boldfaced]
▼
F6 (Bold)

To boldface existing text:

Alt-F4 (Block)
▼
[highlight text to be boldfaced]
▼
F6 (Bold)

REVEAL CODES

[BOLD]	Bold On
[bold]	Bold Off

USAGE

WordPerfect allows you to enhance portions of text with boldfacing by placing the text between a pair of Bold formatting codes. Boldfacing is indicated on the screen by double-intensity or a different color. When printing the boldfaced text, the program will either select a bold version of the font in use or doublestrike the text, depending upon the type of printer you have.

You can also boldface text by using Font (Ctrl-F8), selecting the Appearance option (**2** or **A**) and then selecting the Bold option (**1** or **B**).

To remove boldfacing, locate either the [BOLD] or [bold] code in the Reveal Codes screen and delete it. You only have to delete one of the pair to delete both and remove the boldfacing.

When the cursor is located on a boldfaced character in the text, the number at the Pos indicator is shown in the same attribute used by your monitor to display bold text (double-intensity or a new color). As soon as the cursor is moved ahead of or behind the Bold code, this number returns to the normal attribute. Thus, you can refer to the Pos indicator to locate a Bold code for deletion without using the Reveal Codes screen.

When you are about to delete a Bold code in this way (either on purpose or unintentionally), WordPerfect displays the prompt

> Delete [Bold]? (Y/N) No

You must type **Y** for Yes to delete—if you simply press Enter, the boldfacing will remain.

SEE ALSO

> Base Font
> Cartridges and Fonts
> Font

CANCELING A COMMAND

Terminates almost any WordPerfect command that is being carried out.

KEY SEQUENCE

F1 (Cancel)

USAGE

You can use F1 almost any time you wish to cancel the command you have initiated. There are a few exceptions. For example, merge operations are canceled by pressing Merge R (F9). In certain cases, you can press the Esc key two or more times to cancel a particular command.

When you have not initiated a WordPerfect command, the Cancel key has the function of undeleting text. For information about this use of Cancel, see **Undelete**.

SEE ALSO

Esc Key
Keyboard Layout
Undelete

CANCELING PRINTING

See **Print Job, Cancel**.

CARTRIDGES AND FONTS

Allows you to select the fonts you want to use in the document.

KEY SEQUENCE

To select fonts:

Shift-F7 (Print)
▼
S – **S**elect Printer
▼
[highlight the printer that uses the fonts]
▼
3 – **E**dit
▼
5 – **C**artridges and Fonts
▼
[highlight Cartridge Fonts *or* Soft Fonts*]*
▼
1 Select **F**onts
▼
[mark fonts with ∗ if they will be present when job begins
or with ✛ if WordPerfect must load them during print job]
▼
F7 (Exit) *five times*

To designate where the soft fonts are located:

Shift-F7 (Print)
▼
S – **S**elect Printer
▼

[highlight the printer that uses the fonts]

▼

3 − **E**dit

▼

7 − Path for **D**ownloadable
Fonts and Printer
Command Files *<drive/directory path>* **Enter**

▼

F7 (Exit) *three times*

USAGE

If your printer can use different cartridges or soft fonts, you need to select them before you use them in the document (by selecting a new base font, selecting a new initial font for the document, or changing the size or appearance on the Font menu). The Cartridges and Fonts menu will show you the number of cartridges that the selected printer supports, if any. It will also show you how much memory is available for downloading soft fonts. At the bottom of the screen, there are three options:

1 Select **F**onts; **2** Change **Q**uantity; **N N**ame search: 1

If your laser printer has more than 512K of memory, select the Quantity option (**2** or **Q**). Enter the amount of additional memory in kilobytes above the standard configuration for your printer (512K for the LaserJet), plus the amount of memory available for soft fonts, shown on the screen. For example, if you equip your LaserJet with 1.5Mb of total memory (1Mb or 1024K additional), you enter **1374** for the quantity—1024K extra memory plus the 350K currently available for soft fonts.

To make changes to the font selections, WordPerfect must have access to the printer definition files. Make sure that you have the appropriate Printer disk available or have set the path for the printer files correctly before attempting to select new fonts.

To select cartridge fonts, be sure that the highlight cursor is on *Cartridges* and then choose the Select Fonts option (**1** or **F**). Mark the cartridges you wish to use by highlighting them and typing an asterisk (*). Press Exit (F7) twice and WordPerfect will update the printer definition file.

To select soft (downloadable) fonts, move the highlight cursor to Soft Fonts and then choose the Select Fonts option (**1** or **F**). To quickly locate the font you want to add from the list, use Name Search by pressing F2 and typing in the first few letters of the font name.

Mark with an asterisk (*) all of the fonts that will be present (downloaded) before the print job begins. Mark all of the fonts that will be downloaded during the print job with a plus (+). Press Exit (F7) twice and WordPerfect will update the printer definition file.

If you have marked fonts that are to be downloaded by WordPerfect during the print job, you must indicate the directory that contains the fonts. Note that before printing you must download any fonts marked with *, using the Initialize Printer option on the Print menu (Shift-F7 I). To indicate the directory containing the soft font files, select the Path for Downloadable Fonts and Printer Command Files option (**7** or **D**) and enter the complete path name.

The fonts you have selected will appear on the Base Font menu and may be used in the document by selecting either a new initial font for the printer, a new initial font for the document, a new base font, or a new size or appearance (see **Base Font**, **Font**, and **Initial Settings**).

To unmark fonts, repeat the procedure for editing the fonts for the selected printer. If you marked a font with an asterisk (*), highlight it again and type another * to unmark it. If you marked the font with a plus (+), type + again to unmark it.

SEE ALSO

Base Font
Font
Printer Selection

CASE CONVERSION

Converts a marked block of text to uppercase or lowercase letters.

KEY SEQUENCE

Alt-F4 (Block)
▼
[highlight text to be converted]
▼
Shift-F3 (Switch)
▼
1 Uppercase; **2 L**owercase

USAGE

To convert a block of text to all uppercase or all lowercase letters, you simply mark it as a block with Block (Alt-F4) and then select Switch (Shift-F3). To convert the marked text to uppercase, select the Uppercase option by typing **1** or **U**. To convert it to lowercase, select the Lowercase option by typing **2** or **L**.

Note that converting text to lowercase will not affect a capital letter at the beginning of a sentence. For example

...and John Smith. He...

becomes

...and john smith. He...

CENTER

Centers text on a line between the left and right margins.

KEY SEQUENCE

To center text as you type it:

Shift-F6 (Center)
▼
<text to be centered> **Enter**

To center existing text:

Alt-F4 (Block)
▼
[highlight text to be centered]
▼
Shift-F6 (Center)
▼
[Cntr]? (Y/N) **Yes**

REVEAL CODES

[Cntr]	Centering On
[C/A/Flrt]	Centering Off

USAGE

To center text on a line between the left and right margin settings, press Shift-F6 (Center), type the text, and press the Enter key. To center text after it has been entered, mark the text (this can include several lines) with Block (Alt-F4) and then select Center (Shift-F6). WordPerfect will display the prompt

[Cntr]? (Y/N) No

To have the marked text centered, simply type **Y** for Yes.

To remove centering, locate either the [Cntr] or [C/A/Flrt] code in the Reveal Codes screen and delete it.

SEE ALSO

Block Operations
Flush Right

CENTER PAGE (TOP TO BOTTOM)

Centers text on a page between the top and bottom margins.

KEY SEQUENCE

Home Home Home ↑
▼
Shift-F8 (Format)
▼
2 – **P**age
▼
1 – **C**enter Page (top to bottom) **Y**
▼
F7 (Exit)

REVEAL CODES

[Center Pg]   Center Page Top to Bottom

USAGE

The Center Page (Top to Bottom) command is used when you want to print less than an entire page of text so that it is centered vertically between your top and bottom margins. This is most often used for title sheets of reports and papers.

When using this command, you must remember to position the cursor at the very top of the page before entering the [Center Pg] code.

Most often, when you want text centered vertically, you also want it centered horizontally (see **Center**).

To remove centering on the page, locate and delete the [Center Pg] code in the Reveal Codes screen.

SEE ALSO

Center

CODES

Instruct the printer on how to format the text and graphics in your document.

KEY SEQUENCE

Alt-F3 (Reveal Codes)
▼
[view or edit codes and text in the Reveal Codes screen]
▼
Alt-F3 (Reveal Codes)

REVEAL CODES

See **Appendix D** for a complete list of WordPerfect's hidden codes.

USAGE

WordPerfect enters hidden formatting codes into your document as you use various commands. These codes are then sent to your printer when you print the document. They instruct the printer on how to accomplish various formatting changes in the document.

Some codes, like those used to boldface and underline text, are inserted in pairs, with one code turning on the effect and the other one turning it off.

WordPerfect keeps the formatting codes hidden from view on the editing screen. To see them, you must press Reveal Codes (Alt-F3). This causes the program to split the screen into two windows. The lower window shows the text with all of the codes inserted by WordPerfect commands. WordPerfect indicates the position of the cursor in the Reveal Codes screen by highlighting the code or character. When using Reveal Codes, you can use all of the standard Word-Perfect editing features (including Undelete). When you want the Reveal Codes screen to disappear, press Reveal Codes (Alt-F3) a second time.

Most of the time you use the Reveal Codes screen to locate the position of a code that you wish to delete or change (you can't always tell when the cursor is on a code just by looking at the regular editing screen). To quickly locate the position of a code, you can use WordPerfect's Search feature (see **Search: Searching for Codes**).

You can prevent a formatting change that you have introduced in the document by locating and deleting the code in the Reveal Codes screen. If the cursor is located on the code, press the Del key to remove it. If the cursor is after the code, press the Backspace key to remove it. If you delete a code in error, press Cancel (F1) and select the Restore option (**1** or **R**).

Appendix D shows you all of the hidden codes used in WordPerfect.

SEE ALSO

Appendix D: WordPerfect's Hidden Codes

COLORS/FONTS/ATTRIBUTES

Allows you to change the way particular text attributes are displayed on your screen.

KEY SEQUENCE

Shift-F1 (Setup)

▼

3 – Display

▼

2 – Colors/Fonts/Attributes

▼

*[select colors/fonts/attributes from menu(s)—
varies according to display card and monitor]*

▼

Shift-F3 (Switch) to set Doc 2

▼

F7 (Exit)

USAGE

Colors/Fonts/Attributes allows you to choose how the 16 font attributes available from the Size and Appearance menus (accessed with Font—Ctrl-F8), as well as the attribute used to show a marked block of text, are displayed on your screen. The on-screen display selected for each attribute is independent of the way it will be produced by your printer.

The settings selected with the Colors/Fonts/Attributes option are in effect each time you start WordPerfect. The settings assigned to the Doc 1 screen are saved independently of those for the Doc 2 screen. After selecting your settings for the Doc 1 screen, you can use Switch (Shift-F3) to make the selections for the Doc 2 screen. Use Move (Ctrl-F4) to copy the settings from Doc 1 to Doc 2 and vice versa. After you use Switch and Move, WordPerfect will display the prompt

Copy attributes from other document? (Y/N) No

Type **Y** for Yes to have the settings from one document window copied to the other.

The choices available for displaying different attributes are determined by the type of display card and monitor you are using. The differences are outlined in the following sections.

Monochrome

If you are using a monochrome monitor with a display card other than the Hercules Graphics Card Plus (with RamFont capabilities—see below), you can only set the attributes using underlining, double-intensity (bold), blinking, and inverse video (blocked). When you select the Colors/Fonts/Attributes option from the Display menu of the Setup key, you are presented immediately with the Set Attributes screen. Here, you may alter some of the default settings by changing the Y(es) or N(o) settings for each attribute. You can use the space bar to toggle between Y and N when changing a particular attribute. As you make a change, you can see its effect by looking at the sample in the far right column of the table.

Color

If you have a color monitor, you can set different foreground/background color combinations to represent different attributes. The number of color combinations available depends upon the type of color display card you are using. If you are using an EGA (with sufficient memory) or VGA card, you can select among five different fonts (for showing italics, underline, small caps, etc.), or increase the number of displayable characters from 256 to 512. When you use these options (instead of Normal Font Only), the number of colors is limited to eight.

When using the Colors/Fonts/Attributes option for a color system, you can modify the Fast Text Display option. If you set this to Yes, WordPerfect will rewrite the screen faster, although you may experience "snow" on the screen.

If you have a CGA, PC3270, or MCGA (or EGA with limited memory or in a mode that displays more than 25 lines), you select colors for each attribute on the Set Screen Colors menu by assigning new foreground and/or background colors. To set a new color combination, move to the foreground color and type the letter of a listed color, then move to the background color and type its letter. As you make the change, the Sample column will immediately reflect it.

If you have an EGA (with sufficient memory) or VGA card, you select one of the fonts available by typing an asterisk (*). If the asterisk doesn't appear, there is a problem in loading the appropriate .FRS file (make sure that all .FRS files that begin with EGA have been copied to your WordPerfect directory).

When you select the Screen Colors option (**1** or **S**), you set the color combinations just as described for the CGA card. If you have selected a font, you assign it to an attribute by typing **Y** for Yes or **N** for No (or use the space bar to toggle between the two) in the appropriate column.

Hercules Graphics Cards with RamFont

If you have a Hercules Graphics Card Plus or InColor Card with RamFont, when you select the Colors/Fonts/Attributes option you are presented with the following menu that includes three Font/Color options (when you select one of these options, the program marks it with an asterisk.)

1 – **S**creen Attributes
2 – 12 Fonts, 256 Characters
3 – 6 Fonts, 512 Characters
4 – **N**ormal Font only

Choose option 2 to use 12 fonts with 256 characters or option 3 to use 6 fonts with 512 characters. If you select option 4, Normal Font Only, your display will act as though you have a standard Hercules Graphics card (even if you have a color monitor) and you must follow the procedure for a monochrome system (see **Monochrome** above).

After selecting the number of fonts, select option 1 if you wish to change any of the predefined attributes. There are five capabilities that you can set for certain attributes, starting with Font. To change the number of the font, you can type a number between 1 and 6 if using 6 fonts or 1–9 and A–C if you are using 12 fonts. You can also use the space bar or the plus (+) and minus (–) keys on the numeric pad to cycle through available font choices. Of course, you can change the other capabilities as well as the font for certain attributes.

NOTE

Changing the screen colors in no way affects the colors used in printing. If you have a color printer, select the Print Color option on the Font menu (see **Print Color**).

SEE ALSO

Display, Setup: Graphics Screen Type
Font: Size and Appearance

COLUMNS, TEXT (NEWSPAPER AND PARALLEL)

Allows you to format your text using either newspaper or parallel columns.

KEY SEQUENCE

To define newspaper or parallel text columns:

Alt-F7 (Math/Columns)
▼
4 Column **D**ef
▼
1 – **T**ype
2 – **N**umber of Columns
3 – **D**istance Between Columns
4 – **M**argins
▼
F7 (Exit)

To turn text columns on and off in the document:

Alt-F7 (Math/Columns)
▼
3 Column On/Off

To change the display of text columns on the screen:

Shift-F1 (Setup)
▼
3 – **D**isplay
▼
8 – **S**ide-by-side Columns Display **Y** or **N**
▼
F7 (Exit)

REVEAL CODES

[Col Def]	Column Definition
[Col Off]	End of Text Columns
[Col On]	Beginning of Text Columns

USAGE

WordPerfect can automatically format two different types of text columns: *newspaper* (sometimes called "winding" or "snaking" columns) and *parallel* (or "comparison") columns. Neither of these is to be confused with tabular columns, which are set simply by pressing Tab to go the next tab stop. Newspaper columns are used with continuous text (as in a newsletter), for which it does not matter where the material in the column ends, because the program wraps the text to the top of the next column. Parallel columns are used when the material consists of separate items that should remain together on a page (such as scripts).

There are several basic steps involved in using either type of text column:

1. Position the cursor at the beginning of the area to be formatted in columns or anywhere before this point in the document.
2. Define the columns.
3. Turn on the columns.
4. Enter the text for the columns.
5. Turn off the columns.

Defining the Columns

The steps involved in defining Newspaper and Parallel columns are very similar.

1. Press Alt-F7 (Math/Columns).
2. Select the Column Def option (**4** or **D**).
3. Select the Type option (**1** or **T**). WordPerfect displays the options

   Column Type: **1 N**ewspaper; **2 P**arallel; **3** Parallel with **B**lock Protect: 0

4. Select the appropriate column type: **1** or **N** for newspaper, **2** or **P** for parallel (without block protection), or **3** or **B** for parallel with block protection.
5. Select the Number option (**2** or **N**) and enter the number of columns you want (the default is 2 and you can set up to 24).
6. WordPerfect automatically calculates the distance between columns depending upon the number and the margin settings. If you wish to override this distance, select the Distance Between Columns option (**3** or **D**) and enter the distance you want to use.
7. WordPerfect automatically calculates the left and right margin settings for the columns depending upon the number of columns, the distance between them, and the margin settings. If you wish to have unequal columns, select the Margins option (**4** or **M**) and the the left and right margin settings for the column (or columns) you wish to change.
8. Press Exit (F7) to save your column definition.

When you define text columns, WordPerfect inserts a [Col Def] code in your document. This code includes the number (but not the type) of columns followed by the left and right margin setting of each column defined.

Turning On the Columns

After defining the columns, you are returned to the Math/Columns menu. If you wish to use your columns at the cursor's present position, select the Column On/Off option (**3** or **C**). If you wish to use the columns somewhere later on in the document, exit from this menu, move the cursor to the place where you want your columns to begin, and then return to this option. When you turn on columns, WordPerfect inserts the code [Col On] in the document.

You can't use the Column On/Off option on the Math/Columns menu until after you have defined your columns. If you have defined several different columns in a document, WordPerfect will use the one whose [Col Def] code immediately precedes the [Col On] code.

Editing the Text Columns

When typing or editing the text for your columns, you can use most Word-Perfect editing features. However, you can't sort, add footnotes, or change the margin settings. In addition, movement between columns is a little different in Column mode; these techniques are summarized in Table V.1. The delete keys work within a single column. This means that pressing Delete to the End of Page (Ctrl-Page Down) deletes from the cursor to the end of the column.

KEY SEQUENCE	RESULT
Ctrl-Home → or ←	Moves cursor between columns
Ctrl-Home Home ←	Moves to the first column
Ctrl-Home Home →	Moves to the last column
→	Moves to the first character of the next column when the cursor is on the last character in one column
←	Moves to the last character of the previous column when the cursor is on the first character in one column
Ctrl-Enter	Ends a column and moves to the next column; In a rightmost newspaper-style column, also creates a page break

Note: Other cursor control key sequences work as they do in editing mode and scroll all columns simultaneously.

TABLE V.1: Cursor Movement in Column Mode

You can use Move (Ctrl-F4) to cut or copy a sentence or paragraph in a single column. However, to cut or copy an entire column (equivalent to a page), you must use Block (Alt-F4) with Block Move or Copy. Do not try to use the Tabular Column option to move a column, as a text column is not defined by Tab stops and can't be properly retrieved as a tabular column.

NEWSPAPER COLUMNS

When entering text in newspaper-style columns, WordPerfect inserts a Soft Page code [SPg] when you reach the bottom margin of the page and the cursor moves to the top of the next column. To end a column before you reach the bottom margin, press Ctrl-Enter (Hard Page) to insert a Hard Page code [HPg]. To shorten the length of all newspaper columns on the page, increase the bottom margin.

PARALLEL COLUMNS

When entering text in parallel columns, you press Ctrl-Enter (Hard Page) to move to the next column across. When you press Ctrl-Enter after entering the text for the last column, the cursor returns to the beginning of the first column. If you are using parallel columns without block protection, the codes

[Col Off]
[HRt]
[Col On]

are inserted into the document at this point. If you are using parallel columns with block protection, the codes

[Block Pro:Off][Col Off]
[Hrt]
[Block Pro:On][Col On]

are inserted into the document. All items between the [Block Pro:On] and [Block Pro:Off] codes are kept together on a page. If the material will be split across pages by a soft page break [SPg], WordPerfect will move it all to the next page.

Turning Off the Columns

When you are finished entering your columns and wish to return to the normal format of your document, you need to turn off the columns. To do this, press Alt-F7 (Math/Columns) and select the Column On/Off option (**3** or **C**). WordPerfect inserts a [Col Off] code in your document at the cursor's position.

Changing the Display of Columns

When working with text columns, you can speed up scrolling and rewriting the screen by having WordPerfect display each column on a separate page (as opposed to side by side, the default). To turn off the side-by-side display, press Shift-F1 (Setup), select the Display option (**3** or **D**), select the Side-by-side Columns Display option (**8** or **S**), type **N** to change Yes to No, and press Enter and F7 (Exit). To change the display back to side-by-side, repeat this procedure, this time typing **Y** for Yes.

To delete columns in a document, locate and delete the [Col Def] code in the Reveal Codes screen.

SEE ALSO

Tabs (for creating tabular columns)

COMPOSE

Allows you to create digraphs and diacriticals or select a special symbol or character from one of WordPerfect's character sets.

KEY SEQUENCE

To create a digraph or diacritical:

Ctrl-2 (Compose)

▼

<first character> <second character>

To select a character from one of WordPerfect's character sets:

Ctrl-2 (Compose)

▼

<character set number>, <character number> **Enter**

REVEAL CODES

[*<compose char>*: *<char set num>*, *<char code num>*]

where *compose char* is the special character like ➞, *char set num* is the character set number like 6, and *char code num* is the number of that character in the set like 21. Note that this hidden code only appears when you move the cursor on the Compose character in the Reveal Codes window. For example, if you create the right arrow symbol with compose and position the cursor on it in the Reveal Codes window, you will see

[→:6,21]

displayed in the Reveal Codes screen.

USAGE

You can use Compose (Ctrl-2, not to be confused with Ctrl-F2, Spell) to create digraphs like æ or diacriticals like é or ñ. To produce such characters, you press Compose (Ctrl-2) and then enter the two characters that make up the special character. For example, to produce æ, you follow these steps:

1. Press Ctrl-2 (Compose).
2. Type **ae** (or **ea**—the order in which the characters are entered doesn't matter).

As soon as you type the *a* and the *e,* the æ will appear at the cursor's position. However, the fact that you can create these special characters on your screen doesn't mean that your printer can reproduce them. This depends upon the printer and fonts that you are using.

You can also use the Compose feature to produce specific characters in one of the many characters sets created by WordPerfect. Each set is assigned a number, as is each character in that set. To view the character sets, you need to retrieve the document CHARACTR.DOC on the Conversion disk. You can also retrieve the document CHARMAP.TST to see which of these characters your printer can produce.

To enter a character from one of these sets, you follow these steps:

1. Press Ctrl-2 (Compose).
2. Enter the number of the character set.
3. Type a comma, enter the number of the character in that set, and press Enter.

For example, to enter the ½ symbol, which is character 17 of character set 4, you press Ctrl-2 (Compose), then enter **4,17** and press Enter. If your printer can't produce the character you entered with Compose, you will see a solid rectangle instead of the desired character in your document.

To remove the character, delete it as you would any other character in the document.

NOTE

You can use Ctrl-V instead of Ctrl-2 when using the Compose feature. When you press Ctrl-V, WordPerfect responds with

Key =

You then enter the compose sequence as described in the Usage section above and press the Enter key.

SEE ALSO

Keyboard Layout
Overstrike

CONCORDANCE

See **Indexes: Creating a Concordance File.**

CONDITIONAL END OF PAGE

Ensures that a specific number of lines of text remain together on a page.

KEY SEQUENCE

[move the cursor to the line above the lines to keep together]

▼

Shift-F8 (Format)

▼

4 – Other

▼

2 – Conditional End of Page

▼

Number of Lines to Keep Together: *<number of lines>*

▼

F7 (Exit)

REVEAL CODES

[Cndl EOP]   Conditional End of Page

USAGE

The Conditional End of Page command is used to keep a group of lines together on a page. Once the group of lines is marked, if subsequent changes to an earlier part of the document result in a soft page break within the block, WordPerfect will move the entire block to the beginning of the next page (resulting in a shorter previous page).

To use the Conditional End of Page command, you must count up the number of lines you want to keep together. Before you begin the command procedure, locate the cursor somewhere on the line above those that are always to remain together. Then, follow the key sequence shown above. To remove the conditional end of page, locate and delete the [Cndl EOP] code in the Reveal Codes screen.

NOTE

You can also use Block Protect to accomplish the same thing. When you use this command, you don't have to know the number of lines involved, as you indicate the text to stay on a page by marking it as a block.

SEE ALSO

Block Protection
Widow/Orphan Protection

COPYING FILES

Allows you to copy files between disks and directories from within Word-Perfect.

KEY SEQUENCE

To copy a single file located in the current directory:

F5 (List Files) **Enter**

▼

[highlight file]

▼

8 Copy

▼

Copy this file to: *<drive letter/path name>* **Enter**

To copy multiple files located in the current directory:

F5 (List Files) **Enter**

▼

*[type * before each file to be copied]*

▼

8 Copy

▼

Copy marked files? (Y/N) **Y**

▼

Copy all files to: *<drive letter/path name>* **Enter**

USAGE

WordPerfect allows you to copy files to a new disk or directory from the List Files menu. To copy a single file, highlight the name on the List Files screen and select the Copy option (**8** or **C**). WordPerfect will display the prompt

> Copy this file to:

Enter the drive letter (as in **B**:) if you want to copy the file to a new disk. Enter the entire path name (as in **C:\WP\LTRS**), if you want to copy it to a new directory.

To copy multiple files at one time, mark each file by highlighting it and typing an asterisk (*). To copy all of the files in the list, press Alt-F5 and select the Copy option. The prompt

> Copy marked files? (Y/N) No

will appear. Type **Y** for Yes, designate the drive/directory for these copies in response to the prompt

> Copy all files to:

and press Enter.

SEE ALSO

Directories: Changing Directories
List Files

CURSOR MOVEMENT

Allows you to position the cursor (indicating where text or formatting codes are entered) through the document.

KEY SEQUENCE

Refer to Table V.2.

USAGE

WordPerfect has many key combinations that move the cursor through a document, as shown in Table V.2. However, you can only use these techniques to move through existing text or codes. WordPerfect will not allow you to move the cursor beyond the last text character or formatting code.

TO MOVE	KEY SEQUENCE
Character by character	← or →
Word by word	Ctrl-← or Ctrl-→
To the beginning of a line	Home ←
To the end of a line	Home → or End
To the end of the sentence	Ctrl-Home .
To the next occurrence of a character	Ctrl-Home <*character*>
To the top of the screen	Home ↑ or − (minus)
To the bottom of the screen	Home ↓ or + (plus)
To previous screens	Home ↑ or − (minus) repeatedly
To following screens	Home ↓ or + (plus) repeatedly
To the previous page	PgUp
To the next page	PgDn
To the top of the page	Ctrl-Home ↑
To the bottom of the page	Ctrl-Home ↓
To a specified page	Ctrl-Home <*page number*> Enter
To the last cursor position before the cursor movement command	Ctrl-Home Ctrl-Home
To the beginning of the last-defined block	Ctrl-Home Alt-F4
To the beginning of the document	Home Home ↑
To the end of the document	Home Home ↓

TABLE V.2: WordPerfect's Cursor Movement Techniques

Arrow Keys

WordPerfect uses the four arrow keys to move the cursor one character at a time in the four directions. If you have the original IBM PC, PC/XT, or PC/AT keyboard, these keys are combined with the numeric keypad. If you have the IBM enhanced keyboard, these keys exist both on the numeric keypad and separately; you may use either set of arrow keys to move the cursor provided that Num Lock isn't engaged (indicated by the flashing Pos indicator on the status line and an indicator light on some keyboards).

Word Right/Left

To go to the beginning of the next word to the right, press Ctrl-→. To go to the beginning of the next word to the left, press Ctrl-←.

Home

You press Home plus one of the arrow keys to move the cursor to the limits of the editing screen: Home-→ to go to the end of the line; Home-← to the beginning; Home-↑ to go to the top of the screen; and Home-↓ to the bottom. You can also move the cursor to the end of the line by simply pressing the End key.

To go to the very beginning of the document, before any codes, you press Home three times followed by the ↑ key. To go to the very end of the document, press Home three times followed by ↓.

Screen Up/Down

To move the cursor by screens and scroll the text, you use the Screen Up key, which is the minus key (–) on the numeric keypad, or the Screen Down key, which is the plus key (+) on the numeric keypad. The first time you press Screen Up, it takes the cursor to the top of the screen. The second time and succeeding times, it scrolls the text down by screenfuls. The Screen Down key works the same way, only in the opposite direction. Note that you can't use the Screen Up and Screen Down keys if you have engaged Num Lock to enter numbers in the document from the numeric keypad.

Page Up/Down

The Page Up key on the cursor pad moves the cursor to the top of previous page. The Page Down key moves it to the beginning of the following page.

Go To

Go To (Ctrl-Home) moves the cursor to the next occurrence of a specific character, to a specific page or text column, or to the previous cursor position (see **Go To**).

SEE ALSO

Esc Key
Go To

CURSOR SPEED

Allows you to increase or decrease the rate at which certain keys are repeated.

KEY SEQUENCE

Shift-F1 (Setup)
▼
2 – Cursor Speed
▼
1 15; **2** 20; **3** 30; **4** 40; **5** 50; **6 N**ormal
▼
F7 (Exit)

USAGE

Many keys in WordPerfect, like the arrow keys, Screen Up/Down, Page Up/Down, and all the ordinary character keys, repeat when you hold them down. The Cursor Speed option on the Setup menu allows you increase or decrease the rate of the repetition. This rate is measured in characters per second. The normal speed (selected with the Normal option) is the characters per second considered normal for your keyboard. You can increase this up to 50 characters per second. When you select a new rate, it remains in effect each time you use Word-Perfect.

NOTE

The Cursor Speed option is incompatible with some memory- resident programs. Also, you may find that this feature doesn't work properly on some IBM-compatible computers. See **WordPerfect Startup Options** for information on starting the program using the /NC startup option, which disables this feature.

CUT AND COPY TEXT

Allows you to move or copy text within a document or between two documents.

KEY SEQUENCE

To move or copy a sentence, paragraph, or page:

Ctrl-F4 (Move)
▼
1 Sentence; **2 P**aragraph; **3 P**age
▼
1 Move; **2 C**opy
▼
[move cursor to place where text is to be moved or copied] **Enter**

To move or copy a marked block, column, or rectangle:

Alt-F4 (Block)

▼

[highlight block of text with cursor keys]

▼

Ctrl-F4 (Move)

▼

1 **B**lock; **2** Tabular **C**olumn; **3** **R**ectangle

▼

1 **M**ove; **2** **C**opy

▼

[move cursor to place where text is to be moved or copied] **Enter**

USAGE

WordPerfect provides you with two methods for moving or copying text. When you move text, it is cut from its original position and relocated in the new position you indicate. When you copy text, it remains in its original position and is copied to the new position you indicate. To move or copy text between document windows, press Shift-F3 (Switch) before pressing Enter to retrieve the text.

If you want to move or copy a tabular column (see **Marking a Tabular Column**), a rectangle (see **Marking a Rectangle**), or any block that is not an entire sentence, paragraph, or page, you need to mark the block before you move or copy it.

Text that has been moved or copied remains in a special place in the computer's memory (known as a *buffer*) even after it has been retrieved the first time. To retrieve another copy of the text elsewhere in the document, you take these steps:

1. Relocate the cursor to the place where you want the second copy to appear.
2. Press Ctrl-F4 (Move).
3. Select the Retrieve option by typing **4** or **R**.
4. Select the appropriate option: **1** or **B** for Block (use this option even if you cut or copied an entire sentence, paragraph, or page); **2** or **C** for tabular column; or **3** or **R** for rectangle.

You can also do this by pressing Shift-F10 (Retrieve) and then the Enter key.

Marking a Tabular Column

To mark a tabular column for moving or copying, you must have each column separated by at least one tab stop. Move the cursor to the first tab stop in the first line of the column. Press Block, then move the cursor to the beginning of the column in the last line. Then press Move and select the Tabular Column option. WordPerfect will highlight just the column. Finally, choose either the Copy or Move option and complete the procedure by moving the cursor to the column's new position and pressing Enter.

Marking a Rectangle

A rectangular block is marked for moving or copying from corner to corner. To mark a rectangle, position the cursor at one corner—either the upper-left or the lower-right—and press Block. Then move the cursor to the opposite corner and press Move. Select the Rectangle option (**3** or **R**), choose either Copy or Move, and complete the procedure by moving the cursor to the rectangle's new position and pressing Enter.

To abandon the move or copy operation that you have initiated, press F1 (Cancel). If the marked block disappears from your editing screen when you use Cancel, press Ctrl-F4 (Move) and select the Retrieve and Block (or Column or Rectangle) options to have it reappear in its original position.

SEE ALSO

Appending a Block
Deleting Text: Deleting a Block

DASHES

Prevents hyphenated words from being separated between two lines when the hyphenated text is at the end of a line.

KEY SEQUENCE

To create a single dash:

Home -

To create a double dash:

Home - -

REVEAL CODES

-          Dash (*same as* Soft Hyphen)

-[-]   Double Dash

USAGE

When you hyphenate a word without using WordPerfect's Hyphenation feature, the program uses a hard hyphen that is always printed. If this word passes beyond the right margin on the line, it will be broken across the line. To prevent this from happening (as when using mathematical expressions or equations), you enter a dash by pressing Home before the hyphen key instead of the hyphen key alone. For example, to keep the expression

n–1

together on a line under all circumstances, you type **n**, press Home followed by the hyphen key, and then type **1**. This can be used when typing telephone numbers, ranges of pages or years, and so on—expressions that are harder to read when split across lines.

The dash in WordPerfect is not the same as the en dash often used in typesetting when printing mathematical expressions in preference to the shorter hyphen. (The en dash is so named because it takes up approximately the same amount of space as the character *n* in the font being used.) To create an en dash, you must use the Compose key (Ctrl-2) and then type **4,33** and press Enter. However, many printers can't print this special character; if yours can't, the resulting character will be masked by a solid rectangle on your screen.

To create a double dash, you press Home followed by two hyphens. However, nothing prevents a double dash from being split at the hyphens. The double dash is not the same as the em dash used in typesetting (so-called because it takes up approximately the same amount of space as the character *m* in the font being used). A double dash is printed with space between the hyphens that is not present in an em dash. To print an em dash (if your printer is capable), use the Compose Key (Ctrl-2) and then type **4,34** and press Enter.

Be aware that the en and em dashes are not treated like hard hyphens; that is, words, phrases, or numbers separated by them will not be wrapped to a new line when they extend beyond the right margin.

SEE ALSO

Compose
Hyphenation

DATE, INSERTING THE

Inserts the current date either as text or as a function that is updated when the document is retrieved or printed.

KEY SEQUENCE

To enter the date text or Date code in the document:

Shift-F5 (Date/Outline)

▼

1 Date **T**ext; **2** Date **C**ode

To change the date format:

Shift-F5 (Date/Outline)

▼

3 Date **F**ormat

▼

Date format: *<date format codes>* **Enter**

▼

F7 (Exit)

To change the default date format permanently:

Shift-F1 (Setup)

▼

5 — **I**nitial Settings

▼

2 — **D**ate Format

▼

Date format: *<date format codes>* **Enter**

▼

F7 (Exit)

REVEAL CODES

[Date]   Date/Time Function

USAGE

You can use the Date Text and Date Code options on the Date/Outline menu (Shift-F5) to insert the current date and/or time in your document. If you select the Date Text option (**1** or **T**), the date is entered as text and doesn't change. If you select the Date Code option (**2** or **C**), the date is entered as a function code that is updated whenever you retrieve or print the document.

You can format the date in a variety of ways by using the Date Format option (**3** or **F**). Table V.3 summarizes the format codes and shows you examples of their use. To change the default format code (3 1, 4), follow the steps shown in the key sequence and then enter the codes as shown in Table V.3.

To insert the current date or time during a merge, use the ^D merge code (see **Merge Operations: Merge Codes**).

PATTERN	FORMAT CODES	EXAMPLE
For dates without leading zeros:		
Month DD, YYYY	3 1, 4	March 1, 1989
Weekday Month DD, YYYY	6 3 1, 4	Tuesday March 1, 1989
MM/DD/YYYY	2/1/4	3/1/1989
MM/DD/YY	2/1/5	3/1/89
DD/MM/YY	1/2/5	1/3/89
Report Date: MM/DD/YY	Report Date: 2/1/5	Report Date: 3/1/89
For dates with leading zeros:		
Month, DD, YYYY	3 %1, 4	March 01, 1989
MM/DD/YY	%2/%1/5	03/01/89
For time without leading zeros:		
HH:MM AM/PM	8:9 0	1:7 PM
HH:MM (24 hr. clock)	7:9	13:7
For time with leading zeros:		
HH:MM AM/PM	%8:%9 0	01:07 PM
For date and time:		
MM/DD/YY - HH:MM AM/PM	%2/%1/5 - 8:%9 0	03/01/89 - 1:07 PM

TABLE V.3: Date Format Options

To remove the date inserted as text, delete it as you would any text in Word-Perfect. To remove the Date code, locate and delete the [Date] code in the Reveal Codes screen.

SEE ALSO

Merge Operations: Merge Codes

DECIMAL/ALIGN CHARACTER

Allows you to enter a new character for the decimal point (and tab alignment character) and thousands separator.

KEY SEQUENCE

Shift-F8 (Format)

▼

4 – Other

▼

3 – Decimal/Align Character *<character>* **Enter**
Thousands' Separator *<character>* **Enter**

▼

F7 (Exit)

REVEAL CODES

[Decml Align Char]   Decimal Character or Thousands Separator

USAGE

WordPerfect uses the period as the decimal and alignment character and the comma as the thousands separator. To change these, follow the key sequence shown above. A change to the decimal/align character affects how Tab Align and totals calculated with the Math feature work.

SEE ALSO

Math
Tab Align

DELETING FILES

Allows you to delete files from within WordPerfect without exiting to DOS.

KEY SEQUENCE

To delete a single file in the current directory:

F5 (List Files) **Enter**

▼

[highlight file name]

▼

2 Delete

▼

Delete <*file name*>? (Y/N) **Y**

To delete several files in the current directory at one time:

F5 (List Files) **Enter**

▼

*[enter * before each file to be deleted]*

▼

2 Delete

▼

Delete marked files? (Y/N) **Y**

USAGE

By using the Delete option on the List Files menu, you can delete unneeded document files from within WordPerfect without having to use the DOS delete commands.

To delete a document form the List Files menu, press F5, and enter a new drive/directory if the files aren't in the current directory; otherwise, just press Enter. Move the highlight cursor to the file to be deleted. If you want to delete several files, mark each one by typing an asterisk (*) by its name. Then select the Delete option (**2** or **D**) and confirm the deletion by typing **Y** for Yes.

You can't restore a deleted file in WordPerfect as you can deleted text. Therefore, use the Delete option on List Files with care. If you do delete a file in error, turn to DOS utilities like Norton Utilities or Mace Utilities to restore the file.

SEE ALSO

Directories: Changing Directories

DELETING TEXT

Allows you to delete any amount of text in the document.

KEY SEQUENCE

See Table V.4.

TO DELETE	PRESS
Character by character	Backspace (deletes to left of cursor); Del (deletes character or space the cursor is on)
Word by word	Ctrl-Backspace
Several words	Esc *n* (*n* = number of words to left of the cursor) Ctrl-Backspace
The word to the left of the cursor	Ctrl-← Ctrl-Backspace
The word to the right of the cursor	Ctrl-→ Ctrl-Backspace
From the cursor left to the beginning of a word	Home Backspace
From the cursor right to the end of a word	Home Del
To the end of a line	Ctrl-End
A marked page	Ctrl-PgDn
A sentence	Ctrl-F4 S D
A paragraph	Ctrl-F4 P D
A page	Ctrl-F4 A D
A marked block	Alt-F4 Backspace or Del Y

TABLE V.4: Methods for Deleting Text in WordPerfect

USAGE

WordPerfect includes a wide variety of methods for deleting text in the document or formatting codes in the Reveal Codes screen (see **Codes**). All methods are summarized in Table V.4 and the most common are discussed in the following sections.

To restore the text you just deleted, press Cancel (F1) and select the Restore option (**1** or **R**).

Backspace   Press the Backspace key to delete the character or code to the left of the cursor's position.

Del(ete) Key   Press the Del key to delete the character or code at the cursor's position.

Delete Block   Press the Backspace or Del key and type **Y** for Yes in response to the prompt

  Delete Block? (Y/N) No

to delete a marked block of text (see **Block Operations**).

Delete Word   Press Ctrl-Backspace to delete the word the cursor is on. If the cursor is positioned on a space between words when you press Ctrl-Backspace, the word to the left of the cursor is removed.

Delete to End of Line   Press Ctrl-End to delete the text and codes from the cursor's position to the end of the line.

Delete to End of Page   Press Ctrl-PgDn and type **Y** for Yes in response to the prompt

  Delete Remainder of page? (Y/N) No

to delete from the cursor's position to the end of the page.

Delete to Word Boundary   Press Home Backspace to delete left of the cursor's position to the word boundary (a space). Press Home Del to delete right of the cursor's position to the word boundary (a space).

SEE ALSO

Codes
Undelete

DIRECTORIES

Allows you to create and delete directories from within WordPerfect and to change the current (or default) directory.

KEY SEQUENCE

To create a new directory:

F5 (List Files) =
or
F5 (List Files) **Enter 7–O**ther Directory
▼
<drive/directory path name> **Enter**
▼
Create *<drive/directory path name>*? (Y/N) **Y**

To make an existing directory current (the default):

F5 (List Files) =
or
F5 (List Files) **Enter 7 – O**ther Directory
▼
New directory = *<drive/directory path name>* **Enter**
▼
Dir: *<drive/directory path name>**.*
▼
Cancel (**F1**) – to return to screen
or **Enter** – to obtain a directory listing

To delete a directory (after removing all of its files):

F5 (List Files) **Enter**
▼
[highlight directory name]
▼
2 – Delete
▼
Delete *<drive/directory path name>*? (Y/N) **Yes**

USAGE

WordPerfect allows you to manage your document files by saving them in different directories. Most often these directories contain your documents and are organized as subdirectories of the WordPerfect directory (such as C:\WP50\Files) that contains the WordPerfect program files. You can create and remove such directories from within WordPerfect instead of resorting to the DOS Make Directory commands. However, WordPerfect won't let you delete any directory until you have removed all of the files within it (see **Deleting Files**).

Creating Directories

To create a new directory, you perform the procedure to change directories (outlined in the key sequence above). When WordPerfect finds that the directory doesn't exist, it prompts you to create it. If you type **Y** for Yes, the program creates the directory for you.

PATH NAMES

When entering the path name for the directory, begin with the drive letter and a colon (such as **B:**, **C:**, or **D:**) if it is on another drive and then list all of the directories in the hierarchy, separated by the back slash (\). If the directory is on the same disk, you need only enter the directory names separated by back slashes.

Changing Directories

You can change the current (or default) directory in WordPerfect using List Files (F5) from either the editing screen or the List Files menu. To change the directory from the editing screen, press List Files (F5) and type = . Then enter the new drive/directory path in response to the *New directory* = prompt and press Enter. You can edit the current path name that is placed after this prompt; you don't have to retype it from scratch unless the new one is totally different.

WordPerfect responds by showing you the new default directory, terminated by *.* (the global wild cards for listing all files in the directory). To return to the editing screen, press Cancel (F1). To obtain a listing of all of the files in the new default directory, press Enter.

If you don't know the name of the directory or where it is located on the path, you can change the default directory using the Other Directory option on the List Files menu by pressing List Files (F5) and Enter. If the name of the desired directory appears at the top of the list, move the highlight cursor to it. If it is located on a level above that of the current directory, highlight .. *<PARENT>* *<DIR>* and press Enter twice. Then locate and highlight the directory name on the new list. If the desired directory is a subdirectory of one shown on the list, highlight that directory, press Enter twice, then move the highlight cursor to its name on the new list. Select the Other Directory option (**7** or **O**), and Word-Perfect will supply the path to the highlighted directory as the new directory to change to; to accept it press Enter. To return to the editing screen, press F1 (Cancel) twice. To obtain a directory listing of all of the files in the new default directory, press Enter.

Deleting Directories

To delete a directory, first make sure that there are no files in it. You can do this by changing to the directory and listing the files as outlined above. With the highlight cursor on the directory name, select the Delete option (**2** or **D**) on the List Files menu (F5 Enter) and answer Yes to the prompt to delete the directory.

SEE ALSO

Deleting Files
Looking at the Contents of Files and Directories

DISPLAY PITCH

Adjusts the amount of space that one character occupies on the display screen.

KEY SEQUENCE

Shift-F8 (Format)
▼
3 – **D**ocument
▼
1 – **D**isplay Pitch - Automatic **Y** *or* **N**
Width *<width>* **Enter**
▼
F7 (Exit)

USAGE

WordPerfect displays all characters on the screen in a monospaced pitch of 10 characters per inch, regardless of what font you are using. Sometimes, when you're setting up complex tables or using the Advance feature, some characters will overlap and therefore not be visible on the screen. To help you see the spacing between characters, you can change the display pitch on the Document menu, accessed from Format—Shift-F8.

There are two options attached to Display Pitch: Automatic, which is set to Yes or No, and Width, which allows you to enter a measurement for increasing or decreasing the display pitch. When Automatic is set to Yes, you can only decrease the Width setting, to display the text closer together. If you set Automatic to No, you can increase the Width setting, to display the text farther apart. Doing this may make it necessary to scroll the text horizontally, as it may expand the line length past the right edge of the screen.

You can change the display pitch from anywhere in the document; the new pitch affects the entire document. To return the document to the normal display width of one-tenth of an inch, return to the Display Pitch option and enter **Y** for the Auto setting and **.1** as the Width measurement.

SEE ALSO

Units of Measurement

DISPLAY, SETUP

Enables you change the settings for a variety of screen display options.

KEY SEQUENCE

Shift-F1 (Setup)

▼

3 – **D**isplay

▼

1 – **A**utomatically Format and Rewrite
2 – **C**olors/Fonts/Attributes
3 – **D**isplay Document Comments
4 – **F**ilename on the Status Line
5 – **G**raphics Screen Type
6 – **H**ard Return Display Character
7 – **M**enu Letter Display
8 – **S**ide-by-side Columns Display
9 – **V**iew Document in Black & White

▼

F7 (Exit)

USAGE

The Setup Display menu allows you to change a number of default options having to do with the editing display screen. The purpose of each option is outlined below.

Automatically Format and Rewrite

The default for the Automatically Format and Rewrite option is Yes. This means that WordPerfect rewrites the screen and reformats the text as you edit it (however, word wrap still happens only when you use ↑ or ↓ to move to a new line or one of the other cursor movement techniques to move somewhere else in the text).

If you change this option to No, the program rewrites the screen and reformats the text only when you scroll through enough of the text that WordPerfect is forced to rewrite the screen or when you press Ctrl-F3 (Screen) and select the Rewrite option (**1** or **R**). You can also force the screen to be rewritten at any time by pressing Ctrl-F3 twice.

Colors/Fonts/Attributes

This option allows you to select the way various attributes, like boldfacing, underlining, marked block, and others, are displayed on the screen. The options available from this menu vary according to the display card and monitor you are using. See **Color/Fonts/Attributes** for details on selecting new attributes.

Display Document Comments

If you change the default of Yes to No for this option, all comments you have entered in the document will no longer be visible. Although they can't be seen, they still exist in the document. See **Document Comments** for information on how to enter comments in the document.

Filename on Status Line

After you save your document the first time, WordPerfect displays the document file name in the lower left corner of the editing screen (unless you switch to Typeover). To suppress this display, change this setting from Yes to No.

Graphics Screen Type

WordPerfect automatically selects the correct graphics driver for the display card and monitor installed in your system. However, you may need to use this option when you have two monitors connected to your system and wish to change to a new one. When you select this option (**5** or **G**), the program displays a listing of the various screen types it supports. To change the screen type, move the highlight cursor to the driver name and choose it by entering **1** or **S**. The currently selected screen type is marked with an asterisk (*) before its name.

If the graphics screen type you wish to use is not shown on the list, you may find it on the Fonts/Graphics disk. All screen type files have the extension .WPD. To make a new screen driver available, copy the appropriate .WPD file from the Fonts/Graphics disk to the directory that contains the WP.EXE (WordPerfect startup) file and then return to this menu to select it.

Hard Return Display Character

When you press Enter to end a paragraph or short line in WordPerfect, the program inserts a Hard Return code [HRt] in the document. However, because WordPerfect uses a space as the default hard return display character, you can't see the location of hard returns on the editing screen.

To make hard returns visible, you select this option (**6** or **H**) and enter the character to be used. If you want to use a character that can be entered directly from the keyboard (like <), just type it in. If you want to use a character that can't be entered directly (like ¶), use Compose (Ctrl-2) and the appropriate character set numbers to enter it (see **Compose**).

To restore the hard return to the default of a space, return to this option and press the space bar before pressing Enter and F7 (Exit).

Menu Letter Display

To let you know which letter of a menu option name can be pressed to select the option, WordPerfect displays this letter in bold (either double-intensity or the color selected for boldfacing). You can change this attribute to any of the 16 size and appearance choices on the Font menu (see **Font**). To change the menu letter display, select this option (**7** or **M**). WordPerfect displays the menu choices

1 Size; **2 A**ppearance; **3 N**ormal: 0

To select a new size for the menu letters, choose the Size option and select the desired size from this menu. To change the appearance of the menu letter, select the Appearance option and select the desired appearance (e.g, underlining, italics, etc.). To have WordPerfect use no special enhancement for the menu letters (so you won't be able to tell which letter can be used), select the Normal option.

Side-by-Side Columns Display

When working with text columns (newspaper or parallel), WordPerfect displays the columns side by side on the screen as they will be printed. However, you can scroll through columns more quickly if they are displayed as separate pages on the screen. To turn off the side-by-side column display, change this option from Yes to No. See **Columns, Text (Newspaper and Parallel)** for more information on working with text columns.

View Document in Black & White

If you have a color monitor, you can select the View Document in Black & White option (**9** or **V**) and change No to Yes by typing **Y** and pressing Enter to make the View Document page display appear more like the printed page. After you activate this Display option and then use View Document on the Print menu (Shift-F7 V), the text and graphics on the page will appear in black, and the representation of the paper will appear in white, instead of the same foreground and background colors that you have set up for the document editing screen, as is normally the case. Note that activating this Display option has no effect on the color choices made for the display of text and special attributes in the normal editing screen. If you have a monochrome monitor, turning on this Display option has no effect on the View Document display.

SEE ALSO

Colors/Fonts/Attributes
Columns, Text (Newspaper and Parallel)
Compose
Document Comments
Hard Return
Rewrite, Screen

DOCUMENT COMMENTS

Places nonprinting comments in your document.

KEY SEQUENCE

To create or edit a comment or convert a comment to text:

Ctrl-F5 (Text In/Out)

▼

5 — Comments

▼

1 Create; **2 E**dit; **3** Convert to **T**ext

To convert text to a comment:

Alt-F4 (Block)
▼
[highlight text to be placed in comment]
▼
Ctrl-F5 (Text In/Out)
▼
Create a comment? (Y/N) **Y**

To turn on and off the display of comments in the document:

Shift-F1 (Setup)
▼
3 – **D**isplay
▼
3 – **D**isplay Document Comments **Y** *or* **N**
▼
F7 (Exit)

REVEAL CODES

[Comment]   Document Comment

USAGE

WordPerfect allows you to enter nonprinting comments anywhere in the text of your document. These comments can be used as reminders of editing changes that still remain to be done. You can use the Search feature to quickly locate them in the text because WordPerfect inserts the code [Comment] in the document when you create a comment (see **Search: Searching for Codes**).

On the editing screen, the text entered as a comment is displayed within a double-lined box. If you create the comment in the middle of a line, the comment box will split the sentence on different lines, although the cursor will bypass the comment box when moving from the part of the sentence before the comment to the part after it.

WordPerfect allows you to convert the text entered into a comment box into document text, which will be printed. To do this, you follow the procedure for editing a comment except that you select the Convert to Text option (**3** or **T**) on the Comment menu. The box surrounding the comment disappears, and Word-Perfect reformats the text as required.

You can also convert document text to comment text, so that it is no longer part of the document, nor is it printed, as indicated in the key sequence. When you do this, the prompt

Create a comment? (Y/N) No

will appear. When you type **Y** for Yes, the text will be enclosed in a comment box.

To remove a comment from the document, locate and delete the [Comment] code in the Reveal Codes screen.

SEE ALSO

Document Summary

DOCUMENT COMPARE

Compares the copy of your document on the editing screen with the disk version and marks the differences.

KEY SEQUENCE

To compare a document on screen with a document on disk:

Alt-F5 (Mark Text)

▼

6 – **G**enerate

▼

2 – **C**ompare Screen and Disk Document
and Add Redline and Strikeout

▼

Other Document: <*file name*> **Enter**

To remove all redline markings and strikeout text added when using Document Compare:

Alt-F5 (Mark Text)

▼

6 – **G**enerate

▼

1 – **R**emove Redline Markings and Strikeout Text from Document

▼

Delete redline markings and strikeout text? (Y/N) **Y**

REVEAL CODES

[REDLN]	Redline On
[redln]	Redline Off
[STKOUT]	Strikeout On
[stkout]	Strikeout Off

USAGE

This feature checks the document on the editing screen against any version of the document on disk. This feature compares only phrases in the two documents and automatically indicates any discrepancies between the two by marking the document on your screen. WordPerfect considers a phrase to be any text between markers, including any punctuation marks, hard returns, hard page breaks, Footnote and Endnote codes, and the end of the document.

If phrases that don't exist in the disk version have been added to the document on screen, WordPerfect redlines the text in the screen version. If phrases that still exist in the disk version no longer exist in the document on screen, the program marks the text with strikeout. If phrases have been moved in the document on screen from their position in the disk version, WordPerfect inserts

THE FOLLOWING TEXT WAS MOVED

on a line before the text and

THE PRECEDING TEXT WAS MOVED

on a line after the text. These messages are displayed in strikeout, and the text in between them may be displayed in either redline or strikeout, depending on the version in which it exists.

After running the Document Compare procedure as outlined by the key sequence above, you can locate the Redline codes and strikeout text by using the Search feature (see **Search: Searching for Codes**). After examining the changes, you can remove all Redline and Strikeout codes as indicated in the key sequence.

SEE ALSO

Redline/Strikeout

DOCUMENT, FORMAT

See **Format**.

DOCUMENT SUMMARY

Enables you to add a nonprinting summary to your document.

KEY SEQUENCE

To create or edit a document summary:

Shift-F8 (Format)

▼

3 – **D**ocument
▼
5 – **S**ummary
▼
1 – **D**escriptive Filename
2 – **S**ubject/Account
3 – **A**uthor
4 – **T**ypist
5 – **C**omments
▼
F7 (Exit)

To create a document summary on Save/Exit or change subject search text:

Shift-F1 (Setup)
▼
5 – Initial Settings
▼
3 – Document **S**ummary
▼
1 – **C**reate on Save/Exit **Y** *or* **N**
2 – **S**ubject Search Text <*search text*> **Enter**
▼
F7 (Exit)

USAGE

You can add a document summary to any document that you create in Word-Perfect. The document summary can be added or edited from any place within the document. Unlike version 4.2, WordPerfect 5.0 no longer inserts a Document Summary code in the document and, therefore, provides you with no way to remove a document summary once it has been created. The document summary is never printed. The only way to obtain a hard copy of the summary is to use Shift-PrtSc when the Document Summary menu is on the editing screen.

The document summary can include the following statistics on the document (note that the first two are entered automatically by WordPerfect and the rest are entered by you):

- The system file name—the program inserts *Not Named Yet* if the document has never been saved.
- The date that the document was created (WordPerfect uses the current date as supplied by DOS). This date doesn't change when you save editing changes on subsequent dates.

- A descriptive file name that can contain up to 40 characters. If you enter a descriptive file name and no system file name has yet been assigned, the first part of the descriptive name is used as the system file name, and this name will be suggested as the file name the first time you save the document.

- The subject of the document or account assigned to it. If the Subject Search Text characters defined for the document summary (the default characters are *RE:*) occur within the first 400 characters of the document, the word or phrase following them is automatically inserted after the Subject/Account heading in the document summary. You can also enter your own word or phrase.

- The initials of the typist and/or author of the document.

- Comments containing up to 780 characters. The first 400 characters in the document are automatically displayed in the comment box.

If you wish to keep document summaries for all documents that you create, you can have WordPerfect automatically prompt you to create a summary the first time you save the document or exit the program. This procedure is outlined in the key sequence above.

Locating a File Using Its Document Summary Statistics

When you use the Look option (**5** or **L**) on the List Files menu (F5 Enter) to view the contents of a document that contains a document summary, the summary statistics are always the first text displayed on the screen. You can also use the Word Search option on the List Files menu to locate a file according to particular statistics in the document summary.

If you select the Conditions option (**4** or **C**) under Word Search (**9** or **W**), you can enter the matching conditions for any of the document summary statistics, including a range of creation dates (see **Word Search** for more information).

To make it easier to locate documents of a particular subject-type using Word Search, you should enter a consistent subject description or account number for the Subject/Account statistic. If the characters *RE:* occur in the first 400 characters of the document, the program will automatically enter the word or phrase that follows (up to hard return). You can change this default subject search text from the Setup menu (refer to the key sequence above) to enter a more suitable search word or phrase. Then, you can locate the files that contain the search text by entering it after the Subject/Account heading in the Word Search Conditions menu.

SEE ALSO

Looking at the Contents of Files and Directories
Word Search

Esc Key

Repeats a character (other than a number) or cursor movement key pressed a specified number of times.

KEY SEQUENCE

To repeat a character or cursor movement for the default repeat value:

Esc *<character or cursor movement key>*

To repeat a character or cursor movement for a new repeat value:

Esc *<number of times to repeat> <character or cursor movement key>*

To reset the default repeat value for the Esc key:

Shift-F1 (Setup)

▼

5 — Initial Settings

▼

5 — Repeat Value *<repeat number>* **Enter**

▼

F7 (Exit)

USAGE

The Esc(ape) key in WordPerfect is used primarily to repeat a keyboard character (other than a number) or a cursor movement command. It is only secondarily used to cancel the current WordPerfect command (see **Cancel**). When you press the Esc key, WordPerfect displays the prompt

Repeat Value = 8

If the next key you press is a keyboard character other than a number (like !), WordPerfect will enter that character eight times (entering !!!!!!!!). If the next key you press is a cursor movement key (like ↓ or PgDn), WordPerfect will repeat the cursor movement eight times (moving eight lines or pages down).

You can vary the number of times a character or cursor command is repeated by entering a new repeat number before typing the character or pressing the cursor movement key. WordPerfect uses the new repeat value only that one time and then returns to the default number.

To change the default repeat value permanently, you change the repeat value from the Setup menu (Shift-F1) as outlined in the key sequence.

NOTE

If you press the Del(ete) key after pressing Esc, WordPerfect will delete the next eight characters from the cursor's position to the right. If you press the space bar after the Esc key, it will insert eight spaces.

SEE ALSO

Cancel

EXIT

Quits WordPerfect and returns to DOS or clears the document editing screen to begin a new document.

KEY SEQUENCE

F7 (Exit)

▼

Save document? (Y/N) **Yes**

▼

Document to be saved: *<file name>* **Enter**

▼

Replace *<file name>* (Y/N) **N**o or **Y**es

▼

Exit WordPerfect? (Y/N) **N**o or **Y**es

USAGE

Exit (F7) is used to clear the current editing screen when you want to begin a new document, or to quit WordPerfect when you are finished using the word processor. You also use Exit to leave menus such as Setup, Format, and so on, and after entering the text of headers, footers, footnotes, and endnotes.

Saving and Exiting

When you press Exit during normal document editing, you see the prompt

Save document? (Y/N) Yes

Press Enter to accept the default setting of Yes, unless you wish to abandon the document and any editing you have made to it (thereby exiting without saving the document). When you press Enter, WordPerfect will prompt you for the name of the document. Enter the document name if you haven't saved it before (see **Save Text**) and press Enter. If you have already saved the document at least once, the prompt will contain the document name. If you want to save the document under a new name, type it in or edit the existing name. If you want to save it under the same name, simply press Enter. WordPerfect will respond with the prompt

Replace *<file name>*? (Y/N) No

If you change your mind and decide to rename the document, press Enter. Otherwise, type **Y** for Yes. After the document is saved, WordPerfect will prompt you either to exit the current document editing screen (if you are using both Doc 1 and Doc 2) or to exit WordPerfect. The default response is No, so that you can press Enter to remain in the current editing screen. If you decide you don't want to have your document cleared from the editing screen, press Cancel (F1) to retain it and return to editing its text.

If you answer Yes to exiting WordPerfect, you will be returned to DOS or to the WordPerfect Library shell, if you use this utility. If you answer Yes to exiting the current document editing screen (either Doc 1 or Doc 2), you will be returned to the other editing screen. If you answer No to exiting WordPerfect or the current document editing screen, you will remain in it, and you can begin creating a new document (using the WordPerfect formatting defaults) or retrieve another document for editing.

Quitting WordPerfect Without Using Exit

In WordPerfect it is important that you exit the program properly before you turn off the computer. WordPerfect automatically keeps special files, referred to as *overflow files,* that are not emptied and closed until you press F7 (Exit).

If you simply use Save (F10), and then turn off the power, WordPerfect will detect the presence of these files the next time you start the program and will beep and display this prompt on the initial startup screen:

Are other copies of WordPerfect currently running? (Y/N)

Responding No tells WordPerfect to erase the contents of the overflow files and move on to the standard editing screen.

SEE ALSO

Go To DOS/Shell
Save

Fast Save (Unformatted)

Saves an unformatted version of your document at a faster rate.

KEY SEQUENCE

Shift-F1 (Setup)
▼
4 — Fast Save (unformatted) **Y** *or* **N**
▼
F7 (Exit)

USAGE

Fast Save saves a copy of the document on the editing screen without formatting it when you use Save (F10) or Exit (F7) and save before quitting. A document which has been fast-saved, however, can't be printed from disk unless the cursor was located at the very end of the document when you saved it.

If you aren't concerned with the time it takes to save your document and want to be able to use any of WordPerfect's printing methods at any time, you can leave the Fast Save option turned off.

If you use Fast Save and find that you can't print a document on disk because of it, retrieve the document, press Home Home ↓, and save it again. Then, issue the command to print it from disk.

SEE ALSO

Printing: Printing a Document on Disk

FLUSH RIGHT

Aligns your text flush with the right margin setting.

KEY SEQUENCE

To align text flush right as you type it:

Alt-F6 (Flush Right)

▼

<text> **Enter**

To align existing text flush right:

Alt-F4 (Block)

▼

[highlight all lines to be flush right]

▼

Alt-F6 (Flush Right)

▼

[Flsh Rt]? (Y/N) **Yes**

REVEAL CODES

[Flsh Rt]	Flush Right On
[C/A/Flrt]	Flush Right Off

USAGE

To align text on a line with the right margin setting, follow the key sequence shown above, To right-align text after it has been entered (this can include several lines), mark the text to be flush right with Block (Alt-F4) and then select Flush Right (Alt-F6). WordPerfect will display the prompt

[Flsh Rt]? (Y/N) No

To have the marked text right-aligned, simply type **Y** for Yes.

To remove the right alignment, locate and delete the [Flsh Rt] or [C/A/Flrt] code in the Reveal Codes screen.

SEE ALSO

Center

FONT

Allows you to change the size or appearance of the current fonts used in your document.

KEY SEQUENCE

To change the size of a font:

Ctrl-F8 (Font)

▾

1 Size

▾

1 Supscrpt; **2 S**ubscpt; **3 F**ine; **4 S**mall; **5 L**arge; **6 V**ry Large; **7 E**xt Large

To change the appearance of a font:

Ctrl-F8 (Font)

▾

2 Appearance

▾

1 Bold **2 U**ndrln **3 D**bl Und **4 I**talc **5 O**utln **6 S**hadw **7 S**m Cap **8 R**edln **9 S**tkout

To return to the initial font defined for the selected printer:

Ctrl-F8 (Font)

▾

3 Normal

REVEAL CODES

Size:

[SUPRSCPT]	Superscript On
[suprscpt]	Superscript Off
[SUBSCPT]	Subscript On
[subscpt]	Subscript Off
[FINE]	Fine Print On
[fine]	Fine Print Off
[SMALL]	Small Print On
[small]	Small Print Off
[LARGE]	Large Print On
[large]	Large Print Off
[VRY LARGE]	Very Large Print On
[vry large]	Very Large Print Off
[EXT LARGE]	Extra Large Print On
[ext large]	Extra Large Print Off

Appearance:

[BOLD]	Bold On
[bold]	Bold Off
[UND]	Underline On
[und]	Underline Off
[DBL UND]	Double Underline On
[dbl und]	Double Underline Off
[ITALC]	Italics On
[italc]	Italics Off
[OUTLN]	Outline On
[outln]	Outline Off
[SHADW]	Shadow On
[shadw]	Shadow Off
[SM CAP]	Small Caps On
[sm cap]	Small Caps Off
[REDLN]	Redline On

[redln]	Redline Off
[STKOUT]	Strikeout On
[stkout]	Strikeout Off

USAGE

Font (Ctrl-F8) controls a variety of options, all of which affect the way your text appears when printed. This section contains information on how to enhance the currently selected font by changing either its size or its appearance. For information on changing the current font, see **Base Font**. For information on using Font to select colors for printing, see **Print Color**. In addition, the options Bold, Undrln, Redln, and Stkout on the Appearance menu are discussed under their own reference entries in this book (see **Bold**, **Underline**, and **Redline/Strikeout**).

All of the options on the Size and Appearance menus accessed from Font (Ctrl-F8) insert a pair of formatting codes (see **Appendix C**) and place the cursor between them. You are then free to enter the text that you want enhanced by the particular attribute selected. To return to the normal text font, you either press the → key once to move the cursor beyond the last code of the pair or select the Normal option (**3** or **N**) on the Font menu (this does the same thing as pressing →). To apply one of these attributes to existing text, mark it as a block using Alt-F4 (Block) before selecting the appropriate Size or Appearance menu option.

To delete any size or appearance attributes assigned to text, locate the pair of codes in the Reveal Codes screen and delete either one of them.

Changing the Size of the Font

When you select the Size option (**1** or **S**) on Font, you are presented with seven options. The first two are used for superscripting and subscripting characters. Superscripted text is printed a half-line above the baseline of the normal text, while subscripted text is printed a half-line below. To change the amount of adjustment up or down, use the Advance feature (see **Advance**).

The five remaining size options are used to change only the size of the current font. The actual point size or pitch used to produce the text assigned the attributes Fine, Small, Large, Very Large, and Extra Large depends upon the capabilities of the printer that is currently selected and the range of fonts that have been installed for that printer.

When you change the size of the text using one of these options, WordPerfect automatically adjusts the line spacing to accommodate the larger or smaller size. To overrule this adjustment, you need to use the Line Height option on the Line Format menu (see **Line Height**).

Changing the Appearance of the Font

When you select the Appearance option (**2** or **A**) on the Font menu, you are presented with nine options to enhance your text. The first two attributes, Bold and Undrln, can also be accessed by pressing F6 or F8 respectively (see **Bold** and **Underline**). The remaining attributes can only be accessed from this menu.

The attributes of double underlining (Dbl Und), italics (Italc), outline, shadow, and small caps can't be produced by every printer. To determine whether your printer is capable of producing these effects, print the PRINTER.TST file that is supplied with the program. If you select an enhancement that your printer doesn't support, WordPerfect will ignore it (unless you have specified italics, in which case the program will substitute underlining).

NOTES

The Small Caps option (Sm Cap) produces all uppercase letters in a smaller font size. They are most commonly used with acronyms and with times like 9:00 A.M. When entering text after selecting the Sm Cap option, you don't need to use the Shift key to capitalize the text.

See **Color/Fonts/Attributes** for ways that you can define how these size and appearance attributes are displayed on your editing screen.

SEE ALSO

Base Font
Bold
Cartridges and Fonts
Colors/Fonts/Attributes
Line Height
Print Color
Redline/Strikeout
Underline

FOOTNOTES AND ENDNOTES

Allows you to add footnotes that appear at the bottom of the page or endnotes that appear at a place of your choice in the document.

KEY SEQUENCE

Ctrl-F7 (Footnote)
▼
1 Footnote; **2 E**ndnote
▼
1 Create; **2 E**dit; **3 N**ew Number; **4 O**ptions

REVEAL CODES

[Endnote]	Endnote
[Endnote Placement]	Endnote Placement
[End Opt]	Endnote Options
[Footnote]	Footnote
[Ftn Opt]	Footnote/Endnote Options
[Note Num]	Footnote/Endnote Reference

USAGE

Notes to the text are automatically numbered for you in WordPerfect. If you want the text of the note to appear on the same page as its reference number, you create a footnote. If you want the text of all of the notes to appear together somewhere in the document, you create an endnote.

The text of footnotes and endnotes is not shown in the text, only their reference numbers. To see the notes before printing, you must use the View Document option on the Print menu (see **View Document**).

Creating Notes

To create a footnote or endnote in the text, follow these steps:

1. Move the cursor to the position where you want the footnote or endnote reference number to appear.
2. Press Ctrl-F7 (Footnote).
3. Select either the Footnote (**1** or **F**) or Endnote (**2** or **E**) option.
4. Select the Create option, **1** or **C**.
5. Type the text of your note (insert a space between the number on the note editing screen and the text).
6. Press F7 (Exit) when you are finished entering the note text.

To delete a footnote or endnote from the document, locate and delete the [Footnote] or [Endnote] code in the Reveal Codes screen.

New Number

WordPerfect automatically begins footnote and endnote numbering from 1. To change the starting number for all notes or to renumber a series of notes from a particular place in the document, you use the New Number option (**3** or **N**) on the Footnote or Endnote menu. This feature is especially useful if the document that contains the notes is a subdocument (like a chapter of a book) of a master document that requires sequential numbering of the notes in all the documents to be printed together (see **Master Document**).

To enter a new starting note number, follow these steps:

1. Move the cursor to the place in the document where the notes are to be renumbered (the top of the document if all notes are to be renumbered).
2. Press Ctrl-F7 (Footnote).
3. Select either the Footnote (**1** or **F**) or Endnote (**2** or **E**) option.
4. Select the New Number option, **3** or **N**.
5. Enter the new starting number and press Enter.
6. Press Ctrl-F3 (Screen) and Enter to have the notes renumbered.

WordPerfect inserts a [New Ftn Num] or [New End Num] code in the document at the cursor's position when you use this option.

Endnote Placement

When using endnotes in the document, you designate where the text of the endnotes is to appear by using the Endnote Placement option (**3** or **P** when you press Footnote). If you don't locate the cursor and use the Endnote Placement option to specify where in your document the endnotes are to be inserted, WordPerfect will automatically place them at the end of your document.

When you use the Endnote Placement option, WordPerfect inserts an [Endnote Placement] code at the cursor's position and prompts you with

Restart endnote numbering? (Y/N) Yes

If you choose to restart the endnote numbering from 1, press Enter to answer Yes to this prompt (WordPerfect inserts the code [New End Num:1] in the document). If you want to retain sequential numbering from the last endnote number, type **N** for No. After you respond to this prompt, WordPerfect inserts the following comment in the text:

Endnote Placement.
It is not known how much space endnotes will occupy here.
Generate to determine.

It also automatically inserts a hard page break after this comment.

To generate the endnotes at this point, you select Mark Text (Alt-F5), select Generate (**6** or **G**), select Generate Tables, Indexes, Automatic References, etc. (**5** or **G**) and then press Enter to the prompt.

Existing tables, lists, and indexes will be replaced. Continue? (Y/N) Yes

After the endnotes are generated, you will see the comment

Endnote Placement

on the screen. This comment will take up as much space as is required to print all of the endnotes up to that point in the document. To view your endnotes, use the View Document option (**6** or **V**) on the Print menu (Shift-F7).

If you want the text of your endnotes to appear on a new page, be sure to insert a hard page break (Ctrl-Enter) before the Endnote Placement comment box.

Changing the Formatting of Notes

When printing your footnotes and endnotes, WordPerfect makes certain assumptions as to how they are to be formatted. You can, however, control their formatting by using Options (**4** or **O**) on the Footnote or Endnote menu.

When specifying the spacing within footnotes or endnotes, enter **1** for single spacing, **1.5** for one-and-a-half spacing, **2** for double spacing, and so on. You specify the spacing between notes and the amount of note to keep together on a page by entering a measurement in inches.

To change the style of the numbers in the text or note for footnotes or endnotes, you select the appropriate options and enter the commands to insert the attributes that you wish to use. Note that you can insert graphics into a note if you select the Character type for the graphics box (see **Graphics**).

When you select the option to change the numbering method for footnotes or endnotes, you are presented with these options:

1 Numbers; **2 L**etters; **3 C**haracters: 0

When you select Characters, you can specify up to five different characters to be used. After all of the characters you entered are used, WordPerfect will double and then triple them, if necessary.

For footnotes, you may designate that your footnotes be renumbered on each new page or change the type of line separator used to demarcate the footnote from the body of the text. When you select Line Separating Text and Footnotes, you are presented with the options:

1 No Line; **2** 2-inch Line; **3 M**argin to Margin

The footnote option Print Continued Messages can be used to have WordPerfect print a *Continued...* message on the last line of any footnote that is split across pages (this message will also be printed on the first line of the note on the following page). You can use the Footnotes at Bottom of Page option (No) to have the footnotes moved up on a short page so that they are printed right under the body of the text rather than at the very bottom of the page with multiple blank lines separating the footnotes from the text.

SEE ALSO

Graphics
Mark Text
Master Document
View Document

FORCE ODD/EVEN PAGE

Forces the page to be numbered with either an odd or even number.

KEY SEQUENCE

Shift-F8 (Format)
▼
2 – Page
▼
2 – Force Odd/Even Page
▼
1 Odd; **2 E**ven
▼
F7 (Exit)

REVEAL CODES

[Force:Even]	Force Even Page
[Force:Odd]	Force Odd Page

USAGE

You can use the Force Odd/Even Page feature to ensure that a particular page will always be given either an odd or even page number (see **Page Numbering** for information on adding page numbers to a document). To use this command, position the cursor at the top of the page that is always to have either an odd or even page number.

The Force Odd/Even Page feature can be used in documents that are to be reproduced on both sides of the paper, to guarantee that a particular page is always either a left-hand (even-numbered) page or a right-hand (odd-numbered) page. When you use this feature, the program inserts either a [Force:Odd] or [Force:Even] formatting code at the cursor's position.

WordPerfect will renumber the page only if its number will be the opposite of the type specified by the Force Odd/Even Page code. For example, if you insert a [Force:Even] code at the top of page 1, it will be renumbered to page 2. However, if this code occurs at the top of page 6, it will not be renumbered. Any change to the page number due to the Force Odd/Even Page code is reflected in Pg indicator on the status line.

To return to regular page numbering, locate and delete the [Force] code in the Reveal Codes screen.

SEE ALSO

Headers and Footers
Page Numbering

FORMAT

Controls most aspects of the document format using four submenus: Line, Page, Document, and Other.

KEY SEQUENCE

See Figure V.1.

USAGE

All of the formatting options (with the exception of font changes—see **Font**) are accessed from Format (Shift-F8). Figure V.1 shows the four Format submenus (Line, Page, Document, and Other) and lists all of the options available on each one. To find information about a particular formatting option on these submenus, look it up under the name of the option listed in Figure V.1.

```
Format

    1 - Line
            Hyphenation               Line Spacing
            Justification             Margins Left/Right
            Line Height               Tab Set
            Line Numbering            Widow/Orphan Protection

    2 - Page
            Center Page (top to bottom)  New Page Number
            Force Odd/Even Page          Page Number Position
            Headers and Footers          Paper Size/Type
            Margins Top/Bottom           Suppress

    3 - Document
            Display Pitch             Redline Method
            Initial Codes             Summary

    4 - Other
            Advance                   Overstrike
            Conditional End of Page   Printer Functions
            Decimal Characters        Underline Spaces/Tabs
            Language

    Selection: 0
```

FIGURE V.1: The Format menu.

FORMS

Allows you to set up a form definition and then use it to print all or part of your document.

KEY SEQUENCE

To define, modify, or delete a form:

Shift-F7 (Print)

▼

S — **S**elect Printer

▼

[highlight printer to print form]

▼

3 — **E**dit

▼

4 — **F**orms

▼

1 Add; **2 D**elete; **3 E**dit

▼

F7 (Exit)

To use a form definition:

Shift-F8 (Format)

▼

2 — **P**age

▼

8 — **P**aper **S**ize
Type

▼

F7 (Exit)

REVEAL CODES

[Paper Sz/Typ] Paper Size and Type

USAGE

You use the Forms feature on the Select Printer Forms menu to create a form definition, which stipulates such settings as the paper size and type, orientation, offsets, and location of the paper (type of feed or bin number). You can then apply this form definition to a document by specifying the paper size and type it uses on the Page Format menu.

WordPerfect comes with three predefined forms: Standard letter size in either portrait (narrow), or landscape (wide) mode, Envelope, and [ALL OTHERS] (invoked when you use any other paper size or type). You can modify the settings of these forms or add new definitions to the list. To remove a form definition, select the Delete option (**2** or **D**) on the Printer Select: Forms menu.

Creating a Form Definition

As indicated by the key sequence, the form definitions that you create are part of the printer definition. When you select the Add option on the Printer Select: Forms menu, you are presented with two full-screen menus: the Form Type menu, and the Forms menu. When you select the Edit option, you are presented only with the second Forms menu, where you make the modifications to the selected definition.

When adding a new form definition, you must first specify the type of form to be used. The Form Type menu contains the name of seven frequently used forms. To select one of these, simply enter its mnemonic letter or number. If you want to add your own form description, select the Other option (**9** or **O**) and enter its name.

After indicating the type of form to be used, you are presented with the options in the Forms menu. Here, you indicate the paper size, orientation of the text on the form, whether or not it is initially present, its location (that is, type of feed or bin number), and any special page offsets to be used.

If you need to modify the size of the form, select the Form Size option (**1** or **S**). If none of the predefined size options that appear will do, select the Other option (the letter *O,* not zero) and enter the width and length.

To modify the placement of the text on the page, select the Orientation option (**2** or **O**). You have three choices:

1 Portrait; **2 L**andscape; **3 B**oth: 0

If you select Portrait, the text will run parallel to the insertion edge of the form. If you select Landscape, it will run perpendicular to the insertion edge. Select Both only when your printer allows you to manually determine the direction of the insertion edge. For example, to print the text in portrait mode on an $8^{1}/_{2}$'' × 11'' page, you insert the short edge ($8^{1}/_{2}$'') in the feeder. To print the text in landscape mode, you insert the long edge (11'') in the feeder.

The setting of the third option, Initially Present, should be Yes if the form will be present when the printing begins. If this is not the case, as is true when you must change the type of paper in a bin before printing a form, you should change this setting to No.

The Location option (**4** or **L**) determines the type of paper feed; it has three options attached to it:

1 Continuous; **2 B**in Number; **3 M**anual: 0

If your printer has a sheet feeder with multiple bins, select the Bin Number option and enter its number.

The Page Offsets option (**5** or **P**) is used when the printhead must be positioned in relation to the position of the top and left edge of the paper when the form is loaded in the printer before the printing begins. You can enter either positive or negative offsets for the Top and Side settings. Enter positive offsets for forms that are inserted with their top edge above or their left edge to the right of the printhead position. Enter negative offsets for forms which are inserted with their top edge below or to the right of the printhead position. Note that top and left margin settings for the document are added to the offsets that you specify.

After creating or editing a form definition, always use Exit (F7) instead of Cancel (F1) when leaving the menus. That way, WordPerfect will update the printer definition file with the form's information.

Using a Form Definition

To use a form definition to print your document, you select the appropriate paper size and type from the Page Format menu (refer to the key sequence at the beginning of this entry). After you select the Paper Size option (**8** or **S**) on this menu, you are presented with a full-screen menu that contains several size options. Select the size option here that is appropriate for the form definition you want to use.

After you select the paper size, the Paper Type menu appears. To select a form definition that you named (and defined), choose the Other option (**8** or **O**). This takes you to the Defined Form Types screen, with three options:

1 Select; **2 O**ther; **3 N**ame Search: 1

The screen shows you an alphabetical list of the forms you have defined. Move the cursor to highlight the appropriate name and type **1** or **S** or press Enter.

If WordPerfect can't match the paper size and type requested against one of the predefined form definitions, you will see an asterisk (*) in front of the paper size setting on the Page menu and the message

(*requested form is unavailable)

will be displayed beneath the paper type setting. The program will still go ahead and print the document using the paper size specified; however, it will not use any of the formatting instructions attached to the form definition.

SEE ALSO

Page Size/Type

Go To

Moves the cursor to a specific character, page, or text column, or to the previous cursor position.

KEY SEQUENCE

To go to the next occurrence of a character:

Ctrl-Home (Go To) *<character>*

To go to a specific page in the document:

Ctrl-Home (Go To) *<page number>* **Enter**

To return to the previous cursor position:

Ctrl-Home Ctrl-Home

To move the cursor between text columns:

Ctrl-Home (Go To) → or ←

USAGE

The Go To feature (Ctrl-Home) is used in combination with a particular character or page number to move directly to that character or the top of that page. For example, to move to the next occurrence of a hard return (end of paragraph) in the document, you press Ctrl-Home and press the Enter key. To go to the next period (end of sentence), press Ctrl-Home and type a period. To move directly to the top of a specific page, press Ctrl-Home, type the page number, and press Enter.

To return the cursor to its previous position in the document, you press Ctrl-Home twice. This is very useful when you're moving a block of text to a new place in the document and you wish to return immediately to the place from which the block was moved.

SEE ALSO

Cursor Movement

Go To DOS/Shell

Allows you to exit WordPerfect temporarily to go to DOS or the WordPerfect Library Shell if you run WordPerfect under this utility.

KEY SEQUENCE

Ctrl-F1 (Shell)
▼
1 Go to DOS
▼
<DOS commands>
▼
EXIT Enter (to return to WordPerfect)

USAGE

The Go To DOS or Shell feature allows you to leave WordPerfect temporarily and enter DOS commands while the word processor is still loaded in memory. When in DOS, you can issue commands to perform maintenance tasks like copying, renaming files, or formatting disks, as well as to run other software applications. However, when you go to DOS and try to run another program, you may find that your computer doesn't have sufficient memory to load the new program along with WordPerfect. Also, you should not use this feature to load a RAM-resident utility (sometimes called a TSR) like SideKick. Always exit WordPerfect before loading this type of software.

When you have finished executing your commands at the DOS prompt and are ready to return to WordPerfect, type the word **EXIT** (don't press the Exit key—F7) and press Enter. This will return you immediately to the editing screen and any document you have on it.

If you started WordPerfect from the WordPerfect Library shell, you will be returned to the Library Shell menu when you use the Go To DOS feature. From there, you can go to the DOS prompt by selecting the Go to DOS command on the Shell menu (it too uses the key sequence Ctrl-F1 1). When you are finished with DOS, type **EXIT** to return to the Library Shell menu. To return to WordPerfect, type the program letter you have assigned to WordPerfect 5.0.

GRAPHICS

Allows you to combine graphics created by other programs with the text of your document or to draw rules in the document.

KEY SEQUENCE

To create or edit a graphics box:

Alt-F9 (Graphics)
▼
1 Figure; **2 T**able; **3 T**ext **B**ox; **4 U**ser-Defined
▼
1 Create; **2 E**dit; **3 N**ew Number; **4 O**ptions

To create a Horizontal or Vertical Line graphic:

Alt-F9 (Graphics)

▼

5 Line

▼

1 Horizontal Line *or* **2 V**ertical Line

▼

1 — **H**orizontal Position
2 — **V**ertical Position★
3 — **L**ength of Line
4 — **W**idth of Line
5 — **G**ray Shading (% of black)

★The Vertical Position option appears only when you create a vertical line.

REVEAL CODES

[Box Num]	Caption in Graphics Box (*inserted inside of Box code*)
[Fig Opt]	Figure Box Options
[Figure]	Figure Box
[HLine]	Horizontal Line
[New End Num]	New Endnote Number
[New Fig Num]	New Figure Box Number
[New Ftn Num]	New Footnote Number
[New Tab Num]	New Table Box Number
[New Txt Num]	New Text Box Number
[New Usr Num]	New User-Defined Box Number
[Table]	Table Box
[Tbl Opt]	Table Box Options
[Text Box]	Text Box
[Txt Opt]	Text Box Options
[Usr Box]	User Box
[Usr Opt]	User Box Options
[VLine]	Vertical Line

USAGE

You can use Graphics (Alt-F9) to import a variety of illustrations or graphs created with other graphics programs, as well as digitized images created with scanners, and place them directly in the text of your document. Refer to the Graphics Programs section of the Appendix to your WordPerfect user guide for details on the graphics programs supported. You can also use the Graphics feature to draw vertical and horizontal lines (rules).

In order to insert a graphic image in a document, you must first create a box to contain it. WordPerfect supports four different box types: Figure boxes for any type of graphic image, Table boxes for tables of numbers, Text boxes for any text that is set off from the body of the document (such as sidebars), and User-Defined boxes for any other type of image.

You can use graphics boxes in the body of your document and in its headers, footers, footnotes, and endnotes. If you want to insert a graphics box in a style that you are creating, the box must either be empty or contain only text.

Defining a Graphics Box

After selecting the appropriate type of box for your graphic, you select the Create option (**1** or **C**). You will see a list of menu options that is similar for all types of graphics boxes.

FILENAME

To retrieve a file that contains an image or graph created with another program, select the Filename option (**1** or **F**) and type in the name of the file, including its extension. Be sure to include the complete path name if the graphics file isn't located in the current directory. Note that you don't have to specify the file at the time you create the graphics box to contain it. You can do this later by selecting the Edit option from the box menu, designating the number, and then choosing the Filename option from the Definition screen.

CAPTION

If you want to add a caption to your figure or table, select the Caption option (**2** or **C**). This brings you to an editing screen much like the ones used to enter headers and footers. The screen contains the name of the box followed by its number. You may delete this text. If you retain the number, it will automatically be updated if you later define or delete graphics boxes (of the same type) that precede it in the document.

TYPE

There are three possible types of graphics box associated with the Type option (**3** or **T**): Paragraph, which keeps the graphics box adjacent to the paragraph text; Page, which is affixed to a stationary position on the page; and Character, which is treated like a single character. WordPerfect will always wrap the text of a line that contains a Character box so it is below the boundary of the box, on the next line. Note that Character boxes are the only type that may be added to footnotes and endnotes.

VERTICAL AND HORIZONTAL POSITION

The Vertical Position (**4** or **V**) and Horizontal Position (**5** or **H**) options allow you to control the placement of the graphics box on the page. The settings available for them differ according to the type of graphics box chosen.

For the Paragraph type, the vertical position setting represents the vertical distance from the first line of the paragraph. The default is 0", which places the graphic even with the paragraph's first line. For the page type, you can align the box vertically with the top or bottom margin, center it on the page, or enter an offset measured from the top edge of the page. If you select Full Page, the graphics box expands to the margin settings for that page. For the character type, you can have the graphics box positioned so that the text of the line it's on is aligned with the top, center, or bottom of the box.

You can position the Paragraph type of graphics box horizontally so that it aligns with the left or right edge, or is centered between the edges of the area that contains its associated paragraph text. As long as the Wrap Text Around Box option is set to Yes (see below), the text of the paragraph will wrap around the graphics box. In addition, you can have the box fill this entire area from left to right by choosing the Both Left & Right option.

For the Page type, you have three options for setting the horizontal position of the graphics box: Margins, which allows you to left-align, right-align, center, or expand the box to left and right margins; Columns, which allows you to select a text column or range of columns (see **Columns, Text [Newspaper and Parallel]**), using the same alignment options as with Margins; and Set Position, which allows you to position the box a specific measurement in from the left edge of the page. When using the Column option, you can designate a range of text columns by entering their column numbers separated by a hyphen (as in *2–3*).

When using the character type of graphics box, you don't assign a horizontal position because WordPerfect automatically places the box to the left of the character that contains the cursor at the time you define it.

SIZE

Use the Size option (**6** or **S**) to modify the size of the graphics box. When you select this option, you have three choices:

1 Width (auto height); **2 H**eight (auto width);
3 Both Width and Height: 0

If you want to set both dimensions for the graphics box, select Both Width and Height (**3** or **B**), then enter the two dimensions. WordPerfect will automatically calculate the opposite dimension if you change the width of the box with the Width option (**1** or **W**) or the height with the Height option (**2** or **H**).

WRAP TEXT AROUND BOX

WordPerfect will flow the text around the borders of the graphics box if the Wrap Text Around Box option (**7** or **W**) is set to Yes. On the editing screen, it draws the outline of the graphics box (without displaying the illustration or graph) as you enter the text of the document. If you change this setting to No, the text will go through the graphic and the box outline will not appear on the editing screen. You can preview the positioning of the text around the graphics box by using the View Document feature (see **View Document**).

EDIT

Use the Edit option (**8** or **E**) to enter or edit the text for the graphics box or to modify the position or size of an illustration imported from the graphics file designated in the Filename option (see **Filename** above).

When the graphics box contains only text, you can enter or edit as you would any other text in WordPerfect after selecting the Edit option. You can change the font, size, alignment, or attributes of the text by using the appropriate WordPerfect commands.

When the graphics box contains an illustration or graph created in another program, and you select the Edit option, WordPerfect displays it in graphics mode (if your computer has a graphics card) on the screen surrounded by an outline representing the size and shape of the graphics box that contains it. From here, you can modify its size, its position, or both. Note that you can't add text to an illustration or graph when editing it; this must be done in the program that produced the graphics file.

To move the graphic image in the box, you can press any of the four cursor movement keys. To enlarge the image in the box, you press PgUp; to shrink it, you press PgDn. You can change its proportions by selecting the Scale option and entering a Y-scale (or vertical scale) percentage and an X-scale (horizontal) percentage. To rotate the image clockwise, press the Screen Up key (– on the numeric keypad). To rotate the image counterclockwise, press the Screen Down key (+ on the numeric keypad). You can also rotate the image by selecting the Rotate option and entering the percentage of rotation (where 100% is 360 degrees). When using this option, you can also designate that the image be flipped, by answering Yes to the *Mirror Image? (Y/N)* question that appears after a percentage is entered.

The % Change option is activated by pressing the Ins (Insert) key. The percentage of change affects the amount that the image is moved, scaled, or rotated when applying the techniques discussed above. You can choose among 1%, 5%, 10%, or 25% change by pressing the Ins key until the percentage you want to use appears in the lower right corner of the screen.

You can use the Invert option (4) on the Edit screen to reverse the image if it is a bitmap graphic rather than a line drawing. When you use it, each white dot (or *pixel*) is changed to black and each black dot to white. Graphics imported from .WPG files (the clip art files included with WordPerfect) and .PIC files (which contain Lotus 1-2-3 graphs) are considered line drawings and, therefore, can't be inverted, while EPS (Encapsulated PostScript) and TIFF (Tagged Image File Format— created by scanners) files can be inverted.

After you have made all the desired modifications to your graphic, press F7 (Exit) to return to the Definition screen. If you want to return the image to the original settings, press the Go To key combination, Ctrl-Home.

Adjusting the Settings for a Graphics Box

WordPerfect allows you to modify many of the default settings for the graphics boxes you insert in the document. These include the style of the border of the graphics, the inside space between the image and the borders of the box, the outside space between the text and the borders of the box, level numbering methods, the position of the caption, and the gray shading used in the box.

To change any of these settings, you move the cursor to the place in the document that contains your graphics box, press Alt- F9 (Graphics), select the option that corresponds to the type of box used there, and then select Options by pressing **4** or **O**. When you change any of the options, they affect the style of any of the graphics boxes of the same type from the position of the cursor when you made the changes forward in the document.

Creating Horizontal and Vertical Lines

WordPerfect's Graphics feature allows you to create horizontal and vertical lines (rules) of various thicknesses. Use these lines instead of those created with the Line Draw feature when you need to draw rules that use a proportionally spaced font, as lines created with Line Draw will not print correctly unless you are using a monospaced font. To draw a rule in the document, position the cursor on the line where you want the rule to start and follow the key sequence shown at the beginning of this entry.

WordPerfect can draw either a vertical line that extends up and down part of or the entire length of the page or a horizontal line that extends across part of or the entire width of the page. After selecting the type of line you want, you are presented with line options that allow you to specify the horizontal position (and vertical position if you are creating a vertical line), the length of the line, its thickness, and the amount of gray shading to be applied to it (100% is black).

When specifying the horizontal position of a horizontal line, you can have it aligned with the left or right margin or centered between them. You can also position the line by entering an offset measurement from the left edge of the page or have it extend from the left to the right margin.

When specifying the horizontal position for a vertical line, you can have it drawn slightly ahead of the left margin or after the right margin, or drawn between columns (indicated by number). You can also position the line by entering an offset measurement from the left edge of the page. You can specify the vertical position of the line as centered between the top and bottom margins (Full Page), aligned with either the top or bottom margin, or placed at a specific distance from the top of the page.

Use the Length of Line option to determine how long the rule is to be. If you have specified a horizontal rule whose position is Left and Right, the line length is automatically calculated by the margin settings. For other horizontal lines, the default length (which you can override) is determined by the cursor's position when you created the line.

The Width of Line option allows you to specify how thick the line is to be. To enter this measurement in points, even if the measurement is given in inches by default, follow the number with a *p*.

The Gray Shading option allows you to draw rules in other gradations that are not totally black. To decrease the contrast of the line, enter a percentage (10% is the lowest shading you can specify).

SEE ALSO

Line Draw
View Document

Hard Page Break

See **Page Break, Soft and Hard**.

Hard Return

Terminates paragraphs and short lines of text or enters blank lines.

KEY SEQUENCE

Enter

REVEAL CODES

[HRt]	Hard Return (Enter)
[ISRt]	Invisible Soft Return
[SRt]	Soft Return

USAGE

You use the Enter key to terminate a paragraph of text, to terminate a short line that does not extend as far as the right margin, or to add blank lines to a document. When you press Enter, WordPerfect places an invisible hard return in the document, shown by the code [HRt] in the Reveal Codes screen.

When entering the text of a paragraph, you don't press Enter to begin a new line when you come to the right margin setting, as is the case when using a typewriter. WordPerfect automatically wraps any text that extends beyond the right margin to the next line. At the end of a line where word wrap occurs, the program inserts a soft return, whose code appears as [SRt] in the Reveal Codes screen.

To separate the text of one paragraph into two paragraphs, you locate the cursor on the first character to be in the new paragraph and press Enter (it doesn't matter whether you are in Insert or Typeover mode). To join two paragraphs together, you locate the cursor at the beginning of the second paragraph and press the Backspace key to delete the [HRt] code. To make it easier to locate these Hard Return codes, you can choose a character to display their location on the editing screen (see **Display, Setup: Hard Return Display Character**).

You can manually insert an invisible soft return by pressing Home Enter before you type a phrase that occurs within the hyphenation zone to cause word wrap to take place. When you do this, WordPerfect inserts an [ISRt] code into the document at the cursor's position and wraps to the next line any following text that extends beyond the right margin. Use the invisible soft return to control where a line breaks when you don't want a word or term to be hyphenated. If you add text that changes where the line ends, WordPerfect reformats the line by pushing the [ISRt] code down to the next line. This makes it unnecessary to remove the invisible soft return in order to have the text of your paragraph properly reformatted.

SEE ALSO

Display, Setup: Hard Return Display Character

HARD SPACE

Prevents individual words from being separated by word wrap.

KEY SEQUENCE

Home-space bar

REVEAL CODES

[ ]   Hard Space

USAGE

The hard space, entered between two words by pressing the Home key before pressing the space bar, prevents WordPerfect from separating those words by word wrap. It can be used as the space character in any phrase that should never be separated by word wrap. A hard space code appears as [ ] in the Reveal Codes screen. To convert a hard space to a regular space (subject to word wrap), locate this code, delete it, and press the space bar.

HEADERS AND FOOTERS

Enters running heads at the top or bottom of the pages of your document.

KEY SEQUENCE

Shift-F8 (Format)
▼
2 – Page
▼
3 – Headers *or*
4 – Footers
▼
1 Header **A**; **2** Header **B** *or*
1 Footer **A**; **2** Footer **B**
▼

1 Discontinue; **2** Every **P**age; **3 O**dd Pages; **4** Even Pages; **5 E**dit

▼

< enter or edit text of header or footer >

▼

F7 (Exit)

REVEAL CODES

[Footer A]	First footer
[Footer B]	Second footer
[Header A]	First header
[Header B]	Second header

USAGE

WordPerfect allows you to create up to two different headers (running heads printed at the top of the page) and two different footers (running heads printed at the bottom of the page) in your document. You can have these headings printed on every page, or just on even or odd pages of the document. Before adding a header or footer to your document (as outlined in the key sequence), position the cursor at the top of the first page that the header or footer is to appear on.

You create two headers (or footers) A and B if you want their text to alternate on even- and odd-numbered pages of a bound document. When using two headers or footers on every page, place one flush left and the other flush right or place them on separate lines.

When creating a header or footer, after selecting its number and type, you are presented with a full editing screen on which to enter the text of the header (or footer). Your header or footer can use as many lines as you need. You can also add any text enhancements (such as boldface or a new font) or formatting (such as centering or flush right) that you wish. To insert automatic page numbering into your headers and footers, press Ctrl-B (or Ctrl-N) at the position in the header or footer where you want the page number to appear.

Headers begin printing on the first line below the top margin, and WordPerfect places 0.16" between the last line of the header and the body of the text. Footers begin printing on the first line above the bottom margin, and the program places 0.16" between the first line of the footer and the body of the text.

To see how your headers and footers will appear when printed, use the View Document feature. To discontinue a header or footer from a specific page to the end of the document, select the Discontinue option after selecting the appropriate header or footer on the Page menu. To suppress a header or footer on a specific page, use the Supress (this page only) option (see **Suppress Page Format**). To edit the text of a header, select its header or footer number and use the Edit option on the Header or Footer menu.

To delete a header or footer, locate and delete the [Header/Footer] code associ-ated with it. WordPerfect displays the first 50 characters of the header or footer in the Reveal Codes screen.

SEE ALSO

Suppress Page Format
View Document

HELP

Gives you on-line help about a function key or WordPerfect command.

KEY SEQUENCE

To get help on the function keys:

F3 *<function key or combination>*

▾

Enter *or* **space bar**

To get help on a WordPerfect command:

F3 *<first letter of the command>*

▾

Enter *or* **space bar**

To display the WordPerfect function key template:

F3 F3

▾

Enter *or* **space bar**

USAGE

WordPerfect's on-line help is available any time you are working with the pro-gram. To get help about the use of a particular function key or key combination, press F3 (Help) followed by those function keys. To get help about a particular feature by name, press F3 followed by the initial letter of the feature name (such as **S** to get help on Styles). When a letter has more than one Help screen, type **1** to display another screen of entries for that letter. After locating the name of the feature on the Help screen, press the function keys indicated to obtain informa-tion about the feature's use.

To display a diagram of the function key assignments in WordPerfect, press F3 twice. To exit Help, you simply press Enter or the space bar (pressing F1— Cancel—simply gives you a screen of help on the Cancel feature.

If you wish to reassign the Help key to F1 as it is commonly assigned by other programs, select the ALTRNAT keyboard that is supplied with your program (see **Keyboard Layout**). This keyboard reassigns the Cancel function to the Esc key and the Esc key function to F3.

SEE ALSO

Keyboard Layout

HYPHENATION

Hyphenates words according to WordPerfect's hyphenation rules, either automatically or at your discretion.

KEY SEQUENCE

To turn hyphenation on or off:

Shift-F8 (Format)
▼
1 — Line
▼
1 — Hyphenation
▼
1 Off; **2 M**anual; **3 A**uto
▼
F7 (Exit)

To change the hyphenation zone:

Shift-F8 (Format)
▼
1 — Line
▼
2 — Hyphenation **Z**one — Left <*left zone %*> **Enter**
Right <*right zone %*> **Enter**
▼
F7 (Exit)

REVEAL CODES

/	Cancel Hyphenation
-	Soft Hyphen
[Hyph Off]	Hyphenation Off

[Hyph On]	Hyphenation On
[HZone]	Hyphenation Zone

USAGE

WordPerfect uses three different types of hyphens:

- Soft hyphens, which the program enters; these are not printed if the document is edited and the word no longer requires hyphenation.
- Hard hyphens, which you enter by pressing the hyphen key (-). These will appear on the screen and in print whenever the word appears. A line can break after a hard hyphen.
- Nonbreaking hyphens, which you specify by pressing Home and then pressing the hyphen key (-). This prevents a hyphenated word from being split between two lines.

Soft hyphens are inserted by pressing Ctrl and the hyphen key or when you use the program's Hyphenation feature. The default setting for WordPerfect's Hyphenation feature is off. If you want to use the program's Hyphenation command, you must turn it on and choose between manual and automatic hyphenation as outlined in the key sequence above.

With manual hyphenation, WordPerfect will beep (if the Beep on Hyphenation option is set to Yes—see **Beep Options**) each time a word extends beyond the right margin and starts at or before the left hyphenation zone. You will then see this prompt:

Position hyphen; Press ESC

To the right of this prompt you will see the word as WordPerfect will hyphenate it if you press Esc. To change the place where the word is hyphenated, use the arrow keys to move the hyphen to the position where you want the word to break; then press Esc. If you do not want the word to be hyphenated, press F1 (Cancel).

When automatic hyphenation is on, WordPerfect will hyphenate any word that starts at or before the hyphenation zone and extends beyond the right margin, without giving you a chance to change the place where it is hyphenated.

The Hyphenation Zone option on the Line format menu (**2** or **Z**) is used to change the settings that determine how often WordPerfect will hyphenate a word. If a word begins before or at the left zone boundary and continues past the right zone boundary, WordPerfect will either prompt you for a place to insert a hyphen (if you are using manual hyphenation) or will immediately hyphenate the word (if you are using automatic hyphenation).

The left and right hyphenation zone boundaries are as set as a percentage of the line length. This means that the default setting of 10% for the left boundary is 0.6'' and that of 4% for the right boundary is 0.24'', if the line length is currently

6". To have WordPerfect hyphenate more frequently, decrease the size of the hyphenation zone. To have the program hyphenate less frequently, increase the size of the hyphenation zone.

WordPerfect makes all hyphenation suggestions and decisions according to its own hyphenation rules. You can purchase various foreign language hyphenation modules from WordPerfect Corporation. To have the program use one of these language hyphenation modules, you need to change the Language code on the Other format menu (see **Language**). You indicate where the hyphenation dictionary (or dictionaries) is located by using the Location of Auxiliary Files option on the Setup menu (see **Location of Auxiliary Files**).

SEE ALSO

Beep Options
Dashes
Language
Location of Auxiliary Files

Importing and Exporting DOS Text Files

See **Text In/Out**.

→Indent

Sets a temporary left margin and aligns all text to this indent until you press Enter.

KEY SEQUENCE

F4 (→Indent)

▼

<*text*> **Enter**

REVEAL CODES

[→Indent]   Left Indent

USAGE

For a left indent, press F4 (→Indent) at the beginning of your paragraph. It is then indented ½ inch from the left margin, or to the measurement of the first tab stop if you have reset tabs. Press F4 a second time to indent the paragraph 1 inch (or to the next tab stop), a third time to indent it 1½ inches, and so forth. If you press F4 at the beginning of an existing paragraph, it will be reformatted. When you press F4 at the beginning of a paragraph you are typing, it will be indented as you type until you press Enter again to signal the beginning of a new paragraph. To indent only the first line in a paragraph, use the Tab key instead of F4.

To remove an indentation, locate and delete the [→Indent] code in the Reveal Codes screen.

SEE ALSO

→Indent←
Margin Release
Tabs

→INDENT←

Sets temporary left and right margins and aligns all text to these indents until you press Enter.

KEY SEQUENCE

Shift-F4 (→Indent←)

▼

<*text*> **Enter**

REVEAL CODES

[→Indent←]   Left/Right Indent

USAGE

For a left and right indent, press Shift-F4 (→Indent←). The paragraph will be indented ½ inch from the left and right margins, or to the first tab setting for both sides. Continue to press Shift-F4 to indent the paragraph in increments of ½ inch or to the tab settings. To indent only the first line in a paragraph, use the Tab key. To delete a left and right indent, locate and delete the [→Indent←] code in the Reveal Codes screen.

SEE ALSO

→Indent
Tabs

INDEXES

Generates an index from entries marked in the document or stored in a concordance file.

KEY SEQUENCE

To mark an entry for the index:

Alt-F4 (Block)
▼
[highlight text to be indexed]
▼
Alt-F5 (Mark Text)
▼
3 Index
▼
Index Heading: **Enter** *to use displayed text*
or <index heading> **Enter**
▼
Subheading: **Enter** *to use displayed text*
or <subheading> **Enter**

To define the style of the index:

Alt-F5 (Mark Text)
▼
5 Define
▼
3 — Define Index
▼
Concordance Filename (Enter = none): **Enter** or *<filename>* **Enter**
▼
1 — **N**o Page Numbers
2 — **P**age Numbers Follow Entries
3 — **(**Page Numbers) Follow Entries
4 — **F**lush Right Page Numbers
5 — Flush Right Page Numbers with **L**eaders

To generate an index:

Alt-F5 (Mark Text)
▼
6 Generate
▼

5 – Generate Tables, Indexes, Automatic References, etc.

▼

Existing tables, lists, and indexes will be replaced.
Continue? (Y/N) **Enter** *or any key except N*

REVEAL CODES

[Def Mark:Index]	Index Definition
[EndDef]	End of Index, List, or Table of Contents
[Index]	Index Entry

USAGE

To create an index, you must first mark the items to be included in it, then define its style and generate it. To mark items for an index:

1. Locate the word or phrase you wish to include in the index. Position the cursor on it or on the space following it. If you are indexing a phrase, you must first mark it by pressing Alt-F4 (Block) and highlighting the phrase.

2. Press Alt-F5 (Mark Text) and then select the Index option (*3* or **I**). The following prompt appears:

   Index Heading:

   This prompt is followed by the phrase you marked or the word the cursor is on. If you want the entry to appear in the index just as it does where it is highlighted, press Enter. WordPerfect automatically capitalizes the first letter of an index heading, and it lowercases subheading entries unless the word was capitalized in the text. If you want the word or phrase to appear differently in the index, type it or edit it as you wish it to appear.

3. The program then prompts you for a subheading. If you accepted the default word or phrase as the heading, you can type a subheading or simply press Enter for no subheading. If you entered a different word or phrase for the heading, WordPerfect will present that word or phrase as the default subheading. You can press Enter to accept it, type over the word WordPerfect presents and substitute the one you wish to use, or delete the subheading if you do not want one.

4. Repeat this process for each word or phrase you want to include in your index.

Creating a Concordance File

A concordance file is simply a list of all the words and phrases that you wish WordPerfect to search for and mark as index entries. To use a concordance file, you specify its file name when you define the style of your index.

To create a concordance file, you need to start a new document and enter the words or phrases you want to use in the index as headings or as subheadings. Press Enter after you enter each one. Then, if you are using subheadings, go back and mark each entry with the appropriate index marks by pressing Alt-F5 (Mark Text) and selecting the Index option (you will need to block phrases first). Otherwise, all entries will be headings. You can then generate the index.

Defining the Style of an Index

WordPerfect allows you to choose among several formatting styles for the indexes it generates. To define the style for an index, follow the steps as outlined in the key sequence. After you select the Define and Index options, you see the following prompt:

Concordance filename (Enter = none):

Type the name of the concordance file, if you are using one; otherwise, press Enter.

Then you select the option number corresponding to the style you wish to use as shown in the key sequence section. If you want a columnar index, you must insert the column codes and turn the Columns feature on in the text (with Alt-F7) just before the [DefMark:Index] code that indicates where the index has been defined.

A [Def Mark] code is inserted in the document when you press F7 (Exit) after selecting a numbering style for the index. This marks the position where the index will be generated (see below).

Generating Tables, Lists, and Indexes

After marking the index entries and indicating the style of the index, you are ready to generate the index. After selecting the Generate (**6** or **G**) and Generate Tables, Indexes, Automatic References, etc. (**5** or **G**) options, you receive the prompt

Existing tables, lists, and indexes will be replaced. Continue? (Y/N)

To have WordPerfect generate the index, type **Y** or press any key besides *N*. If you have previously generated an index for the document, it will be completely replaced unless you type **N**. The index is generated at the [Def Mark] code in the document, and the program automatically inserts an [End Def] mark at the end of the index.

SEE ALSO

Lists
Mark Text
Tables of Contents

INITIAL SETTINGS

Allows you to modify the initial settings for the WordPerfect program or just the current document.

KEY SEQUENCE

To change the initial (default) settings for the program:

Shift-F1 (Setup)

▼

5 – **I**nitial Settings

▼

1 – **B**eep Options
2 – **D**ate Format
3 – Document **S**ummary
4 – **I**nitial Codes
5 – **R**epeat Value
6 – Table of **A**uthorities

To change the initial format settings for the current document only:

Shift-F8 (Format)

▼

3 – **D**ocument

▼

2 – Initial **C**odes

▼

Shift-F8 (Format)

▼

<*menu option and new setting*> **F7** (Exit)

▼

F7 (Exit) *twice*

To change the initial font for the current document only:

Shift-F8 (Format)

▼

3 – **D**ocument

▼

3 – Initial **F**ont

▼

[highlight the name of the font]

▼

1 Select

▼

F7 (Exit)

USAGE

WordPerfect allows you to change the default settings that remain in effect each time you use the program or to change the format default settings just for the document you are creating.

To change the default settings for the program, you select Shift-F1 (Setup) and the Initial Settings option (**5** or **I**). Then select the number or letter of the option you wish to reset. Information on changing the default settings for Beep Options, Date Format, Document Summary, Repeat Value (see **Esc Key**), and Table of Authorities can be found under those reference entries in this quide. Refer to **Appendix D** for a list of the default settings in effect when you install WordPerfect.

To change the initial format settings or font for the current document only, you choose the Initial Codes option on the Document menu (as indicated in the key sequence). The Initial Codes option takes you to a split screen that shows the Reveal Codes screen in the lower half. Then, you press Shift-F8 (Format) and select the appopriate format menu (Line, Page, Document, or Other) and change all of the default settings as you want them for the document on the editing screen.

After you finish making the desired changes on the menus and press F7, you will see their formatting codes in the Reveal Codes screen. When you press F7 again, these formatting changes will be added to the document. When you press F7 a third time to return to the editing screen, the cursor will automatically be located at the beginning of the document. However, if you then open the Reveal Codes screen, none of the formatting codes seen earlier will appear. To return to your previous position in the document, press Ctrl-Home (Go To) twice.

You also use this method when using the Initial Codes option on the Initial Settings menu to change the format settings that you want in effect in each time you start WordPerfect. All changes to the initial settings are stored with the document when you save it. Changes made to the settings for the current document preempt those made to the program, just as formatting changes made within the document preempt those made for the document. This means that they will remain in effect even if you retrieve the document on another computer whose copy of WordPerfect has different format defaults in effect.

SEE ALSO

Base Font
Beep Options
Date, Inserting the
Document Summary
Esc Key
Printer, Select
Table of Authorities

INSERT

See **Typeover**.

ITALICS

See **Font**.

JUSTIFICATION

Turns on or off right justification in the document.

KEY SEQUENCE

To turn on or off right justification in the document:

Shift-F8 (Format)

▼

1 — **L**ine

▼

3 — **J**ustification **N** *or* **Y**

▼

F7 (Exit)

To compress or expand the word spacing:

Shift-F8 (Format)

▼

4 — **O**ther

▼

6 — **P**rinter Functions

▼

4 — **W**ord Spacing **J**ustification

Compressed to (0%–100%) <*compression %*> **Enter**

Expanded to (100%–unlimited) <*expansion %*> **Enter**

▼

F7 (Exit)

REVEAL CODES

[Just Lim]	Word/Letter Spacing Justification Limits
[Just Off]	Justification Off
[Just On]	Justification On

USAGE

By default, justification is on when you begin a new document in Word-Perfect. This means that the program will align the right margin of each line by adjusting the spacing between its words. The program can't display justification on the editing screen (the right margin always appears ragged). To see justification and the spacing between words in each line, you need to use the View Document feature.

You can turn off justification for the entire document or just part of it. Position the cursor in the document where you want the change to begin and follow the steps indicated in the key sequence. To turn it off for the entire document, be sure to position the cursor at the beginning of the document (Home Home ↑) before following the key sequence. You can also turn off justification for the whole document by using the Initial Codes option on the Document format menu (see **Initial Settings**).

When you select No for the Justification option from the Format Line menu, WordPerfect inserts a [Just Off] code in the document. You can return to the default of justification by locating and deleting this code in the Reveal Codes screen.

WordPerfect provides two methods for controlling the spacing between words when justification is used. You can turn on WordPerfect's Hyphenation feature and adjust the size of the hyphenation zone (see **Hyphenation**) to reduce the amount of space between words. This is especially useful when you have a short line length, as when using newspaper and parallel columns. You can also adjust the word spacing from the Printer Functions menu (as indicated in the key sequence). The Word Spacing Justification option allows you to modify the minimum and maximum range within which WordPerfect can fit justified text. With a proportionally spaced font, the optimal spacing between words is built into the font (expressed by percentage as 100%). Use the Compressed To option to set the minimum word spacing percentage and the Expanded To option to set the maximum word spacing percentage allowed. When one of these limits is reached, WordPerfect begins to adjust the spacing between letters in the words themselves (see **Word/Letter Spacing**).

SEE ALSO

Hyphenation
Initial Settings
View Document
Word/Letter Spacing

KERNING

Turns on or off automatic kerning, which tightens the letter spacing between specific pairs of letters in a font.

KEY SEQUENCE

Shift-F8 (Format)
▼
4 – **O**ther
▼
6 – **P**rinter Functions
▼
1 – **K**erning **Y** *or* **N**
▼
F7 (Exit)

REVEAL CODES

[Kern Off]   Kerning Off
[Kern On]   Kerning On

USAGE

When you turn on kerning in a document, WordPerfect reduces space between specific letter pairs in a font from the cursor's position forward in the document. Kerning combinations are determined by the kerning table contained in the printer definition file (ending in .PRS) used by the selected printer (see **Printer, Select**).

When you turn kerning on in a document, WordPerfect inserts a [Kern:On] code in the document at the cursor's position. If you decide not to use kerning in the final printed document, locate and delete this code in the Reveal Codes screen.

SEE ALSO

Justification
Word/Letter Spacing

KEYBOARD LAYOUT

Allows you to assign new functions or characters to any key on the keyboard.

KEY SEQUENCE

To create a keyboard layout:

Shift-F1 (Setup)
▼
6 – **K**eyboard Layout
▼
4 – **C**reate
▼

Keyboard Filename: <*name for keyboard*> **Enter**

▼

Key: **4 C**reate

▼

Key: <*key to be redefined*>

▼

1 – Description <*key description*> **Enter**

2 – Action <*new key definition*> **Enter**

▼

F7 (Exit)

To edit a key's function:

Shift-F1 (Setup)

▼

6 – Keyboard Layout

▼

[highlight name of keyboard]

▼

5 Edit

▼

Key: **1 E**dit; **2 D**elete; **3 M**ove; **4 C**reate; Macro: **5 S**ave; **6 R**etrieve

▼

F7 (Exit)

To select a keyboard layout:

Shift-F1 (Setup)

▼

6 – Keyboard Layout

▼

[highlight name of keyboard]

▼

1 Select

▼

F7 (Exit)

USAGE

You can use the Keyboard Layout feature to change the function of any key on the keyboard. The reassigned key functions are then saved under a file name, which can be selected as indicated in the key sequence. When you select a new keyboard layout, it remains in effect each time you start WordPerfect. To return to the original keyboard layout, select the Original option (**6** or **O**) from the Keyboard Layout menu.

Editing Keyboard Definitions

WordPerfect comes with three predefined keyboard layouts, ALTRNAT, ENHANCED, and MACROS, that you can use as is or edit. To view or change the reassignments made to individual keys, select the Edit option (**5** or **E**) on the Keyboard Layout menu. To modify a key definition, move the highlight bar to the name of the key and select the Edit option (**1** or **E**). This takes you to an edit screen very similar to the one used to modify macros (see **Macros**). To modify the key's function, then select the Action option (**2** or **A**). This positions the cursor inside the key definition window. Once there, you can use the regular WordPerfect editing and cursor movement keys to modify the text or the functions listed there.

To add a new function as part of a key definition, press Ctrl-V or Ctrl-F10 (Macro Define), followed by the function key or key combination to be added. For instance, to add centering to a key definition, you select the Action option, position the cursor in the definition window at the place where centering is to happen, press Ctrl-V, and then Shift-F6. WordPerfect will place the code {Center} in the definition window at the cursor's position. As when editing macros, you must be sure to press Ctrl- F10 a second time if you used it instead of Ctrl-V to enter the function key code. This toggles you back into editing mode so that the editing and cursor movement keys work as usual.

When reassigning a key's function, you can also use the macro commands available in WordPerfect. You add a macro command by pressing Ctrl-PgUp once the cursor is in the definition screen, highlighting the name of the macro command, and then pressing Enter (see **Chapter 16** for a list of the macro programming commands).

After you are finished reassigning the function of the key, press F7 (Exit) to save the definition and exit the key modification screen.

When editing a keyboard layout, you can also delete (**2** or **D**) or move (**3** or **M**) a key definition, or create (**4** or **C**) a new key definition. In addition, you can use the Save option (**5** or **S**) to store a key definition as a macro by highlighting the key, typing **5** or **,**) and entering a macro name. That way, you can invoke the key definition as you would any WordPerfect macro, even if the keyboard layout is not currently selected (see **Macros**).

Finally, you can assign a macro definition to a particular key by typing **6** or **R**, pressing the key or key combination, and then entering the name of the macro to be assigned to it. This option allows you to map macro definitions to specific Ctrl- letter key combinations. For example, if you have defined a macro named *backup,* which makes a backup of the current directory, you can use this option to map its function to the key combination Ctrl-B so that you can make a backup simply by pressing Ctrl-B rather than having to press Alt-F10, type **backup,** and then press Enter.

Creating a New Keyboard Definition

Creating a new keyboard layout involves many of the same steps as editing an existing one. After you select the Create option (**4** or **C**), you are prompted to enter a name for the keyboard. After naming it, you go on to define the function of the individual keys and key combinations that you wish to add to it. Each key definition is given a description and an action.

You can create all sorts of specialized keyboards to meet your needs. You can add special math/science or foreign language symbols to the keyboard using the Compose feature (see **Compose**). You can rearrange the WordPerfect function keys so that they match some other word processing system. For instance, a user familiar with WordStar could map Ctrl-Backspace onto Ctrl-T so that Ctrl-T deletes the current word as it does in that word processor. You can also create a keyboard that uses a particular set of macros. For instance, you could set up a merge keyboard that assigns a set of specialized merge macros to familiar keys.

NOTE

The Keyboard Layout feature replaces the Ctrl/Alt key mapping in version 4.2.

SEE ALSO

Compose
Location of Auxiliary Files
Macros

LANGUAGE

Allows you to switch between different language versions of the spelling, thesaurus, and hyphenation dictionaries.

KEY SEQUENCE

Shift-F8 (Format)

▼

4 – **O**ther

▼

4 – Language *<Language code>* **Enter**

▼

F7 (Exit)

REVEAL CODES

[Lang]   Language

USAGE

WordPerfect comes with an English language version of the spelling and the-saurus dictionaries. You can, however, purchase foreign language versions of these dictionaries, as well as special hyphenation dictionaries, from WordPerfect Corporation. To have WordPerfect use one of these versions instead of American English, you must change the Language code default from US (for United States) to its code.

SEE ALSO

Location of Auxiliary Files

LINE DRAW

Allows you to draw straight lines and boxes in the document.

KEY SEQUENCE

Ctrl-F3 (Screen)

▼

2 — Line Draw

▼

1 | ; **2** | | ; **3** *; **4** Change; **5** Erase; **6** Move

▼

F7 (Exit) or **F1** (Cancel)

USAGE

To draw simple graphics in WordPerfect, press Ctrl-F3 (Screen) and select the Line Draw option (**2** or **L**). When you are in WordPerfect's Line Draw mode, the following menu appears:

1 | ; **2** | | ; **3** *; **4** Change; **5** Erase; **6** Move: 1

When you are in Line Draw mode, the option you have selected appears at the end of the menu line. Selecting option **1**, **2**, or **3** allows you to choose among draw-ing single lines, double lines, or asterisks. Selecting option **4** allows you to select up to eight different types of alternate drawing characters. In addition, you can use any of the characters that your printer can print (see **Compose**). If you select option **5**, the cursor will erase each character it passes through. Selecting option **6** allows you to move the cursor through your drawing without changing anything.

To enter text in drawings you have created, you should be in Typeover mode. If you remain in Insert mode, which is WordPerfect's default setting, lines will be pushed to the right as you type, and pressing Enter, Tab, or the space bar will insert spaces into your graphics. You can also type text for your graphics first, then enter Line Draw mode and draw lines around the text you have already entered.

To exit Line Draw mode and enter text, press F7 (Exit) or F1 (Cancel). Pressing F1 does not erase any drawings you have created.

NOTE

When creating horizontal and vertical rules for a desktop publishing application, use the Line option on the Graphics menu (Alt-F9), rather than the Line Draw feature.

SEE ALSO

Graphics: Creating Horizontal and Vertical Lines

LINE FORMAT

See **Format**.

LINE HEIGHT

Allows you to fix the amount of space placed between the baseline of one line and the baseline of the next line in the document.

KEY SEQUENCE

Shift-F8 (Format)

▼

1 — Line

▼

4 — Line Height

▼

1 Auto
2 Fixed *<distance between baselines>* **Enter**

▼

F7 (Exit)

REVEAL CODES

[Ln Height:Auto]   Line Height Auto
[Ln Height: <*num*">] Line Height Fixed

USAGE

WordPerfect automatically adjusts the line height—that is, the measurement from the baseline of one line of text to the baseline of the following line of text—to accommodate the largest font used in the line. If you wish to override this automatic adjustment and enter a fixed line height for all of the lines in a part or all of the document, you use the Line Height option on the Line format menu. After you select the Fixed option (as indicated in the key sequence), enter the distance between baselines. You can enter this measurement in points, inches, or centimeters. If you enter the number of points, and inches is the default unit of measurement, be sure to end the number with *p*— WordPerfect will automatically convert this number into corresponding inches (see **Units of Measure**).

When you change the line height measurement, WordPerfect inserts a [Ln Height:] code in the document at the cursor's position. The line height will then be changed from that point forward in the document, although the difference in the line spacing will not be visible on the editing screen. (To see the effect that changing the line height has on your text, you must use the View Document feature.) To return to automatic line height later on in the text, position the cursor at the beginning of the line where the new line height is to begin, repeat the key sequence, and select the Auto option.

SEE ALSO

Line Spacing

LINE NUMBERING

Numbers the lines in the printed version of the document.

KEY SEQUENCE

Shift-F8 (Format)
▼
1 — **L**ine
▼
5 — Line **N**umbering **Y**
▼

1 — **C**ount Blank Lines
2 — **N**umber Every n Lines, where n is
3 — **P**osition of Number from Left Edge
4 — **S**tarting Number
5 — **R**estart Numbering on Each Page
▼
F7 (Exit)

REVEAL CODES

[Ln Num:Off]   Line Numbering Off

[Ln Num:On]   Line Numbering On

USAGE

WordPerfect allows you to specify that lines be automatically numbered in the documents you create. Although the line numbers do not appear on the editing screen, they will be present when your document is printed or when you preview it (see **View Document**).

To number the lines in a document, move the cursor to the first position at the top of the page where you want line numbering to begin. To turn on line numbering at the cursor position, follow the key sequence shown above and type **Y** after choosing the Line Numbering option. To later turn line numbering off, you type **N** in response to this option. You can also locate and delete the [Ln Num:On] code in the Reveal Codes screen.

When you turn on line numbering, you are presented with five suboptions, which are discussed below.

Count Blank Lines   You can select whether to include blank lines in the line count. If you want blank lines to be skipped, select the Count Blank Lines option (**1** or **C**) and type **N**. WordPerfect automatically includes blank lines as it numbers lines unless you tell it not to. The count does not include blank lines in double-spaced text, however.

Number Every **n** *Lines*   The Number Every *n* Lines, Where *n* Is option allows you to specify the increment for line numbering. For example, suppose you want to number only every other line or every fifth line. To do so, enter the number of lines you want WordPerfect to skip before it numbers the next line. To have the program number every five lines, enter **5**; WordPerfect will count all the lines but will number only lines 5, 10, 15, 20, and so forth.

Position of Number from Left Edge   The Position of Number from Left Edge option allows you to indicate where you want WordPerfect to print the line numbers. Enter the distance from the left margin in inches.

Starting Number   WordPerfect begins line numbering with 1 on each new page unless you change the Starting Number option and enter a new starting number.

Restart Numbering on Each Page   If you want line numbering to continue sequentially throughout your document, enter **N** for the Restart Number on Each Page option.

SEE ALSO

Outlining
Paragraph Numbering
View Document

LINE SPACING

Allows you to change the line spacing in half-line increments.

KEY SEQUENCE

Shift-F8 (Format)
▾
1 — Line
▾
6 — Line **S**pacing *<spacing number>* **Enter**
▾
F7 (Exit)

REVEAL CODES

[Ln Spacing]   Line Spacing

USAGE

The default for WordPerfect is single spacing. To change to another spacing from the cursor's position forward in the document, place the cursor where you want the new spacing to begin and follow the key sequence as shown above.

You can enter the spacing number in half-line increments (such as 1.5). Word-Perfect displays double spacing (and larger whole number spacing like triple, quadruple, and so on) on the screen. To return to the default of single spacing, locate and delete the [Ln Spacing] code in the Reveal Codes screen.

SEE ALSO

Line Height

LIST FILES

Allows you to obtain an alphabetical listing of all of the files in the current directory and perform common maintenance tasks on them.

KEY SEQUENCE

F5 (List Files) **Enter**

▼

1 Retrieve; **2** Delete; **3** Move/Rename; **4** Print; **5** Text In; **6** Look;
7 Other Directory; **8 C**opy; **9 W**ord Search; **N N**ame Search

▼

F1 (Cancel) *or* **space bar** *or* **O**

USAGE

List Files (F5) allows you to obtain a directory listing of files, retrieve or print a particular document, or make a new data directory or drive current. In addition, you can carry out many tasks that you would otherwise have to do in DOS, such as deleting and renaming files, creating directories, and copying files to a new disk or directory. For information on using such options on the List Files menu, refer to the individual reference entry in this book under the option name.

When you press F5, WordPerfect displays the path name of the current directory at the bottom of the editing screen. If you press Enter, it will display a new screen showing an alphabetical list of all program files in that directory as well as the List Files menu.

To move through the list of file names on the List Files screen, use the ↑, ↓, PgUp, and PgDn keys. To move directly to the last file name in the list, press Home Home ↓. To move to the first file, press Home Home ↑. To move between columns, use the ← and → keys.

To locate a particular file quickly, type **N** and start typing the first few characters of its name to activate the Name Search feature. The program tries to match the letters entered with files in the listing and moves the highlight directly to the first match. Press Enter or one of the arrow keys to exit from Name Search.

If you want to view the contents of a different directory, you can edit the displayed path name or enter the path name of the directory you wish to view. If you will be working in a different directory during the current session, you can change the default directory (see **Directories**). Once you have made a particular directory current, all of the documents you create and save will automatically be located in it.

Press Esc, F1 (Cancel), F7 (Exit) or **0** to return to your document after viewing the List Files screen.

SEE ALSO

Copying Files
Deleting Files
Directories
Looking at the Contents of Files and Directories
Name Search
Printing
Renaming a Document
Retrieve
Text In/Out
Word Search

LISTS

Generates lists from marked entries in your document.

KEY SEQUENCE

To mark an entry for the list:

Alt-F4 (Block)
▼
[highlight text to be listed]
▼
Alt-F5 (Mark Text)
▼
2 List
▼
List Number: *<number between 1 and 5>*

To define the style of the list:

Alt-F5 (Mark Text)
▼

5 Define

▼

2 — Define **L**ist

▼

List Number (1–9): <*list number*>

▼

1 — **N**o Page Numbers
2 — **P**age Numbers Follow Entries
3 — (Page Numbers) Follow Entries
4 — **F**lush Right Page Numbers
5 — Flush Right Page Numbers with **L**eaders

▼

F7 (Exit)

To generate a list:

Alt-F5 (Mark Text)

▼

6 Generate

▼

5 — **G**enerate Tables, Indexes, Automatic References, etc.

▼

Existing tables, lists, and indexes will be replaced.
Continue? (Y/N) **Enter** *or any key except N*

REVEAL CODES

[Def Mark:List]	List Definition
[EndDef]	End of Index, List, or Table of Contents
[Mark:List]	List Entry

USAGE

You can mark up to five separate lists in a document, but an item may belong to only one list. For each item that you want to include in a list, follow these steps:

1. Press Alt-F4 and use the cursor movement keys to mark the list item as a block.
2. Press Alt-F5 (Mark Text), then select the List option (**2** or **L**).
3. When the List# prompt appears, enter the number of the list (from 1 to 5).

When you mark a list entry with this method, WordPerfect places a [Mark:List,#] and [End Mark:List,#] code around the marked text. To delete the entry from the list, you need only to locate and delete the [Mark:List #] code for that entry in the Reveal Codes screen.

In addition to the five lists you mark yourself, WordPerfect automatically maintains separate predefined lists of the captions for figures, tables, Text boxes, and User-Defined boxes created with the Graphics feature (see **Graphics**); these are assigned to the list numbers 6 through 9 respectively. For example, to create a list composed of all of the captions for the Text boxes in a document, you simply define the style for list 8 and generate it. There is no need to mark any of the captions assigned to each of these text boxes as you do with the first five lists.

Defining the Style of the List

WordPerfect allows you to choose among several formatting styles for the lists it generates. To define the style for a list, follow the steps as outlined in the key sequence. After you select the Define and List options and indicate the number of the list (1–9), you select the option number corresponding to the style you wish to use.

A [Def Mark] code is inserted in the document when you press F7 (Exit) after selecting a style for the list. This marks the position where the list will be generated (see below). Therefore, most often you will want to position the cursor at the end of the document before you define the list style to have it generated there.

Generating Tables, Lists, and Indexes

After marking the list entries (if you are creating a list from 1 through 5) and indicating the style of the list, you are ready to generate it. After selecting the Generate (**6** or **G**) and Generate Tables, Indexes, Automatic References, etc. (**5** or **G**) options, you receive the prompt

Existing tables, lists, and indexes will be replaced. Continue? (Y/N)

To have WordPerfect generate the list, type **Y** or press any key besides *N*. If you have previously generated an index for the document, it will be completely replaced unless you type **N**. The list is generated at the [Def Mark] code in the document, and the program automatically inserts an [End Def] mark at the end of the list.

SEE ALSO

Graphics
Mark Text

Location of Auxiliary Files

Allows you to indicate to the program where the WordPerfect spelling, thesaurus, and hyphenation dictionaries, as well as the backup, printer, macro, style, and keyboard files, are located.

KEY SEQUENCE

Shift-F1 (Setup)
▼
7 — Location of Auxiliary Files
▼
1 — **B**ackup Directory
2 — **H**yphenation Module(s)
3 — **K**eyboard/Macro Files
4 — **M**ain Dictionary(s)
5 — **P**rinter Files
6 — Style **L**ibrary Filename
7 — **S**upplementary Dictionary(s)
8 — **T**hesaurus
▼
F7 (Exit)

USAGE

You use the Location of Auxiliary Files option on the Setup menu when you first install WordPerfect to indicate where you keep the program's spelling, thesaurus, and hyphenation dictionaries. In addition, you need to use it to indicate what directory will contain the backup files that the program will make if you use the Backup feature (see **Backup, Timed and Original Document**) as well as the printer definition files installed for the printer you use (see **Printer, Select**).

As you work with WordPerfect, you also use this option to indicate the name of the directory that will contain the macro/keyboard layout files (see **Macros** and **Keyboard Layout**), supplementary spelling dictionaries, and style library files that you create (see **Styles**).

When using this option to indicate the location of a particular file or group of files, you select the appropriate option and enter the full path name, including the drive letter and the directory path.

SEE ALSO

Backup, Timed and Original Document
Directories

Hyphenation
Keyboard Layout
Macros
Speller
Style Sheets
Thesaurus

LOCKING A FILE

Allows you to protect a document with a password.

KEY SEQUENCE

To add or change a password:

Ctrl-F5 (Text In/Out)

▼

2 Password

▼

1 Add/Change

▼

Enter Password: *<password>* **Enter**

▼

Re-Enter Password: *<password>* **Enter**

To delete password protection:

Ctrl-F5 (Text In/Out)

▼

2 Password

▼

2 Remove

USAGE

To lock the file that is displayed on the screen, follow the key sequence and select the Add/Change option. You will then be prompted to enter the password twice. The password can contain up to 24 characters. WordPerfect does not display the password on the screen, so it asks you to enter it twice to protect against typing errors. If the password you enter each time is not the same, you will receive an error message and must begin the file-locking procedure all over again.

As soon as you save the document after assigning a password, it will be saved with the document. Thereafter, you will have to enter the password in order to retrieve, copy, move, or rename the document as well as to print it from disk. If you aren't able to enter the password correctly, you will not be able to retrieve or print it ever again.

Once you have retrieved a locked file, you can edit it just like any other Word-Perfect document. If you wish to remove a password from a file after retrieving, you simply press Ctrl-F5 (Text In/Out) and select the Remove option (**2** or **R**). The next time you save the document, it will be saved without the password, which will no longer be required when you retrieve the file or print it from disk.

LOOKING AT THE CONTENTS OF FILES AND DIRECTORIES

Enables you to look at the contents of a file to determine whether it is the one you want to retrieve.

KEY SEQUENCE

F5 (List Files) **Enter**

▼

[highlight the name of the file to view]

▼

6 Look

▼

F7 (Exit)

USAGE

By selecting the Look option (**6** or **L**) on the List Files menu, you can display the contents of the file whose name is currently highlighted. This feature is helpful when you need to view the contents of a file to see if it is the document you want to edit or print.

When you highlight the name of a file and press Enter (or type **6** or **L**), Word-Perfect displays the first part of the document on the screen. If you have added a document summary to the file, you will see its statistics at the top of the screen. You can scroll through the document using any of the standard cursor keys. To return to the List Files menu after viewing the contents of the file, press F7 (Exit).

You can also use the Look option to temporarily view a new directory and locate the documents listed there. Highlight the name of the directory whose listing you wish to see and press Enter (or **6** or **L** and Enter).

SEE ALSO

Directories

MACROS

Enables you to record keystrokes and replay them at any time by entering the macro name under which they are stored.

KEY SEQUENCE

To define a macro:

Ctrl-F10 (Macro Define)

▼

Define macro: *<macro name>* **Enter**

▼

Description: *<description of macro>* **Enter**

▼

<keystrokes to be recorded> **Enter**

▼

Ctrl-F10 (Macro Define)

To edit an existing macro:

Ctrl-F10 (Macro Define)

▼

Define macro: *<macro name>* **Enter**

▼

2 Edit

▼

1 – Description *<new description>* **Enter**
2 – Action *[edit keystrokes as required]*

▼

F7 (Exit)

To replace an existing macro:

Ctrl-F10 (Macro Define)

▼

Define macro: *<macro name>* **Enter**

▼

1 Replace

▼

Description: *<new description of macro>* **Enter**

▼

<new keystrokes to be recorded>

▼

Ctrl-F10 (Macro Define)

To execute an Alt-key macro:

Alt-*<letter assigned to macro>*

To execute all other macros:

Alt-F10 (Macro) *<macro name>* **Enter**

USAGE

A macro is a recorded sequence of keystrokes that you save in a file and can use repeatedly. Macros can consist of text that you do not want to retype, such as standard paragraphs in a contract or form letter, or they can be complex sequences of commands, such as those that set up a document's format, save the document, and print it. You can even combine text and commands within macros so that you do not have to perform tedious, repetitious procedures, such as searching for formatting codes throughout a document and changing them to other codes.

You can set up macros that repeat themselves, as well as macros that call other macros. In addition, you can specify that a macro be executed only if a certain condition is met.

Creating Macros

The subject of macros is extensive. This section presents the rules you need to follow while creating macros but does not make additional suggestions of how you can use them in your work. For complete information on creating and using macros, refer to Chapter 16.

To create a macro:

1. Press Ctrl-F10 (Macro Define) to begin the macro definition. Word-Perfect will display the prompt

   Define Macro:

   Enter a macro name from one to eight characters long, with no spaces between characters, followed by Enter, or press the Alt key in combination with a letter from **A** to **Z**, or simply press the Enter key.

2. WordPerfect will then display the prompt

   Description:

   You may then enter a description of the macro's function, if you wish. It can consist of up to 39 characters. Then press Enter.

3. WordPerfect then displays the prompt *Macro Def,* which you'll see at the bottom of the screen until you terminate the macro definition. Enter all of the keystrokes that you want to include in the macro.

4. Press Ctrl-F10 a second time to terminate the macro definition. Word-Perfect automatically saves the definition in a file. The program appends the extension .WPM to the end of the file name you assigned to the macro. Macro files are automatically saved in the directory that you indicate as the Keyboard/Macro Files directory or in the directory that contains the WordPerfect program files, if you haven't yet specified such a directory (see **Location of Auxiliary Files**).

Executing Macros

To execute a macro whose name consists of one to eight characters, press Alt-F10. WordPerfect displays the following prompt:

Macro:

Enter the name of the macro and press Enter.

To execute a macro that uses the Alt key and a letter from A to Z, you simply press Alt in combination with the letter key you assigned to the macro.

To execute a macro that was named with the Enter key, press Alt-F10 and press Enter. To terminate any macro before it is finished, press F1 (Cancel).

Replacing and Editing Macros

If a macro that you have defined does not work as you intended, you can redefine or edit it. To do either, press Ctrl-F10 (Macro Define) and enter the same name you used when you originally defined the macro. WordPerfect will display the prompt

<macro name>.WPM is Already Defined. **1 R**eplace; **2 E**dit: 0

where *macro name* is the name you entered. To redefine the macro, select the Replace option (**1** or **R**) and reenter the keystrokes you want recorded. Press Ctrl-F10 to terminate and save the new definition when you are finished.

To edit the description or contents of a macro, select the Edit option (**2** or **E**). This takes you to the Macro Editor, which has two options, Description (**1** or **D**) and Action (**2** or **A**). To change the macro's description, select the Description option, edit the comment line, and press Enter. To edit the contents of the macro, select the Action option (**2** or **A**). This places the cursor inside the macro editing window, which displays the keystrokes already saved in the macro.

Macro programming commands and standard WordPerfect editing commands entered into the macro are both represented by a command or feature name enclosed in a pair of braces. For example, you might see the macro command {BELL}, which sounds the bell, or the editing command {Underline}, which underlines text.

To move the cursor, insert new text, or delete existing text or codes in the Macro Editor, you use the WordPerfect editing and cursor movement keys as usual. However, if you wish to add new WordPerfect commands to the macro, you must press Ctrl-V or Ctrl-F10 (Macro Define) before you press the appropriate function key(s). If you use Ctrl-F10 to enter the Function Key mode, you must press it again to reenter Edit mode before you use any of the editing or cursor movement keys. Otherwise, WordPerfect will insert their codes into the macro (such as {Left} when you press ←) rather than performing their usual function (to move the cursor one character to the left). To insert a macro programming command in a macro, press Ctrl-PgUp. This displays a list of commands that you can scroll through. Move the highlight cursor to the one you wish to use and press Enter to insert it into the macro.

Once you have finished editing the contents of a macro, press F7 (Exit) to save the new definition and return to the document editing screen. Press F1 (Cancel) if you wish to abandon any editing to the macro.

Enhancing Macros

You can insert a pause into a macro so that you can enter data from the keyboard while the macro is being executed. This makes it possible to write a "general" macro that can be used to accept variable data. For example, you can have a macro that creates a form letter, pausing for you to enter the address and salutation.

To enter a pause for input into a macro, begin the definition of the macro as described above and then press Ctrl-PgUp at the point where you want to insert the pause. The following menu options will appear at the bottom of the screen:

1 Pause; **2 D**isplay; **3 A**ssign; **4 C**omment: 0

Select the Pause option (**1** or **P**) and then press Enter and continue with the definition of your macro. When you execute a macro that contains a pause (or pauses) for input, the macro will execute all keystrokes up to the place where you entered the pause and then beep to signal that it has paused. To resume macro execution after you have entered your text, press Enter.

To make a macro's operation visible on the screen, you select the Display option (**2** or **D**) after pressing Ctrl-PgUp. The prompt

Display execution? ? (Y/N) No

will appear on the screen. Type **Y** to have the menu options on the document editing screen briefly displayed as WordPerfect commands are selected.

Chaining Macros

A macro can be started from within another macro, or a macro can be made to loop continuously by calling itself. To chain one macro to another, enter the second macro's name at the end of the first macro by pressing Alt-F10 followed by the name of the macro (if you are chaining an Alt macro, you must still press Alt-F10 before pressing Alt and the appropriate letter). You can also chain a macro by selecting the {CHAIN} command in the Macro Editor, entering the name of the macro, and entering a tilde (˜).

When two macros are chained together in this way, all of the keystrokes in the first macro are executed before the keystrokes in the second are executed. By including a search procedure that locates text that you want the macro to process, you can make a macro automatically repeat until it has operated on all occurrences of the search string.

Nesting Macros

You can nest an Alt macro inside of another macro by pressing Alt followed by the appropriate letter key (this time, you don't press Alt-F10 before you press Alt and the letter key). You can also nest a macro by selecting the {NEST} command in the Macro Editor, entering the macro name, and typing a tilde (˜).

When an Alt macro is nested inside another macro, WordPerfect executes the Alt macro's commands as soon as it comes to its name in the sequence of executing the commands in the first macro. After all of the commands in the Alt macro have been executed, WordPerfect resumes execution of any commands that come after the Alt macro name in the original macro.

The Macro Command Language

WordPerfect now includes sophisticated macro programming commands, which you access by pressing Ctrl-PgUp in the Macro Editor. You will find more information about these commands in Chapter 16.

Converting Macros Created in Version 4.2

WordPerfect 4.2 macros carry the extension .MAC and can't be run under WordPerfect 5.0. You can, however, successfully convert some macros using the MACROCNV.EXE utility (located on the Conversion disk). To convert a 4.2 macro to 5.0 form, go to DOS (you can use the Go To DOS feature) and make the drive/directory that contains this file current, then type

MACROCNV <*macro name*>

and press Enter (enter the full path name if the .MAC file is located on another disk or in a different directory). You don't have to include the .MAC extension as part of the file name. If you are trying to convert an Alt macro, be sure that you don't enter a space between the letters *ALT* and the letter of the key used when you type the macro name (that is, type **ALTP**, not **ALT   P**).

The macro conversion utility will convert as many of the keystrokes in the 4.2 macro into their 5.0 counterparts as possible. It will also rename the macro during conversion by replacing its .MAC extension with .WPM (it won't change the macro name). After the macro has been converted, the utility will display a screenful of statistics. The number of commands that couldn't be successfully converted will be indicated. Also, you will find that these unconverted keystrokes have been changed to comments (by enclosing them in semicolons—used to denote comments in 5.0 macros) when you edit the contents with the Macro Editor.

Because of the degree of change to the menu structure in version 5.0, you will find very few macros that don't require some degree of manual reworking. Nevertheless, the MACROCNV utility will allow you to transfer the basic structure of the 4.2 macro over to 5.0, and you can then use the Macro Editor to make all necessary manual changes.

SEE ALSO

Keyboard Layout

MARGIN RELEASE

Moves the cursor one tab stop to the left.

KEY SEQUENCE

To release the margin:

Shift-Tab (Margin Release)

To create a hanging indentation:

F4 (→Indent) **Shift-Tab** (Margin Release)

REVEAL CODES

[←Mar Rel]   Margin Release

USAGE

To move the cursor one tab stop to the right, you press the Tab key. To move the cursor one tab stop to the left, you press the Margin Release, Shift-Tab. When you use Margin Release to move left, WordPerfect inserts a [←Mar Rel] code in the document in front of the [Tab] code. If you delete this code, only, the [Tab] code will remain, and any text will be indented to its stop.

You can use the Margin Release with Indent to create a hanging indentation. To do this, press F4 to indent the paragraph and then press Shift-Tab to remove the indentation for the first line only. Succeeding lines will be indented, as in the following example:

> Hanging indents are often useful when you want to call attention to paragraphs in a series. Sometimes this style of indentation is referred to as an *outdent.*

To delete a hanging indentation, locate and delete the [←Mar Rel] and [→Indent] codes in the Reveal Codes screen.

SEE ALSO

→Indent
→Indent←
Tabs

MARGINS, LEFT AND RIGHT

Allows you to change the left and right margins of your document.

KEY SEQUENCE

Shift-F8 (Format)
▼
1 — Line
▼
7 — Margins - Left *<distance from left edge>* **Enter**
Right *<distance from right edge>* **Enter**
▼
F7 (Exit)

REVEAL CODES

[L/R Mar]   Left and Right Margins

USAGE

To change the left and right margins for a document, position the cursor at the beginning of the line where you want the new margins to begin and follow the key sequence. The left margin setting is given as the distance from the left edge of the paper, and the right margin setting is given as the distance from the right edge of the paper. Any change to these settings takes effect from the cursor's position forward in the document. To set new left and right margins for the entire document, be sure that the cursor is at the beginning of the file (press Home Home ↑ to get there) before you change them.

WordPerfect automatically adjusts the line length for the current font to maintain the left and right margin settings in effect. Therefore, there is no need to change the left and right margin settings when you change the size of the font in the document.

When you change the left and right margin settings in a document, WordPerfect inserts an [L/R Mar] code that includes their new settings. To revert to the default left and right margin settings of 1'' each, locate this code in the Reveal Codes screen and delete it.

SEE ALSO

Forms
Margins, Top and Bottom
Page Size/Type

MARGINS, TOP AND BOTTOM

Allows you to change the top and bottom margins of your document.

KEY SEQUENCE

Shift-F8 (Format)
▼
2 – Page
▼
5 – Margins - Top *<distance from top edge>* **Enter**
Bottom *<distance from bottom edge>* **Enter**
▼
F7 (Exit)

REVEAL CODES

[T/B Mar]   Top and Bottom Margins

USAGE

To change the top and bottom margins for a document, position the cursor at the beginning of the page where you want the margins to change and follow the key sequence. The top margin setting is given as the distance from the top edge of the paper and the bottom margin setting is given as the distance from the bottom edge of the paper. Any change to these settings takes effect from the cursor's position forward in the document. To set new top and bottom margins for the entire document, be sure that the cursor is at the beginning of the file (press Home Home ↑ to get there) before you change them.

WordPerfect maintains the top and bottom margin settings in effect by automatically adjusting the number of lines per page according to the fonts and line heights used. Therefore, there is no need to change the top and bottom margin settings when you change the sizes of fonts or the line height(s) in the document.

When you change the top and bottom margin settings in a document, WordPerfect inserts a [T/B Mar] code that includes their new settings. To revert to the default top and bottom margin settings of 1'' each, locate and delete this code in the Reveal Codes screen.

SEE ALSO

Forms
Line Height
Margins, Left and Right
Page Size/Type

MARK TEXT

Compares documents, removes redline markings and strikeout text, and creates automatic references, master documents, indexes, lists, tables of authorities, and tables of contents.

KEY SEQUENCE

To access the Mark Text menu:

Alt-F5 (Mark Text)
▼
1 Auto **Ref**; **2 S**ubdoc; **3 I**ndex; **4** To**A** Short Form;
5 Define; **6 G**enerate

To mark a table of contents, list, index, or table of authorities reference:

Alt-F4 (Block)
▼

[highlight text to be marked]
▼
Alt-F5 (Mark Text)
▼
1 To**C**; **2 List**; **3 Index**; **4** To**A**

USAGE

Mark Text is used for automatic references, master documents, document comparison, redline and strikeout removal, outlining, paragraph numbering, indexes and concordances, and tables of contents and authorities. When you press Alt-F5, you see the options shown at the top of the key sequence section. If you have already marked text as a block, the options are slightly different (as shown at the bottom of the key sequence section), because they are designed to allow you to designate which category the marked text is to be in.

For specific information on how Mark Text is used in WordPerfect, refer to the individual reference entries shown in the See Also section below.

SEE ALSO

Automatic Reference
Document Compare
Indexes
Lists
Master Document
Redline/Strikeout
Tables of Authorities
Tables of Contents

MASTER DOCUMENT

Allows you to create a master document containing separate documents (specified as subdocuments) that are to be printed together.

KEY SEQUENCE

To insert a subdocument in the master document:

Alt-F5 (Mark Text)
▼
2 Subdoc
▼
Subdoc filename: *<name of file to be inserted>* **Enter**

To expand the master document:

Alt-F5 (Mark Text)

▼

6 Generate

▼

3 – Expand Master Document

To condense the master document:

Alt-F5 (Mark Text)

▼

6 Generate

▼

4 – Condense the Master Document

▼

Save Subdocs? (Y/N) **N** or **Y**

REVEAL CODES

[Subdoc]	Subdocument
[Subdoc:End]	End Subdocument Text
[Subdoc:Start]	Start Subdocument Text

USAGE

The Master Document feature allows you to join any number of separate WordPerfect files together so that they are treated as one long document for the purposes of printing and automated references. This feature is most useful when you are creating a long document that consists of a number of discrete sections or parts. For example, you could use this feature to construct a master document for a training manual that is created from separate WordPerfect documents containing the introduction and each section of the manual. By keeping each section in a separate document, you make it easier and more efficient to edit its text. However, because each document is tied to a master document, you can generate a table of contents, list of figures, and index for the entire manual and print it as though it had been created as a single document.

Each WordPerfect document that is tied to the master document is considered a subdocument. To create a master document, you insert Subdocument codes into the master document, indicating where the text of each subdocument is to be inserted. To insert this code, you simply position the cursor in the master document where the text of a subdocument is to occur and follow the steps outlined in the key sequence. When prompted to enter the subdocument file name, type the name of the document. When you press Enter, WordPerfect displays the name of the subdocument, enclosed in a single-line box. It also enters a [Subdoc:] code into the master document. If you ever want to delete a subdocument from a master document, locate this code in the Reveal Codes screen and delete it—the box containing the subdocument's name in the document editing screen will then disappear.

The master document can contain its own text as well as the Subdocument codes that you enter. If you want to edit the text of a subdocument from within the master document, you can do so by expanding the master document to include the text of all subdocuments within it. Just follow the steps outlined in the key sequence section.

When the master document is expanded, the [Subdoc:] code is replaced by [Subdoc: Start] and [Subdoc: End] codes, which are placed before and after the text of the document (and which are visible on the document editing screen, enclosed in single-line boxes). Once a master document is expanded, you can edit any of its text, including that within the [Subdoc: Start] and [Subdoc: End] codes.

When you use the Exit (F7) or Save (F10) functions on an expanded master document, you receive the prompt

Document is expanded, Condense it? (Y/N) Yes

Press Enter to condense it before saving it. Type **N** to save it in expanded form. If you press Enter, you receive a second prompt,

Save Subdocs? (Y/N) Yes

Press Enter to save any editing changes in the subdocument files before the master document is condensed. Type **N** if you don't want to update the subdocuments with the changes you have made.

You can also condense a master document at any time before saving it. When you condense a master document, as indicated in the key sequence, the text of the subdocuments is replaced with the appropriate [Subdoc] codes. When you give the command to condense the master document, you receive the same prompt to save the subdocuments just as you do when you save the master document.

During editing, be careful that you don't delete any of the [Subdoc: Start] or [Subdoc: End] codes. If you do, WordPerfect won't be able to replace the text that belongs to those codes with the [Subdoc] code. Therefore, the subdocument's text will remain expanded in the master document. In such a case, delete the subdocument text that can't be condensed and then reinsert the file as a subdocument.

You must expand the master document before you print it, if you want all of the text contained in the subdocument to be included in the printout. If you forget to expand the master document before printing, the printout will contain the Subdocument codes instead of the text stored in the subdocuments.

Prior to generating tables of contents, lists, and indexes for a master document, you should expand it just as with printing. If you forget to expand the master document before generating one of these automatic references, Word-Perfect will automatically expand it for you. If this happens, WordPerfect will display the prompt

Update Subdocs? (Y/N) Yes

Press Enter to save the subdocuments before condensing the master document. Type **N** if you don't want the changes saved to them.

SEE ALSO

Indexes
Lists
Tables of Contents

MATH

Performs calculations on numbers in your document.

KEY SEQUENCE

To turn the Math feature on and off:

Alt-F7 (Math/Columns)

▼

1 Math On/Off

To define Math columns:

Alt-F7 (Math/Columns)

▼

2 Math D**ef**

▼

<type of columns, negative number display, number of decimal places, and formulas to be used>

▼

F7 (Exit)

REVEAL CODES

!	Formula Calculation
+	Calculate Subtotal
=	Calculate Total
*	Calculate Grand Total

[Math Def]	Definition of Math Columns
[Math Off]	End of Math
[Math On]	Beginning of Math
[t]	Subtotal Entry
[T]	Total Entry

USAGE

You can use WordPerfect as a calculator for simple mathematical functions such as addition, subtraction, multiplication, and division. The program can calculate totals, subtotals, and grand totals on numbers down columns. In addition, you can write formulas that perform mathematical operations across columns of numbers.

Turning Math On

To get totals, subtotals, and grand totals from simple columns of numbers (not predefined as Math columns):

1. Clear and then reset the tabs (see **Tabs**). When Math mode is on, Word-Perfect aligns tabs on the decimal/alignment character, which is the period (.) unless you change it (see **Decimal/Align Character**).

2. To turn the Math feature on, Press Alt-F7 (Math/Columns) and select the Math On option (**1** or **M**). The following prompt appears in the lower left corner of the screen:

   Math

3. Press the Tab key to move to the first column, then enter the numbers you wish to work with. When you press the period (.) to indicate a decimal point, the numbers will align on that decimal point. When Math mode is on, Word-Perfect treats the tab stop as a decimal tab, like the Tab Align key.

4. Wherever you want a subtotal to be calculated in that column, insert a plus sign (+), either from the numeric keypad or from the top row of your keyboard. WordPerfect will subtotal each number in the column after the previous plus sign. Where you want a total of the subtotals, enter an equal sign (=). If you want any numbers to be considered as subtotals or totals even if no calculation has been performed on them—which may be useful if you are working with imported data on which totals and subtotals have already been calculated—enter **t** before any additional subtotals and **T** before any additional totals. If you want to calculate a grand total—the total of all the totals—enter an asterisk (*).

5. To tell WordPerfect to make the calculations you have specified, press Alt-F7 (Math/Columns) and select the Calculate option (**2** or **A**). (You can select this option at any time to have the program perform calculations—for example, as you enter the numbers.) WordPerfect displays double question marks (*??*) if it cannot make a calculation. If this occurs, recheck your Math Definition screen to make sure that the column references in any formulas you have written are correct.

6. Turn Math mode off by selecting the Math Off option (**1** or **M**) from the Math/Columns menu.

When Math mode is on, you move between columns by using a combination of the Ctrl key and the → and ← keys. Pressing Home ← after the Ctrl-Home (Go To) sequence takes you to the beginning of the first text column.

Defining Math Columns

If you want to perform calculations across columns of numbers, you need to define Math columns.

For each column, you define three things: the type of column (calculation, text, numeric, or total), the symbol to be used with negative numbers (either parentheses or the minus sign), and the number of decimal places that are to be displayed (0–4). To do this, press Alt-F7 and select the Math Def option (**2** or **E**) to use the Math Definition screen. Each row under the letters A through X corresponds to a column.

All columns are predefined as Numeric columns (type 2). To change a column's definition, move the cursor to its letter by using the arrow keys. Enter **0** if the column is to contain a formula, enter **1** if the column is to contain only text, and enter **3** if the column is to contain a total calculated from other columns. If you have defined the column as type 0, the cursor moves down to the Calculation Formulas section of the screen to allow you to enter the formula for the calculation. Only four columns can be defined for calculations. Press F7 to exit to the menu and save the definition. Press F1 to cancel.

Displaying Totals in Separate Columns

If you have defined Math columns, you can display subtotals, totals, and grand totals in separate columns. To do so, you simply define the column or columns that you wish to hold the total calculations as total columns (type 3) and type the + , = , or * symbol in your document in the column where you want the calculation to appear.

Using Special Operators for Row Calculations

To use certain special operators in computing the totals and averages of rows, define the column that is to hold these special operators as a Calculation column (type 0). Then, when the cursor moves to the Calculation Formulas area of the Math Definition screen, enter any one of the special operators listed here.

- The addition symbol (+) calculates the total of all the numbers in the row that are in Numeric columns (type 2).
- The + / symbol calculates the average of all the numbers in the row that are in Numeric columns (type 2).
- The = symbol calculates the total of all the numbers in the row that are in Total columns (type 3).
- The = / symbol calculates the average of all the numbers in the row that are in Total columns (type 3).

These special operators work on numbers to their right and left, across the entire row—not just on numbers to the left.

Revising Math Definitions

You will often want to change the definitions of math columns so that you can add new columns of data, delete columns, or move columns to new locations. With your cursor positioned before the [Math On] code in the Reveal Codes screen, you can delete the old [Math Def] code. Then press Alt-F7 (Math/Columns) and select the Math Def option (**2** or **E**) to change any column definitions that you wish. Recalculate by using the new definition before you move to another part of your document.

If you want to revise a Math Definitions screen that you have already defined, position the cursor to the right of the [MathDef] code before you press Alt-F7 and select the Math Def option. You can then use the cursor movement keys to position the cursor on the settings you wish to change. To edit a formula, place the cursor on the *0* that defines the column holding the formula and reenter **0**. The cursor will move to the Calculation Formulas section of the screen, where you can edit the formula or delete it by pressing F1 (Cancel).

Remember that if you add, delete, or move columns, you will also need to revise the formulas that involve them.

SEE ALSO

Decimal/Align Character
Tabs

MERGE OPERATIONS

Merges data stored in lists in a secondary document into the appropriate places in a primary document.

KEY SEQUENCE

To designate a field from the secondary file to be merged in the primary file:

Shift-F9 (Merge Codes)

▼

^F

▼

Field: *<enter field number>* **Enter**

To insert other Merge codes:

Shift-F9 (Merge Codes)

▼

^C; ^D; ^E; ^F; ^G; ^N; ^O; ^P; ^Q; ^S; ^T; ^U; ^V

To separate fields in the secondary file with Merge R:

F9 (Merge R)

To separate fields in the secondary file with Merge E:

Shift-F9 (Merge Codes)

▼

^E

To perform a merge:

Ctrl-F9 (Merge/Sort)

▼

1 Merge

▼

Primary File: *<name of primary file>* **Enter**

▼

Secondary File: *<name of secondary file>* **Enter**

USAGE

Merge operations in WordPerfect can become quite complex, as the program contains many sophisticated merge features. This reference entry briefly summarizes the rules for working with merge operations. Refer to Chapter 11 for complete information on performing merges.

To perform a basic merge operation, such as a form letter, you usually create and use two separate files: a secondary file that contains all of the data to be substituted into each merged document (such as names and addresses), and a primary file (such as a letter) that indicates by special codes where each item from the secondary file is to be placed.

When the program performs the merge, it takes each record that you have specified from the secondary file and inserts its contents into the appropriate place in the primary file, creating a new merge file consisting of one filled-out standard document for each record.

The same record can be used more than once in a primary file. In addition, you do not have to use each record in the secondary file but can use only those that your primary file requires. You also can use several different primary files with the same secondary merge file. For example, you might want to prepare a form letter to go out to all your customers and use that same set of customer data to generate a set of mailing labels.

However, if you do not need to save the variable data to use again, you can skip the process of creating the secondary file and instead enter each variable item from the keyboard as it is needed. You do this by using the ^C code, which instructs WordPerfect to pause for input from the keyboard. Whenever the program encounters this code in your primary document, it will wait for you to type information into the document. (For details about each of the special Merge codes, see **Merge Codes** below.)

The Primary File

Any primary file you use must indicate where the contents (or fields) of the records in the secondary merge file are to be inserted. You do this by pressing Shift-F9, typing **F**, entering the number of the field (n), and pressing Enter. Each time the program encounters an n in a primary file, it inserts the corresponding data from the nth field in the record that is current in the secondary merge file. For example, if the code were 1, WordPerfect would insert the contents of the first field in the current record. WordPerfect numbers fields sequentially beginning with 1 for the first data item.

If you are not using a secondary file but are instead entering data from the keyboard, enter a ^C Merge code at each point in the document where you want to insert variable data.

CREATING A PRIMARY FILE

To create a primary merge file:

1. Begin a new document, such as a letter. Enter all of the text that is not to vary from merge document to merge document.

2. Indicate any places where you want information to be supplied from the secondary merge file by entering an ^F code; enter a ^C code for input from the keyboard.

You can type a question mark (?) at the end of the field number after you enter the ^F Merge code to keep the program from inserting blank spaces or lines for empty fields. In fact, if you want to make sure that no blank lines are printed and do not want to bother with keeping track of which fields may be blank, you can simply enter **?** after each code as you enter it. That way, if there are any blank fields in your records, you can be sure that WordPerfect will not leave blanks for them.

WordPerfect places the field number inside a pair of caret symbols (^) in the document. For instance, if you enter **2** after the Field prompt, it will appear as ^F2^ in the text when you press Enter. To delete a field from the primary file, you must delete the entire field designation, including the caret symbols.

The Secondary File

The secondary merge file contains the data that will be inserted into the final merged documents. To prepare a secondary merge file, which is basically a database consisting of records and fields, you must follow a certain set of rules so that the program can accurately locate the data you want to use:

- Each item of data (field) must start on a separate line.
- Each line must be terminated by a Merge R code, which indicates the end of a field. To insert this code, press F9.
- Each record must end with a Merge End code, which indicates the end of a record. To insert this code, press Shift-F9 and type **E**. WordPerfect will insert ^E and a hard page break into the document.
- Each record must have the same number of fields, although some of them can be empty. This way, WordPerfect can always locate the correct data for, say, item 9, which would be in the ninth field. If records had variable numbers of fields, that data would not always be in the field with the same number.
- A field can contain more than one line of data. For example, you can use a field to contain an entire standard paragraph or clause in a contract and simply insert it each time it is needed.
- A field can contain several different items of information, as long as you are willing to use this information as a unit. For example, a field may contain a complete street address, such as *2345 Polk St.,* or a name, such as *Rev. Evelyn Barker,* but you will not be able to break that unit into smaller units in your final documents.

You can also begin a secondary merge file with a dummy record that indicates all of the fields in each record. This record does not actually contain data; instead, you can use it as you set up your primary document to see which fields contain what information.

CREATING A SECONDARY FILE

To create a secondary merge file:

1. Begin each information item (field) on its own line and terminate it with a Merge R code. Even if you do not have information for a particular field, you must still press F9 to enter a Merge R code to mark its position in the record because each record in the secondary file must contain the same number of fields.

2. Indicate where each record to be used in the merge operation ends by entering a Merge E code on a separate line.

The following two records illustrate the correct usage of the ^R and ^E codes:

```
Woody Nelson^R
Creative Enterprises^R
115 South St.^R
Orem, UT 84057^R
^E
= = = = = = = = = = = = = = = = = = = = = = = = = = = = = = =
Toby Wilson^R
^R
1205 East 15th Ave.^R
Berkeley, CA 94704^R
^E
= = = = = = = = = = = = = = = = = = = = = = = = = = = = = =
```

Performing a Merge

To perform a merge operation, press Ctrl-F9 (Merge/Sort) and select the Merge option (**1** or **M**). You are then prompted to enter the name of the primary merge file to use:

Primary file:

Enter the file name of your primary merge file and press Enter. You are then prompted to enter the name of the secondary merge file:

Secondary file:

As soon as you enter the name of the file containing the secondary merge data you wish to use, WordPerfect begins the merge operation.

While data from the two files are being processed and the new file is being generated, you will see the message *Merging* displayed in the lower left corner of the screen. When the merge operation is completed, the cursor will be at the end of the file. Scroll through the file to make sure that the correct data are in each field; then save the file.

You can abort a merge operation at any time before it is finished by pressing F1 (Cancel). This causes WordPerfect to stop merging and to write any letters or forms that have been completed to the screen. (This is useful if you are using a large secondary file and you do not need to print documents for all the records.) To reexecute the merge operation, press F7 (Exit) and answer **N** to the prompt about saving the new document. You can then edit either the primary or secondary merge file and reissue the Merge command.

WordPerfect doesn't automatically save a newly created merge file. When WordPerfect completes a merge, it sends the merged file (all of it, including any separate documents it contains) to the screen and simply holds it in RAM. If you have a large number of records in your secondary merge file, it is possible to run out of RAM before WordPerfect generates all of the merged copies. If this occurs, the program stops the merge operation when no more memory is available and processes only part of your secondary merge file.

You can get around this limitation by using the technique WordPerfect calls *merging to the printer*. A special code, ^T, instructs the program to send each standard document to the printer as it is completed and then to clear its contents from RAM. If you are working with a large number of records, you may want to use this technique. However, when you merge to the printer, you are no longer performing a simple merge, and you may need to insert additional codes that tell WordPerfect specifically which primary and secondary file to use for each merge, which records to use, and so forth (see **Merge Codes** below).

Merge Codes

WordPerfect offers many optional Merge codes that you can use to adapt the merge operation to special requirements. To insert a Merge code in a document, press Shift-F9 (Merge Codes) followed by the letter of the code.

THE ^C (CONSOLE) MERGE OPTION

The ^C code temporarily halts the merge operation in progress, allowing you to enter data for a field directly from the keyboard into the merge documents being created. To continue the merge operation once you have finished adding text, press F9. You insert the Merge code into your primary or secondary document by pressing Shift-F9 and typing **C**.

The ^C pause is often combined with paired ^O Merge codes, primarily to keep a user-created message prompt or menu options on the screen and to allow you to enter your response. Insert the ^C code immediately after the final ^O Merge code.

For example, to create the prompt

Enter name of addressee:

you would enter it as

^OEnter name of addressee:^O^C

The ^C code can also be combined with the ^G, ^P, and ^S Merge codes, primarily to allow you to specify the name of a macro or a primary or secondary file to use. In this case, it is entered within any of these paired codes.

THE ^D (DATE) MERGE OPTION

The ^D code inserts the system date (the date entered in DOS when you start the computer) into your merge file. Usually you will use this code to insert the date in a primary merge file instead of entering the date manually or with Word-Perfect's Date Insert function (see **Date, Inserting the**). When you execute the merge operation, WordPerfect will substitute the full date wherever ^D appears. This date is automatically updated to the current date each time you execute a merge operation using a primary document that contains it. To enter this Merge code into your merge file, press Shift-F9 and type **D**.

THE ^G (GO TO MACRO) MERGE OPTION

The ^G Merge code is always paired. Between the pair of ^G codes, you place the name of the macro that is to be executed when the merge operation terminates. For example, if you want the macro Alt-M to be executed as soon as the merge operation called for in a primary file is complete, enter

^GALTM^G

in the primary file. If your macro does not use the Alt key with a single alphabetical letter, you enter its name between the ^G codes. To enter these codes, press Shift-F9 and type **G**, enter the name of the macro (do not enter the .WPM file extension), and press Shift-F9 and type **G** again.

You can enter only one macro in a merge file.

THE ^N (NEXT RECORD) MERGE OPTION

When you merge to the printer (by using the ^T code), the ^N Merge code tells WordPerfect to use the next record in the designated secondary file. If the program does not find a next record in the file, WordPerfect terminates the current merge operation. To enter the ^N Merge code, press Shift-F9 and type **N**.

You can place the ^N code above a particular record in the secondary file to cause WordPerfect to skip that record in the merge operation.

THE ^O (ON-SCREEN MESSAGE) MERGE OPTION

The ^O Merge code is always paired. Between the pair of ^O codes, you place the text of the message or prompt you want displayed in the lower left corner of the screen. To enter these Merge codes, press Shift-F9, type **O**, enter the text of your message as well as any other Merge codes to be included, and press Shift-F9 and type **O** again.

The ^O code is combined with a ^C pause code to keep a message on the screen until you type the data and press F9. For example, if you enter

^OEnter the date of sale: ^O^C

in a primary file when you perform the merge operation, WordPerfect will pause the operation and display

Enter the date of sale

on the last line of the screen in double intensity. This message will remain on screen until the user presses F9.

The ^O codes can also be used to display a menu of options on the screen by including the menu, with all of its options, between a pair of ^O Merge codes. Also within the ^O codes you could include a pair of ^G codes (to execute the macro associated with the menu selection) plus a ^C code (to allow the user to indicate a selection).

THE ^P (PRIMARY FILE) MERGE OPTION

When you merge to the printer (with the ^T code), WordPerfect neither assumes that you are using the same primary file throughout the merge nor automatically merges all records in the secondary file.

The ^P code designates the primary file to be used. It is always paired. Between the pair of ^P Merge codes, you place the complete name of the primary merge file that you want to use. If you do not specify a file name between the pair of ^P codes to switch to a different primary file, WordPerfect uses the current primary file. To insert these codes, press Shift-F9 and type **P**, enter the file name (if you are using other than the current file), and press Shift-F9 and type **P** again.

You can combine ^P Merge codes with the ^T and ^N codes to cause the current merge operation to continue until all of the records in the designated secondary file are processed.

For example, you might want to send each merged document to the printer as it is created, clear it from memory, advance to the next record, and use the same primary document. In such a case, you enter these codes at the end of the primary document:

^T^N^P^P

THE ^Q (QUIT) MERGE OPTION

The ^Q Merge code terminates a merge operation. You may enter this code into either a primary or secondary merge file. However, most often you will use it to restrict the records to be processed in a merge operation. In such a case, you place the code in the secondary merge file on its own line immediately before the beginning (first field) of the first record that you do not want included. When WordPerfect encounters this Merge code, it terminates the merge operation, thus ignoring all records that come after the ^Q code. To enter the ^Q Merge code, press Shift-F9 and type **Q**.

THE ^S (SECONDARY FILE) MERGE OPTION

The ^S Merge code is always paired. Between the pair of ^S codes, you place the complete name of the secondary merge file that you want inserted. If you do not specify a file name between the pair of ^S codes, WordPerfect uses the current secondary file. To insert these codes, press Shift-F9 and type **S**, enter the file name, and press Shift-F9 and type **S** again.

You use the ^S Merge codes to designate a new secondary file to be used during the current merge operation. Enter the complete file name between a pair of ^S codes in the primary file at the place where new data are to be substituted.

When WordPerfect encounters the ^S codes, it uses the designated secondary document in the merge operation and follows the codes it contains until its merge operations are complete.

THE ^T (TYPE) MERGE OPTION

The ^T Merge code sends all of the text that has been merged up to the location of the code directly to the printer. After the text is sent to the printer, it is cleared from the computer's memory.

This code is used to print each merged document as it is generated. To enter the ^T code, press Shift-F9 and type **T**.

Usually you will combine the ^T Merge code with the ^N code and a pair of ^P codes. This combination, ^T^N^P^P, ensures that each record in the second document is processed, and prevents extra form feeds from being inserted between the documents as they are printed.

The ^U (Update) Merge Option

The ^U Merge code rewrites the screen, causing the merge document that is currently being generated to be displayed on the screen. To enter this code, press Shift-F9 and type **U**.

This option is often combined with the ^O, ^C, and ^P Merge codes. It is used for applications in which the merged document is assembled from several merge files.

The ^V (Insert Code) Merge Option

The ^V Merge code is always paired. It inserts any Merge codes enclosed within a pair of ^V codes into the document currently being created. You enter these codes by pressing Shift- F9, typing **V**, pressing Shift-F9 again, typing the letter of the Merge code to be inserted, pressing Shift-F9, and typing **V** a second time.

The ^V code is quite useful for setting up a complex merge operation that adds records that you can transfer to an existing secondary merge document. To summarize the process briefly, by combining the ^O and ^C Merge codes with the ^V code, you can essentially automate the procedure of adding records to any of your secondary merge files. The ^V code (which stands for *Insert,* the usual assignment for *Ctrl-V*) inserts Merge codes into the file you are creating. This is sometimes called a *dual merge.*

Move/Rename File

Allows you to move a file to a new directory or rename it.

KEY SEQUENCE

F5 (List Files) **Enter**

▼

[highlight file to move or rename]

▼

3 Move/Rename

▼

<new path name to move and/or file name to rename > **Enter**

USAGE

The Move/Rename option (**3** or **M**) on the List Files menu allows you to rename files in the directory listing or to move them to a new disk or directory on your hard disk. When you select this option after highlighting the file to be moved or renamed (as indicated in the key sequence), you receive the prompt

New name:

followed by the current file name. To rename it, just edit or retype the file name. To move it to a new directory, edit the path name and leave the file name as is. To move a file and rename it simultaneously, edit both the path name and the file name. After making these changes, press Enter. If you renamed the document, the new name will appear in the directory listing after you press Enter. If you moved the document, its name will no longer appear in the listing (you must change directories to see it).

You can use the Move/Rename option to relocate multiple files in one operation. Mark all of the files to be moved with an asterisk (*) by moving the cursor highlight to each one and typing * (you can mark all of the files in the List Files listing at one time by pressing Alt-F5). After marking the files to be moved, select the Move/Rename option (**3** or **M**), enter the name of the drive/directory that they are to be moved to, and press Enter.

SEE ALSO

Copying Files

MOVE TEXT

See **Cut and Copy Text**.

NAME SEARCH

Moves the highlight cursor directly to the file or font name whose initial characters match those you enter.

KEY SEQUENCE

To locate a file or font from a list on a menu screen:

N Name Search *or* **F2** (→Search)

▾

<character(s) to search for>

▾

Enter *or arrow key to exit*

USAGE

The Name Search feature positions the highlight cursor on the first file or font whose name matches the character or characters entered. It enables you to locate and select a particular file or font in a long listing with just a few keystrokes.

You can initiate a name search on the List Files screen by typing **N** or by pressing F2 (→Search). Even on a screen like the Cartridges and Fonts screen that doesn't list a Name Search option, you can initiate such a search by pressing F2. As you type your first character, the highlight cursor jumps to a file or font name that matches that character. As you continue to type characters, the search narrows, moving the highlight to the first file whose name begins with the matching characters. To exit a name search, press Enter or one of the four arrow keys.

SEE ALSO

Word Search

OUTLINING

Creates an outline by automatically numbering paragraphs as you enter each level.

KEY SEQUENCE

To create an outline:

Shift-F5 (Date/Outline)

▼

4 Outline (*to turn on*)

▼

Enter *<text for level 1>* **Enter**

▼

Tab *<text for next level>* **Enter**

▼

4 Outline (*to turn off*)

To define the outlining style:

Shift-F5 (Date/Outline)

▼

6 Define

▼

1 − Start Paragraph Numbering
(in legal style)

2 – **P**aragraph
3 – **O**utline
4 – **L**egal (1.1.1)
5 – **B**ullets
6 – **U**ser-Defined

▼

F7 (Exit)

REVEAL CODES

[Par Num]	Paragraph Number
[Par Num Def]	Paragraph Numbering Definition

USAGE

After you have turned on Outline mode, each time you enter characters or a space and then press Enter, a new outline number is generated in your text. To generate a number at a lower level, press the Tab key after pressing Enter.

While you are in Outline mode, the prompt

Outline

appears in the lower left corner of your screen. To turn off Outline mode, press Shift-F5 (Date/Outline) and select the Outline option (**4** or **O**), again. Outline mode must be on (the Outline message must be visible on the screen) in order for automatic outline numbering to work.

To indent text without entering an outline number or letter when you are in Outline mode, press the space bar before you press the Tab key. You can also use →Indent (F4) or →Indent← (Shift-F4) to indent text without inserting outline numbers.

Defining the Style of Paragraph/Outline Numbering

WordPerfect's default outlining style (which is option **3**, Outline, on the Paragraph Numbering Definition screen) is as follows:

I.
    A.
        1.
            a.
                (1)
                    (a)
                        i)
                            a)

You can use more than eight levels; the eighth-level definition is used for the levels after the eighth, and each level is indented one additional tab stop. There are also three other numbering styles built into the program: paragraph style, which uses the system 1., a., i., (1), (a), (i), 1), a); legal style, which numbers each paragraph and level sequentially as 1, 1.1, 1.1.1, and so forth, and bullet style, which uses a system of symbols that not all printers can produce. You can also change the system of numbering and punctuation by using the User-Defined option (**6** or **U**) and specifying a custom style.

SEE ALSO

Line Numbering
Paragraph Numbering

OVERSTRIKE

Prints two (or more) characters or fonts in the same position.

KEY SEQUENCE

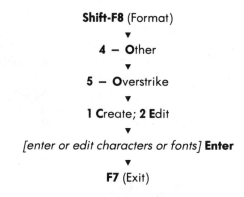

Shift-F8 (Format)
▼
4 – Other
▼
5 – Overstrike
▼
1 Create; **2 E**dit
▼
[enter or edit characters or fonts] **Enter**
▼
F7 (Exit)

REVEAL CODES

[Ovrstk]   Overstrike Preceding Character

USAGE

You can use the Overstrike feature to create composite characters such as foreign language characters that use accent marks or special math/science symbols. This is helpful if your printer is unable to print characters in WordPerfect's character sets created with the Compose feature (see **Compose**). You can also use

Overstrike to have your printer combine attributes available from the Font, Size, or Color menus that appear when you press Ctrl-F8 (Font).

When you enter the characters and/or font attributes for Overstrike (as shown in the key sequence), you see all of the characters and attribute codes as you enter them. When you press F7 (Exit) to return to the editing screen, you see there only the last character entered. WordPerfect prints all of the characters and attributes included in the Overstrike definition in the same position in the document.

To edit a composite character created with Overstrike, bring up the Reveal Codes screen with Alt-F3, position the cursor immediately following the [Ovrstk] code, and select the Edit option (**2** or **E**) as indicated in the key sequence. Enter the new characters and/or attributes, press Enter, and then press F7 (Exit) to return to the editing screen.

To delete a composite character created with Overstrike, locate and delete the appropriate [Ovrstk] code in the Reveal Codes screen.

SEE ALSO

Compose

PAGE BREAK, SOFT AND HARD

Divides pages automatically according to the top and bottom margins, the size of the page, and the printer selected (soft page break), or ends a page at the discretion of the user (hard page break).

KEY SEQUENCE

To enter a hard page break in the document:

Ctrl-Enter

REVEAL CODES

[Hpg]   Hard Page (Ctrl-Enter)

[Spg]   Soft Page

USAGE

WordPerfect automatically adjusts soft page breaks as you edit your document. They are displayed as a line of dashes on the screen. To change the placement of a soft page break, change the top and bottom margins, or delete lines of text on the page.

You insert hard page breaks by pressing Ctrl-Enter at the point where you want a page break to occur. For example, you might want to end a short page at the end of one section of a report so that the next main topic would begin a new page. Hard page breaks are represented by a line of equal signs across the screen.

Hard page breaks are also used to indicate the end of a column when you are using WordPerfect's Columns feature.

To delete a hard page break, position the cursor next to the line of equal signs that represents it and press Backspace or Delete, or locate and delete the [HPg] code in the Reveal Codes screen.

SEE ALSO

Columns
Conditional End of Page
Widow/Orphan Protection

PAGE FORMAT

See **Format**.

PAGE NUMBERING

Adds page numbers that are automatically updated when you make editing changes that affect pagination.

KEY SEQUENCE

To turn on and off page numbering:

Shift-F8 (Format)
▼
2 — **P**age
▼
7 — **P**age Numbering
▼
<page number position, 1–8> or
9 — **N**o Page Numbers
▼
F7 (Exit)

To select a new starting page number:

Shift-F8 (Format)
▼
2 — Page
▼
9 — New Page Number *<page number>* **Enter**
▼
F7 (Exit)

REVEAL CODES

[Pg Num]	New Page Number
[Pg Numbering]	Page Number Position

USAGE

You can turn on page numbering at any point in your document by using the Page Numbering option (**7** or **P**) on the Page Format menu as indicated in the key sequence. When you select Page Numbering, you will see the Page Numbering Position menu, from which you can select where you want page numbers to appear on the page. Choose options **1–3** and **5–7** for page numbers to appear in the same place on every page. Options **4** and **8** will insert page numbers in different locations on alternating left and right pages. Option **9** turns off page numbering.

When you return to your document by pressing F7 (Exit), you will not see page numbers on the screen, but they will appear when the document is printed. You can use the View Document feature to view page numbers in position on the screen.

You can also turn on page numbering by inserting the code ^B in the headers or footers in your document. For example, if you want a header to contain page numbers, enter ^**B** (Ctrl-B) at the position where you want the page number to occur. To specify the position of page numbers in headers and footers, press Alt-F6 (Flush Right) or Shift-F6 (Center) before you enter the ^**B**.

To start page numbering with a number that you specify, use the New Page Number option (**9** or **N**) on the Page Format menu. If you have saved parts of a document in separate files, this option enables you to number the pages sequentially. When you type the number that you want numbering to start with, you can use either Arabic numerals (1, 2, 3, etc.) or Roman numerals (i, ii, iii, etc.).

When you begin numbering with a new page number, you will see the change reflected on the status line.

Be sure to move the cursor to the beginning of the page where you want numbering to start when you use either the Page Numbering or New Page Number option.

To suppress page numbering on any given page, use the Suppress option (**9** or **U**) of the Page Format menu. To turn off page numbering, use option **9** or **N** (No Page Numbers) on the Page Numbering Position menu.

SEE ALSO

Headers and Footers
Suppress Page Format

PAGE SIZE/TYPE

Instructs WordPerfect to use a new page size or form definition in printing.

KEY SEQUENCE

Shift-F8 (Format)
▼
2 ― Page
▼
8 ― Paper **S**ize *<paper size option, 1–9 or O>* **Enter**
Type *<paper type option, 1–8>* **Enter**
▼
F7 (Exit)

REVEAL CODES

[Paper Sz/Typ]   Paper Size and Type

USAGE

Depending on your printer's capabilities, you can use the Paper Size/Type option (**8** or **S**) on the Page Format menu, as indicated by the key sequence, to instruct WordPerfect to format pages for a specific paper size, such as 8.5 by 14 inches (legal) or 5.5 by 5.8 inches (half sheet), and different types of paper, such as bond, letterhead, or transparency masters.

When you use the Paper Size/Type option, you first select the paper size and then the type from the list of options. For example, if your document is an envelope, you would select the Paper Size/Type option (**8** or **S**) and then select Envelopes (**5** or **E**) for the paper size; then select the Envelopes option (**5** or **E** from the Paper Type submenu shown below.

1-Standard

2-Bond

3-**L**etterhead

4-**L**abels

5-**E**nvelope

6-**T**ransparency

7-**C**ardstock

8-**O**ther

You can use the Other option (**O**) on the Paper Size menu to enter the dimensions for a custom paper size if it is not listed and if your printer is capable of handling it.

When the program reaches a Paper Size/Type code in your document, it matches it with either a predefined form definition that your printer supports or a form definition that you have set up by using the Forms option (**F** or **4**) on the Select Printer Edit menu.

SEE ALSO

Forms

PARAGRAPH NUMBERING

Automatically numbers paragraphs as you enter them.

KEY SEQUENCE

Shift-F5 (Date/Outline)

▼

5 Para Num

▼

Paragraph Level (Press Enter for Automatic): *<level number, 1–8>* or **Enter**

▼

<text of paragraph> **Enter**

REVEAL CODES

[Par Num]	Paragraph Number
[Par Num Def]	Paragraph Numbering Definition

USAGE

To number paragraphs automatically, press Shift-F5 (Date/Outline) and select the Paragraph Number option (**5** or **P**). You will be prompted to enter a paragraph level number or to simply press Enter for automatic paragraph numbering. When you press Enter, WordPerfect will insert a paragraph number. Each level of numbering is associated with a tab stop. To enter progressively lower levels of paragraph numbers, press the Tab key until you reach the level you want. Then press Shift-F5, select the Paragraph Number option, and press Enter.

You can also use *fixed numbering,* in which a particular numbering style will be inserted no matter which tab stop you are on. To use fixed numbering, enter the level (1–8) you want to use when you are prompted for the paragraph level.

Defining the Style of Paragraph Numbering

WordPerfect is preset to use the outline style of numbering (I., A., 1., etc.). It also has a built-in paragraph numbering style (1., a., i., etc.) and a legal numbering style (1., 1.1., 1.1.1., etc.). To select the paragraph or legal numbering style:

1. Press Shift-F5 (Date/Outline) and select the Define option (**6** or **D**).

2. When the Paragraph Numbering Definition screen appears, select a numbering style from the options on the screen or create a style of your own by entering any combination of styles and symbols from the choices available.

SEE ALSO

Line Numbering
Outlining

PITCH AND FONT

See **Font**.

PREVIEW DOCUMENT

See **View Document**.

PRINT COLOR

Allows you to select the color of the text (when printed), if you have a color printer.

KEY SEQUENCE

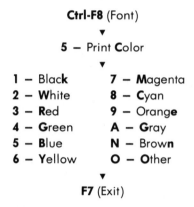

Ctrl-F8 (Font)
▼
5 — Print Color
▼

1 – Black	7 – Magenta
2 – White	8 – Cyan
3 – Red	9 – Orange
4 – Green	A – Gray
5 – Blue	N – Brown
6 – Yellow	O – Other

▼
F7 (Exit)

REVEAL CODES

[Color]   Print Color

USAGE

If you have a color printer, you can use the Print Color option (**5** or **C**) on the Font menu (Ctrl-F8) to select different colors of text for the printed page. For example, you might want to print cover sheets for each section of a document or chapter of a book in a different color, or you might want to highlight a specific section of text by printing it in color.

To return to black printing after having selected a different color, select the Black option (**1** or **K**) from the list of color options and press F7 (Exit).

To specify a custom color, you can select the Other option (**O**) and enter an intensity percentage for red, green, and blue.

The Print Color option controls the color the document is printed in, not the color of the characters on the screen. To change the screen colors, use the Colors/Fonts/Attributes command.

PRINT FORMAT

See **Font** *and* **Format**.

PRINT JOB, CANCEL

Allows you to remove a print job from the print queue.

KEY SEQUENCE

Shift-F7 (Print)
▼
4 — **C**ontrol Printer
▼
1 Cancel Job(s) <*job number*> or
* Y (*to cancel all jobs*)
▼
F7 (Exit)

USAGE

Selecting the Cancel Job(s) option (**1** or **C**) while the Control Printer screen is displayed allows you to cancel a specific print job in the print queue. When WordPerfect prompts you for the job to cancel, enter the job number of the document that is being printed or the job you want to cancel and press Enter. You may need to press Enter again if your printer does not respond. If you are using a large printer buffer, several seconds may elapse before your printer stops printing what has already been sent to it. To cancel all print jobs, enter an asterisk (*), answer **Y** to the prompt *Cancel all print jobs?*, and press Enter.

If you cancel all print jobs, you may get a message informing you that you will need to initialize your printer before you can continue printing. You may also have to adjust the paper in the printer before you print another job.

SEE ALSO

Printer Control
Print Job, Display
Print Job, Rush

PRINT JOB, DISPLAY

Allows you to see the remaining print jobs in the queue beyond the three displayed on the Control Printer screen.

KEY SEQUENCE

Shift-F7 (Print)
▼
4 — **C**ontrol Printer
▼

3 Display Job(s)

▼

<any key>

▼

F7 (Exit)

USAGE

Each time you send a document to the printer, WordPerfect assigns it a job number. The first three print jobs are listed on the Control Printer screen; an *Additional jobs not shown* message indicates that there are additional print jobs that are not listed on the Control Printer screen. You can use the Display Jobs option (**3** or **D**) to see all of the current print jobs, if there are more than three.

Viewing the print job numbers is useful if you are selecting a print job to cancel or bring to the head of the print queue.

SEE ALSO

Print Job, Cancel
Print Job, Rush

PRINT JOB, RUSH

Allows you to select a print job to be sent to the top of the queue.

KEY SEQUENCE

Shift-F7 (Print)

▼

4 — Control Printer

▼

2 Rush Job

▼

<any key>

▼

F7 (Exit)

USAGE

To move a print job to the head of the queue, select the Rush Job option (**4** or **C**) from the Control Printer screen. WordPerfect will prompt you for the number of the job to rush. Enter the job number and press Enter. If you answer **Y** to the

Interrupt prompt, WordPerfect will immediately print your rush job and then resume printing the job it was working on. If you answer **N**, it will print the rush job as soon as the current job is finished.

If the job you want to rush is a new print job that you haven't yet sent to the printer, first send it to the printer in the normal way; then select the Rush Job option and enter the job number for that job.

SEE ALSO

Print Job, Cancel
Print Job, Display

PRINT OPTIONS

See **Binding**, **Print Quality**, *and* **Printer, Select**.

PRINT QUALITY

Allows you to specify the print quality to be used for text and graphics as well as to print graphics separate from the text in your document.

KEY SEQUENCE

To change the graphics print quality or to print text only:

Shift-F7 (Print)
▼
G — **G**raphics Quality
▼
1 Do **N**ot Print; **2** **D**raft; **3** **M**edium; **4** **H**igh

To change the text print quality or to print graphics only:

Shift-F7 (Print)
▼
T — **T**ext Quality
▼
1 Do **N**ot Print; **2** **D**raft; **3** **M**edium; **4** **H**igh

USAGE

The Graphics Quality and Text Quality options on the Print menu control the quality of document printing (draft, medium, and high) for the text and graphic images in your document. You can use these options to prepare rough drafts of documents and to print graphics, which take longer to print, separately from the text. You can select a different print quality for both text and graphics. WordPerfect prints color graphics in black and white, using shading for the color areas.

Your printer may be capable of printing both text and graphics, but not at the same time. If this is the case, you can use the Do Not Print option (**1** or **N**) after selecting the Graphics Quality option to print just the text. Then reinsert the paper in the printer and print just the graphics by selecting the Do Not Print option after choosing the Text Quality option.

Print Quality settings apply to every print job until you change them again or quit WordPerfect.

NOTE

If your graphics do not print completely on a laser printer, you may need additional memory. Graphic images take up a large amount of memory.

PRINTER COMMAND

Inserts special printer formatting commands that are sent to the printer when your document is printed.

KEY SEQUENCE

Shift-F8 (Format)
▼
4 – Other
▼
6 – Printer Functions
▼
2 – Printer Command
▼
1 Command; **2 F**ilename
▼
<*printer command codes or filename*> **Enter**
▼
F7 (Exit)

REVEAL CODES

[Ptr Cmnd]   Printer Command

USAGE

You can use the Other option (**4** or **O**) on the Format menu (Shift-F8) to display the Printer Functions menu and insert special printer codes, turning on special effects that your printer is capable of producing. However, WordPerfect 5.0 can provide most common printer features directly.

To use special printing effects that WordPerfect does not support directly, you must insert a code that WordPerfect sends to your printer to tell it what to do. These codes are specific to each printer, and you must consult your printer manual for a list of the codes used.

To issue a printer command, enter the ASCII code for the printing effect you want. You cannot enter ASCII codes less than 32 or greater than 126 directly from the keyboard, but instead must enter their decimal equivalents, enclosed in angle brackets. ASCII codes are case-sensitive; uppercase *A* (ASCII code 065) is not the same as lowercase *a* (ASCII code 097), for example.

For example, to enter the sequence *Esc* # for your printer, you do not enter the letters *esc* or press the Esc key. Instead, you enter the decimal ASCII equivalent of Esc, 27, enclosed in angle brackets and followed by the # symbol. To do this, you select the Command option as indicated in the key sequence and then enter <27># after the Cmnd: prompt. The format code entered for this printer command (visible only when you use Reveal Codes) will appear as

[Ptr Cmnd: <27>#]

You will not see printer commands on the screen, but they will be sent to the printer when you print your document.

PRINTER CONTROL

Allows you to examine and make modifications to the jobs in the printer queue, as well as to start and stop printing.

KEY SEQUENCE

Shift-F7 (Print)

▼

4 — **C**ontrol Printer

▼

1 Cancel Job(s); **2 R**ush Job; **3 D**isplay Jobs; **4 G**o (start printer); **5 S**top

USAGE

To control the printing process as it is going on, you select the Control Printer option (**4** or **C**) from the Print menu. Doing this brings you to the Control

Printer screen, where you may cancel specific print jobs, start a rush print job, display print jobs, restart the printer after it has been stopped, or stop the printer without canceling print jobs.

After you have temporarily stopped the printer, you can start it again by using the Go option (**4** or **G**) on this menu.

SEE ALSO

Print Job, Cancel
Print Job, Display
Print Job, Rush
Printing, Stop

PRINTER FUNCTIONS

See **Justification**, **Kerning**, **Printer Command**, *and* **Word/Letter Spacing**.

PRINTER, SELECT

Allows you to install a printer, edit a printer definition, or select a new printer.

KEY SEQUENCE

To select a new printer:

Shift-F7 (Printer)
▼
S — **S**elect Printer
▼
[highlight the name of the printer]
▼
1 Select
▼
F7 (Exit)

To install a new printer:

Shift-F7 (Printer)
▼
S — **S**elect Printer
▼
2 Additional Printers
▼

1 Select; **2 O**ther Disk; **3 H**elp; **4 L**ist Printer Files; **N N**ame Search

▼

F7 (Exit)

To edit a printer definition:

Shift-F7 (Printer)

▼

S — **S**elect Printer

▼

[highlight of the name of the printer]

▼

3 Edit

▼

1 — **N**ame
2 — **P**ort
3 — **S**heet Feeder
4 — **F**orms
5 — **C**artridges and Fonts
6 — **I**nitial Font
7 — **P**ath for **D**ownloadable
Fonts and Printer
Command Files

▼

F7 (Exit)

USAGE

WordPerfect saves the printer selection you have made for each document with that document. To select a printer for the document, press Shift-F7 (Print) and choose the Select Printer option (**1** or **S**). The program will display a list of printers that you have installed, and an asterisk (*) will appear next to the name of the currently selected printer. You can move the highlighting to the printer you want to use and press Enter to select it, or select an option from the following menu:

1 Select; **2 A**dditional Printers; **3 E**dit; **4 C**opy; **5 D**elete; **6 H**elp: 1

Installing a New Printer

If the printer you want to use is not displayed, use the Additional Printers option (**2** or **A**) to install it. If the program cannot find the additional printer files, use the Other Disk option (**2** or **O**) to direct it to the drive or directory containing the additional printer files. The printer drivers are on Printer disks 1 through 4. The program will display a list of the printer drivers on each disk. When you see the printer you want to install, move the cursor to highlight its name; then press Enter. The Name Search option (**N**) allows you to search for a specific printer's name. When you select a printer, WordPerfect will display the printer definition file (with the .PRS extension) used by this printer. Press Enter again to have the program copy this file (see **Establishing a Printer Definition**).

Viewing Installed Printers

As you are selecting new printers, you may want to review the list of printers you have already installed. The List Printer Files option (**4** or **L**) on the Additional Printers submenu allows you to view a list of the printers that you have already installed. WordPerfect keeps information about printer drivers in files with an .ALL extension. Once a printer file is created, its definition is kept in a file with a .PRS extension, which is what you see listed on this screen.

Establishing a Printer Definition

After you have selected a new printer, you will see the Printer Helps and Hints screen, which contains information about the specific printer you are installing. Press F7 (Exit) to go to the next menu, where you can change the printer's name, specify which port it is connected to, select a sheet feeder, select forms, specify cartridges and fonts, set the default font that the printer is to use, and specify a path for downloadable fonts and printer command files.

Establishing Printer Settings

The Name option (**1** or **N**) allows you to change the name that appears on the Printer Selection menu. You can enter up to 36 characters for a new name.

The Port option (**2** or **P**) is used to indicate the port your printer is connected to. The default setting is LPT1, the first parallel printer port. If the printer whose definition you just chose is connected to another parallel port, select option 2. You will see a menu listing LPT ports 1 through 3 and COM ports 1 through 4. If your printer is connected to a different port, select the Other option (**8** or **O**) and specify the device name.

When defining a printer that uses a serial port, you will see a screen that indicates the baud rate, parity, number of stop bits, character length, and type of hardware handshaking (XON/XOFF) that your printer normally uses. If you are using different settings, select them and change them. All of the settings possible for your printer should be in your printer manual.

Use the Sheet Feeder option (**3** or **S**) if you are using a sheet feeder to feed paper into your printer. Select the sheet feeder that you are using; then choose the Select option (**1** or **S**). A Helps and Hints screen will appear after you have selected the sheet feeder, and the sheet feeder definition will be copied into the .PRS file that is being created for your printer definition.

The Forms option (**4** or **F**) indicates the location of the paper sizes and types you intend to use with the printer (see **Forms**). The Cartridges and Fonts option (**5** or **C**) indicates the fonts and cartridges you plan to use with the printer (see **Cartridges and Fonts**). The Initial Font option (**6** or **I**) indicates the current default font to be used with that printer. The font selected as the initial font will be used each time you start a new document. To override it, you can use the Initial Font option on the Document Format menu (see **Initial Settings**) or change it through the Base Font option (see **Base Font**). The last option (**7** or **D**) is used to indicate the path name for the subdirectory in which you are storing downloadable fonts or printer command files (see **Cartridges and Fonts** and **Printer Command**).

Editing Printer Definitions

The Edit and Copy options (options **3** or **E** and **4** or **C**) of the Select Printers menu allow you to copy and then modify an existing printer definition. For example, you might want to set up the same physical printer with two different definitions under different names. The first definition might specify a different default font or sheet feeder from the second definition, and you could quickly choose either "printer" by selecting its name from the list of installed printers.

You also use the Select Printer option to delete a printer from the list of installed printers by choosing the Delete option (**5** or **D**). However, you cannot delete the printer definition that is currently selected; to delete it, select a different printer first. To get additional help about the specific printers you have installed, use the Help option (**6** or **H**). To get help with a sheet feeder, press Shift-F3 (Switch) when you are viewing the Printer Help screen.

SEE ALSO

Cartridges and Fonts
Forms
Printing

PRINTING

Prints all or part of a document using the selected printer.

KEY SEQUENCE

To print the current page or entire document on your editing screen:

Shift-F7 (Print)

▼

1 – **F**ull Document

2 – **P**age

To print a document on disk:

Shift-F7 (Print)

▼

3 – **D**ocument on Disk

▼

Document on disk: *<file name>* **Enter**

▼

Page(s): **Enter** *(to print all)* or
<range or selected page numbers> **Enter**

To print a document on disk from the List Files menu:

F5 (List Files) **Enter**

▼

[highlight name of file to be printed]

▼

4 Print

▼

Page(s): **Enter** *(to print all)* or
<range or selected page numbers> **Enter**

USAGE

WordPerfect allows you to print documents in a variety of ways. You can print the document that is currently in RAM (displayed on the screen) or you can print a saved document through the Control Printer screen. In addition, you can print through the List Files screen (F5), or you can print a block of text that you have marked with Block (Alt-F4).

When you press Shift-F7, the Print menu appears. (You can also press Ctrl-PrtSc to bring up this menu.) To print the text of the entire document on the screen, select the Full Text option (**1** or **F**). To print the current page, select the Page option (**2** or **P**).

To print a document that has been saved on disk, you select the Document on Disk option (**3** or **D**), from the Print menu and enter the file name of the saved document. Press Enter to print the whole document, or enter the pages you want to print. To enter the page range, you type the starting and ending page numbers, separated by a dash, over the *(All)* that appears after the Page(s) prompt. To print from a specific page to the end of the document, you enter the starting page number followed by a dash. To print from the beginning of the document up to and including a specific page, you enter a dash followed by the ending page number. When entering any of these combinations, be sure not to enter any spaces between the numbers and the dash or commas used.

Table V.5 shows the various combinations that can be entered at the Page(s) prompt and the results of each.

Note that if you have used the Fast Save option (see **Fast Save: Unformatted**) to save a document, you cannot print it from disk unless you had moved the cursor to the end of the document before you saved it. You must retrieve the document to the screen and then print it.

If you did not select a printer when you installed WordPerfect, when you print a document for the first time, you will need to select the printer you want to use. WordPerfect saves the printer selection you have made for each document with that document. To select a printer for the document, press Shift-F7 and choose the Select Printer option. When you select a different printer for a document, it is reformatted for that printer. To print a document formatted for a printer other than the one that is attached to your computer, select the printer you want the document to be formatted for. Then print it from disk (using the Document on Disk option on the Print menu or the Print option on the List Files screen) without retrieving it to the screen. This technique lets you get a hard copy of a document formatted for a printer that is not available—for example, if you are working at home with a dot matrix printer but will print a final draft of your document on a laser printer at work.

If the document you are retrieving has been formatted for a printer that you have not installed (for example, if you are exchanging files with other Word-Perfect users), you will see a message indicating that WordPerfect cannot find that particular printer (.PRS) file. It will format the document for your default printer in that case.

ENTRY	RESULT
Page(s): 4	Prints only page 4 of the document.
Page(s): 6,12	Prints pages 6 and 12 of the document.
Page(s): 2–6,17	Prints pages 2 through 6 and page 17 of the document.
Page(s): 10–	Prints from page 10 to the end of the document.
Page(s): –5	Prints from the beginning of the document through page 5.
Page(s): x–xii	Prints Roman numeral pages 10 through 12.
Page(s): iv,2–5,iv–x	Prints the first Roman numeral page iv, Arabic numeral pages 2 through 5, and finally the second Roman numeral pages iv through x.

TABLE V.5: Entering Pages to Be Printed

Other Print Options

If your printer supports type-through printing, you can also use the Print menu's Type Through feature (**5** or **Y**) to print as though your keyboard were a typewriter, either one character or one line at a time.

The View Document option (**6** or **V**) lets you preview your document by pages to see how it will appear when printed. Headers, footers, notes, graphics, and page numbers will be displayed on the previewed pages.

The Initialize Printer option (**7** or **I**) is used when you download soft fonts. When you choose this option, the fonts you have marked as present when the print job begins (using *) with the Cartridges and Fonts option are downloaded to the printer you have selected.

All of these options are discussed in separate sections. Refer to the See Also list at the end of this entry.

Changing Print Options

Before you print a document, you can temporarily modify the print options that control the printer used, the number of copies printed, the binding width, and the quality of text and graphics. To do this, you select one of the options from the lower half of the Print menu:

S - **S**elect Printer
B - **B**inding Width
N - **N**umber of Copies
G - **G**raphics Quality
T - **T**ext Quality

(Note: The Select Printer and Binding options are discussed in their own separate sections, and the Graphics Quality and Text Quality options are discussed in the **Print Quality** section.)

Use the Number of Copies option (**N**) to specify the number of copies of a document to be printed while you work on other documents or begin a new one.

Printing from the List Files Screen

To print a document listed on the List Files screen, move the cursor highlight to the document's name and select the Print option (**4** or **P**) on the List Files menu.

To have WordPerfect consecutively print (batch-print) a group of documents listed on this screen, you must mark each document to be printed by highlighting it and then typing an asterisk (*) to mark it. After you have marked all of the document files you wish to print, select the Print option. When you respond **Y** to the prompt to print the marked files, WordPerfect begins printing the documents in the order in which they were marked. The program places all marked files in its print queue in the order they were marked.

If you need to use printer control at any time, you can press Shift-F7 and enter **4** or **C** to go to the Control Printer screen.

To print documents in other subdirectories, highlight the directory name and press Enter twice, then highlight the document file you want to print and select the Print option. Again, if you want to print a group of files listed in this subdirectory, mark all of the files with an asterisk. To return to the current directory, highlight *<PARENT> <DIR>* and press Enter.

SEE ALSO

Cartridges and Fonts
Fast Save: Unformatted
Fonts
Printer Control
Printer, Select
Type Through
View Document

PRINTING, STOP

Halts the current printing job.

KEY SEQUENCE

Shift-F7 (Print)
▼
4 – Control Printer
▼
5 Stop
▼
[fix printing problem]
▼
4 Go (start printer)
▼
F7 (Exit)

USAGE

You may need to stop the printer temporarily to insert a new ribbon or clear a paper jam. To do so, choose the Stop option (**5** or **S**) from the Control Printer screen. This interrupts printing but does not cancel the job. After you have stopped the printer, select the Go option (**4** or **G**) to start it again. If printing does not resume as soon as you type **4** or **G**, check the message area of the Control Printer screen. You may need to reposition the paper in the printer, for example.

SEE ALSO

Print Job, Cancel

PRINTING TO DISK

Saves a copy of the document on disk in DOS text or ASCII format.

KEY SEQUENCE

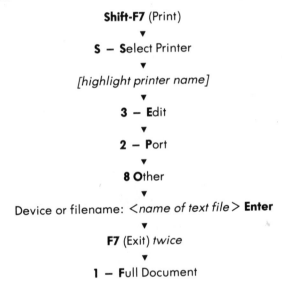

Shift-F7 (Print)
▼
S — **S**elect Printer
▼
[highlight printer name]
▼
3 — **E**dit
▼
2 — **P**ort
▼
8 Other
▼
Device or filename: *<name of text file>* **Enter**
▼
F7 (Exit) *twice*
▼
1 — **F**ull Document

USAGE

WordPerfect can output a document file to a new disk file rather than to your printer; this is known as printing to a disk. The new disk file created with this operation is essentially a DOS text (ASCII) file that also contains all of the printing control codes required to print it as it was formatted by WordPerfect. To save a file as a DOS text file without the formatting codes, you use the Text In/Out key (Ctrl-F5).

When you follow the key sequence shown above, the DOS text file can be printed from the DOS operating system without having a copy of WordPerfect running. This allows you to print WordPerfect documents on a printer attached to another computer that does not even have WordPerfect on it.

As indicated in the key sequence, you need to select the printer name that represents the type of printer that will be used to print the file. Remember that the correct printer definition may differ from the one you use to print documents on the printer (or printers) attached to your computer.

After you specify the printer port, you will need to select the Other option (**8** or **O**) and then type a file name under which the DOS text file version of your document will be stored. If you do not specify a new path name, WordPerfect will save the document in the default directory. When naming the file, you can use the same file name and add the extension .TXT to differentiate it from the original document file.

To obtain a hard copy of the DOS text file, you can use the DOS COPY or PRINT command. (Use COPY if you have temporarily exited from Word-Perfect to DOS.)

SEE ALSO

Text In/Out

REDLINE/STRIKEOUT

Allows you to mark text that has been added to the document with redlining and text that has been deleted from it with strikeout.

KEY SEQUENCE

To redline or strike out text as you type it:

Ctrl-F8 (Font)

▼

2 – **A**ppearance

▼

8 – **R**edln
9 – **S**tkout

▼

<*text*> →

To redline or strike out existing text:

Alt-F4 (Block)

▼

[highlight text]

▼

Ctrl-F8 (Font)
▼
2 Appearance
▼
8 — Redln
9 — Stkout

To select a new redline method:

Shift-F8 (Format)
▼
3 — Document
▼
3 — Redline Method
▼
1 Printer Dependent; **2 L**eft; **3 A**lternating
▼
F7 (Exit)

To removing redline markings and strikeout text from the document:

Alt-F5 (Mark Text)
▼
6 — Generate
▼
1 Remove Redline Markings and Strikeout Text from Document
▼
F7 (Exit)

REVEAL CODES

[REDLN]	Redline On
[redln]	Redline Off
[STKOUT]	Strikeout On
[stkout]	Strikeout Off

USAGE

Redlining and strikeout are useful features for marking sections of text that have been altered so that others can review the changes quickly without having to check the entire document.

To mark text for redlining (most printers do this by placing a vertical bar in the left margin), you select the Redline option. When you have finished typing the text you wish to highlight, press the → key to move beyond the second [redln] format code, or press Ctrl-F8 (Font) and select the Normal option (**3** or **N**) to turn off redlining.

To redline text you have already typed, mark the text as a block before you turn on redlining. The way WordPerfect represents redlining on the screen varies according to the type of monitor you are using. It may not be the same way that it will appear in the printed document.

To strike out existing text, mark the text as a block and then select the Strikeout option (**9** or **S**) from the Appearance submenu of Font.

Changing the Redlining Method

You can choose Printer Dependent, Left, or Alternating as the method of redlining. If you choose Printer Dependent, redlining will appear as your printer has defined it; you can test-print a redlined paragraph to see how this appears. The Left option marks redlined text with a horizontal bar in the left margin. The Alternating option marks redlined text on even pages in the left margin and redlined text on odd pages in the right margin.

Deleting Struck-Out Text and Removing Redlining

Before you issue the final version of a document, you will probably want to delete text that has been struck out and remove redlining marks. To do so, press Alt-F5 (Mark Text), choose the Generate option (**6** or **G**) and choose the Remove Redline Markings and Strikeout Text from Document option (**1** or **R**). When you type **Y** in response to the prompt, all text between the [STKOUT] and [stkout] codes will be deleted, and the Redline and Strikeout codes will be removed from the document.

SEE ALSO

Document Compare

RENAMING A DOCUMENT

See **Move/Rename File**.

REPEAT VALUE

See **Esc Key**.

RETRIEVE

Retrieves a document on disk or the last text that was cut or copied.

KEY SEQUENCE

To retrieve a document while in the editing screen:

Shift-F10 (Retrieve)

▼

Document to be retrieved: *<document name>* **Enter**

To retrieve the text most recently cut or copied from the current document:

Shift-F10 (Retrieve)

▼

Document to be retrieved: **Enter**

To retrieve a document from the List Files menu:

F5 (List Files) **Enter**

▼

[highlight name of file to be retrieved]

▼

1 **R**etrieve

USAGE

Retrieve (Shift-F10) is used to retrieve a saved document. Press Shift-F10 and enter the name of the document; then press Enter.

If you do not enter a document name but instead press Enter at the prompt, the last text you moved or copied from a document you have been working on in the current session will be inserted at the cursor position, so you can paste a selection several times by using this feature.

You can also retrieve documents from the List Files menu, by selecting its Retrieve option (**1** or **R**). If you retrieve a document while you are working on another document, you see the prompt

Retrieve into current document? (Y/N) No

If you type **Y**, the retrieved document will be inserted at the current cursor position, *added to* the current document.

To retrieve a DOS text file, use Text In/Out (Ctrl-F5).

SEE ALSO

Text In/Out

REVEAL CODES

See **Codes**.

REWRITE, SCREEN

Turns off and on automatic screen rewriting.

KEY SEQUENCE

Ctrl-F3 (Screen)

▼

0 Rewrite *or* **Enter** *or* **Ctrl-F3** (Screen)

USAGE

WordPerfect normally rewrites the screen as you enter and edit text so that what you see on the screen resembles what you get in your printed documents. You can temporarily turn off automatic screen formatting to speed up the program's operation if you are working with graphics or complex screen displays.

When you have turned automatic formatting off, you can rewrite the screen by simply pressing Ctrl-F3 (Screen) twice.

SEE ALSO

Display, Setup: Automatically Format and Rewrite

RULER, ON-SCREEN

See **Windows**.

SAVE

Saves a document on disk under the name you assign to it.

KEY SEQUENCE

F10 (Save)

▼

Document to be saved: *<file name>* **Enter**

USAGE

To save a file you are working on and then return to it, press F10 (Save). WordPerfect will prompt you for a file name if you have not saved the file before. Enter a name of up to eight characters with an optional three-character extension (include a directory and drive designation if you want to save the file somewhere other than the current drive and/or directory); then press Enter.

If you have saved the file previously, WordPerfect will provide its file name when you press Save. To save the file under the same name, press Enter and respond **Y** to the prompt

>Replace *<file name>*? (Y/N)No

to indicate that you *do* want to replace the original version of the file with the edited version you are now saving. The default setting is No, which allows you to leave the existing file intact and save the new version under another name. If you want to rename the file in order to keep two versions of a document, press Enter to accept the No setting. WordPerfect will allow you to enter a new file name. Enter the new name (including a drive and directory designation, if you do not want to use the current ones) or edit the existing name; then press Enter.

To cancel a save sequence, use the Cancel key (F1).

SEE ALSO

Exit: Saving and Exiting
Text In/Out

SCREEN KEY

See **Line Draw**; **Rewrite, Screen**; *and* **Windows**.

SEARCH

Locates the next occurrence in the document of specified text or formatting codes.

KEY SEQUENCE

To perform a forward search:

F2 (→Search)

▼

–> Srch: *<search text or function keys>*

▼

F2 (→Search)

To perform a backward (reverse) search:

Shift-F2 (←Search) *or* **F2** ↑

▼

<– Srch: *<search text or function keys>*

▼

F2 (→Search)

USAGE

When you press F2 (Forward Search), the prompt

–> Srch:

appears at the bottom of your screen. The rightward direction of the arrow indicates that WordPerfect will search for your string of characters from the cursor's present position to the end of the document. After you have entered the search string, press F2 or Esc to carry out the search.

You can include up to 59 characters in the search string. WordPerfect ignores case (capitalization) differences in a search as long as the search string is entered in all lowercase letters. To make a search case-sensitive, enter it using the appropriate capital letters. If you enter characters in uppercase, WordPerfect will search for those characters only as capital letters.

If WordPerfect does not find a match for your search string, it will display the message * *Not Found* *, and the cursor will not move from its original position. In such a case, you can press F2 again and retype or edit the search string.

After WordPerfect finds the first occurrence of your search string, you must repeat the Search command to locate any subsequent occurrences. To reissue the command without changing the search string, press F2 twice. To edit the search string before performing the search again, press F2 once, make your changes, and then press F2 again.

For example, if you enter

file list

WordPerfect will find all occurrences of *File List, file list, file List,* and *File list.* If you do not enter a space before *file* and after *list,* WordPerfect will also return any occurrences of the two words together within other words, such as "re*file list*-ings." To have WordPerfect search for an entire word by itself, enter a space before and after it.

If you enter

FILE LIST

WordPerfect will search for *FILE LIST* in uppercase letters only.

Canceling a Search Operation

To abort a search operation after entering the search string, press F1 (Cancel). To return to the place in your document where you were before you began a search operation, press Ctrl-Home (Go To) twice.

Using Wild Cards in a Search

You can substitute ^X (Ctrl-X) for any character when searching for words or phrases in your documents. For example, a search for

no^X

returns *now, not, nor, non,* and so forth. It also returns words that contain *now, not, nor, non,* and so forth, such as *nowadays, notable, nonapplicable, enormous, denoted,* and *anonymous.* To enter the wild card (^X), press Ctrl-V Ctrl-X. Also note that you cannot use ^X at the beginning of a search string. Using ^X as a wild card is useful if you do not remember the exact spelling of the word you wish to find. If you want to limit WordPerfect's search to complete words, you must enter spaces before and after the search string. However, note that this method will not locate words that have a punctuation mark immediately following them.

Extended Searches

When WordPerfect performs a standard search operation, it does not look for matches to your search string in any headers, footers, footnotes, endnotes, graphics box captions, or text boxes that you have added to the document. However, you can perform an extended search operation to include these elements. To do this, press Home before you press F2 to perform a forward search.

Searching in Reverse

You can instruct WordPerfect to search backward through your document to the beginning by pressing Shift-F2 instead of F2 (or by pressing ↑ when the Search prompt is displayed). When you press Shift-F2, WordPerfect responds with this prompt:

<- Srch:

The leftward direction of the arrow shows you that WordPerfect will search from the cursor's present position toward the beginning of the document. After you enter your search string, press Search (F2) to initiate the reverse search. To perform the reverse search operation to locate a previous occurrence, press Shift-F2. To change directions and perform a forward search using the same search string, press the ↓ key when the Search prompt is displayed. You can always change the direction of a search by pressing ↓ or ↑ when you see this prompt.

You can also have WordPerfect perform an extended reverse search by pressing Home before you press Shift-F2 and enter your search string.

Searching for Format Codes

You can also use WordPerfect's Search feature to locate a particular formatting code. (This feature also works while you are using Reveal Codes.) To indicate the code to be searched for, press the appropriate function key or key combination (including, if applicable, the number of the menu option) instead of typing an alphanumeric search string in response to the Search prompt. For instance, to perform a forward search to find the first occurrence of a hard page break, press F2 and then press Ctrl- Enter. In response, the program will display the format code as the search string:

-> Srch: [HPg]

When the code is located, the cursor will be positioned immediately after it.

You can also use this technique to find format codes that require the use of menu options. For example, to search for a [Col On] code, press F2, then press Alt-F7 (Math/Columns) and type **C**.

If you press the key that generates a paired code twice, the Search function will locate the second formatting code of a pair, such as the [und] in [UND][und] or the [bold] in [BOLD][bold], so that, for example, you can replace an underlined word or phrase with a boldfaced version of that same word or phrase. If you perform a regular search for one of these paired codes, WordPerfect locates the first uppercase code. However, if you press the key that generates the code twice, the program will locate the second (lowercase) code, which allows you to locate the beginning of a bold word or phrase, mark it as a block, locate its end, and change it to another style or attribute, such as underline or italics.

For example, to search for an [und] code, you press F2 and then press Underline (F8) twice. Press ← twice; then press Del to remove the [UND] code. (If you do not delete the first code, the program will locate only codes with no text between them.)

For a list of the codes that WordPerfect uses, see **Appendix C**.

SEE ALSO

Search and Replace

SEARCH AND REPLACE

Locates the next occurrence of specified text or formatting codes and replaces them with new text or codes.

KEY SEQUENCE

Alt-F2 (Replace)
▼
w/Confirm? (Y/N) **Y** *or* **N**
▼
Srch: *<search text or codes>* **F2** (→Search)
▼
Replace with: *<replacement text or codes>* **F2** (→Search)

USAGE

You can search for words or phrases and replace them with substitute words or phrases that you specify. You can search for up to 59 characters and replace them with as many as 59 characters, including spaces. In version 5.0, you can search and replace backward by pressing ↑ before entering the search string.

To perform a search-and-replace operation, press Alt-F2 (Replace). For an extended replacement that includes headers, footers, endnotes, footnotes, graphics box captions, and text boxes, press Home before you press Alt-F2. Word-Perfect then asks you whether you want to confirm each replacement:

w/Confirm? (Y/N) N

If you enter **Y**, WordPerfect will ask you to confirm whether you want to make the replacement each time it finds the word or phrase you specified (the *search string*). If you press Enter to accept the No default selection, WordPerfect will replace each occurrence of the search string without prompting you.

After you select whether to confirm, you are prompted to enter the search string. Press F2 after you enter it. WordPerfect then prompts you to enter the replacement string. You can enter text as well as the following formatting codes if you want them to be inserted in your document:

Appearance	Left-Right Indent
Center Page	Margin Release
Center	Math On/Off
Columns On/Off	Math Operators
Font	Merge Code
Hard Space	Size
Hyphen	Soft Hyphen
Hyphenation Cancel	Tab
Indent	Tab Align
Justification On/Off	Widow/Orphan On/Off

If you do not enter a replacement, WordPerfect will delete all occurrences of the phrase or codes you are searching for.

After you have entered the replacement string, press F2 to begin the search-and-replace operation.

Press F1 (Cancel) to end a search-and-replace operation.

SEE ALSO

Search

Setup

Allows you to customize the way WordPerfect works by changing many of its default settings.

KEY SEQUENCE

Shift-F1 (Setup)

▼

1 — **B**ackup
2 — **C**ursor Speed
3 — **D**isplay
4 — **F**ast Save
5 — **I**nitial Settings
6 — **K**eyboard Layout
7 — **L**ocation of Auxiliary Files
8 — **U**nits of Measure

USAGE

You use Setup (Shift-F1) to customize the way WordPerfect works for your own particular needs. Changes you make by using this key remain in effect each time you use WordPerfect. To change settings temporarily as you use the program, use the Format key (Shift-F8).

All of the Setup options are discussed in their own separate sections in this reference.

NOTE

The Setup options associated with Shift-F1 take the place of the WP/S startup command in version 4.2.

SEE ALSO

> Backup, Timed and Original Document
> Beep Options
> Colors/Fonts/Attributes
> Cursor Speed
> Display, Setup
> Document Comments
> Fast Save (Unformatted)
> Initial Settings
> Keyboard Layout
> Location of Auxiliary Files
> Units of Measure

SHEET FEEDERS

See **Printer, Select**.

SHELL

See **Go To DOS/Shell**.

SORT AND SELECT

Allows you to select and sort lines of text, paragraphs, or secondary merge file records.

KEY SEQUENCE

Ctrl-F9 (Merge/Sort)

▼

2 — Sort

▼

Input file to sort: **Enter** (*for screen*) or
 <*file name*> **Enter**

▼

Output file for sort: **Enter** (*for screen*) or
 <*file name*> **Enter**

▼

1 Perform Action; **2 V**iew; **3 K**eys; **4 S**elect; **5 A**ction; **6 O**rder; **7 T**ype

USAGE

WordPerfect's Sort feature allows you to perform three kinds of sorting. Each kind calls for its own special formatting:

- For a line sort, data is organized into columns and rows, as in a spreadsheet. Each row forms a record, and each column is separated by a tab.
- For a paragraph sort, the data to be sorted is separated by two (or more) hard returns or a hard page break (Ctrl-Enter).
- For a merge sort, the data is in a secondary merge file. Each field is terminated by a Merge R code (^R), and each record in the file is terminated by a Merge E code (^E).

To sort a file by any of these three methods, you press Ctrl-F9 (Merge/Sort) and select the Sort option (**2** or **S**). You will then be prompted for the name of the input file to sort. If you press Enter to accept the default selection (Screen), WordPerfect will sort the file that's in RAM. To sort a file that's on disk, enter the complete file name and press Enter.

You are then prompted to indicate where you want the sorted data output. WordPerfect will suggest *(Screen)* as the output destination. If you wish to save the data in a disk file, enter the file name.

You can also mark a block of text and sort the items in it.

Selecting the Type of Sort

You are then presented with the Sort by Line screen. Sort by Line is the default sort type. To perform a different kind of sort, select the Type option (**7** or **T**). When you do, you are presented with these options:

Sorting Type: **1 M**erge; **2 L**ine; **3 P**aragraph: 0

To select Merge Sort, enter **1** or **M**. To select Paragraph Sort, enter **3** or **P**.

Ascending Versus Descending Order

The default sorting order used by WordPerfect is ascending. To change the sort order, select the Order option (**6** or **O**) from the Sort menu. When you do, you are presented with these options:

Sorting Order: **1 A**scending; **2 D**escending: 0

Defining the Sort Keys

To sort data in a file, you must designate the key, or keys, on which to sort it. WordPerfect lets you define up to nine keys for any one sorting operation.

To define the sort key, or keys, to be used, you select the Keys option (**3** or **K**) from the Sort menu. You then define the type of data that will be sorted (alphanumeric or numeric), indicate the field and/or word to be used as the key (fields and words are numbered beginning with 1 from left to right, with words being separated by spaces), and specify the line number to be used (for a paragraph or merge sort).

When you have defined the type of sort, the sort order, and the sort keys to be used, you select Perform Action (**1** or **P**) to sort your data. As soon as WordPerfect has sorted your data, the Sort window will disappear, and you will be returned to the full-screen document window.

Selecting the Records to Be Sorted

WordPerfect also allows you to set up conditions that select only certain records. To use the Select feature, you must first define the sort keys that you wish to use. Then choose the Select option (**4** or **S**) from the Sort menu. Enter the condition that must be met, followed by the number of the key to which the condition is applied. When entering the condition, you type the appropriate logical operator after the key number (see Table V.6), followed by a value. For example:

Key1 > = 650.00*Key1 < = 2500.00

specifies those records in which Key1 (an amount-due field) is between $650.00 and $2500.00. The asterisk (*) indicates the logical AND operator.

After you enter your selection condition, press F7 (Exit) to return to the Sort menu. Select Perform Action (**1** or **P**) to have WordPerfect select and sort your records.

SYMBOL	FUNCTION	EXAMPLE
=	Equal to	key1 = IL
<>	Not equal to	key1 <>CA
>	Greater than	key1 >M
<	Less than	key2<50.00
>=	Greater than or equal to	key1 >= 74500
<=	Less than or equal to	key2<= H
*	Logical AND	key1 = IL * key2<60600
+	Logical OR	key1 = IL + key3>1000.00
g	Global selection	keyg = Mary

TABLE V.6: Symbols and Logical Operators Used in Sorting Records

WordPerfect also lets you select records without sorting them. To do this, you still must define the necessary keys and enter the selection condition as previously described. However, before you select Perform Action, select the Action option (**5** or **A**). When you do this, WordPerfect presents these options:

Action: **1 S**elect and Sort; **2** Select **O**nly: 0

Select the Select Only option (**2** or **O**). When you choose the Perform Action option, WordPerfect will eliminate all records that do not meet the selection condition, although their arrangement will be unchanged from the order in which they were originally entered.

Changing the Sorting Sequence

To change the sorting sequence, press Ctrl-F9 and select Sort Order (**3** or **O**). You are then presented with these options:

Sort Order: **1 US**/European; **2 S**candinavian: 0

To select the Scandinavian sorting sequence, which contains more that 26 letters, press **2** or **S**. To return to the US/European sorting sequence (the normal dictionary sort order for languages using the Roman alphabet without any foreign-language characters), press **1** or **U**.

SEE ALSO

Merge Operations

SPELLER

Allows you to check the spelling of a word, a block of text, or an entire document.

KEY SEQUENCE

Ctrl-F2 (Spell)

▼

1 Word; **2** Page; **3** Document; **4 N**ew Sup. Dictionary; **5 L**ookup; **6 C**ount

USAGE

WordPerfect's Spell key (Ctrl-F2) allows you to check your documents for typographical errors and misspellings. Its main dictionary contains over 100,000 words, and it automatically creates a supplemental dictionary that contains all the words you add to the dictionary as you write.

If you are using the Speller on a floppy disk system, you must first insert the Speller disk into drive B.

You can choose whether to check the word the cursor is on, the current page, or the entire document. You can also check the spelling in text you have marked with Block (Alt-F4).

Checking a Word

To check the spelling of the word the cursor is on, press Ctrl-F2 (Spell) and select Word (**1** or **W**). If the cursor moves to the next word, the current word is spelled correctly. If the spelling is incorrect, WordPerfect will present a list of any possible alternatives. Press the letter corresponding to the word you wish to use or, if the correct alternative is not displayed, press → to begin editing the word manually.

Checking a Page

To check for misspellings and typographical errors only on the page on which the cursor appears, use the Page option (**2** or **P**). You may want to do this if you have checked the entire document and then made corrections or additions to a certain page.

Checking a Document

The Document option (**3** or **D**) allows you to check your entire document, including headers, footers, footnotes, and endnotes.

Changing Dictionaries

By selecting the New Sup. Dictionary option (**4** or **N**), you can specify that WordPerfect check a custom dictionary that you have created. To create a new supplemental dictionary, you simply create a new document containing the words you want to include, each separated by a hard return. *Make sure that the words are spelled correctly.* When you save the document, give it a name, such as LEGAL.SUP, that helps you remember that it is a supplemental dictionary. Then enter that name when you are prompted for the name of a supplemental dictionary after selecting this option.

To create custom main dictionaries, you use the Speller Utility, a separate program that is available on the Speller/Thesaurus disk.

You can specify the directory in which your dictionaries are stored by using the Location of Auxiliary Files option on the Setup menu.

Looking Up an Alternative Spelling

To look up alternative spellings of a word, select the Lookup option (**5** or **L**) and type a word or word pattern at the prompt. WordPerfect then presents all the close combinations of that pattern it can find in its dictionaries.

When you look up a word, you can use the question mark (?) and asterisk (*) wild-card characters in place of letters you are unsure of. The question mark stands for any one letter, and the asterisk represents a sequence of letters. For example, type **rec??ve** to see whether *receive* is spelled as *receive* or *recieve*.

Using the Ignore Numbers Option

To have WordPerfect ignore subsequent occurrences of words with numbers in them like *B1* or *F10*, choose the Ignore Numbers option (**6**) on the Speller menu when the program stops at the first occurrence of a letter/number combination. The Speller automatically skips any numbers that are used alone in the text.

Using the Speller

When you use the Speller, WordPerfect checks your document for words it does not recognize. When it encounters one of these, it presents the message *Not Found* and displays a list of possible spellings (if it finds any near matches). You can simply press the letter corresponding to the correct word; WordPerfect inserts it into the document for you.

If you select the Ignore Numbers option, the Speller ignores numbers, so that it will not query alphanumeric words, such as *F3*.

WordPerfect's Speller also locates words that occur twice in a row and presents the following menu:

Double word: **1 2 S**kip; **3** Delete 2nd; **4** Edit; **5** Disable Double Word Checking

You can press **3** to delete the second occurrence, or you can leave the words in place (press **1** or **2**). Disable Double Word Checking (**5**) allows you to turn this feature off so that the program does not query you at double words.

Once you've selected the Page or Document option of the Speller, the standard menu you see when a word is being queried contains five options:

1 Skip Once; **2** Skip; **3** Add Word; **4** Edit; **5** Look Up

SKIPPING A WORD

If you instruct the Speller to skip a word once (option **1**), it will query you the next time it locates the pattern in your document. Use Skip (option **2**) if you want to keep a certain spelling in this document but do not want to add it to the dictionary. You will not be queried on that spelling again during the current session with the Speller.

ADDING A WORD

To add a word that is being queried—such as a proper name or a specialized term—to the dictionary as you are correcting a document, select Add Word (option **3**). WordPerfect will then add it to the supplemental dictionary that is automatically created as you use the Speller.

You can also add words to the supplemental dictionary directly by retrieving the file WP{WP}US.SUP and typing each word that you wish to add, separated by a hard return. Be sure to save the file under the same name after you have added words to it. (While you have the file on the screen, you can also correct any misspelled words that may have been inadvertently added to the supplemental dictionary.)

EDITING A WORD

If you choose Edit (option **4**), you may edit the word that is presented or simply use the → or ← key to move from that word to the part of the sentence or paragraph that you wish to edit. While you are working with the Speller, only the → and ← keys, along with Backspace and Del, are available as cursor movement keys. You cannot use most of the other cursor movement techniques, such as Go To (Ctrl-Home), or End. You can change from Insert to Typeover mode, however.

After you have edited a word in your document, press F7 (Exit) to return to the Speller.

LOOKING UP A WORD

By selecting this option while you are checking a document, you can enter a word that you wish WordPerfect to look up. Type a word or word pattern at the prompt. WordPerfect then presents all of the close matches to the word that it can find in its dictionaries.

Exiting from the Speller

To exit from the Speller, press F1 (Cancel). The program will present a count of the text it has checked up to that point. Save your document if you want the changes introduced with the Speller to be incorporated into the saved version.

SEE ALSO

Location of Auxiliary Files
Thesaurus

STYLES

Allows you to store formatting commands as styles that can be applied to various parts of your document.

KEY SEQUENCE

To create or edit a style:

Alt-F8 (Style)

▼

3 Create *or* **4 E**dit

▼

1 — Name
2 — Type
3 — Description
4 — Codes
5 — Enter★

▼

F7 (Exit)

The Enter option is used only with the Paired type of style; this option disappears from the menu when you select the Open option for Type.

To apply a style to new text you enter in the document:

[position cursor where you want to apply style]

▼

Alt-F8 (Style)

▼

[highlight style name]

▼

1 On

▼

<text>

▼

2 Off *or* **Enter** *(if you defined Enter as Off)*

To apply a style to existing text in the document:

[position cursor at beginning of text to be formatted]

▼

Alt-F4 (Block)

▼

[highlight text to be formatted]

▼

Alt-F8 (Style)

▼

[highlight style name]

▼

1 On

REVEAL CODES

[Open Style]	Open Style
[Style Off]	Paired Style Off
[Style On]	Paired Style On

USAGE

With version 5.0 of WordPerfect, you can set up styles for each element in your document and use the style instead of formatting text as you type. For example, you can use one style for quotations, and you can define other styles for each level of heading you are using in your documents. For instance, if you want all level-1 headings to be boldfaced and centered, you can define that style. Then, when you are typing a level-1 heading in your text, you can simply turn on the style instead of pressing F6 for bold and Shift-F6 for center. If you work with complex design elements, such as multicolumn formats and a variety of type styles, this feature can save you many keystrokes throughout a document.

Style Types

You can use two different types of styles in WordPerfect: *paired* and *open*. In a paired style, the codes are turned on and then turned off at the end of the text element, such as turning off bold at the end of the heading or returning to normal size after a quotation in smaller type. Open styles are not turned off, so they are appropriate for setting the style of an entire document, such as margins, justification, line spacing, and so forth.

Creating a Style Sheet

To create a style:

1. Press Alt-F8 (Style). The Style menu will appear.

2. Select the Create option (**1** or **C**); then select Name (**1** or **N**).

3. Enter a descriptive name for the style, such as **1 head** (for level-1 headings). You can use up to 11 characters.

4. To select whether the style is to be paired or open, select Type (**2** or **T**); then select Open or Paired. When you select the Open style type, the Enter option (**5** or **E**) disappears.

5. To enter a description of the style you are creating, select Description (**3** or **D**); then enter a short description (up to 54 characters) of the style.

6. You can use both text and codes in a style. To indicate to WordPerfect which codes you want generated when you use this style, select Codes (**4** or **C**) and press the appropriate keys to generate the codes. For example, if you want level-1 heads to be centered and boldfaced, press Shift-F6 (Center) and F6 (Bold). If you are defining a paired style, type the codes that are to be used when the style is turned on *before* the [Comment] on the screen. Move the cursor past the comment and then type the codes that you want WordPerfect to generate when the style is turned off *after* the [Comment]. For example, to insert boldfacing codes, press F6 (Bold) to generate the [BOLD] code; then press → to move past the [Comment]. Press F6 again to generate the [bold] code. If the style is being used to mark text—as for an index or table of contents heading— press Alt-F4 (Block) before the [Comment], move the cursor past the [Comment], and then press the appropriate keys to generate the correct Mark Text code. For example, to mark a heading for a level-1 table of contents entry, you would press Alt-F5, choose ToC, and enter **1** for level 1. Press F7 (Exit) when you have defined the style.

7. If you are creating a paired style, you can assign a new function to the Enter key by choosing Enter (**5** or **E**) and selecting an option for the way the Enter key is to function. You can choose to have the Enter key turn off the style (**2** or **F**), or you can have it turn the style on and then turn it off again (**3** or **O**). Press F7 (Exit) to return to the Style menu.

For a quick way to create a style in an existing document, mark as a block (Alt-F4) the codes that generate the style you want to define; then press Alt-F8 (Style) and select the Create option (**3** or **C**). When you type **4** or **C** for Codes, you will see that WordPerfect has created a paired style from the codes you have highlighted. You can then edit these codes. Be sure to name your new style so that you can remember what it does.

Editing a Style

After you have created a style, you can use the Style menu's Edit option (**4** or **E**) to edit it:

1. Press Alt-F8 (Style) and highlight the style you want to change.
2. Choose Edit (**4** or **E**) and edit the style.
3. Press F7 (Exit) when you have finished editing the style.

WordPerfect automatically changes the codes in your document to conform to the edited style after you have changed it.

To delete a style, highlight it and select Delete (**5** or **D**); then type **Y** to confirm the deletion.

Applying a Style

To use an open style you have created, press Alt-F8 (Style), use the arrow keys to move the cursor to the style, and select On (**1** or **O**). Then type the text that you want to appear in that style. When you apply an open style, it will affect the entire document from the cursor's position forward.

If you are applying a paired style, press Alt-F8 (Style), use the arrow keys to move the cursor to the style, then select On. When you reach the end of the text you want to have in that style, press Alt-F8 and select Off. Or, if you have assigned the Off or Off/On option to the Enter key, press Enter to turn off the style.

If you are using a paired style, you can also block the text you want to apply the style to and then apply the style as described above. WordPerfect automatically inserts the [Style On] and [Style Off] codes around the blocked text.

Saving and Retrieving Styles

The styles you define for a document are saved with the document. You can save the styles as a separate document, however, so that you can apply them to several different documents without having to define styles in each one. To do this, choose Save (**6** or **S**) from the Style menu and enter a name for the list of styles displayed on the screen. Then, to retrieve those styles into another document, choose the Retrieve option (**7** or **R**) from the Style menu and enter the name of the style list.

If you retrieve a style list into a document that already has a list of styles, you will be prompted as to whether you want to replace the document's existing styles with the new ones that you are retrieving. Type **N** to retrieve only the styles that have different names from the ones in the current document, or type **Y** to replace the list on the screen with the list you are retrieving.

Creating a Style Library

You can create a library of all the different styles you use. If you press Alt-F8 (Style) and you have not defined specific styles for a document, WordPerfect retrieves the style library. To create the style library, you must first use Setup (Shift-F1) and indicate the library's path name by using the Location of Auxiliary Files option. Then, after you have created a list of styles for the style library, select option **6** (Save) from the Style menu and enter the path name of the style library.

Once you have created a style library, you can update it with new styles by selecting Update (**7** or **U** on the Style menu), adding new styles or editing existing ones, and selecting Save (**6** or **S**) to save it again.

SEE ALSO

Setup

SUPERSCRIPT/SUBSCRIPT

See **Font**.

SUPPRESS PAGE FORMAT

Allows you to suppress the printing of page numbers or headers and footers for the current page.

KEY SEQUENCE

Shift-F8 (Format)
▼
2 — Page
▼

9 – Suppress (this page only)

▼

1 – Suppress **A**ll Page Numbers, Headers, and Footers
2 – **S**uppress Headers and Footers
3 – Print Page Numbers at **B**ottom Center
4 – Suppress **P**age Number
5 – Suppress **H**eader A
6 – Suppress He**a**der B
7 – Suppress **F**ooter A
8 – Suppress F**o**oter B

▼

F7 F7 (Exit)

REVEAL CODES

[Suppress]   Suppress Page Format

USAGE

To suppress headers, footers, and/or page numbers on a single page, position the cursor at the top of the page (just under the dashed line that marks the page break on your screen). Then press Shift-F8 and select the Page option (**2** or **P**) followed by Suppress for Current Page Only (**9** or **U**). Then select the features (or the combination of features) you want to suppress.

To restore a suppressed format, locate the page with the [Suppress] code and delete that code.

SEE ALSO

Headers and Footers
Page Numbering

SWITCH DOCUMENT

Switches between the Doc 1 and Doc 2 editing screens.

KEY SEQUENCE

Shift-F3 (Switch)

USAGE

If the *Block on* message is not displayed (indicating that text has not been marked as a block), pressing Shift-F3 (Switch) switches you to a second document window. Pressing it a second time returns you to the original document window. You can work with another document or another version of the same document in each window.

NOTE

If you have marked text as a block, pressing Switch displays the Conversion menu so that you can switch to uppercase or lowercase.

SEE ALSO

Case Conversion
Windows

TAB ALIGN

Aligns text on or around the next tab stop using the decimal/align character in effect.

KEY SEQUENCE

Ctrl-F6 (Tab Align)

REVEAL CODES

[Align]	Tab Align On
[C/A/Flrt]	Tab Align Off

USAGE

The Tab Align command (Ctrl-F6) aligns text on or around a tab setting using the alignment character that is in effect. WordPerfect uses the period as the alignment character unless you specify another character or symbol. You can use the Tab Align command with any tab stop that is in effect.

Characters that you type after pressing Tab Align are inserted to the left of the cursor, and the cursor remains stationary at the tab stop until you type the alignment character.

To change the alignment character from the period to another character—for example, the colon (:)—follow these steps:

1. Press Shift-F8 (Format) and choose the Other option (**4** or **O**).

2. Choose Decimal/Align Char (**3** or **D**) and enter the character you want to use as the alignment character— in this case, the colon (:). Press Enter, then press F7 (Exit) to return to your document.

3. To then align your text on the colon, press the Tab key until you are only one tab stop away from where you want the text aligned.

4. Press Ctrl-F6. The cursor will advance to the next tab stop, and you will see this message at the bottom of the screen:

Align Char = :

As you type your text, it will be entered from right to left, just as it is when you use a right-justified or decimal tab. As soon as you type the alignment character—in this case, the colon— the *Align Char = :* message disappears, and any text you then type is entered from left to right as though you were using a left-justified tab. Pressing Tab again or pressing Enter leaves text aligned and simply moves the cursor.

To return text that was aligned with the Tab Align command to the previous tab stop, access the Reveal Codes screen (Alt-F3) and delete the [Align] or [C/A/Flrt] formatting codes that surround the aligned text. If you press Backspace when the cursor is located on one of these codes, you will see a message asking you to confirm the deletion. If you wish to retain the current alignment, press Enter. If you do not, type **Y**.

SEE ALSO

Decimal/Align Character

TABLES OF AUTHORITIES

Allows you generate in a legal document a list of citations that is automatically maintained by WordPerfect.

KEY SEQUENCE

To mark the full form for the table:

Alt-F4 (Block)

▼

[highlight text to be cited]

▼

Alt-F5 (Mark Text)

▼

4 ToA

▼

ToA Section Number (Press Enter for Short Form only):
<section number between 1 and 16> **Enter**

▼

[edit blocked text] F7

▼

Short Form: *<short form name>* **Enter**

To define the style of the table of authorities:

Alt-F5 (Mark Text)

▼

5 Define

▼

4 — Define Table of **A**uthorities

▼

Section Number (1–16): *<section number>* **Enter**

▼

1 — **D**ot Leaders
2 — **U**nderlining Allowed
3 — **B**lank Line Between Authorities

▼

F7 (Exit)

To generate a table of authorities:

Alt-F5 (Mark Text)

▼

6 Generate

▼

5 — **G**enerate Tables, Indexes, Automatic References, etc.

▼

Existing tables, lists, and indexes will be replaced.
Continue? (Y/N) **Enter** *or any key except N*

REVEAL CODES

[Full Form]	Table of Authorities, Full Form
[ToA]	Table of Authorities

USAGE

Tables of authorities are used in legal documents as lists of citations. Creating them involves essentially the same three steps as creating tables of contents: (1) marking the citations, (2) defining the style, and (3) generating the table.

You can divide a table of authorities into 16 sections, such as statutes, regulations, treaties, and so forth. Within each section, WordPerfect sorts the authorities alphanumerically.

Marking Citations for a Table of Authorities

To mark citations for inclusion in a table of authorities:

1. Move to the beginning of the document. You can press F2 (Search) or Home F2 (Extended Search) and specify the citation you wish to find in the document, or simply move to the first occurrence of the citation.

2. Mark the first occurrence of the citation in its full form by pressing Alt-F4 (Block) and highlighting the entire citation.

3. Press Alt-F5 (Mark Text) and select the ToA option (**4** or **A**).

4. The following prompt appears:

    ToA Section Number (Press Enter for Short Form Only):

    For the first occurrence of the citation, enter the number of the section in which you want the citation to be listed in the table of authorities. If this is not the first occurrence and you have already defined a short form, simply press Enter to have WordPerfect mark the citation and its section number for you.

5. For the first occurrence of the citation, WordPerfect presents you with an editing screen in which you can edit the full form of the citation. The text can be up to 30 lines long, and you can use different character styles (bold, italics, and so forth), different fonts, and formats such as indentation.

6. When you have edited the full form of the citation, press F7 (Exit). Word-Perfect then presents you with a suggested short form (the first 40 characters of the full form) on the prompt line. You can shorten the short form even further or accept the program's suggestion by simply pressing Enter. The short form must be unique for each citation.

7. Search for the next occurrence of the citation by using Search (F2) to move directly to it.

8. When the program stops at the next occurrence of the citation, press Alt-F5 (Mark Text) and select ToA Short Form (**4** or **A**). The program displays the short form you have defined. Press Enter to accept it and mark the citation in the document.

Defining the Style of a Table of Authorities

To define the style of a table of authorities:

1. Move the cursor to the location where you want the table of authorities to be generated, usually at the beginning of the document.

2. Press Ctrl-Enter to insert a hard page break. Renumber the first text page as page 1 so that references will be accurate. Position the cursor on the

new page and type the heading you want for the table, such as **Table of Authorities**; press Enter twice to move to a new line.

3. Define each section as you want it to be included in the table. Enter the section name (such as **CASES** or **STATUTES**). Press Alt-F6 (Flush Right) to align the heading *Page:* at the right margin and enter **Page:**. Press Enter to move to a new line to separate the heading from the entries that will be generated. Then press Alt-F5 (Mark Text) and select Define (**5** or **D**). Select Define Table of Authorities (**4** or **A**), enter the section number at the prompt, and press Enter.

4. Select the style you wish to use in that section from the options that appear. You can choose whether to use dot leaders, allow underlining, and allow space between citations. Press Enter to return to the document.

5. Repeat steps 3 and 4 for each section.

If you don't start with a new page number between the definition of the table of authorities and the first text that has been marked for inclusion in the table, your page number references may not be accurate, and WordPerfect will warn you if it does not find a New Page Number code.

Generating a Table of Authorities

After you have marked text for your table of authorities and defined the style of the sections, you can generate the table itself, as shown in the key sequence.

The table will be generated at the [Def Mark] code where you defined the document. If your computer does not have sufficient RAM to hold the entire table in memory, you may be asked to close the Doc 2 window so that WordPerfect can use more memory for generating the table.

To delete a table of authorities, be sure to delete both the [Def Mark] code and the [End Def] code marking the end of the table. If WordPerfect finds a [Def Mark] code but no [End Def] code, it will continue to generate a table of authorities each time you generate your tables and lists.

Editing a Table of Authorities

To edit the full form of a citation in a table of authorities after you have generated the table, position the cursor to the right of the code for the full form in the Reveal Codes screen. Then select Define (**5** or **D**) from the Mark Text menu (Alt-F5), and select Edit Table of Authorities Full Form (**5** or **E**).

The citation will be displayed on the screen. After you have edited it, press F7 (Exit). Then enter the section number to which this citation belongs and press Enter.

You must then generate a new table of authorities to update the changes you have made.

SEE ALSO

Mark Text
Page Numbering

TABLES OF CONTENTS

Allows you to generate from entries in your document a table of contents that is automatically maintained by WordPerfect.

KEY SEQUENCE

To mark an entry for the table of contents:

Alt-F4 (Block)
▼
[highlight text to be included]
▼
Alt-F5 (Mark Text)
▼
1 ToC
▼
ToC Level: *<level number between 1 and 5>* **Enter**

To define the style of the table of contents:

Alt-F5 (Mark Text)
▼
5 Define
▼
1 — Define Table of Contents
▼
1 — **N**umber of Levels
2 — **D**isplay Last Level in Wrapped Format
3 — **P**age Number Position — Level 1
                                                     Level 2
                                                     Level 3
                                                     Level 4
                                                     Level 5

▼
F7 (Exit)

To generate a table of contents:

Alt-F5 (Mark Text)

▼

6 Generate

▼

5 – Generate Tables, Indexes, Automatic References, etc.

▼

Existing tables, lists, and indexes will be replaced.
Continue? (Y/N) **Enter** *or any key except N*

REVEAL CODES

[Def Mark:ToC]	Table of Contents Definition
[EndDef]	End of Index, List, or Table of Contents
[Mark:ToC]	Table of Contents Entry

USAGE

Creating a table of contents consists of three basic steps: (1) marking the headings, (2) defining the style, and (3) generating the table.

Marking Text for a Table of Contents

You can mark up to five levels of headings to be included in a table of contents. For each heading you want included in the table of contents, follow these steps:

1. Press Alt-F4 to mark the heading as a block.
2. Press Alt-F5 (Mark Text). The following prompt appears:

   Mark for: **1** To**C**; **2 L**ist; **3 I**ndex; **4** To**A**: 0

3. Select the ToC option (**1** or **C**). The following prompt appears:

   ToC Level:

4. Enter the level of the heading (from 1 to 5).
5. Repeat steps 1 through 4 for each item you want to include in the table of contents.

WordPerfect inserts [Mark] and [End Mark] codes around each entry as you mark it. To remove the markings so that an item will not be included in the table of contents, delete the [Mark] code.

Defining the Style of a Table of Contents

When you define the style of a table of contents, WordPerfect creates the table at that point in your document. For this reason, go to the beginning of your document, press Ctrl-Enter to create a new, blank page, and type any heading you may want for the contents page, such as **Contents**. Then press Enter to add space between the heading and the table entries that will be generated at that point.

To define the format of the contents page (required before you can generate a table of contents):

1. Press Alt-F5 (Mark Text) and select the Define option (**5** or **D**).
2. Select Define Table of Contents (**1** or **C**). The Table of Contents Definition screen appears.
3. Select Number of Levels (**1** or **N**) and enter the number of heading levels you are using in the table of contents (1–5).
4. Select Display Last Level in Wrapped Format (**2** or **D**) and type **Y** if you want the last level of entries to be wrapped on one line, rather than listed vertically. If you enter **Y**, WordPerfect displays the headings with the last level as one wrapped line and the headings and page numbers separated by semicolons. The default is No.
5. Select Page Number Position (**3** or **P**) and enter a numbering style for each level.

Choose option **1** or **N** to print headings only, with no page numbers. If you choose option **2** or **3** (or **P** or **(**), page numbers will occur next to headings, and with option **3** or **(** they will be in parentheses. Options **4** and **5** (or **F** and **L**) place page numbers flush right, with or without dot leaders.

Generating a Table of Contents

After you have marked text for your table of contents, created a page for it, and defined its style, you can generate the table itself, as shown in the key sequence.

The table will be generated at the [Def Mark] code where you defined the document. If your computer does not have sufficient RAM to hold the entire table in memory, you may be asked to close the Doc 2 window so that WordPerfect can use more memory for generating the table.

To delete a table of contents, be sure to delete both the [Def Mark] code and the [End Def] code marking the end of the table. If WordPerfect finds a [Def Mark] code but no [End Def] code, it will continue to generate a table of contents each time you generate your tables and lists.

If you edit your document so that page breaks change, be sure to generate a new table of contents. WordPerfect does not automatically update tables of contents as page changes occur.

SEE ALSO

Automatic Reference
Lists
Mark Text

TABS

Allows you to change the tab settings in your document.

KEY SEQUENCE

To enter equally spaced tabs:

Shift-F8 (Format)

▼

1 — Line

▼

8 — Tab Set

▼

<start position>, <increment spacing> **Enter**

▼

F7 F7 (Exit)

To clear all tabs and set different kinds of tabs individually:

Shift-F8 (Format)

▼

1 — Line

▼

8 — Tab Set

▼

Ctrl-End (Delete EOF)

▼

[move cursor to desired position(s) on ruler]

▼

Left; **C**enter; **R**ight; **D**ecimal; **.** = Dot Leader

▼

F7 (Exit)

REVEAL CODES

[Tab]   Tab
[Tab Set]   Tab Set

USAGE

WordPerfect is preset with left-justified tabs every ½ inch up to position 8.5''. To move to the next tab setting, use the Tab key.

To set individual tabs, press Shift-F8 (Format) and select the Line option (**1** or **L**). Select Tab Set (**8** or **T**), and the Tab Set menu will appear. To select a new tab stop, move the cursor to the position on the ruler line where you want the new tab and type **L** for a left-justified tab, **R** for a right-justified tab, **C** for a centered tab, **D** for a decimal tab, or **.** (period) for a dot-leader tab. You can indicate that dot leaders be used with left, right, or decimal tabs by moving the cursor to the L, R, or C tab that has already been set and typing a period. As you type, when you press Tab and the next tab has been set as a dot-leader tab, you will see the dot leaders appear on your screen.

Table V.7 illustrates the various types of tabs you can set.

You may use the space bar or the → key to position the cursor on the tab ruler line to see where these tabs appear in relation to your text. You can also type the number of the position where you want a tab and press Enter. For example, to set a tab at the 6.3'' mark, type **6.3** and press Enter.

To delete the existing tabs and set new ones, press Home Home ← to move to the beginning of the line; then press Ctrl-End to delete the existing tab settings. You do not need to delete old tab settings before you set new ones, however.

To delete a single tab, move to the setting on the line; then press Backspace or Delete.

To return to your document without setting tabs after you have displayed the Tab Set menu, press F1 (Cancel).

Setting Evenly Spaced Tabs

You can also specify that WordPerfect set tabs in evenly spaced increments. To do this, press Shift-F8, type **1** or **L**, type **8** or **T**, move the cursor to the beginning of the line, and press Ctrl-End to delete the existing tab settings. Then move the cursor to the first tab stop that you want to set and type **L**, **R**, **C**, or **D** to establish the style of the evenly spaced tabs you are setting (left, right, centered, or decimal). If you are using the default of left-justified tabs, you do not have to take this step.

Then type the number of the character position where you want tabs to start, type a comma, then type the increment by which you want them to be spaced. Finally, press F7 (Exit) twice to return to the document.

TAB TYPE	HOW SET	EXAMPLE
Left-justified	L	First Quarter .....L.............
Right-justified	R	First Quarter ....R...........
Centered	C	First Quarter ....C...........
Decimal	D	$1,256.00 ....D...........
Dot-leader left	.L	Benefits.............Section 1.11 L......................L..........
Dot-leader right	.R	Benefits...Section 1.11 L......................R..........
Dot-leader decimal	.D	Benefits.....Section 1.11 L......................D..........
Dot-leader centered	.C	......First Quarter...... ....C...........

TABLE V.7: Types of Tabs Supported by WordPerfect

For example, to set decimal tabs every inch starting one inch from the left margin, you would type **D** at the 1'' position and then type

1,1

and press Enter.

SEE ALSO

Tab Align

TEXT IN/OUT

Allows you to retrieve a DOS text (ASCII) file into WordPerfect; to save a document as a DOS text, generic, or WordPerfect 4.2 file; to create document comments; and to assign passwords to documents.

KEY SEQUENCE

To retrieve or save a DOS text file:

Ctrl-F5 (Text In/Out)
▼
1 — DOS **T**ext
▼
1 Save; **2 R**etrieve (CR/LF to [HRt]); **3 R**etrieve (CR/LF to [SRt] in HZone)
▼
<*file name*> **Enter**

To retrieve a DOS text file from List Files:

F5 (List Files) **Enter**
▼
[highlight file to be retrieved]
▼
5 Text In
▼
(DOS) Retrieve <*file name*>? (Y/N) **Yes**

To save a document as a generic or WordPerfect 4.2 file:

Ctrl-F5 (Text In/Out)
▼
3 — Save **G**eneric *or*
4 — Save **WP** 4.2
▼
<*file name*> **Enter**

USAGE

The Text In/Out key (Ctrl-F5) allows you to bring DOS text files into Word-Perfect, to save WordPerfect documents in DOS text file format, to assign password protection to files (see **Locking a File**), to save WordPerfect 5.0 files in WordPerfect 4.2 format, to save WordPerfect documents in a generic word processor format, and to create document comments (see **Document Comments**).

Importing and Exporting DOS Text Files

To convert a document to DOS text file (ASCII) format within WordPerfect or to retrieve a document in DOS text format, you use the DOS Text option (**1** or **T**) on the Text In/Out menu (Ctrl-F5). When you select this option, the following menu will appear:

1 Save; **2 R**etrieve (CR/LF to [HRt]); **3 R**etrieve (CR/LF to [SRt] in HZone): 0

If you select Save (**1** or **S**), your current WordPerfect document is converted to a DOS text file. In this format, most of the codes that WordPerfect uses to control formatting are removed. Some WordPerfect codes that control indenting, centering, paragraph numbering, and the Date function are converted to ASCII codes, however. All of your document except footnotes and endnotes will be converted.

To retrieve a document that is in DOS text file format, use option **2** or **3** (or **R** or **E**) instead of using the Retrieve command (Shift-F10). When you press **2** or **R**, carriage returns and line feeds in the DOS text document are converted to hard returns in WordPerfect, so you get a line-for-line conversion. If you are bringing in data from programs such as Lotus 1-2-3 or dBASE III or lines of programming code for which you want to use WordPerfect as a text editor, choose this option, which preserves the column and row format. You may also want to set your margins wider before you import the document to make sure that wide rows are kept intact.

If you use option **3**, carriage returns and line feeds in the DOS text document are converted to soft returns when they occur in the hyphenation zone, so hard returns will not occur in the middle of a paragraph in the imported document. You should use this option for word-wrapped text. You may want to set your margins in WordPerfect as close as possible to those of the DOS text file so that the same line breaks occur.

Retrieving a DOS Text File from List Files

You can also use the Text In option (**5** or **T**) on the List Files menu (F5) to retrieve DOS text files. It is the same as the Retrieve (CR/LF to [HRt]) option on the Text In/Out key.

Converting Documents to a Generic Word Processor Format

You can convert a WordPerfect document to a generic word processor format by using the Save Generic option (**3** or **G**) on the Text In/Out menu. In this format, special WordPerfect format codes are not saved, but the overall text format is maintained. Footnotes and endnotes are not converted, however. In place of the codes that indicate centering, indenting, flush-right text, and soft returns, spaces are inserted, and <CR><LF> (carriage return–line feed) codes are inserted in place of hard returns.

Converting Documents to WordPerfect 4.2 Format

In addition, you will notice on this menu that you can use Save WP 4.2 (**4** or **W**) to convert documents you create in WordPerfect 5.0 into WordPerfect 4.2

format so that they can be used by others who do not have version 5.0. You will be asked to enter a name for the new document; use a different name from that of the current document so that you do not overwrite it.

However, some 4.2 codes, such as Font Change codes, do not have equivalents in version 5.0. If you have such codes in your 5.0 document, you can use a special file called STANDARD.CRS, located on the Conversion disk, to manually change the codes.

SEE ALSO

Document Comments
List Files
Locking a File
Printing to Disk

THESAURUS

Allows you to look for synonyms for any word in the text of your document.

KEY SEQUENCE

[position cursor on word to be looked up]

▼

Alt-F1 (Thesaurus)

▼

1 Replace Word; **2** View Doc; **3** Look Up Word; **4** Clear Column

USAGE

On a floppy disk system, you must first insert the Thesaurus disk into drive B. Since WordPerfect normally looks for the Thesaurus on the default drive, this means you must also change the Thesaurus default drive to B by using the Setup menu. When you have finished using the Thesaurus, replace your data disk in drive B and save any changes. On a hard disk system, the Thesaurus is installed in the default directory during the installation process, and no special instructions are needed.

There are several ways to look up a word:

- Move the cursor to the word in your document and press Alt-F1 (Thesaurus).
- If you are already in the Thesaurus, select View Doc (option **2**), move the cursor to the word you want to look up, and press Alt-F1 (Thesaurus).

- If the word you want to look up is not displayed on the screen, press Alt-F1 (to start the Thesaurus), select Look Up Word (option **3**), and then enter the word.

While you are using the Thesaurus, you will see a few lines of your document at the top of the screen, along with three columns of alternatives, grouped into nouns, verbs, adjectives, and adverbs, as well as antonyms—words of opposite meaning. Any word preceded by a dot is a *headword,* which indicates that you can look up further references to that word by pressing the accompanying letter. At the bottom of the screen is a menu that allows you to replace words, view more of your document, and look up other words.

Replacing a Word

Replace Word (option **1**) allows you to replace the highlighted word in your document with any of the suggested words (with accompanying letters) that appear on the Thesaurus screen. Enter **1** followed by the letter corresponding to the word you wish to use. You can move between the columns of words by using the ← and → keys; the letters will follow the cursor, allowing you to select more words. The ↑ and ↓ keys as well as the PgUp and PgDn keys scroll the columns vertically. The Home Home ↑ and Home Home ↓ key combinations take you to the beginning and end of the Thesaurus entry.

To view groups of related words, type the letter corresponding to any of the headwords (those with dots to their left).

Viewing a Document

The View Doc option (**2**) allows you to return to view your document—for example, to get a better idea of the context in which the word was used. When you are in the document, you can use the cursor movement keys to scroll through the text. After using View Doc, you can return to the Thesaurus screen you were viewing before by pressing F7 (Exit), or you can press Alt-F1 again to look up another word in the Thesaurus.

Looking Up a Word

Look Up Word (option **3**) directs the Thesaurus to look up a word. After you press **3**, WordPerfect will prompt you to enter the word you want to look up.

Clearing a Column

If your screen becomes cluttered with too many alternative words, you can use the Clear Column option (**4**) to clear the column the cursor is in, making room for more synonyms of another headword.

SEE ALSO

Speller

Typeover

Toggles between the default Insert mode and Typeover mode.

KEY SEQUENCE

Ins

USAGE

WordPerfect is preset for Insert mode, which means that characters you type are inserted on the screen, with existing characters being pushed to the right of the cursor. To use Typeover mode, in which characters you type replace the characters on the screen, press Ins. A *Typeover* message appears at the bottom of the screen when Typeover is on. To return to Insert mode, press Ins again.

Pressing Tab in Typeover mode does not insert a tab but simply moves the cursor to the next tab stop.

To define a macro in which the typing mode changes, use WordPerfect's Forced Typeover mode (Home Ins) or Forced Insert mode (Home Home Ins). Otherwise, each time you execute the macro, WordPerfect will use the mode you were in when you recorded the macro.

Type Through

Allows you to use your printer as a typewriter so that any character or line you type is immediately printed.

KEY SEQUENCE

Shift-F7 (Print)
▼
5 — Type Through
▼
1 Line; **2** Character
▼
<characters or line>
▼
F7 (Exit)

USAGE

WordPerfect's Type Through feature allows you to use your keyboard as you would a typewriter. The text you type is not saved, however, but is sent directly to the printer, so you need to position the paper so that the printhead is on the first line to be printed.

To use the Type Through feature, press Shift-F7 and choose Type Through (**5** or **Y**). Then select Line (**1** or **L**) or Character (**2** or **C**). Use the Line option if you want the characters you type to be sent to the printer only when you press Enter. Choose the Character option if you want each character to go to the printer as it is typed; remember, however, that you cannot correct characters if you use this option.

When you use Type Through, you are placed in a special Type Through screen. The line at the top of the screen displays the previously typed line. You cannot edit it, but if you press Ctrl-F4 (Move) it will be copied to the bottom line, which can be edited. You can enter up to 200 characters per line; lines that are too wide to be displayed on the screen will move to the left as you type.

While in Type Through mode, you can use the space bar to move the cursor to the right. You can also use the arrow keys to move the cursor right or left, and Home with the → or ← key moves the cursor to the beginning or end of a line. Pressing Shift-F8 (Format) allows you to insert printer commands. Press F7 (Exit) or F1 (Cancel) to return to the regular editing screen.

UNDELETE

Restores any of the last three deletions at the cursor's position.

KEY SEQUENCE

F1 (Cancel)

▼

1 Restore; **2 P**revious Deletion

USAGE

If WordPerfect is not carrying out a command, the Cancel key (F1) functions as an Undelete key. The following prompt appears along with the most recently deleted text:

Undelete: **1 R**estore; **2 P**revious Deletion: 0

Entering **1** or **R** restores the displayed text to your document; entering **2** or **P** displays the text that was deleted prior to that deletion. Three levels of deletions can be displayed and restored. After the third most recently deleted text is displayed, pressing **2** or **P** displays the first deletion again. Pressing **1** or **R** restores the displayed deletion to your document.

SEE ALSO

Cancel

UNDERLINE

Underlines selected portions of text.

KEY SEQUENCE

To underline new text:

F8 (Underline)

▼

<text to be underlined>

▼

F8 (Underline) or →

To underline existing text:

Alt-F4 (Block)

▼

[highlight text to be underlined]

▼

F8 (Underline)

To change the underlining of spaces and tabs:

Shift-F8 (Format)

▼

4 - Other

▼

7 - Underline - Spaces **Y** *or* **N Enter**
Tabs **Y** *or* **N Enter**

▼

F7 (Exit)

REVEAL CODES

[UND]	Underline On
[und]	Underline Off
[Undrln]	Underlining Spaces/Tabs

USAGE

To underline new text, press F8 before you type. After you press F8, the Pos indicator appears underlined, indicating that text you type will be underlined. To turn underlining off, press F8 again. You can also indicate a block of existing text to be underlined (by pressing Alt-F4 and marking the block).

You can also underline text by pressing Ctrl-F8 (Font), selecting Appearance (**2** or **A**), and selecting Undrln (**2** or **U**).

WordPerfect is preset to underline spaces between words but not spaces created by pressing the Tab key. To change these settings, choose Other (**4** or **O**) from the Format menu (Shift-F8); then select Underline (**7** or **U**).

To use double underlining in a document, press Ctrl-F8 (Font), select Appearance (**2** or **A**), and then select Double Underline (**3** or **D**). You will not see the double underline on the screen unless you have a graphics card such as the Hercules Graphics Card Plus, but it will appear in your document when it is printed.

SEE ALSO

Font: Changing the Appearance of the Font

UNITS OF MEASURE

Allows you to choose the basic units of measure used by WordPerfect.

KEY SEQUENCE

Shift-F1 (Setup)

▼

8 — Units of Measure

▼

1 — Display and Entry of Numbers
for Margins, Tabs, etc.

2 — Status Line Display

▼

F7 (Exit)

USAGE

WordPerfect 5.0 is preset to display measurements entered for menu options and on the status line (for the Ln and Pos indicators) in inches displayed with the " mark, but you can change the default unit of measurement to inches displayed with the abbreviation *i,* centimeters (*c*), points (*p*), or "WordPerfect 4.2 units" (*u*), which means that vertical measurements will be in terms of lines and horizontal measurements will be in terms of columns. (The size of a line or a column will vary with the font you are using.)

After you have set a default unit of measurement, the program will convert any values you enter in other units of measurement to the default unit. (If you enter measurements in WordPerfect 4.2 units, indicate vertical measurements with *v,* as in **8v** for 8 lines, and horizontal measurements with *h,* as in **8h** for 8 columns.) For example, if you have chosen '' for the display and entry of numbers, margins, and tabs, you can still enter a value in points by following the number with *p.* To set a fixed line height of 14 points, you would enter **14p** and WordPerfect would automatically convert it to 0.19'' on the menu screen.

You can also choose a different style for the way information is displayed on the status line. WordPerfect is preset to display the cursor's vertical and horizontal location in inches (''), but you can specify points (especially useful for many desktop publishing applications), centimeters, or ''WordPerfect 4.2 units'' (lines and columns).

To change the default unit of measure, press Shift-F1 (Setup), then select Units of Measure (**8** or **U**). For each option that you want to change, select it on the Units of Measure menu; then type **i** or '' for inches, **c** for centimeters, **p** for points, or **u** for WordPerfect 4.2 units. Then press F7 (Exit).

After you have changed the default unit of measure, they will be used each time you start WordPerfect.

VIEW DOCUMENT

Allows you to preview the way the document will appear when printed.

KEY SEQUENCE

Shift-F7 (Print)

▼

6 — View Document

▼

1 100% **2** 200% **3** Full Page **4** Facing Pages

▼

F7 (Exit)

USAGE

Choosing View Document (**6** or **V**) from the Print menu (Shift- F7) allows you to see how your document will appear when it is printed, complete with text elements that are not normally visible on the screen, such as page numbers and headers. You can select the 100% option (**1**) to view the document in its actual size, 200% (**2**) to see it at twice its actual size, or Full Page (**3**) to view the page. If you select the Facing Pages option (**4**), you will see odd-numbered pages on the right and even-numbered pages on the left.

Once you have displayed a page or pages, you can use the cursor movement keys to scroll through the document, or use the PgUp, PgDn, Screen Up, and Screen Down keys.

To see the previewed pages in reverse video, press Shift-F3 (Switch) while you are in the View Document screen.

To return to your document after previewing it, press F7 (Exit).

SEE ALSO

Display, Setup: View Document in Black & White
Graphics

WIDOW/ORPHAN PROTECTION

Prevents either the first or last line of a paragraph from being separated from the rest of the paragraph by a soft page break.

KEY SEQUENCE

Shift-F8 (Format)

▼

1 — Line

▼

9 — Widow/Orphan Protection Y *or* **N**

▼

F7 (Exit)

REVEAL CODES

[W/O Off]	Widow/Orphan Off
[W/O On]	Widow/Orphan On

USAGE

The Widow/Orphan Protection option instructs the program not to leave the first line of text in a paragraph by itself as the last line of a page (a widow) or the last line of a paragraph as the first line of a page (an orphan). Widow lines are forced to the next page, while orphan lines get one more line added from the previous page.

To turn on widow/orphan protection for an entire document, move the cursor to the beginning. Then press Format (Shift-F8) and select the Line option (**1** or **L**). Select Widow/Orphan Protection (**9** or **W**) and enter **Y**. This option is a toggle; to turn off widow/orphan protection, type **N**.

SEE ALSO

Block Protect
Conditional End of Page
Page Break, Soft and Hard

WINDOWS

Allows you to split the editing screen into two windows to view the text in the Doc 1 and Doc 2 editing areas simultaneously.

KEY SEQUENCE

Ctrl-F3 (Screen)

▼

1 Window

▼

Number of lines in this window: <*number*> **Enter** *or* ↑ **Enter**

USAGE

To split the screen into two windows, select Window (**1** or **W**) from the Screen key menu (Ctrl-F3). WordPerfect will prompt you for the number of lines of text you want to see in the current window. The screen can display up to 24 lines, so you can enter any combination that adds up to 24. For example, to see 12 lines in each window, enter **12**; to see 18 lines in one window and 6 in the other, enter **18**.

You can also use the ↑ and ↓ keys to move the cursor to the position where you want the split to occur and then press Enter. The window will be split at the cursor position.

To move back and forth between windows, press Shift-F3 (Switch). To remove the split screen and return to a full-screen display, press Ctrl-F3, select Windows, and this time enter **0** or **24** as the number of lines you want displayed. The second document will still be in memory, and you can return to it at any time by pressing Shift-F3 (Switch).

You can view the same document in each of the two windows by retrieving it into both windows—for example, if you want to see the beginning and end of a long document at the same time. Both documents will have the same file name, however, so you will have to keep track of which version you want to have as the final saved version.

SEE ALSO

Switch

WORD COUNT

See **Speller**.

WORD/LETTER SPACING

Allows you to adjust the spacing between letters of a word and/or between words in a line.

KEY SEQUENCE

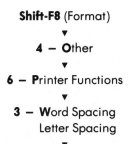

Shift-F8 (Format)

▼

4 – **O**ther

▼

6 – **P**rinter Functions

▼

3 – **W**ord Spacing
Letter Spacing

▼

Word Spacing: **1 N**ormal; **2 O**ptimal; **3 P**ercent of Optimal; **4 S**et Pitch
Letter Spacing: **1 N**ormal; **2 O**ptimal; **3 P**ercent of Optimal; **4 S**et Pitch

▼

F7 (Exit)

REVEAL CODES

[Wrd/Ltr Spacing]   Word and Letter Spacing

USAGE

WordPerfect's Word/Letter Spacing option allows you to adjust the spacing between words and between letters within words. When you justify text, for example, you may want to adjust the amount of space that the program adds between words to make the line of text come out even with the right margin. Letter spacing is normally used to add spaces between letters, creating a visual effect that is widely seen in company logos and on business cards, for example.

To change the word or letter spacing, press Shift-F8 (Format) and select Other (**4** or **O**). Then select Printer Functions (**6** or **P**) and choose Word Spacing/Letter Spacing (**3** or **W**) from the menu that appears. You can then select a setting for word spacing, letter spacing, or both.

The Normal setting (**1** or **N**) sets spacing between words as well as letters to the amount recommended by the manufacturer of your printer. Optimal (**2** or **O**), which is the default, produces the setting that appears best according to the manufacturer of WordPerfect. The Optimal and Normal settings are often, but not always, the same.

If you want to specify the amount of space to be used between words and letters, choose Percent of Optimal (**3** or **P**) and enter a percentage. Percentages less than 100% reduce the amount of space, while percentages greater than 100% enlarge it. Normally, you will not want to change the default setting unless you want to create special typographic effects.

If you want to adjust the spacing between words and letters in terms of pitch (characters per inch), use the Set Pitch option (**4** or **S**) and enter the pitch you want to use. WordPerfect then calculates the correct Percent of Optimal setting needed to generate that pitch in the font you are currently using.

SEE ALSO

Justification
Kerning

WORDPERFECT STARTUP OPTIONS

Allows you to start WordPerfect with a specific document on the editing screen or to start the program using any of its startup options.

KEY SEQUENCE

To start WordPerfect and retrieve a document:

WP *<file name>* **Enter**

To start WordPerfect with a specific startup option:

WP / *<startup option>* **Enter**

USAGE

WordPerfect has various setup options that you can add to the basic **WP** start-up command.

Retrieving a Document at Startup

If you want to start working on a particular document immediately, you can include its file name as part of the startup command. For example, to edit a document named RPT87 located in a directory named \WP50\FILES, give the startup command as

```
WP \WP50\FILES\RPT87
```

If the file is in your default directory, you do not have to give its full path name.

Invoking a Macro at Startup

You can also start WordPerfect and have it invoke a macro as soon as the program starts. For example, if you know that the first thing you need to do when WordPerfect is loaded is to change the current directory and you have created a change-directory macro named CD, you can enter the startup command as

```
WP/M-CD
```

You can start WordPerfect with any macro that has been saved in the directory that WordPerfect uses on startup. If the macro is an Alt-key macro, enter its name exactly as it is saved in your data directory. For example, to invoke a macro named Alt-Y when you start WordPerfect, enter the startup command as

```
WP/M-ALTY
```

Resetting Default Values

The /X startup option tells WordPerfect to restore all the default values that can be changed through the Setup key (Shift- F1). If you are sharing a workstation with other users, you may want to start WordPerfect with this option to make sure that the regular default values are in effect.

Redirecting Overflow Files

Overflow files, which are temporary files containing parts of the document you are currently working on, are normally saved in the drive or directory that WordPerfect uses at startup. You can instruct WordPerfect to save them in a new drive or directory by appending **/D-** (followed by the drive letter and path names, if required), to the WordPerfect startup command. For example, to save overflow files in the same directory (named SALESUM) as the document you are working on, you can start WordPerfect with this command:

```
WP/D-C:\WP50\SALESUM
```

This instructs WordPerfect to save overflow files in a subdirectory named SALE-SUM under the WP directory on drive C.

Not only overflow files but also buffers and temporary macros will be redirected to this new drive and/or directory. Practically, this means that if you are using WordPerfect on a system with two disk drives and start it using both the /D- and /R options (as discussed in the following section), you can remove the WordPerfect System disk from drive A as you work with the program and replace it with a second data disk. In such a case, you would give the startup command as:

A:WP/D-B/R

Overflow files will then be saved on the data disk in drive B along with the documents you are creating and editing. The disk in drive A could then hold macros that you wish to use during the work session, for example.

Using the RAM Option

If your computer has at least 300K of unused expanded memory, you can run WordPerfect with the RAM option. When this option is specified as a part of the startup command, WordPerfect loads all of its menus, error messages, and overlay files from the WordPerfect System disk into RAM. Because the program does not have to read these files from the System disk, it runs faster.

To start the program on a hard disk system using this option, you would enter

WP/R

If you use the /R option with the /D option on a system with two disk drives, you can even remove the WordPerfect System disk during operation, as discussed in the previous section.

Setting Timed Backups for One Session

You can start WordPerfect with a timed backup feature that will be in effect only for the current session. For example, to start WordPerfect and specify a timed backup at 10-minute intervals, enter

WP/B-10

and press the Enter key.

The optimal number of minutes between backups depends on your location and the frequency of power interruptions in your area. If an electrical storm is threatening, you may want to set a very small interval between backups, such as 5 or 10 minutes. The inconvenience caused when WordPerfect interrupts your work to save the document is slight compared to the time it takes to retype a long section of text.

Using the Non-flash Option

There are two circumstances under which you use this option:

- If you are using an IBM-compatible computer.
- If you have loaded WordPerfect from a window program.

If you are using an IBM-compatible computer and your screen goes blank from time to time, start WordPerfect with this option. Likewise, use it in the startup command that the window program uses to load WordPerfect if you have any screen difficulties when using a window program. To start WordPerfect with the Non-flash option, enter the startup command as

    WP/NF

Starting WordPerfect When TSR's Are Running

Some TSR (terminate and stay resident) programs such as SideKick may conflict with WordPerfect's operation. Three startup options may be used if you are having difficulty running WordPerfect concurrently with a TSR program.

- **/NC** disables the cursor speed feature. If WordPerfect does not start when you are running a TSR program, try starting it with this option.
- **/NE** restricts the use of expanded memory so that more memory is available to the TSR program.
- **/NK** disables certain keyboard functions that several TSR programs do not recognize. If WordPerfect starts but locks up when you are running a TSR program, try starting it with this option.

Setting the Screen Size

The /SS option allows you to set the screen size. WordPerfect normally detects the screen size of the monitor you are using, but if for some reason it doesn't, try starting it with this option and setting the actual screen size.

Combining Startup Options

You can combine all startup options. For example, if you want to speed up the program by using the /R option and set a timed backup interval of 10 minutes while retrieving a document named REPORT89 at the same time, you would enter the command as **WP/R/B-15 REPORT89**. Just remember not to enter spaces between the slashes and to enter a hyphen between the option letter and any particular required entry such as a macro name or number of minutes. The command

WP/R/B-15/M-CD

starts WordPerfect with the RAM option, specifies a timed backup at 15-minute intervals, and invokes a macro named CD.

Restoring Setup Defaults

Starting WordPerfect with the /X option restores the program's initial default setup values for the current session only. When you exit WordPerfect, any changes you have made through the Setup key (Shift-F1) are restored.

SEE ALSO

Setup

WORD SEARCH

Locates all of the files in the current directory that contain a specified word or phrase.

KEY SEQUENCE

To perform a word search:

F5 (List Files) **Enter**

▼

9 Word Search

▼

1 Doc Summary; **2 F**irst Page; **3 E**ntire Doc

▼

Word Pattern: *<word(s) or phrase(s)>* **Enter**

To set the search conditions:

F5 (List Files) **Enter**

▼

9 Word Search

▼

4 Conditions

▼

1 – Perform Search on
2 – Undo Last Search
3 – Reset Search Conditions
4 – File **D**ate
    From (MM/DD/YY):
    To (MM/DD/YY):
5 – First Page
6 – Entire Doc
7 – Document **S**ummary
    Creation Date (e.g. Nov)
    Descriptive Name
    Subject/Account
    Author
    Typist
    Comments

▼

F7 (Exit)

USAGE

The Word Search option (**9** or **W**) of the List Files menu (F5) allows you to search through all the files in one directory or through the files you have explicitly marked with an asterisk (*) to find a specific word or phrase (up to 20 characters).

After WordPerfect locates the files that contain what you are searching for, it marks them with an asterisk on the List Files screen. You can use the Look option to view their contents and determine which of them are the documents you are seeking. You can also retrieve a marked file to the editing screen.

To return to the List Files screen with the marked files still displayed after using the Look option, press F7 (Exit). To return to List Files with the marked files displayed after retrieving a file, press F5 (List Files) twice.

Setting Search Options

After you select Word Search, you will see the following menu:

1 Document Summary; **2 F**irst Page; **3 E**ntire Document; **4 C**onditions:0

Select Document Summary (**1** or **D**) for a word, phrase, or pattern only in the document summaries of the files you have marked or of all the files in the directory, if you haven't marked any particular ones.

Select First Page (**2** or **F**) to search through only the first page or the first 4000 characters of each file.

Select Entire Document (**3** or **E**) to search through all the files you have marked or all the files in the directory.

Select Condition (**4** or **C**) to enter specialized search conditions, as discussed below.

Setting Search Conditions

If you select Conditions, you will see the Conditions menu. You can then choose the conditions that the files must meet.

The Perform Search On option (**1** or **P**) lists the number of files that will be searched. After the search has finished, this number changes to the number of files that the search located. To start a search after selecting other search conditions, select this option.

To repeat a search on the same group of files, select Undo Last Search (**2** or **U**). Normally, if you were searching through ten files and WordPerfect located what you were searching for in two files, the next search you carried out would be on the two files that it located. Selecting this option changes the number of files that are to be included in the search to the previous level—in this example, ten files.

Use the Reset Search Conditions option (**3** or **R**) to clear the search conditions and enter new ones for the next search.

File Date (**4** or **D**) allows you to specify that files created on or between certain dates be included in the search. You can enter the date with or without leading zeroes—as **01/02/89** or as **1/2/89**, for example. To enter a single month or an entire year, use the form **1//89** or **//89**.

Options **5** through **7** are the same as the options on the Word Search menu; they are presented here to allow you to specify searches and carry them out from the same screen.

Entering Patterns for Word Searches

When you search a directory for a file containing a specific word or phrase that contains spaces, you must enter the word or phrase to be searched for in quotation marks.

You can search for an exact phrase by adding a blank space after the last letter and before the last quotation mark. You can also enter an exact phrase to be searched for by pressing Ctrl- Enter before typing the phrase.

You can also use wild cards to enlarge the search pattern. For example, if you are searching for a file containing an address for a company and you are sure that its name began with *South* but do not remember whether its full name is *Southwest-ern, Southeastern,* or *Southern,* you can enter the word pattern as **South∗**.

To search for a phrase beginning with one pattern and ending with another, enter it as **"South∗Industries"**. This will locate all phrases starting with *South* and ending with *Industries,* such as *Southern Industries, Southwestern Industries, south of the industries,* and so forth. Uppercase and lowercase are considered to be the same.

Using Logical Operators with Word Search

You can further expand or restrict a word search by using semicolons and blank spaces (which stand for *and*) or commas (which stand for *or*). For example, to search for files that contain both the word *invoice* and the phrase *past due,* you enter

```
invoice;"past due"
```

To search for files that contain either the word *invoice* or the phrase *past due,* enter

```
invoice,"past due"
```

To search for files that contain either the word *invoice* or the phrase *past due* in com-bination with the word *October,* enter

```
invoice,"past due";October
```

SEE ALSO

Document Summary
Name Search

APPENDICES

IMPORTING AND EXPORTING DOCUMENTS

As you work with WordPerfect, you may want to set up documents you create so they can be used with other programs. You may, for example, want to give a document on disk to another department in your company that does not use WordPerfect but instead uses WordStar or some other word processing program. Likewise, you may sometimes want to import text from other word processing programs or data from spreadsheet or database management programs such as Lotus 1-2-3 or dBASE III Plus. You may, for example, want to include spreadsheet data in a table in a report you are writing, or you may want to bring data into WordPerfect to use in graphics you create with the Line Draw feature. In addition, if you use WordPerfect's mail merge facility, you may want to import database data for use in a WordPerfect merge file.

WordPerfect contains a Text In/Out menu for converting WordPerfect text to DOS text file format (also called ASCII format). A separate Convert program, provided on the Learning disk, converts WordPerfect text directly to several formats used by other popular word processing programs. It also allows you to import spreadsheet data saved in data interchange format (DIF) and to accept data from dBASE and WordStar mail merge files. In addition, you can send text to a DOS text file so that you can print it using the DOS PRINT command.

This appendix discusses how to import text and data into WordPerfect and prepare WordPerfect documents for exportation to other programs.

EXPORTING WORDPERFECT DOCUMENTS AS DOS TEXT FILES

Converting a file to a DOS text file (a file in ASCII format) allows text created by one program to be used in other programs. When text is converted to DOS text file format, it loses the special formatting codes that the original word processing program inserted. When a WordPerfect document is converted to a DOS text file, soft returns and soft page breaks are converted to hard returns, and hard returns become carriage return–line feeds.

You can use the Convert utility, a special program run outside of WordPerfect, to convert WordPerfect documents directly to certain other specific formats. Within WordPerfect's Text In/Out menu (Ctrl-F5), there is also a Save Generic option that preserves much of the original formatting. If you are converting a WordPerfect document for use by another word processing program not supported by the Convert utility, you should try using this format. Before you decide to convert a document to a DOS text file or to the generic word processor format, check whether one of the direct conversions on the Convert menu is suitable for the programs you are using. (See "Using the Convert Program" later in this chapter for instructions on how to use the Convert utility to convert documents to other formats.)

Converting Documents to DOS Text Files

If you select DOS Text (**1** or **T**) on the Text In/Out menu (Ctrl-F5), you will see a submenu from which you can choose Save (**1** or **S**). You will be prompted for a new file name to give the document on the screen as it is saved in DOS text file format. To avoid overwriting the WordPerfect version of your document, use a different name, or add an extension such as .TXT.

When you use this option, the WordPerfect document on the screen is converted to a DOS text file. In this format, most of the codes that WordPerfect inserted to control formatting are removed. The WordPerfect codes that control indenting, centering, paragraph numbering, and the Date function are converted to ASCII text, however. Your entire document except its footnotes and endnotes will be converted.

To view your document in DOS text file format, you can exit to DOS (by pressing Ctrl-F1 G) and issue the TYPE command with the name of your file. For example, to view a DOS text file named REPORT, you enter **TYPE REPORT** at the A> or C> prompt. Using the TYPE command is a good way to see whether your document has been converted successfully to DOS text file format.

You can convert your WordPerfect document to a generic word processor format by using option **3** or **G** on the Text In/Out menu. In this format, special WordPerfect formatting codes are not saved, but the overall text format is maintained. Footnotes and endnotes are not converted, however. In place of the codes that indicate centering, indenting, flush right alignment, and soft returns, spaces are inserted, and <CR><LF> (carriage return–line feed) codes are inserted in place of hard returns. Consult the documentation of the other program you plan to use the document with to see what format it will accept.

In addition, you will notice on the Text In/Out menu that you can convert documents you create in WordPerfect 5.0 into WordPerfect 4.2 format. If you are working in an office in which one department has not upgraded to WordPerfect 5.0, you may wish to use this option to prepare documents for that department.

Whenever you convert documents, you should save them with an optional extension that identifies the format they are in. If you save a document in another format with the same name under which you saved it in WordPerfect format, the WordPerfect document will be overwritten, and you will have to convert it back in order to use it again within WordPerfect. You may want to save documents you have converted to DOS text file format with the extension .TXT or .ASC or save documents converted to WordStar with the extension .WSD.

If you are planning to convert a document for use in WordStar or MultiMate, you should use WordPerfect's Convert program instead.

IMPORTING DOS TEXT FILES (ASCII DOCUMENTS)

Normally, when you retrieve into WordPerfect a document that is in DOS text file format, the end of each line contains a hard return ([HRt]). This is fine if you are importing lines of programming code or data that is in columns and rows. However, if you are importing text, the [HRt] at the end of each line makes the text difficult to reformat. You can use either of two options—one that places hard returns at the ends of lines or one that places soft returns at the ends of lines if they occur within the hyphenation zone.

If the WordPerfect document into which you are importing a DOS text file has margins narrower than the incoming DOS text file, the program will insert soft returns at the points where the WordPerfect margins are, and your lines may not be formatted as you prefer. For this reason, be sure to set margins in WordPerfect at 0″ and 8″ before importing the file if you want the text to appear line for line as it was in the other program.

Because DOS text files contain tabs that are set every eight spaces, you may also want to set similar tabs in your WordPerfect document before you import the file. This step is usually not necessary, but if you have any difficulty with the format of the incoming file once it is in WordPerfect, exit the document, set tabs at every eight spaces in a new document, and retrieve the DOS text file again.

Retrieving a DOS Text File

When you retrieve a document saved as a DOS text file, you first choose DOS Text (**1** or **T**) from the Text In/Out menu. You then have two options. Option **2** or **R** converts carriage return–line feed entries into hard returns in WordPerfect; option **3** or **E** converts carriage return–line feed entries into soft returns if they occur within the hyphenation zone. If you are bringing in data that is in columns and rows, such as Lotus 1-2-3 or dBASE III files or lines of programming code for which you want to use WordPerfect as a text editor, you should use option **2** or **R**, which preserves the column and row format. You should also use this option to bring in DOS batch files to revise them. If you are bringing in text that has been word-wrapped, you should use option **3** or **E**.

If the file you are importing uses wide margins (as files in 80-column format do, for instance), you may want to set your margins in WordPerfect to be wider than the incoming file so that the format of the incoming document is preserved.

You can also use the Text In option (**5** or **T**) on the List Files menu (F5) to retrieve DOS text files. To do so, highlight the name of the DOS text file, select Text In, and press Enter. WordPerfect converts the file into WordPerfect format and inserts it at the position of the cursor on the editing screen.

> *Note:* Using Retrieve (**2** or **R**) on the Text In/Out menu is the same as using the Text In option (**5** or **T**) on the List Files menu. Carriage return–line feeds are converted to hard returns in either case.

WordPerfect's Convert Program

WordPerfect also gives you a special Convert program that converts documents in selected formats directly to WordPerfect format and vice versa. When you use the Convert program, most formatting and text attributes, such as bold-facing, are converted into the appropriate codes for the new document. If the program to which you are converting a WordPerfect document can use any of the formats supported by the Convert program, you should usually convert using those formats instead of the DOS (ASCII) text file format because you lose most text formatting attributes when you convert a file to a DOS text file.

In addition, you may want to use a format on the Convert program as an intermediate step in converting a document to WordPerfect format. For example, as you will see later, converting a Lotus 1-2-3 database directly to a DIF file may present problems if you plan to use the database as a WordPerfect secondary merge file. However, if you first convert the Lotus 1-2-3 database to dBASE (as a .DBF file), you can then import the dBASE file directly into Word-Perfect and use it as a secondary merge file in mail merge applications.

The Convert program allows you to bring in two types of files: files containing text, such as documents from other word processing programs and tables of data from other spreadsheet programs, and files containing data, such as data from a database program that you wish to use in mail merge applications. When you use the Convert program, you see the menu in Figure A.1.

You can import documents from the following formats into WordPerfect:

- Revisable-Form-Text or Final-Form-Text, also called document content architecture (DCA), which is used by IBM mainframes for transferring documents created on microcomputers. Conversion to this format preserves many formatting commands. Many popular word processing programs have added DCA to their own conversion programs, so you may be able to convert a document in another program first to DCA and then

```
Name of Input File? ch2
Name of Output File? ch2.wsd

1 WordPerfect to another format
2 Revisable-Form-Text (IBM DCA Format) to WordPerfect
3 Navy DIF Standard to WordPerfect
4 WordStar 3.3 to WordPerfect
5 MultiMate 3.22 to WordPerfect
6 Seven-Bit Transfer Format to WordPerfect
7 WordPerfect 4.2 to WordPerfect 5.0
8 Mail Merge to WordPerfect Secondary Merge
9 WordPerfect Secondary Merge to Spreadsheet DIF
A Spreadsheet DIF to WordPerfect Secondary Merge

Enter number of Conversion desired _
```

FIGURE A.1: The Convert utility menu. This is a special, external program, located on the Learning disk that comes with WordPerfect. It allows you to convert files directly into many popular formats.

directly to WordPerfect, retaining much of its formatting. Check the documentation of the program from which you are importing a document.

- Navy document interchange format (DIF), which is a form of DIF used for exchanging documents, not spreadsheet data.

- WordStar. Most popular word processing programs can convert their documents directly to this format. However, some formatting codes, such as Tab codes, are not translated. You may also be able to use WordStar format as an intermediate format; try it and see. If tabs are not important in the incoming document, this format may work for you.

- MultiMate. Use this option to import MultiMate documents.

- Seven-bit transfer format, which is used for transferring WordPerfect documents (which contain 8-bit control codes) via modems that lack an 8-bit transfer protocol. Most communications programs provide their own 8-bit transfer protocols, but if the one you are using does not, you can use this option to transfer WordPerfect files. When you use this option, the receiver at the other end uses option **6** on the menu, Seven-Bit Transfer Format, to translate the file back into WordPerfect format.

- ASCII format, as discussed above.

You can also convert documents as follows:

- You can convert WordPerfect 5.0 documents into DCA, WordStar, MultiMate, 7-bit transfer format, ASCII format, and WordPerfect 4.2 format.
- You can convert dBASE, WordStar, or other mail merge files into WordPerfect secondary merge files.
- You can convert WordPerfect secondary merge files into DIF (spreadsheet) format.
- You can convert spreadsheet DIF files into WordPerfect secondary merge files.

See the section "Converting Database and Spreadsheet Files" later in this chapter for considerations involved in working with these types of files.

Using the Convert Program

To use the Convert program, you can copy it into the directory in which the files you wish to convert are stored, or you can call it from another directory.

1. At the DOS prompt, A> or C>, enter **CONVERT** (use its path name if it's in another directory) and press Enter. (You can run this utility by using WordPerfect's Shell command, Ctrl-F1 G.) The menu shown in Figure A.1 appears.

2. Type the name of the file you want to convert (the input file); then press Enter.

3. Type the name of the output file—the one you wish the input file to be converted to—then press Enter. The names must be different; you can use a 3-letter extension, such as .WSD for WordStar, to indicate the format to which the file has been converted. You can also indicate a drive letter—for example, to output the converted file to a disk in drive B.

4. WordPerfect then displays the Convert menu. Enter the number corresponding to the current format of the input file. For example, if you are converting a WordStar document to WordPerfect, enter **4**.

5. If you are converting a WordPerfect document to another format, enter **1**. You will see the menu shown in Figure A.2. Enter the number corresponding to the format you want the converted file to use. For example, to convert a WordPerfect document to WordStar format, enter **1 4**.

```
Name of Input File? ch2
Name of Output File? ch2.wsd


1 Revisable-Form-Text (IBM DCA Format)
2 Final-Form-Text (IBM DCA Format)
3 Navy DIF Standard
4 WordStar 3.3
5 MultiMate 3.22
6 Seven-Bit Transfer Format
7 ASCII text file

Enter number of output file format desired _
```

FIGURE A.2: Converting documents to different formats. Unlike when you convert to ASCII format, when you select formats from this menu, formatting codes and text attributes are preserved when the documents are converted.

If you are using the Convert program on a floppy disk system, insert the Convert disk into drive A, insert the disk containing the file you want to convert into drive B, and enter **A:CONVERT** at the DOS prompt to start the Convert program.

CONVERTING DATABASE AND SPREADSHEET FILES

You can bring data into a WordPerfect document as text, which means that you cannot use it in mail merge applications; as a *delimited* file, which means that each field and record is separated by a special character so that WordPerfect can convert it to its secondary merge format; or as a DIF file. The following sections discuss considerations involved in importing data.

Importing Data as Text

Importing spreadsheet or database data to be used as text—most often, as tables—in WordPerfect may produce unsatisfactory results if you have not taken a few necessary steps before converting the document. For example, when you export a wide Lotus 1-2-3 file in ASCII format (by printing it to a disk using the /Print File command in Lotus), you first need to reset your margins in WordPerfect if you do not want the table broken at the existing margins. Spreadsheet data often comprises monthly figures, which means that you will have 12 columns of numbers, plus perhaps 1 column of labels and 1 column of totals. If each column contains a four-digit number as well as a decimal point and two digits for cents, you are obviously going to need either a wider margin than the one you normally use, or a smaller font. When your margins are not set wide enough to hold the incoming data, WordPerfect wraps extra data that extends beyond the right margin. For this reason, you should split wide spreadsheets into smaller segments within the spreadsheet program before you bring them into WordPerfect. You should also set any margins that you have specified in the other program to zero so that the table of data will appear at the left margin in WordPerfect.

Likewise, if you are importing tables of data from a database program, you should create a report and sort or extract data so that it is arranged as you want it before you bring it into WordPerfect.

Importing Data for Use in Mail Merge Operations

Before you can merge database data into a document such as a form letter in WordPerfect, you need to convert the data into WordPerfect's secondary merge format. In this format, each field is terminated by the ^R code, and the end of each record is indicated by the ^E code on a line by itself (see Chapter 11 for additional information about Merge codes). In database files used for mail merge operations, fields and records are arranged by using *delimiters,* which are special characters that indicate the ends of fields and records.

When you use the Convert program with this type of file (option **8** on the Convert menu), it will prompt you for the character that separates fields, the character that separates records, and any characters that should be removed from the incoming file. You will need to type the character or enter its ASCII code equivalent in curly braces. For example, if a space is used to separate fields in the incoming data, you can press the space bar or enter {32}. If a carriage return–line feed separates records, you enter {13}{10}, which is the ASCII code for <CR><LF>. In addition, most delimited files use quotation marks around labels to distinguish them from values. You should mark these as characters to be removed by typing " when you are prompted for characters to delete.

Options **8** and **A** on the Convert menu convert mail merge files and spreadsheet DIF files, respectively, from other programs directly into WordPerfect secondary merge files. Option **9** converts WordPerfect secondary merge files into spreadsheet DIF format. You can use option **9** when you need to export WordPerfect mail merge files to another program format.

In dBASE II or III, you can convert (copy) files to type DELIMITED, which is mail merge format. If you are using dBASE III Plus, you can convert (copy) files to type DIF. In dBASE II or III, you use the command

.COPY TO <*file name*> DELIMITED

The program automatically adds the .TXT extension for you. You will need to specify the file name with the .TXT extension when you use the Convert program. You must also respond to the prompts to indicate the field and record delimiters and to remove quotation marks, as previously mentioned.

When you bring a delimited (mail merge) file into WordPerfect from dBASE II or III, you must reposition the codes that separate records (see "DELIM: A Macro to Reformat Delimited Files" later in this chapter).

If you are translating a file to DIF, the program will translate the whole file. If all you want is a few records, you must first prepare a report containing only those records. When you convert a DIF file, the field names are also converted, and you must manually remove them before you use the file as a WordPerfect secondary merge file. They will be listed at the beginning of the file.

In dBASE III Plus, you can convert files directly to DIF and bring them in as WordPerfect secondary merge files. All the WordPerfect codes required will be in their correct places, and all you will have to do is remove the field names at the beginning of the file.

The command for translating a file to DIF is

.COPY TO <*file name*> DIF

The program automatically adds a .DIF extension; you will need to specify the file name with that extension when you use the Convert program.

DELIM: A Macro to Reformat Delimited Files

Fields in files that are brought into WordPerfect's secondary merge format must be separated by ^R codes, and the ^E code must appear on a separate line to indicate the end of each record. The ^E code should be followed by a hard page break. The macro shown in Figure A.3 searches for each ^E code and inserts a hard page break after it. The macro repeats itself until no more ^E codes are found.

Converting Lotus 1-2-3 Databases
to WordPerfect Secondary Merge Files

You can convert Lotus 1-2-3 databases for use in WordPerfect mail merge operations, but you will need to take an intermediate step if the database contains numeric fields or date fields. The DIF format was designed for spreadsheet-to-spreadsheet conversions, and values are translated in the format in which the program stores them internally. The receiving program, which is usually another spreadsheet, normally reformats values back into its own format. Because Lotus 1-2-3 stores data to a precision of 15 places, the data you import directly in a DIF

```
Macro: Edit

        File            DELIM.WPM

   1 - Description      inserts hard page break after ^E codes

   2 - Action


   {DISPLAY OFF}{Search}{Merge Codes}e{Search}{HPg}{Macro}delim{Enter}




    Selection: 0
```

FIGURE A.3: Searching for ^E codes to insert hard page breaks. This macro automatically converts imported delimited files to the proper format.

file is largely useless for mail merge applications. It is formatted in scientific notation. In addition, dates, which are stored as serial numbers, lose their formatting when imported in a DIF file.

If you have access to dBASE II, dBASE III, or dBASE III Plus, you can solve this problem without having to reenter each number and date manually. First translate your Lotus 1-2-3 database to a dBASE database file, using the Lotus 1-2-3 Translate utility. Then copy the resulting dBASE (.DBF) file to either a DIF file (if you have dBASE III Plus) or a delimited file format (dBASE II or III) and bring it into WordPerfect using the appropriate option on the Convert utility.

If you do not have access to dBASE, you should check whether any database management program you do have access to supports importation of Lotus 1-2-3 worksheets (most do) and can also create ASCII delimited files from the program's database format. For example, Paradox's ExportImport option allows you to import a Lotus 1-2-3 worksheet and to create an ASCII delimited file from the resulting database. You can also do the same thing using the R:base 5000 or R:BASE System V FileGateway program.

If you do not have access to an intermediate program that can perform these types of translations, you will have to manually reenter numbers and dates in the Word-Perfect secondary merge files in order to use them. Using the Lotus 1-2-3/Print File command to create an ASCII file and then the Mail Merge to WordPerfect Secondary Merge command will not accomplish the desired results.

This conversion procedure works because the resulting .PRN file, though in ASCII code, is not delimited by any characters except spaces. Because of the way values are formatted in the Lotus 1-2-3 worksheet, the number of spaces between individual fields in the Print file varies. A Mail Merge to WordPerfect Secondary Merge conversion will work only if each field is separated by a single space and no field contains any internal spaces within its text. In such a case, you can tell WordPerfect to use the space ({32}) as the field delimiter, and a successful translation will result.

Transferring Files Between IBM and Macintosh WordPerfect

If you have access to a Macintosh, you are probably aware of its superior graphics capabilities and range of fonts. WordPerfect Corporation makes a version of Word-Perfect for the Macintosh, so if you have both machines available you can create the text of a document in IBM WordPerfect and transfer it to Macintosh WordPerfect for graphics enhancements. WordPerfect for the Macintosh can convert documents in IBM WordPerfect format, but if you are not using 3½-inch floppy disks with your IBM or IBM-compatible computer, the first problem is how to get the document from the IBM to the Mac, which uses 3½-inch floppies. And even if you do have it on a 3½-inch disk, how do you get it into a format that the Macintosh can read? Once you get the file there and get it in some form that the Macintosh can recognize, it's simple to convert it to WordPerfect Macintosh format.

Note: You may need to save your WordPerfect 5.0 document in WordPerfect 4.2 format before you can transfer it to Macintosh WordPerfect. Check with WordPerfect Corporation to see whether Macintosh WordPerfect accepts version 5.0 documents by the time you read this.

Non-Network Connections

If you're part of a network, such as TOPS, you should have no problem transferring files between a Macintosh and an IBM computer. However, if you're not part of a network, there are three different things you can do to get the files from one computer to another:

- Purchase a PC-compatible disk drive that will read the 5¼-inch floppies into your Macintosh.

- Run communications programs on both computers and use a special cable to connect the two machines.

- Run communications programs on both computers and connect them via modem over the phone lines.

PC-Compatible Disk Drives

The simplest solution is to obtain a PC-compatible drive for the Macintosh, but this is also the most expensive solution. Several manufacturers offer PC-compatible drives that allow you to copy disk files between the 3½-inch and the 5¼-inch disk types. For example, Dayna Communications' DaynaFile is a PC drive that can run on any Mac with an SCSI port. It comes with its own translators. There are many other manufacturers of PC-compatible drives.

Connecting an IBM PC and a Macintosh

You can also obtain a special cable (called a *null modem* cable, available from your dealer) to connect both computers. (Be sure to get the correct type of cable, either the PC style or the AT style.) You'll also need two communications programs—one that runs on your Mac and another for your PC. The PC program should support the file transfer protocol called XMODEM, and it should be capable of transmitting at 9,600 or 19,200 baud. (The word *protocol* refers to settings that control how the sending and receiving computers interact with each other.) ProComm and PC-Talk will both do this, and you can get them as shareware from most computer bulletin boards, including CompuServe.

On your Mac, you should be running a communications program that will transfer at 9,600 or 19,200 baud and allow you to disable MacBinary. Most communications programs for the Macintosh, such as MacTerminal and Micro-Phone, will do this.

Converting IBM WordPerfect Documents to Macintosh WordPerfect

Once you have connected both machines with the cable, you can send IBM WordPerfect documents to a Macintosh by taking these steps:

1. Set both communications programs to 9,600 or 19,200 baud, no parity, 8 data bits, and 1 stop bit. In ProComm, this is setting 12.

2. On the Macintosh side, disable MacBinary. This choice is probably a File Transfer setting on the Settings menu.

3. On the IBM side, select Upload or Send File with XMODEM as the protocol and enter the file name of the DOS file you want to send to the Macintosh.

4. On the Macintosh side, select the Receive XMODEM command.

5. Press Enter to send the file from the IBM to the Macintosh (or use the appropriate command in your communications program). The document will appear as an icon on your Macintosh's screen.

6. Start WordPerfect on the Macintosh.

7. Press Command-L for File Management.

8. Select Open from the File menu; then select the document's name.

Note: If you're not using version 1.01 or greater of Macintosh WordPerfect, the procedure is different. To open an IBM WordPerfect document, use the File Management window (Command-L); then select the document's name and click File/Folder Info. You'll need to click on Drive if the document is on a disk in the floppy drive. Delete what's in the Creator box and type **SSIW**, using uppercase letters. Then delete what's in the Type box and type **WPPC**. Finally, click OK.

You can now use the document that was created on the IBM just as though you had created it on the Macintosh. However, you'll probably want to make some font changes, since fonts aren't translated from machine to machine. Secondary merge files are translated in both directions, so you can do mass mailings on either machine.

Converting Macintosh WordPerfect Documents to IBM WordPerfect

To convert a document to IBM WordPerfect format, display it on your Macintosh screen. Then choose Save As from the File menu and click the IBM WordPerfect Format button. Name the document; then click Save. Remember, if the document is going to DOS, you've got an eight-character limit plus a three-character extension. WordPerfect doesn't require any extension, but you may want to add one to help you identify the source of the document, like CHAPTER2.MAC.

Then you can use the same setup—in reverse—that was just discussed for transferring Macintosh and IBM files. Set the communications program on the IBM to receive an XMODEM file (your choice may be called ''downloading'') and choose Send XMODEM in your Macintosh communications program.

Communicating via Modem

If your Mac and your IBM aren't close to each other—maybe one's at home and the other's at work—you can connect them via modem to transfer Word-Perfect files. You'll need to connect a modem to each computer and have a person at each end when you send a file. As communications settings, choose no parity, 8 data bits, and 1 stop bit. Set up for 1,200 or 2,400 baud, depending on what your modem can handle.

Give the person on the other end a call and tell them there's a file transfer coming so that they can start their communications program. Then have your communications program dial the other computer's number.

When you've made the connection with the other computer, you can transfer documents just as though both computers were connected via cable, as described earlier. As each file is transferred, you'll probably see an indication of how much has been transferred and what portion is waiting to be transferred.

Of course, you can transfer files from IBM to IBM this same way. However, in this case you should note that if your communications programs do not support eight-bit transfer and you have to use seven-bit instead, you'll need to use WordPerfect's Convert program on the files, as described earlier in this appendix. First, convert the files to seven-bit format by using the Convert program at the sending end (type **CONVERT** *filename newfilename* **1 6** at the DOS prompt); then, at the receiving end, convert them back to WordPerfect format (type **CONVERT** *filename newfilename* 6 at the DOS prompt).

CONVERTING WORDPERFECT 4.2
FEATURES TO WORDPERFECT 5.0

WordPerfect 4.2 documents are automatically converted to 5.0 format when you retrieve them into 5.0. However, some of the 4.2 codes have no equivalent in WordPerfect 5.0. These codes include those for font and pitch changes, sheet feeder bin numbers, and ASCII characters (but only if you have changed them to another ASCII character). Font Change codes are replaced in 5.0 by Attribute On and Off codes, such as [ITALC] for italics on and [italc] for italics off. Sheet feeder bin numbers are represented in 5.0 by Paper Size/Type codes. Extended ASCII characters are generated in WordPerfect 5.0 by using the Compose feature (Ctrl-2, as discussed in Chapter 14).

If you retrieve a WordPerfect 4.2 document that contains any of these unconvertible codes into WordPerfect 5.0, you will see Comment boxes on the screen, like those in Figure A.4. If you no longer want to change fonts at those points in your document, you can simply delete the Comment boxes. If you do want to change fonts, you can delete the comments, press Ctrl-F8 (Font), and insert the necessary font changes on a case-by-case basis, depending on which font on the current printer produces the font you were using in 4.2.

However, if you have quite a few 4.2 documents that contain several Font Change, Bin Number, Paper Size, or special nondisplayable character codes and you plan to work with them in version 5.0, you should take the time to set up a special .CRS conversion file that will automatically replace the equivalent 4.2 codes with WordPerfect 5.0 codes each time you retrieve a 4.2 document. You will need to do this for each printer you are using.

Basically, what you do is retrieve a file called STANDARD.CRS and edit it so that WordPerfect knows which codes to replace with 5.0 codes. You then name the STANDARD.CRS file with the name of the .PRS printer file you are currently using, but with the .CRS extension. For example, if you are using an

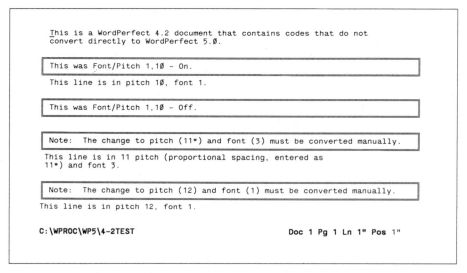

```
     This is a WordPerfect 4.2 document that contains codes that do not
     convert directly to WordPerfect 5.Ø.

    ┌─────────────────────────────────────────────────────────────────────┐
    │ This was Font/Pitch 1,1Ø - On.                                      │
    └─────────────────────────────────────────────────────────────────────┘
     This line is in pitch 1Ø, font 1.

    ┌─────────────────────────────────────────────────────────────────────┐
    │ This was Font/Pitch 1,1Ø - Off.                                     │
    └─────────────────────────────────────────────────────────────────────┘

    ┌─────────────────────────────────────────────────────────────────────┐
    │ Note:  The change to pitch (11*) and font (3) must be converted manually. │
    └─────────────────────────────────────────────────────────────────────┘
     This line is in 11 pitch (proportional spacing, entered as
     11*) and font 3.

    ┌─────────────────────────────────────────────────────────────────────┐
    │ Note:  The change to pitch (12) and font (1) must be converted manually. │
    └─────────────────────────────────────────────────────────────────────┘
     This line is in pitch 12, font 1.


     C:\WPROC\WP5\4-2TEST                          Doc 1 Pg 1 Ln 1" Pos 1"
```

FIGURE A.4: A test document after conversion. This test document was prepared to demonstrate converting WordPerfect 4.2 codes to WordPerfect 5.0.

Epson FX-85 printer, you would rename the edited STANDARD.CRS file EPFX85.CRS upon saving it. (To see the exact name of the .PRS file you are using, press Shift-F7, type **S** for Select, and choose **E** for Edit.) You can then convert the 4.2 document by using the Convert program. (Do not follow the instructions in the manual that say you can simply retrieve the document!)

In the following example, we will examine how you use the STANDARD.CRS file to convert Font Change codes from WordPerfect 4.2 to 5.0.

1. Retrieve the STANDARD.CRS file (Figure A.5) into your Doc 1 window.

2. Retrieve the 4.2 file you are converting into your Doc 2 window. That way, you can see which codes need to be converted. For example, in the test document in Figure A.4, there were Font Change codes for font 1, pitch 10; font 3, pitch 11*; and font 1, pitch 12. The Comment boxes for the last two changes indicate that you will have to change them manually, but when you run the document through the Convert program, WordPerfect will make best-guess substitution for you.

3. After you have determined which Font Change codes you need to convert—and have ascertained which effect you originally intended in WordPerfect 4.2 (it's easy to forget which codes control which fonts)— return to the STANDARD.CRS file and edit it so that the correct codes are generated on the right side of the equal sign (=) for that code.

```
FO 1,10 =
┌─────────────────────────────────────────────────────────────────┐
│ This was Font/Pitch 1,10 - On.                                    │
└─────────────────────────────────────────────────────────────────┘
FF 1,10 =
┌─────────────────────────────────────────────────────────────────┐
│ This was Font/Pitch 1,10 - Off.                                   │
└─────────────────────────────────────────────────────────────────┘
FO 2,10 =
┌─────────────────────────────────────────────────────────────────┐
│ This was Font/Pitch 2,10 - On.                                    │
└─────────────────────────────────────────────────────────────────┘
FF 2,10 =
┌─────────────────────────────────────────────────────────────────┐
│ This was Font/Pitch 2,10 - Off.                                   │
└─────────────────────────────────────────────────────────────────┘
FO 2,12 =
┌─────────────────────────────────────────────────────────────────┐
│ This was Font/Pitch 2,12 - On.                                    │
└─────────────────────────────────────────────────────────────────┘
C:\WPROC\WP5\STANDARD.CRS                          Doc 1 Pg 1 Ln 1" Pos 1"
```

FIGURE A.5: The STANDARD.CRS file. It indicates the codes that represent 4.2 commands on the left side of the equal sign; you need to generate the 5.0 equivalents that you want to use on the right side of the equal sign.

In the STANDARD.CRS file, *FO* stands for *Font On* and *FF* stands for *Font Off*. Although there were no Font Off codes in WordPerfect 4.2, you will need to indicate the appropriate codes in the STANDARD.CRS file. For example, if you want font 1, pitch 10 to be italics, you will need to generate the version 5.0 [ITALC] code as FO = [ITALC] and the [italc] code as FF = [italc]. The fastest way to do this is to use block marking (Alt-F4) so that the codes are positioned correctly.

4. Press Alt-F3 (Reveal Codes) so that you can see what is going on. Then position the cursor after the equal sign and press Alt-F4. Highlight to the next equal sign in the FF line by pressing ↓, as illustrated in Figure A.6. Then press Ctrl-F8 (Font), choose option **2** or **A** (Appearance), and choose option **4** or **I** to generate the [ITALC] and [italc] codes in the correct places. You can then delete the [Comment] codes, as Figure A.7 illustrates. This helps you remember which codes you have replaced with 5.0 codes if you should retrieve the file later to indicate more conversion codes. The [Comment] boxes that you leave in place will not cause any trouble.

Repeat this process for all the Font Change codes that you are using in the version 4.2 document. If you are switching to a different font by using WordPerfect 5.0's Base Font option, don't use blocking. Instead, edit the codes so that the FO

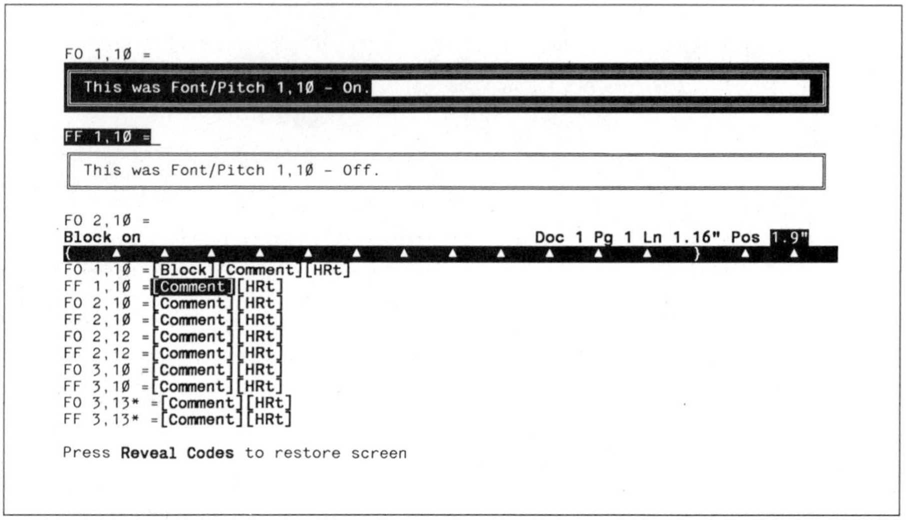

FIGURE A.6: A shortcut. Use block marking to indicate the Attribute On and Off codes quickly.

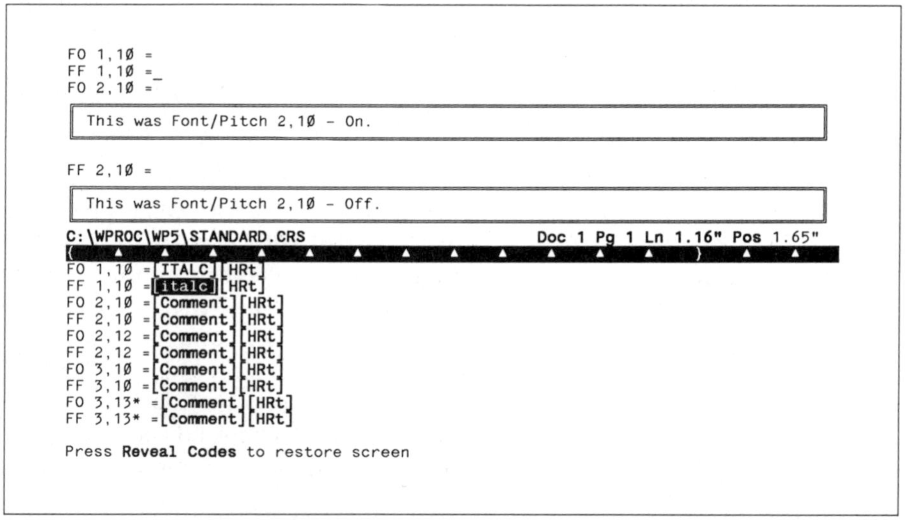

FIGURE A.7: Placing the codes. After the appropriate codes are in place—in this case, [ITALC] and [italc] for Font On (FO =) and Font Off (FF =)—you can delete the [Comment] boxes.

code is the one for the font that is to be turned on and the FF code is for the normal font in your text. For example, to turn on Elite and return to Pica you would edit the codes as

FO 2,10 = [Font:Elite]
FF 2,10 = [Font:Pica]

by pressing Ctrl-F8 F and choosing each font. Choosing Normal has no effect since the program does not know what that font is at this point. In addition, go to the end of the STANDARD.CRS document and insert a Paper Size/Type code at the SZ = position by pressing Shift-F8, choosing Page (**2** or **P**), pressing **8** or **S** for Paper Size/Type, and then typing **1** and **1** for standard 8.5-by-11-inch paper. (If you are printing on a different size of paper, insert the correct code for it.) If there is a Sheet Feeder Bin Number code in the WordPerfect 4.2 document and you change it to a Paper Size/Type code, WordPerfect will automatically insert the paper size at the SZ = code at the end of the STANDARD.CRS file.

If you have used a special nondisplayable character, such as a trademark symbol in the 4.2 document, you will also need to indicate its new character set number and character number in WordPerfect 5.0. At the CH position, type the font number and decimal value of the character that was in the 4.2 document; then, on the other side of the equal sign, press Ctrl-2 (Compose) and type the character set and number of the character in WordPerfect 5.0. You will not see the character on the screen.

5. When you have indicated all of the equivalent codes, save the STANDARD.CRS file under the name of the printer file that you are using but with the .CRS extension. For example, if you are using an HP LaserJet, enter the name as HPLASERJ.CRS (see the preceding discussion for how to determine the exact .PRS file name).

6. You can now exit from the Doc 2 window, which contains your 4.2 document, because the next time you see it, it will be converted. Then go to DOS (Shift-F1 **G**) and enter the command **CONVERT** to run the Convert program.

7. When the Convert program comes up, enter the name of the 4.2 file, including any path name if you have not already copied it into your default directory. Then enter the name you wish to convert it as. You may want to give it a .5 extension so that you can keep track of which file is which if you use the same file name.

8. Choose option **7**, WordPerfect 4.2 to WordPerfect 5.0, from the Convert menu. When you are prompted, enter the name of the *PRINTER*.CRS file you just created.

When WordPerfect completes the conversion, you will see a *Converted* message on your screen. Return to WordPerfect by typing **EXIT** if you used Ctrl-F1 G to leave WordPerfect. Then retrieve the converted file.

Your work is not quite over, as you can see in the test document in Figure A.8. Although the font 1, pitch 10 line was correctly converted to italics and the other two lines were converted to Pica and Elite, WordPerfect also changed margins when it changed font and pitch, so you will need to delete the extra [L/R Mar] codes from the resulting 5.0 document. Press Alt-F2 (Replace), press Enter to replace without confirmation, and then press Shift-F8 and type **L** and then **M** to generate the [L/R Mar] code. Press F2 again at the Replace prompt to replace those codes with nothing (delete them).

At this point, your document should be reformatted correctly in WordPerfect 5.0, as Figure A.9 illustrates. If there were codes that the program indicated must be changed manually, it has made a best guess for the printer you are using. Test-print a sample page to see if those settings are suitable for your document. If they are not, you can search for the [Font:] codes and manually substitute the font, size, or appearance change you want at that location. You may also want to delete any remaining comments, but they won't be printed, so you can leave them in place if you like.

Once you have done this for one document, the other WordPerfect 4.2 documents you retrieve into WordPerfect will automatically have their unconvertible codes substituted. If you see any Comment boxes in other 4.2 documents that

```
      This is a WordPerfect 4.2 document that contains codes that do
      not convert directly to WordPerfect 5.0.

      This line is in pitch 10, font 1.

   This line is in 11 pitch (proportional spacing, entered as
   11*) and font 3.

   This line is in pitch 12, font 1.


C:\WPROC\WP5\5-0CONV                          Doc 1 Pg 1 Ln 1.16" Pos 1"
[Paper Sz/Typ:8.5" x 11",Standard]This is a WordPerfect 4.2 document that contai
ns codes that do[SRt]
not convert directly to WordPerfect 5.0.[HRt]
[HRt]
[ITALC][L/R Mar:1",1"]This line is in pitch 10, font 1.[HRt]
[italc][Font:Pica][L/R Mar:0.83",1.68"][HRt]
This line is in 11 pitch (proportional spacing, entered as[SRt]
11*) and font 3.[HRt]
[HRt]
[Font:Elite][L/R Mar:0.83",2.25"]This line is in pitch 12, font 1.[HRt]

   Press Reveal Codes to restore screen
```

FIGURE A.8: Correcting margin changes. After you use the Convert program and retrieve the document, you will still have to correct for WordPerfect 4.2's additional margin changes.

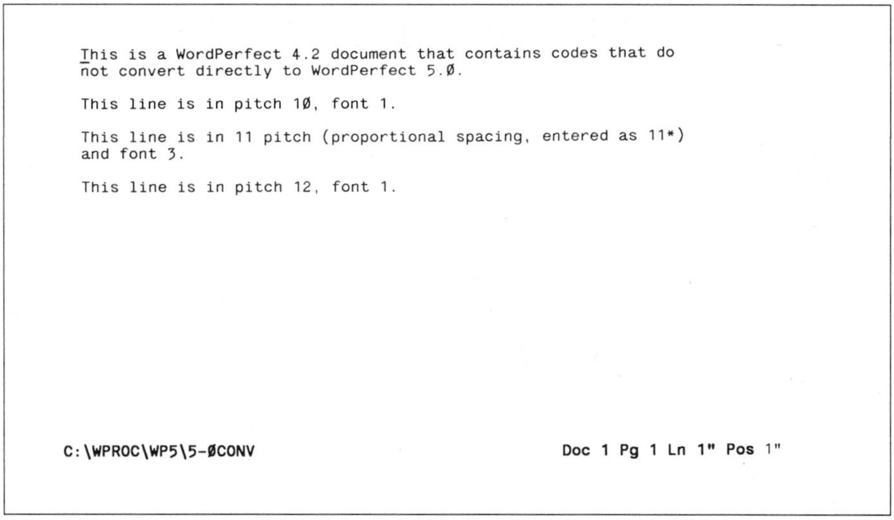

```
This is a WordPerfect 4.2 document that contains codes that do
not convert directly to WordPerfect 5.Ø.

This line is in pitch 1Ø, font 1.

This line is in 11 pitch (proportional spacing, entered as 11*)
and font 3.

This line is in pitch 12, font 1.




C:\WPROC\WP5\5-ØCONV                         Doc 1 Pg 1 Ln 1" Pos 1"
```

FIGURE A.9: The final step. After you delete the extra [L/R Mar] codes and check to make sure that the font substitutions are what you want, your document is ready.

you have retrieved into 5.0., you can retrieve the *PRINTER*.CRS file that you just created and substitute the correct codes in it.

One last word on the subject: If you retrieve a 4.2 document into 5.0 and it is not formatted as you expect, it could be because version 5.0 automatically reformats a document for the printer you have selected. If you do not see any Comment boxes indicating codes that cannot be converted automatically, this is probably what is happening. However, you can select a printer that is not attached to your computer; WordPerfect will not know the difference unless you actually try to print a document. If you are editing a document that you know was formatted for another printer, just select that printer instead of the one that you have connected to your computer. You may need to insert one of the Printer disks so that WordPerfect can locate the appropriate .PRS file.

WORDPERFECT CHARACTER SETS

Character Set 0

```
                    1                   2
    0 1 2 3 4 5 6 7 8 9 0 1 2 3 4 5 6 7 8 9 0 1 2 3 4 5 6 7 8 9
  0
 30       ! " ? $ % & ' ( ) * + , - . / 0 1 2 3 4 5 6 7 8 9 : ;
 60 < = > ? @ A B C D E F G H I J K L M N O P Q R S T U V W X Y
 90 Z [ \ ] ^ _ ` a b c d e f g h i j k l m n o p q r s t u v w
120 x y z { ¦ } ~
```

Character Set 1

```
                    1                   2
    0 1 2 3 4 5 6 7 8 9 0 1 2 3 4 5 6 7 8 9 0 1 2 3 4 5 6 7 8 9
  0 ` ˙ ˜ ^ ¯ ´ ¨ ˘ ˛ , , , ˳ ˳ ° ˳ " ˳ ˇ ˴ — ˘ ß ı ȷ Á á Â â
 30 Ä ä À à Å å Æ æ Ç ç É é Ê ê Ë ë È è Í í Î î Ï ï Ì ì Ñ ñ Ó ó
 60 Ô ô Ö ö Ò ò Ú ú Û û Ü ü Ù ù Ÿ ÿ Ã ã Đ đ Ø ø Õ õ Ý ý Ð ð Þ þ
 90 Ă ă Ā ā Ą ą Ć ć Č č Ĉ ĉ Ċ ċ Ď ď Ě ě Ė ė Ē ē Ę ę Ǵ ǵ Ğ ğ Ĝ ĝ
120 Ģ ģ Ĝ ĝ Ġ ġ Ĥ ĥ Ħ ħ -ı i ı Ī ī Į į ı̨ ı̨ Ĩ ĩ Ĳ ĳ Ĵ ĵ Ķ ķ Ĺ ĺ Ľ ľ Ļ ļ
150 Ŀ ŀ Ł ł Ń ń Ņ ň Ň ň Ņ ņ Ö ö Ō ō Œ œ Ŕ ŕ Ř ř Ŗ ŗ Ś ś Š š Ş ş
180 Ŝ ŝ Ť ť Ţ ţ Ŧ ŧ Ŭ ŭ Ǘ ǘ Ū ū Ų ų Ů ů Ũ ũ Ŵ ŵ Ŷ ŷ Ź ź Ž ž Ż ż
210 Ŋ ŋ Đ đ Ŀ Ĩ ĩ Ŕ ŕ Š š Ť ť Ŷ ŷ Ỳ ỳ Ď ď Ơ ơ Ư ư
```

Character Set 2

```
                    1                   2
    0 1 2 3 4 5 6 7 8 9 0 1 2 3 4 5 6 7 8 9 0 1 2 3 4 5 6 7 8 9
  0 . ¨ ˙ ° ' ˟ = ˗ K ˌ ⌐ ˌ ˌ ˌ ⌐ ˌ ˌ ⌐ ˌ | ˡ ˘ ˌ ˙
```

Character Set 3

```
          0 1 2 3 4 5 6 7 8 9 0 1 2 3 4 5 6 7 8 9 0 1 2 3 4 5 6 7 8 9
 0  ▓ ▌ ▐ ▌ ▐ │ ▀ ▎ ▄ ─ ─ │ ┌ ┐ ┘ └ ├ ┬ ┤ ┴ ┼ ─ │ ┌ ┐ ┘ ┴ ┬ ┤ ┼
30  ┌ ┐ ┘ └ ┌ ┐ ┘ └ ├ ┬ ┤ ┴ ├ ┬ ┤ ┼ ┼ ─ ' ' , ─ ' · , ─ ─ │ ┤
60  ├ ├ ┼ ┬ ┬ ┬ ┬ ┤ ┤ ┤ ┴ ┴ ┴ ┼ ┼ ┼ ┼ ┼ ┼ ┼ ┼ ┼
```

Character Set 4

```
          0 1 2 3 4 5 6 7 8 9 0 1 2 3 4 5 6 7 8 9 0 1 2 3 4 5 6 7 8 9
 0  ● ○ ◻ ■ · ★ ¶ § ¡ ¿ « » £ ¥ ₨ ƒ ª º ½ ¼ ¢ ² ⁿ ® © ¤ ¾ ³ ′ ‚ ‘
30  “ ” „ – — ‹ › ○ □ † ‡ ™ ℠ ℞ ● ○ ■ ▪ □ ▫ – ﬀ ﬃ ﬄ ﬁ ﬂ … $ ₣ ₲
60  ₵ £ , „ ⅓ ⅔ ⅛ ⅜ ⅝ ⅞ Ⓜ Ⓟ Ⓤ % ‰ ‱ № — ¹
```

Character Set 5

```
          0 1 2 3 4 5 6 7 8 9 0 1 2 3 4 5 6 7 8 9 0 1 2 3 4 5 6 7 8 9
 0  ♥ ♦ ♣ ♠ ♂ ♀ ☼ ☺ ● ♪ ♫ ▬ ⌂ ‼ √ ↕ ⌐ ∟ ◻ ◙ ↵ ☞ ☜ ✔ □ ⊠ ☹ # ♭ ♮
30  ϖ ⊙ ☒ ₵ ‿
```

Character Set 6

```
          0 1 2 3 4 5 6 7 8 9 0 1 2 3 4 5 6 7 8 9 0 1 2 3 4 5 6 7 8 9
  0  − ± ≤ ≥ ∝ / ∕ \ ÷ ∓ │ ⟨ ⟩ ~ ≈ ≡ ∈ ∩ ‖ Σ ∞ ¬ → ← ↑ ↓ ↔ ↕ ▶ ◀ ▲
 30  ▼ · · ∘ • Å ˙ μ × ∫ ∏ ∓ ∇ ∂ ′ ″ ¯ e ℓ ℏ ℑ ℜ ℘ ⇄ ⇆ ⇒ ⇑ ⇓
 60  ⇔ ⇕ ↗ ↘ ↖ ↙ ∪ ⊂ ⊃ ⊆ ⊇ ∅ ⌈ ⌉ ⌊ ⌋ ≪ ≫ ∠ ⊗ ⊕ ⊖ ⊕ ⊙ ∧ ∨ ⊻ ⊤ ⊥
 90  ⌒ ⊢ ⊣ ⊡ ∎ ◇ ◆ ⟦ ⟧ ≠ ≢ ∵ ∴ ∷ ⏀ ℒ ℭ ℨ ℘ ○ △ ◇ ★ ‴ ∐ ≈ ≡ < ≤ >
120  ≥ ∃ ∀ ⋘ ⋙ ⋓ ⊊ ⊋ ⊓ ⊔ ⊏ ⊑ ⌐ ⊐ ⊒ △ ▽ ◁ ▷ ⋈ ⌣ ⌢ ◯ ⇀ ↼ ⇁ ↽ ⇌
150  ⟶ ⟵ ⇋ ⇄ ↿ ↾ ⇃ ⇂ ⊩ ⊪ ∪ ∩ ⊂ ⊃ ◉ ⊛ ⊝ ℧ ⊿ ◁ ◁ ▷ ▵ ▿ ⋔ ≐ ≒ ⇄ ⋇
180  ⊨ ≜ ∤ ∣ ★ ≺ ⋠ ≻ ⋡ ∤ ≇ ∦ ⋢ ∤ ⋤ ⋣ ⋥ ⫴ ⫵ ⊅ ⊄ Ⱶ ⱶ ⊥ ⋈ ∤ ☀ ⊐ ∉
210  ⊕ ℰ ℐ ℂ ℑ ℕ ℝ ⨎ ⌐
```

Character Set 7

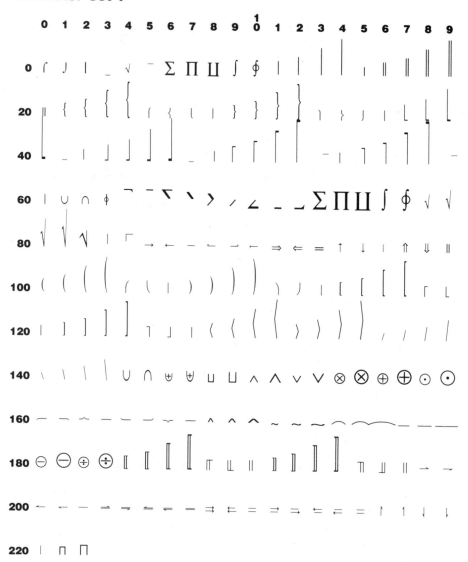

Character Set 8

	0	1	2	3	4	5	6	7	8	9	10	11	12	13	14	15	16	17	18	19	20	21	22	23	24	25	26	27	28	29
0	A	α	B	β	Β	Β	Γ	γ	Δ	δ	E	ε	Z	ζ	H	η	Θ	θ	I	ι	K	κ	Λ	λ	M	μ	N	ν	Ξ	ξ
30	O	o	Π	π	P	ρ	Σ	σ	Σ	ς	T	τ	Υ	υ	Φ	φ	X	χ	Ψ	ψ	Ω	ω	ά	´	ή	ΐ	ΰ	ö	ύ	ϋ
60	ώ	ε	θ	κ	ϖ	ρ	Υ	φ	ω	;	·	´	`		ˆ	ˉ	˘	`	´				˝	˙	̈	̓		˙	̔	̔
90	̔	̔	̔	̓	̔	̔	̔	à	â	ά	ᾷ	ᾶ	ᾳ	ᾷ	ᾶ	ᾳ	ᾷ	ᾶ	ᾳ	ᾷ	ᾶ	ᾳ	ᾷ	ᾶ	ᾳ	ᾷ	è	έ	ề	ế
120	ὲ	έ	ὴ	ή	ῆ	ῃ	ῄ	ῂ	ῇ	ῆ	ῃ	ῄ	ῂ	ῇ	ῆ	ῃ	ῄ	ῂ	ῇ	ῆ	ῃ	ῄ	ῂ	ῇ	ì	î	ΐ	ῖ	ὶ	ί
150	ῗ	ΐ	ΐ	ῖ	ῗ	ò	ό	ὄ	ὂ	ὃ	ὅ	ὂ	ὃ	ὺ	ύ	ῦ	ὓ	ὒ	ὕ	ῧ	ῦ	ὒ	ῧ	ὼ	ώ	ῴ	ῶ	ῲ	ῳ
180	ὠ	ὡ	ῴ	ῶ	ῲ	ῳ	ῷ	ῶ	ῳ	ῷ	ῶ	ῳ	´	,	ϛ	Ϝ	ϙ	ϡ												

Character Set 9

	0	1	2	3	4	5	6	7	8	9	10	11	12	13	14	15	16	17	18	19	20	21	22	23	24	25	26	27	28	29
0	א	ב	ג	ד	ה	ו	ז	ח	ט	י	כ	ך	ל	מ	ם	נ	ן	ס	ע	פ	ף	צ	ץ	ק	ר	ש	ת	בּ	כּ	
30	ף	ֱ	ֲ	ֳ	ָ	ַ	ֶ	ֵ	ֹ	ֻ	ּ	ׁ	ׂ	ֿ	־															

Character Set 10

	0	1	2	3	4	5	6	7	8	9	10	11	12	13	14	15	16	17	18	19	20	21	22	23	24	25	26	27	28	29
0	А	а	Б	б	В	в	Г	г	Д	д	Е	е	Ё	ё	Ж	ж	З	з	И	и	Й	й	К	к	Л	л	М	м	Н	н
30	О	о	П	п	Р	р	С	с	Т	т	У	у	Ф	ф	Х	х	Ц	ц	Ч	ч	Ш	ш	Щ	щ	Ъ	ъ	Ы	ы	Ь	ь
60	Э	э	Ю	ю	Я	я	Ґ	ґ	Ђ	ђ	Ѓ	ѓ	Є	є	Ѕ	ѕ	І	і	Ї	ї	Ј	ј	Љ	љ	Њ	њ	Ћ	ћ	Ќ	ќ
90	Ў	ў	Џ	џ	Ѣ	ѣ	Ѳ	ѳ	Ѵ	ѵ	Ѫ	ѫ																		

Character Set 11 (Hiragana)

	0	1	2	3	4	5	6	7	8	9	10	11	12	13	14	15	16	17	18	19	20	21	22	23	24	25	26	27	28	29
0	ぁ	あ	ぃ	い	ぅ	う	っ	や	ゃ	ゅ	ゆ	よ		が	け	あ	い	う	え	お	か	き	く	け	こ	が	ぎ	ぐ	げ	ご
30	さ	し	す	せ	そ	ざ	じ	ず	ぜ	ぞ	た	ち	っ	つ	て	と	だ	ぢ	づ	で	ど	な	に	ぬ	ね	の	は	ひ	ふ	へ
60	ほ	ば	び	ぶ	べ	ぼ	ぱ	ぴ	ぷ	ぺ	ぽ	ま	み	む	め	も	や	ゆ	よ	ら	り	る	れ	ろ	わ	を	ん	〔	〕	【
90	】	「	」	『	』	。	、	ゝ	ゞ	゛	゜	ー		・																

Character Set 11 (Katakana)

	0	1	2	3	4	5	6	7	8	9	10	11	12	13	14	15	16	17	18	19	20	21	22	23	24	25	26	27	28	29
0	ァ	ア	ィ	イ	ゥ	ウ	ェ	エ	ォ	オ	ッ	ャ	ュ	ョ	ヮ	ヴ	カ	ケ	ア	イ	ウ	エ	オ	カ	キ	ク	ケ	コ	ガ	ギ
30	グ	ゲ	ゴ	サ	シ	ス	セ	ソ	ザ	ジ	ズ	ゼ	ゾ	タ	チ	ツ	テ	ト	ダ	ヂ	ヅ	デ	ド	ナ	ニ	ヌ	ネ	ノ	ハ	ヒ
60	フ	ヘ	ホ	バ	ビ	ブ	ベ	ボ	パ	ピ	プ	ペ	ポ	マ	ミ	ム	メ	モ	ヤ	ユ	ヨ	ラ	リ	ル	レ	ロ	ワ	ヲ	ン	〔
90	〕	【	】	「	」	。	、	ヽ	ヾ	゛	゜	ー		・																

Character Set 12

Character Set 12 is a user-defined character set.

WORDPERFECT'S HIDDEN CODES

CODE	MEANING
—	Cursor Position
[ ]	Hard Space
-	Hyphen Character
•	Soft Hyphen
[-]	Hard Hyphen
[/]	Cancel Hyphenation
!	Formula Calculation
+	Calculate Subtotal
=	Calculate Total
*	Calculate Grand Total
[AdvDn]	Advance Down
[AdvLft]	Advance Left
[AdvRgt]	Advance Right
[AdvToLn]	Advance to Line
[AdvToPos]	Advance to (Column) Position
[AdvUp]	Advance Up
[Align]	Tab Align
[Block]	Beginning of Block
[Block Pro]	Block Protection
[BOLD]	Bold
[Box Num]	Caption in Graphics Box (inserted inside of Box code)
[C/A/Flrt]	End of Tab Align or Flush Right
[Center Pg]	Center Page Top to Bottom
[Cndl EOP]	Conditional End of Page
[Cntr]	Center
[Col Def]	Column Definition
[Col Off]	End of Text Columns
[Col On]	Beginning of Text Columns
[Color]	Print Color

CODE	MEANING
[Comment]	Document Comment
[Date]	Date/Time Function
[DBL UND]	Double Underline
[Decml Align Char]	Decimal Character or Thousands Separator
[Def Mark:Index]	Index Definition
[Def Mark:List]	List Definition
[Def Mark:ToC]	Table of Contents Definition
[End Opt]	Endnote Options
[EndDef]	End of Index, List, or Table of Contents
[Endnote]	Endnote
[Endnote Placement]	Endnote Placement
[EXT LARGE]	Extra Large Print
[Fig Opt]	Figure Box Options
[Figure]	Figure Box
[FINE]	Fine Print
[Flsh Rt]	Flush Right
[Font]	Base Font
[Footer]	Footer
[Footnote]	Footnote
[Force]	Force Odd/Even Page
[Form]	Form (Printer Selection)
[Form Typ]	Form Type
[Ftn Opt]	Footnote/Endnote Options
[Full Form]	Table of Authorities, Full Form
[Header]	Header
[HLine]	Horizontal Line
[HPg]	Hard Page Break
[HRt]	Hard Return
[Hyph Off]	Hyphenation Off
[Hyph On]	Hyphenation On
[HZone]	Hyphenation Zone
[→Indent]	Indent

CODE	MEANING
[→Indent←]	Left/Right Indent
[Index]	Index Entry
[ISRt]	Invisible Soft Return
[ITALC]	Italics
[Just Lim]	Word/Letter Spacing Justification Limits
[Just Off]	Left-Justified/Ragged-Right
[Just On]	Right Justification
[Kern]	Kerning
[Lang]	Language
[LARGE]	Large Print
[Line Height]	Leading (Line Height)
[Ln Num]	Line Numbering
[L/R Mar]	Left and Right Margins
[←Mar Rel]	Left Margin Release
[Mark:List]	List Entry
[Mark:ToC]	Table of Contents Entry
[Math Def]	Definition of Math Columns
[Math Off]	End of Math
[Math On]	Beginning of Math
[New End Num]	New Endnote Number
[New Fig Num]	New Figure Box Number
[New Ftn Num]	New Footnote Number
[New Tab Num]	New Table Box Number
[New Txt Num]	New Text Box Number
[New Usr Num]	New User-Defined Box Number
[Note Num]	Footnote/Endnote Reference (inserted inside Footnote or Endnote code)
[Ovrstk]	Overstrike Preceding Character
[Paper Sz/Typ]	Paper Size and Type
[Par Num]	Paragraph Number
[Par Num Def]	Paragraph Numbering Definition
[Pg Num]	New Page Number
[Pg Numbering]	Page Number Position

CODE	MEANING
[Ptr Cmnd]	Printer Command
[REDLN]	Redline
[Ref]	Reference (Automatic Reference)
[SHADW]	Shadow
[SM CAP]	Small Caps
[SMALL]	Small Print
[SPg]	Soft Page Break
[SRt]	Soft Return
[STKOUT]	Strikeout
[Style Off]	Style Off
[Style On]	Style On
[Subdoc]	Subdocument (Master Documents)
[SUBSCRPT]	Subscript
[Suppress]	Suppress Page Format
[SUPRSCRPT]	Superscript
[t]	Subtotal Entry
[T]	Total Entry
[Tab]	Tab
[Tab Set]	Tab Set
[Table]	Table Box
[Target]	Target (Auto Reference)
[T/B Mar]	Top and Bottom Margins
[Tbl Opt]	Table Box Options
[Text Box]	Text Box
[Txt Opt]	Text Box Options
[UND]	Underlining
[Usr Box]	User Box
[Usr Opt]	User Box Options
[VLine]	Vertical Line
[VRY LARGE]	Very Large Print
[W/O Off]	Widow/Orphan Off
[W/O On]	Widow/Orphan On
[Wrd/Ltr Spacing]	Word and Letter Spacing

WordPerfect's
Default Settings

FEATURE	DEFAULT SETTING
Automatically Reformat and Rewrite	On
Backup Options	
— Timed	Off
— Original	Off
Beep Options	
— on Error	Off
— on Hyphenation	On
— on Search Failure	Off
Center Page, Top to Bottom	Off
Cursor Speed	30 cps
Date Format	3 1,4
Decimal/Align Character	. (period)
— Thousands Separator	, (comma)
Display Comments	On
Display Pitch	Auto
Document Summary	
— on Save/Exit	Off
— Subject Search	RE:
Fast Save	Off
File Name on Status Line	On
Force Odd/Even Page	Off
Hard Return Display Character	Space
Hyphenation	Off
Hyphenation Zone	
— Left	10%
— Right	4%
Justification	On
Kerning	Off
Line Height	Auto
Line Spacing	1 (single)

FEATURE	DEFAULT SETTING
Margins	
— Left	1″
— Right	1″
— Top	1″
— Bottom	1″
Menu Letter Display	Bold
Page Number Position	No page numbers
Paper	
— Size	8½″ × 11″
— Type	Standard
Redline Format	Printer-dependent
Repeat Value	8
Side-by-Side Display of Columns	On
Tab Set	Every .5″
Table of Authorities Format	
— Dot Leaders	On
— Underlining	Off
— Blank Lines	On
Typeover	Off
Underline	
— Spaces	On
— Tabs	Off
Units of Measure	
— Display and Entry of Numbers	″ (inches)
— Status Line Display	″ (inches)
Widow/Orphan Protection	Off
Word Spacing	Optimal
Letter Spacing	Optimal
Word Spacing Justification Limits	
— Compressed to	60%
— Expanded to	400%

HIERARCHY OF FORMATTING CODES AND FONT CHANGES

When you save a document in WordPerfect, the program saves the text along with the format settings that you have selected for it. In addition, the program saves information about the printer that is selected when you create the document and about the font (or fonts) chosen.

FORMATTING A DOCUMENT

WordPerfect 5.0 allows you to format your document in any of three ways:

- Use the program's default format settings, which are in effect any time a new document is started.
- Change the default format settings for the document that is being created.
- Change the default format settings as needed for particular sections of the document.

Table E.1 shows the hierarchy of the formatting codes that can be used to change the default format settings.

Setting New Formatting Defaults for the Program

To change the program defaults for all *new* documents that you create, you use the Setup key (Shift-F1), select the Initial Settings option (**5** or **I**), and then

---

Formatting Codes (Shift-F8 L, P, D, *or* O)

▲

Document Initial Codes (Shift-F8 D C)

▲

Setup Initial Codes (Shift-F1 I I)

TABLE E.1: Hierarchy of Formatting Codes

select the Initial Codes option (**4** or **I**). This takes you to a screen resembling the blank editing screen with the Reveal Codes window visible below. To make changes to various format settings, you then press the Format key (Shift-F8), select the appropriate menu (Line, Page, Document, or Other), and choose the appropriate format option(s). After you select new values and press F7 (Exit), WordPerfect returns you to the Setup Initial Codes screen, where the Reveal Codes window displays any hidden codes used by WordPerfect to put the new settings into effect. After pressing F7 twice more, you are returned to the document editing screen. All new documents will be formatted according to the settings you have chosen.

If you open the Reveal Codes window (Alt-F3) in the document editing screen, however, you will not see any hidden codes reflecting the new values you have chosen. Although formatting codes are stored as part of the document header of each new file, they can't be viewed from the document editing screen, even in the Reveal Codes screen. The only way to view these codes is by returning to the Setup Initial Codes screen.

Changes made to the program's default format settings do not affect any documents that were created before you made the change on the Setup Initial Codes screen.

Setting New Format Defaults for the Document

If you want to change the default format settings for the entire document you are creating or editing, you can do so by modifying the document initial codes. Any new values put into effect at this level override the current program defaults and are saved along with the text of the document.

To change a formatting default for the current document, you press Shift-F8 (Format), select the Document menu (**3** or **D**), and then select the Initial Codes option (**2** or **C**). This takes you to a blank split screen showing the Reveal Codes window (identical to the Setup Initial Codes screen). To change the default format settings for your document, you then press Shift-F8 and select the appropriate Format menu and formatting option(s). After entering the new value(s) and pressing F7, you are returned to the Document Initial Codes screen, where you can see the hidden codes containing the new values that you have selected.

However, just as with the setup initial codes, if you open the Reveal Codes window in the document editing screen, you will not see any hidden codes reflecting the new values you have chosen for the document. Although codes reflecting the changes are stored as part of the header of the current document when it is saved, the only way to view them is by returning to the Document Initial Codes screen.

All of the changes made to the document initial codes are in effect only as long as you are working on the document for which you made them. As soon as you save the document and clear the editing screen, the default format settings in effect for the program take over once again.

Overriding Document or Program Defaults

You don't have to use the Initial Codes option on the Document menu to change WordPerfect's default format settings. Instead, you can change a setting simply by selecting the appropriate option and changing the value on one of the Format menus accessed by the Format key (Shift-F8). When you change a format setting directly from the Line or Page menu, WordPerfect inserts in the document a hidden code that you can view and *delete* when you open the Reveal Codes window in the document. As with new settings made on the Document Initial Codes screen, these changes are saved with the document. Any changes made at this level override not only those made on the Setup Initial Codes screen but also those made on the Document Initial Codes screen.

You should change the default settings for a document from the Document Initial Codes screen instead of directly from the appropriate Format menu when you want to prevent an inexperienced user from mistakenly deleting the formatting codes in the document. Formatting codes that are set through the Document Initial Codes screen can only be deleted by returning to this screen.

Of course, you can't rely on changing the format settings from the Document Initial Codes screen when they are to affect just part of the document, as when changing from single spacing to double spacing and back again. Formatting changes that affect only part of the document must be set from the Format menu. Formatting changes made from the Document Initial Codes screen always affect the entire document from beginning to end, unless they are overridden by a hidden code inserted from the Format menu.

CHANGING FONTS IN A DOCUMENT

Font changes, like format changes, can be made at different levels. Table E.2 shows the hierarchy of font changes used by WordPerfect. WordPerfect 5.0 allows you to select the font to be used in any of three ways:

- Use the printer's initial font, which is in effect any time a new document is started.

- Change the document initial font, which determines the font used for the entire document that is being created.

- Change the base font as needed for particular sections of the document.

Base Font (Ctrl-F8 F)
▲
Document Initial Font (Shift-F8 D F)
▲
Printer Initial Font (Shift-F7 S E I)

TABLE E.2: Hierarchy of Font Changes

When you begin a new document, WordPerfect automatically uses the font designated as the initial font for your printer. For example, if you create a document using the Epson FX-80 as your selected printer, WordPerfect will choose 10 CPI as the printer initial font.

If you want to change the printer initial font for all new documents, you press Shift-F7 (Print), then choose the Select option (**S**) and the Edit option (**3** or **E**). This brings you to the Printer Edit screen. From its menu, you then select the Initial Font option (**6** or **I**). You are presented with a list of the fonts installed for your printer (see Chapter 5 for information on installing fonts). To select a new printer initial font, you move the highlight cursor to the name of the font you wish to use and choose the Select option on this menu (**1** or **S**). After pressing F7 three times, you are returned to the document editing screen.

For example, if you want to make 12 CPI the initial font for your Epson FX-80 printer, you press Shift-F7 S E I. Next, you move the highlight cursor to *12 CPI* on the menu, choose the Select option, and press F7 three times to return to the document editing screen. When you start a new document, it will be formatted for 12 characters per inch instead of 10 (that is, it will be printed in Pica instead of Elite type). However, any documents that you created before this change will still use 10 characters per inch when you edit them or print them from the screen.

You can change the font just for the document you are working on by using the Initial Font option (**3** or **F**) on the Document menu (Shift-F8 D). You select the new font to use just as you do from the Printer Edit screen: highlight the name of the font on the list of available fonts and then choose the Select option (**1** or **S**). If you change the document initial font for your Epson printer to 12 CPI, it will be used only in the document you are currently creating or editing. When you begin a new document, the initial font will go back to 10 CPI (assuming that you haven't changed it from the Printer Edit screen).

When you change either the printer initial font or the document initial font, WordPerfect saves this information as part of the document header. However, in either case, this Font Change code will not be visible when you open the Reveal Codes screen in the document.

You can also change the font in a document by using the Base Font option (**4** or **F**) on the Font key (Ctrl-F8). A font change made at this level overrides any change made to either the document initial font or the printer initial font. When you select a new base font, WordPerfect inserts a Font Change code that is visible and can be *deleted* in the Reveal Codes window.

THE BITSTREAM FONTWARE INSTALLATION KIT

The Bitstream Fontware Installation Kit is available free from WordPerfect Corporation. This kit allows you to make fonts in different sizes and styles that can be produced by a large number of laser printers. The kit also includes three typefaces: Bitstream Charter, Dutch (the Bitstream version of Times Roman), and Swiss (the Bitstream version of Helvetica). You must have a hard disk in order to use the Fontware program.

After creating the styles and sizes of the fonts that you want to use in Word-Perfect and installing them for the printer you are using, you can use them in your documents. You can also purchase other typefaces besides the three supplied free with this kit by ordering them directly from Bitstream, Inc. You can then use the Fontware program to install these typefaces so they can be used with WordPerfect.

You can use the Bitstream Fontware Installation Kit with HP PCL (Hewlett-Packard printer command language) and PostScript PDL (PostScript page description language) laser printers. If you are using an HP PCL printer, you must specify both the type style and the sizes for the fonts you make with the Fontware program. If you are using a PostScript PDL printer, you must specify only the type style; you specify the type size when selecting the font in Word-Perfect. The following HP PCL printers can use this product:

AST Turbolaser

Dataproducts LZR 1230

Destiny Laseract 1

HP LaserJet Plus, 500 Plus, 2000, and Series II

Kyocera F series

LaserPro Silver Express

Mannesmann-Tally MT910

NEC Silentwriter 860 +

Okidata Laserline 6

Olympia Laserstar 6

Panasonic KX-P 4450

Quadram Quadlaser

These are the PostScript PDL printers that can use it:

Apple LaserWriter, LaserWriter Plus, II-NT, and II-NTX
AST TurboLaser PS
IBM Personal Page Printer
NEC Silentwriter 890
QMS PS-810, PS Jet +, and PS II
Texas Instruments 2106 and 2115

INSTALLING THE BITSTREAM FONTWARE INSTALLATION KIT

The Bitstream Fontware Installation Kit comes on six 5¼-inch disks, three of which contain the kit itself and three of which contain the free Fontware typefaces. If you request the kit in 3½-inch format, it comes on four disks, two of which contain the kit itself and two of which contain the free Fontware typefaces.

Before you install the Fontware program, make backup copies of all these disks (see Chapter 1 if necessary). Then, use the backup copies to install the kit.

Before installing the Bitstream Fontware program, you must have first installed WordPerfect (see Chapter 1) and copied the .ALL file that contains the printer definition file for your printer into the directory from which you start WordPerfect. If you are using an HP PCL printer, this file is WPRINT1.ALL, located on the Printer1 disk. If you are using a PostScript PDL printer, this file is probably WPRINT2.ALL, located on the Printer2 disk. (Note that if you use 3½-inch disks, both these files are located on the Printer1/Printer2 disk.)

To copy the .ALL file, follow these steps:

1. Make current the directory from which WordPerfect is started. For example, if you use C:\WP50 as the startup directory, type

   CD C:\WP50

   at the C> prompt.

2. Place the Printer1 or Printer2 disk in drive A of your computer.

3. If the printer definition file for your laser printer is contained in the file WPRINT1.ALL, type

   COPY A:WPRINT1.ALL

   and press Enter. If the printer definition file for your laser printer is contained in the file WPRINT2.ALL, type

   COPY A:WPRINT2.ALL

   and press Enter.

After you have copied the appropriate .ALL file, you can begin the installation of the program files. There are three directories that you must specify during installation: the directory that will contain the Fontware program and typefaces, the directory from which you start WordPerfect (and which now contains the appropriate .ALL file), and the directory that will contain the fonts that you make for your printer.

If you use other soft fonts and have created a directory that contains them, like C:\FONTS, you can specify this as the directory that contains the soft fonts. If you haven't set up a special directory, you can use the name of the directory from which you start WordPerfect, like C:\WP50. Note that you don't have to create a special Fontware directory before running the installation program; the program will do this automatically for you. However, the directory that is to contain the soft fonts must already exist before you install the Fontware program.

To install the Bitstream Fontware program, follow these steps:

1. Place the disk labeled *Diskette 1* (of those marked *Bitstream Fontware Installation Kit*) in drive A.

2. At the DOS prompt, Type

   A:FONTWARE

   and press Enter.

The opening screen of the installation program will ask if you see more than two colors. If you have a monochrome monitor, type **N**. If you have a color monitor and see more than two colors, type **Y**. The Fontware Main Menu shown in Figure F.1 will then appear. The Set Up Fontware option will already be highlighted. Press the Enter key to begin the installation procedure.

Figure F.2 shows you the screen that appears next. Here, you enter the full path name of the three directories described earlier.

1. At the For Fontware prompt, type in the name of the directory that will contain the Fontware program. In Figure F.2, that directory is called C:\FONTWARE.

2. Press Enter to go to the For WordPerfect prompt. Here, type in the name of the directory from which you start WordPerfect, such as **C:\WP50**.

3. Press Enter again to go to the For Printer prompt. Here, you type in the name of the directory that is to contain the fonts you will make with the Bitstream Fontware program. In this figure, it is called C:\FONTS, representing a directory that also contains soft fonts made by other manufacturers.

4. After checking the directories that you have entered on this screen, type **Y** to continue installing the Bitstream Fontware program.

```
┌──────────────────────── Fontware Main Menu ─────────────────────────┐
│                                                                     │
│     ┌───────────────────────────────────────────────────────┐      │
│     │                                                        │      │
│     │          ▐ Set Up Fontware ▌                           │      │
│     │                                                        │      │
│     │          View Control Panel                            │      │
│     │                                                        │      │
│     │          Add/Delete Fontware Typefaces     ─           │      │
│     │                                                        │      │
│     │          Make Fonts              ─                     │      │
│     │                                                        │      │
│     └───────────────────────────────────────────────────────┘      │
│     ┌───────────────────────────────────────────────────────┐      │
│     │ Guides you through first-time setup of your Fontware   │      │
│     │ program.                                               │      │
│     └───────────────────────────────────────────────────────┘      │
│     ▐ ↑↓ to point        ◄─┘ to choose        Ctrl-Q to quit ▌     │
└─────────────────────────────────────────────────────────────────────┘
```

FIGURE F.1: The Fontware Main Menu.

```
┌─────────────────────── Fontware Control Panel ──────────────────────┐
│                                                                     │
│  ┌── Directories ──────────────────────────────────────────┐       │
│  │ For Fontware    : C:\FONTWARE                            │       │
│  │ For WordPerfect: C:\WP5Ø                                 │       │
│  │ ▐ For Printer   : C:\FONTS                             ▌ │       │
│  │                                                          │       │
│  │                                                          │       │
│  │                                                          │       │
│  │                                                          │       │
│  └──────────────────────────────────────────────────────────┘       │
│  ┌──────────────────────────────────────────────────────────┐       │
│  │ Directory for downloadable font files.                   │       │
│  │ To choose the directory shown, press <Enter>.  If you    │       │
│  │ would like the font files in a different directory, type │       │
│  │ the directory name and press <Enter>.                    │       │
│  └──────────────────────────────────────────────────────────┘       │
│  ▐ ◄─┘ for next item     Esc to go back     Ctrl-Q to quit ▌       │
└─────────────────────────────────────────────────────────────────────┘
```

FIGURE F.2: Designating the directories for the Fontware Installation files, the WordPerfect startup, and the fonts that are to be created with the kit.

The Installation program will now copy all of the Fontware program files that it needs. You will be prompted periodically to enter a new disk as required. All of these files will be copied into the directory that you entered at the For Fontware prompt.

Indicating the Printer, Orientation, and Character Set

After these files are copied, you will be prompted to indicate the type of laser printer you have. Use the cursor keys to move to the name of the printer and press the Enter key (see Figure F.3).

If your printer uses the HP PCL language, a pop-up menu will prompt you to indicate the orientation for the fonts you are about to make. You can choose portrait, landscape, or both portrait and landscape. If you don't need to make fonts that print in landscape mode, select portrait mode by pressing the Enter key. Otherwise, move the highlight cursor to *Landscape* or *Both Portrait and Landscape* and then press Enter.

Next, you are prompted to indicate the character set to be used by the fonts you are about to create. If you have an HP LaserJet Series II or compatible, you can choose between ASCII and HP Roman 8. The ASCII character set is smaller; it contains only the letters and punctuation used by English. If you need to print foreign-language accent marks, select the HP Roman 8 character set. If you are using a LaserWriter Plus or compatible, you can choose between the ASCII and WP PostScript character sets. The WP PostScript character set is analogous to the Roman 8 character set for the LaserJet Series II; it includes special characters and accent marks not found in the smaller ASCII character set.

Figure F.4 shows the screen at this point in the installation. In this example, the HP LaserJet Series II in portrait mode with the Roman 8 character set has been chosen. Look over your screen. If the directories, model, and character set are correct, press F10 to continue.

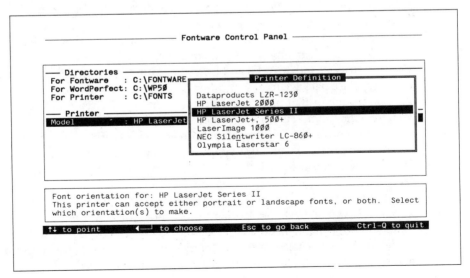

FIGURE F.3: Designating the HP LaserJet Series II as the printer to use.

```
┌─────────────────────────────────────────────────────────────────┐
│                                                                   │
│  ─────────────── Fontware Control Panel ───────────────           │
│                                                                   │
│  ┌─ Directories ───────────────────────────────────────┐         │
│  │ For Fontware    : C:\FONTWARE                        │         │
│  │ For WordPerfect: C:\WP5Ø                             │         │
│  │ For Printer     : C:\FONTS                           │         │
│  │                                                       │         │
│  │ ─ Printer ──────────────────────────────────         │         │
│  │ Model          : HP LaserJet Series II (portrait)    │         │
│  │ Character Set  : HP Roman 8                           │         │
│  │                           ─                           │         │
│  │                                                       │         │
│  │                                                       │         │
│  └───────────────────────────────────────────────────────┘       │
│                                                                   │
│  ┌─────────────────────────────────────────────────────┐         │
│  │ Your Control Panel is now complete.                  │         │
│  │ To accept these choices, press <F1Ø>.  To change any entry, press <Esc>. │
│  └─────────────────────────────────────────────────────┘         │
│  ▌ F1Ø to accept          Esc to go back          Ctrl-Q to quit ▐│
│                                                                   │
└─────────────────────────────────────────────────────────────────┘
```

FIGURE F.4: Completed Fontware Control Panel.

Making Fonts

The next step is to select the typefaces for which you will create fonts. You can choose Bitstream Charter, Dutch, or Swiss, or you can make fonts for all three of these typefaces. This is done from the Fontware Typefaces menu that appears on your screen when you press F10. (If this menu doesn't appear, choose the Add/Delete Fontware Typefaces option on the Fontware Main Menu.)

To select the typefaces, you need to have the Bitstream Fontware disks available. To make Bitstream Charter Roman fonts, place the disk labeled *Bitstream Charter* in drive A and press F3 and Enter. Because Bitstream does not include the entire typeface package free, you can only choose the roman (upright) type from the pop-up menu that appears. To create fonts in Bitstream Charter Roman, you press the Enter key. An arrow then appears to the left of *Roman*. Press F10 to have the program copy this typeface onto your hard disk.

After the program copies the typeface to your hard disk, you can replace the Bitstream Charter disk with the disk containing either the Dutch or Swiss typeface. For example, if you wish to create fonts for the Dutch typeface, you place this disk in drive A and press F3 and the Enter key. The pop-up menu that then appears allows you to choose Roman, Italic, Bold, or Bold Italic. To select one of these, move the highlight cursor to it and press Enter. Again, an arrow appears to the left of the style chosen. Select all of the styles you want to use in this manner and then press F10 to have the typeface copied to your hard disk.

You can repeat this procedure for each style on the menu or switch to the Swiss typeface disk and select new styles for that typeface. Figure F.5 shows you the menu typeface selections that appear for the Swiss typeface. Bitstream Charter Roman and Dutch Bold Italic have already been selected and copied.

After selecting all of the typefaces and type styles for which to make fonts, you must indicate which fonts to make. To do this, press F10 to continue. This brings up the Fontware Make Fonts menu similar to the one shown in Figure F.6. This menu shows you how many typefaces are available.

If you are using an HP PCL laser printer, you must indicate the point sizes to be created for each of the available typefaces. If you are using a PostScript PDL printer, you don't specify the type size from this menu. Instead, you indicate the size when selecting the font for use in WordPerfect. To select a typeface, move the highlight cursor to it and press Enter. The word *Yes* will appear to the right of the typeface. Select all of the typefaces for which you want fonts made and then press F10.

When deciding which sizes of the typeface to make, you must consider how much free space you have available on your hard disk. The larger the type size, the more storage space required. Also, fonts for the HP Roman 8 and WP Post-Script character sets require more space than those using the ASCII character set due to their extra characters.

If the amount of free space is strictly limited, make only the sizes that you will need in producing a specific document. Then, after printing the document in

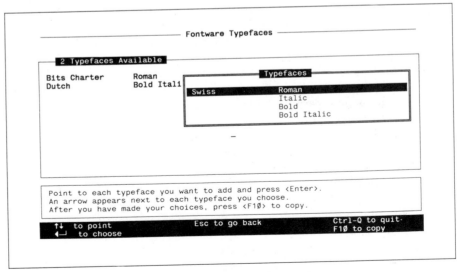

FIGURE F.5: Selecting a Swiss type style for which to make fonts.

```
┌──────────────────────────────────────────────────────────────────────┐
│                                                                        │
│                       ─── Fontware Make Fonts ───                      │
│                                                                        │
│           ┌─────────────────────┐   ┌─────────┐                        │
│           │ 3 Typefaces Available│  │ Printer │                        │
│           ┌──────────────────────┘  └──────────┐──────────────────┐   │
│           │                         │ Point Size Selection │        │   │
│           │ Bits Charter    Roman   │ 10 12 14 16 24                │   │
│           │ Dutch           Bold Italic                             │   │
│           │ Swiss           Bold Italic                             │   │
│           │                         │                                │   │
│           │                         │                                │   │
│           │                         │                                │   │
│           │                         │                                │   │
│           │                         │                                │   │
│           │                         │                                │   │
│           │                         │                                │   │
│           │                         │                                │   │
│           ├─────────────────────────┼────────────────────────────────┤ │
│           │ WordPerfect Style: Normal│ Enter each size you want, followed by a │
│           │ Recommended Size : 6 and up│ space.  You may enter fractional sizes │
│           │ Recommended Use  : Text  │ as decimal values.  Example: 9 10.5 12.25│
│           ├─────────────────────────────────────────────────────────┤ │
│           │ ◄─┘  to accept sizes     Esc to go back      Ctrl-Q to quit│
│           │ F1 help                                      F9 paste      │
│                                                                        │
└──────────────────────────────────────────────────────────────────────┘
```

FIGURE F.6: Specifying the types sizes to be made for each available typeface.

WordPerfect, use its Move/Rename option to move the Font files to a floppy disk. Then, exit WordPerfect and run the Fontware program to create new fonts in the sizes needed to produce the next document or project.

To indicate the sizes to make, you enter the point size. The smallest type size is 6 points for most printers. Check the information on the bottom of the screen to see what the smallest type size is for the font you are making. You can enter type sizes using decimals. When specifying multiple sizes, separate the point size numbers with a space. You can copy the last sequence of point sizes to a new typeface by moving the highlight cursor to the typeface and pressing F9.

After indicating the type sizes for each available typeface, press F10. A box indicating the time needed to create the fonts and indicating whether you have sufficient disk space appears on this screen, as shown in Figure F.7. Note that the time estimate is extremely optimistic; it will almost always take longer than indicated to make the fonts.

If this box indicates that you don't have enough disk space, type **N**, delete some of the sizes chosen earlier, and press F10 again. When everything is as you want it on this menu and you receive the message that available disk space is okay, type **Y** to have the program make your fonts. After your fonts are made, the Fontware program will end and you will be returned to the DOS prompt.

Returning to the Fontware Program

At any time after installing the Fontware program, you can return to it to select new typefaces and make new fonts for them. To restart the program, make

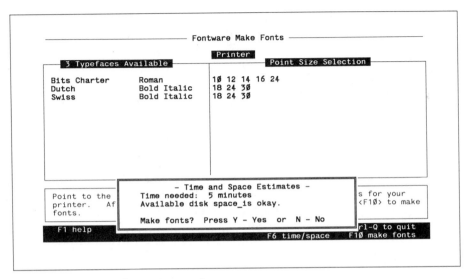

FIGURE F.7: The Time and Space Estimates box.

its directory current, type the command

FONTWARE

and press Enter. The Fontware Main Menu will appear automatically after the opening screen. To add new typefaces or delete existing ones, move the highlight cursor to the Add/Delete Fontware Typefaces option and press Enter. To make new type sizes for a typeface that has already been selected, move the highlight cursor to the Make Fonts option and press Enter.

INSTALLING BITSTREAM FONTS IN WORDPERFECT

Before you can use the fonts that you have made with the Fontware program, you must install them for your printer. The procedure for installing soft fonts for a laser printer is covered in some detail in Chapter 5. The following information only highlights the general procedure that must be followed.

After starting WordPerfect, press Shift-F7 (Print). If necessary, move the highlight cursor to the name of the printer for which you made the Bitstream fonts and choose the Select option (**S**). Then, choose the Edit option (**3** or **E**). At the Select Printer screen, make sure that the directory listed at the Path for Downloadable Fonts and Printer Command Files option is the same as the directory that you indicated at the For Printer prompt on the Fontware Control Panel. If not, select this option (**7** or **D**) and type in the path name exactly as you entered it when installing the Fontware program.

Next, select the Cartridges and Fonts option (**5** or **C**) on the Printer Edit menu. Highlight *Soft Fonts* (if necessary) and then choose the Select Fonts option

(**1** or **S**). The next screen that appears shows all of the soft fonts that are available for your printer. Bitstream soft font listings are preceded by *(FW)*. If you don't see them on your screen, press F2 and then type **(FW** to execute a Name Search. This should take you to the first part of the listing of the fonts that you made with the Fontware program. Mark each font you wish to use with either an asterisk (*) or a plus sign (+) as shown in Figure F.8. Mark the font with an asterisk if it is to be downloaded before you print the document. Otherwise, mark it with a plus sign.

After marking all of the fonts you wish to use, press F7 twice. WordPerfect will then update the fonts that have now been installed for your printer. Press F7 twice more and you will be returned to the Print screen. If you marked any fonts with an asterisk and you wish to use them in printing documents during the current work session, select the Initialize option (**7** or **I**). Then press F7 one last time to return to the document editing screen.

USING BITSTREAM FONTS IN A DOCUMENT

Once Bitstream fonts are installed for your printer, you can use them in documents just as you would any resident fonts. Figures F.9 and F.10 show you printed samples using fonts made with the Fontware program and installed for the HP LaserJet Series II. To select 10 point Bitstream Charter, you press Ctrl-F8 (Font) and select the Base Font option (**4** or **F**). The Charter fonts are listed

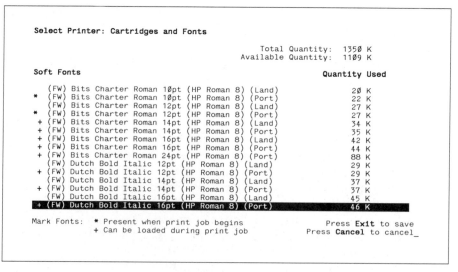

FIGURE F.8: Installing the Bitstream fonts for the HP LaserJet Series II.

This sentence is printed in 10 point Bitstream Charter Roman.

This sentence is printed in 12 point Bitstream Charter Roman.

This sentence is printed in 14 point Bitstream Charter Roman.

This sentence is printed in 16 point Bitstream Charter Roman.

This sentence is printed in 24 point Bitstream Charter Roman.

FIGURE F.9: Sample printout using Bitstream Charter in various point sizes.

This sentence is printed in 18 point Dutch Bold Italic.

This sentence is printed in 24 point Dutch Bold Italic.

This sentence is printed in 30 point Dutch Bold Italic.

FIGURE F.10: Sample printout using Bitstream Dutch Bold Italic in various point sizes.

under *Bits Charter* at the top of the list. You move the highlight cursor to it and then choose the Select option (**1** or **S**). You can continue to select new fonts for your document from among those you installed, either by changing the font size from the Font Size menu (Ctrl-F8 S) or by changing the base font (Ctrl-F8 F).

USING THE PRINTER
DEFINITION PROGRAM

T he Printer Definition program supplied with WordPerfect allows you to make modifications to an existing printer definition or to create a new one for a printer that is not currently supported by the program. The Printer Definition program file is named PTR.EXE and is located on the PTR Program disk (if you use 3½-inch disks, this file is on the Fonts/Graphics/PTR Program disk).

This appendix covers only basic information on using this program to customize a printer definition. For complete information on all aspects of the Printer Definition program, you can purchase the *WordPerfect Printer Definition Program, A Technical Reference* directly from WordPerfect Corporation. This manual explains the Printer Definition program in detail. Consider this documentation essential if you plan to make extensive changes to a printer definition or to create a new printer definition file for a model of printer not currently supported.

WordPerfect 5.0 comes with printer definitions for a great number of printers. The information describing how WordPerfect communicates with your model of printer is contained in the printer's own printer definition file. The printer definitions are stored as .PRS (for *Printer Resource*) files. In turn, a number of related .PRS files are stored in a larger file that carries the file extension .ALL. The .ALL files are named after the number of the Printer disk on which they are located, as follows:

.ALL FILE NAME	PRINTER DISK	PRINTER DEFINITIONS
WPRINT1.ALL	Printer1	Disk Laser printer definitions
WPRINT2.ALL	Printer2	Disk Daisy wheel and Post-Script printer definitions
WPRINT3.ALL	Printer3	Disk Dot matrix printer definitions
WPRINT4.ALL	Printer4	Disk Printer definitions for older printer models no longer manufactured

Note that if you are using 3½-inch disks, the WPRINT1.ALL and WPRINT2-.ALL files are combined on one disk called Printer1/Printer2.

The Printer Definition program can be used to modify the settings for a particular .PRS file or for an entire .ALL file. Most of the time when customizing particular features, you will change the definition only for the specific .PRS file used by your printer.

You should *never* use the Printer Definition program to modify any of the original printer definition files that are supplied on the master Printer disks (the disks that came with the program). Instead, you should make a copy of the Printer disk you need and modify its .ALL or .PRS file.

If you are customizing a .PRS file, start by copying the existing file installed with WordPerfect and renaming it (this procedure is covered in detail in Chapter 7). Then modify this new .PRS file with the Printer Definition program. Once you have selected the file in WordPerfect and tested out the changes, you can remove the .PRS file that you originally installed, if you wish.

STARTING THE PRINTER DEFINITION PROGRAM

To start the Printer Definition program on a two-disk-drive system, follow these steps:

1. Place your working copy of the PTR Program disk in drive A.
2. Place the disk containing a copy of the appropriate .ALL or .PRS file in drive B.
3. Type **B:** and press Enter to make drive B the default.
4. Type **A:PTR** and press Enter to start the Printer Definition program.

To start the Printer Definition program on a hard disk, follow these steps:

1. Copy the files on the PTR Program disk into a directory on your hard disk. For example, to copy the Printer Definition files to your Word-Perfect startup directory, you would place the PTR Program disk in drive A and type

   ```
   COPY A:*.* C:\WP50
   ```

   Substitute the correct startup directory path name if it is something other than C:\WP50.
2. Type **PTR** and press Enter to start the Printer Definition program. The directory into which you copied the Printer Definition program files must be the current one when you enter this startup command.

Starting the Printer Definition Program with a Particular Printer File

You can alter the Printer Definition program startup command so that it loads a particular .ALL or .PRS file on startup. For example, if you wanted to modify the WPRINT3.ALL file on a two-disk system, you would make drive B current, type

    A:PTR WPRINT3.ALL

and press Enter. If you wanted to edit the EPFX80.PRS file copied to a floppy disk when starting the program on a hard disk, you would type

    PTR A:EPFX80.PRS

and press the Enter key.

When you start the program with a particular .ALL file, as indicated in the first example, the Printer Definition program screen lists all of the .PRS files found in the .ALL file, as shown in Figure G.1. When you start the program using a particular .PRS file, only the name of that printer definition appears on the screen.

Specifying the Printer Definition Files to Edit

If you start the Printer Definition program without entering a file name to use, the initial screen for the program won't list any printer definition files. To retrieve a particular .ALL or .PRS file, you press Shift-F10 (Retrieve) and enter the name (and path, if necessary) of the file to be edited. On the screen, you will see the name of the printer you specified, with the cursor at the beginning of the name.

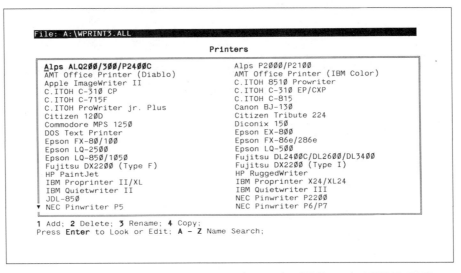

FIGURE G.1: Initial Printer Definition program screen showing the .PRS files in the WPRINT3. ALL file.

Getting On-Line Help

You can obtain on-line help for the Printer Definition program if you copy the PTR.HLP file onto the same disk or into the same directory that contains the PTR.EXE file. When you press F3, the program displays a template showing the function key assignments, as shown in Figure G.2.

Press Ctrl-F3 (Screen Help) to obtain a screen listing of help topics in alphabetical order. If you press Alt-F3 (Item Help), the cursor will move to the correct topic within this list. Once in the Help screen, you can use ↑ or ↓ to move to a new topic. You can press the Screen Help or Item Help key after selecting any menu option in the program to get more information on how the option is used.

The Printer Definition program has many levels of menus, just as WordPerfect does. To select an option and go to the next menu level, you press the Enter key. To exit a menu and return to the previous level, you press F7. To quit the program from almost any level, you press Alt-F7. You will then be asked if you want to save the printer definition file (using the same process that WordPerfect does when you save and exit using the F7 key).

Locating and Selecting the Printer Definition to Edit

To quickly locate and select a particular printer contained in the .ALL file, you can use Name Search by typing the first few characters of the printer's name, or you can use the cursor movement keys as they are used in WordPerfect itself. With Name Search, the cursor will jump to the first printer name that

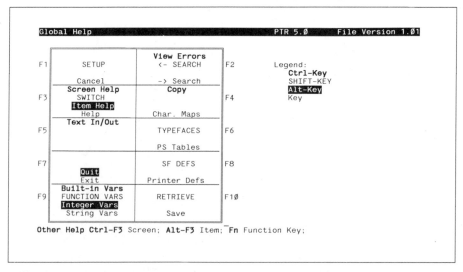

FIGURE G.2: Function key template for the Printer Definition program.

matches the characters typed. In addition to locating the cursor at the beginning of the printer's name, the program displays the name of the currently selected printer definition in bold letters. Once you have located the name of the printer whose definition you want to examine or edit, you can press the Enter key twice (the first time to exit Name Search and the second time to select the Look or Edit option).

If you wish to go directly to a specific screen for the selected printer definition, you can also do so by pressing the appropriate function key. For example, if you want to examine the Character Map screen for the selected printer, you press F4. If you want to view the Proportional Spacing tables for the printer, press F6. You can press F8 (Printer Definitions) to return to the list of printer definitions on the screen.

EDITING A PRINTER DEFINITION

As stated earlier, you can use the Printer Definition program to edit either an .ALL file or a .PRS file. Certain changes, such as those made to the automatic font changes and substitute fonts (discussed below), should be made only to the .PRS file, while others should be made to the .ALL file. Consult the *WordPerfect Printer Definition Program, A Technical Reference* for complete information on what kinds of modifications to make to .PRS files and what kinds to make to the .ALL files that create them.

After you edit an .ALL file and save the changes to it, all new values it contains should be copied to the .PRS files that use its information as soon as you return to WordPerfect, select the printer (Shift-F7 S), and choose the Update option (**7** or **U**).

In this appendix, we will look at two kinds of modifications that can be made to an existing printer definition file. Both of these modifications should be made to a copy of the .PRS file rather than to the .ALL file that contains them.

The first involves the automatic font changes (referred to as *AFC's*) and the substitute fonts used by the program. AFC's determine which fonts are used when you select the size and certain appearance attributes. Substitute fonts describe the fonts that are used if a particular character in the selected font is not included in its character set. It also indicates the priority in which these substitute fonts are to be used.

The second kind of modification involves creating kerning tables. When kerning is turned on and the font is used, the values entered in the kerning table indicate which letter pairs are to be affected and how much they are to be kerned (see Chapter 5 for a discussion of kerning).

Editing the Automatic Font Changes and Substitute Fonts

Before making changes to the automatic font changes or substitute fonts for a printer definition, you should create a new .PRS file and select all of the fonts

you own for it in WordPerfect. In the following discussions, we will use the HP
LaserJet Series II as the sample printer. Before using the Printer Definition program, make a copy of the .PRS file as follows:

1. Press Shift-F7 and choose the Select option (**S**).

2. Select the Additional Printers option (**2** or **A**).

3. Highlight *HP LaserJet Series II* from the list of printers and choose Select (**1**
   or **S**).

4. Edit the existing file name HPLASEII.PRS at the Printer Filename
   prompt and press Enter. (In this example, it was changed to HPL.PRS.)

5. You will see the "Updating font" message and the Help screen for this
   printer. Press F7 to go to the Printer Edit screen.

6. Select the Name option (**1** or **N**) and edit the name of the printer. (In this
   example, HP LaserJet II Kern was used.)

7. Select the Cartridges and Fonts option (**5** or **C**).

8. Choose the Select Fonts option (**1** or **F**) and mark with an asterisk all of the
   cartridges that are used.

9. Press F7, move the highlight cursor down to *Soft Fonts,* and choose the
   Select Fonts option (**1** or **F**) again.

10. Mark all of your soft fonts with a plus sign (rather than an asterisk, which
    subtracts the amount of printer memory required from the total available).

11. Press F7 twice. The "Updating font" message is displayed and all of the
    fonts marked are updated in the .PRS file.

12. Select the Path for Downloadable Fonts and Printer Command Files
    option (**7** or **D**) and enter the directory that contains the soft fonts.

13. Press F7 until you are returned to the document editing screen.

After creating the new .PRS file in this manner, you can exit WordPerfect and
start the Printer Definition program. Note that the Printer Definition program
can't be run with the Go to DOS feature (Ctrl-F1 G). You must exit Word-
Perfect.

Start the Printer Definition program from DOS using the new .PRS file. For
example, on a hard disk you type

    PTR HPL.PRS

and press Enter. When the initial screen of the Printer Definition program comes
up, you see *HP LaserJet Series II* as the only printer displayed. In the upper-left

corner after the File prompt, you see that the program is using

C:\WP50\HPL.PRS

As this printer is already selected, you press Enter to edit it. A list of options for editing is then displayed, as shown in Figure G.3. To make changes to the AFC's and substitute font selections, you need to choose the Fonts option. Because Name Search is operative, you can do this by typing **f**. The cursor will jump to *Fonts*. Press the Enter key twice to get to the Fonts screen.

The Font screen shows you all of the fonts that you selected for this printer definition file. (In this example, all of the soft fonts available for the HP LaserJet Series II were selected). As you could tell from the Sorting message that appears when you select the Fonts option, the font names are arranged alphabetically. To locate a font, you can use the WordPerfect cursor movement keys or use the Search feature.

In this example, we will change the AFC's for the Helvetica 10 point font supplied by Hewlett-Packard. This font is part of the AC soft font set. To locate it quickly, you press F2, type the search string

(AC) helv 10

and press F2 again. This places the cursor on *(AC) Helv 10pt* as shown in Figure G.4. Once you have selected a font by locating the cursor on it, you can go on to the next set of options by pressing Enter.

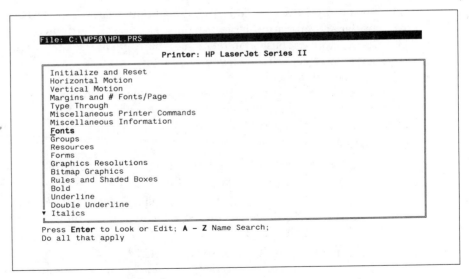

FIGURE G.3: Selecting Fonts for editing.

```
File: C:\WP5Ø\HPL.PRS

                        Printer: HP LaserJet Series II
                                      Fonts
┌──────────────────────────────────────────────────────────────────┐
▲  Solid Line Draw 1Ø pitch (Land)
│  (A/C/L/Q) Courier Italic 1Ø pitch
│  (AC) Helv Ø6pt
│  (AC) Helv Ø6pt (Land)
│  (AC) Helv Ø6pt Bold
│  (AC) Helv Ø6pt Bold (Land)
│  (AC) Helv Ø6pt Italic
│  (AC) Helv Ø6pt Italic (Land)
│  (AC) Helv Ø8pt
│  (AC) Helv Ø8pt (Land)
│  (AC) Helv Ø8pt Bold
│  (AC) Helv Ø8pt Bold (Land)
│  (AC) Helv Ø8pt Italic
│  (AC) Helv Ø8pt Italic (Land)
│  (AC) Helv 1Øpt
│  (AC) Helv 1Øpt (Land)
▼  (AC) Helv 1Øpt Bold
└──────────────────────────────────────────────────────────────────┘
  1 Add; 2 Delete; 3 Rename;
  Press Enter to Look or Edit; A - Z Name Search;
```

FIGURE G.4: Selecting the Helvetica 10 point font in the AC set by Hewlett-Packard.

Figure G.5 shows you the options that appear after you select a font for editing. We want to examine and edit the AFC's for Helvetica 10 point in the AC set. To select the Automatic Font Changes option, just type **A**. Then press the Enter key twice to go on to the first Automatic Font Changes screen shown in Figure G.6.

In this screen, you see the fonts that are automatically selected when you use the extra large, very large, large, small, and fine size attributes (Ctrl-F8 S). These sizes are all established in relation to the 10-point size that would be used as the base font. Below the sizes, you can see the fonts that are used when italics or bold is selected in the document.

To see how you go about changing the font that is used when you specify an attribute, we will outline the steps necessary to change the font for extra large print. This will be changed from Helvetica 24 point to Helvetica 30 point in the AE soft font set.

1. As the Extra Large Print option is currently selected, press the Enter key to view the list of fonts used with this printer.

2. In the screen that appears, the cursor will be located on *(AE) Helv 24pt* and you will see that the font is preceded by an asterisk, indicating that this is the font currently used to produce extra large print.

3. Press the ↓ key until the cursor is on *(AE) Helv 30pt* and type an asterisk (*). The asterisk now precedes *(AE) Helv 30pt,* indicating that this is now the selected font.

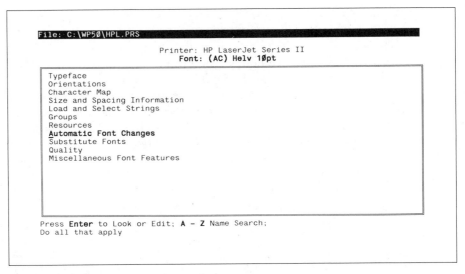

```
File: C:\WP5Ø\HPL.PRS

                      Printer: HP LaserJet Series II
                           Font: (AC) Helv 1Øpt

  ┌──────────────────────────────────────────────────────────────────┐
  │ Typeface                                                           │
  │ Orientations                                                       │
  │ Character Map                                                      │
  │ Size and Spacing Information                                      │
  │ Load and Select Strings                                          │
  │ Groups                                                            │
  │ Resources                                                         │
  │ Automatic Font Changes                                           │
  │ Substitute Fonts                                                  │
  │ Quality                                                           │
  │ Miscellaneous Font Features                                      │
  │                                                                    │
  │                                                                    │
  │                                                                    │
  │                                                                    │
  └──────────────────────────────────────────────────────────────────┘
  Press Enter to Look or Edit; A - Z Name Search;
  Do all that apply
```

FIGURE G.5: Selecting the Automatic Font Changes option.

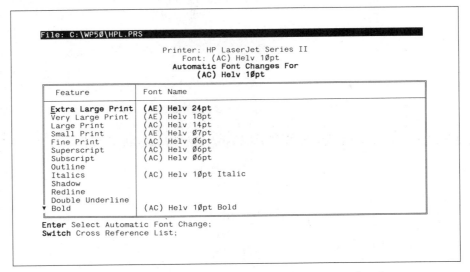

```
File: C:\WP5Ø\HPL.PRS

                      Printer: HP LaserJet Series II
                           Font: (AC) Helv 1Øpt
                       Automatic Font Changes For
                            (AC) Helv 1Øpt

  ┌────────────────────┬─────────────────────────────────────────────┐
  │ Feature            │ Font Name                                    │
  ├────────────────────┼─────────────────────────────────────────────┤
  │ Extra Large Print  │ (AE) Helv 24pt                               │
  │ Very Large Print   │ (AE) Helv 18pt                               │
  │ Large Print        │ (AC) Helv 14pt                               │
  │ Small Print        │ (AE) Helv Ø7pt                               │
  │ Fine Print         │ (AC) Helv Ø6pt                               │
  │ Superscript        │ (AC) Helv Ø6pt                               │
  │ Subscript          │ (AC) Helv Ø6pt                               │
  │ Outline            │                                              │
  │ Italics            │ (AC) Helv 1Øpt Italic                        │
  │ Shadow             │                                              │
  │ Redline            │                                              │
  │ Double Underline   │                                              │
  │ ▼ Bold             │ (AC) Helv 1Øpt Bold                          │
  └────────────────────┴─────────────────────────────────────────────┘
  Enter Select Automatic Font Change;
  Switch Cross Reference List;
```

FIGURE G.6: The first Automatic Font Changes screen for Helvetica 10 point in the AC set.

4. Press F7 to return to the Automatic Font Changes screen. You will now see *(AE) Helv 30pt* listed after *Extra Large Print* as shown in Figure G.7.

Once you save this .PRS file and select this modified printer definition in WordPerfect, extra large type will be printed in 30-point size instead of 24-point size any time you use Helvetica 10 point in the AC set as the base font. You can continue selecting new fonts in this manner for each of the other size attributes on the Automatic Font Changes screen.

There are other AFC's besides the size attributes, italics, and bold that are selected for this font. If you press ↓ until you reach the bottom of this screen, you can scroll up other selections. In Figure G.8, you can see that the (AE) Helv 07pt font is used to produce small caps and the Solid Line Draw 10 pitch is used to perform line drawing. Notice that below *Small Caps,* the categories starting with *ASCII* and ending with *Greek* (there are more below *Greek* not shown in this figure) refer to the various WordPerfect character sets (see Appendix B). With this font, the only AFC listed for the character sets is Solid Line Draw 10 pitch across from the Box Draw category.

You can also add new fonts to categories that are currently empty. For example, if you have the Bitstream Fontware package (see Appendix F), you could use it to make a Swiss 10 point font that uses the Roman 8 character set. Because the Roman 8 character set includes certain foreign-language symbols missing from the Helvetica AC set, you could then select the (FW) Swiss 10pt (HP Roman 8) (Port) font as the AFC for the Multinational 1 category. That way, when you use the Compose feature to produce more common foreign-language symbols in the Multinational 1 character set and have specified Helvetica 10 point as the base font, WordPerfect will print the special characters from the Swiss 10 point font that includes them. After making all of the modifications to the AFC's for the font, you can return to the Fonts submenu by pressing F7.

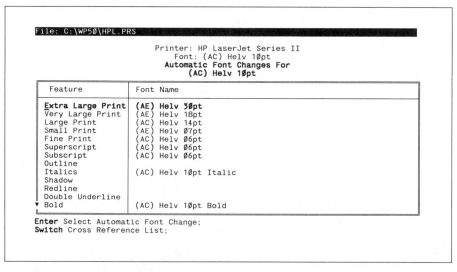

Feature	Font Name
Extra Large Print	(AE) Helv 30pt
Very Large Print	(AE) Helv 18pt
Large Print	(AC) Helv 14pt
Small Print	(AE) Helv 07pt
Fine Print	(AC) Helv 06pt
Superscript	(AC) Helv 06pt
Subscript	(AC) Helv 06pt
Outline	
Italics	(AC) Helv 10pt Italic
Shadow	
Redline	
Double Underline	
▼ Bold	(AC) Helv 10pt Bold

File: C:\WP50\HPL.PRS

Printer: HP LaserJet Series II
Font: (AC) Helv 10pt
Automatic Font Changes For
(AC) Helv 10pt

Enter Select Automatic Font Change;
Switch Cross Reference List;

FIGURE G.7: The Automatic Font Changes screen after increasing the size of the font used to produce extra large print.

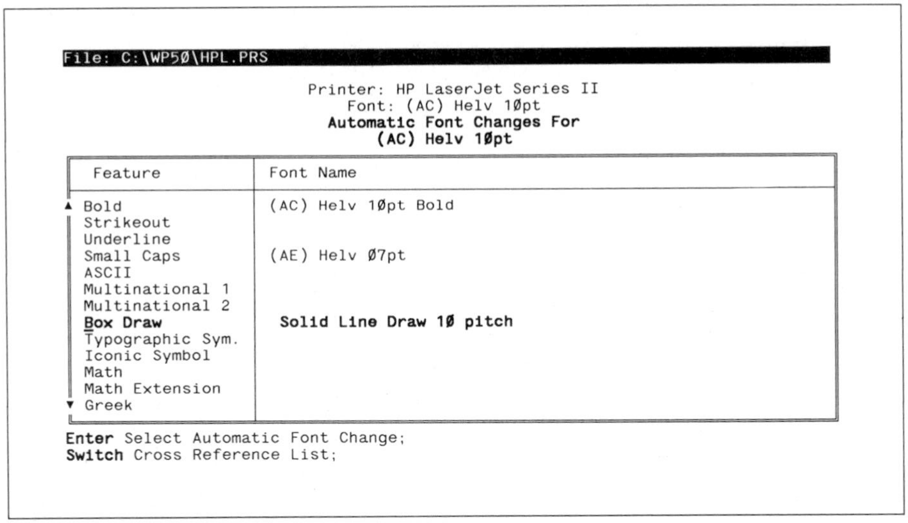

```
┌──────────────────────────────────────────────────────────────────┐
│ File: C:\WP5Ø\HPL.PRS                                              │
│                        Printer: HP LaserJet Series II              │
│                           Font: (AC) Helv 1Øpt                     │
│                        Automatic Font Changes For                  │
│                             (AC) Helv 1Øpt                         │
│   ┌──────────────────────┬───────────────────────────────────┐    │
│   │  Feature             │ Font Name                         │    │
│   ├──────────────────────┼───────────────────────────────────┤    │
│ ▲ │  Bold                │ (AC) Helv 1Øpt Bold               │    │
│ │ │  Strikeout           │                                   │    │
│ │ │  Underline           │                                   │    │
│ │ │  Small Caps          │ (AE) Helv Ø7pt                    │    │
│ │ │  ASCII               │                                   │    │
│ │ │  Multinational 1     │                                   │    │
│ │ │  Multinational 2     │                                   │    │
│ │ │  Box Draw            │ Solid Line Draw 1Ø pitch          │    │
│ │ │  Typographic Sym.    │                                   │    │
│ │ │  Iconic Symbol       │                                   │    │
│ │ │  Math                │                                   │    │
│ │ │  Math Extension      │                                   │    │
│ ▼ │  Greek               │                                   │    │
│   └──────────────────────┴───────────────────────────────────┘    │
│   Enter Select Automatic Font Change;                              │
│   Switch Cross Reference List;                                     │
│                                                                    │
└──────────────────────────────────────────────────────────────────┘
```

FIGURE G.8: The second part of the Automatic Font Changes screen, showing the AFC's for Small Caps and Box Draw.

In addition to modifying the AFC's for a font, you can also modify the substitute fonts that it uses. The fonts selected on the substitute fonts screen tell Word-Perfect which fonts are to be searched to find a character that isn't included in the current font. It also indicates the order (by number) in which the substitute fonts are to be searched. If the character isn't located in the substitute font marked *1,* then WordPerfect searches for it in the substitute font marked *2,* and so on. You can indicate up to nine priority levels, meaning that up to nine different fonts will be searched. However, the more substitute fonts you mark, the slower the print-ing process may be, as WordPerfect has to search (and sometimes download) each substitute font in looking for the character.

To see the list of substitute fonts, you select the Substitute Fonts option on the Fonts submenu (refer to Figure G.5). Figure G.9 shows you the first substitute font for the Helvetica 10 point font in the AC set. As you can see from this figure, Word-Perfect will first search the Helvetica 10 point font in the AD soft font set if a charac-ter used in the document is not found in the AC set. There are two more substitute fonts (not shown in Figure G.9) that are selected: (DA) Letter Gothic 12pt 12 pitch (Math8) is marked *2* and (SB) Century Schoolbook 10pt is marked *3.*

To change the order of the substitute fonts, you move the cursor to the name of the font you want to use and then type in its new priority number over the existing one. The other priority numbers will change to accommodate this renumbering. If you want to remove a substitute font, you move to it and type **0** as the priority num-ber. If you want to add a new substitute font, you move to it and type the new pri-ority number. After making your changes to the substitute fonts, you press F7 to return to the Fonts submenu.

```
┌─────────────────────────────────────────────────────────────────────────┐
│  File: C:\WP50\HPL.PRS                                                     │
│                        Printer: HP LaserJet Series II                     │
│                            Font: (AC) Helv 10pt                           │
│                              Substitute Fonts                             │
│    ┌──────────────────┬──────────────────────────────────────────────┐   │
│    │    Priority      │  Font Name                                    │   │
│    ├──────────────────┼──────────────────────────────────────────────┤   │
│  ▲ │                  │  (AD) Helv 06pt Bold (Land)                   │   │
│  │ │                  │  (AD) Helv 06pt Italic                        │   │
│  │ │                  │  (AD) Helv 06pt Italic (Land)                 │   │
│  │ │                  │  (AD) Helv 08pt                               │   │
│  │ │                  │  (AD) Helv 08pt (Land)                        │   │
│  │ │                  │  (AD) Helv 08pt Bold                          │   │
│  │ │                  │  (AD) Helv 08pt Bold (Land)                   │   │
│  │ │                  │  (AD) Helv 08pt Italic                        │   │
│  │ │                  │  (AD) Helv 08pt Italic (Land)                 │   │
│  │ │       ▐1▌        │  (AD) Helv 10pt                               │   │
│  │ │                  │  (AD) Helv 10pt (Land)                        │   │
│  │ │                  │  (AD) Helv 10pt Bold                          │   │
│  ▼ │                  │  (AD) Helv 10pt Bold (Land)                   │   │
│    │                  │  (AD) Helv 10pt Italic                        │   │
│    └──────────────────┴──────────────────────────────────────────────┘   │
│                                                                           │
│  Enter Priority (1 highest, * after others), Backspace to Clear           │
│                                                                           │
└─────────────────────────────────────────────────────────────────────────┘
```

FIGURE G.9: The first substitute font for Helvetica 10 point in the AC set.

Creating Kerning Tables

You can also create kerning tables for the fonts you use with your printer. WordPerfect supplies very few kerning tables, especially for soft fonts used on the HP LaserJet printer. However, you can use the Printer Definition program to create your own tables, using a process of trial and error to determine the optimum spacing adjustment. Remember that kerning is the procedure of reducing the amount of space between specific letter pairs that appear too far apart when regular letter spacing is used (refer to Chapter 5 for examples of typical kern pairs and more information on kerning).

To create kern pairs for a font, you select the Fonts option and then the name of the font for which you want to create the kerning table. To illustrate this procedure, we have chosen the Helvetica 30 point font (which is now used to print extra large type when Helvetica 10 point is chosen as the base font). After selecting this font, you select the Size and Spacing Information option on the Fonts submenu.

Figure G.10 shows you the screen that appears when you select this option and press Enter. Kerning is done from the Proportional Spacing table. To select this option, press the PgDn key (this option will be displayed in bold) and press Enter. This takes you to a list of Proportional Spacing tables for many different fonts. However, the correct table for the font that you chose earlier (Helvetica 30 point in this case) will be marked with an asterisk, indicating that it is the currently selected table. To view the values for this table, you simply press the Enter key again.

```
┌──────────────────────────────────────────────────────────────────────┐
│ File: C:\WP50\HPL.PRS                                                  │
│                    Printer: HP LaserJet Series II                      │
│                       Font: (AE) Helv 30pt                             │
│                    Size and Spacing Information                        │
│  ┌──────────────────────────────────────────────────────────────────┐ │
│  │ Point Size (1 Point = 1/72 Inch)                     29          │ │
│  │ Font Cell Height (Points)                            29          │ │
│  │ Default Leading (Points)                             2.9         │ │
│  │ PS Table Width Scaling Factor                        1           │ │
│  │ Optimal Character Width (% of Font Width)            100         │ │
│  │ Optimal Space Width (% of Font Width)                60          │ │
│  │ Character Cell Adjust (± 1200ths)                    0           │ │
│  │ Baseline Bias Factor (Points)                        0           │ │
│  │ Horizontal Spacing Units                             1/300       │ │
│  │ Vertical Spacing Units                               1/300       │ │
│  │ Proportional Spacing Table: HP AF Helv30R                        │ │
│  ├──────────────────────────────────────────────────────────────────┤ │
│  │         PS Table Information (change in PS Table)                │ │
│  │ Average PS Table Width (PS Table Units):   69/300               │ │
│  │ Average Scaled Width (PS Table Units):     69/300               │ │
│  │ Point Size PS Table Was Created for:   29                        │ │
│  └──────────────────────────────────────────────────────────────────┘ │
│  Enter Values                                                          │
│  Press Enter to Edit                                                   │
│                                                                        │
└──────────────────────────────────────────────────────────────────────┘
```

FIGURE G.10: Size and Spacing Information sceen for the Helvetica 30 point font.

This takes you to the screen shown in Figure G.11. The Proportional Spacing table for a font contains columns displaying the WordPerfect character set code numbers, the character produced, a description of the character, the width of the character, any adjustment factor to be applied to it, and whether or not kern pairs have been defined for it.

The width of the character is shown in horizontal spacing units, which differ from printer to printer. Because the HP LaserJet can print up to 300 dots per inch, there are 300 units. As you can see from Figure G.11, the first character in this Helvetica 30 point font is the space, and it takes up 31 of these units (31/300 is approximately equal to 1/10 inch).

To create kern pairs for characters, you need to move the cursor over to the column marked *Kern?* and then select the first character of the kern pair. In this example, we will outline the steps for creating two common kern pairs, *Yo* and *y.*, for this font. To create kerning values for *Yo*, follow these steps:

1. Press the → key twice to locate the highlight cursor in the *Kern?* column.

2. Press ↓ until the cursor is on the letter *Y* (uppercase), which has the character set numbers 0,89.

3. Press the Enter key to select *Y* as the first character of the kern pair.

4. This takes you to a new screen that shows the first character of the kern pair at the top. Press the ↓ key until the cursor is on the second letter, *o,* which has the number 0,111. Then press Enter.

```
File: C:\WP50\HPL.PRS

                    Printer: HP LaserJet Series II
                         Font: (AE) Helv 30pt
                      Size and Spacing Information
                 Proportional Spacing Table: HP AF Helv30R

 Number Description                                  Width   Adjust   Kern?

   0,32    (Space)                          `          31              ▄▄
   0,33  ! (Exclamation Point)                         40              ---
   0,34  " (Neutral Double Quote)                      41              ---
   0,35  # (Number/Pound)                              95              ---
   0,36  $ (Dollars)                                   68              ---
   0,37  % (Percent)                                  105              ---
   0,38  & (Ampersand)                                 85              ---
   0,39  ' (Neutral Single Quote)                      31              ---
   0,40  ( (Left Parenthesis)                          42              ---
   0,41  ) (Right Parenthesis)                         42              ---
 ▼ 0,42  * (Asterisk)                                  62              ---

 Units: Printer Motion Units                    Point Size: 29

Press Enter to Edit Kern Adjust Values
```

FIGURE G.11: First part of the Proportional Spacing table for the Helvetica 30 point font.

5. Type in **−12** as the kerning adjustment value, as shown in Figure G.12, and press Enter. If you had any other characters you wanted kerned with *Y,* you would now select them and enter their kerning adjustment values.

6. Press F7 to return to the Proportional Spacing table. Notice that the *Kern?* column for the *Y* now displays ◄──┘, indicating that kern pairs have been created using *Y* as the first character. You can now go on and select other letters, such as *y, W,* and others that require kerning when paired with particular letters.

When you enter a kerning adjustment value, you enter a negative number to indicate that the printer is to advance to the left before printing the second character of the kern pair. How much you adjust the printing depends upon the size of the font and the amount of white space normally left between the characters when printing in that typeface. The number you enter represents the number of horizontal spacing units to move. In this example, we have told the printer to move .04 inch (−12 ÷ 300 = −.04) to the left before printing the *o* after the *Y.*

> *Note:* Don't forget the negative sign when entering kerning adjustment values for the second letter of a kern pair or WordPerfect will increase the space between the letters. Positive values indicate the amount of space to move to the right.

To create a second kern pair that moves the period (.) closer to the letter *y,* you would follow similar steps. This time you would select the *y* (lowercase) on the

Proportional Spacing table and then select the period as the second character. After selecting the period, you would enter **−10** as the kerning adjustment value.

Figure G.13 shows you the effect of using the two new kern pairs. In the first sample sentence, automatic kerning is still off. In the second sentence, automatic kerning has been turned on (Shift-F8 O P K Y).

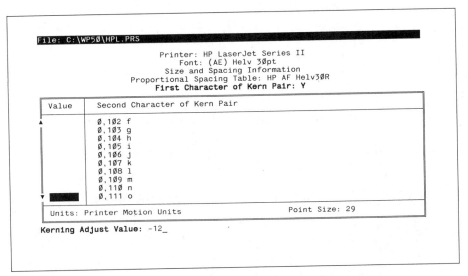

```
File: C:\WP50\HPL.PRS

                      Printer: HP LaserJet Series II
                         Font: (AE) Helv 30pt
                      Size and Spacing Information
                 Proportional Spacing Table: HP AF Helv30R
                    First Character of Kern Pair: Y

   ┌─────────┬──────────────────────────────────────────────┐
   │ Value   │ Second Character of Kern Pair                │
   │         │                                              │
 ▲ │         │    0,102 f                                   │
   │         │    0,103 g                                   │
   │         │    0,104 h                                   │
   │         │    0,105 i                                   │
   │         │    0,106 j                                   │
   │         │    0,107 k                                   │
   │         │    0,108 l                                   │
   │         │    0,109 m                                   │
   │         │    0,110 n                                   │
 ▼ │         │    0,111 o                                   │
   ├─────────┴──────────────────────────────────────────────┤
   │ Units: Printer Motion Units          Point Size: 29    │
   └────────────────────────────────────────────────────────┘

 Kerning Adjust Value: -12_
```

FIGURE G.12: Entering the kerning adjustment value for the kern pair *Yo.*

You go, I'll stay.

You go, I'll stay.

FIGURE G.13: Two sample sentences printed in Helvetica 30 point using the AE soft font set with and without automatic kerning. In the second sentence, which uses automatic kerning, the amount of adjustment to the space between the *Y* and *o* in *You* and between the *y* and the period in *y.* is controlled by the kern pairs created for the modified HP LaserJet Series II printer definition.

Saving a Modified Printer Definition

When you have finished making all of the changes to the printer definition file, you can press Alt-F7 to save them (you can also press F7 continuously to back out of the program). You will be prompted to save the file. When you press Enter or type **Y**, the program will first perform a consistency check. If you have selected conflicting or nonvalid values, the program will save these in a file called PRS.ERR. If the program informs you that information is being saved in this file, you should remain in the program and view the file's contents by pressing Ctrl-F2 (View Errors). You can then take care of the errors and resave the .PRS file.

After performing the consistency check, the program prompts you for the name of the file. It will supply the original file name as the default. If you want to save the modified .PRS file under a new file name, edit the file name before pressing Enter. If you choose to save the file under the same name, you will receive the Replace prompt, as you do when saving and exiting from Word-Perfect. After saving the file, you will be prompted to exit the Printer Definition program.

USING A MODIFIED PRINTER DEFINITION FILE

To use a printer definition that you have modified and saved, you need to start WordPerfect, press Shift-F7 (Print), and choose the Select Printer option (**S**). Then move the highlight cursor to the name of the printer that contains the modified .PRS file. For instance, in our example the new printer definition was named HP LaserJet II Kern to differentiate it from the HP LaserJet Series II definition, which uses the original HPLASEII.PRS file as configured by Word-Perfect. To use the modified definition, you highlight *HP LaserJet II Kern* on the Print Select Printer menu and then choose the Select option (**1** or **S**).

Note: If the modified .PRS file is on a floppy disk, copy it to the startup directory or special printer directory (if you created one).

INDEX

Page numbers that are italicized refer to information presented in tables.

SYBEX Computer Books
are different.

Here is why . . .

At SYBEX, each book is designed with you in mind. Every manuscript is carefully selected and supervised by our editors, who are themselves computer experts. We publish the best authors, whose technical expertise is matched by an ability to write clearly and to communicate effectively. Programs are thoroughly tested for accuracy by our technical staff. Our computerized production department goes to great lengths to make sure that each book is well-designed.

In the pursuit of timeliness, SYBEX has achieved many publishing firsts. SYBEX was among the first to integrate personal computers used by authors and staff into the publishing process. SYBEX was the first to publish books on the CP/M operating system, microprocessor interfacing techniques, word processing, and many more topics.

Expertise in computers and dedication to the highest quality product have made SYBEX a world leader in computer book publishing. Translated into fourteen languages, SYBEX books have helped millions of people around the world to get the most from their computers. We hope we have helped you, too.

For a complete catalog of our publications:

SYBEX, Inc. 2021 Challenger Drive, #100, Alameda, CA 94501
Tel: (415) 523-8233/(800) 227-2346   Telex: 336311
Fax: (415) 523-2373

COMMANDS AND FUNCTIONS—LISTED ALPHABETICALLY

COMMAND	KEY SEQUENCE	PAGE	COMMAND	KEY SEQUENCE	PAGE
Advance left (or right) a specified amount	Shift-F8 O A L (or R)	705	Endnote placement	Ctrl-F7 P	768
Advance to a specified line	Shift-F8 O A I	705	Endnotes, create, edit options	Ctrl-F7 E	767
Advance to a specified position	Shift-F8 O A P	705	Exit to DOS temporarily	Ctrl-F1 G	775
Advance up (or down) a specified amount	Shift-F8 O A U (or D)	705	Exit key (exit from WordPerfect)	F7	760
Append block to disk file	Alt-F4 Ctrl-F4 B A	706	Extra large text	Ctrl-F8 S E	765
Automatically format/rewrite	Shift-F1 D A	751	File management	F5 Enter	807
Automatic reference	Alt-F5 R	707	Fine text	Ctrl-F8 S F	765
Backup files	Shift-F1 B	710	Flush Right key	Alt-F6	762
Base font	Ctrl-F8 F	711	Font appearance	Ctrl-F8 A	766
Binding width	Shift-F7 B	712	Font key	Ctrl-F8	763
Block cut/copy	Alt-F4 Ctrl-F4 B M (or C)	739	Font size	Ctrl-F8 S	765
Block key	Alt-F4	713	Fonts (install)	Shift-F7 S E C	718
Block protection	Alt-F4 Shift-F8	715	Footnote key	Ctrl-F7 F	766
Bold	F6 (or Ctrl-F8 A B)	716	Format	Shift-F8	771
Calculate (with math on)	Alt-F7 A	828	Forms	Shift-F7 S E F	772
Cancel job(s)	Shift-F7 C C	849	Generate list, index, and tables	Alt-F5 G G	809
Cancel key	F1	717	Go (start printer)	Shift-F7 C G	855
Case conversion	Alt-F4 Shift-F3	720	Go To key	Ctrl-Home	775
Center key	Shift-F6	721	Graphics figure	Alt-F9 F	776
Center page top to bottom	Shift-F8 P C	722	Graphics table	Alt-F9 T	776
Change default drive	F5 =	747	Graphics text box	Alt-F9 B	776
Colors/fonts/attributes	Shift-F1 D C	724	Graphics user-defined box	Alt-F9 U	776
Column cut or copy	Alt-F4 Ctrl-F4 C M (or C)	739	Hard page break	Ctrl-Enter	843
Columns (define)	Alt-F7 D	728	Hard return	Enter	783
Compare screen and disk documents	Alt-F5 G C	755	Hard return display character	Shift-F1 D H	752
Compose	Ctrl-2 or Ctrl-V	731	Hard space	Home space bar	784
Conditional end of page	Shift-F8 O C	733	Headers (or footers)	Shift-F8 P H (or F)	784
Copy file	F5 Enter C	734	Help key	F3	786
Cursor speed	Shift-F1 C	737	Horizontal line (graphics)	Alt-F9 L H	781
Date code	Shift-F5 C	742	Hyphen character (hard)	Home - (hyphen)	788
Date format	Shift-F5 F	742	Hyphenation on/off	Shift-F8 L Y	787
Date text	Shift-F5 T	742	Hyphenation zone (set)	Shift-F8 L Z	787
Date/Outline key	Shift-F5	741	Import DOS text file	Ctrl-F5 T (or F5 Enter T)	899
Decimal/align character	Shift-F8 O D	743	Indent key	F4	789
Define list, index, table of authorities, table of contents	Alt-F5 D	822	Index (mark word for)	Alt-F5 I	791
Delete character at cursor	Del	746	Initial codes (document)	Shift-F8 D C	794
Delete character left of cursor	Backspace	746	Initial codes (setup)	Shift-F1 I I	794
Delete characters to right of cursor within word	Home Del	746	Initial font (document)	Shift-F8 D F	794
Delete file	F5 Enter D	744	Initial font (printer)	Shift-F7 S E I	856
Delete to end of line	Ctrl-End	746	Italics	Ctrl-F8 A I	766
Delete to end of page	Ctrl-PgDn	746	Justification off (on)	Shift-F8 L J N (or Y)	796
Delete word	Ctrl-Backspace	746	Kerning	Shift-F8 O P K	797
Disk directory (change)	F5 Enter O	747	Keyboard layout	Shift-F1 K	798
Display columns side by side	Shift-F1 D S	731	Language	Shift-F8 O L	801
Display pitch	Shift-F8 D D	749	Left/Right Indent key	Shift-F4	790
Document comments	Ctrl-F5 C	753	Line draw	Ctrl-F3 L	802
Document comments (display)	Shift-F1 D D	754	Line format	Shift-F8 L	771
Document summary	Shift-F8 D S	756	Line height (leading)	Shift-F8 L H F	803
Double underline	Ctrl-F8 A D	766	Line numbering	Shift-F8 L N	804
End of field	F9	832	Line spacing	Shift-F8 L S	806
End of record (merge E)	Shift-F9 E	832	List Files key	F5	807
			List (mark text for list)	Alt-F4 Alt-F5 L	808
			Location of auxiliary files	Shift-F1 L	811
			Look at contents of a disk file	F5 Enter L	813
			Macro Define key	Ctrl-F10	815